FIFTY-STATE SURVEY | 2026

The Law of Class Action

CLASS ACTIONS & DERIVATIVE SUITS COMMITTEE

AMERICAN BAR ASSOCIATION
Litigation Section

Cover design by ABA Design

Printed in the United States of America.

29 28 27 26 25 5 4 3 2 1

ISBN 978-1-63905-745-0
e-ISBN 978-1-63905-746-7

CONTENTS

PREFACE

This survey was prepared by attorneys in the various states, under the auspices of the American Bar Association's Litigation Section Class Actions and Derivative Suits Subcommittee on State Laws, co-chaired by Fabrice Vincent and Dennis Egan.

Elizabeth J. Cabraser, *Executive Editor*, is a founding partner of the national plaintiffs' firm Lieff Cabraser Heimann & Bernstein, LLP. She represents plaintiffs in complex civil litigation primarily in the areas of class actions, mass torts, products liability, securities and investment fraud, and consumer fraud, as well as through pro bono representation of plaintiffs in civil rights and human rights litigation. Ms. Cabraser is regarded as a national authority in complex civil litigation, including class certification, class notice, settlement, the structuring of class trials, and appellate issues. Under Ms. Cabraser's leadership, Lieff Cabraser has developed into one of the country's largest and most successful plaintiffs' law firms.

Ms. Cabraser is Editor-in-Chief of *California Class Actions Practice and Procedures* (Lexis-Nexis). She has served as court-appointed lead, co-lead, or class counsel in scores of federal multi-district and state coordinated proceedings, and has participated in the design, structure and conduct of eight nationwide class action trials. Ms. Cabraser has held leadership roles in cases that resulted in landmark settlements, verdicts, and precedent-setting rulings, including multi-state tobacco, Fen-Phen (diet drugs), and Holocaust cases. She currently serves in key leadership roles in two of the most high-profile civil cases in the nation: the Toyota sudden acceleration and BP Gulf Oil spill law.

Fabrice N. Vincent, *Executive Editor*, is a partner at Lieff Cabraser Heimann & Bernstein, LLP. A graduate from Cornell Law School (J.D., cum laude, 1992), Mr. Vincent's practice focuses on class actions, personal injury/torts, defective products, wrongful deaths, medical malpractice, and environmental and toxic torts. He has been recognized by *Law & Politics* as a "Northern California Super Lawyer" for many years and has written extensively on current issues in litigation including in *California Class Actions Practice and Procedures*.

Fred B. Burnside, *Coordinating Editor*, is a partner in the Seattle office of Davis Wright Tremaine LLP, co-chairs the firm's Class Action Defense Group, and is Deputy Chair of the firm's Litigation Department. Mr. Burnside's practice focuses on class action defense, with an emphasis on consumer class actions in state and federal courts.

Jahan C. Sagafi, *Coordinating Editor*, is a partner with Outten & Golden LLP and manager of its San Francisco office, where he represents employees and consumers in class actions in federal and state trial and appellate courts.

Howard S. Suskin, *Coordinating Editor*, is a partner in Jenner & Block, LLC's Chicago office, and serves as Chair of the firm's Class Action Litigation Practice Group. Mr. Suskin practices primarily in the areas of class action litigation, professional liability litigation, and securities litigation.

Dennis K. Egan, *Editor Emeritus*, is an attorney at the law firm Kotz, Sangster, Wysocki and Berg, PC located in Detroit, Michigan. His practice is concentrated in the representation of national and regional securities broker/dealers in defending customer lawsuits and arbitrations as well as regulatory enforcement actions. Mr. Egan serves as co-chair of the State Laws Subcommittee of the Litigation Section's Class Actions and Derivative Suits Committee and is also an active member of the Broker/Dealer Litigation Subcommittee of the Litigation Section's Federal Regulation of Securities Committee. He has been recognized by *Law & Politics* as a "Michigan Super Lawyer" in the field of Securities Litigation.

Thomas R. Grande, *Editor Emeritus*, is the principal of Grande Law Offices in Honolulu, Hawaii, where he represents consumers in group and class actions in state and federal court and plaintiffs in cases brought under the state and federal false claims acts. He is a past officer and director of the Consumer Lawyers of Hawaii and was awarded the Outstanding Delivery of Legal Services Award by Hawaii Lawyers Care.

INTRODUCTION

The power of internet and other modern technologies allows class members to follow and participate in class action litigation like never before. The internet empowers class counsel to easily and cost effectively communicate with the entire class, giving stronger voices to class members and creating participation opportunities that, in turn, allows reviewing courts broad feedback and information supporting informed and sophisticated decisions on case management issues, class certification and proposed settlements. Increasingly, class action practice centers upon our federal courts, which have risen to the challenge of the 2020 pandemic by using technology, including video hearings and video appearances, to advance cases despite nationwide sheltering in place and unprecedented reductions in travel.

In 1985, the United States Supreme Court held in *Phillips Petroleum Co. v. Shutts*, 472 U.S. 797 (1985), that state courts can, within certain due process constraints, adjudicate claims of non-resident class members. This ruling opened the door for state courts to entertain multi-state and nationwide class actions that had traditionally been filed in federal forums. While some state courts proved more hospitable than others to multi-state class actions, the succeeding decade witnessed a significant increase in the number of multi-state class actions being adjudicated in the state courts.

The trend toward increasing Supreme Court involvement in major class actions was fueled by several factors, not the least of which was the perception that state courts offered a more flexible forum for adjudication of both certification and liability issues, as well as for approval of class-wide settlements. This was only partly accurate, since most states address class certification and other class action procedural issues, such as class notice and class action settlement approval, under statutes or rules that rely heavily upon, and are often identical to, Fed. R. Civ. P. 23 itself. However, differences in substantive laws, standards of proof, and statutes of limitations meant that claims that might have been barred in a class member's home jurisdiction could nevertheless be adjudicated in a multi-state class certified by a state court in a different jurisdiction.

Accompanying the shift of much class action litigation from federal to state forums was an increase in the number of competing class actions, i.e., the filing of separate class action complaints, commenced in different courts and by different plaintiffs, asserting essentially identical claims against the same defendant.

The appeal of state court forums for class actions was enhanced when the United States Supreme Court ruled that state courts have subject matter jurisdiction to resolve nationwide class actions and that class settlements reached in state courts have preclusive effect even over federal claims that were not litigated in the state forum. *Matsushita v. Epstein*, 516 U.S. 367 (1996). The following year, the Supreme Court in *Amchem Products, Inc. v. Windsor*, 521 U.S. 591 (1997), confirmed that settlement classes are not exempt from the requirements of Rule 23 in a decision which, though technically applicable to both federal and state courts, reinforced the view that parties seeking approval for multi-state settlement classes might encounter fewer obstacles in state than in federal courts.

The 2005 enactment of the Class Action Fairness Act (CAFA) added a new dynamic to the state vs. federal equation. CAFA exponentially expanded federal diversity jurisdiction over cases brought as class actions by, *inter alia*, amending 28 U.S.C §§ 1332 and 1445. Under these provisions of CAFA, parties have a broader right to file class action claims in, or remove them to, federal court, including claims that previously would have been outside the federal courts' diversity jurisdiction. For example, class members' individual claims need not meet the $75,000 traditional federal diversity jurisdiction threshold. Cases brought as class actions in which any unnamed class member is of diverse citizenship from any defendant, and involving over $5 million in controversy, may be filed in or removed to federal court under the expanded diversity jurisdiction provisions of 28 U.S.C. § 1332(d)(1)(11).

The U.S. Supreme Court's decision in *TransUnion LLC v. Ramirez*, 141 S. Ct. 2190 (2021), could potentially result in an increasing role of state courts in consumer class actions alleging violations of federal consumer laws. In *TransUnion LLC v. Ramirez*, Justice Brett Kavanaugh, writing for the majority, tightened the *Spokeo* test for federal class action plaintiffs seeking monetary damages for alleged violations of federal consumer laws, ruling that Article III of the U.S. Constitution requires a concrete injury, not simply an increased risk of harm. Justice Thomas, in a dissent joined by Justices Stephen Breyer, Elena Kagan, and Sonia Sotomayor, observed and wrote that, "by declaring that federal courts lack jurisdiction, the court has thus ensured that state courts will exercise exclusive jurisdiction over these sorts of class actions." Thus, many believe and predict that the TransUnion decision may open the doors to state courts for reinvigorated prosecution and litigation of class actions alleging violations of federal consumer laws in cases where the "concreteness" of the harm alleged is unclear.

A thorough and thoughtful understanding of the workings of the relevant state class action rules and case law will be an important component of either side's decision on filing in, or removal to, federal court. Additionally, and notwithstanding the CAFA-fueled substantial increase in federal forum selection for state-law-based class actions that formerly did not qualify for federal court jurisdiction (either through original federal filing by plaintiffs; or, more frequently, by removal of state-filed class actions to federal court by defendants), the states' class action jurisprudence remains highly relevant. This is particularly true for the more populous or influential states, such as California, Massachusetts, Ohio, Illinois, Texas, and Florida, which have a longstanding class action tradition, a highly developed class action jurisprudence, may have specialized Rules of Court for class actions and other complex cases, and which, the sea change wrought by CAFA notwithstanding, will likely continue to preside over a substantial number of significant class action cases.

The issuance by state courts of a number of key issues summarized in this survey and the Supreme Court's rulings in *Smith, et al. v. Bayer Corp.*, 131 S. Ct. 2368 (2011), and in *TransUnion LLC v. Ramirez*, 141 S. Ct. 2190 (2021), demonstrate the continuing important role of state courts and their class action-related decisions. In *Smith*, the Supreme Court found that the federal court's rejection of Rule 23 certification did not preclude later adjudication in state court of a consumer's class certification motion because federal and state certification rules are not identical and because the state court plaintiff was not a party to the federal suit.

Significantly impacting the scope of class action claims potentially litigable in the state courts is the United States Supreme Court's 2013 opinion in *American Express Co. v. Italian Colors Restaurant* holding that contractual arbitration clauses containing class action waivers are enforceable notwithstanding potentially prohibitive transaction costs in arbitrating individual claims one by one. The impact of arbitration on class certification is an especially active and volatile area.

In 2014, the state courts continued to address the procedural and enforceability issues following from arbitration clauses, such as whether courts, or arbitrators, are to decide whether claims can be arbitrated on a class basis. *See, e.g.*, *Sandquist v. Lebo Automotive, Inc.*, 228 Cal. App. 4th 615 (Cal. App. June 25, 2014) (reversing dismissal of class action in favor of arbitrator determination on class certification). This area will continue to be active and produce a variety of outcomes in the future.

Of late, the United States Supreme Court has turned a critical eye upon the bounds of personal jurisdiction. In *Bristol-Myers Squibb v. Superior Court of California*, 137 S. Ct. 1773 (2017) (*BMS*), the Court explicitly limited the scope of adjudication of mass tort actions by state courts in states where no defendant resides, finding adjudication under those circumstances incompatible with the Fourteenth Amendment due process clause. The Court further clarified that specific personal jurisdiction principles apply to nonresident plaintiffs whose claims have been joined with those of in-state plaintiffs and held that state courts cannot assert jurisdiction over such claims unless each nonresident plaintiff can establish a connection between the forum and their specific claims at issue. It will be interesting to see how the Supreme Court addresses related issues when they come before it.

Amendments to Federal Rule 23(c) modernizing the class notice requirements and to Rule 23(e) providing courts with more specific guidance on the class action settlement approval process, which became effective in December 2018, are just beginning to impact class action practice and practitioners are well-advised to internalize them and update their notice and settlement strategies and techniques.

In the past several years virtually all federal circuits have endorsed the use of Rule 23(c)(4) "issue" classes to surgically certify specific common questions of law or fact. *See, e.g., Martin v. Behr Dayton Thermal Products LLC*, 896 F.3d 405, 413 (C.A.6 (Ohio), 2018); *In re Behr Dayton Thermal Products Litigation*, 2022 WL 3328407, at *3 (S.D. Ohio, 2022) (identifying the seven questions certified for 23(c)(4) class treatment).

—Elizabeth Cabraser and Fabrice Vincent

ALABAMA

1. COMPARISON WITH RULE 23 OF THE FEDERAL RULES OF CIVIL PROCEDURE

Rule 23 of the Alabama Rules of Civil Procedure is essentially identical to Rule 23 of the Federal Rules of Civil Procedure as it appeared prior to the amendments of 1998. The language contained in section 23(e) of the federal rule is more detailed than section 23(e) of the Alabama rule. Moreover, the 1998 amendment to the federal rules added section 23(f), which permits interlocutory appeals of certification rulings. As noted below, the Alabama Legislature in 1999 enacted legislation providing for a right of appeal from such decisions. Ala. Code § 6-5-642. There also is no corollary to sections 23(g) and (h) of the federal rule in Alabama's rule. Nevertheless, decisions under the federal rule have been described by the Alabama Supreme Court as "authoritative" in cases governed by the Alabama rule. *Wyeth, Inc. v. Blue Cross & Blue Shield of Ala.*, 42 So. 3d 1216, 1221 (Ala. 2010), citing *Mitchell v. H & R Block, Inc.*, 783 So. 2d 812, 816 (Ala. 2000); *Ryan v. Patterson*, 23 So. 3d 12, 17 (Ala. 2009); *Reynolds Metals Co. v. Hill,* 825 So. 2d 100, 104 n.1 (Ala. 2002), citing *Cutler v. Orkin Exterminating Co.*, 770 So. 2d 67 (Ala. 2000); *Adams v. Robertson*, 676 So. 2d 1265, 1268 (Ala. 1995), writ dismissed, 520 U.S. 83, 117 S. Ct. 1028, 137 L. Ed. 2d 203 (1997).

2. OTHER LEGISLATION IMPACTING ON CLASS ACTIONS

In 1999, the Alabama Legislature enacted, and the Governor signed into law, two bills addressing class action issues. Those statutes should be read carefully because they include provisions that govern important procedures for class actions in Alabama, including certain deadlines, a planning conference, potential stays of certain types of discovery, requirements for any class-certification order, and appeals. As codified, they provide as follows:

Ala. Code § 6-5-641. *Certification of classes*

(a) No class of civil litigants shall be certified or recognized by any court of the State of Alabama unless there shall have been compliance with the procedures for certification of the class set forth in this article.

(b) As soon as practicable after the commencement of an action in which claims or defenses are purported to be asserted on behalf of or against a class, or as soon as practicable after such assertions in an amended pleading but in no event prior to the time allowed by law for each party (including, but not limited to, counterclaim, cross-claim and third-party defendants) to file an answer or other pleading responsive to the complaint, counterclaim, cross-claim, or third party claim, the court shall hold a conference among all named parties to the action for the purpose of establishing a schedule, in the same manner and to the same extent contemplated by Ala. R. Civ. P. 16, for any discovery in which the parties may wish to engage which is both (1) allowed by Ala. R. Civ. P. 26-37, and (2) germane to the issue of whether the requested class should or should not be certified. At this conference, the court may set a date for a hearing on the issue of class certification, but such hearing may not be set sooner than 90 days after the date on which the court issues its scheduling order pursuant to the conference unless a shorter time is agreed to by all parties.

(c) Upon motion of any party, the court shall, except for good cause shown and even then only if the interests of justice require that it not do so, stay all discovery directed solely to the merits of the claims or defenses in the action until the court shall have made its decision regarding certification of the class. In considering such a motion, the court shall consider whether any prejudice to the plaintiff exists because of the filing by the defendant of a Rule 56 motion for summary judgment, prior to the court's decision regarding class certification.

(d) The court shall, on motion of any party, hold a full evidentiary hearing on class certification. The hearing shall be recorded, and all named parties to the action shall be given notice of the date, time, and place of the hearing by written notification given to the party's attorney (or if appearing *pro se*, to the party) no later than 60 days prior to the date set for the hearing. At the hearing, the parties shall be allowed to present, in the same manner as at trial, any admissible evidence in support of or in opposition to the certification of the class.

(e) When deciding whether a requested class is to be certified, the court shall determine, by employing a rigorous analysis, if the party or parties requesting class certification have proved its or their entitlement to class certification under Ala. R. Civ. P. 23. The burden of coming forward with such proof shall at all times be on the party or parties seeking certification, and if such proof shall not have been adduced, the court shall not order certification of the class. In making this determination, the court shall analyze all factors required by Ala. R. Civ. P. 23 for certification of a class and shall not order certification unless all such factors shall have been established. In announcing its determination, the court shall place in the record of the action a written order addressing all such factors and specifying the evidence, or lack of evidence, on which the court has based its decision with regard to whether each such factor has been established. In so doing, the court may treat a factor as having been established if all parties to the action have so stipulated on the record and if the court shall be satisfied that such factor could be proven to have been established.

(f) Nothing in this act shall affect, or be construed to affect, Ala. R. Civ. P. 12 or Ala. R. Civ. P. 56, including the provisions of Rule 56(f).

Ala. Code § 6-5-642. ***Appeal of certification order***

A Court's order certifying a class or refusing to certify a class action shall be appealable in the same manner as a final order to the appellate court which would otherwise have jurisdiction over the appeal from a final order in the action. Such appeal may only be filed within 42 days of the order certifying or refusing to certify the class. The filing of such appeal, the failure to file an appeal, or the affirmance of the certification or denial order shall in no way affect the right of any party, after the entry of final judgment, to appeal the earlier certification of, or refusal to certify, the class. If the appeal is not the first appeal taken by the party, the subsequent appeal shall be based upon the record at the time of the final judgment and shall be considered by the court only to the extent that either the facts or controlling law relevant to certification have changed from that which existed or controlled at the time of the earlier certification or refusal to certify. During the pendency of any such appeal, the action in the trial court shall be stayed in all respects. Following adjudication on appeal (or, if the initial appeal is to an intermediate appellate court, adjudication of the action on any writ of certiorari granted by the Supreme Court of Alabama), if the class is not to be certified, the stay in the trial court shall automatically dissolve and the trial court may proceed to adjudicate any remaining individual claims or defenses. If, after such appeal or procedure on writ of certiorari, the class is to be certified, the stay shall likewise dissolve and the trial court shall proceed with adjudication on the merits, except that the trial court shall at all times prior to the entry of a final order retain jurisdiction to revisit the certification issues upon motion of a party and to order decertification of the class if during the litigation of the case it shall become evident to the court that the action is no longer reasonably maintainable as a class action pursuant to the factors enumerated in Ala. R. Civ. P. 23(b).

3. CASE LAW INTERPRETING RULE 23

In order to qualify for class treatment, claims must satisfy all of the requirements of Rule 23(a) and all of the requirements of at least one subsection of Rule 23(b), and the named plaintiff must have standing to bring the claims. *Wyeth, Inc. v. Blue Cross & Blue Shield of Ala.*, 42 So. 3d 1216, 1219 (Ala. 2010), citing *Smart Prof'l Photocopy Corp. v. Childers-Sims*, 850 So. 2d 1245, 1248-49 (Ala. 2002); *Ryan v. Patterson*, 23 So. 3d 12, 17 (Ala. 2009), citing *Smart Prof'l Photocopy Corp.*, 850 So. 2d at 1248-49; *Houston County Health Care Auth. v. Williams*, 961 So. 2d 795, 803, 805 (Ala. 2006); *Univ. Fed. Ins. Co. v. Grayson*, 878 So. 2d 280, 285 (Ala. 2003); *Ex parte Exide Corp.*, 678 So. 2d 773, 774 (Ala. 1996); *Ex parte Blue Cross & Blue Shield of Ala.*, 582 So. 2d 469, 474-76 (Ala. 1991); *Rowan v. First Bank of Boaz*, 476 So. 2d 44, 46 (Ala. 1985). The burden is on the party seeking certification to demonstrate that all requirements have been met. *Latham v. Dep't of Corr.*, 927 So. 2d 815, 822 (Ala. 2005); *Rowan v. First Bank of Boaz*, 476 So. 2d at 46. Except in exceptional circumstances, the movant must demonstrate by sufficient, admissible evidence, and not simply through its pleadings, that the Rule 23 requirements are met. *Ex parte Citicorp Acceptance Co.*, 715 So. 2d 199, 203-04 (Ala. 1997); *Ex parte Green Tree Fin. Corp.*, 684 So. 2d 1302, 1307-09 (Ala. 1996); *Ex parte Blue Cross & Blue Shield of Ala.*, 582 So. 2d at 483. Moreover, a court may certify for class treatment only claims that have been properly alleged in the complaint. *Univ. Fed. Ins. Co. v. Grayson*, 878 So. 2d at 294; *Allstate Ins. Co. v. Ware*, 824 So. 2d 739, 745 (Ala. 2002).

The U.S. Supreme Court held in 1982 that a trial court must engage in a "rigorous analysis" in determining whether claims for which class treatment is sought do, in fact, meet the requirements of the federal rule. *Gen. Tel. Co. of the Southwest v. Falcon,* 457 U.S. 147, 161 (1982). Grounded in constitutional due process concerns, the demand for a rigorous analysis of how the evidence supports the conclusion that Rule 23 requirements have been met is reflected in the decisions of the Supreme Court of Alabama and in the 1999 amendments to the Alabama Code. *See* Ala. Code § 6-5-641(e); *Perdue v. Green,* 127 So. 3d 343 (Ala. 2013); *Eufaula Hosp. Corp. v. Lawrence*, 32 So. 3d 30, 34 (Ala. 2009), quoting *Mayflower Nat'l Life Ins. Co. v. Thomas*, 894 So. 2d 637, 641 (Ala. 2004); *Mitchell v. H & R Block, Inc.*, 783 So. 2d 812, 817 (Ala. 2000); *see also Gen. Motors Acceptance Corp. v. City of Red Bay,* 825 So. 2d 746, 748-50 (Ala. 2002); *Allstate Ins. Co. v. Ware*, 824 So. 2d at 745-46; *Ex parte Am. Bankers Life Assurance Co. of Fla.*, 715 So. 2d 186, 187-89 (Ala. 1997); *Rowan v. First Bank of Boaz*, 476 So. 2d at 45-46.

Section 6-5-641(e) expressly requires the trial court to issue "a written order addressing all such factors and specifying the evidence, or lack of evidence, on which the court has based its decision with regard to whether each such factor has been established." Where a defendant asserts affirmative defenses or compulsory counterclaims against members of an alleged class, the trial court must consider and address in its certification order the impact of such defenses and counterclaims in determining whether the requirements of Rule 23 have been met. *Gen. Motors Acceptance Corp. v. Massey*, 893 So. 2d 314, 319-20 (Ala. 2004); *U-Haul Co. of Ala., Inc. v. Johnson*, 893 So. 2d 307, 311-12 (Ala. 2004); *Compass Bank v. Snow*, 823 So. 2d 667, 678 (Ala. 2001). A court is also required to conduct a rigorous analysis of claims and parties added by plaintiff after a class has been certified to determine whether they are appropriate for class treatment. *Ex parte Caremark RX, Inc.*, 956 So. 2d 1117, 1126 (Ala. 2006). A court, however, is not always required to conduct a pre-certification evidentiary hearing. *See Perdue v. Green*, 127 So. 3d 343 (Ala. 2013) (citing *Ex Parte First Nat'l Bank of Jasper*, 717 So. 2d 342, 346 (Ala. 1997)).

In reaching its decision, the trial court may rely on facts to which all parties stipulate, if the court is satisfied that such facts could be proven. Ala. Code 6-5-641(e). Where the parties stipulate to relevant facts supporting certification, the statutory language "still requires the trial court to independently assess the factor to some degree." *Disch v. Hicks,* 900 So. 2d at 406. The court must also ensure that all parties have the opportunity to be heard on the motion for class certification. *Id.* In *Bill Heard Chevrolet Company v. Thomas*, 819 So. 2d 34 (Ala. 2001), the Supreme Court of Alabama reversed class certification because defendants had not been provided an adequate opportunity to contest certification. The court also took the opportunity to discourage the practice of entering a certification order drafted by counsel. *Bill Heard Chevrolet Co. v. Thomas*, 819 So. 2d at 41. In *CIT Communication Finance Corporation v. McFadden, Lyon & Rouse, L.L.C.*, 37 So. 3d 114 (Ala. 2009), the Supreme Court of Alabama affirmed the trial court's class-certification order even though the order was drafted by the plaintiff's counsel, but again strongly discouraged the practice. 37 So. 3d at 121-22. In the holding, the court noted that its decision in *Bill Heard* was based on factors other than the trial court's failure to draft its own order, such as the failure to provide the defendants with an opportunity to present their evidence in opposition to the proposed order. *Id.* These factors were not present in *CIT Communication Finance Corporation. Id.*

4. APPELLATE REVIEW

An order certifying a class will be reviewed by the appellate court for abuse of discretion, but the appellate court will review *de novo* the question of whether the trial court applied the correct legal standard in reaching the decision to grant certification. *Perdue v. Green*, 127 So. 3d 343 (Ala. 2013); *Baldwin Mutual Ins. Co. v. Edwards*, 63 So. 3d 1268, 1271 (Ala. 2010); *Wyeth, Inc. v. Blue Cross & Blue Shield of Ala.*, 42 So. 3d 1216, 1218-19 (Ala. 2010); *Ryan v. Patterson*, 23 So. 3d 12, 17 (Ala. 2009); *Univ. Fed. Credit Union v. Grayson,* 878 So. 2d 280, 286 (Ala. 2003); *Funliner of Ala., L.L.C. v. Pickard*, 873 So. 2d 198, 206 (Ala. 2003). It is an abuse of discretion for the trial court to certify a class when the movant fails to meet its burden of showing sufficient evidence that the claims meet all of the Rule 23 requirements. *Univ. Fed. Credit Union v. Grayson*, 878 So. 2d at 286. A trial court also abuses its discretion by failing to conduct a new class certification hearing when the movant materially changes the class definition. *Baldwin Mutual Ins. Co. v. Edwards*, 63 So. 3d at 1272; *Baldwin Mut. Ins. Co. v. McCain*, 176 So. 3d 1195 (Ala. 2015).

5. RULE 23 REQUIREMENTS

a. Rule 23(a)

i. Numerosity. The test is whether the number of members in the class is so numerous as to make joinder impracticable. Ala. R. Civ. P. 23(a)(1); *State Farm Fire & Casualty Co. v. W.R. Evans*, 956 So. 2d 390 (Ala. 2006); *Latham v. Dep't of Corr.*, 927 So. 2d 815 (Ala. 2005). No hard threshold has been established for the minimum number of class members necessary to meet this requirement. The class may not be so broadly defined as to include individuals who, on the evidence presented, were not damaged by the allegedly wrongful behavior at issue. *Ex parte Central Bank of the South*, 675 So. 2d 403 (Ala. 1996); *Ex parte Gold Kist, Inc.*, 646 So. 2d 1339 (Ala. 1994).

ii. Commonality. Commonality requires only that there be common questions of law or fact. Ala. R. Civ. P. 23(a)(2); *Univ. Fed. Credit Union v. Grayson,* 878 So. 2d 280 (Ala. 2003). Where essentially identical representations are made at different times to different class members but share a common thread and are redressable under the same theory of recovery, the test of commonality may be met. *Harbor Ins. Co. v. Blackwelder*, 554 So. 2d 329, 335 (Ala. 1989). In *General Motors Acceptance Corporation v. Dubose*, 834 So. 2d 67 (Ala. 2002), the court found that ambiguity in a lease contract precludes a finding of commonality because the ambiguity requires a determination of how each class member would interpret the lease language. 834 So. 2d at 71. On the other hand, in *CIT Communication Finance Corporation v. McFadden, Lyon, & Rouse, L.L.C.*, 37 So. 3d 114 (Ala. 2009), the court found that a class, which claimed that the defendant breached an unambiguous lease agreement, satisfied the commonality requirement for class certification because there would be no need for individualized evidence. 37 So. 3d at 23; *see also Hall v. Envtl. Litig. Grp., P.C.*, 248 So. 3d 949 (Ala. 2017). In *Barnhart v. Ingalls*, 275 So. 3d 1112 (Ala. 2018), however, the court held that, if common questions of law or fact predominate, the commonality requirement is satisfied, even if there would be a need for individualized evidence on an issue such as damages.

iii. Adequacy/Typicality. A class representative must be a member of the class he seeks to represent. *Ex parte Prudential Ins. Co. of Am.*, 721 So. 2d 1135 (Ala. 1998) (citing *Amason v. First State Bank of Lineville*, 369 So. 2d 547 (Ala. 1979)). Typicality is met if the named plaintiff's alleged injury "arises from or is directly related to a wrong to a class and that wrong to the class includes the wrong to the plaintiff." *Warehouse Home Furnishing Distrib., Inc. v. Whitson*, 709 So. 2d 1144, 1149 (Ala. 1997). The "relationship between the injury to the class representative and the conduct affecting the entire class of plaintiffs must be sufficient for the court to properly attribute a collective nature to the challenged conduct." *Id.* at 1149. The Alabama Court of Civil Appeals, however, has stated that "[t]ypicality may be satisfied even if there are factual distinctions between the claims of the named plaintiffs and those other class members." *Dickson Campers, Inc. v. City of Mobile*, 37 So. 3d 134, 147-48 (Ala. Civ. App. 2007). The Supreme Court of Alabama went farther in *Barnhart v. Ingalls*, 275 So. 3d 1112 (Ala. 2018), holding that a defect in the named plaintiff's claim, such as vulnerability to a statute of limitations defense, would not necessarily be fatal, at least not when other class members might also be vulnerable to the same defense. *But cf. Baldwin Mutual Ins. Co. v. McCain*, 260 So. 3d 801 (Ala. 2018) (holding that class representative could not meet the typicality and adequacy requirement when class representative appeared to be the only member of the class subject to a unique defense of res judicata). A class representative must suffer at least some injury similar to that of the class in order to satisfy the typicality requirement. *Banker v. Circuit City Stores, Inc.,* 7 So. 3d 992, 999 (Ala. 2008) (affirming the trial court's denial of class certification based on holding that named plaintiff's claims were not "typical of the putative class because [he] had not suffered any damage from the alleged wrongful conduct out of which" the class's claims arise). The named plaintiff should be able to understand the underlying theory of the claims and have no conflict of interest with absent class members. *Warehouse Home Furnishing Distrib., Inc. v. Whitson*, 709 So. 2d at 1149; *Cutler v. Orkin Exterminating Co.*, 770 So. 2d 67 (Ala. 2000) (holding named plaintiffs who did not have arbitration agreements with defendant could not adequately represent class members who signed arbitration provisions); *compare Dickson Campers, Inc. v. City of Mobile*, 37 So. 3d at 148 (holding trial court erred in denying class certification based on lack of typicality because, regardless of "[w]hether the businesses passed on the taxes to their customers or not, [the putative class members] all had the same legal claims against the City based on the same allegation that the taxes were invalid"). A named plaintiff may fail to meet the adequacy requirement if he fails to assert claims available to the class, but only if such failure has a detrimental effect on the claims or rights of absent class members. *See Regions Bank v. Lee*, 905 So. 2d 765 (Ala. 2004).

In 2003, the Supreme Court of Alabama vacated certification of defendant classes for lack of typicality, finding the juridical link theory insufficient to meet the typicality requirement where plaintiff class members alleged similar transactions, but with different defendants in the putative defendant class. *Funliner of Ala., L.L.C. v. Pickard,* 873 So. 2d at 217.

b. Rule 23(b)

The trial court must make clear, in its order certifying a class, which of the Rule 23(b) subsection's criteria are met in the case. *Ex parte Green Tree Fin. Corp.* 684 So. 2d 1302 (Ala. 1996).

i. Rule 23(b)(1)(A) and (1)(B). The requirements under Rule 23(b)(1) are met if separate actions by class members would create a risk of (A) inconsistent or varying adjudications with respect to individual class members that would establish incompatible standards of conduct for the party opposing the class, or (B) adjudications with respect to individual class members that would, as a practical matter, be dispositive of the interests of the other members not parties to the adjudications or substantially impair or impede their ability to protect their interests. Ala. R. Civ. P. 23(b)(1)(A) and (1)(B); *Ex parte Holland*, 692 So. 2d 811 (Ala. 1997).

Mandatory classes have been approved for challenging the validity of ordinances and taxes and actions by trust administrators. *See, e.g., Town of Eclectic v. Mays*, 547 So. 2d 96 (Ala. 1989); *Eagerton v. Williams*, 433 So. 2d 436 (Ala. 1983); *First Ala. Bank of Montgomery, N.A. v. Martin*, 381 So. 2d 32 (Ala. 1980). Although evidence of a limited fund against which class members and others may draw for compensatory and punitive damages can be a proper basis for finding the Rule 23(b)(1) requirement to be met, this requirement is not met when there is insufficient evidence of the defendant's financial condition and the test would require improper speculation on the part of the trial court as to the amount of compensatory and punitive damages a jury might award. *Ex parte Holland*, 692 So. 2d 811. It has been held to be an abuse of discretion for a trial court to certify a class under this prong of Rule 23 when the putative class seeks monetary damages. *Funliner of Ala., L.L.C. v. Pickard*, 873 So. 2d 198 (Ala. 2003) (holding that Rule 23(b)(1) "does not apply to actions seeking compensatory damages but is for actions in which only declaratory or injunctive relief is sought"). The court has also noted that the fact that a claim ultimately results in a monetary damage award does not prevent certification under Rule 23(b)(1) or (b)(2). *Perdue v. Green*, 127 So. 3d 343 (Ala. 2013); (citing *First Alabama Bank of Montgomery, N.A. v. Martin*, 425 So. 415, 423 (Ala. 1982)).

ii. Rule 23(b)(2). Where the relief sought is primarily equitable or injunctive in nature, the inclusion of a claim or settlement for money damages does not bar certification as a non-opt-out class under Rule 23(b)(2). *Warehouse Home Furnishing Distrib., Inc. v. Whitson*, 709 So. 2d 1144 (Ala. 1997); *Adams v. Robertson*, 676 So. 2d 1265 (Ala. 1995). Certification under this provision of Rule 23 will be reversed as an abuse of discretion, however, if monetary damages predominate over the equitable relief sought and do not flow out of a group injury. *Funliner of Ala., L.L.C. v. Pickard*, 873 So. 2d at 208-09; *Warehouse Home Furnishing Distrib., Inc. v. Whitson*, 709 So. 2d at 1151; *Adams v. Robertson*, 676 So. 2d at 1271. Three factors are to be considered in determining whether money damages predominate or are incidental for purposes of class certification: whether such damages (1) are of a kind to which class members would be automatically entitled; (2) can be computed by objective standards, and not standards dependent upon intangible and subjective differences of each class member's circumstances; and (3) would require additional hearings to determine. *Ryan v. Patterson*, 23 So. 3d 12, 21 (Ala. 2009). If a case meets the requirements of both Rule 23(b)(2) and Rule 23(b)(3), certification under (b)(2) is preferred. *Warehouse Home Furnishing Distrib., Inc. v. Whitson*, 709 So. 2d at 1151.

iii. Rule 23(b)(3). Rule 23(b)(3) encompasses the tests of predominance, manageability, and superiority. *Smart Prof'l Photocopy Corp. v. Childers-Sims*, 850 So. 2d 1245 (Ala. 2002). The test of predominance has been described as "whether proposed classes are sufficiently cohesive to warrant adjudication by representation." *Voyager Ins. Companies v. Whitson*, 867 So. 2d 1065, 1071 (Ala. 2003). Under Rule 23(b)(3), putative class representatives must demonstrate that the questions of law or fact common to the members of the class predominate over any questions affecting only individual members, and that a class action is superior to other available methods for the fair and efficient adjudication of the controversy. *Gen. Motors Acceptance Corp. v. Massey*, 893 So. 2d 314 (Ala. 2004). The Supreme Court of Alabama has upheld a trial court's denial of class certification for failure to meet the requirements of predominance, manageability, and superiority in a bait-and-switch consumer fraud action, *Butler v. Audio/Video Affiliates, Inc.*, 611 So. 2d 330 (Ala. 1992), and has vacated other certifications for lack of sufficient evidence generally. *See, e.g., Houston County Health Care Auth. v. Williams*, 961 So. 2d 795 (Ala. 2006); *Ex parte Green Tree Fin. Corp.*, 684 So. 2d 1302 (Ala. 1996).

Where the theory of recovery would require the court to inquire into the state of mind of individual class members, certification is not appropriate because individual issues predominate and class treatment is not the superior method for resolving the claims. *Avis Rent A Car Sys., Inc. v. Heilman*, 876 So. 2d 1111 (Ala. 2003); *Funliner of Ala., L.L.C. v. Pickard*, 873 So. 2d 198 (Ala. 2003) (unjust enrichment); *Smart Prof'l Photocopy Corp. v. Childers-Sims*, 850 So. 2d 1245 (unjust enrichment, money paid by mistake, and money had and received). In *State Farm Fire & Casualty Co. v. W.R. Evans*, 956 So. 2d 390 (Ala. 2006), the Supreme Court of Alabama vacated the trial court's class certification order on the plaintiffs' unjust enrichment and money had and received claims because the individual inquiries required to establish mistake on the part of the defendant would predominate over the common claims. 956 So. 2d at 401-03.

Where claims arise from terms of a written contract that are uniform for all class members, certification may be appropriate. *CIT Commc'n Fin. Corp. v. McFadden, Lyon, & Rouse, L.L.C.*, 37 So. 3d 114 (Ala. 2009); *Alfa Life Ins. Corp. v. Johnson*, 822 So. 2d 400 (Ala. 2001). A threshold issue in such cases, however, is whether the uniform contract terms are ambiguous. *Univ. Fed. Credit Union v. Grayson*, 878 So. 2d 280, 292-93 (Ala. 2003). A finding of ambiguity in the contract language will defeat predominance if the ambiguity necessitates individual inquiry into how class members interpreted or understood the ambiguous terms or otherwise requires consideration of extrinsic evidence unique to individual transactions. *Avis Rent A Car Sys., Inc. v. Heilman*, 876 So. 2d 1111; *Reynolds Metals Co. v. Hill*, 825 So. 2d 100 (Ala. 2002); *Compass Bank v. Snow*, 823 So. 2d 667 (Ala. 2001); *Mann v. GTE Mobilnet of Birmingham, Inc.*, 730 So. 2d 150 (Ala. 1999); *Lackey v. Central Bank of the South*, 710 So. 2d 419 (Ala. 1998). Predominance may also be defeated if individual inquiry is required into the circumstances surrounding the creation or performance of the contracts. *Alfa Life Ins. Corp. v. Hughes*, 861 So. 2d 1088 (Ala. 2003); *see also Nat'l Security Fire & Casualty Co. v. DeWitt*, 85 So. 3d 355 (Ala. 2011) (holding that the predominance and superiority requirements of Rule 23(b)(3) were not met in a breach-of-contract action where litigation over the defendant's alleged non-performance would likely involve the presentation of evidence regarding thousands of individual claims); *Eufaula Hosp. Corp. v. Lawrence*, 32 So. 3d 30 (Ala. 2009) (holding that the individualized determinations necessary to calculate a reasonable charge for medical services rendered by the defendants overwhelmed class cohesiveness for the plaintiffs' breach of contract claims).

While not barring certification of fraud claims *per se*, the Supreme Court of Alabama has noted that certification of such claims under Rule 23(b)(3) is difficult, given the necessity of individualized evidence of representations made, reliance (or lack thereof), and facts giving rise to a duty to disclose. *Houston County Health Care Auth. v. Williams*, 961 So. 2d 795, 804 (Ala. 2006); *Regions Bank v. Lee*, 905 So. 2d 765 (Ala. 2004); *Univ. Fed. Credit Union v. Grayson,* 878 So. 2d 280; *Alfa Life Ins. Corp. v. Hughes*, 861 So. 2d 1088; *Voyager Ins. Companies v. Whitson*, 867 So. 2d 1065 (Ala. 2003); *Reynolds Metal Co. v. Hill,* 825 So. 2d 100; *Ex parte Household Retail Services, Inc.*, 744 So. 2d. 871 (Ala. 1999) ("this Court has not thus far adopted a blanket prohibition against the certification of a fraud class action"); *Ex parte Gov't Employees Ins. Co.*, 729 So. 2d 299 (Ala. 1999); *Ex parte Exxon Corp*., 725 So. 2d 930, 933, n.3 (Ala. 1998); *Ex parte AmSouth Bancorporation,* 717 So. 2d 357 (Ala. 1998). The court will consider whether proof of reliance in a case involves predominating individual issues of fact and, in so doing, it will use the same standard as federal courts—namely, whether there was a material variation in the representations made or in the kinds or degrees of reliance by the persons to whom they were addressed. *Ex parte Household Retail Services, Inc.*, 744 So. 2d. 871, 881 (Ala. 1999). In *CVS Caremark Corp. v. Lauriello*, 175 So. 3d 596 (Ala. 2014), the Supreme Court of Alabama affirmed the certification of a fraud claim as a nationwide class action, finding that the unique facts of the case rendered questions of variation in the representations made or in the kinds or degrees of reliance by individual class members irrelevant. In that case, the class-based fraud claim rested upon alleged misrepresentations made to counsel in the settlement of a prior class action to induce counsel to accept a reduced settlement offer. Because the representations were made to a class's agents, the court found the case to be distinguishable from those in which the reliance of individual class members was at issue.

The Supreme Court of Alabama has also held that the predominance of individual issues precludes certification on claims of negligent or wanton supervision and training. *Univ. Fed. Credit Union v. Grayson,* 878 So. 2d 280; *Voyager Ins. Companies v. Whitson*, 867 So. 2d 1065; *Alfa Life Ins. Corp. v. Hughes*, 861 So. 2d 1088. Similarly, absent evidence that would support a finding of a class-wide fiduciary duty, claims for breach of such a duty are not susceptible to class treatment because of the necessity of making individual inquiries in order to determine the existence of a fiduciary relationship. *Univ. Fed. Credit Union v. Grayson*, 878 So. 2d 280.

In undertaking an analysis under Rule 23(b)(3), a trial court may not consider the merits of plaintiffs' claims because class certification is a procedural issue distinct from the merits. *Mitchell v. H & R Block, Inc*., 783 So. 2d 812 (Ala. 2000). The court should, however, analyze the elements of the causes of action and defenses asserted in order to determine whether the requirements of Rule 23 can be met. *Univ. Fed. Credit Union v. Grayson,* 878 So. 2d 280; *Smart Prof'l Photocopy Corp. v. Childers-Sims,* 850 So. 2d 1245 (Ala. 2002).

6. MISCELLANEOUS COMMENTS

a. Arbitration and Class Actions

In 1998, the Supreme Court of Alabama held that class-wide arbitration is not permitted absent an arbitration agreement permitting the disposition of claims in that manner. *Med Ctr. Cars, Inc. v. Smith*, 727 So. 2d 9, 33 (Ala. 1998). The court concluded that to require arbitration on a class-wide basis without such an agreement would alter the terms of the parties' contract. *Id.*

In 2002, the Supreme Court of Alabama reversed an order compelling arbitration of a consumer claim on the grounds that, under *Med Center Cars, Inc. v. Smith*, the arbitration agreement would bar the consumer from bringing claims on behalf of a class and that such a prohibition under the facts of that case rendered the arbitration agreement unconscionable. *Leonard v. Terminix Int'l Co., L.P.*, 854 So. 2d 529 (Ala. 2002), *reh'g denied*, 854 So. 2d 529 (Ala. 2003). The court concluded that, because the cost of bringing an individual claim exceeded the potential recovery, the prohibition on a class action combined with other limitations on recoverable damages deprived the plaintiffs of any meaningful remedy. *Id.* In *Univ. Toyota & Univ. Chevrolet Buick GMC v. Hardeman*, 228 So. 3d 394 (Ala. 2017), however, the court again held that plaintiffs had no right to engage in class-action arbitration proceedings unless the arbitration agreement so provided. The court also observed that, although plaintiffs in that case had not argued that the arbitration agreements are unconscionable or otherwise invalid either because they do not specifically provide for class-action arbitration or because the chosen forum does not conduct class-action arbitration, "federal and state caselaw is clear . . . that such arguments have no merit." *Id.* at n.2; *see also Chambers v. Groome Transp. of Alabama,* 41 F. Supp. 3d 1327, 1353 (M.D. Ala. 2014) (discussing generally the effect of a valid arbitration agreement's silence as to the availability of class-wide relief in the arbitration forum, the court wrote that "the fact that it may 'be more efficient to proceed as a class' is not to say that the prohibition of class-action procedures is unconscionable under Alabama law"). Much may depend on whether the parties agreed to submit the question of arbitrability—namely, whether class-wide arbitration is or is not available—to the arbitrator. *See, e.g., Ala. Psychiatric Servs. P.C. v. Lazenby*, 2019 Ala. LEXIS 60; 2019 WL 2560096 (Ala. June 21, 2019).

b. Competing Class Actions

When competing class action complaints are filed in different courts, asserting essentially identical claims against a common defendant, the first case to be filed with class action allegations takes precedence and (at least as to competing actions pending in Alabama state courts) will preclude certification of similar or overlapping classes in other cases. *Ex parte The BOC Group, Inc.*, 823 So. 2d 1270 (Ala. 2001); *Grimes v. Liberty Nat'l Life Ins. Co.*, 726 So. 2d 615 (Ala. 1998); *Ex parte Harris,* 711 So. 2d 467 (Ala. 1998); *Ex parte First Nat'l Bank of Jasper*, 717 So. 2d 342 (Ala. 1997). Whether later-filed individual actions are to be abated depends on "a reasoned balance of the equities in each particular case." *Ex parte State Mut. Ins. Co.*, 715 So. 2d 207, 219 (Ala. 1997). In *Ex parte Speedee Cash of Ala., Inc.*, 806 So 2d 389 (Ala. 2001), the court found that when two potential class actions involved at least one identical issue of substantive law and had a common defendant, a stay of the second-filed suit was needed to prevent the risk of inconsistent adjudication on the common issue. In *Ex parte AmSouth Bank*, 735 So. 2d 1151 (Ala. 1999), the court extended this rule to a situation in which the first-filed case was pending in a federal court in Alabama.

c. Settlement of Class Actions

Pursuant to Rule 23(e), there can be no settlement of a class action without the trial court's approval, and the burden is on the proponents of the settlement to show that it is "fair, adequate, and reasonable." *Adams v. Robertson*, 676 So. 2d 1265, 1272-73 (Ala. 1995). In determining whether to approve a settlement, a trial court may consider the following factors: (1) the likelihood of success at trial; (2) the range of possible recovery; (3) the point on or below the range of possible recovery at which the settlement is fair, adequate, and reasonable; (4) the complexity, expense, and duration of the litigation; (5) the substance and amount of opposition to the settlement; (6) the stage of the proceedings at which the settlement was achieved; (7) the financial ability of the defendant(s) to withstand a greater judgment and the potential for a judgment or judgments in an amount or amounts likely to trigger due process considerations relating to punitive damages; and (8) whether proper notice was given. *Id.* at 1273; *see also Perdue v. Green*, 127 So. 3d 343, 356 (Ala. 2013); Even where a trial court properly considers these factors, however, the court will exceed its discretion by approving a settlement agreement that is "adverse to the enactments of the legislature, and is, therefore, illegal and void." *Perdue v. Green*, 127 So. 3d at 356, 358.

In 2004, the Supreme Court of Alabama held that the statutory language requiring the court to conduct a rigorous analysis before certifying a class, Ala. Code § 6-5-641(e), applies to certification of a settlement class just as it does to a class that is certified in a fully adversarial proceeding. *Disch v. Hicks,* 900 So. 2d 399, 405 (Ala. 2004). This applies even though the parties stipulate to factors pertinent to the Rule 23 analysis. *Id.* at 406. Section 6-5-641(e)'s requirement of a comprehensive written order from the trial court applies to orders certifying settlement classes as well as to orders certifying classes where certification is contested by the parties. *Disch v. Hicks*, 900 So. 2d at 406–08.

d. Class Actions and Individual Claims

A class action settlement, whether in state or federal court, can serve as a prior judgment on the merits for purposes of *res judicata. Ala. Dept. of Transp. v. Price*, 854 So. 2d 59 (Ala. 2003); *Providian Nat'l Bank v. Pritchett*, 846 So. 2d 1072 (Ala. 2002); *see also Pharmacia Corp. v. Suggs*, 932 So. 2d 95 (Ala 2005) (holding that plaintiffs' acceptance of settlement in related federal class action mooted their individual claims in state court action and, in turn, deprived state court of subject-matter jurisdiction); *Solomon v. Liberty Nat'l Life Ins. Co.*, 953 So. 2d 1211 (Ala. 2006) (holding that, due to court's continuing jurisdiction, later filed individual action constituted an impermissible collateral attack on settlement). The court will, however, look at the terms of the class notice and release language in determining whether specific claims are barred or released by the settlement. *Id.* In *AmerUs Life Insurance Co. v. Smith*, 937 So. 2d 510 (Ala. 2006), the Supreme Court of Alabama held that although plaintiffs had not opted out of the class settlement and were bound to the terms of the release, they were not precluded from asserting claims that did not fall within the description of those claims barred by the release. 937 So. 2d at 515.

In *Ex parte Green Tree Acceptance, Inc.*, 767 So. 2d 1097 (Ala. 2000), the Supreme Court of Alabama held that a defendant seeking to abate a later-filed individual action must seek relief from the court having jurisdiction over the earlier-filed class action rather than the court in which the individual action was pending, especially given the failure to plead a defense based on abatement. In *New York Life Insurance Co. v. Griffin*, 794 So. 2d 1072 (Ala. 2001), the Supreme Court of Alabama held that because the plaintiff had been a member of a settlement class and had not opted out, he was precluded from subsequently asserting similar claims in an individual action. In *Greene v. Jefferson County Comm'n,* 13 So. 3d 901 (Ala. 2008), the Supreme Court of Alabama held that members of several subclasses in a previous class action lawsuit were barred from maintaining a new class action asserting similar claims. 13 So. 3d at 912-13.

The Supreme Court of Alabama recently held that when a class representative settles his or her individual claims after a class has been certified, the remaining class members still "should have the opportunity to determine whether a new named plaintiff should be certified." *Ala. Mut. Ins. Corp. v. City of Vernon*, 2013 Ala. LEXIS 146, *12–13 (Ala. 2013) (quoting *Corbitt v. Mangum*, 523 So. 2d 348, 351 (Ala. 1981) ("[w]hen the . . . court certified the propriety of the class action, the class of unnamed persons described in the certification acquired a legal status separate from the interest asserted by [the named representative]. Consequently . . . the claims of the class were not extinguished because [the named representative's] claim subsequently failed.") (citations omitted)). It is for the trial court, however, to decide "whether to allow the class members to amend their complaint and substitute a new named plaintiff." *Id.* Further, if a new class representative is substituted, the trial court must then "determine whether that plaintiff meets the adequacy requirements in Rule 23(a), Ala. R. Civ. P., so as to represent the class." *Id.*

e. Certification of Multi-state Classes

Although multi-state classes are not prohibited in Alabama courts, the trial court must conduct a rigorous analysis of the choice-of-law issues raised by a motion to certify a multi-state class. *Ex parte Exxon Corp.*, 725 So. 2d 930 (Ala. 1998). If adjudication of class members' claims in a Rule 23(b)(3) case would require application of the laws of multiple states, then the court must further determine whether such application would defeat predominance, superiority, and manageability. *Id.; Ex parte Green Tree Fin. Corp.*, 723 So. 2d 6 (Ala. 1998); *Mut. Sav. Life Ins. Co. v. James River Corp. of Va.*, 716 So. 2d 1172 (Ala. 1998); *see also Wyeth, Inc. v. Blue Cross & Blue Shield of Ala.*, 42 So. 3d 1216, 1225-26 (Ala. 2010) (vacating the trial court's order that certified a nationwide class of plaintiffs' unjust enrichment claims, because the plaintiffs failed to establish that common questions of law predominated their claims).

f. Pre-certification Discovery

Section 6-5-641(c) provides for a stay of all discovery related *solely* to the merits of the claims or defenses, upon motion of any party, until after the court makes a decision as to class certification. Ala. Code § 6-5-641(c). The effect of this provision is to shift the burden from the responding party to the requesting party who, in opposing the motion to stay, must "show at least one way that the requested discovery is directed to the issues of class certification." *Ex parte CIT Commc'n Fin. Corp.,* 897 So. 2d 296, 301 (Ala. 2004).

g. Attorneys' Fees

Alabama courts may apply either the common-fund or common-benefit theory to award attorneys' fees in class actions. *Ala. Alcoholic Beverage Control Bd. v. City of Pelham*, 855 So. 2d 1070 (Ala. 2003); *City of Birmingham v. Horn*, 810 So. 2d 667 (Ala. 2001).

In *Union Fidelity Life Insurance Co. v. McCurdy*, 781 So. 2d 186 (Ala. 2001), the Supreme Court of Alabama held that the trial court committed an abuse of discretion in using a common-fund theory to award class counsel $915,000 as part of a class settlement. While the potential class recovery was $4.5 million, the court received only 113 claims, resulting in disbursements of approximately $4,500. *Union Fid. Life Ins. Co. v. McCurdy*, 781 So. 2d 186. In light of such low class member participation, the common-fund theory was deemed inappropriate and an alternative lodestar method should have been employed. *Id.* Further, the lack of class member participation must be given great weight in any lodestar calculation and warrants against a significant multiplier. *Id.*

In *Lawler v. Johnson*, No. 1151347, ___ So. 3d ___, 2017 WL 4707517 (Ala. Oct. 20, 2017), the Supreme Court of Alabama vacated a $124 million attorneys' fee award in connection with a class action settlement. The court first held that objectors need not have been intervenors to have standing to appeal the denial of their objections to a class settlement, adopting the rationale of the

U.S. Supreme Court in *Devlin v. Scardelletti*, 536 U.S. 1 (2002), and applying that ruling to all class actions, not just to those in which class members do not have the right to opt out. The court took issue with the trial court's having required objections to class counsel's fee request before the fee application was required to be filed, the short time period between the filing of the fee application and the approval hearing, and the lack of specific information in the fee application regarding the amount of time expended by class counsel and the nature of the work that was done.

h. *Ex Parte* Certifications

In the 1990s, some Alabama trial courts made a practice of issuing *ex parte* or "conditional" certifications, entered at the outset of a case and often without notice to the defendant, as a means of dealing with competing class actions. *Ex parte Voyager Guar. Ins. Co.*, 669 So. 2d 198, 200 (Ala. Civ. App. 1995). Such certifications are no longer available in trial courts as a means of avoiding the rigorous analysis required under *General Telephone Co. of the Southwest v. Falcon*, 457 U.S. 147 (1982). *Ex parte Frontier Corp.*, 709 So. 2d 1197 (Ala. 1998); *Ex parte Citicorp Acceptance Co., Inc.*, 715 So. 2d 199 (Ala. 1997). Classes may be certified only upon a determination by the trial court, after a full evidentiary demonstration and legal analysis, that all of the requirements of Rule 23 have been met. *Ex parte Mercury Fin. Corp. of Ala.*, 715 So. 2d 196, 198 (Ala. 1997); *see also Ex parte Fed. Express Corp.*, 718 So. 2d 13 (Ala. 1998); *Ex parte Prudential Ins. Co. of Am.*, 721 So. 2d 1135 (Ala. 1998); *Ex parte First Nat'l Bank of Jasper*, 717 So. 2d 342 (Ala. 1997).

7. CONTACTING ABSENT CLASS MEMBERS

Alabama state courts have not addressed communications with putative absent class members under Rule 23. Alabama federal courts, however, have acknowledged the general right to contact putative class members under Rule 23, while recognizing the court's right to limit such contacts when abuse occurs. *Cox Nuclear Medicine v. Gold Cup Coffee Services, Inc.*, 214 F.R.D. 696, 697 (S.D. Alabama 2003); *Edwards v. Accredited Home Lenders*, 2008 WL 176364, at *1 (S.D. Ala. April 11, 2008).[1] Courts should not restrict communications with putative class members without a clear record evidencing that the communications have the potential to be abusive and interfere with the rights of the parties. *See Cox Nuclear Medicine*, 214 F.R.D. at 697 (citing *Gulf Oil Co. v. Bernard*, 452 U.S. 89, 101 (1981)). Specifically, the moving party must present evidence that: (1) a particular form of communication has occurred or is threatened to occur; and (2) the communication is abusive and threatens the proper functioning of the litigation. *Id.* at 697–98. The following Alabama federal cases are instructive:

- In *Cox Nuclear Medicine v. Gold Cup Coffee Services, Inc.*, the court denied the plaintiff's request for an order requiring the defendant to show cause why the court should not impose sanctions for its contacts with putative class members—sending letters to its customers informing them of the product's defect and offering a check, which if cashed released the defendant form liability. 14 F.R.D. at 697–98. The court held that the defendant's failure to mention the class action in its letters was not abusive because the action did not seek damages greater than what the defendant proposed in the contact. *Id.* at 699.

[1] Under Alabama law, decisions under Rule 23 of the Federal Rules of Civil Procedure are persuasive because the state and federal rules are almost identical. Wyeth, Inc. v. Blue Cross & Blue Shield of Ala., 42 So. 3d 1216, 1221 (Ala. 2010).

- In *Edwards v. Accredited Home Lenders*, defendants filed a motion to modify the protective order to limit plaintiffs' communications with putative absent class members. 2008 WL 176364, at *1 (S.D. Ala. April 11, 2008). Defendants sought to impose a requirement of seven days' notice of the proposed communication to the opposing side. *Id.* at *2. The court denied the motion because defendants did not show evidence of abuse such that the court would have good cause to limit the communications in this manner. *Id.* at *3.

Additionally, Alabama federal courts have addressed party contact with putative class members under section 216(b) of Title 29 of the United States Code, which authorizes opt-in collective actions as part of the Fair Labor Standards Act. *See Longcrier v. HL-A Co.*, 595 F. Supp. 2d 1218, 1221 (S.D. Alabama 2008). These courts have analogized such contacts to those under Rule 23 and have taken similar actions, such as refusing to restrict the communications without a clear record of abuse and issuing protective orders when such evidence is present. *See Logcrier*, 595 F. Supp. 2d at 1225–28 (holding defendant's contacts to be abusive and issuing a protective order limiting defendant's future communications with potential class members); *West v. Mando America Corp.*, No. 3:08-CV-570-WKW, 2009 WL 4493442, at *2 (M.D. Ala. Oct. 2, 2008) (denying defendant's motion to restrict plaintiff's contact with potential plaintiffs because the advertisements were "not misleading").

RULE 23 OF THE ALABAMA RULES OF CIVIL PROCEDURE

RULE 23. CLASS ACTIONS

(a) *Prerequisites to a class action.* One or more members of a class may sue or be sued as representative parties on behalf of all only if (1) the class is so numerous that joinder of all members is impracticable, (2) there are questions of law or fact common to the class, (3) the claims or defenses of the representative parties are typical of the claims or defenses of the class, and (4) the representative parties will fairly and adequately protect the interests of the class.

(b) *Class actions maintainable.* An action may be maintained as a class action if the prerequisites of subdivision (a) are satisfied, and in addition:

(1) the prosecution of separate actions by or against individual members of the class would create a risk of

(A) inconsistent or varying adjudications with respect to individual members of the class which would establish incompatible standards of conduct for the party opposing the class, or

(B) adjudications with respect to individual members of the class which would as a practical matter be dispositive of the interests of the other members not parties to the adjudications or substantially impair or impede their ability to protect their interests; or

(2) the party opposing the class has acted or refused to act on grounds generally applicable to the class, thereby making appropriate final injunctive relief or corresponding declaratory relief with respect to the class as a whole; or

(3) the court finds that the questions of law or fact common to the members of the class predominate over any questions affecting only individual members, and that a class action is superior to other available methods for the fair and efficient adjudication of the controversy. The matters pertinent to the findings include: (A) the interest of members of the class in individually controlling the prosecution or defense of separate actions; (B) the extent and nature of any litigation concerning the controversy already commenced by or against members of the class; (C) the desirability or undesirability of concentrating the litigation of the claims in the particular forum; (D) the difficulties likely to be encountered in the management of a class action.

(c) *Determination by order whether class action to be maintained; notice; judgment; actions conducted partially as class actions.*

(1) At an early practicable time, consistent with Alabama statutory law, the court shall determine by order whether an action brought as a class action is to be so maintained. An order that grants or denies class certification may be altered or amended before final judgment.

(2) For any class certified under Rule 23(b)(1) or (b)(2), the court may direct appropriate notice to the class. For any class certified under Rule 23(b)(3) – or upon ordering notice under Rule 23(e) to a class proposed to be certified for purposes of settlement under

Rule 23(b)(3) – the court must direct to class members of the class the best notice that is practicable under the circumstances, including individual notice to all members who can be identified through reasonable effort. The notice may be by one or more of the following: United States mail, electronic means, or other appropriate means. The notice shall advise each member that (A) the court will exclude the member from the class if the member so requests by a specified date; (B) the judgment, whether favorable or not, will include all members who do not request exclusion; and (C) any member who does not request exclusion may, if the member desires, enter an appearance through counsel.

(3) The judgment in an action maintained as a class action under subdivision (b)(1) or (b)(2), whether or not favorable to the class, shall include and describe those whom the court finds to be members of the class. The judgment in an action maintained as a class action under subdivision (b)(3), whether or not favorable to the class, shall include and specify or describe those to whom the notice provided in subdivision (c)(2) was directed, and who have not requested exclusion, and whom the court finds to be members of the class.

(4) When appropriate (A) an action may be brought or maintained as a class action with respect to particular issues, or (B) a class may be divided into subclasses and each subclass treated as a class, and the provisions of this rule shall then be construed and applied accordingly.

(d) *Orders in conduct of actions.* In the conduct of actions to which this rule applies, the court may make appropriate orders: (1) determining the course of proceedings or prescribing measures to prevent undue repetition or complication in the presentation of evidence or argument; (2) requiring, for the protection of the members of the class or otherwise for the fair conduct of the action, that notice be given in such manner as the court may direct to some or all of the members of any step in the action, or of the proposed extent of the judgment, or of the opportunity of members to signify whether they consider the representation fair and adequate, to intervene and present claims or defenses, or otherwise to come into the action; (3) imposing conditions on the representative parties or on the intervenors; (4) requiring that the pleadings be amended to eliminate therefrom allegations as to representation of absent persons, and that the action proceed accordingly; (5) dealing with similar procedural matters. The order may be combined with an order under Rule 16, and may be altered or amended as may be desirable from time to time.

(e) *Settlement, voluntary dismissal, or compromise.* The claims, issues, or defenses of a certified class – or a class proposed to be certified for purposes of settlement – may be settled, voluntarily dismissed, or compromised only with the court's approval, and notice of the proposed dismissal or compromise shall be given to all members of the class in such manner as the court directs.

(dc) District court rule. Rule 23 does not apply in the district courts. (Amended eff. 10195.)

This chapter has been updated by Jim Pewitt. Jim has extensive experience in complex business litigation. He is currently the managing member of James P. Pewitt, LLC, in Birmingham, Alabama.

ALASKA

1. COMPARISON OF ALASKA RULE OF CIVIL PROCEDURE 23 WITH FEDERAL RULE OF CIVIL PROCEDURE 23

The provisions of Alaska Rule of Civil Procedure 23(a)–(e) are largely identical to those of Federal Rule of Civil Procedure 23(a)–(e), except insofar as certain stylistic changes were made to the federal rule in 2007. Two substantive differences should be noted.

First, Alaska has not adopted a version of Fed. R. Civ. P. 23(f) allowing a ***discretionary*** appeal of a class action ruling.

Second, while most of Alaska Rule 23 closely parallels Federal Rule of Civil Procedure 23, Alaska Rule 23(e) diverges. As adopted in 1976, Alaska Rule 23(e) consists of one relatively brief sentence: "A class action shall not be dismissed or compromised without the approval of the court and notice of the proposed dismissal or compromise shall be given to all members of the class in such manner as the court directs."

In contrast, the current version of Fed. R. Civ. P. 23(e) is relatively lengthy, with multiple subparts detailing procedural requirements for the parties' provision of information to the court, the court's explanation of grounds for its decision to give notice, approval of the proposal or settlement at issue, identification of any agreements made in connection with the proposal, and additional procedures granting class members new opportunities to object or be excluded. *See Triem v. Kake Tribal Corp.,* Unpublished Memorandum Opinion and Judgment, 2024 WL 181538 (Jan. 17, 2024).

2. CASE LAW INTERPRETING RULE 23

a. Rule 23(a)

i. Numerosity. In *State Dep't of Revenue v. Andrade*, 23 P.3d 58, 67 (Alaska 2001), the Alaska Supreme Court affirmed the trial court's holding that the numerosity requirement was met in a class action with at least twenty named plaintiffs who asserted that there were potentially hundreds of other similarly situated individuals affected by the challenged agency action.

ii. Commonality. The commonality requirement is not fulfilled unless the questions which may be jointly tried are "sufficiently numerous and substantial to make the class action advantageous to the judicial process as well as to the litigants." *Alsop v. State*, 586 P.2d 1236, 1241 (Alaska 1978). In *Alsop*, the Alaska Supreme Court held a class action to be inappropriate on commonality grounds where property owners sought a declaratory judgment that they were owed reimbursement by the state for decreased access to their property caused by proposed highway construction, because each plaintiff had to individually prove his own detriment and damages. *Id.* at 1241.

In a class action for declaratory and injunctive relief seeking to declare unconstitutional systematic discrimination against certain categories of legal aliens in the eligibility statute for the Alaska

Permanent Fund Dividend, the Alaska Supreme Court found the constitutional questions to predominate over the individual claims of class members, therefore satisfying the commonality requirement for maintaining a class action. *Andrade,* 23 P.2d at 68.

iii. Typicality. The claims of the class representative and the other class members must be based on the same legal or factual theory to satisfy the typicality requirement. *Adams v. Pipeline Union 798*, 699 P.2d 343, 348 (Alaska 1985). The Alaska Supreme Court noted that the juridical link doctrine may be used to provide an exception to the Rule 23(a) determination of typicality. *Neese v. Lithia Chrysler Jeep of Anchorage, Inc.*, 210 P.3d 1213, 1220 (Alaska 2009).

iv. Adequacy. The determination of adequacy of representation under Civil Rule 23(a)(4) is a question of fact which will not be reversed unless clearly erroneous. *State v. Alex*, 646 P.2d 203, 214 (Alaska 1982). The Alaska Supreme Court noted that the juridical link doctrine may be used to provide an exception to the Rule 23(a) determination of adequacy. *Neese*, 210 P.3d at 1220. Inadequacy of representation requires that an existing party show "collusion, adversity of interest, possible nonfeasance, or incompetence." *Hertz v. Cleary*, 835 P.2d 438, 442 (Alaska 1992) (citing *State v. Weidner*, 684 P.2d 103, 113 (Alaska 1984)); *see also Adams v. Pipeline Union*, 699 P.2d at 348 n.7. The interests of the named class representatives will not be found to be antagonistic to the interests of the other members of the class unless the antagonism involves the subject matter of the lawsuit. *State v. Alex*, 646 P.2d at 214. The Alaska Supreme Court has also noted that in a suit to strike down a statute as unconstitutional, the requirement of adequate representation "loses vitality" because the finding of unconstitutionality will affect everyone. *Id.* In *Andrade,* 23 P.3d at 68, the Alaska Supreme Court clarified its holding in *State v. Alex,* stating: "But *Alex* did not hold that the concern for adequate representation disappears when the class action challenges the constitutionality of a statute. It merely accorded less weight to that factor in these circumstances."

In 2009, the Alaska Supreme Court clarified that the proper procedure for when a class plaintiff lacks individual standing is to dismiss the complaint, not deny the class for inadequate representation. *Neese v. Lithia Chrysler Jeep of Anchorage, Inc.*, 210 P.3d 1213, 1222 (Alaska 2009).

In *Hertz v. Cleary*, 835 P.2d 438, 443 n.3 (Alaska 1992), the Alaska Supreme Court observed that a *pro se* litigant may not represent a class. The Court reaffirmed this rule in *Hallam v. Holland America Line, Inc.*, 27 P.3d 751, 754 (Alaska 2001). Similarly, in *Hertz v. State, Dep't of Corr.*, 230 P.3d 663, 2010 WL 53112 (Alaska 2010), the Alaska Supreme Court held that a *pro se* prisoner who was a member of a settlement class did not represent the class when he filed a subsequent motion challenging a Department of Corrections decision that allegedly violated a provision of the settlement agreement. The settlement agreement had included a provision that an inmate could not represent the class without an attorney or permission from the court to proceed *pro se*. The prisoner never requested permission to proceed *pro se*, and the superior court never ruled on the prisoner's motion for court-appointed counsel.

In *Hallam v. Alaska Travel Adventures*, 2004 WL 1535161 (Alaska 2004), a later suit brought by the same *pro se* plaintiff as *Hallam v. Holland America Line*, the Supreme Court rejected the plaintiff's claim that the trial court should have conditionally certified the class pending his retention of counsel; while the trial court may *consider* a request for conditional certification under those circumstances, it is not required to do so "when there is no evidence that an attorney is willing or available to represent the class."

In another suit brought by the same *pro se* plaintiff, *Hallam v. Alaska Airlines, Inc.*, 91 P.3d 279, 287–88 (Alaska 2004), in which he was denied the right to assert consumer fraud and antitrust claims against an airline on behalf of a class, the Court did note that a named plaintiff is generally allowed to proceed with his claims on an individual basis even if class certification is denied. The class claims at issue in *Hallam*, however, were not maintainable even on an individual basis because of preemption by the federal Airline Deregulation Act.

b. Rule 23(b)

i. Rule 23(b)(1). In *State v. Alex*, 646 P.2d 203, 213 n.10 (Alaska 1982), a class action brought by commercial fishermen to challenge the constitutionality of a state assessment on salmon sales, the Alaska Supreme Court apparently disapproved the trial court's reliance on Rule 23(b)(3), holding that "this type of suit fits within Rule 23(b)(2), and possibly also within Rule 23(b)(1)."

ii. Rule 23(b)(2). In *State, Dep't of Revenue v. Andrade*, 23 P.3d 58, 68 (Alaska 2001), the Alaska Supreme Court held that class certification was appropriate under Civil Rule 23(b)(2) where a class of aliens sought declaratory and injunctive relief in a suit challenging the constitutionality of the eligibility requirements for dividends from the Alaska Permanent Fund. In *State v. Alex*, 646 P.2d 203, 213 n.10 (Alaska 1982), a class action brought by commercial fishermen to challenge the constitutionality of a state assessment on salmon sales, the Alaska Supreme Court held that "this type of suit fits within Rule 23(b)(2), and possibly also within Rule 23(b)(1)."

iii. Rule 23(b)(3). In *Bartek v. State, Dep't of Natural Res., Div. of Forestry*, 31 P.3d 100, 104 (Alaska 2001), the Alaska Supreme Court noted the trial court's use of Rule 23(b)(3) to certify a class of property owners suing the State for damage from a wildfire but remanded the case for reconsideration of whether the requirements of Rule 23 had been met.

c. Rule 23(e)

i. Rule 23(e). In *Triem v. Kake Tribal Corp.*, Unpublished Memorandum Opinion and Judgment, 2024 WL 181538 (Jan. 17, 2024), the Alaska Supreme Court noted the differences between Alaska Rule 23(e) and its federal analog. Alaska Rule 23(e) consists of one relatively brief sentence: "A class action shall not be dismissed or compromised without the approval of the court and notice of the proposed dismissal or compromise shall be given to all members of the class in such manner as the court directs." In contrast, the current version of Federal Rule 23(e) is relatively lengthy, with multiple subparts detailing procedural requirements for the parties' provision of information to the court, the court's explanation of grounds for its decision to give notice, approval of the proposal or settlement at issue, identification of any agreements made in connection with the proposal, and additional procedures granting class members new opportunities to object or be excluded.

d. Other Cases of Interest

i. Constitutional law. In 2007, the Alaska Supreme Court decided a class action case involving entitlement to pension cost of living adjustments of public employees moving out of state. *Pub. Employees Ret. Sys. v. Gallant*, 153 P.3d 346 (Alaska 2007). In *PERS v. Gallant*, a retired public employee who retired out of state, and retired public school employees planning to move out of state, brought class action claims against the administrators of the Public Employees' Retirement System (PERS) and Teachers' Retirement System, and the State, alleging that the residency requirement for cost of living adjustment (COLA) violated state and federal constitutions. The Superior Court granted plaintiffs' motion for summary judgment, but on appeal the Alaska Supreme Court held that COLA's residency retirement did not violate the equal protection clause of the Alaska Constitution.

In *Heitz v. State, Dep't of Health & Soc. Serv.*, 215 P.3d 302 (Alaska 2009), a foster parent brought a class action suit against the Office of Children's Services to challenge its process for recouping alleged overpayments. The Alaska Supreme Court held that foster parents have a due process property interest in foster care maintenance reimbursements and that OCS was required to provide foster parents with notice and an opportunity to contest such decisions prior to recoupment.

Also in 2009, the Alaska Supreme Court decided *Hageland Aviation Serv., Inc. v. Harms*, 210 P.3d 444 (Alaska 2009), where a pilot brought a class action claim against his employer for unpaid overtime wages under the Alaska Wage and Hour Act. The Alaska Legislature amended the Act in 2005, which retroactively exempted pilots from the Act's overtime compensation. The Supreme Court, noting that Act purposefully eliminated the pilots' claims, as well as claims of two other similar class actions, held that the Act took the pilots' vested property interests in violation of the Alaska Constitution's takings clause.

ii. Exhaustion of administrative remedies. In *State, Dep't of Revenue v. Andrade*, 23 P.2d 58, 66–67 (Alaska 2001), the Alaska Supreme Court upheld the superior court's dismissal of an exhaustion of administrative remedies defense. *Andrade* involved claims by legal aliens who were denied Permanent Fund Dividends by the Alaska Department of Revenue. Among the class plaintiffs, only the Andrade family had pursued an administrative appeal to the Alaska Department of Revenue. On appeal to the superior court, the State argued that the claims of all class plaintiffs except the Andrades should be dismissed for failure to exhaust administrative remedies. The Alaska Supreme Court held that the exhaustion requirement was excused for other class plaintiffs because in the Andrades' case the Department of Revenue refused to decide their constitutional challenges. The pursuit of administrative relief was therefore futile. "Where a claim calls upon the superior court to review only the validity of a statute, exhaustion of administrative remedies is not required." *Id.* at 67 (citation and informal quotes omitted).

iii. Tolling of statute of limitations. In *Nolan v. Sea Airmotive, Inc.*, 627 P.2d 1035, 1039–46 (Alaska 1981), the Alaska Supreme Court held that the filing of a class action complaint tolled the statute of limitations for all putative members of a class, notwithstanding a statutory provision requiring that plaintiffs in Wage and Hour Act cases be specifically named in order to toll the statute. In *Fred Meyer of Alaska, Inc. v. Adams*, 963 P.2d 1025, 1028–30 (Alaska 1998), the Alaska Supreme Court held that the statute of limitations on wage claims remained tolled by the filing of a class action complaint even though class certification was initially denied.

In *Fred Meyer of Alaska, Inc. v. Bailey*, 100 P.3d 881, 885–86 (Alaska 2004), the Alaska Supreme Court held that the statute of limitations on an employee's Wage and Hour Act claim continued to be equitably tolled even after he had opted out of a class action, because he had been threatened with retaliation if he remained in the class. The Court held that the equitable tolling ended when the threat was lifted.

iv. Timing of class certification. In two 1982 cases, the Alaska Supreme Court held that a decision on the merits may be made before class certification. In *Gold Bondholders Protective Council v. Atchison, Topeka and Santa Fe Ry. Co.*, 649 P.2d 947 (Alaska 1982), the Alaska Supreme Court held that the trial court had the discretion to rule upon a motion to dismiss prior to ruling on class certification. The Alaska Supreme Court also held in *State v. Alex*, 646 P.2d at 213–14, that by initiating summary judgment proceedings while their motion for certification was pending, the plaintiffs waived any right to have their class certified before a determination on the merits; thus, the trial court did not err in ruling on the summary judgment motion while the class certification was pending.

In *Neese v. Lithia Chrysler Jeep of Anchorage, Inc.*, 210 P.3d 1213, 1222 (Alaska 2009), the Supreme Court held that the trial court's decision to address whether consumers who had brought a class action suit against several car dealerships before addressing whether to grant class certification was justified because standing is an inherent prerequisite to a class certification inquiry.

v. Review of class certification. In *State, Dep't of Revenue v. Andrade,* 23 P.2d 58, 65 (Alaska 2001), the Alaska Supreme Court held that it will review the decision to grant or deny class certification under the abuse of discretion standard. The abuse of discretion standard also applies to review of a decision on a motion to amend class certification or to redefine the class, *Hanson v. Kake Tribal Corp.*, 939 P.2d 1320, 1330 (Alaska 1997), and in reviewing approval of a class action settlement, *Weiss v. State*, 939 P.2d 380, 386 (Alaska 1997).

In *Shook v. Alyeska Pipeline Serv. Co.*, 51 P.3d 935, 937–38 (Alaska 2002), the Alaska Supreme Court reversed the trial court's decertification of a class in a wage and hour case. The Supreme Court held that it would be an abuse of discretion to reach the merits of the case in deciding to decertify a class.

In *Bartek v. State, Dep't of Natural Res., Div. of Forestry*, 31 P.2d 100, 103 (Alaska 2001), the Alaska Supreme Court held that it was within the discretion of the superior court to decide whether to hold an evidentiary hearing or permit discovery before granting class certification.

The Alaska Supreme Court upheld a denial of a motion to expand a class. In *Hanson v. Kake Tribal Org.*, 939 P.2d 1320 (Alaska 1997), after plaintiffs were granted partial summary judgment and shortly before trial, they moved to expand their class. The trial judge said he would grant the motion to expand the class on condition that the partial summary judgment order was withdrawn. The plaintiffs declined and appealed. The Alaska Supreme Court upheld the trial judge's decision to deny the motion to expand and the condition of withdrawal of summary judgment because expanding the class would have broadened the scope of the lawsuit.

vi. Opt-outs. To determine the sufficiency of an opt-out notice, the Alaska Supreme Court looks to the rules governing class actions. *Neese v. State*, 218 P.3d 983, 990 (Alaska 2009). The Supreme Court determined that Civil Rule 23 applied to procedural aspects of the case: Rule 23(c)(2) set the standard for notice to members of a class, and the Rule 23(e) standard for settlement notices applied.

In *Comm'r, Alaska Dept. of Health & Soc. Serv. v. Anthony*, 709 P.2d 491, 492 (Alaska 1985), the Alaska Supreme Court held that when prisoners had tardily, but without objection, exercised their right to opt out of a class action suit and later brought their own individual suits over prison conditions, the State could not raise the tardiness of their class-action opt outs as a defense to the individual suits.

The Alaska Supreme Court determined that the doctrine of *res judicata* would not preclude consumers from asserting a private, class action cause of action even though they had opted out of separate litigation of substantially the same issues brought by the State Attorney General. *Neese v. State*, 218 P.3d at 989 (Alaska 2009).

vii. Settlement. In *Hertz v. Cleary*, 835 P.2d 438 (Alaska 1992), the Alaska Supreme Court held that a class member's motion to intervene and challenge provisions of a settlement was untimely when the motion to intervene was made after settlement discussions were substantially completed. Later, in *Hertz v. State, Dep't of Corr.*, 230 P.3d 663, 2010 WL 53112 (Alaska 2010), the Alaska Supreme Court held that a *pro se* prisoner who was a member of the *Cleary* settlement class did not represent the class when he filed a subsequent motion challenging a decision of the Department of Corrections that allegedly violated a provision of the settlement agreement. The settlement agreement had included a provision that an inmate could not represent the class without an attorney or permission from the court to proceed *pro se*. The prisoner never requested permission to proceed *pro se*, and the superior court never ruled on the prisoner's motion for court-appointed counsel. In a later case arising out of the same settlement agreement, *Wigglesworth v. State of Alaska*, 393 P.3d

422 (Alaska 2017), the Alaska Supreme Court held that a prior judgment that had declined to terminate settlement agreement on constitutional grounds was the law of the case and was not subject to reconsideration absent certain findings.

In *Weiss v. State*, 939 P.2d 380 (Alaska 1997), *cert. denied*, 118 S. Ct. 366 (1997), the Alaska Supreme Court affirmed the trial court's use of the federal seven-factor framework adopted by *Class Plaintiffs v. City of Seattle*, 955 F.2d 1268, 1291 (9th Cir. 1992), for determining whether a settlement was fair, adequate, and reasonable. *Id.* at 386–87. In response to allegations of settlement collusion, the *Weiss* court held that in absence of evidence to the contrary, a presumption of correctness and arms-length negotiations applies to the review of settlement negotiations. *Id.* at 399, citing Herbert B. Newberg & Alba Conte, 2 *Newberg on Class Actions*, 11.28 at 11–59 (1992). With respect to a Rule 23(e) notice of proposed settlement, the *Weiss* court held that the notice should be "brief and reasonably clear to the minimally sophisticated layperson," and where multiple parties oppose the settlement, the court may insist that the notice be neutral in tone. *Id.* at 400–01.

In *Riley v. Simon*, 790 P.2d 1339, 1342 (Alaska 1990), the Alaska Supreme Court held that due process claims for failure to notify potential class members of a proposed settlement pursuant to Rule 23(e) are reviewed under a harmless error standard where independent grounds for exclusion exist.

In *Smith v. Cleary*, 24 P.2d 1245, 1249 (Alaska 2001), the Alaska Supreme Court held that consent decrees in class actions are to be construed by the normal principles that apply to contract interpretation. In *Barber v. State of Alaska, Department of Corrections*, 393 P.3d 412 (Alaska 2017), and in *Atenor v. State of Alaska, Department of Corrections*, 462 P.3d 1 (Alaska 2020), the court reiterated that normal principles of contract interpretation govern the interpretation of a class action settlement agreement.

In *Neese v. State*, 218 P.3d at 989, the Alaska Supreme Court held that consumers who opted out of a class settlement simultaneously forfeited any potential remaining interest they may have had in the consent judgment, thereby prohibiting them from becoming parties to the consent judgment. The Supreme Court noted that allowing intervention by consumers who opted out would delay execution of the consent judgment and relief to customers who chose to remain parties to the consent judgment. *Id.* at 993.

In *Triem v. Kake Tribal Corp.*, Unpublished Memorandum Opinion and Judgment, 2024 WL 181538 (Jan. 17, 2024), the Alaska Supreme Court held that Rule 23(d) does not require a fairness hearing and does not establish a universal requirement or "duty" demanding a fairness hearing. The portions of Alaska Civil Rule 23(d) that are applicable to a fairness hearing are permissive, not mandatory: "the court *may* make appropriate orders . . . requiring . . . that notice be given *in such manner as the court may direct* to *some or all of the members* of any step in the action, or . . . the opportunity of members to signify whether they consider the representation fair and adequate." Likewise, Alaska Civil Rule 23(e) does not require a fairness hearing. Federal Civil Rule 23(e)(2) requires a fairness hearing before a court may approve a proposal that "would bind class members." The federal rule includes a relatively detailed list of topics the court must consider in determining whether the proposal is "fair, reasonable, and adequate." But Alaska Rule 23(e) does not. A trial court *may* in its discretion apply federal precedent in a fairness analysis under Rule 23(e). But Alaska has declined to mandate such an analysis under Alaska Rule 23(e).

viii. Attorneys' fees. In a published memorandum opinion, *Turner v. Alaska Commc'n Sys. Long Distance, Inc.*, 70 P.3d 1096 (Alaska 2003), the Alaska Supreme Court disapproved language in a proposed class notice that would have advised absent class members that they could be held liable for a portion of the defendants' attorneys' fees if the class did not prevail. The Supreme Court held that absent class members who stood to gain only small monetary compensation and who remained passive throughout the litigation could not be held liable for a successful defendant's attorney's fees. A subsequent opinion explained the Court's rationale more fully. *See Turner v. Alaska Commc'n Sys. Long Distance, Inc.*, 78 P.3d 264 (Alaska 2003). However, in *Catalina Yachts v. Pierce*, 105 P.3d 125, 131 (Alaska 2005), the Supreme Court emphasized, in *dicta*, that *Turner* was not intended to relieve named class members from liability for attorney's fees.

In *Monzingo v. Alaska Air Group, Inc.*, 112 P.3d 655, 664–68 (Alaska 2005), a case decided against the plaintiff on summary judgment before it could be certified as a class action, the Alaska Supreme Court held that the trial court had abused its discretion in awarding the prevailing defendant a portion of the attorney's fees it had incurred in litigating class certification issues. The Supreme Court pointed out that a named plaintiff in a class action case that seeks a small amount of individual relief could be deterred from pursuing relief on a class-wide basis if, by so doing, he was exposed to "high attorney's fees for litigation that goes beyond that required to adjudicate the merits of his own case." The Court held, therefore, that fee awards against named plaintiffs in class action cases warranted "greater scrutiny and a delicate balancing of the relevant equitable factors articulated in" Alaska Civil Rule 82. The Court concluded that named plaintiffs should not "ordinarily" be held liable for attorney's fees that fall beyond those necessary to litigate the merits of their own individual claims, although it placed the burden on the named plaintiff, as the non-prevailing party, to demonstrate that a "downward variance" from the presumptive amounts required under Rule 82 was justified under "case-specific circumstances."

In *Albrecht v. Alaska Trustee, LLC*, 286 P.3d 1059, 1065 (Alaska 2013), the Alaska Supreme Court, relying on *Monzingo*, held that a named plaintiff in a class action case should not ordinarily be held liable for attorney's fees incurred by the prevailing party in fighting class certification or otherwise litigating the structure of a class action, reasoning that such efforts "are motivated by a desire to discourage claims by others." The Court remanded the case to the superior court to determine whether the named plaintiff had carried her burden of demonstrating that she had no "financial incentive to act as a class representative" and was therefore entitled to the downward variance in the attorney's fees award under Rule 82.

In *Anchorage Police & Fire Ret. Sys. v. Gallion*, 65 P.3d 876, 880–84 (Alaska 2003), the Alaska Supreme Court affirmed the trial court's finding that the defendant had committed indirect criminal contempt by violating that part of an order approving a class action settlement that required the defendant to distribute to all class members the trial court's explanation of its award of attorneys' fees to class counsel.

In *Air Logistics of Alaska, Inc. v. Throop*, 181 P.3d 1084 (Alaska 2008), the Alaska Supreme Court provided some additional clarity with respect to attorneys' fees awards in class actions. First, a superior court may—but is not required to—use a two-step method to determine Civil Rule 82 fees: (1) determine the compensable value of the services the attorneys rendered to the class, and (2) apply Rule 82 to that amount to decide how much the losing party should pay. Second, the Superior Court erred when it failed to include certain payments that were made prior to the summary judgment ruling as part of the money judgment when awarding attorneys' fees. All payments that were a result of the litigation should be included, though some are subject to different fee schedules depending on whether or not they were contested. Third, the Superior Court did not abuse its discretion in failing to award full fees for work relating to class certification or class representation, including where the bulk of counsel's efforts were unproductive.

In *State, Dep't of Health & Soc. Serv. v. Okuley*, 214 P.3d 247 (Alaska 2009), attorneys represented on a pro bono basis a class of persons wrongly denied Interim Assistance benefits by the State of Alaska. The Alaska Supreme Court examined in detail the methods by which courts may award reasonable attorney fees under the common fund doctrine. First, the Supreme Court noted that the superior court must apply a three-part test to determine if the common fund is properly applied: "(1) the class of beneficiaries is sufficiently identifiable, (2) the benefits can be accurately traced, and (3) the fee can be shifted with some exactitude to those benefitting." *Id.* at 251 n.12 (quoting *Edwards v. Alaska Pulp Corp.*, 920 P.2d 751, 756 n.9 (Alaska 1996)). Second, the Supreme Court adopted the twelve *Johnson-Kerr* factors, also found in Alaska Bar Rule 35(a), which courts should consider in determining reasonable fee awards. *Id.* at n.13. Third, the Supreme Court noted that a court may calculate attorneys' fees by either the percentage of the fund method or the modified lodestar method, either of which may be modified based on various factors. *Id.* at 250 n.10. The Supreme Court found that the trial court, in using the percentage of the fund method, carefully analyzed the fee award and "recognized and fulfilled its fiduciary duty to the class to scrutinize the fee request." *Id.* at 252. Additionally, the Supreme Court held that because the class was certified under Rule 23(b)(2), due process did not require that class members receive notice of the fee request. *Id.* at 257.

In *Krone v. State, Dep't of Health and Soc. Serv.*, 222 P.3d 250, 257 (Alaska 2009), the Alaska Supreme Court held that class representatives who prevail on constitutional claims are entitled to an award of full reasonable attorney's fees and that neither Rule 82 nor the previous public interest litigation exception to Rule 82 governed. The Supreme Court also held that the method of determining reasonable attorney's fees was not limited to a calculation of actual reasonable hours worked multiplied by reasonable hourly rates and noted that AS § 09.60.010(c)(1) does not suggest such a limitation even though the statute abrogated a judicially created public interest litigation framework that provided some litigants with full attorney's fees or protection against adverse fee awards. *Id.* An appropriate method to determining "actual" fees might include an objective valuation of the attorney's services, which could include multiplying reasonable hourly rates by the actual reasonable hours worked, and/or considering "value-enhancing factors such as risk premiums and encouraging representation in similar cases." *Id.* The Supreme Court noted that the legislative history of AS § 09.60.010(c)(1) "reflects a consensus that successful constitutional claimants were to continue being treated in the same general manner as successful public interest litigants." *Id.* at 258.

In *State, Commercial Fisheries Entry Comm'n v. Carlson*, 270 P.3d 755, 766–67 (Alaska 2012), the Alaska Supreme Court affirmed the trial court's award of attorneys' fees to the class under Rule 82 even though many of the original plaintiffs could not be considered prevailing parties because they were excluded from the class. The defendant State argued the trial court abused its discretion by not adjusting the award of attorneys' fees to reflect the "mixed results achieved by class counsel." Holding the trial court did not abuse its discretion, the Alaska Supreme Court reasoned that "[a]lthough some original class members will not receive a refund, the prevailing party here is the class itself, which won a substantial award."

In *Rusch v. Southeast Alaska Regional Health Consortium*, 563 P.3d 2 (Alaska 2025), the court reiterated its holding in *State, Dep't of Health & Soc. Serv. v. Okuley*, 214 P.3d 247 (Alaska 2009), that the court has "permitted enhanced fees in . . . class action cases because of the risk of nonpayment and the sound policy of encouraging capable representation."

ix. Standing. In *Neese v. Lithia Chrysler Jeep of Anchorage, Inc.*, 210 P.3d 1213, 1219 (Alaska 2009), the Alaska Supreme Court held that consumers in a class-action suit brought against four vehicle dealerships owned by the same umbrella company lacked interest-injury standing with respect to two of the dealerships. The consumers failed to allege that they had suffered any actual injury from those specific dealerships and also failed to name the umbrella corporation as a defendant. *Id.* The Supreme Court noted that the juridical link doctrine has no bearing on the issue of standing and would not excuse the consumers from the requirement that, as class representatives, they must have individual standing in order to bring the suit. *Id.* at 1220–21. The Supreme Court also noted, however, that standing is an inherent prerequisite to any inquiry about class certification, and it found that the Trial Court properly considered the issue of whether the consumers had standing prior to granting class certification. *Id.* at 1221–22.

In *Law Project for Psychiatric Rights, Inc. v. State,* 239 P.3d 1252 (Alaska 2010), the court held that the plaintiff could not establish "citizen-taxpayer standing," and the fact that hypothetical class members "who are more directly affected have chosen not to sue despite their ability to do so does not confer citizen-taxpayer standing on an inappropriate plaintiff." 239 P.3d 1252, 1256 (quoting *Keller v. French*, 205 P.3d 299, 303 (Alaska 2009)).

In *Triem v. Kake Tribal Corp.*, 513 P.3d 994 (Alaska 2022), the Alaska Supreme Court considered a challenge brought by a former class representative and class counsel to the release of a debt owed by a corporation arising out of the settlement of a class action. The background of the case is covered in a prior decision of the court, *Hanson v. Kake Tribal Corp.*, 939 P.2d 1320 (Alaska 1997). In *Triem*, the court held that the former class representative and class counsel lacked standing to appeal the lower court's order forgiving the corporation's debt. The court found that additional briefing by the parties was required on whether Rule 23(d)–(e) applied to a motion to forgive a corporation's debt to a class arising out of a judgment and, if so, whether the rule's requirements were met in this case.

x. Juridical link doctrine. The juridical link doctrine is used to determine the typicality and adequacy requirements of Rule 23 and is an exception to the general principle that "a plaintiff who has no cause of action against the defendant cannot 'fairly and adequately protect the interests' of those who do have such causes of action." *Neese v. Lithia Chrysler Jeep of Anchorage, Inc.*, 210 P.3d 1213, 1220 (Alaska 2009). "[T]his general principle does not apply if or when 'all defendants are juridically related in a manner that suggests a single resolution of the dispute would be expeditious.'" *Id.* (quoting *La Mar v. H&B Novelty & Loan Co.*, 489 F.2d 461, 466 (9th Cir. 1973)).

In *Neese*, consumers brought a class action suit against four car dealerships owned by a common owner, although none of the class representatives had purchased cars at two of the dealerships. The Alaska Supreme Court declined to apply the juridical link doctrine to the issue of standing, noting that although a few courts had done so, "that approach is incorrect because it was intended to be applied only in the context of class certification." *Id.* The Supreme Court also noted, however, that the juridical link doctrine might be available as "an exception for *defendant classes* whose conduct is standardized by a common link to an agreement, contract or enforced system which acts to standardize the factual underpinnings of the claims and to insure the assertion of defenses common to the class." *Id.* at 1221.

xi. Amended complaints. In *Neese v. Lithia Chrysler Jeep of Anchorage, Inc.*, the Supreme Court found that the trial court erred by refusing to allow plaintiff consumers an opportunity to bring in new class representatives to remedy their lack of standing against two or the four named defendants. *Neese*, 210 P.3d at 1224.

However, in *Weimer v. Cont'l Car & Truck, LLC*, 237 P.3d 610 (Alaska 2010), the Supreme Court found that a district court was not in error when it denied the request of a plaintiff who was barred by a statute of limitation from amending his complaint to include non-barred class members. 237 P. 3d 610, 617. Another named plaintiff, possessing the standing that Weimer lacked, could easily have brought the class claim. *Id.* at 616. The Supreme Court distinguished *Weimer* from *Neese*, as the plaintiff in *Weimer* was a sole plaintiff who failed to assert a viable claim against the sole defendant. *Id.* at 617. Furthermore, because no named plaintiff or defendant remained after the court entered final judgment, Weimer's case did not raise concerns about "piecemeal appeals." *Id.*

In *Law Project for Psychiatric Rights, Inc. v. State,* 239 P.3d 1252 (Alaska 2010), the Alaska

Supreme Court again upheld a trial court's denial of a plaintiff's motion to amend to add a named plaintiff with standing, after finding that LPPR was not the appropriate litigant. 239 P.3d 1252, 1254, 1256. The Court did not expound upon its reasoning for upholding the denial and made no reference to *Neese*.

xii. Res judicata. In *Ferguson v. State of Alaska, Department of Corrections*, 816 P.2d 134 (Alaska 1991), the Alaska Supreme Court held that claim preclusion is applied in subsequent litigation to an absent class member only if the class representatives adequately protected the absent class member's interest (cited with approval in an unpublished opinion, *Rosales v. Icicle Seafoods*, Supreme Court No. S-16373, 2017 WL 3122390 (Alaska 2017)).

xiii. Other issues. In *Hudson v. Citibank (South Dakota) NA*, 387 P.3d 42 (Alaska 2016), a bank's arbitration clause required that claims be brought on an individual, not class, basis. After a claimant brought a class action alleging violations by the bank of the Unfair Trade Practices Act, the superior court rendered a ruling on the scope and applicability of the arbitration clause. On appeal, the Alaska Supreme Court held that the issue of the scope and application of the arbitration clause and the availability of injunctive relief should have, instead, been first referred to the arbitrator for determination. In *Metcalfe v. State of Alaska*, 382 P.3d 1168 (Alaska 2016), the plaintiff brought claims against the state involving his retirement benefits both on his own behalf and on behalf of a putative class. The superior court dismissed his claim as time barred prior to certification of the class. The Alaska Supreme Court reversed that ruling on appeal but declined to reach the substantive issues raised by the declaratory judgment complaint on the basis that such a ruling would resolve the issue for the plaintiff, but not for anyone else in the putative class, and could lead to inconsistent results. The court remanded the matter back to the superior court to resolve both the class action issues and the remaining declaratory judgment issues in the first instance.

In *Department of Family and Community Services, Office of Children's Services v. Z.C., through her next friend, Lorenz Kaufman*, 2025 WL 943116, __ P.3d ___ (2025), the court held that field preemption did not bar the class action claims asserted in this case. Field preemption exists where the states are precluded from regulating conduct in a field that Congress, acting within its proper authority, has determined must be regulated by its exclusive governance.

ALASKA RULES OF CIVIL PROCEDURE, RULE 23

(a) Prerequisites to a Class Action. One or more members of a class may sue or be sued as representative parties on behalf of all only if (1) the class is so numerous that joinder of all members is impracticable, (2) there are questions of law or fact common to the class, (3) the claims or defenses of the representative parties are typical of the claims or defenses of the class, and (4) the representative parties will fairly and adequately protect the interests of the class.

(b) Class Actions Maintainable. An action may be maintained as a class action if the prerequisites of subdivision (a) are satisfied, and in addition:

(1) The prosecution of separate actions by or against individual members of the class would create a risk of

(A) Inconsistent or varying adjudications with respect to individual members of the class which would establish incompatible standards of conduct for the party opposing the class, or

(B) Adjudications with respect to individual members of the class which would as a practical matter be dispositive of the interests of the other members not parties to the adjudications or substantially impair or impede their ability to protect their interests; or

(2) The party opposing the class has acted or refuses to act on grounds generally applicable to the class, thereby making appropriate final injunctive relief or corresponding declaratory relief with respect to the class as a whole; or

(3) The court finds that the questions of law or fact common to the members of the class predominate over any questions affecting only individual members, and that a class action is superior to other available methods for the fair and efficient adjudication of the controversy. The matters pertinent to the finding include: (A) the interest of members of the class in individually controlling the prosecution or defense of separate actions; (B) the extent and nature of any litigation concerning the controversy already commenced by or against members of the class; (C) the desirability or undesirability of concentrating the litigation of the claims in the particular forum; (D) the difficulties likely to be encountered in the management of a class action.

(c) Determination by Order Whether Class Action to Be Maintained—Notice—Judgment—Actions Conducted Partially as Class Actions.

(1) As soon as practicable after the commencement of an action brought as a class action, the court shall determine by order whether it is to be so maintained. An order under this subdivision may be conditional, and may be altered or amended before the decision on the merits.

(2) In any class action maintained under subdivision (b)(3), the court shall direct to the members of the class the best notice practicable under the circumstances, including individual notice to all members who can be identified through reasonable effort. The notice shall advise each member that (A) the court will exclude the member from the

class if the member so requests by a specified date; (B) the judgment, whether favorable or not, will include all members who do not request exclusion; and (C) any member who does not request exclusion may, if the member desires, enter an appearance through his counsel.

(3) The judgment in an action maintained as a class action under subdivision (b)(1) or (b)(2), whether or not favorable to the class, shall include and describe those whom the court finds to be members of the class. The judgment in the action maintained as a class action under subdivision (b)(3), whether or not favorable to the class, shall include and specify or describe those to whom the notice provided in subdivision (c)(2) was directed, and who have not requested exclusion, and whom the court finds to be members of the class.

(4) When appropriate (A) an action may be brought or maintained as a class action with respect to particular issues, or (B) a class may be divided into subclasses and each subclass treated as a class, and the provisions of this rule shall then be construed and applied accordingly.

(d) Orders in Conduct of Actions. In the conduct of actions to which this rule applies, the court may make appropriate orders: (1) determining the course of proceedings or prescribing measures to prevent undue repetition or complication in the presentation of evidence or argument; (2) requiring, for the protection of the members of the class or otherwise for the fair conduct of the action, that notice be given in such manner as the court may direct to some or all of the members of any step in the action, or of the proposed extent of the judgment, or of the opportunity of members to signify whether they consider the representation fair and adequate, to intervene and present claims or defenses, or otherwise to come into the action; (3) imposing conditions on the representative parties or on intervenors; (4) requiring that the pleadings be amended to eliminate therefrom allegations as to representation of absent persons, and that the action proceed accordingly; (5) dealing with similar procedural matters. The orders may be combined with an order under Rule 16, and may be altered or amended as may be desirable from time to time.

(e) Dismissal or Compromise. A class action shall not be dismissed or compromised without the approval of the court, and notice of the proposed dismissal or compromise shall be given to all members of the class in such manner as the court directs.

[Amended effective October 15, 1999.]

This chapter was prepared by Jeff Feldman of the University of Washington School of Law.

ARIZONA

1. COMPARISON WITH FED. R. CIV. P. 23

Rule 23 of the Arizona Rules of Civil Procedure is largely the same as the corresponding federal rule, with the exception of Arizona's Rule 23(c)(1), which requires an early hearing on class certification motions, in addition to a written order containing reasoning and evidentiary findings, and Arizona's Rule 23(f), which presumes that discovery and proceedings will be stayed while any appeal is pending. Most recently, as amended effective January 1, 2021, the Arizona Rule requires new notice and approval procedures for class settlements to comport with the Federal Rule. Revised Rule 23(e) tracks the Federal Rule and also provides a mechanism to suspend a pending appeal to allow the trial court to approve certain payments following a class member objection.

As with all Arizona Rules of Civil Procedure, because the Arizona Rules were patterned after the Federal Rules, federal decisions are "authoritative," though not "binding" authority. *See, e.g., Lennon v. First Nat'l Bank*, 518 P.2d 1230, 1232 n.3 (Ariz. Ct. App. 1974) ("[F]ederal cases construing Fed. R. Civ. P. Rule 23, while not controlling, are authoritative"); *see also Johnson v. Svidergol*, 757 P.2d 609, 611 (Ariz. Ct. App. 1988) ("Although federal decisions interpreting federal rules of civil procedure, which are identical to our state rules, are not controlling, they are persuasive."). As a result, counsel should review federal cases for authority on issues that have not been directly addressed by the state courts. As a matter of practice, Ninth Circuit cases generally carry the greatest weight in the Arizona state courts.

2. ENACTMENT OF A.R.S. § 12-1871, *ET SEQ.* AND RELATED CHANGES TO ARIZ. R. CIV. P. 23

Arizona statutes, effective September 13, 2013, and codified as A.R.S. §§ 12-1871 through 12-1873, marked the legislature's effort to modify class certification procedure for all actions filed after the effective date of the statute. A.R.S. § 12-1871 provides that "(A) after the commencement of an action that is brought as a class action *and after a hearing*, the court shall determine by order whether the action is to be maintained as a class action. The court may condition, alter, amend or withdraw its order at any time before the decision on the merits. (B) If the court finds that an action should be maintained as a class action, the court shall certify the action *in writing*, shall *set forth its reasons* as to why the action should be maintained as a class action and shall *describe all evidence* in support of its determination." A.R.S. § 12-1871 (emphasis added).

Second, A.R.S. § 12-1872 provides that the trial court may make widespread orders "in the conduct of class actions."[1] While A.R.S. § 12-1872 did not result in the change of any part of Rule

[1] A.R.S. § 12-1872 provides that, "In the conduct of class actions, the court may make orders that: 1) Determine the course of the proceedings or that prescribe measures to prevent undue repetition or complication in the presentation of evidence or argument. 2) For the protection of the class members or for the fair conduct of the action, require that notice be given in any manner the court directs to some or all of the members of any step in the action, of the proposed entry of judgment or of the

23, it demonstrates the legislature's intent to vest the trial court with wide authority to guide the class action process.

Last, A.R.S. § 12-1873 makes trial court class certification decisions immediately appealable. The section provides that "(A) The court's certification or refusal to certify a class action is appealable in the same manner as a final order or judgment. (B) If an appeal is filed pursuant to this section, all discovery and other proceedings shall be stayed except that on motion of a party, the court may permit discovery proceedings to continue during the pendency of the appeal. (C) An appeal filed pursuant to subsection A of this section shall be entitled to preference." A.R.S. § 12-1873.

To conform Arizona's rules to the new statutes, the Arizona Supreme Court, on its own initiative, amended Rule 23 on an expedited basis pursuant to Ariz. Sup. Ct. R. 28(G). Thereafter, in 2017, the Court adopted an amended, restructured rule to bring Arizona's rule in line with its federal counterpart. On August 26, 2020, the Court amended Rule 23 to incorporate changes to the federal counterpart's 2018 revisions to its notice and settlement procedures. Arizona's revisions took effect on January 1, 2021, and while the rule remains generally in line with its federal counterpart, it continues to contain the aspects intended to comply with A.R.S. §§ 12-1871 through 12-1873.

a. Rule 23(c)(1)—Requiring Hearing and Written Findings

Prior to statutory and rule changes, Arizona courts were not required to hold evidentiary hearings or make specific findings of fact and conclusions of law prior to certifying a class; reliance on pleadings and other pretrial materials was sufficient. *See, e.g., London v. Green Acres Trust,* 765 P.2d 542 (Ariz. Ct. App. 1988). With the revision of Rule 23(c)(1), the trial court must "hold a hearing and determine by order whether to certify the action as a class action." Ariz. R. Civ. P. 23(c)(1). The revised rule also requires the court to enter an order setting forth its reasons and describing the evidence in support of its determination. *Id.* The rule also provides that the order "may be conditioned, altered, amended or withdrawn before the final judgment." As a case develops, therefore, it is appropriate for a court to revisit whether class treatment should continue. *See Garza v. Gama*, 2016 Ariz. App. LEXIS 170, 173 Ariz. Adv. Rep. 21, ¶ 7 (Ariz. Ct. App. July 12, 2016) (*Garza II*) (holding the trial court had not abused its discretion when, after all but one claim had been dismissed, the trial court chose to reconsider "whether common questions continued to predominate and whether the case, now with some 80,000 class members, continued to be manageable.").

b. Rule 23(f)—Appealability and Stay Pending Appeal

Historically, orders denying class certification were not appealable, and could only be challenged by special action procedure. *Garza v. Swift Transp. Co., Inc.*, 213 P.3d 1008, 1012, 1014 (Ariz. 2009) (*Garza I*) (overruling *Reader v. Magma-Superior Copper Co.*, 494 P.2d 708 (Ariz. 1972) (*Reader I*), which held that a denial of a class certification is appealable). But with the enactment of A.R.S. § 12-1873, parties now have a non-discretionary right to an interlocutory appeal of an order certifying or denying class action status in the same manner as a final order or judgment. Compliance with Rule 54(b) or 54(c) is therefore not required to make an A.R.S. § 12-1873 ruling appealable. *Brumett*

---

opportunity of members to signify whether they consider the representation to be fair and adequate, to intervene and present claims and defenses or otherwise to come into the action. 3) Impose conditions on the representative parties or on intervenors. 4) Require that the pleadings be amended to eliminate allegations as to representation of absent persons and that the action proceed accordingly. 5) Deal with similar procedural matters. 6) Combine with any other appropriate pretrial order."

v. MGA Home Healthcare, LLC, et al., 240 Ariz. 420, 380 P.3d 659 (Ariz. Ct. App. 2016). All proceedings are presumptively stayed while the appeal is pending, distinguishing Arizona's rule from the federal version of Rule 23(f). Ariz. R. Civ. P. 23(f) provides that while an appeal is pending under A.R.S. § 12-1873 "all discovery and other proceedings shall be stayed" unless the court allows discovery to continue following the motion of a party. *Id.*

3. CASE LAW INTERPRETING RULE 23

All the requirements of Rule 23(a) and the requirements of at least one section of Rule 23(b) must be met in order for a class to be certified. *London,* 765 P.2d at 541; *Lennon,* 518 P.2d at 1234. Rule 23(a) also requires that the plaintiff be a member of the proposed class, and that a definable class exist. *Lennon,* 518 P.2d at 1232. The burden is on the plaintiff to demonstrate compliance with all the requirements of Rule 23. *Id.* The plaintiff must also have a personal stake, and therefore standing, at the time that the action is brought. *Id.* at 1232–33. The trial court is granted discretion in determining whether a class should be certified, and an order granting or denying certification is reversible only for an abuse of that discretion. *Godbey v. Roosevelt Sch. Dist. No. 66,* 638 P.2d 235, 238 (Ariz. Ct. App. 1981).

a. Rule 23(a)

i. Rule 23(a)(1)—Numerosity. There has been no definitive test established in Arizona to determine when the numerosity requirement has been met. *London*, 765 P.2d at 542 ("There is no bright line rule regarding the number of class members that will satisfy the numerosity prerequisite of rule 23"). The courts generally follow the language of Rule 23(a)(1) and determine whether the members of the class are so numerous that joinder would be impracticable. *Lennon*, 518 P.2d at 1233. The class cannot, however, be so numerous as to be undefinable. Indeed, the Arizona Supreme Court rejected the certification of a plaintiff class consisting of all persons who breathed polluted air because, *inter alia*, the class was so large and undefinable that the court found that a class could not be defined, or even managed, without the predominance of individual issues and a resort to "fluid recovery" damages, both of which were concepts rejected by the court. *Reader v. Magma-Superior Copper Co.*, 515 P.2d 860, 861–62 (Ariz. 1973) (*Reader II*). Where plaintiff had identified twenty potential class members, with only one residing in Arizona, sufficient numerosity was not present. *Ferrara v. 21st Century North America Ins. Co.*, 245 Ariz. 377, 382, 429 P.3d 1171, 1176 (Ariz. Ct. App. 2018), *rev. den.* (Mar. 6, 2019). Where plaintiff had a list of 10,000 likely class members, but had yet to identify a precise number, the court found sufficient numerosity. *Qasimyar v. Maricopa County*, Ariz. App. LEXIS 167, *11 (Ariz. Ct. App. Feb. 11, 2021).[2]

ii. Rule 23(a)(2)—Commonality. For purposes of subsection (a)(2), commonality is met in any situation in which there are common questions of law and fact. The claims of the class members need not be identical. *Lennon*, 518 P.2d at 1233. The affirmative defenses of the defendant need not be common to all class members. *Phx. Law Enf't Ass'n v. City of Phoenix*, Ariz. App. LEXIS 464,

[2] Caution should be exercised in citing *Qasimyar* in light of the limitations on citing memorandum decisions as precedent in Arizona state courts. *See* Ariz. R. S. Ct. 111. A memorandum decision may be cited for persuasive value "only if it was issued on or after January 1, 2015 [and] no opinion adequately addresses the issue before the court[.]" Ariz. R. S. Ct. 111(c)(1)(C).

*16–17 (Ariz. Ct. App. April 22, 2021).[3] If the requirements of Rule 23(a)(2) are not met, it logically follows that the requirements of subsection (a)(3) and (a)(4) are not met. *Reader II*, 515 P.2d at 862.

Where the purported class implicates multiple states' laws it will be incumbent upon the party seeking class treatment to provide an extensive analysis of state law variations. *Ferrara*, 245 Ariz. 377 at 381, 429 P.3d at 1175 (Ariz. Ct. App. 2018) (recognizing requirement of detailed analysis in case that implicated law of thirty-three states (where the laws of twenty-seven of those states appeared to differ from Arizona law), ultimately finding that plaintiff did not meet burden to demonstrate that state law variances did not "pose insuperable obstacles").

iii. Rule 23(a)(3)—Typicality. As noted above, a class representative must be a member of the class that he or she seeks to represent. *Lennon*, 518 P.2d at 1232. To be a member of the class, the class representative must "have suffered or be threatened with the same injury alleged on behalf of the class." *Id.* (citation omitted). The Arizona Supreme Court has held on at least one occasion that even if the claims of the purported class representative arise out of the same conduct as the claims of absent class members, differences in the extent, type, and quantification of damages can make compliance with the typicality requirement of subsection (a)(3) impossible. *Reader II,* 515 P.2d at 862. At the same time, however, the courts have held that the fact that the class members may seek different amounts or types of damages does not render the class representative's claim "atypical." *See Godbey,* 638 P.2d at 238–39 (explaining that individual class members' claims are not atypical if they seek different amounts of money and represent different categories of a central claim); *cf. Lennon*, 518 P.2d at 1232 (determining that plaintiff could not represent class of plaintiffs who "were charged illegal fees" by bank, but could only represent those who were charged illegal fees based upon the use of a specific bank product, because class members who did not complain based upon use of specific product were not "similarly situated").

Of the various tests used by the federal courts in determining "typicality," the Arizona courts have yet to adopt a definitive test. *See Godbey*, 638 P.2d at 239. The *Lennon* court summarized some tests used by the federal courts, but did not adopt any one test. 518 P.2d at 1233 ("Some courts have held that the typicality requirement is satisfied when common questions of law or fact exist. . . . Others have held a representative's claim typical if the interests of the representative are not antagonistic to those of absent class members. . . . Still others require the representative to demonstrate that absent class members have suffered the same grievances of which he complains. . . . Under each of the above tests, we find Mrs. Lennon's claim to be typical of the remainder of the asserted class.") (citations omitted). Thus, counsel can adopt any of these tests in arguing or opposing certification until the Arizona courts decide on which of the tests is appropriate under Arizona law. In any event, courts have stated that the typicality requirement should be liberally construed. *Godbey,* 638 P.2d at 240 ("[W]e believe the requirements of Rule 23(b)(3) (and Rule 23(a)(3), to the extent they overlap) should be liberally construed"). *See also ESI Ergonomics Solutions, LLC v. United Artists Theatre Circuit, Inc.*, 50 P.3d 844, 848 (Ariz. Ct. App. 2002) (quoting *Godbey*).

iv. Rule 23(a)(4)—Adequacy. Adequacy is determined by reference to both the adequacy of the named class plaintiff and the expertise of counsel in charge of the litigation. The cases reveal that there is less specific focus on the named plaintiff, but a more careful analysis of the qualifications of counsel and the absence of any antagonistic interests between the members of the class and the named plaintiff. *See Lennon*, 518 P.2d at 1233–34. "Potential dissatisfaction with an outcome is not a conflict of interest addressed by Rule 23(a)(4)." *Phx. Law Enf't Ass'n*, Ariz. App. LEXIS 464 at

[3] *See supra* note 2 (regarding memo decisions).

*18. Further, some antagonistic interests can be resolved by individual class members opting out of the class. *Qasimyar*, Ariz. App. LEXIS 167 at *16.

b. Rule 23(b)

i. Subsections (b)(1)(A) and (b)(1)(B). There are no Arizona decisions that analyze the requirements for certification under either of these subsections, except to say that the potential of the class action to be dispositive to all claims is not a Rule 23(b)(1)(B) reason to certify the claimants as a class. *Phx. Law Enf't Ass'n*, Ariz. App. LEXIS 464 at *25.

In *Godbey*, the class was initially brought and certified as a class action under Rule 23(b)(1) and (2), but as the court noted, on appeal the parties merged the requirements of the subsections, and also briefed the issues as if proceeding under Rule 23(b)(3). Therefore, the court reviewed the issues under Rule 23(b)(3). 638 P.2d at 239.

ii. Subsection (b)(2). There is also little authority analyzing the specific requirements of certification of classes under subsection (b)(2), although classes have been certified under that subsection of the Rule. *See, e.g., Arnold v. Ariz. Dep't of Health Servs.*, 775 P.2d 521, 523 (Ariz. 1989) (special action suit brought to compel treatment for chronically mentally ill under Arizona Constitution); *see also State v. Boykin*, 508 P.2d 1151, 1154 (Ariz. 1973) (*Boykin I*) (holding that class action challenging overtime practices of police department was "properly a class action" without any discussion of which part of subsection (b) was relied upon). In the majority of cases in which injunctive relief has been sought, however, damages are also requested, and certification has been ordered or denied under the auspices of Rule 23(b)(3). *See, e.g., A.J. Bayless Mkts., Inc. v. Superior Court*, 700 P.2d 1385, 1385 (Ariz. Ct. App. 1985) (certification pursuant to subsection (b)(3) when plaintiffs sought both damages and injunctive relief for gender discrimination in violation of federal and Arizona law).

iii. Subsection (b)(3)

Predominance of common issues of law and fact. The Arizona courts have determined that common issues of law and fact can "predominate" in a class action even though the individual members of the class may be entitled to different amounts of monetary relief. *Godbey*, 638 P.2d at 239. In addition, even if a defendant in a class action has counterclaims against each of the members of the class, common issues will predominate so long as the counterclaims are sufficiently common in nature and scope as to permit mass determination of liability. *Lennon*, 518 P.2d at 1235. But the Arizona court of appeals has acknowledged that while "[d]enial of class action status based upon manageability concerns is disfavored," the presence of individual affirmative defenses "could create individual questions that might make a class action unmanageable." *Garza II*, 2016 Ariz. App. LEXIS 170 at *6, *9, 743 Ariz. Adv. Rep. 21, ¶¶ 14, 18 (holding that there was insufficient evidentiary support for the affirmative defenses pleaded, so manageability was not a bona fide concern in the case at bar). The case law suggests that the issue of predominance is inextricably intertwined with the issue of manageability, and that the questions should be addressed together. *Id.* For example, in *Reader II*, the court found that a class should not be certified for all those who had "occasion to . . . breathe and visualize air" polluted by the defendants both because the plaintiff could not show that common issues predominated over individual issues that would arise (depending on the age, location, duration of exposure, etc., of each individual plaintiff) and because administering such an undefined and massive class would be "unmanageable." 515 P.2d at 860–61. Class certification was denied in *Osuna v. Wal-Mart Stores, Inc.*, No. C20014319, 2004 WL 3255430, at *7 (Ariz. Super.

Ct. Dec. 23, 2004),[4] where individualized questions as to both liability and damages precluded a finding of predominance. Plaintiff sought to bring unjust enrichment claims on behalf of a class of employees who had allegedly worked "off the clock" without compensation. *Id.* The court found that because an "individualized inquiry is necessary to examine the unique circumstances surrounding each alleged occurrence of unjust enrichment" a class action was not a superior method of adjudication. *Id.* The court also rejected plaintiff's proposal that damages could be calculated in the aggregate, finding that no "reasonable methodology" had been presented to the court to render individual awards to class members. *Id.* at *8. While noting that "plaintiff-specific [statute of] limitations issues do not necessarily prevent class certification," the court of appeals was nevertheless persuaded that individualized statutes of limitations for putative class members' tort and contract claims arising out of a failed golf course development "could create issues sufficient to preclude class certification." *Angelo v. Stewart Title & Trust of Phoenix, Inc.*, No. 1CA-CV 15-0689, 2017 WL 410903, at *3 (Ariz. Ct. App. Div. 1 Jan. 31, 2017). The appellate court therefore affirmed the trial court's determination that plaintiffs had not met their burden to demonstrate that class treatment was warranted. *Id.* at *4.

Interests of individual class members in controlling litigation and desirability of concentrating litigation in one forum. These two factors under subsection (b)(3) are generally considered together by the courts. The principal factor considered is the relative size of the individual claims. If the claims of the individual members would be small so that it would be unlikely that each member would bring his or her individual claim, the courts have found that it is "desirable" that the litigation be focused in a single forum and that the class action vehicle outweighs any interests that individual class members might have in controlling litigation. *See Godbey,* 638 P.2d at 240; *Lennon*, 518 P.2d at 1234 n.4.

Manageability. Again, the focus of the Arizona courts on the manageability of a class action under subsection (b)(3) is generally inextricably intertwined with the issues of commonality, typicality, and predominance. *Reader II,* 515 P.2d at 861–62; *Lennon*, 518 P.2d at 1234–35. An action is generally found to be manageable so long as the claims of the named plaintiff are "typical" of the class, and the individual issues, potential counterclaims, and other factors do not render the administration of the action unwieldy such that the action would degenerate into individual trials on individual claims and/or counterclaims. *Lennon*, 518 P.2d at 1235; *Godbey*, 638 P.2d at 240. The appellate courts have generally upheld the "manageability" determinations of trial courts in certifying class actions, although the courts may find such a determination an abuse of discretion if the size of the class, the nature of the claims, and determination of damages would be so focused on individual issues that the administration of the case as a class action would be virtually impossible. *Reader II*, 515 P.2d at 861–62. In *Garza II*, the court of appeals rejected the trial court's holding that conflicts of law issues had rendered a class unmanageable, substituting its own choice of law analysis on *de novo* review. *Garza II*, 2016 Ariz. App. LEXIS 170 at *9, 743 Ariz. Adv. Rep. 21, ¶ 16 (applying Arizona law uniformly to all remaining claims).

Other litigation concerning the controversy. In analyzing this factor, Arizona courts determine "whether there is so much pre-existing litigation that a class action would be unproductive." *ESI Ergonomics*, 50 P.3d 844 at 848 (citation omitted). The absence of individual lawsuits weighs generally in favor finding superiority of class adjudication. *Id.* The lack of other suits may indicate that people are unaware that they have a claim; a class action educates individuals about their rights

4 *See supra* note 2 (regarding memo decisions).

and protects those rights. *Id.* The lack of other suits also is consistent with situations where a claim is not economically feasible, such as where the potential recovery is so small that the costs of litigating would exceed the benefit even if the claim is victorious. *Id.* The lack of other suits also weighs in favor of another factor in the superiority analysis—the interest of class members in controlling their own litigation—because it suggests that members of the putative class would have no such interest. *Id.* at 849. The *ESI* court concluded that the trial court abused its discretion when it improperly applied the "other litigation" factor by construing the lack of other lawsuits as weighing against superiority.

4. MISCELLANEOUS COMMENTS

a. Standing

Arizona's Supreme Court held as a matter of first impression that a plaintiff did not have standing to assert a class claim against defendants where she did not possess individual claims against those defendants. *Fernandez v. Takata Seat Belts, Inc.*, 108 P.3d 917, 920 (Ariz. 2005) (en banc) ("[T]he proper inquiry in a class action lawsuit must initially focus on whether the plaintiff has an individual claim against the defendant. If she does not, she cannot maintain a class action against that defendant."); *see also Karbal v. Ariz. Dep't of Revenue*, 158 P.3d 243, 246 (Ariz. Ct. App. 2007) (holding consumer did not have standing to challenge state transaction privilege taxes on behalf of class of consumers where the legal incidence of the tax fell on sellers, not consumers, even if the sellers did ultimately pass on the cost of the tax). The *Takata* court acknowledged that Arizona's standing requirement was not a constitutional mandate because Arizona lacks a counterpart to the "case or controversy" requirement of the federal constitution, but standing nevertheless remained a prudential prerequisite to suit. 108 P.3d at 919. Arizona law therefore requires that a plaintiff suffer a "distinct and palpable injury" that is "fairly traceable" to the defendant before bringing an action. *Id.* The court rejected plaintiff's argument that the "juridical link" doctrine conferred an exception to Arizona's standing requirement. *Id.* at 920–21. The court discussed the application of the doctrine in other jurisdictions, both state and federal, and held that "[e]ven if we were to adopt the juridical link doctrine," the doctrine did not confer standing in this case because plaintiff had not alleged a conspiracy or concerted action among the defendants, nor had she claimed that they shared a legal relationship. *Id.* at 921.

b. Exhaustion of Administrative Remedies

The Arizona courts have held that individual claimants who must first exhaust administrative remedies are not excused from that requirement by bringing the action under Rule 23. *Estate of Bohn v. Waddell*, 848 P.2d 324, 336 (Ariz. Ct. App. 1992) (holding trial court did not abuse its discretion when it denied class certification of a class consisting of claimants, none of whom had made an attempt to exhaust administrative remedies); *Kerr v. Killian*, 65 P.3d 434, 445 (Ariz. Ct. App. 2001) (finding trial court within its discretion in declining to certify a class of employees who had failed to file any form of administrative refund claim). The courts have held, however, that administrative exhaustion requirements may be satisfied by filing a class action type administrative claim, and then later appealing a denial of that claim to Superior Court. *Andrew S. Arena, Inc. v. Superior Court*, 788 P.2d 1174, 1177 (Ariz. 1990). The Arizona Supreme Court affirmed the "class exhaustion" principle in *Arizona Dep't of Revenue v. Dougherty*, 29 P.3d 862, 869 (Ariz. 2001), holding that "the class device is a suitable vehicle for exhaustion of administrative remedies when not expressly prohibited by statute." The *Dougherty* court interpreted *Arena* as allowing a claim against a public entity to be presented as a class claim. If the claim is denied by the agency, the court may entertain a class action on the claim, even though each member of the putative class has not exhausted administrative remedies on an individual basis.

c. Arizona's Notice of Claim Statute

Asserting class, rather than individual, claims against a public entity or employee does not exempt plaintiffs from their burden to comply with all the requirements of A.R.S. § 12-821.01, Arizona's Notice of Claim statute. *City of Phoenix v. Fields*, 201 P.3d 529, 531 (Ariz. 2009). A.R.S. § 12-821.01 requires that a notice of claim include "a specific amount for which the claim can be settled and the facts supporting that amount." *Id.* Although the *Fields* court recognized that a putative class representative could not yet "make a claim on behalf of the class," the court noted that "nothing prevents [such representatives] from including in their notice the specific amounts for which they would settle their individual claims." *Fields*, 201 P.3d at 534. Thus, a "class claim meets the settlement demand requirement of § 12.821.01(A) if it identifies the amount for which an individual putative class representative would settle his own claim and puts the governmental entity on notice of the claimant's intention to pursue a class action if his claim does not settle." *Id.*

However, the *Fields* court found defendant's Notice of Claim defense waived where defendant either fails to affirmatively plead the defense, or if affirmatively pled, the defendant takes "substantial action to litigate the merits of the claim that would not have been necessary had the entity promptly raised the defense." *Id.* at 536 (holding that the defendant waived its Notice of Claim defense because it "substantially participated in this litigation before raising their notice of claim statute defenses").

d. Class Notice

The Arizona courts have held that the manner and means of notice to the class is left to the discretion of the trial judge, and that the trial court's determination will not be disturbed absent an abuse of discretion. *State v. Boykin,* 538 P.2d 383, 388 (Ariz. 1975) (*Boykin II*). The type and manner of notice, however, must comply in all respects to the requirements of due process. *A.J. Bayless Markets*, 700 P.2d at 1388. Thus, if means of providing notice are available, yet not ordered by the trial court, the trial court's determination with respect to proper notice will be reversed as an abuse of discretion. *See id.* at 1389 (trial court abused its discretion "by refusing to pursue further attempts at actual notice before resorting to notice by publication").

e. Attorneys' Fees

Rule 23(h) allows a court to award reasonable attorneys' fees and costs where otherwise authorized by law or the parties' contract. Counsel for plaintiffs in class actions should consider, before commencing an action, the availability of attorneys' fees, especially in injunctive actions or actions against a public entity. The Arizona Supreme Court has rejected the notion that the trial court has "inherent power" to award fees in a class action. *Boykin II*, 538 P.2d at 387–88. Fees are regularly awarded, however, in "common fund" type cases. *See Burke v. Ariz. State Ret. Sys.*, 77 P.3d 444, 447 (Ariz. Ct. App. 2003); *Ladewig v. Ariz. Dep't of Revenue*, 63 P.3d 1089, 1091 (Ariz. T.C. 2003). Under the common fund doctrine, attorneys' fees are paid out of the common fund (generally the damages owed to and recovered on behalf of the class, which is ultimately divided among class members), so that the fees are paid by and allocated among the prevailing class members, not shifted to the losing party. *Burke*, 77 P.3d at 448–49. The doctrine thus provides for "fee-spreading," *not* "fee-shifting." *Id.* at 448. The common fund doctrine is an exception to the rule that attorneys' fees in Arizona are awarded pursuant only to statute or contract. *Charles I. Friedman, P.C. v. Microsoft Corp.*, 141 P.3d 824, 831 (Ariz. Ct. App. 2006). Therefore, where the payment of attorneys' fees is authorized by a statute or a contract, the common fund doctrine does not apply. *Cf. id.* at 831–32 (allowing lodestar enhancement where parties' settlement agreement provided for application of common fund doctrine in a fee-shifting context). When "arising out of contract," class actions may be appropriately deemed contested actions for which fee-shifting is authorized by Ariz. Rev. Stat. § 341.01. *Leflet v. Redwood Fire and Cas. Ins. Co.*, 247 P.3d 180, 186 (Ariz. Ct. App. 2011). "Special considerations" may apply to such awards, however, because "the tactical management of litigation [by class members] is usually more attenuated than that of traditional named parties." *Id.* Finally, the Arizona Supreme Court has held that attorneys' fees may be awarded under the state's private attorney general doctrine where the successful class solely sought non-monetary relief. *Ansley v. Banner Health Network, et al.*, 459 P.3d 55, 65 (Ariz. 2020).

f. Special Actions

Arizona has abolished the distinction between actions for *mandamus, certiorari* and prohibition in favor of a single type of action termed a "special action." These may be brought under a variety of circumstances. In the class action context, however, it is important to note that the courts have held that a special action may be brought in Superior Court under the auspices of Rule 23, but that a claimant cannot bring an original jurisdiction action in the Supreme Court as a class action. *Arnold*, 775 P.2d at 534–35.

g. Private Securities Litigation

Arizona has adopted legislation mirroring the federal Private Securities Litigation Reform Act of 1995, 15 U.S.C. § 78u-4 *et seq*. Arizona's statute, found at A.R.S. §§ 44-2081 to 44-2087, applies to all private actions arising under Arizona securities law. For any private action brought as a plaintiff class action under Arizona *or* federal rules of civil procedure, the plaintiff is required to comply with specific requirements which mirror those in 15 U.S.C. § 78u-4(a)(2). For instance, each plaintiff seeking to serve as a class representative must file with the complaint a sworn certification and must publish notice to members of the purported class. *See* A.R.S. § 44-2081(B), (D). The court then appoints a "lead plaintiff" in accordance with procedures which mirror those in 15 U.S.C. § 78u-4(a)(3). *See* A.R.S. § 44-2081(E), (F).

h. Venue

Counsel bringing or defending a putative class action should give due consideration to the issue of venue. The Arizona Court of Appeals has dismissed a putative class action for improper venue. *Amparano v. ASARCO, Inc*., 93 P.3d 1086, 1088–91 (Ariz. Ct. App. 2004). Under the venue statute, A.R.S. § 12-401, venue generally lies in the county where a defendant resides, unless the action falls within one of nineteen statutory exceptions. *Amparano*, 93 P.3d at 1091. The exception at issue in *Amparano* states that all actions concerning real property "shall be brought in the county in which the real property or a part thereof is located." A.R.S. § 12-401(12). In *Amparano*, several plaintiffs filed a putative class action alleging, among other things, that the defendant's mining operations caused damage to their real property. The named plaintiffs resided in two different counties. The court granted the defendant's motion to dismiss for improper venue, holding that because the named plaintiffs' real property was located in more than one county, *there was no correct venue* for the action under A.R.S. § 12-401(12). *Amparano*, 93 P.3d at 1091.

i. Tolling the Statute of Limitations Period

The U.S. Supreme Court held, in *American Pipe & Constr. Co. v. Utah*, 414 U.S. 538 (1974), that commencement of a class action tolls the applicable statute of limitations for individual suits as to all members of the class. The Arizona Supreme Court has expressly declined to decide whether *American Pipe* intra-jurisdictional tolling operated to toll a statute of limitations. *Albano v. Shea Homes Ltd. P'ship*, 254 P.3d 360, 364 (Ariz. 2011) ("We assume without deciding that the filing of a class action in Arizona tolls the applicable statute of limitations for non-named class members until class certification is denied."). Likewise, construing Arizona law, a federal district court has suggested that a filed class action tolls the statute of limitations for claimants only within the same state and forum in which the class action is filed. *Newport v. Dell, Inc.*, No. CV-08-0096-TUC-CKJ(JCG), 2008 WL 4347311, *4–5 (D. Ariz. Aug. 21, 2008).

Recently, in a matter of first impression, the Arizona Court of Appeals declined to adopt *American Pipe* cross-jurisdictional tolling of a statute of limitations. *Rader v. Greenberg Traurig, LLP*, No. 1 CA-CV 14-0299, 2015 WL 3875331 (Ariz. Ct. App. June 23, 2015). The Appellants in *Rader* opted out of a certified federal class action that had a preliminarily approved settlement and subsequently filed suit in Arizona state court. *Id.* at 1. The *Rader* court reasoned that because Arizona's general civil savings statute, A.R.S. § 12-504, does not contemplate *American Pipe* tolling, it would not be "consonant with Arizona's legislative scheme . . . [to] adopt cross-jurisdictional tolling by case law." *Rader*, No. 1 CA-CV 14-0299 at *7. A.R.S. § 12-504 was codified by the Legislature in response to an Arizona Supreme Court case which allowed for an equitable exception to a statutory limitations period adopted by the Legislature, in lieu of a general civil savings statute in Arizona. *See Hosogai v. Kadota*, 700 P.2d 1327, 1331 (1985). Therefore, the *Rader* court was unwilling "to adopt a doctrine broader than what the Legislature adopted in a statute enacted in response to a call by the Arizona Supreme Court." *Rader*, No. 1 CA-CV 14-0299 at *7. Additionally, the *Rader* court explained that "whether class certification is granted may be an important consideration in addressing subsequent tolling requests[,]" noting that few state court cases have "adopted cross-jurisdictional tolling when class certification was granted and class members elected to opt out to press their own individual claims." *Id.* at 6.

With respect to events that can terminate the *American Pipe* tolling effect, the *Newport* court suggested that the tolling effect expires for "all asserted members of the class," when "class certification is denied." *Newport*, No. CV-08-0096-TUC-CKJ(JCG) at *4 (quoting *Crown, Cork & Seal Co., Inc. v. Parker*, 462 U.S. 345, 354 (1983)). Additionally, a federal district court sitting in Maryland but interpreting Arizona law has held that the tolling effect for individual claims of class members ends "when a purported class member ceases to be a member of a putative class." *Daisy Mountain Fire Dist. v. Microsoft Corp.*, 547 F. Supp. 2d 475, 480, 482–83, 486 (D. Md. 2008) (holding that a political subdivision of the State of Arizona ceased to be a member of the putative class when the class representative filed an amended complaint that excluded the political subdivision from the class).

The Ninth Circuit has found conflicting evidence on whether and how an Arizona court would apply *American Pipe* to toll a statute of repose and certified the question to the Arizona Supreme

Court. *Albano v. Shea Homes Ltd. P'ship*, 634 F.3d 524, 532–34; 540–41 (9th Cir. 2011) (asking if a motion for class certification tolls a statute of repose and if so whether a court can "weigh the equities of the case in determining whether, and to what extent, an action is tolled"). The Arizona Supreme Court answered that question by holding that it would not apply *American Pipe* to toll a statute of repose. *Albano v. Shea Homes Ltd. P'ship*, 254 P.3d 360, 366 (Ariz. 2011). The court found that while *American Pipe* applied to statutes that are generally considered procedural in nature, it did not apply to statutes creating substantive rights, such as statutes of repose. *Id.* A.R.S. § 12-552, as a statute of repose, granted a substantive right—"immunity [from suit] based on a legislative balance of the respective rights of plaintiffs and defendants"—and that it could not subsequently overrun by a procedural rule. *Resolution Trust Corp. v. Olson*, 768 F. Supp. 283, 285 (D. Ariz. 1991). The idea of applying *American Pipe* was not "consonant with the legislative scheme," which sought specifically to foreclose the possibility of suit after the statutory period of eight years. *Id.* (citing *American Pipe*, 414 U.S. at 557–58).

j. Communication with Absent Class Members

The propriety of *ex parte* contact with putative or absent class members has not been specifically addressed in Arizona.

k. Final Consideration

Although the rules and case law governing class actions in Arizona are generally consistent with federal case law and interpretations, out-of-state counsel should always consult Arizona counsel experienced with class actions before filing or defending a class action in state court. Some of the interpretations given various provisions of Rule 23 are somewhat inconsistent with decisions in at least some of the federal courts, and familiarity with other specific statutes, rules of practice and local courts and judges is very important in the prosecution or defense of class actions in the state courts.

RULE 23 OF THE ARIZONA RULES OF CIVIL PROCEDURE

RULE 23. CLASS ACTIONS (REFS & ANNOS)

Rule 23(a). Prerequisites.

One or more members of a class may sue or be sued as representative parties on behalf of all members only if (1) the class is so numerous that joinder of all members is impracticable, (2) there are questions of law or fact common to the class, (3) the claims or defenses of the representative parties are typical of the claims or defenses of the class, and (4) the representative parties will fairly and adequately protect the interests of the class.

Rule 23(b). Types of Class Actions.

A class action may be maintained if Rule 23(a) is satisfied and if:

(1) prosecuting separate actions by or against individual members of the class would create a risk of:

(A) inconsistent or varying adjudications with respect to individual class members that would establish incompatible standards of conduct for the party opposing the class; or

(B) adjudications with respect to individual class members that, as a practical matter, would be dispositive of the interests of the other members not parties to the individual adjudications or would substantially impair or impede the other members' ability to protect their interests;

(2) the party opposing the class has acted or refused to act on grounds that apply generally to the class, so that final injunctive relief or corresponding declaratory relief is appropriate for the class as a whole; or

(3) the court finds that the questions of law or fact common to class members predominate over any questions affecting only individual members, and that a class action is superior to other available methods for fairly and efficiently adjudicating the controversy. The matters pertinent to these findings include:

(A) the class members' interests in individually controlling the prosecution or defense of separate actions;

(B) the extent and nature of any litigation concerning the controversy already begun by or against class members;

(C) the desirability or undesirability of concentrating the litigation of the claims in the particular forum; and

(D) the likely difficulties in managing a class action.

Rule 23(c). Certification Order; Notice to Class Members; Judgment; Issues Classes; Subclasses.

(1) Certification Order.

(A) When to Issue. At an early practicable date after a person sues or is sued as a class representative, the court must hold a hearing and determine by order whether to certify the action as a class action.

(B) Defining the Class; Appointing Class Counsel. An order that certifies a class action must:

(i) define the class and the class claims, issues, or defenses;

(ii) appoint class counsel under Rule 23(g);

(iii) set forth the court's reasons for maintaining the class as a class action; and

(iv) describe the evidence supporting the court's determination.

(C) Altering or Amending the Order. An order that grants or denies class certification may be conditioned, altered, amended, or withdrawn before final judgment.

(2) Notice.

(A) For (b)(1) or (b)(2) Classes. For any class certified under Rule 23(b)(1) or (b)(2), the court may direct appropriate notice to the class.

(B) For (b)(3) Classes. For any class certified under Rule 23(b)(3) – or upon ordering notice under Rule 23(e)(1) to a class proposed to be certified for purposes of settlement under Rule 23(b)(3) – the court must direct to class members the best notice that is practicable under the circumstances, including individual notice to all members who can be identified through reasonable effort. The notice may be by one or more of the following: United States mail, electronic means, or other appropriate means. The notice must clearly and concisely state in plain, easily understood language:

(i) the nature of the action;

(ii) the definition of the class certified;

(iii) the class claims, issues, or defenses;

(iv) that a class member may enter an appearance through an attorney if the member so desires;

(v) that the court will exclude from the class any member who requests exclusion;

(vi) the time and manner for requesting exclusion; and

(vii) the binding effect of a class judgment on members under Rule 23(c)(3).

(3) Judgment. Whether or not favorable to the class, the judgment in a class action must:

(A) for any class certified under Rule 23(b)(1) or (b)(2), include and describe those whom the court finds to be class members; and

(B) for any class certified under Rule 23(b)(3), include and specify or describe those to whom the Rule 23(c)(2) notice was directed, who have not requested exclusion, and whom the court finds to be class members.

(4) Particular Issues. When appropriate, an action may be brought or maintained as a class action with respect to particular issues,

(5) Subclasses. When appropriate, a class may be divided into subclasses that are each treated as a class under this rule.

Rule 23(d). Conducting the Action.

(1) Generally. In conducting an action under this rule, the court may issue orders that:

(A) determine the course of proceedings or prescribe measures to prevent undue repetition or complication in presenting evidence or argument;

(B) require – to protect class members and to fairly conduct the action – appropriate notice to some or all class members of:

(i) any step in the action;

(ii) the proposed extent of the judgment; or

(iii) the members' opportunity to signify whether they consider the representation fair and adequate, to intervene and present claims or defenses, or to otherwise come into the action;

(C) impose conditions on the representative parties or on intervenors;

(D) require that the pleadings be amended to eliminate allegations about representation of absent persons and that the action proceed accordingly; or

(E) deal with similar procedural matters.

(2) Combining and Amending Orders. An order under Rule 23(d)(1) may be altered or amended from time to time and may be combined with an order under Rule 16.

Rule 23(e). Settlement, Voluntary Dismissal, or Compromise.

The claims, issues, or defenses of a certified class – or a class proposed to be certified for purposes of settlement – may be settled, voluntarily dismissed, or compromised only with the court's approval. The following procedures apply to a proposed settlement, voluntary dismissal, or compromise:

(1) Notice to the Class.

(A) Information that Parties Must Provide to the Court. The parties must provide the court with information sufficient to enable it to determine whether to give notice of the proposal to the class.

(B) Grounds for a Decision to Give Notice. The court must direct notice in a reasonable manner to all class members who would be bound by the proposal if giving notice is justified by the parties' showing that the court will likely be able to:

(i) approve the proposal under Rule 23(e)(2); and

(ii) certify the class for purposes of judgment on the proposal.

(2) Approval of the Proposal. If the proposal would bind class members, the court may approve it only after a hearing and only on finding that it is fair, reasonable, and adequate after considering whether:

(A) the class representatives and class counsel have adequately represented the class;

(B) the proposal was negotiated at arm's length;

(C) the relief provided for the class is adequate, taking into account:

(i) the costs, risks, and delay of trial and appeal;

(ii) the effectiveness of any proposed method of distributing relief to the class, including the method of processing class-member claims;

(iii) the terms of any proposed award of attorney's fees, including timing of payment; and

(iv) any agreement required to be identified under Rule 23(e)(3); and

(D) the proposal treats class members equitably relative to each other.

(3) Identifying Agreements. The parties seeking approval must file a statement identifying any agreement made in connection with the proposal.

(4) New Opportunity to Be Excluded. If the class action was previously certified under Rule 23(b)(3), the court may refuse to approve a settlement unless it affords a new opportunity to request exclusion by individual class members who had an earlier opportunity to request exclusion but did not do so.

(5) Class-Member Objections.

(A) Generally. Any class member may object to the proposal if it requires court approval under Rule 23(e). The objection must state whether it applies only to the objector, to a specific subset of the class, or to the entire class, and also state with the grounds for the objection.

(B) Court Approval Required for Payment in Connection with an Objection. Unless approved by the court after a hearing, no payment or other consideration may be provided in connection with:

(i) forgoing or withdrawing an objection; or

(ii) forgoing, dismissing, or abandoning an appeal from a judgment approving the proposal.

(C) Procedure for Approval After an Appeal. If approval under Rule 23(e)(5)(B) has not been obtained before a notice of appeal is filed, the following procedure applies as to any motion for approval under Rule 23(e)(5)(B) while the appeal remains pending:

(i) Relief Pending Appeal. In addressing the motion, the court may:

(a) defer considering the motion;

(b) deny the motion; or

(c) state either that it would grant the motion if the Court of Appeals remands for that purpose or that the motion raises a substantial issue.

(ii) Motion to the Court of Appeals. If the court states that it would grant the motion or that the motion raises a substantial issue, the movant must promptly move the Court of Appeals under Arizona Rule of Civil Appellate Procedure 3(b) to suspend the appeal and to revest jurisdiction in the superior court to allow the superior court to consider the motion under Rule 23(e)(5)(B).

(iii) Remand. The superior court may decide the motion if the Court of Appeals remands for that purpose.

Rule 23(f). Appeals.

The court's order certifying or denying class action status is appealable in the same manner as a final order or judgment. During the pendency of an appeal under A.R.S. § 12-1873, all discovery and other proceedings are stayed, but the court may, on motion, permit discovery to continue.

Rule 23(g) Class Counsel.

(1) Appointing Class Counsel. Unless a statute provides otherwise, a court that certifies a class must appoint class counsel. In appointing class counsel, the court:

(A) must consider:

(i) the work counsel has done in identifying or investigating potential claims in the action;

(ii) counsel's experience in handling class actions, other complex litigation, and the types of claims asserted in the action;

(iii) counsel's knowledge of the applicable law; and

(iv) the resources that counsel will commit to representing the class;

(B) may consider any other matter pertinent to counsel's ability to fairly and adequately represent the interests of the class;

(C) may order potential class counsel to provide information on any subject pertinent to the appointment and to propose terms for attorney's fees and nontaxable costs;

(D) may include in the appointing order provisions about the award of attorney's fees or nontaxable costs under Rule 23(h); and

(E) may make further orders in connection with the appointment.

(2) Standard for Appointing Class Counsel. When one applicant seeks appointment as class counsel, the court may appoint that applicant only if the applicant is adequate under Rule

23(g)(1) and (4). If more than one adequate applicant seeks appointment, the court must appoint the applicant best able to represent the interests of the class.

(3) Interim Counsel. The court may designate interim counsel to act on behalf of a putative class before determining whether to certify the action as a class action.

(4) Duty of Class Counsel. Class counsel must fairly and adequately represent the interests of the class.

Rule 23(h) Attorney's Fees and Nontaxable Costs.

In a certified class action, the court may award reasonable attorney's fees and nontaxable costs that are authorized by law or by the parties' agreement. The following procedures apply:

(1) Subject to the provisions of this rule, a claim for an award must be made by motion under Rule 54(g) at a time the court sets. Notice of the motion must be served on all parties and, for motions by class counsel, directed to class members in a reasonable manner.

(2) A class member, or a party from whom payment is sought, may object to the motion.

(3) The court may hold a hearing and must find the facts and state its legal conclusions under Rule 52(a).

Rule 23(i) Disposition of Residual Funds in Class Action Cases.

(1) "Residual Funds" are:

(A) the funds that remain after the payment of all approved class member claims, expenses, litigation costs, attorneys' fees, and other court-approved disbursements to implement the relief granted, or

(B) if it is impossible or economically impractical to distribute the settlement or judgment funds to the class at all, the funds remaining after the payment of all approved expenses, litigation costs, attorneys' fees, and other court-approved disbursements to implement the relief granted.

Nothing in this rule is intended to limit the trial court from approving a settlement or order that does not create residual funds.

(2) Any order entering a judgment or approving a proposed compromise or settlement of a class action certified under this rule that establishes a process for identifying and compensating members of the class, or where such process is impossible or economically impractical, may provide for the disbursement of residual funds. In matters where residual funds remain and are not subject to statutory directives, unless the parties jointly direct otherwise, the residual funds shall be disbursed to the Arizona Foundation for Legal Services and Education to grant to Arizona legal services nonprofit entities for use, in accordance with judicial instructions for the award, toward the provision of legal services and access to the justice system for low-income residents of Arizona.

By Nicole Maroulakos Goodwin, a Shareholder with Greenberg Traurig, LLP, in Phoenix, Arizona. Ms. Goodwin focuses her practice on commercial litigation in state and federal court, including business tort, real estate, contract, and health care litigation.

ARKANSAS

Class actions in Arkansas are governed by Rule 23 of the Arkansas Rules of Civil Procedure. While the language of Arkansas Rule 23 largely mirrors the Federal Rule, there are two notable exceptions: (1) the Arkansas Rule does not subdivide subsection (b) into three separate types of class actions as does Federal Rule 23(b), and (2) the Arkansas Rule omits subsections (f) through (h) found in the Federal Rule. Despite these differences, the Arkansas Supreme Court has said that "we will interpret Ark. R. Civ. P. 23 in the same manner the federal courts interpret the comparable Fed. R. Civ. P. 23." *Fraley v. Williams Ford Tractor and Equip. Co.*, 339 Ark. 322, 336, 5 S.W.3d 423, 432 (1999).

1. ARKANSAS RULE OF CIVIL PROCEDURE RULE 23

"(a) *Prerequisites to Class Action.* One or more members of a class may sue or be sued as representative parties on behalf of all only if (1) the class is so numerous that joinder of all members is impracticable, (2) there are questions of law or fact common to the class, (3) the claims or defenses of the representative parties are typical of the claims or defenses of the class, and (4) the representative parties and their counsel will fairly and adequately protect the interests of the class.

(b) *Class Actions Maintainable.* An action may be maintained as a class action if the prerequisites of subdivision (a) are satisfied, and the court finds that the questions of law or fact common to the members of the class predominate over any questions affecting only individual members, and that a class action is superior to other available methods for the fair and efficient adjudication of the controversy. At an early practicable time after the commencement of an action brought as a class action, the court shall determine by order whether it is to be so maintained. For purposes of this subdivision, "practicable" means reasonably capable of being accomplished. An order under this section may be altered or amended at any time before the court enters final judgment. An order certifying a class action must define the class and the class claims, issues, or defenses.

(c) *Notice.* (1) In any class action in which monetary relief is sought, including actions for damages and restitution, the court shall direct to the members of the class the best notice practicable under the circumstances, including individual notice to all members who can be identified through reasonable effort.

(2) The notice must concisely and clearly state in plain, easily understood language:

- the nature of the action;
- the definition of the class certified;
- the class claims, issues, or defenses;
- that a class member may enter an appearance and participate in person or through counsel if the member so desires;
- that the court will exclude from the class any member who requests exclusion, stating when and how members may elect to be excluded; and
- the binding effect of a class judgment on class members.

(3) In any class action in which no monetary relief is sought, the court may require any notice it deems appropriate in the circumstances.

(4) The cost of any notice shall be borne by the representative parties; provided, however, that the court may shift all or part of the cost to the opposing party or parties if the case is settled or the class representative substantially prevails on the merits.

(d) *Orders in Conduct of Actions*. In the conduct of actions to which this rule applies, the court may make appropriate orders: (1) determining the course of proceedings or prescribing measures to prevent undue repetition or complication in the presentation of evidence or argument; (2) requiring, for the protection of the members of the class or otherwise for the fair conduct of the action, that notice be given in such manner as the court may direct to some or all of the members of any step in the action, or of the proposed extent of the judgment, or of the opportunity of the members to signify whether they consider the representation fair and adequate, to intervene and present claims or defenses, or otherwise come into the action; (3) imposing conditions on the representative parties or on intervenors; (4) requiring that the pleadings be amended to eliminate therefrom allegations as to representation of absent persons, and that the action proceed accordingly; (5) dividing the class into subclasses, treating each subclass as a class, and construing and applying the provisions of this rule accordingly; and (6) dealing with similar procedural matters. The orders may be combined with an order under Rule 16 and may be altered or amended from time to time as may be desirable.

(e) *Dismissal or Compromise*. (1) The court must approve any settlement, voluntary dismissal, or compromise of the claims, issues, or defenses of a certified class. The court must direct notice in a reasonable manner to all class members who would be bound by a proposed settlement, voluntary dismissal, or compromise. The court may approve any such resolution that would bind class members only after a hearing and on finding that the settlement, voluntary dismissal, or compromise is fair, reasonable, and adequate.

(2) The parties seeking approval of a settlement, voluntary dismissal, or compromise must file a statement identifying any agreement made in connection with the proposed settlement, voluntary dismissal, or compromise.

(3) The court may refuse to approve a settlement unless it affords a new opportunity to request exclusion to individual class members who had an earlier opportunity to request exclusion but did not do so.

(4) Any class member may object to a proposed settlement, voluntary dismissal, or compromise that requires court approval. An objection may be withdrawn only with the court's approval."

2. CASE LAW INTERPRETING RULE 23

a. Source: Reporter's Notes

[Reprinted from the Reporter's Notes published with AR Order 07.]

"All parts of the Rule have been revised [by amendments in 2006]. Many of these changes echo recent amendments to Federal Rule of Civil Procedure 23, while others incorporate the holding of recent Arkansas decisions and current Arkansas practice. With a few exceptions, the changes are technical and do not change Arkansas law.

Another prerequisite—the adequacy of class counsel—has been added to subdivision (a). This addition conforms the Rule to Arkansas law. *E.g., Mega Life & Health Insurance Co. v. Jacola*, 330 Ark. 261, 275, 975 S.W.2d 898, 904 (1997). Relevant factors for the circuit court's evaluation of class counsel include: counsel's work identifying and investigating potential claims, counsel's experience in handling class actions, complex litigation, and claims of the type asserted; counsel's knowledge of the applicable law; and the resources counsel will commit to representing the class. *See generally* Fed. R. Civ. P. 23(g) (outlining the requirements in appointing class counsel). Unless a showing is made to the contrary, however, Arkansas law presumes that the class representative's counsel "will vigorously and competently pursue the litigation." *USA Check Cashers of Little Rock, Inc. v. Island*, 349 Ark. 71, 80, 76 S.W.3d 243, 247 (2002).

Subdivision (b) on the timing of the circuit court's certification decision has been amended. The former rule required a certification decision as soon as practicable after the lawsuit commenced. That requirement, however, neither captured the prevailing practice nor recognized the good reasons for delaying the certification decision, such as the need for limited discovery on the Rule 23(a) prerequisites. The revised Rule requires a decision on certification at an early practicable time, which is the current standard in the federal Rule. That standard gives the circuit court and the parties some flexibility, while leaving intact the settled Arkansas law that the court may not inquire into the merits at the certification stage. *E.g., Speights v. Stewart Title Guaranty Co., Inc.*, 358 Ark. 59, 186 S.W.3d 715 (2004) (Supplemental Opinion Denying Rehearing).

The amendment deletes the phrase "may be conditional" from the part of subdivision (b) authorizing the circuit court to alter or amend a certification order. The deleted phrase is superfluous; the Arkansas cases on point have emphasized the circuit court's power to reconsider, affirm, alter, modify, or withdraw certification. *E.g., Fraley v. Williams Ford Tractor and Equipment Co.*, 339 Ark. 322, 347, 5 S.W.3d 423, 438-39 (1999). All of these actions spring from the power to alter or amend a certification order. This change brings the Arkansas Rule back into conformity with the federal Rule.

The amendment also replaces the phrase "before the decision on the merits" in subdivision (b) with the phrase "at any time before the court enters final judgment." This change follows an amendment to the federal Rule; it better reflects the duration of the circuit court's authority to modify its certification decision; and it should give the circuit court greater flexibility to deal with developments late in the litigation but before final judgment.

A new sentence has been added to the end of subdivision (b). As the cases make plain, the certification order must define the class in sufficiently definite terms so that the court and the parties may identify the class members. *E.g., Ferguson v. Kroger*, 343 Ark. 627, 631-32, 37 S.W.3d 590, 593 (2001). Identifying the claims, issues, and defenses will likewise help in identifying class members and expedite the resolution of the litigation. The amendment tracks existing Arkansas law and the federal Rule. This amendment does not alter the precedent holding that the circuit court is not required to perform a rigorous analysis of the case at the certification stage. *E.g., THE/FRE, Inc. v. Martin*, 349 Ark. 507, 514, 78 S.W.3d 723, 727 (2002).[1] But the circuit court must "undertake enough of an analysis to enable [the appellate court] to conduct a meaningful review." *See Lenders Title Co. v. Chandler*, 353 Ark. 339, 349, 107 S.W.3d 157, 162 (2003).

Subdivision (c) on notice has been rewritten and divided into subparts. The changes specify the contents of the notice in clearer terms, make a plain-statement requirement for the notice explicit, and bring the Arkansas Rule in line with the comparable federal Rule. A provision explicitly authorizing the circuit court to require notice in class actions where no monetary relief is sought has also been added. All these revisions are technical and do not change Arkansas law.

A new sentence (5) has been added to subdivision (d) to recognize the circuit court's authority

---

[1] This position was reinforced by the Supreme Court in *Beverly Enterprises-Arkansas, Inc. v. Thomas*, 370 Ark. 310, 322, 259 S.W.3d 445, 453 (2007) when the Court distinguished the case before it from *Kohn v. American Housing Foundation, Inc.*, 178 F.R.D. 536 (D. Colo. 1998), stating that "[t]he Kohn case, though, is distinguishable from the instant case in that the federal district court used a 'rigorous analysis' under Federal Rule 23 in determining whether the certification criteria had been met. This Court does not require that the circuit court conduct a 'rigorous analysis' under our Rule 23."

to create subclasses. The Arkansas cases have assumed this authority, and implicitly approved it, for almost twenty years. *E.g., Int'l Union of Ethical, Radio and Machine Workers v. Hudson*, 295 Ark. 107, 117, 747 S.W.2d 81, 86-87 (1988); *State Farm Fire & Casualty Co. v. Ledbetter*, 355 Ark. 28, 35-36, 1295 S.W.3d 815, 820-21 (2003). The federal Rule authorizes subclasses, which are often useful. This change conforms the Rule to current Arkansas practice. Former sentence (5) has been renumbered as (6).

Subdivision (e) about dismissal and compromise has been rewritten. With some exceptions, the revised Rule restates Arkansas law in the clearer terms of Federal Rule of Civil Procedure 23(e) and incorporates current Arkansas practice. For example, proposed settlements are evaluated now for fairness, reasonableness, and adequacy. *Ballard v. Martin*, 349 Ark. 564, 79 S.W.3d 838 (2002). Subdivision (1) also requires the circuit court to hold a fairness hearing before approving any proposed settlement. This is a new requirement, though fairness hearings are routine in most class actions. Subdivision (2) requires the parties seeking approval of any settlement to file a statement identifying side agreements. This new requirement will promote fairness in settlements and mirrors the federal Rule. Subdivision (3) gives the circuit court discretion to open a second opt-out window if the circumstances justify it. The federal Rule contains this option, and it merely recognizes the circuit court's power to fashion all appropriate relief as part of approving any proposed settlement. Finally, subdivision (4) requires court approval before an objection may be withdrawn. Objections often can, and should be, resolved by the parties. This new requirement, also drawn from the federal Rule, will help the circuit court insure the fairness of those resolutions in light of the overall proposed settlement of the litigation."

b. Additional Analysis

Three of the best cases for a general understanding of class action practice under Rule 23 in Arkansas are *Fraley v. Williams Ford Tractor and Equip. Co.*, 339 Ark. 322, 5 S.W.3d 423 (1999); *Gen. Motors Corp. v. Bryant*, 374 Ark. 38, 285 S.W.3d 634 (2008); and *Industrial Welding Supplies of Hattiesburg, LLC v. Pinson*, 2017 Ark. 315, 530 S.W.3d 854 (2017). These cases provide an overview of the six elements governing class certification in Arkansas courts. Arkansas law is "well-settled that the six requirements for class action certification include: (1) numerosity, (2) commonality, (3) typicality, (4) adequacy, (5) predominance, and (6) superiority." *Teris, L.L.C. v. Chandler*, 375 Ark. 70, 76, 289 S.W.3d 63, 67 (2008) (citing *Gen. Motors*, 374 Ark. at 42, 285 S.W.3d at 637); *see also Union Pac. R.R. v. Vickers*, 2009 Ark. 259, at 6, 308 S.W.3d 573, 577; *Diamante, LLC v. Dye,* 2013 Ark. 501, at 10, 430 S.W.3d 710, 718 (discussing the adequacy requirement and evaluating commonality and typicality); *Hotels.com, L.P. v. Pine Bluff Advert. & Promotion Com'n*, 2013 Ark. 392, at 11, 430 S.W.3d 56, 62 (determining whether the predominance element was satisfied); *Stephens Prod. Co. v. Mainer*, 2019 Ark. 118, at 4, 571 S.W.3d 905, 908 (discussing the numerosity and superiority requirements and evaluating whether such requirements were satisfied); *Infinity Healthcare Mgmt. of Ark., LLC v. Boyd*, 2019 Ark. 346, 588 S.W.3d 22 (affirming class certification following evaluation of all six elements); *Altice USA, Inc.* v. *City of Gurdon*, 2024 Ark. App. 228, 688 S.W.3d 441 (considering the requirements to satisfy the predominance and superiority requirements). All six elements must be present before class certification is appropriate, and where one is lacking, the court will deny certification without considering the other elements. *See Faigin v. Diamante*, 2012 Ark. 8, at 7–8, 386 S.W.3d 372, 377–78. In addition, the court must be able to objectively identify members of the class. *GGNSC Arkadelphia, LLC v. Lamb*, 2015 Ark. 253, at 9, 465 S.W.3d 826, 831.

Class certification is within the "broad discretion" of the trial court, and "[the Arkansas Supreme

Court] will not reverse a circuit court's decision to grant or deny class certification absent an abuse of discretion." *Vickers*, 2009 Ark. 259, at 7, 308 S.W.3d at 577. To find an abuse of discretion, the reviewing court will focus on "the evidence contained in the record to determine whether it supports the circuit court's decision." *Id.* at 7, 308 S.W.3d at 577; *see also Philip Morris Cos., Inc. v. Miner*, 2015 Ark. 73, at 3, 462 S.W.3d 313, 316 (citing *Asbury Auto Grp., Inc. v. Palasack*, 366 Ark. 601, 604, 237 S.W.3d 462, 465 (2006)). The Supreme Court of Arkansas has stated that a court abuses its discretion when it acts "improvidently, thoughtlessly, or without due consideration." *City of Conway v. Shumate*, 2017 Ark. 36, at 7, 511 S.W.3d 319, 325 (citing *Bank of the Ozarks v. Cossey*, 2015 Ark. 367, at 8, 471 S.W.3d 203, 209). Further, a circuit court abuses its discretion when it issues an order certifying a class action lawsuit under Rule 23 without defining the class claims, issues, or defenses, and when the order fails to provide any analysis of the six Rule 23 elements. *Agents Mut. Ins. Co. v. Benham*, 2020 Ark. 39, at 4–5, 591 S.W.3d 799, 802; *Koppers, Inc. v. Trotter*, 2019 Ark. 134, at 5, 572 S.W.3d 372, 375–76.

Arkansas views class certification as a procedural question that will not include any consideration of the merits of the case. *See Carquest of Hot Springs, Inc. v. Gen. Parts, Inc.*, 367 Ark. 218, 223, 238 S.W.3d 916, 920 (2006); *see also Teris*, 375 Ark. at 76, 289 S.W.3d at 67–68 (citing *Carquest*, 367 Ark. at 223, 238 S.W.3d at 920); *Advance Am. Servicing of Ark., Inc. v. McGinnis*, 2009 Ark. 151, at 4, 300 S.W.3d 487, 491. A reviewing court "may not consider whether the plaintiffs will ultimately prevail or even whether they have a cause of action." *Ark. Media, LLC v. Bobbitt*, 2010 Ark. 76, at 6, 360 S.W.3d 129, 134; *Rosenow v. Alltel Corp.*, 2010 Ark. 26, at 8–9, 358 S.W.3d 879, 886 (reversing denial of class certification because analysis of potential damages was an improper merits-based determination). The court's "focus is 'whether the requirements of Rule 23 are met' and 'it is totally immaterial whether the petition will succeed on the merits or even if it states a cause of action.'" *Philip Morris*, 2015 Ark. 73, at 3, 462 S.W.3d at 316 (quoting *Am. Abstract & Title Co. v. Rice*, 358 Ark. 1, 9, 186 S.W.3d 705, 710 (2004)). "[A]n impermissible consideration of the merits . . . at the class certification stage" is reversible error. *Carquest*, 367 Ark. at 224, 238 S.W.3d at 920 (citations omitted). *But see Faigin v. Diamante*, 2012 Ark. 8, at 6–7, 386 S.W.3d 372, 377 (affirming denial of class certification, even though "the circuit court abused its discretion by basing part of its decision . . . upon the [in]ability of the proposed class to withstand a Rule 12(b)(6) motion," because "this was not the sole basis of the circuit court's ruling, and even if it had been, this court can affirm if the right result is reached even if it is for a different reason").

The Arkansas Supreme Court prohibits class definitions that require inquiry into the underlying merits to determine who is an appropriate class member. *Sw. Bell Yellow Pages, Inc. v. Pipkin Enters., Inc.*, 359 Ark. 402, 407, 198 S.W.3d 115, 118 (2004); *see also Walker v. Wilmoe Corp.*, 2017 Ark. 340, at 4, 531 S.W.3d 387, 390. Fact inquiries aimed at identifying potential class members "[do] not require delving into the merits" and are permissible. *Baptist Health v. Hutson*, 2011 Ark. 210, at 6, 382 S.W.3d 662, 667 (holding that "determining whether the person is legally responsible for the charges for services or goods received" from the defendant "does not require delving into the individual merits of each claim"). In 2010, the Court confirmed that *res judicata* is an impermissible, merits-intensive inquiry at the class certification stage. *United Am. Ins. Co. v. Smith*, 2010 Ark. 468, at 18, 371 S.W.3d 685, 696.

In June 2008, the Arkansas Supreme Court restated that class certification is strictly procedural. *See Gen. Motors Corp. v. Bryant*, 374 Ark. 38, 42, 285 S.W.3d 634, 638 (2008). In *General Motors*, the Court affirmed class certification notwithstanding substantial differences among state laws. With regard to the differing state laws, the Court noted the circuit court's finding that there was "no greater merits-intensive determination than the one regarding choice of law," and stated that decertification of the class was always an option if applying other state laws subsequently created problems. *Id.* at

43–44, 285 S.W.3d at 639. The Court found class certification proper because of two predominating questions: whether the vehicles contained a defectively designed parking brake system and whether General Motors concealed that defect. *Id.* at 49, 285 S.W.3d at 642.

General Motors highlights two important features of Arkansas class action practice. First, it reiterates the basic rule that the predominance requirement under Arkansas law simply requires preliminary, overarching issues of liability and wrongdoing common to all class members. *Id.* at 44, 285 S.W.3d at 639; *see also Kersten v. State Farm Mut. Auto. Ins. Co.*, 2013 Ark. 124, at 8, 426 S.W.3d 455, 460 ("The starting point in examining the predominance requirement is whether a common wrong has been alleged against the defendant. . . ."); *Philip Morris*, 2015 Ark. 73, at 6, 462 S.W.3d at 317 ("The predominance element can be satisfied if the preliminary, common issues may be resolved before any individual issues."); *Vickers*, 2009 Ark. 259, at 10, 308 S.W.3d at 578; *City of Conway v. Shumate*, 2017 Ark. 36, at 7, 511 S.W.3d 319, 325 (citing *United Am. Ins.*, 2010 Ark. 468, at 10, 371 S.W.3d at 692 ("Predominance is a more stringent requirement than commonality.")). The relevant predominance inquiry, as the Court has repeatedly stated, is whether "there [are] issues that [are] common to each member of the class that [can] be resolved before any of the individual issues." *Vickers*, 2009 Ark. 259, at 17–18, 308 S.W.3d at 582 (reversing class certification); *see also Teris,* 375 Ark. at 82, 289 S.W.3d at 71 (stating that the "ultimate question to be resolved . . . is whether there are overarching issues that can be addressed before resolving individual issues"); *Hotels.com, L.P.,* 2013 Ark. 392, at 14, 430 S.W.3d at 64. Varying fact patterns or degrees of injury and damage will not defeat predominance or typicality as long as there is a common wrong alleged against the defendant. *Campbell v. Asbury Auto., Inc.*, 2011 Ark. 157, at 15–16, 381 S.W.3d 21, 33; *see also Kersten*, 2013 Ark. 124, at 6, 426 S.W.3d at 459–60 (focus of the typicality requirement is on the conduct of the alleged wrongdoer rather than the alleged injury); *Hutson*, 2011 Ark. 210, at 7, 382 S.W.3d at 667. However, despite the seemingly low bar set by these pronouncements, "class certification is inappropriate where there is 'no one set of operative facts [that] establishes liability' [citation omitted]." *Vickers*, 2009 Ark. 259, at 15, 308 S.W.3d at 581; *see also Ark. Dept. of Veterans Affairs v. Mallett*, 2015 Ark. 428, at 6–7, 474 S.W.3d 861, 865 (finding that the predominance requirement was not satisfied when plaintiff employees worked a diverse group of positions, from food preparation technicians to security officers, and determination of employer's liability would require highly individualized inquiry as to each employee's hours worked during a given week).

Second, *General Motors* illuminates the Arkansas Supreme Court's view that individual issues may be properly resolved in a decertified stage of a bifurcated class action proceeding. 374 Ark. at 44, 285 S.W.3d at 639; *see also Vickers*, 2009 Ark. 259, at 10, 308 S.W.3d at 579; *Teris*, 375 Ark. at 81–82, 289 S.W.3d at 71; *DIRECTV, Inc. v. Murray*, 2012 Ark. 366, at 16, 423 S.W.3d 555, 565 (raising defenses against individual members of the class will not defeat certification); *Lambert & Lambert Investors, Inc. v. Harris*, 2016 Ark. 24, at 6, 480 S.W.3d 138, 142 ("If a case involves preliminary, common issues of liability and wrongdoing that affect all class members, the predominance requirement of Rule 23 is satisfied, even if the circuit court must subsequently determine individual damages issues in bifurcated proceedings"). As the Court has explained, "a bifurcated process of certifying a class to resolve preliminary, common issues and then decertifying the class to resolve individual issues . . . is consistent with Rule 23." *Teris*, 375 Ark. at 81–82, 289 S.W.3d at 71; *see also Lamb*, 2015 Ark. 253, at 11, 465 S.W.3d at 832; *Philip Morris*, 2015 Ark. 73, at 7, 462 S.W.3d at 318 ("[A]ny individual issues regarding causation and damages can be addressed, if necessary, using the bifurcated approach."). "Rule 23 specifically contemplates the ability of the circuit court to decertify a class if it becomes too unwieldy and states: 'An order under this section may be altered or amended at any time before the court enters final judgment.'" *Teris*, 375 Ark. at 85–86, 289 S.W.3d at 74; *see also Philip Morris*, 2015 Ark. 73, at 11–12, 462 S.W.3d at 320 ("[T]o the extent that causation and reliance require individual inquiries, the circuit court can decertify the class in a bifurcated proceeding."). Further, the *Teris* opinion explains that "real efficiency can be had if common, predominating questions of law or fact are first decided, with cases then splintering for the trial of individual issues[.]" 375 Ark. at 85, 289 S.W.3d at 73.

In 2010, the Arkansas Supreme Court issued two decisions regarding the role of potential damages in the Rule 23 analysis. In *Arkansas Media, LLC v. Bobbitt*, the Court held that a "lack of remedy by itself" will not defeat a finding of superiority. 2010 Ark. 76, at 13, 360 S.W.3d 129, 138. In *Rosenow v. Alltel Corp.*, the Court held that the trial court's consideration of potential damages and potential damage setoffs was an improper merits-based analysis and an abuse of discretion. 2010 Ark. 26, at 8–12, 358 S.W.3d 879, 885–88 (reversing denial of class certification because of merits-based determination).

The Court also established that challenges to the scope of a proposed class are not grounds for denial of class certification under Rule 23 unless the proposed class is "excessively broad." *Compare United Amer. Ins. Co.*, 2010 Ark. 468, at 18–20, 371 S.W.3d. at 696–97 (affirming class certification of all persons in five states that made specific purchases between 1998 and 2009 despite lack of evidence of any disputed action or harm after 2006), *with Faigin v. Diamante*, 2012 Ark. 8, at 7, 386 S.W.3d 372, 377 (denying class certification of more than 300 lot owners where the underlying cause of action involved foreclosure and only seven of the lot owners were in foreclosure: "The fact that other lot owners in the subdivisions might share one or more concerns with the [proposed class representatives] is not the same as sharing an element in the underlying cause of action. The procedural posture of this case requires that the members of the proposed class share a common defense to the complaint in foreclosure. . . .").

In *Beverly Enters. Ark., Inc. v. Thomas*, the Arkansas Supreme Court affirmed a trial court's decision to certify a class of nursing home residents for purposes of bringing statutory and contractual claims and suggested that its decision would likely be different if the trial court had certified the class to allow the residents to pursue negligence claims. 370 Ark. 310, 322, 259 S.W.3d 445, 453 (2007). In reaching its decision, the Court relied upon *Fleming v. Barnwell Nursing Home & Health Facilities, Inc.*, 309 A.D.2d 1132, 766 N.Y.S.2d 241 (2003).

Similarly, the Court has indicated "that it is more inclined to approve class certification in mass-accident cases than in products-liability or toxic-tort cases." *Teris*, 375 Ark. at 82, 289 S.W.3d at 71 (citing *Baker v. Wyeth-Ayerst Labs. Div.*, 338 Ark. 242, 992 S.W.2d 797 (1999)).

It is within the trial court's discretion to deny amendments to class action complaints once the class is certified. *Asbury Auto.*, 2011 Ark. 157, at 11, 381 S.W.3d at 31.

In February 2020, the Arkansas Supreme Court clarified that a defendant waives the right to compel class notice under Rule 23(c) when it files a motion for summary judgment before compelling class notice. *See City of Ft. Smith v. Merriott*, 2020 Ark. 94, at 5, 593 S.W.3d 481, 484. However, a defendant retains the right to compel class notice if its motion for summary judgment is denied and the court makes no findings on the merits. *Id.* at 7–8, 593 S.W.3d at 485–86. *But see Nat'l Enters., Inc. v. Kessler*, 363 Ark. 167, 213 S.W.3d 597 (2005).

Rule 23(b) of the Arkansas Rules of Civil Procedure requires a trial court to make specific findings in a class certification order. ("An order certifying a class action must define the class and the class claims, issues, or defenses.") Similarly. Ark. R. Civ. P. 52(a) also requires the trial court to enter specific findings of fact and conclusions of law with respect to the court's ruling on class certification when a party makes a timely request. Absent a trial court making these findings, the burden falls on the litigants to request them. A party's failure to make such a request previously constituted a waiver of the Rule 23(b) requirements. *Jacola*, 330 Ark. at 268, 975 S.W.2d at 900. More recently, the Arkansas Supreme Court has recognized that the burden falls on the trial court to enter the required findings, and absent those findings, a class certification order should be remanded and may not be considered on appeal. *Pinson*, 2017 Ark. 315, 530 S.W.3d 854.

Upon receiving a Rule 52(a) request for specific findings, the trial court need only make brief, definite, pertinent findings and conclusions upon the contested matters. *BPS Inc. v. Richardson*, 341 Ark. 834, 849, 20 S.W.3d 403, 411 (2000). If a timely request is made by a party, the trial court's failure to make specific findings of fact and conclusions of law is an abuse of discretion. *Id.* at 850, 20 S.W.3d at 412. The trial court must undertake enough of an analysis to enable the appellate court to conduct a meaningful review of certification issues on appeal, which requires more than a cursory mention of the six criteria or bare conclusions that those criteria have been satisfied. *Chandler*, 353 Ark. at 349, 107 S.W.3d at 162; *Lenders Title Co. v. Chandler*, 358 Ark. 66, 77, 186 S.W.3d 695, 701 (2004). In 2019, the Arkansas Supreme Court announced that where Rule 52 is invoked, a trial court must enter specific findings of fact and conclusions of law for all six elements found in Rule 23, regardless of whether class certification is granted or denied. *Conley v. Boll Weevil Pawn Co.*, 2019 Ark. 31, at 6, 566 S.W.3d 125, 129.

Trial judges must set out clear findings of fact to sustain a class under Rule 23. In *Baptist Health v. Haynes*, the Arkansas Supreme Court reversed and remanded a trial court's order certifying a class due to insufficient findings of the criteria necessary for class certification because "the order does not explain what the common issues of law or fact are, nor does it explain how or why those common issues predominate, or why a class action is a superior method of adjudicating the plaintiffs' claims." 367 Ark. 382, 389, 240 S.W.3d 576, 582 (2006).

Arkansas trial courts are allowed to address pre-certification communication with potential class members if problems are brought to the court's attention. In *Fraley v. Williams Ford Tractor and Equip. Co.*, the Arkansas Supreme Court held that pre-certification communications with potential class members which attempt to substantially reduce member participation in the class action, or which otherwise indicate a likelihood of coercion or a serious potential for harm to the interests of the class, should be restricted or prohibited. 339 Ark. 322, 340, 5 S.W.3d 423, 434–35 (1999) (adopting the reasoning of the federal court in *Hampton Hardware, Inc. v. Cotter & Co., Inc.*, 156 F.R.D. 630 (N.D. Tex. 1994)).

In 2011, the Arkansas Supreme Court held that Arkansas courts have subject matter jurisdiction to review all class action settlements, including those that are reached before a suit is initiated and filed with the court. *Hunter v. Runyan*, 2011 Ark. 43, at 14, 382 S.W.3d 643, 651. Such review is required for each class action settlement. *Id.* at 11, 382 S.W.3d at 650.

The *Hunter* court also clarified that Arkansas law requires all class actions to allow opt-out rights. *Id.* at 15, 382 S.W.3d at 652. Unlike the federal rule, there are no mandatory classes under Rule 23(b)(2). *Id.* at 15, 382 S.W.3d at 652. Lastly, the *Hunter* court held that unnamed members of a class, whose request to intervene has not been granted, have no standing to appeal the final approval of class action settlement, even if they objected to the settlement. *Id.* at 15, 382 S.W.3d at 652; *see also DeJulius v. Sumner*, 373 Ark. 156, 160, 282 S.W.3d 753, 756 (2008).

Rule 2(a)(9) of the Arkansas Rules of Appellate Procedure is analogous to subsection (f) of Federal Rule 23 and provides that an order granting or denying class certification can be appealed as a matter of right. The trial court cannot require a supersedeas bond on appeal from a class certification order, and a petition for a writ of certiorari is a permissible remedy for the trial court's error in requiring such a bond. *Beverly Enters.-Ark., Inc. v. Cir. Ct. of Indep. Cnty.*, 367 Ark. 13, 16–17, 238 S.W.3d 108, 110–11 (2006).

This chapter was prepared by Byron J. Walker and Ryan Smith. Walker is a member of Rose Law Firm, a Professional Association. His practice focuses on complex business and regulatory litigation at the pretrial, trial, and appellate levels. Smith also is a member of Rose Law Firm. He practices in the area of business and commercial litigation.

CALIFORNIA

California's operative general class action statute, Code of Civil Procedure § 382, was enacted in 1872 as part of California's Field Code and has remained essentially unchanged. California's second class action statute, the Consumer Legal Remedies Act, is found at Civil Code §§ 1750, *et seq.*, and lists 23 prohibited acts, violations of which form the basis for class actions seeking damages and a wide variety of other remedies. In addition, California's Unfair Competition Law (UCL), Business and Professions Code §§ 17200, *et seq.*, permits anyone who incurs injury-in-fact to seek equitable forms of redress for group harms, including injunction, disgorgement, and restitution, through a class action.

1. STATEWIDE COURT RULES GOVERNING CLASS ACTIONS

Effective January 1, 2002, the California Judicial Council adopted a comprehensive system of uniform statewide Management of Class Action Rules (Cal. Rules of Ct., Rules 3.760-3.771.). These Rules supersede a patchwork of disparate local rules from Los Angeles, San Francisco, and San Diego counties. From the form of the complaint to the judgment, the new Rules provide a uniform procedure governing most aspects of class actions in California. The 12 new Rules of Court do not appear to change the existing substantive certification criteria that govern class actions in California, but instead codify the "best practices" of federal and state courts in addressing issues of discovery, certification, notice, and settlement to provide guidance to practitioners and courts for the effective management of class cases. These Rules "apply to each class action brought under Civil Code § 1750, *et seq.*, or Code of Civil Procedure § 382 until the court finds the action is not maintainable as a class action or revokes a prior class certification." (Cal. Rules of Ct., Rule 3.760(a).)

The Rules preempt local rules relating to pleadings, demurrers, ex parte applications, motions, discovery, provisional remedies, and the form and format of filings. As a result, all local rules on these matters concerning these fields are null and void unless otherwise permitted or required by statute or Judicial Council Rule. (Cal. Rules of Ct., Rule 981.1(a).) There are some exceptions, most significantly for local rules enacted under the Trial Court Delay Reduction Act. (Cal. Rules of Ct., Rule 981.1(b); *see* Gov. Code §§ 68600, *et seq.*) A former exception for local rules governing class actions was repealed effective January 1, 2002. (*See* former Cal. Rules of Ct., Rule 981.1(c).) Practitioners should familiarize themselves with these Rules, which prescribe procedures that differ markedly from federal practice in a number of respects, including class notice.

Rule 3.760 (Application) states that class actions brought under Civil Code § 1750, *et seq.*, or Code of Civil Procedure § 382 fall under the scope of Rules 3.760-3.771. Governing the contents of the complaint, Rule 3.761 (Form of Complaint) requires, *inter alia*, that the complaint include a description detailing how the case meets the requirements for class certification.

Rule 3.762 (Case Conference) directs the parties to consider case conferences to discuss class issues, discovery, hearings, and other matters, but prohibits presentation of evidence at such meetings. Should such a case conference occur, Rule 3.763 (Conference Order) allows the court, at its discretion, to make scheduling and other case management orders.

Rule 3.764 (Motion to Certify or Decertify a Class or Amend or Modify an Order Certifying a Class) allows both plaintiffs and defendants to file a motion to determine class issues. When the court certifies, amends, or modifies the class (Rule 3.765, Class Action Order), the court must issue an order containing a description of the class and any subclasses. Additionally, Rule 3.766 (Notice to Class Members) describes the procedures for determining the manner, content, and cost of any notice sent or published to inform absent class members of class certification. Under Rule 3.767 (Orders in the Conduct of Class Actions), the court has great flexibility in making a variety of orders regulating the conduct of the class action.

Marking a substantial departure from prior authority, Rule 3.768 (Discovery from Unnamed Class Members) recognizes for the first time the defendant's right to pursue discovery from unnamed class members, so long as the class has been certified. The other new Rules largely track prior law. For example, any settlement, as to any cause of action or any party, requires judicial review and approval under Rule 3.769 (Settlement of Class Actions). Rule 3.770 (Dismissal of Class Actions), in addition to mandating court approval for a dismissal—whether of an entire class action, a cause of action, or a party—requires that the facts on which the parties rely must be properly documented. Rule 3.771 (Judgment) states that the judgment must include the court's description of class members. This Rule also requires that proper notice be given.

2. CALIFORNIA'S CLASS ACTION ACT

California's primary class action statute, Code of Civil Procedure § 382, is a flexible tool that has been used to litigate and resolve complex cases in many different contexts. Section 382 states:

> [W]hen the question is one of a common or general interest, of many persons, or when the parties are numerous, and it is impracticable to bring them all before the court, one or more may sue or defend for the benefit of all.

To obtain certification under Code of Civil Procedure § 382, two primary requirements must be satisfied:

1. There must be an ascertainable class; and
2. There must be a well-defined community of interest in the questions of law or fact affecting the parties to be represented. (*Sav-On Drug Stores, Inc. v. Superior Court* (2004) 34 Cal. 4th 319 [17 Cal. Rptr. 3d 906] (*Sav-On*); *Richmond v. Dart Industries, Inc.* (1981) 29 Cal. 3d 482, 470 [174 Cal. Rptr. 506] (*Dart Indus.*); *Daar v. Yellow Cab* (1967) 67 Cal. 2d 695, 704 [63 Cal. Rptr. 724] (*Daar*); Judicial Council of California, *Deskbook on the Management of Complex Civil Litigation* (2003) § 3.71.)

A class is ascertainable, as required for certification, if the class definition is sufficiently clear and objective so that a court will be able to use it to determine membership of persons or entities in the class at the remedy phase. (*See Daar, supra*, 67 Cal. 2d at 704–06 (holding class including all customers of Yellow Cab Company cabs for four-year period was ascertainable); *see also Hicks v. Kaufman and Broad Home Corp.* (2001) 89 Cal. App. 4th 908 [107 Cal. Rptr. 2d 761] (class consisting of owners of homes with defective foundations located in specified housing developments constructed and marketed by defendant was precise, objective, and determinable, in part, from public records and defendant's records).) The primary concern of the courts in requiring ascertainability is to be able to identify the class members bound by class adjudication. (*Daar, supra,* 67 Cal. 2d at

704–06; *see generally Newberg on Class Actions* (4th ed. 2002) § 6.14, 614–20 (explaining ascertainability is a matter of clear and objective class definition with implications for binding class members).)

Acertainability is a low threshold. The California Supreme Court in *Noel v. Thrifty Payless* (2019) 445 P.3d 626 explained that a class is ascertainable "when it is defined in terms of objective characteristics and common transactional facts that make the ultimate identification of class members possible when that identification becomes necessary." *Id.* at 643. The court rejected the line of authority proposing a stricter view of ascertainability, which would call for an examination into (1) class definition, (2) the size of the class, and (3) the means of identifying class members. *See e.g.*, *Reyes v. Board of Supervisors* (1987) 196 Cal. App. 3d 1263, 1271. The *Noel* court held that no "additional requirement that the identification of class members must occur without unreasonable expense or time" should be "read[] into the ascertainability element." *Id.* at 646 (rejecting *Sotelo v. MediaNews Grp., Inc.* (2012) 207 Cal. App. 4th 639, 648–50). In addition, a representative plaintiff in a class action need not describe "how notice of the action will be communicated to individual class members" or prove that class members will receive individual notice of action. *Id.* at 644, 646. Class members must only demonstrate that the class is defined in "objective terms that make the eventual identification of class members possible." *Id.* at 642.

There is a federal circuit divide as to the ascertainability standard, with the Fifth, Sixth, Seventh, Eighth, and Ninth circuits applying a less stringent standard, which requires only that the court be able to "resolve the question of whether class members are included or excluded from the class by reference to objective criteria." (*See, e.g.*, *Briseno v. ConAgra Foods* (9th Cir. 2017) 844 F.3d 1121, 1131; *Rikos v. Procter & Gamble Co.* (6th Cir. 2015) 799 F.3d 497, 525), and the First, Second, Third, Fourth, and Eleventh circuits applying a higher standard, which requires a plaintiff to show that (1) the class is "defined with reference to objective criteria"; and (2) there is "a reliable and administratively feasible mechanism for determining whether putative class members fall within the class definition." (*See, e.g.*, *Byrd v. Aaron's Inc.* (3d Cir. 2015) 784 F.3d 154, 163.)

"The community of interest requirement involves three factors: (1) predominant common questions of law or fact; (2) class representatives with claims or defenses typical of the class; and (3) class representatives who can adequately represent the class." (*Linder v. Thrifty Oil Co.* (2000) 23 Cal. 4th 429, 435 [97 Cal. Rptr. 2d 179] (citations and quotations omitted).) (*Linder*) In *Sav-On*, the operating managers and assistant managers of the Sav-On drugstore chain moved for class certification in an overtime action. The trial court certified two sub-classes of operating and assistant managers. The Court of Appeal reversed, holding that under the circumstances of the case, the common legal issue of whether the Sav-On managers were exempt from wage and hour rules involved individual factual questions that predominated over common issues. (97 Cal. App. 4th 1070; 118 Cal. Rptr. 2d 792, 800.) The common legal question, according to the Court of Appeal, was whether the proposed class members spent more than half of their time on tasks that are characterized as "exempt"—that is, tasks that are primarily intellectual, managerial, or require discretionary judgment. The California Supreme Court unanimously reversed, and reinstated the class certification, finding that whether the operating and assistant managers spent more than 50% of their time performing non-managerial tasks is a predominating common issue. (*Sav-On, supra*, 34 Cal. 4th at 327.) For other examples of California predominance analysis, *compare Cipro Cases I and II* (2004) 121 Cal. App. 4th 402 [17 Cal. Rptr. 3d 1] (affirming class certification in antitrust indirect purchaser case, finding common issues of alleged anticompetitive behavior appropriate for class treatment) with *Global Minerals & Metals Corp. v. Superior Court* (2003) 113 Cal. App. 4th 836 [7 Cal. Rpt. 3d 28] (vacating antitrust class certification decision where plaintiffs were indirect purchasers and sellers of various copper products alleged to have been price-fixed). *See also Lebrilla v. Farmers Group,*

Inc. (2004) 119 Cal. App. 4th 1070 [16 Cal. Rptr. 3d 25] (reversing order denying class certification and finding that imitation crash parts were uniformly not of like kind and quality as original equipment parts); *but see Malmquist v. City of Folsom* (2024) 101 Cal. App. 5th 1186, 1203 (affirming denial of class certification because the question of whether the city's water was a substantial factor in causing leaks in copper pipes and damaging property would require individualized proof).

Recent decisions provide more examples of how California courts analyze the predominance requirement. One appellate court held that individual issues predominated for plaintiffs' meal break claim because defendant's operating units had different approaches to meal periods. *Bartoni v. Am. Med. Response West*, 11 Cal. App. 5th 1084, 1102 (2017). In contrast, another court held that common questions predominated when defendant had a policy of requiring all employees to sign on-duty meal agreements and allowing client preference to dictate whether an employee had an off-duty or on-duty meal period, instead of determining as the employer whether the nature of the work prevented its employees from having an off-duty meal period. *Lubin v. Wackenhut Corp.*, 5 Cal. App. 5th 926, 941 (2016). Conversely, in *Salazar v. See's Candy Shops, Inc.*, 64 Cal. App. 5th 85, 93 (2021), the court affirmed denial of class certification, holding that employee timekeeping records were insufficient to demonstrate predominance because individual testimony was required to determine whether employees voluntarily worked through their breaks. Another court affirmed denial of class certification because plaintiffs provided no common proof that putative class members were required to work overtime. *Kizer v. Tristar Risk Mgmt.*, 13 Cal. App. 5th 830, 834 (2017). In another case denying class certification, the Court found that plaintiffs' double-blind survey, the sole evidence provided to determine liability, afforded no fair, manageable way to establish liability on common proof. *McCleery v. Allstate Ins. Co.*, 37 Cal. App. 5th 434, 456 (2019). And in a decision setting out a new test for employment status, the California Supreme Court found commonality satisfied by the question of whether work performed by delivery drivers occurred in the usual course of the hiring company's business, and by the question of whether the drivers were engaged in an independently established trade such that their categorization as independent contractors was improper. *Dynamex Operations W. v. Superior Court*, 4 Cal. 5th 903 (2018).

In determining whether the class action requirements are met, California courts also consider the following factors:

1. Numerosity—whether the class is so numerous that joinder of all members individually would be impractical;
2. Commonality—whether issues of law and fact common to the class predominate over individual issues;
3. Typicality—whether the claims of the representative plaintiff are typical of the class claims generally;
4. Adequacy of representation—whether the representative plaintiff will fairly and adequately protect the interests of the class members; and
5. Superiority—whether a class action would be a fair and more efficient means of resolving the dispute.[1]

(*Daar, supra*, 67 Cal. 2d at 709; *B.W.I. Custom Kitchen v. Owens-Illinois* (1981) 191 Cal. App. 3d 1341, 1347-55 [235 Cal. Rptr. 228]; *Lazar v. Hertz Corp.* (1983) 143 Cal. App. 3d 128 [191 Cal.

---

[1] Superiority is demonstrated where the class action "both eliminates the possibility of repetitious litigation and provides small claimants with a method of obtaining redress for claims which would otherwise be too small to warrant individual litigation." *Dart Indus., supra*, 29 Cal. 3d at 469.

Rptr. 849].)

While California's legislature has never formally adopted Rule 23 of the Federal Rules of Civil Procedure (except for claims under California Consumer Legal Remedies Act, Civil Code § 1781, which incorporates most of Rule 23's actual language), the California Supreme Court has effectively tapped it as a resource, both by direct reliance upon the Rule and upon federal decisions interpreting it. (*Linder, supra*, 23 Cal. 4th at 437–38, *modified by Linder*, 23 Cal. 4th 1079; *City of San Jose v. Superior Court* (1974) 12 Cal. 3d 447 [115 Cal. Rptr. 797] (denying class status to airport neighbors asserting damages for diminution of market value).) In practice, California trial courts look to Rule 23 for guidance on class certification criteria, and most practitioners allege and brief the Rule 23 criteria in addressing Code of Civil Procedure § 382 ascertainability and community of interest standards.

Although § 382 of the Code of Civil Procedure is silent on the question of the availability of "mandatory" class certification, such as provided under Rule 23(b)(1) and 23(b)(2), California Courts regularly rely upon these federal provisions to certify claims in appropriate circumstances, principally for claims rooted in equity. (*See, e.g., Bell v. American Title Ins. Co.* (1991) 226 Cal. App. 3d 1589, 1603-1606 [277 Cal. Rptr. 583] (approving class certification, under Rule 23(b)(2), of claims arising from alleged title insurance fee abuses).) In *Bell*, for example, the California Court of Appeals adopted the federal judiciary's preference for Rule 23(b)(1) and/or (b)(2) class certification over 23(b)(3) certification, when the court has a choice. (*Id.* at 1608.) California practitioners should, however, avoid undue emphasis on federal law when California law suffices. (*See, e.g., Stephen v. Enterprise Rent-A-Car* (1991) 235 Cal. App. 3d 806, 814 [1 Cal. Rptr. 2d 130] ("[i]t is only in the absence of relevant state precedent that courts turn to federal law and Rule 23 for guidance").) Notably, under Rule 1856(b)-(e), the Court has discretion whether or not to allow notice to and/or exclusion from the Class under the particular circumstances of the cases, making notice much more flexible under California practice than it is even under recently revised Federal Rule 23(c).

In *Linder*, the California Supreme Court reiterated the position consistent with federal law that class certification is a procedural matter and is to be made without regard to the merits of the case. (*Linder, supra*, 23 Cal. 4th at 439–40.) The *Linder* court rejected the defendant's invitation to add an additional barrier to class certification by requiring trial courts to evaluate the merits of the underlying claims prior to certifying a class, noting that pre-certification merits challenges are already permitted by standard demurrer and pre-trial motion practice and suggesting that a merits challenge may be included in the certification proceeding only in exceptional circumstances. (*Id.* at 445.) (*See also Sav-On, supra*, 34 Cal. 4th at 326; *Fireside Bank v. Superior Court* (2007) 40 Cal. 4th 1069 [56 Cal. Rptr. 3d 861].)

The question of whether a particular action meets the requirements of Code of Civil Procedure § 382 rests within the sound discretion of the trial court. (*Kagan* v. *Gibraltar Sav. & Loan Assoc.* (1984) 35 Cal. 3d 582, 595 [200 Cal. Rptr. 38].) However, as demonstrated in *Hicks v. Kaufman and Broad Home Corp.* (2001) 89 Cal. App. 4th 908 [107 Cal. Rptr. 2d 761] (*Hicks*), the denial of class certification is an appealable order. (*See also Dart Indus., supra*, 29 Cal. 3d at 470.) According to *Daar v. Yellow Cab Co.* (1967) 67 Cal. 2d 695, 69, denying class certification is "tantamount to a dismissal of the action as to all members of the class other than plaintiff" and "'prevents further proceedings as effectually as would any formal judgment.'" (*Herrscher v. Herrscher, supra,* 41 Cal.2d at 303–04; *see Southern Pac. R.R. Co. v. Willett* (1932) 216 Cal. 387, 390 [14 P.2d 526] as cited in *Daar.*) As a result, the denial of certification of a class effectively sounds the death knell for the claims of many class members. As illustrated in *Hicks*, the trial court's denial of class certification can deprive class members of the possibility of a remedy because many class action suits involve claims that are not substantial enough to warrant individual litigation. In *Blue Chip Stamps v. Superior Court of Los Angeles County* (1976) 18 Cal. 3d 381 [134 Cal. Rptr. 393], Justice Tobriner emphasizes this point in his separate concurring opinion, stating that "a company which wrongfully exacts a dollar from each of millions of customers will reap a handsome profit; the class action is often the only effective way to halt and redress such exploitation. The problems which arise in the management of a class action involving numerous small claims do not justify a judicial policy that would permit the defendant to retain the benefits of its wrongful conduct and to continue that conduct with impunity." Tobriner's opinion has been quoted repeatedly, including the decisions in *Murphy v. Check n' Go of California, Inc.* (2007) 156 Cal. App. 4th 138 [67 Cal. Rptr. 3d 120], *Discover Bank v. Superior Court* (2005) 36 Cal. 4th 148 [30 Cal. Rptr. 3d 76, 113 P.3d 1100], and *Linder*.

In *Hicks*, the court of appeals reversed a trial court and instructed it to certify a class of defective home foundation claims for homeowners pursuing relief under theories of breach of express and implied warranty while upholding the decision not to certify tort claims for strict liability and negligence because of the economic loss rule. Further, the court held that "proof of breach of warranty does not require proof the product has malfunctioned but only that it contains an inherent defect which is substantially certain to result in malfunction during the useful life of the product. The question whether an inherently defective product is presently functioning as warranted goes to the remedy for the breach, not proof of the breach itself." (*Hicks, supra,* 89 Cal. App. 4th at 917–18.)[2] The court also rejected the contention that the representative plaintiffs were inadequate for seeking only economic damages, and not consequential compensation damages (such as harm to carpets or tiles, etc.) on the grounds that the court has multiple options including issue certification, analogous to and recognized under Fed. Rules Civ. Proc., Rule 23(c)(4), which empowers trial courts with flexibility to even certify limited issues for class treatment. (*Hicks* at 925–26 (footnotes omitted)).

In *Lockheed Martin Corp. v. Superior Court of San Bernardino County* (2003) 29 Cal. 4th 1096 [131 Cal. Rptr. 2d 1], the California Supreme Court upheld a writ directing the trial court to vacate certification of a class for medical monitoring. The plaintiffs had alleged that seven different defendants had contaminated the City of Redlands' municipal drinking water supply with twelve different toxic chemicals over a period of forty years and plaintiffs requested that defendants fund medical monitoring on behalf of a class of over fifty thousand class members for forty different medical conditions. In *Lockheed*, the Supreme Court acknowledged evidence that many Redlands residents were exposed to toxic chemicals during the class period but stated that evidence of exposure alone in that case did not support a finding that medical monitoring was a reasonably necessary response, especially because the toxic exposures would be so disparate among the class members. (*Id.* at p. 1109.) Therefore, the Supreme Court held that plaintiffs did not provide substantial evidence to resolve possible dosage issues with common proof because "each class member's actual toxic dosage would remain relevant to some degree." (*Id.*)

In *Lockheed*, the California Supreme Court unanimously refused to recognize the existence of any "per se or categorical bar" to any type of classwide medical monitoring claim "susceptible to common proof." (*Lockheed, supra*, 29 Cal. 4th at 1104–05.) The key holding in *Lockheed* reaffirms the overarching standard for determining whether any case qualifies for class treatment. *Lockheed* rejected a stricter standard for certification in medical monitoring or tort cases, instead repeating the

---

[2] *See also* American Honda Motor Co., Inc. v. Superior Court, 199 Cal. App. 4th 1367, 1375 [132 Cal. Rptr. 3d 91] (2011) (clarifying that "[a] breach of warranty cannot result if the product operates as it was intended to and does not malfunction during its useful life.") (*citing* Daugherty v. American Honda Motor Co., Inc. (2006) 144 Cal. App. 4th 824, 831–832 [51 Cal. Rptr. 3d 118])).

universal standard first articulated in *Collins v. Rocha* (1972) 7 Cal. 3d 232, 238 [102 Cal. Rptr. 1]: "The ultimate question in every case . . . is whether . . . the issues which may be jointly tried, when compared with those requiring separate adjudication, are so numerous or substantial that the maintenance of a class action would be advantageous to the judicial process and to the litigants." (*Lockheed, supra,* 131 Cal. Rptr. 2d at 7.) This requirement is the touchstone of class certification jurisprudence in California and provides the context within which each of the specific certification factors enumerated in §§ 382, 1781, the Rules of Court, and case law must be considered.

Under the right circumstances, class certification of medical monitoring claims is enjoying increasing support from the courts and from leading scientists because of its important public policy principles, prevention of serious injury and/or death from early detection and treatment. (*See, e.g., In re Diet Drugs Prods. Liab. Litig.*, 1999 U.S. Dist. LEXIS 13228 (E.D. Pa. Aug. 26, 1999) [granting nationwide medical monitoring Class Certification for persons nationwide exposed for more than 60 days to Pondimin and/or Redux]; Studdart et al., *Medical Monitoring for Pharmaceutical Injuries: Tort Law for the Public's Health?* (February 19, 2003) 289 JAMA 889 ["Medical monitoring arms the courts with a new mechanism for addressing harms proactively rather than reactively, which could yield new victories for public health."]).

In *Duran v. U.S. Bank Nat'l Ass'n*, No. S200923, 2014 WL 2219042 (Cal. May 29, 2014), a much-awaited and important decision, the California Supreme Court followed the middle-of-the-road course seen in prior recent decisions, such as *Brinker*. On the one hand, the court reiterated the availability of representative testimony to determine liability and damages. On the other hand, the court held that class action trial management plans that incorporate representative testimony and random sampling are subject to a preliminary assessment to determine the level of variability within the class and to permit litigation of relevant affirmative defenses. *Cf. Tyson Foods, Inc. v. Bouaphakeo*, 136 S. Ct. 1036 (2016) (holding that representative evidence from a sample can be used to show predominance of common questions of law and fact, depending on the purpose for which the sample is being introduced and on the underlying cause of action). *But see McCleery v. Allstate*, 37 Cal. App. 5th 434 (2019) (denying class certification because plaintiffs' liability and damage calculations were solely based on the evidence of an expert witness relying on an anonymous double-blind survey).

3. *CY PRES*/FLUID RECOVERY

California courts have endorsed the principle of *cy pres* and the mechanism of fluid recovery in class actions, by which settlement or judgment proceeds are dedicated to charitable or nonprofit organizations. (*State of California v. Levi Strauss & Co.*, 41 Cal. 3d 460, 224 Cal. Rptr. 605 (1986). *Cy pres*, which means "as near as possible," has been utilized by courts "where class members are difficult to identify, or where they change constantly, or where there are unclaimed funds." (Herbert B. Newberg & Alba Conte, *Newberg on Class* Actions § 10:16 n.1 (4th ed. 2002).)

In *Cundiff v. Verizon California, Inc.*, 167 Cal. App. 4th 718, 84 Cal. Rptr. 3d 377 (2008), the court of appeal held that the procedure for distribution of unpaid residue applies not only to circumstances in which a common fund is created, but also to claims-made settlements. In this case the court of appeal reversed the trial court's decision that the Code of Civ. Proc. Sec. 384 does not apply to the "claims made settlement" and held instead that Sec. 384's definition of "unpaid residue" includes uncashed and returned settlement checks.

Typically, the residue remaining in a class fund is distributed *cy pres* after claims have been paid to individual class members, but the California courts have expressly endorsed the dedication of the entirety of a class action settlement to *cy pres* benefits, where the circumstances of the case or the nature of the settlement render individual distribution impractical or cost-ineffective. (*In re Vitamin Cases*, 107 Cal. App. 4th 820, 132 Cal. Rptr. 2d 425 (2003) (affirming *cy pres* treatment of the entirety of a $38 million consumer class settlement).) In *Principles of the Law of Aggregate Litigation* (American Law Institute 2010), the American Law Institute proposes a rule limiting *cy pres* to "circumstances in which direct distribution to individual class members is not economically feasible, or where funds remain after class members are given a full opportunity to make a claim." (*Aggregate Litigation*, § 3.07, entitled "Cy Pres Settlements"). Additional alternatives to *cy pres* or fluid distribution that the court may consider to distribute unclaimed funds are to escheat them to the government and revert them to defendants. (*Six Mexican Workers v. Arizona Citrus Growers* 904 F.2d 1301, 1305 (9th Cir. 1990).)

Under California law, the *cy pres* distribution must aim to "further the purposes of the underlying causes of action" or "promote justice for all Californians." (Cal. Code Civ. Proc. § 384.) Similarly, in federal courts, the *cy pres* distribution must aim at benefiting the class or be related to the underlying claims. The Ninth Circuit set aside two settlements for failing to meet this standard: First, in *Nachshin v. AOL, LLC*, 663 F.3d 1034, 1040 (9th Cir. 2011), the Ninth Circuit found that while the *cy pres* distributions were made on behalf of a nationwide plaintiff class, they were improperly distributed to geographically isolated and substantively unrelated charities. Second, in *Dennis v. Kellogg Co.*, 2012 U.S. App. LEXIS 14385, at *15–20 (9th Cir. July 13, 2012, No. 11-55674), the *cy pres* recipients—unspecified charities that feed the indigent—were not sufficiently related to the plaintiffs' allegation that Kellogg falsely stated that its cereal was scientifically proven to improve children's cognitive functions.

4. CALIFORNIA'S CONSUMERS LEGAL REMEDIES ACT

The Consumers Legal Remedies Act, Civil Code §§ 1750 *et seq.* (CLRA), was enacted in 1970 and "established a nonexclusive statutory remedy for 'unfair methods of competition and unfair or deceptive acts or practices undertaken by any person in a transaction intended to result or which results in the sale or lease of goods or services to any consumer. . . .'" (*Reveles v. Toyota by the Bay* (1997) 57 Cal. App. 4th 1139, 1154 [67 Cal. Rptr. 2d 543], *quoting Gallin v. Superior Court* (1991) 230 Cal. App. 3d 541, 545–46 [281 Cal. Rptr. 304].) The CLRA's key provision is Civil Code § 1781, which permits a consumer action to be maintained as a class action, and mandates certification of the class if the enumerated requirements are met. The standards are:

- It is impracticable to bring all members of the class before the court.
- The questions of law or fact common to the class are substantially similar and predominate over the questions affecting the individual members.
- The claims or defenses of the representative plaintiffs are typical of the claims or defenses of the class.
- The representative plaintiffs will fairly and adequately protect the interests of the class.

(Civ. Code § 1781.) If these tests are met, and the claims presented fall within one of the 23 acts specifically prohibited by Civil Code §§ 1770(a)(1)–(23), class certification "shall" be granted. (Civ. Code § 1781(b).) The determination of whether class certification requirements were met lies, again, within the trial court's discretion. (*Petherbridge v. Altadena Federal Sav. and Loan Ass'n* (1974) 37 Cal. App. 3d 193, 199 [112 Cal. Rptr. 144].) The court is empowered to order either party to give notice to the class if a matter is certified. (Civ. Code § 1781(d).) In consumer matters, defendants ordinarily are required to pay for notice. (*See, e.g., Civil Service Emp. Ins. Co.* v. *Superior Court of*

City and County of San Francisco (1978) 22 Cal. 3d 362, 365 [149 Cal. Rptr. 360].)

The third standard may be met regardless of whether the plaintiffs' damage claims are identical or varied. According to *Rose v. City of Hayward, supra,* 126 Cal. App. 4th at 934, "the law unequivocally provides that each class member may establish damages independently without threatening the integrity of the class action." This rule was established in *Vasquez v. Superior Court* (1971) 4 Cal. 3d 800, which states that "the mere fact that, ultimately, each class member will be required to establish his individual damages does not preclude the maintenance of a class action." It goes on to say that "the fact that some matters bearing on the right to a recovery in a purported class action may require separate proof by each class member will not preclude maintenance of the action as a class action, so long as the issues that may be jointly tried, as compared to those requiring separate adjudication, justify the maintenance of the suit as a class action." As a result, each plaintiff may have a different claim without jeopardizing the class action status of the plaintiffs.

The fourth requirement has caused a great deal of discussion. This is due primarily to the fact that some defendants choose to settle with the representative plaintiffs, raising concern that the representative plaintiffs may no longer fairly and adequately represent the remaining class members. Deciding whether a plaintiff who has already received individual benefits should be allowed to continue as the case's representative plaintiff is up to the trial court. (*La Sala v. American Sav. & Loan Assn.* (1971) 5 Cal. 3d 864, 871–72 [97 Cal. Rptr. 849] (*Sala*).) In making its determination, "the trial court may take into account that the named plaintiffs have already obtained their individual benefits from the action; plaintiffs who have nothing at stake often will not devote sufficient energy to the prosecution of the action; further, the receipt of benefits by the named plaintiffs may sometimes create a conflict of interest between the class and its would-be representatives. On the other hand, [. . .] the court may find that the named plaintiffs will continue fairly to represent the class, and, therefore, permit them to continue the class litigation." (*Id.* at 871–72.) As evidenced by the analysis of Reed's *Legislating for the Consumer: An Insider's Analysis of the Consumers Legal Remedies Act* (1971) 2 Pacific L.J. 1, 19, the drafters of CLRA intentionally sought to bar the "picking off" of prospective class action plaintiffs through settlements:

> The most important point in connection with the settlement of class actions is that settlement with the named plaintiffs will not preclude them from further prosecuting the action on behalf of the remaining members of the class. Note that § 1782(c) precludes the further maintenance of the action only if *all* the described conditions are shown to exist. Those conditions require settlement with all reasonably identifiable members of the class. The term 'maintained' in § 1782 (c) was deliberately and carefully chosen just as the term 'commenced' was deliberately avoided. *The intent was to make certain that a person can commence a class action 30 days after he has made a demand on behalf of the class even if the merchant has offered to settle his particular claim in accordance with § 1782(b)*. An action so commenced may not be maintained, however, if the conditions for settlement with the class have been met. It is evident that construction of § 1782(c) so as to preclude a person from maintaining any action if his particular claim had been settled would destroy class actions under the statute. That most certainly was not the intent of the legislature. (Italics added.)

In cases where defendants and representative plaintiffs come to an agreement, the trial court must take great care to determine whether the representative plaintiff is still willing and able to capably represent the interests of the remaining plaintiffs. In contrast, if the defendant did not voluntarily offer plaintiffs a settlement, then the "pick off" exception to mootness does not apply.

Schoshinski v. City of Los Angeles (2017), 9 Cal. App. 5th 780, 804.

A wide variety of potential remedies are available under the CLRA, including actual damages, punitive damages, injunctive relief, restitution, civil penalties of $5,000 for each plaintiff or class member for acts injurious to "Senior Citizens" and/or "Disabled Persons" and "any other relief that the court deems proper." (Civ. Code §§ 1780(a)(1)–(5) & (b).) Only "consumers" who have actually suffered damage from the prohibited practice may sue under the CLRA. (*Kagan v. Gibraltar Sav. & Loan Assn., supra,* 35 Cal. 3d at 593 ("we interpret broadly the requirement of § 1780 that a consumer 'suffer any damage' to include the infringement of any legal right as defined by § 1770").)

The CLRA's class action procedures are narrower than those under Code of Civil Procedure § 382, since the California courts do not read the provisions of Rule 23(b)(1) and (2) into the CLRA, as they do with § 382. (*See also* Stern, Bus. & Prof. C. § 17200 Practice (2004) §§ 10:69 *et seq.*) However, class certification under CLRA § 1781 is more flexible than under Rule 23, since class claims brought under the CLRA do *not* require a showing of superiority or substantial benefit to the public for certification. (Civ. Code § 1781(b); *Hogya v. Superior Court* (1977) 75 Cal. App. 3d 122, 136 [142 Cal. Rptr. 325] (CLRA's purpose would be undermined if class certification could be denied based upon trial court's own assessment of the presence or absence of a public benefit resulting from certification); *cf. Caro v. Procter & Gamble Co.* (1993) 18 Cal. App. 4th 644, 654-55 [22 Cal. Rptr. 2d 419] (upholding denial of class certification, under Code of Civil Procedure § 382, of an orange juice mislabeling action where trial court observed a lack of substantial public benefit).) Where class claims brought under the CLRA are joined with other claims, certification of the CLRA claims is governed by Civil Code § 1781, while certification of the remaining claims is governed by § 382.

Notably, as a pre-condition to the initiation and maintenance of a damages action, Civil Code § 1782 requires a minimum of 30 days' notice to the intended defendant, during which period the intended defendant may correct the alleged wrongs, or plan to correct them within a reasonable period, and thereby prevent a CLRA damages claim. (Civ. Code § 1782(b); *Kagan v. Gibraltar Sav. & Loan Ass'n, supra,* 35 Cal. 3d at 590. *See Valdez v. Seidner-Miller, Inc.*, 33 Cal. App. 5th 600 (Cal. Ct. App. 2019) (holding that when "30 days after receipt of the notice" falls on Saturday, Sunday, or other holiday, the defendant has until the following business day to respond).) In practice, plaintiffs often file a CLRA class action seeking equitable relief and send the statutory demand letter simultaneously; thereafter, if the defendant does not correct the practice complained of, the existing equitable relief complaint is amended to add a damages claim.

California law supports the proposition that to prove class-wide "causation" under the CLRA, individual proof of subjective reliance need not be shown to satisfy the causation element of a claim because an inference of common reliance arises where material information has been uniformly concealed from, or not disclosed to, the class as a whole. The propriety of inferring common reliance from the materiality of a misrepresentation or concealment that was broadly disseminated to the class as a whole was most recently reaffirmed in *McAdams v. Monier, Inc.* (2010) 182 Cal. App. 4th 174 [105 Cal. Rptr. 3d 704] (manufacturer's failure to disclose product defect supported inference of common reliance) and *Massachusetts Mutual Life Ins. Co. v. Superior Court* (2002) 97 Cal. App. 4th 1282 [119 Cal. Rptr. 2d 190]. A practitioner must always bear in mind, however, that "such an inference will not arise where the record will not permit it." (*Id.* at 1294 [distinguishing the court's refusal to infer reliance in *Caro v. Procter & Gamble Co., supra*, 18 Cal. App. 4th 644].) Thus, the class plaintiffs must be prepared to present evidence, obtained through investigation and discovery, that the defendant made uniform misrepresentations to, or uniformly withheld or concealed information from, the class as a whole. Once broad dissemination of common (mis)information to the class has been established, "the ultimate question of whether the undisclosed [or affirmatively misrepresented] information was material [is] a common question of fact suitable for treatment in a class action." (*Massachusetts Mutual Life Ins. Co. v. Superior Court, supra,* 97 Cal. App. 4th at 1294.) For a Ninth Circuit decision addressing and confirming class certification under the CLRA, *see Chamberlan v. Ford Motor Co.* (9th Cir. 2005) 402 F.3d 952.

5. CALIFORNIA'S UNFAIR COMPETITION LAW

California's unfair business practices law is found at Business and Professions Code §§ 17200, *et seq.*, and its companion Deceptive, False, and Misleading Advertising Law is codified at §§ 17500, *et seq.* Although not formally named by the legislature, the statutes are commonly referred to as the Unfair Competition Law (UCL). The roots of the UCL go back to 1933 when the California legislature first rejected the rule of *caveat emptor* by amending Civil Code § 3369 to prohibit acts of unfair competition. The California Supreme Court has repeatedly recognized the broad remedial purposes of the statute. (*Stop Youth Addiction, Inc. v. Lucky Stores* (1998) 17 Cal. 4th 553, 578 [71 Cal. Rptr. 2d 731].) In *Stop Youth Addiction*, the California Supreme Court endorsed § 17200 as a vehicle to redress group harm occasioned by any unfair business practice, including the violation of other laws. (*Id.* at 573–78.)

Previously, under the UCL's expansive statutory provisions, any person could act as a private attorney general on behalf of the general public and obtain broad equitable relief in the form of injunctions and/or restitution without the expense or delays attendant to class certification. (*Stop Youth Addiction, supra,* 17 Cal. 4th at 573–78.) Notably, in *Cortez v. Purolator Air Filtration Products* (2000) 23 Cal. 4th 163 [96 Cal. Rptr. 2d 518], the California Supreme Court recognized that restitution was not strictly limited to the recovery of funds that have actually been in the possession of the plaintiff but suggested, instead, that the concept of restitution extends to recovery of funds acquired by any illegal means. (*Id.* at 170–79.) In so holding, the court approved collective equitable relief to the class in the form of restitution of unpaid overtime wages owed to workers, in recognition of the principle that restitution includes enforcement of obligations to pay funds owed. (*Id.*)

On November 2, 2004, the California electorate passed Proposition 64. Among other things, Proposition 64 requires that a plaintiff pursuing a § 17200 claim allege an actual injury to him, her, or itself, and not sue on behalf of the general public as a private attorney general. As amended, § 17204 now reads in pertinent part:

> Actions for any relief pursuant to this chapter shall be prosecuted exclusively . . . by . . . or upon the complaint of any board, officer, person, corporation or association or by any person who has suffered injury in fact and has lost money or property as a result of such unfair competition.

The California Supreme Court ruled that Proposition 64 applies to cases that were filed before the revisions to § 17204 became effective. (*Californians for Disability Rights v. Mervyn's, LLC* (2006) 39 Cal. 4th 223 [46 Cal. Rptr. 3d 57].) The California Supreme Court clarified that Proposition 64 does not eliminate the ability of private plaintiffs to seek broad-ranging public injunctive relief, so any arbitration provision that purports to preclude public injunctive relief in any forum is void as contrary to public policy. *McGill v. Citibank, N.A.* (2017) 2 Cal. 5th 945, 952. Class certification is not required for UCL and FAL claims seeking injunctive relief to prevent future wrongful business practices that will injure the public. (*Id.* at 960.)

The California Supreme Court decision in *In re Tobacco II Cases* (2009) 46 Cal. 4th 298 [93 Cal. Rptr. 3d 559], addressed the question of who in a UCL class action must comply with Proposition 64's standing requirements. The Court, analogizing Prop 64's standing requirements to standing requirements in Federal Rule 23 class actions, held that only the class representatives, and not all absent class members, must meet the standing requirements set by Proposition 64. It found that holding otherwise would "undermine the guarantee made by Proposition 64's proponents that the initiative would not undermine the efficacy of the UCL as a means of protecting consumer rights, because requiring all unnamed members of a class action to individually establish standing would effectively eliminate the class action lawsuit as a vehicle for the vindication of such rights." (*Id.* at 321.) The Court also found that while the "as a result of" language imposed a reliance requirement in deceptive practice cases, the "the plaintiff need not demonstrate [that the misrepresentation] was the only cause" of the injury. (*Id.* at 326.) In *Kwikset Corp. v. Superior Court* (2011) 51 Cal. 4th 310, 330 [120 Cal. Rptr. 3d 741], the California Supreme Court clarified that while a plaintiff must allege "economic injury" that is caused by a deceptive practice to meet Proposition 64's standing requirements, this requirement is met by alleging that the plaintiff would not have bought the product but for the misrepresentation.[3] *See e.g.*, *Veera v. Banana Republic, LLC*, 6 Cal. App. 5th 907, 910 (Cal. App. 2d Dist. 2016) (reversing summary judgment, holding that plaintiffs who bought items from defendant at full price due to misleading advertising had standing to bring claims under the UCL, FAL, and CLRA because they suffered economic harm from the difference between the advertised price and the actual price paid). The Court suggested in both *Tobacco II* and *Kwikset* that the causation requirement may not apply in certain cases alleging "unfair" or "unlawful" practices. (*See Tobacco II*, *supra*, 46 Cal. 4th at 325, n.17; *Kwikset, supra*, 51 Cal. 4th at 326, n.9.)

Recent state and federal decisions applying *Tobacco II*'s and *Kwikset*'s holdings regarding standing, or addressing class certification in light of these holdings, include *Nelson v. Pearson Ford* (2010) 186 Cal. App. 4th 983 [112 Cal. Rptr. 3d 607] (illegal charges caused economic injury); *Durell v. Sharp Healthcare* (2010) 183 Cal. App. 4th 1350 [108 Cal. Rptr. 3d 682] (no standing where plaintiff failed to allege reliance); *Hale v. Sharp Healthcare* (2010) 183 Cal. App. 4th 1383 [108 Cal. Rptr. 3d 669] (reliance properly pled); *Pfizer v. Superior Court* (2010) 182 Cal. App. 4th 622 [105 Cal. Rptr. 3d 795] (class certification reversed where class members were not exposed to misrepresentations); *Knapp v. AT&T Wireless Services, Inc.* (2011) 195 Cal. App. 4th 932 [124 Cal. Rptr. 3d 565] (same); *Davis-Miller v. Automobile Club of Southern California* (2011) 201 Cal. App. 4th 106 [134 Cal. Rptr. 3d 551] (same); *Mazza v. Am. Honda Motor Co.* (9th Cir. 2012) 666 F.3d 581 (same); *Tucker v. Pacific Bell Mobile Servs.* (Aug. 7, 2012, A132619) 2012 Cal. App. LEXIS 866 (demurrer on class allegations upheld based on *Knapp*); *Stearns v. Ticketmaster Corp.* (9th Cir. 2011) 655 F.3d 1013 (reversing denial of class certification on ground that unnamed class members need not prove standing under either the UCL or Article III); *POM Wonderful LLC v. Coca-Cola Co.* (9th Cir. 2012) 679 F.3d 1170, 1178 (district court erroneously interpreted "lost money or property" language to require the plaintiff to show entitlement to restitution in UCL injunctive relief claim); *Chavez v. Blue Sky Beverage Co.* (N.D. Cal. 2010) 268 F.R.D. 365 (granting class certification); *Estrella v. Freedom Fin. Network* (N.D. Cal. June 2, 2010, No. C 09-03156) 2010 U.S. Dist. LEXIS 61236 (same).

The California Supreme Court addressed the relief available under the UCL in *Korea Supply Co. v. Lockheed Martin Corp.* (2003) 29 Cal. 4th 1134 [131 Cal. Rptr. 2d 29]. The court confirmed that although plaintiffs cannot seek damages under the UCL, their right to restitution includes recovery of money that a defendant took directly from them as well as of money in which they had an

---

[3] The Court also noted that there were "innumerable" other ways in which "economic injury" may be present: "A plaintiff may (1) surrender in a transaction more, or acquire in a transaction less, than he or she otherwise would have; (2) have a present or future property interest diminished; (3) be deprived of money or property to which he or she has a cognizable claim; or (4) be required to enter into a transaction, costing money or property, that would otherwise have been unnecessary." *Kwikset, supra,* 51 Cal. 4th at 323.

ownership interest. (*Id.* at 1145.) However, the court held that a plaintiff in *an individual action* had no right to the *non-restitutionary* disgorgement of profits. (*Id.* at 1140.) In *Korea Supply*, this limited the remedies available to the plaintiff, who alleged that it lost a commission it would have received on a potential contract with the Korean government because a competitor secured the contract by offering government officials bribes and sexual favors. The California Supreme Court held that even if the competitor's actions violated the UCL, the plaintiff could not recover the profits of the competitor or its own lost commission. (*Id.* at 1152.) Those measures of relief could not be properly characterized as "restitution." (*Id.*) The court nevertheless indicated that in *class actions* the plaintiffs might be entitled to even this sort of non-restitutionary disgorgement of profits. (*Id.* at 1148, fn.6.)

In *Corbett v. Superior Court* (2002) 101 Cal. App. 4th 649 [125 Cal. Rptr. 2d 46], the court of appeal held that a UCL claim permits fluid recovery as long as it is part of a certified class action where notice is provided to the class. In the absence of formal class certification, however, UCL plaintiffs can only obtain restitution for injured persons who actually make a claim; plaintiffs may not obtain the type of "fluid fund" or "cy pres" recovery that is permitted in a formal class action. (*Kraus v. Trinity Management Services, Inc.* (2000) 23 Cal. 4th 116 [96 Cal. Rptr. 2d 485], *rehg. den.* (2000) 2000 Cal. LEXIS 5863 [2000 Cal. Daily Op. Service 6063].) Similarly, because restitution, even liberally construed, does not encompass actual damages, practitioners should, in appropriate cases, consider combining injunctive/equitable UCL claims along with class claims for damages. (*See also Dean Witter Reynolds, Inc. v. Superior Court* (1989) 211 Cal. App. 3d 758, 774 [259 Cal. Rptr. 789] (exclusion of compensatory damages claims from the UCL is "consistent with the overarching legislative concern to provide a streamlined procedure for the prevention of ongoing or threatened acts of unfair competition.").)

The California legislature amended the UCL in 1992 to expand the definition of unfair competition to include "any" unlawful, unfair, or fraudulent business "act or practice." (Bus. & Prof. Code § 17200 (Historical and Statutory Notes).) This "borrowing provision" of the UCL permits a cause of action to be maintained if a challenged practice violates some other law, even if that law does not provide a private right of action. (*Stop Youth Addiction, supra*, 17 Cal. 4th at 573–75 (rejecting defendants' contention that underlying penal code violations are exclusively reserved for governmental prosecution).) Moreover, even if a practice is not illegal, it may be unfair or deceptive. (*See, e.g., Committee on Children's Television, Inc. v. General Foods Corp.* (1983) 35 Cal. 3d 197 [197 Cal. Rptr. 783] (*Committee on Children's Television*).)

In *Committee on Children's Television*, the Supreme Court of California reversed the trial court's grant of a demurrer to claims brought in connection with alleged misrepresentations involving sugared breakfast cereals and, in so doing, recognized the UCL's broad prohibition against unfair or deceptive practices, stating that to obtain injunctive relief, it is "necessary only to show that 'members of the public are likely to be deceived.'" (*Committee on Children's Television, supra,* 35 Cal. 3d at 211). Moreover, the California Supreme Court observed that a trial court "may also order restitution without individualized proof of deception, reliance, and injury if it 'determines that such is remedy is necessary to prevent the use or employment of the unfair practice. . . . '" (*Id., citing Fletcher v. Security Pacific National Bank* (1979) 23 Cal. 3d 442, 453 [153 Cal. Rptr. 28]; *see also In re Tobacco II Cases, supra,* 46 Cal. 4th at 320 (distinguishing standard of proving entitlement to restitution with standard of proving standing under the UCL).) Significantly, 1992 amendments to the UCL also expanded the scope of injunctive relief to encompass past activity and out-of-state activity, so long as the problematic action emanated from California. (Bus. & Prof. Code § 17203 (Historical and Statutory Notes).)

The broad scope of the UCL and its particular suitability to class treatment were recognized in *Prata v. Superior Court* (2001) 91 Cal. App. 4th 1128 [111 Cal. Rptr. 2d 296] (*Prata*). *Prata* was brought under the UCL as a proposed class action on behalf of Bank One customers for false and misleading advertising from its "Same-as-Cash" program. (*Id.*) The trial court granted summary adjudication in favor of Bank One on the UCL claims, finding that the existence of 19 different advertisements, different locales, and multiple merchants would be unmanageable as a class action. (*Id.* at 1134–35.) However, the court of appeal granted plaintiff's petition for a writ of mandate on the grounds that the trial court abused its discretion in applying the wrong legal standards under § 17200, and directed the trial court to vacate its ruling that plaintiff could not bring a representative action, finding that no individualized inquiry was required in order to find a violation of § 17200. According to the Court: "The burden of proof is modest: the representative plaintiff must show that members of the public are likely to be deceived by the practice. It was therefore not necessary for the trial court to determine which advertisements, disclosures, or representations actually were relied upon by members of the public who participated in Bank One's 'Same-As-Cash' promotion to determine liability." (*Id.* at 1144) (citations omitted).)

The *Prata* court also detailed some of the myriad ways in which the general public could be deceived under the UCL: "By their breadth, [§§ 17200 and 17500] encompass not only those advertisements which have been deceived or misled because they are untrue, but also those which may be accurate on some level, but will nonetheless tend to mislead or deceive. . . . A perfectly true statement couched in such a manner that it is likely to mislead or deceive the consumer, such as by failure to disclose other relevant information, is actionable under these §§." (*Prata, supra,* 91 Cal. App. 4th at 1137, *citing Day v. AT&T Corp.* (1968) 63 Cal. App. 4th 325, 332–33 [74 Cal. Rptr. 2d 55].). *Massachusetts Mutual Life Ins. Co. v. Superior Court, supra,* 97 Cal. App. 4th 1282, reaffirms *Prata's* holding that reliance is not an element of a UCL claim.

In *Rose v. Bank of America* (2013) 57 Cal. 4th 390 [20913 Cal. LEXIS 6521], the Supreme Court held that the UCL is not a mere enforcement mechanism and, instead, provides its own distinct and limited equitable remedies for unlawful business practices predicated upon violations of other laws, including federal laws so long as the UCL claims are not federally preempted. Similarly in *Zhang v. Superior Court* (2013) 57 Cal. 4th 364 [2013 Cal. LEXIS 6520], the Supreme Court held that California's unfair insurance practice act (UIPA)—which bars a private right of action—does not bar a UCL claim based on independent common law bad faith grounds even, if the alleged conduct also violates the UIPA. The UCL and FAL do not provide a right to jury trial since the UCL was enacted to create new rights and remedies not available under common law, and because the relief available is primarily equitable in nature. (*Nationwide Biweekly Administration, Inc. v. Superior Court* (2020) 9 Cal. 5th 279, 327 [261 Cal. Rptr. 3d 713, 746, 462 P.3d 461, 489].).

6. CLASS ACTION BANS IN ARBITRATION CLAUSES

In *AT&T Mobility, LLC v. Concepcion* (2011) 563 U.S. 333, the United States Supreme Court held that California's "*Discover Bank* rule" was preempted by the Federal Arbitration Act (FAA). The *Discover Bank* rule provided that class action bans in arbitration clauses were unenforceable where (1) the ban is in a contract of adhesion; (2) the dispute involves small individual damages; and (3) the plaintiff alleges a deliberate scheme to cheat large numbers of consumers out of small sums of money. (*Discover Bank, supra*, 36 Cal. 4th at 162–63.)

In *American Express v. Italian Colors Restaurant* (2013) 570 U.S. 228, the Court reaffirmed the enforceability of arbitration clauses containing class action waivers. The Court found that claims under antitrust laws can be arbitrated and whether class actions are the only practical way for antitrust laws to be enforced was immaterial. The Court rejected the merchants' "effective vindication" argument, finding that nothing in the arbitration clause at issue prevented the merchants from asserting their statutory rights in individual arbitration—what mattered was the right to pursue the claim, not whether it is costly to do so. (*Id.* at 238 n.5 ("The FAA's command to enforce arbitration agreements trumps any interest in ensuring the prosecution of low-value claims.").) Then, in *Epic Systems Corp. v. Lewis* (2018) 138 S. Ct. 1612, 1619, the Court once again confirmed that arbitration agreements providing for individualized proceedings must be enforced, despite the FAA's savings clause and the National Labor Relations Act's (NLRA) establishment of a substantive right for employees to engage in concerted activity like class action litigation.

Before *Italian Colors*, California courts had broadly recognized that generally applicable contract defenses to arbitration clauses, such as unconscionability, survived *Concepcion*. (*See, e.g., Mission Viejo Emergency Med. Assoc. v. Beta Healthcare Group* (2011) 197 Cal. App. 4th 1146, 1158 [128 Cal. Rptr. 3d 330] (disagreeing that *Concepcion* "preempts all California law relating to unconscionability" and finding that it "simply does not go that far"); *Kilgore v. KeyBank, N.A.* (9th Cir. 2012) 673 F.3d 947, 963 ("*Concepcion* did not overthrow the common law contract defense of unconscionability whenever an arbitration clause is involved.").) Several courts applying California law also determined that *Concepcion* did not overrule the "one-sided" or "overly harsh" unconscionability test set forth by the California Supreme Court in *Armendariz v. Foundation Health Psychcare Services, Inc.* (2000) 24 Cal. 4th 83 [99 Cal. Rptr. 2d 745]. In *Samaniego v. Empire Today, LLC* (2012) 205 Cal. App. 4th 1138, 1147–48 [140 Cal. Rptr. 3d 492], for example, the court found an arbitration provision to be unconscionable because it shortened the statute of limitations, contained a one-sided fee shifting provision, and exempted from arbitration claims typically brought by employers. Additionally, the court in *Unimax Express, Inc. v. Cosco N. Am., Inc.* (C.D. Cal. Nov. 28, 2011, No. 11-02947) 2011 U.S. Dist. LEXIS 136110, at *11–12, held that a provision requiring notice of a billing dispute within thirty days of the improper charges unfairly burdened the invoiced party. (*See also McIntosh v. Powdered, Inc.* (June 8, 2011, No. A129063) 2011 Cal. App. Unpub. LEXIS 4366, at *34–35 (one-sided term allowing employer, but not employees, to take injunctive relief claims to court was unconscionable).

After *Italian Colors*, the California Supreme Court issued a 70-page opinion, in *Sonic-Calabasas v. Moreno* (2013) 57 Cal. 4th 1109, confirming the continued viability of California's unconscionability defense to mandatory arbitration clauses. The *Sonic-Calabasas* majority opinion held that, "After *Concepcion*, unconscionability remains a valid defense to a petition to compel arbitration." The Court focused on rules that make arbitration potentially too expensive or time consuming for consumers and held that such obstacles can preclude mandatory arbitration.

Since *Sonic-Calabasas*, California courts continue to find overly unconscionable arbitration agreements unenforceable. *See Penilla v. Westmont Corp.* (2016) 3 Cal. App. 5th 205, 208 (finding procedural unconscionability due to pressure to sign agreement and failure to translate it into Spanish, finding substantive unconscionability due to prohibitively high arbitration costs, shortened limitations periods, and limitations on remedies, and holding that severance was inappropriate due to permeation). *See also Magno v. Coll. Network, Inc.* (2016) 1 Cal. App. 5th 277, 285, 288, 292 (finding procedural unconscionability because plaintiffs were young, had to rush through the signing process, had no ability to negotiate, and did not separately initial or sign the arbitration agreement, finding substantive unconscionability due to shortened limitations period and forum selection clause requiring arbitration thousands of miles away, and holding that severance was inappropriate).

The Ninth Circuit in *Chavarria v. Ralphs Grocery Company* (2013) 733 F.3d 916 confirmed the continuing viability of unconscionability under California law as a potential defense to mandatory arbitration. The Court found the grocery company's arbitration policy procedurally unconscionable because it was a condition of employment on a "'take it or leave it' basis" and the terms were not provided to the plaintiff until three weeks after she had agreed to be bound by it. The Ninth

Circuit also held the arbitration policy was substantively unconscionable because the policy's arbitrator selection process would always produce an arbitrator proposed by the defendant and the fee apportionment provision would price employees out of the dispute. The Court deemed this arrangement to be so one sided it "shocked the conscience." The Ninth Circuit further held that California's acceptance of unconscionability defenses was not preempted by the FAA, or *Italian Colors*, because its unconscionability provisions apply to contracts generally and do not, in practice, impact arbitration agreements disproportionately.

An unconscionability defense under California state law, however, is not impenetrable. A California Supreme Court decision recently held that three challenged arbitration provisions were not unconscionable and found that the defendant was under no obligation to highlight the arbitration clause in its contract. (*Sanchez v. Valencia Holding Co., LLC* (2015) 61 Cal. 4th 899 [353 P.3d 741].) The three enforceable provisions were: (1) limitations on the parties' appeal rights; (2) requiring the appealing party to pay the appeal costs, absent any showing that the costs were unaffordable; and (3) retaining the parties' rights to self-help remedies, such as repossession. (*Id.* at 916, 921, 922.) The Court concluded that commerce depends on the enforceability of a written contract, and that a party cannot avoid a contractual obligation by complaining in retrospect that it was a "bad bargain." (*Id.* at 911.)

Other courts, while acknowledging that *Armendariz* remains good law, have also determined certain one-sided terms in arbitration clauses are not unconscionable. In *Grabowski v. C.H. Robinson Co.* (S.D. Cal. 2011) 817 F. Supp. 2d 1159, 1173, for example, the court held that a one-sided provision allowing the employer, but not the employee, to bring certain claims in court was not unconscionable. Other courts have found one-sided terms to be overcome by arbitration opt-out provisions that purportedly eliminate procedural unconscionability. (*See, e.g., Meyer v. T-Mobile USA Inc.* (N.D. Cal. 2011) 836 F. Supp. 2d 994, 1004.) Still other courts have dealt with one-sided terms by severing them from the arbitration clause. (*See, e.g., Quevedo v. Macy's, Inc.* (C.D. Cal. 2011) 798 F. Supp. 2d 1122, 1139.) *See also Farrar v. Direct Commerce, Inc.* (2017) 9 Cal. App. 5th 1257, 1261 (compelling arbitration because unconscionable term could be severed).

The United States Supreme Court's recent decision in *Viking River Cruises, Inc. v. Moriana*, 142 S. Ct. 1906 (2022), addressed the extent to which claims under the Private Attorney General Act, Labor Code §§ 2699 *et seq.* (PAGA), can be compelled to individual arbitration. In *Viking River*, the Supreme Court differentiated between claims for PAGA civil penalties based on Labor Code violations committed against the plaintiff personally and claims based on violations committed against other employees. (*Id.* at 1916.) The Court held as a matter of FAA preemption that PAGA plaintiffs may be compelled to arbitrate their individual PAGA claims if they are subject to a mandatory arbitration agreement that is construed to require arbitration of only the individual component of the plaintiff's PAGA claim, but that the FAA does not allow an arbitration agreement to strip a plaintiff of state statutory rights—including the right to assert PAGA claims in at least some forum. (*Id.* at 1921, 1924–25.) *Viking River* presented several state law questions to be resolved by California courts. (*Id.* at 1925 (Sotomayor, J., concurring) ("[T]he Court reasons, based on available guidance from California courts, that Moriana lacks 'statutory standing' under PAGA to litigate her 'non-individual' claims separately in state court. Of course, if this Court's understanding of state law is wrong, California courts . . . will have the last word." (citation omitted)).)

The California Supreme Court resolved key issues in *Adolph v. Uber Techs., Inc.*, 14 Cal. 5th 1104 (2023), holding that PAGA plaintiffs have standing under PAGA to pursue their "non-individual" representative action claims in court even after being compelled to "individual" arbitration. The California high court reaffirmed that the only two elements of PAGA standing are that the plaintiff was (1) employed by the alleged violator, and (2) the victim of one or more of the alleged violations.

Id. at *15–16. Such standing "is not affected by enforcement of an agreement to adjudicate a plaintiff's individual claim in another forum." *Id.* at *18. As such, if an employer's arbitration agreement requires its employees to split their PAGA claims between arbitration and court, those employees retain standing to prosecute both components of their claims in the required forums. *Id.* at *22. *See also Johnson v. Lowe's Home Centers* 93 F.4th 459 (9th Cir. 2024) (holding that *Adolph* is consistent with *Viking River*); *Barrera v. Apple American Group* 95 Cal. App. 5th 63 (2023) (same). Alternatively, plaintiffs who are bound by arbitration agreements can choose to forgo their individual claims and pursue only representative PAGA claims; employees are not required to bring individual claims to have PAGA standing. *Balderas v. Fresh Start Harvesting, Inc.* 101 Cal. App. 533 (2024).

The California Supreme Court will soon resolve an appellate split regarding whether a PAGA plaintiff can pursue purely representative PAGA relief for others, disavowing their individual PAGA claim (a so-called "headless" PAGA action). *See Parra Rodriguez v. Packers Sanitation Svcs. Ltd., LLC*, 2025 Cal. App. LEXIS 103 (2025) (allowed); *Balderas v. Fresh Start Harvesting, Inc.*, 101 Cal. App. 5th 533 (2024) (allowed); *Leeper v. Shipt, Inc.* (2024) 107 Cal. App. 5th 1001, 1009 (not allowed). The question is now pending before the California Supreme Court in *Leeper*.

In July 2024, the California Legislature amended the PAGA statute. In addition to making various substantive changes, the revision required that a given plaintiff have "personally suffered each of the violations alleged," Cal. Lab. Code § 2699(c)(1), overturning the rule that a plaintiff could pursue claims for various alleged violations so long as they had suffered at least one of the violations.

Who decides whether class arbitration is available in an arbitration agreement, the court or an arbitrator, depends on the parties' agreement. (*Sandquist v. Lebo Auto., Inc.* (2016) 1 Cal. 5th 233, 241) There is no state or federal law presumption to the contrary; rather, the decision of what to submit to an arbitrator is a matter of contractual agreement by the parties. (*Id.* at 260 (disapproving *Kinecta Alternative Financial Solutions, Inc. v. Superior Court* (2012) 205 Cal. App. 4th 506 [140 Cal. Rptr. 3d 347]; *Garden Fresh Restaurant Corp. v. Superior Court* (2014) 231 Cal. App. 4th 678 [180 Cal. Rptr. 3d 89]).) *See also Nguyen v. Applied Med. Res. Corp.* (2016) 4 Cal. App. 5th 232, 240 (vacating order dismissing class claims to allow arbitrator to decide whether the arbitration clause permits arbitration on a class-wide basis).

California courts have recently reaffirmed the principle that a nonparty to an arbitration agreement cannot compel arbitration unless they prove that the agreement was "expressly . . . intended to benefit them." *Jarboe v. Hanlees Auto Grp.*, 53 Cal. App. 5th 539, 550 (2020); *see also DMS Servs., LLC v. Superior Ct.*, 205 Cal. App. 4th 1346, 1352 (2012) ("One must be a party to an arbitration agreement to be bound by it or invoke it."); *Jensen v. U-Haul Co. of California*, 18 Cal. App. 5th 295, 301 (2017) (noting that a non-signatory may be required to arbitrate a claim if (1) a benefit was conferred, or (2) a preexisting relationship existed).

Practitioners should continue to be cautious when citing or otherwise relying on historic California decisions and/or statutes obviating or avoiding application of mandatory arbitration agreements cases, as such decisions and/or authority will continue to provoke potential controversy, new decisions, and additional nuances.

7. CHOICE OF LAW

In *Washington Mutual Bank v. Superior Court* (2001) 24 Cal. 4th 906 [103 Cal. Rptr. 2d 320] (*Washington Mutual*), the California Supreme Court reversed the judgment of the court of appeal and remanded with directions to the trial court to vacate its nationwide class certification order in a forced placed mortgage-hazard insurance action, pending further analysis of choice-of-law issues and renewed manageability consideration. (*Id.* at 928.) In reversing the trial court's order of nationwide class certification, the California Supreme Court chided the trial court for failing to first determine the "force and effect of contractual agreements that, according the defendant, would require the application of different states' laws in the action." (*Id.* at 911.) The trial court's failure to decide, prior to certifying the class, what law applied to the claims of more than 25,000 mortgagors class members nationwide, mandated reversal and reconsideration of choice-of-law and manageability issue. (*Id.* at 915, *citing Clothesrigger, Inc.* v. *GTE Corp.* (1987) 191 Cal. App. 3d 605, 619 [236 Cal. Rptr. 605].)

Notably, the California Supreme Court held in *Washington Mutual* that choice-of-law provisions in contracts of adhesion deserve no special exemption or analysis since the applicable choice-of-law analysis already mandates a reasonability examination and cannot contravene fundamental California policy. (*Washington Mutual, supra,* 24 Cal. 4th at 917.) Further, the California Supreme Court rejected the court of appeal's suggestion that consumers deserved special treatment in the choice-of-law analysis to prevent California businesses from otherwise avoiding involvement in nationwide class actions, quoting *City of San Jose v. Superior Court*, *supra*, 12 Cal. 3d 447 for the proposition that "[c]lass actions are provided only as a means to enforce substantive law. Altering the substantive law to accommodate procedure would be to confuse the means with the ends—to sacrifice the goal for the going." (*Washington Mutual, supra,* at 918, *quoting City of San Jose v. Superior Court, supra*, 12 Cal. 3d at 462.) Where laws of multiple states are found applicable, the California Supreme Court in *Washington Mutual* expressly preserved the possibility of class certification utilizing discernible legal groupings and subclasses so long as the trial courts analyze class certification manageability in the context of review of variations among the state laws and their effect upon predominance and "whether litigation of a nationwide class may be managed fairly and efficiently." *Washington Mutual, supra,* at 922. Citing a number of federal decisions involving multistate class actions under Rule 23(b)(3), the Court reminded the trial court that it is incumbent upon the class action proponent to prove each element of class certification.

Public policy goals trumped the contracts' choice of law provisions in *America Online v. Superior Court of Alameda County* (2001) 90 Cal. App. 4th 1 [108 Cal. Rptr. 2d 699], where the court of appeals upheld a trial court's refusal to stay or dismiss consumer class action claims that America Online argued were barred by contractual choice of law rules specifying application of Virginia law, which does not allow consumer lawsuits to be brought as class actions. Instead, the court held that enforcing the forum selection clause would have violated California public policy by eviscerating important legal rights afforded to California consumers and that the unavailability of class relief in Virginia was sufficient to preclude enforcement of the forum selection clause. (*Id.* at 15–16.) Similarly, choice of law agreements cannot be used to circumvent the Ending Forced Arbitration of Sexual Assault and Sexual Harassment Act, 9 U.S.C. §§ 401–402 (EFAA). (*Casey v. Superior Court* (2025) 108 Cal. App. 5th 575, 580 [329 Cal.Rptr.3d 518, 522] ["[T]he EFAA preempts attempts under state law to compel arbitration of cases relating to a sexual harassment dispute, and parties cannot contract around the law by way of a choice-of-law provision."]).

For recent federal decisions on California's choice of law doctrine in the UCL/CLRA class certification context, *compare Mazza, supra,* 666 F.3d at 594 (application of California law to a nationwide class improper even though defendant headquartered in California and misrepresentations emanated from California because transactions occurred elsewhere) with *Chavez, supra,* 268 F.R.D. at 379 (California law applicable to nationwide class where defendant headquartered in California and conduct emanated from California).

The California legislature has also enacted additional restrictions on choice-of-law provisions. Under Civ. Code § 1799.208, effective January 1, 2025, a seller cannot require that a consumer arbitrate claims outside of California or under the laws of another state. This ensures that disputes arising in California are adjudicated within the state, under California law. The statute enables contracts to be voided at the consumer's discretion and provides the opportunity for consumers to recover attorney fees for doing so.

8. CLASS ACTION SETTLEMENTS

In *Wershba v. Apple Computer, Inc.* (2001) 91 Cal. App. 4th 224 [110 Cal. Rptr. 2d 145] (*Wershba*), a class action settlement followed the plaintiffs' filing of UCL and CLRA claims on behalf of Apple customers nationwide after the withdrawal of promised levels of free technical support. The appellate court upheld the settlement, approving the trial court's notice plan and lodestar/multiplier attorneys' fee analysis and rejected claims of prejudice to absent class members. Settlement Class Notice, including claim forms, releases and instructions, were mailed and/or e-mailed to approximately 2.4 million class members, posted on Apple's web site and published in *USA Today* and *MacWorld.* The notice advised class members of the means to opt-out and object to the proposed settlement, including its class certification provision and attorneys' fee award payments. 363 class members opted out of the nationwide settlement and 20 class members objected, of which only two appeared at the hearing.

Utilizing an abuse of discretion standard, the court of appeals agreed that all class certification requirements were met and rejected the contention that the interests of various class member subgroups were in conflict and the two class representatives inadequate to protect the class. Instead, the appellate court agreed that all class members suffered a common alleged wrong by virtue of deprivation of promised free technical support and that the settlement terms adequately addressed the interests of the various sub-groups. (*Wershba v. Apple Computer, Inc., supra,* 91 Cal. App. 4th at 248.)

The *Wershba* court accepted the objectors' contention that the settlement's tender at the time of class certification triggered heightened scrutiny due to the absence of adversary certification but was satisfied that the normal fairness review sufficed to protect the class against fraud and collusion. (*Wershba v. Apple Computer, Inc., supra,* 91 Cal. App. 4th at 239, citing comparable federal cases.) The trial court's denial of discovery to objectors, requested only one week before the hearing, was upheld in light of the court's discretion to allow pre-fairness hearing discovery upon a proper motion and hearing. The court rejected objectors' contention that the trial court violated due process and choice of law principles in certifying the nationwide class under California law. Instead, the court was satisfied that California's role as the origin of all of the representations to justify the constitutional application of California law to the claims of the nationwide class. (*Id.* at 241, *citing Clothesrigger, Inc. v. GTE Corp., supra*, 191 Cal. App. 3d at 613.) Rejecting the contention that some of the other states' laws offered materially benefited residents of these states, the court found that, "in fact California's consumer protection laws are among the strongest in the country." Finally, the court stated, "Even though there may be differences in consumer protection laws from state to state, this is not necessarily fatal to a finding that there is a predominance of common issues among a nationwide class. As the Ninth Circuit has observed, state consumer protection laws are relatively homogeneous: 'the idiosyncratic differences between state consumer protection laws are not sufficiently substantive to predominate over the shared claims: and do not preclude certification of a nationwide settlement class.'" (*Wershba v. Apple Computer, Inc., supra,* 91 Cal. App. 4th at 244, *quoting Hanlon v. Chrysler Corp.* (1998) 150 F. 3d 1011, 1022–23.)

Appellate review of a trial court's order pertaining to settlement must be conducted under a deferential abuse of discretion standard. (*7-Eleven Owners for Fair Franchising v. The Southland Corp.* (2000) 85 Cal. App. 4th 1135, 1156 [102 Cal. Rptr. 2d 777]).)

a. Attorneys' Fees

The California Supreme Court recently reaffirmed the propriety of calculating fees as a percentage of the common fund made available to the class. *Laffitte v. Robert Half Int'l Inc.* (2016) 1 Cal. 5th 480, 485. The court affirmed the fee award of one-third of the common fund, holding that trial courts have further discretion to conduct a lodestar cross-check or forgo the lodestar analysis and use other means to evaluate the reasonableness of the requested fee percentage. *Id.* at 506. The mandate from *Serrano v. Priest* (1977) 20 Cal. 3d 25, 48 (*Serrano III*) that the lodestar be used as the "starting point of every fee award" is only applicable to fees awarded under the private attorney general theory, not for common funds created or preserved by litigation. *Id.* at 498–99.

b. Standing to Appeal a Class Settlement Requires Intervention

In *Hernandez v. Restoration Hardware, Inc.*, 4 Cal. 5th 260, 270 (2018), the California Supreme Court held that class members need to intervene in the action to have standing to appeal any aspect of the settlement.

In contrast, the United States Supreme Court recently resolved a split of federal authority and unequivocally rejected intervention as a prerequisite for class member appeal and, instead, held that any class member who appears and objects before the trial court has standing to appeal:

> What is most important to this case is that nonnamed class members are parties to the proceedings in the sense of being bound by the settlement. It is this feature of class action litigation that requires that class members be allowed to appeal the approval of a settlement when they have objected at the fairness hearing. To hold otherwise would deprive nonnamed class members of the power to preserve their own interests in a settlement that will ultimately bind them, despite their expressed objections before the trial court.

(*Devlin v. Scardelletti et al.* (2002) 2002 U.S. Lexis 4215, 4217 [70 U.S.L.W. 4496].) Thus, class members must both move to intervene and object to the settlement to preserve all appellate rights.

9. ORDER DENYING CLASS CERTIFICATION IS IMMEDIATELY APPEALABLE

An order denying a class certification motion, unlike one granting certification, is immediately appealable because the order has the death knell effect of making further proceedings in the action impracticable. (*Daar, supra,* 67 Cal. 2d at 699.) Unless the motion is specifically denied without prejudice to re-asserting it, a plaintiff who fails to appeal from an order denying class certification can lose the right to attack it. (*Safaie v. Jacuzzi Whirlpool Bath, Inc.* (2011) 192 Cal. App. 4th 1160 [122 Cal. Rptr. 3d 344].)

a. Exception for Stayed PAGA Claims

However, dismissal of class claims is not appealable where the plaintiff continues to pursue a PAGA claim and individual arbitration, because there is no de facto final judgment for absent plaintiffs and thus no death knell effect. *Young v. Remx, Inc.* (2016) 2 Cal. App. 5th 630, 633. *See also Nguyen v. Applied Med. Res. Corp.* (2016) 4 Cal. App. 5th 232, 240.

b. Pre-Certification Discovery

California courts recognize the parties' right to conduct appropriate pre-certification discovery. (*Best Buy Stores, L.P. v. Superior Court* (2006) 137 Cal. App. 4th 772 [40 Cal. Rptr. 3d 578]; *Bartold v. Glendale Federal Bank* (2000) 81 Cal. App. 4th 816, 827 [97 Cal. Rptr. 2d 226] ("[D]ue process requires 'an opportunity to conduct discovery on class action issues before . . . documents in support of or in opposition to the motion must be filed . . .'") quoting *Carabini v. Superior Court* (1994) 26 Cal. App. 4th 239, 243–44 [31 Cal. Rptr. 2d 520]; *see also Atari, Inc. v. Superior Court* (1985) 166 Cal. App. 3d 867, 870 [212 Cal. Rptr. 773] (determination of whether common questions predominate over individual ones "cannot realistically be made until the parties have had a chance to conduct reasonable investigation"). However, California courts recognize the need to protect unnamed class members from routine discovery, recognizing that "to the extent the absent class members are compelled to participate in the trial of the lawsuit, the effectiveness of the class action device is destroyed." (*Danzig v. Superior Court* (1978) 87 Cal. App. 3d 604, 608–12 [151 Cal. Rptr. 185].)

Rule 3.768 explicitly recognizes discovery from unnamed class members, following class certification. A list of factors for the court to consider when such discovery is contested is likely to produce a fair balance between the interests of the parties and absent class members. (Cal. Rules of Ct., Rule 3.768.) Individual class members will likely continue to enjoy judicial protection from overbroad, cumulative or harassing discovery.

The scope of discovery for PAGA claims mirrors that in class actions. In *Williams v. Superior Court* (2018) 3 Cal. 5th 531, the California Supreme Court held that the contact information of employees the PAGA plaintiff sought to represent was discoverable for the same reasons that it would be in a conventional wage and hour class action.

10. MISCELLANEOUS

a. Tolling

The California Supreme Court has embraced the tolling principle set forth in *American Pipe & Construction Co. v. Utah*, 414 U.S. 538 (1974). *Fierro v. Landry's Rest., Inc.*, 32 Cal. App. 5th 276, 285 (2019). "If class certification is denied, the statute of limitations is tolled from the time of commencement of the suit to the time of denial of certification for all purported members of the class who either make timely motions to intervene in the surviving individual action or who timely file their individual actions." *Jolly v. Eli Lilly & Co.*, 751 P.2d 923, 933 (1988). In *Hildebrandt v. Staples the Off. Superstore, LLC*, 58 Cal. App. 5th 128, 145 (2020), the court clarified that the main concern is "the *prejudice* that would arise if defendants did not receive *adequate notice* of the substantive claims and generic identity of potential plaintiffs 'within the statutory period of limitation so that they might preserve their defense.'" 58 Cal. App. 5th 128, 142–43 (2020) (citing *Jolly*, 751 P.2d at 936–37). Specifically, the relevant policy consideration is "protection of the class action device." *Id. American Pipe* tolling, however, "does not apply to any later class claims that may be asserted by the purported class member who files a new action." *Fierro*, 32 Cal. App. 5th at 285. "If the purported class member files a new class action after the expiration of the applicable statute of limitations on the class's claim, then the claim is barred." *Id.* In short, the filing of a class action only "tolls the running of the applicable statutes of limitations as to the *individual claims* of all putative class members until class certification is denied." *Id.*

b. Overlapping Representative Actions and Reverse Auctions ("Plaintiff Shopping")

A reverse auction, also called plaintiff shopping, is a defendant's attempt to settle for the lowest possible price by selecting the weakest among multiple plaintiffs to secure a release of all claims being pursued by all plaintiffs in overlapping representative actions. *See Reynolds v. Beneficial Nat'l Bank*, 288 F.3d 277, 282 (7th Cir. 2002) (Posner, J.) (defining a reverse auction as "the practice whereby the defendant in a series of class actions picks the most ineffectual class lawyers to negotiate a settlement with in the hope that the district court will approve a weak settlement that will preclude other claims against the defendant"); 4 William B. Rubenstein, *Newberg on Class Actions* § 13:57 (5th ed. 2018) (explaining the primary" problem in the reverse auction situation is that the class's interests have been sold out, and class members will get less than the full value of their claims; ("Standards and Guidelines for Litigating and Settling Consumer Class Actions, 299 F.R.D. 160 (3d ed. 2014]") (In a reverse auction] a defendant proposes a cheap settlement and shops around among plaintiffs 'counsel until the defendant finds a lawyer willing to settle on its terms. The potential for collusion and abuse is obvious if a lawyer agrees to a bad deal in order to secure fees."). Two commentators have identified certain" yellow flags "of reverse auctions for courts to protect against:

> First is the situation in which the judge observes evidence of a reverse auction settlement. Markers of a reverse auction include the presence of overlapping class actions involving similar claims against the same defendant; settlement discussions initiated by the defendant; settlement bargaining limited to one of the competing groups of plaintiffs' attorneys; settlement with the group of attorneys who present a less substantial threat of carrying the case forward to trial; lack of an extended process of settlement bargaining; agreements that promote the award of lucrative and potentially justified attorneys' fees; and sudden expansion of the scope of the settled case (for example, by converting the action from a statewide to a nationwide class).

Jonathan R. Macey & Geoffrey P. Miller, *Judicial Review of Class Action Settlements*, 1 J. Legal Analysis 167, 191–94 (2009); *cf. Dalchau v. Fastaff, LLC*, No. 17-cv-01584-WHO, 2018 WL 1709925, at *4 (N.D. Cal. Apr. 9, 2018) (Orrick, J.) (considering the timing of a settlement, "the way in which it came about," and the lack of "vigorous[] litigat[ion]" of classwide claims in the settling case in concluding that a settlement "plausibly reflect[s] an attempt on the part of [the defendant] to undercut [the plaintiff] in the instant action" and escape liability). It is important to recognize that the conditions of a reverse auction are structural in nature, resulting from a breakdown in the typical bilateral posture of plaintiff and defendant through the presence of another plaintiff willing to bid against the plaintiff. No finding of subjective factors such as collusion, mendacity, or unethical behavior is required.

A reverse auction is most harmful when the disparity in bargaining position strengths of multiple sets of lawyers is most extreme – either because one case is in a stronger procedural posture (e.g., greater discovery, further developed, or poised for a key decision that exposes the defendant to risk) or because one case is prosecuted by plaintiffs' counsel in a stronger position (e.g., more qualified, more experienced, more resources, etc.). If a defendant is exposed to liability from a plaintiff in a strong position, and it then negotiates a settlement with the weaker plaintiff, this is a strong sign that a reverse auction has occurred. *See, e.g.*, *Litty v. Merrill Lynch & Co., Inc.*, No. 14 Civ. 425, 2015 WL 4698475, at *10 (C.D. Cal. Apr. 27, 2015) (denying preliminary approval of settlement that had appearance of reverse auction "in light of the settlement amount, Plaintiff's weak negotiating position, and Defendants' effort to settle three separate cases with Plaintiff"); *Galeener v. Source Refrigeration & HVAC, Inc.*, No. 13-cv-04960-VC (N.D. Cal.).

Approval of reverse auction settlements creates perverse incentives in representative cases. Namely, it "signals to the unscrupulous plaintiffs' attorney that by filing a parallel, shadow action . . . , [he or she] can underbid the original plaintiffs' attorney team that researched, prepared and filed the action." John C. Coffee, Jr., *Class Wars: The Dilemma of the Mass Tort Class Action*, 95 Colum. L. Rev. 1343, 1371 (1995) (exploring the issue). Reverse auctions are more likely where there are cases in different forums (e.g., state and federal) or where there is limited case management. Gaps and uncertainties create a powerful incentive for unscrupulous plaintiffs' lawyers to file copycat lawsuits and unscrupulous defendants to exploit competition by pitting plaintiffs against each other. Without careful judicial management, this incentive structure can lead to increasingly clogged dockets, wasted judicial resources, erosion of PAGA's and Rule 23's purposes, and inefficient use of plaintiffs' resources. *See In re Checking Account Overdraft Litig.*, 859 F. Supp. 2d 1313, 1324 (S.D. Fla. 2012) ("Competing lawsuits involving the same parties and the same issues in separate jurisdictions waste judicial resources and can lead to conflicting results.").

Therefore, where a court receives a proposed settlement in case A that would release claims asserted in case B, where case B is another representative action (e.g., a class action or PAGA action) that is in a stronger position, some commentators have proposed a principle of "prudential deference," whereby the court stays case A so that case B can further develop. This allows for the stronger plaintiff to proceed and possibly increase the value of the case, often resulting in a higher-value settlement. If case B founders, the settlement in case A remains as a type of insurance, and the court can, if appropriate, approve it.

To avoid the conditions that can lead to a reverse auction, courts should clarify leadership structures, using procedures analogous to Fed. R. Civ. P. 23(g) (appointment of interim class counsel) at the earliest feasible moment in the case. This can prevent later-filed cases from improperly subverting earlier-filed cases. If plaintiffs' counsel in a later-filed case seeks to take the reins from interim lead counsel, they can bring a motion for the leadership structure to be adjusted.

The California Supreme Court recently held that a PAGA plaintiff who has disclaimed reliance on any "personal interest" in their individual capacity does not satisfy the interest requirement for intervention under Cal. Civ. Proc. Section 387 and therefore cannot intervene in a PAGA action to object to a proposed settlement that purports to settle overlapping PAGA claims, even when there is evidence of a reverse auction. *See Turrieta v. Lyft, Inc.*, S27172 (Cal. 2024). The court did not address whether a PAGA plaintiff may intervene in such circumstances if they seek to vindicate their own personal interests.

Recently, the California Employment Lawyers Association (CELA) published a policy governing reverse auctions, including recommendations for how courts, parties, and mediators should address circumstances with overlapping claims in multiple representative actions. *See* Cal. Emp. Law. Ass'n, CELA Reverse Auctions Policy (2020) (available at www.CELA.org/ReverseAuctions). The policy recommends best practices for determining early on whether a new case overlaps with a preexisting one, resolving such overlaps through cooperative approaches or court resolution of competing leadership proposals, securing coordination to minimize opportunities for plaintiff shopping, mediating, and settling cases appropriately, etc. *Id.*

11. COMMUNICATIONS WITH ABSENT CLASS MEMBERS

a. Basic Principles

There is a wealth of authority in California governing parties' communications with potential class members pre- and post-certification. As a starting point, California prohibits communication with represented parties. *See* Cal. R. Prof. C. 2100(A). So a defendant may not communicate with class members about the litigation post-certification. Pre-certification, potential class members are generally not deemed to be represented by plaintiff's counsel. *See Babbitt v. Albertson's Inc.*, No. C-92-1883 SBA (PJH), 1993 WL 128089, at *2 (N.D. Cal. Jan. 28, 1993); *In re McKesson HBOC, Inc. Sec. Litig.*, 126 F. Supp. 2d 1239, 1245 (N.D.Cal. 2000); *but see Pollar v. Judson Steel Corp.*, 1984 U.S. Dist. LEXIS 19765, 1984 WL 161273 (N.D. Cal. Feb. 3, 1984). (As discussed in the introduction, some authorities suggest that there is a constructive attorney-client relationship.) However, pre-certification communications will still be improper if they are false, misleading, confusing, or coercive.

California Courts routinely sanction improper communications by either party. *See, e.g.*, *Quezada v. Schneider Logistics Transloading & Distribution*, No. 12-2188 CAS (DTBx) (C.D. Cal. March 25, 2013) (prohibiting defendant's communications with class members, striking defendant's 106 declarations, and ordering curative notice); *Wright v. Adventures Rolling Cross Country, Inc.*, No. 12-0982 EMC, 2012 U.S. Dist. LEXIS 83505 (N.D. Cal. June 15, 2012) (granting corrective notice and prohibiting defendants from contacting potential class members); *Li v. A Perfect Day Franchise, Inc.*, 270 F.R.D. 509, 518 (N.D. Cal. Sept. 29, 2010) (ordering corrective notice); *Fleury v. Richemont N. Am., Inc.*, No. C-05-4525 EMC, 2007 U.S. Dist. LEXIS 62763 (N.D. Cal. Aug. 15, 2007) (limiting limits on proposed class representative's communications based on his prior misleading statements); *Mevorah v. Wells Fargo Home Mortg., Inc.*, No. C-05-1175, 2005 U.S. Dist. LEXIS 28615, 2005 WL 4813532 (N.D. Cal. Nov. 17, 2005) (finding defendant's pre-certification interviews to be misleading and improper because they failed to advise employees of (1) the pendency of the litigation and (2) the potentially adverse nature of the corporation's interest and the employees' interests, and ordering defendant to disclose information regarding all employees contacted for interviews, and to give an opportunity for plaintiff to depose them); *Veliz v. Cintas Corp.*, No. C-03-1180, 2004 WL 2623909, at *3 (N.D. Cal. Nov. 12, 2004) (requiring defendant to pay costs of corrective notice sent to current employees who had received letter from defendant disparaging lawsuit); *Babbitt v. Alberstson's, Inc.*, No. C-92-1883, 1993 WL 150300 (N.D. Cal. March 31, 1993) (requiring courtesy copies of communications be sent to plaintiff's counsel); *Pollar v. Judson Steel Corp.*, 1984 U.S. Dist. LEXIS 19765, 1984 WL 161273 (N.D. Cal. Feb. 3, 1984) (finding employer's pre-certification newspaper ad was misleading because it did not disclose the existence of the class action lawsuit or identify plaintiff's counsel).

Importantly, California also requires that counsel for an organization make clear that they represent the organization when dealing with the "organization's directors, officers, employees, members, shareholders, or other constituents" if the organization's interests "are *or may become* adverse" to the individual's. Cal. R. Prof. C. 3-600(D) (emphasis added). In addition, counsel should also refrain from leading the individuals to believe that confidential information shared with counsel will not be used by the organization. *Id.*

b. Defendant's Counsel

Defendant's counsel needs to avoid engaging in communications that a court might view as misleading or coercive, such as encouraging opt-outs. (Note that at least one court has ordered plaintiff's counsel to provide a defendant with a pre-certification class list. *See, e.g.*, *Castaneda v. Burger King Corp.*, No. C 08-4262 WHA (JL), 2009 WL 2382688, at *7–8 (N.D. Cal. July 31, 2009).) The courts have presented some general contours of what is a proper communication:

1. The communication should include the plaintiff's claims, contact information for the plaintiff's

counsel, and the status of the case, although it can be allowably partisan if even-handed for the most part, and attach the complaint.[4]

2. The communication should inform the potential class members that they have a right to an attorney, that defense counsel represents the defendant, and that class members are not required to speak with defense counsel.[5]
3. It must state that an appeals court has "vetted and approved the theory of the case," if that is true.[6]
4. It must explain that the defendant may be adverse to potential class members, and that any statements may be used to oppose class certification or liability.[7]

c. Plaintiff's Counsel

Plaintiff's counsel should of course comply with all ethical solicitation rules and limitations, as governed by California Rule of Professional Conduct 1-400(C). It is important to note that plaintiffs' counsel are free to investigate the claims of their client[s], which includes affirmatively contacting potential class members and explaining the litigation to them.

As a general matter, because plaintiff's counsel is seeking to advance the interests of potential class members and is usually at an informational disadvantage relative to the defendant, communications with potential class members are often an important discovery tool. Plaintiff's counsel's common request to discover the names and contact information of potential class members is perfectly appropriate. *Pioneer Electronics*, 40 Cal. 4th at 373. "Contact information regarding the identity of potential class members is generally discoverable, so that the lead plaintiff may learn the names of other persons who might assist in prosecuting the case. *Pioneer Electronics (USA), Inc. v. Superior Court*, 40 Cal. 4th 360, 373 (2007). Class lists are often required to be produced pre-certification, to allow plaintiff's counsel to identify witnesses or substitute class representatives. *See, e.g.*, *Holman v. Experian Info Solutions, Inc.*, No. C 11-0180 CW, 2012 U.S. Dist. LEXIS 59401, at *48 (N.D. Cal. Apr. 27, 2012) ("Numerous courts in the Northern District of California have allowed pre-certification discovery of putative class members' confidential information subject to a protective order, without requiring prior notice to the putative class members."); *Currie-White v. Blockbuster, Inc.*, No. C 09–2593 MMC (MEJ), 2010 WL 1526314, at *4 (N.D. Cal. Apr. 15, 2010); *Artis v. Deere & Co.*, No. 10–5289 WHA (MEJ), 276 F.R.D. 348, 2011 WL 2580621, at *4–5 (N.D. Cal. June 29, 2011); *Bottoni v. Sallie Mae, Inc.*, No. 10-03602 LB, 2012 WL 8304347 (N.D. Cal. June 1, 2012); *Khalilpour v. Cellco P'ship*, No. C 09-02712 CW (MEJ), 2010 U.S. Dist. LEXIS 43885, at *6–7, 2010 WL 1267749, at *4 (N.D. Cal. Apr. 1, 2010) (ordering production of class members' names, addresses, and phone numbers in a consumer class action, pre-certification, without opt-out process); *York v. Starbucks Corp.*, No. 08-7919-GAF (PJWx), 2009 U.S. Dist. LEXIS 92274, at *3

---

[4] *See* Cty. of Santa Clara v. Astra USA, Inc., No. C 05-03740 WHA, 2010 WL 2724512, at *4 (N.D. Cal. July 8, 2010); In re M.L. Stern Overtime Litig., 250 F.R.D. 492, 498–99 (S.D. Cal. 2008); Maddock v. KB Holmes, Inc., 248 F.R.D. 229, 237 (C.D. Cal. 2007); MCL 4th § 21.12.

[5] *See Castaneda*, 2009 WL 2382688, at *1; *Babbitt*, 1993 WL 128089, at *7; *Maddock*, 248 F.R.D. at 237.

[6] *See Cty. of Santa Clara*, 2010 WL 2724512, at *4.

[7] *See* Mevorah v. Wells Fargo Home Mortg., Inc., No. C 05-1175 MHP, 2005 WL 4813532, at *5 (N.D. Cal. Nov. 17, 2005); *see also Maddock*, 248 F.R.D. at 237.

(C.D. Cal. June 20, 2009); *Putnam v. Eli Lilly & Co.*, 508 F. Supp. 2d 812, 814 (C.D. Cal. 2007) (ordering production of names, addresses, and telephone numbers).

Sometimes courts require notice to the class members to allow them to opt out of the list. *See, e.g.*, *Pioneer Electronics*, 40 Cal. 4th at 523–24; *Crab Addison, Inc. v. Super. Ct.*, 169 Cal. App. 4th 958, 970, 975 (2009); *Belaire-West Landscape, Inc. v. Superior Court*, 149 Cal. App. 4th 554, 561 (2007)' *Salazar v. Avis Budget Grp., Inc.*, No. 07cv64-IEG (WMc), 2007 WL 2990281, at *1, *3 (S.D. Cal. Oct. 10, 2007); *cf. Puerto v. Superior Court*, 158 Cal. App. 4th 1242 (2008) (finding that trial court abused its discretion in requiring an *opt-in* procedure before class member witness information was produced).

12. CONCLUSION

California's class action statute predates the current federal Rule 23. California class action jurisprudence embraces and synthesizes Rule 23 and its jurisprudence and applies the principles of representative actions to a broad array of consumer contexts. The California Judicial Council has enacted new Rules of Court that meld the provisions of Rule 23, current California practice and jurisprudence, and many of the best aspects of the San Francisco and Los Angeles County Superior Courts' local class action rules. The Council has produced a single comprehensive set of statewide Rules to be given uniform application, and to provide procedural requirements from inception of the class action through settlement, trial, and judgment.

CALIFORNIA CLASS ACTION STATUTES

CAL. CODE OF CIV. PROC. § 382. NONCONSENT TO JOINDER AS PLAINTIFF; REPRESENTATIVE ACTIONS

If the consent of any one who should have been joined as plaintiff cannot be obtained, he or she may be made a defendant, the reason thereof being stated in the complaint; and when the question is one of a common or general interest, of many persons, or when the parties are numerous, and it is impracticable to bring them all before the court, one or more may sue or defend for the benefit of all.

CAL. CIV. CODE § 1781. CONSUMER'S CLASS ACTION; CONDITIONS; NOTICES; JUDGMENT

(a) Any consumer entitled to bring an action under Section 1780 may, if the unlawful method, act, or practice has caused damage to other consumers similarly situated, bring an action on behalf of himself and such other consumers to recover damages or obtain other relief as provided for in Section 1780.

(b) The court shall permit the suit to be maintained on behalf of all members of the represented class if all of the following conditions exist:

(1) It is impracticable to bring all members of the class before the court.

(2) The questions of law or fact common to the class are substantially similar and predominate over the questions affecting the individual members.

(3) The claims or defenses of the representative plaintiffs are typical of the claims or defenses of the class.

(4) The representative plaintiffs will fairly and adequately protect the interests of the class.

(c) If notice of the time and place of the hearing is served upon the other parties at least 10 days prior thereto, the court shall hold a hearing, upon motion of any party to the action which is supported by affidavit of any person or persons having knowledge of the facts, to determine if any of the following apply to the action:

(1) A class action pursuant to subdivision (b) is proper.

(2) Published notice pursuant to subdivision (d) is necessary to adjudicate the claims of the class.

(3) The action is without merit or there is no defense to the action.

A motion based upon Section 437c of the Code of Civil Procedure shall not be granted in any action commenced as a class action pursuant to subdivision (a).

(d) If the action is permitted as a class action, the court may direct either party to notify each member of the class of the action. The party required to serve notice may, with the consent of the court, if personal notification is unreasonably expensive or it appears that all members of the class cannot be notified personally, give notice as prescribed herein by publication in accordance with Section 6064 of the Government Code in a newspaper of general circulation in the county in which the transaction occurred.

(e) The notice required by subdivision (d) shall include the following:

(1) The court will exclude the member notified from the class if he so requests by a specified date.

(2) The judgment, whether favorable or not, will include all members who do not request exclusion.

(3) Any member who does not request exclusion, may, if he desires, enter an appearance through counsel.

(f) A class action shall not be dismissed, settled, or compromised without the approval of the court, and notice of the proposed dismissal, settlement, or compromise shall be given in such manner as the court directs to each member who was given notice pursuant to subdivision (d) and did not request exclusion.

(g) The judgment in a class action shall describe those to whom the notice was directed and who have not requested exclusion and those the court finds to be members of the class. The best possible notice of the judgment shall be given in such manner as the court directs to each member who was personally served with notice pursuant to subdivision (d) and did not request exclusion.

CALIFORNIA RULES OF COURT; MANAGEMENT OF CLASS ACTIONS, RULES OF COURT 1850-1861

RULE 3.760 APPLICATION

(a) ***Class actions*** The rules in the Chapter apply to each class action brought under Civil Code § 1750 *et seq.*, or Code of Civil Procedure § 382 until the court finds the action is not maintainable as a class action or revokes a prior class certification.

(b) ***Relief from compliance with rules*** The court, on its own motion or on motion of any named party, may grant relief from compliance with the rules in this chapter in an appropriate case. (*Adopted, eff.* Jan. 1, 2002; *amended, eff.* Jan. 1, 2007.)

RULE 3.761. FORM OF COMPLAINT

(a) ***Caption of pleadings*** A complaint for or against a class party must include in the caption the designation "CLASS ACTION." This designation must be in capital letters on the first page of the complaint, immediately below the case number but above the description of the nature of the complaint.

(b) ***Heading and class action allegations*** The complaint in a class action must contain a separate heading entitled "CLASS ACTION ALLEGATIONS," under which the plaintiff describes how the requirements for class certification are met. (*Adopted, eff.* Jan. 1, 2007.)

RULE 3.762. CASE CONFERENCE

(a) ***Purpose*** One or more conferences between the court and counsel for the parties may be held to discuss class issues, conduct and scheduling of discovery, scheduling of hearings, and other matters. No evidence may be presented at the conference, but counsel must be fully prepared to discuss class issues and must possess authority to enter into stipulations.

(b) ***Notice by the parties*** Notice of the conference may be given by any party. If notice is given by a named plaintiff, notice must be served on all named parties to the action. If notice is given by a defendant, notice must be served only on the parties who have appeared. Within 10 calendar days after receipt of the notice, the plaintiff must serve a copy on each named party who has not appeared in the action and must file a declaration of service. If the plaintiff is unable to serve any party, the plaintiff must file a declaration stating the reasons for failure of service.

(c) ***Notice by the court*** The court may give notice of the conference to the plaintiff. Within 10 calendar days after receipt of the notice given by the court, the plaintiff must serve a copy of the notice on all parties who have been served in the action, whether they have appeared or not, and must file a declaration of service. If the plaintiff is unable to serve any party, the plaintiff must file a declaration stating the reasons for failure of service.

(d) ***Timing of notice*** The notice must be filed and served on the parties at least 20 calendar days before the scheduled date of the conference.

(e) ***Timing of conference*** A conference may be held at any time after the first defendant has appeared. Before selecting a conference date, the party noticing the conference must: (1) Obtain prior approval from the clerk of the department assigned to hear the class action and (2) Make reasonable efforts to accommodate the schedules of all parties entitled to receive notice under (b). (*Adopted, eff.* Jan. 1, 2002; *amended, eff.* Jan. 1, 2007.)

RULE 3.763. CONFERENCE ORDER

At the conclusion of the conference, the court may make an order:

(1) Approving any stipulations of the parties;

(2) Establishing a schedule for discovery;

(3) Setting the date for the hearing on class certification;

(4) Setting the dates for any subsequent conferences; and

(5) Addressing any other matters related to management of the case.

(*Adopted, eff.* Jan. 1, 2002.)

RULE 3.764. MOTION TO CERTIFY OR DECERTIFY A CLASS OR AMEND OR MODIFY AN ORDER CERTIFYING A CLASS

(a) ***Purpose*** Any party may file a motion to:

(1) Certify a class;

(2) Determine the existence of and certify subclasses;

(3) Amend or modify an order certifying a class; or

(4) Decertify a class.

(b) ***Timing of motion, hearing, extension, deferral*** A motion for class certification should be filed when practicable. In its discretion, the court may establish a deadline for the filing of the motion, as part of the case conference or as part of other case management proceedings. Any such deadline must take into account discovery proceedings that may be necessary to the filing of the motion.

(c) ***Format and filing of motion***

(1) *Time for service of papers.* Notice of a motion to certify or decertify a class or to amend or modify a certification order must be filed and served on all parties to the action at least 28 calendar days before the date appointed for hearing. Any opposition to the motion must be served and filed at least 14 calendar days before the noticed or continued hearing, unless the court for good cause orders otherwise. Any reply to the opposition must be served and filed at least 5 calendar days before the noticed or continued date of the hearing, unless the court for good cause orders otherwise. The provisions of Code of Civil Procedure § 1005 otherwise apply.

(2) *Length of papers.* An opening or responding memorandum filed in support of or in opposition to a motion for class certification must not exceed 20 pages. A reply memorandum must not exceed 15 pages. The provisions of rule 3.1113 otherwise apply.

(3) *Documents in support.* The documents in support of a motion for class certification consist of the notice of motion; a memorandum; evidence in support of the motion in the form of declarations of counsel, class representatives, or other appropriate declarants; and any requests for judicial notice.

(4) *Documents in opposition.* The documents in opposition to the motion consist of the opposing party's memorandum; the opposing party's evidence in opposition to the motion, including any declarations of counsel or other appropriate declarants; and any requests for judicial notice.

(d) ***Presentation of evidence*** Evidence to be considered at the hearing must be presented in accordance with rule 3.1306.

(e) ***Stipulations*** The parties should endeavor to resolve any uncontroverted issues by written stipulation before the hearing. If all class issues are resolved by stipulation of the named parties and approved by the court before the hearing, no hearing on class certification is necessary. (*Adopted, eff.* Jan. 1, 2002; *amended, eff.* Jan. 1. 2007.)

RULE 3.765. CLASS ACTION ORDER

(a) ***Class described*** An order certifying, amending, or modifying a class must contain a description of the class and any subclasses.

(b) ***Limited issues and subclasses*** When appropriate, an action may be maintained as a class action limited to particular issues. A class may be divided into subclasses. (*Adopted, eff.* Jan. 1, 2002.)

RULE 3.766. NOTICE TO CLASS MEMBERS

(a) ***Party to provide notice*** If the class is certified, the court may require either party to notify the class of the action in the manner specified by the court.

(b) ***Statement regarding class notice*** The class proponent must submit a statement regarding class notice and a proposed notice to class members. The statement must include the following items:

(1) Whether notice is necessary;

(2) Whether class members may exclude themselves from the action;

(3) The time and manner in which notice should be given;

(4) A proposal for which parties should bear the costs of notice; and,

(5) If cost shifting or sharing is proposed under subdivision (4), an estimate of the cost involved in giving notice.

(c) ***Order*** Upon certification of a class, or as soon thereafter as practicable, the court must make an order determining:

(1) Whether notice to class members is necessary;

(2) Whether class members may exclude themselves from the action;

(3) The time and manner of notice;

(4) The content of the notice; and

(5) The parties responsible for the cost of notice.

(d) ***Content of class notice*** The content of the class notice is subject to court approval. If class members are to be given the right to request exclusion from the class, the notice must include the following:

(1) A brief explanation of the case, including the basic contentions or denials of the parties;

(2) A statement that the court will exclude the member from the class if the member so requests by a specified date;

(3) A procedure for the member to follow in requesting exclusion from the class;

(4) A statement that the judgment, whether favorable or not, will bind all members who do not request exclusion; and

(5) A statement that any member who does not request exclusion may, if the member so desires, enter an appearance through counsel.

(e) ***Manner of giving notice*** In determining the manner of the notice, the court must consider:

(1) The interests of the class;

(2) The type of relief requested;

(3) The stake of the individual class members;

(4) The cost of notifying class members;

(5) The resources of the parties;

(6) The possible prejudice to class members who do not receive notice; and

(7) The res judicata effect on class members.

If personal notification is unreasonably expensive or the stake of individual class members is insubstantial, or if it appears that all members of the class cannot be notified personally, the court may order a means of notice reasonably calculated to apprise the class members of the pendency of the action-for example, publication in a newspaper or magazine; broadcasting on television, radio, or the Internet; or posting or distribution through a trade or professional association, union, or public interest group. (*Adopted, eff.* Jan. 1, 2002.)

RULE 3.767. ORDERS IN THE CONDUCT OF CLASS ACTIONS

(a) **Court orders.** In the conduct of a class action the court may make orders that:

(1) Require that some or all of the members of the class be given notice in such manner as the court may direct of any action in the proceeding, or of their opportunity to seek to appear and indicate whether they consider the representation fair and adequate, or of the proposed extent of the judgment;

(2) Impose conditions on the representative parties or on interveners;

(3) Require that the pleadings be amended to eliminate allegations as to representation of absent persons, and that the action proceed accordingly;

(4) Facilitate the management of class actions through consolidation, severance, coordination, bifurcation, intervention, or joinder; and

(5) Address similar procedural matters.

(b) **Amended orders.** The orders may be altered or amended as necessary. (*Adopted, eff.* Jan. 1, 2002; *amended eff.* Jan. 1, 2007.)

RULE 3.768. DISCOVERY FROM UNNAMED CLASS MEMBERS

(a) ***Types of discovery permitted*** The following types of discovery may be sought, through service of a subpoena and without a court order, from a member of a class who is not a party representative or who has not appeared:

(1) An oral deposition;

(2) A written deposition; and

(3) A deposition for production of business records and things.

(b) ***Motion for protective order*** A party representative, deponent, or other affected person may move for a protective order to preclude or limit the discovery.

(c) ***Interrogatories require court order*** party may not serve interrogatories on a member of a class who is not a party representative or who has not appeared, without a court order.

(d) ***Determination by court*** In deciding whether to allow the discovery requested under (a) or (c), the court must consider, among other relevant factors:

(1) The timing of the request;

(2) The subject matter to be covered;

(3) The materiality of the information being sought;

(4) The likelihood that class members have such information;

(5) The possibility of reaching factual stipulations that eliminate the need for such discovery;

(6) Whether class representatives are seeking discovery on the subject to be covered; and

(7) Whether discovery will result in annoyance, oppression, or undue burden or expense for the members of the class.

(*Adopted, eff.* Jan. 1, 2002; *amended eff.* Jan. 1, 2007.)

RULE 3.769. SETTLEMENT OF CLASS ACTIONS

(a) ***Court approval; after hearing*** A settlement or compromise of an entire class action, or of a cause of action in a class action, or as to a party, requires the approval of the court after hearing.

(b) ***Attorney's fees*** Any agreement, express or implied, that has been entered into with respect to the payment of attorney's fees or the submission of an application for the approval of attorney's fees must be set forth in full in any application for approval of the dismissal or settlement of an action that has been certified as a class action.

(c) ***Preliminary approval of settlement*** Any party to a settlement agreement may serve and file a written notice of motion for preliminary approval of the settlement. The settlement agreement and proposed notice to class members must be filed with the motion, and the proposed order must be lodged with the motion.

(d) ***Order certifying provisional settlement class*** The court may make an order approving or denying certification of a provisional settlement class after the preliminary settlement hearing.

(e) ***Order for final approval hearing*** If the court grants preliminary approval, its order must include the time, date, and place of the final approval hearing; the notice to be given to the class; and any other matters deemed necessary for the proper conduct of a settlement hearing.

(f) ***Notice to class of final approval hearing*** If the court has certified the action as a class action, notice of the final approval hearing must be given to the class members in the manner specified by the court. The notice must contain an explanation of the proposed settlement and procedures for class members to follow in filing written objections to it and in arranging to appear at the settlement hearing and state any objections to the proposed settlement.

(g) ***Conduct of final approval hearing*** Before final approval, the court must conduct an inquiry into the fairness of the proposed settlement.

(h) ***Judgment and retention of jurisdiction to enforce*** If the court approves the settlement agreement after the final approval hearing, the court must make and enter judgment. The judgment must include a provision for the retention of the court's jurisdiction over the parties to enforce the terms of the judgment. The court may not enter an order dismissing the action at the same time as, or after, entry of judgment. (Rule 3.769 amended effective January 1, 2009; adopted as rule 1859 effective January 1, 2002; previously amended and renumbered effective January 1, 2007.)

RULE 3.770. DISMISSAL OF CLASS ACTIONS

(a) ***Court approval of dismissal*** A dismissal of an entire class action, or of any party or cause of action in a class action, requires court approval. The court may not grant a request to dismiss a class action if the court has entered judgment following final approval of a settlement. Requests for dismissal must be accompanied by a declaration setting forth the facts on which the party relies. The declaration must clearly state whether consideration, direct or indirect, is being given for the dismissal and must describe the consideration in detail.

(b) ***Hearing on request for dismissal*** The court may grant the request without a hearing. If the request is disapproved, notice of tentative disapproval must be sent to the attorneys of record. Any party may seek, within 15 calendar days of the service of the notice of tentative disapproval, a hearing on the request. If no hearing is sought within that period, the request for dismissal will be deemed denied.

(c) ***Notice to class of dismissal*** If the court has certified the class, and notice of the pendency of the action has been provided to class members, notice of the dismissal must be given to the class in the manner specified by the court. If the court has not ruled on class certification, or if notice of the pendency of the action has not been provided to class members in a case in which such notice was required, notice of the proposed dismissal may be given in the manner and to those class members specified by the court, or the action may be dismissed without notice to the class members if the court finds that the dismissal will not prejudice them. (Rule 3.770 amended effective January 1, 2009; adopted as rule 365 effective January 1, 1984; previously amended and renumbered as rule 1860 effective January 1, 2002, and as rule 3.770 effective January 1, 2007.)

RULE 3.771. JUDGMENT

(a) ***Class members to be included in judgment*** The judgment in an action maintained as a class action must include and describe those whom the court finds to be members of the class.

(b) ***Notice of judgment to class*** Notice of the judgment must be given to the class in the manner specified. (Formerly Rule 1861, *adopted, eff.* Jan. 1, 2007. Renumbered Rule 3.771 and *amended, eff.* Jan. 1, 2007.)

By Elizabeth J. Cabraser and Fabrice Vincent, partners, Lieff, Cabraser, Heimann & Bernstein, LLP; and Jahan C. Sagafi, partner, Outten & Golden, LLP. Any opinions expressed herein are the authors', and not necessarily those of their firm or their clients.

COLORADO

1. COMPARISON WITH RULE 23 OF THE FEDERAL RULES OF CIVIL PROCEDURE

Rule 23 of the Colorado Rules of Civil Procedure is "virtually" identical to Rule 23 of the Federal Rules of Civil Procedure. As a result, the Colorado courts look to federal decisions for "guidance" in interpreting the Colorado Rule. *State v. Buckley Powder Co.*, 945 P.2d 841, 844 (Colo. 1997); *Mountain States Tel. & Tel. Co. v. Dist. Ct.*, 778 P.2d 667, 671 (Colo. 1989); *Higley v. Kidder, Peabody Co.*, 920 P.2d 884 (Colo. App. 1996); *Rosenthal v. Dean Witter Reynolds, Inc.*, 883 P.2d 522, 531 (Colo. App. 1994), *aff'd in part, rev'd in part*, 908 P.2d 1095 (Colo. 1995). Like the Federal Rule, Colorado Rule 23 "should be liberally construed in light of [the] policy favoring the maintenance of class actions." *Jackson v. Unocal Corp.*, 262 P.3d 874, 881 & 883–84 (Colo. 2011); *Hicks v. Colo. Hamburger Co., Inc.*, 527 P.3d 451, 456 (Colo. App. 2022) (citing *Jackson,* 296 P.3d at 880–81), *cert. denied*, 2023 WL 3061390 (Apr. 23, 2023).

2. CASE LAW INTERPRETING RULE 23

The threshold requirements for class certification under Colorado Rule 23 are such that a class may be certified "only if all requirements are met." *Borwick v. Bober*, 529 P.2d 1351, 1353 (Colo. App. 1974). The proponent of class certification bears the burden of demonstrating that all prerequisites for certification were met. *Livingston v. U.S. Bank*, 58 P.3d 1088, 1090 (Colo. App. 2002). A sufficient factual basis for class certification may be established by use of the pleadings, affidavits, discovery responses, and other evidence to show that all requirements are met. *Levine v. Empire Sav. & Loan Ass'n*, 592 P.2d 410, 413 (Colo. 1979). Ordinarily, the proponent of a class will be given an opportunity to obtain discovery on class issues and present evidence at a hearing. A trial court may, however, require some "minimal showing of substance of the class" before permitting discovery or granting an evidentiary hearing. *Id.*; *Clark v. Farmers Ins. Exch.*, 117 P.3d 26, 31 (Colo. App. 2004). To defeat certification of a class, the opponents also must come forward with sufficient evidence. *Villa Sierra Condo. Ass'n v. Field Corp.*, 787 P.2d 661, 666 (Colo. App. 1990). A trial court must rigorously analyze the evidence and determine to its satisfaction that each requirement of C.R.C.P. 23 is met. *Jackson,* 262 P.3d at 877 & 881. In conducting a rigorous analysis the trial court may consider any factual or legal dispute relevant to the requirements of C.R.C.P. 23, including those that incidentally overlap with the merits and including disputed expert testimony. *Id.* at 885. The trial court should not resolve factual or legal disputes to "screen out or prejudge the merits" and need not determine whether expert testimony will be admissible at trial or whether an expert will ultimately prevail at trial on the merits. *Id.* at 885–86. The trial court has a continuing obligation to review whether proceeding as a class action is appropriate and an order on the maintainability of a class "may be conditional, and may be altered or amended before the decision on the merits." *Farmers Ins. Exch. v. Benzing*, 206 P.3d 812, 818 (Colo. 2009); *see also Jackson*, 262 P.3d at 881–83.

The decision to certify a class, as well as to decertify a class, lies within the trial court's broad discretion and will not be reversed unless it was manifestly arbitrary, unreasonable, or unfair. *Benzing*, 206 P.3d at 817–18. An abuse of discretion may also occur if the trial court applies the incorrect legal standard. *Jackson,* 262 P.3d at 880. In sum, so long as the trial court rigorously analyzes the evidence, it retains the discretion to determine whether the evidence supports each element of C.R.C.P. 23. *BP America Prod. Co. v. Patterson*, 263 P.3d 103, 108 (Colo. 2011). However, if class certification rests purely on a question of law, the Court of Appeals reviews the trial court decision de novo. *Colo. Hamburger Co., Inc.*, 527 P.3d at 456.

a. Rule 23(a)

i. Identity of the class. The definition of the class is an essential prerequisite to maintaining a class action. *Jackson*, 262 P.3d at 887. A proposed class definition must be sufficiently definite so that it is administratively feasible to ascertain whether or not a particular individual is a member of the class. *BP America Prod. Co.*, 263 P.3d 114. The proposed class definition must specify a particular group that was harmed during a particular time frame and facilitate a court's ability to ascertain the class's membership in some objective manner. *Jackson*, 262 P.3d at 887. A class representative must be part of the class and possess the same interest and suffer the same injury as the class members. *Garcia v. Medved Chevrolet, Inc.*, 263 P.3d 92, 103 (Colo. 2011).

ii. Numerosity. The basic standard is whether the number of putative class members is so large as to make joinder impracticable. *LaBerenz v. Am. Fam. Mut. Ins. Co.*, 181 P.3d 328, 335–36 (Colo. App. 2007). No specific number of class members is required and the number of class members in the reported cases varies greatly. *See, e.g., Kuhn v. State Dep't of Revenue*, 817 P.2d 101, 105 (Colo. 1991); *Mountain States Tel. & Tel. Co.*, 778 P.2d at 671; *Cherry Hills Farms, Inc. v. City of Cherry Hills Village*, 670 P.2d 779, 783 (Colo. 1983). "In determining whether the numerosity requirement is met, a court may consider reasonable inferences that can be drawn from the facts before it," and may find the numerosity requirement satisfied "where the exact size of the class is unknown but general knowledge and common sense indicate that it is large." *LaBerenz*, 181 P.3d at 334–35. However, to be included for purposes of numerosity, each class member must have suffered an injury. *Id.* at 337.

iii. Commonality. There must be questions of law or fact that are common to the class; however, there may be varying fact situations among individual members of the class, "as long as the claims of the plaintiffs and other class members are based on the same legal or remedial theory." *LaBerenz*, 181 P.3d at 338.

iv. Typicality. The claims or defenses of the class representative must be "typical of the claims or defenses of the class." C.R.C.P. 23(a)(3). "Typicality requires that the class representative's claims reflect those of the class and that the class claims are encompassed within the representative's claims." *Benzing v. Farmers Ins. Exch.*, 179 P.3d 103, 111 (Colo. App. 2007), *rev'd on other grounds*, 206 P.3d 812 (Colo. 2009); *Reyher v. State Farm Mut. Auto. Ins. Co.*, 230 P.3d 1244, 1256 (Colo. App. 2009), *rev'd on other grounds*, 266 P.3d 383 (Colo. 2011.) (finding typicality where the alleged unlawful conduct by the insurance company was directed at all insureds and health care providers). Colorado courts may find typicality lacking if the class representative "brings into the controversy considerations unique to that individual." *Robinson v. Lynmar Racquet Club, Inc.*, 851 P.2d 274, 279 (Colo. App. 1993); *Ammons v. Am. Family Mut. Ins. Co.*, 897 P.2d 860, 863–864 (Colo. App. 1995).

v. Adequacy of representation. The named plaintiffs must be able to "fairly and adequately protect the interests" of the class. The adequacy of both prospective class representatives and class counsel are reviewed by the courts, which also analyze whether would-be class representatives have conflicts of interest vis-à-vis the class. *Kuhn*, 817 P.2d at 106. "Variations in entitlement to damages among the named plaintiffs and class members do not constitute a conflict of interest" that will defeat adequacy. *Reyher*, 230 P.3d at 1257. "Where a named plaintiff has been found not to be a proper class representative, however, the court should consider remedying the problem by substituting a new class representative." *Benzing*, 179 P.3d at 111, *rev'd on other grounds*, 206 P.3d 812 (Colo. 2009).

b. Rule 23(b)

Before a class is certified, it must meet all of the Rule 23(a) requirements and at least one of the Rule 23(b) criteria. *Buckley Powder*, 945 P.2d at 844.

i. Rule 23(b)(1)(A) and (1)(B). A class action may be maintained where separate lawsuits involving class members could result in inconsistent outcomes or "establish incompatible standards of conduct" with respect to the opposing party. Class actions under subsection (b)(1)(B) may be maintained where individual lawsuits would "as a practical matter be dispositive of the interests" of non-parties or substantially impair those interests.

ii. Rule 23(b)(2). Class actions may be brought under this section where declaratory or injunctive relief is sought against a party whose conduct affects the class generally. Where the class members seek declaratory or injunctive relief as well as damages, the court must make a determination as to whether the case is predominantly a (b)(2) case or predominantly a (b)(3) case. Rule 23(b)(2) certification is not prohibited where damages are sought in addition to injunctive and declaratory relief, so long as the damages are incidental to the primary relief sought. *Town of Breckenridge v. Egencia*, LLC, 442 P.3d 969, 983 (Colo. App. 2018). If the court concludes that the plaintiffs seek primarily damages, the case will be classified as a (b)(3) case and all (b)(3) requirements will apply. *Buckley Powder*, 945 P.2d at 845; *Goebel v. Colo. Dep't of Inst.*, 764 P.2d 785, 795 (Colo. 1988). The Colorado Supreme Court has rejected "need" as a requirement for certification of a (b)(2) class. *Buckley Powder*, 945 P.2d at 845–46. Class certification is proper under Rule 23(b)(2) where the plaintiff seeks to declare unconstitutional a statute and implementing regulation. *Whiteside v. Smith*, 67 P.3d 1240, 1243–44 (Colo. 2003).

iii. Rule 23(b)(3). *Predominance.* The court must find that there are questions of law of fact common to the members of the class which "predominate" over individual issues. It is not necessary for the common issues to be "determinative of defendant's liability," but they must be "central" issues. *Villa Sierra Condo. Ass'n*, 787 P.2d at 665; *Toothman v. Freeborn & Peters,* 80 P.3d 804, 809, 814 (Colo. App. 2002). The predominance inquiry is a "fact driven, pragmatic inquiry." *Patterson v. BP America Prod. Co.*, 360 P.3d 211 226 (Colo. App. 2015). *Often* the issue most relevant to this inquiry is whether the plaintiff advances a theory by which to prove or disprove an element on a simultaneous classwide basis and obviates the need to examine each class member's individual positions. *Jackson*, 262 P.3d 889; *BP American Prod. Co.*, 263 P.3d at 109. Where individual issues predominate over common issues, the trial court should deny certification. *Livingston v. U.S. Bank, N.A.*, 58 P.3d 1088, 1090–91 (Colo. App. 2002); *Colo. Hamburger Co.*, 527 P.3d at 458–59. Neither variations in damages suffered by class members nor the existence of some affirmative defenses particular to an individual class member prevent class certification as a matter of law. *Id* at 890. *See* *also Jackson v. Unocal Corp.*, 231 P.3d 12, 26–27 (Colo. App. 2009), *rev'd on other grounds, Jackson*, 262 P.3d 874 (Colo. 2011) (describing role of trial court in evaluating predominance).

Where a defendant alleges that the elements of reliance, causation, and injury create individualized issues precluding class certification, the trial court must conduct a rigorous analysis to determine whether common issues predominate. Common circumstantial evidence of an omission or nondisclosure of a material fact may support an inference of ignorance and reliance. *BP American Prod. Co.*, 263 P.3d at 111. And common circumstantial evidence may support an inference of causation and injury. *Garcia*, 263 P.3d at 98–102. However, a defendant may introduce evidence rebutting a classwide inference. *BP America Prod. Co.*, 263 P.3d at 111; *Garcia*, 263 P.3d at 102. In a notable decision, in which a petition for writ of certiorari to the Colorado Supreme Court was recently denied, the Colorado Court of Appeals held that an inference of reliance may be rebutted by evidence that a reasonable putative class member would have made the same decision, even if the information had been disclosed. *Maxwell v. United Serv. Auto. Ass'n*, 342 P.3d 474, (Colo. App. 2014), *cert. denied*, 2015 WL 337582 (Colo. 2015). The court, noting that direct evidence is often unavailable to defendants in a class action case, also held that defendants may use circumstantial evidence or indirect evidence to rebut the inference of reliance in a fraudulent concealment case. *Id.* at 25; *Colo. Hamburger Co.*, 527 P.3d at 459. But *cf. BP America Prod. Co.,* 360 P.3d at 227–28, where the Colorado Court of Appeals held that evidence that some class members should have known or had reason to inquire about concealed facts is not actual knowledge sufficient to rebut classwide inference of fraudulent concealment. A trial court's failure to consider a defendant's evidence that refutes classwide theories of inferred reliance, causation and injury constitutes reversible error. *Garcia*, 263 P.3d at 100–02; *State Farm Mut. Auto. Ins. Co. v. Reyher*, 266 P.3d 383, 388 (Colo. 2011).

Superiority. The trial court is given broad discretion to determine whether certification of a class is the "superior means to adjudicate the case." Need [for a class action] is one of many factors which the trial court may consider in making that decision." *Buckley Powder*, 945 P.2d at 845. "In considering the issue of predominance or superiority, whether a case should be certified is a fact-driven, pragmatic inquiry guided by the objective of judicial efficiency and the need to provide a forum for the vindication of dispersed losses." *Medina v. Conseco Annuity Assurance Co.*, 121 P.3d 345, 348 (Colo. App. 2005). Although a court may not "decide the substantive claims and defenses of the parties" when considering whether to certify a class under Rule 23(b)(3), "[s]ome inquiry into the plaintiff's theory of the case . . . is necessary to ensure that common class issues predominate over individual ones." *Benzing*, 206 P.3d at 820. "The requirement of predominance is met where the plaintiff advances a theory by which to prove or disprove an element on a simultaneous, class-wide basis, since such proof obviates the need to examine each class member's individual position." *Id.* (internal quotations and citations omitted).

The existence of a statutory scheme for refunding taxes collected under an unconstitutional tax statute did not preclude class action relief where the court found that a class action was "superior" to the statutory scheme. *Buckley Powder Co. v. State*, 70 P.3d 547, 554 (Colo. App. 2002) ("The fact intensive superiority inquiry seeks to determine the best mechanism for identifying claimants and processing their claims."). However, where plaintiff complained about seven different types of insurance policies with different language, "individual issues predominate[d] over common issues of law and fact, and [] a class action [wa]s not the superior method for resolving plaintiff's claim." *Medina*, 121 P.3d at 348. If the parties can "obtain the same relief without class certification, then a class is not the superior method . . . and certification should be denied." *Buckley Powder Co.,* 70 P.3d at 554. A need for some proof of individual damages does not bar certification. *Toothman*, 80 P.3d at 809, 814–16. A class may be permitted to prove aggregate damages, with individual damages proceedings to take place at a later time. *Buckley Powder Co.*, 70 P.3d at 554. Class action certification is considered "particularly appropriate for proceedings involving alleged violations of securities laws." *Toothman*, 80 P.3d at 809. However, a "fraud on the market" theory will not support class certification where plaintiffs rely on alleged omissions made in face-to-face transactions, or where the claims concern products sold in an inefficient market. *Benzing*, 206 P.3d at 820 (rejecting "fraud on the market" theory with respect to claims of deceptive trade practices in insurance industry).

c. Rule 23(c)(1)

After entering a class certification order, a trial court may consider other evidence and subsequent developments in the case to modify the order, redefine the class, create subclasses, or enter other case management orders. Colo. R. Civ. P. 23(c)(1)(4); *Goebel,* 764 P.2d at 794; *Villa Sierra Condo. Ass'n*, 787 P.2d at 667. Generally, "trial courts should not consider decertification without the discovery of new facts or changes in the law or positions of the parties." *Benzing*, 206 P.3d at 819. However, the court at all times must ensure that the class action requirements are met. *Id.* "In particular, where there is evidence that the court may be required to undertake individualized inquiries to resolve issues of liability, the court retains the discretion to modify or decertify the class." *Id.*

d. Rule 23(d)

The trial court is given discretion to manage class actions, including "authority to protect putative class members against abusive practices that harm their interests in the action and compromise the viability of maintaining the class action." *Air Commc'n & Satellite, Inc. v. Echostar Satellite Corp.*, 38 P.3d 1246, 1253 (Colo. 2002).

Although the plaintiff must normally submit a proposal to certify a class, a court may *sua sponte* act to create subclasses under appropriate circumstances or may certify only as to common (but not as to individual) issues. *Toothman,* 80 P.3d at 817. A court is permitted by Rule 23(c) and (d) to restructure classes where necessary, either on motion of a party or on its own motion. *Buckley Powder Co.*, 70 P.3d at 555–56; *see also Medina*, 121 P.3d at 349 (noting that the "burden is on plaintiff, not the court, to suggest certification of smaller class or creation of subclasses") (citing Alba Conte, Herbert B. Newberg, *Newberg on Class Actions* § 4:25 (2002)).

e. Rule 23(e)

Following federal law, the Colorado Court of Appeals has held that in evaluating a proposed settlement under C.R.C.P. 23(e), the trial court must determine whether the settlement is fair, adequate and reasonable. *Higley*, 920 P.2d at 891. Factors that may govern the trial court's analysis include the strength of plaintiff's case, the risk, expense, complexity and likely duration of further litigation, the risk of maintaining class action status throughout the trial, the amount offered in settlement, the extent of discovery completed, the experience and views of class counsel and the reaction of class members to the proposed settlement. *Id.* A trial court's approval of a class action settlement will not be overturned absent a showing of "a clear abuse of discretion." *Id.*

f. Rule 23(f)

For many years, Colorado courts held that orders denying class certification were final and subject to immediate appeal. *Levine v. Empire Sav. & Loan Ass'n*, 557 P.2d 386, 387 (Colo. 1976). Effective July 1, 2003, Colorado Rule 23 was amended to permit discretionary appeals of orders granting or denying class certification pursuant to the procedures set forth in C.R.S. § 13-20-901. In *Clark v. Farmers Insurance Exchange*, 117 P.3d 26 (Colo. App. 2004), the Colorado Court of Appeals outlined a non-exclusive, five-factor test for courts to apply in deciding whether to permit an interlocutory appeal. Those factors are: (1) the "death knell" factor, or whether the class certification ruling is likely dispositive of the litigation; (2) the substantial weakness factor, or whether the trial court's ruling likely constitutes an abuse of discretion; (3) whether the appeal will permit resolution of a legal issue important to the litigation, as well as important in itself; (4) the nature and status of the litigation, including the status of discovery, the pendency of relevant motions, and the length of time the matter has been pending; and (5) whether future events may make intermediate appellate review more or less appropriate. *Id.* at 29–32. However, the Court of Appeals has held that "where a *named plaintiff* chooses not to file an interlocutory appeal of an *order denying* class certification under [C.R.S.] § 13-20-901(1), the plaintiff does *not* waiver the right to appeal that order by requesting and obtaining a C.R.C.P. 54(b) certification of final judgment . . ." *Devora v. Strodtman*, 282 P.3d 528, 533 (Colo. App. 2012) (emphasis added).

3. MISCELLANEOUS COMMENTS

a. Cost of Notice to Class Members

Although the named representative must usually bear the cost of notice to class members, the Colorado Supreme Court in unusual circumstances has placed the burden on the defendant. *Mountain States Tel. & Tel. Co.*, 778 P.2d at 673, 676 ("content neutral" notice included with telephone bills).

b. Objections to Settlement by Class Members

Class members other than named plaintiffs have standing to appeal an order approving a settlement if they intervene in the action or if a motion to intervene is improperly denied. *Higley*, 920 P.2d at 889–90.

c. Status of Settlement Class Claiming Breach of Settlement Agreement

A class that has been certified by the Court to facilitate a class-wide settlement survives the dismissal of the settled lawsuit and survives through the life of the settlement agreement. *EnCana Oil & Gas, Inc. v. Miller*, 405 P.3d 488 (Colo. App. 2017).

d. Damages Recovery Is Common Fund for Payment of Attorneys' Fees

A damage recovery by a class is a common fund out of which attorneys' fees will be paid; the attorneys' right to payment from the common fund is a substantive right. *Kuhn v. State*, 924 P.2d 1053, 1057–60 (Colo. 1996); *Brody v. Hellman*, 167 P.3d 192, 198 (Colo. App. 2007) (engaging in extensive analysis of reasonableness of common fund award of attorney's fees). A pre-existing fee arrangement may assist a court in determining the attorney's fee expectations, but is only one factor the court considers in assessing reasonableness. *Brody*, 167 P.3d at 199. A common fund remedy may be employed in a case against a governmental entity. *Buckley Powder Co.*, 70 P.3d at 558.

e. Effect of Previous Certification of Settlement Classes on Certification of Class as to Remaining Defendants

The fact that a court has certified settlement classes with respect to some defendants in a case is not determinative as to certification of classes with regard to non-settling defendants because litigation management issues do not arise where classes are certified for settlement purposes. *Toothman*, 80 P.3d at 809–10.

f. In Class Actions against Public Entities, Fees That Plaintiffs' Attorneys May Receive from Award Are Limited by Statute

The limitation in C.R.S. § 1317203, which limits attorneys' fees awarded in class actions against public entities to an amount not more than $250,000, is unambiguous, enforceable, and constitutional. *Buckley Powder Co.*, 70 P.3d at 561–63.

g. Claim and Issue Preclusion

Class actions for injunctive relief certified pursuant to Rule 23(b)(2) do not preclude subsequent suits for damages by class members, although such suits would be precluded if the class had been certified under Rule 23(b)(3). *Jahn ex. rel. Jahn v. ORCR, Inc.*, 92 P.3d 984, 988 (Colo. 2004). The Court reasoned that due process required that class members must be adequately represented and given notice that their claims may be lost before they are bound to a class judgment. Since class certification under Rule 23(b)(2) requires adequate representation, but not individual notice, members of 23(b)(2) classes who do not receive notice are not precluded from filing subsequent damages suits. *Id.* at 989, 991–92.

Issue preclusion may bar a plaintiff from seeking class certification, where the plaintiff's attorney had previously been denied class certification on behalf of another plaintiff and the other requirements for issue preclusion are satisfied. *Goldsworthy v. Am. Family Mut. Ins. Co.*, 2009 P.3d 1108 (Colo. 2008), *cert. denied*, 2009 WL 1585992 (Colo. 2009).

h. Tolling of Limitations Periods

In *Rosenthal v. Dean Witter Reynolds, Inc.*, Colorado adopted the rule articulated by the United States Supreme Court in *American Pipe & Construction Co. v. Utah*, 414 U.S. 538 (1974). *Rosenthal*, 883 P.2d at 531. Under this rule, the commencement of a class action tolls the limitation period for all putative members of the class until class certification is denied. At that point, class members may file their own suit or intervene as plaintiffs in the pending action. *Id. Rosenthal* also addressed whether the limitations period would be tolled with respect to a class member who sought to become a class representative after the limitations period had passed. The court concluded that "as long as the party seeking to act as a class representative does not commence a new, separate suit as a class representative, but merely seeks to maintain the currently pending and timely filed action as a class action and act as class representative, the statute of repose does not apply." *Id.* at 531.

i. Entry of Judgment

Rule 23(c)(3) requires that the judgment in a class action must "include and describe those whom the court finds to be members of the class," and must "specify or describe those to whom the notice

. . . was directed, and who have not requested exclusion." C.R.C.P. 23(c)(3). A court's failure to comply with these requirements, however, does not preclude the entry of a final judgment or suspend the time in which to file an appeal. *Goodwin v. Homeland Cent. Ins. Co.*, 172 P.3d 938, 945 (Colo. App. 2007).

j. Communications with Absent Class Members

There is a single case in Colorado concerning a defendants' communications with absent class members. In *Air Communications & Satellite Inc. v. Echostar Satellite Corp.*, 38 P.3d 1246 (Colo. 2002), plaintiff, a retailer of defendant's products and services, filed a putative class action on behalf of other retailers alleging breach of contract and other claims. Prior to class certification, defendant sent the putative class members new retailer agreements that purported to waive claims asserted in the class action lawsuit. The named plaintiff moved for emergency relief under C.R.C.P 23(d). The district court issued an order requiring the mailing of corrective notice and prohibiting defendant from communicating with the putative class without prior approval from the court. On appeal, the Supreme Court of Colorado held that the district court did not abuse its discretion in requiring corrective notice. *Id.* at 1248, 1251. However, the court did abuse its discretion in requiring prior review of future, precertification, communications with putative class members. *Id.* The Colorado Supreme Court reasoned that trial courts have extensive authority to limit communications between defendants and class members *after* certification of a class, but that the authority to limit communications *before* certification is narrower. *Id.* at 1252. Generally, a defendant may communicate with prospective class members regarding a pending class action prior to class certification. *Id.* at 1252. However, the trial court has the authority to protect putative class members against abusive practices that harm their interests in the action and compromise the viability of maintaining the class action while the court proceeds through the necessary and appropriate steps for deciding whether to certify a class. *Id.* at 1253. Trial courts have the authority under C.R.C.P. 23(d) to require corrective action. *Id.* However, a trial court must balance defendants' and putative class members' interests and make specific findings of fact to restrain future, pre-certification, communications. *Id.* at 1255. The Colorado Supreme Court has articulated standards to guide trial courts in considering restrictions on future communications. A trial court must consider the following factors for formulating restrictions on future communications with putative class members: "(1) the severity and likelihood of perceived harm; (2) the precision with which the order is drawn; (3) the availability of a less onerous alternative; and (4) the duration of the order." *Id.* at 1256 (citations omitted).

Addressing plaintiffs' communications with absent class members, the Colorado Court of Appeals in *BKP, Inc. v. Killmer, Lane & Newman, LLP*, 506 P.3d 84 (Colo. App. 2021), *cert. granted*, No. 21SC930, 2022 WL 17585946 (Colo. Dec. 12, 2022), held that the litigation privilege did not shield attorneys for the class from liability for making defamatory statements at a press conference publicizing the filing of their class action complaint. The court's holding was based on its finding that the defamatory statements were not related to the class action because the communications were not necessary to inform putative class members of the lawsuit; the identity of the class could be ascertained through discovery.

RULE 23 OF THE COLORADO RULES OF CIVIL PROCEDURE

RULE 23. CLASS ACTIONS

(a) *Prerequisites to Class Action* One or more members of a class may sue or be sued as representative parties on behalf of all only if: (1) The class is so numerous that joinder of all members is impracticable; (2) there are questions of law or fact common to the class; (3) the claims or defenses of the representative parties are typical of the claims or defenses of the class; and (4) the representative parties will fairly and adequately protect the interests of the class.

(b) *Class Actions Maintainable* Any action may be maintained as a class action if the prerequisites of section (a) are satisfied, and in addition:

(1) The prosecution of separate actions by or against individual members of the class would create a risk of:

(A) Inconsistent or varying adjudications with respect to individual members of the class which would establish incompatible standards of conduct for the party opposing the class; or

(B) Adjudications with respect to individual members of the class which would as a practical matter be dispositive of the interests of the other members not parties to the adjudications or substantially impair or impede their ability to protect their interest; or

(2) The party opposing the class has acted or refused to act on grounds generally applicable to the class, thereby making appropriate final injunctive relief or corresponding declaratory relief with respect to the class as a whole; or

(3) The court finds that the questions of law or fact common to the members of the class predominate over any questions affecting only individual members, and that a class action is superior to other available methods for the fair and efficient adjudication of the controversy. The matters pertinent to the findings include:

(A) The interest of members of the class in individually controlling the prosecution or defense of separate actions;

(B) The extent and nature of any litigation concerning the controversy already commenced by or against members of the class;

(C) The desirability or undesirability of concentrating the litigation of the claims in the particular forum;

(D) The difficulties likely to be encountered in the management of class action.

(c) *Determination by Order Whether Class Action to Be Maintained; Notice; Judgment; Actions Conducted Partially as Class Actions*

(1) As soon as practicable after the commencement of an action brought as a class action, the court shall determine by order whether it is to be so maintained. An order under this section (c) may be conditional, and may be altered or amended before the decision

on the merits.

(2) In any class action maintained under subsection (b)(3), the court shall direct to the members of the class the best notice practicable under the circumstances, including individual notice to all members who can be identified through reasonable effort. The notice shall advise each member that: (A) The court will exclude him from the class if he so requests by a specified date; (B) the judgment, whether favorable or not, will include all members who do not request exclusion; and (C) any member who does not request exclusion may, if he desires, enter an appearance through his counsel.

(3) The judgment in an action maintained as a class action under subsections (b)(1) or (b)(2), whether or not favorable to the class, shall include and describe those whom the court finds to be members of the class. The judgment in an action maintained as a class action under subsection (b)(3), whether or not favorable to the class, shall include and specify or describe those to whom the notice provided in subsection (c)(2) was directed, and who have not requested exclusion, and whom the court finds to be members of the class.

(4) When appropriate: (A) An action may be brought or maintained as a class action with respect to particular issues, or (B) a class may be divided into subclasses and each subclass treated as a class, and the provisions of this Rule shall then be construed and applied accordingly.

(d) *Orders in Conduct of Actions* In the conduct of actions to which this Rule applies, the court may make appropriate orders:

(1) Determining the course of proceedings or prescribing measures to prevent undue repetition or complication in the presentation of evidence or argument;

(2) Requiring, for the protection of the members of the class or otherwise for the fair conduct of the action, the notice be given in such manner as the court may direct to some or all of the members of any step in the action, or of the proposed extent of the judgment, or of the opportunity of members to signify whether they consider the representation fair and adequate, to intervene and present claims or defenses, or otherwise to come into the action;

(3) Imposing conditions on the representative parties or on intervenors;

(4) Requiring that the pleadings be amended to eliminate therefrom allegations as to representation of absent persons, and that the action proceed accordingly;

(5) Dealing with similar procedural matters. The orders may be combined with an order under Rule 16, and may be altered or amended as may be desirable from time to time.

(e) *Dismissal or Compromise* A class action shall not be dismissed or compromised without the approval of the court, and notice of the proposed dismissal or compromise shall be given to all members of the class in such manner as the court directs.

(f) *Appeals* An appeal from an order granting or denying class certification under this rule may be allowed pursuant to the procedures set forth in C.R.S. § 13-20-901 (2003).

This chapter was prepared by Jessica P. Marsh of Williams Weese Pepple & Ferguson, PC, in Denver.

CONNECTICUT

1. COMPARISON OF CONNECTICUT'S RULES WITH RULE 23 OF THE FEDERAL RULES OF CIVIL PROCEDURE

Class actions in Connecticut are governed by Connecticut Practice Book §§ 9-7 through 9-10 and Conn. Gen. Stat. § 52-105. Connecticut Practice Book § 9-7 is identical in substance to Rule 23(a) of the Federal Rules of Civil Procedure, requiring proof of numerosity of potential claimants, commonality and typicality of issues of law and fact, and adequacy of representation.

Similarly, Connecticut Practice Book § 9-8 is identical in substance to Federal Rule 23(b), requiring that one of the following three conditions be met in addition to the requirements of § 9-7: (1) that prosecution of separate actions by individual members would create a risk of inconsistent adjudications or adjudications dispositive of the interests of other members who are not parties to the adjudications, (2) that the party opposing the class has acted in such a way that is generally applicable to all members of the class, thereby making final injunctive relief or corresponding declaratory relief with respect to the class as a whole appropriate, or (3) that there is a predominance of common issues of law or fact and superiority of a class action over other forms of adjudication. Both the state and federal rules include the same non-exhaustive list of four factors that a court should consider when determining whether or not the predominance and superiority requirements have been met.

Practice Book § 9-9 adopts the substance of Federal Rule 23(c), (d), (e), (f), (g), and (h). Section 9-9(a) mirrors Rule 23(c), requiring that the court issue its certification decision at an "early practicable time," which, if granted, must define the class, class claims, issues, or defenses, appoint class counsel, and give the court authority to amend such order before final judgment. The provision also requires notice to the class and, in classes certified under § 9-8(3), requires notice, including individual notice, to all known members and specifies certain criteria that must be contained within that notice. Both the federal and Connecticut rules state that a judgment shall apply to the entire class but also that classes can be certified with respect to certain issues or subclasses may be created. Section 9-9(b), the counterpart to Rule 23(d), gives the court authority to make orders that: (1) prescribe measures to prevent undue repetition in the presentation of evidence and arguments, (2) require that notice be given to some or all members of the class regarding steps taken in the proceeding, (3) impose conditions on parties, (4) require that pleadings be amended as the litigation progresses, or (5) deal with similar procedural matters. Section 9-9(c), like Rule 23(e), requires the approval of the court for withdrawal or compromise of an action in which the class has been certified and specifies procedures the court must follow, including notice of a proposed dismissal or compromise to be given to all class members who would be bound by it. Unlike Rule 23(e), however, § 9-9(c) expressly states that court approval is not required for the settlement or voluntary withdrawal of a putative class action prior to class certification.

Sections 9-9(d) and (e) correspond to Federal Rule 23(g), addressing the appointment of class counsel and factors the court must take into consideration in appointing class counsel. Section 9-9(f) and Rule 23(h) are also virtually identical in the way they handle requests for attorney's fees.

Section 9-9, subsection (g), which became effective on January 1, 2015, addresses the court's discretion regarding "residual funds" left over after all claims, costs, and fees are satisfied. Under these circumstances, the court can approve a settlement that leaves no residual funds, designate recipients of such funds, or disburse the funds to organizations that provide legal services for the poor in Connecticut pursuant to Conn. Gen. Stat. § 51-81c.

The first and third sentences of Practice Book § 9-10, concerning orders to ensure adequate representation, while not verbatim, are essentially the same as Federal Rule 23(d)(1)(C) and (d)(1)(D), respectively, although § 9-10 also allows the court to require security in addition to any orders. The second sentence of § 9-10 of the Connecticut rule is comparable to Federal Rule 23(d)(1)(B). Unlike Federal Rule 23(c)(2)(B), which mandates notice of the pendency of a Rule 23(b)(3) class action, the second sentence of Practice Book § 9-10 provides that a Connecticut court *may* order that notice be given of the pendency of the action.

Partial class actions may be brought in state court, even though the Practice Book rules do not expressly provide for partial class actions as Rule 23 does. Connecticut has also not adopted provisions similar to Federal Rule 23(f) regarding discretionary interlocutory review of denial of class certification.

The only direct statutory provision for class actions in general, Conn. Gen. Stat. § 52-105, provides that a class action may be brought "[w]hen the persons who might be made parties are very numerous." Accordingly, the Practice Book rules offer more detailed guidance than the statute.

2. CASE LAW INTERPRETING CLASS ACTION RULE §§ 9-7 THROUGH 9-10

a. General Principles

In determining whether to certify a class, a court is required to take the substantive allegations of the complaint as true and must decide whether the requirements for class certification have been met. *Collins v. Anthem Health Plans, Inc.*, 275 Conn. 309, 321, 880 A.2d 106, 113 (2005) (*Collins II*) (citing *Collins v. Anthem Health Plans, Inc.*, 266 Conn. 12, 24, 836 A.2d 1124, 1134 (2003) (*Collins I*)); *Rivera v. Veterans Mem. Med. Ctr.*, 262 Conn. 730, 743, 818 A.2d 731, 740 (2003). "[A] trial court should not assume the truth of the plaintiff's allegations if the allegations bear on an issue of class certification. . . . But inquiries into the merits of a plaintiff's case should be performed only to the extent necessary to ensure the plaintiff has met the requirements of the class action rules." *Rodriguez v. Kaiaffa, LLC*, 337 Conn. 248, 262, 253 A.3d 13, 26 (2020). Any "doubts regarding the propriety of class certification should be resolved in favor of certification." *Collins II*, 275 Conn. at 321, 880 A.2d at 113 (quoting *Rivera*, 262 Conn. at 743, 818 A.2d at 740). While plaintiffs bear the burden of proving that they satisfy the elements for class certification, "they need not prove that their claims ultimately will succeed." *Rivera*, 262 Conn. at 746, 818 A.2d at 741. The court "has broad discretion in determining whether a suit should proceed as a class action." *Neighborhood Builders, Inc. v. Madison*, 294 Conn. 651, 662, 986 A.2d 278, 285 (2010) (citation omitted); *Macomber v. Travelers Prop. & Cas. Corp.*, 277 Conn. 617, 626, 894 A.2d 240, 249 (2006) (quoting *In re Visa Check/Mastermoney Antitrust Litig.*, 280 F.3d 124, 132 (2d Cir. 2001)); *Ahmad v. Yale-New Haven Hosp., Inc.*, 104 Conn. App. 380, 384, 933 A.2d 1208, 1213 (2007). While the court may consider, *sua sponte*, whether to modify the scope of the proposed class, it is under no affirmative obligation to do so. *Collier v. Adar Hartford Realty, LLC*, 349 Conn. 822, 843–45, 322 A.3d 1041, 1056–57 (2024).

Since the requirements set forth in §§ 9-7 through 9-10 of the Connecticut Practice Book are substantially similar to the requirements for class certification under Rule 23 of the Federal Rules of

Civil Procedure, a Connecticut state court may use federal case law in aid of its construction of the Connecticut certification requirements. *Collins II*, 275 Conn. at 322-23, 880 A.2d at 114 (citing *Collins I*, 266 Conn. at 32, 836 A.2d at 1139); *Rivera,* 262 Conn. at 737-38, 818 A.2d at 736-37. Also, the Connecticut Supreme Court has adopted an approach similar to that of the federal rule, "which permits the trial court to revisit the issue of class certification throughout the proceedings." *Rivera*, 262 Conn. at 739, 818 A.2d at 738. Like Rule 23, Practice Book §§ 9-7 and 9-8 are designed to increase efficiencies in civil litigation by preventing proliferation of lawsuits and duplicative efforts and expenses. *Collins I*, 266 Conn. at 25-26, 836 A.2d at 1134, 1135 (quoting *Rivera*, 262 Conn. at 735, 818 A.2d at 735).

Nevertheless, one Superior Court has held that reliance on federal decisions for guidance should be limited to class certification issues and should not extend into the doctrine of standing. *Taylor v. Hartford Fin. Servs. Grp., Inc.*, No. X07HHDCV166072110S, 2017 WL 5014868, at *1 (Conn. Super. Ct. Sept. 26, 2017). In *Taylor*, the court denied the defendant's motion to dismiss the class action complaint for lack of standing in which the defendant argued that the plaintiff failed to allege sufficient facts to establish plausible claims under the standard set forth in *Bell Atlantic Corp. v. Twombly*, 550 U.S. 544 (2007). While acknowledging that Connecticut courts use federal class action case law as a guide, the court held that standing was not a class action question and, in any event, that Connecticut has not adopted the *Twombly* plausibility test for standing. *Taylor*, 2017 WL 5014868, at *1.

For a class to be certified in Connecticut courts, the plaintiff bears the burden of demonstrating that all the prerequisites set out in Practice Book §§ 9-7 and 9-8 are satisfied. *Arduini v. Automobile Ins. Co. of Hartford*, 23 Conn. App. 585, 589 A.2d 152, 154 (1990); *Thames River Apt. Tenants v. New London Hous. Auth.*, No. X04CV064006233S, 2007 WL 4305525, at *8 (Conn. Super. Ct. Nov. 13, 2007); *Machado v. City of New Haven*, No. CV044004852, 2006 WL 2734257, at *3 (Conn. Super. Ct. Sept. 11, 2006). Section 9-7 requires that a potential class demonstrate (1) numerosity, (2) commonality, (3) typicality, and (4) adequacy of representation before certification will be granted, and Section 9-8 additionally requires that common questions of law or fact predominate and that a class action is superior in terms of judicial fairness and efficiency to other available adjudicative methods. *See* §§ (b) and (c) *infra.* In determining whether a plaintiff has met his or her burden, the Connecticut Supreme Court follows the lead of federal courts, directing its trial courts to undertake a "rigorous analysis." *Rodriguez*, 373 Conn. at 256, 253 A.3d 13 at 23; *Standard Petrol Co. v. Faugno Acquisition*, 330 Conn. 40, 48, 191 A.3d 147, 157 (2018) (internal citation and quotation marks omitted); *Neighborhood Builders, Inc.*, 294 Conn. at 656, 986 A.2d 278; *Marr v. WMX Tech., Inc.*, 244 Conn. 676, 680, 711 A.2d 700 (1998).

For decisions engaging in detailed analyses of these requirements, *see, e.g., Rodriguez*, 337 Conn. at 255–88, 253 A.3d at 22–41 (regarding commonality, typicality, and § 9-8 factors); *Standard Petrol Co.*, 330 Conn. at 52–75, 191 A.3d at 159–71 (2018) (regarding all four § 9-7 factors as well as the § 9-8 factors of predominance and superiority); *Artie's Auto Body, Inc. v. Hartford Fire Ins. Co.*, 287 Conn. 208, 215–36 (2008) (regarding predominance) (*Artie's I*); *Macomber*, 277 Conn. at 628–32, 894 A.2d at 250–52 (2006) (regarding typicality and adequacy of representation); *Collins II*, 275 Conn. at 323–33, 880 A.2d at 114–19 (regarding commonality, adequacy of representation, and predominance); *Ahmad*, 104 Conn. App. at 386–91 (regarding predominance); *Asia Moreland v. C&L Diners, LLC,* No. X07CV196113453S, 2021 WL 4777020, at *1–6 (Conn. Super. Ct. Aug. 25, 2021) (regarding all four § 9-7 factors as well as the § 9-8 factors of predominance and superiority); *Chandler v. Ruby Tuesday, Inc.*, No. X07CV196106450S, 2021 WL 1251103, at *2 (Conn. Super. Ct. Jan. 22, 2021) (regarding commonality, typicality, and adequacy of representation); *Diaz v. Griffin Health Servs. Corp.*, No. X01CV156029965S, 2020 WL 8130207, at *3–9 (Conn. Super.

Ct. Nov. 23, 2020) (regarding commonality and § 9-8 factors); *Gold v. Rowland*, No. CV020813759S, 2011 WL 6976499, at *4–12 (Conn. Super. Ct. Dec. 13, 2011) (regarding typicality, adequacy of representation, and predominance); *Moore v. Midland Credit Mgmt.*, No. X04CV034005909S, 2007 WL 4171562, at *2–7 (Conn. Super. Ct. Nov. 5, 2007) (regarding all four § 9-7 factors as well as the § 9-8 factors of predominance and superiority); *Neighborhood Builders, Inc. v. Town of Madison*, No. X01CV044005268S, 2007 WL 3257469, at *3–14 (Conn. Super. Ct. Oct. 12, 2007) (same); *Peruta v. Outback Steakhouse of Fla., Inc.*, 50 Conn. Supp. 51, 54–68, 913 A.2d 1160, 1164–72 (Conn. Super. Ct. Aug. 24, 2006) (regarding all four § 9-7 factors and predominance); *Agrella v. Ford Motor Co.*, No. X01CV020184712S, 2006 WL 1493823, at *2–4 (Conn. Super. Ct. May 18, 2006) (same); *Town of New Hartford v. Conn. Res. Recovery Auth.*, No. UWYCV040185580SX02, 2006 WL 853217, at *3–15 (Conn. Super. Ct. Mar. 21, 2006) (regarding all §§ 9-7 and 9-8 factors); *Palmer v. Friendly Ice Cream Corp.*, No. X07CV044001612S, 2006 WL 361339, at *1–5 (Conn. Super. Ct. Jan. 25, 2006) (regarding all four § 9-7 factors and predominance); *Macomber v. Travelers Prop. & Cas.*, No. X03CV990496761S, 2004 WL 1559183, at *10 (Conn. Super. Ct. May 26, 2004), *rev'd sub nom. Macomber*, 277 Conn. 617, 894 A.2d 240 (2006) (same).

b. Section 9-7. Prerequisites to Class Actions

Connecticut Practice Book § 9-7 provides that, for one or more members of a class to sue or be sued as representatives on behalf of all the other members, four prerequisites must be met. While "it is necessary, or at least proper, to set forth the requisite elements of a class action in a complaint," *Baker v. Town of Cheshire*, No. CV075013602, 2008 WL 1971495, at *11 (Conn. Super. Ct. Apr. 24, 2008), alleging a separate cause of action for a class action does not appear to be required. *Brower v. Family Practice of Litchfield, LLC*, No. X02CV064013153S, 2007 WL 2428988, at *5 (Conn. Super. Ct. Aug. 10, 2007) (stating that a complaint is "sufficiently pled with regard to [the] three [named] plaintiffs" and, therefore, motion to strike complaint for failure to state a cause of action for class action is premature).

i. Numerosity. While the plaintiff is not required to provide the court with an exact class size, the plaintiff is required to show "some evidence or a reasonable estimate" of the number of members in a class. *Stebbins v. Doncasters, Inc.*, No. X07CV990072908S, 2000 WL 1058864, at *3 (Conn. Super. Ct. July 14, 2000) (quoting *Campbell v. New Milford Bd. of Educ.*, 36 Conn. Supp. 357, 360, 423 A.2d 900 (Conn. Super. Ct. Aug. 12, 1980)). While mere speculation or conclusory allegations as to the size of the class will not justify certification, *see Arduini*, 23 Conn. App. at 591, 583 A.2d at 155; *Rivera v. Rowland*, No. CV95545629, 1996 WL 677452, at *2 (Conn. Super. Ct. Nov. 8, 1996), "an estimate based on reasonable inferences drawn from available facts satisfies the requirement—particularly where . . . more precise information is within the defendant's control." *Peruta*, 50 Conn. Supp. at 54, 913 A.2d at 1164. Statistics may support a finding of numerosity but are unlikely to be sufficient without evidence of specific individuals who qualify for the class, "or other strong and reliable indicia of numerosity." *See Parker v. Colgate-Palmolive Co.*, No. X08CV030193798, 2004 WL 3090652, at *3–5 (Conn. Super. Ct. Nov. 29, 2004) (holding almost total reliance on statistical extrapolations was too close to speculation). Once the appropriate size of the class is fairly determined, "[t]he fact that an unknown percentage of class members might wish to opt out of the case is immaterial." *Palmer*, 2006 WL 361339, at *2.

There is no "magic" number of people involved in an action that automatically fulfills the numerosity requirement. Generally, however, numbers that are amenable to a simple joinder of parties are too small for certification as a class. *See Arduini*, 23 Conn. App. at 590, 583 A.2d at 154 (10–11 people too small for class certification); *Villano v. Constantinou*, No. X07CV010077486S, 2003 WL 21101527, at *1–2 (Conn. Super. Ct. May 2, 2003) (certification denied where petitioners identified only 20 members of one subclass and 9 members of another). Even larger numbers of parties can be deemed more suitable for joinder than for class certification. For example, as the court in *Town of New Hartford* recognized, "many cases with a potential class membership in excess of 40 result in the denial of class certification because joinder is not impracticable. . . ." 2006 WL 853217, at *5 (citing cases from the Southern District of New York, District of Hawaii, and Connecticut denying certification to classes of 57 and 54, 200, and 118 members, respectively). Nevertheless, a class consisting of as few as 40 members *can* be sufficiently numerous for class certification. *See id.* at *10–11 ("The United States Court of Appeals for the Second Circuit has stated that 'the difficulty in joining as few as 40 class members should raise a presumption that joinder is impracticable.'") (quoting *Robidoux v. Celani*, 987 F.2d 931, 935 (2d Cir. 1993)); *Dougan v. Sikorsky Airline Corp.*, No. X03CV126033069, 2016 WL 921779, at *5 (Conn. Super. Ct. Feb. 11, 2016) (a proposed class of 40 members was sufficient to satisfy the numerosity requirement for class certification) *vacated sub nom.*, *Dougan v. Sikorsky Aircraft Corp.*, No. X03HHDCV126033069S, 2017 WL 7806431, at *7 (Conn. Super. Ct. Mar. 28, 2017) ("[T]he court's decision granting the defendants' 2016 motions for summary judgment does not permit, as a matter of law, the class certification decision to stand. Accordingly, pursuant to Practice Book § 9-9(a)(1)(C), the court hereby vacates the class certification decision. . . ."); *Artie's Auto Body, Inc. v. Hartford Fire Ins. Co.*, No. X08CV030196141S, 2009 WL 3087209, at *5 (Conn. Super. Aug. 26, 2009) (finding subclass of 54 meets numerosity requirement when members are spread throughout state). *See also Moore*, 2007 WL 4171562, at *2–8 (class of 100 or more numerous enough for certification); *Artie's Autobody, Inc. v. Hartford Fire Ins. Co.*, No. X08CV030196141S, 2006 WL 2730143, at *3 (Conn. Super. Ct. Aug. 30, 2006) (noting that "a respected commentary on class action law suggests a presumption of sufficient impracticability and numerosity should arise when the putative class exceeds 40 members[,] 1 Conte & Newberg, *Newberg on Class Actions*, § 3.5 (4th ed. 2002)," the court held that a potential class in the hundreds met the numerosity requirements); *Hastedt v. Remodeling Contrs. Ass'n, Inc.*, No. XO6CV990156058S, 2000 WL 371466, at *2 (Conn. Super. Ct. Apr. 3, 2000) ("A class of 80 or 90 members clearly would be so numerous as to make joinder impracticable."); *Campbell*, 36 Conn. Supp. at 361, 423 A.2d at 903 (class of 450–800 members numerous enough for certification).

Courts may consider more than just the number of people in the class in determining the practicability of joinder: "Courts should not be so rigid as to depend upon mere numbers as a guideline on the practicability of joinder; a determination of practicability should depend upon all the circumstances surrounding a case." *Town of New Hartford*, 2006 WL 853217, at *4 (quoting *Demarco v. Edens*, 390 F.2d 836, 845 (2d Cir. 1968)). For instance, courts may consider such additional factors as the geographic location of potential class members, the judicial economy of avoiding individual suits, and the class members' resources and abilities to bring individual actions. *See Hong Pham v. Starkowski,* No. HHDCV095034410S, 2009 WL 5698062, at *9 (Conn. Super. Ct. Dec. 18, 2009), *rev'd*, 300 Conn. 412, 16 A.3d 635 (2011) (considering members' English language skills, level of legal sophistication, and disabled or elderly status in deciding to certify class); *Thames River Apt. Tenants*, 2007 WL 4305525, at *3 (finding the indigency of class members rendered joinder unsuitable despite geographic proximity); *Town of New Hartford,* 2006 WL 853217, at *14–15 (noting that centralized location of class members in Connecticut and high level of members' sophistication favored joinder, but ultimately granting certification due to likely tainting of potential class members caused by defendant's misleading statements to them). *See also Liss v. Milford Partners*, No. X07CV044001734S, 2005 WL 1433924, at *2 (Conn. Super. Ct. May 26, 2005) (individuals in a potentially small class of less than 40 had already obtained individual counsel and so judicial economy would not be assisted through certification of a class); *Parker*, 2004 WL 3090652, at *5 (holding that class of Connecticut claimants was not so geographically dispersed as to make joinder impracticable).

Courts may also consider potential class members' willingness to participate in the action. *See Mason v. Barbieri*, No. X04HHDCV085035997S, 2016 WL 2891522, at *3 (Conn. Super. Ct. Apr. 28, 2016) (a failure to show that any of the 377 proposed class members were interested in pursuing litigation prevented a determination as to whether joinder was impracticable); *Kennynick, LLC v. Standard Petroleum Co.*, No. FSTCV095009985S, 2015 WL 5806772, at *3 (Conn. Super. Ct. Aug. 31, 2015) ("Plaintiffs must show that potential class members have an interest in participating in the action").

ii. Commonality. Commonality does not require a complete identity of legal and factual issues among all members of the class. Commonality only requires that there *exists* some common question of law or fact among the members, not that it predominates. *Town of New Hartford*, 2006 WL 853217, at *11 (citing *Campbell*, 36 Conn. Supp. at 362, 423 A.2d at 904). The need for individual treatment of members of the class on the issue of damages does not defeat commonality. *Marr*, 244 Conn. at 683, 711 A.2d at 703; *Moore*, 2007 WL 4171562, at *6–8. Anticipating modification of this approach, the Connecticut Superior Court noted that the U.S. Supreme Court's holding in *Wal-Mart Stores, Inc. v. Dukes*, 131 S. Ct. 2541, 2551 (2011), cautioned that courts should not define the common questions too broadly in finding commonality. *Sal's Glass Co. v. Duplicating Methods Co.*, No. HHDCV106016006S, 2013 WL 1407500, at *3 (Conn. Super. Ct. Mar. 11, 2013). In *Wal-Mart Stores, Inc.*, the Supreme Court found that "claims must depend upon a common contention. . . . That common contention, moreover, must be of such a nature that it is capable of classwide resolution—which means that determination of its truth or falsity will resolve an issue that is central to the validity of each one of the claims in one stroke." 131 S. Ct. at 2551. *See also Diaz*, 2020 WL 8130207, at *8–9 (concluding that professional negligence claims requiring determination of the appropriate institutional standard of care met the commonality requirement for class certification but that recklessness claims "focus[ing] on specific acts of misuse" of medical equipment did not meet the commonality standard).

iii. Typicality. The injury to the representative of the class must be typical of, and directly related to, the injury to the class as a whole, so that "each class member's claim arises from the same course of events, and each class member makes similar legal arguments to prove the defendant's liability." *Collins I*, 266 Conn. at 34, 836 A.2d at 1140 (citation omitted). While typicality does not require the named representatives and the class members to base their claims on identical factual allegations, the question of law or fact in dispute must hold the same degree of centrality in each claim. *Id.*; *see also Robichaud v. Hewlett Packard Co.*, 82 Conn. App. 848, 854, 848 A.2d 495, 499 (2004) (claims not typical where "they do not share with the members of the proposed class a characteristic that is central to the claim asserted"). For instance, "class certification is inappropriate where a putative class representative is subject to unique defenses which threaten to become the focus of the litigation." *Macomber*, 277 Conn. at 629–30, 894 A.2d at 251 (internal citations omitted). Additionally, typicality requires the named representative to have individual standing to raise the claims of the class. *Viglione Heating and Cooling, Inc. v. AIU Ins. Co.*, No. UWYCV085007892SX02, 2010 WL 797192, at *2 (Conn. Super. Ct. Feb. 5, 2010) ("What [a plaintiff] may not achieve himself, he may not accomplish as a representative of the class.") (quoting *Macomber*, 227 Conn. at 632, 894 A.2d 240). The Connecticut Supreme Court has held that whether a defendant is the incorrect party to a class action does not need to be decided by a trial court to determine a plaintiff class representative's standing at the class certification stage. Rather, that is an issue of misjoinder. *Rodriguez*, 337 Conn. at 274, 253 A.3d at 33. The Court stated that "[i]f the defendants are the incorrect parties to [the] action, they must file a motion to strike." *Id.*

iv. Adequacy. The requirement of Practice Book § 9-7(4) that the named representatives be able to fairly and adequately protect the interests of the entire class is meant to "address[] concerns about the competency of class counsel and conflicts of interest. The adequacy requirement is met when the representatives: (1) have common interests with the unnamed class members; and (2) will vigorously prosecute the class action through qualified counsel." *Collins II*, 275 Conn. at 326, 880 A.2d at 116 (internal citations and quotation marks omitted). In other words, the court must be satisfied that there are no antagonistic claims or interests among class members that would fracture the class and present a conflict of interest between the named representatives' counsel and other class members and that the representatives' counsel are properly qualified to litigate the class action. *Agrella*, 2006 WL 1493823, at *3. "It is axiomatic that no party can fairly or adequately represent the interests of the absent class if he is also motivated by interests adverse to the class as a whole." *McNerney v. Carvel.*, No. CV00579244, 2001 WL 267653, at *4 (Conn. Super. Ct. Feb. 23, 2001) (quoting *McQuillan v. Engelman*, No. X06CV990153482S, 2000 WL 226410, at *1–3 (Conn. Super. Ct. Feb. 10, 2000) (citation omitted)). *See also Thames River Apt. Tenants*, 2007 WL 4305525, at *5 (finding a possible conflict regarding personal injury damages, but no conflict present when limiting relief to injunctive relief); *Saphir v. Neustadt*, 37 Conn. Supp. 46, 48–49, 429 A.2d 972, 973 (Conn. Super. Ct. July 28, 1980) (striking class action allegations of pro se plaintiff). The Connecticut Supreme Court has recognized reasoned authority that takes a nuanced approach, noting "[p]erfect symmetry of interest is not required and not every discrepancy among the interests of class members renders a putative class action untenable. Only conflicts that are fundamental to the suit and that go to the heart of the litigation prevent a plaintiff from meeting the . . . adequacy requirement. . . . Put another way, to forestall class certification the intraclass conflict must be so substantial as to overbalance the common interests of the class members as a whole." *Standard Petrol Co*, 330 Conn. at 57–58, 191 A.3d at 162 (quoting *Matamoros v. Starbucks Corp.*, 699 F.3d 129, 138 (1st Cir. 2012)). Moreover, courts have recognized that the possibility of such a conflict diminishes when class members have a right to opt out of the class. *Standard Petrol Co*, 330 Conn. at 58, 191 A.3d at 162 (citing *Matamoros*, 699 F.3d at 139; *Smilow v. Southwestern Bell Mobile Systems, Inc.*, 323 F.3d 32, 43 (1st Cir. 2003); and *Carder Buick-Olds Co. v. Reynolds & Reynolds, Inc.*, 148 Ohio App. 3d 635, 643, 775 N.E.2d 531 (2002)).

Nevertheless, attorneys may pursue mutually conflicting theories of liability even when success on one theory would benefit some class members while success on the other theory would benefit the other class members. *Gold,* 2011 WL 6976499, at *7. When the court's determination of which theory prevails does not depend on "extrinsic evidence or the ingenuity of counsel" but rather on the interpretation of documents "not subject to adversary manipulation," typicality and adequacy of representation are satisfied. *Id.* at *22 (finding the class has "a strong common interest in pursuing both theories simultaneously" since by just pleading one, they would waive the other).

If any problems arise regarding the adequacy of the representation of a class, the court is empowered under Practice Book § 9-10 to order an amendment to the pleadings eliminating all reference to absent parties. *See Campbell*, 36 Conn. Supp. at 373, 423 A.2d at 909. Alternatively, a court may order the division of a class into subclasses if "the interests of one group are antagonistic to another." *Artie's Auto Body, Inc. v. Hartford Fire Ins. Co.*, No. X08CV030196141S, 2008 WL 5218614, at *2 (Conn. Super. Ct. Nov. 12, 2008) (*Artie's II*) (citing 7B Wright, Miller and Kane, *Federal Practice and Civil Procedure* § 1790 (2d ed. 2003)). It is unnecessary to divide a class "merely because different groups have alternative legal theories for recovery or because those groups have different factual bases for relief." *Id.* Rather, subclasses are appropriate when the class contains members with "conflicting or antagonistic interests." *Id.* While subclasses may cure conflicts between or among class members, "a class with subgroups that are so incompatible as to be on opposite sides of the case is not feasible." *Id.* The Connecticut Supreme Court has certified a subclass that seeks additional damages not sought by the rest of the class where the affirmative answer to the class-wide claim is a prerequisite to recovery for the damages sought by the subclass. *Diaz*, 2020 WL 8130207, at *9 (certifying subclass of putative class members seeking emotional distress damages for professional negligence who will be "subject to individualized determination of proximate cause for their emotional distress claim in the event the entire class prevails on the central claim").

c. Section 9-8. Class Actions Maintainable

In order for a class action to be certified, a court must find, in addition to the four prerequisites of Practice Book § 9-7, that one of three conditions listed is also met: (1) that prosecution of separate actions by individual members would create a risk of inconsistent adjudications or be dispositive of the interests of other members who are not parties to the adjudications, (2) that the party opposing the class has acted in such a way that is generally applicable to all of the members of the class, thereby making final injunctive relief or corresponding declaratory relief with respect to the class as a whole appropriate, or (3) that questions of law or fact common to the members of the class predominate over any questions affecting only individual members and that a class action is superior to other methods of adjudication. Practice Book § 9-8.

The third requirement has generated the most judicial analysis because before 2010 it was the only requirement of § 9-8. Even before the requirements of predominance and superiority were incorporated into § 9-8, the Connecticut Supreme Court used the four factors set forth in Rule 23(b)(3) of the Federal Rules of Civil Procedure to assess whether these requirements had been satisfied. *Collins I*, 266 Conn. at 48–49, 56–57, 836 A.2d at 1147, 1152. Those factors are:

> (A) the interest of members of the class in individually controlling the prosecution or defense of separate actions; (B) the extent and nature of any litigation concerning the controversy already commenced by or against members of the class; (C) the desirability or undesirability of concentrating the litigation of the claims in the particular forum; (D) the difficulties likely to be encountered in the management of a class action.

Id. at 48–49, 836 A.2d at 1147 (quoting Fed. R. Civ. P. 23(b)(3)).

i. Predominance. The requirement of predominance is "far more demanding" than that of commonality. *Id.* at 48 (quoting *Amchem Prods., Inc. v. Windsor*, 521 U.S. 591, 624, 138 L. Ed. 2d 689 (1997)). "A more searching merits inquiry may be necessary in considering whether common questions *predominate* over individual questions, of course, because the predominance element of the class certification analysis relates to the nature of the actual proof necessary to establish the claims." *Rodriguez*, 337 Conn. at 265, 253 A.3d at 28 (emphasis in original). Predominance does not require a complete unanimity of common questions as to all class members. *Campbell*, 36 Conn. Supp. at 368–69, 423 A.2d at 907. For example, "the presence of individualized damages issues does not prevent a finding that the common issues in the case predominate . . . , [p]articularly when damages can be computed according to some formula, statistical analysis, or other easy or essentially mechanical methods." *Rodriguez*, 337 Conn. at 253, 253 A.3d at 41 (stating that the necessity for an individualized question of damages "generally does not defeat predominance"); *Collins II*, 275 Conn. at 330–31, 880 A.2d at 118 (internal citations and quotation marks omitted); *Gold*, 2011 WL

6976499, at *10 (even when plaintiffs' damages would vary, predominance is met when a common set of rules and standards would govern the calculation of each award).

If, however, liability regarding each member of the class must proceed on an individualized basis, class certification will not be granted. *Collier v. Adar Hartford Realty, LLC*, 349 Conn. 822, 840, 322 A.3d 1041, 1054 (2024) (no predominance where plaintiffs in action against a housing development sought certification for all past tenants going back to 2004, which would require individualized proof of each class member's damages because the record lacked generalized evidence from before 2015); *Ahmad*, 104 Conn. App. at 388–91, 933 A.2d 1214–16; *Collier v. Adar Hartford Realty, LLC*, No. X07HHDCV196115255S, 2022 WL 18054024, at *9 (Conn. Super. Ct. Nov. 21, 2022) (no predominance where "generalized proof will not suffice to establish the conditions present in each apartment"); *Diaz*, 2020 WL 8130207, at *8–9 (no predominance where determinations of specific acts needed to determine liability for recklessness); *BThrifty, LLC v. Comcast Spotlight, LLC*, No. X07CV106013996S, 2012 WL 800762, at *4 (Conn. Super. Ct. Feb. 16, 2012) (no predominance where "each potential class member's contract must be examined separately to determine the specifics and whether the elements of breach of contract . . . have been proven"); *Weathers v. Condor Capital Corp.*, No. X01CV020169144S, 2009 WL 2507129, at *7 (Conn. Super. Ct. July 30, 2009) (no predominance where examination of each class member's file would be required to determine liability); *Parker*, 2004 WL 3090652, at *9–10 (class certification denied where issues subject to individualized proof predominated over issues subject to generalized proof); *Granito v. IBM*, No. X07CV020080440S, 2004 WL 424063, at *1–2 (Conn. Super. Ct. Feb. 17, 2004) (no predominance where individual hearings needed to decide liability, causation, and damages). *Compare to Artie's I*, 287 Conn. at 233-35, 947 A.2d at 338–39 (concluding that expert's suggested method of determining causation and ascertainable loss was sufficient for predominance); *Collier v. Adar Hartford Realty, LLC*, No. X07-HHD-CV-19-6115255-S, 2025 WL 10664624, at *19 (Apr. 1, 2025) (on remand, the court granted plaintiff's motion for class certification when the class was narrowed to those tenants who lived at the defendant's housing development after 2014, when generalized evidence of damages was available).

"Only when common questions of law or fact 'will be the object of most of the efforts of the litigants and the court' will the predominance test be satisfied." *Collins II*, 275 Conn. at 332, 880 A.2d at 119 (citation omitted). *See also McNerney*, 2001 WL 267653, at *7 ("When common questions represent a significant aspect of a case so that they can be resolved for all class members in a single suit, predominance exists.") (quoting *Walsh v. Nat'l Safety Assocs., Inc.*, 44 Conn. Supp. 569, 588–89, 695 A.2d 1095 (Conn. Super. Ct. Feb. 9, 1996), *aff'd*, 241 Conn. 278, 694 A.2d 795 (1997)).

Courts, therefore, conduct the following three-point inquiry when determining whether common questions predominate: (1) What are the elements of the causes of action sought to be asserted on behalf of the class? (2) Could generalized evidence be offered to prove those elements on a class-wide basis, or will individualized proof be needed to establish each class member's entitlement to monetary or injunctive relief? (3) How do the common issues that are subject to generalized proof weigh against the issues requiring individualized proof? *Collins II*, 275 Conn. at 331–32, 880 A.2d at 118–19; *Artie's I*, 287 Conn. at 215–17, 947 A.2d at 328–29.

ii. Superiority. In assessing the superiority requirement, Connecticut courts may consider the same non-exhaustive list of factors found in Federal Rule 23(b)(3) as used in determining predominance. *Collins I*, 266 Conn. at 56–57, 836 A.2d at 1152 (superiority requirement met where class was not so large as to present manageability issues, judicial economy would be lost if each class member were required to bring individual action challenging same conduct, and incentive for each class member to bring individual action was relatively small). The predominance and superiority criteria are intertwined so that, "[i]f the predominance criterion is satisfied, courts generally will find that the class action is a superior mechanism even if it presents management difficulties." *Collins II*, 275 Conn. at 347, 880 A.2d at 127 (citation omitted). *See also Lawrence Mall of New Haven v. City of West Haven*, No. CV030478088, 2004 WL 237926, at *9 (Conn. Super. Ct. Jan. 20, 2004) ("Where . . . common issues predominate and parties are numerous, the superiority of a class action over individual suits is obvious and has been recognized by the courts.") (quoting *Campbell*, 36 Conn. Supp. at 370, 423 A.2d at 908).

Superiority is also generally found where "the certification of the class would avoid inconsistent verdicts, and would promote judicial economy because all of the cases would be heard in one central location[,] [a]ll witnesses would testify once in a trial instead of, perhaps, numerous times, and all exhibits could be contained in one location." *Town of New Hartford*, 2006 WL 853217, at *15. Additionally, class actions are often superior where some class members' economic injuries are too miniscule to justify the commencement of individual actions, certification will minimize the proliferation of lawsuits that might otherwise result, and duplicative adjudicative efforts and litigation expenses can be avoided. *Lawrence Mall*, 2004 WL 237926, at *9. *See also Parker*, 2004 WL 3090652, at *10 ("A class action provides a superior means for claimants of small amounts to prosecute their cases.").

For a case discussing certification of a class on the second ground (as well as the third), see *Tuohy v. Town of Groton*, No. CV126018123S, 2013 WL 3970235, at *6 (Conn. Super. Ct. July 16, 2013) (finding that the town of Groton had acted "on grounds generally applicable to the class" and that the plaintiffs were seeking both injunctive and declaratory relief).

d. Section 9-9. Dismissal or Compromise of Class Action

"The Connecticut class action rule also requires court approval of any withdrawal [of a certified class] action due to a settlement and may require notice of such proposed dismissal, compromise or settlement to be given to absent members." *Hennessey v. Connecticut Valley Fitness Ctrs., Inc.*, No. CV980504488S, 2001 WL 1199840, at *5 (Conn. Super. Ct. Sept. 12, 2001) (citing Practice Book §§ 9-9 and 9-10). "The court may approve a settlement, withdrawal, or compromise that would bind class members only after a hearing and a finding that the settlement, withdrawal, or compromise is fair, reasonable, and adequate." *Bushansky v. Phoenix Cos., Inc.*, No. X08FSTCV156027891S, 2017 WL 1194768, at *2 (Conn. Super. Ct. Feb. 23, 2017) (quoting Practice Book § 9-9(c)(1)(C)). For a denial of a motion to approve a class settlement, *see Gray v. Found. Health Sys., Inc.*, No. X06CV990158549S, 2004 WL 945137, at *1–11 (Conn. Super. Ct. Apr. 21, 2004) (considering nine factors in determining that proposed settlement was not sufficiently fair, reasonable and adequate: (1) complexity, expense and likely duration of litigation; (2) reaction of class to settlement; (3) stage of proceedings and amount of discovery completed; (4) risks of establishing liability; (5) risks of establishing damages; (6) risks of maintaining class action through trial; (7) ability of defendants to withstand greater judgment; (8) range of reasonableness of settlement fund in light of best possible recovery; and (9) range of reasonableness of settlement fund in light of attendant risks of litigation). For a case approving a settlement as fair, reasonable, and adequate, as well as discussing the notice requirements of § 9-9, *see Rabinowitz v. City of Hartford*, No. HHDCV075008403S, 2014 WL 5356392, at *1 (Conn. Super. Ct. Sept. 17, 2014).

Courts are especially scrutinizing proposed settlements in "deal litigation," which is a type of class action brought by shareholders challenging corporate mergers and which seeks to force companies to issue additional disclosures regarding a proposed merger. In a typical case, some shareholders of the company being sold in the proposed merger will allege a breach of fiduciary duty on the part of the board of directors for selling the company at an inadequate price and by means of a flawed sales process. After the company issues proxy statements to solicit a vote of the shareholders, plaintiffs are likely to amend their complaints to allege a deficiency in the proxy statements, claiming that it prevents shareholders from making an informed decision before voting on the sale. Plaintiffs will then demand additional disclosures to settle the case and allow the sale to move forward. In deal litigation, the parties often propose "disclosure settlements," "in which the primary, if not sole, benefit to stockholders is the provision of additional disclosures as a supplement to previously filed proxy statements in exchange for a release of claims." *Stein v. UIL Holdings Corp.*, No. X08FSTCV156025536S, 2017 WL 1656891, at *3 (Conn. Super. Ct. Apr. 10, 2017). The *Stein* court followed the example of other jurisdictions that have expressed skepticism toward disclosure settlements. *See, e.g.*, *In re Trulia, Inc. Stockholder Litig.*, 129 A.3d 884 (Del. Ch. 2016); *In re Walgreen Co. Stockholder Litig.*, 832 F.3d 718 (7th Cir. 2016). Thus, with respect to whether a "disclosure settlement" is "fair, reasonable and adequate," "practitioners should expect that disclosure settlements are likely to be met with continued disfavor . . . *unless* the supplemental disclosures address a plainly material misrepresentation or omission, *and the subject matter of the proposed release is narrowly circumscribed to encompass nothing more than disclosure claims and fiduciary duty claims concerning the sales process, if the record shows that such claims have been investigated sufficiently*." *Stein*, 2017 WL 1656891, at *3 (emphasis in original) (citing *Trulia*, A.3d at 898-99). *See also Bushansky*, 2017 WL 1194768, at *3 ("This court must focus specifically on the 'get' that the shareholders received in the form of additional disclosures and the 'give' that the shareholders surrender in the form of the particular release."). For the denial of a "disclosure settlement," *see Stein*, 2017 WL 1656891, at *1. For the approval of a "disclosure settlement," *see Bushansky*, 2017 WL 1194768, at *1.

The offer of compromise mechanism under Practice Book §§ 17-14 *et seq.* and Connecticut General Statutes § 52-192a applies to class actions. *See Paetzold v. Metro. Dist. Comm'n*, 2019 WL 5856462, at *2 (Conn. Super. Ct. Oct. 24, 2019) ("So the offer of compromise mechanism does apply to class actions. It is overlaid by the class action procedures that would apply. It is affected by those procedures, but not defeated by them."). Practice Book §§ 17-14 through 17-18 and Connecticut General Statutes § 52-192a provide that a plaintiff may file an offer of compromise and, if the defendant does not accept the offer and if the plaintiff obtains a judgment equal to or greater than the amount in the offer of compromise, the court shall add eight percent annual interest to the amount of the judgment. In *Paetzold*, the plaintiff filed an offer of compromise, and the defendant filed a motion to strike the offer, arguing that the mechanism should not apply to class actions because it is uniquely difficult for a defendant to respond to an offer of compromise in a class action. In denying the motion to strike, the court reasoned that the "mechanism says nothing about applying the mechanism only to cases where it is easy for the defendant to make up its mind whether to accept." *Id.* The court rejected the defendant's request for an extension of the 30-day deadline to respond to the offer until after the opt-out period, stating that the number of class members opting out of a class action settlement is usually negligible. "[T]he opt-outs are never enough to change a determination whether to settle and may be easily dealt with during the approval or judgment process if needed." *Id.* The court, nevertheless, granted the defendant an extension of another 30 days to respond because the initial 30-day period had expired during the pendency of the motion to strike. *Id.*

3. APPEALS

In 2004, the Connecticut Appellate Court held that a judgment on the merits against a person claiming to be a representative of a purported class does not render moot an appeal challenging the denial of class certification or deprive the person of standing to bring the appeal. *Robichaud*, 82 Conn. App.

at 851–52, 848 A.2d at 498.

The Connecticut Supreme Court held in 2003 that a decision to decertify a class is an appealable final judgment. *Rivera*, 262 Conn. at 731–32, 818 A.2d at 733. The *Rivera* Court held that, once certified, a class should be decertified only where it is clear that changed circumstances make continued class action treatment improper. *Id.* at 740, 818 A.2d at 738.

In contrast, the Connecticut Supreme Court held in 2008 that a denial of class certification is not a final judgment for the purposes of appeal because it is not separate and distinct from the underlying action and does not cause the loss of a statutory or constitutional right. *Palmer v. Friendly Ice Cream Corp.*, 285 Conn. 462, 469–82, 940 A.2d 742, 747–55 (2008); *Bucchere v. Brinker Int'l, Inc.*, 287 Conn. 704, 706, 950 A.2d 493, 493–94 (2008) (per curiam). Despite the Connecticut practice of looking to federal case law for guidance on class action issues, the Supreme Court held that recent revision of Rule 23(f) of the Federal Rules of Civil Procedure did not provide grounds for interlocutory appeals from denials of class certification in Connecticut courts, even on a discretionary basis, because there still was no Connecticut statutory authority to do so. *Palmer*, 285 Conn. at 474–75, 940 A.2d at 750–51. Thus, the tolling of the statute of limitations for the benefit of the putative class ends as soon as certification is denied. *Liss v. Milford Partners., Inc.*, No. X07CV044025123S, 2008 WL 642686, at *4 (Conn. Super. Ct. Feb. 20, 2008).

4. MISCELLANEOUS

As a practical matter, class actions should normally qualify for the Connecticut Complex Litigation Docket, a special statewide docket of cases "that have many parties and common questions of law or fact." Practice Book § 23-13. Other factors considered in an application for case referral to the Complex Litigation Docket are legally intricate issues and the possibility of millions of dollars in damages or a lengthy trial. Cases on the Complex Litigation Docket are assigned to one of several judges on the Complex Litigation Docket for the entire case rather than to whatever judge is available for motions and trial on the regular civil docket.

With regard to the numerosity prerequisite of Practice Book § 9-7(1), even when the majority of factors, including geographic location of the putative class members, the class members' level of sophistication, and judicial economy, arguably favor joinder (and, thus, denial of class certification), certification may be warranted if the defendant has engaged in misleading conduct toward potential class members. *See Town of New Hartford*, 2006 WL 853217, at *10 (where defendant made statements to potential class members misleading them into believing that they would face increased costs by joining suit, court found that joinder would be difficult, if not impossible, and, therefore, certification was warranted).

When notice of class certification is given, Practice Book § 9-9(a)(2)(B)(v) provides that it must establish a way to "exclude from the class any member who requests exclusion. . . ." *Roberts v. Verde Energy, USA, Inc.*, No. X07HHDCV156060160S, 2017 WL 6601993, at *3 (Conn. Super. Ct. Dec. 6, 2017) (internal quotation marks omitted). While the rule does not expressly state that the "opt-out" approach is exclusive, it may be the best method in a case "where the complexity of claims and the size of the individual amounts at stake may artificially depress participation and the significance of any remedy, thereby irrationally diluting the public benefit that might be gained from deterring any trade practice or other violations. . . ." *See id.* at *1–3 (certifying potential class of thousands of residential and small business customers who may have been overcharged by electric company in violation of contract and state statute).

Partial class actions may be brought in state court, even though the Practice Book rules do not expressly provide for partial class actions. *Collins I*, 266 Conn. at 25–27, 836 A.2d at 1135–36. Note that Rule 23(c)(4) of the Federal Rules does specifically authorize partial class actions.

Evidence offered in state court to support or oppose a motion for class certification must comply with the Connecticut Code of Evidence. *Robichaud v. Hewlett-Packard Co.*, No. X01CV010165706S, 2002 WL 31505640, at *1 (Conn. Super. Ct. Oct. 25, 2002) (noting, in contrast, that the federal rule does not require that evidence comply with the Federal Rules of Evidence when ruling on class certification).

In *Rigat v. GAF Materials Corp.*, No. CV010095029, 2002 WL 237339, at *4–5 (Conn. Super. Ct. Jan. 25, 2002), the court held that plaintiff was bound by the terms of an Alabama class action settlement which became the subject of a court judgment despite lack of actual notice of the Alabama class action. The standard for class notice is "best practicable," and the Alabama court's holding that the notice given to class members "was the best practicable under the circumstances" and complied with applicable state and federal law meant that the judgment must be afforded full faith and credit and given *res judicata* effect.

A motion to strike has been recognized as the appropriate method for testing the sufficiency of allegations establishing the basis and suitability of a class action. *See, e.g.*, *Machado*, 2006 WL 2734257, at *2–3; *Kubas v. Hartford Fin. Servs. Co.*, No. X07CV000073192S, 2000 WL 1170237, at *1 (Conn. Super. Ct. July 19, 2000); *Saphir*, 37 Conn. Supp. at 48, 429 A.2d at 973. One Connecticut court has noted, "motions to defeat certification prior to the completion of discovery are generally regarded with disfavor." *Diaz v. Griffin Health Services Corp.*, No. X10CV156029965S, 2017 WL 960792, at *6 (Conn. Super. Ct. Jan. 31, 2017) (quoting 3 *Newberg on Class Actions* § 7.22, 114 (5th ed. 2013)). Consequently, if a motion to strike is made at such a juncture, the movant carries the "heavy burden [to] demonstrate[e] from the face of plaintiffs' complaint that it will be impossible to certify the [class] alleged by the plaintiffs regardless of the facts the plaintiffs may be able to prove." *Diaz*, 2017 WL 960792, at *6 (alterations in original) (quoting *Bryant v. Food Lion, Inc.*, 774 F. Supp. 1484, 1495 (D.S.C. 1991)).

In *Grimes v. Hous. Auth.*, 242 Conn. 236, 243, 698 A.2d 302, 306 (1997), the Connecticut Supreme Court adopted the rule in *Am. Pipe & Construction Co. v. Utah*, 414 U.S. 538, 554, 94 S. Ct. 756, 38 L. Ed. 2d 713 (1974), that "the commencement of a class action suspends the applicable statute of limitations as to all asserted members of the class who would have been parties had the suit been permitted to continue as a class action."

It has been held that Conn. Gen. Stat. § 52-105, which permits a class action, only applies to civil actions, *Jones v. Foote*, 165 Conn. 516, 520–21, 338 A.2d 467, 469 (1973), and, therefore, does not apply to, *e.g.*, administrative appeals, *id.*, or probate proceedings, *Mahakian* v. *Kalamian*, 13 Conn. Supp. 327, 329 (Conn. Super. Ct. May 8, 1945).

With respect to the defense of a class action and the effect of defenses on the propriety of class certification requirements, the Connecticut Supreme Court observed that there does not appear to be a uniform view as to whether the defendant should bear the burden of production while a plaintiff retains the ultimate burden of persuasion or whether the plaintiff should bear both burdens. *Standard Petrol Co*, 330 Conn. at 71, 191 A.3d at 169. The defendant's articulation of its defense must provide a plaintiff with a sufficient basis to be able to address how a defense might bear on class certification requirements. *See id.* 330 Conn. at 72–74, 191 A.3d at 170–71.

The Connecticut Supreme Court has held that a certification order that defines the plaintiff class by reference to a general description of a corporate defendant rather than its legal name does not constitute improper certification of a class in violation of Practice Book § 9-9 if the class definition clearly identifies the defendant in a manner "rendering readily ascertainable and verifiable the individuals" who comprise the plaintiff class. *Rodriguez*, 337 Conn. at 289, 253 A.3d at 42 ("[I]ndividuals . . . will easily recognize whether they qualify as a class member based on their [relationship to the named defendant as generally described] during the stated time period, and their eligibility as such will be subject to definitive verification.").

5. CONTACTING ABSENT CLASS MEMBERS

In Connecticut, there is no state court decision on the issue of whether opposing counsel may ethically communicate with absent putative class members. In a 2011 Informal Opinion, however, the Connecticut Bar Association Professional Ethics Committee concluded that "unless and until the class is certified by the Court, the Requesting Attorney may contact the putative class members." CBA Informal Op. 2011-09. The Professional Ethics Committee noted that its research did not reveal any Connecticut authority regarding the permissibility of communications with putative class members. *Id.* Despite the lack of Connecticut authority on this issue, the Professional Ethics Committee opined that:

> The mere fact that an attorney has filed an action and unilaterally asked the court to appoint him or her as the class' attorney, does not—without more—establish an attorney-client relationship between that attorney and members of the proposed class such that the proposed class members cannot be contacted by attorneys for defendants in that action. Accordingly, the Committee agrees with the majority rule that putative class members are not represented until the class is certified.

Id. While communications between opposing counsel and putative class members are permissible, "counsel may seek to place reasonable restrictions on such contact." *Id.* (citing *Gulf Oil v. Bernard*, 452 U.S. 89, 101–04 (1981)).

In *A&R Body Specialty & Collision Works, Inc. v. Progressive Cas. Ins. Co.*, No. CIV. 3:07CV929 WWE, 2012 WL 3854954, at *2 (D. Conn. Sept. 5, 2012), the United States District Court for the District of Connecticut relied on the Connecticut Bar Association Professional Ethics Committee's Informal Opinion 2011-09 in determining what restrictions to impose on an opposing counsel's communication with putative class members. The district court explained that "Federal Rule of Civil Procedure 23(d)(1)(C) gives the Court discretion to impose conditions on the parties in class action suits . . . includ[ing] regulating communications between counsel and putative class members." *Id.*

While courts can regulate communications, the communications should only be limited when there is "a clear record and specific findings that reflect a weighing of the need for limitation and the potential interference with the rights of the parties." *Austen v. Catterton Partners V, LP*, 831 F. Supp. 2d 559, 563 (D. Conn. 2011) (citing *Gulf Oil*, 452 U.S. at 101–02). "Any such order must 'limit[] speech as little as possible, consistent with the rights of the parties under the circumstances' [and] . . . in crafting any such order, the Court must pay 'attention to whether [a particular] restraint is justified by a likelihood of serious abuses.'" *Id.* at 564 (quoting *Gulf Oil*, 452 U.S. at 104).

Additionally, as summarized in *Austen*, the Second Circuit has held that "*ex parte* communications between defense counsel and putative class members, even *ex parte* settlement negotiations, are not abusive communications that warrant limitations absent indications in the record of the need for limitations." *Austen*, 831 F. Supp. 2d at 565 (citing *Weight Watchers of Philadelphia, Inc. v. Weight Watchers Int'l, Inc.*, 455 F.2d 770, 775 (2d Cir. 1972), and *Christensen v. Kiewit-Murdock Inv. Corp.*, 815 F.2d 206, 213 (2d Cir. 1987)).

CONNECTICUT STATUTES AND RULES

CONN. GEN. STAT. § 52-105. NUMEROUS PARTIES MAY BE REPRESENTED BY ONE

When the persons who might be made parties are very numerous, so that it would be impracticable or unreasonably expensive to make them all parties, one or more may sue or be sued or may be authorized by the court to defend for the benefit of all.

CONNECTICUT'S UNFAIR TRADE PRACTICES ACT

Two sections under Connecticut's Unfair Trade Practices Act ("CUTPA") pertain to class actions:

Conn. Gen. Stat. § 42-110g states in pertinent part:

Action for damages. Class actions. Costs and fees. Equitable relief. Jury trial.

(a) Any person who suffers any ascertainable loss of money or property, real or personal, as a result of the use or employment of a method, act or practice prohibited by section 42-110b, may bring an action in the judicial district in which the plaintiff or defendant resides or has his principal place of business or is doing business, to recover actual damages. . . .

(b) Persons entitled to bring an action under subsection (a) of this section may, pursuant to rules established by the judges of the Superior Court, bring a class action on behalf of themselves and other persons similarly situated who are residents of this state or injured in this state to recover damages.

* * *

(d) . . . In a class action in which there is no monetary recovery, but other relief is granted on behalf of a class, the court may award, to the plaintiff, in addition to other relief provided in this section, costs and reasonable attorneys' fees. In any action brought under this section, the court may, in its discretion, order, in addition to damages or in lieu of damages, injunctive or other equitable relief.

* * *

(f) An action under this section may not be brought more than three years after the occurrence of a violation of this chapter.

Conn. Gen. Stat. § 42-110h states:

Class actions.

As soon as practicable after the commencement of an action brought as a class action, the court shall determine by order whether it is to be so maintained. An order under this section may be conditional, and it may be amended before decision on the merits. An order issued under this section shall be immediately appealable by either party.

Class actions are also permissible under Conn. Gen. Stat. § 12-242kk, pertaining to condemnation; Conn. Gen. Stat. § 36a-683 (incorporating 15 U.S.C. § 1640), pertaining to disclosure by creditors; and § 36a-855, pertaining to student loan servicers. Conn. Gen. Stat. § 31-68(a)(3) adds two additional hurdles for class actions in restaurant waitstaff minimum wage cases.

CONN. RULES FOR THE SUPERIOR COURT, PRACTICE BOOK §§ 9-7 THROUGH 9-10

§ 9-7. Class Actions—Prerequisites to Class Actions

One or more members of a class may sue or be sued as representative parties on behalf of all only if (1) the class is so numerous that joinder of all members is impracticable, (2) there are questions of law or fact common to the class, (3) the claims or defenses of the representative parties are typical of the claims or defenses of the class, and (4) the representative parties will fairly and adequately protect the interests of the class.

§ 9-8. Class Actions—Class Actions Maintainable

An action may be maintained as a class action if the prerequisites of Section 9-7 are satisfied, and in addition:

(1) the prosecution of separate actions by or against individual members of the class would create a risk of: (A) inconsistent or varying adjudications with respect to individual members of the class which would establish incompatible standards of conduct for the party opposing the class; or (B) adjudications with respect to individual members of the class which would, as a practical matter, be dispositive of the interests of the other members who are not parties to the adjudications or substantially impair or impede their ability to protect their interests, or

(2) the party opposing the class has acted or refused to act on grounds generally applicable to the class, thereby making appropriate final injunctive relief or corresponding declaratory relief with respect to the class as a whole; or

(3) the court finds that the questions of law or fact common to the members of the class predominate over any questions affecting only individual members and that a class action is superior to other available methods for the fair and efficient adjudication of the controversy. The matters pertinent to the findings include: (A) the interest of members of the class in individually controlling the prosecution or defense of separate actions; (B) the extent and nature of any litigation concerning the controversy already commenced by or against members of the class; (C) the desirability or undesirability of concentrating the litigation of the claims in the particular forum; (D) the difficulties likely to be encountered in the management of class action.

§ 9-9. Class Actions—Procedure for Class Certification and Management of Class

(a) (1) (A) When a person sues or is sued as a representative of a class, the court must, at an early practicable time, determine by order whether to certify the action as a class action.

(B) An order certifying a class action must define the class and the class claims, issues or defenses, and must appoint class counsel.

(C) An order under Section 9-9 (a) (1) (A) may be altered or amended before final judgment.

(2) (A) For any class certified under Section 9-8 (1) or (2), the court must direct notice to the class.

(B) For any class certified under Section 9-8 (3), the court must direct to class members the best notice practicable under the circumstances, including individual notice to all members who can be identified through reasonable effort. The notice must concisely and clearly state in plain, easily understood language:

(i) the nature of the action;

(ii) the definition of the class certified;

(iii) the class claims, issues or defenses;

(iv) that a class member may enter an appearance through counsel if the member so desires;

(v) that the court will exclude from the class any member who requests exclusion, stating when and how members may elect to be excluded; and

(vi) the binding effect of a class judgment on class members under Section 9-8 (3).

(3) The judgment in an action maintained as a class action under Section 9-8 (1) or (2), whether or not favorable to the class, shall include and describe those whom the court finds to be members of the class. The judgment in an action maintained as a class action under Section 9-8 (3), whether or not favorable to the class, shall include and specify or describe those to whom the notice provided in Section 9-9 (a) (2) (B) was directed, and who have not requested exclusion, and whom the court finds to be members of the class.

(4) When appropriate, (A) an action may be brought or maintained as a class action with respect to particular issues, or (B) a class may be divided into subclasses and each subclass treated as a class, and the provisions of Sections 9-7 and 9-8 shall then be construed and applied accordingly.

(b) In the conduct of actions to which Sections 9-7 et seq. apply, the court may make appropriate orders:

(1) determining the course of proceedings or prescribing measures to prevent undue repetition or complication in the presentation of evidence or argument;

(2) requiring, for the protection of the members of the class or otherwise for the fair conduct of the action, that notice be given in such manner as the court may direct to some or all of the members of:

(A) any step in the action;

(B) the proposed extent of the judgment; or

(C) the opportunity of members to signify whether they consider the representation fair and adequate, to intervene and to present claims or defenses, or otherwise to come into the action;

(3) imposing conditions on the representative parties or on interveners;

(4) requiring that the pleadings be amended to eliminate therefrom allegations as to representation of absent persons, and that the action proceed accordingly;

(5) dealing with similar procedural matters. The orders may be altered or amended as may be desirable from time to time.

(c) (1) (A) The court must approve any settlement, withdrawal, or compromise of the claims, issues, or defense of a certified class. Court approval is not required for settlement, withdrawal or compromise of a claim in which a class has been alleged but no class has been certified.

(B) The court must direct notice in a reasonable manner to all class members who would be bound by a proposed settlement, withdrawal or compromise.

(C) The court may approve a settlement, withdrawal, or compromise that would bind class members only after a hearing and on finding that the settlement, withdrawal, or compromise is fair, reasonable, and adequate.

(2) The parties seeking approval of a settlement, withdrawal, or compromise of an action in which a class has been certified must file a statement identifying any agreement made in connection with the proposed settlement, withdrawal or compromise.

(3) In an action previously certified as a class action under Section 9-8 (3), the court may refuse to approve a settlement unless it affords a new opportunity to request exclusion to individual class members who had an earlier opportunity to request exclusion but did not do so.

(4) (A) Any class member may object to a proposed settlement, withdrawal or compromise that requires court approval under (c) (1) (A).

(B) An objection made under (c) (4) (A) may be withdrawn only with the court's approval.

(d) Unless a statute provides otherwise, a court that certifies a class must appoint class counsel. An attorney appointed to serve as class counsel must fairly and adequately represent the interests of the class.

(1) In appointing class counsel, the court must consider:

(A) the work counsel has done in identifying or investigating potential claims in the action;

(B) counsel's experience in handling class actions, other complex litigation, and claims of the type asserted in the action;

(C) counsel's knowledge of the applicable law; and

(D) the resources counsel will commit to representing the class.

(2) The court may:

(A) consider any other matter pertinent to counsel's ability to represent the interests of the class fairly and adequately;

(B) direct potential class counsel to provide information on any subject pertinent to the appointment and to propose terms for attorney's fees and nontaxable costs; and

(C) make further orders in connection with the appointment.

(e) The court may designate interim counsel to act on behalf of the putative class before determining whether to certify the action as a class action. When there is one applicant for appointment as class counsel, the court may appoint that applicant only if the applicant is adequate under subsection (d). If more than one adequate applicant seeks appointment as class counsel, the court must appoint the applicant best able to represent the interests of the class. The order appointing class counsel may include provisions about the award of attorney's fees or nontaxable costs under subsection (f).

(f) In an action certified as a class action, the court may award reasonable attorney's fees and nontaxable costs authorized by law or by consent of the parties as follows:

(1) a request for an award of attorney's fees and nontaxable costs must be made by motion subject to the provisions of this subdivision, at a time set by the court. Notice of the motion must be served on all parties and, for motions by class counsel, directed to class members in a reasonable manner.

(2) A class member or a party from whom payment is sought, may object to the motion.

(3) The court may hold a hearing and must find the facts and state its conclusions of law on such motion.

(g) (1) "Residual funds" are funds that remain after the payment of approved class member claims, expenses, litigation costs, attorney's fees, and other court-approved disbursements made to implement the relief granted. Nothing in this rule is intended to limit the parties to a class action from recommending, or the trial court from approving, a settlement that does not create residual funds.

(2) Any order, judgment or approved settlement in a class action that establishes a process for identifying and compensating members of the class may designate the recipient or recipients of any such residual funds that may remain after the claims payment process has been completed. In the absence of such designation, the residual funds shall be disbursed to the organization administering the program for the use of interest on lawyers' client funds pursuant to General Statutes § 51-81c for the purpose of funding those organizations that provide legal services for the poor in Connecticut.

§ 9-10. CLASS ACTIONS—ORDERS TO ENSURE ADEQUATE REPRESENTATION

The judicial authority at any stage of an action under this section may require such security and impose such terms as shall fairly and adequately protect the interests of the class in whose behalf the action is brought or defended. It may order that notice be given, in such manner as it may direct, of the pendency of the action, of a proposed settlement, of entry of judgment, or of any other proceedings in the action, including notice to the absent persons that they may come in and present claims and defenses if they so desire. Whenever the representation appears to the judicial authority inadequate fairly to protect the interests of absent parties who may be bound by the judgment, it may at any time prior to judgment order an amendment of the pleadings, eliminating therefrom all reference to representation of absent persons, and it shall order entry of judgment in such form as to affect only the parties to the action and those adequately represented.

The Connecticut chapter was prepared by Richard S. Order, Esq., a shareholder in the Litigation Department of Updike, Kelly & Spellacy, P.C., in Hartford, Connecticut, www.uks.com, with assistance from summer associate Isabelle R. Kirschbaum.

DELAWARE

1. COMPARISON OF DELAWARE RULES WITH RULE 23 OF THE FEDERAL RULES OF CIVIL PROCEDURE

Delaware continues to maintain separate law and equity courts. The law court at the trial level is the Superior Court; the equity court is the Court of Chancery. The class action rules in the Superior Court and the Court of Chancery are similar to Fed. R. Civ. P. 23. *O'Malley v. Boris*, C.A. No. 15735, 2001 WL 50204 (Del. Ch. Jan. 11, 2001). Because of the similarity between the state rules and Fed. R. Civ. P. 23, federal case law and the Advisory Committee's notes are considered persuasive authority in Delaware state court actions. *Noerr v. Greenwood*, C.A. No. 14320-NC, 2002 WL 31720734, at *5 (Del. Ch. Nov. 22, 2002); *Nottingham Partners v. Dana*, 564 A.2d 1089, 1094 (Del. 1989). Federal decisions interpreting Fed. R. Civ. P. 23 provide guidance when applying and construing the rule. *Boris*, 2001 WL 50204, at *3. Note however, that Delaware does not have a counterpart to Fed. R. Civ. P. 23(f), which permits an interlocutory appeal from an order denying class certification.

Court of Chancery Rule 23 was amended in September 2023 to align its language in certain respects to the Fed. R. Civ. P. 23. The 2023 amendments also align Rule 23 with current practices in certain respects. The changes include the new Rule 23(d), which establishes the procedure and standards for appointment of class counsel, and new Rule 23(g), which provides the court with a framework for determining a reasonable attorney fee and expense award. Rule 23(f), which governs dismissal and settlement of class actions, was revised to align the rule with current practice and the federal rule. The comment to the 2023 revisions states that other than these revisions, no substantive change in the interpretation of Rule 23 was intended and that prior Delaware authorities interpretating the rule remain applicable.

In 2024, Rule 23(f)(1) was amended following revision to Rule 15 in order to renumber a cross reference from Rule 15(aaa) to Rule 15(a)(5).

2. SUMMARY OF CASE LAW INTERPRETING COURT OF CHANCERY AND SUPERIOR COURT RULE 23

a. Rule 23(a)

i. Numerosity. Precise enumeration of class members is not required and there is no "magic" number for determining whether joinder is impracticable. *Zimmerman v. Home Shopping Network, Inc.*, C.A. Nos. 10911 & 10919, 1990 WL 118363 (Del. Ch. Aug. 14, 1990) (certifying class of purchasers of debentures which were originally sold to 140 purchasers). The court should consider the circumstances surrounding the case and not just the number of class members. *Mentis v. Del. Am. Life Ins. Co.*, C.A. No. 98C-12-023, 2000 WL 973299, at *3 (Del. Super. May 30, 2000). The "number of potential class members is not, in itself, determinative of this analysis." *Id.* Other factors are considered including geographical diversity of the class members, the nature of the action, the size of individual claims, the relief sought and the ease of identifying class members. *Id.* Classes with as few as forty members may be sufficient; usually anything over one hundred will satisfy the numerosity requirement. *Leon N. Weiner & Assocs., Inc. v. Krapf*, 584 A.2d 1220 (Del. 1991); *Mentis*, 2000 WL 973299, at *3 (usually, more than 40 members is adequate); *Dubroff v. Wren Holdings, LLC*, C.A. No. 3940, 2010 WL 3294219 (Del. Ch. Aug. 20, 2010); *Buttonwood Tree Value Partners, L.P. v. R.L. Polk & Co.*, C.A. No. 9250-VCG, 2022 WL 2255258, at *6 (Del. Ch. June 23, 2022) (58 to 64 members sufficient). A class size of fewer than twenty-five members is not permitted unless special circumstances justify class certification. *Erickson v. Centennial Beauregard Cellular L.L.C.*, C.A. No. 19974, 2003 WL 1878583, at *3 (Del. Ch. Apr. 11, 2003). To date, most Delaware class actions have been brought on behalf of stockholders of nationally traded securities and numerosity is often inferred from the aggregate dollar value of the securities sold. *See, e.g.*, *Van de Walle v. Salomon Bros., Inc.*, C.A. No. 9894, 1997 WL 633288 (Del. Ch. Oct. 2, 1997) (fair to assume that class consists of hundreds of purchasers where eight million shares were sold in offering that raised over $165 million). If the factors establishing numerosity are present, numerosity will not be defeated simply because some of the putative class members have the financial wherewithal to proceed on their own. *Smith v. Hercules, Inc.*, C.A. No. 01C-08-291, 2003 WL 1580603, at *5 (Del. Super. Jan. 31, 2003).

ii. Commonality. Commonality is satisfied "where the question of law linking the class members is substantially related to the resolution of the litigation even though the individuals are not identically situated." *Weiner*, 584 A.2d at 1225 (citation omitted); *CME Grp., Inc. v. Chi. Bd. of Options Exch. Inc.*, C.A. No. 2369, 2009 WL 1547510 (Del. Ch. June 3, 2009) (certifying settlement class that included members segregated into groups based on their interest in the company). Additionally, the requirement will normally be satisfied "if the named plaintiffs share at least one question of fact or law with the grievances of the prospective class." *Mentis*, 2000 WL 973299, at *3. In *Weiner*, the court held that the commonality requirement was satisfied in a defendant class action against 203 property owners arising out of a common deed restriction. *Weiner*, 584 A.2d at 1225–26. In *Oliver v. Boston Univ.*, C.A. No. 16570, 2002 WL 385553 (Del. Ch. Feb. 28, 2002), the court did not certify a class of stockholders because the class included those who held stock several years prior to the challenged merger, and those who did not own stock when the merger was consummated. The court held that there were no questions of law or fact common to all members of the purported class, thus the class lacked commonality. *Id.* at *4.

The commonality requirement does not necessarily prohibit certification where class members may have conflicting claims. *In re Phila. Stock Exch., Inc.*, 945 A.2d 1123, 1141 (Del. 2008) (affirming certification of a settlement class of shareholders that included individuals that currently owned or previously owned stock where the class could be subdivided at a later time to take conflicts into account). It also does not prohibit certification where damages are so different as to not be subject to class certification. Commonality was found for medical providers and insureds who sued an automobile insurance company claiming medical reimbursement models were unlawful, even though each class members' damages would be unique, because the plaintiffs sought only a declaratory judgment and ruling that insurance policies were breached by use of reimbursement models. *Green v. GEICO Gen. Ins. Co.*, 2019 WL 4039609 (Del. Super. Aug. 27, 2019). The possibility that some class members may have benefited by the transaction being challenged, because class members owned stock in multiple transacting entities, does not necessarily defeat commonality, especially in cases involving publicly-traded companies. *In re Straight Path Commc'ns Inc. Consol. S'holder Litig.*, C.A. No. CV 2017-0486-SG, 2022 WL 2236192, at *5–6 (Del. Ch. June 14, 2022).

Neither equitable nor common law fraud claims are maintainable as a class action because individual questions of law or fact, particularly as to the element of justifiable reliance, predominate over common questions of law or fact. *Gaffin v. Teledyne, Inc.*, 611 A.2d 467, 472 (Del. 1992); *Manzo v. Rite Aid Corp.*, C.A. No. 18451-NC, 2002 WL 31926606, at *4 (Del. Ch. Dec. 19, 2002), *aff'd*, 825 A.2d 239 (Del. 2003); *see also In re Countrywide Corp. S'holders Litig.*, C.A. No. 3464, 2009 WL 846019 (Del. Ch. Mar. 31, 2009) (allegedly fraudulent statements in speech are not subject to class action because element of justifiable reliance on the statements is inherently individual); *Dubroff*, 2010 WL 3294219, at *1 (denying class certification for lack of commonality because Delaware requires reliance and causation for a claim of breach of the duty of disclosure where no stockholder action is sought).

Similarly, commonality does not exist when proposed class members' claims are based upon common questions, but resolving those questions for each class member requires a look at individualized facts. *First State Orthopedics v. Liberty Mut. Ins. Co.*, 2020 WL 764149, at *5–6 (Del. Super. Ct. Feb. 13, 2020).

iii. Typicality. The test of typicality is that the legal and factual position of the class representative must not be markedly different from those of putative class members. *Weiner*, 584 A.2d at 1225; *Paine Webber R&D Partners, L.P. v. Centocor Inc.*, C.A. No. 96C-04-194, 1997 WL 719096 (Del. Super. Oct. 9, 1997). The typicality requirement is satisfied if the representative's claim or defense arises from the same series of events or course of conduct that gives rise to the claims of other members of the class and is based on the same legal theory. *Weiner*, 584 A.2d at 1226; *Boris*, 2001 WL 50204, at *3. A class representative's claims are considered typical if they do not require substantially more or less proof than would the claims of putative class members. *Singer v. Magnavox Co.*, C.A. No. 4929, 1978 WL 4651 (Del. Ch. Dec. 14, 1978). Differences in the amount of damages that may be awarded among the putative class members will not defeat typicality. *Smith*, 2003 WL 1580603, at *8.

The trading strategies of a hedge fund do not make them atypical for class certification purposes. *Regal Entm't Grp. v. Amaranth LLC*, 894 A.2d 1104, 1111–12 (Del. Ch. 2006).

iv. Adequacy. It is of "cardinal importance" for a trial court to expressly find that the named plaintiff can "fairly and adequately protect the interest of the class." *Phila. Stock Exch.*, 945 A.2d at 1144. Adequacy of representation is a factual question. *In re Best Lock Corp. S'holder Litig.*, 845 A.2d 1057, 1093 (Del. Ch. 2001); *Price v. Wilmington Tr. Co.*, 730 A.2d 1236, 1238 (Del. Ch. 1997). The issue is whether the class representative is competent to represent the entire class. *Prezant v. De Angelis*, 636 A.2d 915, 923 (Del. 1994). When determining the adequacy of representation, the court considers the quality of the plaintiff's case as well as the caliber of the legal representation. *Alston v. State*, C.A. No. 01C-09-030, 2002 WL 184247 (Del. Super. Jan. 28, 2002) (holding that a pro se plaintiff is not an adequate representative for the class considering the complicated legal matters that class actions encompass). The adequacy requirement may bar a plaintiff from pursuing overlapping individual and class claims when there is a "meaningful risk" that the plaintiff would favor his or her own interests over that of the class. *Pope v. Hycroft Mining Corp.*, C.A. No. 2022-0957-LWW, 2024 WL 3352852, at *2 (Del. Ch. July 9, 2024).

The fact that class counsel plays a dominant role does not mean that the class representative is inadequate. *In re Infinity Broad. Corp. S'holders Litig.*, 802 A.2d 285, 291 (Del. 2002). A class representative may be adequate despite having little to no knowledge of the facts of the case at the outset of the litigation. *Buttonwood*, 2022 WL 2255258, at *10.

Topics that may require consideration in assessing adequacy include (1) when did the representative acquire stock, (2) whether it has since continuously held an equity position, (3) whether there is some personal agenda unrelated to the claims or best interest of the nominal defendant and its shareholders, and (4) whether the plaintiff may be subject to any defenses not applicable to shareholders in general. *Cal. Public Emps.' Ret. Sys. v. Coulter*, C.A. No. 19191-NC, 2004 WL 1238443, at *4 (Del. Ch. May 26, 2004). In stockholder class action litigation, a plaintiff's sale of its stock prior to consummation of the transaction at issue does not make the plaintiff a per se inadequate class representative. *In re Celera Corp. S'holder Litig.*, 59 A.3d 418 (Del. 2012) (affirming the Court of Chancery's certification of a shareholder that sold its stock after the merger at issue was announced but before the transaction was consummated as a class representative). Likewise, a "fast filing" stockholder that files a stockholder suit without first bringing an 8 *Del. C.* § 220 books and records action is not a presumptively inadequate class representative. *Pyott v. La. Mun. Police Emps.' Ret. Sys.*, 74 A.3d 612, 618 (Del. 2013). But, "as a policy matter, trading by representative plaintiffs on the basis of information obtained through litigation is unacceptable and undermines the integrity of the litigation process." *In re Straight Path Commc'ns Inc. Con. S'holder Litig.*, 2022 WL 728844, at *9 (Del. Ch. Mar. 11, 2022). The requirement that the class representative adequately represent the interests of the class is similar to the typicality requirement, but it focuses more directly on whether the proposed class representative has any conflict of interest with the class. *Best Lock*, 845 A.2d at 1093. The Court of Chancery has indicated that the existence of a litigation funding agreement is relevant to the adequacy analysis due to concerns over the funders' "potential to exercise control over the litigation in a manner that may give rise to a conflict." *Burkhart v. Genworth Fin.*, 2024 WL 3888109, at *3–4 (Del. Ch. Aug. 21, 2024).

The Court of Chancery has noted that it is premature to rule on the adequacy of a class plaintiff when considering a 12(b)(6) motion to dismiss. *Samuels v. CCUR Holdings, Inc.*, No. CV 2021-0358-PAF, 2022 WL 1744438, at *5 n.42 (Del. Ch. May 31, 2022), cert. denied, (Del. Ch. 2022), and appeal refused, No. 216, 2022, 2022 WL 2902826 (Del. July 22, 2022).

Close scrutiny is given to the adequacy requirement in defendant class actions because of the risk that plaintiff will seek a weak adversary to represent the class. *Weiner*, 584 A.2d at 1224. A hedge fund may adequately represent a defendant class. *Regal*, 894 A.2d at 1110. In *Regal*, the defendant hedge fund publicly disputed the method by which plaintiff Regal, an issuer of a series of convertible notes, calculated the number of common shares that a noteholder would receive on conversion. *Id.* at 1105–06. Regal sought a declaration that its calculation method was correct. *Id.* at 1106. The court explained that certification of a defendant class was appropriate there in order to protect Regal from "inconsistent claims by similarly situated Noteholders." *Id.* Conflicts of interest may render a proposed defendant class representative inadequate. *Buttonwood*, 2022 WL 2255258, at *13 (denying certification of a proposed defendant class representative where that individual also served as the fiduciary of a trust that was also a member of the plaintiff class).

b. Rule 23(aa)

Rule 23(aa) (added in 2007) prohibits fee splitting or fee sharing with the class plaintiff and requires that persons seeking to serve as representative party file an affidavit stating that they have not received, been promised, and will not accept compensation other than that expressly permitted by the rule (*e.g.*, a pro rata share of the class award, out-of-pocket costs and expenses). Rule 23(e) also requires the filing of a similar affidavit at the time judicial approval of a settlement is sought.

In rare instances, the Court of Chancery has also permitted a bonus payment known as a "plaintiff's award" to compensate for extraordinary service to the class. *Raider v. Sunderland*, C.A. No. 19357, 2006 WL 75310, at *1 (Del. Ch. Jan. 4, 2006). To determine whether such an award is appropriate, the court has examined four factors: (1) whether the time and expertise provided by the class plaintiff went "well beyond" that provided by a typical plaintiff; (2) whether the class as a whole received a benefit in addition to the final settlement because of the class plaintiff's efforts; (3) whether the class plaintiff stood to receive only a small pro-rata recovery; and (4) whether notice was provided to the class. *Id.* at *2.

c. Rule 23(b)

i. Rule 23(b)(1)(A). Certification is appropriate under Rule 23(b)(1)(A) when a determination of the rights of all parties is necessary to avoid inconsistent or varying adjudications. *Weiner*, 584 A.2d at 1226. The fact that the relief sought is monetary will not, on its own, defeat certification under Rule 23(b)(1). *Noerr*, 2002 WL 31720734, at *5. In *Weiner*, the court ruled that certification of a defendant class consisting of over 200 property owners was appropriate under (b)(1)(A) because of the risk of the plaintiffs suing each landowner individually and obtaining inconsistent results. Generally, actions challenging the exercise of fiduciary duties in corporate transactions are properly certified under Rule 23(b)(1). *Weiner*, 584 A.2d at 1226; *In re AXA Fin., Inc. S'holders Litig.*, C.A. No. 18268, 2002 WL 1283674 (Del. Ch. May 22, 2002); *see Turner v. Bernstein*, 768 A.2d 24 (Del. Ch. 2000); *CME*, 2009 WL 1547510, at *5.

ii. Rule 23(b)(1)(B). Under (b)(1)(B), the focus is on the effect separate actions would have on the ability of other parties to protect their interests. *Paine Webber*, 1997 WL 63318, at *6.

iii. Rule 23(b)(2). This section is used for cases seeking classwide injunctive or corresponding declaratory relief. *Nottingham Partners*, 564 A.2d at 1095. Courts have discretionary power under Rule 23(b)(2) to allow members to opt out of the class. *Id.* at 1098. If a declaratory judgment in an individual action will bind the party opposing the proposed class and injunctive relief is unwarranted, class certification under Rule 23(b)(2) may be unnecessary. *First State Orthopaedics, P.A. v. Emps. Ins. Co. of Wausau*, 2022 WL 18228287, at *3 (Del. Super. Dec. 29, 2022).

The distinctions between Rule 23(b)(1) and (b)(2) are not well defined and the categories are not mutually exclusive. *In re Lawson Software, Inc. S'holder Litig.*, C.A. No. 6443, 2011 WL 2185613, at *1 (Del. Ch. May 27, 2011) (citing *In re Countrywide Corp. S'holders Litig.*, C.A. No. 3464, 2009 WL 846019, at *11 (Del. Ch. Mar. 31, 2009)). Delaware courts traditionally view "'actions challenging the propriety of director conduct in carrying out corporate transactions [as] properly certifiable under both subdivisions (b)(1) and (b)(2).'" *Lawson*, 2011 2185613, at *1 (quoting *In re Cox Radio, Inc. S'holders Litig.*, C.A. No. 4461, 2010 WL 1806616, at *8 (Del. Ch. May 6, 2010)). Under either Rule 23(b)(1) or (b)(2), "certification of a mandatory (*i.e.*, non-opt out) class is appropriate, and decisions are *res judicata* as to the entire class." *Lawson*, 2011 WL 2185613, at *1 (internal citations and quotations omitted).

The "main difference between Rule 23(b)(2) and Rule 23(b)(3) certification lies in the remedy sought; the former seeks a court order to control the defendant's behavior or to establish the plaintiff's legal rights and the latter seeks monetary damages." *First State Orthopaedics P.A. v. Liberty Mut. Ins. Co.*, 2020 WL 6875219, at *5 (Del. Super. Nov. 20, 2020). Nonetheless, a request for money damages does not preclude certification under Rule 23(b)(2) so long as it is not the predominant remedy. *Nottingham Partners*, 564 A.2d at 1095.

iv. Rule 23(b)(3). This section is used primarily for class-wide suits seeking money damages. *Ala. By-Prods. Corp. v. CEDE & Co.*, 657 A.2d 254, 261 (Del. 1995). Mere obstacles in calculating class damages should not preclude class certification. *Benning v. Wit Cap. Group, Inc.*, 792 A.2d 188 (Del. 2001) (TABLE). Certification of a class based on oral misrepresentations is generally denied because such representations are likely to vary from purchaser to purchaser and thus involve predominantly individual questions. *Mentis*, 2000 WL 973299, at *7. Non-disclosure mass tort cases (*i.e.*, those without a common connection such as a single-event disaster) are not suitable for class treatment because individual issues relating to causation predominate over common issues. *Muttart v. Am. Mortg. & Guar. Co.*, C.A. No. 96C-09-263, 1998 WL 110067 (Del. Super. Feb. 9, 1998). When the fact of damage must be proven on an individual basis, the predominance requirement is not satisfied. *Wit Capital Group, Inc. v. Benning*, 897 A.2d 172, 185–86 (Del. 2006). For example, in *Wit*, investors alleged that they were wrongfully denied the opportunity to purchase IPO shares. *Id.* at 185. Because some of the investors may have ended up selling their investments for less than the IPO price, they were not injured, so therefore there was no injury-in-fact common to all class members. *Id.* The court rejected that a lost investment opportunity was an injury-in-fact. *Id.* at 186.

3. MISCELLANEOUS COMMENTS

Settlement classes are permissible, but the trial court must explicitly determine that all the requirements of Rule 23 are satisfied. *Prezant*, 636 A.2d 915. This determination is the first in a series of steps the court takes in considering whether to approve a settlement. *In re AMC Ent. Holdings, Inc. S'holder Litig.*, 299 A.3d 501, 507 (Del. Ch. July 21, 2023). Without deciding the merits of the case, the court "must assess the nature of the claims asserted and the defenses that might be raised and then apply its own business judgment to determine whether the proposed settlement is fair and reasonable." *CME*, 2009 WL 1547510, at *5. "Of particular importance is the balance between the strength of the claims being compromised against the benefits secured for the class by the settlement." *Blank v. Belzberg*, 858 A.2d 336, 340 (Del. Ch. 2003). Although Delaware law favors settlement over litigation, in a class action suit, the court must vigilantly protect the interests of the unrepresented class. *Gatz v. Ponsoldt*, C.A. No. 174, 2009 WL 1743760, at *2 (Del. Ch. June 12, 2009). As such, the court will not approve a settlement where the record is inadequate and inconsistent. *In re Prime Hospitality, Inc. S'holders Litig.*, C.A. No. 652-N, 2005 WL 1138738, at *7 (Del. Ch. May 4, 2005). Where the court rejects a settlement, it need not reach the issue of class certification. *AMC*, 299 A.3d at 537 & n.203.

Bifurcation of class action settlements is permissible. *Phila. Stock Exch.*, 945 A.2d at 1135–36 (affirming the Court of Chancery's bifurcation of complex allocation issues from issues relating to the adequacy and fairness of the aggregate settlement amount).

A class certification order may be modified following trial. In *In re Sears Hometown and Outlet Stores, Inc. Stockholder Litigation*, the Court of Chancery modified the definition of the class to divide the class into subclasses: dissenting class members who had exercised appraisal rights and had not received merger consideration, and nondissenting class members who had already received merger consideration. The only difference between the subclasses was an offset in damages. 332 A.3d 1088, 1108–09 (Del. Ch. 2025).

State court settlements of stockholder class actions usually include a release of federal securities law claims. *In re Countrywide Corp. S'holders Litig.*, C.A. No. 3464, 2009 WL 2595739 (Del. Ch. Aug. 24, 2009), *aff'd sub. nom. Ark. Teacher Ret. Sys. v. Caiafa*, 996 A.2d 321 (Del. 2010). This occurs even if the federal claims could not be brought in state court in the first instance, *i.e.*, claims under the Securities Exchange Act of 1934. *See, e.g.*, *In re MCA, Inc. S'holders Litig.*, C.A. No. 11740, 1993 WL 43024 (Del. Ch. Feb. 16, 1993), *aff'd*, 633 A.2d 370 (Del. 1993) (TABLE). The settlement in *MCA* was challenged in the Ninth Circuit and led to the United States Supreme Court's decision in *Matsushita Elec. Indus. Co. v. Epstein*, 516 U.S. 367 (1996), wherein the Supreme Court held that the final judgment in the Delaware settlement was entitled to full faith and credit. The scope of release, however, is limited to claims "based on the 'same identical factual predicate' or the 'same set of operative facts.'" *Phila. Stock Exch.*, 945 A.2d at 1146 (citing *UniSuper, Ltd. v. News Corp.*, 898 A.2d 344, 347 (Del. Ch. 2006)). If a settlement releases a defendant from claims based on tangential facts or facts that have not yet occurred, then the release is too broad and precluded on substantive due process grounds. *Id.* (citing *UniSuper*, 898 A.2d at 347). A release must be limited to claims based on the property interest giving rise to the claims in the complaint, or rights appurtenant to that interest. *AMC*, 299 A.3d at 508, 530–31. Likewise, a release will not be permitted where it would adversely impact a pending action based on other closely interrelated transactions such that the claims in the different actions are not sufficiently segregable. *Off v. Ross*, C.A. No. 3468, 2008 WL 5053448, at *12–14 (Del. Ch. Nov. 26, 2008). This is particularly so where the class in question is a mandatory class with no opportunity to opt-out. *Marie Raymond Revocable Trust v. MAT Five LLC*, 980 A.2d 388, 407 (Del. Ch. 2008).

Pursuant to Court of Chancery general practice, settling parties must provide notice of settlement to class members between 30 and 45 days prior to the settlement hearing. *In re Coleman Co., Inc. S'holders Litig.*, 750 A.2d 1202, 1210 (Del. Ch. 1999). The deadline to determine whether to opt out of the settlement may be less than 30 days. *See MAT Five*, 980 A.2d at 409 (holding that 30 days notice and 20 days to determine whether to opt out is sufficient). Notice to putative class members is also required if claims on behalf of a putative class are being dismissed as moot and defendants agree to pay to plaintiff's counsel a mootness fee award, because of the "risk of buy off" presented by the proposed fee payment. *See In re Advanced Mammography Sys., Inc. S'holders Litig.*, 1996 WL 633409, at *1 (Del. Ch. Oct. 30, 1996); *In re Zalicus, Inc. Stockholders Litig.*, 2015 WL 226109 (Del. Ch. Jan. 16, 2015).

Class counsel may present a proposed settlement over the objections of the named plaintiffs. *In re M&F Worldwide Corp. S'holders Litig.*, 799 A.2d 1164 (Del. Ch. 2002). Once class representatives object to a settlement negotiated on their behalf, "class counsel may continue to represent the remaining class representatives and the class, as long as the interest of the class in continued representation by experienced counsel is not outweighed by the actual prejudice to the objectors being opposed by their former counsel." *Id.* at 1176 (quoting *Lazy Oil Co. v. Witco Corp.*, 166 F.3d 581, 590 (3d Cir. 1999)). Any plaintiff that objects to a settlement is limited on appeal to the arguments raised before the trial court. *See Phila. Stock Exch.*, 945 A.2d at 1134 (declining to address the merits of objections on appeal that were not initially presented to the Court of Chancery).

There are hundreds of cases addressing settlements of stockholder class action suits and awards of attorneys' fees. When awarding fees in class action litigation, the courts consider several factors, including: the results achieved, the amount of time and effort applied to the case, the complexities of the litigation, the skill and ability of counsel, and the contingent nature of the case. *Sugarland Indus., Inc. v. Thomas*, 420 A.2d 142, 147–50 (Del. 1980); *Crowhorn v. Nationwide Mut. Ins. Co.*, 836 A.2d 558, 565 (Del. Ch. 2003); *see also Goodrich v. E.F. Hutton Group, Inc.*, 681 A.2d 1039, 1050 (Del. 1996). The primary factor is the benefit conferred to the class because fee awards are usually based on a percentage of that benefit. *United Vanguard Fund, Inc. v. Takecare, Inc.*, 693 A.2d 1076, 1079 (Del. 1997); *see also Ala. Elec. Pension Fund v. Brown*, 941 A.2d 1011, 1015 (Del. 2007). "Higher percentages are warranted when cases progress further or go the distance to post-trial adjudication." *Brinckerhoff v. Tex. E. Prods. Pipeline Co.*, 986 A.2d 370, 396 (Del. Ch. 2010). Delaware courts do not reduce the percentage awarded as the size of the recovery increases, unlike some other courts that apply a declining-percentage method for calculating attorneys' fees in large or so-called "mega-fund" cases. *In re Dell Techs. Inc. Class V Stockholders Litig.*, 300 A.3d 679, 687 (Del. Ch. 2023), *as revised* (Aug. 21, 2023), *aff'd* __ A.3d __, 2024 WL 3811075 (Del. Aug. 14, 2024).

Counsel for Delaware plaintiffs are entitled to a rebuttable presumption of a "causal relationship between the benefit and a timely filed suit." *Infinity Broad. Corp.*, 802 A.2d at 290. Attorneys that litigate the matter in other jurisdictions may share in a Delaware fee award "if their efforts elsewhere conferred a benefit realized as part of the Delaware settlement." *Id.* at 291. These attorneys, however, are not entitled to the same presumption and must instead substantiate their contribution to the result achieved. *Ala. Elec. Pension Fund*, 941 A.2d at 1015. Counsel who litigate successfully on behalf of specific stockholders, but who do not subsequently take steps to benefit an entire class, lack standing to obtain a fee award even where their efforts incidentally confer a class-wide benefit. *See In re Orchard Enters., Inc. Stockholder Litig.*, C.A. No. 7840, 2014 WL 4181912, at *13 (Del. Ch. Aug. 22, 2014).

The court may reduce a fee award where no appreciable risk is taken by the plaintiffs' attorneys. *In re Cox Commc'ns, Inc. S'holders Litig.*, 879 A.2d 604, 642 (Del. Ch. 2005). In *Cox*, the court reduced the agreed upon fee by approximately 74 percent, stating that no risk premium should be awarded in a going private transaction with a controlling shareholder where there was a negotiable proposal by defendant and a settlement of the case at the same price and terms accepted by a special committee. *Id.* To obtain court approval of a proposed settlement where the only benefits obtained are supplemental disclosures regarding a subject transaction, plaintiff's counsel must be able to demonstrate that those supplemental disclosures are "plainly material," meaning that it should not be a "close call" that the information is material as defined by Delaware law. *In re Trulia, Inc. Stockholder Litig.*, 129 A.3d 884, 898 (Del. Ch. 2016).

Arbitration agreements, even adhesion contracts, can effectively waive the ability to file a class action. *Edelist v. MBNA Am. Bank*, 790 A.2d 1249, 1260 (Del. Super. 2001).

The Court of Chancery will shift a portion of defendant's attorneys' fees to plaintiff when plaintiff conducts a class action in bad faith. *Beck v. Atl. Coast PLC*, 868 A.2d 840 (Del. Ch. 2005).

When multiple plaintiffs' firms are competing for the position of lead counsel in a consolidated class action, the Court of Chancery considers several factors in determining the leadership structure including: (1) the quality of the pleadings that appears best able to represent the interests of the class, (2) the relative economic stakes of the competing litigants in the outcome of the lawsuit, and (3) the enthusiasm or vigor with which the various contestants have prosecuted the lawsuit. *TWC Tech. Ltd. P'ship v. Intermedia Commc'ns, Inc.*, C.A. Nos. 18336, 18289 & 18293, 2000 WL 1654504, at *4 (Del. Ch. Oct. 17, 2000); *see Hirt v. U.S. Timberlands Serv. Co.*, C.A. No. 19575, 2002 WL 1558342, at *2 (Del. Ch. July 3, 2002).

In the context of a short-form merger where plaintiff alleges disclosure violations in the notice provided pursuant to 8 Del. C. § 253, class certification depends on the nature of the violation. *Berger v. Pubco Corp.*, 976 A.2d 132, 145 (Del. 2009). If only a technical and non-prejudicial violation of the statute occurs, minority shareholders may be required to opt-in to the class. *Gilliland v. Motorola, Inc.*, 873 A.2d 305 (Del. Ch. 2005). Class certification at that stage is premature. *Id.* On the other hand, a substantive disclosure violation does not require minority stockholders to opt-in. *Berger*, 976 A.2d at 145. Under those circumstances, minority stockholders are entitled to participate in a "quasi-appraisal" class action to recover the difference between fair value and the merger price of their shares. *Id.*

Delaware does not permit defendants to "pick off" a class representative plaintiff by compelling settlement to moot his claims in an effort to eliminate standing even if defendants' action is taken prior to class certification. *Stratton v. Am. Indep. Ins. Co.*, C.A. No. 08C-12-012, 2011 WL 2083933 (Del. Super. May 11, 2011).

4. CASE LAW INVOLVING THE TOLLING OF LIMITATIONS PERIODS DURING THE PENDENCY OF A CLASS ACTION

In Delaware, the statute of limitations for claims is tolled during the pendency of a class action. *Dow Chem. Corp. v. Blanco*, 67 A.3d 392 (Del. 2013) (holding as a matter of first impression that the statute of limitations was tolled in Delaware while a class action was pending in Texas); *Dubroff v. Wren Holdings*, C.A. Nos. 3940 & 6067, 2011 WL 5137175 (Del. Ch. Oct. 28, 2011). This is because, without a tolling rule, "'all class members would be forced to intervene to preserve their claims, and one of the major goals of class action litigation—to simplify litigation involving a large number of class members with similar claims—would be defeated.'" *Dubroff*, 2011 WL 5137175, at *13 (quoting *Devlin v. Scardelletti,* 536 U.S. 1, 10 (2002)). The court in *Dubroff* did not decide whether the "limitations period should run between the time when a claim of a purported class representative is dismissed and when class certification is decided." *Id.* It recognized, however, that the federal rule, which the court views as persuasive, is that "'[o]nce the statute of limitations has been tolled, it remains tolled for all members of the putative class until class certification is denied.'" *Id.* (quoting *Crown, Cork & Seal Co. v. Parker*, 462 U.S. 345, 354 (1983)); *see also Marquinez v. Dow Chem. Co.*, 183 A.3d 704 (Del. 2018) (holding that a dismissal on grounds of *forum non conveniens* and consequent denial as moot of "all pending motions," including a motion for class certification, did not end the class action tolling period).

In *Harman v. Masoneilan Int'l, Inc.*, 442 A.2d 487, 501 (Del. 1982), the Delaware Supreme Court declined to apply the doctrine of laches to a minority shareholder who filed suit against a majority shareholder one month after the decertification of a class action suit in New York State court. The plaintiff relied on *Am. Pipe* as authority that the filing of a class action tolls the running of a statute of limitations on the class members' claims. *Id.* at 503 n.27. The Delaware Supreme Court did not decide the tolling issue, but instead ruled that plaintiff's claim was not barred as a matter of law by laches because laches requires a finding of unreasonable delay, which can only be determined after discovery or at trial. *Id.* at 503.

RULES OF THE COURT OF CHANCERY OF THE STATE OF DELAWARE DEL. CT. CH. R. 23 (2024)

RULE 23. CLASS ACTIONS

(a) Prerequisites. One or more members of a class may sue or be sued as representative parties on behalf of all members only if:

(1) the class is so numerous that joinder of all members is impracticable;

(2) there are questions of law or fact common to the class;

(3) the claims or defenses of the representative parties are typical of the claims or defenses of the class; and

(4) the representative parties will fairly and adequately protect the interests of the class.

(aa) Affidavit from Representative Party.

(1) A person seeking to serve as a representative party must file an affidavit within 10 days after filing any of the following:

(A) a complaint;

(B) a motion to intervene; or

(C) a motion seeking appointment as a representative party.

(2) The affidavit must state that the person has not received, been promised, or been offered-and will not accept-any form of compensation, directly or indirectly, for serving as a representative party, except for:

(A) any damages or other relief that the Court may award the person as a class member;

(B) any fees, costs, or other payments that the Court expressly approves to be paid to or on behalf of the person; or

(C) reimbursement from the person's attorneys of actual and reasonable out-of-pocket expenditures incurred in prosecuting the action.

(b) Types of Class Actions.

A class action may be maintained if Rule 23(a) is satisfied and if:

(1) prosecuting separate actions by or against individual class members would create a risk of:

(A) inconsistent or varying adjudications with respect to individual class members that would establish incompatible standards of conduct for the party opposing the class; or

(B) adjudications with respect to individual class members that, as a practical matter, would be dispositive of the interests of the other members not parties to the individual adjudications or would substantially impair or impede their ability to protect their interests;

(2) the party opposing the class has acted or refused to act on grounds that apply generally to the class, so that final injunctive relief or corresponding declaratory relief is appropriate with respect to the class as a whole; or

(3) the Court finds that the questions of law or fact common to class members predominate over any questions affecting only individual members, and that a class action is superior to other available methods for fairly and efficiently adjudicating the controversy. The matters pertinent to these findings include:

(A) the class members' interests in individually controlling the prosecution or defense of separate actions;

(B) the extent and nature of any litigation concerning the controversy already begun by or against class members;

(C) the desirability or undesirability of concentrating the litigation of the claims in the particular forum; and

(D) the likely difficulties in managing a class action.

(c) Certification Order; Notice; Judgment; Subclasses.

(1) Certification Order. A class action must be certified by order. The order must define the class and identify a representative party. The order may be altered or amended before final judgment.

(2) Notice.

(A) For (b)(1) or (b)(2) Classes. In any class action certified under Rule 23(b)(1) or (b)(2), the Court may direct appropriate notice to the class members.

(B) For (b)(3) Classes. In any class action certified under Rule 23(b)(3), the Court must direct to the class members the best notice that is practicable under the circumstances, including individual notice to all members who can be identified through reasonable effort. The notice must advise each member:

(i) that the Court will exclude from the class any member who requests exclusion by a specified date;

(ii) of the binding effect of a judgment, whether favorable or not, on members who do not request exclusion; and

(iii) that a class member who does not request exclusion may enter an appearance through counsel if the member so desires.

(3) Judgment. Whether or not favorable to the class, the judgment must:

(A) in an action maintained as a class action under Rule 23(b)(1) or Rule 23(b)(2), include and describe those whom the Court finds to be class members; and

(B) in an action maintained as a class action under Rule 23(b)(3), include and specify or describe those to whom the Rule 23(c)(2) notice was directed, who have not requested exclusion, and whom the Court finds to be class members.

(4) Particular Issues. When appropriate, an action may be brought or maintained as a class action with respect to particular issues.

(5) Subclasses. When appropriate, a class may be divided into subclasses that are each treated as a class under this rule.

(d) Class Counsel.

(1) Duty of Class Counsel. Class counsel must fairly and adequately represent the interests of the class.

(2) Interim Counsel. The Court may designate interim counsel to act on behalf of a putative class before determining whether to certify the action as a class action. Interim counsel has the same duty as class counsel to fairly and adequately represent the interests of the class.

(3) Appointing Class Counsel. Unless a statute provides otherwise, the Court must appoint class counsel when certifying a class and may make further orders in connection with that appointment. If only one applicant seeks appointment and the applicant cannot provide adequate representation, then the Court may not certify the class.

(4) Disputed Appointments. The Court may resolve disputes over the appointment of class or interim counsel, including who can best represent the interests of the class.

(A) When selecting class or interim counsel, the Court may consider:

(i) counsel's competence and experience;

(ii) counsel's access to the resources necessary to represent the class;

(iii) the quality of the pleading;

(iv) counsel's performance in the litigation to date;

(v) the proposed leadership structure;

(vi) the relative economic stakes of the representative parties;

(vii) any conflicts between counsel or the representative parties and members of the class; and

(viii) any other matter pertinent to the ability of counsel or the representative party to fairly and adequately represent the interests of the class.

(B) The Court may:

(i) order any applicant to provide information on any subject pertinent to the application and to propose terms for attorney's fees and expenses; and

(ii) include in the appointing order provisions about the award of attorney's fees or expenses under Rule 23(g).

(e) Conducting the Action.

(1) In General. In conducting an action under this rule, the Court may issue orders that:

(A) determine the course of proceedings or prescribe measures to prevent undue repetition or complication in presenting evidence or argument;

(B) require-to protect class members and fairly conduct the action-giving notice to some or all class members of:

(i) any step in the action;

(ii) the proposed extent of the judgment; or

(iii) the members' opportunity to signify whether they consider the representation fair and adequate, to intervene and present claims or defenses, or otherwise to come into the action;

(C) impose conditions on the representative parties or on intervenors;

(D) require that the pleadings be amended to eliminate allegations about representation of absent persons and that the action proceed accordingly; or

(E) deal with similar procedural matters.

(2) Amending and Combining Orders. An order under Rule 23(e)(1) may be altered or amended from time to time and may be combined with an order under Rule 16.

(f) Dismissal or Settlement.

(1) In General. Subject to Rule 15(a)(5), a class action may be dismissed or settled only if the Court approves the terms of the proposed dismissal or settlement.

(2) Required Submissions. The parties submitting the proposed dismissal or settlement must file:

(A) a further affidavit from each representative party that meets the requirements of Rule 23(aa)(2);

(B) if a dismissal, a proposed form of order stating the terms on which the action will be dismissed; and

(C) if a settlement, the definitive agreement governing the settlement.

(3) Notice. Notice of the proposed dismissal or settlement must be given to all class members in the manner directed by the Court.

(A) Dismissal Without Notice. But the Court may order dismissal without notice if the dismissal is to be without prejudice to the class or with prejudice to the plaintiff only.

(B) Information About Notice. The parties must provide the Court with information sufficient to rule on whether to require notice and in what form.

(C) Means of Notice. Notice may be given by any appropriate means approved by the Court, including first-class U.S. mail, email, or publication.

(D) Contents of Notice. Unless the Court orders otherwise, the notice of a proposed dismissal or settlement must clearly and concisely state, in plain, easily understood language:

(i) the location, date, and time of any hearing;

(ii) the nature of the action;

(iii) the definition of the class;

(iv) a summary of the claims, issues, defenses, and relief that the class action sought;

(v) a description of the terms of the proposed dismissal or settlement;

(vi) any award of attorney's fees or expenses, or any representative-party award, that will be sought if the proposed dismissal or settlement is approved;

(vii) instructions for objectors;

(viii) that additional information can be obtained by contacting class counsel;

(ix) how to contact class counsel; and

(x) not to contact the Court with questions about the terms of the proposed dismissal or settlement.

(4) Class-Member Objections.

(A) In General. Any class member may object to the proposed dismissal or settlement of a class action. The objection must state with specificity the grounds for and purpose of the objection and state whether it applies only to the objector, to a specific subset of the class, or to the entire class.

(B) Court Approval Required for Payment in Connection with an Objection. Unless approved by the Court after a hearing, no payment or other consideration may be provided in connection with:

(i) forgoing or withdrawing an objection; or

(ii) forgoing, dismissing, or abandoning an appeal from the judgment approving the proposed dismissal or settlement.

(C) Taking over Case After Providing Adequate Security. The Court may allow an objector to substitute as a representative party if:

(i) the objector satisfies the requirements for a representative party in Rule 23; and

(ii) if the proposed dismissal or settlement would provide relief to the class, the objector provides adequate security.

(5) Approval of the Proposal. If the proposed dismissal or settlement would bind class members, the Court may approve it only after a hearing and only on finding that it is reasonable after considering whether:

(A) the representative party and class counsel have adequately represented the class;

(B) adequate notice of the hearing was provided;

(C) the proposed dismissal or settlement was negotiated at arm's length; and

(D) the relief provided for the class falls within a range of reasonableness, taking into account:

(i) the strength of the claims;

(ii) the costs, risks, and delay of trial and appeal;

(iii) the scope of the release; and

(iv) any objections to the proposed dismissal or settlement.

(6) Disposition of Residual Settlement Funds.

(A) Any order approving a settlement under this rule that establishes a process for compensating class members must provide for the disbursement of residual settlement funds, if any.

(B) The Court may direct that residual settlement funds be redistributed to identified class members. But if redistribution is uneconomic, the Court may approve a transfer of the funds to the Combined Campaign for Justice or a similar organization.

(g) Attorney's Fees and Expenses; Representative-Party Awards.

(1) In a class action, the Court may award reasonable attorney's fees and expenses to class counsel.

(2) Any person from whom payment is sought may oppose the award, and any class member may object as provided in Rule 23(f)(4).

(3) Any counsel who will share in the award of attorney's fees and expenses must submit an affidavit documenting their fees and expenses.

(4) The Court may authorize class counsel to pay a reasonable award to a representative party out of any award of attorney's fees.

RULES OF CIVIL PROCEDURE FOR THE SUPERIOR COURT OF THE STATE OF DELAWARE Del. Super. Ct. Civ. R. 23 (2004)

RULE 23. CLASS ACTIONS

(a) *Requisites to class action.* One or more members of a class may sue or be sued as representative parties on behalf of all only if (1) the class is so numerous that joinder of all members is impracticable, (2) there are questions of law or fact common to the class, (3) the claims or defenses of the representative parties are typical of the claims or defenses of the class, and (4) the representative parties will fairly and adequately protect the interests of the class.

(b) *Class actions maintainable*. An action may be maintained as a class action if the prerequisites of paragraph (a) are satisfied, and in addition:

(1) The prosecution of separate actions by or against individual members of the class would create a risk of:

(A) Inconsistent or varying adjudications with respect to individual members of the class which would establish incompatible standards of conduct for the party opposing the class, or

(B) Adjudications with respect to individual members of the class which would as a practical matter be dispositive of the interests of the other members not parties to the adjudications or substantially impair or impede their ability to protect their interests; or

(2) The party opposing the class has acted or refused to act on grounds generally applicable to the class, thereby making appropriate final injunctive relief or corresponding declaratory relief with respect to the class as a whole; or

(3) The Court finds that the questions of law or fact common to the members of the class predominate over any questions affecting only individual members, and that a class action is superior to other available methods for the fair and efficient adjudication of the controversy. The matter pertinent to the findings include:

(A) The interest of members of the class in individually controlling the prosecution or defense of separate actions;

(B) The extent and nature of any litigation concerning the controversy already commenced by or against members of the class;

(C) The desirability or undesirability of concentrating the litigation of the claims in the particular forum;

(D) The difficulties likely to be encountered in the management of a class action.

(c) *Determination by order whether class action to be maintained; notice; judgment; actions conducted partially as class actions.*

(1) As soon as practicable after the commencement of an action brought as a class action, the Court shall determine by order whether it is to be so maintained. An order under this paragraph may be conditional, and may be altered or amended before the decision on the merits.

(2) In any class action maintained under paragraph (b)(3), the Court shall direct to the members of the class the best notice practicable under the circumstances, including individual notice to all members who can be identified through reasonable effort. The notice shall advise each member that:

(A) The Court will exclude him from the class if he so requests by a specified date;

(B) The judgment, whether favorable or not, will include all members who do not request exclusion; and

(C) Any member who does not request exclusion may, if he desires, enter an appearance through his counsel.

(3) The judgment in an action maintained as a class action under paragraph (b)(1) or (b)(2), whether or not favorable to the class, shall include and describe those whom the Court finds to be members of the class. The judgment in an action maintained as a class action under paragraph (b)(3), whether or not favorable to the class, shall include and specify or describe those to whom the notice provided in paragraph (c)(2) was directed, and who have not requested exclusion, and whom the Court finds to be members of the class.

(4) When appropriate (A) an action may be brought or maintained as a class action with respect to particular issues, or (B) a class may be divided into subclasses and each subclass treated as a class, and the provisions of this rule shall then be construed and applied accordingly.

(d) *Orders in conduct of actions*. In the conduct of actions to which this rule applies, the Court may make appropriate orders: (1) Determining the course of proceedings or prescribing measures to prevent undue repetition or complication in the presentation of evidence or argument; (2) requiring, for the protection of the members of the class or otherwise for the fair conduct of the action, that notice be given in such manner as the Court directs to some or all of the members of any step in the action, or of the proposed extent of the judgment, or of the opportunity of members to signify whether they consider the representation fair and adequate, to intervene and present claims or defenses, or otherwise to come into the action; (3) imposing conditions on the representative parties or on intervenors; (4) requiring that the pleadings be amended to eliminate therefrom allegations as to representation of absent persons, and that the action proceed accordingly; (5) dealing with similar procedural matters. The orders may be combined with an order under Rule 16, and may be altered or amended as may be desirable from time to time.

(e) *Dismissal or compromise*. A class action shall not be dismissed or compromised without the approval of the Court, and notice by mail, publication or otherwise of the proposed dismissal or compromise shall be given to all members of the class in such manner as the Court directs; except that if the dismissal is to be without prejudice to the class or with prejudice to the plaintiff only, then such dismissal shall be ordered without notice thereof if there is a showing that no compensation in any form has passed directly or indirectly from any of the defendants to the plaintiff or plaintiff's attorney and that no promise to give any such compensation has been made. (Added, effective Sept. 30, 1994.)

The Delaware chapter was prepared by Bruce E. Jameson, Eric J. Juray, John G. Day, and Caitlin E. Whetham of Prickett, Jones & Elliott, PA in Wilmington, Delaware. The authors acknowledge and are grateful for the contributions of Elizabeth M. McGeever to versions of this chapter published in prior years.

DISTRICT OF COLUMBIA

1. COMPARISON WITH RULE 23 OF THE FEDERAL RULES OF CIVIL PROCEDURE

District of Columbia Superior Court Rule 23 is substantially identical to Federal Rule of Civil Procedure 23. *See* Super. Ct. Civ. R. 23 (2019). However, Superior Court Rule 23-I includes several supplemental provisions to the general class action rule. *See* D.C. Super. Ct. Civ. R. 23-I (2017).

Rule 23-I outlines the specific procedures for bringing class actions in the District of Columbia. The complaint must contain "class action allegations," and Rule 23-I(a) specifies the allegations that must be included in a proper pleading. These allegations include the size of the class and the questions of law or fact that are common to the class. Rule 23-I(a)(2)(A), (C).

One significant departure from the federal rule requires that plaintiffs file a request for certification of class action status within 90 days after filing the complaint. Super. Ct. Civ. R. 23-I(b). However, the court has the discretion to extend this period. While moving for certification under Rule 23(b)(3), plaintiffs are required to propose how notice will be accomplished and how the costs of the notice will be covered. Super. Ct. Civ. R. 23-I(c). The defendant can move at any time to strike the class action allegations or to dismiss the complaint. Super. Ct. Civ. R. 23-I(b). Like in the federal rule, the court can alter or amend its order granting or denying class certification before the final judgment. Super. Ct. Civ. R. 23(c)(1)(C).

2. CASE LAW INTERPRETING DISTRICT OF COLUMBIA RULE 23

The trial court has discretion in determining whether a proposed class is proper. *Yarmolinsky v. Perpetual Am. Fed. Sav. and Loan Assoc.*, 451 A.2d 92, 94 (D.C. 1982)*; see Cowan v. Youssef*, 687 A.2d 594, 602 (D.C. 1996) ("[W]hen the trial court conducts a thorough review of the request for class certification, as it did here, we will not reverse its decision even if we would have ruled differently."). The party seeking certification has the burden of establishing that the cause of action meets all the requirements for certification. *Goss v. Med. Serv. of D.C.*, 462 A.2d 442, 446 (D.C. 1983).

Matters relevant to the court's findings include: the interest of members of the class in individually controlling separate actions; the extent and nature of litigation concerning the controversy the members of the class already commenced; the advantages or disadvantages of concentrating the litigation of the claims in the chosen forum; and the obstacles likely to be encountered in management of the class action. *Yarmolinsky*, 451 A.2d at 94.

a. Rule 23(a)

i. Numerosity. An allegation of numerosity can be sufficient when the case has the potential for many plaintiffs. *Reed v. Philip Morris, Inc.,* No. 96-5070, 1997 WL 538921, at *3 (D.C. Super. Ct. Aug. 18, 1997) (finding the allegation of numerosity sufficient in a tobacco personal injury case, even though it was the only case pending in D.C. Superior Court, because the case had a potential for a large number of plaintiffs). The "Court need only find an approximation of the size of the class" and "[a]bsent unique circumstances, numerosity is satisfied when a proposed class has at least forty members." *Ait-Hamadi v. Ristorante La Perla of Washington,* No. 2016-CA002467, 2017 D.C. Super. LEXIS 1, at *10 (D.C. Super. Ct. Mar. 7, 2017) (quoting *Coleman v. District of Columbia*, 306 F.R.D. 68, 76 (D.D.C. 2015)). Therefore, an assertion from a knowledgeable party that a putative class contained "as many as fifty" members was sufficient to satisfy the numerosity requirement where that allegation was not controverted by evidence from the defendant. *Id.* Nonetheless, if the class definition is so overbroad as to include a majority of plaintiffs who would not identify themselves as having a claim and it is unclear whether those with a colorable claim would be sufficient to satisfy the numerosity requirement, a class will not be certified. *See Parkhurst v. D.C. Water & Sewer Auth.*, No. 2009-CA000971, 2013 D.C. Super. LEXIS 4, at *17–27 (D.C. Super Ct. April 8, 2013). In assessing the impracticability of joinder, courts consider "the size of the individual claims, the potential financial resources of the Proposed Class members and the alleged ability of claimants to institute individual suits." *Juana v. Rudrakalash LLC*, No. 2019-CA-005732-B, 2023 WL 9116580, at *3 (D.C. Super Ct. Aug. 18, 2023) (numerosity satisfied where class included at least 25 "non-tipped hourly workers who may have limited resources to pursue litigation individually").

ii. Commonality. Commonality will be satisfied in cases where there is common evidence of liability as to the proposed class, even if class member's damages can only be determined through individualized inquiry. *Chaney v. Capitol Park Assocs., LP*, No. 12-CA-5582, 2014 D.C. Super. LEXIS 8, at *5 (D.C. Super. Ct. Feb. 19, 2014). *See also Ford v. ChartOne, Inc.*, 908 A.2d 72, 85–86 (D.C. 2006) (noting that "[f]actual variations among the class members will not defeat the commonality requirement, so long as a single aspect or feature of the claim is common to all proposed class members"). Commonality requires a common contention "the truth or falsity of which will resolve an issue that is central to the validity of each one of the claims in one stroke." *Ait-Hamadi,* 2017 D.C. Super. LEXIS 1, at *14. However, where questions of liability also entail individualized inquiries, the requirement of commonality will not be satisfied simply because there are some overlapping common questions. *See, e.g., Cowan*, 687 A.2d at 602–03 (holding that apartment building tenants did not satisfy the requirements for a class action when the individual heating and air conditioning systems in each apartment would be at issue); *Goss,* 462 A.2d at 446 (holding that a determination of the necessity of medical treatment for each insured plaintiff required individualized review); *FDS Rest., Inc. v. All Plumbing Inc.*, No. 16-CV-1009, 2020 D.C. App. LEXIS 111, at *44–45 (D.C. Mar. 26, 2020) (holding that class certification was not warranted where vicarious liability would have to be determined with respect to each individual plaintiff)

iii. Adequacy/Typicality. Factual variations among plaintiffs' claims will not defeat a claim of typicality. *Yarmolinsky*, 451 A.2d at 94. Similarly, evidence that the named representatives have a greater interest in the prosecution of the case than the unnamed class members does not rise to the level of animus necessary to render the representatives inadequate. *Chaney*, 2014 D.C. Super. LEXIS 8, at *10. However, "where it is predictable that a major focus of the litigation will be on an arguable defense unique to the named plaintiff, class certification [will] be denied." *Id. See also Parkhurst*, No. 2009-CA000971, 2013 D.C. Super. LEXIS at *29–36 (where named plaintiffs' claims may depend on acts or omissions that materially differ from those that caused absent class member injuries, plaintiffs cannot carry their burden of establishing typicality or adequacy).

In general, where a lead plaintiff "has no viable claim of her own, she cannot represent any class of claimants." *Allen v. Dist. of Columbia*, 312 A.3d 207, 208, 211–12 (D.C. 2024) (summarily affirming denial of class certification where lead plaintiff's claim failed to survive summary judgment). However, because the District of Columbia's local courts were established by Congress pursuant to Article I and so are not constitutionally bound by the Article III standing requirement that applies in federal courts, "a public interest organization that has organizational standing to bring a consumer class action claim [pursuant to statute], but which has not itself suffered an injury that would otherwise be required to make it a member of the putative class, may serve as a class representative under Rule 23(a)." *Travelers United, Inc. v. Sonesta Int'l Hotels Corp.*, No. 2023-CAB-005254, 2024 WL 5004842, at *1, 4–9, 11 (D.C. Super. Ct. Jan. 6, 2024) (certifying class represented by public interest organization that "does not actually have its own injury or independent claim"), *request to certify interlocutory appeal denied*, 2025 WL 848605 (D.C. Super. Ct. Mar. 12, 2025); *see Travelers United, Inc. v. Hyatt Hotels Corp.*, 761 F. Supp. 3d 97, 114 (D.D.C. 2025). Courts assessing typicality in such cases may ask not whether the lead plaintiff's claim is typical of the class members' claims, but instead whether "the case presents a typical challenge to [the allegedly wrongful] practice." *Sonesta*, 2024 WL 5004842, at *11.

b. Rule 23(b)

i. Rule 23(b)(1)(A) and (1)(B). Authorizes class action treatment when either "inconsistent or varying adjudications . . . would establish incompatible standards" or "adjudications with respect to individual members . . . would as a practical matter be dispositive of the interests of the other members. . . ."

ii. Rule 23(b)(2). Provides injunctive or declaratory relief when the defendant has acted or refused to act on grounds applicable to the class as a whole. *See Apartment and Office Bldg. Ass'n of Met. Wash. v. Wash.*, 343 A.2d 323, 327 n.8 (D.C. 1975). Injunctive relief is also available to plaintiffs acting in a representative capacity without seeking class certification under Rule 23 where the plaintiff establishes a claim under the District of Columbia Consumer Protection Procedures Act (CPPA) and the plaintiff does not have a claim for monetary damages. *See Margolis v. U-Haul Int'l, Inc.*, No. 2007-CA005245 B, 2009 D.C. Super. LEXIS 8, at *4, *11, *25 (D.C. Super. Ct. Dec. 17, 2009).

iii. Rule 23(b)(3). Class certification should be granted where there are significant common issues and the alternative would be a large number of individual cases that would strain judicial resources. *Chaney*, 2014 D.C. Super. LEXIS 8, at *15. A class action is also superior where the "typical claims of class members are far too small for the individual class members to maintain individual actions." *Id.* (internal citation omitted). If "the defendant's activities present 'a common course of conduct' so that the issue of statutory liability is common to the class, the fact that damages . . . may vary for each party does not require that the class be terminated as being beyond the scope of Rule 23 (b)(3)." *Ait-Hamadi,* 2017 D.C. Super. LEXIS 1, at *28 (citation omitted). Similarly, even as to questions of liability, "[t]he existence of individual questions that are ministerial in nature or otherwise easy to resolve does not defeat a certification petition." *Id.* Where application of the law will turn on individual factual determinations, however, denial of class certification is appropriate. *Cowan*, 687 A.2d at 602.

c. Rule 23(c)(4)

Rule 23(c)(4)[1] permits the trial court to certify a class only with respect to particular issues. This does not, however, render Rule 23(b)(3)'s predominance requirement irrelevant for certification under Rule 23(c)(4). *See Parkhurst*, 2013 D.C. Super. LEXIS at *37–49. Specifically, a class cannot be certified under Rule 23(c)(4) where severing causation and damages issues for later "mini-trials" would still leave a class with a plethora of individual liability issues and where the proposed class would be so overinclusive that a great many class members would undisputedly have suffered no damages. *See id.* at *16–27, *37–49. The District will generally follow federal law in interpreting its identical statute on this point. *See generally id.* (citing federal case law without distinguishing District of Columbia law throughout opinion).

d. Rule 23(f)

Rule 23(f) authorizes the Court of Appeals to permit an interlocutory appeal from the grant or denial of class action certification only when the trial judge includes a statement in the ruling order endorsing an immediate appeal. *Ford v. ChartOne Inc*., 834 A.2d 875, 879–81 (D.C. 2003). Pursuant to D.C. Code § 11-721(d), the Court of Appeals has discretion to permit an interlocutory appeal only when the trial judge's ruling order certifies that the case involves a controlling question of law, there is substantial ground for a difference of opinion, and an immediate appeal of the ruling or order may materially advance the ultimate termination of the litigation or case. *Id.* The trial judge's certification "is an indispensable precondition" for the Court of Appeals to exercise its discretion to permit an interlocutory appeal. *Id.* at 879.

3. MISCELLANEOUS COMMENTS

a. Burden of Certification

The party seeking certification has the burden of establishing that the cause of action meets all the requirements for certification. *See Levant v. Whitely*, 755 A.2d 1036, 1049 (D.C. 2000) (under Rule 23, the burden of proving adequacy rests on the plaintiff); *Goss,* 462 A.2d at 446. Where the proposed class definition is found to be deficient, the court is not necessarily required to allow plaintiff(s) to redefine the class. *See, e.g., FDS Rest., Inc.,* 2020 D.C. App. LEXIS at *45–46 (trial court did not abuse its discretion when ruling that Plaintiff could not seek certification of a more limited "fallback" alternative class definition because it had waived the argument by failing to raise that possibility in any of its three previous motions to certify a class nor in the three previous lengthy hearings on class certification).

b. Ethical Duties in Mass Representation

Attorneys who represented individuals in an incipient class action do not owe any duty to unnamed members where the class was never certified. *See Taylor v. Akin, Gump, Strauss, Hauer & Feld*, 859 A.2d 142, 149 (D.C. 2004) (citation omitted). Thus, even where a putative plaintiff played an affirmative role in the early stages of litigation, if that plaintiff was unnamed in any resulting suit and not encompassed by a later-certified class, class counsel owed neither a duty of notice to the plaintiff nor any other professional duty to represent that plaintiff's claim. *Id.*

---

[1] This rule was previously codified as Rule 23(c)(4)(A).

c. Types of Relief

Whenever a bona fide (b)(2) class also seeks individual monetary relief, the trial court has discretion to adopt a "hybrid" approach and "certify a (b)(2) class with respect to the claims for declaratory or injunctive relief and a (b)(3) class with respect to the claims for monetary relief." *Ford v. ChartOne Inc.*, 908 A.2d 72, 87 n.15 (D.C. 2006) (citing *Eubanks v. Billington,* 110 F.3d 87, 96 (D.C. Cir. 1997)). This hybrid approach grants class members (b)(3) protections "including the right to opt out . . . at the monetary relief stage." *Id.*

d. Rule 23 and the CPPA

The District of Columbia Consumer Protection Procedures Act (CPPA) allows consumers to bring suit under the statute for unlawful trade practices on behalf of themselves and the general public. Plaintiffs suing in a representative capacity for damages under the CPPA must still satisfy traditional Rule 23 requirements, such as notice and opt-out procedures. *See Rotunda v. Marriott Int'l, Inc.*, 123 A.3d 980, 986 (D.C. 2015). The requirement for CPPA suits to comply with Rule 23 applies to suits for class-wide damages, but not necessarily suits seeking only injunctive relief, individual damages, or punitive damages. *Animal Legal Defense Fund v. Hormel Foods Corp.*, 258 A.3d 174, 190 (D.C. 2021); *see Nat'l Consumers League v. Starbucks Corp.*, No. 24-00421 (AHA), 2025 WL 315141, at *2–3 (D.D.C. Jan. 28, 2025); *Clean Label Project Found. v. Mead Johnson & Co.*, No. 20-cv-3231, 2023 WL 2733723, at *2–4 (D.D.C. Mar. 31, 2023).

Chapter authors Benjamin Brown and Aaron J. Marks are with Cohen, Milstein, Sellers & Toll, P.L.L.C., and work on class actions for plaintiffs in the field of antitrust.

FLORIDA

1. COMPARISON WITH RULE 23 OF THE FEDERAL RULES OF CIVIL PROCEDURE

Florida Rule of Civil Procedure 1.220 governs traditional class actions. The Supreme Court of Florida amended the Rule in 1980 to bring it in line with modern practice and the federal class action rule, Federal Rule of Civil Procedure 23. *In re Rules of Civil Procedure*, 391 So. 2d 165 (Fla. 1980). Florida Rule of Civil Procedure 1.221 governs class actions by or against homeowners' associations and condominium associations relating to certain matters, while Florida Rule of Civil Procedure 1.222 governs class actions by or against mobile homeowners' associations. Both Rule 1.221 and Rule 1.222 expressly provide "An action under this rule shall not be subject to the requirements of rule 1.220."

The most notable difference between Florida Rule of Civil Procedure 1.220 and Federal Rule of Civil Procedure 23 is Florida's specific pleading requirement, as set forth in subsection 1.220(c). Florida requires that the complaint include the designation "Class Representation" in the caption and requires a specific recitation of the various prerequisites to class representation in a separate section titled "Class Representation Allegations." Fla. R. Civ. P. 1.220(c). Rules 1.221 and 1.222 presume that an action brought by or against one of the associations to which they apply that fairly fits within the types of actions specified within them satisfy all of those requirements. Florida courts have held that trial courts have discretion to impose requirements similar to those set forth in Rule 1.220 in proper cases. *E.g., Amber Glades, Inc., v. Leisure Assocs. Ltd. P'ship*, 893 So. 2d 620, 626–27 (Fla. 2d DCA 2005) (Trial court authorized to require notice to members of class and opportunity to opt out in Rule 1.222 case where some members of the class could be adverse to majority of members).

2. CASE LAW INTERPRETING RULE 1.220

A class action complaint must explain the necessity of bringing the action as a class suit; explain the plaintiff's right to represent the class; allege that the plaintiff brought suit on behalf of himself and all others similarly situated; allege the existence of a class, described with some degree of certainty; allege that members of the class are so numerous as to make it impracticable to bring them all before the court; make it clear that the plaintiff adequately represents the class; and show that the interests of the plaintiff are coextensive with the interests of the other members of the class. Fla. R. Civ. P. 1.220(a); *Harrell v. Hess Oil & Chem. Corp.*, 287 So. 2d 291, 293–94 (Fla. 1973).

The plaintiff must plead and prove each element required by Rule 1.220. *Seminole Cty. v. Tivoli Orlando Assocs. Ltd.*, 920 So. 2d 818, 822 (Fla. 5th DCA 2006). The Third District Court of Appeal's ruling in *State Farm Mutual Insurance Co. v. Kendrick*, 822 So. 2d 516, 517–18 (Fla. 3d DCA 2002), provides an example of an appellate court reversing a lower court's order certifying a class due to the plaintiff's failure to meet the requirements imposed by Rule 1.220(a). The appellate court carefully analyzed the record and found that the plaintiff had not proven numerosity, commonality, typicality, and adequacy.

Florida courts must rigorously analyze all requests for class certification and may look beyond the pleadings to "determine how disputed issues might be addressed on a classwide basis." *Earnest v. Amoco Oil Co.*, 859 So. 2d 1255, 1258 (Fla. 1st DCA 2003). *But see Sweeney v. Integon Gen. Ins. Corp.*, 806 So. 2d 605, 606 (Fla. 4th DCA 2002) (reversing the trial court's order dismissing the plaintiff's complaint for failure to state a cause of action, holding that it was error for the lower court to go beyond the four corners of the complaint and conclude that the plaintiff could not possibly establish the truth of his allegations).

"The very purpose of a class suit is to save a multiplicity of suits, to reduce the expense of litigation, to make legal processes more effective and expeditious, and to make available a remedy that would not otherwise exist." *City of Opa-Locka, Fla. v. Suarez*, 314 So. 3d 675, 681 (Fla. 3d DCA 2021) (quoting *Tenney v. City of Miami Beach*, 11 So. 2d 188, 189 (Fla. 1942)).

3. PREREQUISITES TO CLASS REPRESENTATION

Rule 1.220

a. Rule 1.220(a)(1). Numerosity and Impracticability of Joinder

"Numerosity alone does not create the existence of a class." *Paradise Shores Apartments, Inc. v. Practical Maint. Co.*, 344 So. 2d 299, 303 (Fla. 2d DCA 1977). Where a plaintiff brings a class action alleging that persons constituting a class are so numerous as to make it impractical to bring them all before the court, he must do more than merely plead the language of the rule. He must allege facts showing numerosity with a fair degree of certainty. *City of Lakeland v. Chase Nat'l Co.*, 32 So. 2d 833, 838 (Fla. 1947); *see Maner Props. Inc. v. Siksay*, 489 So. 2d 842, 844–45 (Fla. 4th DCA 1986), *abrogated on other grounds by Holiday Pines Prop. Owners Ass'n v. Wetherington*, 557 So. 2d 243 (Fla. 4th DCA 1990) (finding that the plaintiff's evidence of 352 class members satisfied the numerosity requirement and showed that separate joinder would be impractical).

The number of class members is only one factor to consider when determining whether the numerosity requirement is satisfied. "The judgment as to whether a given number is sufficient is not susceptible to hard and fast standards since 'numerosity' is tied to 'impracticability' of joinder under specific circumstances." *Smith v. Glen Cove Apartments Condos. Master Ass'n, Inc.*, 847 So. 2d 1107, 1110 (Fla. 4th DCA 2003) (quoting *Fifth Moorings Condo., Inc. v. Shere*, 81 F.R.D. 712, 715–16 (S.D. Fla. 1979)).

In *Canal Insurance Co. v. Gibraltar Budget Plan, Inc.*, 41 So. 3d 375, 377–78 (Fla. 4th DCA 2010), the Fourth District Court of Appeal denied certification on numerosity grounds, finding that the plaintiffs failed to provide sufficient proof supporting its allegation of 169 potential class members.

Where the plaintiff alleges a main class and one or more subclasses, the plaintiff must allege and prove that each subclass is, standing alone, sufficiently numerous to warrant certification. "The establishment of numerosity as to the primary or main class is not necessarily sufficient to establish numerosity with respect to the subclass." *Hartwood Reserve Homeowners Ass'n, Inc. v. Allen*, 207 So. 3d 997, 999–1000 (Fla. 5th DCA 2016).

In cases involving fewer than 50 members, courts must consider additional factors, including "1) [the] judicial economy arising from avoiding multiple actions; 2) the geographic dispersion of members of the proposed class; 3) the financial resources of those members; 4) the ability of the members to file individual suits[;] and 5) requests for prospective relief that may have an effect on future class members." *Braun v. Campbell*, 827 So. 2d 261, 266 (Fla. 5th DCA 2002) (citing *Ansari v. N.Y. Univ.*, 179 F.R.D. 112, 114–15 (S.D.N.Y. 1998)).

Even a moderately large proposed class which appears to be adequately defined and clearly ascertainable will fail if it is overbroad. *Leibell v. Miami-Dade County*, 84 So. 3d 1078, 1083 (Fla. 3d DCA 2012). In *Leibell*, Florida's Third District Court of Appeal upheld the trial court's denial of class certification where, out of the proposed class of 1400 members, there was only evidence that one had protested the program fee at issue, and the evidence showed that many more of the proposed class members did not wish to seek the remedies sought by the one protesting member in her lawsuit.

To be numerous, the proposed class must include members who suffered injury or actual damage. *See Lucarelli Pizza & Deli v. Posen Constr., Inc.*, 173 So. 3d 1092, 1094 (Fla. 2d DCA 2015).

b. Rule 1.220(a)(2). Commonality

A plaintiff may maintain a class action suit where the subject of the action presents questions of common or general interest and all class members have a similar interest in obtaining the relief sought or the question involved. *Colonial Penn Ins. Co. v. Magnetic Imaging Sys. I, Ltd.*, 694 So. 2d 852, 853 (Fla. 3d DCA 1997); *see also Arvida/JMB Partners v. Council of Vills., Inc.*, 733 So. 2d 1026, 1030 (Fla. 4th DCA 1998). Class members must have some right of recovery based on the same essential facts. Plaintiffs may plead claims that arose out of the same actions by the defendant but within different factual contexts as a class action if they present questions of common interest.

"The primary concern in the consideration of commonality is whether the representative's claim arises from the same practice of course of conduct that gave rise to the remaining claims and whether the claims are based on the same legal theory." *Sosa v. Safeway Premium Fin. Co.*, 73 So. 3d 91, 107 (Fla. 2011). "The threshold of the commonality requirement is not high. A mere factual difference between class members does not necessarily preclude satisfaction of the commonality requirement. Individualized damage inquiries will also not preclude class certification. . . . More specifically the commonality prong only requires that resolution of a class action affect all or a substantial number of the class members, and that the subject of the class action presents a question of *common or general interest*. Furthermore, the commonality requirement is satisfied if the common or general interest of the class members is the object of the action, the result sought, or the general question implicated in the action. This core of the commonality requirement is satisfied if the questions linking the class members are substantially related to the resolution of the litigation, even if the individuals are not identically situated." *Id.* (emphasis in original; citations omitted)

Florida's Third District Court of Appeal has held that class action claims that are based on widely divergent facts and present "a multitude of varied claims" under various contracts or agreements such as insurance policies are unsuitable for class treatment. *Kendrick*, 822 So. 2d at 516.

But in *Shoma Development Corp. v. Vazquez*, 749 So. 2d 1287, 1288–89 (Fla. 3d DCA 2000), the court upheld certification of a class based upon breach of contract claims. The court observed that while it could not certify fraud claims, all class members signed a similar form of contract with the home builder making class treatment appropriate.

Florida's Second District Court of Appeal held that one of three classes certified in a complex antitrust case contained conflicts of interest. The class included both sellers and purchasers of replacement parts. Because the court found that the conduct challenged in the lawsuit benefited class members who sell replacement parts and harmed those who buy replacement parts, those who benefited from the alleged conduct could not adequately represent the interests of those harmed by the same conduct. Therefore, the court reversed a finding of class certification and remanded to the trial court to give the plaintiffs an opportunity to reformulate the class definitions. *Océ Printing Sys. USA, Inc. v. Mailers Data Servs., Inc.*, 760 So. 2d 1037 (Fla. 2d DCA 2000).

In *Ortiz v. Ford Motor Co.*, 909 So. 2d 479, 481 (Fla. 3d DCA 2005), the class representative pursued an unjust enrichment claim against Ford, alleging that he overpaid for his Ford Explorer due to Ford's concealment of a design defect that allegedly caused those vehicles to roll over. The court found no commonality. Although common factual issues existed, the claims required an individualized determination of whether each class member received a warning about rollovers, and if so, how they interpreted that warning and how that may have impacted the purchase price.

Similarly in *Brown-Peterkin v. Williamson*, 307 So. 3d 45, 51 (Fla. 4th DCA 2020), the court affirmed the denial of certification after a commonality analysis, where the insurer defendant's sales procedures changed over time and affected class members differently depending upon when they purchased their policy.

The Fourth District Court of Appeal recognized commonality in *Olen Properties Corp. v. Moss*, 981 So. 2d 515, 520 (Fla. 4th DCA 2008). A former tenant brought a class action against her landlord after the landlord charged an early cancellation fee equal to one month's rent. The tenant argued that the landlord had not taken into account the re-renting of the unit, resulting in greater damages to early cancellation renters than the landlord actually sustained. The tenant also argued that the landlord improperly charged liquidated damages rather than actual damages. After the trial court certified the class, the landlord appealed, arguing that because different fees were charged for different renters based on their particular circumstances, no commonality existed. The Fourth District Court of Appeal disagreed, holding that "the issue is not whether the . . . fees were the same, but whether or not [the landlord's] practice of charging liquidated damages rather than actual damages violated Florida law or whether [the landlord was] required to credit tenants' accounts with rent it received from reletting the premises."

The Second District Court of Appeal also recognized commonality in *Morgan v. Coats*, 33 So. 3d 59, 64–65 (Fla. 2d DCA 2010), where detention guards brought a class action against the sheriff for uncompensated half-hour meal breaks. The guards were required to remain on call at the jail and were usually interrupted during meal breaks to handle disturbances. The trial court denied certification holding, among other reasons, that each guard's claim was based on different factual circumstances and would require unique proof. The Second District Court of Appeal disagreed, holding that the "sheriff engaged in a similar course of conduct with all detention deputies . . . [namely the] failure to pay the . . . deputies for their meal periods . . ." The court reasoned that a single scheme harmed the entire class in a common way and the only variance between class members dealt with individualized damages to each class member which, alone, cannot preclude class certification.

At the class certification stage, courts may "consider the application of defenses in analyzing the commonality element." *Easter v. City of Orlando*, __ So. 3d __ (Fla. 5th DCA 2018).

c. Rule 1.220(a)(3). Typicality

"Typicality 'compels an examination of the relationship of the class representative's claim to the claims of the class members.'" *Seminole County*, 920 So. 2d at 822.

"The test for typicality is not demanding and focuses generally on the similarities between the class representative and the putative class members. Mere factual differences between the class representative's claims and the claims of the class members will not defeat typicality. Rather, the typicality requirement is satisfied when there is a strong similarity in the legal theories upon which those claims are based and when the claims of the class representative and class members are not antagonistic to one another." *Sosa*, 73 So. 3d at 114–15 (citations omitted).

"Typicality is defeated if the defendant has a unique defense to the class representative's claim." *Brown-Peterkin v. Williamson*, 307 So. 3d 45, 51 (Fla. 4th DCA 2020).

In *Atlanta Casualty Co. v. Open MRI of Pinellas, Inc.*, 911 So. 2d 135, 138 (Fla. 2d DCA 2005), the court reversed class certification where the purported class representative's claims were not typical of the other class members.

"A difference in the extent of damages [between class members] does not preclude a finding of typicality." *CVE Master Mgmt. Co. v. Ventnor B Condo. Ass'n, Inc.*, 140 So. 3d 1074, 1079 (Fla. 4th DCA 2014).

In *Wyeth, Inc. v. Gottlieb*, 930 So. 2d 635, 643 (Fla. 3d DCA 2006), the Third District Court of Appeal held that the class representative's claims were not typical where factual differences among the class members' claims and the defenses that defendant could assert varied depending on each plaintiff's individual circumstances and conditions. Similarly, in *Miami Automotive Retail, Inc. v. Baldwin*, 97 So. 3d 846, 853–54 (Fla. 3d DCA 2012), the Third District Court of Appeal reversed class certification where the defendant had unique defenses to the class representative's claim that would "preoccupy the named plaintiff to the detriment of the interest of absent class members."

In *Baptist Hospital, Inc. v. Baker*, 84 So. 3d 1200, 1205 (Fla. 1st DCA 2012), the First District Court of Appeal held that the class representative's claims were not typical where the class included members who could bring additional claims based on injuries not suffered by the class representative. The fact that the class representative's damages might vary in amount from those of the other class members does not necessarily defeat typicality on its own; "the 'key inquiry' on typicality is 'whether the class representative is part of the class and possesses the same interest and suffers the same injury as the class members.'" *Id.* (quoting *Sosa*, 73 So. 3d at 114).

In *Olen Properties Corp.*, 981 So. 2d at 520, the Fourth District Court of Appeal held that the plaintiffs' claims were typical. The defendant landlord argued that the factual reasons for charging liquidated damages to each member the class (a group of former renters) differed for each class member. The Fourth District Court of Appeal held that the renters' claims nevertheless were typical, holding that "the mere presence of factual differences will not defeat typicality" (citing *Broin v. Phillip Morris Cos.*, 641 So. 2d 888, 892 (Fla. 3d DCA 1994)).

The Second District Court of Appeal also found typicality in *Morgan*, 33 So. 3d at 65–66, where detention deputy guards brought a class action against the sheriff for uncompensated half-hour meal breaks. The Second District Court of Appeal overturned the trial court's denial of certification, finding that typicality was met because the class representative "possessed the same interest and had suffered the same type of injury as the rest of the class members." The court also dismissed any argument that variance in the severity of each class members' injury would bar a finding of typicality among the class.

d. Rule 1.220(a)(4). Adequacy of Representation

"A trial court's inquiry concerning whether the adequacy requirement is satisfied contains two prongs. The first prong concerns the qualifications, experience, and ability of class counsel to conduct the litigation. The second prong pertains to whether the class representative's interests are antagonistic to the interests of the class members." *Sosa*, 73 So. 3d at 115.

The named representatives meet the adequacy of representation requirement if they have interests in common with the proposed class members and show that they will properly prosecute the case. *Colonial Penn Ins. Co.*, 694 So. 2d at 852.

Plaintiffs must introduce some evidence of class counsel's prior class action litigation experience and ability to absorb the costs of such litigation. *CVE Master Mgmt. Co.*, 140 So. 3d at 1079–80.

The adequacy of class representation presents a fact issue within the trial court's discretion. The appellate courts will not disturb the trial court's determination of the named plaintiffs' qualifications to adequately represent a class, absent a clear showing of abuse of discretion. *McFadden v. Staley*, 687 So. 2d 357, 359 (Fla. 4th DCA 1997).

"Satisfaction of the commonality and typicality requirements provides 'strong evidence that the named plaintiffs adequately represent the class." *Discount Sleep of Ocala, LLC v. City of Ocala*, 245 So. 3d 842, 853 (Fla. 5th DCA 2018). Although it is expected that representatives maintain a "minimal level of interest in the action," a representative is not required to attend or testify at an evidentiary hearing on class issues. *See id.* at 854 n.4.

In line with its previous opinion in *Taran v. Blue Cross Blue Shield of Florida, Inc.*, 685 So. 2d 1004 (Fla. 3d DCA 1997), the Third District Court of Appeal upheld a lower court's granting of summary judgment in favor of a class action defendant because the purported class representative suffered no damages. *Ramon v. Aries Ins. Co.*, 769 So. 2d 1053 (Fla. 3d DCA 2000). The insurance company already repaid the money that the plaintiff claimed to have lost prior to class certification. *See also Neighborhood Health P'Ship, Inc. v. Fischer*, 913 So. 2d 703, 705–06 (Fla. 3d DCA 2005) (holding that class representative had no standing in breach of contract action where he had no claim for damages).

The *Ramon* case contains some interesting language from the court discussing the requirements that a proposed class representative must meet to qualify as "adequate." The court cites portions of the plaintiff's deposition transcript stating that he had no knowledge of any others similarly situated and that he personally conducted no investigation. The court suggested that a plaintiff should do more before a court considers class certification. Otherwise, "'certification of a large class may so increase the defendant's potential damages liability and litigation costs that he may find it economically prudent to settle and to abandon a meritorious defense.' For this reason, 'class actions create the opportunity for a kind of legalized blackmail.'" *Id.* at 1056 (citations omitted).

On the other hand, in *Allstate Indemnity Co. v. De La Rosa*, 800 So. 2d 245, 246 (Fla. 3d DCA 2001), the Third District Court of Appeal confirmed the general principle that a defendant may not attempt to "pick off" potential class action representatives by paying their claims in full. However, the determination of whether the defendant has attempted to do so remains within the trial court's discretion.

In *Graham v. State Farm Fire and Casualty Co.*, 813 So. 2d 273, 274 (Fla. 5th DCA 2002), the Fifth District Court of Appeal held that the plaintiff policyholders had no standing to assert class action claims against the insurer, which paid off their claims with interest two years prior to the filing of the class action. The opinion clarified that courts will look to the time of class certification as the point for considering whether a defendant is attempting to "pick off" a potential class action litigant.

In *Marco Island Civic Ass'n v. Mazzini*, 805 So. 2d 928 (Fla. 2d DCA 2001), a doctor brought a class action seeking a declaratory judgment naming a particular resident as the representative of a class of resident defendants. In examining class certification, the appellate court held that where a potential defendant class representative has no legal representation, that purported class representative is not adequate for purposes of Rule 1.220(a). The appellate court also held that the trial court erred as a matter of law in determining that class representation by a pro se defendant is superior to other available methods for adjudicating the issue presented.

In *Wyeth, Inc.*, 930 So. 2d at 639–43, the court examined the merits (or lack thereof) of the class representative's underlying claim and found that she was not an adequate class representative.

In *Grosso v. Fidelity National Title Insurance Co.*, 983 So. 2d 1165, 1173 (Fla. 3d DCA 2008), the Third District Court of Appeal reversed an order granting class certification and approving a class settlement, and remanded the case to the trial court with instructions to determine whether the class representative's incentive to settle was influenced by her own personal gain. The class representative stood to receive approximately 100 times more than the individual class members in the settlement.

City of Tampa v. Addison, 979 So. 2d 246, 253–56 (Fla. 2d DCA 2007), involved the certification of a *defendant* class. A group of attorneys challenged the constitutionality of the City of Tampa's occupational license tax. The attorneys moved for the certification of a plaintiff's class and a class of defendant municipalities and counties that levied a similar tax. The trial court granted the certification of both classes. On appeal, the City challenged the certification of the defendant class, arguing that the plaintiffs failed to prove that the City's attorneys could adequately represent the other members of the defendant class. The Second District Court of Appeal applied heightened scrutiny to the certification of the defendant class, but nonetheless held that the plaintiffs had met their burden of proving that the City's attorneys could adequately represent the other defendant municipalities and counties.

In *Miami Automotive Retail, Inc. v. Baldwin*, 97 So. 3d 846, 854–55 (Fla. 3d DCA 2012), the Third District Court of Appeal reversed the certification of a class on adequacy grounds. The class representative's husband had previously been disqualified as class counsel after counsel's two former law firms asserted charging liens for costs associated with the case, and where counsel had been sanctioned for communicating with potential class members. Moreover, the representative failed to offer any evidence that she could pay outstanding costs.

Rule 1.221

e. Limits on Class Actions by or against Condominium Associations

Rule 1.221 provides in pertinent part:

> A homeowners' or condominium association, after control of such association is obtained by homeowners or unit owners other than the developer, may institute, maintain, settle, or appeal actions or hearings in its name on behalf of all association members concerning matters of common interest to the members, including, but not limited to: (1) the common property, area, or elements; (2) the roof or structural components of a building, or other improvements (in the case of homeowners' associations, being specifically limited to those improvements for which the association is responsible); (3) mechanical, electrical, or plumbing elements serving a property or an improvement or building (in the case of homeowners' associations, being specifically limited to those elements for which the association is responsible); (4) representations of the developer pertaining to any existing or proposed commonly used facility; (5) protests of ad valorem taxes on commonly used facilities; and, in the case of homeowners' associations; (6) defense of actions in eminent domain or prosecution of inverse condemnation actions. If an association has the authority to maintain a class action under this rule, the association may be joined in an action as representative of that class with reference to litigation and disputes involving the matters for which the association could bring a class action under this rule. Nothing herein limits any statutory or common law right of any individual homeowner or unit owner, or class of such owners, to bring any action that may otherwise be available.

This language, based upon statutory language, Chs. 718, 720, Fla. Stat., relating to the powers of condominium associations and homeowners' associations, authorizes such association, after the developer of the project has turned over control, to bring or defend a class action on behalf of all of the homeowners or unit owners other than the developer for any "matter of common interest to the members," including but not limited to the 6 enumerated types of claims. *Four Jay's Constr., Inc., v. Marina at the Bluffs Condo. Ass'n*, 846 So. 2d 555, 558 (Fla. 4th DCA 2003); *Kesl, Inc. v. Racquet Club of Deer Creek II Condo., Inc.*, 574 So.2d 251, 253 (Fla. 4th DCA 1991); *Juno by the Sea Condo. Apts., Inc. v. Juno by the Sea N. Condo. Ass'n,* 418 So.2d 1190, 1191 (Fla. 4th DCA 1982).

As noted, *supra* at 1, class actions under this rule are not subject to any of the requirements of Rule 1.220. An evidentiary hearing is not required. *See Biza Corp. v. Galway Bay Mobile Homeowners Ass'n, Inc.*, 304 So. 3d 1227, 1232 (Fla. 3d DCA 2019). Indeed, Rule 1.221 was promulgated, in large part, to overcome the difficulties created by Rule 1.220. *Eberwein v. Coral Pine Condo. I*, 431 So. 2d 616, 617–18 (Fla. 4th DCA 1983).

Rule 1.222

f. Limits on Class Actions by or against Mobile Homeowners' Associations

Rule 1.222 provides in pertinent part:

> A mobile homeowners' association may institute, maintain, settle, or appeal actions or hearings in its name on behalf of all homeowners concerning matters of common interest, including, but not limited to: the common property; structural components of a building or other improvements; mechanical, electrical, and plumbing elements serving the park property; and protests of ad valorem taxes on commonly used facilities. If the association has the authority to maintain a class action under this rule, the association may be joined in an action as representative of that class with reference to litigation and disputes involving the matters for which the association could bring a class action under this rule. Nothing herein limits any statutory or common law right of any individual homeowner or class of homeowners to bring any action which may otherwise be available.

This language, based upon statutory language, Ch. 723, Fla. Stat., relating to the powers of mobile homeowners' associations, authorizes such association to bring or defend a class action on behalf of all of the mobile homeowners other than the mobile home park owner for any "matter of common interest to the members," including but not limited to the 6 enumerated types of claims. *Lanca Homeowners, Inc., v. Lantana Cascade of Palm Beach, Ltd.*, 541 So. 2d 1121, 1123 (Fla. 1988); *Amber Glades, Inc., v. Leisure Assocs. Ltd. P'ship, supra.*

As noted *supra* in Section 3(e), class actions under this rule are not subject to any of the requirements of Rule 1.220.

4. RULE 1.220(B)—CLAIMS AND DEFENSES MAINTAINABLE

a. Prerequisites under Rule 1.220(b)(1)

In *Océ Printing Systems*, 760 So. 2d at 1043, the Second District Court of Appeal affirmed the trial court's certification pursuant to Rule 1.220(b)(1)(A) based on the threat of inconsistent adjudications of individual plaintiffs' claims. The court held that the Rule does not require a finding that inconsistent adjudications actually occurred, only that they could occur.

In *Cheatwood v. Barry University, Inc.*, 2001 WL 1769914, at *12–13 (Fla. Cir. Ct. Dec. 26, 2001), a Florida circuit court held that class certification based on Rule 1.220(b)(1)(A), which applies where inconsistent or varying adjudications would lead to incompatible standards of conduct for the party opposing the class, is appropriate "only under narrowly limited circumstances." (quoting *Hall v. Burger King Corp.*, 1992 WL 372354, at *10 (S.D. Fla. 1992)). The Rule "applies only where 'a party is obliged by law to treat the members of a class alike (a utility acting toward customers; a government imposing tax), or where the party must treat all alike as a practical necessity (a riparian owner using water as against downriver owners)." *Id.* at *12 (citing *Georgine v. AmChem Prods., Inc.*, 521 U.S. 591, 614 (1997)). The circuit court also declined to certify a class based on Rule 1.220(b)(1)(B), which applies where "adjudications concerning individual members of the class which would, as a practical matter, be dispositive of the interests of other members of the class who are not parties to the adjudication to protect their interests," because plaintiffs failed to provide any support for such a contention. *Id.* at *13. Rule 1.220(b)(1)(B) typically applies only in limited funds cases. *Id.* (citing *AmChem*, 521 U.S. at 614). Note that although *Cheatwood* is instructive, as a trial court opinion has no binding affect outside of the circuit from which it came.

b. Rule 1.220(b)(2). Injunctive or Declaratory Relief

Under Rule 1.220(b)(2) and its federal analog, declaratory or injunctive relief must be the predominant remedy requested for the class. *Freedom Life Ins. Co. v. Wallant*, 891 So. 2d 1109, 1117–18 (Fla. 4th DCA 2004); *see also Powers v. Gov't Emp. Ins. Co.*, 192 F.R.D. 313, 318 (S.D. Fla. 1998).

In *Océ Printing Systems*, 760 So. 2d at 1037, the Second District Court of Appeal upheld class certification of claims seeking solely injunctive relief. The complaint in question contained six counts, only one of which sought to permanently enjoin the defendants from engaging in anticompetitive conduct. The court observed that certification was proper because the plaintiffs sought actual injunctive relief rather than monetary damages through an injunction to disgorge profits. *Id.*

In *Ferreiro v. Phila. Indem. Ins. Co.*, 928 So. 2d 374, 377 (Fla. 3d DCA 2006), the plaintiff previously had received a declaratory judgment in her favor holding that the defendant insurance company was required to inform her that uninsured motorist coverage was available. She then sought certification on behalf of a class. The trial court held that given the previous judgment in her favor, she had no standing to represent the class. The Third District Court of Appeal reversed, finding that because a final judgment had not been rendered on the plaintiff's claims for damages or the insurance company's liability, her individual claims remained pending and gave her standing to represent a class.

Monetary relief may be sought in the context of Rule 1.220(b)(2) provided that monetary relief is incidental to the injunctive or declaratory relief sought. *See Discount Sleep of Ocala, LLC*, 245 So. 3d at 855.

Where plaintiffs pursue claims for injunctive relief under 1.220(b)(2) while pursuing separate claims for monetary damages under Rule 1.220(b)(3), the latter claims do not require an inquiry into whether monetary relief is incidental to the separate injunctive or declaratory relief. *See Gundel v. AV Homes, Inc.*, 290 So. 3d 1080, 1087 (Fla. 2d DCA 2020).

c. Rule 1.220(b)(3). Predominance

Rule 1.220(b)(3)'s "predominance" inquiry tests whether the proposed class is sufficiently cohesive to warrant adjudication by class representation. *Chase Manhattan Mortg. Corp. v. Porcher*, 898 So. 2d 153, 157 (Fla. 4th DCA 2005) (reversing certification where individualized question of whether each borrower sent payment within the grace period would predominate).

To establish predominance, the plaintiff must provide some basis in fact to show class injury or establish that common questions of law or fact common to the class predominate over questions of law or fact affecting only some individual class members. *Earnest*, 859 So. 2d at 1260 (holding that predominance not met where expert testimony was admittedly speculative).

Common questions must not only exist, they must "predominate and pervade." *Sosa*, 73 So. 3d at 111.

The predominance requirement requires a "proof-based inquiry." *Mosaic Fertilizer, LLC v. Curd*, 259 So. 3d 239, 244 (Fla. 2d DCA 2018). "A proponent of certification must demonstrate a 'reasonable methodology for generalized proof of class-wide impact' whereby 'proving his or her individual case . . . necessarily proves the cases of the other class members.'" *Id.* (quoting *Sosa*, 73 So. 3d at 112).

Courts may consider merits-based evidence if relevant to the issue of whether to certify a class. *Ocean Harbor Cas. Ins. v. MSPA Claims, 1*, 261 So. 3d 637, 641 (Fla. 3d DCA 2018); *see also Angelo v. Parker*, 275 So. 3d 752, 755 (Fla. 1st DCA 2019) ("Rule 1.220 requires the court to consider the law applicable to the claims and the substance of the claims before ruling on a motion to certify a class.").

"Predominance exists where common questions can be answered by the use of computerized software systems." *Velez*, 2023 WL 2589411 at *5.

Logistical and analytical difficulties in calculating individual class members' damages do not necessarily predominate over common issues. *City of Opa-Locka, Fla. v. Suarez*, 314 So. 3d 675, 680–81 (Fla. 3d DCA 2021) ("The focus of a class certification hearing is not on the merits of the claims, or whether the class representatives will prevail at trial, but 'whether a litigant's claim is suited for class certification' and whether the proposed class provides 'a superior method for the fair and efficient adjudication of the controversy.'" (quoting *Sosa*, 73 So. 3d at 105–06)).

In *Commonwealth Land Title Ins. Co. v. Higgins*, 58 So. 3d 280, 283 (Fla. 1st DCA 2011), the First District Court of Appeal affirmed the certification of a class despite the fact that plaintiffs did not present conclusive evidence of predominance at the class merits stage. The court held that it may be enough for plaintiffs to present a theory that, if correct, would result in common issues predominating. If that theory later proves incorrect, then the trial court can always modify or decertify the class.

In *Stone v. Compuserve Interactive Servs.*, 804 So. 2d 383, 388–89 (Fla. 4th DCA 2001), the Fourth District Court of Appeal affirmed the denial of class certification where integral questions of law and fact differed for various members of the putative class.

In *Bouchard Transportation Co. v. Updegraff*, 807 So. 2d 768 (Fla. 2d DCA 2002), the appellate court addressed three separate certified classes that related to an oil spill off the Florida coast. Classes were composed of businesses, residents, and nonresident tourists. In examining the requirements of Rule 1.220(b), the court found that individual questions of law predominated over common questions. This case illustrates the importance of carefully defining a class to avoid potential conflicts and individualized issues.

In *Engle v. Liggett Group, Inc.*, 945 So. 2d 1246, 1267–71 (Fla. 2006), the Supreme Court of Florida affirmed the district court's finding that individualized issues such as causation, comparative fault and damages predominated in plaintiffs' class action against tobacco companies. Although it decertified the class, the Supreme Court let certain factual findings not related to such individualized issues stand, holding that class members could incorporate these findings into individual damages actions.

In *Morgan*, 33 So. 3d at 65–66, the Second District Court of Appeal found predominance where detention deputy guards brought a class action against the sheriff for uncompensated half-hour meal breaks. The Second District Court of Appeal held that predominance was met because each claim was based on the same legal theory and alleged misconduct. Therefore, if the class representative could prove his claim each of the class members' claims would also be proven thereby satisfying the predominance prong.

The Second District Court of Appeal affirmed the denial of class certification in *Hess Corp. v. Grillasca,* 27 So. 3d 684, 686–89 (Fla. 2d DCA 2009), where a purported class action was brought against Hess for placing holds on customers' bank accounts when the customers purchased gasoline with their debit cards. The court found that each class member was affected in unique ways by the alleged harm such as the length and amount of their holds, whether the customer was notified of the potential hold on their accounts and whether they had sustained any damages from the hold. Moreover, the Second District Court of Appeal held that the class action trial would have devolved into multiple mini-trials addressing the differences in claims.

The Third District Court of Appeal reversed the certification of a class on predominance grounds in *Miami Automotive Retail, Inc.*, 97 So. 3d at 855–59, where the class representative's claim of deceptive and unfair trade practices was based on specific oral representations and negotiations she had with the car dealer defendant. To satisfy the predominance requirement, the plaintiff would have had "to allege that similar representations she claims were made to her were also made to the other class members." "Where the facts necessary to determine liability are based upon the defendant's interactions with specific plaintiffs, individual issues predominate over class-wide proof."

The Third District Court of Appeal also reversed the certification of a class on predominance grounds in *Alderwoods Group, Inc. v. Garcia*, 119 So. 3d 497 (Fla. 3d DCA 2013). The court held that plaintiffs' claims for intentional infliction of emotional distress, gross negligence, and tortious interference required "highly individualized proof" and therefore were not amenable to class treatment.

In the deceptive and unfair trade practices context, predominance cannot be shown where "the individual knowledge and experience of the consumer is an important element of the cause of action and its defense, [because] there can be no class-wide proof that injury was not reasonably avoidable." *Porsche Cars N. Am., Inc. v. Diamond*, 140 So. 3d 1090, 1099 (Fla. 3d DCA 2014).

"[T]he existence of affirmative defenses does not undermine the predominance of the common issues." *Concert Plantation, LLC v. Dorso*, 352 So. 3d 914, 917 (Fla. 2d DCA2022) (citing *Tyson Foods, Inc. v. Bouaphakeo*, 577 U.S. 442, 453–54 (2016)).

d. Rule 1.220(b)(3). Superiority

A class action must be superior to other potential methods for a fair and efficient adjudication of the issues. *Ortiz*, 909 So. 2d at 481.

"Three factors for courts to consider when deciding whether a class action is the superior method of adjudicating a controversy are (1) whether a class action would provide the class members with the only economically viable remedy; (2) whether there is a likelihood that the individual claims are large enough to justify the expense of separate litigation; and (3) whether a class action cause of action is manageable." *Sosa*, 73 So. 3d at 116.

"To find superiority, a court must find all other methods of resolving the issues in a case to be inferior to a class action." *Discount Sleep of Ocala, LLC*, 245 So. 3d at 856.

The plaintiffs satisfied the superiority requirement of Rule 1.220(b)(3) in an action brought against a developer based on the developer's alleged fraud in bringing quiet title actions against class members who had purchased lots from the developer. *Est. of Bobinger v. Deltona Corp.*, 563 So. 2d 739, 746 (Fla. 2d DCA 1990). *But see Volkswagen of Am., Inc. v. Sugarman*, 909 So. 2d 923, 924 (Fla. 3d DCA 2005) (finding that a class action was not superior to individual suits given the need to litigate substantially different factual issues).

Tobacco class actions involve "uniquely individualized" claims that cannot satisfy the predominance and superiority requirements of Florida's class action rules. *Liggett Grp., Inc. v. Engle*, 853 So. 2d 434, 444 (Fla. 3d DCA 2003) (decertifying the class and reversing the largest punitive damages verdict in American history), *approved in part, quashed in part and remanded, Engle v. Liggett Grp., Inc.*, 945 So. 2d 1246 (Fla. 2006).

In *Morgan*, 33 So. 3d at 65–66, the Second District Court of Appeal found superiority where detention deputy guards brought a class action against the sheriff for uncompensated half-hour meal breaks. The trial court denied certification holding that, among other reasons, the class representative failed the superiority test as "individualized inquiries would be necessary for each claim and that 'any realization of judicial economy as proposed by [the class representative] would come at the expense of the due process right of [the sheriff].'" The Second District Court of Appeal overturned, holding that superiority was present as individualized litigation expenses would not be justified because there were approximately 1,000 potential class members each seeking compensation for small amounts of uncompensated time stemming from one common misconduct. The court further reasoned that class certification would not only save litigation expenses but would also conserve judicial resources.

e. Rule 1.220(b)(3). Manageability

A court must consider any difficulties likely to be encountered in the management of the claim on behalf of the class. The courts will not certify broad classes containing numerous members from many different states, especially if the class threatens to overwhelm the court's resources. *R.J. Reynolds Tobacco Co. v. Engle*, 672 So. 2d 39, 41–42 (Fla. 3d DCA 1996). Instead, the proposed class will be reduced to manageable proportions.

f. Rule 1.220(b)(3). Ascertainability

Class members must be identifiable through a "manageable process that does not require much, if any, individual inquiry." *BJ's Wholesale Club, Inc. v. Bugliaro*, 273 So. 3d 1119, 1122 (Fla. 3d DCA 2019) (quoting *Karhu v. Vital Pharms., Inc.*, 621 Fed App'x 945, 946 (11th Cir. 2015)).

5. RULE 1.220(C)—PLEADING REQUIREMENTS

Every pleading alleging the existence of a class must include a specific recitation of facts addressing each of the requirements of Rule 1.220(c). *Seminole*, 920 So. 2d at 822 (holding that the plaintiff's allegations failed to meet the standard set forth in Rule 1.220(c)); *Dade Cnty. Police Benevolent Ass'n, Inc. v. Metro. Dade County*, 452 So. 2d 6, 9 (Fla. 3d DCA 1984) (same).

"[W]here a complaint states a cause of action but is not maintainable as a class action, the portions of the complaint relating to the class action should be stricken." *Fla. Dep't of Transp. v. Tropical Trailer Leasing, LLC*, 308 S. 3d 242, 248 (Fla. 1st DCA 2020).

6. RULE 1.220(D)—DETERMINATION OF CLASS REPRESENTATION; NOTICE; JUDGMENT; CLAIM OR DEFENSE MAINTAINED PARTLY ON BEHALF OF CLASS

a. Rule 1.220(d)(1). Requirements of Order Granting or Denying Class Certification

In *Sosa*, 73 So. 3d at 117–18, the Supreme Court of Florida held that the trial court "render an order on class certification as soon as practicable, with that order separately detailing the trial court's factual findings and conclusions of law, and, if proceeding with a class, specifically designating the applicable section of rule 1.220."

A trial court's order granting or denying class certification should be remanded if devoid of the specific factual or legal findings required by Rule 1.220(d)(1). *See Seminole*, 920 So. 2d at 824.

An order granting certification must include a claim-by-claim analysis, but unlike federal law, an order denying certification does not. *See Bawtinhimer v. D.R. Horton, Inc.*, 161 So. 3d 539, 540 (Fla. 5th DCA 2014).

b. Rule 1.220(d)(1). Reconsideration of Certification

Under Rule 1.220(d)(1), a trial court can reconsider the prior certification of a class if subsequent developments alter the previous certification ruling. *Heikes v. Republic Ins. Co.*, 866 So. 2d 97, 99 (Fla. 4th DCA 2004). However, the Rule was not designed to allow an appellate court to decertify a class contrary to its previous affirmance of class certification. *See Engle*, 945 So. 2d at 1266.

Rule 1.220(d)(1) requires that an order granting or denying certification "state under which subdivision of [Rule 1.220(b)] the claim or defense is to be maintained." In *Tampa Service Co. v. Hartigan*, 966 So. 2d 465, 466 (Fla. 4th DCA 2007), the Fourth District Court of Appeal held that although the trial court's certification order did not specifically name the subsections under which the class was maintainable, the order complied with Rule 1.220(d) because its language adequately tracked the language of the subsections relied upon.

"Under Florida Rule of Civil Procedure Rule 1.220(d)(1), a class-certification order may be altered or amended at any time before entry of a judgment on the merits." *Liggett Grp., Inc.*, 853 So. 2d at 442; *see also Canal Ins. Co.*, 41 So. 3d at 377 (holding that trial courts may redefine a proposed class to allow utilization of class action mechanism).

c. Rule 1.220(d)(1). Time for Seeking Class Certification

Under Rule 1.220(d)(1), plaintiff must seek a determination of class certification "as soon as practicable after service of any pleading alleging the existence of a class under this rule." In *Osborne v. Emmer,* 184 So. 3d 637, 639 (Fla. 4th DCA 2016), the Fourth DCA affirmed the dismissal of a class action in which plaintiff had failed to move for certification after five years.

d. Rule 1.220(d)(2). Notice Requirement

Rule 1.220(d)(2) states that the party asserting a class's existence generally pays the initial costs of providing notice. However, the courts have broad discretion to impose those costs on the defending party where doing so "provides the most economically viable means of assuring efficient and cost-effective notification." *Fla. Dep't of Agric. & Consumer Servs. v. Cox*, 947 So. 2d 561, 563 (Fla. 4th DCA 2006) (quoting *Sears, Roebuck and Co. v. Labora*, 670 So. 2d 1025, 1026 (Fla. 3d DCA 1996)).

In *Combined Servs., Inc. v. City of Opa-Locka,* 394 So. 3d 98 (Fla. 3d DCA 2024), the appellate court affirmed the trial court's rejection of a late opt-out request where the class notice was mailed to more than 12,000 class members and posted to a public website, thereby satisfying Florida Rule of Civil Procedure 1.220(d)(2).

e. Rule 1.220(d)(4). Particularized Issues and Subclasses

Rule 1.220(d)(4)(A) states that class claims may be maintained as to particular issues and may be divided into subclasses. Citing Rule 1.220(d)(4)(A) and its Federal analog, the Supreme Court of Florida separated liability and damages phases of a tobacco class action, and "certifi[ed] treatment of liability while leaving damages to be determined on an individual basis." *Engle*, 945 So. 2d at 1268; *see also Philip Morris USA, Inc v. Douglas*, 110 So. 3d 419, 433–34 (Fla. 2013) (reapproving process of bifurcating common issues from individualized ones).

Absent a motion to amend the complaint, a class definition may not be expanded once it has been proposed. *Fla. Dep't of Transp. v. Tropical Trailer Leasing, LLC*, 229 So. 3d 1251, 1254–55 (Fla. 1st DCA 2017). *Accord Combined Servs., Inc. v. City of Opa-Locka,* 394 So. 3d 98 (Fla. 3d DCA 2024) (affirming settlement that permissibly amended class definition to correct fail-safe issue by objectively including all residential and commercial accountholders active during the class period). "Trial courts abuse their discretion when they certify a class that is broader than the class defined in the complaint." *Id.* at 1255.

7. RULE 1.220(E)—DISMISSAL OR COMPROMISE

Under Rule 1.220(e), notice must be provided to the court and to class members before a dismissal or settlement is entered. However, unlike its federal analog, Fed. R. Civ. P. 23(e)(4)(a), the Florida rule does not specifically address a class member's right to object to the proposed dismissal or settlement. *Litvak v. Scylla Props., LLC*, 946 So. 2d 1165, 1176 n.13 (Fla. 1st DCA 2006).

In *Fung v. Florida Joint Underwriters Ass'n*, 840 So. 2d 1101, 1103 (Fla. 3d DCA 2003), the court held that where the parties to a class action have fully negotiated a settlement agreement, the trial court may either accept or reject the settlement but may not rewrite it over either party's objection. *See also Hameroff v. Pub. Med. Assistance Tr. Fund*, 911 So. 2d 827, 830 (Fla. 1st DCA 2005) ("Any concerns that the trial court may have had with the settlement's inequities should have been made known to the parties prior to the settlement's approval.").

In *Grosso*, 983 So. 2d at 1170, the Third District Court of Appeal held that where the parties seek simultaneously the certification of a class and the approval of a settlement, the trial court must "apply heightened scrutiny and . . . take a more active role as a guardian of the interest of the absent class members." Moreover, a notice of settlement cannot be misleading, and must provide the class members with essential information. *Id.* at *8; *see also Nelson v. Wakulla County*, 985 So. 2d 564, 576–77 (Fla. 1st DCA 2008).

8. MISCELLANEOUS COMMENTS

a. Offer of Judgment Statute Applicable to Class Actions

Florida's offer of judgment statute provides that in a civil action for damages, if a defendant files an offer of judgment that the plaintiff does not accept within 30 days, the defendant can recover its reasonable costs and attorney's fees if the judgment is one of no liability or is at least 25 percent less than the offer. Fla. Stat. § 768.79 (2018). Although it noted the existence of valid and legitimate concerns when applying the offer of judgment statute to class action representatives, the court in *Oruga Corp. v. AT&T Wireless of Florida, Inc.*, 712 So. 2d 1141, 1143–44 (Fla. 3d DCA 1998), held that class actions are not exempt from the coverage of the statute, which plainly and unambiguously states that it applies to any civil action for damages.

After *Oruga*, the Supreme Court of Florida amended Section 768.79's procedural analog, Fla. R. Civ. P 1.442. *Amendments to the Fla. Rules of Civil Procedure*, 773 So. 2d 1098 (Fla. 2000). Rule 1.442 now states that: "In any case in which the existence of a class is alleged, the time for acceptance of a proposal for settlement is extended to 30 days after the date the order granting or denying certification is filed." Before the amendment, proposed representative plaintiffs could receive more than their actual damages, and have only thirty days to accept the proposal. Defendants therefore could place pressure upon the representative to accept an early offer and, as a result, eliminate a class action before certification. Now, proposed representatives can honor their commitment to the proposed class and know whether a class has been certified before deciding whether to accept a proposal for settlement.

b. No Class Maintainable on Fraud Claims Based on Separate Contracts

To sustain a fraud claim in Florida, a litigant must establish an intentional material misrepresentation on which he relied to his detriment. The Supreme Court of Florida, in *Lance v. Wade*, 457 So. 2d 1008, 1009, 1011 (Fla. 1984), prohibited a fraud class action based upon separate contracts where each class member had his own separate and distinct contract. The court held that each person must make an individual determination as to which contractual terms are important to him. What one purchaser may rely upon in entering a contract may not be material to another purchaser.

A more recent decision strengthened the *Lance* holding by prohibiting class action relief from separate contracts on the basis of fraud, regardless of the genesis of the fraud and whether it was based on misrepresentations or omissions. *Humana, Inc. v. Castillo*, 728 So. 2d 261, 265 (Fla. 2d DCA 1999).

The Third District Court of Appeal reversed a class certification order against a home builder because the claims certified were based upon fraud. *Shoma Dev. Corp.*, 749 So. 2d at 1287. The court reiterated the Supreme Court of Florida's holdings in *Osceola Groves v. Wiley*, 78 So. 2d 700, 702 (Fla. 1955), and *Lance*, 457 So. 2d at 1008, which held that claims for fraud are replete with individual issues and cannot be certified. Although the class members cited a 1994 tobacco case, *Broin v. Phillip Morris Cos.*, 641 So. 2d 888 (Fla. 3d DCA 1994), to support class certification, the Third District Court of Appeal distinguished *Broin* as involving claims for the inhalation of second-hand cigarette smoke by flight attendants in airplane cabins, as opposed to individual fraudulent contracts. The court stated that allegedly fraudulent activities of a home builder would be more analogous to the circumstances in *Lance* and that a class should not be certified.

In *Chateau Communities, Inc. v. Ludtke*, 783 So. 2d 1227, 1230 (Fla. 5th DCA 2001), the court reaffirmed the general rule espoused in *Lance*, that fraud claims cannot be brought in a class action because such claims contain distinct facts and require proof of matters unique to each plaintiff. Bringing a class action based upon fraud in Florida thus remains an all but impossible task. Importantly, the Third District Court of Appeal recently found that to recover in a class action based upon claims arising under the Florida Deceptive and Unfair Trade Practices Act (FDUTPA), Fla. Stat. 501.201 *et. seq.*, it is not necessary that the class demonstrate actual reliance. Therefore, the existence of individual questions of reliance does not bar class certification. *Latman v. Costa Cruise Lines, N.V.*, 758 So. 2d 699,

703 (Fla. 3d DCA 2000); *see also Davis v. Powertel, Inc.*, 776 So. 2d 971, 974–75 (Fla. 1st DCA 2000). *But see Rollins, Inc. v. Butland*, 951 So. 2d 860, 876 (Fla. 2d DCA 2006) (overturning class certification of FDUTPA claims where claims involved complex contractual agreements and extended periods of performance).

c. Class Action Counterclaims

Rule 1.220 "permits the assertion of class actions by way of counterclaims." *Cabrera v. U.S. Bank Nat'l Ass'n*, 81 So. 3d 516, 521 (Fla. 4th DCA 2019).

The certification of a compulsory class counterclaim is not prohibited as a matter of law. If a counterclaim would be compulsory in a standard lawsuit, then the court must consider the same factors required to determine whether to certify a standard class action. *Key Club Assocs., L.P. v. Mayer*, 718 So. 2d 346, 346–47 (Fla. 2d DCA 1998).

d. National Class Certification Involving Florida State Law Claims

In 1999, the Fourth District Court of Appeal upheld certification of a national class in a case brought against a cruise line pursuant to Florida's Unfair and Deceptive Trade Practices Act. The case alleged that a cruise line imposed improper port charges. Applying the significant relationship test, the court found that the cruise line had significant connections to Florida and certified the class. *Renaissance Cruises, Inc. v. Glassman*, 738 So. 2d 436 (Fla. 4th DCA 1999); *see also Latman*, 758 So. 2d at 699 (reversing trial court's order denying class certification where plaintiff alleged violations of the Florida Deceptive and Unfair Trade Practices Act (FDUTPA) because of the cruise line's alleged failure to disclose that it would retain portions of the port charges); *Premier Cruise Lines, Ltd. v. Picaut*, 746 So. 2d 1132, 1133–34 (Fla. 5th DCA 1999) (certifying a class under the Florida Deceptive and Unfair Trade Practices Act when a cruise company kept part of the port charges for itself).

In contrast, the Second District Court of Appeal reversed a class certification order certifying three nationwide classes based upon Florida state laws. The court reasoned that the language of the Florida Anti-Trust Act of 1980 and FDUTPA limited those statutes' application to residents of Florida. But the Second District Court of Appeal remanded the case to the trial court to determine whether any certification could be appropriate. *Océ Printing Sys.*, 760 So. 2d at 1037.

In *Hutson v. Rexall Sundown, Inc.*, 837 So. 2d 1090, 1094 (Fla. 4th DCA 2003), the Fourth District Court of Appeal affirmed the trial court's denial of a nationwide class certification in a deceptive trade practices action against a calcium products manufacturer. The court held that certification was improper because the manufacturer's alleged marketing violations occurred throughout the country, requiring the application of at least fifty different consumer protection laws.

Florida courts may stay a putative national class action filed in Florida until the resolution of a "substantially identical" national class action filed in another state's courts. *J.M. Smucker Co. v. Rudge*, 877 So. 2d 820, 821–22 (Fla. 3d DCA 2004) (staying national class action filed in Florida pending resolution of substantially identical class action filed in Illinois); *see also Beckford v. Gen. Motors Corp.*, 919 So. 2d 612, 613 (Fla. 3d DCA 2006) (staying Florida class action pending previously filed federal class action).

e. Discovery

The Fifth District Court of Appeal has found that a defendant is entitled to a protective order staying discovery on the merits of a plaintiff's claims until class certification has been determined. *Policastro v. Stelk*, 780 So. 2d 989, 991 (Fla. 5th DCA 2001); *see also Richardson v. Gyves*, 874 So. 2d 658, 659 (Fla. 4th DCA 2004) (Klein, J., concurring) (stating in dicta that courts in the Fourth District Court of Appeal must follow *Policastro*). The court reasoned that no class action may proceed until there is a named plaintiff with standing to represent the class. The court held that Florida Rule of Civil Procedure 1.220(d)(l), which permits discovery prior to class certification, does not include merits discovery. Moreover, if a court determines that a plaintiff has no standing or if class certification otherwise was inappropriate, the plaintiff would then have no right to pursue discovery on behalf of a class that he/she does not represent. *See also Miami-Dade County v. E. Partners, LLC*, 298 So. 3d 1185, 1187 (Fla. 3d DCA 2020) (quashing order compelling merits discovery where question of class representative's standing had not been resolved).

In *Florida Power & Light v. Thomas*, 838 So. 2d 1240 (Fla. 1st DCA 2003), the appellate court denied FPL's petition for common law certiorari of the trial court's order denying its motion for a protective order. FPL sought to bifurcate class certification discovery from merits discovery, and to stay merits discovery. The trial court denied the motion and the First District Court of Appeal affirmed, holding that FPL failed to carry its burden of showing that without the protective order, it would suffer irreparable harm. It may be error for a trial court to stay pre-certification discovery that seeks information needed to satisfy class pleading requirements. *See Williams Island Ventures, LLC v. de la Mora*, 246 So. 3d 471 (Fla. 3d DCA 2018). In *Williams*, the plaintiffs sought information in support of their class pleadings that could only be obtained from the defendant through discovery. The defendant moved to stay discovery, which the trial court granted. The trial court then dismissed the plaintiffs' case with prejudice for failing to state a claim. The Third DCA reversed, finding that the plaintiffs could have satisfied their class action pleading requirements had they obtained the information through discovery.

f. Forum Selection Clauses and Other Contractual Provisions

In *America Online, Inc. v. Booker*, 781 So. 2d 423, 425 (Fla. 3d DCA 2001), the Third District Court of Appeal dealt with certification and a contractual forum selection provision. The court held that the unavailability of a class action procedure in the transferee forum was not sufficient, standing alone, to render an otherwise valid forum-selection clause unenforceable. Based upon this rationale, Florida plaintiffs cannot circumvent or defeat otherwise valid provisions requiring suit in other states simply by asserting claims on behalf of a purported class.

In *Bellsouth Mobility, LLC v. Christopher*, 819 So. 2d 171, 172 (Fla. 4th DCA 2002), the Fourth District Court of Appeal held that arbitration clauses and other contractual provisions that attempt to limit consumer relief while maintaining unfair advantages for the company or corporation are unconscionable.

In *America Online, Inc. v. Pasieka*, 870 So. 2d 170, 171–72 (Fla. 1st DCA 2004), the First District Court of Appeal refused to give effect to a forum selection clause requiring a suit to be filed in Virginia, where the plaintiff's class complaint included claims under FDUTPA and the Florida Free Gift Advertising Law (FFGAL). The court held that the purpose and effectiveness of FDUTPA and FFGAL would be undermined considerably if the case was sent elsewhere.

In *Fonte v. AT&T Wireless Services, Inc.*, 903 So. 2d 1019, 1024–25 (Fla. 4th DCA 2005), the court upheld a contractual class action waiver provision, citing the numerous alternative legal remedies available to the plaintiff.

In *Eglin v. Fed. Credit Union v. Baird*, 400 So. 3d 643 (Fla. 1st DCA 2024), the court did not enforce an arbitration provision "in a hyperlink buried in a routine monthly account statement email" and failed to mention the waiver contained within the hyperlink.

g. Attorneys' Fees

Florida has adopted the common fund doctrine. *See Truman J. Costello P.A. v. City of Cape Coral*, 693 So. 2d 48 (Fla. 2d DCA 1997).

Florida does not recognize the substantial benefit doctrine. *See id.*

In *Tripp Construction, Inc. v. Verde*, 789 So. 2d 1171 (Fla. 3d DCA 2001), the court reversed an award of attorney's fees to class counsel based upon Fla. R. Civ. P. 1.380(c). The plaintiffs served requests for admission asking the defendant to admit that the subject homes violated applicable building codes. The defendant denied the requests for admission and the case went to trial. At trial, the plaintiffs submitted uncontroverted evidence that the homes were in violation of the building codes, and a verdict was entered in favor of the class. The trial court awarded attorney's fees to the class from the date which the defendant denied the requests for admission. The Third District Court of Appeal reversed this decision, holding that while the class was entitled to attorney's fees, the amount must be determined based upon the time expended by counsel to prove those facts that the defendant failed to admit.

In *North County Co. v. Bologna*, 816 So. 2d 842, 843–44 (Fla. 4th DCA 2002), the trial court certified a class and approved a form notification to members of the class that included an "opt-out" provision. The defendant then proceeded to contact most of the class members and warned them that they should opt out of the class or else suffer thousands of dollars of losses in attorney's fees. Upon request, the trial court granted a motion for attorney's fees against the defendant for abuse of the notification process; however, the Fourth District Court of Appeal reversed, holding that a factual finding of bad faith, vexatiousness, wantonness or oppression is required before a motion for attorney's fees due to an alleged abuse of the class action notification process is granted.

h. Appellate Issues

Fla. R. App. P. 9.130(a) governs the appeal of an order certifying a class.

An order certifying a class is reviewed for abuse of discretion. *Sosa*, 73 So. 3d at 98; *Pinellas Cnty. Sch. Bd. v. Crowley*, 911 So. 2d 881, 882 (Fla. 2d DCA 2005) (affirming certification of class claims on behalf of black students in public school system).

Doubts about class certification should be resolved in favor of certification. *Sears Home Improvement Prods., Inc. v. Porterfield*, 949 So. 2d 318, 319 (Fla. 1st DCA 2007); *Chase Manhattan Mortg. Corp. v. Porcher*, 898 So. 2d 153, 157 (Fla. 4th DCA 2005).

In *Faulk v. Air Products and Chemicals, Inc.*, 798 So. 2d 820, 821 (Fla. 1st DCA 2001), the appellate court affirmed a denial of a motion for class certification. Interestingly, in the interlocutory appeal process, the plaintiffs also requested that the appellate court rule that the lower court erred in denying the plaintiffs' motion to amend the complaint to add punitive damages. The appellate court confirmed that, pursuant to Florida Rule of Appellate Procedure 9.130(a), the court has no jurisdiction to review rulings or orders not listed within the rule during an interlocutory appeal.

Similarly, the Third District Court of Appeal dismissed an appeal for lack of jurisdiction in *Phillip Morris, Inc. v. Jett*, 802 So. 2d 353, 355–56 (Fla. 3d DCA 2001). In that case, the defendant wished to appeal certain findings involving the enforcement of a previously approved settlement agreement. The appellate court ruled that jurisdiction remains in the trial court to make such orders as may be necessary to enforce its judgment. Therefore, the appellate court has no jurisdiction to review the individual damage trials of class members until final orders are entered.

In *American Medical Security v. Addison*, 802 So. 2d 357, 358 (Fla. 4th DCA 2001), the defendants attempted to raise issues involving alleged errors in the trial court's denial of their motions to dismiss during an interlocutory appeal of the trial court's certification of the class. The appellate court reaffirmed that it would not address alleged errors in the motion to dismiss during an interlocutory appeal of class certification. *See also United Servs. Auto Ass'n v. Modregon*, 818 So. 2d 562, 563 (Fla. 2d DCA 2002), *abrogation on other grounds recognized by Burnett v. Clarendon Select Ins. Co.*, 920 So. 2d 188, 189 (Fla. 2d DCA 2006) (holding that pursuant to Florida Rule of Appellate Procedure 9.130, a motion to dismiss is not an appealable interlocutory order).

In *Florida Power & Light v. Thomas*, 838 So. 2d at 1240, the court dismissed a party's petition for common law certiorari for lack of jurisdiction. The court held that a party seeking a protective order bears the burden of presenting evidence to the trial court showing that the requested discovery would be unduly burdensome. If that burden is not met, then the petition fails for lack of jurisdiction.

Since it is unclear that any order "certifying a class" is necessary under either Rule 1.221 or Rule 1.222, it is unclear that interlocutory appellate review is available in class actions governed by them. Thus, if a party were desirous of interlocutory review, it would behoove the party to ask the trial court to exercise its discretion and certify the class represented, especially where there is some question whether all of the members of the association in question have the same interest in prosecuting or defending the case. See, *Amber Glades, Inc., v. Leisure Assocs. Ltd. P'ship, supra* (questioning whether Fla. R. App. P. 9.130 applies to class actions under Rule 1.222 since no Rule 1.220 certification order is required).

i. PIP Benefits

In *Cannarella v. Allstate Indemnity Co.*, 809 So. 2d 73, 74–75 (Fla. 2d DCA 2002), the Second District Court of Appeal confirmed that PIP benefits are not untimely paid until 30 days after the insurer receives notice of the loss. Accordingly, the court affirmed a summary judgment in favor of Allstate holding that no interest is due to class plaintiffs until the thirty-first day after notice is provided. *See also United Auto. Ins. Co. v. Stat Techs., Inc.*, 787 So. 2d 920 (Fla. 3d DCA 2001).

In 2003, the Florida Legislature amended the PIP Statute, which now requires PIP claimants to send a demand letter to their insurers. Fla. Stat. § 627.736(11) (2003). This requirement applies to "all actions filed on or after August 1, 2003." Ch. 2003-411, § 16, Laws of Fla. Arguably, a class plaintiff must now show that all members of a putative class have met this demand letter requirement.

In *United Automobile Insurance Co. v. Diagnostics of South Florida., Inc.*, 921 So. 2d 23, 25–26 (Fla. 3d DCA 2006), the court held that the class representative had no standing to represent the class where the deductible had not been paid, relieving the insurance company of making PIP payments.

j. Notice, Due Process and Hearing

In *Ernie Haire Ford, Inc. v. Gilley*, 903 So. 2d 956, 959 (Fla. 2d DCA 2005), the court reversed class certification on notice and due process grounds where the trial court certified the class without setting a hearing on the motion or considering evidence. *See also Seminole*, 920 So. 2d at 824 (reversing class certification where, among other things, trial court failed to conduct an evidentiary hearing).

However, in *Sosa*, 73 So. 3d at 105, the Supreme Court of Florida stated "[a]lthough rule 1.220 does not demand it, and certainly not all situations require it, a trial court may conduct an evidentiary hearing to evaluate the basis for class certification when there may be questions with regard to" predominance and superiority.

k. Class Cut-off Date

Where the trial court certified and then recertified a class, the recertification date was the proper cutoff date for determining class membership. *Engle*, 945 So. 2d at 1275.

l. Dismissal of Class Claims with Prejudice

Unless it clearly appears that amendment of a class action claim would be futile, a trial court's refusal to allow an amendment is an abuse of discretion. *Murga v. United Prop. & Cas. Ins. Co.*, 941 So. 2d 482, 482–83 (Fla. 3d DCA 2006).

m. Jurisdiction

In Florida, circuit courts have jurisdiction over all matters with an amount in controversy exceeding $15,000. In *Hernando County v. Mornana*, 979 So. 2d 276, 278 (Fla. 5th DCA 2008), the Fifth District Court of Appeal held that the amount of the claim of the entire class determines the dollar amount at issue for jurisdictional purposes. Thus, if the aggregated individual claims exceed $15,000, then jurisdiction vests in the circuit court.

Before a putative class action may be transferred from circuit to county court based on the amount in controversy, the circuit court should determine whether the requirements of a class action have been met. *Diamond v. Elvis Towing, Inc.*, 268 So. 3d 249, 251–52 (Fla. 2d DCA 2019).

n. Class Action Waivers in Consumer Contracts

In *S.D.S. Autos, Inc. v. Chrzanowski*, 976 So. 2d 600, 610 (Fla. 1st DCA 2007), the District Court of Appeal "join[ed] numerous other courts [around the country] in declining to enforce bans on class relief in consumer contracts that give rise to claims under consumer protection statutes." *But see AT&T Mobility LLC v. Concepcion*, 563 U.S. 333, 131 S. Ct. 1740 (2011) (holding that Federal Arbitration Act (FAA) preempted a California ruling that class waivers in consumer arbitration agreements are unconscionable); *McKenzie Check Advance of Fla. v. Betts*, 112 So. 3d 1176, 1183–84 (Fla. 2013) (applying *Concepcion* and enforcing class action waiver provision in consumer contract).

In *Anderson v. Maronda Homes, Inc. of Florida*, 98 So. 3d 127, 130–31 (Fla. 2d DCA 2012), the Second District Court of Appeal found that in cases not involving explicit class action waivers like the one in *AT&T Mobility*, contract interpretation may be required to determine whether class arbitration is allowed. In general, "[b]eyond peradventure, 'a party may not be compelled under the FAA to submit to class arbitration unless there is a contractual basis for concluding that the party *agreed* to do so.'" *Id.* at 130 (quoting *Stolt-Nielsen S.A. v. AnimalFeeds Int'l Corp.*, 130 S. Ct. 1758, 1775 (2010)). As such, "[a]ssent to class arbitration is needed; agreement cannot be inferred from silence." *Id.* However, "[i]t is not impossible to conjure up a situation where a class waiver so thoroughly vitiates the ability to vindicate rights that the waiver cannot stand." *Id.* at 131.

Reasonable notice of a class action waiver must have been provided to class members and cannot be applied retroactively to claims that have already accrued. *Eglin Fed. Credit Union v. Baird*, 400 So. 3d 643 (Fla. 1st DCA 2024).

o. Conflict of Interest of Class Counsel

"Because of inevitable tension between large numbers of class members, class action litigation often leads to conflicts of interest." *Broin v. Phillip Morris Cos.*, 84 So. 3d 1107, 1111 (Fla. 3d DCA 2012), *quashed by Young v. Achenbach*, 136 So. 3d 575 (Fla. 2014) (rejecting application of the federal court balancing test to determine whether attorney disqualification is warranted, in favor of Florida Rules of Professional Conduct). A common dilemma in class actions occurs when one or more class representatives object to a settlement, thus becoming adverse parties to the remaining class representatives and the rest of the class. Applying the usual rules on attorney-client relations, the class counsel could easily be disqualified in such situations, a result that would undermine many fair and reasonable settlements. "In light of these concerns, the [Third Circuit] fashioned a balancing test: '[I]n the class action context, once some class representatives object to a settlement negotiated on their behalf, class counsel may continue to represent the remaining class representatives and the class, as long as the interest of the class in continued representation by experienced counsel is not outweighed by the actual prejudice to the objectors of being opposed by their former counsel.'" *Id.* (quoting *Lazy Oil Co. v. Witco Corp.*, 166 F.3d 581, 590 (3d Cir. 1999)).

p. Opt-outs

"[A] party who opts out of a class action retains the right to proceed individually, but not to launch a competing class action of opt-outs seeking the same relief resolved on a class basis in a prior lawsuit." *Bay Area Injury Rehab Specialists Holdings, Inc. v. United Servs. Auto. Ass'n*, 173 So. 3d 1004 (Fla. 2d DCA 2015).

q. Defendant Classes

Defendant classes may be certified where common questions predominate and each named plaintiff has a claim against each defendant class member, or where the defendant class members are related by a conspiracy or "juridicial link." *See Inphynet Contracting Servs., Inc. v. Matthews*, 196 So. 3d 449, 459 (Fla. 4th DCA 2016); *Addison*, 979 So. 2d at 253–56 (reversing certification of defendant class and holding that common regulatory scheme affecting private defendants does not confer standing over defendant class) (distinguishing *Addison*, 979 So. 2d at 254).

r. Direct Versus Derivative Standing

Putative class of shareholders must allege and prove direct injury under Florida's two-part inquiry into direct versus derivative standing. *See Arbitrage Fund v. Petty*, 307 So. 3d 119, 124–28 (Fla. 3d DCA 2020) (citing *Dinuro Invs., LLC v. Camacho*, 141 So. 3d 731 (Fla. 3d DCA 2014)).

s. Class Representative's Standing

"[T]he class representative must illustrate that a case or controversy exists between him or her and the defendant, and that this case or controversy will continue throughout the existence of the litigation. . . . If it is shown that the plaintiff who seeks class certification suffered no injury and, thus, has no cause of action against the defendant, the class should not be certified." *Pet Supermarket, Inc. v. Eldridge*, 360 So. 3d 1201, 1205–06 (Fla. 3d DCA 2023) (citations omitted).

RULE 1. 220: FLORIDA

1. TEXT OF RULE 1.220 OF THE FLORIDA RULES OF CIVIL PROCEDURE

Rule 1.220. Class actions

(a) *Prerequisites to class representation.* Before any claim or defense may be maintained on behalf of a class by one party or more suing or being sued as the representative of all the members of a class, the court shall first conclude that (1) the members of the class are so numerous that separate joinder of each member is impracticable, (2) the claim or defense of the representative party raises questions of law or fact common to the questions of law or fact raised by the claim or defense of each member of the class, (3) the claim or defense of the representative party is typical of the claim or defense of each member of the class, and (4) the representative party can fairly and adequately protect and represent the interests of each member of the class.

(b) *Claims and defenses maintainable.* A claim or defense may be maintained on behalf of a class if the court concludes that the prerequisites of subdivision (a) are satisfied, and that:

(1) the prosecution of separate claims or defenses by or against individual members of the class would create a risk of either:

(A) inconsistent or varying adjudications concerning individual members of the class which would establish incompatible standards of conduct for the party opposing the class; or

(B) adjudications concerning individual members of the class which would, as a practical matter, be dispositive of the interests of other members of the class who are not parties to the adjudications, or substantially impair or impede the ability of other members of the class who are not parties to the adjudications to protect their interests; or

(2) the party opposing the class has acted or refused to act on grounds generally applicable to all the members of the class, thereby making final injunctive relief or declaratory relief concerning the class as a whole appropriate; or

(3) the claim or defense is not maintainable under either subdivision (b)(1) or (b)(2), but the questions of law or fact common to the claim or defense of the representative party and the claim or defense of each member of the class predominate over any question of law or fact affecting only individual members of the class, and class representation is superior to other available methods for the fair and efficient adjudication of the controversy. The conclusions shall be derived from consideration of all relevant facts and circumstances, including (A) the respective interests of each member of the class in individually controlling the prosecution of separate claims or defenses, (B) the nature and extent of any pending litigation to which any member of the class is a party and in which any question of law or fact controverted in the subject action is to be adjudicated, (C) the desirability or undesirability of concentrating the litigation in the forum where the subject action is instituted, and (D) the difficulties likely to be encountered in the management of the claim or defense on behalf of a class.

(c) *Pleading requirements.* Any pleading, counterclaim, or crossclaim alleging the existence of a class shall contain the following:

(1) Next to its caption the designation: "Class Representation."

(2) Under a separate heading, designated as "Class Representation Allegations," specific recitation of:

(A) the particular provision of subdivision (b) under which it is claimed that the claim or defense is maintainable on behalf of a class;

(B) the questions of law or fact that are common to the claim or defense of the representative party and the claim or defense of each member of the class;

(C) the particular facts and circumstances that show the claim or defense advanced by the representative party is typical of the claim or defense of each member of the class;

(D) (i) the approximate number of class members, (ii) a definition of the alleged class, and (iii) the particular facts and circumstances that show the representative party will fairly and adequately protect and represent the interests of each member of the class; and

(E) the particular facts and circumstances that support the conclusions required of the court in determining that the action may be maintained as a class action pursuant to the particular provision of subdivision (b) under which it is claimed that the claim or defense is maintainable on behalf of a class.

(d) *Determination of class representation; notice; judgment: claim or defense maintained partly on behalf of a class.*

(1) As soon as practicable after service of any pleading alleging the existence of a class under this rule and before service of an order for pretrial conference or a notice for trial, after hearing the court shall enter an order determining whether the claim or defense is maintainable on behalf of a class on the application of any party or on the court's initiative. Irrespective of whether the court determines that the claim or defense is maintainable on behalf of a class, the order shall separately state the findings of fact and conclusions of law upon which the determination is based. In making the determination the court (A) may allow the claim or defense to be so maintained, and, if so, shall state under which subsection of subdivision (b) the claim or defense is to be maintained, (B) may disallow the class representation and strike the class representation allegations, or (C) may order postponement of the determination pending the completion of discovery concerning whether the claim or defense is maintainable on behalf of a class. If the court rules that the claim or defense shall be maintained on behalf of a class under subdivision (b)(3), the order shall also provide for the notice required by subdivision (d)(2). If the court rules that the claim or defense shall be maintained on behalf of a class under subdivision (b)(1) or subdivision (b)(2), the order shall also provide for the notice required by subdivision (d)(2), except when a showing is made that the notice is not required, the court may provide for another kind of notice to the class as is appropriate. When the court orders postponement of its

determination, the court shall also establish a date, if possible, for further consideration and final disposition of the motion. An order under this subsection may be conditional and may be altered or amended before entry of a judgment on the merits of the action.

(2) As soon as is practicable after the court determines that a claim or defense is maintainable on behalf of a class, notice of the pendency of the claim or defense shall be given by the party asserting the existence of the class to all the members of the class. The notice shall be given to each member of the class who can be identified and located through reasonable effort and shall be given to the other members of the class in the manner determined by the court to be most practicable under the circumstances. Unless otherwise ordered by the court, the party asserting the existence of the class shall initially pay for the cost of giving notice. The notice shall inform each member of the class that (A) any member of the class who files a statement with the court by the date specified in the notice asking to be excluded shall be excluded from the class, (B) the judgment, whether favorable or not, will include all members who do not request exclusion, and (C) any member who does not request exclusion may make a separate appearance within the time specified in the notice.

(3) The judgment determining a claim or defense maintained on behalf of a class under subdivision (b)(1) or (b)(2), whether or not favorable to the class, shall include and describe those persons whom the court finds to be members of the class. The judgment determining a claim or defense maintained on behalf of a class under subdivision (b)(3), whether or not favorable to the class, shall include and identify those to whom the notice provided in subdivision (d)(2) was directed, who have not requested exclusion and whom the court finds to be members of the class.

(4) When appropriate, (A) a claim or defense may be brought or maintained on behalf of a class concerning particular issues, or (B) class representation may be divided into subclasses, and each subclass may be treated as a separate and distinct class and the provisions of this rule shall be applied accordingly.

(e) *Dismissal or compromise*. After a claim or defense is determined to be maintainable on behalf of a class under subdivision (d), the claim or defense shall not be voluntarily withdrawn, dismissed, or compromised without approval of the court after notice and hearing. Notice of any proposed voluntary withdrawal, dismissal, or compromise shall be given to all members of the class as the court directs.

Amended 347 So. 2d 599 at 608; Oct. 9, 1980, effective Jan. 1, 1981 (391 So. 2d 165). Amended July 16, 1992, effective Jan 1, 1993 (604 So. 2d 1110).

2. TEXT OF RULE 1.221 OF THE FLORIDA RULES OF CIVIL PROCEDURE

A homeowners' or condominium association, after control of such association is obtained by homeowners or unit owners other than the developer, may institute, maintain, settle, or appeal actions or hearings in its name on behalf of all association members concerning matters of common interest to the members, including, but not limited to: (1) the common property, area, or elements; (2) the roof or structural components of a building, or other improvements (in the case of homeowners' associations, being specifically limited to those improvements for which the association is responsible); (3) mechanical, electrical, or plumbing elements serving a property or an improvement or building (in the case of homeowners' associations, being specifically limited to those elements for which the association is responsible); (4) representations of the developer pertaining to any existing or proposed commonly used facility; (5) protests of ad valorem taxes on commonly used facilities; and, in the case of homeowners' associations; (6) defense of actions in eminent domain or prosecution of inverse condemnation actions. If an association has the authority to maintain a class action under this rule, the association may be joined in an action as representative of that class with reference to litigation and disputes involving the matters for which the association could bring a class action under this rule. Nothing herein limits any statutory or common law right of any individual homeowner or unit owner, or class of such owners, to bring any action that may otherwise be available. An action under this rule shall not be subject to the requirements of rule 1.220.

Credits

Added Oct. 9, 1980, effective Jan. 1, 1981 (391 So. 2d 165). Amended July 16, 1992, effective Jan. 1, 1993 (604 So. 2d 1110); Sept. 27, 2007, effective Jan. 1, 2008 (966 So. 2d 943).

Editors' Notes

COMMITTEE NOTES

1980 Adoption. The present rule relating to condominium associations [1.220(b)] is left intact but renumbered as rule 1.221.

2007 Amendment. Consistent with amendments to section 720.303(1), Florida Statutes, homeowners' associations have been added to the rule.

3. TEXT OF RULE 1.222 OF THE FLORIDA RULES OF CIVIL PROCEDURE

A mobile homeowners' association may institute, maintain, settle, or appeal actions or hearings in its name on behalf of all homeowners concerning matters of common interest, including, but not limited to: the common property; structural components of a building or other improvements; mechanical, electrical, and plumbing elements serving the park property; and protests of ad valorem taxes on commonly used facilities. If the association has the authority to maintain a class action under this rule, the association may be joined in an action as representative of that class with reference to litigation and disputes involving the matters for which the association could bring a class action under this rule. Nothing herein limits any statutory or common law right of any individual homeowner or class of homeowners to bring any action which may otherwise be available. An action under this rule shall not be subject to the requirements of rule 1.220.

1988 Editor's Note: Rule 1.222 was adopted in Lanca Homeowners, Inc. v. Lantana Cascade of Palm Beach, Ltd., 541 So. 2d 1121 (Fla. 1988).

The Florida portion of this ABA Class Action Survey was edited by Jason Kellogg, Esq., a partner at Levine Kellogg Lehman Schneider + Grossman, LLP in Miami, Florida. Portions relating to Florida Rules of Civil Procedure 1.221 and 1.222 were edited by Edward A. Marod, Esq., an equity shareholder at Gunster Yoakley & Stewart, P.A. in West Palm Beach, Florida.

GEORGIA

1. COMPARISON OF O.C.G.A. § 9-11-23 TO FEDERAL RULE OF CIVIL PROCEDURE 23

Georgia enacted a revised class action statute effective July 1, 2003, and applicable to actions filed on or after that date. O.C.G.A. § 9-11-23. When enacted, the statute was nearly identical to the Federal Rule 23 at the time. This 2003 enactment brought Georgia textually in line with the class action rules and statutes of most other jurisdictions, although in practice Georgia parties litigated class action issues as if the standardized text had been implemented years before. Federal Rule 23 was significantly revised on December 1, 2003, yet Georgia has not adopted those revisions. Effective April 22, 2005, Georgia continued to chart its own course by substantially revising Georgia's Rule 23(f), which established special procedures for putative class action litigants during the period prior to the court's decision on certification.

As was the case even before these various revisions, Georgia courts may look to federal authority for guidance when making class certification determinations. *Sta-Power Indus. Inc. v. Avant*, 216 S.E.2d 897, 900 (Ga. Ct. App. 1975). *See also Atlanta Postal Credit Union v. Cosby*, 912 S.E.2d 137, 144 n.5 (Ga. Ct. App. 2025); *Georgia–Pacific Consumer Products, LP v. Ratner*, 762 S.E.2d 419, 421 n.3 (Ga. 2014) ("when Georgia courts interpret and apply OCGA § 9-11-23, they commonly look to decisions of the federal courts interpreting and applying [Federal] Rule 23"); *Ansley Walk Condo. Ass'n v. Atlanta Dev. Auth.*, 867 S.E.2d 600, 604 (Ga. Ct. App. 2021) ("[b]ecause OCGA § 9-11-23 is based on Rule 23 of the Federal Rules of Civil Procedure, it is appropriate that we look to federal cases interpreting that rule for guidance").

2. CASE LAW INTERPRETING O.C.G.A. § 9-11-23

A plaintiff seeking to represent a class must do more than draft a complaint; instead, he or she must show that the class members have suffered the same injury, which does not mean merely that they have all suffered a violation of the same provision of law. *Rite Aid of Ga., Inc. v. Peacock*, 726 S.E.2d 577, 579 (citing *Wal-Mart Stores, Inc. v. Dukes*, 131 S. Ct. 2541, 2551 (2011)).

When a class action is filed, the statute of limitations for the action is tolled for all asserted members of the class during the pendency of the action. *State of Ga. v. Private Truck Council of Am., Inc.*, 371 S.E.2d 378, 380 (Ga. 1988). The tolling of the statute of limitations permits class members to rely on the class action to protect their rights without concern that the statute of limitations on their individual claims will have run should class certification ultimately be denied. *Id.*

A putative class plaintiff must affirmatively move for class certification: merely pleading a class action is insufficient. *City of Atlanta v. Miller*, 569 S.E.2d 907, 910 (Ga. Ct. App. 2002). Prior to the entry of a pretrial order, a party seeking class certification must obtain leave of court before any amendment to the party's pleadings that might have the effect of compromising any putative class claim. *Murphy v. Hope*, 195 S.E.2d 24, 25 (Ga. 1972).

In Georgia, the movant for class certification bears the burden of establishing its right to class certification. *Jones v. Douglas County*, 418 S.E.2d 19, 25 (Ga. 1992). A party seeking class certification must affirmatively demonstrate his or her compliance with Rule 23(a). *Rite Aid*, 726 S.E.2d at 579 (citing *Dukes*, 131 S. Ct. at 2551). The entire point of a burden of proof is that, if doubts remain about whether the standard is satisfied, the party with the burden of proof loses. All else being equal, the presumption is against class certification because class actions are an exception to our constitutional tradition of individual litigation. The party seeking class certification has a burden of proof, not a burden of pleading. *Vest Monroe, LLC v. Doe*, 906 S.E.2d 406, 410 (Ga. 2024) (quoting *Brown v. Electrolux Home Products*, 817 F3d 1225, 1233–34 (11th Cir. 2016) (emphasis in original)).

Georgia's class action statute neither directs a plaintiff to move for class certification within a specified time, nor does it prevent a defendant from requesting an order denying class certification or a court from acting on its own initiative. *Fuller v. Heartwood 11, LLC*, 687 S.E.2d 287, 290 (Ga. Ct. App. 2009), *cert. denied sub nom Vesta Holdings I, LLC v. Fuller,* 2010 Ga. LEXIS 361 (Ga. Apr. 19, 2010). The decision to certify an action as a class action may be made upon the motion of the proponent or the opponent of the class action or upon the court's own initiative. *Id.* at 291. A trial court is expected to actively manage a case to ensure that the certification decision is not unjustifiably delayed. *Id.* O.C.G.A. § 9-11-23 places a shared obligation upon the litigants and the court to ensure that the question of class certification is timely resolved. *Id.*

In the absence of a local rule governing the timely filing of a motion for class certification, a court may not deny an otherwise proper motion *solely* on the basis that it was untimely. *Id.* Rather, the court must determine, considering the factors set forth below, whether the delay resulted in any actual prejudice to the litigants or to the class. *Id.* at 291–92. Then, in its order on the motion for class certification, the court must set forth in writing factual findings supporting its decision. *Id.* at 292. The purposes served by requiring the certification of a class "as soon as practicable" include timely identifying the legal issues and trial strategies involved in a case, in determining who will be bound by a judgment, and in expeditiously and efficiently managing the litigation from discovery through appellate review. *Id.* Legitimate reasons for delay include resolving legal issues that may be dispositive of the action against a named individual without binding the proposed class and conducting discovery on the certification issue so that the court will have sufficient information when deciding whether to certify the class. *Id.*

When two or more competing class actions exist, Georgia courts apply a first-to-judgment analysis to determine the primacy, and thus the *res judicata* effect, among them. *Smith v. AirTouch Cellular of Ga., Inc.*, 534 S.E.2d 832, 835–36 (Ga. Ct. App. 2000), *cert. denied*, 2000 Ga. LEXIS 740 (Oct. 6, 2000).

Absent class members have been held not to be opposing parties for the purposes of compulsory counterclaims. *Earthlink, Inc. v. Eaves*, 666 S.E.2d 420, 425 (Ga. Ct. App. 2008). There is no jurisdiction over absent class members until the court certifies a class. *Id.*

It does not appear that Georgia's appellate courts have had occasion to consider the boundaries, if any, to be placed on communications with putative class members. *But see Eastside Baptist Church v. Vicinanza*, 603 S.E.2d 681 (Ga. Ct. App. 2004) (vacating an injunction that prohibited the defendant from contacting putative class members because the trial judge who entered it had an "undisputed conflict of interest"). However, one source of relevant considerations may be found in the Local Rules for the U.S. District Court for the Northern District of Georgia. *See* N.D. Ga. L.R. 23.1(C).

The proper way to test class action treatment is a motion under O.C.G.A. § 9-11-23(c)(1), not a motion to dismiss under O.C.G.A. § 9-11-12(b)(6). *Glynn County v. Coleman*, 779 S.E.2d 753,755

(Ga. Ct. App. 2015) (citing 3B Moore's Federal Practice P 23.50, 23–421), *cert. denied,* 2016 Ga. LEXIS 189 (Feb. 22, 2016). While a defendant can certainly seek a ruling on a dispositive motion before certification of a class, it cannot use a dispositive motion as a vehicle to deny class certification. *Id.* (citing 5-23 Moore's Federal Practice—Civil § 23.81 (court may rule on dispositive motion before deciding whether to certify class)). Generally, in determining the propriety of class certification the first issue to be resolved is not whether the plaintiff has stated a cause of action or will prevail on the merits, but is instead whether the requirements for class certification have been satisfied. *Sta-Power*, 216 S.E.2d at 900. Any assertion that the named plaintiff cannot prevail on his claims does not comprise an appropriate basis for denying class certification. *Village Auto Ins. Co. v. Rush*, 649 S.E.2d 862, 866–67 (Ga. Ct. App. 2007), *cert. denied*, 2008 Ga. LEXIS 72 (Jan. 7, 2008). Merit-based disputes are not ripe for resolution at the class certification stage, particularly where no dispositive motions have been filed, argued, or ruled on below, and merits discovery has not concluded. *Id.*; *see also Peck v. Lanier Golf Club, Inc.*, 680 S.E.2d 595, 598 (Ga. Ct. App. 2009) (reversing court order dismissing case where trial court found, in effect, that the class certification requirements were moot because there was no merit to the action).

The certification process should proceed unless litigation of the defense impacts the statutory prerequisites, such as commonality or predominance. *See, e.g.*, *Cosby*, 912 S.E.2d at 143 (citing *Lon Smith & Assocs. v. Key*, 527 S.W.3d 604, 630–31 (Ct. App. Tx. 2017) (although affirmative defense may require evaluation of individual issues, it does not preclude certification where the defense involves "proof common to the defendants")). The Georgia Court of Appeals has suggested that the existence of an arbitration clause would not preclude class certification, because certification requires only that the plaintiff meet the statutory requirements. *Cosby*, 912 S.E.2d at 143. A trial court could consider whether an arbitration provision barred the class action suit on a class-wide basis, and in any event, the application of an arbitration defense would involve answers and proof common to the class. *Id.* at 144. *See also Bickerstaff v. SunTrust Bank*, 788 S.E.2d 787, 795 (2016) (noting that trial court would consider whether members had opted out of arbitration agreement after class certification stage).

Similarly, the Georgia Court of Appeals has rejected the claim that a notice provision warranted dismissal of a class action complaint. *Atlanta Postal Credit Union v. Holiday*, 885 S.E.2d 196, 204 (2023). The argument that the plaintiff has not satisfied a notice requirement is a defense that the plaintiff is not required to affirmatively disprove in the complaint. *Id.* For the same reasons applicable to the arbitration clause, the Court of Appeals has concluded that a potential notice defense does not automatically preclude class certification. *Cosby*, 912 S.E.2d at 144.

Although a motion to dismiss is not the proper vehicle to challenge class certification, motions to dismiss have been used to successfully challenge the case merits before a trial court reaches class certification issues. *Carnett's, Inc. v. Hammond*, 610 S.E.2d 529, 532 (Ga. 2005) (proper for court to reach issues that are both merits issues and class issues). For example, if a trial court lacks subject matter jurisdiction, then the court must consider jurisdiction first, whether raised in a motion to dismiss or *sua sponte*. *Patterson v. Ellerbee*, 603 S.E.2d 308, 310 (Ga. Ct. App. 2004). Where the court lacks jurisdiction, the question of class action certification becomes irrelevant because the trial court would have no power to make that determination. *Id.*; *see also Perkins v. Georgia Dept. of Medical Assistance*, 555 S.E.2d 500, 503 (Ga. Ct. App. 2001) (res judicata barred named plaintiff's claims); *Dryvit Sys., Inc. v. Stein*, 568 S.E.2d 569, 571 (Ga. Ct. App. 2002) (statutes of limitation precluded named plaintiff's claims). Further, there are certain subject matter areas in which class actions are precluded, and in those cases the merits issues may be addressed first. For instance, an action for a tax refund may not be brought by the taxpayer on behalf of a class consisting of other taxpayers who are alleged to be similarly situated. *Georgia Department of Revenue v. Roof*, 690 S.E.2d 442 (Ga.

Ct. App. 2010) (citing O.C.G.A. § 48-2-35(c)(5) as "constitut[ing] a legislative overruling of the Court of Appeal's holding in *City of Atlanta v. Barnes*, 276 Ga. 449 . . . (2003), that a class action was a permissible means for a taxpayer to pursue a tax refund action").

In ruling on class certification, a court may appropriately consider the merits of the action to the degree necessary to determine whether the requirements of O.C.G.A. § 9-11-23 have been satisfied.

Whether a case should be allowed to proceed as a class action involves intensely practical considerations, most of which are purely factual or fact-intensive. Each case must be decided on its own facts, on the basis of practicalities and prudential considerations. *Vest Monroe*, 906 S.E.2d at 410 (quoting *Trevizo v. Adams*, 455 F.3d 1155, 1163 (10th Cir. 2006)); *Gay v. B.H. Transfer Co.*, 652 S.E.2d 200, 202 (Ga. Ct. App. 2007) (error for court to find Rule 23 factors moot because there was no merit to the action); *Premier Paving GP, Inc. v. IOU Central, Inc.*, 852 S.E.2d 586, 588–89 (Ga. Ct. App. 2021) (reversing dismissal and denial of class certification based solely on the merits: "[T]hese merits question may be considered to the extent—but only to the extent—that they are relevant to determination whether the prerequisites for class certificate are satisfied.").

For example, when a named plaintiff defines a putative class to encompass elements of her cause of action, a trial court is required to look at issues that will also be considered in examining the merits of her claims to determine whether class certification would be proper. *McGarry v. Cingular Wireless, LLC*, 599 S.E.2d 34, 35 (Ga. Ct. App. 2004). Also relevant to when the merits may be addressed is whether the key question in the case is a purely legal one, where no discovery or resolution of factual issues is necessary to decide it. *See, e.g., Miller v. Deal*, 761 S.E.2d 274, 280 at n.12 (2014) (holding class certification unavailable after deciding issue—whether putative class members had categorical right to appointed counsel—that was "both a merits question and a class question").

Sometimes it may be necessary for the court to probe behind the pleadings before coming to rest on the certification question, and certification is proper only if the trial court is satisfied, after a rigorous analysis, that the prerequisites of Rule 23(a) have been satisfied. *Rite Aid*, 726 S.E.2d at 579 (citing *Dukes*, 131 S. Ct. at 2551). Frequently that rigorous analysis will entail some overlap with the merits of the plaintiff's underlying claim. *Id.* The class determination generally involves considerations that are enmeshed in the factual and legal issues comprising the plaintiff's cause of action. *Id. See also Miller v. Deal*, 761 S.E.2d at 280, n.12.

A Georgia trial judge holds broad discretion regarding whether to allow a case to proceed as a class action. *Ford Motor Credit Co. v. London*, 332 S.E.2d 345, 347 (Ga. Ct. App. 1985). Decisions regarding class certification fall within the trial court's discretion and will be upheld on appeal absent abuse of that discretion. *Village Auto*, 649 S.E.2d at 864. *But see Griffin Industries, Inc. v.* Green, 677 S.E.2d 310 (Ga. Ct. App. 2009) (questioning whether standard of review should be *de novo* as a matter of law upon the facts as found by the trial court), *cert. denied* 2009 Ga. LEXIS 791 (Ga. Sept. 28, 2009). Moreover, Georgia's courts of appeal will not reverse the factual findings in a trial court's class certification order unless they are clearly erroneous. *Village Auto*, 649 S.E.2d at 864. Under the "clearly erroneous" test, factual findings must be affirmed if supported by any evidence. *Id.* Implicit in this deferential standard of review is a recognition of the fact-intensive basis of the certification inquiry and of the trial court's inherent power to manage and control pending litigation. *See Resource Life Insurance Co. v. Buckner*, 698 S.E.2d 19, 29 (Ga. Ct. App. 2010). Critically, the fact that an appellate court may have reached a different conclusion in deciding whether to certify a class, had the question been put to that court in the first instance, is of no consequence. *Vest Monroe*, 906 S.E.2d at 411.

The Georgia Court of Appeals has tacitly approved of a trial court employing a special master to make recommended findings of fact and conclusions of law regarding class certification issues.

Brenntag Mid South, Inc. v. Smart, 710 S.E.2d 569 (Ga. Ct. App. 2011).

Pursuant to the amended § 9-11-23, Georgia's appellate courts may in their discretion permit an appeal of an order granting or denying class certification. *See* O.C.G.A. § 9-11-23(g). Under O.C.G.A. § 9-11-23(g), such an order may be challenged only by an appeal "filed within 30 days of the order certifying or refusing to certify the class." *Id.* Thus, litigants cannot thereafter appeal a class certification order, such as waiting until after entry of final judgment in the underlying case to raise such a challenge. *See Jones v. Forest Lake Village Homeowners Assoc., Inc.*, 696 S.E.2d 453, 458 (Ga. Ct. App. 2010).

Where a trial court does not determine to grant class action status to a suit, the action rests upon the underlying action of the representative plaintiff as its individual action. *Perkins*, 555 S.E.2d at 503.

According to the Georgia Court of Appeals, certification orders are "inherently tentative" in that a trial court retains jurisdiction to modify or vacate them as may be warranted by subsequent events in the litigation. *J.M.I.C. Life Ins. Co. v. Toole*, 634 S.E.2d 123, 129 (Ga. Ct. App. 2006), *cert. denied*, 2006 Ga. LEXIS 916 (Oct. 30, 2006). It has been held that a trial court does not abuse its discretion where it modifies the class definition after a subsequent event in the litigation, such as the parties engaging in discovery, and before a decision on the merits. *SunTrust Bank v. Bickerstaff*, 913 S.E.2d 51, 60 (Ga. 2025).

Prior to the 2003 amendment to O.C.G.A. § 9-11-23, Georgia's class action statute did not expressly provide for sub-classing. Georgia's appellate courts, however, drew from the federal rules when construing Georgia's statute and found "bifurcation of classes" appropriate under certain circumstances. *State Farm Mutual Auto. Ins. Co. v. Mabry*, 556 S.E.2d 114, 117 (Ga. 2001). The amended O.C.G.A. § 9-11-23 contemplates sub-classing at § 9-11-23(c)(4)(b).

As in most other jurisdictions, to certify a class a Georgia court must find that each of the four Rule 23(a) prerequisites have been satisfied, as well as at least one of the 23(b) criteria. *See* O.C.G.A. § 9-11-23. To satisfy these requirements, it is not enough for a plaintiff simply to allege that they are satisfied; rather, the plaintiff must come forward with evidence to prove satisfaction of the statutory requirements. *Cagle v. Portfolio Recovery Assoc.*, 889 S.E.2d 181, 184–85 (Ga. Ct. App. 2023); *Ratner*, 762 S.E.2d at 422–23 (citing *Dukes*, 131 S. Ct. at 2550–52). If a plaintiff fails to meet even one of the threshold requirements of OCGA § 9-11-23 (a), there is no need to consider any of the other requirements of the statute, and the request for certification must fail. *Bowden v. Med. Ctr., Inc.*, 845 S.E.2d 555, 560 (Ga. 2020).

Georgia courts deciding whether to certify a class must enter a written order addressing these factors and specifying the findings of fact and conclusions of law on which the court has based its decision. *See* O.C.G.A. § 9-11-23(f)(3). The court may rely upon the stipulations of the parties as to whether certain factors have been established. *Id.* The Georgia Court of Appeals has noted federal court authority that the rules of evidence are not strictly enforced at the class certification stage because of the preliminary nature of the proceedings. *See, e.g., City of Roswell v. Bible*, 833 S.E.2d 537, 541–42 (Ga. Ct. App. 2019) (citing *City of Rome v. Hotels.com*, No. 4:05-CV-249-HLM, 2911 WL 13228684 at *4 (N.D. Ga. Mar. 21, 2011); *Fisher v. Ciba Specialty Chems. Corp.*, 238 F.R.D 273 (S.D. Ala. 2006)). *See also Rice v. Fulton County*, 897 S.E.2d 491, 497 (2024) (the credibility and admissibility of evidence "are issues we do not consider at the class certification stage").

Georgia appellate courts will vacate and remand orders certifying a class that lack the specificity required by Rule 23(f)(3). *See, e.g., Griffin Indus., Inc. v. Green*, 635 S.E.2d 231 (Ga. Ct. App. 2006); *see also McDonald Oil Co. v. Cianocchi*, 648 S.E.2d 154, 155–56 (Ga. Ct. App. 2007) (vacating a certification order based in part on the trial court's failure to hold a hearing). Even so, an order denying class certification, that does not separately address each of the Rule 23 factors, may be acceptable if the factors not satisfied are sufficiently discussed in the order. *Roland v. Ford Motor Co., Inc.*, 655 S.E.2d 259, 263 (Ga. Ct. App. 2007), *cert. denied*, 2008 Ga. LEXIS 270 (Mar. 10, 2008).

On review of an order denying class certification, Georgia appellate courts will consider the factual findings as adopted by the trial court and affirm them unless clearly erroneous, and will review the conclusions of law for an abuse of discretion. *Brenntag Mid South, Inc.*, 710 S.E.2d at 574.

Judgments entered with respect to certified class must comply with O.C.G.A. § 9-11-23(c)(3). The failure of a judgment to account for persons excluded from the class may result in an appellate court vacating the judgment and remanding the case. *See, e.g., American Home Servs., Inc. v. A Fast Sign Co., Inc.*, 747 S.E.2d 205, 207 (Ga. Ct. App. 2013), *cert. denied*, 2014 Ga. LEXIS 438 (May 19, 2014).

The following paragraphs summarize other key considerations in Georgia class action practice.

a. Numerosity

Numerosity is the threshold factor, the *sine qua non* for class actions. *American Debt Found., Inc. v. Hodzic*, 720 S.E.2d 283, 285 (Ga. Ct. App. 2011); *see also Murphy*, 195 S.E.2d at 25. In order to satisfy this requirement, the plaintiff need not allege the exact number and identity of the class members but must only establish that joinder is impracticable through some evidence or reasonable estimate of the number of purported class members. *Brenntag Mid South, Inc.*, 710 S.E.2d at 574 (finding no abuse of discretion in trial court defining class by geographic boundaries in alleged chemical release case). Additionally, the class simply must meet a minimum standard of definiteness which will allow the trial court to determine membership in the proposed class. *Id.*

A named plaintiff seeking class certification must first demonstrate that the proposed class is adequately defined and clearly ascertainable. *Atlanta Impound, Inc. v. Attia*, 913 S.E.2d 869, 873 (Ga. Ct. App. 2025) (quoting *Cherry v. Dometic Corp.*, 986 F.3d 1296, 1302 (11th Cir. 2021) ("Ascertainability is an implied prerequisite of [OCGA § 9-11-23]."")). There is no requirement that every class member, other than the named plaintiffs, be identified at the outset of the litigation; instead, a class definition is necessary only to establish that the class does, in fact, exist and that its members will be identifiable. *Bible*, 833 S.E.2d at 544 (citing *Campos v. ChoicePoint, Inc.*, 237 F.R.D. 478, 488 (N.D. Ga. 2006)). The trial court must simply establish that the class is clearly ascertainable, i.e., capable of being determined. *See id.* Significantly, administrative feasibility is not an inherent aspect of, nor is it a prerequisite to, establishing ascertainability. *Atlanta Impound, Inc.*, 913 S.E.2d at 873. Instead, a proposed class is ascertainable if it is adequately defined such that its membership is capable of determination. *Id.* at 873–74.

Although mere allegations of numerosity are insufficient to meet this prerequisite, a plaintiff need not show the precise number of members in the class. *Cagle*, 889 S.E.2d at 185 (quoting *Vega v. T-Mobile USA, Inc.*, 564 F.3d 1256, 1267 (11th Cir. 2009)). But even so, a plaintiff still bears the burden of "making some showing, affording the [trial] court the means to make a supported factual finding, that the class actually certified meets the numerosity requirement." *Cagle*, 889 S.E.2d at 185. Indeed, "[m]ere speculation as to the number of class members—even if such speculation is a bet worth making—cannot support a finding of numerosity." *Id.* Thus, for example, when a putative class is some subset of a larger pool, the trial court may not infer numerosity from the number in the larger pool alone. *Id.* at 186 (finding lack of numerosity where the only conclusion that could be drawn from the plaintiff's evidence "was that the number of class members would be equal to or less than 39,496 and equal to or greater than zero").

The concept of numerosity applies to the number of *putative* class members, and does not require that the actual number of class members be determined before a class is certified. *Bickerstaff*, 788 S.E.2d at 795 (emphasis in original) (holding that contractual time-limit for opting out of arbitration provision was tolled by filing of class action, and that putative class members' ability to opt-out of class after certification did not defeat numerosity). All putative class members benefit from the class representative's filing of the complaint just as if each member had filed the complaint himself or herself. *Id.* at 794. That a putative class representative cannot bind the putative class members before certification does not equate to numerosity lacking. *Id.*

Although the focus of the numerosity requirement generally concerns whether joinder of proposed class members is impractical and not whether the number of proposed class members is too few, the Georgia Court of Appeals has recognized that the Eleventh Circuit Court of Appeals has, at least in general terms, found that a class of fewer than 21 members is inadequate. *American Debt Found., Inc.*, 720 S.E.2d at 285–86. On the other hand, impracticability of joinder is generally presumed if the class includes more than 40 members. *Id.* at 286. Parties seeking class certification do not need to know the precise number of class members but they must make reasonable estimates with support as to the size of the proposed class. *Bible*, 833 S.E.2d at 543 (citing *In re Checking Account Overdraft Litig.*, 286 F.R.D. 645, 651 (S.D. Fla. 2012) (generally less than 21 is inadequate, more than 40 is sufficient)).

To make this determination, Georgia courts look not only to the number of putative members but also at all other relevant factors; for example, the geographical dispersion of the class, the ease with which class members may be identified, the nature of the action, and the size of each plaintiff's claim. *American Debt Found., Inc.*, 720 S.E.2d at 287. Georgia's class action statute requires at least a minimal causal connection between the numerosity of the potential plaintiffs and the impracticability of their joinder. *Id.*

Upon a finding that the "numerousness" of parties makes it impracticable without great delay and other inconveniences to join them all, which would obstruct and probably defeat the purposes of justice, the trial court may consider whether it represents a proper case to proceed as a class action. *Id.* at 285.

b. Commonality

Traditionally, commonality has referred to the group characteristics of the class as a whole, while typicality refers to the individual characteristics of the named plaintiff in relation to the class. *Brenntag Mid South, Inc.*, 710 S.E.2d at 575. However, Georgia courts also have recognized that the commonality and typicality requirements of Rule 23(a) tend to merge. *Rite Aid*, 726 S.E.2d at 581. In considering whether common questions will predominate, Georgia Courts look to the specific claims asserted. *Endochoice Holdings, Inc. v. Raczewski*, 830 S.E.2d 597, 603–04 (Ga. Ct. App. 2019).

Prior to the U.S. Supreme Court's *Dukes* decision, Georgia courts generally held that before the class certification decision, plaintiffs needed only to present information on commonality sufficient to establish the existence of such common issues. However, then as now they were not required to establish that they would ultimately prevail on the merits. *Griffin Indus., Inc.*, 635 S.E.2d at 233 (finding common issues relating to operation of agricultural plant). *See also State Farm Mut. Auto. Ins. Co. v. Mabry*, 556 S.E.2d 114, 117 (Ga. 2001) (finding common issues in insurer's handling of certain vehicle damages claims); *UNUM Life Ins. Co. of Am. v. Crutchfield*, 568 S.E.2d 767, 769 (Ga. Ct. App. 2002) (finding common issues related to operation of insurer's computer program and stating that "claims arising from interpretation of form agreements are considered to be 'classic' cases for treatment as a class action"). The commonality requirement did not require that all questions of law and fact were common to every member of the class; rather, the rule as interpreted at that time required only that resolution of the common questions affected all or a substantial number of the class members. *Brenntag Mid South, Inc.*, 710 S.E.2d at 575.

Post-*Dukes*, to establish the sort of commonality that O.C.G.A. § 9-11-23(a)(2) requires, a plaintiff is required to show that the class members have suffered the "same injury." *Bowden,* 845 S.E.2d at 561; *Ratner*, 762 S.E.2d at 423 (citing *Dukes*, 131 S. Ct. at 2551) (reversing class certification after examining evidence that plaintiffs submitted toward proving on a classwide basis that area by which the class was defined was in fact contaminated with hydrogen sulfide gas from nearby sludge fields). To do so, a plaintiff must point to a "common contention" that each member of the class has suffered the same instance or course of wrongful conduct, and the plaintiff also must show that this "common contention" is capable of classwide resolution—which means that determination of its truth or falsity will resolve an issue that is central to the validity of each one of the claims in one stroke. *Ratner*, 762 S.E.2d at 423.

At class certification, a plaintiff need not prove the merit of her or his "common contention"—that is, the plaintiff need not definitively prove that each and every member of the class did, in fact, suffer the "same injury." *Id.* at n.12. But the plaintiff must show that the "common contention" is capable of being proved at once for the whole class. *Id.* To do that, the plaintiff must point to some evidence by which the plaintiff could prove the merit of the "common contention." *Id.*

Establishing commonality is a "relatively low bar" and "even a single common question will do." *Doe v. Vest Monroe, LLC*, 890 S.E.2d 439, 444 (2023) (reversed on other grounds, *Vest Monroe*, 906 S.E.2d 406) (quoting *Dukes*, 564 U.S. at 359). The focus of the commonality inquiry is not on the strength of each plaintiff's claim, but instead is on whether the defendant's conduct was common as to all the class members. *Vest Monroe*, 893 S.E.2d at 444. The principal requirement of *Dukes* is merely a single common contention that enables the class action to generate common answers apt to drive the resolution of the litigation. *Id.* These common answers may indeed relate to the injurious effects experienced by the class members, but they may also relate to the defendant's injurious conduct. *Id.* (quoting *In re Deepwater Horizon*, 739 F3d 790, 811 (5th Cir. 2014)).

Variations in state law will not defeat commonality where the variations would not have any legal significance—i.e., they would not necessitate the application of a different set of legal principles. *See Resource Life Insurance Co. v. Buckner*, 698 S.E.2d at 30–31.

c. Typicality

A class representative must be part of the class and possess the same interest and suffer the same injury as the class members. *Vest Monroe*, 906 S.E.2d at 411 (affirming trial court's finding that typicality was lacking) (quoting *Gen. Tel. Co. of the Southwest v. Falcon*, 457 U. S. 147, 156 (1982)). In other words, there must be a nexus between the class representative's claims or defenses and the common questions of fact or law which unite the class. *Vest Monroe*, 906 S.E.2d at 411 (quoting *Kornberg v. Carnival Cruise Lines*, 741 F.2d 1332, 1337 (11th Cir. 1984)). A sufficient nexus is established if the claims or defenses of the class and the class representative arise from the same event or pattern or practice and are based on the same legal theory. *Id.* Typicality, however, does not require identical claims or defenses. *Id.* A factual variation will not render a class representative's claim atypical unless the factual position of the representative markedly differs from that of other members of the class. *Id.* Typicality derives its independent legal significance from its ability to screen out class actions in which the legal or factual position of the representatives is markedly different from that of other members of the class even though common issues of law or fact are present. *Vest Monroe*, 906 S.E.2d at 413 (quoting *Marcus v. BMW of North America*, 687 F.3d 583, 598 (3d Cir. 2012)). Where the qualitative nature of a putative class representative's claims, and the proof thereof, is materially different (in contrast to when the class members are quantitatively more injured than the putative representative and thus would be entitled to more damages), resolution of the putative representative's claims would not necessarily resolve the claims of the class members belonging to the other group, thus defeating typicality. *Vest Monroe*, 906 S.E.2d at 413 (emphasis in original).

The typicality requirement under O.C.G.A. § 9-11-23(a) is satisfied upon a showing that the defendant "committed the same unlawful acts in the same method against an entire class." *Liberty Lending Servs. v. Canada*, 668 S.E.2d 3, 10 (Ga. Ct. App. 2008). A purported class representative must show that her claims are typical of those of the putative class members. *Life Ins. Co. of Ga. v. Meeks*, 617 S.E.2d 179 (Ga. Ct. App. 2005) (named plaintiff's claims against insurer for medical treatment reimbursement ruled atypical of putative class member claims). In other words, to be typical, a class representative must possess the same interest and suffer the same injury as the class members. *See, e.g., Deal v. Miller*, 739 S.E.2d 487, 492 (Ga. Ct. App. 2013), *affirmed*, 761 S.E.2d 274 (Ga. 2014). The Court of Appeals in *City of Roswell v. Bible* explained that the typicality test centers on whether other members have the same or similar injury, whether the action is based on conduct which is not unique to the named class plaintiffs, and whether other class members have been injured by the same course of conduct. *Bible*, 833 S.E.2d at 544 (citing *In re Checking Account Overdraft Litig.*, 286 F.R.D. 645, 653 (S.D. Fla. 2012)). This test is not demanding and is satisfied if the claims or defenses of the class and the class representative arise from the same event or pattern or practice and are based on the same legal theory. *Id.* (citing *Ault v. Walt Disney World Co.*, 692 F.3d 1212, 1216 (11th Cir. 2012)). The typicality requirement may be satisfied despite substantial factual differences when there is a strong similarity of legal theories. *Id.* at 6 (citing *Local 703, I.B. of T. Grocery & Food Employees Welfare Fund v. Regions Financial Corp.*, 762 F.3d 1248, 1260 (11th Cir. 2014)).

Typicality measures whether a sufficient nexus exists between the claims of the named representatives and those of the class at large. *Brenntag Mid South, Inc.*, 710 S.E.2d at 575. A sufficient nexus is established if the claims or defenses of the class and the class representatives arise from the same event or pattern or practice and are based on the same legal theory. *Id.*

The Georgia Supreme Court has observed that the whole class action scheme is based upon the premise that a member of a class may act as a representative of the other purported class members. *Bickerstaff*, 788 S.E.2d at 792–93. Georgia law provides that contractual obligations may be performed by an agent, where personal skill is not required, and the law of agency provides generally that whatever one may do himself may be done by an agent. *Id.* at 793 (citing O.C.G.A. §§ 13-4-20 and 10-6-5). The representative in a class action is an agent for the class members, and the class action is a device by which that representative is an agent for persons who have not appeared or given even tacit consent. *Id.* The satisfaction of a precondition for suit by the class plaintiff typically avoids the necessity for each class member to satisfy the precondition individually. *Id.* at 794. Consistent with the law of agency, members of the class who do not opt-out thereby ratify the filing of the complaint, and that ratification will relate back to the date that the complaint was filed. *Id.* at 795 (citing *American Pipe and Constr. Co. v. Utah*, 414 U.S. 538 (1974)).

A Georgia court may also look to whether the putative class plaintiff acquiesced in the conduct about which he complains. *See, e.g., Lewis v. Knology, Inc.*, 799 S.E.2d 247, 253 (Ga. Ct. App. 2017), *cert. denied* (Sept. 13, 2017) (considering whether plaintiff had acquiesced in corporate merger); *Peacock*, 726 S.E.2d 577 (noting that plaintiff complained about sale of pharmacy records but sought to have prescriptions filled at defendant new pharmacy).

The Georgia Supreme Court's *Bickerstaff* decision gave credence to numerous Georgia Court of Appeals decisions that held, presumably but not expressly pursuant to the "typicality" analysis, that a named plaintiff's satisfaction of prerequisites to suit (such as *ante litem* notice) may be sufficient to satisfy the requirement for other unnamed class members generally. *See, e.g., City of Atlanta v. Benator*, 714 S.E.2d 109, 112 (Ga. Ct. App. 2011); *Schorr v. Countrywide Home Loans, Inc.*, 697 S.E.2d 827, 829 (Ga. 2010) (pre-suit written demand requirement in context of O.C.G.A. § 44-14-3); *Barnes v. City of Atlanta*, 637 S.E.2d 4, 6 (Ga. 2006) (tax refund class action); *Resource Life Insurance*, 698 S.E.2d 19 at 28 (in putative class action involving claims based on insurance policy language, the filing of the class action itself served as sufficient notice to the insurer where the policy language required insureds to provide notice but the language does not give rise to a condition precedent). *See also Homes of Ga., Inc. v. Humana Employers Health Plan of Ga., Inc.*, 640 S.E.2d 313, 316 (Ga. Ct. App. 2006) (holding that class allegations of certain violations of the Georgia Insurance Code do not require the exhaustion of administrative remedies), *cert. denied*, 2007 Ga. LEXIS 339 (Ga. Apr. 24, 2007). *But see Mack v. Georgia Auto Pawn, Inc.*, 585 S.E.2d 661 (Ga. Ct. App. 2003) (in context of notice and good faith offer requirements of the Georgia Pawnshop Act, holding that where a Georgia statute requires *ante litem* notice prior to suit, a putative class representative is incapable of providing notice on behalf of a putative class and class certification will be denied on that basis).

d. Adequacy of Representation

Georgia courts must also consider the ability of the named plaintiff to represent the class. A named plaintiff bears the burden to demonstrate her adequacy to represent the proposed class, which burden includes showing that she is a member of the class that she seeks to represent. *McGarry*, 599 S.E.2d at 36. Where a plaintiff's participation is so minimal that they virtually have abdicated to their attorneys the conduct of the case, the plaintiff is inadequate. *Lewis*, 799 S.E.2d 247, 250 (citing *London v. Wal-Mart Stores, Inc.*, 340 F.3d 1246, 1254 (11th Cir. 2003)). To examine the adequacy of a proposed class representative, the Georgia Court of Appeals has considered the person's knowledge of the law firms representing her, her familiarity with her counsel, whether she knew of or had negotiated her counsel's fees, her knowledge of the basis for her claims, and whether she had appeared at the hearing on class certification to provide evidence in support of her proposed representation of the class. *Id.* at 251. *See also Raczewski*, 830 S.E.2d at 602–03 (adequacy showing sufficient where testimony and evidence demonstrated named plaintiffs had sufficient knowledge and understanding of the claims, and each had shown a sufficient degree of participation in the litigation).

The Georgia Court of Appeals has declined to find named plaintiffs inadequate where they abandoned certain claims, the statutes of limitation had not run, and potential class members who wished to pursue the abandoned claims had the option of opting out of the class and pursuing the claims individually. *Id.* at 603.

But more recently, the Georgia Court of Appeals has found that where the named plaintiffs "unequivocally waived" emotional distress claims to facilitate class certification, that waiver created an insurmountable conflict in terms of their adequacy to represent the class. *Pride Medical, Inc. v. Doe*, 879 S.E.2d 845 (2022). The Court of Appeals in *Pride Medical* reasoned that a plaintiff cannot be allowed to represent a class where he has opted to pursue certain claims on a classwide basis while jeopardizing the class members' ability to subsequently pursue other claims. *Id.* at 849–50. Thus, where a plaintiff seeks to "throw away" recovery for emotional distress damages that could be a major component of each class member's recovery, he is not an adequate class representative and thus certification is inappropriate. *Id.* at 850.

Other important aspects of adequate representation are whether the plaintiff's counsel is experienced and competent, and whether the plaintiff's interests are antagonistic to those of the class. *Jones,* 418 S.E.2d at 24. The class certification movant's burden includes an evidentiary showing that other putative class members share in the movant's alleged dissatisfaction. *Id.* at 25. Georgia courts also will examine whether class counsel pose any conflicts of interest. *Duffy v. The Landings Assoc., Inc.*, 563 S.E.2d 174, 176 (Ga. Ct. App. 2002) (wherein named alleged class representative was member of law firm seeking to represent the class).

It is improper for a court to simply label circumstances as being potential conflicts of interest without explaining why the conflict might exist. *Gay*, 652 S.E.2d at 202–03 (rejecting conflict of interest finding that was based on mere reference to a motion for attorneys' fees filed by defendant against named plaintiffs and their attorneys).

The entity seeking to represent the alleged class also must mail an initial notice of the alleged class action to each member of such class. *Hill v. General Finance Corp. of Ga.*, 241 S.E.2d 282, 285 (Ga. Ct. App. 1977); *Ford Motor Credit*, 332 S.E.2d at 348. Consequently, one factor to be considered in determining class certification is the named plaintiff's financial responsibility for costs that he or she must bear. *Id.*

When the named plaintiff has no valid claim against the defendant, he is not eligible to represent the purported class. *Life Ins. Co. of Ga.*, 617 S.E.2d at 185. However, any argument that a named plaintiff is not an adequate representative because he will not ultimately prevail on his claim does not comprise an appropriate basis for denying class certification. *Taylor Auto Group v. Jessie*, 527 S.E.2d 256, 258 (Ga. Ct. App. 1999), *cert. denied*, 2000 Ga. LEXIS 464 (Ga. May 26, 2000).

e. Predominance

The Rule 23(b)(3) predominance inquiry tests whether proposed classes are sufficiently cohesive to warrant adjudication by representation. *Brenntag Mid South, Inc.*, 710 S.E.2d at 576. A plaintiff may satisfy this requirement by showing that issues subject to class-wide proof predominate over issues requiring proof that is unique to the individual class members. *Id.*

When plaintiffs seek to assert rights merely common to the putative class, class certification will be denied if individualized issues predominate over common issues. *Stevens v. Thomas*, 361 S.E.2d 800, 804 (Ga. 1987); *Tanner v. Brasher*, 326 S.E.2d 218, 221 (Ga. 1985) ("[w]here the resolution of individual questions plays . . . an integral part in the determination of liability, a class action suit is inappropriate"); *Bowden*, 845 S.E.2d at 562 (commonality found lacking where, "at the level of specificity required to actually resolve the class claims, any commonality breaks down into an individualized inquiry").

The predominance inquiry requires a court to consider how a trial on the merits would be conducted if a class were certified to ensure that what is purportedly a class case will remain so once put before a jury, based upon the nature of the evidence that the plaintiff will have to present to prove the classwide claims. *Perez v. Atlanta Check Cashers, Inc.*, 692 S.E.2d 670, 676–77 (Ga. Ct. App. 2010).

Common issues of fact and law predominate if they have a direct impact on every class member's effort to establish liability and on every class member's entitlement to injunctive and monetary relief. *Rollins, Inc. v. Warren*, 653 S.E.2d 794, 797 (Ga. Ct. App. 2007), *cert. denied*, 2008 Ga. LEXIS 216 (Feb. 25, 2008). As long as common issues predominate, a class may be certified even if some individual questions of law or fact exist. *Village Auto Ins. Co.,* 649 S.E.2d at 866.

The predominance inquiry focuses on the legal or factual questions that qualify each class member's cause as a genuine controversy and is far more demanding than the commonality requirement;

whether an issue predominates can be determined only after considering what value the resolution of the class-wide issue will have in each class member's underlying cause of action. *Diallo v. American Intercontinental University, Inc.*, 687 S.E.2d 278, 283 (Ga. Ct. App. 2009).

To determine whether the requirement of predominance is satisfied, a court must first identify the parties' claims and defenses and their elements. *Ansley Walk Condo. Ass'n*, 867 S.E.2d at 604 (quoting *Brown v. Electrolux Home Products*, 817 F.3d 1225, 1234 (11th Cir. 2016)). The court should then classify these issues as common questions or individual questions by predicting how the parties will prove them at trial. *Id. See also Roland*, 655 S.E.2d at 263 (individualized issues predominated as to elements of alleged breaches of contract, warranty, and implied warranty of merchantability).

Where, after adjudication of the class-wide issues, plaintiffs must still introduce a great deal of individualized proof or argue a number of individualized legal points to establish most or all of the elements of their individual claims, such claims are not suitable for class certification under Rule 23(b)(3). *Rollins, Inc.*, 653 S.E.2d at 797.

Consistent with *Walmart Stores, Inc. v. Dukes*, the Georgia Supreme Court has explained that what matters to class certification is not the raising of common questions—even in droves—but rather the capacity of a class-wide proceeding to generate common answers apt to drive the resolution of the litigation. *Bowden*, 845 S.E.2d at 561 (commonality lacking in case challenging reasonableness of hospital liens, where ultimate reasonableness of charges hinged on looking at the specific bills in question and analyzing them against numerous factors); *MCG Health, Inc. v. Perry*, 755 S.E.2d 341, 343–44 (Ga. Ct. App. 2014) (class certification reversed in case involving insurers' hospital liens upon injured patients' causes of action against the tortfeasors) (quoting *Dukes*, 131 S. Ct. at 2551). Dissimilarities within the proposed class are what have the potential to impede the generation of common answers. 755 S.E.2d at 344. In other words, a common question is not enough when the *answer* may vary with each class member and is determinative of whether the member is properly part of the class. *Bowden*, 845 S.E.2d at 561 (emphasis in original); *see also Rollins, Inc.*, 653 S.E.2d at 797 (same principle, applied in the context of breach of contract claims).

A class action is not authorized when the issue presented must be resolved on a case-by-case basis and the resolution of individual questions plays an integral part in the determination of liability. *Bowden*, 845 S.E.2d at 561–62; *Duffy*, 563 S.E.2d at 176; *Carnett's, Inc.*, 610 S.E.2d at 532 (commonality lacking where movant failed to prove that all putative class members were similarly situated in satisfying one element of alleged statutory violation); *Life Ins. Co. of Ga.*, 617 S.E.2d at 185 (abuse of discretion to certify class where many individualized suits would be necessary, even if one or two common issues could be resolved class-wide). Further, Georgia appellate courts have refused to condone the certification of a class when the circumstances surrounding a member's actual response to the defendant's allegedly wrongful act could vary widely. *Rite Aid*, 726 S.E.2d at 580.

The presence of individualized damages issues does not prevent a finding that the common issues in the case predominate. *Ansley Walk Condo. Ass'n*, 867 S.E.2d 600, 606 (2021) (quoting *Brown*, 817 F.3d at 1239). The black letter rule is that individual damage calculations generally do not defeat a finding that common issues predominate. *Id.* Although damages often raise numerous individual questions, predominance is a qualitative rather than a quantitative concept. *Id.* It is not determined simply by counting noses; that is, determining whether there are more common issues or more individual issues, regardless of relative importance. *Id.*

No matter how individualized the issue of damages may be, determination of damages may be reserved for individual treatment with the question of liability tried as a class action. *Doe v. Vest Monroe, LLC*, 890 S.E.2d at 444–45 (reversed on other grounds, *Vest Monroe*, 906 S.E.2d 406) (quoting *Glazer v. Whirlpool Corp.*, 722 F.3d 838, 854 (6th Cir. 2013). The legal requirement that class members have all suffered the same injury can be satisfied by an instance of the defendant's injurious conduct, even when the resulting injurious effects—the damages—are diverse. *Doe v. Vest Monroe, LLC*, 890 S.E.2d at 445 (reversed on other grounds, *Vest Monroe*, 906 S.E.2d 406) (quoting *In re Deepwater Horizon*, 739 F.3d at 810). In certain cases, individualized damages issues are, in and of themselves, sufficient to justify a trial court refusing to certify a class. *Hill*, 241 S.E.2d at 285; *Williams v. Cox Enterprises, Inc*., 283 S.E.2d 367, 370 (Ga. Ct. App. 1981). Individual damages defeat predominance when they are accompanied by significant individualized questions going to liability. *Ansley Walk Condo. Ass'n*, 867 S.E.2d at 606 (quoting *Brown*, 817 F.3d at 1240). However, minor variations in amount of damages do not destroy the class when the legal issues are common. *Sta-Power Indus., Inc.*, 216 S.E.2d at 901. Plaintiffs need only come forward with plausible statistical or economic methodologies to demonstrate impact on a class-wide basis. *Fortis Ins. Co. v. Kahn*, 683 S.E.2d 4, 9 (Ga. Ct. App. 2009), *cert. denied sub nom Fortis Benefits Ins. Co. v. Kahn*, 2010 Ga. LEXIS 48 (Ga. Jan. 12, 2010). Particularly where damages can be computed according to some formula, statistical analysis, or other easy or essentially mechanical methods, the fact that damages must be calculated on an individual basis is no impediment to class certification. *Id.*

Moreover, if fraud based on oral misrepresentations is the gravamen of a complaint, then class certification is inappropriate. *Stevens*, 361 S.E.2d at 804. However, the simple fact that reliance is an element in a cause of action is not an absolute bar to class certification. *Liberty Lending Servs.*, 668 S.E.2d at 12 (upholding certification of class claims alleging theft by conversion, theft by deception, and Georgia RICO violations).

With respect to claims of fraud based upon written representations, the reliance element may sometimes be presumed. *Life Ins. Co. of Ga*., 617 S.E.2d at 185. Where the fact that similar written representations are common to all the agreements at issue, the circumstantial evidence that can be used to show reliance is also common to the whole class. *Liberty Lending Servs.*, 668 S.E. 2d at 12. In another instance, the Court of Appeals held that common issues predominated where the defendant allegedly rigged its computer system such that it automatically added undisclosed charges onto the putative class members' accounts. *Village Auto Ins. Co*., 649 S.E.2d 862.

Under certain circumstances, the qualitative analysis necessary to show liability for injuries such as loss of consortium, anxiety, and emotional distress may demonstrate that common questions vital to proving causation must be answered on a highly individualized basis, rendering class certification improper. *Doctors Hospital Surgery Center, L.P. v. Webb,* 704 S.E.2d 185, 188–89 (Ga. Ct. App. 2010).

The presence of counterclaims has been held to be, in and of itself, sufficient to deny class certification. *Hill*, 241 S.E.2d at 285. Similarly, although a defense may arise and may affect different class members differently, this occurrence does not compel a finding that individual issues predominate over common ones. *Fortis Ins. Co*, 683 S.E.2d at 9. So long as a sufficient constellation of common issues binds class members together, variations in the sources and application of a defense will not automatically foreclose class certification. *Id. See also Bible*, 833 S.E.2d at 543 ("unique affirmative defenses will rarely predominate where a common source of conduct is established") (citing *In re Checking Account Overdraft Litig.,* 286 F.R.D. at 656).

Where the defendant's liability can be determined on a class-wide basis because the cause of the disaster is a single course of conduct that is identical for each of the plaintiffs, a class action may be the best-suited vehicle to resolve such a controversy. *Brenntag Mid South, Inc.*, 710 S.E.2d at 576.

The Georgia Court of Appeals has stated that common questions of law and fact may predominate when an action is brought on behalf of purchasers of agreements from a common source, the character of the right sought to be enforced is common, and common relief is sought. *UNUM Life Ins. Co.*, 568 S.E.2d at 769; *Bible*, 833 S.E.2d at 542 ("similar claims arising from the breach of a single contract present a classic case for treatment as a class action"). *See also Holiday*, 885 S.E.2d at 208 ("[F]orm contracts are ideal for class treatment.") (quoting *Venerus v. Avis Budget Car Rental*, 723 Fed. App'x 807, 815 (11th Cir. 2018)).

Where corporate policies constitute the very heart of the plaintiffs' claims, common issues will predominate because those policies would necessarily have to be re-proven by every plaintiff. *Bowden*, 833 S.E.2d at 543 (citing *In re Checking Account Overdraft Litig.*, 286 F.R.D. at 656).

Actions on behalf of defrauded securities purchasers present a particularly desirable situation for a class action. *Raczewski*, 830 S.E.2d at 604 (citing *Avant*, 134 Ga. App. at 954). In other words, where claims are based on an alleged misstatement in the offering materials, the question of whether those materials in fact contained a misstatement usually predominates. *Id.* In that securities claim context, the *Raczewski* Court found that for defendants to prove that common questions do not predominate, they are required to submit evidence sufficient to show the existence of individual investor knowledge sufficient to preclude a finding by the court that common liability issues predominate over individual knowledge issues. *Id.* at 604 (citing *In re Kosmos Energy Ltd. Securities Litig.*, 299 F.R.D. 133, 152 (N.D. Tex. 2014)).

Individualized issues involving multiple states' laws may render class certification improper. *International Business Machines Corp. v. Kemp*, 536 S.E.2d 303 (Ga. Ct. App. 2000). However, the Georgia Court of Appeals has upheld the certification of a class involving the laws of 38 states where (1) the class members executed materially similar form contracts, and (2) the opponent of certification did not come forward with evidence showing that the laws of the different states would yield different results among the class members. *J.M.I.C. Life Ins. Co.*, 634 S.E.2d at 128.

Not all cases involving purchasers of agreements from a common source qualify for class treatment. *UNUM Life Ins. Co.*, 568 S.E.2d at 769. A class action is not authorized where the issue presented must be resolved on a contract-by-contract basis, and where the resolution of individual questions plays such an integral part in the determination of liability. *Aetna Casualty & Surety Co. v. Cantrell*, 399 S.E.2d 237, 239 (Ga. Ct. App. 1990); *see also Life Ins. Co. of Ga.*, 617 S.E.2d at 184–85 (finding certification inappropriate where written contracts varied among putative class members, or where account-by-account analysis would be required); *Rollins, Inc.*, 653 S.E.2d at 798–99 (identifying individualized issues relating to allegedly forged signatures, and to whether putative class members fulfilled affirmative obligations under contract); *Perez v. Atlanta Check Cashers, Inc.*, 692 S.E.2d 670 (Ga. Ct. App. 2010) (individualized issues predominated where questions involved whether putative class members gave authorizations or consents to release of personally identifying information, and where there was no evidence showing lack of consent on a classwide basis).

In the context of personal injury tort claims, the Georgia Court of Appeals affirmed a denial of class certification where the risk exposure varied by putative class member. *R.S.W. v. Emory Healthcare, Inc.*, 659 S.E.2d 680 (Ga. Ct. App. 2008). In *R.S.W.*, the Court found that the answer to the question whether a healthcare provider breached its duty to warn surgery patients was a highly individualized, case-by-case determination that precluded class certification. *Id.* at 683. *See also John E. King and Associates v. Toler*, 675 S.E.2d 492 (Ga. Ct. App. 2009) (class certification reversed where proof of each claim would require evidence of each class member's chiropractic treatment, and claim handling by defendant law firm), *cert. denied,* 2009 Ga. LEXIS 345 (Ga. June 1, 2009).

f. Superiority

The superiority rule requires the courts to balance, in terms of fairness and efficiency, the merits of a class action against those of alternative available methods of adjudication. *Brenntag Mid South, Inc.*, 710 S.E.2d at 577. Thus, the issue is not whether a class action will be difficult to manage; instead, the trial court is to consider the relative advantages of a class action suit over other forms of litigation which might be available. *Id.*

The Georgia Court of Appeals has held that it is insufficient for a court to determine superiority based on merely one of the four superiority factors in O.C.G.A. § 9-11-23(b)(3)(a)-(d). *McGarry*, 599 S.E.2d at 37. That Court also has rejected a "cursory" ruling on superiority where the trial court simply restated the requirement and held that it was not satisfied. *Gay*, 652 S.E.2d at 203. Further, the controlling issue here is not whether a class action will be difficult to manage. *Earthlink, Inc.*, 666 S.E.2d at 424. Instead, the trial court is to consider the relative advantages of a class action over other forms of litigation which might be available. *Id.* A classwide proceeding in this case has the capacity to generate common answers that will drive the resolution of this litigation and renders a class action superior to other available methods for the fair and efficient adjudication of the controversy. *SunTrust Bank v. Bickerstaff*, 824 S.E.2d 717, 724 (Ga. Ct. App. 2019) (citing *Dukes*, 131 S. Ct. 2541, 2551)).

One of the purposes of class litigation must be to prevent burdening the judicial system or the class members with a multiplicity of individual suits. *Life Ins. Co. of Ga.*, 617 S.E.2d at 185. Georgia courts have held class actions to be particularly appropriate in cases involving the sale of unregistered securities. *Trend Star Continental, Ltd. v. Branham*, 469 S.E.2d 750, 751 (Ga. Ct. App. 1996). Superiority also has been found where the claims arose from the events leading to the release of a chemical plume and the resulting evacuation, the damages involved for each class member were relatively small, and the economic reality dictated that the suit proceed as a class action or not at all. *Brenntag Mid South, Inc.*, 710 S.E.2d at 577. *See also Rice v. Fulton County*, 897 S.E.2d at 497 ("[W]here the defendant's liability can be determined on a class-wide basis because the cause of the disaster is a single course of conduct which is identical for each of the plaintiffs, a class action may be the best suited vehicle to resolve such a controversy.") (quoting *Sterling v. Velsicol Chem. Corp.*, 855 F2d 1188, 1197 (III) (6th Cir. 1988)).

However, in the registered securities context, negligent representation cases require that each investor show actual and justifiable reliance on the representation at issue, and this requirement may impact the suitability of a case for class certification. *White v. BDO Seidman, LLP*, 549 S.E.2d 490 (Ga. Ct. App. 2001).

g. Injunctive Relief

Certification under O.C.G.A. § 9-11-23(b)(2) is inappropriate if the predominant relief sought in the action is monetary damages. *Rollins, Inc*., 653 S.E.2d at 800–01. Monetary relief predominates unless it is incidental to requested injunctive or declaratory relief. *Id.* at 801. *See also Doctors Hospital Surgery Center, L.P.,* 704 S.E.2d at 187 (holding that "trial court abused its discretion in granting certification based on the claim for medical monitoring because the recovery of monetary damages [wa]s at the core of this dispute"). Further, monetary damages claims are not merely incidental when the damages claims of each individual putative class member would require detailed, case-by-case fact finding at mini-trials. *Rollins, Inc*., 653 S.E.2d at 802. Declaratory and injunctive relief do not predominate where the purpose of that requested relief is to lay a legal foundation for the recovery of money damages. *Id.* at 801 (reversing Rule 23(b)(2) certification where requested declaratory and injunctive relief "would be little more than an overture to the damages opera").

In determining whether certification under 23(b)(2) is appropriate, a court should not focus on the subjective intentions of the class representatives and their counsel in bringing suit—i.e., it should not focus on whether the primary motive for the litigation was the recovery of monetary damages. *Resource Life Insurance*, 698 S.E.2d at 31–32. Rather, the relevant questions are whether members of the proposed class would benefit from the injunctive relief sought and whether any monetary relief is incidental to the injunctive relief. *Id.* at 32.

The mere fact that putative 23(b)(2) class members seek monetary damages in addition to equitable relief does not automatically mean that those damages are the predominate relief sought. *Id.* at 33. Rather, monetary relief is incidental to injunctive and declaratory relief where damages are capable of computation by means of objective standards and not dependent in any significant way on the intangible, subjective differences of each class member's circumstances. *Id.*

The key to the (b)(2) class is the indivisible nature of the injunctive or declaratory remedy warranted—the notion that the conduct is such that it can be enjoined or declared unlawful only as to all of the class members or as to none of them. *Cosby*, 912 S.E.2d at 145 (citing *Dukes*, 131 S. Ct. at 2257). In other words, Rule 23(b)(2) applies only when a single injunction or declaratory judgment would provide relief to each member of the class. *Id.* It does not authorize class certification when each individual class member would be entitled to a different injunction or declaratory judgment against the defendant. *Id.* Similarly, it does not authorize class certification when each class member would be entitled to an individualized award of monetary damages. *Id.*

h. Class Attorneys' Fees

Georgia adheres to the common-fund doctrine. *See, e.g., Barnes*, 637 S.E.2d at 7–8. The doctrine provides that a person, who at his own expense and for the benefit of persons in addition to himself maintains a successful action for the preservation, protection, or creation of a common fund in which others may share with him, is entitled to reasonable attorneys' fees from the fund as a whole. *Private Truck Council, Inc.*, 258 Ga. at 534–35. The doctrine rests on the perception that persons who obtain the benefit of a lawsuit without contributing to its cost are unjustly enriched at the successful litigant's expense. *Id.* at 535.

i. Settlement Considerations

Class action settlements generally constitute an adjudication on the merits for *res judicata* purposes. For such a settlement to do so, it is sufficient that the merits were or could have been determined pursuant to an appropriate handling of the case. *AirTouch Cellular,* 534 S.E.2d at 836.

It is a well-settled rule that only class members have standing to challenge a class settlement. *American Med. Sec., Inc. v. Parker*, 612 S.E.2d 261, 263 (Ga. 2005). Non-class members whose rights and remedies are not affected by a settlement lack standing to challenge the settlement on an individual basis. *Id.*

When a class settlement has been achieved, Georgia courts are to engage in a "percentage of the fund" analysis to determine appropriate class counsel fees. *Friedrich v. Fid. Nat. Bank*, 545 S.E.2d 107, 109–10 (Ga. Ct. App. 2001) ("we find persuasive the criticisms of the lodestar method").

As a general matter, a Georgia court determining such a fee award must identify a reasonable percentage of the settlement fund to be allocated to class counsel as fees. *Id.* Specifically, a Georgia trial court must articulate its reasons for selecting the percentage upon which a fee award is based. *Id.* at 110. An order awarding such fees must identify the percentage of the fund awarded and all factors on which the court relied and explain how each factor influenced the court's chosen percentage. *Id.*

A Georgia court may draw from a non-exclusive list of factors relevant to class settlement fee awards. *Id.* at 109. Pertinent factors may include:

- The time and labor required to reach the settlement;
- The novelty and difficulty of the questions presented;
- The skill required to perform the legal service properly;
- The preclusion of other employment visited upon settlement class counsel by accepting the case;
- The customary fee in the given legal community;
- Whether the fee as originally agreed was fixed or contingent;
- The time limitations imposed by the client or the circumstances;
- The damages amount involved and the results obtained;
- The experience, reputation, and ability of settlement class counsel;
- The "undesirability" of the case;
- The nature and length of settlement class counsel's relationship with the client;
- Awards in similar cases;
- Significance of class members' and other parties' objections to the settlement terms and requested class counsel fees;
- Non-monetary benefits conferred upon the settlement class;
- The economics involved in prosecuting a class action; and
- Other factors unique to the case-at-hand.

Id. In most instances, there will also be additional factors unique to a particular case which will be relevant to the trial court's consideration. *Id.*

TEXT OF OFFICIAL CODE OF GEORGIA ANNOTATED § 9-11-23 (2025)

§ 9-11-23. CLASS ACTIONS

(a) One or more members of a class may sue or be sued as representative parties on behalf of all only if:

(1) The class is so numerous that joinder of all members is impracticable;

(2) There are questions of law or fact common to the class;

(3) The claims or defenses of the representative parties are typical of the claims or defenses of the class; and

(4) The representative parties will fairly and adequately protect the interests of the class.

(b) An action may be maintained as a class action if the prerequisites of subsection (a) of this Code section are satisfied, and, in addition:

(1) The prosecution of separate actions by or against individual members of the class would create a risk of:

(A) Inconsistent or varying adjudications with respect to individual members of the class which would establish incompatible standards of conduct for the party opposing the class; or

(B) Adjudications with respect to individual members of the class which would as a practical matter be dispositive of the interests of the other members not parties to the adjudications or substantially impair or impede their ability to protect their interests;

(2) The party opposing the class has acted or refused to act on grounds generally applicable to the class, thereby making appropriate final injunctive relief or corresponding declaratory relief with respect to the class as a whole; or

(3) The court finds that the questions of law or fact common to the members of the class predominate over any questions affecting only individual members, and that a class action is superior to other available methods for the fair and efficient adjudication of the controversy. The matters pertinent to the findings include:

(A) The interest of members of the class in individually controlling the prosecution or defense of separate actions;

(B) The extent and nature of any litigation concerning the controversy already commenced by or against members of the class;

(C) The desirability or undesirability of concentrating the litigation of the claims in the particular forum; and

(D) The difficulties likely to be encountered in the management of a class action.

(c) (1) As soon as practicable after the commencement of an action brought as a class action, the court shall determine by order whether it is to be so maintained. An order under this subsection may be conditional, and may be altered or amended before the decision on the merits.

(2) In any class action maintained under paragraph (3) of subsection (b) of this Code section, the court shall direct to the members of the class the best notice practicable under the circumstances, including individual notice to all members who can be identified through reasonable effort. The notice shall advise each member that:

(A) The court will exclude the member from the class if the member so requests by a specified date;

(B) The judgment, whether favorable or not, will include all members who do not request exclusion; and

(C) Any member who does not request exclusion may, if the member desires, enter an appearance through counsel.

(3) The judgment in an action maintained as a class action under paragraph (1) or (2) of subsection (b) of this Code section, whether or not favorable to the class, shall include and describe those whom the court finds to be members of the class. The judgment in an action maintained as a class action under paragraph (3) of subsection (b) of this Code section, whether or not favorable to the class, shall include and specify or describe those to whom the notice provided in paragraph (2) of subsection (b) of this Code section was directed, and who have not requested exclusion, and whom the court finds to be members of the class.

(4) When appropriate:

(A) An action may be brought or maintained as a class action with respect to particular issues; or

(B) A class may be divided into subclasses and each subclass treated as a class, and the provisions of this rule shall then be construed and applied accordingly.

(d) In the conduct of actions to which this rule applies, the court may make appropriate orders:

(1) Determining the course of proceedings or prescribing measures to prevent undue repetition or complication in the presentation of evidence or argument;

(2) Requiring, for the protection of the members of the class or otherwise for the fair conduct of the action, that notice be given in such manner as the court may direct to some or all of the members of any step in the action, or of the proposed extent of the judgment, or of the opportunity of members to signify whether they consider the representation fair and adequate, to intervene and present claims or defenses, or otherwise to come into the action;

(3) Imposing conditions on the representative parties or on intervenors; and

(4) Requiring that the pleadings be amended to eliminate therefrom allegations as to representation of absent persons, and that the action proceed accordingly. The orders may be combined with other orders, and may be altered or amended by the court as may be desirable from time to time.

(e) A class action shall not be dismissed or compromised without the approval of the court, and notice of the proposed dismissal or compromise shall be given to all members of the class in such manner as the court directs.

(f) (1) After the commencement of an action in which claims or defenses are purported to be asserted on behalf of or against a class, the court shall hold a conference among all named parties to the action for the purpose of establishing a schedule for any discovery germane to the issue of whether the requested class should or should not be certified. At this conference, the court shall set a date for a hearing on the issue of class certification. Except for good cause shown, such hearing may not be set sooner than 90 days nor later than 180 days after the date on which the court issues its scheduling order pursuant to the conference. If evidence is presented by affidavit, the parties shall have an opportunity to cross-examine affiants as to such testimony offered by affidavit.

(2) Except for good cause shown, the court shall stay all discovery directed solely to the merits of the claims or defenses in the action until the court has issued its written decision regarding certification of the class.

(3) When deciding whether a requested class is to be certified, the court shall enter a written order addressing whether the factors required by this Code section for certification of a class have been met and specifying the findings of fact and conclusions of law on which the court has based its decision with regard to whether each such factor has been established. In so doing, the court may treat a factor as having been established if all parties to the action have so stipulated on the record.

(4) Nothing in this Code section shall affect, or be construed to affect, any provision of Code Section 9-11-12 or Code Section 9-11-56.

(g) A court's order certifying a class or refusing to certify a class shall be appealable in the same manner as a final order to the appellate court which would otherwise have jurisdiction over the appeal from a final order in the action. The appellate courts shall expedite resolution of any appeals taken under this Code section. Such appeal may only be filed within 30 days of the order certifying or refusing to certify the class. During the pendency of any such appeal, the action in the trial court shall be stayed in all respects.

Chapter author Kevin A. Maxim is the principal and shareholder in The Maxim Law Firm, P.C. in Atlanta. He is a member of both the Georgia and Alabama Bars. He has substantial experience in litigating class actions, and the firm's business litigation practice focuses on issues arising from contracts, real estate, the internet, fraud, insurance, and trade secrets.

HAWAII

1. COMPARISON WITH RULE 23 OF THE FEDERAL RULES OF CIVIL PROCEDURE

Rule 23 of the Hawaii Rules of Civil Procedure (HRCP) is almost identical to Fed. R. Civ. P. 23 as it existed prior to the 1998 amendments. Hawaii has never adopted the changes that were made to the federal rule in 1998, 2003, 2007, and 2018.

On January 11, 2011, Hawaii adopted a new subsection (f) to govern money that cannot be successfully distributed to class members—"residual funds." Subsection (f) provides the court with discretion to approve distribution of residual funds to recipients "as agreed to by the parties, including nonprofit tax exempt organizations eligible to receive assistance from the indigent legal assistance fund under Hawaii Revised Statutes ("HRS") § 607-5.7 (or any successor provision) or the Hawaii Justice Foundation, for distribution to one or more such organizations." HRCP 23(f).

In 1998, the federal version of Rule 23 was amended to allow for interlocutory appeals at the sole discretion of the appellate court. In contrast, under Hawaii law, the only avenue for interlocutory appeal of a class certification order is to obtain trial court permission under HRS § 641-1(b) or HRCP Rule 54 (b), as applicable. *Jacober v. Sunn*, 5 Haw. App. 20, 674 P.2d 1024 (1984) (Class action plaintiffs sought declaratory, injunctive, and monetary relief, and the lower court retained jurisdiction to decide and award monetary relief after issuing orders for declaratory and injunctive relief; the lower court's decision and order was, thus, interlocutory and not appealable without the court's permission.).

In 2003, Fed. R. Civ. P. 23 was amended by changes to subparagraphs (c) and (e), and the addition of subparagraphs (g) and (h). None of these changes have been made to the Hawaii version of Rule 23. Subparagraph (c) changed the timing of class certification from "as soon as practicable" to "at an early practicable time" in order to reflect "prevailing practice" and allow for delay when appropriate. Fed. R. Civ. 23 (advisory committee notes to 2003 amendment). Hawaii retains the original language. The federal standards for settlement or compromise in subparagraph (e) were also changed in 2003 and 2018. The amended version of Fed. R. Civ. P. 23(e) expressly allows settlement prior to class certification without court approval. Hawaii retains the original language, which by use of the ambiguous phrase "class action," supported some decisions that held that an individual settlement prior to class certification required judicial approval. *See* Manual for Complex Litigation, 3d ed., § 30.41 (Federal Judicial Center 1995). However, no published Hawaii decision has ever considered this language, so it is not clear whether a Hawaii court would interpret Hawaii's version of Rule 23(e) consistently with the revised federal version. The 2003 amendments to the federal rule also included the addition of subparagraph (g), governing appointment of class counsel, and (h), detailing the procedures for submission of requests for attorney fees by class counsel. Similarly, the 2018 amendments to the federal rule further clarified the procedures and standards for class action settlements. While Hawaii has never adopted these changes, there are also no published Hawaii decisions that are inconsistent with these amended criteria. There is, therefore, no reason to presume the criteria relevant to issues relating to appointment of class counsel, fee submissions, and settlement would be substantially different in Hawaii than in federal courts since 2003. Thus, practitioners can expect Hawaii courts to continue to look to federal case law for guidance where there is no Hawaii case law on point. *Kalima v. State of Hawaii*, 148 Haw. 129, 144, 468 P.3d 143, 158 (2020); *Stallard v. Consolidated Maui, Inc.*, 103 Haw. 468, 475, 83 P.3d 731, 738 (2004).

2. HAWAII CASE LAW INTERPRETING RULE 23

Whether a suit shall be allowed to proceed as a class action is a question of fact to be determined by the trial court within its discretion. *Life of Land v. Burns*, 59 Haw. 244, 580 P.2d 405 (1978). The trial court has broad discretion in deciding whether to certify a class. *Levi v. University of Hawaii*, 67 Haw. 90, 679 P.2d 129 (1984); *Akau v. Olohana Corp.*, 65 Haw. 383, 652 P.2d 1130 (1982); *Filipo v. Chang*, 62 Haw. 626, 618 P.2d 295 (1980). Discretionary authority is normally undisturbed on review. *Levi, supra*. An appellate court will overrule only if the court below has misconstrued or misapplied the tests of HRCP Rule 23. *Akau, supra*. But if the record does disclose a possible misapprehension or misapplication of Rule 23's criteria, the Hawaii Supreme Court will conduct a careful review of the rule's application to the facts involved, especially when questions respecting the adequacy of representation are raised. *Kemp v. State of Hawaii Child Support Enforcement Agency*, 111 Haw. 367, 384, 141 P.3d 1014, 1031 (2006); *Life of Land v. Land Use Comm'n*, 63 Haw. 166, 623 P.2d 431 (1981) (*see* Section 3.a., *infra*, for a brief discussion of this defendant class action).

In *Life of Land v. Land Use Comm'n*, the Supreme Court of Hawaii recognized that the pragmatic objectives of class actions include economies of time, effort, and expense, as well as uniformity of decision for persons similarly situated. *Id.* at 179, 623 P.2d at 432. But the desirable economies and uniformity are not procurable at the expense of fairness to absentees. *Id.* Concern for due procedure is as relevant as considerations of convenience, expense, and uniformity in the allowance or disallowance of class actions. *Id.* The trial court has a definite obligation to protect the interests of absent class members at all stages of litigation. *Montalvo v. Chang*, 64 Haw. 345, 641 P.2d 1321 (1982) (overruled on other grounds discussed in Section 3.g., *infra*). The party seeking to certify a class has the burden of establishing that all four requirements of Rule 23(a) have been met and must further show a situation suitable for the maintenance of a class action under at least one subpart of Rule 23(b). *Life of Land v. Land Use Comm'n*, 63 Haw. at 180, 623 P.2d at 433. The party seeking to certify a class bears this burden even if the class sought to be created is a defendant class. *Life of Land v. Burns, supra*.

The burden of addressing the certification issue in a timely fashion rests on all parties to the case, and the language "as soon as practicable" clearly contemplates that the class determination should be made before the decision on the merits. *Levi*, 67 Haw. at 92, 679 P.2d at 131. In *Levi*, since defendant, like plaintiff, was under a duty to settle the class certification as soon as practicable, the Court held that defendant should be estopped from complaining about staleness. *Id.* (*See* Section 3.b., *infra*, for more discussion of the timeliness of certification under the heading, No Nunc Pro Tunc Certification.)

a. Rule 23(a)

i. Numerosity. Rule 23(a) provides a class suit is only maintainable where "the class is so numerous that joinder of all members is impracticable." "The focal point of inquiry thereunder is 'Who Are The Proposed Class,' and the specific criteria are that its members be identifiable and their possible joinder impracticable." *Life of Land v. Land Use Comm'n*, 63 Haw. at 182, 623 P.2d at 444 (citing *Moore's Federal Practice*). The Supreme Court of Hawaii found no error in the trial court's approval of the "numerosity" element of a proposed defendant class of 150 members. *Id.* The Supreme Court of Hawaii also found that the trial court did not abuse its discretion in denying certification when the proposed class contained approximately 16 members. *Levi, supra.*

ii. Commonality. Rule 23(a)'s subpart (2) requires the presence of "questions of law or fact common to the class." "The inquiry here focuses on 'What Are the Claims or Defenses of the Class,' and the pertinent criterion is the presence of common claims or defenses extending throughout the class." *Life of Land v. Land Use Comm'n*, 63 Haw. at 182, 623 P.2d at 444 (citing *Moore's Federal Practice*). While there are overtones of due process in the "commonality" test, the inquiries generated thereby are more directly concerned with the establishment of predictable economies of time, effort, expense, and uniformity of decision. *Id.*

iii. Typicality/Adequacy. The third and fourth prerequisites under Rule 23(a) are primarily structured to assure due process for absentees. *Id.* at 183, 623 P.2d at 444. The Supreme Court of Hawaii has determined that the "typicality" requirement of subpart (a)(3) is designed to be read in conjunction with the requirement of (a)(4) that there be fair and adequate representation of the entire class. *Id.* The "typicality" requirement can be equated with an absence of conflicts of interest. *Id.* at 183, 623 P.2d at 445. When claims or defenses among class members and representatives are coextensive, there is a probability of fair and adequate representation; when they are potentially conflicting, absentees are unlikely to be afforded representation consistent with notions of fairness and justice. *Id.* at 184, 623 P.2d at 445. For example, a class certification is improper if colorable defenses may derive from specific circumstances rather than from those circumstances common to the putative class. *Id.* Also, if there is an indication that the representative may be particularly interested in a claim or defense unique to him or a subclass, the court is justified in denying class certification on the grounds of inadequate representation. *Id.* But in the absence of some evidence of an actual conflict, the mere fact that the class representative was the sister of a partner in one of two law firms representing the class would not render the class representative inadequate. *Nakamura v. Countrywide Home Loans, Inc.*, 122 Haw. 238, 247, 225 P.3d 680, 689 (Haw. App. 2010). Finally, to be adequate a class representative must "possess the same interest and suffer the same injury as the class members." *Kemp*, 111 Haw. at 385, 141 P.3d at 1032 (quoting *AmChem Products, Inc. v. Windsor*, 521 U.S. 591, 625–26 (1997)). But this does not mean that "incidental factual differences between" the class representative's claim and the claims of the class will bar class certification. *Nakamura*, 122 Haw. at 245, 225 P.3d at 687. Thus, a plaintiff was adequate to represent a class including persons employed at both the hotel where he worked and another hotel with a different owner where all class members' claims were based on the same legal and factual bases and the same company operated both hotels. *Gurrobat v. HTH Corp.*, 133 Haw. 1, 15–16, 323 P.3d 792, 806–07 (2014).

iv. Predominance/Superiority. "The Rule 23(b)(3) predominance requirement 'tests whether proposed classes are sufficiently cohesive to warrant adjudication by representation.'" *Nakamura*, 122 Haw. at 247, 225 P.3d at 689 (quoting *Amchem*, 521 U.S. at 623). A class against a mortgage lender for violation of the Hawaii Deceptive Acts and Practices Act (H.R.S. § 480-2) arising from alleged omissions and false statements in the charging of certain fees satisfied the predominance and superiority requirements because the dispositive issue in such cases "is whether the alleged deceptive practice 'is likely to mislead consumers acting reasonably under the circumstances.'" *Id.* (quoting *Courbat v. Dahana Ranch, Inc.*, 111 Haw. 254, 262, 141 P.3d 427, 435 (2006)). Thus, "proof of the essential elements of H.R.S. § 480-2 do not require individual treatment because the dispositive question revolves around [the defendant's] alleged deceptive practices and not individual Class member transactions." *Id.*, 122 Haw. at 248, 225 P.3d at 690.

b. Rule 23(b)(1), (b)(2), and (b)(3)

Generally, if declaratory and injunctive relief are sought, class actions are processed under Rule 23(b)(2). *Jacober*, 5 Haw. App. at 25, 674 P.2d at 1027. Cases for damages usually proceed under either subpart (b)(1) or (b)(3). In *Jacober*, declaratory, injunctive, and monetary relief were all three permissibly sought under Rule 23(b)(2). *Id.*

The standards of specificity for classes under subpart (b)(2) are less stringent than under (b)(3) because only the latter requires individual notice to members and the ability of members to be excluded from the class as described in subpart (c)(2). *Akau, supra.* Although (b)(2) allows less specificity, all class members must have standing, and a class description which is too indefinite could include members who have no standing. *Id.* In *Akau*, the standing requirement was satisfied because the court found that all of the members of the (b)(2) class had suffered an injury in fact. 65 Haw. at 393, 652 P. 2d at 1137. The court also found that the class definition in *Akau* satisfied the specificity requirements of (b)(2).

3. MISCELLANEOUS COMMENTS

a. Defendant Classes

The Supreme Court of Hawaii holds that "defendant class actions demand greater attention to the due process rights of absent class members for a defendant class is more than likely to be represented by a reluctant representative." *Life of Land v. Land Use Comm'n*, 63 Haw. at 180, 623 P.2d at 443. The Supreme Court of Hawaii recognizes that Rule 23 ostensibly treats defendant class actions no differently from plaintiff class actions but points out that defendant class actions are still relatively uncommon and often distrusted. *Id.* The Court notes that this distrust centers on the perceived difficulty of affording absent members of a defendant class adequate representation. *Id.* The Supreme Court of Hawaii does not subscribe to the view that an absent defendant can never be adequately represented but, instead, considers defendant actions viable and valuable procedural instruments in complex litigation in which the rights of numerous parties are adjudicated. *Id.* Nonetheless, in *Life of Land v. Land Use Comm'n*, the Court found that the requirements of Rule 23(a) had not been satisfied.

b. No Nunc Pro Tunc Certification

The Supreme Court of Hawaii holds that the trial court lacks the power to enter a class certification order nunc pro tunc when the motion seeking class certification was filed one year after entry of judgment. *Koolauloa Welfare Rights Group v. State of Hawaii*, 65 Haw. 341, 652 P.2d 185 (1982). In that case, the stipulation pursuant to which judgment was entered provided for certification, but no determination was made and no order entered prior to the judgment. The Supreme Court of Hawaii held that the motion seeking class certification which was filed one year after the judgment was barred by Hawaii Rule of Civil Procedure 60(b) unless it was a "clerical mistake." The Supreme Court held that, whatever kind of mistake it was that caused the untimely motion to certify the class, it was not a clerical mistake, and there was no power on the part of the court below to enter the order certifying the class. The Court went on to hold that Rule 23(c)(1) clearly contemplates that the class determination will be made before the decision on the merits. Because there was no certification before the decision on the merits, there was no class at the time the stipulation and judgment were entered.

c. Class Actions and Statutes of Limitations

The Supreme Court of Hawaii has adopted the rule enunciated in *American Pipe and Constr. Co. v. Utah*, 414 U.S. 538 (1974), and clarified in *Crown, Cork and Seal Co., Inc. v. Parker*, 462 U.S. 345 (1983), that the commencement of a class action suspends the applicable statute of limitations as to all asserted members of a class who would have been parties had the suit continued as a class action. *Levi*, 67 Haw. at 93, 679 P.2d at 132; *see also Fratinardo v. Employees' Ret. Sys. of the State of Hawaii*, 121 Haw. 462, 469, 220 P.3d 1043, 1050 (Haw. App. 2009). To hold otherwise would be to encourage intervention and filings of separate actions in the event class certification might be denied, thus creating the multiplicity of actions that class suits were designed to avoid. *Id.* Tolling lasts from the date the class action is filed until it is clear no class will be maintained. *In re Manuel*, 526 P.3d 267, 280 (Haw. 2023). Thus, where the trial court denies class certification, but the named plaintiff appeals, tolling continues during the appeal. *Id.* Tolling applies to later filed claims where the earlier action's complaint provided the defendant with "the essential information necessary to determine both the subject matter and size of the prospective litigation." *Coles v. City and Cnty. of Honolulu*, 517 P.3d 750, 853 (Haw. 2022) (quoting *Am. Pipe*, 414 U.S. at 555).

Class action tolling applies cross-jurisdictionally, so that a putative class action filed in another jurisdiction operates to suspend the statute of limitations for purposes of a later action filed in Hawaii. *Patrickson v. Dole Food Co., Inc.*, 137 Haw. 217, 226, 368 P.3d 959, 968 (2015). In *Patrickson*, the trial court denied class certification and later entered summary judgment against the plaintiffs' individual claims. *Id.* at 222, 368 P.3d at 964. The plaintiffs appealed summary judgment but not denial of class certification, so the court did not reach the question of whether tolling applied to the class claims or just the individual claims. *Id.* Several years later, the United States Supreme Court held that class action tolling applies to individual claims but does not apply to claims brought on behalf of a class. *China Agritech, Inc. v. Resh*, 548 U.S. 732 (2018). Whether the Hawaii Supreme Court would follow *China Agritech* is an open question.

d. Damages

The Supreme Court of Hawaii has held that "class action damages must be capable of measurement across the entire class." *Kalima, supra*. Nevertheless, if the fact of damages is proved on a classwide basis, a "more liberal rule is allowed in determining the amount" for each class member. *Id.* Thus, for a class of people who were deprived of their right to homesteads by the state, the trial court did not err in adopting a model that calculated individual class member damages based on the rental value of a single representative lot for each year during the claims period. *Id.* at 160, 468 P.3d at 146.

e. Settlement

In matters litigated as class actions, the general rule is that a judicially-approved settlement is binding upon the members of the class who have not opted out. *Alden v. Kona Palisades, Inc.*, 3 Haw. App. 47, 641 P.2d 330 (1982). In *Koolauloa Welfare Rights Group*, *supra*, the notice of a proposed compromise, given under subsection (e) of this rule, was defective because it did not describe the basis for the complaint, the relief being sought therein, or the relief being given by the compromise. Since there is no way a person reading the notice would have known that his or her rights were being affected by the compromise, that settlement was not binding.

f. Standing of Class Members

Each class member must have standing as defined by Hawaii law, but Hawaii courts are not subject to a "cases or controversies" limitation like that imposed upon the federal judiciary by Article III, § 2 of the United States Constitution. *Life of Land v. Land Use Comm'n*, 63 Haw. at 171, 623 P.2d at 438. The Supreme Court of Hawaii adopted instead the injury in fact test. *Id.* at 175, 623 P.2d at 441. For example, the Court has allowed persons who show aesthetic and environmental injury standing to sue so long as their aesthetic and environmental interests are "personal" and "special," or a property interest is also affected. *Id.* Moreover, a member of the public has standing to sue to enforce the rights of the public even though his injury is not different in kind from the public's generally, if he can show that he has suffered an injury in fact and the concerns of a multiplicity of suits are satisfied by any means, including a class action. *Akau, supra.* The Supreme Court points out that its decisions have afforded standing on a basis at least coextensive with federal doctrine when harm to public interests is alleged. *Life of Land v. Land Use Comm'n*, 63 Haw. at 176, 623 P.2d at 441. This is not to suggest, however, that Hawaii's standing requirements will follow every twist or turn in the development of federal doctrine. *Id.* The Supreme Court's touchstone on standing issues is "the needs of justice." *Id.*

g. Standing of Class Representative

A class representative has standing to represent a class even if the class includes members with claims against different defendants so long as "the legal and factual bases underlying his claims are coextensive with those of all other class members." *Gurrobat, supra.*

h. Shareholder's Actions

A personal action alleging injury to shareholders as shareholders, and not to the corporation, may be brought by representative shareholders on behalf of all of them as a class action under Rule 23. *Chambrella v. Rutledge*, 69 Haw. 271, 740 P.2d 1008 (1987); *see also* HRCP Rule 23.1, *infra.*

i. Attorneys' Fees

In 2000, the Hawaii Supreme Court changed the way that attorneys' fees are calculated in Hawaii class actions which result in a common fund. *Chun v. Board of Trustees of the Employees Ret. Sys. of the State of Hawaii*, 92 Haw. 432, 445, 992 P.2d 127, 140 (2000) (*Chun I*) (overruling *Montalvo, supra*). In *Chun I*, the Court remanded the case, ruling that in common fund cases, the circuit court may decide whether to employ the percentage method or the lodestar method of calculating attorneys' fees. Prior to *Chun I*, trial courts were required to use the lodestar method. *See Montalvo*, 64 Haw. at 358–59, 641 P.2d at 1331. In *Chun I*, the Court explained that *Montalvo* is overruled only insofar as it dictates that the lodestar method alone may be used to calculate attorneys' fees in common fund cases. The Court will continue to follow *Montalvo's* explication of the mechanics of the lodestar method. In 2005, *Chun v. Board of Trustees of the Employees Ret. Sys. of the State of Hawaii* (*Chun II*), returned to the Supreme Court after the circuit court awarded attorneys' fees on remand. 106 Hawaii 416, 106 P.2d 339 (2005). The Supreme Court held that the circuit court did not abuse its discretion in ordering that attorneys' fees be set at 25 percent of the common fund because no controlling precedent required the circuit court to do otherwise. *Id.* at 434–39, 106 P.2 357–62.

j. Residual Funds

HRCP 23(f) expressly grants the court discretion to approve the distribution of funds that cannot be successfully distributed to class members to charitable organizations.

The Hawaii section was prepared by Robert Hatch, who is a partner at Bronster Fujichaku Robbins in Honolulu, Hawaii.

IDAHO

1. COMPARISON WITH RULE 23 OF THE FEDERAL RULES OF CIVIL PROCEDURE

The Idaho Rule of Civil Procedure governing class actions was amended effective July 1, 2016, to move from Rule 23 to Rules 77–79. This was part of a larger renumbering, with the result that the class action rules are grouped with other special proceedings. The Idaho Rules are substantially similar, except for their location, to the federal rule though Idaho does not have an analog to Fed. R. Civ. P. 23(f). The Idaho Supreme Court considers "federal authority . . . relevant" because the Idaho rules on class actions were based on the federal rules. *O'Boskey v. First Fed. Sav. & Loan Ass'n of Boise*, 112 Idaho 1002, 1005 n.2, 739 P.2d 301, 304 n.2 (1987).

2. RULE 77 OF THE IDAHO RULES OF CIVIL PROCEDURE (FORMERLY RULE 23)

Class actions are generally favored where the interests of absent class members can be adequately represented by the named plaintiff and the requirements of the rule are met. *Bush v. Upper Valley Telecable Co.*, 96 Idaho 83, 89, 524 P.2d 1055, 1061 (1974).

Certification of a class action is governed by the Idaho Rules of Civil Procedure, *Bettwieser v N.Y. Irrigation Dist.*, 154 Idaho 317, 324, 297 P.3d 1124, 1141 (2013), and in particular Rule 77, *Zeyen v. Pocatello/Chubbock Sch. Dist. No. 25*, 165 Idaho 690, 697, 451 P.3d 25, 32 (2019). To certify a lawsuit as a class action, the trial court must find that all four factors in Rule 77(a) (at the time Rule 23(a)) exist and that at least one factor in Rule 77(b) (at the time Rule 23(b)) exists. *BHA Invs., Inc. v. City of Boise*, 141 Idaho 168, 171–72, 108 P.3d 315, 318–19 (2004). If the court finds that a necessary factor is absent, the court need not address the other factors. *Id.*

3. RULE 77(A) OF THE IDAHO RULES OF CIVIL PROCEDURE (FORMERLY RULE 23(A))

The first factor in Rule 77(a) (at the time Rule 23(a)) is that "the class is so numerous that joinder of all members is impracticable." *BHA Invs., Inc. v. City of Boise*, 141 Idaho 168, 172, 108 P.3d 315, 319 (2004). In *BHA Investments,* the Idaho Supreme Court found that the "district court did not abuse its discretion in deciding that seventeen known entities located within the City did not constitute a class that was so numerous that joinder of all members is impracticable." *Id.*

A plaintiff is not required to file a case as a class action simply because the right he seeks to establish is also held by a number of other individuals, but instead is allowed to choose to bring an individual action. *Camp Easton Forever, Inc. v. Inland Nw. Council BSA*, 156 Idaho 893, 898, 332 P.3d 805, 810 (2014); *Middlekauff v. Lake Cascade, Inc.*, 110 Idaho 909, 915, 719 P.2d 1169, 1175 (1986). Rule 77(a) *et seq.* (at the time Rule 23(a) *et seq.*) merely establish the conditions under which one "or more members of a class *may* sue or be sued as representative party on behalf of all." *Id.* (emphasis in the original; citation omitted).

When class members seek only declaratory and injunctive relief, requiring "individual harm to each of the unnamed class members . . . contradicts the general principles of a class action suit" and a trial is not required "to examine the viability or bases of class members' claims." *Tucker v. State*, 168 Idaho 570, 584, 484 P.3d 851, 865 (2021) (quoting *Rodriguez v. Hayes*, 591 F.3d 1105, 1125 (9th Cir. 2010)) (*Tucker II*). The "efficiencies of a class action would be thwarted if routine discovery of absent class members [was] permitted." *Id.* (quoting *In re Carbon Dioxide Indus. Antitrust Litig.*, 155 F.R.D. 209, 212 (M.D. Fla. 1993)) (alteration in the original).

4. RULE 77(B) OF THE IDAHO RULES OF CIVIL PROCEDURE (FORMERLY RULE 23(B))

a. Rule 77(b)(1) and (2)

Class actions may be used to obtain declaratory and injunctive relief. *See, e.g., O'Boskey v. First Fed. Sav. & Loan Ass'n of Boise*, 112 Idaho 1002, 739 P.2d 301 (1987). A class action may be used to confirm or adjudicate rights that will be enforceable for or against similarly situated persons. *Twin Lakes Improvement Ass'n, Inc. v. E. Greenacres Irrigation Dist.*, 90 Idaho 281, 287, 409 P.2d 390, 392 (1965).

b. Rule 77(b)(3)

Where adjudication of class claims would require individual mini-trials to determine harm, causation, and damages with respect to individual class members, adjudication as a class action pursuant to Rule 77(b)(3) (at the time Rule 23(b)(3)) is inappropriate. *Pope v. Intermountain Gas Co.*, 103 Idaho 217, 238–39, 646 P.2d 988, 1010–11 (1982).

5. RULE 77(C) OF THE IDAHO RULES OF CIVIL PROCEDURE (FORMERLY RULE 23(C))

The appellate court reviews class certification orders for abuse of discretion. *Pope v. Intermountain Gas Co.*, 103 Idaho 217, 237, 646 P.2d 988, 1008 (1982). However, if the lower court failed to provide an analysis of the factors required by Rule 77 (at the time Rule 23), the appellate court will conduct an independent review of the record. *Id.*

An order of the Idaho Industrial Commission that adjudged and decreed that the Commission did not have authority to entertain class actions was a dismissal on jurisdictional grounds, and therefore a final order of the Commission, properly appealable to the Idaho Supreme Court. *Monroe v. Chapman*, 105 Idaho 269, 270 n.1, 668 P.2d 1000, 1001 n.1 (1983) (although the Commission had subject matter jurisdiction, because the Commission had not adopted a class action rule, it had no authority over class).

6. RULE 77(D) OF THE IDAHO RULES OF CIVIL PROCEDURE (FORMERLY RULE 23(D))

The Idaho Supreme Court held that an amended complaint filed after class certification did not revive the timeliness of the defendant's request for a jury trial. *Hayden Lake Fire Prot. Dist. v. Alcorn*, 141 Idaho 388, 396–97, 111 P.3d 73, 81–82 (2005), overruled on other grounds by *Farber v. Idaho State Ins. Fund* (*Farber II*), 152 Idaho 495, 272 P.3d 467 (2012). The Supreme Court recognized the right of intervenors in a class action to request a jury trial after the time had expired but distinguished other parties. An intervenor has a right to demand a jury trial upon intervention because, unlike the existing parties in the suit, it has not had the opportunity to assert that right. *Id.* (citing *United States v. Cal. Mobile Home Park Mgmt. Co.*, 107 F.3d 1374, 1378–79 (9th Cir. 1997); *United States v. Country Club Garden Owners Ass'n, Inc.*, 159 F.R.D. 400, 404–05 (E.D.N.Y. 1995)).

7. RULE 78 OF THE IDAHO RULES OF CIVIL PROCEDURE (FORMERLY RULE 23(F))

A stockholder's derivative action is an action brought by one or more stockholders of a corporation to enforce a corporate right or remedy a wrong to the corporation in cases where the corporation fails and refuses (because it is controlled by the wrongdoers or for other reasons) to take appropriate action for its own protection. *McCann v. McCann*, 138 Idaho 228, 233, 61 P.3d 585, 590 (2002) (quoting 19 Am. Jur. 2d *Corporations* § 2250, 151–52 (1986)).

In a derivative action, the "complaint shall . . . allege with particularity the efforts, if any, made by the plaintiff to obtain the action which plaintiff desires from the directors . . . and the reasons for the plaintiff's failure to obtain the action or for not making the effort." Idaho R. Civ. P. 78; *Orrock v. Appleton*, 147 Idaho 613, 618, 213 P.3d 398, 403 (2009) (emphasis omitted). In *Orrock*, the plaintiff did not make a demand on the Micron Board of Directors that they investigate a claim of price fixing. 147 Idaho at 618, 213 P.3d at 403. The Idaho Supreme Court reaffirmed the federal courts' interpretation of Rule 78 (at the time Rule 23(f)) that a demand upon the board is a precondition to a shareholder derivative suit. *Id.*

In a shareholder derivative suit, "To prevent abuse . . . equity courts established as a precondition 'for the suit' that the shareholder demonstrate 'that the corporation itself had refused to proceed after suitable demand, unless excused by extraordinary conditions.'" *Id.* (quoting *Kamen v. Kemper Fin. Servs., Inc.*, 500 U.S. 90, 95–96, 101, 111 S. Ct. 1711, 1716, 114 L. Ed. 2d 152, 163 (1991)). The demand requirement "affords the directors an opportunity to exercise their reasonable business judgment." *Id.* (quoting *Daily Income Fund, Inc. v. Fox*, 464 U.S. 523, 533, 104 S. Ct. 831, 836–37, 78 L. Ed. 2d 645, 653 (1984)). The "function of the demand doctrine in delimiting the respective powers of the individual shareholder and of the directors to control corporate litigation clearly is a matter of 'substance,' not 'procedure.'" *Id.* (quoting *Kamen*, 500 U.S. at 96–97, 111 S. Ct. at 1716, 114 L. Ed. 2d at 163–64).

Orrock argued that a demand would have been futile. The complaint was dismissed for failure to state a cause of action because it lacked any factual allegation supporting a futility excuse. The *Orrock* court did not discuss *McCann*, 138 Idaho at 236, 61 P.3d at 593 ("legislature's intent [was] to no longer recognize 'futility' as an exception to the requirement of demand as a condition preceding the institution of a shareholder's derivative action").

8. RULE 79 OF THE IDAHO RULES OF CIVIL PROCEDURE (FORMERLY RULE 23(G))

An association can be a class action defendant. *Gardner v. Sch. Dist. No. 55,* 108 Idaho 434, 440, 700 P.2d 56, 62 (1985) (lower court applied Rule 79 (at the time Rule 23(g)) to the Blackfoot Education Association).

9. TOLLING OF THE STATUTE OF LIMITATIONS FOR PUTATIVE CLASS MEMBERS

The pendency of a class proceeding tolls the statute of limitations for putative class members. *Pope v. Intermountain Gas Co.*, 103 Idaho 217, 239 n.28, 646 P.2d 988, 1010 n.28 (1982); *Am. Pipe & Constr. Co. v. Utah*, 414 U.S. 538, 554, 94 S. Ct. 756, 766, 38 L. Ed. 2d 713 (1974).

In *American Pipe and Construction*, a class action was filed just before the statute of limitations expired, and then the trial court declined to certify the class. 414 U.S. at 541–43, 94 S. Ct. at 760–61. Eight days later, class members sought to intervene in the same action to assert the same claims as the class would have asserted. 414 U.S. at 543–44, 94 S. Ct. at 761–62. The U.S. Supreme Court tolled the statute of limitations, holding that "the commencement of a class action suspends the applicable statute of limitations as to all asserted members of the class who would have been parties had the suit been permitted to continue as a class action." 414 U.S. at 554, 94 S. Ct. at 766. The U.S. Supreme Court stated that the purpose behind the statute of limitations is to protect the defendants from a plaintiff who has "slept on his rights," and the class litigation in that case had notified the defendant both of the substantive claims against it and the identity of claimants. 414 U.S. at 554–55, 94 S. Ct. at 766–67 (citation omitted).

10. INSURANCE ISSUES

A single deductible applies to all the claims in a class action rather than a deductible for each class member's claims. *City of Idaho Falls v. Home Indem. Co.*, 126 Idaho 604, 609, 888 P.2d 383, 388 (1995) (citing *Previews, Inc. v. Cal. Union Ins. Co.,* 640 F.2d 1026 (9th Cir. 1981) (ambiguity in the insurance policy of whether the deductible applied to each class member resolved against the insurer thus applying only a single deductible for the class action)).

11. CHOICE OF LAW

Idaho procedural law applies even if the Idaho court is applying another jurisdiction's substantive law based on application of choice of law. *Orrock v. Appleton*, 147 Idaho 613, 617–18, 213 P.3d 398, 402–03 (2009); *see, e.g., Sword v. Sweet*, 140 Idaho 242, 247, 92 P.3d 492, 497 (2004).

12. ONE-WAY INTERVENTION

In class actions, the rules of procedure contemplate that ordinarily the class will be determined and given notice early in the proceedings and prior to deciding the merits. *See* Idaho R. Civ. P. 77(c); *see also Eisen v. Carlisle & Jacquelin*, 417 U.S. 156, 177–78, 94 S. Ct. 2140, 2152–53, 40 L. Ed. 2d 732 (1974); *Anderson v. Air West Inc. (In re Consol. Pretrial Proceedings in Air W. Sec. Litig.)*,

73 F.R.D. 12, 14–15 (N.D. Cal. 1976). Otherwise, potential class members could await the determination of the merits prior to deciding whether to participate in the class and be bound by the judgment. *Anderson*, 73 F.R.D. at 14–15. But that rule can be waived by the defendant seeking a merits determination before certification. *O'Boskey v. First Fed. Sav. & Loan Ass'n of Boise*, 112 Idaho 1002, 1005, 739 P.2d 301, 304 (1987).

13. EDUCATIONAL ISSUES

The Constitutionally Based Educational Claims Act (CBECA), Idaho Code §§ 6-2201 to 2216, requires that a plaintiff first sue the local school district before suing the State of Idaho. In *Joki v. Idaho*, 162 Idaho 5, 11, 394 P.3d 48, 54 (2017), the Idaho Supreme Court rejected the argument that this nullifies Rule 77 governing class actions. The Supreme Court ruled that the argument that CBECA unconstitutionally altered the Idaho Rules of Civil Procedure is "unavailing." *Id.*

14. STANDING

Those seeking to certify a class must first show that they have standing. *Zeyen v. Pocatello/Chubbock Sch. Dist. No. 25*, 165 Idaho 690, 697, 451 P.3d 25, 32 (2019). Idaho has adopted the constitutionally based federal justiciability standard. *Id.* For class actions, standing is met "if at least one named plaintiff satisfies the requirements of standing against every named defendant." *Zeyen*, 165 Idaho at 698, 451 P.3d at 33 (quoting *Tucker v. Idaho*, 162 Idaho 11, 19, 394 P.3d 54, 62 (2017)).

15. MERE ALLEGATION THAT CLAIMS BROUGHT ON BEHALF OF A CLASS

In *Bradbury v. City of Lewiston*, 172 Idaho 393, 533 P.3d 606, 2024 (2023), the plaintiff stated in his complaint he brought his petition on "the behalf of all residents of Lewiston rate payers." *Id.* However, he did not (i) join any parties to the action, (ii) file his petition as a class action, or (iii) ask the trial court "to certify the action as a class action." *Id.* The Idaho Supreme Court held that this was not a class action and that the plaintiff had "filed this lawsuit on his own behalf and for no one else." *Id.*

16. MISCELLANEOUS CLASS ACTIONS ALLOWED

Joinder of parties by class action has been used in cases involving, for example, claims of antitrust violations, *Pope v. Intermountain Gas Co.*, 103 Idaho 217, 221 n.7, 646 P.2d 988, 992 n.7 (1982) (noting joinder allowed by trial court); violations of rate schedules, *Bush v. Upper Valley Telecable Co.*, 96 Idaho 83, 524 P.2d 1055 (1974); right to tax refunds, *Ware v. Idaho State Tax Comm'n*, 98 Idaho 477, 567 P.2d 423 (1977); wrongful imposition of assumption fees by a mortgagee, *O'Boskey v. First Fed. Sav. & Loan Ass'n of Boise*, 112 Idaho 1002, 739 P.2d 301 (1987); and management of public insurance funds, *Hayden Lake Fire Prot. Dist. v. Alcorn*, 141 Idaho 388, 111 P.3d 73, 76 (2005), overruled on other grounds by *Farber v. Idaho State Ins. Fund*, 152 Idaho 495, 272 P.3d 467 (2012).

In *Farber v. Idaho State Insurance Fund*, 147 Idaho 307, 208 P.3d 289 (2009), the Idaho Supreme Court certified a class of about 30,000 Idaho employers who paid annual premiums of $2,500 or less to the fund for workers' compensation insurance from the policy year beginning in 2001 onward (i.e., the majority of the fund's policyholders). The Supreme Court enforced a statute which requires a pro rata distribution of excess premiums rather than limiting the distribution to employees who paid more than $2,500 in premiums. *Farber I*, 147 Idaho at 311–12, 208 P.3d at 293–94; *see also Farber II*, 152 Idaho 495, 272 P.3d 467 (appeal after remand).

RULE 77. CLASS ACTIONS

(a) Prerequisites to a Class Action. One or more members of a class may sue or be sued as representative parties on behalf of all only if:

(1) the class is so numerous that joinder of all members is impracticable;

(2) there are questions of law or fact common to the class;

(3) the claims or defenses of the representative parties are typical of the claims or defenses of the class; and

(4) the representative parties will fairly and adequately protect the interests of the class.

(b) Types of Class Actions. A class action may be maintained if subdivision (a) is satisfied and if:

(1) prosecuting separate actions by or against individual class members would create a risk of:

(A) inconsistent or varying adjudications with respect to individual class members that would establish incompatible standards of conduct for the party opposing the class; or

(B) adjudications with respect to individual class members that, as a practical matter, would be dispositive of the interests of the other members not parties to the adjudications or would substantially impair or impede their ability to protect their interests; or

(2) the party opposing the class has acted or refused to act on grounds generally applicable to the class, so that final injunctive relief or corresponding declaratory relief is appropriate respecting the class as a whole; or

(3) the court finds that the questions of law or fact common to class members predominate over any questions affecting only individual members, and that a class action is superior to other available methods for the fairly and efficiently adjudicating the controversy. The matters pertinent to these findings include:

(A) the class members' interests in individually controlling the prosecution or defense of separate actions;

(B) the extent and nature of any litigation concerning the controversy already begun by or against class members;

(C) the desirability or undesirability of concentrating the litigation of the claims in the particular forum; and

(D) the difficulties in managing a class action.

(c) Certification Order; Notice to Class Members; Judgment; Issues Classes; Subclasses.

(1) *Certification Order.*

(A) Time to Issue. At an early practicable time after a person sues or is sued as a class representative, the court must determine by order whether to certify the action as a class action.

(B) Defining the Class; Appointing Class Counsel. An order that certifies a class action must define the class and the class claims, issues, or defenses, and must appoint class counsel under subdivision (g).

(C) Altering or Amending the Order. An order that grants or denies class certification may be altered or amended before final judgment.

(2) *Notice.*

(A) For (b)(1) or (b)(2) Classes. For any class certified under subdivision (b)(1) or (b)(2), the court may direct appropriate notice to the class.

(B) For (b)(3) Classes. For any class certified under subdivision (b)(3), the court must direct to class members the best notice that is practicable under the circumstances, including individual notice to all members who can be identified through reasonable effort. The notice must clearly and concisely state in plain, easily understood language:

(i) the nature of the action;

(ii) the definition of the class certified;

(iii) the class claims, issues, or defenses;

(iv) that a class member may enter an appearance through an attorney if the member so desires;

(v) that the court will exclude from the class any member who requests exclusion;

(vi) that the judgment, whether favorable or not, must include all members who do not request exclusion;

(vii) the time and manner for requesting exclusion; and

(viii) the binding effect of a class judgment on members under subdivision(c)(3).

(3) *Judgment.* Whether or not favorable to the class, the judgment in a class action must:

(A) for any class certified under subdivisions (b)(1) or (b)(2), include and describe those whom the court finds to be class members; and

(B) for any class certified under subdivision (b)(3), include and specify or describe those to whom the subdivision (c)(2) notice was directed, who have not requested exclusion, and whom the court finds to be class members.

(4) *Particular Issues.* When appropriate, an action may be brought or maintained as a class action with respect to particular issues.

(5) *Subclasses.* When appropriate, a class may be divided into subclasses that are each treated as a class under this rule.

(d) Conducting the Action.

(1) *In General.* In conducting an action under this rule, the court may issue orders that:

(A) determine the course of proceedings or prescribe measures to prevent undue repetition or complication in presenting evidence or argument;

(B) require—to protect class members and fairly conduct the action—giving appropriate notice to some or all class members of:

(i) any step in the action;

(ii) the proposed extent of the judgment; or

(iii) the members' opportunity to signify whether they consider the representation fair and adequate, to intervene and present claims or defenses, or to otherwise come into the action;

(C) impose conditions on the representative parties or on intervenors;

(D) require that the pleadings be amended to eliminate allegations about representation of absent persons and that the action proceed accordingly; or

(E) deal with similar procedural matters.

(2) *Combining and Amending Orders.* An order under subdivision (d)(1) may be altered or amended from time to time and may be combined with an order under Rule 16.

(e) Settlement, Voluntary Dismissal, or Compromise. The claims, issues, or defenses of a certified class may be settled, voluntarily dismissed, or compromised only with the court's approval. The following procedures apply to a proposed settlement, voluntary dismissal, or compromise:

(1) the court must direct notice in a reasonable manner to all class members who would be bound by the proposal;

(2) if the proposal would bind class members, the court may approve it only after a hearing and on finding that it is fair, reasonable, and adequate;

(3) the parties seeking approval must file a statement identifying any agreement made in connection with the proposal;

(4) if the class action was previously certified under subdivision (b)(3), the court may refuse to approve a settlement unless it affords a new opportunity to request exclusion to individual class members who had an earlier opportunity to request exclusion but did not do so;

(5) any class member may object to the proposal if it requires court approval under this subdivision (e); the objection may be withdrawn only with the court's approval.

(f) Reserved.

(g) Class Counsel.

(1) *Appointing Class Counsel.* Unless a statute provides otherwise, a court that certifies a class must appoint class counsel. In appointing class counsel, the court:

(A) must consider:

(i) the work counsel has done in identifying or investigating potential claims in the action;

(ii) counsel's experience in handling class actions, other complex litigation, and the types of claims asserted in the action;

(iii) counsel's knowledge of the applicable law; and

(iv) the resources that counsel will commit to representing the class;

(B) may consider any other matter pertinent to counsel's ability to fairly and adequately represent the interests of the class;

(C) may order potential class counsel to provide information on any subject pertinent to the appointment and to propose terms for attorney's fees and nontaxable costs;

(D) may include in the appointing order provisions about the award of attorney's fees or nontaxable costs under Rule 23(h); and

(E) may make further orders in connection with the appointment.

(2) *Standard for Appointing Class Counsel.* When one applicant seeks appointment as class counsel, the court may appoint that applicant only if the applicant is adequate under Rule 77(g)(1) and (4). If more than one adequate applicant seeks appointment, the court must appoint the applicant best able to represent the interests of the class.

(3) *Interim Counsel.* The court may designate interim counsel to act on behalf of a putative class before determining whether to certify the action as a class action.

(4) *Duty of Class Counsel.* Class counsel must fairly and adequately represent the interests of the class

(h) Attorney's Fees and Nontaxable Costs. In a certified class action, the court may award reasonable attorney's fees and nontaxable costs that are authorized by law or by the parties' agreement. The following procedures apply:

(1) a claim for an award must be made by motion under Rule 54, subject to the provisions of this subdivision (h), at a time the court sets. Notice of the motion must be served on all parties and, for motions by class counsel, directed to class members in a reasonable manner;

(2) a class member, or a party from whom payment is sought, may object to the motion;

(3) the court may hold a hearing and must find the facts and state its legal conclusions under Rule 52(a);

(4) the court may refer issues related to the amount of the award to a special master.

RULE 78. DERIVATIVE ACTIONS

(a) Prerequisites. This rule applies when one or more shareholders or members of a corporation or an unincorporated association bring a derivative action to enforce a right that the corporation or association may properly assert but has failed to enforce. The derivative action may not be maintained if it appears that the plaintiff does not fairly and adequately represent the interests of shareholders or members who are similarly situated in enforcing the right of the corporation or association.

(b) Pleading Requirements. The complaint must be verified and must:

(1) allege that the plaintiff was a shareholder or member at the time of the transaction complained of, or that the plaintiff's share or membership later devolved on it by operation of law;

(2) allege that the action is not a collusive one to confer jurisdiction that the court would otherwise lack; and

(3) state with particularity:

(A) any effort by the plaintiff to obtain the desired action from the directors or comparable authority and, if necessary, from the shareholders or members; and

(B) the reasons for not obtaining the action or not making the effort.

(c) Settlement, Dismissal, and Compromise. A derivative action may be settled, voluntarily dismissed, or compromised only with the court's approval. Notice of a proposed settlement, voluntary dismissal, or compromise must be given to shareholders or members in the manner that the court orders.

RULE 79. ACTION RELATING TO UNINCORPORATED ASSOCIATIONS

This rule applies to an action brought by or against the members of an unincorporated association as a class by naming certain members as representative parties. The action may be maintained only if it appears that those parties will fairly and adequately protect the interests of the association and its members. In conducting the action, the court may issue any appropriate orders corresponding with those in Rule 77 (d), and the procedure for settlement, voluntary dismissal, or compromise must correspond with the procedure in Rule 77 (e).

Peter G. Barton is an Idaho District Judge in Boise, Idaho. He handles civil cases exceeding $10,000 and felony cases. Mr. Barton earned his B.S.E. degree from Duke University and his J.D. degree from Harvard Law School. He has been the Idaho reporter since 2015.

ILLINOIS

1. 735 ILCS 5/2-801—PREREQUISITES FOR MAINTENANCE OF A CLASS ACTION

The full text of the Illinois class action statute is provided at the end of this chapter. Class certification in Illinois is governed by Section 2-801 of the Illinois Code of Civil Procedure (735 ILCS 5/2-801), which is patterned after Rule 23 of the Federal Rules of Civil Procedure. *Avery v. State Farm Mut. Auto. Ins. Co.*, 216 Ill. 2d 100, 835 N.E.2d 801 (2005), *cert. denied*, 126 S. Ct. 1470, 164 L. Ed. 2d 248 (2006). Given the relationship between these two provisions, federal decisions interpreting Rule 23 are persuasive authority with regard to questions of class certification in Illinois. *Id.*

Under Section 2-801, a class may be certified only if the proponent establishes the four prerequisites set forth in the statute:

A. Numerosity (the class is so numerous that joinder of all members is impracticable);
B. Commonality (there are questions of fact or law common to the class, which common questions predominate over any questions affecting only individual members);
C. Adequacy of representation (the representative parties will fairly and adequately protect the interest of the class); and
D. Appropriateness (the class action is an appropriate method for the fair and efficient adjudication of the controversy).

The Illinois Supreme Court, by and through its holding in *Avery,* reaffirmed the necessity of these four elements. *See also Walczak v. Onyx Acceptance Corporation*, 365 Ill. App. 3d 664, 850 N.E.2d 357 (1st Dist. 2006) (wherein the Appellate Court discusses these four prerequisites and provides numerous citations to Illinois cases regarding same). The Appellate Court continues to rely upon this four-part test of certification. *S37 Management, Inc. v. Advance Refrigeration Co.*, 961 N.E.2d 6 (1st Dist. 2011).

A comparison of the Illinois statute 735 ILCS 5/2-801 with Fed. R. Civ. P. 23 reveals that Illinois has no express provisions analogous to Fed. R. Civ. P. 23(b)(1) (risk of inconsistent adjudications or impairing the interests of non-parties) or Fed. R. Civ. P. 23(b)(2) (appropriateness of final injunctive relief or declaratory relief). Further, the superiority requirements of the Illinois statute are less stringent than Fed. R. Civ. P. 23(b)(3). However, notwithstanding the absence of (b)(1) and (b)(2) equivalents, Illinois courts have included (b)(1) and (b)(2) criteria in certifying classes. *See, e.g., Rodriguez v. Credit System Specialists, Inc.,* 17 Ill. App. 3d 606, 308 N.E.2d 342 (1st Dist. 1991).

2. PLEADING REQUIREMENTS

Illinois is a fact-pleading jurisdiction, mandating that plaintiffs allege facts sufficient to bring their claims within the scope of the cause of action being asserted. *See Anderson v. Vanden Dorpel*, 172

Ill. 2d 399, 408 (1996). The relevant question in deciding whether a class action has been adequately pleaded is whether the complaint contains allegations which implicate, or bring the complaint within, the prerequisites of the class action statute. *Weiss v. Waterhouse Securities, Inc.*, 208 Ill. 2d 439, 804 N.E.2d 536 (2004). The plaintiff need not *establish* the statutory prerequisites to survive a motion to dismiss class claims but may state the complaint's factual allegations broadly enough to include the *possible* existence of a class action claim under the Illinois statute. *Id.* at 450–51. Hence, while the Illinois class action statute does not require plaintiffs to plead facts establishing a class action, the Illinois Supreme Court has held that a plaintiff must allege facts sufficient to satisfy the statutory prerequisites for a class action. *Id., see also Akinyemi v. JP Morgan Chase Bank, NA.*, 391 Ill. App. 3d 334, 339, 908 N.E.2d 163 (1st Dist. 2009). Class action allegations may be stricken as insufficient, via a motion on the pleadings under 735 ILCS 5/2-615.

3. CERTIFICATION HEARING

Certification hearings do not pertain to the merits of the controversy. *Chultem v. Ticor Title Insurance Co.*, 401 Ill. App. 3d 226, 238, 927 N.E.2d 289 (1st Dist. 2010), *leave to appeal denied* 237 Ill. 2d 553, 938 N.E.2d 519 (Ill. 2010); *Cruz v. Unilock Chicago, Inc.*, 383 Ill. App. 3d 752, 775, 892 N.E.2d 78 (2d Dist. 2008). Rather, the scope of the hearing is whether the requirements of Section 2-801 have been met. *Id., see also Szabo v. Bridgeport Machines, Inc.,* 249 F.3d 672, 667 (7th Cir. 2001); *Eggleston v. Chicago Journeyman Plumber's Local Union No. 130*, 657 F.2d 890, 895 (7th Cir. 1981). The trial court is to conduct a rigorous analysis as to the issues as to certification. *Stefanski v. City of Chicago*, 2015 Ill. App. (1st) 132844. *Clark v. TAP Pharmaceutical Products Inc.,* 343 Ill. App. 3d 538, 545 (5th Dist. 2003). Where the question of certification is close, there is a preference for certifying. *Clark*, 343 Ill. App. 3d at 542–45; *S37 Management, Inc. v. Advance Refrigeration Co.*, 961 N.E.2d 6 (1st Dist. 2011). The party moving for class certification has the burden of establishing its propriety. *CE Design Ltd. v. C&T Pizza, Inc.*, 2015 Ill. App. (1st) 131465.

The courts are split regarding whether the complaint's allegations must be accepted as true for the purpose of certification. *Clark, Ramirez, Chultem,* and *S37 Management, Inc.* support the proposition that they must be accepted as true. The Second District Court of Appeals, in contrast, has held that the trial court may consider any matters of law or fact properly presented by the record including pleadings, depositions, affidavits, answers to interrogatories, and any evidence adduced at the hearing on the motion to decide certification. *Cruz, supra,* (citing *Szabo v. Bridgeport Machines, Inc.,* 249 F.3d 672 (7th Cir. 2001)); *see also Enzenbacher v. Browning-Ferris Industries of Illinois, Inc.* 332 Ill. App. 3d 1079, 1078, 774 N.E.2d 858 (2d Dist. 2002).

The United States District Court for the Northern District of Illinois provided guidance with respect to the interplay of standing and class certification in *Muir v. Nature's Bounty, Inc.*, Case No. 15-9835 (N.D. Ill. Sept. 28, 2017) In *Muir,* The Northern District dismissed the nationwide class claims because Muir could not maintain a nationwide class applying the law of Illinois. In the case, plaintiff Michael Muir filed a putative class action against Nature's Bounty for claims related to an alleged misrepresentation regarding an ingredient's prevalence in the supplement. Nature's Bounty is a natural supplement manufacturer. His claims alleged damages both in Illinois and on a national level. The court dismissed the proposed nationwide and multi-state consumer classes while allowing the Illinois class to proceed to a hearing on certification.

The granting of class certification to a class is not the end of the proverbial road to the plaintiff. The emergence of facts, even those uncovered through discovery directed to the defendant *by* the plaintiff, can serve not only to buttress the appropriateness of certification, but also to undermine certification. In *Johnson v. YAHOO! Inc.*, No. 14 CV 2028, 2018 WL 835339 (N.D. Ill. Feb. 13,

2018) the United States District Court for the Northern District of Illinois reversed its own certification when discovery produced *by the defendant* in the case revealed the too many individualized inquiries were present to sustain certification in the Telephone Consumer Protection Act (TCPA) class action. The decertification of class actions is well-known in Federal Court, and with the decision in *Yahoo*, Illinois state practitioners are well-advised to understand that certification is not "set in stone" since it is generally granted *before* fact discovery and that Illinois courts will certainly rely on *Yahoo* in reaching decisions in this regard.

4. INTERLOCUTORY APPEALS AND APPELLATE REVIEW

Illinois Supreme Court Rule 306(a)(8) allows a party to petition the Illinois Appellate Court for leave to appeal from a trial court order denying or granting class action certification. A certification decision is not reviewed *de novo*, but for an abuse of discretion. *Weiss v. Waterhouse Securities, Inc.*, 208 Ill. 2d 439, 804 N.E.2d 536 (2004). The filing of a motion for reconsideration does not toll the time for filing an interlocutory appeal. *Ellis v. AAR Parts Trading, Inc.*, 357 Ill. App. 3d 723, 828 N.E.2d 726 (1st Dist. 2005).

A decision regarding class certification is within the sound discretion of the trial court and will not be disturbed absent abuse of discretion or application of permissible legal criteria. *Smith v. Illinois Central RR Co.*, 223 Ill. 2d 441, 447, 860 N.E.2d 332, 336 (2006). The review does not involve a *de novo* evaluation of the facts alleged and the facts of record. *Health Cost Controls v. Sevilla,* 365 Ill. App. 3d 795, 805 (1st Dist. 2006); *see also Cruz v. Unilock Chicago, Inc.*, 383 Ill. App. 3d 752, 892 N.E.2d 78 (2d Dist. 2008).

Decisions regarding class certification are within the sound discretion of the trial court and should be overturned only where the trial court clearly abused its discretion or applied impermissible legal criteria. *Avery v. State Farm Mutual Automobile Ins. Co.*, 216 Ill. 2d 100, 835 N.E.2d 801, (2005). However, a trial court's discretion in deciding whether to certify a class action is not unlimited and is bounded by, and must be exercised within, the framework of the civil procedure rules governing class actions. *Id.*; *see also Broussard v. Meineke Discount Muffler Shops, Inc.*, 155 F.3d 331, 344 (4th Cir. 1998). While a trial court has broad discretion in deciding whether to certify a class, this discretion must be exercised within the framework of Fed. R. Civ. P. 23. *Avery*, 835 N.E.2d at 820; *Broussard*, 155 F.3d at 344.

The Court of Appeals has also held that the trial court lacks authority, under Supreme Court Rule 306, to extend the petitioner's time for the filing of an interlocutory appeal regarding class certification. *De Bouse v. Bayer AG*, 385 Ill. App. 3d 812, 896 N.E.2d 882 (5th Dist. 2008), *reversed on other grounds*, 235 Ill. 2d 544, 922 N.E.2d 309 (Ill. 2009). In *De Bouse*, the trial court, recognizing that the clerk of court had failed to serve an executed copy of its order granting class certification to the defendant within the 30-day window in which defendant would have otherwise possessed the right to appeal pursuant to Rule 306(a)(8), granted the defendant's request to vacate its order, and re-entered it to restart the appeal clock. The Court of Appeals, however, found that the trial court lacked the jurisdiction to grant such an order, noting that a motion to file a late appeal should have been filed in the Court of Appeals. Furthermore, the Court of Appeals determined that the extension was not warranted because "the parties bear the responsibility to monitor the status of the case and that this responsibility is not lessened where the circuit court fails to give notice of the entry of the order." *Id.* at 823. Hence, the *De Bouse* court dismissed the Rule 306(a)(8) appeal of class certification for lack of jurisdiction finding that it was not timely filed.

5. NUMEROSITY/IMPRACTICALITY OF JOINDER—SECTION 801(1)

As noted, the Illinois statute requires that a class be "so numerous that joinder of all members is impractical." The potential number of class members need only be great enough to render separate litigation impractical. *See McCabe v. Burgess*, 57 Ill. App. 3d 450, 373 N.E.2d 327 (4th Dist. 1978).

The impracticability of joinder depends on several factors in addition to mere numbers. The Illinois statute and Fed. R. Civ. P. 23 use the same language. Among the factors taken into consideration are (1) the amount of a plaintiff's claim, (2) the ability of putative class members to bring suit on their own behalf; (3) the likelihood that they might do so, and (4) the geographic location of putative class members. *See Steinberg v. Chicago Med. School*, 69 Ill. 2d 320, 371 N.E.2d 634 (1977). Illinois courts have certified relatively small classes. *See, e.g., Kulins v. Malco A. Microdot Co.*, 121 Ill. App. 3d 520, 459 N.E.2d 1038 (1st Dist. 1984) (certification of a class that ultimately consisted of 19 members was not an abuse of discretion).

The question of numerosity for purposes of maintaining a class action depends on the particular facts of each case, and no arbitrary rules regarding the size of classes have been established. Illinois courts construing the numerosity requirement may follow federal practice under Rule 23, due to its similar language. *In re Rosewell*, 236 Ill. App. 3d 165, 603 N.E.2d 681, 686 (1st Dist. 1992). The plaintiff need not demonstrate a precise figure for the class size. A good faith non-speculative estimate will suffice. *Arenson v. Whitehall Convalescence and Nursing Home Inc.*, 164 F.R.D. 659, 662 (N.D. 1996). Plaintiffs need only demonstrate that the class is sufficiently numerous to make joinder of all the members impracticable. *Ramirez v. Midway Moving and Storage, Inc.,* 378 Ill. App. 3d 51, 880 N.E.2d 653 (1st Dist. 2007).

6. COMMONALITY/TYPICALITY—SECTION 801(2)

The Illinois statute does not have the typicality requirement of Fed. R. Civ. P. 23(a)(3); however, Illinois law mirrors Fed. R. Civ. P. 23(b)(3) (and 23(a)(2)) with respect to commonality. There must be common elements of law or fact. In a class action, it is appropriate to litigate questions of law and fact common to all members of a class and, after determination of common questions, to determine in an ancillary proceeding question that may be peculiar to individual class members. *McCabe v. Burgess*, 57 Ill. App. 3d 450, 373 N.E.2d 327 (4th Dist. 1978). While there need not be both a common question of fact and a common question of law, there must be a common question that predominates over individual questions. *Miner v. Gillette Co.*, 87 Ill. 2d 7, 17 (1981), and *Health Cost Controls v. Sevilla*, 365 Ill. App. 3d 795, 850 N.E.2d 851 (1st Dist. 2006).

In Illinois, an issue is "predominant" if it disposes of an entire controversy, leaving only minor issues to be resolved in individual circumstances. *Waters v. City of Chicago*, 95 Ill. App. 3d 919, 420 N.E.2d 599 (1st Dist. 1981). The Illinois Supreme Court in *Weiss v. Waterhouse Securities, Inc.*, 208 Ill. 2d 439, 450, 804 N.E.2d 536, 543 (2004), stated that "the test for whether common questions predominate is whether the successful adjudication of the plaintiffs' claim will establish a right to recovery in the class members." However, the *Weiss* Court cautioned that this test ("successful adjudication") is to be used in the class certification context, but not in the context of a motion to dismiss, because (as noted above) "establishing" a right of recovery in class members is not required at the pleading stage. *Id.* A class action complaint need only properly *allege* a class action, not *establish* a right of recovery, to survive a motion to dismiss.

Prior to *Avery v. State Farm, supra,* it was clear that a plaintiff could meet his/her commonality requirement through an allegation (and eventual offer of proof) that there was *one* common issue of fact *or* law that predominates over all other issues. *Gordon v. Boden*, 224 Ill. App. 3d 195, 586

N.E.2d 461 (1st Dist. 1991) (citing *Miner v. Gillette Co.*, 87 Ill. 2d 7, 428 N.E.2d 478 (1981)); *see also Steinberg v. Chicago Med. School*, 69 Ill. 2d 320, 371 N.E.2d 634 (1977); *Smith v. Illinois Central Railroad Company*, 363 Ill. App. 3d 944, 845 N.E.2d 703 (5th Dist. 2005); and *Lee v. Allstate Life Insurance Company*, 361 Ill. App. 3d 970, 838 N.E.2d 15 (2d Dist. 2005). That is, it was recognized that a class action could not be defeated by the mere existence of some individual issues when common questions of fact or law predominated. *Chultem v. Ticor Title Insurance Co.*, 401 Ill. App. 3d 226, 238, 927 N.E.2d 289 (1st Dist. 2010), *leave to appeal denied* 237 Ill. 2d 553, 938 N.E.2d 519 (Ill. 2010). Emphasizing this fact, the Illinois Court of Appeals has held: "the existence of individual issues, a separate determination of individual damages, multiple theories of recovery, or even the inability of some class members to obtain relief because of a particular individual factor will not, standing alone, defeat class certification if the common questions of fact or law are otherwise predominant." *Purcell and Wardrope, Chartered v. Hertz Corp.,* 175 Ill. App. 3d 1069, 530 N.E.2d 994, 998 (1st Dist. 1988) (citing *Miner v. Gillette Co.*, 87 Ill. 2d 7, 428 N.E.2d 478 (1981)). The Appellate Court, as recent as 2012, continues to recognize that "[A] class action will not be defeated solely because of some factual variations among class members' grievances." *See Hooker v. Retirement Bd. of the Firemen's Annuity and Benefit Fund of Chicago*, 972 N.E.2d 189, 197 (Ill. App. Ct. 1st Dist. 2012) (1st Dist. 2012). Likewise, the Appellate Court continues to find that "[w]here liability is premised on a common practice uniformly applied . . . it is proper for the trial court to find the plaintiff's claims present questions of fact and law, common to the class, that predominate over questions affecting only individual members of the class." *S37 Management, Inc. v. Advance Refrigeration Co.*, 961 N.E.2d 6, 16 (1st Dist. 2011).

Avery v. State Farm, supra, however, established that certain factual variations will defeat "commonality." In *Avery,* the plaintiff asserted a class action against State Farm over its alleged use of non-OEM (original equipment manufacturer) parts in repairing policy holders' automobiles involved in accidents. The trial court certified a nationwide class despite State Farm contention that it used different contracts in different states, which contained materially different parts requirements. The trial court granted certification, in part, by relying on testimony from a State Farm property consultant who testified State Farm's "basic philosophy" was to restore a policyholder's car to its "pre-loss" condition throughout the United States. The trial court reasoned that this "uniform practice," and whether it was breached, was a question of fact or law common to all class members, and that this common interest predominated over questions affecting individual class members.

The jury awarded the plaintiff class $456,180,000. The trial court awarded an additional $130 million in disgorgement damages and $600 million in punitive damages for violations of the Illinois Consumer Fraud Act, raising the award to $1,186,180,000. The Court of Appeals affirmed with one exception. *Avery v. State Farm Mutual Automobile Ins. Co.*, 321 Ill. App. 3d 269, 746 N.E.2d 1242 (5th Dist. 2001). That is, it eliminated the $130 million in disgorgement damages as a double recovery, lowering the damages to $1,056,180,000.

The Illinois Supreme Court, however, reversed on numerous grounds. Relevant to this discussion, the Court declined to accept plaintiffs' argument permitting the "commonality" requirement to be met through the establishment of a "uniform practice." Instead, the Court examined each State Farm contract at issue. Finding that the State Farm contracts had materially different language regarding State Farm's duty to repair policy holder's autos, the Court held that the "commonality and predominance" requirements of section 2-801 could not be met and reversed the certification of a nationwide contract class. 216 Ill.2d at 135, 835 N.E.2d at 824. As noted by the Second District, "In *Avery*, the individual issues of determining the wording of each separate and distinct contract that each class member agreed to and its legal effect outweighed any conceivable common issues." *Cruz v. Unilock Chicago, Inc.*, 383 Ill. App. 3d 752, 892 N.E.2d 78 (2d Dist. 2008).

As a side note, the *Avery* Court went on to hold that State Farm's use of non-OEM parts was not a breach of any of its contracts, as the use of non-OEM parts did not constitute compensable damage (a review of the *Avery* Court's reasoning on damages is indispensable for anyone involved in Illinois class action litigation). In addition, the *Avery* Court reversed the lower court's holding regarding the Illinois Consumer Fraud Act count, which is discussed below. Finally, it is worthy of note that the dissent argued, in language not often seen in Illinois Supreme Court opinions, that *Avery* signaled the Illinois judiciary's new hostility to class actions in general.

Illinois Supreme Court opinions following *Avery* have evidenced this new hostility. *See Gridley v. State Farm*, 217 Ill. 2d 158, 840 N.E.2d 269 (2005), and *Price v. Philip Morris, Inc.*, 219 Ill. 2d 182, 848 N.E.2d 1 (2005) (plurality opinion) *cert den'd* 127 S. Ct. 685, 75 U.S. 3281, 166 L. Ed. 2d 517 (2006). *Gridley* involved State Farm's alleged practice of obtaining "clean" titles to vehicles it had previously declared "total losses." The *Gridley* Court reversed the trial and appellate courts and remanded with instructions that the trial court grant State Farm's motion to dismiss on *forum non conveniens* grounds. *Price* involved Philip Morris' sale of "light" cigarettes. The *Price* Court reversed the trial court's decision finding the cigarette maker liable for fraud in violation of the Illinois Consumer Fraud Act (CFA) and remanded with instructions that the case be dismissed. The *Price* Court reasoned that section 10b(1) of the CFA barred liability because the Federal Trade Commission (FTC) had authorized cigarette makers to use terms like "low," "reduced," and "light" in their advertising if accompanied by clear and conspicuous disclosure of tar and nicotine contents. As in *Avery,* Justice Freeman dissented and was joined by Justice Kilbride.

The Supreme Court has continued to mold the commonality requirement consistent with that expressed in *Avery, Gridley,* and *Price,* emphasizing that there must be "predominant" questions of law or fact under Section 801(2). *Smith v. Ill. Cent. R.R. Co.*, 223 Ill. 2d 441, 860 N.E.2d 332 (2006). In *Smith*, the plaintiffs filed suit against Illinois Central Railroad Company, on behalf of themselves and those who sustained damage as a result of a train derailment. Plaintiffs alleged negligence, nuisance, and trespass. The trial court granted plaintiffs' motion to certify the class action and the Appellate Court affirmed. The Illinois Supreme Court, however, reversed the lower courts and made two significant holdings. First, it reaffirmed that the Illinois class action statute is patterned after Federal Rule of Civil Procedure 23(b)(3) and quoted, with approval, from a Texas Supreme Court opinion, as follows: "the purpose of the predominance requirement is to ensure that the proposed class is sufficiently cohesive to warrant adjudication by representation . . ." and that, "the test for predominance is not whether the common issues outnumber the individual ones, but whether common or individual issues will be the object of most of the efforts of the litigants and the court." *Smith* at 448–49 (citing *Southwestern Refining Co. v. Bernal*, 22 S.W.3d 425, 434, 43 Tex. Sup. Ct. J. 706 (Tex. 2000)). Second, it held that liability for the derailment could not be equated to alleged health consequences arising from chemical exposure resulting from the derailment. That is, because the majority of the damages did not arise from the derailment itself, but instead were caused by exposure to the spilled chemicals, proximate causation would involve highly individualized variables, including whether and to what extent, which chemicals each member was exposed to, location at the time of exposure, age, activity, medical history and credibility. In light of this, the *Smith* Court held that because individual issues of proximate causation and damages would consume the great bulk of the time at trial that common issues of fact did not predominate. *See also, Byer Clinic and Chiropractic, Ltd. v. Kapraun* 48 N.E.3d 244 (1st Dist. 2016) (holding that commonality is not satisfied when the proposed class representative attempts to fill the shoes of two sets of plaintiffs that were allegedly damaged on two separate occasions six full months apart from each other by the same defendant under the umbrella of the Federal Telephone Consumer Protection Act (TCPA)).

In *Bremis v. Safeco Ins. Co. of America*, 407 Ill. App. 3d 1164, 948 N.E.2d 1054 (5th Dist. 2011), the Appellate Court again held that certain factual variations would defeat commonality. In *Bremis,* the plaintiff was a physician who treated a patient insured by Safeco. He asserted a class action on behalf of: "All persons insured by Safeco property and casualty insurance companies . . . (and their assignee medical providers), who . . . submitted one or more claims for payment of medical expenses . . . had their claim(s) adjusted and reviewed by computer bill review software incorporating Ingenix 'MDR modules;' and . . . received or were tendered payment in an amount less than the submitted medical expense due to charges purportedly exceeding the usual, customary or reasonable amount, based upon the Ingenix 'MDR modules.'" The *Bremis* Court held that there was no commonality because the question of "usual and customary" charges was an individual question that would need to be answered by each claimant. In addition, the court found that the question of the assignment versus an authorization for payment was a potential individualized issue that could prevent commonality. Hence, the class claim failed.

While the possibility of setoffs or counterclaims may reduce damage awards these claims do not defeat commonality or affect liability. *Walczak v. Onyx Acceptance Corp.*, 365 Ill. App. 3d 664, 678, 850 N.E.2d 357 (1st Dist. 2006) (citing with approval *Haynes v. Logan Furniture Mart, Inc.*, 503 F.2d 1161, 1165 n.4 (7th Cir. 1974)). Moreover, it should be noted that class members against whom a defendant's counterclaim might apply may simply opt out of the class. 735 ILCS 5/2-804.

Although the Illinois class action statute does not have the "typicality" requirement of Fed. R. Civ. P. 23(a)(3), typicality should not be ignored. In particular, the U.S Supreme Court has held that "[t]he commonality and typicality requirements of Rule 23(a) tend to merge. Both serve as guideposts for determining whether under the particular circumstances maintenance of a class action is economical. . . . Those requirements therefore also tend to merge with the adequacy-of-representation requirement." *Gen. Tel. Co. of Southwest v. Falcon*, 457 U.S. 147, 102 S. Ct. 2364, 72 L. Ed. 2d 740 (1982).

7. ADEQUATE REPRESENTATION—SECTION 801(3)

"The purpose of the adequate representation requirement is to ensure that all class members will receive proper, efficient, and appropriate protection of their interests in the presentation of the claim." *P.J.'s Concrete Pumping Service, Inc. v. Nextel West Corp.*, 345 Ill. App. 3d 992, 1004, 803 N.E.2d 1020 (2d Dist. 2004). The test of adequate representation is whether the interests of the named parties are the same as the interests of those who are not named. *Cruz v. Unilock Chi., Inc.*, 383 Ill. App. 3d 752, 778, 892 N.E.2d 78, 103 (2d Dist. 2008) (citing *P.J.'s*, 345 Ill. App. 3d at 1004.

The Illinois statute requires that the representative plaintiff be a member of the class he represents. *McCabe v. Burgess*, 57 Ill. App. 3d 450, 373 N.E.2d 327 (4th Dist. 1978), *Faison v. RTFX, Inc.*, 2014 IL App (1st) 121893 (1st Dist. 2014). The purpose of the adequate representation requirement is to ensure that all class members will receive proper, efficient, and appropriate protection of their interests in the presentation of the claim. *Gordon v. Boden*, 224 Ill. App. 3d 195, 586 N.E.2d 461 (1st Dist. 1991) (citing *Purcell & Wardrope, Chtd. v. Hertz Corp.,* 175 Ill. App. 3d 1069, 530 N.E.2d 994, 1000 (1st Dist. 1988)). The adequacy requirement is satisfied if the plaintiff's interests are not antagonistic to the class interests, the case is not collusive, and the plaintiff's attorneys are experienced, qualified, and able to conduct the case. *Spirek v. State Farm Mut. Auto Ins. Co.,* 65 Ill. App. 3d 440, 382 N.E.2d 111, 119 (1st Dist. 1978). A class representative that is no longer part of the putative class is not an adequate representative. *Evans v. Godinez*, 2014 IL App (4th) 130686 (4th Dist. 2014).

In *Steinberg v. System Software Assoc., Inc.,* 306 Ill. App. 3d 157, 713 N.E.2d 709 (1st Dist.

1999), the First District Court of Appeals held that exclusion of plaintiffs in a competing class action in federal court was not necessarily an abuse of discretion. However, should a sole plaintiff (where the class action motion is pending) or a sole class representative (in a certified class) be found inadequate or no longer adequate, the court "must allow a reasonable period of time for substitution of other class members as the class representatives." *Hillenbrand v. Meyer Medical Group SC*, 308 Ill. App. 3d 381, 720 N.E.2d 287, 296 (1st Dist. 1999); *In re Discovery Zone Securities Litigation*, 169 F.R.D. 104, 109 (N.D. Ill. 1996).

A distinction between standing and adequacy of representation was made in *Moran Transportation Corp. v. Stroger*, 303 Ill. App. 3d 459, 708 N.E.2d 508 (1st Dist. 1999). In *Moran,* the trial court found that the plaintiffs lacked standing to bring the claims they sought to assert, because they did not qualify for the tax-exemption in question, but nevertheless proceeded to grant a class certification motion. The *Moran* Court reversed this finding (holding that those taxpayers who did not qualify for exemption nevertheless possessed standing. That Court, however, denied certification because the lower court had not properly evaluated the elements required for certification, including representation.

Several Illinois cases have been concerned with the timing of a tender to the named class representatives and its effect and this matter was settled by the Illinois Supreme Court in *Ballard RN Ctr., Inc. v. Kohll's Pharm. & Homecare, Inc.*, 48 N.E.3d 1060 (2015). *Ballard* decided with finality that the plaintiff's filing of a Motion for Class Certification contemporaneously with the initial complaint was not in fact a countless shell and did preclude mootness after the defendant tendered relief to the named plaintiff in the putative class. The practice of tendering relief to the named plaintiff in a class is a practice that has drawn a great deal of criticism in the Federal Circuits; however, the decision in *Ballard* was one of first impression before Illinois' highest court. The Seventh Circuit has already settled the matter for its practitioners in *Chapman v. First Index, Inc*., 796 F.3d 783, 787 (7th Cir. 2015), stating "to the extent that [it] hold[s] that a defendant's offer of full compensation moots the litigation or otherwise ends the Article III case or controversy," thus eliminating all together the "pick off" strategy. *Id*. The *Ballard* decision thus causes what can be described as a split between Illinois jurisprudence with Seventh Circuit jurisprudence and as such should be carefully considered when handling cases under Illinois class action law. The Supreme Court has ruled prior to *Ballard* that where the claims of the named representatives have been resolved, they are not proper parties who would fairly and adequately protect the interest of the class they purport to represent. *Wheatley v. Board of Education of Township High School District 205*, 99 Ill. 2d 481, 459 N.E.2d 1364 (1984). Given this, full tender to a named representative prior to the filing of a certification motion, renders the representative's action moot. *Hayman v. Autohaus on Edens, Inc.,* 315 Ill. App. 3d 1075, 734 N.E.2d 1012 (1st Dist. 2000). *Yu v. International Business Machines Corp.*, 314 Ill. App. 3d 892, 732 N.E.2d 1173 (1st Dist. 2000); *see also Arriola v. Time Insurance Co.*, 323 Ill. App. 3d 138, 751 N.E.2d 221 (1st Dist. 2001) (summary judgment granted in favor of defendant where defendant made tender and plaintiff had not filed a motion to certify the class); *Bruemmer v. Compaq Computer Corp*., 329 Ill. App. 3d 755, 768 N.E. 2d 276 (1st Dist. 2002) (plaintiff failed to seek class certification which resulted in the claim being rendered moot upon defendant's post-litigation tender); *Cohen v. Compact Power Systems, LLC,* 382 Ill. App. 3d 104, 887 N.E.2d 668 (1st Dist. 2008) (summary judgment granted to defendant where defendant made tender and plaintiff had not filed a motion to certify); *Akinyemi v. JP Morgan Chase Bank, NA*., 391 Ill. App. 3d 334, 339, 908 N.E.2d 163 (1st Dist. 2009) (summary judgment granted to defendant who made tender prior to the filing of a class certification motion). The Supreme Court, in *Barber v. American Airlines, Inc.,* 241 Ill. 2d 450, 948 N.E.2d 1042 (Ill. 2011), rejected the "pick-off" exception to *Wheatley, supra*, recognized in *Gelb v. Air Con Refrigeration & Heating, Inc.*, 326 Ill. App. 3d 809, 761 N.E.2d 265 (1st Dist.

2001) (wherein the court held that tender before plaintiff had a reasonable opportunity to file a motion for class certification did not moot the claim) and *Barber v. American Airlines, Inc.*, 398 Ill. App. 3d 868, 925 N.E.2d 1240 (1st Dist. 2010) (wherein the court held that the defendant's unilateral act of refunding the claimed amount did not moot the claim prior to the filing of a class certification motion), as it was contrary to the explicit holding of *Wheatley. See Barber,* 241 Ill. 2d at 459; *see also Gatreaux v. DKW Enterprises, LLC*, 958 N.E.2d 1088, 1093 (1st Dist. 2011) (wherein the court observed "[i]n its decision in *Barber* . . . the supreme court explicitly rejected the 'pick off' exception and reaffirmed the viability of the 'pick off' rule"). Significantly, the Appellate Court, in *Gatreaux*, held that it is the timing of the tender that determines mootness; plaintiff's refusal of said tender is irrelevant. *Id.* at 1099–1100. In light of these cases, a plaintiff is advised to file for class certification simultaneously with the filing of the complaint or as soon as possible, to avoid the very real potential that class claims are mooted by a defendant's tender to named representatives.

It is important, however, that class counsel be sure that a Motion for Class Certification is more than a countless "shell" motion as it is clear that such a motion will not suffice to comply with the protections of *Barbar as Ballard RN Ctr., Inc. v. Kohll's Pharm. & Homecare, Inc.*, 2014 IL App. (1st) 131543 (1st Dist. 2014), discussed in greater detail below, does not eliminate the "pick off" strategy, but instad affirms the aforementioned tactic. The Supreme Court ruled that a Motion for Class Certification filed at the same time as the initial Class Complaint did not prevent the Defendant from making a tender offer and mooting the class thus keeping the onus on the plaintiff to move for certification as early as possible and with proper pleading standards achieved. The class counsel in *Barbar* did not make any factual allegations in the initial Motion and stated that a subsequent supporting memorandum would be filed and failed to ever do so. Based on these facts, and the fact that the class representative did not have any knowledge of a class at the time the Motion for Certification was filed, the First District agreed with the Defendants that the tender offer was valid and that the class was moot. *Ballard* at P60.

Also pertaining to tender, it is important to note that where there has been tender and acceptance of the plaintiff's compensatory damages, but at the same time there is an outstanding claim seeking attorneys' fees and a pending motion for certification, the trial court must rule on the pending motion for certification prior to ruling on any motion to dismiss based on mootness. *Hillenbrand v. Meyer Med. Group*, 308 Ill. App. 3d 381, 391, 720 N.E.2d 287, 296 (1st Dist. 1999) (citing to *Franks v. Bowman Transportation Co.*, 424 U.S. 747, 753 (1976), and *Susman v. Lincoln American Corp.*, 587 F.2d 866, 870 (7th Cir. 1978)). In fact, a named plaintiff in a putative class action cannot accept a tender without first obtaining permission from the court. *See* 735 ILCS 5/2-806, *infra* (class actions are not to be compromised except with the approval of the court). Hence, the acceptance of a tender without such court permission would be a nullity. Furthermore, this rule is logical because without it there would be a danger that a putative class action could be brought with the primary purpose of promoting a larger settlement of an individual claim. Likewise, a defendant should not be allowed to dilute a putative class (and certainly not a certified class) without first obtaining permission of the court because "To hold otherwise would allow a party to simply tender payment to the named plaintiffs, in each class action filed against it, prior to the trial court's ruling on their motion for class certification." *Hillenbrand,* 720 N.E.2d at 296.

The Appellate Court in *Jensen v. Bayer AG*, 371 Ill. App. 3d 682, 862 N.E.2d 1091 (1st Dist. 2007), discussed adequacy of class representation regarding a CFA claim. In *Jensen*, the plaintiff/representative asserted that the defendant's medication was defective and breached an implied warranty. The Illinois trial court granted summary judgment to the defendants and denied class certification. The Appellate Court affirmed both rulings finding that the medication in question was marketed directly to doctors. Hence, there was no representation made to the plaintiff. Furthermore, the plaintiff did not have sufficient privity of contract to make a proper breach of implied warranty claim. Thus, the plaintiff could not be considered an acceptable class representative and class certification was properly denied. Echoing this holding, the First District Court of Appeals has held that a class action cannot be certified if the named class representative lacks a valid cause of action. *Cwik v. Topinka*, 328 Ill. Dec. 766, 905 N.E.2d 300 (1st Dist. 2009) *affirmed on other grounds,* 237 Ill. 2d 409, 930 N.E.2d 990 (Ill. 2010), *cert. denied* 131 S. Ct. 476, 178 L. Ed. 2d 290 (U.S. 2010).

A tender offer is not a foolproof tool to mooting a valid class, however. In *G.M. Sign, Inc. v. Swiderski Elecs., Inc.*, 2014 IL App. (2d) 130711 (2d Dist. 2014), the Second District Court of Appeals noted that a tender is an unconditional offer of payment consisting of the actual production of a sum not less than the amount due on a particular obligation. Further, the tender must be without conditions to which the creditor can have a valid objection, or which will be prejudicial to his [or her] rights. *G.M. Sign, Inc. v. Swiderski Elecs., Inc.*, at 28. In *GM Sign*, the defendant made a tender offer to the class representative that was only valid until the trial court ruled on certification. The Second District reversed the circuit court in finding that the offer was not a legitimate tender.

8. FAIR AND EFFICIENT ADJUDICATION OF CONTROVERSY—SECTION 801(4)

Illinois law considers whether a class action can best secure economies of time, effort and expense; promote uniformity; or accomplish other ends of equity and justice that class actions seek to obtain. *Gordon v. Boden*, 224 Ill. App. 3d 195, 586 N.E.2d 461 (1st Dist. 1991). Illinois law considers class actions appropriate when separate suits could result in the establishment of inconsistent standards of conduct for persons opposing a class or when a separate suit could affect the rights of other members of the class. *Rodriguez v. Credit System Specialists, Inc.,* 17 Ill. App. 3d 606, 308 N.E.2d 342 (1st Dist. 1991).

Illinois cases also recognize that the availability of the class action device can benefit persons whose claims are so small as to discourage the filing of individual actions. *See, e.g., Smyth v. Kaspar Am. State Bank*, 9 Ill. 2d 27, 136 N.E.2d 796, 805 (1956) (quoting *Weeks v. Bareco Oil Co.*, 125 F.2d 84 (7th Cir. 1941)) (to allow a defendant to contest liability against small claimants in separate suits would, in many cases, give defendants an advantage that would essentially close the door of justice to all claimants). Conversely, it has been held that class treatment is not justified where the recovery sought is "too trivial to justify an imposition upon the administration of civil justice." *Hayman v. Autohaus on Edens, Inc.,* 315 Ill. App. 3d 1075, 734 N.E.2d 1012 (1st Dist. 2000) (*dicta* rejecting continued prosecution of a class action where class representative's damages amounted to three days' interest on $299). As a general rule, the Appellate Court has held that: "Where the first three requirements for class certification have been satisfied, the fourth requirement may be considered fulfilled as well." *Ramirez v. Midway Moving and Storage, Inc.,* 378 Ill. App. 3d 51, 880 N.E.2d 653 (1st Dist. 2007) (citing *Walczak*, 365 Ill. App. 3d at 679).

In *Fakhoury v. Pappas*, 395 Ill. App. 3d 302, 912 N.E.2d 1161, 334 Ill. Dec. 273 (1st Dist. 2009), the Appellate Court found that class certification was a fair and efficient method of addressing claims that the country treasurer had miscalculated interest owed on property tax refunds, despite a statute barring class action complaints for those seeking tax refunds. In *Fakhoury*, the court granted class certification as equitable relief, after the main claims were resolved, to correct a problem common to a class of individuals. Hence, the court determined that class action was "an efficient, fair and effective means of resolving this issue." *Id.* at 312, 316.

To provide context, in *Ballard RN Ctr., Inc. v. Kohll's Pharm. & Homecare, Inc.*, 2014 Ill. App. (1st) 131543 (1st Dist. 2014), the First District Appellate Court had the occasion to analyze the appropriateness requirement in the backdrop of the Federal Telephone Consumer Protection Act (TCPA). On March 3, 2010, plaintiff Ballard RN Center, Inc. (Ballard) allegedly received an unsolicited one-page fax from defendant Kohll's, which advertised corporate flu shot services. Discovery showed that on March 3, 2010, Kohll's sent the fax at issue to a total of 4,760 fax numbers and successfully transmitted it to 4,142 of them. In *Ballard*, the circuit court granted class certification to the putative class under TCPA and the Illinois Consumer Fraud Act. On appeal, the defendant argued that a class action was not an appropriate means to resolve the claim and that the class representative was not adequate.

As to appropriateness, the First District Court of Appeals agreed with the circuit court finding that the legislative history of the TCPA belies the assertion that class action lawsuits in TCPA cases are against congressional intent, and that the TCPA was first enacted in 1991. In 2005, Congress amended the TCPA by enacting the Junk Fax Prevention Act of 2005 (JFPA) (47 U.S.C. § 609 (2006)). At the time the JFPA was enacted, there had been numerous class action lawsuits certified under the TCPA. *See, e.g., ESI Ergonomic Solutions, LLC v. United Artists Theatre Circuit, Inc.*, 203 Ariz. 94, 50 P.3d 844 (Ariz. Ct. App. 2002); *Core Funding Group, LLC v. Young*, 792 N.E.2d 547 (Ind. Ct. App. 2003). Nevertheless, Congress did not take any action to prohibit or narrow the scope of class action lawsuits under the TCPA. The First District Court accordingly held it is apparent that the legislature has acquiesced in courts' construction of the statute allowing for class action lawsuits. *See Charles v. Seigfried*, 165 Ill. 2d 482, 492, 651 N.E.2d 154, 209 Ill. Dec. 226 (1995); *Ballard*, at 41.

As noted in paragraph 8 above, the decision of the Illinois Supreme Court in *Ballard* should not be construed as challenging the validity of the so called "pick off" strategy to defeating a potential class action however as pursuant to the standing requirements in Article III and subsequent mooting of certain class actions can still occur. *Ballard* simply validates the tactic employed by plaintiffs' attorneys to file a motion for class certification as soon as reasonably possible in the state court process.

While the link to Section 801(4) requirements is attenuated, the pursuit of TCPA claims in Illinois were examined by the United States District Court for the Northern District of Illinois in *Alpha Tech Pet, Inc. v. LaGasse*, LLC, No. 16-cv-513 (N.D. Ill. Nov. 3, 2017). In *LaGasse*, the Northern District granted the defendant's Motion to Deny Class Certification based on a decision out of the D.C. Circuit finding that solicited faxes do not require an opt-out notice.

9. NOTICE TO THE CLASS—SECTION 803

As to notice, the Illinois statute provides that "upon a determination that an action may be maintained as a class action, or any time during the conduct of the action, the court in its discretion may order such notice that it deems necessary to protect the interest of the class and the parties." 735 ILCS 5/2-803. This is not an absolute requirement of notice. Rather, whether notice is to be given at all, and the kind of notice to be given, are matters of discretion for the trial court. This discretion is obviously limited by due process considerations, which do not require individual notice in all circumstances. *Carrao v. Health Care Serv. Corp.*, 118 Ill. App. 3d 417, 454 N.E.2d 781 (1st Dist. 1983).

> The giving of notice to other members of the class is not mandatory, and thus the class members have no clear right to notice; in fact, determination of whether an action may be maintained as a class action and determination of whether notice must be given, and in what manner and to whom, are separate discretionary determinations which the trial court must make, and thus notice is not a common question prerequisite for

maintenance of a class action.

McCabe v. Burgess, 57 Ill. App. 3d 450, 373 N.E.2d 327 (4th Dist. 1978).

In several recent cases, Illinois courts have approved notice by publication only where the class was exceedingly large and the damages of individual class members were moderate. *See, e.g., Avery v. State Farm Mut. Auto. Ins. Co.*, 321 Ill. App. 3d 269, 746 N.E.2d 1242 (5th Dist. 2001), *rev'd on other grounds, Avery v. State Farm Mutual Automobile Ins. Co.*, 216 Ill. 2d 100, 835 N.E.2d 801 (2005).

No Illinois case has discussed whether or not notice is required where the relief, if granted to the class representatives, will automatically inure to the benefit of the punitive class members. For example, in a case where the easement for the peaceful and quite enjoyment of a cemetery is trespassed upon, if the only relief sought is the abatement of the trespass, is it necessary that there be some sort of notice directed to all easement holders. It is suggested under such circumstances due process should not require notice.

Illinois Courts have also held that notice to each perspective class member communicated by fax also satisfies Section 803 notice requirements. *Shaun Fauley, Sabon, Inc. v. Metropolitan Life Ins. Co.*, 52 N.E.3d 427 (2d Dist. 2016).

10. EXCLUSION—SECTION 804

Under 735 ILCS 5/2-804, putative class members have the right to opt out of (i.e., be excluded from) the class and accordingly the possibility of a counterclaim against particular class members does not defeat class certification. *Walczak,* 365 Ill. App. 3d at 681. Emphasizing the finality of the option, the Appellate Court has held that putative class members who fail to opt-out are bound by any ensuing settlement agreement, thus, *res judicata* bar new claims. *Currie v. Wisconsin Central, LTD*, 961 N.E.2d 296, 309 (1st Dist. 2011). In addition, the *Currie* Court made it clear that filing an individual suit is not a substitute for opting out. *Id.*

No Illinois court has addressed whether opt-out rights must be afforded under circumstances such as those covered by Federal Rule of Civil Procedure 23(b)(1) or (2) even though Illinois courts appear to recognize class actions that would be certified under those sections of Rule 23.

11. BINDING EFFECT OF JUDGMENTS IN CLASS CASES—SECTION 805

Judgments entered in an action certified for class treatment are binding on all class members as defined by the court, excluding any persons who are properly excluded under subsection 2-804(b) of the Act. 735 ILCS 5/2-805.

12. DISMISSAL OR COMPROMISE OF CLASS CASES—SECTION 806

735 ILCS 5/2-806 requires "that any action brought as a class action shall not be compromised or dismissed except with the approval of the court and, unless excused for good cause shown, upon notice as the court may direct." This assures that the cost of representation is shared by all class members. *Mills v. Elec. Auto-Lite Co.*, 396 U.S. 375, 393–94, 24 L. Ed. 2d 593, 607 (1970).

13. RESIDUAL FUNDS IN A COMMON FUND—SECTION 807

Illinois law has long recognized the doctrine of fluid recovery (*cy pres*) and permitted its use in class action cases where it was not feasible to distribute all of the funds to identifiable class members. *Gordon v. Boden*, 224 Ill. App. 3d 195, 586 N.E.2d 461 (1st Dist. 1991). In further recognition of this doctrine, the Illinois Legislature has recently codified and expanded this practice through its enactment of 735 ILCS 5/2-807. Significantly, this section, which took effect on July 1, 2008, requires all judgments and/or orders approving proposed settlement of class actions to establish a process for the distribution of residual funds to one or more "eligible organizations," as defined by the section. This section, however, does not apply to class actions against the State of Illinois or its political subdivisions.

14. VENUE

In *Boxdorfer v. DaimlerChrysler Corp.*, 339 Ill. App. 3d 335, 790 N.E.2d 391 (5th Dist. 2003), the Illinois Appellate Court held that where "all the alleged acts of a failure to disclose defects on the part of the defendant did not take place in Madison County, but, rather, took place in Michigan, where the cars had been designed, manufactured and sold by the defendant" that venue for a consumer fraud claim was not proper in Madison County and, thus, transferred the case to Sangamon County; the location of the defendant's registered agent. In *Rensing v. Merck and Company, Inc., et al.*, 367 Ill. App. 3d 1046, 857 N.E.2d 702 (5th Dist. 2006), the Appellate Court applied a similar logic. In that case, the defendant advertised or promoted a pharmaceutical, which the plaintiff purchased and ingested in St. Clair County, where plaintiff filed suit under the Illinois Consumer Fraud Act. The *Rensing* Court, however, transferred venue to Cook County, where the defendant's registered agent was located.

With respect to jurisdiction, the United States District Court for the Norther District of Illinois established that the requirements established in the landmark United States Supreme Court Decision in *Bristol-Myers Squibb Co. v. Superior Court of California*, 137 S. Ct. 1773 (2017), applied to jurisdiction determinations in class actions including those in Illinois. In *Bristol-Myers*, 86 California residents and 592 residents of other states sued Bristol-Myers, a company headquartered in New York and incorporated in Delaware, in a mass tort action in California state court alleging the company's drug Plavix caused injuries. The drug company argued that the national plaintiffs did not have a strong enough nexus to California to pursue their claims there. The Northern District squared itself with the *Bristol-Myers* Court and applied the same reasoning to denying nationwide certification of an Illinois consumer fraud claim. In *DeBernardis v. NBTY, Inc.* No. 1:17-cv-06125 (N.D. Ill. Jan. 18, 2018). The Northern District found that the nationwide putative class members did not share a strong enough nexus with Illinois for the full class to be certified in Illinois. Developments will be ongoing in the wake of *Bristol-Myers.*

15. ATTORNEYS' FEES

The Illinois Supreme Court has long recognized the common fund method of determining attorneys' fees (which provides for the recoupment of attorney fees as a percentage on the common fund). Interestingly, the Illinois Supreme Court disapproved of the common fund method for two decades, limiting fee determinations to the lodestar method (a court determined reasonable number of attorney hours multiplied by the significance of other pertinent considerations, such as the contingency nature of the proceeding, the complexity of the litigation, and the benefits that were conferred upon the class members). *Flynn v. Kucharski,* 59 Ill. 2d 61, 319 N.E.2d 1 (1974); *Brundidge v. Glendale Federal Bank*, 168 Ill. 2d 235, 239, 659 N.E.2d 909 (1995). However, in 1995, the Illinois Supreme Court abrogated the *Flynn* limitation, holding that fees could be determined by either method and impliedly encouraged the use of the common fund method. *Brundidge*, 168 Ill. 2d at 246. The U.S. Seventh Circuit Court of Appeals and Illinois courts have each recognized that the Illinois common fund doctrine is not preempted by ERISA. *Primax Recoveries, Inc., v. Sevilla*, 324 F.3d 544, 549–50 (7th Cir. 2003), and *Health Cost Controls v. Sevilla*, 365 Ill. App. 3d 795, 850 N.E.2d 851 (1st Dist. 2006).

In *Langone v. Schad, Diamond and Shedden, PC.*, 406 Ill. App. 3d 820, 835–36 (1st Dist. 2010), the court examined a dispute between law firms regarding attorney fees from a class action settlement. The court determined that the plaintiff firm could not claim attorney fees from the settlement fund because it had failed to follow the court's direction to submit detailed time records to support claimed fees and/or to dispute the court's distribution.

As a side note, the Illinois Appellate Court determined in *In re Chicago Flood Litigation*, 289 Ill. App. 3d 937, 682 N.E.2d 421 (1st Dist. 1997), that there was no basis for imposing obligations under the *quantum meruit* doctrine to opt-out plaintiffs for the payment of attorney fees to class counsel.

16. STANDING TO OBJECT

An objector need not intervene as a pre-condition to appeal an order approving a class action settlement. *Rosen v. Ingersoll-Rand Company, et al.*, 372 Ill. App. 3d 440, 865 N.E.2d 451 (1st Dist. 2007) (citing with approval *Devlin v. Scardelletti,* 536 U.S. 1, 14, 122 S. Ct. 2005, 153 L. Ed. 2d 27 (2002)). However, non-intervening parties may waive their standing to object to the settlement by failing to comply with reasonable requirements set forth in the notice. *Rosen,* 372 Ill. App. 3d at 448.

17. DECERTIFICATION OF A CLASS ACTION

In *Mashal v. The City of Chicago,* 981 N.E.2d 951, 367 Ill. Dec. 223 (Ill. 2012), the Illinois Supreme Court addressed the 735 ILCS 5/2-802(a) provision, which permits courts to "amend" certification orders "before a decision on the merits." In an issue of first impression, the Court found that: "a 'decision on the merits' is a complete determination of liability on a claim based on the facts disclosed by the evidence, and which establishes a right to recover in at least one class member, but which is something short of a final judgment." *Id.* at *44. The Court, however, has held that an order setting aside an earlier determination of class certification would be improper if based merely upon the court's "feelings of error regarding the original certification." *Barliant v. Follett Corp.*, 74 Ill. 2d 226, 231, 384 N.E.2d 316 (1978); *Rosolowski v. Clark Refining and Marketing*, 383 Ill. App. 3d 420, 890 N.E.2d 1011 (1st Dist. 2008). Instead, the *Barliant* Court held that only "clearly changed circumstances" could support a decision to decertify a class. *Id.* In *Wenikoff v. Health Care Service Corp.*, 376 Ill. App. 3d 228, 877 N.E.2d 11 (1st Dist. 2007), the Illinois Appellate Court interpreted and applied the *Barliant* holding, finding that that decertification requires a "significant difference" in circumstances and will not be supported by trivial changes. In fact, the *Wenikoff* Court held that a newly discovered issue, which barred the representative plaintiff's recovery, did not amount to a "significant" change in circumstances and did not support the decertification of the class. *Wenikoff, supra* at 232–33.

18. MISCELLANEOUS

a. Clauses Compelling Arbitration and Barring Class Action

Illinois courts tend to include appraisal clauses, such as those found in automobile insurance policies, within the broader category of arbitration clauses. *See, e.g., Hanke v. American International Southern Insurance Company,* 335 Ill. App. 3d 1164, 1169, 782 N.E.2d 328, 332 (5th Dist. 2002); *Travis v. American Manufacturers Mutual Insurance Company*, 335 Ill. App. 3d 1171, 1177, 782 N.E.2d 322, 327 (5th Dist. 2002); *Austin v. Illinois Farmers Ins. Co.*, 351 Ill. App. 3d 931, 938, 815 N.E.2d 435, 441 (5th Dist. 2004). The increasing use of arbitration clauses and appraisal clauses has caused Illinois courts to examine whether class claims may be forced into arbitration and/or whether clauses barring class actions are unconscionable.

The threshold question when examining the enforceability of an arbitration clause is to determine which statute applies—Section 1 of the Illinois Uniform Arbitration Act (710 ILCS 5/1) (West 2004) or Section 2 of the Federal Arbitration Act. *Tortoriello v. Gerald Nissan of North Aurora, Inc.*, 379 Ill. App. 3d 214, 224–25, 882 N.E.2d 157 (2d Dist. 2008). Illinois courts have repeatedly found that state law governs contracts to arbitrate, even where the contract at issue involves interstate commerce. *Tortoriello*, Ill. App. 3d at 225 (citing *Glazer's Distributors of Illinois, Inc. v. NWS—Illinois, LLC*, 376 Ill. App. 3d 411, 876 N.E.2d 203 (1st Dist. 2007)); *see also Ragan v. AT&T Corp.*, 355 Ill. App. 3d 1143, 1148, 824 N.E.2d 1183, 1187 (5th Dist. 2005); *Cohen v. Blockbuster Entertainment, Inc.*, 338 Ill. App. 3d 171, 787 N.E.2d 846 (1st Dist. 2003) (*Blockbuster I*).

Who determines the arbitration clause's validity is a significant question. *Tortoriello, supra* at 226. The Illinois appellate court has repeatedly held: "The issue of whether a contract to arbitrate exists must be determined by the court, not an arbitrator." *Bahuriak v. Bill Kay Chrysler Plymouth, Inc.*, 337 Ill. App. 3d 714, 786 N.E.2d 1045 (2d Dist. 2003); *see also Green Tree Financial Corp. v. Bazzle*, 539 U.S. 444, 451, 123 S. Ct. 2402, 156 L. Ed. 2d 414 (2003); *Zobrist v. Verizon Wireless*, 354 Ill. App. 3d 1139, 1143, 822 N.E.2d 536, 537 (5th Dist. 2004); *Austin v. Illinois Farmers Ins. Co.*, 351 Ill. App. 3d 931, 815 N.E.2d 435 (5th Dist. 2004); and 710 ILCS 5/2(b) ("[o]n application, the court may stay an arbitration proceeding commenced or threatened on a showing that there is no agreement to arbitrate"). In *Green Tree*, the U.S. Supreme Court determined that: "certain gateway matters, such as whether the parties have a valid arbitration agreement at all or whether a concededly binding arbitration clause applies to a certain type of controversy," are to be decided by the court. *Green Tree, supra* at 452; *see also Austin, supra* at 937. Furthermore, if there is a valid arbitration agreement, the court will support a stay where another action regarding the same subject matter is pending. *See Aventine Renewable Energy, Inc. v. JP Morgan Chase Bank*, 406 Ill. App. 3d 757, 940 N.E.2d 257 (3d Dist. 2010).

The Appellate Court has ruled that a putative class will not require arbitration if it fails due to impossibility. *Quickclick Loans, LLC v. Russell*, 943 N.E.2d 166, 347 Ill. Dec. 876 (1st Dist. 2011). In *Quickclick Loans, LLC,* the arbitration agreement in question required that the parties arbitrate with one of two specified organizations. However, neither organization was available to arbitrate the matter in question. Hence, the agreement failed due to impossibility and did not bar the putative class claim.

In the absence of a challenge to the validity of the arbitration clause, Illinois courts have held that arbitrators are well situated to determine the scope and effect of arbitration clauses. *Tortoriello*, Ill. App. 3d at 227; *see also Kinkel v. Cingular Wireless, LLC*, 357 Ill. App. 3d 556, 828 N.E.2d 812 (1st Dist. 2005), citing *Green Tree*, 539 U.S. at 453. Illinois courts have held that arbitration should be compelled when the arbitration agreement is clear that the dispute is within its scope. *Travis*, 335 Ill. App. 3d at 1177, 782 N.E.2d at 327; *Hanke*, 335 Ill. App. 3d at 1169, 782 N.E.2d at 332; *see also*

Reed v. Doctor's Associates, Inc., 331 Ill. App. 3d 618, 772 N.E.2d 372 (5th Dist. 2002). Disputes that lie outside the scope of an agreement to arbitrate are not arbitral. *Id.* A defendant has the burden of showing that at least some of a plaintiff's claims fall within the scope of an arbitration agreement; the failure of the defendant to meet this initial burden will bar arbitration. *See Cohen v. Blockbuster Entertainment, Inc.*, 351 Ill. App. 3d 772, 777, 814 N.E.2d 933, 937 (1st Dist. 2004) (*Blockbuster II*). If an arbitrator is satisfied that the arbitration clause permits the arbitration to proceed as a class action, then the arbitrator must also decide whether class arbitration is the best method to resolve the case. *Bess v. DirecTV, Inc.* 351 Ill. App. 3d 1148, 1155 815 N.E.2d 455, 460 (5th Dist. 2004) (*Bess I*).

Whether an arbitration clause is unconscionable, and thus unenforceable, is determined by the court. *Tortoriello v. Gerald Nissan of North Aurora, Inc.*, 379 Ill. App. 3d 214, 224–25, 882 N.E.2d 157 (2d Dist. 2008); *Bess v. DirecTV, Inc.*, 381 Ill. App. 3d 229, 885 N.E.2d 488 (5th Dist. 2008) (*Bess II*). A finding of unconscionability may be based upon either procedural or substantive unconscionability. *Razor v. Hyundai Motor America,* 222 Ill. 2d 75, 99, 854 N.E.2d 607, 622 (2006). "Procedural unconscionability refers to a situation where a term is so difficult to find, read, or understand that the plaintiff cannot fairly be said to have been aware he was agreeing to it." *Bess II*, 885 N.E.2d at 495. Interestingly, the *Kinkel* court found that there was "a degree of procedural unconscionability" in the agreement's failure to specify the cost of the arbitration. The *Kinkel* Court did not find this fact to be sufficient to render the arbitration/class action waiver clause procedurally unconscionable but did find that it was "a factor" in determining that the clause was substantively unconscionable. *Kinkel*, 393 Ill. 2d at 27; *see also Keefe v. Allied Home Mortgage Corp.*, 393 Ill. App. 3d 226, 912 N.E.2d 310 (5th Dist. 2009) (following *Kinkel*'s holding).

Substantive unconscionability pertains to the actual terms of the contract and requires an examination of the relative fairness of the obligations assumed. Substantive unconscionability is shown by contract terms so one-sided as to oppress or unfairly surprise an innocent party, an overall imbalance in the obligations and rights imposed by the bargain, and significant cost-price disparity. *Kinkel*, 393 Ill. 2d at 28 (citing *Maxwell v. Fidelity Financial Services, Inc.*, 184 Ariz. 82, 89, 907 P.2d 51, 58 (1995); *see also Keefe,* 393 Ill. App. 3d at 233. In *Kinkel*, the Court held that a prohibition on class arbitration was unconscionable because it was substantively unconscionable because it was so broad that "those allegedly injured would be economically prohibited from ever vindicating their rights in separate lawsuits." *Kinkel*, 828 N.E.2d at 818–20. In *Keefe*, the court found that while the arbitration agreement itself was not unconscionable, the class action waiver it contained was substantively unconscionable, thus the court severed the clause. *Keefe*, 393 Ill. App. 3d at 234. Similarly, in *Blockbuster I, supra*, the Illinois Appellate Court held that the court could consider the amount of the arbitration fee in determining the unconscionability of an arbitration clause containing class action preclusion. Moreover, the Illinois Appellate Court, in *Hutcherson v. Sears Roebuck & Co.*, 342 Ill. App. 3d 109, 793 N.E.2d 886 (1st Dist. 2003), held that a prohibition on class actions was insufficient to render an arbitration clause unconscionable, alone, but should be considered a factor in conjunction with other factors. *See also Rosen v. Saks Inc.*, 343 Ill. App. 3d 1075, 799 N.E.2d 488 (1st Dist. 2003).

In addition, the Illinois Appellate Court has held that consideration and, in particular, mutuality of obligation, is a vital component of the enforceability of an arbitration cause. In *General Motors Acceptance Corp. v. Johnson*, 354 Ill. App. 3d 885, 822 N.E.2d 30 (1st Dist. 2004) the Illinois Appellate Court held that there was proper consideration where both parties signed an arbitration agreement stating that either party could, unilaterally, elect to have their dispute arbitrated. However, in *Vassilkovska v. Woodfield Nissan*, Inc., 294 Ill. Dec. 207, 830 N.E.2d 619 (1st Dist. 2005), the opposite was true. The *Vassilkovska* Court held that an arbitration agreement, wherein the car buyer, but not the car seller, waived her right to pursue a cause of action in court lacked consideration because there was no mutuality of obligation.

Where the circuit court has rendered a decision regarding a motion to compel without an evidentiary hearing and without findings of fact, the standard of review is *de novo. Kinkel v. Cingular Wireless LLC*, 223 Ill. 2d 1, 22, 857 N.E.2d 250 (2006).

b. The Illinois Consumer Fraud and Deceptive Trade Practices Act

In Illinois, class actions frequently assert consumer claims under the Consumer Fraud and Deceptive Trade Practices Act (CFA), 815 ILCS 505 *et seq.* The Illinois Supreme Court has provided recent guidance regarding CFA claims in *Avery v. State Farm Mutual Automobile Ins. Co., supra, and De Bouse v. Bayer AG*, 235 Ill. 2d 544, 922 N.E.2d 309 (Ill. 2009).

In *Avery*, the Court, relying largely upon its holding in *Oliveira v. Amoco Oil Co.,* 201 Ill. 2d 134, 776 N.E.2d 151 (Ill. 2002), held that the CFA requires a plaintiff attempting to represent a consumer class to possess a viable claim of his own, limited to Illinois-based conduct, and to show actual deception and damages. This holding was consistent with prior opinions in *Mulligan v. QVC, Inc.,* 382 Ill. App. 3d 620, 888 N.E.2d 1190 (1st Dist. 2008) (wherein plaintiff's class action CFA claim failed for lack of damages) and *Barbara's Sales, Inc. v. Intel Corp*., 227 Ill. 2d 45, 879 N.E.2d 910 (2007) (wherein plaintiff's class action CFA claim failed because the representation relied upon was not actionable).

In *De Bouse,* the Supreme Court reaffirmed the rule that a plaintiff must be deceived by a statement or omission of the defendant. The plaintiff in *De Bouse* asserted that she could maintain a CFA class action against the defendant for concealment of negative drug testing results without possessing evidence that she received communication from the defendant. The Court found that the absence of such communication was fatal. It held that where plaintiff failed to show that there was communication to her (directly or indirectly), she could not establish the necessary proximate cause for a CFA action. *De Bouse v. Bayer AG*, 235 Ill. 2d 544, 556, 922 N.E.2d 309 (Ill. 2009).

Furthering this line of cases, the Appellate Court for the Fifth District has held that "each and every class member would need to show that reliance on a misrepresentation of fact caused them damage in order to recover under the Consumer Fraud Act, as well as under . . . common law fraud theories . . ." *Lilley v. Career Educ. Corp*., 2012 IL App (5th) 100614-U, P26, 2012 Ill. App. Unpub. LEXIS 2583, 19 (5th Dist. 2012). Because the *Lilley* court found that individual issues of reliance exist, class certification was found to be inappropriate for lack of commonality. *Id.*

It is respectfully suggested that the Illinois Supreme Court's treatment of the Illinois Consumer Fraud Act is inconsistent with the United States Supreme Court's decision in *Bridge v. Phoenix Bond & Indemnity Co.*, 553 U.S. 639, 128 S. Ct. 2131 (2008), wherein the Supreme Court held that reliance was not a necessary element for a claim under RICO. While reliance may be one way to establish causation, causation can be established by other means, and the language of the Illinois act does not require "reliance."

In fact, the United States District Court for the Eastern District of New York, in analyzing the Illinois Consumer Fraud Act, clearly noted Illinois courts have certified classes asserting violations of the ICFA, where the defendant engaged in "uniform" conduct toward the class, and the successful adjudication of the named plaintiff's claims would establish a right to recovery for all class members. *Cook v. Coca-Cola Co.* (*In re Vitamin water Mktg. & Sales Practice Litig.*), 2013 U.S. Dist. LEXIS 98570 (E.D.N.Y. July 10, 2013) (citing *S37 Mgmt., Inc. v. Advance Refrigeration Co.*, 2011 IL App. (1st) 102496, 961 N.E.2d 6, 16, 356 Ill. Dec. 172 (Ill. App. Ct. 2011) (defendant's uniform collection of a "government processing" charge in every invoice justified class certification)). While the *Cook*

Court left the final reliance determination to the transferor court, clearly the *Cook* Court recognized the true nature of the Illinois Consumer Fraud Act and necessity for it to be liberally construed in the class setting.

The dissent in *Lilley* makes a similar point. Therein, Justice Chapman wrote that violation of the CFA as to the representative plaintiff should be sufficient to establish the causation element for the common right to recover for all class members. *Lilley v. Career Educ. Corp., supra*. Justice Chapman stressed that for CFA litigation, which is "a consumer-oriented claim . . . , certification of the class . . . would serve the interests of justice and judicial economy while preserving defendants' due process rights and defenses." *Id.* at P37.

It should be noted that after the United States Supreme Court's ruling in *Bristol-Myers Squibb Co. v. Superior Court of California*, 137 S. Ct. 1773 (2017), coupled with the Northern District's holding in *DeBernardis v. NBTY, Inc.*, No. 1:17-cv-06125 (N.D. Ill. Jan. 18, 2018), both discussed above, the ability of non-Illinois plaintiffs to bring a class action with Illinois will have to achieve a heightened nexus of contact with Illinois.

In *Nelson v. Great Lakes Educational Loan Services Inc.*, 928 F.3d 639 (7th Cir. 2019), the Seventh Circuit further limited the reach of the Illinois Consumer Fraud Act finding that the Illinois state law provisions were pre-empted by the federal Higher Education Act in a case involving a student loan servicing organization allegedly making inadequate disclosures to a borrower. The case will likely have a wide impact on student loan litigation. As of the writing of this chapter, the case has already been cited in the Third and Eleventh Circuits during oral argument.

While not instructive on the elements of the Act, *Quinn v. Specialized Loan Servicing, LLC*, No. 1:16-cv-02021, 2019 WL 5260774 (N.D. Ill. Oct. 17, 2019), was instructive with respect to the waiver of defenses. Following the United States decision *Bristol-Myers Squibb Co. v. Superior Court*, 137 S. Ct. 1773 (2017), the defendants in *Quinn* moved for dismissal on personal jurisdiction grounds since some of the putative class was comprised of individuals outside of Illinois. This defense was raised after the *Myers* decision. The *Quinn* Court did not dismiss ruling that a litigant should raise a defense it wishes to preserve. Thus, any and all defenses to Illinois class actions should be presented strenuously and early in the litigation.

The Act continues to serve as a conduit through which to initiate national class actions involving consumer goods. Many national class actions are filed under the Act while applying Illinois law in far-flung jurisdictions. For example, in *Esquibel et al. v. Colgate-Palmolive Co. and Tom's of Maine, Inc.*, 23-cv-742, S.D.N.Y. (2023) the plaintiffs used the Act to assert a "price premium" claim against a toothpaste manufacturer due to the presence of polyfluoroalkyl substances (PFAS) in the product. While the complaint was filed in the United States District Court for the Southern District of New York, Count V sounded under the Illinois Act. The basis of the claim was not any physical injury, but rather the allegation that, had the plaintiffs known about the chemicals, they would not have paid a premium for what was marketed as a "natural" product. The case was dismissed without prejudice; however, it is indicative of the reach manifest in the tentacles of the Act as applicable to class actions.

c. Breach of Warranty Under the Uniform Commercial Code

In *Connick v. Suzuki Motor Co.*, 174 Ill. 2d 482, 675 N.E.2d 584 (1996), one of the issues presented was what type of notice of breach was a necessary condition precedent to suit, where the claims of the class members were not for personal injury. The Illinois Supreme Court stated that the notice requirement of Section 2-607 of the Uniform Commercial Code required that "the seller be notified that *this particular transaction* is 'troublesome and must be watched.'" *Connick*, 174 Ill. 2d at 489, 675 N.E.2d at 590 (emphasis added). It is respectfully suggested that "this particular transaction" can be construed to mean the distribution of a particular product. However, in *Connick*, the Supreme Court apparently narrowed the notice requirement by stating: "Even if a manufacturer is aware of problems with a particular product line, the notice requirement of Section 2-607 is satisfied only where the manufacturer is somehow apprised of the trouble with the particular product purchased by a particular buyer." The Court failed to address the (perhaps unintended) result of such a holding—that it could eliminate class actions founded on UCC warranty claims. Hopefully, if presented with a fact situation that turns on the effect of its ruling on consumer class actions, the Court will reconsider whether this restriction is appropriate.

d. Preemption and Preclusion

In *Hicks v. Airborne Express*, 367 Ill. App. 3d 1005 (5th Dist. 2006), the Illinois Appellate Court found that the Airline Deregulation Act did not preempt a class' breach of contract action. The complaint, however, was dismissed because the contract between the class and Airborne Express identified the exclusive remedy for failure to deliver packages in a timely manner as the receipt of another flight ready envelope free of charge. Airborne Express had satisfied this remedy provision.

In *Kircher v. Putnam Funds Trust*, 398 Ill. App. 3d 664, 922 N.E.2d 1164 (5th Dist. 2010), investors filed a state of Illinois class action suit against their investment advisors asserting negligence and willful and wanton mismanagement of funds. Removal to federal court was defeated. The Appellate Court, however, found that the state court claim was precluded, pursuant to the Securities Litigation Uniform Standards Act (SLUSA). The *Kircher* Court found that the implicit gravamen of the claim was that the advisors failed to make required disclosures, which satisfied the preclusion provision contained in SLUSA for class action claims.

e. Choice of Law

In *Hall v. Sprint Spectrum*, 376 Ill. App. 3d 822, 876 N.E. 2d 1036 (5th Dist. 2007), the cellular telephone provider's form contained a choice-of-law provision providing for the application of Kansas law. The trial court certified a 48-state class action complaint applying the law of Kansas. The Appellate Court affirmed, giving effect to the contractual choice-of-law provision. It is important to consider the impact of *Bristol-Myers Squibb Co. v. Superior Court*, 137 S. Ct. 1773 (2017), In any choice of law situation after the landmark decision. While not based squarely on choice of law principals, the decision significantly simplified many choice of law issues in Illinois finding that claims that were not sufficiently connected to a particular state cannot qualify for specific personal jurisdiction on their own.

In *Barbara's Sales et al., v. Intel*, 227 Ill. 2d 45, 879 N.E.2d 910 (2007), the plaintiffs argued that California law should be applied on behalf of a nationwide or, alternatively, an Illinois class. The defendant, Intel, whose principal place of business was in California, argued for the application of Illinois law. The trial court concluded that Illinois had no legitimate interest in applying California laws to adjudicate the dispute between a California corporate defendant and Illinois consumers. The Illinois Appellate Court vacated the trial court and remanded with directions to apply California substantive law (and to reconsider its class certification order in light of the applicability of California law). The Illinois Supreme Court, however, reversed the Appellate Court as to choice of law and dismissed the action on other grounds. The *Barbara's Sales* Court explained its choice of law analysis as follows. First, it noted that if the consumer fraud laws were similar in the two states, a choice of law analysis would not be necessary but in this case, was required due to significant differences in the respective laws. *Barbara's Sales*, 227 Ill. 2d at 59–60. Second, again applying the Second

Restatement of Conflicts of Laws, the Court noted that Illinois "appl[ies] the broad principle that the rights and liabilities as to a particular issue are to be governed by the jurisdiction which retains the 'most significant relationship' to the occurrence of the parties." *Barbara's Sales*, 227 Ill. 2d at 61. The Court examined several factors and determined that California possessed no interest in applying its laws to a class based, and who were harmed, primarily in the states of Illinois and Missouri. *Barbara's Sales*, 227 Ill. 2d at 62–64. The Court held that the trial court's application of Illinois law was well justified.

f. Releases

In *Lewis v. Giordano's Enterprises, Inc.*, 397 Ill. App. 3d 581, 921 N.E.2d 740 (1st Dist. 2009), the court addressed a number of issues of first impression. In *Lewis*, a former employee filed a class action claim for violation of the Minimum Wage Law and Wage Payment and Collection Act, asserting that after food deductions were made wages fell below the statutory minimum. The *Lewis* Court found that releases executed after the class claim was filed were void, pursuant to the language of the Act, and that private settlement would frustrate the purpose of the Act.

The appeal of a class action settlement was the subject of *Quick v. Shell Oil Co.*, 404 Ill. App. 3d 277, 937 N.E.2d 255, 344 Ill. Dec. 549 (3d Dist. 2010). The *Quick* Court ruled that the appropriate standard of review for a class action settlement was the abuse of discretion standard. *Id.* at 281.

g. Communication with Absent Class Members

There is no blanket prohibition against communication with absent class members in Illinois. The Illinois Supreme Court has long held that prior restraints upon communication are "the most serious and least tolerable infringement on First Amendment rights." *Kemner v. Monsanto Co.*, 112 Ill. 2d 223, 242–43, 492 N.E.2d 1327 (Ill. 1986). The *Kemner* court further held that such prior restraint would be permitted only if the communication in question posed "a clear and present danger or a serious and imminent threat to the fairness and integrity of the trial." *Id.* at 244.

The Illinois appellate courts have, likewise, recognized that "[t]here is no prohibition against communications . . . with persons who fall within the proposed class prior to class certification." *Jankousky v. Jewel Cos.*, 182 Ill. App. 3d 763, 767 (1st Dist. 1989). The *Jankousky* court, however, acknowledged that communication by the defendant seeking to settle may be limited when such communication would "affect[s] the rights of the nonsettling class members." *Id.*

The only Illinois court case addressing plaintiffs' contact with absent class members implicitly endorses the practice. In *Willeford v. Toys "R" Us-Delaware, Inc.*, 385 Ill. App. 3d 265 (Ill. App. Ct. 5th Dist. 2008), the defendant sought a protective order to avoid revealing names and addresses of patrons injured in their stores, for fear that plaintiffs would contact those revealed for a class action. The *Willeford* court noted that if the only potential harm the defendants could point to was the possibility that the plaintiff could contact class members, it was insufficient justification for the requested relief and denied the request for protective order. *Id.* at 276.

While the Illinois state courts have only tangentially broached this issue, U.S. District Courts in Illinois have addressed it head on. In *Kuhl v. Guitar Ctr. Stores, Inc.*, the U.S. District Court for the Northern District of Illinois acknowledged the U.S. Supreme Court holding in *Gulf Oil Co. v. Bernard*, 452 U.S. 89, 100, 101 S. Ct. 2193, 2202, 68 L. Ed. 2d 693 (1981), and found that "While a court has limited power to restrict communications between defendants and putative class members before the class is even certified . . . such control is designed to prevent abuse of the class action process such as . . . misleading communications and communications which affect a putative class member's decision to participate in the class action." *Kuhl v. Guitar Ctr. Stores, Inc.,* 2008 U.S. Dist. LEXIS 101747, at *3 (N.D. Ill. Dec. 16, 2008). Hence, courts limit communications between parties and potential class members *only* where "based on a clear record and specific findings that reflect a weighing of the need for a limitation and the potential interference with the rights of the parties." *Kuhl,* 2008 U.S. Dist. LEXIS 101747, at *3 (quoting *Gulf Oil*, 452 U.S. at 101, 101 S. Ct. at 2200; *see, also Williams v. Chartwell Fin. Servs*., 204 F.3d 748, 759 (7th Cir. 2000)).

Similarly, the U.S. District Court for the Northern District of Illinois addressed the issue in *Jones v. Nat'l Council of YMCA*, wherein it acknowledged that "[e]ach side has the right to communicate with putative class members." *Jones v. Nat'l Council of YMCA*, 2011 U.S. Dist. LEXIS 36087, at *14 (N.D. Ill. Mar. 31, 2011) (citing *EEOC v. Mitsubishi Motor Mfg. of Am., Inc*., 102 F.3d 869, 870 (7th Cir. 1996)). While the *Jones* Court recognized that FRCP 23(d) authorizes the district court to regulate communications with putative class members, it also cautioned that "[j]udicial intervention is justified only where there is 'a clear record and specific findings that reflect a weighing of the need for a limitation and the potential interference with the rights of the parties.'" *Jones*, 2011 U.S. Dist. LEXIS 36087, at *15 (citation omitted). Finally, the *Jones* court advised that intervention "should result in a carefully drawn order that limits speech as little as possible consistent with the rights of the parties under the circumstances." *Id.*

h. Tolling of the Statute of Limitations

The class action tolling rule allows for the tolling of the applicable statute of limitations for all putative class members under Illinois' relation back doctrine. *Mabry v. Village of Glenwood*, 41 N.E.3d 508 (1st Dist. 2015) (tolling one-year limitations period for claims against village for trespass and negligent operation of sewer system).

i. The Illinois Biometric Information Privacy Act

The Illinois Biometric Information Privacy Act (BIPA), codified at 740 ILCS 14, was enacted in 2008 with the intent to protect online users, particularly those who engage in social media, form the unlawful use of facial geometries in photographs without express consent. Significant class action litigation under the statute began in earnest in 2015 in Illinois spurred on by a private cause of action along with substantial fines and attorneys' fees. Between 2015 and early 2017, roughly 100 class action complaints have been filed in Illinois Courts against a variety of companies. Through the first quarter of 2023, over 180 actions were filed under the BIPA.

The Illinois Supreme Court held that an individual does not have to demonstrate actual "harm" to establish that he or she is "aggrieved" under BIPA in January 2019 which resulted in an increase of filing BIPA class actions. As a result, between 2018 and 2019, over 210 BIPA class actions were filed in Illinois. Most of these cases relate to the use of fingerprint recognition technology for timekeeping in the workplace or other similar biometric facilities. *See Namuwonge v. Kronos, Inc.*, 418 F. Supp. 3d 279 (N.D. Ill. 2019).

The decision giving rise to the spike in BIPA litigation was *Rosenbach v. Six Flags Entertainment Corporation, et al.*, 129 N.E.3d 1197 (Ill. 2019). In *Rosenbach*, the plaintiffs alleged that Six Flags Entertainment and Great America violated BIPA when they fingerprinted the plaintiffs without notice of—or an opportunity to consent to—their biometric collection, storage, use, and destruction policies as required by the statute. The defendants sought to dismiss the action prior to certification and the Trial Court denied the motion leaving two questions to proceed to the Second District on Appeal, *to wit:* (1) whether an individual alleging technical violations of Section 15 of the act (i.e., the notice and consent provisions) is an "aggrieved" person entitled to liquidated damages; and (2) whether an individual alleging those same violations is an "aggrieved" person entitled to injunctive relief under the act. The Second District answered both questions in the negative reasoning that plaintiffs must allege an actual injury, adverse effect, or harm to be "aggrieved" and as such the plaintiffs were not damaged.

In January 2019, the Illinois Supreme Court resolved a split in the Illinois Appellate Court over what it means to be an "aggrieved" which is the operative BIPA language since only aggrieved individuals can bring a claim under the Act. The Illinois Appellate Court split over whether a technical violation of the Act without any actual harm is sufficient to make an individual "aggrieved" with the Second District in *Rosenbach* establishing a narrow definition. The Supreme Court rejected the need for an individual to have suffered actual harm. Instead, the Court held that a person is "aggrieved" under the Act even if his or her biometric information was collected in a manner that did not fully comply with the requirements of the Act and no actual injury is required. This overruled the Second District opinion and paved the way for an increase in filings.

BIPA class action filing has continued at a similar pace of prior years with multiple cases being filed each week. While there have been no recent decisions that overrule prior Illinois jurisprudence, business groups have been asserting continual pressure to modify the Act. Under this pressure, Governor JB Pritzker signed into law a bill introducing some significant modifications that could impact the biometric privacy litigation endemic in Illinois. *See* SB 2979, August 4, 2024. The primary alteration to the Act redefines how violations of the Act are accounted for. Previously, each instance of unauthorized collection could be treated as a separate violation which was the driving force behind the proliferation of class action lawsuits. Under this metric, large classes could result in substantial damages as violations would accrue almost in perpetuity. Under the new amendment, the repeated collection of the same biometric data would instead result in a single, yet continual, violation of the Act.

This modification in the definition of "violation" may reduce the claimed damages under the Act; however, statutory interpretation encompassing legislative intent will serve as the final determining factor in the efficacy of the amendment.

As to Article III standing, on May 5, 2020, the U.S. Court of Appeals for the Seventh Circuit found that the Class Action Fairness Act did apply to a BIPA case meeting the CAFA requirements in *Bryant v. Compass Group USA, Inc.* No. 20-1443 (7th Cir. 2020). The Plaintiff sought removal on the grounds that that the Plaintiff did not suffer injury-in-fact as required to satisfy Article III standing. The Seventh Circuit ultimately sided with the removing Defendant finding that the alleged violation of BIPA's Section 15(b), which imposes consent requirements on the party collecting biometric information, amounted to an injury-in-fact. This decision stemmed from a two-prong analysis: First, the violation amounted to an invasion of the plaintiff's "private domain," which the Court found was akin to trespass. Second, the court held that the defendant's alleged failure to obtain informed consent from the plaintiff equated to an informational injury as well. The Seventh Circuit sided with removal. It is worth noting that this decision could certainly materialize in Plaintiffs' briefs in Illinois Courts when faced with motions to dismiss despite the pyric victory claimed by the removing Defendants in this case.

The Supreme Court has ruled that the applicable statute of limitations applicable to BIPA claims is five years. This ruling overturned, at least in part, the First District ruling below that had placed a one-year limitations period on BIPA claims. *See Tims v. Black Horse Carriers, Inc.*, 2023 IL 127801 (Feb. 2023). This decision brings the Illinois class action landscape in line with many other state and federal district courts that have applied the five-year "catch-all" limitations period, thus significantly expanding the window for claims.

The *Tims* Court started by pointing out that the application of multiple limitations periods as the First District did could confuse potential litigants of the time periods necessary for commencement of litigation. Then, the Court applied the five-year statute of limitations better comported with the intent of the legislature to allow an aggrieved party time to discover and address the violation.

From a duty-to-defend standpoint, the Illinois Supreme Court found in *West Bend Mutual Ins. Co. v. Krishna Schaumburg Tan Inc.*, 2021 IL 125978, that an insurer must defend a tanning salon against a customer's BIPA claims since the putative class alleged a BIPA violation that could be covered under the salon's general liability policy. Defenses at the motion to dismiss stage have been largely unsuccessful. In *McDonald v. Symphony Bronzeville Park, LLC*, 2022 IL 126511 (2022), the Illinois Supreme Court held the Illinois Workers' Compensation Act does not preempt a claim for statutory damages under the Illinois Biometric Information Privacy Act. It further found that damages to an individual's right to privacy are not the type of compensable injuries capable of redress under the Compensation Act. Further, In *Young v. World Wide Tech., LLC*, No. 19-cv-46 (S.D. Ill.), the defense has challenged the constitutionality of BIPA's statutory damages. The basis of this challenge is that such damages are "excessive and disproportionate in light of the absence of any actual harm." A decision has not been issued and the State of Illinois was invited to intervene pursuant to Fed. R. Civ. P. 5.1(b) and Section 2403. Substantial litigation is likely to continue under the BIPA for years to come. A decision has not been issued. Substantial litigation is likely to continue under the BIPA for years to come.

Certain defenses have prevailed. In *Clark v. Microsoft Corporation*, the United States Court of Appeals for the Seventh Circuit partially dismissed a putative class action complaint against Microsoft Corporation under BIPA. The alleged violations arose from training software produced by a third-party company that apparently used facial geometry scans to provide feedback to salespeople on their sales interactions. The Seventh Circuit rejected three of the putative class claims under the BIPA:

- Section 15(a): The Court found that hosting BIPA-protected information on a server is not enough to suggest that Microsoft, through the use of its Azure servers, exercised some degree of control over the information;
- Section 15(b): The Court found that Microsoft did not have enough control over the subject information to require it to receive written consent from the subjects since the data was procured by a third party;
- Section 15(c): The Court found that Microsoft did not receive a benefit from the information stored on its Azure servers from the data procured by a third party and the plaintiffs had not suffered adequate harm;
- Section 15(d): The Court found that Microsoft, by allowing a third party to use its Azure servers, did not disseminate any BIPA-protected information.

See Clark v. Microsoft Corp., No. 1:2023cv00695, Document 33 (N.D. Ill. 2023). The memorandum and order was handed down on August 21, 2023.

Certain exemptions applying to BIPA were also discussed in the Federal Courts. In *Vo v. VSP Retail Dev. Holding, Inc.* No. 19 C 7187, 2020 WL 1445605 (N.D. Ill. 2020), the United States District Court for the Northern District of Illinois found that a company which captured biometric data regarding to eyeglasses was exempt from the BIPA requirements due to the HIPAA exception to the statute. The case was dismissed.

Despite the widespread use of the Act to target large technology companies as well as retail companies across the country, the Act has been expanded in 2022. In *Sosa v. Onfido, Inc.*, 600 F.

Supp. 3d 859 (N.D. Ill. 2022), the U.S. District Court for the Northern District of Illinois found that faceprints *derived* by digital photographs as well as digital markers were covered under the BIPA. Facial recognition and its accompanying metadata have long been a mainstay of the Act; however, *Sosa* appears to be opening the door to "conventional" photographs. The case involved the plaintiff filing suit due to the fact that he did not receive notice that the software collected, stored, or used his faceprint. He did not provide written consent and was not informed about the software's retention or deletion practices for the faceprint.

In *H.K., et al. v. Google LLC*, Case No. CC 20LL00017 (2025), in the Circuit Court of the Ninth Judicial District, McDonough County, Illinois, Google settled a BIPA class action alleging that Google collected and stored biometrics from students using its Google Workspace for Education platform without getting consent from the students or their parents. This $8.74 million settlement is indicitive of the the fact that BIPA claims will continue to be prevalant among Illinois class action cases despite litgation to dull BIPA's impact.

Thus, the case turned not on the technology utilized by the defendant company but rather the lack of notice and consent of the plaintiff and the failure of the company to institute a *written policy* detailing the use of the biometric identifiers.

Effective August 2024, Illinois amended the Act to update the Act's definition of "written release" and significantly limit potential damages. First, the Act as amended provides that a written release now includes electronic signatures. *See* 740 ILCS 14/10. Second, the Act as amended provides that a private entity that collects or discloses a person's biometric data without consent can be found liable only for one BIPA violation per person, limiting the aggrieved party to a single recovery per individual. *See* 740 ILCS 14/20. This amendment overrides the 2023 Illinois Supreme Court holding in *Cothron v. White Castle Systems, Inc.*, which held that certain claims under the Act accrued and could be subject to separate damages for each scan taken without informed consent, and could continue to accrue with each violative transmission. *See* 2023 IL 128004.

The BIPA has been expanding in Illinois over the years since its 2008 enactment with no signs of ceasing. This proliferation has been buttressed by the fact that multiple state and federal courts applying Illinois law have determined that a valid action under the Act may be brought by an individual or class based on the belief of a private citizen who *believes* that they have had their rights violated.

Certain groups within the Illinois legislature have been proposing restrictions to the Act. Presently, cases have successfully been filed and/or settled against:

- Facebook
- Google
- Snap, Inc.
- Applebees
- KFC/Taco Bell/Pizza Hut
- Microsoft
- 7 Eleven
- Giorgio Armani
- OnlyFans.com
- Proctor & Gamble
- Walmart
- Candid Color Systems

j. The Illinois Genetic Information Privacy Act

The Illinois Genetic Information Privacy Act (GIPA) was first enacted in 1998 and amended in 2008 to be brought more closely in line with its federal counterpart, the Genetic Information Nondiscrimination Act (GINA). The legislative intent of the GIPA was to protect information about an individual's genetic material. Said material as defined in the statute pertains not only to the results of genetic tests, but also the genetic tests of family members, and the "manifestation or possible manifestation of a disease or disorder in a family member of the individual." *See* 410 ILCS 513, *et seq*.

Pursuant to GIPA, an employer shall not directly or indirectly:

- solicit, request, require or purchase genetic testing or genetic information of a person or a family member of the person, or administer a genetic test to a person or a family member of the person as a condition of employment, preemployment application, labor organization membership, or licensure;
- affect the terms, conditions, or privileges of employment, preemployment application, labor organization membership, or licensure, or terminate the employment, labor organization membership, or licensure of any person because of genetic testing or genetic information with respect to the employee or family member, or information about a request for or the receipt of genetic testing by such employee or family member of such employee;
- limit, segregate, or classify employees in any way that would deprive or tend to deprive any employee of employment opportunities or otherwise adversely affect the status of the employee as an employee because of genetic testing or genetic information with respect to the employee or a family member, or information about a request for or the receipt of genetic testing or genetic information by such employee or family member of such employee; and
- retaliate through discharge or in any other manner against any person alleging a violation of this Act or participating in any manner in a proceeding under this Act.

See 15 ILCS 513/25(c)(1)–(4).

The GIPA is closely related to the Illinois Biometric Information Privacy Act (BIPA) and, as with the BIPA, is proving to be fertile ground for class actions cases venued in Illinois state and federal courts. Through August 2023, approximately a dozen class action complaints have been filed against various entities.

Although historically there has been a dearth of published judicial decisions applying GIPA, this will likely change in the coming years. In terms of continuing developments, one recent decision by a federal district court found that the federal law on employee benefit plans—the Employee Retirement Income Security Act (ERISA)—preempted the claims of certain plaintiffs representing a proposed class, specifically regarding the employer's alleged violation of the GIPA provision in 410 ILCS 513/25(e) prohibiting use of genetic information in connection with workplace wellness programs. *See Branson v. Caterpillar, Inc.*, No. 23-CV_14329, 2024 WL 3823157 (N.D. Ill. Aug. 14, 2024). The court agreed with the employer that because the wellness program was tied to an employee benefits plan, that provision of GIPA "relates" to an ERISA plan and is preempted. *Id.*

CHAPTER 735 OF THE ILLINOIS COMPILED STATUTES5/2-801 THROUGH 5/2-806

§ 735 ILCS 5/2-801. PREREQUISITES FOR THE MAINTENANCE OF A CLASS ACTION

Sec. 2-801. Prerequisites for the maintenance of a class action. An action may be maintained as a class action in any court of this State and a party may sue or be sued as a representative party of the class only if the court finds:

(1) The class is so numerous that joinder of all members is impracticable.

(2) There are questions of fact or law common to the class, which common questions predominate over any questions affecting only individual members.

(3) The representative parties will fairly and adequately protect the interest of the class.

(4) The class action is an appropriate method for the fair and efficient adjudication of the controversy.

§ 735 ILCS 5/2-802. ORDER AND FINDINGS RELATIVE TO THE CLASS

Sec. 2-802. Order and findings relative to the class.

(a) *Determination of class.* As soon as practicable after the commencement of an action brought as a class action, the court shall determine by order whether it may be so maintained and describe those whom the court finds to be members of the class. This order may be conditional and may be amended before a decision on the merits.

(b) *Class action on limited issues and sub-classes.* When appropriate, an action may be brought or maintained as a class action with respect to particular issues, or divided into sub-classes and each sub-class treated as a class. The provisions of this rule shall then be construed and applied accordingly.

§ 735 ILCS 5/2-803. NOTICE IN CLASS CASES

Sec. 2-803. *Notice in class cases.* Upon a determination that an action may be maintained as a class action, or at any time during the conduct of the action, the court in its discretion may order such notice that it deems necessary to protect the interests of the class and the parties.

An order entered under subsection (a) of Section 2-802 of this Act, determining that an action may be maintained as a class action, may be conditioned upon the giving of such notice as the court deems appropriate.

§ 735 ILCS 5/2-804. INTERVENTION BY AND EXCLUSION OF CLASS MEMBERS

Sec. 2-804. *Intervention by and exclusion of class members*.

(a) *Intervention*. Any class member seeking to intervene or otherwise appear in the action may do so with leave of court and such leave shall be liberally granted except when the court finds that such intervention will disrupt the conduct of the action or otherwise prejudice the rights of the parties or the class.

(b) *Exclusion*. Any class member seeking to be excluded from a class action may request such exclusion and any judgment entered in the action shall not apply to persons who properly request to be excluded.

§ 735 ILCS 5/2-805. JUDGMENTS IN CLASS CASES

Sec. 2-805. *Judgments in class cases.* Any judgment entered in a class action brought under Section 2-801 of this Act shall be binding on all class members, as the class is defined by the court, except those who have been properly excluded from the class under subsection (b) of Section 2-804 of this Act.

§ 735 ILCS 5/2-806. DISMISSAL OR COMPROMISE OF CLASS CASES

Sec. 2-806. *Dismissal or compromise of class cases.* Any action brought as a class action under Section 2-801 of this Act shall not be compromised or dismissed except with the approval of the court and, unless excused for good cause shown, upon notice as the court may direct.

§ 735 ILCS 5/2-807. RESIDUAL FUNDS IN A COMMON FUND CREATED IN A CLASS ACTION

Sec. 2-807. Residual funds in a common fund created in a class action.

(a) *Definitions*. As used in this Section.

"Eligible organization" means a not-for-profit organization that:

(i) has been in existence for no less than 3 years;

(ii) has been tax exempt for no less than 3 years from the payment of federal taxes under Section 501(c)(3) of the Internal Revenue Code;

(iii) is in compliance with registration and filing requirements applicable pursuant to the Charitable Trust Act and the Solicitation for Charity Act; and

(iv) has a principal purpose of promoting or providing services that would be eligible for funding under the Illinois Equal Justice Act.

"Residual funds" means all unclaimed funds, including uncashed checks or other unclaimed payments, that remain in a common fund created in a class action after court-approved payments are made for the following:

(i) class member claims;

(ii) attorney's fees and costs; and

(iii) any reversions to a defendant agreed upon by the parties.

(b) *Settlement.* An order approving a proposed settlement of a class action that results in the creation of a common fund for the benefit of the class shall, consistent with the other Sections of this Part, establish a process for the administration of the settlement and shall provide for the distribution of any residual funds to one or more eligible organizations, except that up to 50% of the residual funds may be distributed to one or more other nonprofit charitable organizations or other organizations that serve the public good if the court finds there is good cause to approve such a distribution as part of a settlement.

(c) *Judgment.* A judgment in favor of the plaintiff in a class action that results in the creation of a common fund for the benefit of the class shall provide for the distribution of any residual funds to one or more eligible organizations.

(d) *State and its political subdivisions.* This Section does not apply to any class action lawsuit against the State of Illinois or any of its political subdivisions.

(e) *Application.* This Section applies to all actions commenced on or after the effective date of this amendatory Act of the 95th General Assembly and to all actions pending on the effective date of this amendatory Act of the 95th General Assembly for which no court order has been entered preliminarily approving a proposed settlement for a class of plaintiffs.

The Illinois chapter is written and updated by Ryan R. Bradley and Kathryn Johnson-Monfort of Heyl, Royster, Voelker & Allen, P.C. Ryan and Kathryn practice in complex civil litigation out of Heyl Royster's Champaign, Illinois, office (www.heylroyster.com).

INDIANA

1. COMPARISON WITH RULE 23 OF THE FEDERAL RULES OF CIVIL PROCEDURE

Rule 23 of the Indiana Rules of Trial Procedure is similar to Rule 23 of the Federal Rules of Civil Procedure prior to the 2003 amendments to the federal rules. In addition, Indiana Trial Rule 23(C)(1) requires that, absent a waiver, the court must conduct a hearing in making a determination as to class certification.[1] While Indiana's Rule 23 lacks the interlocutory appeal mechanism of Federal Rule 23(f), a 2008 amendment to Rule 14(C) of the Indiana Rules of Appellate Procedure permits a party to seek interlocutory appeal of a class certification order within thirty days of its entry. The party seeking interlocutory review must file a motion in the Indiana Court of Appeals asking the Court of Appeals to accept jurisdiction. The Court of Appeals may grant or deny the motion in its discretion. If the Court of Appeals grants the motion, the appellant must file a notice of appeal within fifteen days of the order accepting jurisdiction. Absent an order from the trial court or a judge of the Court of Appeals, an interlocutory appeal of a class certification order does not stay proceedings in the trial court unless the trial court or a judge of the Court of Appeals so orders. Ind. Appellate R. 14(H).

2. INDIANA CLASS ACTION LAW—INDIANA T.R. 23

a. General Principles

Federal decisions are treated as persuasive authority in interpreting Trial Rule 23. *E.g., Associated Med. Networks, Ltd. v. Lewis*, 824 N.E.2d 679, 682 (Ind. 2005); *Hefty v. Certified Settlement Class*, 680 N.E.2d 843, 848 (Ind. 1997); *Perdue v. Murphy*, 915 N.E.2d 498, 505 (Ind. Ct. App. 2009); *Chicago Title Ins. Co. v. Gresh*, 888 N.E.2d 779, 782 (Ind. Ct. App. 2008); *Reel v. Clarian Health Partners, Inc.*, 855 N.E.2d 343, 349 (Ind. Ct. App. 2006) (appeal on remand, 917 N.E.2d 714 (Ind. Ct. App. 2009) *reh'g denied*). "The determination of whether an action is maintainable as a class action is 'committed to the sound discretion of the trial court.'" *Associated Med. Networks, Ltd. v. Lewis*, 824 N.E.2d 679, 682 (Ind. 2005) (*citing N. Ind. Pub. Serv. Co. v. Bolka*, 693 N.E.2d 613, 615 (Ind. Ct. App. 1998), *trans denied*). The trial court has broad discretion in determining whether an action is maintainable as a class action. *E.g., Ind. Bus. Coll. v. Hollowell*, 818 N.E.2d 943, 949 (Ind. Ct. App. 2004); *McCart v. Chief Executive Officer in Charge, Indep. Fed. Credit Union*, 652 N.E.2d 80 (Ind. Ct. App. 1995). The trial court's certification order will be affirmed if it is supported by substantial evidence. *Lewis*, 824 N.E.2d at 682; *Chicago Title Ins. Co. v. Gresh*, 888 N.E.2d 779 (Ind. Ct. App. 2008). Misinterpretation of law, however, will not justify affirmance under the abuse of discretion standard. *Lewis*, 888 N.E.2d at 682; *Chicago Title Ins. Co.*, 888 N.E.2d at 781. The

[1] A hearing to determine class action status constitutes a "trial" sufficient to invoke the waiver provision of the rule for change of judge or county under Indiana law. Ind. T.R. 76(C)(5).

burden of proof for class certification rests upon the movant, and failure to meet any of the mandatory prerequisites will result in a denial of class certification. *Rene ex rel. Rene v. Reed*, 726 N.E.2d 808 (Ind. Ct. App. 2000) (appeal on remand, 751 N.E.2d 736 (Ind. Ct. App. 2001)). A trial court's ruling on class certification is reviewed under an abuse of discretion standard. *E.g., Assoc. Med. Networks, Ltd.*, 824 N.E.2d at 682; *Hefty*, 680 N.E.2d at 843. Class certification orders are not final appealable orders but can only be reviewed if permitted as an interlocutory appeal. *Martin v. Amoco Oil,* 696 N.E.2d 383, 385–86 (Ind. 1998); Ind. Appellate R. 14(C).

The Indiana Supreme Court has addressed settlement classes, holding that the trial court must require a showing of fairness before approving a settlement class. *Hefty*, 680 N.E.2d 843. In one instance, a court approved a settlement even though the majority of class members were opposed to the settlement. *Cmty. Care Ctrs., Inc. v. Ind. Family and Soc. Servs. Admin.,* 716 N.E.2d 519 (Ind. Ct. App. 1999), *reh'g denied.*

b. Rule 23(A) Principles

i. Numerosity. There is no minimum threshold for meeting the numerosity requirement; courts have permitted certification of classes consisting of less than 100 persons. *E.g., Shallenberger v. Hope Lutheran Church*, 449 N.E.2d 1152 (Ind. Ct. App. 1983) (class of 61 persons regarding certificates of deposit); *Kuespert v. State*, 378 N.E.2d 888 (Ind. Ct. App. 1978) (reversing trial court's failure to certify class of 57 limited police employees); *Hatcher v. Smith*, 283 N.E.2d 582 (Ind. Ct. App. 1972) (class action on behalf of 33 firefighters for vacation pay). However, six members is too few. *Union Savings Bank v. Spencer*, 243 N.E.3d 1170, 1178–79 (Ind. Ct. App. 2024). And where a plaintiff expressed an ability to join all 1,536 members of the proposed class, the appellate court upheld the trial court's denial of certification of the claim as a class action. *Jack Gray Transp., Inc. v. Ind. Dep't of State Revenue*, 744 N.E.2d 1071 (Ind. Ct. App. 2001). A plaintiff seeking to certify a class will fail when a court finds that the "number of people who fit the [proposed class] definition is unknown" entirely. *Greer v. Buss*, 918 N.E.2d 607, 619 (Ind. Ct. App. 2009). However, "[p]laintiffs are not required to specify the identities or exact number of persons included in the proposed class, and the fact that the number of class members cannot be determined with precision does not defeat certification." *7-Eleven, Inc. v. Bowens*, 857 N.E.2d 382, 392 (Ind. Ct. App. 2006). A finding of numerosity need only be supported by "common sense assumptions." *Id.* at 391 (quoting *N. Ind. Pub. Serv. Co. v. Bolka*, 693 N.E.2d 613, 616 (Ind. Ct. App. 1998)).

ii. Commonality. Commonality exists if the claims of class members and the individual plaintiff derive from a common nucleus of operative fact. *Edward D. Jones & Co. v. Cole*, 643 N.E.2d 402, 405 (Ind. Ct. App. 1994). A common nucleus of operative fact exists where there is a common course of conduct. *Id.* Various matters have been found to state a common question: breach of trust (*Bank One Indianapolis, N.A. v. Norton*, 557 N.E.2d 1038, 1042 (Ind. Ct. App. 1990)); breach of contract (*Skalbania v. Simmons*, 443 N.E.2d 352 (Ind. Ct. App. 1982)); breach of fiduciary duty (*Id.*); breach of warranty (*Id.*); fraud (*Id.*); Indiana Securities Act (*Edward D. Jones & Co.*, 643 N.E.2d at 404); Indiana RICO (*Id.*); negligence (*Skalbania,* 443 N.E.2d 352); unjust enrichment (*Conagra, Inc. v. Farrington*, 635 N.E.2d 1137 (Ind. Ct. App. 1994)); civil rights (42 USC § 1983) and Individuals with Disabilities Education Act (20 USC § 1401) (*Rene*, 726 N.E.2d at 808); claim for excessive interest charges for payday loans under the Indiana Uniform Consumer Credit Code (*see Livingston v. Fast Cash USA, Inc*., 753 N.E.2d 572 (Ind. 2001) (ruling on certified question from Indiana federal district courts)).

iii. Adequacy of class representative. Whether a plaintiff will adequately and fairly represent the class is a matter of concern for the trial court. *Anderson v. Ind. Dep't of State Revenue*, 758 N.E.2d 597 (Ind. Tax 2001). The burden of proof that the class will be fairly and adequately represented rests with the movant. *Id.* The sufficiency of representation is a question of fact. *Id.* There should be evidence to demonstrate to the trial court that such duties will be discharged. *Kaufmann v. Credithrift Fin., Inc.*, 465 N.E.2d 207 (Ind. Ct. App. 1984). The fact that a plaintiff may be a "professional plaintiff" does not alone disqualify an individual from representing the class. *Id.* Where there are multiple representatives, only one of the representatives need meet the standard. *Conagra*, 635 N.E.2d at 1142.

Where the claims of the named plaintiffs could possibly be foreclosed by the statute of limitations, they could still serve as class representatives since the limitations issue was a defense and not relevant to the certified issue as to whether a breach of trust occurred. *Bank One Indianapolis, N.A.* 557 N.E.2d at 1040–41. *But see Alexander v. PSB Lending Corp.*, 800 N.E.2d 984 (Ind. Ct. App. 2003) (plaintiff lacked standing to bring class action claims in consumer action against defendants class with whom plaintiff did not have direct relationship; declining to apply juridical link doctrine); *Ziegler v. Ind. Dep't of State Revenue,* 797 N.E.2d 881 (Ind. Tax 2003) (class action to recover tax refund would be limited to class members who had complied with statutory requirement to file tax refund claim on an individual basis.)

iv. Adequacy of counsel. An attorney admitted to the practice of law in this state is assumed to be competent to practice in the court as class counsel. *Bank One Indianapolis, N.A.*, 557 N.E.2d at 1044. The trial court is vested with discretion in determining the adequacy of class counsel. *State ex rel. Harris v. Scott Circuit Court*, 437 N.E.2d 952 (Ind. 1982) (replacing out-of state lead counsel with local counsel after dispute concerning distribution of fees).

v. Typicality. Typicality exists if it is shown that the named plaintiff's claims are neither in conflict with nor antagonistic with the claims of the class as a whole. *E.g.*, *7-Eleven, Inc. v. Bowens*, 857 N.E.2d 382, 392 (Ind. Ct. App. 2006); *Edward D. Jones & Co.*, 643 N.E.2d at 407. A plaintiff's claims need not be factually identical with those of putative class members. *7-Eleven, Inc.*, 857 N.E.2d at 392. Typicality may be satisfied if the claims are based on a common legal theory or if they arise from the same course of conduct by the defendant. *Id.*

c. Rule 23(B) Principles

i. 23(B)(1). This rule requires only that a risk of filing of other suits be shown, not that other suits have been filed. *Bank One Indianapolis, N.A.*, 557 N.E.2d at 1044.

ii. 23(B)(1)(A). To qualify under this section, there must be a risk of inconsistent judgments. *Id.* A class action against a bank for breach of trust in managing trust accounts was properly certified under 23(B)(1)(A) since the suit would impact on the future management of other trust accounts and separate actions with the risk of conflicting results that would establish incompatible standards of conduct for the bank. *Id.*

iii. 23(B)(1)(B). This type of class may be certified where an adjudication would as a practical matter be dispositive of the interests of the class or substantially impair or impede their ability to protect their interests. *Bowen v. Sonnenberg*, 411 N.E.2d 390, 398 (Ind. Ct. App. 1980).

iv. 23(B)(2). If the actions of the defendant are generally applicable to the class, this is sufficient to certify a (B)(2) class. *CSX Transp., Inc. v. Rabold*, 593 N.E.2d 1277, 1279 (Ind. Ct. App. 1992). Where a railroad denied it had abandoned certain lands, its refusal to allow class members to recover full use of their properties was generally applicable to the class and supported certification of a (B)(2) class in a quiet title action. *Id.*; *see also Stevens v. Dep't of Pub. Welfare,* 566 N.E.2d 544, 546 (Ind. Ct. App. 1991) (reversing dismissal of (B)(2) class regarding Medicaid reimbursement); *Golitko v. Ind. Dep't of Correction*, 712 N.E.2d 13 (Ind. Ct. App. 1999).

v. 23(B)(3). A (B)(3) class may be certified if common questions of law or fact predominate over individual questions and a class action is superior to other methods of adjudicating the controversy. *Conagra Inc*., 635 N.E.2d at 1143 (upholding certification of class based on defendant's alleged fraudulent conduct in wheat and soybean transactions). There is no precise test for determining whether common questions of law or fact predominate over issues affecting individual members; rather, the court makes a pragmatic assessment of the entire action and all the issues involved. *Lincoln Nat'l Life Ins. Co. v. Bezich*, 33 N.E.3d 1160, (Ind. Ct. App. 2015). Factors that favor a finding of predominance include:

- The substantive elements of class members' claims require the same proof for each class member.
- The proposed class is bound together by a mutual interest in resolving common questions more than it is divided by individual interests.
- The resolution of an issue common to the class would significantly advance the litigation.
- One or more common issues constitute significant parts of each class members' individual cases.
- The common questions are central to all the members' claims.
- The same theory of liability is asserted by or against all class members, and all defendants raise the same basic defenses.

Id. Courts have found predominance in a number of different factual scenarios. *Clark-Floyd Landfill, LLC v. Gonzalez*, 150 N.E.3d 238 (Ind. Ct. App. 2020) (class certified under Rule 23(B)(3) for public nuisance against a landfill); *Conagra Inc*., 635 N.E.2d at 1143; *see also Am. Cyanamid Co. v. Stephen*, 623 N.E.2d 1065, 1074–75 (Ind. Ct. App. 1993) (class certified under Rule 23 (B)(3) on issue of punitive damages, among other issues); *Skalbania,* 443 N.E.2d at 352 (class certified under Rule 23(B)(3) on losses by season ticket holders against hockey team and league for failure to complete the season); *Louisville & Nashville R.R. Co. v. Wollenmann*, 390 N.E.2d 669, 671 (Ind. Ct. App. 1979) (Rule 23(B)(3) class certified for damages suffered after plaintiff class was forced to evacuate due to liquid propane spill).

d. Rule 23(C)—Selected Principles

i. 23(C)(1). The trial court should hold a hearing as soon as possible after the commencement of a class action to determine whether the action should proceed as a class action. *Kuespert,* 378 N.E.2d at 892. Rule 23(C)(1) contemplates that certification may be conditional and may be altered or amended before the decision on the merits. *Id.* at 893.

Rule 23(C)(1) does not absolutely preclude a trial court from hearing a defendant's motion for summary judgment prior to an adjudication on class certification. *Reel v. Clarian Health Partners, Inc*., 855 N.E.2d 343, 356 (Ind. Ct. App. 2006) (appeal on remand, 917 N.E.2d 714 (Ind. Ct. App. 2009) *reh'g denied*). However, a defendant who moves for summary judgment prior to a ruling on class certification and prevails is not protected by *res judicata* from suits by other potential class members. *Id.* at 355–56. Likewise, a defendant who moves for summary judgment prior to a ruling on class certification and is unsuccessful may not later complain about one way intervention when the named plaintiff moves to certify the class.

ii. 23(C)(4). This rule is designed for use where members of a class have divergent interests. *Hendershot v. Carey*, 616 N.E.2d 412, 421 (Ind. Ct. App. 1993) (creating two subclasses of hourly and salaried employees). The rule allows a court to divide a certified class into subclasses and treat each subclass as a separate class. *Id.* An overly broad class definition can be remedied under this provision because the trial court can redefine the class to eliminate overbreadth, sua sponte, if necessary. *Rene*, 726 N.E.2d at 808. Class actions have been certified with subclasses. *Dunn v. Jenkins*, 377 N.E.2d 868 (Ind. 1978) (five subclasses).

e. Other Matters

i. Arbitration. Under Indiana contract law, the party seeking to compel arbitration bears the burden of demonstrating the existence of an enforceable arbitration agreement. *Decker v. Star Fin. Grp., Inc.*, 187 N.E.3d 937, 943 (Ind. Ct. App. 2022). There is no presumption in favor of arbitration when determining whether the parties agreed to arbitrate. *Id.* (quoting *MPact Const. Grp., LLC v. Super. Concrete Constructors, Inc.*, 802 N.E.2d 901, 906 (Ind. 2004) ("imposing on parties a policy favoring arbitration before determining whether they agreed to arbitrate could frustrate the parties' intent and their freedom to contract")). "[I]n general, an arbitration agreement, like a typical contract, requires offer, acceptance of the offer and consideration." *Id.* (internal quotation omitted). Failure to provide reasonable notice of a new arbitration term may preclude a party from demonstrating any enforceable arbitration agreement was formed. *Id.* Likewise, arbitration clauses may not cover a given dispute based upon their plain language. *Fin. Ctr. First Credit Union v. Rivera*, 178 N.E.3d 1245, 1253 (Ind. Ct. App. 2021). And, like other contractual rights, a right to arbitrate may be waived by taking actions inconsistent with such a right. *Id.*

ii. Attorneys' fees. The decision to award attorneys' fees is committed to the discretion of the trial court. *Tioga Pines Living Ctr., Inc. v. Ind. Family and Soc. Servs. Admin.*, 760 N.E.2d 1080 (Ind. Ct. App. 2001; *see Penn Cent. Corp. v. Buchanan*, 712 N.E.2d 508 (Ind. Ct. App. 1999) (a comprehensive discussion of the various methods of computing attorneys' fees in class actions under Indiana law)). In *Citizens Action Coalition of Indiana, Inc. v. PSI Energy, Inc.*, 664 N.E.2d 401,410 (Ind. Ct. App. 1996), the Indiana Court of Appeals recognized that 25 or 30 percent is an appropriate attorney fee award in common fund cases. *See also Cmty. Care Serv. Ctrs., Inc. v. Ind. Family & Soc. Servs. Admin.*, 716 N.E.2d 519, 550 (Ind. Ct. App. 1999) ("general agreement that a range of 25%–30% is justified for attorney fees awards in common fund cases").

iii. Cy pres distribution of residual settlement funds. Under the most recent amendments adding section (F) to Rule 23, orders entering a judgment for a class or approving a settlement class must provide for distribution of residual funds. In matters where the claims process has been exhausted and residual funds remain, not less than 25 percent of the residual funds must be disbursed to the Indiana Bar Foundation to support the activities and programs of the Indiana Pro Bono Commission and its pro bono districts. The court may disburse the balance of any residual funds beyond the minimum percentage to the Indiana Bar Foundation or to any other entity for purposes that have a direct or indirect relationship to the objectives of the underlying litigation or otherwise promote the substantive or procedural interests of members of the certified class.

iv. Intervention. An unnamed member of a pending class cannot intervene unless granted such permission by the court. *City of Hobart v. Baum*, 145 N.E.2d 573 (Ind. 1957).

v. Pre-certification communication with putative class. Trial court's issuance of gag order prohibiting communication between plaintiffs and putative class members was an abuse of discretion in absence of evidence of need to restrict such communications. *Shallenberger v. Hope Lutheran Church*, 449 N.E.2d 1152 (Ind. Ct. App. 1983).

vi. Review of class certification granted under default judgment. Unchallenged default judgment against defendant precludes defendant from challenging on appeal the class certification, upholding default judgment of $250,000 against defendant for violating the Telephone Consumer Protection Act (TCPA) by sending unsolicited advertisements for its services by facsimile. *Core Funding Group, LLC v. Young,* 792 N.E.2d 547 (Ind. Ct. App. 2003), *trans denied.*

vii. Statute of limitations. Indiana follows the *American Pipe* rule that "the commencement of a class action suspends the applicable statute of limitations, until the court's ruling on class certification, as to all asserted members of the class who would have been parties had the suit been permitted to continue as a class action." *Am. Pipe & Constr. Co. v. Utah*, 414 U.S. 538, 554, 94 S. Ct. 756, 766 (1974); *Arnold v. Dirrim*, 398 N.E.2d 426, 439 (Ind. Ct. App. 1979) (holding that statute of limitations was tolled during time between filing of action as class action and certification of class). However, where a claimant did not present a class action tolling argument to the trial court and defendants did not have unequivocal notice of that claim, claimant waived the issue for purposes of appeal. *McGill v. Ling*, 801 N.E.2d 678, 688 (Ind. Ct. App. 2004) *trans. denied.*

3. RECENT LAW REVIEW ARTICLES

David S. Schwartz, *Mandatory Arbitration and Fairness*, 84 NOTRE DAME L. REV. 1247, 1262, 1318–20 (2008) (discussing the abuse of mandatory arbitration clauses as an attempt to limit class actions).

Jessica Erickson, *Corporate Misconduct and the Perfect Storm of Shareholder Litigation*, 84 NOTRE DAME L. REV. 75 (2008) (discussing securities class actions and derivative suits arising out of the same allegations of corporate wrongdoing).

Marissa L. Bracke, Note, *Where Improper Purposes Lead, Inadequate Protections Follow: Integrating the Rule 11 Improper Purpose Inquiry with the Rule 23 Protections for Absent Class Members*, 41 VAL. U.L. REV. 353 (2006).

Thomas E. Willging & Shannon R. Wheatman, *Attorney Choice of Forum in Class Action: What Difference Does It Make?*, 81 NOTRE DAME L. REV. 591 (2006).

4. RECENT DECISIONS INVOLVING CLASS ACTIONS

a. Indiana Decisions

***Gierek v. Anonymous 1*, 250 N.E.3d 378 (Ind. 2025).** Patients who had undergone surgeries brought a class action alleging that the hospital failed to properly sterilize surgical equipment for numerous patients. The trial court denied the patients' motion for class certification on the grounds that it did not have jurisdiction under Indiana's Medical Malpractice Act (MMA) to certify a class. The Indiana Supreme Court reversed. It held that although the MMA applied to the patients' claims, which required pre-suit review by a medical malpractice panel, the trial court nonetheless had jurisdiction to determine the issue of class certification as a "preliminary question" under the MMA before panel review.

***Union Savings Bank v. Spencer*, 243 N.E.3d 1170, 1178–79 (Ind. Ct. App. 2024).** In an action under Indiana's Deceptive Consumer Sales Act, where only six people had been damaged by receiving and paying an incorrect payoff statement amount from their mortgage lender, numerosity was not met for purposes of class certification.

***Members of Medical Licensing Board of Indiana v. Anonymous Plaintiff 1*, 233 N.E.3d 416 (Ind. Ct. App. 2024).** Five women and an organization consisting of religious members brought a preliminary injunction against prosecutors of five counties, alleging that state law criminalizing most abortions violated plaintiffs' rights under Indiana's Religious Freedom Restoration Act (RFRA). The trial court certified the case as a class action under Trial Rules 23(A) and (B)(2) and granted the preliminary injunction. On appeal, the Indiana Court of Appeals affirmed, rejecting arguments that the class was defined in a fail-safe manner and rejecting arguments that the elements for certification were not met where there was a possible diversity of religious views within the class.

***Hoosier Contractors, LLC v. Gardner*, 212 N.E.3d 1234 (Ind. 2023).** Plaintiff who was not damaged by violation of state deceptive consumer sales act lacked standing to represent a class.

***Mellowitz v. Ball State University*, 221 N.E.3d 1214 (Ind. 2023).** The Indiana Supreme Court affirmed the trial court's order, holding that a law restricting class action suits against universities relating to the COVID-19 pandemic does not violate the constitutional separation of powers, did not unconstitutionally take the student's property without just compensation, and did not unconstitutionally impair the student's contract with the university.

***Decker v. Star Fin. Grp., Inc.*, 204 N.E.3d 918 (Ind. 2023).** Bank customers brought class action alleging bank improperly charged overdraft fees, and bank moved to compel individual arbitration. The trial court compelled arbitration, but on interlocutory appeal the Court of Appeals reversed. The Indiana Supreme Court granted transfer. The Court held that the bank failed to prove an "arbitration agreement" was formed where the bank's modification clause permitted it only to "change" terms of the existing agreement but the bank had attempted to later "add" the arbitration clause that was not a subject addressed in the original agreement. The bank therefore had no authority to add the term and therefore arbitration could not be compelled.

***Netflix, Inc. v. City of Fishers*, 212 N.E.3d 188 (Ind. Ct. App. 2023).** Cities brought class action against streaming video service provider for a declaratory judgment requiring the service provider to pay franchise fees to cities. The service provider moved to dismiss for lack of subject matter jurisdiction, arguing that the cities were required to exhaust administrative remedies. The trial court denied the motion. On interlocutory appeal, the Court of Appeals affirmed.

***Butler Motors, Inc. v. Benosky*, 181 N.E.3d 304, 309 (Ind. Ct. App. 2021), *trans. denied*, 186 N.E.3d 579 (Ind. 2022).** Automobile purchasers brought 14 class actions against various auto dealers for charging "document preparation fees" that purchasers alleged violated the Indiana Deceptive Consumer Sales Act (DCSA) and constituted constructive fraud and unjust enrichment. Purchasers also alleged that each entity within a dealer group was liable as an alter ego or through the juridical link doctrine. Dealers moved to dismiss each claim and to dismiss claims against the alter ego defendants. The trial court denied the motions on all grounds, and the Court of Appeals affirmed in all respects. Court held that purchasers stated claims, including claims against alter ego defendants, and that amendment of separate statute did not expressly permit the fees so as to place them in the DCSA's safe harbor.

***Baker v. Pickering*, 178 N.E.3d 347, 354 (Ind. Ct. App. 2021), *reh'g denied* (Dec. 28, 2021), *trans. denied*, 186 N.E.3d 584 (Ind. 2022).** Plaintiff appealed from order compelling individual arbitration, and the Indiana Court of Appeals dismissed the appeal for lack of appellate jurisdiction. The Court held that an order compelling arbitration is not a final appealable order and that, to be appealable, an order compelling arbitration must be converted into a final judgment under Trial Rule 54(B) or must be certified for interlocutory appeal under Appellate Rule 14(B).

***Fin. Ctr. First Credit Union v. Rivera*, 178 N.E.3d 1245, 1253 (Ind. Ct. App. 2021).** Trial court denied motion to compel arbitration and the Indiana Court of Appeals affirmed. The Court held that defendant had waived any right to arbitrate individual counterclaim by litigating and that arbitration clause did not permit arbitration of class claims, which could therefore proceed in court.

***Indiana University v. Thomas*, 167 N.E.3d 724 (Ind. Ct. App. 2021).** University students filed a class action asserting contract and tort claims relating to mold growth in dorms. The trial court certified the class, but the Court of Appeals reversed class certification. The court held that the complaint requested court-ordered remediation but in seeking class certification the theory was that the university breached its contract by conducting remediation.

***Dempsey v. Winski*, 149 N.E.3d 1243 (Ind. Ct. App. 2020).** Taxpayer brought class action for interest not paid on tax credit. The trial court denied class certification and the Court of Appeals affirmed, finding plaintiff did not identify any basis for a finding that anyone other than himself had a tax credit that qualified for interest earned.

***Clark-Floyd Landfill, LLC v. Gonzalez*, 150 N.E.3d 238 (Ind. Ct. App. 2020).** Homeowners filed a nuisance and negligence action against a landfill based on noxious odors emanating from the landfill, which reduced the homeowners' property value and interfered with the quiet use and enjoyment of their properties. The trial court certified the class, and the Court of Appeals affirmed class certification. The Court held that "in making a determination regarding class certification, a trial court may not conduct a preliminary inquiry into the merits of the suit," and it rejected the argument that it should follow any federal authority to the contrary. The court rejected arguments that differences in damages or exposure defeated class certification and it rejected challenges to the form of evidence designated.

***Dempskey v. Winski*, 149 N.E.3d 1243 (Ind. Ct. App. 2020).** A taxpayer brought a class action against the county auditor seeking interest on the overpayment of property taxes, the principal amount of which had already been refunded. The trial court denied the motion and the Court of Appeals affirmed. The court held that the taxpayer failed to present any evidence relating to numerosity when he had had access to records to do so. In particular, the taxpayer failed to identify any other person who had received a refund of the principal of an overpayment. The Court of Appeals held that the trial court was within its discretion to deny the motion based on the lack of evidence.

Celadon Trucking Servs., Inc. v. Wilmoth*, 70 N.E.3d 833 (Ind. Ct. App. 2017), *trans. denied.

Truckers, who were independent contractors, brought a class action against a nationwide transportation company, asserting claims for breach of contract and unjust enrichment and seeking to recover the difference between the "pump price" that the company deducted from the truckers' compensation for fuel charges at gas stations and the lower amount that company actually paid to the gas station for that fuel. The trial court denied the company's motion for judgment on the pleadings, certified a class, and entered summary judgment in favor of the class for $3,302,923.60 plus pre- and post-judgment interest. The Indiana Court of appeals affirmed in all respects, and the Indiana Supreme Court declined to review the judgment.

***Comm'r of Ind. Bureau of Motor Vehicles v. Vawter*, 45 N.E.3d 1200 (Ind. Ct. App. 2015).** A certified class challenged the constitutionality of a state personalized license plate program. In a direct appeal from a trial court summary judgment in favor of the class, the Indiana Supreme Court reversed, holding that phrases on license plates were government speech and therefore were not subject to First Amendment protections or Due Process limitations.

***Lincoln Nat'l Life Ins. Co. v. Bezich* (Ind. Ct. App. 2015).** The plaintiff filed a complaint against Lincoln National Life Insurance Company (Lincoln), alleging three separate counts of breach of contract regarding his variable life insurance policy. The trial court issued an order denying class certification as to Count 1 and Count 2 of the complaint but certified a single-issue class as to Count 3 for the purpose of determining liability. On appeal, the Indiana Court of Appeals affirmed certification of the issue class but reversed the trial court's decision not to certify a class as to Counts 1 and 2. The Court of Appeals held that common issues predominated in interpreting whether Lincoln breached the insurance policy in the manner it determined certain fees.

***Ramsey v. Lightning Corp.*, 991 N.E.2d 132 (Ind. Ct. App. 2013).** The trial court initially certified a class of persons who had been charged an allegedly unlawful document preparation fee on auto sales. Later, the trial court decertified the class when the defendant showed that the only class representative had not actually paid the document preparation fee as part of her transaction. The Court of Appeals affirmed, finding that the trial court did not abuse its discretion because the named representative was not adequate and lacked standing because she had not been charged the challenged fee.

***Bell v. Bryant Co.*, 2 N.E.3d 716 (Ind. Ct. App. 2013).** The Court of Appeals reversed judgment on the pleadings with respect to a class action claim. The Court held that "in order to determine whether certification of the class here is appropriate under T.R. 23, the trial court will be required to consider matters beyond the pleadings. Accordingly, this could not provide a valid basis for granting a T.R. 12(C) judgment on the pleadings in favor of [the defendant]" with respect to the issue of class certification.

Edwards v. Apex 1 Processing, Inc.*, 962 N.E.2d 663 (Ind. Ct. App. 2012), *trans. denied* and *Edwards v. Geneva-Roth Capital, Inc.*, 956 N.E.2d 1195 (Ind. Ct. App. 2011), *reh'g denied & trans. denied. Ms. Edwards brought two class actions under Indiana's Small Loans Act against online payday lenders known as "LoanPoint USA" and "Paycheck Today." The lenders both moved to compel individual arbitration under the Federal Arbitration Act. The trial court denied the motions to compel arbitration based on the general contract law defense of impossibility. The arbitration clauses selected the National Arbitration Forum (NAF) as the mandatory arbitration forum, but the NAF no longer conducts consumer arbitrations. On appeal, the Indiana Court of Appeals affirmed and held that because the choice of forum was integral to the clauses and because the forum was unavailable, the clauses could not be performed based on their own terms and failed for impossibility.

***Goldberg v. Farno,* 953 N.E.2d 1244 (Ind. Ct. App. 2011).** After the trial court had denied certification of a litigation class on superiority grounds, the plaintiff and several defendants entered into a class action settlement agreement, and the trial court granted class certification for purposes of settlement over the objection of one of a non-settling defendant. The Indiana Court of Appeals affirmed. As an issue of first impression, the Court of Appeals adopted the "plain legal prejudice" standard to determine whether a non-settling defendant has standing to object to a partial class action settlement. The Court held that the non-settling defendant lacked standing because the class settlement did not interfere with his contractual rights, did not interfere with his right to seek contribution or indemnification, and did not strip him of a legal claim or cause of action.

***Farno v. Ansure Mortuaries of Ind., LLC,* 953 N.E.2d 1253 (Ind. Ct. App. 2011).** Purchasers of prepaid burial goods brought a putative class action against several defendants for the looting of pre-need trust funds. The trial court denied class certification, finding that the class action was not the superior method to pursue the litigation due to other available methods, which included a lawsuit filed by the Indiana Securities Commissioner. The Court of Appeals affirmed but recognized that the trial court had the inherent power to revisit its class certification decision based on facts that had changed since the initial denial of certification.

***JK Harris & Co., LLC., v. Sandlin,* 942 N.E.2d 875 (Ind. Ct. App. 2011).** Plaintiff brought a class action against JK Harris for its failure to adequately provide tax resolution services and its failure to reimburse funds paid by Plaintiff class. JK Harris failed to answer and so the the trial court certified a class and entered default judgment. JK Harris appealed the certification, stating that Plaintiff had not met the numerosity, commonality, or predominance requirements under Rule 23. The Indiana Court of Appeals affirmed the Trial Court's decision not to set aside the class certification. However, because the Defendant had presented additional evidence, the Court of Appeals remanded the case so that an evidentiary hearing could be conducted to address the proper class definition.

b. Influential Seventh Circuit Decisions

***Butler v. Sears, Roebuck & Co.,* 727 F.3d 796, 801 (7th Cir. 2013) cert. denied, 134 S. Ct. 1277, 188 L. Ed. 2d 298 (U.S. 2014).** In holding that a multi-state class action relating to an alleged defect in washing machines was certifiable under Rule 23, the Seventh Circuit explained that "[i]t would drive a stake through the heart of the class action device, in cases in which damages were sought rather than an injunction or a declaratory judgment, to require that every member of the class have identical damages. If the issues of liability are genuinely common issues, and the damages of individual class members can be readily determined in individual hearings, in settlement negotiations, or by creation of subclasses, the fact that damages are not identical across all class members should not preclude class certification."

RULE 23 OF THE INDIANA RULES OF TRIAL PROCEDURE

RULE 23. CLASS ACTIONS

(a) *Prerequisites to a class action.* One or more members of a class may sue or be sued as representative parties on behalf of all only if:

(1) the class is so numerous that joinder of all members is impracticable;

(2) there are questions of law or fact common to the class;

(3) the claims or defenses of the representative parties are typical of the claims or defenses of the class; and

(4) the representative parties will fairly and adequately protect the interests of the class.

(b) *Class actions maintainable.* An action may be maintained as a class action if the prereuisites of subdivision (A) are satisfied, and in addition:

(1) the prosecution of separate actions by or against individual members of the class would create a risk of:

(A) inconsistent or varying adjudications with respect to individual members of the class which would establish incompatible standards of conduct for the party opposing the class, or

(B) adjudications with respect to individual members of the class which would as a practical matter be dispositive of the interest of the other members not parties to the adjudications or substantially impair or impede their ability to protect their interests; or

(2) the party opposing the class has acted or refused to act on grounds generally applicable to the class, thereby making appropriate final injunctive relief or corresponding declaratory relief with respect to the class as a whole; or

(3) the court finds that the questions of law or fact common to the members of the class predominate over any questions affecting only individual members, and that a class action is superior to other available methods for the fair and efficient adjudication of the controversy. The matters pertinent to the findings include:

(A) the interest of members of the class in individually controlling the prosecution or defense of separate actions;

(B) the extent and nature of any litigation concerning the controversy already commenced by or against members of the class;

(C) the desirability or undesirability of concentrating the litigation of the claims in the particular forum;

(D) the difficulties likely to be encountered in the management of a class action.

(c) *Determination by order whether class action to be maintained—notice—judgment—actions conducted partially as class actions.*

(1) As soon as practicable after the commencement of an action brought as a class action, the court, upon hearing or waiver of hearing, shall determine by order whether it is to be so maintained. An order under this subdivision may be conditional, and may be altered or amended before the decision on the merits.

(2) In any class action maintained under subdivision (B)(3), the court shall direct to the members of the class the best notice practicable under the circumstances, including individual notice to all members who can be identified through reasonable effort. The notice shall advise each member that:

(A) the court will exclude him from the class if he so requests by a specified date;

(B) the judgment, whether favorable or not, will include all members who do not request exclusion; and

(C) any member who does not request exclusion may, if he desires, enter an appearance through his counsel.

(3) The judgment in an action maintained as a class action under subdivision (B)(1) or (B)(2), whether or not favorable to the class, shall include and describe those whom the court finds to be members of the class. The judgment in an action maintained as a class action under subdivision (B)(3), whether or not favorable to the class, shall include and specify or describe those to whom the notice provided in subdivision (C)(2) was directed, and who have not requested exclusion, and whom the court finds to be members of the class.

(4) When appropriate:

(A) an action may be brought or maintained as a class action with respect to particular issues; or

(B) a class may be divided into subclasses and each subclass treated as a class, and the provisions of this rule shall then be construed and applied accordingly.

(d) *Orders in conduct of actions.* In the conduct of actions to which this rule applies, the court may make appropriate orders:

(1) determining the course of proceedings or prescribing measures to prevent undue repetition or complication in the presentation of evidence or argument;

(2) requiring, for the protection of the members of the class or otherwise for the fair conduct of the action, that notice be given in such manner as the court may direct to some or all of the members of any step in the action, or of the proposed extent of the judgment, or of the opportunity of members to signify whether they consider the representation fair and adequate, to intervene and present claims or defenses, or other-wise to come into the action;

(3) imposing conditions on the representative parties or on intervenors;

(4) requiring that the pleadings be amended to eliminate therefrom allegations as to representation of absent persons, and that the action proceed accordingly;

(5) dealing with similar procedural matters.

The orders may be combined with an order under Rule 16, and may be altered or amended as may be desirable from time to time. The court shall allow reasonable attorney's fees and reasonable expenses incurred from a fund recovered for the benefit of a class under this section and the court may apportion such recovery among different attorneys.

(e) *Dismissal or compromise.* A class action shall not be dismissed or compromised without the approval of the court, and notice of the proposed dismissal or compromise shall be given to all members of the class in such manner as the court directs.

(f) *Disposition of Residual Funds.* (1) "Residual Funds" are funds that remain after the payment of all approved class member claims, expenses, litigation costs, attorneys' fees, and other court-approved disbursements to implement the relief granted. Nothing in this rule is intended to limit the trial court from approving a settlement that does not create residual funds. (2) Any order entering a judgment or approving a proposed compromise of a class action certified under this rule that establishes a process for identifying and compensating members of the class shall provide for the disbursement of residual funds, unless otherwise agreed. In matters where the claims process has been exhausted and residual funds remain, not less than fifty percent (50%) of the residual funds shall be disbursed to the Indiana Bar Foundation to support the activities and programs of the Indiana Pro Bono Commission. The court may disburse the balance of any residual funds beyond 29 the minimum percentage to the Indiana Bar Foundation or to any other entity for purposes that have a direct or indirect relationship to the objectives of the underlying litigation or otherwise promote the substantive or procedural interests of members of the certified class.

RULE 14(C) OF THE INDIANA RULES OF APPELLATE PROCEDURE

RULE 14. INTERLOCUTORY APPEALS

(c) *Interlocutory appeals from orders granting or denying class action certification.* The Court of Appeals, in its discretion, may accept jurisdiction over an appeal from an interlocutory order granting or denying class action certification under Ind. Trial Rule 23.

(1) Time for filing motion. A motion requesting that the Court of Appeals accept jurisdiction over an interlocutory appeal from an order granting or denying class action certification shall be filed within thirty (30) days of the entry of the order.

(2) Content of motion. The motion requesting that the Court of Appeals accept jurisdiction shall state:

(A) The date of the order granting or denying class action certification.

(B) The facts necessary for consideration of the motion.

(C) The reasons the Court of Appeals should accept the interlocutory appeal.

(3) Attachments to motion. A copy of the trial court's order granting or denying class action certification shall be attached to the motion requesting that the Court of Appeals

accept jurisdiction over the interlocutory appeal.

(4) Response to motion. Any response to the motion requesting the Court of Appeals to accept jurisdiction shall be filed within fifteen (15) days after service of the motion.

(5) Filing of notice of appeal. The appellant shall file a Notice of Appeal with the Clerk within fifteen (15) days of the Court of Appeals' order accepting jurisdiction over the interlocutory appeal. The Notice of Appeal shall be in the form prescribed by Rule 9, and served in accordance with Rule 9(F)(10). The appellant shall also comply with Rule 9(E).

Richard E. Shevitz is a partner in the Indianapolis firm of Cohen Malad, LLP, and serves as the Chair of the firm's Class Action Practice Group. Vess A. Miller is a partner at Cohen Malad, LLP, and concentrates his practice in class action litigation.

IOWA

Prior to July 1, 1980, the Iowa rule regarding class actions was essentially the same as old Rule 23(a) of the Federal Rules of Civil Procedure, which existed in the federal courts until the substantial revision in 1966 of the federal rule. Hence, prior to July 1, 1980, Iowa state courts were still dealing with the old true, hybrid, spurious class action analysis. Effective July 1, 1980, Iowa adopted the provisions of the Uniform Class Actions Act, which had been approved in 1976 by the National Conference of Commissioners of Uniform State Laws. To date, only North Dakota and Iowa have adopted this Uniform Act.

As one can see from the lengthy Iowa Rules dealing with class actions, *supra*, the Iowa Rules are much more detailed than Rule 23 of the Federal Rules of Civil Procedure. It appears the drafters of the Uniform Act took the 1966 Fed. R. Civ. P. 23 and the case law interpreting and deciding various issues under "new" Fed. R. Civ. 23, and tried to codify what they thought were the best decisions regarding Fed. R. Civ. 23, adding perhaps some of their own ideas. The result of their efforts is much more detailed rules regarding class actions. For example, Rule 1.263, "Criteria considered," has thirteen subparts identifying factors to be given weight by the court in determining whether a class should be permitted. Additionally, there are three required findings in determining whether the representative parties fairly and adequately protect the interests of the class. Moreover, Rule 1.266, "Notice of action," is very detailed regarding the notice and various administrative matters dealing with notice. Rule 1.270, "Counterclaims," deals specifically with what type of counterclaims may be brought in a class action. Rule 1.275, "Attorney's fees," and Rule 1.276, "Arrangements for attorney's fees and expenses," are also very detailed with respect to their subject matter.

Two provisions that are contained in the Rules might be considered unusual by lawyers in other jurisdictions. One is the provision that "(3) An order certifying or refusing to certify an action as a class action is appealable." Rule 1.264, "Order on certification." The other is the provision that "(2) Upon a determination that the costs and litigation expenses of the action cannot reasonably and fairly be defrayed by the representative parties or by other available sources, the court by order may authorize and control the solicitation and expenditure of voluntary contributions for this purpose from members of the class, advances by the attorneys or others, or both, subject to reimbursement from any recovery obtained for the class. The court may order any available funds so contributed or advanced to be applied to the payment of any costs taxed in favor of a party opposing the class." Rule 1.276, "Arrangements for attorney's fees and expenses."

A reading of the Iowa cases shows that the Iowa courts have not been unduly restrictive in granting class certification. Indeed, in *Legg v. West Bank*, 873 N.W.2d 756, 758–59 (Iowa 2016) the Iowa Supreme Court affirmed that Iowa's class actions laws are to be interpreted liberally: "Our class-action rules are remedial in nature and should be liberally construed to favor the maintenance of class actions. *Anderson Contracting, Inc v. DSM Copolymers, Inc*., 776 N. W. 2d 846, 848 (Iowa 2009) (quoting *Comes v. Microsoft Corp*., 696 N.W. 2d 318, 320 (Iowa 2005)." And this apparently was the desire of the drafters of the Model Act. In the Prefatory Note to the Model Act, the drafters stated: "More classes with claims will be seeking redress in the state courts because federal courts have severely restricted the availability of class actions in their forum. Presently, states vary in their treatment of class actions. A strong need exists for states to adopt a uniform class action act." 12 Uniform Laws Annotated, Civil Procedure and Remedial Laws (West 1996) at 100. Although the Iowa Supreme Court has cited federal cases on class certification, Justice Appel wrote a special concurrence to emphasize that in adopting the Uniform Class Actions Act the intention was to create a more generous standard, hence, given "the difference between Iowa law and Federal law on the question of class certification . . . federal class action precedent is of limited value in determining class certification under Iowa law." *Freeman v. Grain Processing Corp.*, 895 N.W.2d 105, 130–31 (Iowa 2017).

"The burden of establishing that a purported class of plaintiffs meets the pre-requisites is, of course, on the plaintiffs." *Vignaroli v. Blue Cross of Iowa*, 360 N.W.2d 741, 744 (Iowa 1985). *See also City of Dubuque v. Iowa Trust*, 519 N.W.2d 786, 791 (Iowa 1994). "A failure of proof on any one of the prerequisites is fatal to class certification. . . . Except where the facts underlying the class are merely speculative, however, the proponent's burden is light. 2 Herbert B. Newberg & Alba Conte, *Newberg on Class Actions* § 720 at 70 (3d ed. 1992)." *City of Dubuque,* 519 N.W.2d at 791. The Iowa Supreme Court "will reverse an order granting or denying certification only if the district court's decision was based upon an abuse of discretion." *Vignaroli,* 360 N.W.2d at 743. In *City of Dubuque*, the court stated that "[r]eversal is appropriate only when the record reveals that the court's decision was based a class initially certified based upon the pleadings on clearly untenable or unreasonable grounds." *City of Dubuque*, 519 N.W.2d at 79; *Anderson Contracting, Inc. v. DSM Copolymers, Inc.,* 776 N.W.2d 846, 848 (Iowa 2009). Similarly, where the trial court decertifies, after discovery, a class initially certified, that decertification decision is reviewed on the abuse of discretion standard. *Vos v. Farm Bureau Life Ins. Co.*, 667 N.W.2d 36, 44 (Iowa 2003).

The Iowa Supreme Court has stated that "adequacy of representation is perhaps the most significant of the prerequisites to a determination of class certification." *Stone v. Pirelli Armstrong Tire Corp*., 497 N.W.2d 843, 846 (Iowa 1993). In *Stone*, the named plaintiff (purported class representative) sued the tire manufacturer and the union for alleged sexual harassment. The Supreme Court affirmed the district court's denial of class certification. The district court concluded that the named plaintiff would not fairly and adequately protect the interests of the class because of her lack of stature among female employees, her lack of credibility, her potential conflict of interest because she was no longer employed at the plant, and her inadequate financial resources. Fifteen Pirelli female employees testified that they did not want to be part of the lawsuit or have the plaintiff represent them in the event they became part of the class. The Supreme Court also noted that there was a potential conflict because the plaintiff was no longer employed by the tire maker, and she would be interested in monetary damages but not interested in the injunctive relief that was a significant portion of the claim. The court also affirmed the denial of class certification based upon the fact that the named plaintiff lacked sufficient financial resources to be an adequate class representative and was concerned that the lawyers advancing the expenses would ultimately end up acquiring a financial interest in the litigation that might interfere with their exercise of independent judgment. Perhaps the most damaging evidence to plaintiff's certification as a class representative was that the court found she lacked credibility because she had admitted in an earlier divorce case in which she was a party that she destroyed unfavorable evidence.

Adequate representation was also an issue in *Vignaroli,* 360 N.W.2d 741 (Iowa 1985). There the Iowa Supreme Court affirmed certification of a class action against an employer and former employer in a suit for severance pay and for alleged diminution of employment benefits. The defendants claimed there were conflicts of interest between the named plaintiffs and the potential class members because some of the employees had left the employment, while others remained and because some of the employees might have no complaints with respect to the defendants' action and have willingly accepted new employment with one of the defendants in lieu of severance pay. Further, the defendants argued that the named plaintiffs were overzealous and, therefore, not proper class representatives. Additionally, the defendants raised lack of financial resources and improper communications, which solicited funds from the purported class members and misrepresented the status, purpose, and effect of the litigation. The Supreme Court, in affirming class certification, stated that not every disagreement between a class representative and members of the class would stand in the way of a class action.

The different result reached in *Stone* versus *Vignaroli* may be the result of two factors. First, in each case the Supreme Court was affirming the trial court's determination regarding certification. In *Stone,* the court affirmed the denial of certification, and in *Vignaroli* the court affirmed the grant of class certification. Obviously, with an abuse-of-discretion standard on appeal, what happens in the trial court may well be determinative of class status. Second, the cases that deny certification for inadequacy of representation of the purported class representative require that there be a significant flaw with the representative, such as the lack of credibility for something like destroying unfavorable evidence in a prior case. *Stone*, 497 N.W.2d 843.

In *Martin v. Amana Refrigeration, Inc*., 435 N.W.2d 364 (Iowa 1989), the Supreme Court affirmed the trial court's certification of the class. The named plaintiff sued for breach of implied warranty in the design and construction of a furnace-water heater. Amana contended that plaintiff's heat modular was still intact and not yet cracked, therefore she could not be a class representative on behalf of those whose heat modulars had cracked. The Iowa Supreme Court affirmed class certification, noting that the fact that her heat module unit was still intact did not prevent her from adequately representing the class for claims for alleged defective design and manufacture. The case also holds that a certification order, although interlocutory, is appealable as a matter of right. In *Martin*, the Supreme Court, in discussing numerosity, cites *Newberg on Class Actions* for the general rule "that if the class is large, then the numbers alone should be dispositive" and that "[f]orty or more has been recognized as the range where numbers alone should suffice to show impracticality of joinder." *Id.* at 368. *See also Legg v. West Bank*, 873 N.W. 2d 756, 759 (Iowa 2016) citing *Dubuque v. Iowa Trust*, 519 N.W. 2d 786, 792, for "[a] class with forty or more members is within the range where impracticability is presumed."

In *Vignaroli* and its progeny, the Iowa Supreme Court has recognized the need for common questions of law or fact to predominate over questions affecting only individual members. *See, e.g.*, *Vignaroli*, 360 N.W.2d at 744–45. Therein, the court recognized and appreciated the difficulty involved in trying a class suit based upon individual, oral representations, but it also stated that "[i]t is not necessary that the individual claims be carbon copies of each other." *Id.* at 745. The Supreme Court also stated that the individual nature of damage claims will not necessarily preclude class action status. *Id.* at 745.

In a case where neighboring property owners sued a wet corn processing mill on the grounds of nuisance, negligence and trespass as a result of pollution emitted from the mill into the atmosphere, the Supreme Court affirmed the trial court's certification of class, with two subcategories based on proximity to the mill. *Freeman v. Grain Processing, infra.* 895 N.W.2d 105 (Iowa 2017). In reviewing whether common issues predominated, the Court noted the trial court's decision had devoted eleven of its forty-seven pages to addressing the predominance issue. *Id.*

In *Chicoine v. Wellmark, Inc.* 22-0303 (Iowa Jan. 26, 2024), class action certification was sought on behalf of approximately 1,300 chiropractors. They claimed Wellmark's administrative agreements with a large number of entities that self-funded healthcare insurance setting a reimbursement rate for chiropractic services violated Iowa's antitrust law. The trial court found the record did not support the claim the class would have been better off "but for" those administrative agreements. The plaintiffs failed to present any evidence supporting the commonality of harm to support their antitrust claim. In contrast, in challenging class action certification, Wellmark presented abundant evidence that individual issues could predominate over common issues based on the possible behavior of self-funded entities and the circumstances of individual chiropractors in absence of the administrative agreement. The Supreme Court noted "'[t]he district court has considerable leeway when deciding whether to certify the class.' *Freeman*, 895 N.W.2d at 115. We conclude that the district court acted within its broad discretion in denying class certification on the grounds that individual questions predominate over common questions on the threshold liability issue of antitrust injury." *Chicoine v. Wellmark, Inc.*, __ N.W.2d at __ (Iowa 2024).

The case of *Roland v. Annett Holdings, Inc*., 940 N.W.2d 752 (Iowa 2020), merits review. There the Iowa Supreme Court reversed as an abuse of discretion the district court's grant and the Court of Appeals' affirmance of class certification. The case began as workers' compensation action. Roland, an over-the-road trucker was a resident of Alabama who sustained a work-related injury. The employer trucking company required truckers sign a Memorandum of Understanding (MOU) stating, if injured, the trucker agreed to Des Moines, Iowa, as the location for modified work duty. The deputy workers' compensation commissioner found the requirement that Roland accept modified duty in Des Moines deprived him of benefits in violation of Iowa Workers' Compensation law. After that finding was sustained in court, Roland filed a class action based on the application of the MOU to resident out-of-state trucker employees. Justice Appeal's lengthy analysis in his dissent reveals the Supreme Court's finding on the class certification issue to be inconsistent with the rules and precedent, however, the Supreme Court's decision may be based less on the class action issue than its application in the workers' compensation context: "[C]lass adjudication of workers' compensation benefits conflicts with Iowa Code 85." *Id.* at 757. "We hold for class-certification purposes, the validity of the MOU must be determined driver-by-driver based on individual factual circumstances." *Id.* at 758.

In *Comes v. Microsoft Corp*., 696 N.W.2d 318 (Iowa 2005), the court rejected Microsoft's contention that the named plaintiffs could not show adequate financial resources to maintain the action. The court observed the plaintiffs' attorneys had applied under rule 1.276 for approval of a fee arrangement and had agreed to advance costs. The *Comes* court quoted the rationale expressed at *Rand v. Monsanto Co*., 926 F.2d 596, 599 (7th Cir. 1991) (Easterbrook, J)—that it would be foolish given the limited stake for a representative plaintiff "to vouch for the entire costs." *Comes,* 696 N.W.2d at 327. The court concluded "in view of Iowa Rule of Civil Procedure 1.276 and its provision for advancement of costs in a class-certification case," the plaintiffs had met the adequate financial requirement showing. *Comes,* 686 N.W.2d at 327.

The Uniform Class Actions Act adopted by Iowa contains a section that tolls the statute of limitations upon the commencement of a class action. The statute of limitations resumes running against a member of the class: upon filing an election of exclusion by that member; upon entry of an order of certification, or of an amendment thereof, eliminating that member from the class; except as to representative parties, upon entry of an order refusing to certify an action as a class action; or upon dismissal of the action without an adjudication on the merits. (*See* Rule 1.277.)

Former Rules 42.6, 42.19, and 42.20 were stricken effective January 24, 1998. Rule 42.6 dealt, in part, with reciprocal multi-state jurisdiction over residents of states that had also passed the Model Act. However, because only two states had adopted the Model Act, it actually restricted Iowa state courts regarding nationwide class actions. *Phillips Petroleum Company v. Shutts*, 472 U.S. 797, 105 S. Ct. 2965, 86 L. Ed. 2d 628 (1985) (allowing state courts, in certain circumstances, to exercise jurisdiction over non-resident class members in state courts) had caused the Commissioners of Uniform State Laws to delete the similar section on the grounds that *Shutts* rendered the section obsolete. Rule 42.19 and

Rule 42.20 were stricken at the same time because they dealt, in part, with the same issue. *See* Committee Comment—1997 contained in the 1999 *Iowa Rules of Court, State and Federal* (West) at 16. *See also* Comment in the new Iowa Rules on Class Actions, *supra*, [after Rule 1.277(4)].

Effective July 1, 2009, the Iowa legislature created a private right of action for "Consumer Frauds" (Chapter 714H). Prior thereto, the Attorney General had exclusive right to bring "Consumer Frauds" actions (714.16). Under the new law, a party must give notice to the Attorney General of the claim, any judgment, and any appeal (714H.6). 714H.7 Class Actions provides:

> A class action lawsuit alleging a violation of this chapter shall not be filed with a court unless it has been approved by the attorney general. The attorney general shall approve the filing of a class action lawsuit alleging a violation of this chapter unless the attorney general determines that the lawsuit is frivolous. This section shall not affect the requirements of any other law or of the Iowa rules of civil procedure relating to class action lawsuits.

The Rules deal with specific types of post-certification communications. All of such post-certification communications require Court approval and/or supervision: Rule 1.266, Notice of action; Rule 1.269, Discovery by or against class members; Rule 1.271, Dismissal or compromise (including notice thereof); Rule 1.276(2), "Upon a determination that the costs and litigation expenses of the action cannot reasonably and fairly be defrayed by the representative parties or by other available sources, the court by order may authorize and control the solicitation and expenditure of voluntary contributions for this purpose from members of the class, advances by the attorneys or others, or both, subject to reimbursement from any recovery obtained for the class."

A reading of the Iowa cases shows that the Iowa courts have not been unduly restrictive in granting class certification. Indeed, in *Legg*, 873 N.W.2d 756, 758–59 (Iowa 2016) the Iowa Supreme Court affirmed that Iowa's class actions laws are to be interpreted liberally: "Our class-action rules are remedial in nature and should be liberally construed to favor the maintenance of class actions. *Anderson Contracting, Inc v. DSM Copolymers, Inc*., 776 N. W. 2d 846, 848 (Iowa 2009) (quoting *Comes v. Microsoft Corp*., 696 N.W. 2d 318, 320 (Iowa 2005)." And this apparently was the desire of the drafters of the Model Act. In the Prefatory Note to the Model Act, the drafters stated: "More classes with claims will be seeking redress in the state courts because federal courts have severely restricted the availability of class actions in their forum. Presently, states vary in their treatment of class actions. A strong need exists for states to adopt a uniform class action act." 12 Uniform Laws Annotated, Civil Procedure and Remedial Laws (West 1996) at l00.

F. CLASS ACTIONS

[Note: In 2002 the Class Action Rules were renumbered; from July 1, 1980 to February 15, 2002 it was Rule 42]

Rule 1.261 Commencement of a class action. One or more members of a class may sue or be sued as representative parties on behalf of all in a class action if both of the following occur:

1.261(1) The class is so numerous or so constituted that joinder of all members, whether or not otherwise required or permitted, is impracticable.

1.261(2) There is a question of law or fact common to the class.

[Report 1980; November 9, 2001, effective February 15, 2002]

Rule 1.262 Certification of class action.

1.262(1) Unless deferred by the court, as soon as practicable after the commencement of a class action the court shall hold a hearing and determine whether or not the action is to be maintained as a class action and by order certify or refuse to certify it as a class action.

1.262(2) The court may certify an action as a class action if it finds all of the following:

a. The requirements of rule 1.261 have been satisfied.

b. A class action should be permitted for the fair and efficient adjudication of the controversy.

c. The representative parties fairly and adequately will protect the interests of the class.

1.262(3) If appropriate, the court may do any of the following:

a. Certify an action as a class action with respect to a particular claim or issue.

b. Certify an action as a class action to obtain one or more forms of relief, equitable, declaratory, or monetary.

c. Divide a class into subclasses and treat each subclass as a class.

[Report 1980; November 9, 2001, effective February 15, 2002]

Rule 1.263 Criteria considered.

1.263(1) In determining whether the class action should be permitted for the fair and efficient adjudication of the controversy, as appropriately limited under rule 1.262(3), the court shall consider and give appropriate weight to the following and other relevant factors:

a. Whether a joint or common interest exists among members of the class.

b. Whether the prosecution of separate actions by or against individual members of the class would create a risk of inconsistent or varying adjudications with respect to individual members of the class that would establish incompatible standards of conduct for a party opposing the class.

c. Whether adjudications with respect to individual members of the class as a practical matter would be dispositive of the interests of other members not parties to the adjudication or substantially impair or impede their ability to protect their interests.

d. Whether a party opposing the class has acted or refused to act on grounds generally applicable to the class, thereby making final injunctive relief or corresponding declaratory relief appropriate with respect to the class as a whole.

e. Whether common questions of law or fact predominate over any questions affecting only individual members.

f. Whether other means of adjudicating the claims and defenses are impracticable or inefficient.

g. Whether a class action offers the most appropriate means of adjudicating the claims and defenses.

h. Whether members who are not representative parties have a substantial interest in individually controlling the prosecution or defense of separate actions.

i. Whether the class action involves a claim that is or has been the subject of a class action, a government action, or other proceeding.

j. Whether it is desirable to bring the class action in another forum.

k. Whether management of the class action poses unusual difficulties.

l. Whether any conflict of laws issues involved pose unusual difficulties.

m. Whether the claims of individual class members are insufficient in the amounts or interests involved, in view of the complexities of the issues and the expenses of the litigation, to afford significant relief to the members of the class.

1.263(2) In determining under rule 1.262(2) that the representative parties fairly and adequately will protect the interests of the class, the court must find all of the following:

a. The attorney for the representative parties will adequately represent the interests of the class.

b. The representative parties do not have a conflict of interest in the maintenance of the class action.

c. The representative parties have or can acquire adequate financial resources, considering rule 1.276, to ensure that the interests of the class will not be harmed.

[Report 1980; October 31, 1997, effective January 24, 1998; November 9, 2001, effective February 15, 2002]

Rule 1.264 Order on certification.

1.264(1) The order of certification shall describe the class and state the following:

a. The relief sought.

b. Whether the action is maintained with respect to particular claims or issues.

c. Whether subclasses have been created.

1.264(2) The order certifying or refusing to certify a class action shall state the reasons for the court's ruling and its findings on the facts listed in rule 1.263(1).

1.264(3) An order certifying or refusing to certify an action as a class action is appealable.

1.264(4) Refusal of certification does not terminate the action, but does preclude it from being maintained as a class action.

[Report 1980; November 9, 2001, effective February 15, 2002]

Rule 1.265 Amendment of certification order.

1.265(1) The court may amend the certification order at any time before entry of judgment on the merits. The amendment may do the following:

a. Establish subclasses.

b. Eliminate from the class any member who was included in the class as certified.

c. Provide for an adjudication limited to certain claims or issues.

d. Change the relief sought.

e. Make any other appropriate change in the order.

1.265(2) If notice of certification has been given pursuant to rule 1.266, the court may order notice of the amendment of the certification order to be given in terms and to any members of the class the court directs.

1.265(3) The reasons for the court's ruling shall be set forth in the amendment of the certification order.

1.265(4) An order amending the certification order is appealable. An order denying the motion of a member of a defendant class, not a representative party, to amend the certification order is appealable if the court certifies it for immediate appeal.

[Report 1980; October 31, 1997, effective January 24,1998; November 9, 2001, effective February 15, 2002]

Rule 1.266 Notice of action.

1.266(1) Following certification the court, by order after hearing, shall direct the giving of notice to the class.

1.266(2) The notice, based on the certification order and any amendment of the order, shall include all of the following:

a. A general description of the action, including the relief sought, and the names and addresses of the representative parties.

b. A statement of the right of a member of the class under rule 1.267 to be excluded from the action by filing an election to be excluded, in the manner specified, by a certain date.

c. A description of possible financial consequences on the class.

d. A general description of any counterclaim being asserted by or against the class, including the relief sought.

e. A statement that the judgment, whether favorable or not, will bind all members of the class who are not excluded from the action.

f. A statement that any member of the class may enter an appearance either personally or through counsel.

g. An address to which inquiries may be directed.

h. Other information the court deems appropriate.

1.266(3) The order shall prescribe the manner of notification to be used and specify the members of the class to be notified. In determining the manner and form of the notice to be given, the court shall consider the interests of the class, the relief requested, the cost of notifying the members of the class, and the possible prejudice to members who do not receive notice.

1.266(4) Each member of the class, not a representative party, whose potential monetary recovery or liability is estimated to exceed $100 shall be given personal or mailed notice if that member's identity and whereabouts can be ascertained by the exercise of reasonable diligence.

1.266(5) For members of the class not given personal or mailed notice under rule 1.266(4), the court shall provide, as a minimum, a means of notice reasonably calculated to apprise the members of the class of the pendency of the action. Techniques calculated to ensure effective communication of information concerning commencement of the action shall be used. The techniques may include personal or mailed notice, notification by means of newspaper, television, radio, posting in public or other places, and distribution through trade, union, public interest, or other appropriate groups.

1.266(6) The plaintiff shall advance the expense of notice under this rule if there is no counterclaim asserted. If a counterclaim is asserted the expense of notice shall be allocated as the court orders in the interest of justice.

1.266(7) The court may order that steps be taken to minimize the expense of notice.

[Report 1980; October 31, 1997, effective January 24, 1998; November 9, 2001, effective February 15, 2002]

Rule 1.267 Exclusion.

1.267(1) A member of a plaintiff class may elect to be excluded from the action unless any of the following occur:

a. The member is a representative party.

b. The certification order contains an affirmative finding under rule 1.263(1)(*a*), (*b*), or (*c*).

c. A counterclaim under rule 1.270 is pending against the member or that member's class or subclass.

1.267(2) Any member of a plaintiff class entitled to be excluded under rule 1.267(1) who files an election to be excluded, in the manner and in the time specified in the notice, is excluded from and not bound by the judgment in the class action.

1.267(3) The elections shall be made a part of the record in the action.

1.267(4) A member of a defendant class may not elect to be excluded.

[Report 1980; October 31,1997, effective January 24, 1998; November 9, 2001, effective February 15, 2002]

Rule 1.268 Conduct of action.

1.268(1) The court on motion of a party or its own motion may make or amend any appropriate order dealing with the conduct of the action including, but not limited to, any of the following:

a. Determining the course of proceedings or prescribing measures to prevent undue repetition or complication in the presentation of evidence or argument.

b. Requiring, for the protection of the members of the class or otherwise for the fair conduct of the action, that notice be given as the court directs, of the following:

(1) Any step in the action.

(2) The proposed extent of the judgment.

(3) The opportunity of members to signify whether they consider the representation fair and adequate, to enter an appearance and present claims or defenses, or otherwise participate in the action.

c. Imposing conditions on the representative parties or on interveners.

d. Inviting the attorney general to participate with respect to the question of adequacy of class representation.

e. Making any other order to ensure that the class action proceeds only with adequate class representation.

f. Making any order to ensure that the class action proceeds only with competent representation by the attorney for the class.

1.268(2) A class member who is not a representative party may appear and be represented by separate counsel.

[Report 1980; November 9, 2001, effective February 15, 2002]

Rule 1.269 Discovery by or against class members.

1.269(1) Discovery may be used only on order of the court against a member of the class who is not a representative party or who has not appeared. In deciding whether discovery should be allowed the court shall consider, among other relevant factors, the timing of the request, the subject matter to be covered, whether representatives of the class are seeking discovery on the subject to be covered, and whether the discovery will result in annoyance, oppression, or undue burden or expense for the member of the class.

1.269(2) Discovery by or against representative parties or those appearing is governed by the rules dealing with discovery by or against a party to a civil action.

[Report 1980; November 9, 2001, effective February 15, 2002]

Rule 1.270 Counterclaims.

1.270(1) A defendant in an action brought by a class may plead as a counterclaim any claim the court certifies as a class action against the plaintiff class. On leave of court, the defendant may plead as a counterclaim a claim against a member of the class or a claim the court certifies as a class action against a subclass.

1.270(2) Any counterclaim in an action brought by a plaintiff class must be asserted before notice is given under rule 1.266.

1.270(3) If a judgment for money is recovered against a party on behalf of a class, the court rendering judgment may stay distribution of any award or execution of any portion of a judgment allocated to a member of the class against whom the losing party has pending an action in or out of state for a judgment for money, and continue the stay so long as the losing party in the class action pursues the pending action with reasonable diligence.

1.270(4) A defendant class may plead as a counterclaim any claim on behalf of the class that the court certifies as a class action against the plaintiff. The court may certify as a class action a counterclaim against the plaintiff on behalf of a subclass or permit a counterclaim by a member of the class. The court shall order that notice of the counterclaim by the class, subclass, or member of the class be given to the members of the class as the court directs, in the interest of justice.

1.270(5) A member of a class or subclass asserting a counterclaim shall be treated as a member of a plaintiff class for the purpose of exclusion under rule 1.267.

1.270(6) The court's refusal to allow, or the defendant's failure to plead, a claim as a counterclaim in a class action does not bar the defendant from asserting the claim in a subsequent action.

[Report 1980; November 9, 2001, effective February 15, 2002]

Rule 1.271 Dismissal or compromise.

1.271(1) Unless certification has been refused under rule 1.262, a class action, without the approval of the court after hearing, may not be:

a. Dismissed voluntarily.

b. Dismissed involuntarily without an adjudication on the merits.

c. Compromised.

1.271(2) If the court has certified the action under rule 1.262, notice of hearing on the proposed dismissal or compromise shall be given to all members of the class in a manner the court directs. If the court has not ruled on certification, notice of hearing on the proposed dismissal or compromise may be ordered by the court which shall specify the persons to be notified and the manner in which notice is to be given.

1.271(3) Notice given under rule 1.271(2) shall include a description of the procedure available for modification of the dismissal or compromise and a full disclosure of the reasons for the dismissal or compromise including, but not limited to, the following:

a. Any payments made or to be made in connection with the dismissal or compromise.

b. The anticipated effect of the dismissal or compromise on the class members.

c. Any agreement made in connection with the dismissal or compromise.

d. A description and evaluation of alternatives considered by the representative parties.

e. An explanation of any other circumstances giving rise to the proposal.

1.271(4) On the hearing of the dismissal or compromise, the court may do any of the following:

a. As to the representative parties or a class certified under rule 1.262, permit dismissal with or without prejudice or approve the compromise.

b. As to a class not certified, permit dismissal without prejudice.

c. Deny the dismissal.

d. Disapprove the compromise.

e. Take other appropriate action for the protection of the class and in the interest of justice.

1.271(5) The cost of notice given under rule 1.271(2) shall be paid by the party seeking dismissal, or as agreed in case of a compromise, unless the court after a hearing orders otherwise.

[Report 1980; November 9, 2001, effective February 15, 2002]

Rule 1.272 Effect of judgment on class. In a class action certified under rule 1.262 in which notice has been given under rule 1.266 or 1.271, a judgment as to the claim or particular claim or issue certified is binding, according to its terms, on any member of the class who has not filed an election of exclusion under rule 1.267. The judgment shall name or describe the members of the class who are bound by its terms.

[Report 1980; November 9, 2001, effective February 15, 2002]

Rule 1.273 Costs.

1.273(1) Only the representative parties and those members of the class who have appeared individually are liable for costs assessed against a plaintiff class.

1.273(2) The court shall apportion the liability for costs assessed against a defendant class.

1.273(3) Expenses of notice advanced under rule 1.266 are taxable as costs in favor of the prevailing party.

[Report 1980; November 9, 2001, effective February 15, 2002]

Rule 1.274 Relief afforded.

1.274(1) The court may award any form of relief consistent with the certification order to which the party in whose favor it is rendered is entitled including equitable, declaratory, monetary, or other relief to individual members of the class or the class in a lump sum or installments.

1.274(2) Damages fixed by a minimum measure of recovery provided by any statute may not be recovered in a class action.

1.274(3) If a class is awarded a judgment for money, the distribution shall be determined as follows:

a. The parties shall list as expeditiously as possible all members of the class whose identity can be determined without expending a disproportionate share of the recovery.

b. The reasonable expense of identification and distribution shall be paid, with the court's approval, from the funds to be distributed.

c. The court may order steps taken to minimize the expense of identification.

d. The court shall supervise, and may grant or stay the whole or any portion of, the execution of the judgment and the collection and distribution of funds to the members of the class as their interests warrant.

e. The court shall determine what amount of the funds available for the payment of the judgment cannot be distributed to members of the class individually because they could not be identified or located or because they did not claim or prove the right to money apportioned to them. The court after a hearing shall distribute that amount, in whole or in part, to one or more states as unclaimed property or to the defendant or to the Iowa Supreme Court Lawyer Trust Account Commission.

f. In determining the amount, if any, to be distributed to a state or to the defendant, the court shall consider the following criteria:

(1) Any unjust enrichment of the defendant.

(2) The willfulness or lack of willfulness on the part of the defendant.

(3) The impact on the defendant of the relief granted.

(4) The pendency of other claims against the defendant.

(5) Any criminal sanction imposed on the defendant.

(6) The loss suffered by the plaintiff class.

g. The court, in order to remedy or alleviate any harm done, may impose conditions respecting the use of the money distributed to the defendant.

h. Any amount to be distributed to a state shall be distributed as unclaimed property to any state in which are located the last-known addresses of the members of the class to whom distribution could not be made. If the last-known addresses cannot be ascertained with reasonable diligence, the court may determine by other means what portion of the unidentified or unlocated members of the class were residents of a state. A state shall receive that portion of the distribution that its residents would have received had they been identified and located. Before entering an order distributing any part of the amount to a state, the court shall give written notice of its intention to make distribution to the attorney general of the state of the residence of any person given notice under rule 1.266 or 1.271 and shall afford the attorney general an opportunity to move for an order requiring payment to the state.

[Report 1980; October 31, 1997, effective January 24, 1998; November 9, 2001, effective February 15, 2002; Court Order September 14, 2017, temporarily effective September 14, 2017, permanently effective November 14, 2017]

Rule 1.275 Attorney's fees.

1.275(1) Attorney's fees for representing a class are subject to control of the court.

1.275(2) If under an applicable provision of law a defendant or defendant class is entitled to attorney's fees from a plaintiff class, only representative parties and those members of the class who have appeared individually are liable for those fees. If a plaintiff is entitled to attorney's fees from a defendant class, the court may apportion the fees among the members of the class.

1.275(3) If a prevailing class recovers a judgment for money or other award that can be divided for the purpose, the court may order reasonable attorney's fees and litigation expenses of the class to be paid from the recovery.

1.275(4) If the prevailing class is entitled to declaratory or equitable relief, the court may order the adverse party to pay to the class its reasonable attorney's fees and litigation expenses, if permitted by law in similar cases not involving a class, or the court finds that the judgment has vindicated an important public interest. However, if any monetary award is also recovered, the court may allow reasonable attorney's fees and litigation expenses only to the extent that a reasonable proportion of that award is insufficient to defray the fees and expenses.

1.275(5) In determining the amount of attorney's fees for a prevailing class the court shall consider all of the following factors:

a. The time and effort expended by the attorney in the litigation, including the nature, extent, and quality of the services rendered.

b. Results achieved and benefits conferred upon the class.

c. The magnitude, complexity, and uniqueness of the litigation.

d. The contingent nature of success.

e. In cases awarding attorney's fees and litigation expenses under rule 1.275(4) because of the vindication of an important public interest, the economic impact on the party against whom the award is made.

f. Appropriate criteria in the Iowa Rules of Professional Conduct.

[Report 1980; November 9, 2001, effective February 15, 2002; April 20, 2005, effective July 1, 2005]

Rule 1.276 Arrangements for attorney's fees and expenses.

1.276(1) Before a hearing under rule 1.262(1) or at any other time the court directs, the representative parties and the attorney for the representative parties shall file with the court, jointly or separately, all of the following:

a. A statement showing any amount paid or promised them by any person for the services rendered or to be rendered in connection with the action or for the costs and expenses of the litigation and the source of all of the amounts.

b. A copy of any written agreement, or a summary of any oral agreement, between the representative parties and their attorney concerning financial arrangements or fees.

c. A copy of any written agreement, or a summary of any oral agreement, by the representative parties or the attorney to share these amounts with any person other than a member, regular associate, or an attorney regularly of counsel with that law firm.

This statement shall be supplemented promptly if additional arrangements are made.

1.276(2) Upon a determination that the costs and litigation expenses of the action cannot reasonably and fairly be defrayed by the representative parties or by other available sources, the court by order may authorize and control the solicitation and expenditure of voluntary contributions for this purpose from members of the class, advances by the attorneys or others, or both, subject to reimbursement from any recovery obtained for the class. The court may order any available funds so contributed or advanced to be applied to the payment of any costs taxed in favor of a party opposing the class.

[Report 1980; October 31, 1997, effective January 24, 1998; November 9, 2001, effective February 15, 2002]

Rule 1.277 Statute of limitations. The statute of limitations is tolled for all class members upon the commencement of an action asserting a class action. The statute of limitations resumes running against a member of a class:

1.277(1) Upon filing an election of exclusion by that member.

1.277(2) Upon entry of an order of certification, or of an amendment thereof, eliminating that member from the class.

1.277(3) Except as to representative parties, upon entry of an order under rule 1.262 refusing to certify an action as a class action.

1.277(4) Upon dismissal of the action without an adjudication on the merits.

[Report 1980; October 31, 1997, effective January 24, 1998; November 9, 2001, effective February 15, 2002]

COMMENT: Former Iowa R. Civ. P. 42.6 was stricken in order to eliminate its restriction on personal jurisdiction over nonresident class members, and to permit exercise of jurisdiction over nonresident class members to the extent permitted by the U.S. and state constitutions as interpreted by the courts Former Iowa R. Civ. P. 42.19 and 42.20 were stricken because the Model Act has been adopted in only two states.

Rule 1.278 Virtual representation. Where persons composing a class which may be increased by others later born, do or may make a claim affecting specific property involved in an action to which all living members of the class are parties, any others later born shall also be deemed to have been parties to the action and bound by any decree rendered therein.

[Report 1943; November 9, 2001, effective February 15, 2002]

Rule 1.279 Shareholder's actions. Shareholders in an incorporated or unincorporated association, who sue to enforce its rights because of its failure to do so, shall support their petition by affidavit, and allege their efforts to have the directors, trustees or other shareholders bring the action or enforce the right, or a sufficient reason for not making such effort.

[Report 1943; November 9, 2001, effective February 15, 2002]

Rules 1.280 Reserved.

Chapter author Susan A. Low practices in Des Moines, Iowa.

KANSAS

1. COMPARISON WITH RULE 23 OF THE FEDERAL RULES OF CIVIL PROCEDURE

Kansas Statutes Annotated (K.S.A.) § 60-223 of the Kansas Rules of Civil Procedure is modeled after Rule 23 of the Federal Rules of Civil Procedure. *Shutts v. Phillips Petroleum Co.,* 222 Kan. 527, 567 P.2d 1292 (1977), *cert. denied,* 434 U.S. 1068, *rehearing denied,* 435 U.S. 961 (1978); *Steele v. Security Benefit Life Ins.*, 226 Kan. 631, 638, 602 P.2d 1305 (1979); *Bigs v. City of Wichita,* 271 Kan. 455, 478, 23 P.3d 855 (2001). The Kansas Supreme Court may find the federal courts' interpretation of Rule 23 persuasive. *Steele*, 226 Kan. at 636, 602 P.2d 1305; *Dragon v. Vanguard Indus.,* 277 Kan. 776, 778, 89 P.3d 908 (2004) (*Dragon I*); *Anderson Off. Supply v. Advanced Med. Ass'n*, 47 Kan. App. 2d 140, 162, 273 P.3d 786, 800 (2012) ("mirrors the Federal Rule"); *Farrar v. Mobil Oil*, 43 Kan. App. 2d 871, 875, 234 P.3d 19 (2010) (Rule 23 "parallels" K.S.A. § 60-223), *rev. denied,* (Nov. 5, 2010); *O'Brien v. Leegin Creative Leather Prods., Inc.*, 294 Kan. 318, 277 P.3d 1062, 1088 (2012) (Kansas class certification statute "modeled after and has traditionally been interpreted like Fed. R. Civ. Proc. 23"). In 2014, K.S.A. §§ 60-456 to 458 were amended to adopt the *Daubert* standard for expert testimony.

"Due to the representative nature of class actions, district courts have a responsibility to oversee such cases in a meaningful matter. In fulfilling this oversight responsibility, district courts have the authority to issue appropriate orders to control the court of the proceedings and to protect the interests of the parties." *In re CEC Entm't, Inc., Stockholder Litig.,* No. 120,324, 2019 WL 4725289, at *6 (Kan. App. 2019) (unpublished) (citing K.S.A. 2018 Supp. 60-223(d)); *see Ross-Williams v. Bennett,* 55 Kan. App. 2d 524, 545, 419 P.3d 608, *rev. denied* Nov. 21, 2018. With the parties' consent, the duty to oversee class litigation includes appointing a special master with broad power to "oversee all proceedings in [the] case other than any trial on the merits and related pre-trial motions, pre-trial briefing, and the pre-trial conference." *In re CEC Entm't, Inc., Stockholder Litig.,* 2019 WL 4725289, at *6. The special master's recommendations are binding unless a party objects to the report within 30 days. *Id.* The district court can review a special master's findings of fact for clear error and conclusions of law *de novo*. *Id.*

Trial judges are afforded substantial discretion in determining whether a class action should be certified. *Steele v. Security Benefit Life Ins.*, 226 Kan. 631, 638, 602 P.2d 1305 (1979); *Bigs v. City of Wichita*, 271 Kan. 455, 477, 23 P.3d 855 (2001); *L. Ruth Fawcett v. Oil Producers, Inc. of Kan.,* 302 Kan. 350, 352 P.3d 1032 (2015) (*Fawcett I*) (reversing summary judgment entered in favor of certified class of royalty owners in oil and gas wells but left intact certification of the class action). The Kansas Court of Appeals further examined the rigorous statutory analysis for class certification and determined the district court did not abuse its discretion because it "thoughtfully considered the parties' arguments" and found the plaintiffs "presented enough evidence to satisfy the class-action requirements." *Cooper Clark Found. v. Oxy USA Inc.*, 58 Kan. App. 2d 335, 366, 469 P.3d 1266 (2020).

But that discretion can be reversed for failure to rigorously analyze the K.S.A. § 60-223 factors or for legal error. *O'Brien v. Leegin Creative Leather Prod., Inc.*, No. 108,988, 2014 WL 1362657 (Kan. App. 2014) (unpublished) (reversing denial of class certification), *rev. denied,* (Aug. 28, 2014); *Ruby v. Atlantic Credit and Fin., Inc.*, No. 110,266, 2014 WL 3294886 (Kan. App. 2014) (unpublished) (reversing district court's two page order certifying class action for failure to rigorously analyze the statutory factors); *Johnson v. MKA Enters., Inc.,* No. 112,049, 2015 WL 4487037 (Kan. App. 2015) (unpublished) (reversing district court's order certifying a consumer car purchaser class action for failing to rigorously analyze K.S.A. § 60-223(b)(1)(A) and (b)(3)).

Kansas state courts have a history of certifying multi-state class actions. *Gray v. Amoco Prod. Co.,* 1 Kan. App. 2d 338, 564 P.2d 579 (1977); *Shutts v. Phillips Petroleum Co.*, 235 Kan. 195, 670 P.2d 1159 (1984); *Sternberger v. Marathon Oil Co.*, 257 Kan. 315, 894 P.2d 788 (1995); *Dragon v. Vanguard Indus.,* 277 Kan. 776, 778, 89 P.3d 908 (2004) (*Dragon I*) (listing cases).

The Kansas Supreme Court also ruled in *Dragon I* that a trial court must conduct a rigorous analysis of the K.S.A. § 60-223 factors based on the movant's *prima facie* evidentiary showing. 277 Kan. 776, 89 P.3d 908 (2004). This adopts the approach taken by some federal courts. *See Critchfield Physical Therapy v. Taranto Grp.*, 293 Kan. 285, 293, 263 P.3d 767, 775 (2012) (affirming "light" or "prima facie" showing, rather than "heavy burden of proof on plaintiffs," and clarifying that a "mini-trial with extensive fact-finding" is not required).

With regards to choice-of-law issues in multi-state class actions, the Kansas Supreme Court also ruled that the party moving for class certification has the burden to show the requirements of Rule 23 can be satisfied under applicable law and that there are no material differences in the various states' law that would defeat manageability by the trial court. *Dragon I*, 277 Kan. At 791–92. If there are procedural or substantive factors affecting the choice of law determinations, plaintiffs should thoroughly brief those issues to the trial court. *Id.* at 790. Ultimately, the *Dragon I* Court reversed the class certification order of a fifty-state class because the trial court failed to consider material conflict of law issues through a conflicts' test (e.g., *lex fori*, *lex loci delecti*, or most significant relationship) to determine whether these conflicts could be managed by the trial court during trial or by subclassing. *Id.* at 790–91.

In *Dragon v. Vanguard Indus., Inc.* (*Dragon II*), the Kansas Supreme Court unanimously reversed the lower court's denial of class certification due to the inadequate record made by the trial court and affirmed that narrowing the class scope and causes of action to gain class certification was proper and appropriate. 282 Kan. 349, 361, 144 P.3d 1279, 1288 (2006) (quoting Comment, *Preserving Adequacy of Representation When Dropping Claims in Class Actions,* 74 UMKC L. Rev. 105, 106 (Fall 2005) ("dropping claims, which may serve valid strategic aims of the class representative, need not threaten the representative's adequacy, and may instead facilitate the purposes of Rule 23")). The Court established that class certification requires a rigorous analysis, mandating findings of fact under a *prima facie* standard and conclusions of law should be entered on each K.S.A. § 60-223 class certification factor. *Dragon II* was remanded for further consideration, and a smaller class was ultimately certified.

In *Farrar v. Mobil Oil Corp.*, the Kansas Court of Appeals held that the proper choice of law for interpreting an oil gas lease is the forum where the relevant property is located (using the test *lex rei sitae*), not where the lease was executed. 43 Kan. App. 2d 871, 879–83, 234 P.3d 19, *rev. denied* (Kan. 2010).

In *Mai v. Catholic Diocese of Wichita*, the Kansas Court of Appeals held that the trial court may adopt a party's proposed findings of fact and conclusions of law entirely. No. 98,298, 2007 WL 4105340, at *4 (Kan. App. 2007) (unpublished).

2. SUMMARY OF CASE LAW INTERPRETING K.S.A. § 60-223

a. Rule 23(a) Requirements

i. Numerosity. There is no set number of class members required. *Shupbach v. Continental Oil Co.*, 193 Kan. 401, 405, 394 P.2d 1, 5 (1964) (allegation of 23 class members sufficient); *Sternberger v. Marathon Oil Co.*, 257 Kan. 315, 344, 894 P.2d 778, 807 (1995) (38 subclass members); *but see Combs v. Devon Energy Prod. Co., LP,* 303 P.3d 1278, at *7 (Kan. App. 2013) (denying class certification for 25 or less class members), *rev. denied* (Dec. 27, 2013).

ii. Commonality. The rule requires the existence of either a common question of fact or a common question of law, not the presence of both. *Shutts v. Phillips Petroleum Co.*, 235 Kan. 195, 212, 679 P.2d 1159 (1984) (*Shutts II*), *aff'd in part, rev'd in part and remanded*, 472 U.S. 797 (1985) (recognizing commonality is stated in the disjunctive). Kansas courts liberally construe this requirement. *Gray v. Amoco Prod. Co.,* 1 Kan. App. 2d 338, 564 P.2d 579 (1977). The trial court does not abuse its discretion in certifying a class action even though each plaintiff may have sustained a different amount of damages. *Bigs v. City of Wichita,* 271 Kan. 455, 478 23 P.3d 855 (2001). Commonality is met even if some class members may have suffered no damages as long as it is not "so many . . . that the integrity of the class is undermined." *Critchfield Physical Therapy v. Taranto Grp.*, 293 Kan. 285, 293, 297, 263 P.3d 767, 775, 778 (2012) (unnecessary to prove "that all or most of the potential class were entitled to damages"). The presence of individual questions, while tending to diminish the weight of facts applicable to the class, does not necessarily defeat a *prima facie* showing the class prerequisites are satisfied. *Dragon v. Vanguard Indus., Inc.*, 277 Kan. 776, 793, 89 P.3d 908 (2004) (*Dragon I*) (citing Newberg § 7:26 and *Helmley v. Ashland Oil, Inc.*, 1 Kan. App. 2d 532, 536–37, 571 P.2d 345, *rev. denied*, 222 Kan. 749 (1977)). The Kansas Court of Appeals affirmed the lower court's ruling in a class action where royalty owners demonstrated enough evidence based on defendant's own documents such that plaintiffs' claims met the requirements for commonality and "were capable of classwide resolution without individual evidence from class members." *Cooper Clark Found. v. Oxy USA Inc.*, 58 Kan. App. 2d 335, 357, 469 P.3d 1266, 1282 (2020), petition denied, (Kan. Nov. 24, 2020). However, "the district court must discern what common legal and factual issues lie at the heart of the dispute" and may consider the merits of the claims to the extent they overlap with determining whether the prerequisites for certification are met. *Johnson v. MKA Enters., Inc.,* No. 112,049, 2015 WL 4487037, at *3 (Kan. App. 2015) (unpublished) (citing *Edington v. R.G. Dickinson and Co.,* 139 F.R.D. 183, 188 (D. Kan. 1991) and *Wal-Mart Stores, Inc. v. Dukes*, 564 U.S. 338, 361 (2011)) (reversing district court's order certifying a consumer class action because "car transactions are individual [not common] events").

iii. Typicality. This requirement overlaps with the adequacy of representation requirement and they are jointly assessed. *Connolly v. Frobenius,* 2 Kan. App. 2d 18, 574 P.2d 971 (1978); *Helmley v. Ashland Oil, Inc.,* 1 Kan. App. 2d 532, 571 P.2d 345 (1977). The "coextensiveness" element does not require identical interests between the class representative and the class, but only a sharing of "common objectives and legal or factual positions." *Helmley*, 1 Kan. App. at 536 (citing 7 Wright & Miller, Fed. Prac. and Proc. Civil, § 1769, at 655).

iv. Adequacy of representation. Adequacy requires (1) the proposed class representative to bear relationship to the class and (2) adequate class counsel. The *Shutts* decisions extensively discuss this element in the context of the procedural due process rights of absent class members living in several states outside of Kansas. *See generally Phillips Petroleum Co. v. Shutts*, 472 U.S. 797, 105 S. Ct. 2965, 86 L. Ed. 2d 628 (1985), *on remand*, 240 Kan. 764, 732 P.2d 1286 (1987); *Shutts v.*

Phillips Petroleum Co., 235 Kan. 195, 679 P.2d 1159 (1984); *Shutts v. Phillips Petroleum Co.*, 222 Kan. 527, 567 P.2d 1292 (1977). *See also Sternberger v. Marathon Oil Co.,* 257 Kan. 315, 894 P.2d 788 (1995).

In *Chamberlain v. Farm Bureau Mut. Ins.*, the Kansas Court of Appeals decided that if a plaintiff voluntarily settles his claim, his case should be dismissed, and it moots any consideration of class certification for lack of standing by the proposed class representative. 36 Kan. App. 2d 163, 137 P.3d 1081 (2006). The trial court had discretion to allow a substitute class representative but did not err by refusing to allow it under these circumstances. *Id.* at 178. But a defendant cannot "buy its way out of a class action" without plaintiff's consent. *Jenkins v. Schalansky*, No. 92,044, 2005 WL 217177, at *4 (Kan. App. 2005) (unpublished), *rev. denied*, June 9, 2005; *Steele v. Sec. Benefit Life Ins.*, 226 Kan. 631, 636–37, 602 P.2d 1305 (1979).

In *Mai v. Catholic Diocese of Wichita*, the Kansas Court of Appeals found that under K.S.A. § 60-223(b) the class representative was inadequate to represent an unincorporated association since the lawsuit was antagonistic to a majority vote of the association. No. 98,298, 2007 WL 4105340, at *5–6 (Kan. App. 2007) (unpublished).

b. Rule 23(b)(1), (2), and (3) Requirements

A class action is superior to thousands of individual small claims actions even though defendant "might benefit if only a small number of plaintiffs found it worth their while to bring suit or were aware of their rights." *Critchfield Physical Therapy v. Taranto Grp.*, 293 Kan. 285, 300–01, 263 P.3d 767, 779–80 (2012). A class action is superior even if class members may be able to recover more in an individual action. *N. Star Cap. Acquisition, LLC v. Budd*, No. 105,060, 2012 WL 98489, *1, *4–6 (Kan. App. 2012) (unpublished) (also amending the class definition on appeal), *rev. denied* (Kan. Feb. 7, 2013).

District courts rejected defendants' claims that the requirements of K.S.A. § 60-223(b)(3) were not met in two consumer antitrust cases in *Bellinder v. Microsoft Corp.*, Nos. 00–C–0855, 00–C–00092, 99-CV-17089, 2001 WL 1397995 (D. Kan. Sept. 7, 2001) and in *Daric Smith v. Phillip Morris Co.,* Case No. 00-CV-26 (Seward Co. Dist. Ct. Nov. 15, 2001).

In re Vitamin Antitrust Litig., an indirect purchaser price-fixing antitrust class action against choline chloride manufacturers, resulted in a certified class under a Rule 23(b)(3) analysis. 2006 WL 4103412 (Kan. Dist. Ct. Mar. 10, 2006). The class certification order lists a compendium of contested Kansas indirect purchaser class actions, all of which have been certified. In the subsequent *In re Vitamin Antirust Litig.*, the district court granted summary judgment on the merits to the class, awarding approximately $12 million in statutory "full consideration" treble damages, attorneys' fees, expenses, and prejudgment interest. 2006 WL 4058904 (Kan. Dist. Ct. Dec. 22, 2006). The Kansas legislature repealed the "full consideration" damages language in 2013. *See* K.S.A. 50-115, Repealed by Laws 2013, ch. 102, § 7, eff. April 18, 2013. This is the first plaintiff's antitrust judgment on the merits rendered in Kansas, and it carefully addressed collateral estoppel law.

A (b)(1) class for *damages* is appropriate. *Critchfield Physical Therapy v. Taranto Grp.*, 293 Kan. 285, 305, 263 P.3d 767, 783 (2012). A (b)(1) or (b)(2) class is considered mandatory and therefore does not require class notice. *Anderson Off. Supply v. Advanced Med. Ass'n*, 47 Kan. App. 2d 140, 162, 273 P.3d 786, 800 (2012) (citing *Wal-Mart Stores, Inc. v. Dukes*, 564 U.S. 338 (2011)). *But see Johnson v. MKA Enters., Inc.,* 353 P.3d 470 (Kan. App. 2015) (unpublished) (reversing district court's order certifying a consumer class action for failing to rigorously analyze K.S.A. 60-223(b)(1)(A) and (b)(3) requirements).

"At the class-certification stage, a plaintiff isn't even required to prove that all or most class members suffered injury." *O'Brien v. Leegin Creative Leather Prod., Inc.,* 2014 WL 1362657, at *11 (*O'Brien II*) (reversing denial of class certification because "the district court did require—that all issues be capable of resolution with common answers—[which] simply isn't the law").

In *Obrien II*, the Kansas Court of Appeals found that K.S.A. § 60-223(b)(3) provides four "matters" that are pertinent to both the predominance and superiority inquiry: "'(A) The class member's interest in individually controlling the prosecution or defense of separate actions; (B) the extent and nature of any litigation concerning the controversy already begun by or against class members; (C) the desirability or undesirability of concentrating the litigation of the claims in the particular forum; and (D) the likely difficulties in managing a class action.'" 2014 WL 1362657, at *12 (Kan. App. 2014) (quoting K.S.A. § 60-223(b)(3)). Where all class members would lose their right to proceed under the Kansas Consumer Protection Act for either actual damages or civil penalties, whichever is greater, plus attorneys' fees, a class action may not be superior to individual actions. *Johnson v. MKA Enters., Inc.*, No. 112,049, 2015 WL 4487037, at *6–7 (Kan. App. 2015) (unpublished).

c. Rule 23(e) Requirements—Settlement

i. Preliminary approval. Following federal law, preliminary approval was granted to an indirect purchaser antitrust settlement in *Williams Foods, Inc. v. Eastman Chem.*, No. 99-C-16680 (Kan. Dist. Ct. Johnson Cnty. May 3, 2001), and in *Candace Todd v. F. Hoffman-La Roche Ltd.,* No. 98-C-4574 (Kan. Dist. Ct. Wyandotte Cnty. June 8, 2001).

ii. Final approval. In *Coulter v. Anadarko Petroleum Corp.*, the Kansas Supreme Court approved a class settlement finding in an opt-out Rule 23(b)(3) type class that (1) class counsel is adequate even if some factual claims or legal theories are not pursued during the litigation but are released in the settlement; (2) the identical factual predicate rule applied in Kansas to release claims that were not actively litigated but later released; (3) class settlements can include contract modifications en masse, including go-forward provisions to resolve future disputes between the class and the defendant and arbitration provisions that prevent all or part of any future disputes returning to court; (4) a settlement class that has been previously certified in a litigated context does not warrant "heightened scrutiny" of the class certification decision; (5) the propriety of the class settlement is considered as a whole, not by consideration of parts of it in isolation; and (6) the district court's decision to approve a class settlement will be reviewed on an abuse of discretion standard including both factual findings and legal conclusions. 296 Kan. 336, 292 P.3d 289 (Jan. 11, 2013) (citing cases). Without specifically adopting a multi-factor approach for the district court to use in analyzing a class settlement as a whole to determine whether the settlement was fair, reasonable, and adequate, the Kansas Supreme Court used the Tenth Circuit four-factor approach. *Id.* at 358–59 (citing *Jones v. Nuclear Pharmacy, Inc.,* 741 F.2d 322, 324 (10th Cir. 1984)). The Kansas Supreme Court affirmed the use of these factors as there was some evidence in the record to support each of the four class settlement factors. *Id.* at 359–66; *see also Chance v. U.S. Tobacco Co.,* 2006 WL 1390382 (Seward Co. Kan. Dist. Ct. March 8, 2006) (setting forth the usual standards adopted by federal courts for final approval of a class settlement for a two-state class). *Premier Pork, Inc. v. Rhone-Poulenc, S.A.* details the usual standards adopted by federal courts for final approval of a class settlement for a Kansas class. 2006 WL 1388464 (Scott Co. Kan. Dist. Ct. Jan. 31, 2006).

iii. Incentive awards. Kansas has approved the use of both percentage of the settlement fund and flat amount as incentive awards. *See, e.g., Freebird, Inc. v. Cimarex Energy Co.*, 46 Kan. App. 2d 631, 645–46, 264 P.3d 500, 511 (2012) (applying three factor test and affirming incentive award of 1 percent of the settlement fund), *rev. denied* (June 13, 2012) and *Premier Pork, Inc. v. Rhone-*

Poulenc, S.A., 2006 WL 1388464 (Scott Co. Kan. Dist. Ct. Jan. 31, 2006) (granting $7,500 incentive award to each of the class representatives along with a final settlement approval, representing 0.92 percent of the settlement fund).

iv. Attorneys' fees. Kansas has approved the use of both percentage of the settlement fund and flat amount as incentive awards. *See, e.g., Freebird, Inc. v. Cimarex Energy Co.*, 46 Kan. App. 2d 631, 645–46, 264 P.3d 500, 511 (2012) (applying three-factor test and affirming incentive award of 1 percent of the settlement fund), *rev. denied* (June 13, 2012), and *Premier Pork, Inc. v. Rhone-Poulenc, S.A.*, 2006 WL 1388464 (Scott Co. Kan. Dist. Ct. Jan. 31, 2006) (granting $7,500 incentive award to each of the class representatives along with a final settlement approval, representing 0.92 percent of the settlement fund).

v. Cy pres award. Cy pres class settlements have been approved by Kansas courts. *See, e.g., Williams Foods, Inc. v. Eastman Chem. Co.*, 2001-2 *Trade Cases* 73,414, 2002 WL 1298887 (Kan. Dist. Ct. Johnson Cnty. Aug. 8, 2001) (granting cy pres award); *Havens Protected "C" Clamps, Inc., d/b/a Able Auto Glass v. Pilkington plc,* Case No. 99C5573 (Kan. Dist. Ct. Wyandotte Cnty. June 25, 2004) (granting cy pres award); *Bellinder v. Microsoft Corp.*, Case No. 99C17089 (Kan. Dist. Ct. Johnson Cnty. June 8, 2004) (approving a combination voucher settlement and cy pres award); *Chance v. U.S. Tobacco Co.*, 2006 WL 1390382 (Kan. Dist. Ct. Seward Cnty. March 8, 2006) (approving coupon settlement); *Premier Pork, Inc. v. Rhone-Poulenc, S.A.*, 2006 WL 1388464 (Kan. Dist. Ct. Scott Cnty. Jan. 31, 2006) (approving combination claim process and cy pres award).

vi. Special master for allocation. Special masters sometimes have been appointed to advise the court on allocation among class members when multiple state class actions are settled together in one suit. *Chance v. U.S. Tobacco Co.*, Case No. 05-CV-112 (Kan. Dist. Ct. Seward Cnty.); *Merriman v. Cabot Corp.*, Case No. 2003-CV-115 (Kan. Dist. Ct. Pratt Cnty. May 20, 2008).

3. MISCELLANEOUS COMMENTS

a. Annihilating Damages

Class actions cannot be avoided by claiming classwide damages would annihilate the defendant because "the threat of catastrophic judgment should not protect parties that violate the law on a large scale." *Critchfield Physical Therapy v. Taranto Grp.*, 293 Kan. 285, 302, 263 P.3d 767, 781 (2012).

b. Communication with Putative Class Members

There is little Kansas law on this subject. After a class is certified, class members cannot generally be contacted by a defendant on the subject matter of the certified class. *Hammond v. City of Junction City, Kansas*, 2002 WL 169370, at *3–4 (D. Kan. Jan. 23, 2002) (unpublished). But before the class is certified, courts weigh the timing and content of the communication and impose restrictions as necessary. *Rankin v. Bd. of Educ. Wichita Pub. Schs.*, 174 F.R.D. 695, 697 (D. Kan. 1997) (barring communication about the class action suit) (citing *Gulf Oil Co. v. Bernard*, 452 U.S. 89 (1981)).

An order certifying a class action and providing class notice serves a similar purpose to a pretrial order: each more closely define the claim(s) involved than what was required initially in the case under notice-pleading rules. *Smith v. Philip Morris Co.*, 50 Kan. App. 2d 535, Syl. ¶ 3, 335 P.3d 644, 659 (2014), *rev. denied* (June 29, 2015). When class certification order and class notice defined the class's claim as conspiracy to fix wholesale price of cigarettes, the certified plaintiff class could not broaden the conspiracy claim to encompass other conduct without seeking modification of the class certification order and providing new notice. *Id.*

c. Contested Class Certifications

Kansas has a long history of certifying contested class actions, particularly in royalty owner litigation and indirect purchaser litigation. *Dragon I*, 277 Kan.776, 787–88, 89 P.3d 908 (2004) (listing contested royalty owner class actions); *In re Vitamin Antitrust Litig.*, 2006 WL 4103412 (Kan. Dist. Ct. Mar. 10, 2006) (listing contested indirect purchaser antitrust class actions); *Lloyd Smith v. Kansas Gas Serv.*, Case No 01-C-29 (Kan. Dist. Ct. Reno Cnty. June 6, 2002) (contested class certified involving real property owners in Reno County, Kansas, who suffered or will suffer diminished property values as a result of natural gas releases in the Yaggy facility); *Farrar v. Mobil Oil Corp.*, 43 Kan. App. 2d 871, 234 P.3d 19, *rev. denied* (Kan. 2010) (royalty owner class certification upheld).

d. Law of the Case

In the class action context, the Supreme Court of Kansas applied the law-of-the-case doctrine to hold that when a second trial or appeal is pursued, the first decision settles the law of the case of all questions in the first appeal and reconsideration will not be given to those settled questions on the second appeal. *L. Ruth Fawcett Tr. v. Oil Producers Inc. of Kansas*, 315 Kan. 259, Syl. ¶ 4, 507 P.3d 1124, 1127 (2022) (*Fawcett II).*

e. Lead Counsel Selection

In *In re Kinder Morgan, Inc. Shareholders Litig.*, the district court, when considering the appointment of lead class counsel, stated "since law firms do not practice law, this Court is much more concerned with the professionalism and experience of the attorneys who would actually be working on this file than it is about the general reputation of a particular law firm." 2006 WL 1843560, at *1 (Kan. Dist. Ct. Shawnee Cnty. June 23, 2006) (setting forth a 17-factor test for individual attorneys).

f. Personal Jurisdiction

In *Merriman v. Crompton Corp.*, a unanimous Kansas Supreme Court resolved a number of personal jurisdiction issues in an antitrust class action: (1) plaintiff must satisfy personal jurisdiction on a *prima facie* evidentiary standard; (2) a foreign corporation applying for authority to do business in Kansas expressly consents to personal jurisdiction; (3) general jurisdiction exists over a foreign corporation doing business in Kansas with systematic and continuous contacts with Kansas; (4) specific jurisdiction exists because out-of-state antitrust conduct is a tortious act involving economic injury in-state; (5) the stream of commerce theory of personal jurisdiction which originated in product liability cases is extended to and applies in an antitrust case; and (6) conspiracy jurisdiction is constitutional since defendants purposefully participate in a conspiracy reasonably expected to reach Kansas consumers. 282 Kan. 433, 146 P.3d 162 (2006). The Court found that direct purchaser sales into the State by one or more defendants showed purposeful availment even if those direct sales could not be traced to the plaintiff's injury because the purposeful nature of the conspiracy provided the nexus between the in-state sale and the plaintiff's injury. *Id.* at 471–72.

g. Removal

i. Without CAFA. In *Havens Protected "C" Clamps, Inc., D/B/A Able Auto Glass, Sol's Glass Company, Inc. v. Pilkington PLC*, the district court denied removal of a state antitrust class action case to federal court and remanded the action to state district court stating that while the claims asserted by the class representatives appeared to exceed $75,000, the claim of at least one class member does not and so the defendants have failed to meet their burden to establish that diversity jurisdiction exists in the case. No. 00-2035-JWL, 2007 WL 382027 (D. Kan. Mar. 28, 2000). This case is largely rendered moot by the Class Action Fairness Act (CAFA) and overruled by *ExxonMobil Corp. v. Allapattah Services, Inc.*, 545 U.S. 546, 125 S. Ct. 2611, 162 L.Ed.2d 502 (2005).

In *Prime Care of Ne. KS, LLC v. Humana Ins.*, the Tenth Circuit vacated the district court's judgment and held that an amendment to state court complaint after CAFA permits removal *only* if the amendment does not relate back. 447 F.3d 1284, 1289 (10th Cir. 2006).

ii. With CAFA. Procedural Removal Issues: *Geismann v. Aestheticare, LLC,* held that a removing defendant can freely amend the grounds and evidence for removal within the 30 days after receiving notice of the removable claim, but under 28 U.S.C. §1653, new grounds are untimely and defendant can only clarify or correct, but not materially change, evidence submitted. 622 F.Supp.2d 1091, 1097–98 (D. Kan. 2008). Removal evidence must be based on personal knowledge, not on an affidavit "to the best of my knowledge" or "on information and belief." *Id.* at 1099, n.8.

Substantive Removal Issues: Amount in Controversy. To include statutory treble damages in the amount in controversy for removal, the removing party must prove "that it more likely than not [that defendant] committed willful violations of the TCPA such that the class may recover treble damages." *Geismann v. Aestheticare, LLC*, 622 F.Supp.2d 1091, 1099–1100 (D. Kan. 2008).

Eatinger v. BP Am. Prod. Co. held that when the state court plaintiff did not affirmatively assert the class claim to be less than $5 million, defendant had a "reasonable probability" burden of proof to carry to avoid remand. 524 F. Supp. 2d 1342 (D. Kan. 2007). *Freebird, Inc. v. Merit Energy Co.* held that when the state court plaintiff did affirmatively assert the class claim to be less than $5 million, that controlled because plaintiff remained "the master of her own claim," unless defendant seeking removal proves "to a legal certainty that plaintiff can recover the jurisdictional amount." 597 F. Supp. 2d 1245, 1248 (D. Kan. 2009) (quoting *Morgan v. Gay*, 471 F.3d 469, 474 (3rd Cir. 2006), and *Frederico v. Home Depot*, 507 F.3d 188 (3rd Cir. 2007), and citing *St. Paul Mercury Indem. Co. v. Red Cab Co.*, 303 U.S. 283 (1938)). A removing defendant's evidence must be "by contentions, interrogatories or admissions in state court; by calculation from the complaint's allegations[;] by reference to the plaintiff's informal estimates or settlement demands[;] or by introducing evidence, in the form of affidavits from the defendant's employees or experts, about how much it would cost to satisfy the plaintiff's demands." *Freebird*, 597 F. Supp. 2d at 1249 (quoting *McPhail v. Deere & Co.*, 529 F.3d 947, 954 (10th Cir. 2008)).

Dart Cherokee Basin Operating Co. v. Owens, a royalty underpayment putative class action filed in Kansas state court, made removal of class actions easier by abrogating Tenth Circuit authority and finding "a defendant's notice of removal need include only a plausible allegation that the amount in controversy exceeds the jurisdictional threshold" of $5 million. 135 S. Ct. 547, 554 (2014). Only when the plaintiff contests the allegation must the defendant come forward with evidence supporting its allegation. "Discovery may be taken with regard to the question" of whether the amount in controversy is met. *Id.*

h. Shareholder Derivative Suits

K.S.A. § 60-223(a) permits derivative actions by shareholders and § 60-223(b) allows class actions relating to unincorporated associations. *See Newton v. Hornblower, Inc.,* 224 Kan. 506, 582 P.2d 1136 (1978); *Richards v. Bryan,* 19 Kan. App. 2d 950, 879 P.2d 638 (1994).

i. Statute of Limitations

A federal district court determined in *In re Vitamins Antitrust Litigation* that (a) claims for violations of the Kansas antitrust laws are governed by the three-year statute of limitations set forth in K.S.A. § 60-512(2); (b) the discovery rule applies to claims for violations of the Kansas antitrust laws; and (c) the fraudulent concealment doctrine also applies to toll the statute of limitations for claims alleging violations of the Kansas antitrust laws. No. MISC99-197, 2000 WL 1524912 (D.D.C. 2000).

In *Farmland Nat'l Beef Packing Co., L.P. v. Stone Container Corp.,* the trial court received a direct purchaser opt-out case on remand from the federal MDL court and considered a statute of limitations motion to dismiss. 2006 WL 2356958 (Kan. Dist. Ct. Seward Cnty. Aug. 3, 2006). The trial court recognized cross-jurisdictional tolling based on the filing of federal court class action and found after such filing, a plaintiff's statute of limitations remains "tolled until the class action is denied or until the Plaintiff opts out of the class." Plaintiff timely opted out. *Id.* at *2 (also recognizing equitable tolling) (quoting and following *Crown, Cork and Seal, Inc. v. Parker,* 462 U.S. 345 (1983)).

In *Seaboard Corp. v. Marsh Inc.*, the Kansas Supreme Court held the Kansas savings statute, K.S.A. § 60-518, applies to save a substantially similar second filed class action in a Kansas state court even if the first filed, but now dismissed, class case that was not filed in a Kansas state court. The Court also found the six-month grace period for re-filing is triggered by the dismissal of the appeal in the first case, not from the district court dismissal date or from the date a client opts out of a class settlement. 295 Kan. 384, 284 P.3d 314 (2012). The second filed class action need not be identical to the first filed class action if it involves the same conduct, transaction, or occurrence and even if all the same defendants are not sued in the second action. Without specifically addressing class action tolling, the Kansas Supreme Court recognized its savings principles and justifications for applying the savings statute were aligned with the *American Pipe & Constr. v. Utah,* 414 U.S. 538 (1974), and *Crown Cork* principles for class action tolling in the federal system.

In *Anderson Off. Supply, Inc. v. Advanced Med. Assocs., P.A.*, the Kansas Court of Appeals held under pendent jurisdiction it could consider a merits issue during a K.S.A. § 60-223(f) interlocutory appeal and decided the four-year statute of limitations under 28 U.S.C. §1658(a) applied to a federal Telephone Consumer Protection Act claim made in Kansas state court rather than a shorter Kansas statute of limitations. 47 Kan. App. 2d 140, 273 P.3d 786 (2012).

In *Cooper Clark Foundation v. Oxy USA Inc.*, the Kansas Court of Appeals determined the statute of limitations affirmative defense would not create individual questions that predominate, because no plaintiff could have known about the deductions concealed by the defendant; as such, the statute of limitations defense created a common question capable of classwide resolution. 58 Kan. App. 2d 335, 360, 469 P.3d 1266 (2020), *petition denied* (Kan. Nov. 24, 2020). Further, this determination of possible classwide resolution was not an abuse of discretion by the district court because the evidence alleged by the plaintiffs' expert "supports an inference of equitable estoppel classwide" based on plaintiffs' reliance, and timely discovery of claims would not have been possible. *Id.* at 363; *see also L. Ruth Fawcett Trust v. Oil Producers, Inc. of Kan.*, 58 Kan. App. 2d 855,

875, 475 P.2d 1268 (2020) (holding, in a class action claim for equitable estoppel, "an inference of reliance by the Class is appropriate where circumstantial evidence [is] used to show reliance is common to the whole Class").

j. Trial

Although a class member may testify about his damages as illustrative, "the jury cannot multiply that individual loss by the number of class members to arrive at the appropriate amount of judgment to award the class." Instead, the Class must prove "total, class-wide damages, rather than the individual damages of each member of the class," usually through expert testimony. *Gilley v. Kansas Gas Serv. Co.*, 85 Kan. 24, 29, 169 P.3d 1064 (2007).

"Large in scope" class action can be tried and, although the 17-week trial was not a "perfect trial," the district court did not err in denying plaintiff's motion for new trial when the jury returned a verdict for the defendant on all counts. *City of Neodesha v. BP Corp. N. Am., Inc.,* 50 Kan. App. 2d 731, 334 P.3d 830 (2014) (certified class of all real property owners in Neodesha, Kansas tried claims for negligence, strict liability, nuisance, trespass, and statutory violation, fraudulent concealment or fraud by silence, breach of fiduciary duty, breach of contract, and declaratory and injunctive relief against defendant BP for contamination of soil and groundwater from its refinery).

SECTION 60-223 OF THE KANSAS STATUTES ANNOTATED

60-223. CLASS ACTIONS

(a) *Prerequisites*. One or more members of a class may sue or be sued as representative parties on behalf of all members only if (1) The class is so numerous that joinder of all members is impracticable; (2) there are questions of law or fact common to the class; (3) the claims or defenses of the representative parties are typical of the claims or defenses of the class; and (4) the representative parties will fairly and adequately protect the interests of the class.

(b) *Types of class actions*. A class action may be maintained if the prerequisites of subsection (a) are satisfied, and if:

(1) Prosecuting separate actions by or against individual members would create a risk of:

(A) Inconsistent or varying adjudications with respect to individual class members that would establish incompatible standards of conduct for the party opposing the class; or

(B) adjudications with respect to individual class members that as a practical matter, would be dispositive of the interests of the other members not parties to the individual adjudications or would substantially impair or impede their ability to protect their interests; or

(2) the party opposing the class has acted or refused to act on grounds that apply generally to the class, so that final injunctive relief or corresponding declaratory relief is appropriate respecting the class as a whole; or

(3) the court finds that the questions of law or fact common to class members predominate over any questions affecting only individual members, and that a class action is superior to other available methods for fairly and efficiently adjudicating the controversy. The matters pertinent to these findings include: (A) The class member's interest in individually controlling the prosecution or defense of separate actions; (B) the extent and nature of any litigation concerning the controversy already begun by or against class members; (C) the desirability or undesirability of concentrating the litigation of the claims in the particular forum; and (D) the likely difficulties in managing a class action.

(c) *Certification order; notice to class members; judgment; issues classes; subclasses.*

(1) Certification order.

(A) Time to issue. At an early practicable time after a person sues or is sued as a class representative, the court must determine by order whether to certify the action as a class action.

(B) Defining the class; appointing class counsel. An order that certifies a class action must define the class and the class claims, issues or defenses, and must appoint class counsel under subsection (g).

(C) Altering or amending the order. An order that grants or denies class certification may be altered or amended before final judgment.

(2) Notice.

(A) For subsection (b)(1) or (b)(2) classes. For any class certified under subsection (b)(1) or (b)(2), the court may direct appropriate notice to the class.

(B) For subsection (b)(3) classes. For any class certified under subsection (b)(3), the court must direct to class members the best notice that is practicable under the circumstances, including individual notice to all members who can be identified through reasonable effort. The notice must clearly and concisely state in plain, easily understood language:

(i) The nature of the action;

(ii) the definition of the class certified;

(iii) the class claims, issues or defenses;

(iv) that a class member may enter an appearance through an attorney if the member so desires;

(v) that the court will exclude from the class any member who requests exclusion;

(vi) the time and manner for requesting exclusion; and

(vii) the binding effect of a class judgment on members under subsection (c)(3).

(3) Judgment. Whether or not favorable to the class, the judgment in a class action must:

(A) In an action maintained as a class action under subsection (b)(1) or (b)(2), include and describe those whom the court finds to be class members; and

(B) in an action maintained as a class action under subsection (b)(3), include and specify or describe those to whom the notice provided in subsection (c)(2) was directed, who have not requested exclusion, and whom the court finds to be class members.

(4) Particular issues. When appropriate, an action may be brought or maintained as a class action with respect to particular issues.

(5) Subclasses. When appropriate, a class may be divided into subclasses that are each treated as a class under this section.

(d) *Conducting the action.*

(1) In general. In conducting an action under this section, the court may issue orders that:

(A) Determine the course of proceedings or prescribe measures to prevent undue repetition or complication in presenting evidence or argument;

(B) require, to protect class members and fairly conduct the action, giving appropriate notice to some or all class members of:

(i) Any step in the action;

(ii) the proposed extent of the judgment; or

(iii) the members' opportunity to signify whether they consider the representation fair and adequate, to intervene and present claims or defenses, or to otherwise come into the action;

(C) impose conditions on the representative parties or on intervenors;

(D) require that the pleadings be amended to eliminate allegations about representation of absent persons and that the action proceed accordingly; or

(E) deal with similar procedural matters.

(2) Combining and amending orders. An order under subsection (d)(1) may be altered or amended from time to time and may be combined with an order under K.S.A. 60-216, and amendments thereto.

(e) *Settlement, voluntary dismissal or compromise*. The claims, issues or defenses of a certified class may be settled, voluntarily dismissed or compromised only with the court's approval. The following procedures apply to a proposed settlement, voluntary dismissal or compromise:

(1) The court must direct notice in a reasonable manner to all class members who would be bound by the proposal;

(2) if the proposal would bind class members, the court may approve it only after a hearing and on finding that it is fair, reasonable and adequate;

(3) the parties seeking approval must file a statement identifying any agreement made in connection with the proposal;

(4) if the class action was previously certified under subsection (b)(3), the court may refuse to approve a settlement unless it affords a new opportunity to request exclusion to individual class members who had an earlier opportunity to request exclusion, but did not do so; and

(5) any class member may object to the proposal if it requires court approval under this subsection (e); the objection may be withdrawn only with the court's approval.

(f) *Appeals*. The court of appeals may permit an appeal from an order granting or denying class action certification under this section if application is made to the court within 14 days after the order is entered. An appeal does not stay proceedings in the district court unless the district judge or the court of appeals so orders.

(g) *Class counsel.*

(1) Appointing class counsel. Unless a statute provides otherwise, a court that certifies a class must appoint class counsel. In appointing class counsel, the court:

(A) Must consider:

(i) The work counsel has done in identifying or investigating potential claims in the action;

(ii) counsel's experience in handling class actions, other complex litigation and the types of claims asserted in the action;

(iii) counsel's knowledge of the applicable law; and

(iv) the resources that counsel will commit to representing the class;

(B) may consider any other matter pertinent to counsel's ability to fairly and adequately represent the interests of the class;

(C) may order potential class counsel to provide information on any subject pertinent to the appointment and to propose terms for attorney's fees and nontaxable costs;

(D) may include in the appointing order provisions about the award of attorney's fees or nontaxable costs under subsection (h); and

(E) may make further orders in connection with the appointment.

(2) Standard for appointing class counsel. When one applicant seeks appointment as class counsel, the court may appoint that applicant only if the applicant is adequate under subsection (g)(1) and (g)(4). If more than one adequate applicant seeks appointment, the court must appoint the applicant best able to represent the interests of the class.

(3) Interim counsel. The court may designate interim counsel to act on behalf of a putative class before determining whether to certify the action as a class action.

(4) Duty of class counsel. Class counsel must fairly and adequately represent the interests of the class.

(h) *Attorney's fees and nontaxable costs.* In a certified class action, the court may award reasonable attorney's fees and nontaxable costs that are authorized by law or by the parties' agreement. The following procedures apply:

(1) A claim for an award must be made by motion, subject to the provisions of this subsection, at a time the court sets. Notice of the motion must be served on all parties and, for motions by class counsel, directed to class members in a reasonable manner;

(2) a class member, or a party from whom payment is sought, may object to the motion;

(3) the court may hold a hearing and must find the facts and state its legal conclusions under subsection (a) of K.S.A. 60-252, and amendments thereto; and

(4) the court may refer issues related to the amount of the award to a special master as provided in K.S.A. 60-253, and amendments thereto.

Amended effective July 1, 1997; July 1, 2004; July 1, 2010.

Chapter author Hammons Hepner is an associate with Sharp Law LLP in Prairie Village, Kansas. Hammons's practices includes class actions and complex litigation in state and federal courts. Elly Lang helped prepare this chapter.

KENTUCKY

1. COMPARISON WITH RULE 23 OF THE FEDERAL RULES OF CIVIL PROCEDURE

Rule 23 of the Kentucky Rules of Civil Procedure is similar to Rule 23 of the Federal Rules of Civil Procedure. *Manning v. Liberty Tire Servs. of Ohio, LLC,* 577 S.W. 3d 102, 109 n.3 (Ky. Ct. App. 2019). CR 23 does include a provision similar to Fed. R. Civ. P. 23(f) at CR 23.06. Kentucky courts look to decisions under the Federal Rule for guidance. *Hensley v. Haynes Trucking*, 549 S.W.3d 430, 436 (Ky. 2018); *Nebraska Alliance Realty Co. v. Brewer*, 529 S.W.3d 307, 311 (Ky. Ct. App. 2017); *Lamar v. Office of Sheriff of Daviess County*, 669 S.W.2d 27, 31 (Ky. Ct. App. 1984); *Bellarmine College v. Hornung*, 662 S.W.2d 847, 848 (Ky. Ct. App. 1983). *See also Curtis Green & Clay Green, Inc. v. Clark*, 318 S.W.3d 98, 105 (Ky. Ct. App. 2010).

2. CASE LAW INTERPRETING RULE 23[1]

The trial court must "probe behind the pleadings," conduct a "rigorous analysis," and have evidentiary support for its conclusions when evaluating class certification. *Hensley*, 549 S.W.3d at 445–46. Additionally, the trial court must make findings of fact, which demonstrate that the requirements of Civil Rule 23.01 have been met, and issue an order outlining its findings. *Rose v. The Council for Better Education, Inc.*, 790 S.W.2d 186, 202 (Ky. 1989); *Pyro Mining Co. v. Ky. Comm'n on Human Rights*, 678 S.W.2d 393, 396 (Ky. 1984); *City of Bromley v. Smith*, 2002 Ky. App. LEXIS 1397, at *7 (Ky. Ct. App. July 5, 2002); *Brockman v. Jones,* 610 S.W.2d 943, 945 (Ky. Ct. App. 1980).

Abuse of discretion is the standard of review for trial court opinions on class certification. *Hensley*, 549 S.W.3d at 444; *Sowders v. Atkins*, 646 S.W.2d 344, 346 (Ky. 1983); *Nebraska Alliance Realty Co.*, 529 S.W.3d at 311; *Hager v. Allstate Ins. Co.*, 2009 Ky. App. Unpub. LEXIS 893, at *16 (Ky. Ct. App. Oct. 16, 2009) (unpublished); *Powell v. James Marine, Inc.*, 2015 Ky. App. Unpub. LEXIS 457, at *9 (Ky. Ct. App. June 19, 2015) (unpublished).

A court abuses its discretion if the decision was "arbitrary, unreasonable, unfair, or unsupported by sound legal principles." *Hensley*, 549 S.W.3d at 444 (quoting *Goodyear Tire & Rubber Co. v. Thompson*, 11 S.W.3d 575, 581 (Ky. 2000); *Nebraska Alliance Realty Co.*, 529 S.W.3d at 311; *Childers Oil Co. v. Reynolds*, 2012 Ky. App. Unpub. LEXIS 386, at *7 (Ky. Ct. App. May 25, 2012) (unpublished) (quoting *Commonwealth v. English*, 993 S.W.2d 941, 945 (Ky. 1999)).

Because appellants bear the burden of demonstrating that the trial court abused its discretion in denying class certification, they must articulate in their appeal the basis for finding that all the requirements of CR 23 have been met, otherwise the appeal fails, even when the trial court's denial of class

[1] Due to the relatively few class actions that have proceeded to trial in Kentucky, and because reported decisions on certification routinely discuss more than one provision of the rule, the reader is encouraged to review all cases cited, rather than focus on only those cases cited in a particular subsection.

certification failed to articulate specific findings in support of its denial. *Powell v. James Marine, Inc.*, 2015 Ky. App. Unpub. LEXIS 457 (Ky. Ct. App. June 19, 2015) (unpublished). "As long as the [trial] court's reasoning stays within the parameters of [CR] 23's requirements for certification of a class, the [trial court's] decision will not be disturbed." *Hensley*, 549 S.W.3d at 444.

A plaintiff must first establish personal standing (actual case or controversy) to assert claims before the court can evaluate adequacy of plaintiff's ability to represent putative class members under Rule 23.01–23.04. *Davis v. Dept. of Revenue of the Fin. & Admin. Cabinet*, 197 S.W.3d 557, 565 (Ky. Ct. App. 2006), *rev'd on other grounds, Dept. of Revenue of Ky. v. Davis,* 128 S. Ct. 1801 (2008). A plaintiff cannot purport to represent a class when his underlying claim lacks legal merit. *Cole v. Warren Cnty.*, 495 S.W.3d 712, 721 (Ky. Ct. App. 2015).

A trial court has subject matter jurisdiction to determine whether class certification is appropriate if it has subject matter jurisdiction over only one claim. *Hensley*, 549 S.W.3d at 439. An erroneous decision with respect to class certification does not deprive a court of jurisdiction where it otherwise has subject matter jurisdiction. *Commonwealth v. White*, 2014 Ky. Unpub. LEXIS 18 (Ky. Mar. 20, 2014) (unpublished). If a proposed class representative plaintiff does not allege damages in excess of the jurisdictional minimum, with the exception of certain specified categories of cases defined by Kentucky statute and common law, dismissal for lack of subject matter jurisdiction is proper. *Cullman Sec. Servs. v. United Propane Gas, Inc.*, 2015 Ky. App. Unpub. LEXIS 744 (Ky. Ct. App. Nov. 13, 2015) (unpublished).

Prior to the amendments to Rule 23 effective January 1, 2011, a trial court's order granting class certification was not subject to immediate appellate review on a writ of mandamus. *Garrad County Bd. of Educ. v. Jackson*, 12 S.W.3d 686 (Ky. 2000). *Accord Merck & Co., Inc. v. Combs,* 2011 Ky. Unpub. LEXIS 29, at *15 (Ky. Mar. 24, 2011) (unpublished) (noting new provision of CR 23.06 now permits immediate right of appeal).

a. Rule 23.01

i. Numerosity. Numerosity requires that the number of members in a class be so numerous as to make joinder impracticable. No precise size or number of class members automatically satisfies the numerosity requirement. *Manning,* 577 S.W.3d at 112; *Hensley*, 549 S.W.3d at 443. The showing required is that it would be extremely difficult or inconvenient to join all class members in the action. *Hensley,* 549 S.W.3d at 443. The Kentucky Court of Appeals held in *Russell County Fiscal Court v. Kelley*, 823 S.W.2d 941, 943 (Ky. Ct. App. 1991) that because the broad definition of the proposed class included multiple entities, there was sufficient evidence to support the trial court's finding that members of the class were so numerous as to make joinder impracticable. Likewise, defining a class in accordance with geographic boundaries is acceptable if evidence is presented supporting the proposed geographic boundaries of the proposed class and the alleged zone of exposure. *Manning*, 577 S.W.3d at 112. However, where a plaintiff provides no evidence of numerosity of the class he seeks to represent, certification is improper. *Sowders*, 646 S.W.2d at 346. In one instance, a Kentucky court certified a class with 74 members. *Keeton v. City of Ashland*, 883 S.W.2d 894, 895 (Ky. Ct. App. 1994). A Kentucky court has also deferred ruling on a class certification motion in light of ongoing mediation procedures with putative class members seeking refund of occupational license fee taxes and denied class certification when less than one dozen putative class members remained. *Coffman v. Ky. Dept. of Educ.*, 2004 WL 178333, at *3 (Ky. Ct. App. Jan. 30, 2004). Numerosity was not met when only 17 proposed class members were specifically identifiable. *Stanifer v. Louisville & Jefferson Cnty. Metro. Sewer Dist.*, 2023 WL 324709 (Ky. App. Jan 20, 2023) (unpublished).

See also Voorhees v. Cortona Partners, LLC, 2022 WL 17839521 (Ky. App. Dec. 22, 2022) (unpublished), *motion for discretionary rev. denied* (Mar. 15, 2023) (numerosity not met when trial court determined 54 drivers could be joined in action).

ii. Commonality. Commonality requires that there be common questions of law or fact. However, the rule does not require that all questions of law and fact be common. *Hensley*, 549 S.W.3d at 443; *Wiley v. Adkins*, 48 S.W.3d 20, 23 (Ky. 2001). In *Wiley*, the Kentucky Supreme Court affirmed certification of class alleging claim for fraud and held that there need not be a complete identity of facts as to each class member, as long as there is a common nucleus of operative facts. *Id.*

The Court of Appeals in *Hager v. Allstate Ins. Co.*, 2009 Ky. App. Unpub. LEXIS 893, at *17 (Ky. Ct. App. Oct. 16, 2009) (unpublished) adopted the Sixth Circuit's view of commonality as stated in *Powers v. Hamilton County Public Defender Comm'n*, 501 F.3d 592, 619 (6th Cir. 2007): "The commonality requirement is satisfied if there is a single factual or legal question common to the entire class." To have standing to sue as a class representative, however, the plaintiff must be a member of the proposed class and possess the same interest and suffer the same injury as the other class members. *Id.*

If a common contention is based upon the same injury to each class member, then a common question exists for purposes of class certification. *Stewart Title Guaranty Co. v. Finney*, 2012 Ky. App. Unpub. LEXIS 817, at *9–12 (Ky. Ct. App. Nov. 2, 2012) (unpublished) (finding that common question of whether title company used discounted rate schedule is not defeated by other factual dissimilarities for class certification purposes).

In a single-disaster, mass tort event, liability can often be resolved on a class basis. *Manning*, 577 S.W.3d at 114. *See also Stanifer*, 2023 WL 324709, at *3.

iii. Adequacy/Typicality. Claims and defenses are considered typical "if they arise from the same event, practice, or course of conduct that gives rise to the claims of other class members and if the claims of the representative are based on the same legal theory." *Hensley*, 549 S.W.3d at 443. The two criteria examined to determine adequacy are: (1) whether there is common interest between the representative and the unnamed class members; and (2) the representative must be willing to vigorously prosecute the action on behalf of the class through qualified counsel. *Id.* at 443. There must not be any significant interests of the representative that are antagonistic or conflicting with the unnamed class members. *Id.* Likewise, single event mass accidents based on the same course of conduct can satisfy the typicality requirement. *Manning*, 577 S.W.3d at 114–15.

Claims or defenses of the representative parties must be typical of the claims or defenses of the class, and the representative party must demonstrate that he will fairly and adequately protect the interest of the class. Plaintiff's interests must be aligned with those of the class to be typical. *Hager v. Allstate Ins. Co.*, 2009 Ky. App. Unpub. LEXIS 893, at *17 (Ky. Ct. App. Oct. 16, 2009) (unpublished) (quoting *Powers v. Hamilton County Public Defender Comm'n*, 501 F.3d 592, 618 (6th Cir. 2007)). A plaintiff's claim is typical if it arises from the same event, practice or course of conduct that gives rise to claims of the class and is based on the same legal theory. *Id. See also Childers Oil Co. v. Reynolds*, 2012 Ky. App. Unpub. LEXIS 386, at *11–14 (Ky. Ct. App. May 25, 2012) (unpublished).

"[The adequacy] prong necessarily requires an analysis of class counsel's ability to adequately protect the class's interest. 'It tests the qualifications of class counsel and the class representatives. It also aims to root out conflicts of interest within the class to ensure that all class members are fairly represented. . . .'" *Summit Med. Grp., Inc. v. Coleman*, 599 S.W.3d 445, 451 (2019) (quoting *Nebraska Alliance*, 529 S.W.3d at 315). Proposed class counsel does not satisfy the adequacy requirement when representing two proposed class representatives with materially different interests. *Compliance Advantage v. Criswell*, 2020 Ky. App. Unpub. LEXIS 346, at *15 (Ky. Ct. App. May 15, 2020) (unpublished). Proposed class representative does not satisfy the adequacy requirement when allowing a case to languish for nearly five years without advancing it beyond the pleading stage. *Summit Med. Grp., Inc. v. Coleman*, 2022 WL 1697800, at *9–10 (Ky. Ct. App. May 27, 2022) (unpublished), *motion for discretionary rev. denied* (Oct. 13, 2022).

In actions where plaintiffs seek only property damage claims and potential personal injury claims are disavowed, the adequacy of representation requirement of CR 23.01(d) is not met. *Little v. Louisville Gas and Electric Co.*, 2020 WL 7295199, at *4 (Ky. Ct. App. Dec. 11, 2020).

b. Rule 23.02(b)

Notice to class members is not required in 23.02(b) class. *Lexington-Fayette Urban County Govt. v. Hayse*, 684 S.W.2d 301, 303 (Ky. Ct. App. 1984).

c. Rule 23.02(c)

In order for common issues to predominate over individual ones, there must be a mutuality of interests among the proposed class members to warrant adjudication of their claims in one action. *Childers Oil Co. v. Reynolds*, 2012 Ky. App. Unpub. LEXIS 386, at *17 (Ky. Ct. App. May 25, 2012) (unpublished). When generalized proof will resolve some of the legal or factual issues and if those issues are more substantial than issues requiring individual proof, then the predominance inquiry is satisfied. *Stewart Title Guaranty Co. v. Finney*, 2012 Ky. App. Unpub. LEXIS 817, at *13–14 (Ky. Ct. App. Nov. 2, 2012) (unpublished). However, if the case would splinter into a series of mini-trials as to certain elements of the claims at issue, then common questions do not predominate and a class action is not the superior method of proceeding. *Merck & Co., Inc. v. Ratliff*, 2012 Ky. App. LEXIS 31, at *20–22 (Ky. Ct. App. Feb. 10, 2012), *motion for discretionary review granted.*

Where there was no evidence indicating date of execution of deed to predecessors of members of a putative defendant class, common questions of law and fact did not predominate over individual issues, and thus, the trial court erred in certifying a 23.02(c) class in a quiet title action where the central issue was the exact date the deed was executed to predecessor in title as to each putative class member. *Trabue v. Tichenor*, 695 S.W.2d 432, 435 (Ky. Ct. App. 1985).

Even in cases where there are common issues of law and fact, there can still be a multitude of individual issues that predominate over the common ones such that the predominance element is not satisfied. *Manning*, 577 S.W.3d at 117. *See also Little v. Louisville Gas and Electric Co.*, 2020 WL 7295199, at *5 (Ky. Ct. App. Dec. 11, 2020).

Although CR 23.02(c) requires that common questions of law and fact predominate, "[i]t is not necessary that there be a complete identity of facts relating to all members as long as there is a common nucleus of operative facts." *Kentucky Farm Bureau Mut. Ins. Co. v. Coates*, 2019 Ky. App. Unpub. LEXIS 762, at *9–10 (Ky. Ct. App. Oct. 25, 2019) (unpublished) (quoting *Wiley v. Adkins*, 48 S.W.3d 20, 23 (Ky. 2001)). A bifurcation of liability and damages is not an abuse of discretion. *Id.*

When plaintiff alleged a variety of injuries from blasting that occurred in different locations over a two-year period, there was insufficient uniformity regarding causation and injury to satisfy 23.02(c) requirements, even where the 23.01 requirements of commonality and typicality were found to exist. *Vance v. Whitig-Turner/Kokosing Joint Venture*, 2022 WL 3329459 (Ky. App. Aug. 12, 2022) (unpublished).

d. Rule 23.05

Court approval is necessary for dismissal or settlement of a class action. A trial court should not rubber-stamp settlement but inquire whether settlement is fair, reasonable, and adequate. Factors for a court to consider when determining whether to approve proposed class action settlement are: (1) likelihood of recovery at trial; (2) amount of discovery completed and stage of proceedings when settlement reached; (3) ability of defendants to withstand greater liability; (4) reasonableness and amount of settlement fund; (5) whether similar segments of the class are treated differently; (6) whether different segments of the class are treated similarly; (7) future expense and likely duration of litigation; (8) number of objections and nature of objections; (9) reaction of class to the settlement; (10) whether settlement was reached after arms-length negotiations; (11) experience of class counsel; and, (12) other benefits of settlement. *Doe v. Roman Catholic Diocese of Covington*, 2006 WL 250694, at *1 (Ky. Cir. Ct. Jan. 31, 2006).

e. Rule 23.08

When reviewing application for attorneys' fees in class actions, a trial court must state findings of fact and conclusions of law supporting its decision. Additionally, when deciding to award fees, the trial court must explain its "reasons for adopting a particular methodology." *College Ret. Equities Fund, Corp. v. Rink,* 2015 Ky. App. Unpub. LEXIS 30, at *7 (Ky. Ct. App. Jan. 16, 2015) (unpublished) (quoting *Moulton v. U.S. Steel Corp.*, 581 F.3d 344, 352 (6th Cir 2009)). Any fee awarded must be reasonable and authorized by law or the parties' agreement. *College Ret. Equities Fund, Corp.*, at *10. Although Kentucky appellate courts have not addressed how a trial court is to determine a reasonable fee, federal courts have used a percentage-of-fund or lodestar method. *Id.* When the record in the case supports a percentage-of-fund method it is not an abuse of the trial court's discretion to use a percentage-of-fund rather than lodestar method. *Id.* at *17–18. A trial court's fee award is reviewed under an abuse of discretion standard due to the trial court's superior understanding of the litigation. *Id.* at *24–25.

3. MISCELLANEOUS COMMENTS

a. Sums of the claims of individual class members may not be aggregated in order to meet the jurisdictional amount requirement for actions brought in Kentucky Circuit Courts. *Lamar v. Office of Sheriff of Daviess County*, 669 S.W.2d 27, 31 (Ky. Ct. App. 1984).

b. A trial court that renders class action judgment cannot predetermine whether judgment is *res judicata. Board of Educ. of Fayette County v. Taulbee*, 706 S.W.2d 827, 830 (Ky. 1986).

c. Class action is an available method for declaratory judgment regarding the validity of a tax assessment or tax rate. *Rosenbalm v. Commercial Bank of Middlesboro*, 838 S.W.2d 423, 429 (Ky. Ct. App. 1992) (quoting *Bischoff v. City of Newport*, 733 S.W.2d 762, 763 (Ky. Ct. App. 1987)). Class action relief is available with respect to taxpayer claims for refunds of alleged unconstitutional tax. *City of Bromley v. Smith*, 149 S.W.3d 403, 406 (Ky. 2004); *City of Bromley v. Smith*, 2008 WL 465829 (Ky. Ct. App. Feb. 22, 2008). Class action is appropriate in taxpayer suits seeking refunds of *ad valorem* taxes. *City of Somerset v. Bell*, 156 S.W.3d 321, 327 (Ky. Ct. App. 2005) (reversing previous decisions holding that class action not appropriate in *ad valorem* refund claims) (Buckingham, J., dissenting), *but see* amendment to KRS 134.590(3) and (6) in 2005, 2005 Ky. Acts 112, § 2, which appears to overrule *City of Somerset* by requiring "each taxpayer individually apply" to receive an *ad valorem* tax refund and bringing into question whether class action is available for *ad valorem* tax refund claims and *City of Bromley v. Smith*, 2008 WL 465829, at *2 (Ky. Ct. App. Feb. 22, 2008) (suggesting that class action relief is not available for *ad valorem* tax, but is available for challenge to constitutionality of flat-rate tax).

d. A class action is an available method for challenging the constitutionality of a state statute. *D.F., et al. v. James C. Codell, III, Sec'y of the Transp. Cabinet, et al.*, 127 S.W.3d 571, 574 (Ky. 2003).

e. An unincorporated association may be sued through use of the class action procedural rule by naming a member of the association and the association. *American Collectors Exchange, Inc. v. Kentucky State Democratic Central Exec. Comm.*, 566 S.W.2d 759, 761 (Ky. Ct. App. 1978).

f. Uncertainty as to an exact amount of damages does not preclude a recovery of damages. *Wiley v. Adkins*, 48 S.W.3d 20, 23 (Ky. 2001).

g. A writ of prohibition is unavailable to a defendant seeking immediate review of a trial court's denial of a motion to dismiss based on *res judicata* effect of final order and judgment in a previous class action settlement in N.J. *The Independent Order of Foresters v. Chauvin*, 175 S.W.3d 610, 611 (Ky. 2005).

h. A trial court judge who *sua sponte* ordered a Settlement Master appointed to oversee claims made in a sex abuse class action settlement to report details on the abusers, abuse, and victims to the state prosecutor did not act outside his jurisdiction in doing so because the order did not improperly modify the terms of the settlement agreement and did not breach any fiduciary duty owed to class members; however, the appellate court ordered that victims' names and contact information were not to be disclosed in the reports. *Doe v. Potter*, 225 S.W.3d 395, 397 (Ky. Ct. App. 2006).

i. In response to disciplinary proceedings initiated against them, attorneys representing class members in settlement of Fen-Phen litigation moved to withdraw their membership to the Kentucky Bar under terms of permanent disbarment after admitting that they failed to inform their clients of the terms of the class action settlement and of fee splitting arrangements with other attorneys, and that they sought contingency fee awards that were more than the amount provided for in their contracts with their clients. Attorneys were held to have violated numerous provisions of the Kentucky Supreme Court Rules, including failure to hold their clients' property separate from their own. Motions were granted and attorneys were ordered to pay all fees associated with disciplinary proceedings. *Gallion v. Ky. Bar Ass'n*, 266 S.W.3d 802 (Ky. 2008); *Cunningham v. Ky. Bar Ass'n*, 266 S.W.3d 808 (Ky. 2008). *See also Ky. Bar Ass'n v. Mills*, 318 S.W.3d 89 (Ky. 2010); *Ky. Bar Ass'n v. Helmers*, 353 S.W.3d 599 (Ky. 2011); *Ky. Bar Ass'n v. Chesley*, 393 S.W.3d 584 (Ky. 2013). A former judge was disbarred in connection with same proceedings after finding that *ex parte* meeting with plaintiffs' attorneys resulted in entry of an order approving fees and expenses that contained numerous false statements. *Ky. Bar Ass'n v. Bamberger*, 354 S.W.3d 576 (Ky. 2011).

j. A request for medical monitoring under negligence and strict liability causes of action without a showing of present physical injury was dismissed for failure to state a claim upon which relief can be granted for plaintiff and putative class. *Wood v. Wyeth-Ayerst Labs.*, 82 S.W.3d 849 (Ky. 2002).

k. Despite losing on the merits of individual claim at the trial court, a litigant has standing to appeal the trial court's earlier denial of class certification. *Hager v. Allstate Ins. Co.*, 2009

Ky. App. Unpub. LEXIS 893, at *12–13 (Ky. Ct. App. Oct. 16, 2009) (unpublished).

l. A question of whether to issue notice when class certification is denied is discretionary with the trial court. *Hager v. Allstate Ins. Co.*, 2009 Ky. App. Unpub. LEXIS 893, at *29 (Ky. Ct. App. Oct. 16, 2009) (unpublished). In exercising its discretion, the trial court should examine what evidence exists of reliance on the pending action and prejudice to the putative class members, as well as cost and judicial economy of any proposed notice. *Id.* Evidence of prejudice includes whether putative class members had actual notice of the action and reasonably relied on the action to protect their interests. *Id.* at *29–30.

m. A named plaintiff must be a member of the class with standing to sue to pursue an action as a class action. *Dunn v. Kentucky Farm Bureau Mutual Ins. Co.,* 2009 Ky. App. Unpub. LEXIS 422, at *8 (Ky. Ct. App. Mar. 27, 2009) (unpublished) (citing *Schlesinger v. Reservists Committee to Stop the War,* 418 U.S. 208, 94 S. Ct. 2925, 41 L. Ed. 706 (1974)). It is not error to dismiss a proposed class complaint and deny effort to file an amended complaint prior to "class discovery" when the named plaintiff does not have a justiciable cause of action. *Swearingen v. Hagyard Davidson McGee Assocs., PLLC*, 641 S.W.3d 186, 196 (Ky. Ct. App. 2022).

n. A class action ban in an arbitration clause is enforceable when challenge to unconscionability of such a provision is based solely on the fact that the dispute involves a large number of *de minimis* claims. *Schnuerle v. Insight Communications Co., L.P.*, 376 S.W.3d 561 (Ky. 2012) (upholding class action waiver provision in arbitration clause governed by Federal Arbitration Act) (citing *AT&T Mobility LLC v. Concepcion*, 563 U.S. 333, 131 S. Ct. 1740, 179 L. Ed. 2d 742 (2011)). Class action plaintiffs who filed suit against an accounting firm were compelled to arbitrate the class claims pursuant to the arbitration provision contained in the engagement letter. *Ernst & Young v. Clark*, 323 S.W.3d 682 (Ky. 2010), *cert. denied*, 131 S. Ct. 1478 (2011).

o. A medical malpractice claim against a physician based on the physician's prescription of pharmaceutical Redux was covered by release in a class action settlement releasing all claims against physicians related solely to their prescription of Redux, even though the release did not release the physicians from independent negligence and culpable conduct, where expert supporting claim did not have any opinions regarding the standard of care that were independent of the prescription of Redux. *Edwards v. Baehler*, 2011 Ky. App. Unpub. LEXIS 112 (Ky. Ct. App. Feb. 18, 2011) (unpublished).

p. When an attorney voluntarily withdraws from a contingency fee case without good cause, the claim for attorney's fee is unwarranted. *Bonar v. Waite, Schneider, Bayless & Chesley Co.,* 373 S.W.3d 419 (Ky. 2012).

q. Although there is not a published Kentucky decision on point, it appears that Kentucky courts would not apply the tolling of federal claims as contemplated in *American Pipe & Constr. Co. v. Utah*, 414 U.S. 538 (1974), cross-jurisdictionally to toll Kentucky state law claims. *Easterly v. Metropolitan Life Ins. Co.*, 2009 Ky. App. Unpub. LEXIS 428 (Ky. Ct. App. Feb. 13, 2009) (unpublished).

r. Kentucky's wage and hour statute, KRS 337.385, does not create a special statutory proceeding, and thus CR 23 is a viable procedural mechanism by which to pursue class actions or representative claims brought pursuant to that statute. *McCann v. Sullivan Univ. Sys.*, 528 S.W.3d 331 (Ky. Aug. 24, 2017).

s. A settlement class member is collaterally estopped from bringing a malpractice action against class counsel after final order and appeal of class action settlement because opportunity to object to the settlement and adequacy of class counsel's representation was available prior to court approval of the class settlement. *Simpson v. Chesley*, 2013 Ky. App. Unpub. LEXIS 934 (Ky. Ct. App. Nov. 27, 2013) (unpublished).

t. A trial court abuses its discretion when it certifies a class where none of the named plaintiffs' claims encompass any of the claims of the subclasses certified. *Bridal Warehouse, Inc. v. Witak*, 2017 Ky. App. Unpub. LEXIS 833, at *19–20 (Ky. Ct. App. 2017) (unpublished).

u. Trial court's use of proposed findings of fact and conclusions of law tendered by plaintiff when ruling on class certification is not an abuse of discretion. *Kentucky Farm Bureau Mut. Ins. Co. v. Coates*, 2019 Ky. App. Unpub. LEXIS 762, at *4–5 (Ky. Ct. App. Oct. 25, 2019) (unpublished).

v. An attorney-client relationship does not exist until a class has been certified and the time for opting out by potential class members has expired. *Doe v. Golden & Walters,* 2019 Ky. App. Unpub. LEXIS 635, at *21 (citing ABA Formal Op. 07-445 (April 11, 2007)) (unpublished).

w. Class defined as "[a]ll real property owners in the Commonwealth of Kentucky on whose real property Defendants committed trespass, nuisance and/or negligent property damage due to the unlawful use of Rainbow Weed Killer pesticides" is an impermissible fail-safe class because it bases class membership on the merits of each individual's claim. *AT&T Corp. v. Feltner*, 2021 WL 2753980, at *3 (Ky. Ct. App. July 2, 2021). Trial court's certification of class was permissible, but four subclasses defined as fail-safe were impermissible, resulting in affirmation of class certification but reversal and remand as to the subclasses for further consideration. *St. Stephen's Cemetery Ass'n v. Seaton*, 2022 WL 16842445 (Ky. App. Nov. 10, 2022) (unpublished), *motion for discretionary rev. denied* (Mar. 15, 2023).

x. Certification of a class is improper when order fails to identify findings of fact that support the requirements of typicality and adequacy of representation mandated by CR 23.01, as well as which provision of CR 23.02 is applicable. *AT&T Corp. v. Feltner*, 2023 WL 6522337 (Ky. Ct. App. Oct. 6, 2023) (unpublished).

y. Trial court did not abuse its discretion in certifying a class of former UK HealthCare patients alleging that collection efforts taken with respect to unpaid medical bill balances were improper because an identical pattern of conduct was at issue. *University of Kentucky v. Long*, 2024 WL 874779 (Ky. Ct. App. March 1, 2024) (unpublished). The issue of sovereign immunity is a threshold question that impacts the ability of the lower court to hear the case, and thus is an appropriate question to be reviewed during a CR 23.06 interlocutory appeal of a class certification decision. *Long, et al. v. Commonwealth of Kentucky, Dept. of Rev., et al.*, __ S.W.3d __, 2025 WL 2388442 (Ky. Aug. 14, 2025).

z. If trial court properly granted summary judgment on individual claims, it is not an abuse of discretion for the trial court to then deny motion for class certification as moot. *Gardner v. GEICO Gen. Ins. Co.*, 2023 WL 3398188 (Ky. Ct. App. May 12, 2023) (unpublished).

TEXT OF RULE 23 OF THE KENTUCKY RULES OF CIVIL PROCEDURE

CR 23 CLASS ACTIONS

CR 23.01 Prerequisites to class action

Subject to the provisions of Rule 23.02, one or more members of a class may sue or be sued as representative parties on behalf of all only if (a) the class is so numerous that joinder of all members is impracticable, (b) there are questions of law or fact common to the class, (c) the claims or defenses of the representative parties are typical of the claims or defenses of the class, and (d) the representative parties will fairly and adequately protect the interests of the class.

HISTORY: Amended eff. 1-1-78; prior amendment eff. 7-1-69; adopted eff. 7-1-53.

CR 23.02 Class actions maintainable

An action may be maintained as a class action if the prerequisites of Rule 23.01 are satisfied, and in addition:

(a) The prosecution of separate actions by or against individual members of the class would create a risk of

(i) inconsistent or varying adjudications with respect to individual members of the class which would establish incompatible standards of conduct for the party opposing the class, or,

(ii) adjudications with respect to individual members of the class which would as a practical matter be dispositive of the interests of the other members not parties to the adjudications or substantially impair or impede their ability to protect their interests; or

(b) the party opposing the class has acted or refused to act on grounds generally applicable to the class, thereby making appropriate final injunctive relief or corresponding declaratory relief with respect to the class as a whole; or

(c) the court finds that the questions of law or fact common to the members of the class predominate over any questions affecting only individual members, and that a class action is superior to other available methods for the fair and efficient adjudication of the controversy. The matters pertinent to the findings include: (i) the interest of members of the class in individually controlling the prosecution or defense of separate actions; (ii) the extent and nature of any litigation concerning the controversy already commenced by or against members of the class; (iii) the desirability or undesirability of concentrating the litigation of the claims in the particular forum; (iv) the difficulties likely to be encountered in the management of a class action.

HISTORY: Amended eff. 1-1-78; adopted eff. 7-1-69.

CR 23.03 Determination by order whether class action to be maintained; notice; judgment; actions conducted partially as class actions

(1) At an early practicable time after a person sues or is sued as a class representative, the court must determine by order whether to certify the action as a class action.

(2) An order that certifies a class action must define the class and the class claims, issues, or defenses, and must appoint class counsel under CR 23.07.

(3) An order that grants or denies class certification may be altered or amended before final judgment.

(4) If an appeal is taken from the Certification Order, as authorized by CR 23.06, notice shall not be given until a final non-appealable order has decided the issue. If no appeal is taken the court, after 11 days from the entry of its Certification Order, shall give notice as follows:

(a) For any class certified under CR 23.02(a) or 23.02(b), the court may direct appropriate notice to the class.

(b) For any class certified under CR 23.02(c), the court must direct to class members the best notice that is practicable under the circumstances, including individual notice to all members who can be identified through reasonable effort. The notice must clearly and concisely state in plain, easily understood language:

(i) the nature of the action;

(ii) the definition of the class certified;

(iii) the class claims, issues, or defenses;

(iv) that a class member may enter an appearance through an attorney if the member so desires;

(v) that the court will exclude from the class any member who requests exclusion by a specified date;

(vi) the time and manner for requesting exclusion; and

(vii) the binding effect of a class judgment, whether favorable or not, on members under CR 23.03.

(5) Whether or not favorable to the class, the judgment in a class action must:

(a) for any class certified under CR 23.02(a) or (b) include and describe those whom the court finds to be class members; and

(b) for any class certified under CR 23.02(c) include and specify or describe those to whom the CR 23.02(c) notice was directed, who have not requested exclusion, and whom the court finds to be class members.

(6) When appropriate, an action may be brought or maintained as a class action with respect to particular issues.

(7) When appropriate, a class may be divided into subclasses that are each treated as a class under this rule.

HISTORY: Amended by Order 2010-09, eff. 1-1-11; prior amendment eff. 1-1-78; adopted eff. 7-1-69.

CR 23.04 Orders in conduct of actions

(1) In conducting an action under CR 23.03, the court may issue orders that:

(a) determine the course of proceedings or prescribe measures to prevent undue repetition or complication in presenting evidence or argument;

(b) require—to protect certified class members and fairly conduct the action—giving appropriate notice to some or all class members of:

(i) any step in the action

(ii) the proposed extent of the judgment; or

(iii) the members' opportunity to signify whether they consider the representation fair and adequate, to intervene and present claims or defenses, or to otherwise come into this action.

(c) impose conditions on the representative parties or on intervenors;

(d) require that the pleadings be amended to eliminate allegations about representation of absent persons and that the action proceed accordingly; or

(e) deal with similar procedural matters.

(2) An order under CR 23.04(1) may be altered or amended from time to time and may be combined with an order under Rule 16.

HISTORY: Amended by Order 2010-09, eff. 1-1-11; prior amendment eff. 1-1-78; adopted eff. 7-1-69.

CR 23.05 Dismissal or compromise

The claims, issues, or defenses of a certified class may be settled, or defenses of a certified class may be settled, voluntarily dismissed, or compromised only with the court's approval. The following procedures apply to a proposed settlement, voluntary dismissal, or compromise:

(1) The court must direct notice in a reasonable manner to all class members who would be bound by the proposal.

(2) If the proposal would bind class members, the court may approve it only after a hearing and on finding that it is fair, reasonable, and adequate.

(3) The parties seeking approval must file a statement identifying any agreement made in connection with the proposal.

(4) If the class action was previously certified under CR 23.02(c), the court may refuse to approve a settlement unless it affords a new opportunity to request exclusion to individual class members who had an earlier opportunity to request exclusion but did not do so.

(5) Any class member may object to the proposal if it requires court approval under this subdivision (5); the objection may be withdrawn only with the court's approval upon a showing of good cause.

(6) Disposition of Residual Funds.

(a) "Residual Funds" are funds that remain after the payment of all approved class member claims, expenses, litigation costs, attorneys' fees, and other court-approved disbursements to implement the relief granted. Nothing in this rule is intended to limit the parties to class action from agreeing to, or the trial court from approving, a settlement that does not create residual funds.

(b) Any order entering a judgment or approving a proposed compromise of a class action certified under this rule that establishes a process for identifying and compensating members of the class shall provide for the disbursement of residual funds. In matters where the claims process has been exhausted and residual funds remain, not less than twenty-five percent (25%) of the residual funds shall be disbursed to the Civil Rule 23 Account maintained by the Kentucky IOLTA Fund Board of Trustees pursuant to Supreme Court Rule 3.830(20). Such funds are to be allocated to the Kentucky Civil Legal Aid Organizations based upon the current poverty formula established by the Legal Services Corporation to support activities and programs that promote access to the civil justice system for low-income residents of Kentucky.

HISTORY: Amended by Order 2013-14, eff. 3-6-14; prior amendments eff. 1-1-14 (Order 2013-14); 1-1-11 (Order 2010-09); adopted 7-1-69.

CR 23.06 Appeals

An order granting or denying class action certification is appealable within 10 days after the order is entered. An appeal does not stay proceedings in the circuit court unless the circuit judge or the Court of Appeals so orders. The matter shall be expedited in the appellate courts.

HISTORY: Adopted by Order 2010-09, eff. 1-1-11.

CR 23.07 Class counsel

(1) Appointing Class Counsel. Unless a statute provides otherwise, a court that certifies a class must appoint class counsel. In appointing class counsel, the court:

(a) must consider:

(i) the work counsel has done in identifying or investigating potential claims in the action;

(ii) counsel's experience in handling class actions, other complex litigation, and the types of claims asserted in the action;

(iii) counsel's knowledge of the applicable law; and

(iv) the resources that counsel will commit to representing the class;

(b) may consider any other matter pertinent to counsel's ability to fairly and adequately represent the interests of the class;

(c) may order potential class counsel to provide information on any subject pertinent to the appointment and to propose terms for attorney's fees and nontaxable costs;

(d) may include in the appointing order provisions about the award of attorney's fees or nontaxable costs under CR 23.08; and

(e) may make further orders in connection with the appointment.

(2) When one applicant seeks appointment as class counsel, the court may appoint that applicant only if the applicant is adequate under CR 23.07(1) and (4). If more than one adequate applicant seeks appointment, the court must appoint the applicant best able to represent the interests of the class.

(3) The court may designate interim counsel to act on behalf of a putative class before determining whether to certify the action as a class action.

(4) Class counsel must fairly and adequately represent the interests of the class.

HISTORY: Adopted by Order 2010-09, eff. 1-1-11.

CR 23.08 Attorney's fees and nontaxable costs

In a certified class action the court shall approve or award reasonable attorney's fees and nontaxable costs that are authorized by law or by the parties' agreement. The following procedures apply:

(1) A claim for an award must be made by motion to be heard at a time the court sets. Notice of the motion must be served on all parties and, for motions by class counsel, directed to class members in a reasonable manner.

(2) A class member, or a party from whom payment is sought, may object to the motion.

(3) The court may hold a hearing and must find the facts and state its legal conclusions under CR 52.01.

(4) The court may refer issues related to the amount of the award to a Commissioner, as provided in CR 53.

HISTORY: Adopted by Order 2010-09, eff. 1-1-11.

Chapter author Marjorie A. Farris is Firm Chair at Stites & Harbison, PLLC, in Louisville, Kentucky. Ms. Farris practices in the area of complex litigation and is co-chair of the firm's class action practice team.

LOUISIANA

1. COMPARISON WITH RULE 23 OF THE FEDERAL RULES OF CIVIL PROCEDURE

For the most part, Louisiana's current class action scheme, which was amended and effective July 1997, is the same as Rule 23 of the Federal Rules of Civil Procedure. *See* La. C.C.P. art. 591; *Doe v. S. Gyms, LLC*, 112 So. 3d 822, 828 (La. 2013). The former procedures for class actions in Louisiana were also very similar to federal law, although the language of the statute was different. *See Ford v. Murphy Oil U.S.A., Inc.*, 795 So. 2d 419 (La. App. 4 Cir. 2001); *McCastle v. Rollins Environmental Services*, 456 So. 2d 612 (La. 1984); *Stevens v. Board of Trustees*, 309 So. 2d 144 (La. 1975); *Williams v. State of Louisiana*, 350 So. 2d 131 (La. 1977). *Stevens* essentially allowed Fed. R. Civ. P. 23(b)(3) class actions in Louisiana. *Ford* relies in part on the ruling in *Amchem Products, Inc. v. Windsor*, 521 U.S. 591 (1997). The case of *Duhe v. Texaco*, 779 So.2d 1070 (La. App. 3 Cir. 2001), arose under the new law. The trial court certified a class relying in part on cases decided under the old law, and the defendant appealed. In affirming the certification of the class, the appellate court held that although Louisiana had changed its law, much of its prior jurisprudence still applied. For a recent discussion of Louisiana's class action law, *see Price v. Martin*, 79 So. 3d 960 (La. 2011).

2. INTERPRETIVE CASE LAW

An appellate court reviews a district court's factual findings regarding class certification under a manifest error standard; however, the "ultimate decision of whether or not to certify the class is reviewed under the abuse of discretion standard." *Dupree v. Lafayette Inc. Co*, 51 So. 3d 673, 680 (La. 2010). Although Louisiana utilized Fed. R. Civ. P. 23 as a guide in amending its class action statutes, there are some provisions of Louisiana's law that are different and/or which there is no analog in Fed. R. Civ. P. 23. Those differences are as follows:

a. La. C.C.P. art. 591

Louisiana Code of Civil Procedure Article 591(A)(5) has no counterpart in Fed. R. Civ. P. 23. La. C.C.P. art. 591(A)(5) provides that one or more class members may sue or be sued on behalf of the class as long as "[t]he class is or may be defined objectively in terms of ascertainable criteria, such that the court may determine the constituency of the class for purposes of conclusiveness of any judgment that may be rendered in the case. . . ." *See Brantley v. City of Gretna*, 347 So. 3d 1147, 1166 (La. App. 5 Cir. 2022) (the fact that members of a class cannot be objectively defined until the ultimate issue of liability is determined will not prevent certification of the class); *see also Sutton Steel & Supply Inc. v. Bell South Mobility, Inc.*, 875 So. 2d 1062 (La. App. 3 Cir. 2004) (finding that because a trial court can redefine the class before a decision on the merits of the common issues, appellate courts often permit certification despite a finding that the definition is inadequate for one reason or another); *Watters v. Department of Social Services*, 929 So. 2d 267 (La. App. 4 Cir. 2006) (unless a decision on the merits has been rendered, an appellate court, on finding the class definition to be vague, may remand the matter to the trial court to allow any inadequacies to be resolved).

In addition to the factors provided for in Fed. R. Civ. P. 23(b)(3), for a finding that "questions of law or fact common to the members of the class predominate over any questions affecting only individual members, and that a class action is superior to other available methods for the fair and efficient adjudication of the controversy," Louisiana has two other factors that are pertinent for such a finding. The additional factors are "[t]he practical ability of individual class members to pursue their claims without class certification" and "[t]he extent to which relief plausibly demanded on behalf of or against the class, including the vindication of such public policies or legal rights as may be implicated, justifies the costs and burdens of class litigation." La. C.C.P. art. 591(B)(3)(e) and (f). Presumably, the first provision deals with those cases in which the individual claims are large enough to be pursued independently, and the second provision deals with those cases in which the individual claims are so small as to make administration of the class impractical. It should be noted that Louisiana courts favor class actions when they involve vindication of the rights of person with negative value lawsuits. *Duhe*, *supra*, 779 So. 2d at 1086; *Clark v. Trus Joist MacMillian*, 836 So. 2d 454 (La. App. 3 Cir. 2002). For a discussion of the procedural steps a trial court must undertake in determining whether to certify a class, *see Baker v. PHC-Minden, L.P.*, 167 So. 3d 528 (La. 2015).

La. C.C.P. art. 591(B) has an additional, significant provision in Subparagraph (4) which provides that "[t]he parties to a settlement [may] request certification under Subparagraph B(3) for the purposes of settlement, even though the requirements of Subparagraph B(3) might not otherwise be met." *See Pollard v. Alpha Technical*, 102 So. 3d 71, 86 (La. App. 4 Cir. 2011) (holding that "satisfaction of all elements of La. C.C.P. art. 591(A) is a prerequisite for an action to be maintained as a settlement class under La. C.C.P. art. 591(B)(4), even though the requirements of La. C.C.P. art. 591(B)(3) need not be met"). Under this provision, settlement classes will presumably be more favored and more easily approved in a Louisiana court than in a federal court. *See Amchem, supra*, 521 U.S. 591; *White v. General Motors*, 718 So. 2d 480 (La. App. 1 Cir. 1998).

Finally, La. C.C.P. art. 591(C) is the last portion of this Article without a counterpart in Fed. R. Civ. P. 23. La. C.C.P. art. 591(C) provides that "[c]ertification shall not be for the purpose of adjudicating claims or defenses dependent for their resolution on proof individual to a member of the class. However, following certification, the court shall retain jurisdiction over claims or defenses dependent for their resolution on proof individual to a member of the class." *See Price v. Martin*, 79 So. 3d 960 (La. 2011). Thus, it follows that "varying degrees of damages . . . [or] class members [that] must individually prove their right to recover" does not prevent the class from being certified. *Brantley v. City of Gretna*, 347 So. 3d 1147, 1159–60, 1167 (La. App. 5 Cir. 2022); *Doe v. Univ. Healthcare Sys., L.L.C.*, 145 So. 3d 557 (La. App. 4 Cir. 2014).

b. La. C.C.P. art. 592

Louisiana Code of Civil Procedure Article 592(A)(1) is counterpart to Fed. R. Civ. P. 23(c)(1). However, while Fed. R. Civ. P. 23(c)(1) provides that an order certifying a class be issued "[a]t an early practicable time," La. C.C.P. art. 592(A)(1) mandates that the proponent of the class file a motion to certify the action as a class action "[w]ithin ninety days after service on all adverse parties of the initial pleading demanding relief on behalf of or against a class." The ninety days can be "extended by stipulation of the parties or on motion for good cause shown." La. C.C.P. art. 592 (A)(1). This statute has been applied literally. *See Sellers v. El Paso Indus. Energy, LP,* 8 So. 3d 723 (La. App. 5 Cir. 2009). Nevertheless, plaintiff is only required to file one motion for class certification within ninety days of the filing of the initial pleading, even if the initial pleading has been amended. *Jones v. Capitol Enterprises, Inc.*, 89 So. 3d 474, 493 (La. App. 4 Cir. 2012).

La. C.C.P. art. 592(A)(2) has no analog in Fed. R. Civ. P. 23. If a proponent fails to file a certification motion within the time delays of La. C.C.P. art. 591(A)(1), any party may file a notice of said failure. After the notice is filed and a hearing is held, the demand for class relief may be stricken. La. C.C.P. art. 592(A)(2). If stricken, the "action may continue between the named parties alone" and the demand for class relief may be "reinstated upon a showing of good cause by the proponent." La. C.C.P. art. 592(A)(2). If a party fails to move for class certification within the time delays, the trial court is given great discretion as to whether the class action petition should be dismissed, and its decision will not be overturned on appeal absent an abuse of discretion. *Crader v. Pinnacle Entertainment, Inc.*, 931 So. 2d 535 (La. App. 3 Cir. 2006); *Sellers*, 8 So. 3d at 728. Notably, dismissal of a class action for failing to move for certification is not considered a "ruling on the merits" and res judicata will not preclude a separate class action by new class representatives. *See Crooks v. LCS Corrections Services, Inc.*, 934 So. 2d 64 (La. App. 1 Cir. 2006).

La. C.C.P. art. 592(A)(3)(a) provides that no motion to certify a class action shall be granted before a hearing on the motion, which shall be held as soon as practicable, but not before (1) all adverse parties have been served with the pleading that demands class relief, made an appearance, or the proponent has made a diligent effort to perfect service, and (2) the parties have had adequate time to conduct discovery on class certification issues. *See Feldheim v. SI-SIFH Corp.*, 715 So. 2d 168 (La. App. 5 Cir. 1998) (parties are allowed time for discovery on pre-certification issues).

Pursuant to La. C.C.P. art. 592(A)(3)(b), at the hearing, the proponent of the class has the burden to satisfy all requirements in La. C.C.P. art. 591.

La. C.C.P. art. 592(A)(3)(c) requires a class action be certified if the court finds that the action is appropriate. However, if the court finds the action is not appropriate as a class action, the action will proceed between the named parties. Either way, such a ruling is subject to appeal and a party may request the court give its findings of fact and reasons for judgment in writing within ten days after notice of the order or judgment. In addition, La. C.C.P. art. 592(A)(3)(d) allows the court, at any time before a decision on the merits of the common issues, to "alter, amend or recall its initial ruling on certification and may enlarge, restrict, or otherwise redefine the constituency of the class or the issues to be maintained in the class action." *See Richardson v. Am. Cyanamid Co.,* 757 So. 2d 135 (La. App. 5 Cir. 2000) (a class action may be decertified at any time before there is a ruling on the merits of the class claims, even if the initial class certification was appealed and affirmed by the appellate court); *Bourgeois v. A.P. Green Indus.*, 39 So. 3d 654 (La. App. 5 Cir. 2010) (denial of class certification is not necessarily res judicata with regard to a newly defined class).

La. C.C.P. art. 592(B)(1–2) specifies the requirements of a notice. The first sentence is identical to the first sentence of Fed. R. Civ. P. 23(c)(2). From there, the statute is different and provides that notice be given as soon as practical after certification but early enough "that a delay . . . for the class members to exercise an option to be excluded from the class will have expired before commencement of the trial on the merits of the common issues." The notice shall include, among the requirements of Fed. R. Civ. P. 23(c)(2)(B), general description of the action, the names and addresses of the representative parties, a statement advising class members that they may be excluded or that they may be required to take further action, address of counsel, and any other information the court finds necessary. La. C.C.P. art. 592(B)(2). Finally, La. C.C.P. art. 592(B)(3) governs who bears the expenses for the notice. *See Orrill v. AIG, Inc.*, 38 So. 3d 457 (La. App. 4 Cir. 2010) (finding settlement notice substantively and procedurally inadequate as over 8,000 notices were returned and no further efforts made to notify these individuals such as a publication in a newspaper or a website should be created).

La. C.C.P. art. 592(E) is analogous to Fed. R. Civ. P. 23(d), however, Subparagraph (E) provides more context as to the specific "similar procedural matters" the court is permitted to order such as "case management orders providing for consolidation, duties of counsel, . . . scheduling of and the delays for pre-certification and post-certification discovery, and other matters which affect the general order of proceedings." *Adams v. CSX Railroad*, 904 So. 2d 13 (La. App. 4 Cir. 2005) (upholding the trial court's order regarding the conduct of trials and the limitation of discovery in a class action where additional trials were required to determine damages).

c. La. C.C.P. art. 593

Louisiana Code of Civil Procedure Article 593 simply provides the venue restrictions for class actions. La. C.C.P. art. 593(A) mandates that an action brought *on behalf of* a class be brought in a parish of proper venue as to the defendant. In *Tramonte v. Daimler Chrysler Corp.*, 760 So. 2d 1192 (La. App. 5 Cir. 2000), the defendant argued that this venue provision limited venue to the defendant's primary place of business. On appeal, the court disagreed and held that Louisiana's supplemental venue articles applied such that venue was also proper in the parish where the contract giving rise to the class action was executed. Similarly, in *Cacamo v. Liberty Mutual Fire Ins. Co.*, 764 So. 2d 41 (La. 2000), the Louisiana Supreme Court held that venue for class actions is to be determined through reference to Louisiana's supplemental venue articles. *See also Thomas v. Mobil Oil Corporation*, 843 So. 2d 504 (La. App. 4 Cir. 2003) (finding venue proper in any parish in which putative class members were injured).

Likewise, La. C.C.P. art. 593(B) provides that an action brought *against* a class be brought in a parish of proper venue as to any of the defendant class members. Interestingly, this Subparagraph makes no mention of an action brought against multiple defendants who are not in a defendant class. *See Strasner v. State of Louisiana*, 762 So. 2d 1206 (La. App. 1 Cir. 2000) (holding that a class action against a group of defendants could not be cumulated in one venue where the defendants were neither jointly or solidarily liable).

d. La. C.C.P. art. 594

Louisiana Code of Civil Procedure Article 594 applies to dismissals or compromises. Subparagraphs (A) and (B) are essentially the same as Fed. R. Civ. P. 23(e). However, La. C.C.P. art. 594(C)–(E), which have no counterpart in Fed. R. Civ. P. 23, provide, respectively, that the court retains authority to review and approve amounts paid as attorney fees pursuant to the settlement, absent an agreement to the contrary, any agreement that provides for attorney fees is subject to judicial approval, and if the settlement requires the creation of a settlement fund, the court can approve the settlement, as long as it is fair, reasonable, and adequate for the class, and issue a final judgment without the prior qualification of representatives of incompetents and absentees. *Ursin v. New Orleans Aviation Board*, 902 So. 2d 508 (La. App. 5 Cir. 2005) (holding that the terms of a settlement are binding and res judicata as to all class members, unless the members opt out of the settlement); *Vekic v. Shell Pipeline Co., L.P.*, 33 So. 3d 182 (La. App. 4 Cir. 2009) (dismissing plaintiff's case in state court on the basis that the plaintiff failed to opt out of the federal court class action settlement). The trial court's approval of a proposed settlement may not be overturned on appeal absent an abuse of discretion. *Orrill, supra*, 38 So. 3d 457.

e. La. C.C.P. art. 595

Louisiana Code of Civil Procedure Article 595 grants the court authority to require plaintiff to furnish security and award expenses to the representative parties. There is no counterpart in Fed. R. Civ. P. 23. Specifically, La. C.C.P. art. 595(A) permits the court to award the parties their "reasonable expenses of litigation, including attorney's fees, when as a result of the class action a fund is made available, or a recovery or compromise is had which is beneficial, to the class." *See Vela v. Plaquemines Parish Gov't*, 811 So. 2d 1263 (La. App. 4 Cir. 2002) (approving attorney's fee award equal to 30 percent of the judgment value); *cf. Thibodeaux v. Conoco Philips Co.*, 952 So. 2d 912 (La. App. 3 Cir. 2007) (any agreement among counsel for attorney's fees and expenses must still comply with Rule 1.5(e) of the Rules of Professional Conduct); *see also Etter v. Hibernia Corp.*, 952 So. 2d 782 (La. App. 2007), (approving attorney's fees as they were negotiated after the settlement had already been agreed upon between the parties); *In re Ungar*, 25 So. 3d 101, 110 (La. 2009) (suspending attorney from the practice of law for failing to advise his clients concerning settlement of a putative class action "in order to facilitate collection of an excessive fee"). In addition, according to La. C.C.P. art. 595(B), any time prior to judgment, but after a contradictory motion, the court can order the plaintiff in a class action to provide security for court costs, which the defendant may later be required to pay.

f. La. C.C.P. art. 596

Louisiana Code of Civil Procedure Article 596 addresses prescription and suspension of class actions. Particularly, the Article provides that the prescription on the "claims arising out of the transactions or occurrences described in a petition brought on behalf of a class is suspended on the filing of the petition as to all members of the class as defined or described therein." If suspended, prescription will continue thirty days after (1) the class member's election form is submitted as to the member who is electing to be excluded from the class, (2) mailing or publication of notice that the class has been modified so as to exclude him pursuant to La. C.C.P. art. 592, or (3) mailing or publication of notice that the class has been dismissed, the demand for relief has been stricken, the court has denied the motion to certify the class, or the court has vacated a prior order certifying the class. La. C.C.P. art. 596(A). Prescription in Louisiana is similar to the statute of limitation in other states. It is significant that this Article uses the word "suspend" rather than "interrupt." If prescription is interrupted, it begins anew, but if suspended, it simply stops and then continues at the point where it stopped. *See Bailey ex rel. Brown v. ExxonMobil Corp.*, 102 So. 3d 167, 176 (La. App. 5 Cir. 2012), (discussing distinction between interruption of prescription and suspension of prescription in the context of Article 596).

The suspension of prescription by a timely-filed class action petition under Article 596 depends on the venue of original filing of the class. If the class is first filed in a Louisiana state court, then prescription is suspended for putative class members and does not begin running against them until one of the three triggers enumerated in Article 596(A) occurs. *Smith v. Transport Services Co. of Illinois*, 148 So. 3d 903 (La. 2014). However, if the class is filed directly in federal court, then there is no "cross jurisdictional tolling" that suspends prescription under Article 596 for later-filed actions in state court. *Quinn v. Louisiana Property Ins. Corp.*, 118 So. 3d 1011, 1020 (La. 2012); *see also Duckworth v. La. Farm Bureau Mut. Ins. Co.*, 125 So. 3d 1057 (La. 2012) (analyzing Article 596 and holding that the filing of an individual lawsuit prior to a ruling on class certification does not forfeit the benefit of suspending prescription).

g. La. C.C.P. art. 597

Finally, Louisiana has a separate article that pertains to a judgment's effect. La. C.C.P. art. 597 provides that "[a] definitive judgment on the merits rendered in a class action concludes all members of the class, whether joined in the action or not, if the members who were joined as parties fairly insured adequate representation of all members of the class." *See Elfer v. Murphy Oil, U.S.A., Inc.*, 811 So. 2d 892 (La. 2002) (granting exceptions of res judicata and *lis pendens* in a class action filed by putative class members to a previously filed class action—regardless of whether they were joined as part of the original class action or not); *Aisola v. Louisiana Citizens Property Ins. Corp.*, 180 So. 3d 266 (La. 2015) (same); *Alonzo v. State, Department of Natural Resources*, 884 So. 2d 634 (La. App. 4 Cir. 2004) (holding that res judicata does not apply to persons who opt out of a class and thus they cannot benefit from the ruling in that class action). For cases rejecting res judicata exceptions, *see Morales v. The Parish of Jefferson, et al.*, 54 So. 3d 669 (La. App. 5 Cir. 2010), and *Estate of Raven v. Lincoln Nat. Life Ins. Co.,* 51 So. 3d 147 (La. App. 5 Cir. 2010).

3. MISCELLANEOUS COMMENTS

a. Arbitration

Louisiana's highest court has adopted a liberal policy favoring arbitration and found that a presumption of arbitrability exists. *Aguillard v. Auction Management Corp.*, 908 So. 2d 1 (La. 2005). However, not all arbitration clauses in a standard form contract are enforceable. *See Sutton Steel & Supply v. BellSouth Mobility, Inc., supra*, 971 So. 2d 1257 (La. App. 3 Cir. 2007) (finding the arbitration provisions of a contract adhesionary and therefore unenforceable); *cf. Hanlon v. Monsanto AG Products, LLC,* 124 So. 3d 535 (La. App. 2 Cir. 2013) (holding that the arbitration clause was not adhesionary); *see also Gunderson v. F.A. Richard & Associates, Inc.*, 937 So. 2d 916 (La. App. 3 Cir. 2006) (finding that some of plaintiffs' claims against certain defendants in a putative class action had to proceed to arbitration under the binding arbitration clause).

b. Intervention

Third persons that are seeking to intervene in pending consolidated actions are not permitted to hijack the original plaintiff's claims and convert them into class actions. *Leger v. Kent*, 817 So. 2d 305 (La. App. 4 Cir. 2002). Thus, such a result can only be accomplished by amending the petition, not by intervening and asserting class action. *Id.* Nevertheless, an adjudication of the original actions will not have a res judicata effect upon the intervenor's claims. *Phillips v. G & H Seed Co., Inc.*, 32 So. 3d 1134 (La. App. 3 Cir. 2010); *see also Opelousas General Hospital Auth. v. Fairpay Solutions, Inc.*, 118 So. 3d 1269 (La. App. 3 Cir. 2013) (holding that a third party seeking to intervene in an action cannot object to a settlement if they are not a class member or cannot intervene because they have no justiciable interest in the resolution).

c. No Class Actions Under the Louisiana Unfair Trade Practices Act

Violations of the Louisiana Unfair Trade Practices Act may not be pursued in a class action. Specifically, La. R.S. 51:1409(A) provides that persons who suffer losses because of an unfair trade practice "may bring an action individually but not in a representative capacity." *See also Indest-Guidry, Ltd. v. Key Office Equipment, Inc.*, 997 So. 2d 796, 810 (La. App. 3 Cir. 2008).

d. *Cy Pres* Awards

Cavalier v. Mobil Oil Corp., 898 So. 2d 584 (La. App. 4 Cir. 2005), is the first Louisiana case to deal with a *cy pres* distribution of a class action settlement. *Cavalier* holds that such a distribution must parallel the intended use of the funds as nearly as possible. Thus, where a class action settlement was for chemical emissions to a particular geographical area, any *cy pres* distribution must be to that same geographical area. *See also Adams v. CSX Railroads*, 80 So. 3d 1160 (La. App. 4 Cir. 2011).

e. Reliance

Reliance issues have been held to defeat predominance on claims of fraud and misrepresentation. *Chiarella v. Sprint Spectrum LP,* 921 So. 2d 106 (La. App. 4 Cir. 2005). For an example of where reliance was found classwide, *see Scott v. American Tobacco Co., Inc*., 949 So. 2d 1266 (La. App. 2007).

f. Numerosity

Courts must conduct a rigorous analysis of the numerosity requirement because the procedural vehicle of a class action is an exception to the rule that parties must be named. *Doe v. Southern Gyms, LLC*, 112 So. 3d 822 (La. 2013). Such an analysis includes evaluating, quantifying, and weighing the La. C.C.P. art. 591(A) factors "to determine to what extent the class action would in each instance promote or detract from the goals of effectuating substantive law, judicial efficiency, and individual fairness." *Id.* at 829; *Brantley v. City of Gretna*, 347 So. 3d 1147, 1158 (La. App. 5 Cir. 2022); *see also Doe v. Univ. Healthcare Sys., L.L.C.,* 145 So. 3d 557 (La. App. 4 Cir. 2014) (finding no abuse of discretion in the trial court's ruling declining to certify a class because the plaintiffs failed to meet the requirements of, *inter alia*, numerosity, but consolidated the cases for coordinated discovery, pre-trial motions, and trial on the basis of judicial efficiency). More than mere allegations of numerosity is needed; proponent of class must have evidence in the record as to this factor, and 15 potential additional putative class members is insufficient to meet this requirement. *See Sanders v. City of Winnfield*, 321 So. 3d 1072, 1085 (La. App. 2 Cir. 2021).

There is no magic number of class members necessary to render joinder impractical and satisfy the numerosity requirement. *Doe v. Southern Gyms,* 112 So. 3d at 830–31; *Lillie v. Stanford Trust Co.*, 235 So. 3d 1139, 1150 (La. App. 1 Cir. 2017). For a discussion of the factors to consider in a numerosity analysis, *see Bagot v. James Holdings, LLC,* 235 So. 3d 1330 (La. App. 5 Cir. 2017).

g. Class Representative

The wife of an attorney for the class is not a proper class representative. *See Guidry v. Dow Chem. Co.*, 108 So. 3d 755 (La. 2013). Further, "the inability to secure but one class representative . . . militates against the commonality requirement." *Albe v. City of New Orleans,* 174 So. 3d 212, 221 (La. App. 4 Cir. 2015).

h. Money Damages in a "(B)(1) Class"

Under La. C.C.P. art. 591(B)(1), Louisiana courts generally do not certify classes when plaintiffs are only seeking monetary damages. *Dupree, supra*, 51 So. 3d at 681. However, in rare situations, such classes have been certified. *Marshall v. Air Liquide-Big Three, Inc.*, 2 So. 3d 541 (La. App. 4 Cir.

2008); *Watters v. Dep't of Social Services*, 929 So. 2d 267 (La. App. 4 Cir. 2006).

i. Taxes

The Louisiana Board of Tax Appeals has jurisdiction to certify and hear a class action. *See St. Martin v. State*, 25 So. 3d 736 (La. 2009).

j. *Lis Pendens;* Multiple, Overlapping Actions

Unnamed, putative class members are "parties" to an action for the purpose of La. C.C.P. art. 531 and are barred by *lis pendens* from bringing a second action that involves the same transaction or occurrence between the same parties in the same capacities. *Saulsbury Industries, Inc. v. Cabot Corp.*, 348 So. 3d 1267, 1268 (La. 2022); *Aisola v. La. Prop. Ins. Corp.,* 180 So. 3d 266 (La. 2015). When two or more actions requesting the certification of a class pursuant to Art. 591 are filed in different Louisiana courts regarding the same transaction or occurrence at the same location and, if certified, would encompass one or more of the same plaintiffs against one or more of the same defendants, the defendant may have the actions transferred to where the transaction or occurrence occurred. La. C.C.P. art. 593.1(A). Likewise, when two or more actions requesting the certification of a class pursuant to Art. 591 are filed in different Louisiana courts regarding the multiple related transactions or occurrences in different locations and, if certified, would encompass one or more of the same plaintiffs against one or more of the same defendants, the defendant may have the actions transferred to the court where the first suit was brought. La. C.C.P. art. 593.1(B).

k. Objectively Definable Class

"The parties seeking certification must be able to establish a definable group of aggrieved persons based on objective criteria derived from the operative facts of the case." *Albe*, 174 So. 3d at 222. Supposition that some members of the class are aggrieved is not sufficient. *Id.*

l. Judicial Interest

Where class certification is denied, judicial interest begins to run from the original date of the filing of the class action petition, not the later date that a former putative class member may file her own action. *Jones v. American Home Assurance Co.,* 317 So. 3d 498 (La. App. 4 Cir. 2018).

m. Special Masters

The costs of a court-appointed special master can be taxed as costs. However, the special master may not charge as part of those taxed-costs expenses the special master incurs to hire a law firm to defend the special master's appointment. The special master shoulders those costs in the interest of maintaining his position as special master, not to benefit the class. La. R.S. 13:4165; *Billieson v. City of New Orleans,* 224 So. 3d 1091 (La. App. 2017).

ARTICLES 591-597 OF THE LOUISIANA CODE OF CIVIL PROCEDURE

ART. 591. PREREQUISITES; MAINTAINABLE CLASS ACTIONS

A. One or more members of a class may sue or be sued as representative parties on behalf of all, only if:

(1) The class is so numerous that joinder of all members is impracticable.

(2) There are questions of law or fact common to the class.

(3) The claims or defenses of the representative parties are typical of the claims or defenses of the class.

(4) The representative parties will fairly and adequately protect the interests of the class.

(5) The class is or may be defined objectively in terms of ascertainable criteria, such that the court may determine the constituency of the class for purposes of the conclusiveness of any judgment that may be rendered in the case. This prerequisite shall not be satisfied if it is necessary for the court to inquire into the merits of each potential class member's cause of action to determine whether an individual falls within the defined class.

B. An action may be maintained as a class action only if all of the prerequisites of Paragraph A of this Article are satisfied, and in addition:

(1) The prosecution of separate actions by or against individual members of the class would create a risk of:

(a) Inconsistent or varying adjudications with respect to individual members of the class which would establish incompatible standards of conduct for the party opposing the class, or

(b) Adjudications with respect to individual members of the class which would as a practical matter be dispositive of the interests of the other members not parties to the adjudications or substantially impair or impede their ability to protect their interests; or

(2) The party opposing the class has acted or refused to act on grounds generally applicable to the class, thereby making appropriate final injunctive relief or corresponding declaratory relief with respect to the class as a whole; or

(3) The court finds that the questions of law or fact common to the members of the class predominate over any questions affecting only individual members, and that a class action is superior to other available methods for the fair and efficient adjudication of the controversy. The matters pertinent to these findings include:

(a) The interest of the members of the class in individually controlling the prosecution or defense of separate actions;

(b) The extent and nature of any litigation concerning the controversy already commenced by or against members of the class;

(c) The desirability or undesirability of concentrating the litigation in the particular forum;

(d) The difficulties likely to be encountered in the management of a class action;

(e) The practical ability of individual class members to pursue their claims without class certification;

(f) The extent to which the relief plausibly demanded on behalf of or against the class, including the vindication of such public policies or legal rights as may be implicated, justifies the costs and burdens of class litigation; or

(4) The parties to a settlement request certification under Subparagraph B(3) for purposes of settlement, even though the requirements of Subparagraph B(3) might not otherwise be met.

C. Certification shall not be for the purpose of adjudicating claims or defenses dependent for their resolution on proof individual to a member of the class. However, following certification, the court shall retain jurisdiction over claims or defenses dependent for their resolution on proof individual to a member of the class.

ART. 592. CERTIFICATION PROCEDURE; NOTICE; JUDGMENT; AND ORDERS

A. (1) Within ninety days after service on all adverse parties of the initial pleading demanding relief on behalf of or against a class, the proponent of the class shall file a motion to certify the action as a class action. The delay for filing the motion may be extended by stipulation of the parties or on motion for good cause shown.

(2) If the proponent fails to file a motion for certification within the delay allowed by Subparagraph (1) of this Paragraph, any adverse party may file a notice of the failure to move for certification. On the filing of such a notice and after hearing thereon, the demand for class relief may be stricken. If the demand for class relief is stricken, the action may continue between the named parties alone. A demand for class relief stricken under this Subparagraph may be reinstated upon a showing of good cause by the proponent.

(3) (a) No motion to certify an action as a class action shall be granted prior to a hearing on the motion. Such hearing shall be held as soon as practicable, but in no event until after both of the following have occurred:

(i) All named adverse parties have been served with the pleading containing the demand for class relief or have made an appearance or, with respect to unserved defendants who have not appeared, the proponent of the class has made due and diligent effort to perfect service of such pleading;

(ii) The parties have had a reasonable opportunity to obtain discovery on class certification issues, on such terms and conditions as the court deems necessary, which may include expert witness testimony or evidence. The admissibility of expert witness testimony or evidence for class certification purposes shall also be governed by Article 1425(F), although the court in its discretion may change the deadlines for filing or hearing a motion as set forth in Article 1425(F) provided such deadlines are prior to or contemporaneous with the class certification hearing.

(b) At the hearing on the motion to certify an action as a class action, the proponent of the class shall have the burden of proof to establish that all requirements of Article 591 have been satisfied

(c) If the court finds that the action should be maintained as a class action, it shall certify the action accordingly. If the court finds that the action should not be maintained as a class action, the action may continue between the named parties. In either event, the court shall give in writing its findings of fact and reasons for judgment provided a request is made not later than ten days after notice of the order or judgment. A suspensive or devolutive appeal, as provided in Article 2081, et seq., may be taken as a matter of right from an order or judgment provided for herein.

(d) In the process of class certification, or at any time thereafter before a decision on the merits of the common issues, the court may alter, amend, or recall its initial ruling on certification and may enlarge, restrict, or otherwise redefine the constituency of the class or the issues to be maintained in the class action.

B. (1) In any class action maintained under Article 591(B)(3), the court shall direct to the members of the class the best notice practicable under the circumstances, including individual notice to all members who can be identified through reasonable effort. This notice, however given, shall be given as soon as practicable after certification, but in any event early enough that a delay provided for the class members to exercise an option to be excluded from the class will have expired before commencement of the trial on the merits of the common issues.

(2) The notice required by Subparagraph (1) of this Paragraph shall include:

(a) A general description of the action, including the relief sought, and the names and addresses of the representative parties, or, where appropriate, the identity and location of the source from which the names and addresses of the representative parties can be obtained.

(b) A statement of the right of the person to be excluded from the action by submitting an election form, including the manner and time for exercising the election.

(c) A statement that the judgment, whether favorable or not, will include all members who do not request exclusion.

(d) A statement that any member who does not request exclusion may, if the member desires, enter an appearance through counsel at that member's expense.

(e) A statement advising the class member that the member may be required to take further action as the court deems necessary, such as submitting a proof of claim in order to participate in any recovery had by the class.

(f) A general description of any counterclaim brought against the class.

(g) The address of counsel to whom inquiries may be directed.

(h) Any other information that the court deems appropriate.

(3) Unless the parties agree otherwise, the proponents of the class shall bear the expense of the notification required by this Paragraph. The court may require the party opposing the class to cooperate in securing the names and addresses of the persons within the class defined by the court for the purpose of providing individual notice, but any additional costs reasonably incurred by the party opposing the class in complying with this order shall be paid by the proponent of the class. The court may tax all or part of the expenses incurred for notification costs.

C. The judgment in an action maintained as a class action under Article 591(B)(1) or (2), whether or not favorable to the class, shall include and describe those whom the court finds to be members of the class. The judgment in an action maintained as a class action under Article 591(B)(3), whether or not favorable to the class, shall include and specify or describe those to whom the notice provided in Paragraph B of this Article was directed, and who have not requested exclusion, and whom the court finds to be members of the class.

D. When appropriate an action may be brought or maintained as a class action with respect to particular issues, or a class may be divided into subclasses and each subclass treated as a class, and the provisions of Article 591 and this Article shall then be construed and applied accordingly.

E. In the conduct of actions to which Article 591 and this Article apply, the court may make any of the following appropriate orders:

(1) Determining the course of proceedings or prescribing measures to prevent undue repetition or complication in the presentation of evidence or argument.

(2) Requiring, for the protection of the members of the class or otherwise for the fair conduct of the action, that notice be given in such manner as the court may direct to members of the class of any step in the action, or of the proposed extent of the judgment, or of the opportunity of members to signify whether they consider the representation fair and adequate, to intervene and present claims or defenses, or otherwise to come into the action.

(3) Imposing conditions on the representative parties or on intervenors.

(4) Requiring that the pleadings be amended to eliminate therefrom allegations as to representation of absent persons, and that the action proceed accordingly.

(5) Dealing with similar procedural matters, including but not limited to case management orders providing for consolidation, duties of counsel, the extent and the scheduling of and the delays for pre-certification and post-certification discovery, and other matters which affect the general order of proceedings; however, the court shall not order the class-wide trial of issues dependent for their resolution on proof individual to a member of the class, including but not limited to the causation of the member's injuries, the amount of the member's special or general damages, the individual knowledge or

reliance of the member, or the applicability to the member of individual claims or defenses.

(6) Any of the orders provided in this Paragraph may be combined with an order pursuant to Article 1551, and may be altered or amended as may be desirable from time to time.

ART. 593. VENUE

A. An action brought on behalf of a class shall be brought in a parish of proper venue as to the defendant.

B. An action brought against a class shall be brought in a parish of proper venue as to any member of the class named as a defendant.

ART. 593.1. CLASS ACTION; LIS PENDENS

A. When two or more actions requesting the certification of a class pursuant to Article 591 are filed in two or more Louisiana courts regarding the same transaction or occurrence at the same location, and such classes, if certified, would encompass one or more of the same plaintiffs suing in the same capacities against one or more of the same defendants in the same capacities, the defendant may, by excepting as provided in Article 925, have all such actions transferred to the district court where the transaction or occurrence occurred.

B. When two or more actions requesting the certification of a class pursuant to Article 591 are filed in two or more Louisiana courts regarding multiple related transactions or occurrences in different locations and such classes, if certified, would encompass one or more of the same plaintiffs suing in the same capacities against one or more of the same defendants in the same capacities, the defendant may, by excepting as provided in Article 925, have all such actions transferred to the district court where the first suit was brought.

ART. 593.2. CLASS ACTIONS; FORUM NON CONVENIENS

Notwithstanding the provisions of Article 123, within thirty days of the certification of a class under Article 591 by a different Louisiana court regarding the same transaction or occurrence and encompassing one or more of the same plaintiffs suing in the same capacities against one or more of the same defendants in the same capacities, any court where a related putative class action is pending may, upon contradictory motion, in the interests of justice and for good cause shown, transfer the putative class action to the district where the related action has been certified.

ART. 594. DISMISSAL OR COMPROMISE

A. (1) An action previously certified as a class action shall not be dismissed or compromised without the approval of the court exercising jurisdiction over the action.

(2) Notice of the proposed dismissal of an action previously certified as a class action shall be provided to all members of the class, together with the terms of any proposed compromise that the named parties have entered into. Notice shall be given in such manner as the court directs.

B. After notice of the proposed compromise has been provided to the members of the class, the court shall order a hearing to determine whether the proposed compromise is fair, reasonable, and adequate for the class. At such hearing, all parties to the action, including members of the class, shall be permitted an opportunity to be heard.

C. The court shall retain the authority to review and approve any amount paid as attorney fees pursuant to the compromise of a class action, notwithstanding any agreement to the contrary.

D. Any agreement entered by the parties to a class action that provides for the payment of attorney fees is subject to judicial approval.

E. If the terms of the proposed compromise provide for the adjudged creation of a settlement fund to be disbursed to and among members of the class in accordance with the terms thereof, the court having jurisdiction over the class action is empowered to approve the compromise settlement of the class action as a whole and issue a final judgment accordingly, following a finding that the compromise is fair, reasonable, and adequate for the class, and to order the distribution of the settlement fund accordingly, without the necessity of prior qualification of representatives of minors, interdicts, successions, or other incompetents or absentees, or prior approval of the terms of the settlement or the distribution thereof by another court; provided, that in such cases the court having jurisdiction over the class action shall include in the orders of settlement and distribution of the settlement fund appropriate provisions to ensure that all funds adjudicated to or for the benefit of such incompetents, successions, or absentees are placed in appropriate safekeeping pending the completion of appointment, qualification, and administrative procedures otherwise applicable in this code to the interests and property of incompetents, successions, and absentees.

ART. 595. AWARD OF EXPENSES OF LITIGATION; SECURITY FOR COSTS

A. The court may allow the representative parties their reasonable expenses of litigation, including attorney's fees, when as a result of the class action a fund is made available, or a recovery or compromise is had which is beneficial, to the class.

B. The court, on contradictory motion at any stage of the proceeding in the trial court prior to judgment, may require the plaintiff in a class action to furnish security for the court costs which a defendant may be compelled to pay. This security for costs may be increased or decreased by the court, on contradictory motion of any interested party, on a showing that the security furnished has become inadequate or excessive.

ART. 596. PRESCRIPTION; SUSPENSION

A. Liberative prescription on the claims arising out of the transactions or occurrences described in a petition brought on behalf of a class is suspended on the filing of the petition as to all members of the class as defined or described therein. Prescription which has been suspended as provided herein, begins to run again:

(1) As to any person electing to be excluded from the class, from the submission of that person's election form;

(2) As to any person excluded from the class pursuant to Article 592, thirty days after mailing or other delivery or publication of a notice to such person that the class has been restricted or otherwise redefined so as to exclude him; or

(3) As to all members, thirty days after mailing or other delivery or *publication* of a notice to the class that the action has been dismissed, that the demand for class relief has been stricken pursuant to Article 592, or that the court has denied a motion to certify the class, or has vacated a previous order certifying the class.

B. The time periods in Subparagraphs (A)(2) and (3) of this Article commence upon the expiration of the delay for taking an appeal if there is no appeal, or when an appeal becomes final and definitive. The notice required by Subparagraphs (A)(2) and (3) of this Article shall contain a statement of the delay periods provided herein.

ART. 597. EFFECT OF JUDGMENT

A definitive judgment on the merits rendered in a class action concludes all members of the class, whether joined in the action or not, if the members who were joined as parties fairly insured adequate representation of all members of the class.

This chapter was prepared by Pearl Robertson and Emma Kingsdorf Schwab of Irpin Avin & Hawkins.

MAINE

1. COMPARISON WITH RULE 23 OF THE FEDERAL RULES OF CIVIL PROCEDURE

Maine Rule of Civil Procedure 23 was modeled after Federal Rule of Procedure 23 but has not been amended to reflect the 1998 and 2003 amendments to the Federal Rule.

2. CASE LAW INTERPRETING MAINE RULE 23

a. The significant written opinions by Maine state judges addressing certification under Maine Rule 23 are the opinions of the trial courts in the following cases

In *Karofsky v. Abbott Laboratories*, CV951009 (Me. Super. Ct., Cum. Cty., Oct. 15, 1997), the court denied a motion to certify a Rule 23(b)(3) class in an antitrust action brought on behalf of indirect, consumer purchasers of brand name prescription drugs. In this lengthy opinion by Justice Saufley, who later became the Chief Justice of Maine's highest court, the court found that the need to establish injury in fact to each class member would likely raise numerous individual issues that would tend to predominate and preclude effective management of the proceedings.

In *Millett v. Atlantic Richfield Co.*, CV-98-555 (Me. Super. Ct., Cum. Cty., Mar. 2, 2000), the court denied a motion to certify 23(b)(2) and 23(b)(3) classes in litigation by private well-owners against alleged promoters of MTBE, a gasoline additive. The court found that claim gerrymandering rendered the action inappropriate, that requests for damages rendered (b)(2) certification inappropriate, and that individual issues would predominate and preclude effective management of the action.

In *Jordan v. MBNA Marketing Systems, Inc.*, CV-00-020 (Me. Super. Ct., Waldo Cty., Aug. 3, 2001), the court denied class certification to employees seeking wage adjustments because substantial variations in each plaintiff's circumstances did not allow a mechanical calculation of damages. In addition, plaintiffs were unable to meet the requirements of either Rule 23(b)(2) because some class members would benefit only from monetary relief or Rule 23(b)(3) because the predominance of individual issues meant a class action would not achieve economies of time, effort, and expense and would not promote uniformity of decision as to similarly situated persons without sacrificing procedural fairness. The court again denied class certification in *Jordan v. MBNA Marketing Sys., Inc.*, CV-00-020 (Me. Super. Ct., Waldo Cty., June 14, 2002), despite a revised class definition because the requirement of typicality under Rule 23(a)(3) could not be met with the wide variety of facts affecting each potential class member's damages.

In *Flippo v. L.L. Bean, Inc.*, CV-00-446 (Me. Super. Ct., Cum. Cty., Apr. 9, 2002), the court certified, under Rule 23(b)(3), a class of all users of L.L. Bean discount coupons who were assessed sales tax on the amount of the purchase prior to deduction of the value of the coupon. The court examined state tax law and determined that, apart from the issue of damages, the principal issues in the cases were common issues shared by all class members. In *Flippo v. L.L. Bean, Inc.*, 2006 ME 62, 898 A.2d 942, the Law Court affirmed in part and vacated in part, but did not address the issue of class action certification.

In *Melnick v. Microsoft Corp.*, CV-99-709 (Me. Super. Ct., Cum. Cty., Aug. 24, 2001), the court followed *Karofsky, supra,* denying class certification in this indirect purchaser antitrust action because the plaintiffs could not meet Rule 23(b) requirements.

In *Pease v. Cherryfield Foods, Inc.*, CV-00-015 (Me. Super. Ct., Knox Cty., Jan. 24, 2001), the court addressed a request to certify a class of wild blueberry growers in a state antitrust action based on an allegation that defendants conspired to fix the field price paid to growers. The court initially denied class certification due solely to a lack of typicality, despite the "strong assumption that claims of representative parties will be typical of absent class members if a common scheme relative to all members of a class is alleged," because the named plaintiffs did not reflect the substantial differences among all commercial Maine blueberry growers. Subsequently, after the addition of new plaintiffs, the court certified a class of commercial growers who grew wild blueberries that were sold directly or indirectly to defendants. *Decision and Order*, dated July 31, 2002. Following a trial and judgment for the plaintiffs, the case was settled before the Law Court was able to opine on any aspects of the class certification.

In *Gerard v. DeCoster*, CV-01-134 (Me. Super. Ct., And. Cty., Jan. 11, 2002), the court without discussion of Rule 23, implicitly found that all of the requirements of subpart (a) and (b)(3) were met by the class of truck drivers and former truck drivers seeking wage adjustments.

In *Everest v. Leviton Manufacturing Co.*, CV-040-612 (Me. Super. Ct., Cum. Cty., June 5, 2007), the court denied class certification under Rules 23(b)(1)(A) and 23(b)(3) to consumer purchasers of electrical outlets proceeding under Maine's Unfair Trade Practices Act, 5 M.R.S.A. §§ 205-A *et seq.*, and on an unjust enrichment cause of action. The court denied certification under Rule 23(b)(1)(A) after concluding that that the defendant would not be held to incompatible standards of conduct merely because separate lawsuits might result in divergent findings of liability. The court also questioned whether Rule 23(b)(1)(A) could ever be used to certify a class when the party adverse to the class does not seek this Rule's protection. The court's rejection of certification under Rule 23(b)(3) was based on its conclusion that because both causes of action involved fact-specific elements, such as reliance and causation, the plaintiffs could not satisfy Rule 23(b)(3)'s predominance and superior method of adjudication requirements.

In *Stenzel v. Dell, Inc.*, CV-03-323 (Me. Super. Ct., Cum. Cty., Mar. 10, 2004), although the court was not called on to apply Maine Rule 23, it took up the issue of the enforceability of an arbitration clause that prohibits class litigation. The case arose out of a consumer contract for purchase of a computer. The court ruled that the plain language of the contract prohibited arbitration of claims on behalf of anyone other than the complaining customer and that the contract was one of adhesion. Applying Texas law, the court held that the clause was enforceable and dismissed the action. In *Stenzel v. Dell, Inc.*, 2005 Me. 37, 870 A.2d 133, the Law Court, also applying Texas law, affirmed.

In *Sabina v. J.P. Morgan Chase Bank, N.A.*, 2015 WL 1756027 (Super. Ct. Cumberland Cty., April 13, 2015), the Court denied a motion to strike class allegations, determining that class certification issues were better addressed through an opposition to a motion for class certification. In so ruling, the Court noted the potential legitimacy of an argument to the effect that the class definition constituted a fail safe class.

In *Manirakiza v. Mayhew*, 2016 WL 4151513 (Me. Super. Ct., Ken. Cty., June 28, 2016), the Court denied for lack of superiority a request for certification of a group of persons denied food supplement benefits by the state on the basis of their status as non-citizens. The Court determined that class certification was "unnecessary" because of the "facts and procedural posture" of the case. Though the Court's exact rationale is not clear, the state had argued that class certification was not necessary because, if it lost, it would apply the Court's interpretation uniformly. It appears that certification was only sought and analyzed under subsection (b)(3).

In *Southwick v. Health Affiliates Maine, LLC*, 2019 WL 6703171 (Me. Super. Ct. Cumberland Cty., Sept. 30, 2019), Justice Horton, who has since joined the Law Court, denied a motion for certification of a class of employees asserting their employer's compensation policy violated Maine wage payment laws. The court reasoned that the central issue in the action was the legality of the compensation policy and determined that it would be appropriate to address this legal issue at the certification stage to save the costs and judicial resources of class litigation. Concluding that the compensation policy did not violate Maine law, the court declined to certify the class because the factual issues relevant to each class member—whether each individual class member agreed to and understood the compensation policy—lacked commonality.

In *Milwood v. Camden National Bank*, 2021 WL 5167685 (Me. B.C.D. Sept. 28, 2021), the court granted summary judgment in favor of the defendant when the plaintiff—a member of a settlement class in an earlier class action against the same defendant regarding bank fees—brought a new putative class action against the bank arising from related fee practices. The court determined that release terms of the earlier class settlement barred a new class action over the bank's overdraft fees and practices. When the plaintiff urged the court to adopt the "identical factual predicate" test to determine whether the class action was barred on res judicata grounds, the court declined to do so, explaining that it was the release from the earlier settlement that was controlling and, further, Maine has not yet adopted the test.

In *Deane v. Central Maine Power Co.*, 2022 WL 1539587 (Me. B.C.D. April 4, 2022), the Business and Consumer Court denied class certification under Rules 23(a) and 23(b) in an intentional infliction of emotional distress (IIED) case. The Court concluded that the injury and causation elements of IIED require individualized inquiries and foreclose finding commonality or typicality under Rules 23(a)(2) and (a)(3). The Court then went on to address predominance under Rule 23(b)(3) and, noting the overlap with the commonality analysis under Rule 23(a)(2), again found that the legal and factual questions at issue in the case were not common to the class. Even if the questions were common, however, the Court seemed to doubt whether common questions could ever predominate over individual ones in the context of an IIED claim. Moreover, the Court declined the plaintiffs' proposed methods for administering the adjudication, concluding that the difficulties inherent to managing an IIED class action could not be overcome through bifurcating the proceedings.

In *Stewart v. The University of Maine System,* 2023 WL 6282733 (Me. Super. Ct. Cumberland Cty., Sept. 18, 2023), the court granted class certification in a COVID-19 tuition refund class action brought on behalf of all students in the University of Maine system (which manages seven schools throughout the state). The court certified three classes: (1) a tuition class comprising all students who paid tuition but had classes moved to online only learning; (2) a "system fee" class comprising students who paid certain student fees related to on-campus activities but were prohibited from attending campus; and (3) an "Orono fee class" of students slated to attend the University of Orono who were charged recreation center fees but prohibited from attending campus. The only remaining claim at class certification was for breach of contract. The court found that an implied contract applicable to each class could be identified in the standard form policies students signed in connection with their enrollment forms, and that differences in marketing materials which could "inform individual class members' understanding of what they would receive from Defendant in return for enrollment and payment of tuition and fees" did not destroy predominance. *Id* at *7. The court's analysis appears to have been based solely on the allegations in the pleadings, which the court took as true for purposes of the class certification decision. It appears the court was not presented with any evidentiary submissions related to the individualized experiences of class members other than the putative class representative.

b. Published opinions by Maine's highest court (the Law Court) in which it appears that requests for class certification were considered in the courts below consist of the following

In *Millett v. Atlantic Richfield Co.*, 2000 Me. 178, 760 A.2d 250, the Law Court refused to hear on interlocutory review plaintiffs' appeal from the denial of their motion to certify a class. Without closing the door entirely on such appeals, the Law Court found that, on the record in this case, neither the death knell doctrine nor other exceptions to the final judgment rule would be satisfied even if the court were to recognize them.

In *Goumas v. State Tax Assessor*, 2000 Me. 79, 750 A.2d 563, the Law Court denied plaintiff's appeal of a dismissal based on res judicata, holding that after a class action is dismissed with prejudice a member of the class cannot relitigate the same cause of action. The Law Court examined the language of the certification to determine the scope of the class action and determined that the same parties were privy to the same cause of action and all other requirements of the doctrine of res judicata were met.

In *Biewald v. State*, 451 A.2d 98 (Me. 1981), the Law Court noted that plaintiffs sought to have the action certified as a class action pursuant to Rule 23 and that "a document in the case file appears to revive such certification." *Id.* at 99 n.1. Because no actual order of certification was entered in the docket, however, the Law Court decided to "treat this appeal as a claim by the individual plaintiffs and not as a class action," sidestepping any review of the decision below to certify. *Id.*

In *Moore v. Canal National Bank*, 409 A.2d 679 (Me. 1979), the plaintiffs sought certification of a class in relationship to a claim alleging violations of the Federal Truth in Lending Act, 15 U.S.C. §§ 1601, *et seq.*, and the Maine Consumer Code, 9A M.R.S.A. (Supp. 197980). In an unpublished opinion, the trial court denied the motion for certification. The reason for the denial was not stated. After reviewing the substantive merits of the plaintiffs' claim (and vacating an order of summary judgment dismissing the claim), the Law Court simply stated that "the trial justice did not abuse his discretion in denying [the motion to certify]." *Moore*, 409 A.2d at 688.

In *Wellman v. Department of Human Services*, 574 A.2d 879 (Me. 1990), the trial court certified a class consisting of "unmarried but acknowledged fathers of minor children who have been ordered to reimburse the [state] for AFDC payments . . ." *Id.* The claim was for monetary, declaratory, and injunctive relief arising out of the practice of the state's Department of Human Services to require class members to reimburse the state for AFDC payments made not only to support the class members' children, but also to support the mothers of the class members' children. In affirming a decision granting the class members injunctive and declaratory relief but denying monetary relief on the grounds of sovereign immunity, the Law Court expressed no views on any Rule 23 issues.

In *Blair v. State Tax Assessor*, 485 A.2d 957 (Me. 1984), it appears that the trial court certified a class consisting of all persons who received state retirement allowances and were subject to income taxation by the state. The complaint challenged a decision of the State Tax Assessor determining that state retirement benefits and allowances in excess of employees' contributions were subject to Maine's income tax. The complaint alleged a breach of "federal and state constitutional rights to due process, freedom of contract, and equal protection. . . ." *Id.* at 958. The opinion indicates nothing further about Rule 23 issues.

In *Hammond v. Temporary Compensation Review Board*, 473 A.2d 1267 (Me. 1984), the plaintiffs sought administrative review of a decision by the Maine Temporary Compensation Review Board lowering twenty-seven employee classifications under the state employee classification system. It appears that the trial court certified a class consisting of all employees in the twenty-seven different classifications that were reduced by the Review Board. Nothing further concerning the class action aspects is mentioned in the opinion.

In *LeGrand v. York County Judge of Probate*, 2017 Me. 167, the Law Court addressed an issue of mootness. *LeGrand* involved an unusual fact pattern. A part-time Maine probate judge had altered the schedule on which he would hear cases. A litigant in one of those cases brought a putative class action seeking reinstatement of the old schedule. The trial court certified a class (without objection by the defendant), and proceeded to rule on the merits, finding for the defendant. By the time of the appeal, the named Plaintiff's probate case had completed. The defendant thus argued on appeal that the case was moot. The Law Court disagreed, relying on the Supreme Court's decisions in *Sosna v. Iowa*, 419 U.S. 393 (1975), and *U.S. Parole Comm'n v. Geraghty*, 445 U.S. 388 (1980), to hold that a putative class action is not moot, even if the individual named Plaintiffs case becomes moot, so long as the individual case was not moot at the time of the filing of the motion for class certification and the claims of at least some members of the putative class continue to be contested.

In *Manirakiza v. Dep't of Health & Human Servs.*, 2018 Me. 10, 177 A.3d 1264, the Law Court summarily affirmed the lower court's denial of class certification, noting simply that it found no error in the trial court's decision. That trial court decision is summarized above.

c. Published opinions by the Law Court that bear on the order of proceedings on the merits and proceedings on class certification consist of the following

In *Beaulieu v. City of Lewiston*, 440 A.2d 334 (Me. 1982), although it appears that the issue of certification was not considered below, the trial court proceeded to rule on the merits of the controversy prior to considering certification; granting summary judgment for the defendant, the court did not reach the issue of certification. *Id.* at 337 n.3. The Law Court simply noted this point in its opinion without comment and proceeded to review the substance of the decision below on the merits. *Id.*

In *McKinnon v. Honeywell International, Inc.*, 2009 Me. 69, 977 A.2d 420, the Law Court affirmed (4–2) a summary judgment in favor of a defendant based on lack of proof of antitrust injury. Without detailed discussion, the Law Court stated that the trial court "correctly dismissed [the plaintiff's] motion to certify the class as moot." *Id.* at ¶ 23, 977 A.2d at 427. The dissenters argued that the motion for class certification should have been decided prior to the decision on the summary judgment motion. There is no indication that the defendant—the party opposing class certification and requesting summary judgment—objected to the court's deciding the merits first, and it therefore remains unclear whether the Law Court would approve the *McKinnon* procedure in such a case.

d. Opinions relating to communications with absent class members

No Maine court has issued a decision dealing with the issue of communications with absent class members. In 2011, Judge Hornby, a former member of Maine's highest court and currently a district judge in the federal court in Maine, issued a one paragraph decision denying a pre-certification request that a defendant make certain unspecified disclosures to the putative class, citing to the standard established by the Supreme Court in *Gulf Oil Co. v. Bernard*, 452 U.S. 89, 101–02 (1981), that any order limiting communications must be supported by "a clear record and specific findings." *See Scovil v. FedEx Ground Package Sys., Inc.*, 2011 WL 3104066 (D. Me. July 25, 2011). The Court granted the request to require three other disclosures, noting that the defendant did not oppose that request.

3. HISTORY OF MAINE RULE OF CIVIL PROCEDURE 23

A discussion of the history of Maine Rule 23, together with the reporter's original notes accompanying the promulgation of Maine Rule 23 in 1959, is set forth in Field, McKusick & Wroth, *Maine Civil Practice* 385 (1970 & 1981 Supp.).

4. OTHER STATUTES AUTHORIZING CLASS ACTION PROCEEDINGS

In addition to Rule 23, Maine has enacted a variety of statutes over the years that allow proceedings to be commenced on behalf of others. The most notable of these are the sections of the Maine Business Corporations Act that provide for shareholder derivative actions. *See* 13C M.R.S.A. §§ 751, *et seq*. and M.R. Civ. P. 23A and 23B.

RULE 23 OF THE MAINE RULES OF CIVIL PROCEDURE

RULE 23. CLASS ACTIONS

(a) *Prerequisites to a class action.* One or more members of a class may sue or be sued as representative parties on behalf of all only if (1) the class is so numerous that joinder of all members is impracticable, (2) there are questions of law or fact common to the class, (3) the claims or defenses of the representative parties are typical of the claims or defenses of the class, and (4) the representative parties will fairly and adequately protect the interests of the class.

(b) *Class actions maintainable.* An action may be maintained as a class action if the prerequisites of subdivision (a) are satisfied, and in addition:

(1) the prosecution of separate actions by or against individual members of the class would create a risk of

(A) inconsistent or varying adjudications with respect to individual members of the class which would establish incompatible standards of conduct for the party opposing the class, or

(B) adjudications with respect to individual members of the class which would as a practical matter be dispositive of the interests of the other members not parties to the adjudications or substantially impair or impede their ability to protect their interests, or

(2) the party opposing the class has acted or refused to act on grounds generally applicable to the class, thereby making appropriate final injunctive relief or corresponding declaratory relief with respect to the class as a whole; or

(3) the court finds that the questions of law or fact common to the members of the class predominate over any questions affecting only individual members, and that a class action is superior to other available methods for the fair and efficient adjudication of the controversy. The matters pertinent to the findings include:

(A) the interest of members of the class in individually controlling the prosecution or defense of separate actions;

(B) the extent and nature of any litigation concerning the controversy already commenced by or against members of the class;

(C) the desirability or undesirability of concentrating the litigation of the claims in the particular forum;

(D) the difficulties likely to be encountered in the management of a class action.

(c) Determination by order whether class action to be maintained; notice; judgment; actions conducted partially as class actions.

(1) As soon as practicable after the commencement of an action brought as a class action, the court shall determine by order whether it is to be so maintained. An order under

this subdivision may be conditional, and may be altered or amended before the decision on the merits.

(2) In any class action maintained under subdivision (b)(3), the court shall direct to the members of the class the best notice practicable under the circumstances, including individual notice to all members who can be identified through reasonable effort. The notice shall advise each member that (A) the court will exclude the member from the class if the member so requests by a specified date; (B) the judgment, whether favorable or not, will include all members who do not request exclusion; and (C) any member who does not request exclusion may, if the member desires, enter an appearance through his counsel.

(3) The judgment in an action maintained as a class action under subdivision (b)(1) or (b)(2), whether or not favorable to the class, shall include and describe those whom the court finds to be members of the class. The judgment in an action maintained as a class action under subdivision (b)(3), whether or not favorable to the class, shall include and specify or describe those to whom the notice provided in subdivision (c)(2) was directed, and who have not requested exclusion, and whom the court finds to be members of the class.

(4) When appropriate (A) an action may be brought or maintained as a class action with respect to particular issues, or (B) a class may be divided into subclasses and each subclass treated as a class, and the provisions of this rule shall then be construed and applied accordingly.

(d) *Orders in conduct of actions.* In the conduct of actions to which this rule applies, the court may make appropriate orders:

(1) determining the course of proceedings or prescribing measures to prevent undue repetition or complication in the presentation of evidence or argument;

(2) requiring, for the protection of the members of the class or otherwise for the fair conduct of the action, that notice be given in such manner as the court may direct to some or all of the members of any step in the action, or of the proposed extent of the judgment, or of the opportunity of members to signify whether they consider the representation fair and adequate, to intervene and present claims or defenses, or otherwise to come into the action;

(3) imposing conditions on the representative parties or on intervenors; requiring that the pleadings be amended to eliminate therefrom allegations as to representation of absent persons, and that the action proceed accordingly;

(4) dealing with similar procedural matters. The orders may be combined with an order under Rule 16, and may be altered or amended as may be desirable from time to time.

(e) *Dismissal or compromise.* A class action shall not be dismissed or compromised without the approval of the court, and notice of the proposed dismissal or compromise shall be given to all members of the class in such manner as the court directs.

This section was prepared by Gavin McCarthy and Matthew Altieri of Pierce Atwood, LLP.

MARYLAND

1. DEVELOPMENT OF MARYLAND RULE 2-231

In 1975 the Appellate Court[1] acknowledged the "dearth of authority" on former Rule 209, finding a single case "only peripherally" addressing class actions. *See Johnson v. Chrysler Credit Corp.*, 26 Md. App. 122, 126, 337 A.2d 210, 212–13 (1975) (citing *Hooks v. Comptroller of Treas.*, 265 Md. 380, 289 A.2d 332 (1972)) (holding that § 348 of Retail Sales Tax Act prohibits taxpayers from bringing action on behalf of others). Over the years, Maryland appellate courts have had an increasing number of opportunities to interpret Rule 2-231 (the opinions of Maryland trial courts do not appear in a regional or state reporter, but class action jurisprudence in Maryland is not robust compared to other states). For this reason, and due to the similarity of FRCP 23 and Maryland 2-231, Maryland courts generally apply the body of law that has developed from the federal court's interpretation of Rule 23. *See Johnson*, 26 Md. App. at 127, 337 A.2d at 213.

The primary purpose of the Maryland class action rule is to "overcome the impracticalities of overtly cumbersome joinder requirements." *Kirkpatrick v. Gilchrist*, 56 Md. App. 242, 249, 467 A.2d 562, 566 (1983). The Kirkpatrick court determined that the trial court abused its discretion in dismissing a case for failure to join necessary parties while plaintiffs' motion for class certification remained pending. *See id.* at 251–52, 467 A.2d at 566–67; *but see Johnson*, 26 Md. App. at 129, 337 A.2d at 214 ("Although in some circumstances the class action may be an important public interest device, in others it contravenes the more traditional notions of an individual's jurisprudential rights. As a potential and perhaps unwilling litigant, an individual must assert affirmatively his right to be left alone, the very articulation of which reveals its incongruity.").

2. COMPARISON WITH RULE 23 OF THE FEDERAL RULES OF CIVIL PROCEDURE

In 1984 Maryland adopted a version of Rule 23 of the Federal Rules of Civil Procedure as its own class action rule, replacing former Rule 209. Maryland Rule 2-231 is nearly identical to pre-1998 Fed. R. Civ. P. 23, but there are some differences beyond the grammatical and organizational:

> In 2019, the Supreme Court issued an Order to amend Rule 2-231, thereby limiting class certification to "only plaintiff classes." Per the Court's Order, "[d]efendant classes shall not be named or certified." This amendment marked a notable split from Rule 23, which contains no such provision limiting class certifications only to plaintiff classes. The subsequent subsections in Rule 2-231 were updated to reflect this amendment.[2]

---

[1] As of December 14, 2022, the Court of Appeals became the Supreme Court of Maryland, and the Court of Special Appeals became the Appellate Court of Maryland.

[2] Note that all of the below-mentioned cases involved the Courts' interpretations of Rule 2-231 prior to the 2019 amendment. Thus, the subsection labels in those opinions do not reflect the Rule's organization as it is today. To maintain consistency

Both Rule 23 and Rule 2-231 provide that an action "may be maintained" as a class action if all the prerequisites of subsection (a) and one prerequisite of subsection (b) of Rule 23, and all the prerequisites of subsection (b) and one prerequisite of subsection (b) of Rule 2-231, are satisfied. Rule 2-231(c) provides that under such circumstances a class action may be maintained "unless justice requires otherwise," while the federal rule contains no such discretionary language.

Rule 2-231(d), which otherwise tracks federal Rule 23(c)(1), requires that the court hold a hearing on the issue of class certification at the request of either party, which the federal rule does not.

Rule 2-231(h) provides that only class representatives shall be treated as parties for purposes of discovery, but that the court may, on motion, allow discovery by or against other members of the class. Rule 23 contains no such provisions regarding discovery.

Rule 23 requires that individual notice be provided to all members who can be identified through reasonable effort, while Rule 2-231(f) states that notice shall be given in the manner the court directs.

Rule 23 requires that notice to (b)(3) class members include the nature of the action, the definition of the class certified, and the class claims, issues, or defenses, while Rule 2-231(f) does not specify such matters be included in the notice.

Rule 23 authorizes a court of appeals to permit an appeal from an order granting or denying a class certification order; Rule 2-231 contains no such provision.

Rule 23 contains provisions regarding the appointment and duties of class counsel and procedures for class counsel to obtain attorney's fees and nontaxable costs. Rule 2-231 does not contain any similar provisions.

Both Rule 23(e) and Rule 2-231(i) require court approval for any dismissal, compromise, or settlement of the class action; however, only Rule 23(e) articulates the procedures a court must apply to a proposed dismissal, compromise, or settlement.

3. CASE LAW INTERPRETING RULE 2-231

a. In General

The provision in the Maryland Rules for class actions does not affect the subject matter jurisdiction of Maryland's trial courts. *Pollokoff v. Maryland Nat'l Bank*, 288 Md. 485, 418 A.2d 1201 (1980). The *Pollokoff* court refused to enlarge the former Superior Court of Baltimore City's jurisdiction, preventing putative class members from aggregating their claims so as to meet that court's $2,500 statutory minimum for jurisdiction. The General Assembly has since abrogated that particular rule, providing in Courts & Judicial Proceedings § 4-402(d)(ii) that the separate claims of proposed members of a class may be aggregated to meet the minimum amount in controversy in the (now-named) circuit courts. *See Gilman v. Wheat, First Sec. Inc.*, 345 Md. 361, 692 A.2d 454 (1997). Putative members of alleged classes whose cumulated claims fail to reach the $5,000 threshold must litigate their claims separately in the district courts, where availability of the class action remains undecided. *See Pollokoff*, 288 Md. at 498, 418 A.2d at 1208; Md. Code Ann., Cts. & Jud. Proc. § 4-402(d)(1)(i)

---

with the most current form of the Rule, the author has substituted the Rule's current subsection labels for the labels that existed at the time the cited opinions were drafted.

(establishing $5,000 threshold). Notwithstanding § 4-402(d)(ii), the rule underlying *Pollokoff* remains: that the jurisdiction of any court is not extended, limited, or affected by any procedural rule, including the class action rule. Md. Rule 1-201(b).

Rule 2-231 is permissive and not mandatory. As a matter of public policy, Maryland permits class actions and allows separate claims of proposed class members to be aggregated to reach the $5,000 jurisdictional minimum, but the policy extends no further. Maryland law does not require a plaintiff who satisfies the requirements of Rule 2-231(b) and (c), but who prefers to pursue a claim as a solitary or co-plaintiff, to file a class action complaint. *Gilman*, 345 Md. at 380, 692 A.2d at 464. The Supreme Court has also held that the adoption of Rule 2-231 did not change the practice of permitting a taxpayer action without the joinder of all other similarly situated taxpayers. *Gardner v. Bd. of County Comm'rs*, 320 Md. 63, 80, 576 A.2d 208, 216 (1990). The Appellate Court held that the circuit court did not abuse its discretion in denying Plaintiff's motion for class certification because "justice requires otherwise," even though class certification prerequisites had probably been met. *Applestein v. Fairfield Resorts, Inc.*, 2009 Md. App. LEXIS 164, *30 (Md. App. July 8, 2009). A class action is not superior to the statutory remedy provided for individual plaintiffs under the Telephone Consumer Protection Act (TCPA). *Id.* at *32. Congress amended the TCPA to provide a private right of action enabling consumers to appear in a small claims court or similar court without an attorney and obtain fair damages. *Id.* at *33.

b. Notification

Albeit under the rubric of the former Rule 209, one Maryland court endorsed the United States Supreme Court's proclamation that, except in cases where the defendant owed class members a preexisting fiduciary duty, the "usual rule is that a plaintiff must initially bear the cost of notice to the class . . . as part of the ordinary burden of financing his own suit." *Johnson*, 26 Md. App. at 128, 337 A.2d at 213 (citing *Eisen v. Carlisle & Jacquelin*, 417 U.S. 156, 178 (1974)).

In *Norman v. Borison*, the Supreme Court affirmed that an absolute privilege adheres to plaintiffs' attorneys' publication of their proposed class action complaint to the press, plaintiffs' attorneys' republication of their federal complaints on the Internet, and plaintiffs' attorneys' verbal statements about their proposed class action to the press. *Norman v. Borison*, 418 Md. 630, 638, 17 A.3d 697, 702 (2011).

The court stated, "[w]e are not prepared to say that plaintiffs are prohibited from promoting preemptively their class action suit, before they have been certified as such, or that they must avoid verbal communications to the press in doing so—provided framing the suit as a 'class action' status is not shown to have been a subterfuge for funneling defamatory statements to the press." *Id.* at 665, 17 A.3d at 717–18.

The court acknowledged that it might have reached a different conclusion if the plaintiffs had not intended to become a class action. *Id.* The court's analysis turned on the fact that the allegedly defamatory statements provided notice to potential class members, in accordance with Maryland Rule 2-231. *Id.* at 644, 17 A.3d at 705. The Court's interpretation of Rule 2-231 was guided by the history and development of Federal Rule of Civil Procedure 23. *Id.* at 660–61, 17 A.3d at 714–15. Thus, the court concluded that early notice provided in a newspaper and by verbal statements to the press is in accordance with the time and form of notice parameters of the state and federal Rules. *Id.* at 664–65, 17 A.3d at 717–18.

Republication of the complaints on the Internet is permissible because the complaints are already public documents when published. *Id.* at 664, 17 A.3d at 717. Moreover, "republication of the complaints served the previously noted and judicially-cognizable purpose—the notification of potential class members of ongoing litigation, in which they may have a stake." *Id.*

c. Predominance of Common Issues

In *Philip Morris, Inc. v. Angeletti*, the Supreme Court found insufficient basis to vacate a certification order under Maryland Rule 2-231(b) but found that the certification order did not withstand scrutiny under Maryland Rule 2-231(c)(3), which requires that common issues "predominate" over individual issues. 358 Md. 689, 752 A.2d 200 (2000). The Supreme Court held that individual issues overwhelmingly predominated over common issues in this mass tort tobacco lawsuit. *Id.* at 760, 752 A.2d at 239, citing with approval *Arch v. American Tobacco Co.*, 175 F.R.D. 469, 486 (E.D. Pa. 1997) ("individual issues raised not only predominate over the common issues but overwhelm the common issues"). The Supreme Court held that the circuit court should have concluded that class certification was "not appropriate in the face of so many individualized, significant issues despite the purported 'qualitative' force of the less numerous common questions." *Phillip Morris, Inc.*, 358 Md. at 762, 752 A.2d at 240.

The Supreme Court rejected the circuit court's plan to allow the "common issues jury" to assess punitive damages for all class members. *Id.* at 777–78, 752 A.2d at 249. "Allowing a single jury to set irrevocably the amount of punitive damages to be imposed relative to and on behalf of several, let alone thousands of individuals, whose actual damages are themselves determined separately from each other, does not enable the jury to properly assess the amount of punitive damages that are appropriate in specific relation to differing amounts of—and reasons for—actual damages." *Id.* The Supreme Court explicitly agreed with the manufacturers' assessment that the proposed procedure "contravenes the bedrock requirements of Maryland substantive law." *Id.*

The Supreme Court further clarified the distinction between individual and common issues of fact or law delineated in *Phillip Morris, Inc.* and reviewed the conditions necessary for meeting the commonality requirement of class certification, e.g., that "questions of law or fact [are] common to the defenses of the class." *Creveling v. Government Employees Insurance Co.*, 376 Md. 72, 88, 828 A.2d 229, 238 (2003) (citing Md. Rule 2-231(b)); *see Phillip Morris, Inc.*, 358 Md. at 760–62, 752 A.2d at 239–40. In *Creveling*, plaintiffs/appellants were injured in automobile accidents, received medical treatment, and made claims to their insurance companies, which were not reimbursed in full. *Creveling*, 376 Md. at 80, 828 A.2d at 233. In April 2001, plaintiffs/appellants filed suit against their insurance companies, alleging breach of contract for failure to pay the full amount of their Personal Injury Protection (PIP), and also asserted claims on behalf of themselves and a class of persons for whom the insurance providers had denied or reduced PIP benefits because of payments from collateral sources. *Id.*

At trial, the circuit court found that the proposed class satisfied the numerosity, typicality, and adequacy of representation requirements of Rule 2-231(b), but failed to satisfy the commonality requirement, stating that the cases "presented liability issues requiring individual inquiry unique to each class member, including whether the medical treatment received was accident related, whether treatment was necessary in light of the injury sustained, and whether the amount sought reflected a reasonable cost for the services provided." *Id.* at 82, 828 A.2d at 234–35. The plaintiffs/appellants appealed the denial of class certification to the Appellate Court and, pursuant to Maryland Rule 8-302, petitioned the Supreme Court for writs of certiorari before the Appellate Court heard the cases. *Id.* at 83, 828 A.2d at 235. The Supreme Court granted certiorari and, in July 2003, ruling on two consolidated cases, affirmed the circuit court's denial of class certification, reasoning that the proposed class failed to meet the commonality prerequisite. *Id.* at 103–04, 828 A.2d at 247–48.

After granting certiorari, the Supreme Court first established the standard of review for an appeal of the denial of class certification. The court stated that the general standard for review regarding whether to certify a class action is abuse of discretion. *Id.* at 90, 828 A.2d at 239; *Phillip Morris, Inc.*, 358 Md. at 726, 752 A.2d at 220. The court declined to adopt an asymmetrical approach of review dependent upon whether the certification was denied or granted and extended to appeals from the denial of certification the same standard of abuse of discretion that it previously had applied to review of the grant of certification. Specifically, the court stated that "this deferential standard appropriately recognizes the factual nature of a class certification inquiry and a trial court's power to manage its docket." *Creveling*, 376 Md. at 91, 828 A.2d at 240.

Upon establishing the standard of review, the Supreme Court analyzed whether class certification could be proper in a case where the common issue of fact or law had been decided previously by the court and, thus, all remaining issues were based on an individual analysis. *Id.* at 94–95, 828 A.2d at 242. The court further stated that the only possible common question presented was "whether the insurer must pay PIP benefits to an insured when an expense is incurred on his or her behalf regardless of whether a collateral source paid the bill." *Id.* at 92, 828 A.2d at 241. This question, however, had been decided previously by the Supreme Court in *Dutta v. State Farm*, 363 Md. 540, 563–64, 769 A.2d 948, 961–62 (2001) (holding that an insurer must pay benefits to the insured regardless of whether a collateral source paid the bill and to withhold the payment as such is illegal); *Creveling*, 376 Md. at 95, 828 A.2d at 242. Accordingly, because the common issue had already been settled, the court held that only individual questions remained, precluding satisfaction of the statutorily mandated prerequisites. *Creveling*, 376 Md. at 95, 828 A.2d at 242. The court held that in such a circumstance the commonality requirement could not be satisfied because the class must have at least one common question of law or fact in dispute. *Id.* at 92, 95, 828 A.2d at 241–42; *see also Phillip Morris, Inc.*, 358 Md. at 734, 752 A.2d at 225.

The court also considered appellants' attempt to satisfy the commonality requirement by asserting that the appellee had waived its right to review the individual issues and, in the alternative, was estopped from reviewing these issues during the remediation process. The court held, however, that the doctrine of waiver is not applicable unless the parties actually intend to relinquish that right and may neither expand nor establish insurance coverage. *Creveling*, 376 Md. at 95–96, 828 A.2d at 243. The court further stated that whether a defense in an insurance claim may be waived depends on whether the defense is based on lack of basic coverage, which may not be waived, or based on the claimant's failure to satisfy a "technical" condition subsequent, which may be waived. *Id.* at 96–97, 828 A.2d at 243 (citing *Insurance Co. of North America v. Coffman*, 52 Md. App. 732, 742–43, 451 A.2d 952, 957 (1982)). Finally, the court held that the individual questions remaining—whether the injuries were related to an accident, whether the treatment was necessary, and whether the costs were reasonable—are "not merely technical conditions that must be satisfied for existing coverage to apply because they define the boundaries of coverage." *Id.* at 99, 828 A.2d at 245. "Waiver of these requirements would change radically the nature of the insurance policies," and, therefore, does not satisfy the statutory prerequisite by making the issues common to the class. *Id.*

The court also declined to order the insurance company to cease review of individual claims during the remediation process, holding that the circumstances for estoppel were not present. *Id.* at 103, 828 A.2d at 247. Appellants alleged that the insurance companies, in denying the claim on one ground, were estopped from reevaluating the claims during the remediation process and arguing other grounds for the denial of coverage. *Id.* at 83, 828 A.2d at 235. In rejecting appellants' arguments, the court held that, without evidence of prejudice or detrimental reliance, insurance companies are not estopped from reviewing the individual claims during the remediation process and "since any prejudice is dubious . . . the trial court did not err by not finding that estoppel operated to dispose of individual issues and create commonality." *Id.* at 103, 828 A.2d at 247.

Additionally, appellees argued that tender of the full amount of the PIP claims rendered the action moot. *Id.* at 83, 828 A.2d at 235. The court declined to rule on this issue, stating that the "trial court properly denied class certification, proposed class members no longer retain an interest in the action. Accordingly, we need not resolve the effect of tenders of relief." *Id.* at 83 n.3, 828 A.2d at 235 n.3. The court did caution, however, that the case "does not constitute an endorsement of tendering payment to named plaintiffs with the goal of annulling class action litigation" and allowing such a practice would preclude the survival of most class actions. *Id.* (citing *Roper v. Consurve, Inc.*, 578 F.2d 1106, 1110 (5th Cir. 1978), *aff'd on other grounds sub nom., Deposit Guarantee National Bank v. Roper*, 445 U.S. 326, 100 S. Ct. 1166, 63 L.Ed. 2d 427 (1980)).

The Appellate Court, relying primarily on *Philip Morris, Inc.*, explained that even where class members' damages are highly fact-specific, the commonality and typicality requirements of class certification can be met when questions of law or fact predominate. *LVNV Funding, LLC v. Finch (Finch II)*, No. 1075, 2017 WL 6388959, at *29–30 (Md. App. Dec. 14, 2017), *vacated on other grounds*, 463 Md. 586, 207 A.3d 202 (2019). In *Finch II*, a class action was brought claiming that LVNV was unjustly enriched through collection actions in violation of the Maryland Collection Agency Licensing Act (MCALA) and Maryland Consumer Debt Collection Act (MCDCA). LVNV, which was in the business of credit card debt collection, argued that the circuit court improperly certified the class where the class members could be distinguished by the circumstances of their payments to LVNV, when their claims in relation to that payment accrued, and whether the underlying debt for which the payment was made was valid. *Id.* at *28. LVNV specifically relied on a decision by the United States Court of Appeals for the Eleventh Circuit, which asserted that unjust enrichment claims are "essentially never appropriate for class-wide adjudication." *Id.* at *29 (citing *Vega v. T-Mobile USA, Inc.*, 564 F.3d 1256, 1274 (11th Cir. 2009). Unlike in *Vega*, each class member's claim in *Finch II* was dependent on the outcome of the same legal question: Did LVNV's collection actions violate the MCDCA and thus was LVNV unjustly enriched. *Id.* at *30. The Court held that the issues raised by LVNV in challenging the class certification would have no legal impact on the substantive issue related to the class's claim. *Id.* at *29. The court also found the typicality requirement was met under the same reasoning. Relying again on *Philip Morris, Inc.*, the court held that the class members seek the same relief relying on the same legal arguments. *Id.* at 30 (citing *Philip Morris, Inc.*, 358 Md. at 738). Because the class members' claims were dependent on the outcome of the legality of LVNV's collection efforts, class certification was appropriate even if the circumstances of each member's injury was highly fact-specific.

The Appellate Court later provided additional detail on the requirements necessary for class certification. *Chavis v. Blibaum Assocs., P.A.*, 246 Md. App. 517, 230 A.3d 188 (2020), *rev'd on other grounds*, 476 Md. 534, 264 A.3d 1254 (2021). In *Chavis*, the Appellate Court affirmed denial of class certification to a group of plaintiffs that defined their class as "[a]ll natural persons against whom [defendant] obtained a judgment that was not satisfied prior to [date] in a [defined lawsuit] and who have since satisfied that judgment," stating that plaintiffs "did not satisfy several of the requirements necessary for class certification." The proposed class lacked the numerosity, commonality, and typicality requirements because "the class definition did not sufficiently address the issues in question or readily identify the members of the class" where the trial court "would have to conduct mini-trials to determine whether the plaintiffs fit into the class." *Id.* 541. The proposed class also lacked adequate class representatives because plaintiffs "offered no evidence to suggest that the class representatives had knowledge of the case or were interested in pursuing the matter and taking on the duties as class representatives." *Id.* at 542. And in *Silver v. Greater Baltimore Medical Center, Inc.*, 248 Md. App. 666, 704–05, 243 A.2d 576, 598–99 (2020), the Appellate Court affirmed the denial of class certification, finding that individual concerns about certain at-issue hospital facility-specific fees reasonably might have outweighed common class-wide issues.

More recently, the Appellate Court provided further guidance on the predominance analysis required under Md. Rule 2-231(c)(3). In *Bennett v. Donaldson Group, LLC*, the Appellate Court reviewed a circuit court decision finding that this predominance requirement had not been met. The circuit court had denied class certification on this basis, finding that each putative class member would be required to establish case-specific elements of his or her case, which would require the examination of individual facts and evidence as to each class member and "essentially engulf the 'common' issues" in the case. *Bennett v. Donaldson Grp., LLC*, No. 1372, 2022 WL 2981494, at *5 (Md. App. July 28, 2022), *cert. denied sub nom.*, 482 Md. 33, 284 A.3d 413 (2022). The Appellate Court agreed, finding that each class member would have to establish that their rental unit was uninhabitable and that there were damages, the amount of damages as determined on an individualized fact-specific basis, and that certain repairs were not performed in a reasonable time and that this breach caused actual damages. Such elements required detailed individual assessments and defeated Mr. Bennett's argument for class certification based on common issues and facts. *Id.* at *5. The Appellate Court also affirmed the lower court's denial of class certification based upon its determination that certain statistical evidence was unreliable and therefore did not adequately establish predominance. *Id.* at *6.

For purposes of establishing collateral estoppel, actual identity of parties is not required in class actions. *Weaver v. Prince George's County*, 34 Md. App. 189, 200, 366 A.2d 1048 (Md. App. 1976), *aff'd*, 281 Md. 349, 379 A.2d 399 (1977) (citing *Hansberry v. Lee*, 311 U.S. 32, 40–41 (1940)).

A case may be certified as a class action for purposes of liability, but not damages, where legislation is passed that constitutes a taking. *State v. Braverman*, 228 Md. App. 239, 137 A.3d 377 (2016), *cert. denied sub nom.*, *Goldberg v. State*, 450 Md. 115, 146 A.3d 469 (2016). "The legislation arguably damaged individual owners in individual ways, so that common questions of law or fact might not predominate over questions affecting only individual members on the issue of damages. Md. Rule 2-231(c)(3)." *Id.* at 248 n.3, 137 A.3d at 382 n.3.

d. Superiority

In *Philip Morris Inc. v. Angeletti*, 358 Md. 689, 752 A.2d 200 (2000), the Supreme Court held that class action treatment was inappropriate for the plaintiffs' claims under the "superiority" requirement of Rule 2-231(c)(3) due to the difficulty in managing an "immature tort." *Id.* at 768–69, 752 A.2d at 243–44 (citing with approval *Arch*, 175 F.R.D. at 494–95). The Supreme Court held that the circuit court abused its discretion on both the "superiority" and "predominance" questions in certifying the classes under Rule 2-231(c)(3). *See generally Anne Arundel Cty. v. Halle Dev., Inc.*, 408 Md. 539, 574, 971 A.2d 214, 235 (2009) (noting that any burden on the class action defendant resulting from class certification is a "secondary consideration" in the superiority analysis because "the superiority required by the statute is not 'superior administrative convenience' exclusively for the defendant, but superiority 'for the fair and efficient adjudication' of the matter"). In a more recent decision, the Appellate Court found that the superiority requirement was not satisfied where a trial would require a jury to resolve disputes concerning fees charged by multiple medical providers over 16 different fee schedules, which caused a significant manageability problem. *See Silver v. Greater Baltimore Medical Center, Inc.*, 248 Md. App. 666, 704–05, 243 A.2d 576, 598–99 (2020).

e. Numerosity

The Circuit Court of Montgomery County in *Worsham v. Americor*, No. 259191-V, 2008 WL 5325400 (Md. Cir. Ct. July 8, 2008), denied a motion for class certification for failing to meet the numerosity prerequisite of Rule 2-231(b). The court held that the plaintiff made no showing regarding the class size, location of members, and amount of each potential member's claim to satisfy the numerosity prerequisite. *Id.* at 4.

In *LaRocca v. The Creig Northrop Team, P.C.*, 217 Md. App. 536 (2014), *rev'd on other grounds*, *Windesheim v. Larocca*, 443 Md. 312, 116 A.3d 954 (2015), the Appellate Court considered the issue of numerosity in a class action arising out of an alleged mortgage fraud scheme. The trial court had denied certification on numerosity grounds after calculating the estimated class size as the number of transactions (20) instead of the number of persons (34). *Id.* at 571. On appeal, the court held that the trial court did not abuse its discretion in finding that the class size consisted of the number of loan transactions and not the number of parties to the loans. *Id.* at 576. Specifically, the court observed that the case involved alleged fraudulent acts arising out of each of the loan transactions, with the alleged fraud committed in relation to each loan, regardless of how many people were co-borrowers for each loan. *Id.*

f. Adequacy

In *Worsham v. Americor*, No. 259191-V, 2008 WL 5325400 (Md. Cir. Ct. July 8, 2008), the trial lcourt highlighted its "independent duty" to assure the adequacy of the named class representative and counsel to protect absent members. *Id.* at 5. Counsel was inadequate even though he had previously litigated similar cases because the case was over three years old and had made little progress. *Id.* Counsel had previously failed to show up for trial, and the two defendants who were actually served had been dismissed. *Id.* Moreover, the court held that a class action was not superior under 2-231(c)(3) because of plaintiff and counsel's inability to manage the class action to a "successful conclusion" or present a plan to reach the trial stage. *Id.* at 7. The court held that, although the Supreme Court had not yet ruled on the issue, the standard of proof for class action prerequisites is a preponderance of the evidence. *Id.* at 3.

The Supreme Court has held that plaintiffs who had no direct contractual relationship to defendants were inadequate class representatives. *Master Fin., Inc. v. Crowder*, 409 Md. 51, 81, 972 A.2d 864, 881 (2009). The Supreme Court affirmed the circuit court's dismissal of the borrower's complaints against the defendants who were not alleged to have purchased loans made to the named plaintiffs because the plaintiffs could not "fairly and adequately protect the interests" of absent class members who might have a relationship with those defendants. *Id.* While affirming the Appellate Court's dismissal of the complaints, the court declined to rely on the plaintiff's lack of standing, as the Appellate Court relied, but rather found the plaintiffs to be inadequate representatives of a class against such defendants. *Id.* Both the Supreme Court and the Appellate Court declined to adopt the "juridical link doctrine" urged by the plaintiffs where "defendants are juridically related in a manner that suggests a single resolution of the dispute would be expeditious." *Id.* at 77, 972 A.2d at 879–80 (quoting *La Mar v. H & B Novelty & Loan Co.*, 489 F.2d 461, 466 (9th Cir. 1973)). In relying on Rule 2-231 and adequacy requirements (rather than of standing), the court stated that it was following federal decisions under Rule 23 requiring defendants that do not have a direct connection with the putative class representatives be linked by allegations of "conspiracy, contract, or uniform law or rule mandating or permitting the same conduct by those defendants." *Id.* at 80, 972 A.2d at 881.

Parties to a class action cannot agree to its certification in the absence of a necessary party. The Supreme Court held that the circuit court should have dismissed a complaint where parties failed to join a required party pursuant to Rule 2-211(a). *Richmond v. Dist. Court of Md.*, 412 Md. 672, 672, 990 A.2d 549, 549 (2010). Appellant class members sought a judgment declaring their right to representation by the Public Defender during their initial appearance before a District Court Commissioner, but they had failed to join the Public Defender as a party in their class action in the circuit court. *Id.* The court ruled that the circuit court should not have permitted the parties to agree that the case met Rule 2-231 requirements without the Public Defender speaking on the issues of whether the case should be a class action and whether the Public Defender is obligated to represent an indigent defendant during an initial appearance before a District Court Commissioner. *Id.*

g. "No-Class-Action" Agreements

In April 2005, the Supreme Court ruled that a "no-class-action" provision within an arbitration agreement is not unconscionable, and thus is enforceable. *Walther v. Sovereign Bank*, 386 Md. 412, 872 A.2d 735 (2005). In *Walther*, plaintiffs obtained a second mortgage on their home from Empire Funding Corporation, which subsequently assigned the note to Sovereign Bank (Sovereign). *Id.* at 419, 872 A.2d at 739. The terms of the loan required plaintiffs to pay several fees, which they later alleged were exorbitant. *Id.* at 418–19, 872 A.2d at 739. In addition, an arbitration provision was included in the loan contract stating that, "any dispute subject to arbitration shall not be adjudicated as a class action or consolidated proceeding." *Id.* at 419, 872 A.2d at 739.

Despite this "no-class-action" arbitration provision, plaintiffs filed a class action in the Circuit Court of Baltimore County alleging that Sovereign had violated the Maryland Secondary Mortgage Loan Law by charging $2,847 in illegal fees. *Id.* at 419, 872 A.2d at 739–40. Sovereign responded to the complaint by filing a petition seeking to compel arbitration and a motion to dismiss or to stay proceedings. *Id.* at 420, 872 A.2d at 740. The circuit court granted the petition to enforce arbitration and stayed plaintiff's original suit. *Id.* On appeal, the Appellate Court affirmed the petition to enforce arbitration, finding that the "no-class-action" provision was not unconscionable. *Id.* at 421, 872 A.2d at 741. Finally, plaintiffs sought relief in the Supreme Court. *Id.* at 422, 872 A.2d at 741.

The Supreme Court found that the "no-class-action" provision was not unconscionable and affirmed the intermediate appellate court's ruling. *Id.* at 449, 872 A.2d at 757. The court noted that both federal and Maryland law favor arbitration agreements. *Id.* at 424–25, 872 A.2d at 742–43. Moreover, the court observed that the Maryland Uniform Arbitration Act closely mirrors the Federal Arbitration Act and provides that a "written agreement to submit any existing controversy to arbitration or a provision in a written contract to submit to arbitration any controversy arising between the parties in the future is valid and enforceable, and is irrevocable, except upon grounds that exist at law or in equity for the revocation of a contract." *Id.* at 424, 872 A.2d at 742. Accordingly, if the arbitration agreement stands as valid and enforceable under contract law, the "no-class-action" provision is also enforceable and is not, in and of itself, unconscionable. *Id.* at 425–26, 872 A.2d at 742.

More recently, the Supreme Court has confirmed that questions as to the existence of a valid agreement to arbitrate, including a limitation upon class action rights, must be decided by a court upon ruling on a motion to compel arbitration, and that it is inappropriate for this issue to be referred to an arbitrator for decision. *Access Funding, LLC v. Linton*, 482 Md. 602, 665, 290 A.3d 112, 149 (2022), *as modified on reconsideration* (Mar. 16, 2023).

h. Class Action Tolling Doctrine

In 2006, the Supreme Court in *Philip Morris USA, Inc. v. Christensen*, 394 Md. 227, 905 A.2d 340 (2006), *abrogated on other grounds*, *Mummert v. Alizadeh*, 435 Md. 207, 77 A.3d 1049 (2013), addressed the issue of whether Maryland would adopt the "class action tolling doctrine" established by the United States Supreme Court with regard to the federal class action rule and followed by many state courts applying similar state rules. The court affirmed the decision of the Appellate Court to adopt the doctrine, holding that statutes of limitations applicable to the claims of unnamed putative class action plaintiffs are tolled during the time between a class action filing and a judicial denial of class certification. *Id.* at 231, 905 A.2d at 342. The court stated that for a plaintiff to take advantage of the tolling doctrine, however, the class action complaint must put the defendants on notice of the individual plaintiff's claims. *Id.* at 261, 905 A.2d at 360.

In *Christensen*, the plaintiff brought wrongful death and survival claims against several tobacco manufacturers who were also defendants in the *Philip Morris Inc. v. Angeletti* class action lawsuit discussed more fully above. *Id.* at 232, 905 A.2d at 343. Plaintiff's decedent, who had been diagnosed with lung cancer caused by smoking, was a putative class member in the *Angeletti* case. In *Angeletti*, however, the Supreme Court vacated the circuit court's certification of class action status. Thereafter, Plaintiff filed the instant suit against the defendant tobacco manufacturers, in an individual capacity. The defendants contended that Plaintiff's claims were barred by the statute of limitations. Plaintiff, however, argued that the court should apply the "class action tolling doctrine" to find the survival claims timely. *Id.* at 234, 905 A.2d at 344.

In its decision to adopt the class action tolling doctrine, the Supreme Court noted that the doctrine helped achieve the purposes of the Maryland class action rule. The class action rule promotes judicial economy and efficiency, and a failure to adopt the doctrine would undermine that rule by encouraging putative class action plaintiffs to file duplicative individual suits to prevent their claims from being time barred following a denial of class action status. *Id.* at 254, 905 A.2d at 356. Thus, the court agreed with the Supreme Court's holding that "the commencement of a class action suspends the applicable statute of limitations as to all asserted members of the class who would have been parties had the suit been permitted to continue as a class action," *Id.* at 247, 905 A.2d at 352 (quoting *American Pipe & Construction Co. v. Utah*, 414 U.S. 538, 554 (1974)), whether an asserted member intervenes in the original action or files an individual suit following the denial of class certification. *Id.* at 254, 905 A.2d at 356.

The court also held that the class action tolling doctrine must be applied in a manner consistent with the purposes of statutes of limitations. For class action tolling to be applied in a manner consistent with those purposes, the court stated that the original class action complaint must provide the defendants with notice of the "number and generic identities of the potential plaintiffs." *Id.* at 256, 905 A.2d at 357 (quoting *American Pipe*, 414 U.S. at 555). In addition, the individual suit must "concern the same evidence, memories, and witnesses as the subject matter of the original class suit." *Id.* (quoting *American Pipe*, 414 U.S. at 562 (Blackmun, J., concurring)).

The court rejected the defendants' argument to exclude "mass torts" from the class action tolling doctrine because there was no reason to assume that individual plaintiffs could not meet the notice requirement in such cases. *Id.* at 260, 905 A.2d at 359. For a plaintiff to meet the notice requirement, the defendants must be able to identify that particular putative class member's claims in the class action complaint, not necessarily every putative class member's claims. *Id.* at 261, 905 A.2d at 360. The court also rejected defendants' argument that plaintiffs should have only thirty days following a class certification denial to file an individual complaint or to intervene. Under such a rule, the court noted, a plaintiff could have less time to bring a suit than if the class action had never been filed. Thus, the court decided that the tolling effect of the doctrine must provide a plaintiff with at least as much time to file a suit as would be provided if the filing of a class action complaint suspended the statute of limitations from the time of filing to the time that certification is denied. *Id.* at 264, 905 A.2d at 362.

The court concluded that Plaintiff's claims were tolled by the filing of the class action, and therefore, Plaintiff's survival action was timely. *Id.* at 265, 905 A.2d at 363. The court found that the preconditions to class action tolling were met because Plaintiff was a member of the putative class, the defendants (except one) were defendants in the class action suit, and Plaintiff's survival claims were asserted in the class action suit. The court stated further that Plaintiff could take advantage of class action tolling because the defendants had sufficient notice of Plaintiff's claims. *Id.* In making this ruling, the court noted that plaintiff actively participated in the class action litigation before the class certification was vacated, by providing an affidavit and giving testimony, thus enabling the defendants to determine that he was a member of the class and to prepare to defend against his claims. *Id. See also Worsham*, 2008 WL 5325400 n.13 (noting that class members would not be harmed by denying class certification because they would likely receive the benefit of the tolling rule).

In 2013, the Appellate Court declined to adopt cross-jurisdictional tolling of the statute of limitations in class action litigation. In *Adedje v. Westat, Inc.*, the court considered a plaintiff whose claims had been dismissed by the United States District Court for the District of Maryland on two previous occasions and who sought to bring a similar claim in Maryland state court. 214 Md. App. 1 (2013). The plaintiff was initially part of a putative class action suit, alleging that Westat had violated the federal Fair Labor Standards Act (FLSA) by failing to pay its employees an overtime rate for any time they worked more than 40 hours per week. *Id.* The federal court denied the initial attempt at class certification and, on November 2, 2010, dismissed the case. *See Syrja v. Westat, Inc.*, 756 F. Supp. 2d 682 (D. Md. 2010); *Adedje,* 214 Md. App. at 7. On December 2, 2010, the plaintiffs then filed individual complaints in the District of Maryland, alleging violations of the FLSA and Maryland's Wage Payment and Collection Law, which were subsequently dismissed in September 2011. *Adedje,* 214 Md. App. at 7–8.

On September 30, 2011, Adedje filed suit again in the Circuit Court for Montgomery County, alleging violations of Maryland's Wage and Hour Law and its Wage Payment and Collection Law. *Id.* at 9–10. Westat filed a motion to dismiss, arguing that Adedje's claim was time barred because (1) her employment ended in 2007 and she failed to allege a Maryland Wage and Hour law claim in her first lawsuit and (2) that equitable tolling did not apply in Maryland. *Id.* at 8–9. The circuit court agreed and granted Westat's Motion to Dismiss, holding that Count I of her complaint under the Wage and Hour law was indeed not tolled because it had never been asserted previously. *Id.* The circuit court held that Count II, Adedje's Wage Payment and Collection Law claim, was also time-barred because even though the Wage Payment and Collection Law claim was asserted in the second federal action and even with the application of the tolling provision of 28 U.S.C. § 1367(d), the statute of limitations expired before the state court lawsuit was filed. *Id.*

On appeal, the issue before the Appellate Court was whether Adedje's claim for overtime wages under the Maryland Wage Payment and Collection Law was barred by the statute of limitations. *Id.* at 11–12. Westat argued that Maryland does not recognize cross-jurisdictional class action tolling and that Adedje only opted into Mr. Syrja's Fair Labor Standards Act class action suit, which did not include the Wage Payment and Collection Law claim. *Id.* at 12–13. The Appellate Court agreed, holding that courts should consider the following factors when determining whether a class action tolling exception applies: "(1) whether the plaintiff was a party to the prior action; (2) whether the action concerns the same facts, claims, defendants, and witnesses as the prior action; (3) whether the defendant was placed on notice of another claim being filed; (4) whether persuasive authority and policy exist that support use of the tolling exception; and (5) whether recognition of the exception harmonizes with the purpose of statutes of limitation." *Id.* at 30.

Applying these factors, the court held that Adedje's Wage Payment and Collection Law claim was time barred for three reasons. *Id.* First, while Adedje was a party to the putative class action suit in federal court, Westat did not have reasonable notice of her state law claims from the filing of a federal class action. *Id.* at 30–32. Second, permitting cross-jurisdictional tolling of the statute of limitations would undermine the goals of statutes of limitations: to prevent courts from litigating stale claims, and to prevent citizens from having to defend their case after their memories have faded. *Id.* Third, a tolling exception was poor public policy because allowing class actions in other courts to halt the limitations period in Maryland would "render [Maryland] the focal point for complainants whose class certifications were denied," and cross-jurisdictional tolling would put Maryland "at the mercy of other jurisdictions, waiting on them to rule on the cases before being able to adjudicate issues in its own courts." *Id.* at 29.

On July 30, 2021, the Supreme Court reexamined the application and scope of the class action tolling doctrine in Maryland. *See Cain v. Midland Funding, LLC*, 475 Md. 4, 53–69, 256 A.3d 765, 793–803 (2021). While the Supreme Court confirmed once more that the class action tolling doctrine remains valid in Maryland, it declined to expand the scope of this doctrine to provide for an additional judicial tolling exception with respect to successive class action cases. *Id.* at 62, 256 A.3d at 799. Specifically, the relevant inquiries before the Supreme Court were (1) whether the class action tolling adopted in *Christensen* applies to successive class action suits, and not just to individual class member claims after class certification is denied; and (2) whether this principle would apply in equal force to cross-jurisdictional claims, such as where the initial putative class action was filed in a federal court or in another state. *Id.* at 62–69, 256 A.3d at 799–803.

As to the former issue, the Supreme Court declined to expand the class action tolling doctrine to include successive class actions. In support of this decision, the Supreme Court relied largely upon the Supreme Court's approach taken in *China Agritech, Inc. v. Resh*, ___ U.S. ___, 138 S. Ct. 1800, 201 L. Ed. 2d 123 (2018). *Id.* at 62–65, 256 A.3d at 799–800. Adopting portions of Justice Ginsburg's opinion in *China Agritech*, the Supreme Court concluded that no persuasive authority or policy considerations would support the recognition of successive class action suits in this context, and that the proposed exception would be inconsistent with principles of judicial economy and efficiency. *Id.* at 64, 256 A.3d at 800. The Court also cautioned that this proposed exception would potentially cause a "rolling tolling" approach to class action litigation that would further frustrate efficiency concerns. *Id.*, 256 A.3d at 800.

As to the latter issue, which impacts only individual suits, the Supreme Court elected to adopt the principle of cross-jurisdictional class action tolling. *Id.* at 65–69, 256 A.3d at 800–03. This issue was explicitly left unsettled following *Christensen*. 394 Md. at 254 n.9, 905 A.2d 340. Examining the issue directly at this time, the Supreme Court found that the same principles that supported intra-jurisdictional class action tolling also weighed in favor of cross-jurisdictional class action tolling. *Id.* at 67, 256 A.3d at 802. The Court concluded that "Maryland recognizes *American Pipe* class action tolling for absent members of putative class actions filed in other state and federal courts." *Id.* at 68, 256 A.3d at 802. It further found that the same factors articulated in *Christensen* for intra-jurisdictional tolling also apply to a court's application of cross-jurisdictional class action tolling in the future. *Id.*, 256 A.3d at 802–03.

i. Dispositive Motions Before Certification

In 2011, in the interests of judicial economy and efficiency, the Appellate Court affirmed that trial courts may address dispositive motions prior to determining class certification issues. *Gomez v. Jackson Hewitt, Inc.*, 198 Md. App. 87, 90, 16 A.3d 261, 263 (2011); *Daughton v. Maryland Auto. Ins. Fund*, 198 Md. App. 524, 18 A.3d 152 (2011).

In *Gomez*, the Appellate Court affirmed the trial court's dismissal of plaintiff's claims where judicial economy dictated that the court make a determination about defendant's motion to dismiss before considering a motion to certify the class. *Id.* Plaintiff claimed that defendant violated Maryland's Credit Services Business Act (CSBA) and Consumer Protection Act by facilitating a refund anticipation loan (RAL) for plaintiff in exchange for payment without the appropriate license to do so. *Id.* at 91, 16 A.3d at 263. Upon the parties' request that the trial court rule on defendant's motion to dismiss before plaintiff filed a motion for class certification, the trial court dismissed the case and plaintiff appealed. *Id.* at 92–93, 16 A.3d at 264. Reviewing the case *de novo*, the Appellate Court found that the CSBA was directed at so-called "credit repair agencies," who charge fees for credit improvement or loan extension services. *Id.* at 112–13, 16 A.3d at 276. The court rejected plaintiff's argument that, by facilitating plaintiff's RAL, defendant "obtained an extension of credit" for plaintiff within the meaning of the CSBA, based on the finding that defendant only charged plaintiff for tax preparation services. *Id.* at 122, 16 A.3d at 282. Accordingly, the Appellate Court held that the CSBA did not apply and affirmed the trial court's dismissal. *Id.* at 120–21, 16 A.3d at 280–81.

Similarly, in *Daughton*, the Appellate Court upheld the trial court's grant of summary judgment to defendant Maryland Automobile Insurance Fund (MAIF), where plaintiff's "complaint sought class action certification, but the court never ruled on that issue." 198 Md. App. 524, 528, 18 A.3d 152, 154 (2011). In this action for breach of contract, plaintiff Daughton alleged that MAIF failed to pay her PIP benefit claim within the statutory 30-day period, and then failed to pay interest on the late benefit payment as required by Maryland law. *Id.* at 527–28, 18 A.3d at 154. MAIF moved for summary judgment on the grounds that it was entitled to sovereign immunity and that, because plaintiff filed suit over two years after her cause of action arose, it was barred by the applicable one-year statute of limitations. *Id.* at 528, 18 A.3d at 154. The trial court granted summary judgment for MAIF as to both of Daughton's claims. *Id.* In affirming the trial court, the Appellate Court concluded that MAIF was an agency or instrumentality of the state, as evidenced by the degree to which it is subject to state control and regulation; whether MAIF functioned in many ways like a traditional, private liability insurance carrier was not determinative. *Id.* at 546, 18 A.3d at 165. As such, defendant enjoyed sovereign immunity, which plaintiff could only have defeated by filing suit within one year of the date that her cause of action arose. *Id.* at 550, 18 A.3d at 167 (*citing* St. Gov. Art. § 12-202). The court, moreover, rejected Daughton's argument that she had an implied private right of action with a longer limitations period pursuant to Ins. Art. § 19-508(c). *Id.* at 547, 18 A.3d at 166. Finally, plaintiff argued that the one-year statute of limitations was tolled when MAIF failed to make the interest payments that plaintiff alleged she was owed. *Id.* The Appellate Court found this argument to be without merit; not only had plaintiff conceded this point at trial, but plaintiff's interpretation of § 12-201 produced the "untenable result" that the limitations period for all breach of contract claims against state agencies or instrumentalities would not begin to run before suit was filed and liability was established. *Id.* at 550–51, 18 A.3d at 167–68. Accordingly, the Appellate Court held that summary judgment in favor of MAIF was appropriate. *Id.* at 551, 18, A.3d at 168.

In 2017, the Appellate Court again addressed whether the court can rule on dispositive motions prior to considering a request for class certification. *See Murray v. Midland Funding, LLC*, 233 Md. App. 254, 263–64, 163 A.3d 271, 277 (2017). Plaintiff argued that the circuit court erred in ruling on Defendant's Motion to Dismiss before considering Plaintiff's request for class certification. *Id.* at 264 n.7, 163 A.3d 277 n.7. The Appellate Court cited Md. Rule 2-231(c), which states the following: "On motion of any party or on the court's own initiative, the court shall determine by order as soon as practicable after commencement of the action whether it is to be maintained as a class action. A hearing shall be granted if requested by any party." *Id.*, 163 A.3d 277 n.7. The Appellate Court emphasized that "the hearing must be held *soon*, but it does not say the hearing must be held *before* a ruling on a motion to dismiss." *Id.*, 163 A.3d 277 n.7. Accordingly, the Appellate Court refused to instruct the circuit court to hold a hearing and rule on Plaintiff's request for class certification prior to ruling on the dispositive Motion to Dismiss. *Id.*, 163 A.3d 277 n.7.

j. Standard for Subsequent Motions Concerning Class Considerations

In 2024, in a matter of first impression, the Supreme Court addressed what standard a trial court should apply to a motion concerning class certification after a trial court ruled on a previous motion concerning the same issues. *See Westminster Mgmt., LLC v. Smith*, 486 Md. 616, 668, 312 A.3d 741, 772 (2024). The Supreme Court agreed that the trial court utilized the correct "material change in circumstances test" when determining whether the merits of the second motion should be considered. *Id.* The Supreme Court reasoned that the material change in circumstances test is "consistent with Md. Rule 2-231" and "strikes an appropriate balance between accommodating changes in circumstances and judicial efficiency." *Id.* A material change in circumstances warranting a trial court's consideration of a second motion for class certification may include: a substantial change in the proposed class definition, new evidence obtained through discovery, an intervening change in the law, a pertinent change in the legal landscape of the case due to plaintiffs altering their claims, or any combination thereof. *Id.* at 670, 312 A.3d at 773. Ultimately, the Supreme Court found that the trial court erred in its application of the material change in circumstances test because new evidence presented before the trial by the movant "constituted a material change in circumstances," such that the trial court should have considered the motion on its merits. *Id.* at 671–73, 312 A.3d at 774–75.

k. Mootness

In 2013, the Supreme Court addressed whether a defendant may moot a putative class action by tendering settlement to the prospective class representative prior to class certification. *Frazier v. Castle Ford, Ltd.*, 430 Md. 144, 148, 59 A.3d 1016, 1018 (2013). In rejecting the bright line rule that tendering individual relief annuls the class action litigation, the Court stated that such a rule was "not a wise one" because "many meritorious class actions will never get off the ground" if a defendant can defeat a class action by satisfying the class representative's claim immediately after suit is filed. *Id.* at 157, 59 A.3d at 1024. Instead of the bright-line rule, the court adopted the following standard: "A tender of individual relief to the putative class representative does not moot a class action if the individual plaintiff has not had a reasonable opportunity to seek class certification, including any necessary discovery." *Id.* at 161, 59 A.3d at 1026.

Frazier arose from a putative class action suit alleging that several hundred customers were sold warranties in which Crystal Ford misrepresented the warranty's duration. *Id.* at 148–50, 59 A.3d at 1018–19. In August 2007, Crystal Ford reimbursed the prospective class representative, Mr. Frazier, for the out-of-pocket expenses incurred for fixing his vehicle and extended his warranty to the original date intended. *Id.* at 150, 59 A.3d at 1019. After tendering the individual damages, Crystal Ford filed a motion for summary judgment and a motion to deny class certification. The circuit court granted both motions, reasoning that Frazier had been made whole and "no longer had an interest to act on behalf of a class." *Id.* at 150–51, 59 A.3d at 1020. The Appellate Court affirmed the circuit court's decision.

In reversing the decisions of the lower courts, the Supreme Court explained that the consequences of tendering individual damages were previously discussed in *Creveling v. GEICO*, 376

Md. 72, 828 A.2d 229 (2003). The court noted, however, that it did not explicitly adopt one of the discussed approaches and instead left for a later case the issue regarding the effect of tendering damages to a potential class representative. *Fraizer*, 430 Md. at 157, 59 A.3d at 1023. In choosing an approach, the court endorsed the Ninth Circuit's holding in *Pitts v. Terrible Herbst, Inc.*, 653 F.3d 1081 (9th Cir. 2011). In *Pitts*, the Ninth Circuit held that a class action is not moot if a defendant "attempts to pick off a prospective class representative before a motion for certification can reasonably be filed." *Frazier*, 430 Md. at 159 (citing *Pitts*, 653 F.3d at 1092). The Ninth Circuit explained that "[o]nly once the denial of class certification is final does the defendant's offer . . . moot the merits of the case because the plaintiff has been offered all that he can possibly recover through litigation." *Pitts*, 653 F.3d at 1092.

In 2014, the Supreme Court again addressed whether a plaintiff can seek class certification if the prospective class representative no longer has a claim for relief from the defendant. *Marshall v. Safeway, Inc.*, 437 Md. 542, 88 A.3d 735 (2014). Using the standard identified in *Frazier*, the court in *Marshall* found that the plaintiff was precluded from seeking class certification because the defendant had already tendered individual damages to the prospective class representative. *Id.* at 563. In *Marshall*, the plaintiff filed a putative class action suit against her employer, Safeway, for incorrectly calculating wages exempt from garnishment. *Id.* at 542. Ten days after the plaintiff filed the class action suit, Safeway corrected its system for calculating wage exemptions and tendered to the plaintiff the amount that was erroneously withheld. *Id.* at 550. Fifteen months after filing the initial complaint, the plaintiff filed a motion for class certification, which the circuit court denied as moot. *Id.* at 551, 555. The Appellate Court affirmed the circuit court's decision. *Id.*

Relying on *Frazier*, the Supreme Court affirmed the circuit court's finding that Marshall had been given reasonable time to seek class certification after receiving damages from Safeway. *Marshall*, 437 Md. at 554. Although *Frazier* established that a defendant's tender of individual relief to the prospective class representative does not moot a class action if the plaintiff has not had reasonable time to move for class certification, the *Marshall* court found that the plaintiff received a reasonable amount of time to do so. *Id.* at 563. Acknowledging that this decision was within the circuit court's discretion, the court noted that Marshall's "motion to certify was filed late—15 months after the action was filed and only three weeks before trial—and, if granted, would make it impossible to conduct the trial as scheduled." *Id.* at 554.

Similarly, the Supreme Court affirmed the circuit court's denial of class certification because Marshall failed to join a necessary party under rule 2-211, in this instance, the garnishing creditor of each member of the class. *Id.* at 565. Per Rule 3-646, garnishing creditors are considered a party to disputes over garnished wages, "a party with a much greater interest in the matter than the employer," according to the court. *Id.* Noting that joining creditors to a suit of over 500 garnishments would be "wholly unworkable," the court acknowledged that the only common issue in the suit was Safeway's improper standard for calculating exempt wages, an issue that was rendered moot. *Id.* Furthermore, because facts unique to each employee would determine the individual damage awards, the circuit court held that issues common to the class did not predominate over individual issues, as required for class certification by Rule 2-231(c)(3). *Marshall*, 437 Md. at 554. Accordingly, the Supreme Court held that the circuit court did not abuse its discretion by denying class certification. *Id.* at 566.

l. Settlement

In 2016, the Appellate Court addressed the standards that the court must apply when approving a class action settlement under Rule 2-231(i). *Shenker v. Polage*, 226 Md. App. 670, 130 A.3d 1171 (2016). In *Shenker*, the Circuit Court for Baltimore City approved a class action settlement of claims against Cole Real Estate Investments, Inc. (CREI), American Realty Capital Properties, Inc. (ARCP), and both companies' directors and officers, relating to their February 2014 merger. Certain CREI shareholders brought derivative and class action claims, alleging that the CREI board breached its fiduciary duties in negotiating and completing due diligence for the merger. The parties reached a settlement that the circuit court approved preliminarily, but before the circuit court conducted its settlement approval hearing, ARCP announced that certain financial results had been misstated and that others were not (yet) reliable. After further negotiations, the parties agreed to an amended settlement that, among other things, released CREI's officers and directors from future liability, but carved the officers and directors of ARCP out of the release. Five class members, including Robert Shenker, objected to the amended settlement, arguing that the release was overbroad because it precluded the objecting shareholders from bringing federal securities claims against CREI's officers and directors.

Because Rule 2-231(i) does not articulate what standard to apply, the court turned to the federal analogue, Rule 23(e), under which courts typically apply a two-step process: "first, by evaluating the procedural fairness of the settlement process, and second, by evaluating the settlement's substantive fairness and adequacy. When reviewing a trial court's decision to approve a class action settlement, 'there is a strong presumption in favor of finding a settlement fair.'" *Id.* at 683–84, 130 A.3d at 1179 (quoting *Decohen v. Abbasi, LLC*, 299 F.R.D. 469, 479 (D. Md. 2014)). Additionally, the trial court's decision is afforded substantial deference, and is reversed only upon clear showing that the court abused its discretion. *Id.* The court determined that, although the trial court did not undertake a step-by-step "Rule 23-style" analysis for settlement approval, the settlement nonetheless complied with both Rule 2-231(i) and Rule 23(e). The trial court was still "well-informed" and it was evident from the written memorandum and from the transcript of the fairness hearing that the circuit court considered and analyzed the settlement in a manner consistent with the requirements of Federal Rule 23(e), and reached its ultimate conclusion that the settlement was "fair, reasonable, and adequate on a fully informed basis." *Id.* at 685, 130 A.3d at 1180. The court reasoned that fairness could be found so long as the settlement was reached "as a result of good faith bargaining at arm's length." *Id.* at 687, 130 A.3d at 1182 (quoting *In re Jiffy Lube Sec. Litig.*, 927 F.2d 155, 159 (4th Cir. 1991)). The court also determined that, where class members relinquish the right to bring suit, the adequacy of the settlement should be evaluated by "weigh[ing] the likelihood of the plaintiff's recovery on the merits against the amount offered in settlement." *Shenker*, 226 Md. App. at 688, 130 A.3d at 1181 (quoting *In re Mid-Atl. Toyota Antitrust Litig.*, 564 F. Supp. 1379, 1384 (D. Md. 1983)). Maryland courts consider the following factors: "(1) the relative strength of the plaintiffs' case on the merits, (2) the existence of any difficulties of proof or strong defenses the plaintiffs are likely to encounter if the case goes to trial, (3) the anticipated duration and expense of additional litigation, (4) the solvency of the defendants and the likelihood of recovery on a litigated judgment, and (5) the degree of opposition to the settlement." *Id.* Lastly, the court determined that the due process concern during judicial review of a class action settlement is "whether class counsel adequately represented the interests of the class." *Id.* at 690–91, 130 A.3d at 1183. The Appellate Court affirmed approval of the settlement because the settlement agreement was both procedurally and substantively fair, and there was no due process concern.

A recent case from the Supreme Court provides a limitation on the terms of a class action settlement: a private class settlement cannot interfere with a state or federal consumer protection agency's actions on its own behalf. *Linton v. Consumer Protection Division*, 467 Md. 502, 225 A.3d 456 (2020). In *Linton*, the Maryland Consumer Protection Division (MCPD) intervened on behalf of a class that sued their assignee of structured settlement annuity benefits. *Id.* A provision in the class-action settlement between the class members and the assignee limited the ability of the MCPD to pursue further claims against the assignee for its violation of Maryland's consumer protection laws. *Id.* The Court noted that while the class members were free to disclaim their own rights, "they have no authority, through a private settlement, whether or not approved by a court, to preclude MCPD from pursuing its own remedies against those who violate the Consumer Protection Act, including a general request for disgorgement/restitution." *Id.* at 520.

m. Attorneys' Fees

Under the "common-fund doctrine," class counsel are paid out of the monetary recovery that they generate for the class. *See, e.g., Hess Constr. Co. v. Bd. of Educ. of Prince George's County*, 341 Md. 155, 166, 669 A.2d 1352 (1996) (stating that an equity court has "the power to direct payment of counsel fees out of a fund that has been created by the efforts of counsel"); *Bowling v. Brown*, 57 Md. App. 248, 268, 469 A.2d 896 (1984) (allowing fees "where a common fund, benefitting the public, has been created as a result of litigation"). The application of the "common-fund doctrine" is vested within the discretion of the trial judge." *Halle Dev., Inc. v. Anne Arundel Cty.*, No. 1299, 2017 WL 5629677, at *15 (Md. Ct. Spec. App. Nov. 22, 2017). Once a common fund is awarded to the class, a particular fee schedule with the named plaintiffs is not controlling as it pertains to the Class as a whole and thus it is within the discretion of the court to determine the percentage of the common fund to be allocated as counsel fees. *Id.* at *15–16. "[B]y definition, the common-fund doctrine requires a fund. *State v. Braverman*, 228 Md. App. 239, 255, 137 A.3d 377, 386 (2016), *cert. denied sub nom., Goldberg v. State*, 450 Md. 115, 146 A.3d 469 (2016). Therefore, when a judgment results in the "invalidation of [a] statute, but not in any actual monetary recovery or fund," the doctrine does not apply. *Id.*

4. INTERESTING CASES

In April 1998, tobacco manufacturers and related entities filed a petition with the Supreme Court for a writ of mandamus requesting that the Supreme Court vacate the certification by the Circuit Court for Baltimore City of two classes of Maryland residents who, as current or former users of tobacco products, sued the manufacturers claiming to have been injured by tobacco use or addicted to nicotine. *Philip Morris Inc. v. Angeletti*, 358 Md. 689, 752 A.2d 200 (2000); *see also Hartford Fire Ins. Co. v. Brown*, No. 355, SEPT.TERM, 2020, 2020 WL 3790868, at *1 (Md. App. July 7, 2020) (noting *Phillip Morris Inc.* as emblematic of the proper use of a writ of mandamus). The circuit court certified for class action treatment under Maryland Rule 2-231(c)(3) eight traditional tort and contract causes of action, a consumer protection claim, and under Rule 2-231(c)(2), a claim for medical monitoring. The circuit court also approved the plaintiffs' proposed litigation plan, a three-phase trial to determine liability in Phase I, followed by the class representatives' trial on causation and damages in Phase II, and the trial of individual class member issues in Phase III.

In deciding the threshold question of whether it had the authority to issue a writ of mandamus vacating the certification order, the Supreme Court found that appellate review of the certification order would be "inadequate and ineffective" in light of the "commitment of such an extraordinary amount of the judicial and other resources of the busiest trial court in the state." *Philip Morris Inc.*, 358 Md. at 714, 752 A.2d at 213. The Class Action Notice Plan accompanying the certification order estimated total class membership at over 750,000. *Id.* at 716 n.11. The court emphasized that this case was not a "garden variety class action litigation" and that appellate reversal of the class certification order after Phase II and III trials would be a "waste of judicial resources . . . without precedent in this State." *Id.* at 716, 752 A.2d at 215. The court held that "the public interest and [the Court's] responsibility in exercising the supreme judicial authority of this State thus compel[s] the exercise of [the] Court's discretion in this extraordinary case." *Id.* at 718, 752 A.2d at 215. *Compare Royal Fin. Serv. v. Eason*, 183 Md. App. 496, 502, 961 A.2d 1161, 1165 (Md. Ct. Spec. App. 2008) (dismissing an appeal based on the certification of a small class seeking damages under Maryland's Secondary Mortgage Loan Laws because the trial court's certification order was not an appealable final judgment and dismissal would not result in an "extraordinary" level of wasted judicial resources because the class involved relatively few members), *with Anne Arundel County v. Cambridge Commons*, 167 Md. App. 219, 230, 892 A.2d 593, 600 (2005) (applying the collateral order doctrine to hear an interlocutory appeal when the class certification order contained allegedly burdensome research and cost provisions with respect to class notice that could not effectively be undone on appeal from final judgment).

The Appellate Court affirmed the general rule that the certification of a class is not an appealable final order and does not satisfy the three requirements of the collateral order doctrine. *Ford Motor Credit Co. v. Ferrell*, 188 Md. App. 704, 709, 982 A.2d 1175, 1178 (Md. Ct. Spec. App. 2009). The court declined to make an exception when presented with what the court called a "garden variety class action." *Id.* at 717, 982 A.2d at 1183. Such class actions, the court observed, always involve a large number of plaintiffs and impose substantial burdens and expenses on defendants. *Id.* at 715, 717, 982 A.2d at 1183. "There is no magic number of potential class members, claims, time, or dollars spent that will render a class certification immediately appealable." *Id.* at 717, 982 A.2d at 1183. The court went on to note: "*FRCP 23(f)* was amended in 1998 to expressly authorize federal courts of appeal to review orders granting or denying class certification." *Id.* at 719, 982 A.2d at 1183. Rule 2-231 lacks a similar provision, suggesting that interlocutory appellate review of class action certification orders is not available in Maryland. *Id.* at 719, 982 A.2d at 1183.

In a 2011 class action suit brought by indigent arrestees in Baltimore County Circuit Court against state and city officials and the Public Defender, seeking injunctive and declaratory relief, the Supreme Court upon reconsideration held that the represented class was entitled under Article 24 of the Maryland Declaration of Rights to be represented at an initial hearing before a Commissioner. *DeWolfe v. Richmond*, 434 Md. 444, 464, 76 A.3d 1019, 1031 (2013).

The plaintiffs represented the class of all indigent persons brought for initial bail hearings and denied representation by counsel at the initial bail hearings, presently and in the future. The plaintiffs looked to the circuit court for a declaration that they and the represented class have the right to be represented by a public defender at bail hearings, under both the federal and state constitutions as well as the Public Defenders Act. *Dewolfe v. Richmond*, 434 Md. 403, 409–10, 76 A.3d 962, 965 (2012). The Supreme Court held that the circuit court did not err in declaring the plaintiffs' entitlement to representation, even though it lacked consideration of the costs associated with the rights declared. *Id.* The court also held that the circuit court's denial of injunctive relief "does not erect a *res judicata* bar to the Plaintiffs' seeking future injunctive relief, as may be necessary to enforce the right to counsel declared by the Circuit Court." *Id.*

Finally, the Supreme Court joined the "the supermajority of states and federal courts" by adopting the *Daubert* standard for determining the admissibility of expert testimony. *Rochkind v Stevenson*, 471 Md. 1, 26, 236 A.3d 630, 644 (2020) ("We adopt *Daubert* [*v. Merrell Dow Pharmaceuticals, Inc.*, 509 U.S. 579 (1993)]."). The factors to be considered in a *Daubert* analysis include "but are not limited to: (1) whether a theory or technique can be (and has been) tested; (2) whether a theory or technique has been subjected to peer review and publication; (3) whether a particular scientific technique has a known or potential rate of error; (4) the existence and maintenance of standards and controls; and (5) whether a theory or technique is generally accepted. . . . (6) whether experts are proposing to testify about matters growing naturally and directly out of research they have conducted independent of the litigation, or whether they have developed their opinions expressly for purposes of testifying; (7) whether the expert has unjustifiably extrapolated from an accepted premise to an unfounded conclusion; (8) whether the expert has adequately accounted for obvious alternative explanations; (9) whether the expert is being as careful as he [or she] would be in his [or her] regular professional work outside his [or her] paid litigation consulting; and (10) whether the field of expertise claimed by the expert is known to reach reliable results for the type of opinion the expert would give." *Id.* at 35–36, 236 A.3d at 650 (citations omitted).

The Maryland chapter was written by Matthew T. Wagman and Bridget Brodie, a Principal and Associate, respectively, in the Washington D.C. and Baltimore offices of Miles & Stockbridge P.C.; and John Parker Sweeney, Andrew J. Narod, and Timothy Willman, litigation Partners and Associate, respectively, in the Washington D.C. office of Bradley Arant Boult Cummings, LLP. The authors extend special thanks to Tyrese K. McNair, a 2024 Summer Associate in the Baltimore office of Miles & Stckbridge P.C., for his contributions to this chapter.

MASSACHUSETTS

1. MASSACHUSETTS LAW PROVIDES FOR TWO DISTINCT TYPES OF CLASS ACTION

Two forms of class action are available under Massachusetts law. Rule 23 of the Massachusetts Rules of Civil Procedure establishes a class action rule of general applicability that is modeled on Fed. R. Civ. P. 23 though, as discussed below, it differs from the federal rule in several material respects. Massachusetts Rule 23 applies to all actions seeking to assert civil claims on behalf of a putative class other than those arising under the Massachusetts unfair and deceptive trade practices statute, Mass. Gen. Laws ch. 93A (Chapter 93A).[1] Class actions asserting claims under Chapter 93A are subject to unique class action provisions applicable to claims brought by consumers, *see* Mass. Gen. Laws ch. 93A, § 9(2), or to claims brought by businesses, *see* Mass. Gen. Laws ch. 93A, § 11. The class action provisions under §§ 9(2) and 11 are similar to each other but differ in several significant ways from both Fed. R. Civ. P. 23 and Mass. R. Civ. P. 23. Both forms of class action under Massachusetts law are discussed below.

2. COMPARISON OF MASS. R. CIV. P. 23 WITH FED R. CIV. P. 23

Rule 23 of the Massachusetts Rules of Civil Procedure is similar in many respects to its federal cognate, Fed. R. Civ. P. 23, but omits certain provisions that are present in the federal rule. Because Mass. R. Civ. P. 23 was modeled on the federal rule, the Supreme Judicial Court (SJC)[2] has held that where the Massachusetts rule omits text used in the federal rule, it reflects a conscious choice by the Legislature not to adopt the associated federal procedure. Massachusetts courts may not judicially incorporate or adopt those omitted federal procedures when applying Mass. R. Civ. P. 23. *See Fletcher v. Cape Cod Gas Co.*, 394 Mass. 595, 602, 477 N.E.2d 116, 121 (1985). Thus, practitioners

[1] Please note that Massachusetts practitioners and the Massachusetts courts (including the Supreme Judicial Court) commonly use the non-Bluebook citation format "G.L. c." to refer to chapters of the Massachusetts General Laws (e.g., citing to Chapter 93A as "G.L. c. 93A" instead of "Mass. Gen. Laws ch. 93A"). Citations appearing in quotations from court opinions will be rendered as set forth in those opinions; otherwise, all citations in this chapter will be rendered in Bluebook format.

[2] The SJC is the highest appellate court in Massachusetts. With limited exceptions not applicable to class action practice, the SJC has discretionary jurisdiction to hear appeals from lower courts. The Superior Court (Mass. Super. Ct.) is the division of the Trial Court authorized to hear class actions. The Appeals Court (Mass. App. Ct.) is the intermediate appellate court with mandatory jurisdiction to hear appeals as of right from judgments in the Superior Court, and discretionary jurisdiction to hear appeals from class certification decisions and other interlocutory orders. If an appellant does not accompany their appeal with "parts of the trial transcript and copies of motions which are essential for review of the issues," the lower court judgment will be affirmed. *Tatulli v. Avalonbay Cmtys., Inc.*, 105 Mass. App. Ct. 1117, 255 N.E.3d 626, 2025 Mass. App. Unpub. LEXIS 156, at *1 (Mass. App. Ct. Mar. 7, 2025) (Mass. App. Ct. R. 23.0 decision (summary disposition); appellant failed to include hearing transcript that explained the motion judge's basis for denying class certification).

should be aware that practice under Mass. R. Civ. P. 23 differs from practice under the federal rule in the following key respects.

First, the Massachusetts rule may be more conducive to vagueness in class definition, due to the omission of the federal rule's provision calling for class certification at "an early practicable time" after commencement of the action. *See Mass. Gen. Hosp. v. Rate Setting Comm'n*, 371 Mass. 705, 713, 359 N.E.2d 41, 47 (1977). One court has suggested that, in certain circumstances, it may be proper to delay defining the class with precision until the time of judgment. *See Cleary v. Comm'r of Pub. Welfare*, 21 Mass. App. Ct. 140, 153, 485 N.E.2d 955, 965 (1985). At the same time, Massachusetts courts have found it premature to address class certification where there has been no discovery, and therefore no factual record with respect to minimum contacts between putative class members and Massachusetts. *See GFS Trust v. Bristol Compressors Int'l*, No. 2012-00134-BLS1, 30 Mass. L. Rptr. 160, 2012 Mass. Super. LEXIS 209, at *11–12 (Mass. Super. Ct. May 23, 2012) (Lauriat, J.); *see also Enemark v. Cadete Enters.*, No. 2011-00574-BLS1, 2012 Mass. Super. LEXIS 217, at *6 (Mass. Super. Ct. June 7, 2012) (Lauriat, J.) (deferring action on motion for class certification for ninety days to allow opportunity for discovery to address whether named plaintiffs could fairly and adequately represent the putative class); *cf. Chambers v. Tufts Associated HMO, Inc.*, No. 1884CV02837-BLS2, 2020 Mass. Super. LEXIS 177, *1 (Mass. Super. Ct. Oct. 22, 2020) (rejecting the argument that the class certification would prejudice the defendant by forcing litigation of essentially individualized claims because the defendant had the opportunity to explore the existence of individual issues during discovery).

Second, Massachusetts Rule 23 makes no allowance for the "limited issue" certification that is expressly permitted by Fed. R. Civ. P. 23(c)(4), which grants federal courts the discretion to certify classes or subclasses as to a subset of the issues presented in the named plaintiff's complaint. *See Fletcher*, 394 Mass. at 602, 477 N.E.2d at 121; *see also Bellermann v. Fitchburg Gas & Elec. Light Co.*, 470 Mass. 43, 54, 18 N.E.3d 1050, 1060 (2014) (citing *Fletcher*, 394 Mass. at 602). Nevertheless, in practice, some Massachusetts trial courts have crafted and certified a narrower class than the one asserted in the plaintiff's complaint. *See, e.g., Weld v. CVS Pharm., Inc.*, No. 98-0897, 11 Mass. L. Rptr. 21, 1999 Mass. Super. LEXIS 439, at *6 (Mass. Super. Ct. Nov. 19, 1999) (Brassard, J.) (declining to certify the class alleged in plaintiffs' complaint —consisting of all CVS pharmacy customers nationwide—and instead certifying a far narrower class, consisting only of Massachusetts CVS customers who received the mailings at issue). Based on the facts and arguments presented in support of class certification, courts will, if supported by the evidence, exercise their discretion to modify the class definition to ensure that a certified class is defined based on objective criteria. *See, e.g., Baranofsky v. Rousselot Peabody*, No. 2084CV00896-BLS2, 2022 Mass. Super. LEXIS 25, *3–6 (Mass. Super. Ct. Jun. 13, 2022).

Third, Mass. R. Civ. P. 23(b) differs from its federal counterpart because it permits certification only if the plaintiffs have met their burden to establish that common questions of fact or law predominate, and that a class action is superior to other available methods for the matter's efficient and fair adjudication (i.e., a class certified under Fed. R. Civ. P. 23(b)(3)). *Fletcher*, 394 Mass. at 599, 477 N.E.2d at 119. As such, it omits the possibility of certification for classes under standards equivalent to Fed. R. Civ. P. 23(b)(1) or (2), where disposition on the merits will affect non-party class members, where numerous persons make claims against a limited fund or resource insufficient to satisfy all claims, or for certification of classes to pursue injunctive relief. *Cf.* Fed. R. Civ. P. 23(b)(1),(2).

Fourth, the Massachusetts rule, unlike its federal counterpart, permits notice to be provided to class members only at the court's discretion, and does not allow absent class members to opt out of the class. *Blake v. Hometown America Communities, Inc.*, 486 Mass. 268, 280 n.13, 158 N.E.3d 18,

32 (2020); *Fletcher*, 394 Mass. at 602, 477 N.E.2d at 121; *Sullivan v. First Mass. Fin. Corp.*, 409 Mass. 783, 790, 569 N.E.2d 814, 819 (1991). As set forth in Part 4 *infra*, the absence of notice and opt out provisions precludes, on due process grounds, the certification of multi-state class actions in Massachusetts state courts in all suits for money damages, unless the named plaintiff can establish that *every* member of the proposed class has sufficient minimum contacts with the state for a Massachusetts court to assert personal jurisdiction over *each* of them without resorting to the notice and opt-out procedures required by Federal Rule 23. *See Moelis v. Berkshire Life Ins. Co.*, 451 Mass. 483, 487, 887 N.E.2d 214, 218–19 (2008) (citing *Phillips Petroleum Co. v. Shutts*, 472 U.S. 797, 811 (1985)); *see also Weitzner v. Cynosure, Inc.*, 85 Mass. App. Ct. 77, 81, 5 N.E.3d 953, 957–58 (2014) (affirming denial of motion to certify national class of "junk fax" recipients, because non-Massachusetts class members had no right to opt out and lacked minimum contacts with the forum).

Further, the lack of an "opt out" provision may, under certain circumstances, nullify the application of claim preclusion principles to class actions. *See Aspinall v. Philip Morris Cos.*, 442 Mass. 381, 397, 813 N.E.2d 476, 489 (2004) (reasoning that claim preclusion principles do not bar class members that proceed in a class action based purely on an economic theory of damages from later seeking personal injury damages in individual lawsuits), *abrogated on other grounds by Tyler v. Michaels Stores Inc.*, 464 Mass. 492, 502–03, 984 N.E.2d 737, 745 (2013); *Longval v. Comm'r of Correction*, 448 Mass. 412, 417–18, 861 N.E.2d 760, 765 (2007) (holding that a class action suit seeking only declaratory or injunctive relief does not bar subsequent individual suits for damages by class members).

3. CASE LAW INTERPRETING SPECIFIC PRONGS OF MASS. R. CIV. P. 23

A litigant seeking to certify a class action must satisfy Mass. R. Civ. P. 23(a) and (b) and must also be a member of the class he or she seeks to represent at the time of certification. *Bellermann* v. *Fitchburg Gas & Elec. Light Co.*, 470 Mass. 43, 52, 18 N.E.3d 1050 (2014); *Gonzalez v. Comm'r of Correction*, 407 Mass. 448, 451, 553 N.E.2d 1295, 1298 (1990); *see Beauchesne v. New England Neurological Assocs., P.C.*, 98 Mass. App. Ct. 716, 726, 159 N.E.3d 728, 738 (2020) (reversing and remanding denial of class action certification where the lower court had improperly dismissed the class representative's individual claim). "[E]ven where there is a separate statutory provision for bringing an action on behalf of others similarly situated, the propriety of a class action is subject to Mass. R. Civ. P. 23." *Shea v. Weston Golf Club*, No. 02-01826, 22 Mass. L. Rptr. 437, 2007 Mass. Super. LEXIS 148, at *6 (Mass. Super. Ct. May 18, 2007) (Fremont-Smith, J.) (citing *Baldassari v. Public Fin. Trust*, 369 Mass. 33, 40, 337 N.E.2d 701, 706 (1975));[3] *see also Chaves v. King Arthur's Lounge, Inc.*, No. 07-2505, 2009 Mass. Super. LEXIS 298, at *21 (Mass. Super. Ct. July 30, 2009) (McIntyre, J.) (Wage Act does not grant automatic class status, so class may be certified on a Wage Act claim only if the requirements of Rule 23 are satisfied).

---

[3] As is discussed in detail below, an exception to the principle stated in *Shea* is the class action provision in Mass. Gen. Laws ch. 93A, § 9(2), which courts interpret to omit the predominance requirement present in Mass. R. Civ. P. 23(b) based on the absence of predominance language in the statute. *See* Kwaak v. Pfizer, Inc., 71 Mass. App. Ct. 293, 298, 881 N.E.2d 812 (2008). Courts have declined to give a similar construction to class action provisions in other statutes that do not implicate Chapter 93A's broad remedial consumer protection purposes. *See, e.g.,* Sagar v. Florenza, 2014 Mass. Super. LEXIS 1, at *2–4 (2014) (Curran, J.) (rejecting argument by analogy that certification of class to pursue claims under the Wage Act should, like certification of a class under Chapter 93A, omit the requirement to establish predominance).

If an individual cannot maintain an action independently, he or she cannot represent a class seeking relief. *Doe v. Governor*, 381 Mass. 702, 704–05, 412 N.E.2d 325, 327 (1980); *see Monell v. Boston Pads, LLC*, 2013 Mass. Super. LEXIS 102, at *22 (Mass. Super. Ct. Jul. 19, 2013) (Cosgrove, J.) (denying certification of class to pursue claims under Mass. Gen. Laws ch. 149, §148B, where plaintiff was not an "employee" for purposes of that statute). These rules recognize that a named plaintiff with a personal stake is more motivated to adequately represent class interests. *Gonzalez*, 407 Mass. at 452, 553 N.E.2d at 1298.

The burden to establish that the requirements of Rule 23 have been met rests with the party or parties seeking class certification. *Bellermann*, 470 Mass. at 52, 18 N.E.3d 1050; *Fletcher v. Cape Cod Gas Co.*, 394 Mass. 595, 597, 477 N.E.2d 116, 118 (1985). A plaintiff, however, does not have the burden of producing evidence sufficient to prove each Rule 23 requirement; rather, a plaintiff must provide "information sufficient to enable the motion judge to make a reasonable judgment" that the class comports with the Rule. *Henry v. Bozzuto Mgmt. Co.*, 98 Mass. App. Ct. 690, 159 N.E.3d 701 (2020) (quoting *Layes v. RHP Props., Inc.*, 95 Mass. App. Ct. 804, 821 (2019) (citation omitted)); *see also Weld v. Glaxo Wellcome, Inc.*, 434 Mass. 81, 87, 746 N.E.2d 522, 528 (2001) (same). Courts have broad discretion concerning class certification, and appeals courts will reverse a trial court's finding only for abuse of discretion—meaning that the certification decision must be "arbitrary, unreasonable, or capricious." *Weld*, 434 Mass. at 85, 746 N.E.2d at 527. The trial judge may not certify a class on the basis of "speculation or generalization regarding satisfaction of the requirements of Rule 23," and has the discretion to hold an evidentiary hearing before deciding a class certification motion. *Id.*; *see also Foster v. Commissioner of Correction (No. 1)*, 484 Mass. 698, 713–14, 146 N.E.3d 372, 388 (2020) ("[T]he Superior Court judge is better positioned to take expert testimony to determine the appropriate definition of [the class] . . . ."). Standing alone, however, a court's failure to hold an evidentiary hearing does not constitute an abuse of discretion. *Id.*

The "decision as to class certification is not immutable and if at any time it appears that for any reason [the representative plaintiff] no longer fairly and adequately protects the interests of the class, class status may be withdrawn or appropriately modified." *Aspinall v. Phillip Morris Cos.*, 442 Mass. 381, 399, 813 N.E.2d 476, 490 n.22 (2004) (quoting *Sch. Comm. of Brockton v. Mass. Comm'n Against Discrimination*, 423 Mass. 7, 14, 666 N.E.2d 468, 473 (1996)), *abrogated on other grounds by Tyler v. Michaels Stores Inc.*, 464 Mass. 492, 502–03, 984 N.E.2d 737, 745 (2013).

a. Rule 23(a)

i. Numerosity. The first prerequisite to class certification is that "the class is so numerous that joinder of all members is impracticable. . . . " Mass. R. Civ. P. 23(a)(1). "The word 'impracticable' in the context of Mass. R. Civ. P. 23 has been interpreted to mean impractical, unwise, or imprudent, rather than impossible or incapable of being performed." *Reynolds v. City Express, Inc.*, 2014 Mass. Super. LEXIS 44, at *37 (Mass. Super. Ct. Jan. 18, 2014) (Locke, J.) (citing *Brophy v. Sch. Comm. of Worcester*, 6 Mass. App. Ct. 731, 735, 383 N.E.2d 521, 524 (1978)). "A determination of impracticability should depend on all circumstances surrounding the case, including the size of the class, geographic dispersion, the nature of relief sought and the practicality of forcing relitigation of a common core of issues." *Owens v. Capobianco*, No. 94-6070, 1995 Mass. Super. LEXIS 717, at *3 (Mass. Super. Ct. Apr. 25, 1995) (McEvoy, J.) (citations omitted).

The Supreme Judicial Court has never attempted to set any minimum number of class members that would be necessary for a class suit. *See* Reporters' Notes to Rule 23, Mass. Ann. Laws Court Rules, Rules of Civ. Procedure (LexisNexis 2012). Along with the number of class members, courts also consider efficiency and judicial economy when making class certification decisions. *Brophy v.*

Sch. Comm. of Worcester, 6 Mass. App. Ct. 731, 735, 383 N.E.2d 521, 524 (1978); *see also Campbell v. Glodis*, No. 2010-0397C, 28 Mass. L. Rptr. 465, 2011 Mass. Super. LEXIS 114, at *8 (Mass. Super. Ct. May 27, 2011) (Inge, J.) (finding numerosity requirement satisfied where class currently consisted of eleven inmates subjected to alleged excessive use of pepper spray, but there may be others, as yet unnamed, who fall within the class, and the joinder of all such plaintiffs "certainly appears impractical, unwise and imprudent" (quotations and citations omitted)); *Chaves v. King Arthur's Lounge, Inc.*, No. 07-2505, 2009 Mass. Super. LEXIS 298, at *22 (Mass. Super. Ct. July 30, 2009) (McIntyre, J.) (class of seventy persons sufficiently large to render individual actions "impracticable"); *Reynolds*, 2014 Mass. Super. LEXIS 44, at *37 (class of at least forty individuals satisfies numerosity requirement); *cf. Norell v. Spring Valley Country Club, Inc.*, No. 1482-CV-00283, 33 Mass. L. Rep. 299, 2016 Mass. Super. LEXIS 33 (Mass. Super. Ct. Mar. 14, 2016) (Hiller, J.) (class size of "more than twenty," without other indicators of impracticability, failed numerosity requirement); *In re OvaScience, Inc.*, No. SUCV-2015-3087-BLS2, 2017 Mass. Super. LEXIS 255, at *6 (Mass. Super. Ct. Nov. 8, 2017) (Sanders, J.) (class of thirteen persons failed the numerosity requirement); *Baranofsky*, 2022 Mass. Super LEXIS 25 at *8 (a proposed class of several thousand people "easily satisfies" the numerosity requirement).

Numerosity cannot be established through mere speculation. In *OvaScience*, the evidence before the court showed that the thirteen members of the putative shareholder class consisted of eleven individuals and two institutional holders. *See* 2017 Mass. Super. LEXIS 255, at *6. Plaintiffs argued that the institutional holders undoubtedly were holders of the shares "in street name" on behalf of tens of thousands of individual beneficial owners of the shares. This supposition, the court held, was insufficient to satisfy the plaintiffs' burden to prove numerosity because the plaintiffs, despite the opportunity to take discovery, had submitted no evidence concerning the number of beneficial holders. Although a plaintiff "need not show the exact number of potential members in order to satisfy the numerosity prerequisite, [the plaintiff] does bear the burden of showing impracticability and mere speculation as to the number of parties involved is not sufficient to satisfy Rule 23(a)(1)." *Id.* at *7 (quoting *Swack v. Credit Suisse First Bos*., 230 F.R.D. 250, 258 (D. Mass. 2005) (quotations omitted)); As a result, plaintiffs failed to satisfy their burden to prove numerosity. *See OvaScience*, 270 Mass. Super. LEXIS 255. Note, however, if plaintiff can establish that there are numerous class members, the inability to identify those class members by name will not preclude a finding of numerosity. *See Gammella v. P.F. Chang's China Bistro, Inc.*, 482 Mass. 1, 12–13, 120 N.E.3d 690, 700–01 (2019) (finding numerosity satisfied where plaintiff identified hundreds of potential class members—but could not provide their names—because the number of people, combined with the fact that the defendant refused to provide their names, "made it reasonable to infer that the number of plaintiffs would satisfy the numerosity requirement").

ii. Commonality. The second prerequisite to class certification is that there "are questions of law or fact common to the class. . . . " Mass. R. Civ. P. 23(a)(2). Each class member's interest does not have to be identical in all respects, but "the interest must arise out of a common relationship to a definite wrong." *Eldridge v. Provident Cos.*, No. 97-1099, 11 Mass. L. Rptr. 417, 2000 Mass. Super. LEXIS 163, at *19 (Mass. Super. Ct. Mar. 6, 2000) (Toomey, J.) (quoting *Spear v. H.V. Greene Co.*, 246 Mass. 259, 266, 140 N.E. 795, 797 (1923)).

Few reported Massachusetts cases address the commonality requirement in any detail. The Supreme Judicial Court has suggested, in dicta, that plaintiffs have commonality if their claims "derive from a common course of conduct on the part of the defendants and present the identical issue." *Aspinall v. Philip Morris Cos., Inc.*, 442 Mass. 381, 392, 813 N.E.2d 476, 486 (2004), *abrogated on other grounds by Tyler v. Michaels Stores Inc.*, 464 Mass. 492, 502–03, 984 N.E.2d 737, 745 (2013); *see also Reynolds v. City Express, Inc.*, 2014 Mass. Super. LEXIS 44, at *38 (Mass. Super. Ct. Jan.

18, 2014) (Locke, J.) (commonality satisfied because all plaintiffs worked for the same company and were required to sign "apparently identical paperwork"). However, the SJC has also affirmed a trial court's ruling that, even if all putative class members were subjected to the same practices by the defendant, commonality is not satisfied if "actual injury to each individual depends upon analysis of discrete facts, which are not common to all 28,500 plaintiffs." *Bellerman v. Fitchburg Gas & Elec. Light Co.*, No. 2009-00023-B, 30 Mass. L. Rptr. 612, 2013 Mass. Super. LEXIS 3, at *16 (Mass. Super. Ct. Jan. 4, 2013) (Wilkins, J.), *aff'd*, 470 Mass. 43, 18 N.E.3d 1050 (2014).

Because the text of Mass. R. Civ. P. 23(a)(2) follows that of Fed. R. Civ. P. 23(a)(2), counsel may look to interpretations of the federal rule for further guidance on commonality. In particular, the federal courts' continuing reexamination of the commonality requirement in the wake of *Wal-Mart Stores, Inc. v. Dukes*, 564 U.S. 338 (2011), should be especially instructive. *See Wal-Mart*, 564 U.S. at 350 (to satisfy the commonality requirement, "claims must depend upon a common contention" that "must be of such a nature that it is capable of class-wide resolution—which means that determination of its truth or falsity will resolve an issue that is central to the validity of each one of the claims in one stroke"). Additionally, while a single transaction or occurrence, or a series of transactions or occurrences, does not appear to be required to satisfy commonality under Rule 23(a), the predominance requirement of section (b) may imply such a requirement. *See* Reporters' Notes to Rule 23, Mass. Ann. Laws Court Rules, Rules of Civ. Procedure (LexisNexis 2012).

iii. Typicality. The third prerequisite to class certification is that "the claims or defenses of the representative parties are typical of the claims or defenses of the class. . . ." Mass. R. Civ. P. 23(a)(3). Typicality "may be satisfied by an allegation that the defendant acted consistently toward the members of a putative class." *Fletcher v. Cape Cod Gas Co.*, 394 Mass. 595, 601, 477 N.E. 2d 116, 121 (1985). There must be a sufficient relationship between the named plaintiff's injury and the conduct affecting the class: "[A] plaintiff representative nominally satisfies the typicality requirement with an allegation that the defendant acted consistently toward the representative and the members of a putative class." *Reynolds v. City Express, Inc.*, 2014 Mass. Super. LEXIS 44, at *39 (Mass. Super. Ct. Jan. 18, 2014) (Locke, J.) (citing *Weld v. Glaxo Wellcome, Inc.*, 434 Mass. 81, 87, 746 N.E. 522, 528–29 (2001)); *Baranofsky*, 2022 Mass. Super LEXIS 25 at *19. Further, the claims of the named plaintiff and those of the class must be based on the same legal theory. *Reynolds*, 2014 Mass. Super. LEXIS 44, at *39 (citing *Weld*, 434 Mass. at 87, 746 N.E. at 528–29). "The word 'typical' does not, however, require that all members of the class be identically situated." Reporters' Notes to Rule 23, Mass. Ann. Laws Court Rules, Rules of Civ. Procedure (LexisNexis 2012).

Subsumed within the typicality requirement is the principle that a would-be class representative, at a minimum, must be a member of the class he or she purports to represent. *See Gonzalez v. Comm'r of Correction*, 407 Mass. 448, 451, 553 N.E.2d 1295, 1298 (1990). This means, among other things, that the named plaintiff must have standing to bring the claims advanced on behalf of the class. *Doe v. Governor*, 381 Mass. 702, 704–05, 412 N.E.2d 325, 327 (1980). A court, however, "will not allow a defendant's voluntary cessation of his allegedly wrongful conduct with respect to [only the] named plaintiffs to moot the case for the entire plaintiff class." *Wolf v. Comm'r of Pub. Welfare*, 367 Mass. 293, 299, 327 N.E.2d 885, 889 (1975); *see also Meaney v. OneBeacon Ins. Group, LLC*, Civ. A. No. 07-1294-BLS2, 2010 Mass. Super. LEXIS 64, *6 (Mass. Super. Ct. Feb. 25, 2009) (Neel, J.) (in putative class action, defendant's tender to named plaintiff of full amount due under contract does not require dismissal of the action or prevent the named plaintiff from continuing to assert claims on behalf of the putative class, even though the named plaintiff is technically no longer a member of that class). Similarly, courts overlook technical mootness where the conduct at issue may be characterized as "capable of repetition, yet evading review." *Gonzalez*, 407 Mass. at 450, 553 N.E.2d at 1297; *see Silva v. Tadisco Services, Inc.*, No. 1684-CV-02778-BLS2, 2018 Mass. Super. LEXIS 23,

*4 (Mass. Super. Ct. Mar. 6, 2018) (Salinger, K.) ("Consumers do not lose the chance to seek an effective private remedy through a c. 93A class action merely because the defendant chooses to pay the entire amount of the named plaintiff's individual claim.").

The Supreme Judicial Court has relaxed the typicality requirement in the context of a class action brought against multiple defendants that engaged in a similar course of conduct *vis-à-vis* members of the putative class. In *Weld v. Glaxo Wellcome, Inc.*, the Supreme Judicial Court held that the trial court did not abuse its discretion by concluding that the named plaintiff's claims were "typical" and certifying the proposed class, even though the named plaintiff personally had standing to assert claims against only one of the four defendants, while the other three defendants had no contact whatsoever with the named plaintiff. 434 Mass. at 87–92, 746 N.E.2d at 529–31. Invoking the "juridical links doctrine," the court reasoned that Rule 23, like the permissive joinder standard contained in Rule 20(a), is a "procedural device that permits collective adjudication of related claims, not a substantive rule that results in joint and several liability." *Id.* at 90–91, 746 N.E.2d at 530–31. Although the absence of any nexus between the named plaintiff and the three other defendants may be a defense that these defendants can assert against the named plaintiff's right to recover from them, this potential defense did not render the named plaintiff's claims atypical for purposes of Rule 23(a)(3). *Id.*

Similarly, in *Foster v. Commissioner of Correction (No. 1)*, the SJC reasoned that basic claims of a heightened risk of contracting COVID-19 brought by a class of incarcerated individuals satisfied the Rule 23 typicality requirement. 484 Mass. 698, 713, 146 N.E.3d 372, 388 (2020). The court concluded that although the named putative class representatives were being housed at different facilities than some other purported absent class members, and thus their risks were not identical, the claims were sufficiently similar to be considered typical and representative of the class interests. *Id.*

iv. Adequacy. The fourth and final prerequisite to class certification is that "the representative parties will fairly and adequately protect the interests of the class." Mass. R. Civ. P. 23(a)(4). Under Rule 23(a)(4) the class representative has the responsibility to protect the interests of all class members. *Spence v. Reeder*, 382 Mass. 398, 409, 416 N.E.2d 914, 921 (1981). Accordingly, "[f]or a plaintiff to be a fair and adequate representative of the class, the plaintiff must have 1) no potential conflicts with the proposed class members and 2) qualified, experienced counsel able to vigorously conduct the proposed litigation." *Eldridge v. Provident Cos.*, No. 97-1099, 11 Mass. L. Rptr. 417, 2000 Mass. Super. LEXIS 163, at *20–21 (Mass. Super. Ct. Mar. 6, 2000) (Toomey, J.) (citing *Andrews v. Bechtel Power Corp.*, 780 F.2d 124, 130 (1st Cir. 1985)).

The "adequacy and vigor of plaintiffs' counsel is the critical element in determining whether the party representative will fairly and adequately protect the class," and the court has an "ongoing duty" to make sure that requirement is complied with at all stages of the litigation. *Weld v. CVS Pharm., Inc.*, No. 98-0897-BLS-2, slip op. at 6, 9 (Mass. Super. Ct. Feb. 23, 2006) (Gants, J.) (citing *Key v. Gillette Co.*, 782 F.2d 5, 7 (1st Cir. 1986)). The adequacy determination "is not immutable and if at any time it appears that for any reason the [representative plaintiff] no longer fairly and adequately represents the class, class status may be withdrawn or appropriately modified." *Aspinall v. Phillip Morris Cos.*, 442 Mass. 381, 399, 813 N.E.2d 476, 490 n.22 (2004) (quoting *Sch. Comm. of Brockton v. Mass. Comm'n Against Discrimination*, 423 Mass. 7, 14, 666 N.E.2d 468, 473 (1996)), *abrogated on other grounds by Tyler v. Michaels Stores Inc.*, 464 Mass. 492, 502–03, 984 N.E.2d 737, 745 (2013); *see Weld*, No. 98-0897-BLS-2, slip op. at 9 (granting motion to decertify class based on inadequacy of the class representative and his counsel after they did "nothing of significance" to prosecute the case for three and a half years); *Weld v. CVS Pharm., Inc.*, Civ. A. No. 98-0897-BLS-2 (Mass. Super. Ct. Dec. 18, 2006) (Gants, J.) (reinstating earlier ruling decertifying the class). The fact that some members of the putative class do not wish to participate in the action does not render the named plaintiff an inadequate representative. *Chaves v. King Arthur's Lounge, Inc.*, No. 07-2505, 2009 Mass. Super. LEXIS 298, at *2425 (Mass. Super. Ct. July 30, 2009) (McIntyre, J.) (in class action brought on behalf of class of exotic dancers, fact that certain absentee class members "do not wish to be involved" and cannot opt out does not render the named plaintiffs inadequate representatives, particularly given that the absentee dancers' economic dependence on the defendant club for employment is "likely a factor" in their "reluctance to litigate").

The adequacy requirement of Rule 23(a)(4) presupposes the existence of a named plaintiff to pursue the class claims. Death of the named plaintiff before class certification is sought or granted terminates an attorney's authority to pursue claims on behalf of the client or the putative class absent authorization by deceased's legal representative. This principle, which applies in actions brought in a client's individual capacity, applies with full force when the named plaintiff dies before a class is certified. *See Kingara v. Secure Home Health Care Inc.*, 489 Mass. 393, 395 (2022). In *Kingara*, after the named plaintiff's death, her counsel, on her own initiative, took steps to attempt to find and substitute a new representative plaintiff in the action. Specifically, she filed a motion requesting that the court (1) order notice to putative class members pursuant to Mass. R. Civ. P. 23(d) informing them of the named plaintiff's death and inviting them to join the action; (2) order the defendants to identify putative class members' names and addresses; and (3) extend tracking order deadlines to allow substitution of a new class representative and complete discovery. *Id.* at 394. Counsel, however, failed to locate the deceased plaintiff's personal representative and, as a result, had not been authorized to act by any party then joined to the action whose interests she represented. *Id.* at 396. Thus, in keeping with the general principle that a deceased plaintiff's counsel has no authority to act on behalf of a deceased plaintiff absent authorization by the deceased's representative, the Supreme Judicial Court held that a deceased plaintiff's counsel could not act on behalf of anyone whose interests were implicated in the putative class action. *Id.* at 396. Had a class already been certified, counsel would have owed a duty to absent class members that would have authorized some unilateral action to avoid prejudice to the class members she would then have represented. Here, however, the absence of a certified class meant that counsel had no authority to act. *Id.*

b. Rule 23(b)

If the four prerequisites of Rule 23(a) are satisfied, Mass. R. Civ. P. 23(b) provides that a lawsuit may be maintained as a class action only if the court finds: (1) "that the questions of law or fact common to the members of the class predominate over any questions affecting only individual members" (the "predominance" requirement), and (2) "that a class action is superior to other available methods for the fair and efficient adjudication of the controversy" (the "superiority" requirement). These predominance and superiority requirements "introduce a highly discretionary element" into the court's analysis. *Baldassari v. Public Fin. Trust*, 369 Mass. 33, 40, 337 N.E.2d 701, 706 (1975). Courts have broad discretion when deciding Rule 23 motions; "a discretion that is particularly extensive when dealing with the superiority requirement of Rule 23(b)." *Berry v. Town of Danvers*, 34 Mass. App. Ct. 507, 515, 613 N.E.2d 108, 112 (1993).

i. Predominance. Construing the predominance requirement under Rule 23(b), the Supreme Judicial Court has framed the issue thus: "Although common questions need not be dispositive of the entire class action . . . their resolution should at least provide a definite signal of the beginning of the end." *Fletcher v. Cape Cod Gas Co.*, 394 Mass. 595, 603, 477 N.E.2d 116, 122 (1985) (quoting *Mertens v. Abbott Lab.*, 99 F.R.D. 38, 41 (D.N.H. 1983)). There is no clear-cut test for this requirement. *See Reynolds v. City Express, Inc.*, 2014 Mass. Super. LEXIS 44, at *41 (Mass. Super. Ct. Jan.

18, 2014) (Locke, J.) ("The predominance requirement is satisfied by a sufficient constellation of common issues between class members and cannot be reduced to a mechanical, single-issue test."). In some cases, personal-injury liability questions have failed to meet this test, *see Fletcher*, 394 Mass. at 603, 477 N.E.2d at 122, as have questions concerning individual inmates' domicile for voting purposes, *see Dane v. Registrars of Voters of Concord*, 374 Mass. 152, 160, 371 N.E.2d 1358, 1364 (1978), and questions that require consideration of individuals' state of mind, *see Schrier v. BankNorth, N.A. Mass.*, 02-1050B, 2004 Mass. Super. LEXIS 625, at *19–20 (Mass. Super. Ct. Dec. 27, 2004) (McCann, J.); *cf. Dessources v. Copart of Conn., Inc.*, No. 03-2164C, 2004 Mass. Super. LEXIS 651, at *4–5 (Mass. Super. Ct. Dec. 8, 2004) (Houston, J.) (raising the same concerns as *Schrier*, but classifying them as failures to satisfy the "commonality and typicality" requirements). On the other hand, the predominance requirement was satisfied in a case alleging that a program operated by the defendants constituted a *per se* invasion of privacy. *Weld v. Glaxo Wellcome, Inc.*, 434 Mass. 81, 90–93, 746 N.E.2d 522, 531–32 (2001).

"Because the salient inquiry is whether the plaintiffs' claims are '*sufficiently* cohesive to warrant adjudication by representation,' no rote formula can determine whether the plaintiffs have met their burden on the question of predominance." *Salvas v. Wal-Mart Stores, Inc.*, 452 Mass. 337, 364, 893 N.E.2d 1187, 1209 (2008) (quoting *Amchem Prods., Inc. v. Windsor*, 521 U.S. 591, 623 (1997)) (emphasis in original). Rather, the predominance requirement introduces a "highly discretionary element" into a motion judge's class certification decision, but that discretion "must be exercised in accord with the purposes sought to be achieved by class actions." *Id* at 363, 893 N.E.2d at 1209 (quotations and citations omitted). As a result, the trial court must "engage in an 'individualized, pragmatic evaluation of the relationship between and the relative significance of the common and individual issues,'" to determine which predominates. *Id.* at 364, 893 N.E.2d at 1209–10 (quoting *In re Relafen Antitrust Litig.*, 231 F.R.D. 52, 70 (D. Mass. 2005)). Applying this standard in *Salvas*, the Supreme Judicial Court reversed the trial court's class decertification order, and held that, even if the number of unharmed class members was not *de minimis*, plaintiffs had satisfied the predominance requirement on the issue of liability because they had asserted claims alleging that all members of the class were subjected to the same unlawful policy (cutting short their rest and meal breaks). *Id.* at 364–72, 893 N.E.2d at 1210–15.

If the proposed class definition requires the court to make a determination on the merits of the claim in order to decide whether a potential claimant is in the class or not, then individualized inquiries predominate and the proposed class fails as an improper "fail-safe class." *See Gammella v. P.F. Chang's China Bistro, Inc.*, 482 Mass. 1, 15 n.18, 120 N.E.3d 690, 702 (2019) (a "fail-safe class . . . is defined so that whether a person qualified as a member depends on whether the person has a valid claim"). "A fail-safe class is impermissible because 'a class member either wins or, by virtue of losing, is defined out of the class and is therefore not bound by the judgment.'" *Id.* (quoting *McCaster v. Darden Restaurants, Inc.*, 845 F.3d 794, 799 (7th Cir. 2017)); *see also Johnson v. Edgar P. Benjamin Healthcare Ctr., Inc.*, No. 1884-CV-00033-BLS2, 2020 Mass. Super. LEXIS 50, at *2–3 (Mass. Super. Ct. Feb. 25, 2020) (denying class certification because proposed class definition of "employees who can show they did not receive all of the pay they were owed because their time records were altered" was a fail-safe class that would require the court to determine which employees have valid claims and which do not to determine the composition of the class).

Questions of causation can be dispositive of predominance, as common issues do not predominate where "causation would have to be resolved on an individual (or small group) basis." *See Bellermann v. Fitchburg Gas & Elec. Light Co.*, 470 Mass. 43, 55, 18 N.E.3d 1050, 1061 (2014). Thus, in *Bellermann*, the Supreme Judicial Court affirmed class-certification denial because, even if defendant's "systemic failures may have had a general tendency to delay" the restoration of power, "it would still remain for each class member to show that those failures caused a prolonged outage on an individual basis," and the "nominal class action would degenerate in practice into multiple lawsuits separately tried." *Id.* (quotations and citations omitted); *see also Marquis v. Google, Inc.*, No. 2011-02808-BLS1, 32 Mass. L. Rptr. 269, 2014 Mass. Super. LEXIS 104, at *42 (Mass. Super. Ct. June 27, 2014) (Kaplan, J.) (denying class certification for claim that a search engine violated the Massachusetts wiretap statute by using an automated email review to deliver targeted advertising, because individualized inquiries would be necessary to determine which class members had and had not been exposed to defendant's disclosures about its advertising practices).

With respect to damages, the fact that individualized inquiries to establish the *amount* of damages that each class member suffered typically will not bar class certification on predominance grounds where there exist "extensive" common issues of fact and law relating to liability. *See Salvas,* 454 Mass. at 364, 893 N.E.2d at 1210 ("Class certification may be appropriate where common issues of law and fact are shown to form the nucleus of a liability claim, even though the appropriateness of class action treatment in the damages phase is an open question."); *see also Woodruff v. Niles Co.*, No. 05-3225, 22 Mass. L. Rptr. 469, 2007 Mass. Super. LEXIS 146, at *8 (Mass. Super. Ct. May 9, 2007) (Hopkins, J.) ("[N]ecessity for individualized inquiries at the damages stage does not preclude class certification where all the other requirements are met.") (citing *Weld*, 434 Mass. at 92, 746 N.E.2d at 531–32). If the amount of damages varies within the class, judges have a number of options, including conditional class certification and bifurcated trials, to address the liability and damages phases. *See Salvas*, 452 Mass. at 368, 893 N.E.2d at 1212 (citing A. Conte & H.B. Newberg, *Class Actions* § 4:32, at 287–88 (4th ed. 2002)).

Even though differences in the *amounts* of class members' damages may not destroy predominance, a class that requires individual determinations as to the *existence* of individual class members' damages will not satisfy Rule 23(b). *See McGilloway v. Safety Ins. Co.*, Nos. 1784CV02089-BLS2 & 1884CV01627-BLS, 2023 Mass. Super. LEXIS 51, at *13–15 (Mass. Super. Ct., Jun. 20, 2023). These two issues, though sometimes confused, are quite distinct. As the court explains in *McGilloway*,

> There is a difference between determining the extent of harm (the question of damages) and deciding whether there was any harm at all (which goes to liability). "While obstacles to calculating damages may not preclude class certification, the putative class must first demonstrate economic loss on a common basis."

Id. at *13 (quoting *Newton v. Merrill Lynch, Pierce, Fenner & Smith, Inc.*, 259 F.3d 154, 189 (3d Cir. 2001)). In *McGilloway*, plaintiffs claimed that insurers improperly failed to pay insureds for lost resale value that their motor vehicles allegedly suffered after being damaged in a collision and then fully repaired. Because determining whether there was any loss in resale value would require individualized class member-specific determinations, the class could not be certified under Rule 23(b). *See id.* at *15.

Some courts have held that class certification is almost never appropriate for breach of express warranty claims, because proof of detrimental reliance and fact of injury rarely, if ever, presents a case in which common issues of fact predominate. *See Hiller v. DaimlerChrysler Corp.*, No. 02-681, 23 Mass. L. Rptr. 202, 2007 Mass. Super. LEXIS 442, at *13 (Mass. Super. Ct. Sept. 25, 2007) (Henry, J.). This is particularly true in products liability cases in which the product at issue must be evaluated by reference to another varying factor, such as when the product is sold in combination with, or as part of, another product—for example, a seatbelt that is installed in a number of different car models. *Id.* at *13 (finding that common issues did not predominate, because the inherent danger of a common seatbelt design could not be evaluated without reference to the particular types of vehicles that used the seatbelt); *see also Holzman v. General Motors Corp.*, No. 02-1368, 2007 Mass. Super. LEXIS 462, at *33–34 (Mass. Super. Ct. Nov. 6, 2007) (Billings, J.) (finding that individualized inquiries predominated in an action alleging that twenty-three different models of jacks, each sold with one or more GM vehicles over one or more model years, were incapable of performing their intended function).

In *West Concord 5-10-1.00 Store, Inc. v. Interstate Mat Corp.*, plaintiffs sought class action certification for a claim under the federal Telephone Consumer Protection Act (TCPA), which allows private actions for statutory damages to be brought under state class action law if the defendant uses "any telephone facsimile machine, computer, or other device to send an unsolicited advertisement to a telephone facsimile machine," unless: (1) a prior business relationship exists between the parties; or (2) the recipient voluntarily makes its fax number available for public distribution. No. 2010-00356-C, 31 Mass. L. Rptr. 58, 2013 Mass. Super. LEXIS 22, at *1 (Mass. Super. Ct. Mar. 5, 2013) (Kottmyer, J.); 47 U.S.C. §§ 227(a)(4), (b)(1)(C). The court held that to succeed under the TCPA, each class member would need to show receipt of an unwanted fax and establish that (1) they did not have a prior relationship to the business and (2) that they did not voluntarily make their fax number available for distribution. *Id.* at *16. Because of the individualized showing required of each plaintiff, the court held that it was not clear that common questions of fact predominated and so denied class certification. *Id.; see also Weitzner v. Cynosure, Inc.*, 85 Mass. App. Ct. 77, 79, 5 N.E.3d 953, 956 (2014) (plaintiff's TCPA claim did not satisfy the predominance requirement because "liability to each class plaintiff turned, in part, on 'whether there was an existing business relationship between an individual class plaintiff and Cynosure or whether Cynosure. . . obtained that plaintiff's facsimile number from a source through which the plaintiff voluntarily agreed to such a distribution'" (internal citation omitted)).

Affirmative defenses should also be considered when evaluating whether common issues predominate. For example, class certification is inappropriate if individualized inquiries will be necessary to resolve a statute of limitations defense. *Moelis v. Berkshire Life Ins. Co.*, 451 Mass. 483, 490–91, 887 N.E.2d 214, 221 (2008) (because each member of the proposed class was subjected to different information about the life insurance policies at issue, the trial court acted within its discretion in finding that individualized inquiries would be necessary to determine when each proposed class member learned or reasonably should have learned that he or she had been harmed).

ii. Superiority. Massachusetts courts balance the benefits and burdens of class actions against alternative means of resolving the controversy. Unlike its federal counterpart, however, Mass. R. Civ. P. 23(b) does not delineate a list of factors for courts to consider under this balancing test. Instead, Massachusetts courts generally consider whether individual suits or "test case" actions make better use of resources and better promote fairness among similarly situated litigants. *See Carpenter v. Suffolk Franklin Sav. Bank*, 370 Mass. 314, 321, 346 N.E.2d 892, 897 (1976). Where common issues predominate, a class action may be the superior option for litigants. *Sniffin v. Prudential Ins. Co. of Am.*, 11 Mass. App. Ct. 714, 724–25, 419 N.E.2d 308, 314–15 (1981). This is particularly so where the class would aggregate numerous small claims whose likely range of recovery would preclude any individual plaintiff from having his or her day in court. *See Weld v. Glaxo Wellcome, Inc.*, 434 Mass. 81, 93, 746 N.E. 522, 532 (2001); *see also Campbell v. Glodis*, No. WOCV2010-0397C, 28 Mass. L. Rptr. 465, 2011 Mass. Super. LEXIS 114, at *14–15 (Mass. Super. Ct. May 27, 2011) (Inge, J.) (superiority satisfied where: (1) the class size "makes joinder impracticable"; (2) the defendant administrators making policy decisions at the jail would "benefit from one uniform determination" of the issues; (3) "maintaining separate causes of action for every possible plaintiff would be unnecessarily costly"; and (4) "there appears to be no special administrative difficulty in determining damages compared with the problems associated with administering countless individual lawsuits"). Further, the Appeals Court has recognized that the cumulative cost to the defendant associated with a class action is not a valid basis for finding that a class action would be inferior to individualized litigation. *See Hazel's Cup & Saucer, LLC v. Around the Globe Travel, Inc.*, 86 Mass. App. Ct. 164, 166–67, 15 N.E.3d 220, 223 (2014) ("[T]he possibility that the class action mechanism may work successfully as it was intended to by the enacting Legislature in providing appropriate redress by aggregating small recoveries [may not] be treated as a factor supporting a conclusion that the class action mechanism would be inferior to individual litigation of those claims.").

On the other hand, if certifying a class action would not dispense with the need for individualized adjudication of liability because of the "need to show causation on a plaintiff-by-plaintiff basis," Rule 23(b)'s superiority requirement is not satisfied. *Bellerman v. Fitchburg Gas & Elec. Light Co.*, No. 2009-00023-B, 30 Mass. L. Rptr. 612, 2013 Mass. Super. LEXIS 3, at *20 (Mass. Super. Ct. Jan. 4, 2013) (Wilkins, J.), *aff'd*, 470 Mass. 43, 18 N.E.3d 1050 (2014). Further, at least one trial court has recognized that, where class certification would have the potential for "ruinous liability" for a small business, would "significantly outweigh the actual harm suffered," and would "create inordinate pressure to settle," the superiority requirement is not satisfied. *West Concord 5-10-1.00 Store, Inc. v. Interstate Mat Corp.*, No. 2010-00356-C, 31 Mass. L. Rptr. 58, 2013 Mass. Super. LEXIS 22, at *19–22 (Mass. Super. Ct. Mar. 5, 2013) (Kottmyer, J.) (denying motion for certification of a class of individuals who received unwanted faxes in violation of the federal Telephone Consumer Protection Act and noting that certification would be for the benefit of the attorneys bringing the case and "not for the benefit of individuals who are truly aggrieved as a result of receiving the faxes").

c. Notice Under Rule 23(b)

Rule 23(d) grants the trial court discretion to "order that notice be given, in such manner as it may direct, of the pendency of the action, of a proposed settlement, of entry of judgment, or of any other proceedings in the action, including notice to the absent persons that they may come in and present claims and defenses if they so desire." Mass. R. Civ. P. 23(d). Thus, although notice to the class is not required, Rule 23(d) grants the trial courts discretion to order notice if circumstances warrant.

In *Kingara v. Secure Home Health Care Inc.*, the Supreme Judicial Court held that the trial court may exercise that discretionary power sua sponte in circumstances where the putative class members would otherwise face significant prejudice. 489 Mass. 393, 396 (2022). In *Kingara*, the named plaintiff died before seeking or obtaining class certification. The deceased's lawyer, without authorization from her legal representative, moved for and obtained an order which, among other things, granted leave to provide notice to the class informing them of plaintiff's death and inviting them to join the action. *Id.* at 394. Although the SJC held that plaintiff's counsel lacked authority to move for the relief sought, *see* Section 3.a.iv., *supra*, the Court nonetheless went on to decide that the trial court had the authority to order notice sua sponte. *See id.* at 396. Such authority is consistent both with the plain language of Rule 23(d) and the absence of any provision in Rule 23 conditioning relief under the rule on the submission of a motion by a party. *See id.* Although Rule 23 grants inherent authority to protect the interests of absent class members, the Supreme Judicial Court held that exercising such authority before class certification is only appropriate if significant prejudice to absent class members is found, such as the potential loss of time-barred claims if a putative class action is dismissed without notice to the class. *See id.* at 398 n.6. Because no such findings had been made below, the SJC remanded to the trial court for further findings concerning the potential prejudice to putative class members in the absence of notice of the named plaintiff's death. *Id* at 398.

4. MULTI-STATE CLASS ACTIONS GENERALLY PRECLUDED IN MASSACHUSETTS STATE COURTS

The most significant differences between Mass. R. Civ. P. 23 and Fed. R. Civ. P. 23—the absence of an "opt out" provision and mandatory notice requirement—work together to preclude, on due process grounds, the certification of most putative multi-state class actions in Massachusetts state courts. *Moelis v. Berkshire Life Ins. Co.*, 451 Mass. 483, 486–87, 887 N.E.2d 214, 218–19 (2008). In *Blake v. Hometown America Communities, Inc.*, however, the court noted that even though Massachusetts does not have an "opt out" or "opt in" provision, judges retain the right to issue practical orders to purported class members as a prerequisite for compensation, if the defendant is found liable. 486 Mass. 268, 285 n.14, 158 N.E.3d 18, 32 n.14 (2020) (citing Mass. Gen. Laws ch. 93A, § 9(2)).

This general prohibition stems from the United States Supreme Court's holding that it violates due process to certify a class that includes members who lack minimum contacts with the forum state, unless the absentee class members receive notice, an opportunity to be heard, *and* an opportunity to opt out of the class. *Phillips Petroleum Co. v. Shutts*, 472 U.S. 797, 811 (1985). Because Mass. R. Civ. P. 23 and Mass. Gen. Laws ch. 93A, §§ 9 and 11 do not permit individuals to opt out of a class action, these due process requirements cannot be satisfied in Massachusetts state court class actions unless the plaintiff can establish that every member of the proposed class has "minimum contacts" with Massachusetts sufficient to grant personal jurisdiction. *Moelis*, 451 Mass. at 487–88, 887 N.E.2d at 218–19; *see also Weitzner v. Cynosure, Inc.*, 85 Mass. App. Ct. 77, 79–81, 5 N.E.3d 953, 957–58 (2014) (same). This general prohibition against national and multi-state classes applies even where the defendant does not oppose class certification. *See Qual-Craft Indus., Inc. v. Realworld Corp.*, No. 98-1186, 10 Mass. L. Rptr. 124, 1999 Mass. Super. LEXIS 204, at *7–8 (Mass. Super. Ct. Mar. 1, 1999) (Connolly, J.) (refusing *sua sponte* to certify a national settlement class requested by both parties). It even applies where absent class members would be left without any remedy due to the expiration of the statute of repose. *Jackie 888, Inc. v. Tokai Pharms., Inc.*, No. 143806, 36 Mass. L. Rptr. 1206, 2019 Mass. Super. LEXIS 1206, at *5–7 (Mass. Super. Ct. Nov. 25, 2019) (Sanders, J.) (denying certification of nationwide class where the statute of repose expired on the claims because "[d]ue process applies to more than just property rights . . . arguably, it embraces the right *not* to participate in litigation—or if one does pursue litigation, to file in the court of one's choice represented by counsel of one's choosing").

Massachusetts courts have posited only two exceptions to this prohibition. First, a national or multi-state class is permissible if the named plaintiff can establish that *every* member of the proposed class has sufficient minimum contacts with the Commonwealth for a Massachusetts court to assert personal jurisdiction over them. *Moelis*, 451 Mass. at 487–88, 887 N.E.2d at 218–19. In *Moelis*, purchasing life insurance policies from an insurance company domiciled in Massachusetts was held insufficient to establish minimum contacts that would support personal jurisdiction over out-of-state class members. *See id.* at 488; *compare Eldridge v. Provident Cos.*, No. 97-1009, 11 Mass. L. Rptr. 417, 2000 Mass. Super. LEXIS 163, at *6–10 (Mass. Super. Ct. Mar. 6, 2000) (Toomey, J.) (holding a multi-state class permissible under Mass. R. Civ. P. 23 because every member of the proposed class had signed a contract to act as sales representatives of an insurance company headquartered in Massachusetts and, therefore, had sufficient minimum contacts with Massachusetts). Likewise, in *In re OvaScience Stockholder Litig.*, the court held that purchasing shares in a corporation domiciled in Massachusetts did not establish sufficient contacts with Massachusetts to support personal jurisdiction over non-Massachusetts class members. No. SUCV2015-3087-BLS2, 2017 Mass. Super. LEXIS 225, at *4–5 (Mass. Super. Ct. Nov. 8, 2017).

Second, courts have suggested in dicta that a national or multi-state class may be permissible when the complaint seeks "predominantly" equitable relief. *See Eldridge*, 2000 Mass. Super. LEXIS 163, at *11. Such an exception would only apply, if at all, where any monetary relief requested is purely "incidental" in nature and flows "automatically" from the injunctive relief sought. *Weld v. CVS Pharm., Inc.*, No. 98-0897, 11 Mass. L. Rptr. 21, 1999 Mass. Super. LEXIS 439, at *9–10 (Mass. Super. Ct. Nov. 19, 1999) (Brassard, J.); *Eldridge*, 2000 Mass. Super. LEXIS 163, at *12. However, no reported decision has ever relied on this rationale to certify a multi-state injunctive relief class under Mass. R. Civ. P. 23 or Mass. Gen. Laws ch. 93A, § §9(2) or 11. *See, e.g., Weitzner*, 85 Mass. App. Ct. at 79, 5 N.E.3d at 958 (finding that injunctive relief did not predominate for class seeking $5 billion in damages under the TCPA's "junk fax" provisions).

5. CONSUMER CLASS ACTIONS UNDER MASS. GEN. LAWS CH. 93A

a. Predominance and Superiority May Be Considered But Are Not Required

The Massachusetts unfair or deceptive trade practices statute, Mass. Gen. Laws ch. 93A, §9(2), provides an additional vehicle for the certification of a consumer class action in Massachusetts state court. The requirements for class certification under this statute are less well-defined than under Mass. R. Civ. P. 23:

> Any persons entitled to bring [a consumer claim under Chapter 93A] may, if the use or employment of the unfair or deceptive act or practice has caused similar injury to numerous other persons similarly situated and if the court finds in a preliminary hearing that he adequately and fairly represents such other persons, bring the action on behalf of himself and such other similarly injured and situated persons; the court shall require that notice of such action be given to unnamed petitioners in the most effective practicable manner. Such action shall not be dismissed, settled or compromised without the approval of the court, and notice of any proposed dismissal, settlement or compromise shall be given to all members of the class of petitioners in such manner as the court directs.

Mass. Gen. Laws ch. 93A, § 9(2).[4] In substance, courts construe § 9(2) to incorporate the four class action prerequisites set forth in Mass. R. Civ. P. 23(a) but, consistent with the text of § 9(2), omit the "predominance" and "superiority" requirements contained in Mass. R. Civ. P. 23(b). In *Baldassari v. Public Fin. Trust*, the Supreme Judicial Court held that these omissions from Chapter 93A were no accident, and that the Legislature intended the class certification requirements under Chapter 93A to be less restrictive than under Mass. R. Civ. P. 23. 369 Mass. 33, 38, 337 N.E.2d 701, 705 (1975); *see also Blake v. Hometown America Communities, Inc.*, 486 Mass. 268, 279 n.9, 158 N.E.3d 18, 30 n.9 (2020); *Feeney v. Dell Inc.*, 454 Mass. 192, 201, 908 N.E.2d 753, 762 (2009) ("[T]he requirements for class certification under the statutory class action provision in [Chapter 93A], § 9(2) are easier to satisfy than under Mass. R. Civ. P. 23.").

That is not to say that courts presumptively certify classes brought under Chapter 93A. Ten

---

[4] The business right of action Chapter 93A, *see* Mass. Gen. L. ch. 93A, § 11, likewise provides that a business that is bringing a claim for violation of Mass. Gen. L. ch. 93A, § 2 "may, if the use or employment of the unfair method of competition or the unfair or deceptive act or practice has caused similar injury to numerous other persons similarly situated and if the court finds in a preliminary hearing that he adequately and fairly represents such other persons, bring the action on behalf of himself and such other similarly injured and situated persons; the court shall require that notice of such action be given to unnamed petitioners in the most effective, practicable manner."

years after *Baldassari*, the Supreme Judicial Court retreated somewhat from its earlier position and held that even if a plaintiff satisfies all of the Rule 23(a) requirements expressly referenced in Chapter 93A, a judge applying Chapter 93A still has the *discretion* to deny class certification based upon the "predominance" and "superiority" considerations articulated in Mass. R. Civ. P. 23(b)—notwithstanding that the Rule 23(b) factors are not mentioned anywhere in Chapter 93A. *See Fletcher v. Cape Cod Gas. Co.*, 394 Mass. 595, 605–06, 477 N.E.2d 116, 122 (1985). The Court also cautioned that this discretion must be balanced against "a pressing need for an effective private remedy for consumers," and that "traditional technicalities are not to be read into the statute in such a way as to impede the accomplishment of substantial justice." *Id.* at 605–06, 477 N.E.2d at 122. As a result of these discretionary considerations, decisions by Massachusetts trial courts have varied in their willingness to deny class certification under Chapter 93A on predominance and superiority grounds. Some courts exercise the discretion granted in *Fletcher* and require that plaintiffs seeking to bring a consumer class action under Chapter 93A satisfy all of the requirements set forth in Mass. R. Civ. P. 23. *See, e.g.*, *Eldridge v. Provident Cos.*, No. 97-1009, 11 Mass. L. Rptr. 417, 2000 Mass. Super. LEXIS 163, at *17–18 (Mass. Super. Ct. Mar. 6, 2000) (Toomey, J.); *Weld v. CVS Pharm., Inc.*, No. 98-0897, 11 Mass. L. Rptr. 21, 1999 Mass. Super. LEXIS 439, at *10 (Mass. Super. Ct. Nov. 19, 1999) (Brassard, J.). In contrast, other courts hold that the considerations set forth in Mass. R. Civ. P. 23(b) have no place in an analysis of whether class certification is appropriate under Chapter 93A. *See, e.g., Olson v. Energy North, Inc.*, No. 98-00228, 9 Mass. L. Rptr. 494, 1999 Mass. Super. LEXIS 45, at *11 (Mass. Super. Ct. Jan. 14, 1999) (Gants, J.).

Over the past twenty years, however, the Supreme Judicial Court's interpretation of §9(2) has evolved from a relatively plaintiff-friendly standard to a more demanding one on the questions of predominance and superiority. The more liberal construction was evident in the Court's 2004 decision in *Aspinall v. Philip Morris Companies*, which reinforced the principle that the Rule 23(b) predominance inquiry is inapplicable to class actions brought under Mass. Gen. Laws ch. 93A, §9(2). *See* 442 Mass. 381, 813 N.E.2d 476 (2004), *abrogated on other grounds by Tyler v. Michaels Stores Inc.*, 464 Mass. 492, 502–03, 984 N.E.2d 737, 745 (2013). There, the Supreme Judicial Court reversed a ruling of a single justice of the Appeals Court decertifying a plaintiff class, which alleged that the defendant tobacco company had committed deceptive acts in violation of Chapter 93A by marketing and selling "light" cigarettes that were advertised as providing low tar and nicotine to smokers, when in fact most smokers would not receive decreased levels of tar and nicotine compared to ordinary cigarettes. *See id.* In the earlier decision decertifying the plaintiff class, the single justice ruled that the Superior Court failed to consider any of the plaintiff class members' individual characteristics, and instead had focused exclusively on the defendant's conduct. *See Aspinall v. Philip Morris Cos.*, No. 02-J-4, 2003 WL 21297272 (Mass. App. Ct. May 27, 2003). Insofar as some members of that plaintiff class did not suffer any harm at all, the single justice concluded that a finding of causation of harm under Chapter 93A would depend on "individualized smoking patterns," which rendered the certified class overbroad and assured that common issues would not predominate. *See id.* at *1, *2, *7.

On direct appellate review, the Supreme Judicial Court reversed the single justice, holding that a class action was "not only an appropriate method" to address plaintiffs' claims "but, pragmatically, the only method whereby [the putative class] can seek redress for the alleged [injury]." *Aspinall,* 442 Mass. at 393, 813 N.E.2d at 486. The Court stressed its own earlier admonition in *Fletcher* that a judge deciding a certification request under Chapter 93A must keep in mind the "pressing need for an effective private remedy for consumers." *Id.* at 391–92, 813 N.E.2d at 485 (quoting *Fletcher*, 394 Mass. at 605–06). To the *Aspinall* court, the absence of a requirement under Chapter 93A to show reliance on an alleged misrepresentation, coupled with economic damages theories that did not rely on individual proof, favored certification of a class bound by defendants' alleged common course of conduct; i.e., "misrepresent[ation] [of] material information concerning the design, function, marketing, toxicity, and tar and nicotine yields" of light cigarettes. *Id.* at 392–93, 813 N.E.2d at 485–86. In addition to clarifying that Chapter 93A does not contain a "predominance" requirement, the *Aspinall* court further cautioned against equating the "similarity requirements" of Rule 23(a) with Chapter 93A's requirement that the parties seeking certification are "similarly situated" and have suffered from "similar injury." *Id.* at 391, 813 N.E.2d at 485; *see also Reynolds v. City Express, Inc.*, 2014 Mass. Super. LEXIS 44, at *43 (Mass. Super. Ct. Jan. 18, 2014) (Locke, J.) (holding that "the discretionary requirements of predominance and superiority under Mass. R. Civ. P. 23(b) are not required for the certification of a G.L. c. 93A class action").

More recently, however, the Supreme Judicial Court reaffirmed that, notwithstanding *Aspinall*, trial courts still have discretion to apply a predominance analysis when considering whether to certify a class pursuant to Chapter 93A. *See Moelis v. Berkshire Life Ins. Co.*, 451 Mass. 483, 490, 887 N.E.2d 214, 220 (2008). In *Moelis*, the Court noted that although § 9(2) does not require the plaintiff to demonstrate predominance and superiority, the trial court has discretion to consider these issues "in determining whether members of the proposed class are 'similarly situated' and have suffered 'similar injury' under §9(2)." *Id.* On that basis, the Court affirmed the trial court's decision to deny certification of a statewide class on the ground that for purposes of resolving the statute of limitations defense, the members of the proposed class were not similarly situated and individualized inquiries would be necessary to determine when each class member learned or reasonably should have learned of his or her claims. *Id.* at 491, 887 N.E.2d at 221. Similarly, in *Bellermann*, the Supreme Judicial Court affirmed the trial court's decision to deny class certification pursuant to Chapter 93A because plaintiffs could not show that all members of the proposed class were "similarly injured" by defendant electric company's delay in restoring power where some putative class members had their power restored relatively quickly and others had long outages. *See Bellermann v. Fitchburg Gas & Elec. Light Co.*, 470 Mass. 43, 57–58, 18 N.E.3d 1050, 1060–61 (2014). Class certification was also denied for the plaintiffs' claim that the electric company's communication failures prevented customers from planning for extended outages, because "[a]s reflected by the variety of ways that the plaintiffs contend they would have responded to better information, this theory of injury would necessitate individualized inquiry regarding the counterfactual mental processes of each class member." *See id.* at 57–58.

b. Causation and Injury May Not Be Presumed

To maintain a class action under Mass. Gen. Laws ch. 93A, § 9(2), plaintiffs may not simply allege the occurrence of an unfair or deceptive act or practice that violated their legal rights but must also "allege and ultimately prove that [the class] has, as a result, suffered a distinct injury or harm that arises from the claimed unfair or deceptive act itself." *Tyler v. Michaels Stores, Inc.*, 464 Mass. 492, 503, 984 N.E.2d 737, 745 (2013) (citing *Hershenow v. Enterprise Rent-A-Car Co.*, 445 Mass. 790, 791, 840 N.E.2d 525, 528–29 (2006)). The burden to prove causation and injury will often entail individualized class member-specific determinations and preclude class certification under § 9(2).

Section 9 of Massachusetts General Laws Chapter 93A does *not* require a plaintiff consumer to allege or prove a "loss of money or property" to be eligible to recover nominal, statutory damages of $25 per violation. *See* Mass. Gen. Laws ch. 93A § 9. The Supreme Judicial Court initially interpreted this amendment as eliminating the requirement that a plaintiff allege any injury beyond the allegedly unfair or deceptive conduct itself. *Leardi v. Brown*, 394 Mass. 151, 160, 474 N.E.2d 1094

(1985) (by eliminating "loss of money or property" requirement, "the Legislature exercised its prerogative to create a legal right, the invasion of which, without more, constitutes an injury"); *see also Aspinall v. Philip Morris Cos.*, 442 Mass. 381, 401–02, 813 N.E.2d 476 (2004) ("[D]eceptive advertising" in violation of ch. 93A, "if proved, effected a per se injury on consumers" of the defectively advertised product within the meaning of § 9(1)). In 2006, however, the SJC ruled in *Hershenow* that even though the plaintiff need not allege a "loss of money or property" to recover damages under Section 9, the plaintiff must allege a "loss" separate and apart from the deception itself that was caused by the unfair or deceptive conduct. *Hershenow*, 445 Mass. at 791, 840 N.E.2d at 528–29. Accordingly, the court affirmed entry of summary judgment in favor of defendant because even though plaintiff sufficiently alleged unfair or deceptive conduct (by reason of the defendant's inclusion of an unlawful collision damage waiver provision in the rental car contract at issue), the plaintiff never suffered any loss because the plaintiff's car was never damaged and, therefore, the illegal contractual provision was never implicated. *See id.*

In its 2013 decision in *Tyler*, the Supreme Judicial Court reaffirmed this causal harm requirement. There, the plaintiff sought nominal damages under § 9 based on the defendant's collection of the plaintiff's zip code at the time of processing a credit card payment, a practice specifically enumerated as an unfair or deceptive act in violation of Chapter 93A. The Court rejected the argument that plaintiff should be entitled to recover nominal damages in the absence of proof that the defendant used the zip code information in some manner that harmed plaintiff—e.g., by using it to locate plaintiff's address to send junk mail—and in doing so expressly abrogated its prior holding in *Leardcai* on this point:

> The invasion of a consumer's legal right (a right, for example, established by a statute or regulation), without more, may be a violation of G.L. c. 93A, §2, and even a *per se* violation of §2, but the fact that there is such a violation does not necessarily mean the consumer has suffered an injury or a loss entitling her to at least nominal damages and attorney's fees; instead, the violation of the legal right that has created the unfair or deceptive act or practice must cause the consumer some kind of separate, identifiable harm arising from the violation itself. To the extent that. . . *Leardi* can be read to signify that "invasion" of a consumer plaintiff's established legal right in a manner that qualifies as an unfair or deceptive act under G.L. c. 93A, §2, automatically entities the plaintiff to at least nominal damages (and attorney's fees), we do not follow the *Leardi* decision.

Tyler, 464 Mass. at 503, 984 N.E.2d at 745–46 (citing *Rhodes v. AIG Dom. Claims, Inc.*, 461 Mass. 486, 496 n.16, 961 N.E.2d 1067 (2012)); *Casavant v. Norwegian Cruise Line Ltd.*, 460 Mass. 500, 504–05, 952 N.E.2d 908 (2011); *Iannacchino v. Ford Motor Co.*, 451 Mass. 623, 632–33, 888 N.E.2d 879 (2008); *Hershenow*, 445 Mass. at 801–02, 840 N.E.2d 526; *see also Layes v. RHP Properties, Inc.*, 95 Mass. App. Ct. 804, 824, 133 N.E. 3d 353, 371 (2019) (reversing class certification order and remanding for trial court to determine "whether there are sufficiently similar injuries across the purported class" which would require proof for each class of "not only the c. 93A violation, but also some kind of 'separate, identifiable harm' resulting from the c. 93A violation").

As a result of *Hershenow* and *Tyler*, a consumer may no longer obtain certification of a Chapter 93A class action based simply on the allegation that the defendant engaged in conduct that was unfair or deceptive toward the proposed class. Now, a plaintiff must also show that he or she will be able to demonstrate that the allegedly unfair or deceptive conduct caused an "actual loss" to the proposed class members—without the need for individualized inquiries. *See, e.g., Kwaak v. Pfizer, Inc.*, 71 Mass. App. Ct. 293, 300–01, 881 N.E.2d 812, 817–18 (2008) (reversing trial court's class certification order under Section 9(2) of Chapter 93A on grounds that individualized inquiries would be necessary to determine which members of the putative class were influenced by the allegedly deceptive advertising campaign about Listerine serving as a substitute for flossing—and therefore may have suffered an injury—and which members of the putative class purchased the Listerine for other reasons); *Dolben Co., Inc. v. Friedmann*, No. 10034, 2008 Mass. App. Div. LEXIS 6, at *16–17 (Mass. App. Div. Jan. 2, 2008) (affirming trial court's finding that chapter 93A claim could not be based on mere allegation that the landlord had committed a code violation by failing to provide tenant with a signed copy of the lease, because the tenant could not show any resulting harm); *Chambers v. Tufts Associated HMO, Inc.*, No. 1884CV02837-BLS2, 2020 Mass. Super. LEXIS 177, *14 (Mass. Super. Ct. Oct. 20, 2020) (rejecting the claim that a "separate and distinct" injury had been sustained by purchasers of health insurance plans with falsely advertised deductibles, when those individuals had not actually spent money on medical services beyond the allegedly misleading deductible amount); *Besseck v. New Eng. Water Heater*, No. 04-4877-BLS1, 2006 Mass. Super. LEXIS 323, at *10 (Mass. Super. Ct. July 5, 2006) (denying motion for class certification under Chapter 93A, where named plaintiffs could not meet Hershenow's requirement to show that they suffered an actual loss from the defendants' allegedly "unfair or deceptive" refusal to remove water heaters from the class members' homes); *Waters v. Earthlink*, 22 Mass. L. Rptr. 527, 2006 Mass. Super. LEXIS 674, at *26 (Mass. Super. Ct. May 10, 2006) (Kane, J.) (denying motion for class certification under Chapter 93A because, even if disruption of internet service was the result of the defendant's unfair or deceptive conduct, under *Hershenow* the plaintiff must show that this disruption caused each member of the class to suffer some actual loss; this would require individualized inquiries, which are incompatible with the class action device); *cf. Salvas v. Wal-Mart Stores, Inc.*, 452 Mass. 337, 364–72, 893 N.E.2d 1187, 1210–15 (2008) (in considering class certification pursuant to Mass. R. Civ. P. 23 as opposed to Chapter 93A, the predominance requirement as to liability may be satisfied in some circumstances even if the number of class members unharmed by the allegedly unlawful conduct is not de minimis).

The *Hershenow* causal harm requirement was narrowly refined in *Iannacchino v. Ford Motor Co.*, 451 Mass. 623, 888 N.E.2d 879 (2008). In that case, the plaintiffs alleged that Ford knowingly manufactured, sold, and failed to recall door latches that did not meet mandatory federal safety requirements, and that Ford issued false safety certifications for these vehicles. The trial court granted a motion for judgment on the pleadings dismissing the plaintiffs' Chapter 93A claim, finding that while the plaintiffs had alleged deceptive conduct, they could not satisfy the *Hershenow* "actual injury" and causation requirements because no plaintiff alleged that he had been in an accident where the door latches failed or had otherwise suffered any actual damages. *Id.* at 628, 888 N.E.2d at 884–85. On direct appellate review, the Supreme Judicial Court rejected this reasoning. Unlike *Hershenow*, in which the plaintiffs did not suffer any injury because they never had to make a claim under the unlawful contract provision during the finite period that the car rental agreement was in place, here the plaintiffs were injured because:

> the purchase price paid by the plaintiffs for their vehicles would entitle them to receive vehicles that complied with those safety standards or that would be recalled if they did not comply. If Ford knowingly sold noncompliant (and therefore potentially unsafe) vehicles or if Ford, after learning of noncompliance, failed to initiate a recall and to pay for the condition to be remedied, the plaintiffs would have paid for more (viz., safety regulation-compliant vehicles) than they received. Such an overpayment would represent an economic loss – measurable by the cost to bring the vehicles into compliance – for which the plaintiffs could seek redress under G.L. c. 93A, §9.

Id. at 630–31, 888 N.E.2d at 886–87. The Supreme Judicial Court nonetheless affirmed the trial court's ruling dismissing the Chapter 93A claim, based upon a finding that plaintiffs had not alleged with sufficient particularity facts to establish that Ford failed to comply with federal safety standards. *Id.* at 631, 888 N.E.2d at 887. Thus, *Iannacchino* suggests that when the defendant's alleged unfair or deceptive conduct involves the sale of a product that is non-compliant with mandatory safety standards, then the class of persons who purchased that product have suffered a loss within the meaning of *Hershenow* because they overpaid for the product. Accordingly, such consumers may maintain a Chapter 93A action without any further showing that each class member suffered an accident-related injury from the defective product. *Id.* at 630–31, 888 N.E.2d at 886–87. Whether and to what extent *Iannacchino* applies outside of the context of inherently dangerous products remains an open question.

The Supreme Judicial Court later clarified the issue of whether a regulatory violation will constitute injury under Chapter 93A. *See Bellermann v. Fitchburg Gas & Elec. Light Co.*, 475 Mass. 67 (2016). There, the Court held that the plaintiffs' alleged overpayment for utility rates, based on the utility's lack of emergency preparedness for winter storms, was not a cognizable injury under 93A. *See id.* at 70. Citing to *Iannacchino* and *Aspinall*, the Court explained:

> In those cases [*Iannacchino* and *Aspinall*] we recognized that, under some circumstances, a consumer may suffer an economic injury by purchasing a product or service that does not comply with applicable regulations. We stated clearly, however, that to meet the injury requirement under G. L. c. 93A, §9 (1) or 11, a plaintiff must have suffered a separate, identifiable harm arising from the regulatory violation that is distinct from the claimed unfair or deceptive conduct itself. By contrast, adoption of the plaintiffs' theory of economic injury would permit class certification under G. L. c. 93A, § §9 (2) and 11, whenever a product (or service) fails to conform to a regulatory requirement and the consumer alleges an economic injury based on overpayment for the product.

Id. at 73 (internal quotations and citations omitted). Comparing the plaintiffs' claims in *Bellermann* to those in *Hershenow*, the Court concluded that an economic injury based on a "potential inadequacy" was insufficient to support class certification under 93A: "Since no severe storm occurred, and no plaintiff lost electric power during the class certification period as a result of [defendant's] asserted lack of planning and preparedness for a nonexistent storm, none of the plaintiffs has demonstrated an economic injury." *Id.* at 76–77. Because that theory of injury was invalid, plaintiffs could not show that class members had sustained a "similar injury" that would permit certification of a consumer class under Section 9(2) of Chapter 93A. *See id.* at 78. That said, a similar *injury* need not also result in similar *damages*. *See Layes v. RHP Properties, Inc.*, 95 Mass. App. Ct. 804, 825 (2019) (finding that the insertion of an illegal clause within lease agreements was a common injury among the residents, even though different residents may have been injured in different ways as a result of that clause).

c. Notice Requirements

Chapter 93A also differs from Mass. R. Civ. P. 23 with respect to notice to the certified plaintiff class. While Rule 23 contains no notice provision, Chapter 93A requires that notice of the class action "be given to unnamed petitioners in the most effective practicable manner." Mass. Gen. Laws ch. 93A, § 9(2). However, Chapter 93A, like Rule 23, does not contain any "opt out" provision. Thus, as is the case under Mass. R. Civ. P. 23, a multistate class action seeking monetary damages may not be certified under Chapter 93A without running afoul of due process requirements. *Moelis v. Berkshire Life Ins. Co.*, 451 Mass. 483, 487, 887 N.E.2d 214, 218–19 (2008) (citing *Phillips Petroleum Co. v. Shutts*, 472 U.S. 797, 811 (1985)).

When feasible, § 9(2) requires individualized notice to class members. *See Aspinall v. Philip Morris Cos.*, No. 98-6002-H, 20 Mass. L. Rptr. 300, 2005 Mass. Super. LEXIS 629, at *5–7 (Mass. Super. Ct. Dec. 7, 2005) (Lauriat, J). If the defendant's participation in serving notice will mitigate costs, the court may, in its discretion, impose some or all of the burden of notice on the defendant. *See id.* at *3.

d. Demand Letter Requirements

Thirty days prior to filing a complaint under Mass. Gen. Laws ch. 93A, § 9, a plaintiff consumer must serve a demand letter upon the defendant(s) "describing the unfair or deceptive act or practice relied upon and the injury suffered." Mass. Gen. Laws ch. 93A, § 9(3). Even when a plaintiff purports to assert a Chapter 93A claim on behalf of a putative class, unless and until a class is certified, the court must evaluate the demand letter's sufficiency based solely on whether it describes the named plaintiff's claims with sufficient particularity. *Richards v. Arteva Specialties S.A.R.L.*, 66 Mass. App. Ct. 726, 732, 850 N.E.2d 1068, 1074 (2006).[5] The Supreme Judicial Court has ruled that if a class is ultimately certified, in most instances there is no need for the service of a new demand letter on behalf of the class. *Baldassari v. Public Fin. Trust*, 369 Mass. 33, 42, 337 N.E.2d 701, 707 (1975) ("Multiple demands for relief need not be filed on behalf of all of the members of the class. If no reasonable tender of settlement is made in response to the first demand [by the named plaintiff], further demands are not likely to serve any useful purpose and are not required."); *see also Bosque v. Wells Fargo Bank, N.A.*, 762 F. Supp. 2d 342, 354 (D. Mass. 2011) ("[U]nder Massachusetts law a demand letter that identifies the particularized injuries of one class representative claimant and gives notice to defendant of the pendency of the class action is sufficient") ; *Ortins v. Lincoln Prop. Co.*, No. 134104, 35 Mass. L. Rptr. 597, 2019 Mass. Super. LEXIS 481, at *20 (Mass. Super. Ct. Aug. 9. 2019) (Barrett, J.) ("plaintiff may commence a Chapter 93A class action claim without specifically identifying the claim as a class action in the demand letter" and "a demand letter need only be made on the plaintiff's own behalf, even if the plaintiff is proposing to represent a class of similarly situated persons"). However, a "separate question" might be presented if the named plaintiff who originally made the demand accepted a tender of settlement by defendants or rejected a reasonable tender of settlement. *Baldassari*, 369 Mass. at 42, 337 N.E.2d at 707; *see also Richards*, 66 Mass. App. Ct. at 738, 850 N.E.2d at 1078 ("If and when a class is certified, it is unclear . . . whether one or more new demand letters would be necessary or even appropriate.").

Note, however, that the demand requirement applicable to consumer Chapter 93A claims is not present in Mass. Gen. L. ch. 93A, § 11. Businesses are not required to send demand before initiating a Chapter 93A lawsuit.

---

[5] In contrast, outside of the Chapter 93A context, "during the period of time between the plaintiffs' assertion that the claim is brought in a representative capacity and the court's certification, a judge should 'treat[] the suit as a class suit for the purposes of dismissal or compromise.'" Meaney v. OneBeacon Ins. Group, LLC, No. 07-1294-BLS2, 25 Mass. L. Rptr. 308, 2009 Mass. Super. LEXIS 61, at *22 (Mass. Super. Ct. Feb. 25, 2009) (Neel, J.) (under Mass. Gen. Laws ch. 232A, §1, defendant must make tender to putative class, and not just named plaintiff, to make a timely tender under the statute) (quoting Wolf v. Comm'r of Pub. Welfare, 367 Mass. 293, 298, 327 N.E.2d 885, 889 (1975)).

e. Contractual Arbitration Provisions Seeking to Bar Consumers from Bringing Chapter 93A Class Actions Are Enforceable

The United States Supreme Court has held that the Federal Arbitration Act's "command to enforce arbitration agreements trumps any interest in ensuring the prosecution of low-value claims" through a class action. *American Express Co. v. Italian Colors Restaurant*, 570 U.S. 228, 238 (2013); *see also AT&T Mobility, LLC v. Concepcion,* 563 U.S. 333 (2011); *Landry v. Transworld Sys. Inc.*, 485 Mass. 334, 337–38, 149 N.E.3d 781, 784–85 (2020). In August 2013, the Supreme Judicial Court held that even though it considers this interpretation of the Federal Arbitration Act to be "untenable," it is "bound to accept that view as a controlling statement of federal law." *Feeney v. Dell*, SJC-11133a, 2013 Mass. LEXIS 635 (Aug. 1, 2013) (*Feeney III*). Accordingly, contractual provisions which require consumers to arbitrate their claims on an individual basis are enforceable. *See id.*

6. CLASS ACTIONS UNDER THE MASSACHUSETTS WAGE ACT

The Massachusetts Wage Act specifically empowers plaintiffs aggrieved by certain statutory violations to prosecute a class action on "behalf of others similarly situated" for injunctive relief, damages, lost wages, and other benefits. Mass. Gen. Laws ch. 149, § 150. However, the Wage Act does not grant automatic class status, so a class may be certified on a Wage Act claim only if the requirements of Rule 23 are otherwise satisfied. *See Gammella v. P.F. Chang's China Bistro, Inc.* 482 Mass. 1, 9, 120 N.E.3d 690, 698 (2019) ("[W]e hold that *rule 23* provides the correct framework for analyzing a certification claim brought under the Wage Act or the minimum fair wage law."). The class certification requirements under § 150 are less stringent than those imposed by Mass. R. Civ. P. 23, so a class that satisfies Rule 23 will necessarily satisfy § 150. *See Escorbor v. Helping Hands Co.*, No. SUCV2015-2053-D, 2017 Mass. Super. LEXIS 162, at *7 (Mass. Super. Ct. Sept. 13, 2017).

If an arbitration agreement is silent as to whether it permits class actions to enforce the Wage Act, an arbitrator has the discretion to permit a plaintiff to bring claims in arbitration on behalf of a class. In *Carey Int'l, Inc. v. Ksikes*, the arbitration agreement at issue neither expressly prohibited nor authorized class proceedings, but provided that the agreement should be interpreted pursuant to Massachusetts law. No. 2011-2467-BLS1, 29 Mass. L. Rptr. 300, 2011 Mass. Super. LEXIS 328 (Dec. 8, 2011) (Fabricant, J.). The arbitrator held that because Massachusetts law favors class actions for the private enforcement of certain statutes, the choice of Massachusetts law evinced the intent to authorize class proceedings in arbitration to enforce the Wage Act. *See id.* The Superior Court confirmed the arbitration award, rejecting the employer's argument that the arbitrator exceeded his authority by permitting the class action to proceed. *Id.* at *7–8.

7. CLASS ACTIONS UNDER THE MASSACHUSETTS TORT CLAIMS ACT

The Massachusetts Tort Claims Act (MTCA) establishes the procedures for asserting tort claims against public employees and municipalities. Mass. Gen. Laws ch. 258, § 2. Specifically, the MTCA establishes that public employers "shall be liable for injury or loss of property or personal injury or death caused by the negligent or wrongful acts or omissions of any public employee while acting within the scope of his office or employment." *Id.* Class actions can be brought against public employers under the MTCA. *Magliacane v. Gardner*, 483 Mass. 842, 855, 138 N.E.3d 347, 360 (2020) ("Because a class action under Mass. R. Civ. P. 23 . . . may be brought against 'a private individual under like circumstances,' and because none of the exceptions precludes class relief, we conclude that a class action may be brought against a public employer under the act.").

Under the MTCA, a plaintiff must provide the public employer notice of the claim in writing by means of a presentment letter that identifies the alleged tort and provides the government the opportunity to investigate and settle claims and prevent future claims. Mass. Gen. Laws. Ch. 258, § 4. The process for bringing a class action claim under the MTCA is comparable to the procedure for consumer claims under Chapter 93A, § 9. *Id.* at 856–57. Demand is proper under the MTCA "where a putative class representative makes a presentment on behalf of a class prior to filing a class action against a public employer under the act." *Id.* Massachusetts courts are known to have addressed class actions under the MTCA only once, and, in that matter, the court found the plaintiff's presentment letter proper where it clearly defined the claimants, "put the city on notice regarding the nature and scope of the class, and it enabled the city to investigate or settle the claims and to take steps to prevent similar claims from arising in the future." *Magliacane*, 483 Mass. at 858. *See also Pisarczyk v. Lynch,* No. 19-P-1769, 2020 Mass. App. Unpub. LEXIS 904, *4 (Mass. App. Ct. Oct. 29, 2020) ("this strict presentment requirement is a statutory prerequisite for recovery under the [a]ct, 'the purpose of which is to allow public employers the opportunity to investigate and settle claims and to prevent future claims through notice to executive officers.'").

8. CONDUCT OF CLASS ACTIONS IN MASSACHUSETTS STATE COURTS

a. Contacts with Absent Class Members

Under Massachusetts law, putative absent class members are not parties represented by counsel, and therefore there is no blanket prohibition against communications with them. *See, e.g., Clark v. Legal Sea Foods, LLC*, 32 Mass. L. Rptr. 375, 2014 Mass. Super. LEXIS 160, at *5 (Mass. Super. Ct. Nov. 6, 2014) (Wilson, J.); *McLaughlin v. Liberty Mut. Ins. Co.*, 224 F.R.D. 295, 297, 2004 U.S. Dist. LEXIS 15964 (D. Mass. 2004); *cf. Fulco v. Continental Cablevision, Inc.*, 789 F. Supp. 45, 47, 1992 U.S. Dist. LEXIS 4287 (D. Mass. 1992) (recognizing that once a class is certified, absent class members are parties represented by class counsel). At least one court, however, has hypothesized that a local rule could preclude precertification communications with putative class members absent court approval. *See McLaughlin*, 224 F.R.D. at 297. In any event, absent local rule or court order, precertification communications with putative class members does not violate SJC Rule § 3:07, Rule 4.2.

Decisions in this area by Massachusetts courts are sparse. Courts have explained that precertification communications should not be limited without a clear record and specific findings tending to show a likelihood of serious abuse, and only then through a narrowly tailored order. *See Chambers v. RDI Logistics, Inc.*, 476 Mass. 95, 111, 65 N.E.3d 1, 15–16 (2016); *Davine v. Golub Corp.*, Civil Action No. 14-30136-MGM, 2014 U.S. Dist. LEXIS 151344, at *4 (D. Mass. 2014) (each citing, inter alia, *Gulf Oil Co. v. Bernard*, 452 U.S. 89 (1981)). In *Chambers*, the first reported Massachusetts appellate court decision to address precertification communication with putative class members, the Massachusetts Supreme Judicial Court adopted the U.S. Supreme Court's guidance in *Gulf Oil* that "a clear record and specific findings that reflect a weighing of the need for a limitation and the potential interference with the rights of the parties," and barring communications "must be justified by a likelihood of serious abuses." 65 N.E.3d at 15 (internal quotation marks and citations omitted). There, the challenged communication—letters from the defendant to its employees, putative class members, enclosing a check that would purportedly release that person's claims—was "not coercive or misleading," because the letters:

- "[C]ontained a citation to the plaintiffs' class action";
- "[F]airly described the status of the case";
- "[E]xplicitly stated that [the defendant] would not consider the employees' decision whether to endorse the check in business dealings unrelated to the matter"; and
- "[A]dvised the recipients that they may wish to consult with an attorney before deciding whether to endorse the check."

Id. at 16. Interestingly, the same general fact pattern was present in *Vargas v. Spirit Delivery & Distribution Services, Inc.*, but there the court was "concerned" that the consequences of opting out and class members' rights was "not fully communicate[d]," and thus ordered the defendant not to send further communications without court approval. Civ. A. No. 4:13-cv-12635-TSH (D. Mass. July 13, 2016).

In its description of the law, *Chambers* does not break new ground. Even before *Chambers*, Massachusetts courts appeared to pay particular attention to the need to narrowly tailor any injunction; for example, prohibiting communications on one topic while permitted communications on any other aspect of the case's merits. *See, e.g., Clark*, 2014 Mass. Super. LEXIS 160, at *3. In that case, during settlement negotiations with the proposed class representative (which precluding filing a class certification motion) over wage act claims, the defendant was enjoined "from having any settlement communications with workers who are part of the putative class in this case," although that injunction was limited to *settlement* communications only. *Id.* at *5, 8 ("This Order shall not preclude Defendant from discussing the merits of the case with non-represented Covered Workers for purposes of responding to Plaintiffs' motion for class certification."). The court identified as relevant factors: the putative class members' ability to retain counsel, how the defendant made the settlement offer ("in a suddenly-called, mandatory meeting, as they reported to work"), the context for the putative members ("given the impending closure of the restaurant, the threat of retaliation and termination"), that the communication did not disclose the existence of "class-wide settlement" discussions, including an upcoming mediation, and that there are mandatory treble damages for the claim at issue (even though it was disclosed in the complaint provided at the meeting). *Id.* at *5–7.

Further, counsel should also consider four other relevant Massachusetts cases:

- In *Davine v. Golub Corp.*, despite the defendant's efforts, one of its managerial employees made a potentially misleading oral communication to three potential class members; because the defendant had already taken corrective action to ensure that the three individuals who heard the communication would not be prejudiced by the communication. 2014 U.S. Dist. LEXIS 151344, at *5.
- In *Sweet v. Superior Steel & Precast Erectors, Inc.*, plaintiff's counsel were allowed to interview putative class members who were defendant's employees, on the conditions that plaintiff's counsel "identify the subject matter of the litigation, the role of plaintiff's counsel and the purpose of the interview," and "explain that the employee can refuse to be interviewed or can request to have individual counsel or the employer's counsel present during the interview." No. 001649, 2001 Mass. Super. LEXIS 667, at *6–7 (Mass. Super. Ct. Mar. 28, 2001) (Butler, J.).
- In *Fulco v. Continental Cablevision, Inc.*, defense counsel were permitted to interview members of a certified class who were defendant's employees on limited topics, only "with each such individual's express written consent to such an interview," and, if the class member requested, with class counsel present. 789 F. Supp. at 47.
- In *Payne v. Goodyear Tire & Rubber Co.*, the court declined to order the defendant

not to communicate with putative class members, in the absence of evidence of actual or inherent coercion on the defendant's part in the course of the communications. 207 F.R.D. at 21–22.

b. Discovery of Absent Class Members

One of the few reported Massachusetts cases to deal with the question of discovery of absent class members is *Aspinall v. Philip Morris Cos.*, No. 98-6002-H, 20 Mass. L. Rptr. 303, 2005 Mass. Super. LEXIS 642 (Mass. Super. Ct. Nov. 22, 2005) (Lauriat, J.). There, in proceedings on remand from the Supreme Judicial Court's decision in a case of the same name, the defendant sought to depose 156 absent class members to investigate whether the beliefs of class members conformed with the plaintiffs' perception of the "reasonable consumer" and to challenge class certification. In response to plaintiffs' objections to this proposed discovery, the trial court considered the question of when absent class member discovery may be had in a class action. The court found that discovery of absent class members will be permitted if: (1) the information sought is relevant to common questions; (2) the discovery is sought in good faith and is not unduly burdensome; and (3) the information is not available from the representative parties. *Id.* at *2. The court noted that there is a "heavy burden" to justify interrogatories and an "even heavier" burden to justify depositions. *Id.* at *3. Given that the defendants sought to take a large number of depositions, the court applied a heightened level of scrutiny to each of the elements.

The defendants sought absent-class-member depositions as to both liability and to support defendants' efforts to decertify the class. The court rejected any discovery relating to decertifying the class, holding that it was not relevant to common questions. As to defendants' substantive defenses, the court held that class discovery was only available as to "whether the beliefs of class members conform to the plaintiffs' perception of the 'reasonable consumer.'" *Id.* at *13. The defendants had sought discovery to show that members of the class did not rely on the alleged misrepresentations, but the court held that these were not relevant to common questions regarding materiality or deceptiveness. *Id.* at *6, 8, 13. However, the court permitted limited discovery regarding whether the absent class members resembled the plaintiff's alleged "reasonable consumer." *Id.* at *13.

The 156 depositions sought were deemed too numerous. The court gave the defendants the option of deposing 25 absent class members for no more than two hours each, or to survey a representative sample of absent class members, provided that the parties could agree on appropriate protocols. *See id.* at *29.

c. Stay of Massachusetts Putative Class Action in Favor of Ongoing Proceedings in Other Jurisdictions

Although this area of law is relatively undeveloped, there is precedent for courts granting motions to stay putative class actions filed in Massachusetts in favor of duplicative proceedings already filed in other jurisdictions. In *Davenport v. Benhamou*, the Superior Court stayed a putative class action lawsuit filed in Middlesex Superior court, pending outcome of five similar class actions filed and consolidated into a single action in Delaware. No. 07-3793-F, 23 Mass. L. Rptr. 436, 2007 Mass. Super. LEXIS 556, at *1–2 (Mass. Super. Ct. Dec. 20, 2007) (Giles, J.). Each suit arose from the same transaction: a merger agreement between 3Com, a Delaware corporation based in Massachusetts, and Diamond II Acquisitions Corp. and Diamond II Holdings, Inc. *Id.* at *3. Although the Superior Court acknowledged a "paucity of guidance" regarding competing state class actions involving the same parties, facts, and proposed class, the court stayed the Massachusetts case, reasoning that (1) there exists a general policy favoring first filed actions; (2) predictability, consistency, and judicial economy favored proceeding with the consolidated Delaware actions, in which the Massachusetts plaintiffs would be class members and adequately represented; and (3) comity between the states favored recognizing Delaware's ability and authority to fully resolve the claims. *Id.* at *4–6.

Similarly, in *Van Emden Mgmt. Corp. v. Marsh & McLennan Cos.*, the trial court granted defendant's motion to stay a putative class action alleging bid-rigging and kickback schemes because, at the time the Massachusetts complaint was filed, numerous other actions involving the same allegations against the same defendants were pending in various jurisdictions throughout the United States, including a consolidated federal action in the District of New Jersey. No. 05-0066-A, 20 Mass. L. Rptr. 79, 2005 Mass. Super. LEXIS 484, at *2–4 (Mass. Super. Ct. Sept. 21, 2005) (MacDonald, J.). In granting the stay, the court rejected plaintiff's argument that "unique aspects of [Chapter] 93A relief, both from a substantive law perspective and procedurally for class certification, [made] the Massachusetts state court forum the most appropriate one . . . ." *Id.* at *5. While stating that it was mindful of the Supreme Judicial Court's emphasis that the "strong state interest in ensuring that 93A's expansive class certification standard be respected in practice," the court nonetheless found that the New Jersey litigation was being closely managed by the presiding federal judge, and accordingly found no risk that Massachusetts' interests would be subverted. *Id.* at *8. Conversely, the court concluded that a denial of the stay would "disrupt the orderly disposition of the national litigation and generate substantial economic costs for all parties involved," and would likely produce inconsistent rulings with respect to discovery, class certification, and substantive matters. *See id.* at *9.

d. Tolling of the Statute of Limitations

Under federal law, the commencement of a putative class action tolls the applicable statutes of limitation as to all asserted members of the class. *Am. Pipe & Constr. Co. v. Utah,* 414 U.S. 538, 554 (1974).

Massachusetts appellate courts have yet to address the question of whether and to what extent the *American Pipe* doctrine applies under Massachusetts law. However, at least one Superior Court decision held that *American Pipe* tolling does apply under Massachusetts law, in certain circumstances. *See Mullally v. Waste Mgmt. of Mass.*, No. 06-882, 2009 Mass. Super. LEXIS 439, *3 (Mass. Super. Ct. May 18, 2009) (Donavan, J.). In *Mullally*, the Superior Court rejected the defendants' argument that the class for tolling purposes is limited to the class as defined in plaintiffs' initial motion for class certification and held that *American Pipe* tolling is applicable to all members of the putative class as defined in the complaint. Ultimately, however, the Superior Court declined to permit tolling, as the complaint "unequivocally narrowed the class definition to include only a subcategory of claimants." *Id.* at *2–3.

e. Settlement Approval

A class action in Massachusetts, whether under Mass. R. Civ. P. 23 or Mass. Gen. Laws ch. 93A, may not be settled without the court's final approval, and notice of any proposed settlement must be provided to all members of the class in the manner the court directs. Mass. R. Civ. P. 23(c); Mass. Gen. Laws ch. 93A, § 9. In determining whether a settlement merits final approval, the court must determine whether the settlement is "fair, reasonable, and adequate." *Sniffin v. Prudential Ins. Co.*,

395 Mass. 415, 421, 480 N.E.2d 294, 297 (1985). "The criteria generally utilized in determining whether a settlement is fair, reasonable, and adequate are: 1. likelihood of recovery, or likelihood of success; 2. amount and nature of discovery or evidence; 3. settlement terms and conditions; 4. recommendations and experience of counsel; 5. future expense and likely duration of litigation; 6. recommendation of neutral parties, if any; 7. number of objectors and nature of objections; and 8. the presence of good faith and the absence of collusion." *Vermont Pure Holdings, Ltd. v. Berry*, No. 06-01814-BLS1, 27 Mass. L. Rptr. 33, 2010 Mass. Super. LEXIS 71, *28–29 (Mass. Super. Ct. Feb. 8, 2010) (quoting 4 *Newberg on Class Actions* § 11:43). Further, even where a class action is filed only for purposes of settlement, the class certification prerequisites must still be met. *Id.* at *30–31 n.6.

A 2008 decision of the Superior Court Business Litigation Session addressed the standards for preliminary approval of a class action settlement. *See In re Mass. Smokeless Tobacco Litig.*, No. 03-5038-BLS1, 23 Mass. L. Rptr. 719, 2008 Mass. Super. LEXIS 126, at *20 (Mass. Super. Ct. April 9, 2008) (Gants, J.) (declining, on public policy grounds, to grant preliminary approval of proposed settlement that called for defendants to pay $2.58 million in coupons, because it would only benefit those class members who continued to use the smokeless tobacco products at issue). Notably, the court determined that preliminary settlement approval—while merely setting in motion the filing of notice requirements, inviting class members to dissent at the final hearing if they feel the settlement is unfair or inadequate—should not be granted if the court fully intends to deny final approval, even if no dissenting class members appear and protest the settlement. *Id.* at *8. In rejecting the proposed settlement, the court emphasized the need to closely scrutinize coupon settlements which provide no value to the class unless the class members actually redeem the coupons and continue to use the product at issue. *Id.* at *10–13.

While Rule 23(c) permits class members to object to a settlement before it is approved, it is unsettled whether such class members have standing to appeal from a settlement that the court approves over their objections if they do not move to intervene prior to the entry of final judgment. That question has not yet appear to have been decided by a Massachusetts court, but is discussed in *Chechowitz v. Autofair, Inc.*, 102 Mass. App. Ct. 1107, 203 N.E.3d 1178, 2023 Mass. App. Unpub. LEXIS 26 (Mass. App. Ct. Jan. 18, 2023). *Chechowitz* was a putative wage and hour class action. After that case was instituted, but before a class was certified, four employees of the defendant filed arbitration demands to pursue separately their own identical wage and hour claims. When the plaintiff and defendant in *Chechowitz* reached agreement on a class settlement, the defendant sought and obtained a stay of the four parallel arbitrations, arguing that the class settlement would resolve those claims. The four employees who had sought arbitration then moved to intervene in the class action. That motion was denied and not appealed. The four then filed objections to the settlement. The court approved the settlement over their objections. The objectors then noticed an appeal from the final settlement approval order. *See id.* at *1–3. In an unreported decision, the Appeals Court affirmed the final settlement approval order on the merits. *Id.* at *5–6.

Before turning to the merits, however, the Appeals Court first addressed whether the objectors even had standing to appeal. "As a general rule, only parties to a lawsuit, or those who properly become parties, may appeal from an adverse judgment." *Id.* at *3 (quoting *Corbett v. Related Cos. Northeast, Inc.*, 424 Mass. 714, 718, 677 N.E.2d 1153 (1997)). According to the panel in *Chechowitz,* in a class action, the "parties" are the named plaintiffs and defendants. Absent court approval to intervene, class members are not parties, and have no right to challenge any other rulings in the action. *Id.* at *4 (citing *Reznik v. Garaffo*, 466 Mass. 1034–35, 999 N.E.2d 1089 (2013)). The Superior Court's denial of the objectors' motion to intervene in *Chechowitz* was appealable. *See id.* at *4 (citing *Reznik*, 466 Mass. 1034, 1034–35, 999 N.E.2d 1089 & n.2 (2013)). Insofar as intervention was denied and not appealed, the Appeals Court stated that "it may be questioned whether the objectors have standing to bring this appeal." *Id.* at *4–5 (citations omitted). Ultimately, the court concluded that it "need not pause to consider that issue, because in any event the objectors' claims are meritless." *Id.* at *5.

The dicta in *Chechowitz* questioning the objectors' standing turns on the premise that, absent a successful motion to intervene, class members are not "parties" and, therefore, lack standing to appeal. However, addressing this very same question, the United States Supreme Court held that "nonnamed class members . . . who have objected in a timely manner to approval of the settlement at the fairness hearing have the power to bring an appeal without first intervening." *Devlin v. Scardelletti*, 536 U.S. 1, 14 (2002). The Supreme Court based its holding on the undisputed interest of class members in a judgment that would legally bind them. *See id.* at 17. Interestingly, because of that undisputed interest, the federal government argued in an amicus submission that intervention should be readily granted, and thus required as prerequisite to appeal. The Supreme Court rejected this position, finding that it imposed a needless formality. *See id.* at 12–13.

Devlin provides a heavy and persuasive counterweight to the dicta in *Chechowitz*. And the absence of an opt-out right under Mass. R. Civ. P. 23 and Chapter 93A arguably makes the appealable interest of an objector to a Massachusetts state court settlement even stronger than that in *Devlin*. But the Supreme Court's construction of federal appellate jurisdiction is not subject to the same deference that Massachusetts courts give to federal courts' construction of federal cognates to the Massachusetts Rules of Civil Procedure. The extent of Massachusetts appellate jurisdiction ultimately rests with the Supreme Judicial Court. Until this question is definitively resolved, an objecting class member who wishes to appeal a final class settlement approval order might want to consider first moving to intervene as a prudent means to preserve the objector's right to appeal.

f. Relationships between and among Class Counsel

The Appeals Court has upheld the enforceability of referral fee agreements in the class action context. *Vita v. Berman De Valerio & Pease, LLP*, 81 Mass. App. Ct. 748, 755-56, 967 N.E.2d 1142, 1149 (2012) (affirming findings that: (1) defendant law firm breached referral agreement when it unilaterally decided to pay the plaintiff only 4 percent of the fees earned in class action settlement, rather than the customary 10 percent the lawyer had contracted for, and (2) defendant's conduct in attempting to coerce the plaintiff into accepting a lower fee constituted a Chapter 93A violation).

However, the Appeals Court has rejected class-action lawyers' attempts to use the courts as a vehicle to resolve strategic disputes among co-counsel. In *Bartle v. Berry*, the court affirmed the dismissal of claims for intentional interference with advantageous relations and civil conspiracy, which were based on the allegation that class action co-counsel had allegedly foiled a settlement opportunity by commencing a separate class action in the midst of settlement negotiations. "Initiating the lawsuits on behalf of the consumer class, regardless of the motive, violated no duty" owed to co-counsel. 80 Mass. App. Ct. 372, 381–84, 953 N.E.2d 243, 251–54 (2011).

g. Moving to Strike or Dismiss Class Claims under Rule 12

Although no Massachusetts appellate decision has addressed the issue, Superior Court decisions have allowed motions under Mass. R. Civ. P. 12 to strike or dismiss class claims. Relying on federal court decisions interpreting Fed. R. Civ. P. 23 and Fed. R. Civ. P. 12(f), the court in *Kantzelis v. Commerce Ins. Co.*, held that "a Massachusetts trial court may dismiss class allegations under Mass. R. Civ. P. 12(f)." No. SUCV2016-3144-BLS1, 2017 Mass. Super. LEXIS 218, at *11 (Mass. Super. Ct. Nov. 13, 2017) (Kaplan, J.) (citing *Manning v. Boston Med. Ctr. Corp.*, 725 F.3d 34 (1st Cir.

2013)). There, because the pleaded claims could only be proven through individualized evidence, the plaintiffs' class allegations did not support a plausible claim for class treatment and warranted granting the motion to strike. *See id.* at *19–21. However, as the Judge Kaplan subsequently stated in *DeOliveira v. Liberty Mut. Ins. Co.*, "motions to strike class claims are disfavored by the courts and should rarely be granted." *Id.* at *3. In *DeOliveira*, unlike *Kantzelis*, the complaint's allegations posited a common course of conduct and did not, on its face, require individualized fact finding to establish class members' claims. Therefore, the motion to strike was denied. *See* No. SUCV2017-0218-BLS1, 2018 Mass. Super. LEXIS 75, at *4–6 (Mass. Super. Ct. May 9, 2018).

TEXT OF RULE 23 OF THE MASSACHUSETTS RULES OF CIVIL PROCEDURE

(a) *Prerequisites to class action.* One or more members of a class may sue or be sued as representative parties on behalf of all only if (1) the class is so numerous that joinder of all members is impracticable, (2) there are questions of law or fact common to the class, (3) the claims or defenses of the representative parties are typical of the claims or defenses of the class, and (4) the representative parties will fairly and adequately protect the interests of the class.

(b) *Class actions maintainable.* An action may be maintained as a class action if the prerequisites of subdivision (a) are satisfied, and the court finds that the questions of law or fact common to the members of the class predominate over any questions affecting only individual members, and that a class action is superior to other available methods for the fair and efficient adjudication of the controversy.

(c) *Dismissal or compromise.* A class action shall not be dismissed or compromised without the approval of the court. The court may require notice of such proposed dismissal or compromise to be given in such manner as the court directs.

(d) *Orders to insure adequate representation.* The court at any stage of an action under this rule may require such security and impose such terms as shall fairly and adequately protect the interests of the class in whose behalf the action is brought or defended. It may order that notice be given, in such manner as it may direct, of the pendency of the action, of a proposed settlement, of entry of judgment, or of any other proceedings in the action, including notice to the absent persons that they may come in and present claims and defenses if they so desire. Whenever the representation appears to the court inadequate fairly to protect the interests of absent parties who may be bound by the judgment, the court may at any time prior to judgment order an amendment of the pleadings, eliminating therefrom all reference to representation of absent persons, and the court shall order entry of judgment in such form as to affect only the parties to the action and those adequately represented.

(e) *Disposition of residual funds*

(1) "Residual Funds" are funds that remain after the payment of all approved class member claims, expenses, litigation costs, attorneys' fees, and other court-approved disbursements to implement the relief granted. Nothing in this rule is intended to limit the parties to a class action from suggesting, or the trial court from approving, a settlement that does not create residual funds.

(2) Any order, judgment or approved compromise in a class action certified under this rule that establishes a process for identifying and compensating members of the class may provide for the disbursement of residual funds. In matters where the claims process has been exhausted and residual funds remain, the residual funds shall be disbursed to one or more nonprofit organizations or foundations (which may include nonprofit organizations that provide legal services to low income persons) which support projects that will benefit the class or similarly situated persons consistent with the objectives and purposes of the underlying causes of action on which relief was based,

or to the Massachusetts IOLTA Committee to support activities and programs that promote access to the civil justice system for low income residents of the Commonwealth of Massachusetts.

(3) Where residual funds may remain, no judgment may enter or compromise be approved unless the plaintiff has given notice to the Massachusetts IOLTA Committee for the limited purpose of allowing the committee to be heard on whether it ought to be a recipient of any or all residual funds.

TEXT OF MASS. GEN. LAWS CH. 93A, § 9(2)

(2) Any persons entitled to bring such action [pursuant to Mass. Gen. Laws ch. 93A, § 9(1)] may, if the use or employment of the unfair or deceptive act or practice has caused similar injury to numerous other persons similarly situated and if the court finds in a preliminary hearing that he adequately and fairly represents such other persons, bring the action on behalf of himself and such other similarly injured and situated persons; the court shall require that notice of such action be given to unnamed petitioners in the most effective practicable manner. Such action shall not be dismissed, settled or compromised without the approval of the court, and notice of any proposed dismissal, settlement or compromise shall be given to all members of the class of petitioners in such manner as the court directs.

TEXT OF MASS. GEN. LAWS CH. 93A, § 11, PARA. 3

Any persons entitled to bring such action [pursuant to Mass. Gen. Laws ch. 93A, § 11] may, if the use or employment of the unfair method of competition or the unfair or deceptive act or practice has caused similar injury to numerous other persons similarly situated and if the court finds in a preliminary hearing that he adequately and fairly represents such other persons, bring the action on behalf of himself and such other similarly injured and situated persons; the court shall require that notice of such action be given to unnamed petitioners in the most effective, practicable manner. Such action shall not be dismissed, settled or compromised without the approval of the court, and notice of any proposed dismissal, settlement or compromise shall be given to all members of the class of petitioners in such a manner as the court directs.

This chapter was prepared by Kevin McGinty and Larry Schoen, Members in the Litigation Section in the Boston office of Mintz, Levin, Cohn, Ferris, Glovsky and Popeo, P.C., and Matthew Stein, Special Counsel in the Litigation Section in Mintz's Boston office. Hannah Bruce and Samantha Schatten, members of Mintz's 2025 Summer Associate class, assisted in preparation of this chapter.

MICHIGAN

1. COMPARISON WITH RULE 23 OF THE FEDERAL RULES OF CIVIL PROCEDURE

Michigan's General Court Rules of 1963 were substantially overhauled in 1983 with the enactment of the Michigan Court Rules. The Michigan Court Rules borrowed from a number of sources, including the Federal Rules of Civil Procedure and other states' rules. MCR 3.501 varies in some respects from Fed. R. Civ. P. 23. For example, the requirements under Fed. R. Civ. P. 23(b)(3) apply to all Michigan class actions. MCR 3.501 also contains explicit provisions on statutes of limitations and the filing of counter claims.

2. CASE LAW INTERPRETING MCR 3.501

After MCR 3.501 was enacted in 1983, for a period of years, there was a limited amount of case law interpreting some of the provisions of the newer rule. Cases under the former rule were deemed useful if the language was carried over from the previous rule. The Michigan appellate courts, recognizing the limited amount of law on some topics, suggested referring to federal cases on class certification. *Neal v. James,* 252 Mich. App. 12, 651 N.W.2d 181 (2002); *Brenner v. Marathon Oil Co.*, 222 Mich. App. 128, 565 N.W.2d 1 (1997); *Adelman v. Compuware Corp.*, 2017 WL 6389899 (Mich. App. Dec. 14, 2017). However, while federal cases may be persuasive, they are not binding. *Bell v. Civil Service Comm.* 2020 WL 4036606 (Mich. App. July 16, 2020), citing *Abela v. Gen. Motors Corp.,* 469 Mich. 603, 677 N.W.2d 325 (2004). In *Henry v. Dow Chem. Co.*, 484 Mich. 483, 772 N.W.2d 301 (2009), the Michigan Supreme Court held that the federal court requirement that the court conduct a "rigorous" analysis of the factors in the relevant class action court rule applies to state courts addressing class actions under MCR 3.501 in the sense that the court should not simply accept bare assertions that the prerequisites for class certification exist. A party seeking class certification is required to provide the certifying court with information sufficient to establish that each prerequisite for class certification in MCR 3.501(A)(1) is in fact satisfied *Erma Rogers Revocable Trust by Plumley v. Erickson Retirement Communities*, 2017 WL 6345742 (Mich. App. Dec. 12, 2017). The Michigan courts do not expressly require a "rigorous analysis" but as a practical matter the courts so diligently review the record presented to determine whether the various prerequisites are met that it may be a distinction without significance.

The Michigan circuit courts have jurisdiction over all class actions without regard to jurisdictional amounts in controversy. *Dix v. American Bankers Life Assurance Co.*, 429 Mich. 410, 415 N.W.2d 206 (1987). In *A&D Dev. v. Michigan Commercial Ins. Mut.,* 301296, 2012 WL 639334 (Mich. Ct. App. Feb. 28, 2012) *appeal denied*, 817 N.W.2d 89 (Mich. 2012), the Court of Appeals reversed a trial court decision sending a class action regarding challenging the use of surplus funds after the conversion of a workers' compensation self-insurance fund into a mutual insurance company to the state Workers' Compensation Agency. State agencies do not possess the authority to hear class action claims in an administrative proceeding, absent an explicit statutory grant of powers or administrative rules permitting the agency to do so. There was no such authority regarding the WCA.

An order certifying a class will only be reversed on appeal if it is clearly erroneous. *Mooahesh v. Department of Treasury*, 195 Mich. App. 551, 492 N.W.2d 246 (1992); *Zine v. Chrysler Corp.*, 236 Mich. App. 261, 600 N.W.2d 384 (1999). But in *Henry v. Dow Chem. Co.*, 484 Mich. 483, 772 N.W.2d 301 (2009), the Michigan Supreme Court clarified, holding that where a party challenges a lower court's factual findings on class certification, a review for clear error is appropriate, and where a party challenges a trial court's exercise of discretion, a review for abuse of discretion is appropriate. Given that the analysis a trial court must undertake in order to determine whether to certify a proposed class may involve making both findings of fact *and* discretionary determinations, *Henry* found it proper to review the trial court's factual findings for clear error and the decisions within the trial court's discretion for abuse of discretion. These standards of review on appeal were reaffirmed in *Schafer v. Kent County*, __ Mich.__; __ N.W. 3d__, 2024 WL 3573500 (July 29, 2024). A preliminary ruling that a class may be certified may not be subject to appeal, but the court of appeals may grant leave to appeal a "permanent"/final class certification order. *Wilson v. Sinai Grace Hospital*, 2004 Mich. App. LEXIS 1099 (Apr. 29, 2004).

In *Fitzpatrick v. Public School Employees Retirement System,* 2011 WL 1902000 (Mich. App. May 19, 2011), the Court of Appeals held that a person appealing an administrative ruling regarding retirement benefits could not add a class action claim when appealing that decision to the circuit courts. The court noted that if petitioner prevailed on the legal issue presented by his petition for review, he (or another similarly situated person) may then properly file a class action complaint for superintending control in the circuit court directing respondents to pay retirement benefits consistent with the legal ruling resolving the substantive issue in petitioner's favor.

a. Rule 3.501(A)

Rule 3.501(A) contains five requirements for a class action, all of which must be satisfied. *A&M Supply Co. v. Microsoft Corp.*, 252 Mich. App. 580, 654 N.W.2d 572 (2002). The requirements must be followed strictly. *Henry v. Dow Chem. Co.*, 484 Mich. 483, 772 N.W.2d 301 (2009). The plaintiff seeking class certification bears the burden of proof. *Henry v. Dow Chem. Co.*, *supra*; *Zine v. Chrysler Corp.*, 236 Mich. App. 261, 600 N.W.2d 384 (1999); *Tinman v. Blue Cross & Blue Shield of Michigan*, 264 Mich. App. 546, 692 N.W.2d 58 (2004). In *Brindley v. Severstal, NA, Inc.*, 485 Mich. 999, 775 N.W.2d 742 (2009), the Michigan Supreme Court remanded the lower court's decision granting class certification despite the Court's belief that the lower court's decision to grant certification was probably not an abuse of discretion. But the lower court had prefaced its decision with a statement that it was required to accept the allegations made in support of the request for certification as true. A court cannot preclude certification of an action as a class action without considering the requirements of this rule. *Salesin v. State Farm Fire & Casualty Co.*, 229 Mich. App. 346, 581 N.W.2d 781 (1998). A party's pleadings will only be sufficient to support certification if they are uncontested or admitted by the other party. *Duskin v. Dept. of Human Services*, 304 Mich. App. 645 (2014). In addressing certification, the court should not question the actual merits of the case. *Id.*

Henry v. Dow Chem. Co., 484 Mich. 483, 772 N.W.2d 301 (2009), also held that a court may base its class certification decision on the pleadings alone *only if* the pleadings set forth sufficient information to satisfy the court that each prerequisite is in fact met. *Accord*, *Duncan v. State*, 300 Mich. App. 176, 832 N.W. 2d 761 (2013). The averments in the pleadings of a party seeking class certification are only sufficient to certify a class if they satisfy the burden on the party seeking certification to prove that the prerequisites are met, such as in cases where the facts necessary to support this finding are uncontested or admitted by the opposing party. *Henry, supra*; *Erma Rogers Revocable Trust by Plumley v. Erickson Retirement Communities*, 2017 WL 6345742 (Mich. App. Dec. 12, 2017).

The trial court does not abuse its discretion by postponing the class certification hearing until discovery is completed. *Duncan v. State*, 300 Mich. App. 176, 832 N.W. 2d 761 (2013).

A threshold requirement is that the proposed class representative is a member of the class. A plaintiff who cannot maintain the cause of action as an individual is not qualified to represent the proposed class. *Camden v. Kaufman*, 240 Mich. App. 389, 613 N.W.2d 335 (2000); *Zine, supra*; *McGill v. Automobile Ass'n of Michigan*, 207 Mich. App. 402, 525 N.W.2d 12 (1994).

Anderson v. Indian Village Manor Associates, LLC, 2002 Mich. App. LEXIS 669 (Apr. 30, 2002) (unpublished), reversed and remanded an order certifying a class of residential apartment building tenants because the lower court granted certification by simply announcing that a class would be certified. There was no analysis of the requirements of MCR 2.305, and the order was likewise terse and cursory. Similarly, in *Rennie v. Marble Head Lime, Inc.*, 2005 Mich. App. LEXIS 1445 (June 16, 2005) (unpublished), the Court of Appeals remanded the case to the lower court for consideration of the issue of adequacy of representation because the lower court record was unclear as to whether the lower court adequately scrutinized plaintiffs' claims regarding adequacy of representation.

In *Keech v. S.R. Jacobson Devel. Co.*, 2006 Mich. App. LEXIS 1813 (June 13, 2006), plaintiffs' participation in the settlement of a national class action against the manufacturer of allegedly defective wood siding barred any claim against defendant builder. The federal settlement expressly applied to "individuals and companies involved in the distribution, installation, construction and first-time sale of structures with siding" and "any third party involved in building, installing or distributing the product."

In *Estes v. Anderson*, 2012 WL 5857283 (Mich. App. Nov. 15, 2012), the court affirmed certification of a class of participants in City of Detroit pension programs suing the plans' trustees over investments made by the plans. Plaintiffs satisfied their obligation to provide the certifying court with information sufficient to establish that each prerequisite for class certification in MCR 3.501(A) was in fact satisfied. The lower court considered the many class action allegations in plaintiffs' complaint, the documentation that plaintiffs submitted to substantiate their motion for class certification, and the parties' many briefs pertaining to certification. In light of the complaint's class action allegations and the evidence plaintiffs appended to their motion for class certification, which the lower court referenced in deciding the motion, the Court of Appeals concluded that (1) the lower court's order adequately explained that the prerequisites for class certification existed in the case; (2) the lower court's order contained no clearly erroneous findings of fact; and (3) the lower court acted within its discretion in entering the order certifying the plaintiff class.

Michigan Ass'n of Chiropractors v. Blue Cross Blue Shield of Michigan, 300 Mich. App. 551, 834 N.W. 2d 138 (2013), involved a lawsuit by a chiropractic association and a chiropractor claiming that defendant insurer had breached provider agreements and a settlement agreement. Plaintiffs successfully moved to certify a class comprised of "all similarly situated chiropractors who have or had Traditional Services or PPO Product Agreements with Blue Cross, are members of the MAC and have been denied lawful reimbursement." On appeal, the Court of Appeals declined to decertify the entire class but had issues with the class definition. The court decertified the class on the complaint count involving retrospective compensatory damages because it would require an individualized examination of what claims were submitted and denied by each chiropractor. The court left the class standing on declaratory relief claims.

In *Hanton v. Hantz Fin'l Services, Inc.*, 306 Mich. App. 654, 858 N.W.2d 481 (2014), *lv. denied*, 497 Mich. 2011, 862 N.W.2d 651 (2015), the court held that the plaintiff trustee was not prohibited from filing a claim against a financial advisor regarding a Ponzi scheme due to the dismissal of another noncertified class action brought by a different plaintiff. In the other case, Raymond Bergin as the plaintiff did not file his motion for class certification on time, so the court granted his 2011 motion to dismiss the case without prejudice on the condition that any rulings and orders made in his case would be deemed final and binding in any refiled case where Bergin was a class representative or member of the class and substantially similar claims were made. When Hanton's case was moved to the same judge, that judge held that Bergin's failure to timely move for class certification barred Hanton's motion. The Court of Appeals reversed, holding that Hanton's status as an unnamed putative class member in the *Bergin* case did not make the court order on Bergin applicable to her. Bergin was not acting a class representative merely because he had filed a complaint. Absent class certification, the class did not exist, and any orders in the case only applied to Bergin.

i. Separate classes. In *Bell v. Civil Service Comm.*, 2020 WL 4036606 (Mich. App. July 16, 2020), the Court of Appeals held it was not error for the lower court to certify two classes of persons who took two versions of an Entry Level Law Enforcement Examination required for applicants to law enforcement positions in the Michigan State Police and the Department of Natural Resources. Defendants claimed the court could not certify multiples classes in the same case absent each class originating from a single class that meets all certification requirements. The Court of Appeals disagreed, noting that MCR 3.501(B)(3)(d)(ii) specifically allows "a proposed class" to be divided into subclasses. Nothing in the language of the court rules prohibited the lower court from certifying two classes in a single suit, where appropriate.

ii. Numerosity. The class must be so numerous that joinder of all members is impracticable. There is no particular minimum number of members necessary to meet the requirement. *Zine, supra*; *Hill v. City of Warren*, 2003 Mich. App. LEXIS 268 (Feb. 4, 2003) (unpublished); *rev'd on other grounds* 469 Mich. 958, 671 N.W.2d 534 (2003); *Duskin v. Dept. of Human Services*, 304 Mich App. 645 (2014). The exact number of members need not be known as long as general knowledge and common sense indicate that the class is large. *Hill, supra*. Because the court cannot determine if joinder of the class members would be impracticable unless it knows that approximate number of members, the plaintiff must adequately define the class so potential members can be identified and must present some evidence of the number of class members or otherwise establish by reasonable estimate the number of class members. *Id.* The presence of at least 350 minority employees affected by a governmental law department reorganization was sufficient. *Neal v. James,* 252 Mich. App. 12, 651 N.W.2d 181 (2002). A class of 700 patients suing a hospital over allegedly inadequate sterilization of endoscopic equipment was sufficiently numerous. *Creech v. W.A. Foote Memorial Hospital*, 2004 Mich. App. LEXIS 1404 (Jun. 8, 2004) (unpublished). The fact that several thousand city-planted trees were causing damage to homeowners' properties supported numerosity because general knowledge and common sense indicated that there were thousands of putative class members. *Hill v. City of Warren*, 276 Mich. App. 299, 740 N.W.2d 706 (2007), *lv. denied*, 480 Mich. 1195, 748 N.W.2d 520 (2008).

In *Erma Rogers Revocable Trust by Plumley v. Erickson Retirement Communities*, 2017 WL 6345742 (Mich. App. Dec. 12, 2017), the court affirmed certification of a class of persons who signed residential independent living apartment agreements regarding defendants' alleged failure to refund deposits as advertised. The number of members of the class as redefined by the lower court was not clear as there were roughly 1,000 persons who were potential members before reductions were made. The court was clear that it did not need to know the exact size of the class.

A school district seeking certification of a class of school districts alleging the right to insurance coverage of Y2K problems failed to demonstrate that a sufficient number of school districts had such problems so as to satisfy the numerosity requirement. *Royal Oak School District v. MASB-SEG Property and Casualty PPL, Inc.*, 2003 Mich. App. LEXIS 2352 (Sept. 16, 2003) (unpublished). A subclass of eight was not sufficiently numerous. *Kennedy Masonry, Inc. v. Associated Builders & Contrs. of Michigan Workers Compensation Fund,* 2004 Mich. App. LEXIS 2943 (Mich. Ct. App. 2004).

In *Keech v. S.R. Jacobson Devel. Co.,* 2006 Mich. App. LEXIS 1814 (June 13, 2006), the Court of Appeal reversed the lower court's certification of a class of purchasers of allegedly defective wood siding because the class representative failed to demonstrate that anyone other than himself was in his alleged subclass. In *Jackson v. Wal-Mart Stores, Inc.,* 2005 Mich. App. LEXIS 2975 (Nov. 29, 2005), the Court of Appeals affirmed the denial of class certification in a case brought by a Wal-Mart employee who claimed that during a six-year period, the company was requiring employees to wrok "off the clock" and was denying paid breaks. The court would not assume that all Wal-Mart employees in Michigan were affected, and plaintiff did not carry his burden of proof regarding numerosity.

Numerosity was not found in *Duskin v. Dep't of Human Servs.*, 2009 Mich. App. LEXIS 1378 (June 11, 2009), where plaintiffs alleged that the state agency discriminatorily denied male, but not female, racial and ethnic minorities a sufficient number of promotions to supervisory and management positions. Although the number of potential class members was sufficiently large on its face (616), not every potential class member had been denied a promotion. The Court of Appeals reversed certification a second time, holding *Duskin v. Dept. of Human Services*, 304 Mich. App. 645 (2014). In that case, while the plaintiff demonstrated that there were 586 minority males in the class, he did not demonstrate that a sizable number of those 586 persons suffered an actual injury. Accordingly, numerosity was not established.

Michigan Ass'n of Chiropractors v. Blue Cross Blue Shield of Michigan, 300 Mich. App. 551, 834 N.W. 2d 138 (2013), involved a lawsuit by a chiropractic association and a chiropractor claiming that defendant insurer had breached provider agreements and a settlement agreement. Plaintiffs successfully moved to certify a class comprised of "all similarly situated chiropractors who have or had Traditional Services or PPO Product Agreements with Blue Cross, are members of the MAC and have been denied lawful reimbursement." The Court of Appeals noted that the lower court only looked at one of the three requirements for a chiropractor to be in the class, i.e., that he or she was a member of plaintiff association but did not examine whether they were signatories to a Blue Cross agreement and had been wrongfully denied reimbursement. Although this was clear error, since the court had limited plaintiffs' claims to declaratory relief, the court held that it could "deemphasize" the need to estimate the number of chiropractors suffering actual harm.

Numerosity existed in *Nowacki v. Dept. of Corrections,* 2014 WL 4088041 (Mich. App. Aug. 19, 2014), *lv. denied,* 498 Mich. 859, 865 N.W.2d. 28 (2015), where 80 male corrections officers were in a class attacking restrictions on the ability to work in certain positions in a women's correctional facility. Plaintiffs claimed that the restrictions were applied too broadly in an effort to purge the facility of male corrections officers. That number was sufficient.

The Court of Appeals affirmed denial of class certification in *Kowalchuk v. City of Jackson*, 2017 WL 2262876 (Mich. App. May 23, 2017), because the plaintiffs failed to establish numerosity. Plaintiffs were property owners who claimed that defendant city's drawing of groundwater out of four wells in a city park deprived the class of their right to reasonably use the groundwater beneath and surrounding their properties. Plaintiffs did not show that a sizable number of persons suffered an actual injury from defendant's use of the groundwater and therefore failed to satisfy the numerosity requirement.

In *Bell v. Civil Service Comm.*, 2020 WL 4036606 (Mich. App. July 16, 2020), two classes of persons challenged two versions of an Entry Level Law Enforcement Examination required for applicants to law enforcement positions in the Michigan State Police and the Department of Natural Resources. Defendants claimed numerosity was not met because plaintiffs could not identify how many putative class members suffered an injury because of the exam. The Court of Appeals disagreed because the class alleged that the test had a disproportionate impact on African American candidates and that all class members took and failed to tests. The fact that unscored writing sections were treated as failures was not improper.

Brown v. VHS of Michigan, Inc., 2021 WL 1157280 (Mich. App. Mar. 25, 2021), addressed certification of a class action brought against a hospital and funeral home regarding the mishandling of stillborn or deceased babies' remains. On review, the Court of Appeals held that numerosity was met by having at least 34 class members.

iii. Commonality. There must be questions of law and fact common to the members of the class that predominate over questions affecting only individual members. This factor is concerned with whether there is a common issue the resolution of which will advance the litigation. *Communications Workers of America, Local 4100 v. Ameritech Services, Inc.*, 2003 Mich. App. LEXIS 1494 (June 24, 2003) (unpublished); *A&M Supply Co. v. Microsoft Corp.*, 252 Mich. App. 580, 654 N.W.2d 572 (2002); *Zine, supra*. The issues in the class that are subject to generalized proof, thus applicable to the case as a whole, must predominate over those issues that are subject only to individualized proof. *Id.* But there is no requirement that all questions necessary for ultimate resolution be common to the members of the class. *A&M Supply Co. v. Microsoft Corp.*, 252 Mich. App. 580, 654 N.W.2d 572 (2002); *Grigg v. Michigan National Bank*, 405 Mich. 148, 274 N.W.2d 752 (1979). In a case involving property damages caused by city-planted trees had the requisite commonality because the individualized determinations of the extent of damage would not predominate over the common question whether defendant city was liable *at all* for damage caused by its trees. *Hill v. City of Warren*, 276 Mich. App. 299, 740 N.W.2d 706 (2007), *lv. denied*, 480 Mich. 1195, 748 N.W.2d 520 (2008).

Commonality is not satisfied if liability is resolved pre-certification, leaving only individualized damages issues to be resolved. *Salesin v. State Farm Fire & Casualty Co.*, 2003 Mich. App. LEXIS 2508 (Oct. 7, 2003).

Certification of a class of female teachers who had been denied maternity-related disability benefits was properly denied because of the presence of seven different collective bargaining agreements during the class period and individual issues, including exhaustion of remedies and mitigation of damages. *Lee v. Board of Education*, 184 Mich. App. 502, 459 N.W.2d 1 (1989). Certification of a class of no-fault auto insureds who had been denied inpatient television and telephone services was reversed on appeal, because whether such services are an allowable expense under Michigan's no-fault statute depended on an individual analysis of the facts and circumstances of each insured. *Hamilton v. AAA Michigan*, 248 Mich. App. 535, 639 N.W. 2d 837 (2001). Similarly, casino patrons alleging wrongful detention by security guards failed to show commonality because liability depended upon individual conduct of patrons and guards. *Stiglmaier v. Detroit Entertainment, L.L.C.*, 2004 Mich. App. LEXIS 2292 (Aug. 31, 2004) (unpublished).

Certification of minority legal personnel in a city law department claiming racial discrimination was reversed in *Neal v. James*, 252 Mich. App. 12, 651 N.W.2d 181 (2002). The only common issue alleged concerned the reorganization of the law department. Under federal precedents, workforce changes made during a reorganization do not satisfy commonality because resolution of the merits will involve a review of each plaintiff's individual qualifications, work performance, and other individual factors.

Similarly, in *Communications Workers of America, Local 4100 v. Ameritech Services, Inc.*, 2003 Mich. App. LEXIS 1494 (June 24, 2003) (unpublished), the Court of Appeals reversed certification of a class of African American telephone technicians who complained that a new performance review program operated in a discriminatory fashion. Commonality was not satisfied because the employees had varied work histories and employment circumstances. Plaintiffs' theories of liability were based upon disparate impact and disparate treatment, the latter subject to different methods of proof. Individualized questions of damages and mitigation also existed.

In *Creech v. W.A. Foote Memorial Hospital*, 2004 Mich App. LEXIS 1404 (June 8, 2004) (unpublished), the Court of Appeals affirmed the lower court's certification of a class of patients which sued a hospital over allegedly inadequate sterilization of endoscopic equipment. Despite some factual variations, common questions such as whether defendant was negligent in its disinfecting process were sufficient to meet the commonality requirement. In *Vandenbroeck v. Commonpoint Mortgage Co.*, 2004 Mich. App. LEXIS 2098 (Aug. 10, 2004) (unpublished), the named plaintiff claimed that defendant mortgage companies had a practice of charging loan discount fees without providing loan discounts. These allegations contained the requisite commonality because the class members were all charged discount fees and did not receive discounted interest rates in exchange.

In *Tinman v. Blue Cross & Blue Shield of Michigan*, 264 Mich. App. 546, 692 N.W.2d 58 (2004), the Court of Appeals reversed the denial of decertification of a class of patients contesting the denial of emergency room benefits based upon the final diagnosis. The court found that individual questions predominated. Rather than being subject to generalized proofs, the evidence of the type of emergency health services and medically necessary services provided, the medical conditions involved and whether they occurred suddenly, the signs and symptoms that manifested those medical conditions, and whether payment was denied for services up to the point of stabilization would all vary from patient to patient.

Commonality was not found in *Kennedy Masonry, Inc. v. Associated Builders & Contrs. of Michigan Workers Compensation Fund,* 2004 Mich. App. LEXIS 2943 (Mich. Ct. App. 2004), where construction companies sued claiming that their self-insured worker compensation carrier improperly escrowed refunds due them. The court held that each individual class member must establish that it is entitled to a surplus refund but for its withdrawal from the fund. But whether a class member was entitled to a surplus distribution depended on a number of facts unique to that particular class member.

In *Peet v. Sweet Onion, Inc.*, 2005 Mich. App. LEXIS 737 (Mar. 17, 2005), the Court of Appeals reversed certification of a class of persons who allegedly became ill after eating food prepared at defendant banquet hall on three different occasions. The common question of fact was whether defendants served contaminated food at each of the three events. Thereafter, questions affecting only individual members of the class would remain, including whether a class member became ill after eating at one of the events, whether the illness was caused by eating food served at the event or by a pathogen from some other source, what symptoms each class member exhibited, the severity and duration of the symptoms, and what damages each class member sustained. These questions would be subject to the particularized proof from each potential victim and would obviously predominate over the simple, common question of fact.

In *Williams v. Terra Energy, Inc.,* 2006 Mich. App. LEXIS 2309 (July 25, 2006), the Court of Appeals for the second time reversed the lower court's certification of a class of oil and gas leaseholders who claimed that the lessee defrauded them out of royalty payments. There was not a single question which if answered would establish class-wide liability. Each lease would have to be examined to determine whether the leaseholder had not received royalty payments. This destroyed commonality and also rendered the class representatives' claims potentially atypical.

Commonality did not exist in a class action brought by tenants against a landlord regarding alleged improper deductions from security deposits because in individual analysis of each tenant's situation would be required. *Maier v. Community Resource Mgmt. Co.*, 2006 Mich. App. LEXIS 708 (Mar. 16, 2006).

In *Jackson v. Wal-Mart Stores, Inc.*, 2005 Mich. App. LEXIS 2975 (Nov. 29, 2005), the Court of Appeals affirmed the denial of class certification in a case brought by a Wal-Mart employee who claimed that during a six-year period, the company was requiring employees to work "off the clock" and was denying paid breaks. Plaintiff based the claim on an equitable theory of implied contract, which would require individualized determinations of whether the company had been unjustly enriched as to each employee.

Commonality was not found in *Duskin v. Dep't of Human Servs.*, 2009 Mich. App. LEXIS 1378 (June 11, 2009), where plaintiffs alleged that the state agency discriminatorily denied male, but not female, racial and ethnic minorities a sufficient number of promotions to supervisory and management positions. While plaintiffs asserted that the class representatives applied for or were available for promotions, but were not chosen for discriminatory reasons, plaintiffs offered no information about the representatives' eligibility and qualifications, what positions they sought, what qualifications the positions required, and whether a less qualified, non-minority or female candidate was promoted instead. And, importantly, plaintiffs failed to explain how the claims of the representative plaintiffs present a question common to the entire class of every minority male employee at DHS. After remand, the Court of Appeals reversed class certification for a second time in *Duskin v. Dept. of Human Services*, 304 Mich. App. 645 (2014). The court held that the class members' claims included an inextricable mix of racial discrimination, ethnic discrimination and gender discrimination claims asserted against different actors and the department as a whole.

Michigan Ass'n of Chiropractors v. Blue Cross Blue Shield of Michigan, 300 Mich. App. 551, 834 N.W.2d 138 (2013), involved a lawsuit by a chiropractic association and a chiro-practor claiming that defendant insurer had breached provider agreements and a settlement agreement. Plaintiffs successfully moved to certify a class comprised of "all similarly situated chiropractors who have or had Traditional Services or PPO Product Agreements with Blue Cross, are members of the MAC and have been denied lawful reimbursement." On appeal, the Court of Appeals declined to decertify the entire class but had issues with the class definition. The court decertified the class on the complaint count involving retrospective compensatory damages because it would require an individualized examination of what claims were submitted and denied by each chiropractor. The court left the class standing on declaratory relief claims. The limitations on the declaratory relief claims forestalled the need for individualized proofs on damages. But the retrospective compensatory damages claims would require an individual inquiry for each class member, destroying commonality.

Commonality existed in *Nowacki v. Dept. of Corrections,* 2014 WL 4088041 (Mich. App. Aug. 19, 2014), *lv. denied,* 498 Mich. 859, 865 N.W.2d. 28 (2015), where 80 male corrections officers were in a class attacking restrictions on the ability to work in certain positions in a women's correctional facility. Plaintiffs claimed that the restrictions were applied too broadly in an effort to purge the facility of male corrections officers. The allegation that the restrictions were applied too broadly was a common issue central to the validity of each claim.

Commonality also existed in *Erma Rogers Revocable Trust by Plumley v. Erickson Retirement Communities*, 2017 WL 6345742 (Mich. App. Dec. 12, 2017), a class action regarding residential independent living agreements. The class members' claims involved the same general facts and theories regarding a common scheme by the defendants to lease units promising a full refund upon reoccupancy. The defendants used common forms that did not vary significantly in content. While differences in individual units or the times when units were vacated may be factors in calculating damages, those differences did not impact the common liability issues in this litigation. The fact that the damages might vary did not prevent certification.

Commonality was also found in *Bell v. Civil Service Comm.*, 2020 WL 4036606 (Mich. App. July 16, 2020), where two classes of persons challenged as discriminatory versions of an Entry Level Law Enforcement Examination required for applicants to law enforcement positions in the Michigan State Police and the Department of Natural Resources. Defendants argued that the writing portion of the 20002 exam was subjectively scored, requiring hundreds of mini-trials. The Court of Appeals held that the use of a standard scoring template, which limited the graders' discretion, preserved commonality. Only damages appropriate for the whole class would be decided at the first stage of trial. There would not be 600 mini-trials on damages.

In *Carter v. Michigan State Police,* 2020 WL 4036516 (Mich. App. July 16, 2020), applicants for the Michigan State Police who received a 2 on a 1–3 scale used in prescreening interviews were required to wait two years to reapply. The class representative received a 2 due to a poor credit history and current past-due bills. He claimed that the interview used subjective criteria that *discriminated* against African-American applicants. The Court of Appeals reversed the lower court's decision that the class lacked commonality. The court found that the question of whether the framework of the prescreening interview, which allowed discretionary ranking based on subjective criteria, discriminates on the basis of race and not by business necessity was a common question to the entire class.

Commonality did not exist in *Brown v. VHS of Michigan, Inc.*, 2021 WL 1157280 (Mich. App. Mar. 25, 2021), which addressed certification of a class action brought against a hospital and funeral home regarding the mishandling of stillborn or deceased babies' remains. While, as a general matter, plaintiffs' claims arose from the deaths of human babies and fetuses, the question of whether the remains were handled properly in accordance with the wishes of the parent was not capable of class-wide resolution. There will be individualized inquiries on the circumstances under which the hospitals took possession of the remains, the parent's directions regarding the same, and the circumstances under which the remains ended up at the particular funeral home. Moreover, plaintiffs' claims for negligence, intentional infliction of emotional distress, and fraud would require individualized proofs.

Commonality did not exist in *Yamaoka v. Sun Communities, Inc.*, No. 355446, 2021 WL 6131166, (Mich. Ct. App. Dec. 28, 2021), where an alleged class of former mobile home owners sued an operator of mobile home parks. Two of the three named plaintiffs failed to make lease payments and left their mobile homes after they moved out. Their mobile homes were seized as abandoned under the terms of their leases. The third named plaintiff was evicted and tried to sell his mobile home but his lease did not have an abandonment provision. The leases required individualized proofs as the lease terms varied.

In *Hogan v. Wayne County*, 2024 WL 2790297 (Mich. App. May 30, 2024), commonality was lacking in an action brought by female jail inmates and detainees alleging harassment and mistreatment at the county jail. Commonality requires common injury demonstrated with generalized proof rather than individual injuries. The declarations filed by plaintiffs described differing experiences. It was not enough to show that all members of the class experienced some type of sexual harassment or racially discriminatory language during strip searches.

iv. Typicality. The proposed class representative must be a member of the class, i.e., a plaintiff who cannot maintain the action as an individual is not qualified to represent a class. *A&M Supply Co. v. Microsoft Corp.*, 252 Mich. App. 580, 654 N.W.2d 572 (2002); *Zine v. Chrysler Corp.*, 236 Mich. App. 261, 600 N.W.2d 384 (1999). The claims or defenses of the representative parties must be typical of the claims or defenses of the class. In an employment discrimination action, *Neal v. James,* 252 Mich. App. 12, 651 N.W.2d 181 (2002); held that plaintiffs did not allege a single policy or practice of discrimination, but rather a set of individual claims for discrimination. But the class representative in *Creech, supra,* made identical claims over inadequately disinfected endoscopic equipment to those of the class. The *Creech* court noted that class action litigation is preferable for claims of injuries resulting from a single disaster or single course of conduct. In *Vandenbroeck v. Commonpoint Mortgage Co.,* 2004 Mich. App., mortgage companies had a practice of charging loan discount fees without providing loan discounts. These allegations contained the requisite typicality because the class representative's claim had the same essential characteristics of the class at large and was based upon the same legal theory.

Typicality was not found in *Duskin v. Dep't of Human Servs.*, 2009 Mich. App. LEXIS 1378 (June 11, 2009), where plaintiffs alleged that the state agency discriminatorily denied male, but not female, racial and ethnic minorities a sufficient number of promotions to supervisory and management positions. Plaintiffs articulated no factual basis to confirm their individual disparate treatment claims and they failed to connect their allegations to the other members of the class. Typicality also fails when it is foreseeable that a defendant will raise specific evidence applicable only to each proposed class representative as to why he or she was not promoted or better trained. In *Duskin v. Dept. of Human Services*, 304 Mich. App. 645 (2014), the Court of Appeals reversed certification a second time, finding that there was no indication that the named representatives had the same essential characteristics regarding *all* the claims concerning *all* the different types and methods of discrimination by the various actors that the class definition and the minority males' allegations encompassed.

In *Henry v. Dow Chem. Co.*, 484 Mich. 483, 772 N.W.2d 301 (2009), the Michigan Supreme Court reversed the lower court's certification of classes of present and former property owners who sued a chemical company relating to dioxin contamination of a floodplain. Regarding typicality, the Court noted that the trial court's analysis consisted of a restatement of the standard; a statement that "plaintiffs contend" that their claims "arise from the same course of conduct" and that "they share common legal and remedial theories"; and a quote from a federal district court case stating that the typicality requirement may be satisfied if "there is a nexus between the class representatives' claims [and] defenses and the common questions of fact or law which unite the class." It was unclear from the trial court's analysis whether it independently determined that the plaintiffs alleged basic questions of law and fact sufficient to support their allegation that their legal remedial theories were typical of those of the class.

Michigan Ass'n of Chiropractors v. Blue Cross Blue Shield of Michigan, 300 Mich. App. 551, 834 N.W.2d 138 (2013), involved a lawsuit by a chiropractic association and a chiropractor claiming that defendant insurer had breached provider agreements and a settlement agreement. Plaintiffs successfully moved to certify a class comprised of "all similarly situated chiropractors who have or had Traditional Services or PPO Product Agreements with Blue Cross, are members of the MAC and have been denied lawful reimbursement." On appeal, the Court of Appeals declined to decertify the entire class but had issues with the class definition. The court decertified the class on the complaint count involving retrospective compensatory damages because it would require an individualized examination of what claims were submitted and denied by each chiropractor. The court left the class standing on declaratory relief claims. The limitations on the declaratory relief claims forestalled the need for individualized proofs on damages. But the retrospective compensatory damages claims would require an individual inquiry for each class member, destroying typicality.

Typicality also existed in *Erma Rogers Revocable Trust by Plumley v. Erickson Retirement Communities*, 2017 WL 6345742 (Mich. App. Dec. 12, 2017), a class action regarding residential independent living agreements. The fact that the class representative did not sign an amendment to accept a discounted refund did not make its claim atypical. Differences in the management companies involved did not affect typicality.

Typicality existed in *Brown v. VHS of Michigan, Inc.*, 2021 WL 1157280 (Mich. App. Mar. 25, 2021), which addressed certification of a class action brought against a hospital and funeral home regarding the mishandling of stillborn or deceased babies' remains. A class action was the most economic method of adjudicating the claims because the claims of the plaintiff and the class members were closely intertwined. Class plaintiff's allegations for the class mirrored her personal accusations.

In *Hogan v. Wayne County*, 2024 WL 2790297 (Mich. App. May 30, 2024), typicality was lacking in a class action by female jail inmates and detainees alleging mistreatment. Claims of certain named plaintiffs were not even typical of those by other named plaintiffs. The incidents described in the plaintiffs' declarations differed widely.

v. Adequacy. The representative parties must fairly and adequately assert and protect the interests of the class. In *Neal v. James,* 252 Mich. App. 12, 651 N.W.2d 181 (2002), plaintiffs did not demonstrate adequacy because of potential conflicts between class members, some of whom were denied promotions, and the presence of highly individualized claims. *Neal* was distinguished in *Nowacki v. Dept. of Corrections,* 2014 WL 4088041 (Mich. App. Aug. 19, 2014), *lv. denied,* 498 Mich. 859, 865 N.W.2d. 28 (2015), where 80 male corrections officers were in a class attacking restrictions on the ability to work in certain positions in a women's correctional facility. Plaintiffs claimed that the restrictions were applied too broadly in an effort to purge the facility of male corrections officers. Defendant cited *Neal* claiming that the class members may have been in competition for the same job. The Court of Appeals distinguished *Neal*, which involved highly individualized claims as to why certain individuals were not hired or promoted. Potential conflicts in *Nowacki* did not go to the core issue in the case, i.e., whether the restrictions were too broadly applied to the male plaintiffs.

In *Wilson v. Sinai Grace Hospital*, 2004 Mich. App. LEXIS 1099 (Apr. 29, 2004) (unpublished), the Court of Appeals held that representatives of a class of patients suing over a 90 day-plus delay in responding to requests for medical records were not rendered inadequate representatives because the hospital subsequently provided the records to the named plaintiffs. They still suffered the same injury suffered by the class members, *i.e*, having to wait an inordinate amount of time to receive records to which they were entitled.

Adequacy was not found in *Duskin v. Dep't of Human Servs.*, 2009 Mich. App. LEXIS 1378 (June 11, 2009), where plaintiffs alleged that the state agency discriminatorily denied male, but not female, racial, and ethnic minorities a sufficient number of promotions to supervisory and management positions. The possibility that a class representative competed for the same promotion sought by a class member created potential conflicts. After remand, the Court of Appeals again reversed certification, including on adequacy grounds in *Duskin v. Dep't of Human Services*, 304 Mich. App. 645 (2014), holding that the class members' generalized statement regarding their goals failed to support either (1) counsel's qualifications or (2) a lack of conflicting interests among the representative parties and class members.

In *Henry v. Dow Chem. Co.*, 484 Mich. 483, 772 N.W.2d 301 (2009), the Michigan Supreme Court reversed the lower court's certification of classes of present and former property owners who sued a chemical company relating to dioxin contamination of a floodplain. Regarding adequacy, the Court stated that the lower court found adequacy by reasoning that "no proof has been submitted to this Court that would indicate that the Plaintiffs herein, the representative parties, would not fairly and adequately assert and protect the interest of the class." In other words, the circuit court did not perform an analysis that sufficiently shows that it independently determined that the plaintiffs would adequately represent the class and also potentially shifted the burden to defendant to show that plaintiffs would *not* adequately represent the class.

Michigan Ass'n of Chiropractors v. Blue Cross Blue Shield of Michigan, 300 Mich. App. 551, 834 N.W.2d 138 (2013), involved a lawsuit by a chiropractic association and a chiropractor claiming that defendant insurer had breached provider agreements and a settlement agreement. Plaintiffs successfully moved to certify a class comprised of "all similarly situated chiropractors who have or had Traditional Services or PPO Product Agreements with Blue Cross, are members of the MAC and have been denied lawful reimbursement." On appeal, the Court of Appeals declined to decertify the entire class but had issues with the class definition. The court decertified the class on the complaint count involving retrospective compensatory damages because it would require an individualized examination of what claims were submitted and denied by each chiropractor. The court left the class standing on declaratory relief claims. The limitations on the declaratory relief claims forestalled the need for individualized proofs on damages. The court found the adequacy requirement met. But the class representative failed to establish that he had exhausted his contractual remedies and did not satisfy the adequacy requirement on the retrospective compensatory damages claim.

Doe v. Henry Ford Health Sys., 308 Mich. App. 592, 865 N.W.2d 138 (2014), held that where the class representative has no individual claims to pursue against the defendants, the representative is not qualified to represent a class. The Court of Appeals found that plaintiff's claims regarding negligence, breach of contract, and invasion of privacy regarding an alleged data breach concerning doctors' visits by 159 patients. The Court of Appeals held that plaintiff's claims against defendants were not cognizable and, therefore, reversed the certification of the class.

Adequacy was challenged in *Brown v. VHS of Michigan, Inc.*, 2021 WL 1157280 (Mich. App. Mar. 25, 2021), which addressed certification of a class action brought against a hospital and funeral home regarding the mishandling of stillborn or deceased babies' remains. Defendants claimed that plaintiff's counsel had not handled a class action before and the class representative had previously donated a stillborn baby whose remains were not mishandled. The court did not find that the lower court erred in finding class counsel adequate. They were experienced and had represented they would get additional assistance if needed. The class representative did not have a conflict rendering her inadequate.

vi. Superiority. Maintenance of the action as a class action must be superior to other available means of adjudication in promoting the convenient administration of justice. The concern is whether the issues are so disparate as to make a class action unmanageable. *Lee v. Board of Education*, 184 Mich. App. 502, 459 N.W.2d 1 (1989); *Dix v. American Bankers Life Assurance Co.*, 429 Mich. 410, 415 N.W.2d 206 (1987). Matters such as the diversity of defenses and counterclaims bear upon whether a class action suit promotes the convenient administration of justice. *Lee, supra; Grigg v. Michigan National Bank*, 405 Mich. 148, 274 N.W.2d 752 (1979). In addressing this factor, the court is to consider, among other factors:

(a) Whether prosecution of separate actions by or against individual members of the class would create a risk of either (i) inconsistent or varying adjudications with respect to individuals that would confront the party opposing the class with incompatible standards of conduct; or (ii), adjudications with respect to individual class members that would as a practical matter be dispositive of the interests of other members not parties to the adjudication or substantially impair or impede their ability to protect their interests.

(b) Whether final equitable or declaratory relief might be appropriate with respect to the class.
(c) Whether the action will be manageable as a class action.
(d) Whether in view of the complexity of the issues or the expense of litigation the separate claims of the individual class members are insufficient in amount to support separate actions.
(e) Whether it is probable that the amount which may be recovered by individual class members will be large enough in relation to the expense and effort of administrating the action to justify a class action.
(f) Whether members of the class have a significant interest in controlling the prosecution or defense of separate actions.

MCR 3.501(A)(2). *A&M Supply Co. v. Microsoft Corp.*, 252 Mich. App. 580, 654 N.W.2d 572 (2002); *Accord, Erma Rogers Revocable Trust by Plumley v. Erickson Retirement Communities*, 2017 WL 6345742 (Mich. App. Dec. 12, 2017).

In *Edgecumbe v. Cessna Aircraft Co.*, 171 Mich. App. 573, 430 N.W.2d 788 (1988), the court of appeals affirmed denial of class certification of a suit over repairs to an allegedly defective camshaft on an airplane. The court of appeals noted that the airplane manufacturer had between 500 and 750 dealers in all fifty states and that the interplay of multiple states' laws on product liability and warranty issues would make litigation in a Michigan court cumbersome. But in *Creech, supra*, the court affirmed certification of a class of patients alleging inadequate sterilization of medical equipment due to satisfaction of the six factors listed above. In *Wilson v. Sinai Grace Hospital*, 2004 Mich. App. LEXIS 1099 (Apr. 29, 2004) (unpublished), the lower court devised an adequate way to notify class members of the class action involving alleged improper sterilization of medical equipment without infringing on patient-physician privilege.

Superiority was lacking in *Duskin v. Dep't of Human Servs.*, 2009 Mich. App. LEXIS 1378 (June 11, 2009), where plaintiffs alleged that the state agency discriminatorily denied male, but not female, racial and ethnic minorities a sufficient number of promotions to supervisory and management positions. Individualized inquiries clearly predominated over any common questions. Further, the defenses to disparate treatment claims involving promotional decisions was specific to each plaintiff, would have required individualized proofs relating to hundreds of claims, and rendered the action unmanageable as a class. It would also be unfair to bind the entire class of plaintiffs to the judgment reached in the case if some minority male employees had viable individual claims of disparate treatment. After remand, in *Duskin v. Dep't of Human Services*, 304 Mich. App. 645 (2014), the court held that plaintiff's failure to establish commonality meant that the superiority element was not satisfied.

In *Nowacki v. Dept. of Corrections,* 2014 WL 4088041 (Mich. App. Aug. 19, 2014), *lv. denied,* 498 Mich. 859, 865 N.W.2d. 28 (2015), 80 male corrections officers were in a class attacking restrictions on the ability to work in certain positions in a women's correctional facility. Plaintiffs claimed that the restrictions were applied too broadly in an effort to purge the facility of male corrections officers. The court held that separation of 80 actions based on the same practice and the same evidence would be duplicative, place an unnecessary burden on the court system and could lead to inconsistent adjudications.

The superiority component was satisfied in *Erma Rogers Revocable Trust by Plumley v. Erickson Retirement Communities*, 2017 WL 6345742 (Mich. App. Dec. 12, 2017), a class action regarding residential independent living agreements. In deciding this factor, the court may consider the practical problems that can arise if the class action is allowed to proceed. The relevant concern is whether the issues are so disparate that a class action would be unmanageable. The court found that the evidence regarding the overall issues were common to all residents. The fact that damages proofs might be individualized did not prevent certification.

Superiority was found in *Brown v. VHS of Michigan, Inc.*, 2021 WL 1157280 (Mich. App. Mar. 25, 2021), which addressed certification of a class action brought against a hospital and funeral home regarding the mishandling of stillborn or deceased babies' remains. The claims were not so disparate as to make the case unmanageable. To try each case separately would have entailed significant duplication of judicial resources.

In *Hogan v. Wayne County*, 2024 WL 2790297 (Mich. App. May 30, 2024), superiority was lacking in a class action by female jail inmates and detainees alleging mistreatment. The disparate issues of law and fact rendered a class action unmanageable.

vii. Opt-out rights. Class members have the right to opt-out of the action subject to the authority of the court to order them to be made parties under other applicable court rules. Court orders regarding whether parties have timely opted out will not be set aside unless clearly erroneous. *Briney v. Kelsey-Hayes,* 2001 Mich. App LEXIS 1192 (Aug. 21, 2001) (unpublished). Michigan class members who failed to opt out of a Minnesota class action despite notice of the class action were barred from bringing an individual action in Michigan. *Brown v. Malt-O-Meal Co.*, 2003 Mich. App. LEXIS 2933 (Nov. 20, 2003) (unpublished).

viii. Intervention rights. Class members have the right to intervene in the action subject to the authority of the court to regulate the orderly course of the action.

ix. Statutory minimum relief cases. An action for a penalty or minimum amount of recovery without regard to actual damages imposed or authorized under a statute may not be maintained as a class action unless the statute specifically authorizes its recovery in a class action.

x. Duties of class counsel. In *Piotrowski v. LaBelle*, 2012 WL 1758703, 2012 Mich. App. LEXIS 980 (Mich. Ct. App. May 17, 2012), the court affirmed the dismissal of a legal malpractice suit brought by an absent class member against class counsel. Plaintiff was a member of a class of female prisoners who were subjected to sexual abuse and misconduct by male prison staff during their incarceration in Michigan state prisons. Plaintiff never took any action to participate in a substantial settlement even though the existence and terms of the settlement were published and circulated on terms approved by the lower court. Defendant class counsel did what was legally adequate and required of her by informing all class members of the settlement. She acted consistently with prevailing Michigan law, and the court's order governing notice of the settlement. Her duty was to use reasonable skill, care, discretion, and judgment to the class she represented, and not to use extraordinary diligence to plaintiff who was a member of the class. The court did not agree that a class counsel is held to a higher duty to individual class members if contact with them is somehow made.

xi. Attorneys' fees. In *Anderson v. Davis*, 2012 WL 6216900 (Mich. App. Dec. 13, 2012), the court affirmed summary disposition of a lawsuit by an attorney seeking to collect a portion of attorneys' fees collected by defendant. Plaintiff, an attorney, had filed a class action and discussed retaining defendant as co-counsel for the class. When class certification was reversed by the Court of Appeals, plaintiff withdrew as class representative and as co-counsel. Defendants ultimately obtained class certification and a settlement. The Court of Appeals affirmed the dismissal of plaintiffs' suit, holding that plaintiff's behavior had been an impediment to the ultimate settlement of the class action. There was nothing in the record to indicate that plaintiff was entitled to any portion of the fees recovered by defendant.

xii. Communications with absent class members. There are no cases addressing the ability of counsel for either side in a class action to communicate with absent class members. As noted above, the Michigan Courts would look to cases under Fed. R. Civ. P. 23 for guidance.

b. Rule 3.501(B). ***Certification procedure***

i. Time limitations. The motion for class certification must be filed within 91 days of the filing of the complaint. The time limit can be extended by stipulation or on motion for cause shown. "Cause" does not mean "good cause." *Tindall v. State of Michigan*, 2003 Mich. App. LEXIS 993 (Apr. 17, 2003). If the plaintiff fails to file the motion within the allowed time, the defendant may file a notice of the failure, upon which the class allegations are stricken. However, the court may address a renewed motion for class certification because the rule does not forbid subsequent motions for certification or mandate any particular timing requirements for bringing them. *Hill v. City of Warren*, 276 Mich. App. 299, 740 N.W.2d 706 (2007), *lv. denied*, 480 Mich. 1195, 748 N.W.2d 520 (2008). Where plaintiff files an amended class action complaint by right under MCR 2.118(A) due to defendants not filing any responsive pleadings, the 91-day period runs from the filing of the amended complaint, not the original complaint. *Badeen v. PAR, Inc.,* 300 Mich. App. 430, 834 N.W.2d 85 (2013); *vacated in part on other grounds*, 496 Mich. 75, 853 N.W.2d 303 (2014). *Badeen* noted that MCR 3.501(B) requires the motion for class certification to be filed within 91 days of the filing of "a complaint that includes class action allegations. . . ." The use of the phrase "a complaint" contemplated that more than one complaint might be filed.

Motions for decertification are treated as distinct and independent motions that implicate the same considerations as a motion to certify a class action, rather than as a motion for reconsideration and, therefore, are not subject to the time limitations on motions for reconsideration. *Tinman v. Blue Cross & Blue Shield of Michigan*, 264 Mich. App. 546, 692 N.W.2d 58 (2004).

Except on motion for good cause, a motion for class certification may not be considered until all defendants are served or all unserved summonses have expired.

ii. Consideration. The court has the option of granting the motion, denying it, or postponing a ruling pending discovery or other preliminary procedures. The court may limit certification to particular issues or forms of relief or may divide the proposed class into separate classes for the purposes of certification or denial or revocation of certification. Any order certifying a class must identify the class.

c. Rule 3.501(C). ***Notice***

The certification motion must include a proposal for notice or state reasons why a determination of notice matters cannot then be made and offer a proposal as to when such determination should be made. The court is to determine as soon as practicable the manner of notice and may postpone notice until after discovery.

The court may require individual written notice to all members who can be identified with reasonable effort. The court may also order notice through another method reasonably calculated to reach the class members, including newspaper or magazine publication, broadcasting, or dissemination through a trade or professional association, union or public interest group. The court is to consider the extent and nature of the class, the relief requested, the cost of notifying the members, the resources of plaintiff, and the possible prejudice to members of the class if notice is not received.

The content of the notice is spelled out in MCR 3.501(C)(5). The notice shall include notice of the right of a member of the class to be excluded from the action.

Plaintiff bears the cost of notice, which may be allowed as a taxable cost.

In *Rennie v. Marble Head Lime, Inc.*, 2005 Mich. App. LEXIS 1445 (June 16, 2005) (unpublished), the Court of Appeals vacated the approval of a class action settlement involving emission of lime dust and particulates where the lower court approved notice solely by publication in three newspapers. Because of the nature of the case, the lower court erred in permitting exclusive reliance on publication to serve notice on the unnamed members of the class in question without stating on the record factual findings and legal conclusions to justify that decision. The court remanded the case for full consideration of the notice issue.

In *Nowacki v. Dep't of Corrections,* 319 Mich. App. 144, 900 N.W.2d 154 (2017). The class's claims were split. The defendants had transferred claims for injunctive and declaratory relief to the Court of Claims, while monetary claims were in the Circuit Court and stayed, where a class had been certified. The court held that the class could dismiss the equitable and declaratory claims in the Court of Claims in order to pursue the monetary claims without advance notice to the putative class. The court agreed with the Court of Claims that the notice of dismissal could be incorporated into the regular class notice. Class members who would choose to opt out of the class could still pursue the equitable and declaratory claims.

d. Rule 3.501(D). *Judgment*

The judgment shall describe the parties bound. A pre-certification judgment only binds the named parties. But unnamed class members are bound by a judgment rendered in a properly certified class action. *SHR Ltd. Partnership v. SWEPI LP*, 2007 Mich. App. LEXIS 184 (Mich. App. Jan. 30, 2007). A motion for summary disposition may be filed and decided before certification. If granted in favor of a party seeking certification, that party is not precluded from then representing the class in the action. A complaint which does not include class allegations may not be amended to include such allegations after the granting of summary disposition. A court may grant summary disposition to defendants before addressing class certification, but that judgment only binds the named parties. *Allen Park Retirees Ass'n, Inc. v. State Dept. of Treasury*, 2016 WL 6992174 (Mich. App. Nov. 29, 2016).

A certified class action may not be dismissed or settled without court approval and notice to the class. In *Brenner v. Marathon Oil Co.*, 222 Mich. App. 128, 565 N.W.2d 1 (1997), the court of appeals reversed the lower court's approval of a class action settlement which was opposed by 87 percent of the class members and the class representatives.

In *Adelman v. Compuware Corp.*, 2017 WL 6389899 (Mich. App. Dec. 14, 2017), the court affirmed approval of the settlement of a shareholder class action which had been objected to by intervening plaintiffs. A trial court may approve a class action settlement if the settlement is fair, reasonable, and adequate. The court of appeals reviewed the trial court's approval of the settlement under an abuse of discretion standard. An evaluation of whether a settlement is fair and reasonable requires balancing the strengths of the claims being compromised against the benefits the settlement provides to the class members. The settlement's proponents bore the burden of persuasion by a preponderance of the evidence. Supplemental disclosures confirmed that all the shareholders were treated equally in the settlement, that a class representative did not receive any preferential or different treatment, that none of the directors obtained a special benefit from the agreement, and that none of the individuals or entities involved in the settlement negotiations had ties to the only bidder for the company. The board was entitled to the protection of the business judgment rule in the absence of demonstrable fraud or breach of the board's fiduciary duties. The court found that the discovery conducted was adequate and that the objectors did not have a likelihood of success on their breach of fiduciary duty claims. The court also had no issue with a "disclosure-only" settlement.

e. Rule 3.501(F). *Statute of limitations*

The commencement of a class action tolls statutes of limitations as to all persons within the proposed class. The statute begins to run again when (1) the opposing party files a notice that plaintiff failed to file a motion for class certification within the required period; (2) class certification is denied; (3) 28 days after notice to the class of the elimination of such person from the class; (4) submission of an opt-out; or (5) final disposition of the action.

In *Cowles v. Bank West*, 476 Mich. 1, 719 N.W.2d 94 (2006), *reh'g denied*, 477 Mich. 1209, 722 N.W.2d 429 (2006), plaintiff had brought the class action in 1998 over the charging of mortgage document preparation fees. She amended the complaint to add a federal Truth in Lending Act claim. But there was an issue as to whether the named plaintiff's TILA claim was time-barred. Another borrower, whose TILA claim was arguably not time-barred, successfully moved to intervene. The lower court dismissed the entire case, holding that the substitute class representative's TILA claim did not relate back to the filing of the original complaint by the original class representative. The Court of Appeals reversed, holding that the court rules on relation-back of amendments applied to class actions and that the TILA claim related to the same conduct or transaction as pleaded in the original complaint. The Michigan Supreme Court affirmed that portion of the Court of Appeals opinion, holding that the filing of a class-action complaint tolls the period of limitations under MCR 3.501(F) for a putative class member's claim when that claim was not pleaded in the initial class-action complaint but arose out of the same factual and legal nexus. The filing of such a complaint is sufficient to toll the period of limitations as long as the defendant has notice of both the claim being brought and the number and generic identities of the potential plaintiffs.

In *Colvin v. Detroit Entertainment, L.L.C.*, 2011 WL 2586321 (Mich. App. June 30, 2011), the Court of Appeals affirmed dismissal of claims brought by casino patrons on statutes of limitations grounds. Plaintiffs attempted to obtain tolling under MCR. 3.301(F) because of class actions filed by other patrons. Class certification was granted by the lower court in those cases, but the Court of Appeals in 2004 reversed the class certification orders. The Court of Appeals held in this case that the statute started to run again upon the entry of the Court of Appeals order reversing the lower court's granting of certification, not when the Michigan Supreme Court denied those plaintiffs' application for leave to appeal the Court of Appeals decision. MCR 3.501(F)(2) provides for the resumption of the running of a statute of limitations "on entry of an order denying certification" and, in this case, such an order was entered.

While claims related to the same conduct will relate back to the first complaint, that does not apply where the amended complaint adds new defendants to the class action. *Neal v. Dept of Corrections*, 2005 Mich. App. LEXIS 342 (Feb. 10, 2005) (unpublished).

f. Rule 3.501(G). *Discovery*

Representative parties and intervenors are subject to discovery in the same manner as any party in a civil action. Absent class members are subject to discovery to the same extent as non-parties and may be ordered to submit to discovery procedures applicable to parties. In *Fitzpatrick v. Public School Employees Retirement System,* 2011 WL 1902000 (Mich. App. May 19, 2011), the Court of Appeals held that a person appealing an administrative ruling regarding retirement benefits could not add a class action claim when appealing that decision to the circuit courts. The Court reversed an order allowing the appellant to take discovery on the numerosity issue.

g. Rule 3.501(H). *Counterclaims*

A party to a class action has the express right to file counterclaims against the class or individual class members. Each of the elements of class certification under MCR 3.501(A) must be satisfied. *Adair v. City of Detroit*, 198 Mich. App. 506, 498 N.W.2d 924 (1993). There is no limitation on the type of counterclaim or the type of recovery sought. MCR 3.501(I)'s prohibition against defendant class actions seeking money from individual members of a defendant class does not apply to counterclaims. *Id.*

A counterclaim against class members other than a representative party must be filed within 56 days after the class member intervenes or submits a claim for distribution of a share of any award recovered in the action, or within such other time as the court directs. If the class notice did not notify the class of a counterclaim, a class member may elect to be excluded from the action.

h. Rule 3.501(I). *Defendant classes*

An action seeking damages against individual members of a defendant class may not be maintained as a class action. Non-public agency or officer class representatives may decline to defend the action in a representative capacity unless the court finds that the convenient administration of justice requires otherwise.

MICHIGAN COURT RULE 3.501

RULE 3.501 CLASS ACTIONS

(A) *Nature of class action*

(1) One or more members of a class may sue or be sued as representative parties on behalf of all members in a class action only if:

(a) the class is so numerous that joinder of all members is impracticable;

(b) there are questions of law or fact common to the members of the class that predominate over questions affecting only individual members;

(c) the claims or defenses of the representative parties are typical of the claims or defenses of the class;

(d) the representative parties will fairly and adequately assert and protect the interests of the class; and

(e) the maintenance of the action as a class action will be superior to other available methods of adjudication in promoting the convenient administration of justice.

(2) In determining whether the maintenance of the action as a class action will be superior to other available methods of adjudication in promoting the convenient administration of justice, the court shall consider among other matters the following factors:

(a) whether the prosecution of separate actions by or against individual members of the class would create a risk of

(i) inconsistent or varying adjudications with respect to individual members of the class that would confront the party opposing the class with incompatible standards of conduct; or

(ii) adjudications with respect to individual members of the class that would as a practical matter be dispositive of the interests of other members not parties to the adjudications or substantially impair or impede their ability to protect their interests;

(b) whether final equitable or declaratory relief might be appropriate with respect to the class;

(c) whether the action will be manageable as a class action;

(d) whether in view of the complexity of the issues or the expense of litigation the separate claims of individual class members are insufficient in amount to support separate actions;

(e) whether it is probable that the amount which may be recovered by individual class members will be large enough in relation to the expense and effort of administering the action to justify a class action; and

(f) whether members of the class have a significant interest in controlling the prosecution or defense of separate actions.

(3) Class members shall have the right to be excluded from the action in the manner provided in this rule, subject to the authority of the court to order them made parties to the action pursuant to other applicable court rules.

(4) Class members have the right to intervene in the action, subject to the authority of the court to regulate the orderly course of the action.

(5) An action for a penalty or minimum amount of recovery without regard to actual damages imposed or authorized by statute may not be maintained as a class action unless the statute specifically authorizes its recovery in a class action.

(B) *Procedure for certification of class action*

(1) *Motion.*

(a) Within 91 days after the filing of a complaint that includes class action allegations, the plaintiff must move for certification that the action may be maintained as a class action.

(b) The time for filing the motion may be extended by order on stipulation of the parties or on motion for cause shown.

(2) *Effect of failure to file motion.* If the plaintiff fails to file a certification motion within the time allowed by subrule (b)(1) the defendant may file a notice of the failure. On the filing of such a notice, the class action allegations are deemed stricken, and the action continues by or against the named parties alone. The class action allegations may be reinstated only if the plaintiff shows that the failure was due to excusable neglect.

(3) *Action by court.*

(a) Except on motion for good cause, the court shall not proceed with consideration of the motion to certify until service of the summons and complaint on all named defendants or until the expiration of any unserved summons under MCR 2.102(D).

(b) The court may allow the action to be maintained as a class action, may deny the motion, or may order that a ruling be postponed pending discovery or other preliminary procedures.

(c) In an order certifying a class action, the court shall set forth a description of the class.

(d) When appropriate the court may order that

(i) the action be maintained as a class action limited to particular issues or forms of relief, or

(ii) a proposed class be divided into separate classes with each treated as a class for purposes of certifying, denying certification, or revoking a certification.

(e) If certification is denied or revoked, the action shall continue by or against the named parties alone.

(C) *Notice to class members*

(1) *Notice requirement.* Notice shall be given as provided in this subrule to persons who are included in a class action by certification or amendment of a prior certification, and to persons who were included in a class action by a prior certification but who are to be excluded from the class by amendment or revocation of the certification.

(2) *Proposals regarding notice.* The plaintiff shall include in the motion for certification a proposal regarding notice covering the matters that must be determined by the court under subrule (C)(3). In lieu of such a proposal, the plaintiff may state reasons why a determination of these matters cannot then be made and offer a proposal as to when such a determination should be made. Such a proposal must also be included in a motion to revoke or amend certification.

(3) *Action by court.* As soon as practicable, the court shall determine how, when, by whom, and to whom the notice shall be given; the content of the notice; and to whom the response to the notice is to be sent. The court may postpone the notice determination until after the parties have had an opportunity for discovery, which the court may limit to matters relevant to the notice determination.

(4) *Manner of giving notice.*

(a) Reasonable notice of the action shall be given to the class in such manner as the court directs.

(b) The court may require individual written notice to all members who can be identified with reasonable effort. In lieu of or in addition to individual notice, the court may require notice to be given through another method reasonably calculated to reach the members of the class. Such methods may include using publication in a newspaper or magazine; broadcasting on television or radio; posting; or distribution through a trade or professional association, union, or public interest group.

(c) In determining the manner of notice, the court shall consider, among other factors,

(i) the extent and nature of the class,

(ii) the relief requested,

(iii) the cost of notifying the members,

(iv) the resources of the plaintiff, and

(v) the possible prejudice to be suffered by members of the class or by others if notice is not received.

(5) *Content of notice.* The notice shall include:

(a) a general description of the action, including the relief sought, and the names and addresses of the representative parties;

(b) a statement of the right of a member of the class to be excluded from the action by submitting an election to be excluded, including the manner and time for exercising the election;

(c) a description of possible financial consequences for the class;

(d) a general description of any counterclaim or notice of intent to assert a counterclaim by or against members of the class, including the relief sought;

(e) a statement that the judgment, whether favorable or not, will bind all members of the class who are not excluded from the action;

(f) a statement that any member of the class may intervene in the action;

(g) the address of counsel to whom inquiries may be directed; and

(h) other information the court deems appropriate.

(6) *Cost of notice.*

(a) The plaintiff shall bear the expense of the notification required by subrule (C)(1). The court may require the defendant to cooperate in the notice process, but any additional costs incurred by the defendant in doing so shall be paid by the plaintiff.

(b) Upon termination of the action, the court may allow as taxable costs the expenses of notification incurred by the prevailing party.

(c) Subrules (C)(6)(a) and (b) shall not apply when a statute provides for a different allocation of the cost of notice in a particular class of actions.

(7) *Additional Notices.* In addition to the notice required by subrule (C)(1), during the course of the action the court may require that notice of any other matter be given in such manner as the court directs to some or all of the members of the class.

(D) *Judgment*

(1) The judgment shall describe the parties bound.

(2) A judgment entered before certification of a class binds only the named parties.

(3) A motion for judgment (including partial judgment) under MCR 2.116 may be filed and decided before the decision on the question of class certification. A judgment entered before certification in favor of a named party does not preclude that party from representing the class in the action if that is otherwise appropriate.

(4) A complaint that does not include class action allegations may not be amended to include such allegations after the granting of judgment or partial judgment under MCR 2.116.

(5) A judgment entered in an action certified as a class action binds all members of the class who have not submitted an election to be excluded, except as otherwise directed by the court.

(6) Residual Funds.

(a) "Residual Funds" are funds that remain after the payment of approved class member claims, expenses, litigation costs, attorney's fees, and other court-approved disbursements made to implement the relief granted in the judgment approving a proposed settlement of a class action.

(b) Nothing in this rule is intended to limit the parties to a class action from proposing a settlement, or the court from entering a judgment approving a settlement, that does not create Residual Funds.

(c) Any judgment approving a proposed settlement of a class action certified under this rule that may result in the existence of Residual Funds shall provide for the disbursement of any such Residual Funds upon the stipulation of the parties and subject to the approval of the court. In matters where the claims process has been exhausted and Residual Funds remain, unless the judgment provides otherwise, the Residual Funds shall be disbursed to the Michigan State Bar Foundation to support activities and programs that promote access to the civil justice system for low income residents of Michigan.

(E) *Dismissal or compromise*

An action certified as a class action may not be dismissed or compromised without the approval of the court, and notice of the proposed dismissal or compromise shall be given to the class in such manner as the court directs.

(F) *Statute of limitations*

(1) The statute of limitations is tolled as to all persons within the class described in the complaint on the commencement of an action asserting a class action.

(2) The statute of limitations resumes running against class members other than representative parties and intervenors:

(a) on the filing of a notice of the plaintiff's failure to move for class certification under subrule (B)(2);

(b) 28 days after notice has been made under subrule (C)(1) of the entry, amendment, or revocation of an order of certification eliminating the person from the class;

(c) on entry of an order denying certification of the action as a class action;

(d) on submission of an election to be excluded;

(e) on final disposition of the action.

(3) If the circumstance that brought about the resumption of the running of the statute is superseded by a further order of the trial court, by reversal on appeal, or otherwise, the statute of limitations shall be deemed to have been tolled continuously from the commencement of the action.

(G) *Discovery*

Representative parties and intervenors are subject to discovery in the same manner as parties in other civil actions. Other class members are subject to discovery in the same manner as persons who are not parties, and may be required to submit to discovery procedures applicable to parties to the extent ordered by the court.

(H) *Counterclaims*

(1) *Right to file counterclaims.* A party to a class action may file counterclaims as in any other action, including counterclaims by or against a class or an individual class member.

(2) *Notice of intent to file counterclaims.* The defendant may file notice of intent to assert counterclaims against absent class members before notice of certification is given under subrule (C)(1), identifying or describing the persons against whom counterclaims may be filed and describing the nature of the counterclaims.

(3) *Time to file.* A counterclaim against a class member other than a representative party must be filed and served within 56 days after the class member intervenes or submits a claim for distribution of a share of any award recovered in the action, whichever is earlier, or within such further time as the court allows.

(4) *Notice to class members.* If the notice of certification given under subrule (C)(1) did not notify potential class members of the counterclaim, each class member against whom a counterclaim is asserted shall be permitted to elect to be excluded from the action. Notice of this right shall be served with the counterclaim.

(5) *Control of action.* The court shall take such steps as are necessary to prevent the pendency of counterclaims from making the action unmanageable as a class action. Such steps include but are not limited to severing counterclaims for separate trial under MCR 2.505(B) or ordering that consideration of the counterclaims be deferred until after determination of the issue of the defendant's liability, at which time the court may hear the counterclaims, remove them to a lower court, change venue, dismiss them without prejudice, or take other appropriate action.

(I) *Defendant classes*

(1) An action that seeks to recover money from individual members of a defendant class may not be maintained as a class action.

(2) A representative of a defendant class, other than a public body or a public officer, may decline to defend the action in a representative capacity unless the court finds that the convenient administration of justice otherwise requires.

Chapter author Dennis K. Egan is a shareholder with the firm of Kotz Sangster Wysocki, PC in Bloomfield Hills, Michigan. He regularly defends corporate clients in defending class actions in state and federal courts. Mr. Egan has served as co-chair of the State Laws Subcommittee of the Litigation Section's Class Actions and Derivative Suits Committee and is a former Executive Editor Emeritus of this Survey.

MINNESOTA

1. COMPARISON WITH RULE 23 OF THE FEDERAL RULES OF CIVIL PROCEDURE

Rules 23.01–23.10 of the Minnesota Rules of Civil Procedure are essentially identical to their federal counterpart, Rule 23 of the Federal Rules of Civil Procedure. Minnesota courts can look to federal precedent in interpreting Minn. R. Civ. P. 23 "because of the substantial similarity between Minnesota's class certification rule and the equivalent federal rule." *Bacon v. Bd. of Pensions of the Evangelical Lutheran Church in Am.*, 930 N.W.2d 437, 440 (Minn. Ct. App. 2019).

2. CASE LAW INTERPRETING MINNESOTA RULE 23

Minnesota courts interpret a class action as a protector of the individual's rights by consolidating the claims into one action. A class action serves to "take care of the smaller guy," and provide relief "where the potential recovery is too small to justify individual litigation." *Peterson v. BASF Corp.*, 618 N.W.2d 821, 826 (Minn. Ct. App. 2000) (internal quotation marks omitted). Often, smaller claims, for example consumer cases, survive only by consolidation when brought against the defendant. "A class action is superior to other methods in promoting the public purpose of protecting those who cannot protect themselves." *Weme v. Freeway Ford, Inc.*, No. EM 02-009737, 2003 WL 23741867, at *8 (Minn. Dist. Ct. Apr. 11, 2003) (citing *Rathbun v. W.T. Grant Co.*, 219 N.W. 2d 641, 653 (Minn. 1974).

a. Rule 23.01

The determination that an action is maintainable as a class action under Minnesota Rule of Civil Procedure 23 is a two-step process. The Court must first determine whether the prerequisites of Rule 23.01 have been met: numerosity, commonality, typicality, and adequacy of representation. When all four prerequisites have been satisfied, the Court must then determine whether one or more of the three criteria set forth in Rule 23.02 are satisfied. The certification requirements of Minnesota Rule 23 must be established by a preponderance of the evidence and factual disputes relevant to Rule 23 requirements must be resolved. *Whitaker v. 3M Co.,* 764 N.W.2d 631, 638 (Minn. Ct. App. 2009).

i. Numerosity. A class must include a sufficiently large number of people such that joinder of all members is impracticable. Minnesota Rule of Civil Procedure 23.01(a) offers no guidance on what constitutes sufficient numerosity. Instead, courts consider such factors as the size of the putative class, the size of the class member's individual claim, the inconvenience of trying individual suits and the nature of the action itself. *Lewy 1990 Tr. ex rel. Lewy v. Inv. Advisors, Inc.*, 650 N.W.2d 445, 452 (Minn. Ct. App. 2002). While there is no bright-line number of class members below which joinder is deemed impracticable, at least one Minnesota court denied certification of a proposed class with fewer than forty members. *See Novack v. Nw. Airlines, Inc.*, 525 N.W.2d 592, 600 (Minn. Ct.

App. 1995). Speculation cannot support a finding of numerosity, but a good faith, reasonable estimate, supported by evidence, will generally suffice. *Lewy*, 650 N.W.2d at 452–53.

ii. Commonality. Class actions must have at least one question of law or fact common to the class. Minn. R. Civ. P. 23.01(b). A common question of fact or law exists when "resolution of the common questions affect all or a substantial number of class members." *Lewy*, 650 N.W.2d at 453 (citing *Jenkins v. Raymark Indus., Inc.*, 782 F.2d 468, 472 (5th Cir. 1986)); *see also Sandusky Wellness Ctr., LLC v. Medtox Sci., Inc.*, 821 F.3d 992, 998 (8th Cir. 2016) (finding that a class met commonality and predominance requirement where common contention, capable of classwide resolution, was whether class members received an unsolicited fax advertisement violating the TCPA). In other words, commonality exists when the subject of dispute has a common cause of action. *Streich v. Am. Fam. Mut. Ins. Co.*, 399 N.W.2d 210, 214 (Minn. Ct. App. 1987) (citing *In re Objections & Def. to Real Prop. Taxes for 1980 Assessment*, 335 N.W.2d 717, 719 (Minn. 1983)). Commonality requires all members of the putative class to be subject to or suffer the same injury as the class representative. *L.K. v. Gregg*, 380 N.W.2d 145, 152 (Minn. Ct. App. 1986). However, it is not the common questions that satisfy the "commonality" requirement, but rather "the capacity of a class-wide proceeding to generate common answers" to drive the resolution of the litigation. *Hoekman v. Educ. Minn.*, 335 F.R.D. 219, 243 (D. Minn. 2020) (citing *Wal-Mart Stores, Inc. v. Dukes*, 564 U.S. 338, 350 (2011)).

iii. Typicality. The claims of the class representative, and the defenses to those claims, must be typical of the claims and defenses of the class as a whole. Minn. R. Civ. P. 23.01(c). The test of typicality is whether the named class representatives "have an interest compatible with that of the class sought to be represented." *Peterson*, 618 N.W.2d at 825; *Streich*, 399 N.W.2d at 215. Typicality is usually satisfied when the representative's claim arises from the same event or is based on the same legal theory as the other class members. *Braun v. Wal-Mart Stores, Inc.*, No. 19-CO-01-9790, 2003 WL 22990114, at *5 (Minn. Dist. Ct. Nov. 3, 2003).

iv. Adequacy of representation. The final requirement is that the class representative must fairly and adequately protect the interests of the class. Minn. R. Civ. P. 23.01(d). Thus, adequacy of representation is closely tied to the typicality requirement. To establish adequacy, a representative's interests must coincide with the interests of other class members. The adequacy inquiry also extends to the class representative's counsel, to ensure that counsel is both (1) sufficiently experienced to handle a class action and (2) will protect the interests of the entire class. *Streich*, 399 N.W.2d at 215. Factors applied when determining adequacy of representation are (1) if the representatives' interests are sufficiently similar to those of absent class members to ensure that the representatives will vigorously prosecute the suit on their behalf; (2) if the attorneys are qualified, experienced, and capable of conducting the litigation; and (3) if the representatives have any conflicting interests with the objective of the class they seek to represent. *Lewy*, 650 N.W.2d at 454.

b. Rule 23.02

Upon satisfaction of all the four prerequisites of Rule 23.01, a party must also satisfy the requirements of Minnesota Rule of Civil Procedure 23.02. The most common type of class action—where the putative class seeks to recover damages—requires a showing of predominance and superiority under Rule 23.02(c).

i. Predominance. Predominance is established where (1) generalized evidence will prove or disprove an element on a class-wide basis (2) without the need to examine each class member's individual circumstances. *See Lewy*, 650 N.W.2d at 455–56; *see also, e.g.*, *In re Zurn Pex Plumbing Prod. Liab. Litig.*, 644 F.3d 604, 618–19 (8th Cir. 2011) (finding common issues predominated both negligence and warranty claims in product liability action); *Blades v. Monsanto Co.*, 400 F.3d 562, 570–75 (8th Cir. 2005) (holding that predominance is satisfied where the putative class members' claims can be proved on a class-wide basis with "common proof").

The predominance inquiry also focuses on whether questions of law are sufficiently common to the claims of class members, and "[i]f the liability issue is common to the class, common questions are held to predominate over individual questions." *Lewy*, 650 N.W.2d at 455–56 (citing *Genden v. Merrill Lynch, Pierce, Fenner & Smith, Inc.*, 114 F.R.D. 48, 52 (S.D.N.Y. 1987)). For example, class certification was granted for a damages class alleging violations of Minnesota's Consumer Fraud Act (MCFA) for a class of insurance policy holders where unique factors presented common questions. *Taqueria El Primo LLC v. Ill. Farmers Ins. Co.* (*Taqueria I*), 577 F. Supp. 3d 970 (D. Minn. 2021). In *Taqueria I*, insureds brought a putative class action against automobile policy insurers, alleging that insurers entered into secret agreements with health care providers that resulted in billing restrictions that breached the insurance contracts and violated Minnesota's No-Fault Insurance Act, the Minnesota Consumer Fraud Act (MCFA), and the Minnesota Uniform Deceptive Trade Practices Act (MDTPA). The court found that the requirements were satisfied to certify a predominance class seeking monetary damages under the MCFA where the plaintiffs alleged that certain billing limitations imposed by defendants were unknown to both consumers and the Department of Commerce, resulting in several possible common questions of materiality, harm, and reliance that would apply to all consumers.

The predominance requirement is not met where each putative class member's entitlement to a remedy depends on facts specific to each class member and "common, aggregation-enabling, issues in the case" are not more prevalent or important than the non-common, aggregation-defeating, individual issues. *Hoekman*, 335 F.R.D. at 258 (D. Minn. 2020) (quoting *Tyson Foods, Inc. v. Bouaphakeo*, 577 U.S. 442, 453 (2016)). The Eighth Circuit has held cases alleging fraud-based violations of Minnesota consumer protection statutes may not be suitable for class certification where the defendant presents evidence that individual non-reliance on the alleged fraud predominates over common questions. *Hudock v. LG Elec. U.S.A., Inc.*, 12 F.4th 773 (8th Cir. 2021) (citing evidence in action alleging untrue statements about the "refresh rate" on television sets that some consumers didn't care about refresh rates when shopping for certain televisions, and therefore the inquiry required "plaintiff-by-plaintiff determinations" as to which television feature motivated individual consumers to purchase televisions, making certification inappropriate); *Johannessohn v. Polaris Indus., Inc.*, 9 F.4th 981 (8th Cir. 2021) (allowing defendants to present evidence challenging individual consumer-plaintiff's reliance on the alleged omissions making individual questions predominate in action alleging fraud-based violations of Minnesota's consumer protection statutes regarding heat defects on all-terrain vehicles); *but see In re Fedex Ground Package Sys., Inc., Emp. Prac. Litig.*, No. 3:05-MD-527 (MDL-1700), 2008 WL 5263376 (N.D. Ind. Dec. 16, 2008) (finding class certification of fraud-based violations of Minnesota consumer protection statutes appropriate because plaintiffs aren't required to present individualized evidence of reliance under Minnesota law).

Furthermore, a question lacks predominance when class certification would result in thousands of "mini-trials," precluding a uniform method for calculating damages. *Kochlin v. Norwest Mortg., Inc.*, No. C3-01-136, 2001 WL 856206, at *4–5 (Minn. Ct. App. July 31, 2001) (citing *Keating v. Philip Morris, Inc.*, 417 N.W.2d 132 (Minn. Ct. App. 1987)). However, individualized issues pertaining to damages do not necessarily defeat predominance. *See Rilley v. MoneyMutual, LLC*, 329 F.R.D. 211 (D. Minn. 2019) (certifying class where the consumers' proposed method for measuring damages required individualized inquiry).

ii. Superiority. Minnesota Rule of Civil Procedure 23.02(c) requires that a class action be "superior to other available methods for the fair and efficient adjudication of the controversy." The Rule directs that courts consider the following factors in evaluating "superiority": "(1) the interest of members of the class in individually controlling the prosecution or defense of separate actions; (2) the extent and nature of any litigation concerning the controversy already commenced by or against members of the class; (3) the desirability or undesirability of concentrating the litigation of the claims in the particular forum; and (4) the difficulties likely to be encountered in the management of a class action." *Id. See, e.g., Peterson*, 618 N.W.2d at 826 ("The purpose of the class action has been to take care of the smaller guy.") However, where a plaintiff can collect attorneys' fees, the expense of litigation may not be a factor supporting superiority. *Gardner v. Equifax Info. Serv.*, No. 06-3102, 2007 WL 2261688, at *6 (D. Minn. Aug. 6, 2007).

The focus on manageability is similar to the concern addressed by the predominance inquiry. That is, whether there are too many "individualized" issues that must be tried such that a class action trial would be unwieldy and impractical. If so, the class action may be denied or narrowed in scope. *See Kochlin*, 2001 WL 856206, at *5. Where the predominance requirement has been satisfied, however, courts may still allow the case to proceed as a class action, absent some significant manageability problem. *Lewy*, 650 N.W.2d at 457 (finding that the necessity of individualized damages calculation was preferable to thousands of individual trials that would test both liability and damages).

iii. Class certification in cases involving injunctive or declaratory relief. A class is also certifiable under Rule 23.02(a) or (b). A class may be certified under 23.02(a) where the prosecution of separate actions by or against individual members of the class would create a risk of inconsistent or varying adjudications with respect to individual members of the class which would establish incompatible standards of conduct for the party opposing the class, or adjudications with respect to individual members of the class which would as a practical matter be dispositive of the interests of the other members not parties to the adjudications or substantially impair or impeded their ability to protect their interests. Minn. R. Civ. P. 23.02(a)(1) – (2); *Bacon*, 930 N.W.2d at 440–41 (holding that a class may be certified under Minn. R. Civ. P. 23.02(a) when the class seeks both equitable and monetary recovery on behalf of class as a whole rather than asserting individualized monetary claims).

A class may be certified under Rule 23.02(b) when a defendant has acted or refused to act on grounds generally applicable to the class and where the relief sought is primarily equitable in nature. Typically, such class actions relate to civil rights, discrimination, the constitutionality of statutes, or other types of declaratory actions. *Streich*, 399 N.W.2d at 216.

3. CLASS NOTICE

For classes certified under Minnesota Rule of Civil Procedure 23.02(c)(3), the court must direct that notice be sent to class members informing them that a class has been certified. Minn. R. Civ. P. 23.03(b)(2). The purpose of the notice process is to inform class members that they have a choice whether to opt out of the class or to remain in the class and to provide sufficient information for class members to make that choice. *Taqueria El Primo LLC v Ill. Farmers Ins. Co.* (*Taqueria II*), 630 F. Supp. 3d 1121, 1130 (D. Minn. 2022).

Notice must plainly and concisely state:

(A) the nature of the action,
(B) the definition of the class certified,

(C) the class claims, issues, or defenses,
(D) that a class member may enter an appearance through counsel if the member so desires,
(E) that the court will exclude from the class any member who requests exclusion, stating when and how members may elect to be excluded, and
(F) the binding effect of a class judgment on class members under Rule 23.03(c).

Minn. R. Civ. P. 23.03(b)(2).

Minnesota rules require the best notice that is practicable under the circumstances, including individual notice to all members who can be identified through reasonable effort. Minn. R. Civ. P. 23.03(b)(2). Notice by email has supplanted notice by U.S. mail as the primary "best notice practicable." *See, e.g.*, *Taqueria II*, 630 F. Supp. 3d at 1126–27 (permitting primary notice by email, followed by a USPS postcard in cases of a "bounce back").

4. RULE 23.06 APPEALS

An application to appeal a class certification order must be filed within 30 days of filing of the order, as set forth in Minnesota Rule of Civil Appellate Procedure 105. Minnesota appellate courts review the district court's decision to certify a class "for an abuse of discretion." *Bacon*, 930 N.W.2d at 440. "[A] district court abuses its discretion if it adopts an incorrect legal rule or misapplies the rule 23 factors." *Id.* at 443.

The standard governing an appellate court's consideration of whether to grant a petition for review was articulated by the Minnesota Supreme Court in *Gordon v. Microsoft Corp*., 645 N.W.2d 393 (Minn. 2002). The Minnesota Supreme Court established a "nonexclusive list of factors" to consider in requests for discretionary review, including (1) whether a questionable class certification order may sound a "death knell" for the case; (2) whether class certification, if granted, places inordinate pressure on the defendant to settle the case; and (3) whether an appeal would provide resolution of an important legal issue. *Id.* at 400–02.

5. COMMUNICATION WITH ABSENT CLASS MEMBERS

Minnesota state courts provide no guidance on the issue of communications with absent or putative class members. There are no published decisions. The Eighth Circuit and the United States District Court for the District of Minnesota have recognized that, once a class is certified, absent class members are parties represented by class counsel under Federal Rule of Civil Procedure 23. *In re Potash Antitrust Litig.*, 896 F. Supp. 916, 920–21 (D. Minn. 1995). The Court in *Potash*, however, did not prohibit defendants from writing to the certified class, but instead required that defendants' communications with class members relating to the merits of the litigation be supervised by the court. *Id.* at 920. Therefore, the court ordered that defendants' anticipated communications with the class concerning the merits of the litigation be provided to the court and class counsel in advance. *Id.*; *see also In re Wholesale Grocery Prod. Antitrust Litig.*, No. 09-MD-2090, 2017 WL 826917, at *5 (D. Minn. Mar. 1, 2017) (stating that once a class is certified, the "judge has ultimate control over communications among the parties, third parties, or their agents and class members on the subject matter of the litigation"). Communications with class members in the ordinary course of business, unrelated to the litigation, are not barred. *Potash,* 896 F. Supp. at 920–21 (citing *Manual for Complex Litigation (Third)* § 30.2 (1995)).

Putative absent class members are not parties represented by counsel, and therefore, there is no blanket prohibition against communications with them. *See, e.g.*, *In re Baycol Prod. Litig.*, No. MDL 1431, 2004 WL 1058105, at *3 (D. Minn. May 3, 2004) (recognizing that defendants have a right to negotiate settlements with prospective class members where no class has been certified); s*ee also Rothe v. Wayzata Nissan LLC.*, No. 02-3233, 2003 WL 21181343 (D. Minn. May 14, 2003) (finding defendant's communication with putative class members permissible where defendant sent a letter along with a $1,000 check as an offer of settlement to 35 putative class members); *In re Target Corp. Customer Data Sec. Breach Litig.*, No. 14-25522, 2015 WL 2165432, at * 2 (D. Minn. May 7, 2015) (refusing to enjoin the settlement proposal to putative class members because even though the terms of the settlement did not appear to be fair or reasonable, there was no serious misconduct to warrant judicial inference).

In addition, the Eighth Circuit has held that a district court may not order restraints on speech under Federal Rule of Civil Procedure 23(d) except when justified by a finding of actual or threatened misconduct of a serious nature. *Great Rivers Co-op of Se. Iowa v. Farmland Indus., Inc.*, 59 F.3d 764 (8th Cir. 1995). In *Great Rivers*, defendant published an opinion piece in its newsletter to potential class members denouncing a class action lawsuit against it. The district court required defendant to publish in its newsletter a rebuttal article by plaintiffs, and "to refrain from communicating anything in the future that could reasonably be taken as an invitation to opt out." *Id.* at 766. Finding that the district court made insufficient findings regarding misrepresentations and the likelihood of serious abuses, the Eighth Circuit reversed the district court's order.

MINNESOTA RULES OF CIVIL PROCEDURE

RULE 23. CLASS ACTIONS

23.01 Prerequisites to a class action

One or more members of a class may sue or be sued as representative parties on behalf of all only if

(a) The class is so numerous that joinder of all members is impracticable;

(b) There are questions of law or fact common to the class;

(c) The claims or defenses of the representative parties are typical of the claims or defenses of the class; and

(d) The representative parties will fairly and adequately protect the interests of the class.

23.02 Class actions maintainable

An action may be maintained as a class action if the prerequisites of Rule 23.01 are satisfied, and in addition:

(a) The prosecution of separate actions by or against individual members of the class would create a risk of

(1) Inconsistent or varying adjudications with respect to individual members of the class which would establish incompatible standards of conduct for the party opposing the class, or

(2) adjudications with respect to individual members of the class which would as a practical matter be dispositive of the interests of the other members not parties to the adjudications or substantially impair or impede their ability to protect their interests; or

(b) the party opposing the class has acted or refused to act on grounds generally applicable to the class, thereby making appropriate final injunctive relief or corresponding declaratory relief with respect to the class as a whole; or

(c) The court finds that the questions of law or fact common to the members of the class predominate over any questions affecting only individual members, and that a class action is superior to other available methods for the fair and efficient adjudication of the controversy. The matters pertinent to the findings include: (1) the interest of members of the class in individually controlling the prosecution or defense of separate actions; (2) the extent and nature of any litigation concerning the controversy already commenced by or against members of the class; (3) the desirability or undesirability of concentrating the litigation of the claims in the particular forum; and (4) the difficulties likely to be encountered in the management of a class action.

23.03 Determination by order whether to certify a class action; appointing class counsel; notice and membership in class; judgment; multiple classes and subclasses

(a) *Certification order.*

(1) When a person sues or is sued as a representative of a class, the court must—at an early practicable time—determine by order whether to certify the action as a class action.

(2) An order certifying a class action must define the class and the class claims, issues, or defenses, and must appoint class counsel under Rule 23.07.

(3) An order under Rule 23.03(a)(1) may be altered or amended before final judgment.

(b) *Notice.*

(1) For any class certified under Rule 23.02(a) or (b), the court may direct appropriate notice to the class.

(2) For any class certified under Rule 23.02(c), the court must direct to class members the best notice practicable under the circumstances, including individual notice to all members who can be identified through reasonable effort. The notice must concisely and clearly state in plain, easily understood language:

(A) The nature of the action,

(B) The definition of the class certified,

(C) The class claims, issues, or defenses,

(D) That a class member may enter an appearance through counsel if the member so desires,

(E) That the court will exclude from the class any member who requests exclusion, stating when and how members may elect to be excluded, and

(F) The binding effect of a class judgment on class members under Rule 23.03(c).

(c) *Identification of class members.* The judgment in an action maintained as a class action under Rule 23.02(a) or (b), whether or not favorable to the class, shall include and describe those whom the court finds to be members of the class. The judgment in an action maintained as a class action under Rule 23.02(c), whether or not favorable to the class, shall include and specify or describe those to whom the notice provided in Rule 23.03(b) was directed, and who have not requested exclusion, and whom the court finds to be members of the class.

(d) *Issue classes and subclasses.* When appropriate (1) an action may be brought or maintained as a class action with respect to particular issues, or (2) a class may be divided into subclasses and each subclass treated as a class; and the provisions of this rule shall then be construed and applied accordingly.

23.04 Orders in conduct of action

In the conduct of actions to which this rule applies, the court may make appropriate orders:

(a) Determining the course of proceedings or prescribing measures to prevent undue repetition or complication in the presentation of evidence or argument;

(b) requiring, for the protection of the members of the class or otherwise for the fair conduct of the action, that notice be given in such manner as the court may direct to some or all members of any step in the action, or of the proposed extent of the judgment, or of the opportunity of members to signify whether they consider the representation fair and adequate, to intervene and present claims or defenses, or otherwise to enter the action;

(c) imposing conditions on the representative parties or intervenors;

(d) requiring that the pleadings be amended to eliminate therefrom allegations as to representation of absent persons, and that the action proceed accordingly; or

(e) dealing with similar procedural matters.

The orders may be combined with an order pursuant to Rule 16, and may be altered or amended whenever necessary.

23.05 Settlement, voluntary dismissal, or compromise

(a) *Court approval.*

(1) A settlement, voluntary dismissal, or compromise of the claims, issues, or defenses or a compromise of the claims, issues, or defenses of a certified class is effective only if approved by the court.

(2) The court must direct notice in a reasonable manner to all class members who would be bound by a proposed settlement, voluntary dismissal, or compromise.

(3) The court may approve a settlement, voluntary dismissal, or compromise that would bind class members only after a hearing and on finding that the settlement, voluntary dismissal, or compromise is fair, reasonable, and adequate.

(b) *Disclosure required.* The parties seeking approval of a settlement, voluntary dismissal, or compromise under Rule 23.05(a) must file a statement identifying any agreement made in connection with the proposed settlement, voluntary dismissal, or compromise.

(c) *Additional opt-out period.* In an action previously certified as a class action under Rule 23.02(c), the court may refuse to approve a settlement unless it affords a new opportunity to request exclusion to individual class members who had an earlier opportunity to request exclusion but did not do so.

(d) *Objection to settlement.*

(1) Any class member may object to a proposed settlement, voluntary dismissal, or compromise that requires court approval under Rule 23.05(a)(1).

(2) An objection made under Rule 23.05(d)(1) may be withdrawn only with the court's approval.

(e) *Distribution of Residual Funds, If Any.*

In the event there are residual funds that remain after payment of all approved class member claims (including any supplemental distributions to the class), expenses, litigation costs, attorney's fees, and other court-approved disbursements, the court shall direct notice regarding the distribution of these funds and establish a deadline by which potential recipients must submit a statement asserting a basis to designate the organization as a recipient of the residual funds. This notice shall be provided as directed by the court to any potential recipient of residual funds identified by the parties or the court and to the State Board of Civil Legal Aid for the purpose of informing qualified legal services programs within the meaning of Minnesota Statutes, section 480.24, subdivision 3. The notice must include the deadline established by the court for submission of statements by potential recipients. Notice given to the State Board of Legal Aid shall be made using the form and delivery method required by State Court Administration.

In approving the distribution or other disposition of residual funds, the district court shall consider all relevant factors, including the recommendations of the parties, the nexus between the nature, purpose, and objectives of the class action and the interests of the class members, and the interests of potential recipients of the residual funds.

23.06 Appeals

The court of appeals may in its discretion permit an appeal from an order of a district court granting or denying class action certification under this rule. An application to appeal must be sought within the time provided in Rule 105 of the Minnesota Rules of Civil Appellate Procedure, and shall be subject to the other provisions of that rule. An appeal does not stay proceedings in the district court unless the district judge or the court of appeals so orders.

23.07 Class counsel

(a) *Appointing class counsel.*

(1) Unless a statute provides otherwise, a court that certifies a class must appoint class counsel.

(2) An attorney appointed to serve as class counsel must fairly and adequately represent the interests of the class.

(3) In appointing class counsel, the court

(A) must consider:

(i) the work counsel has done in identifying or investigating potential claims in the action,

(ii) counsel's experience in handling class actions, other complex litigation, and claims of the type asserted in the action,

(iii) counsel's knowledge of the applicable law, and

(iv) the resources counsel will commit to representing the class;

(B) may consider any other matter pertinent to counsel's ability to fairly and adequately represent the interests of the class;

(C) may direct potential class counsel to provide information on any subject pertinent to the appointment and to propose terms for attorney fees and nontaxable costs; and

(D) may make further orders in connection with the appointment.

(b) *Appointment procedure*

(1) The court may designate interim counsel to act on behalf of the putative class before determining whether to certify the action as a class action.

(2) When there is one applicant for appointment as class counsel, the court may appoint that applicant only if the applicant is adequate under Rule 23.07(a)(2) and (3). If more than one adequate applicant seeks appointment as class counsel, the court must appoint the applicant best able to represent the interests of the class.

(3) The order appointing class counsel may include provisions about the award of attorney fees or nontaxable costs under Rule 23.08.

23.08 Attorney fees award

In an action certified as a class action, the court may award reasonable attorney fees and nontaxable costs authorized by law or by agreement of the parties as follows:

(a) *Motion for award of attorney fees.* A claim for an award of attorney fees and nontaxable costs must be made by motion, subject to the provisions of this subdivision, at a time set by the court. Notice of the motion must be served on all parties and, for motions by class counsel, directed to class members in a reasonable manner.

(b) *Right to object.* A class member, or a party from whom payment is sought, may object to the motion.

(c) *Hearing and findings.* The court may hold a hearing and must find the facts and state its conclusions of law on the motion under Rule 52.01.

(d) *Reference to special master.* The court may refer issues related to the amount of the award to a special master as provided in Rule 53.01(a).

23.09 Derivative actions by shareholders or members

In a derivative action brought by one or more shareholders or members to enforce a right of a corporation or of an unincorporated association, the corporation or association having failed to enforce a right which may properly be asserted by it, the complaint shall allege that the plaintiff was a shareholder or member at the time of the transaction of which the plaintiff complains or that the plaintiff's share or membership thereafter devolved on the plaintiff by operation of law. The complaint shall also allege with particularity the efforts, if any, made by the plaintiff to obtain the desired action from the directors or comparable authority and, if necessary, from the shareholders or members, and the reasons for the plaintiff's failure to obtain the action or for not making the effort. The derivative action may not be maintained if it appears that the plaintiff does not fairly and adequately represent the interest of the shareholders or members similarly situated in enforcing the right of the corporation or association. The action shall not be dismissed or compromised without the approval of the court, and notice of the proposed dismissal or compromise shall be given to shareholders or members in such manner as the court directs.

23.10 Actions relating to unincorporated associations

An action brought by or against the members of an unincorporated association as a class by naming certain members as representative parties may be maintained only if it appears that the representative parties will fairly and adequately protect the interests of the association and its members. In the conduct of the action the court may make appropriate orders corresponding with those described in Rule 23.04 and the procedure for dismissal or compromise of the action shall correspond with that provided in Rule 23.05.

Chapter authors Gordon Rudd and David Cialkowski are partners with Zimmerman Reed LLP, practicing in the area of complex litigation and class actions.

MISSISSIPPI

On May 17, 2018, the Mississippi Supreme Court denied a motion to amend Mississippi Rule of Civil Procedure 23 to permit state court class actions. The Mississippi Rules of Civil Procedure therefore still contain no section permitting class actions. While Rule 23 has been formally enumerated, it merely contains a simple caption: "Rule 23. Class Actions [Omitted]." Miss. R. Civ. P. 23. The Supreme Court of Mississippi recognized that it "intentionally omitted Rule 23, which would have covered class actions." *Marx v. Broom*, 632 So. 2d 1315, 1322 (Miss. 1994). The justification for this omission was a concern that "meaningful reforms had not yet been developed that would make class actions manageable." *American Bankers Ins. Co. of Florida v. Booth*, 830 So. 2d 1205, 1214 (Miss. 2002). The Court did point out, however, that "the rules may be amended" upon the emergence of such reforms. *Id.*

Mississippi has historically recognized class actions brought in chancery courts under their general equity jurisdiction. *See USF&G Ins. Co. of Mississippi v. Walls*, 911 So. 2d 463, 464–66 (Miss. 2005). However, the Supreme Court of Mississippi has recently settled the point that class actions "are not permitted in any legal proceeding in our state," on the basis that (1) there "is no rule or statute which expressly or impliedly provides for class actions" and (2) that the Mississippi Rules of Civil Procedure apply to all civil actions. *Id.* at 467. Impliedly, class actions were permissible in a court of equity up to the time when the Mississippi Rules of Civil Procedure were adopted.

Representing a counterbalance to the absence of a procedural class action mechanism, Mississippi state courts once permitted the liberal joinder of parties. *See, e.g., American Bankers Ins. Co. of Florida v. Alexander*, 818 So. 2d 1073 (2001). Pursuant to amendments in 2004 to the Mississippi Rules of Civil Procedure, however, the Supreme Court of Mississippi proceeded to cast aside liberal joinder by significantly tightening the applicable requirements. The revised Comment to Rule 20 of the Mississippi Rules of Civil Procedure concluded that as a prerequisite for joinder, there must be "a distinct litigable event linking the parties." Miss. R. Civ. P. 20 cmt. The reference to a distinct event was language framed to clarify the term "transaction or occurrence" appearing in Rule 20. *See Jannssen Pharmaceutica, Inc. v. Bailey*, 878 So. 2d 31, 46 (Miss. 2004) (citing Miss. R. Civ. P. 20 and cmt. thereto).

Perhaps the key case in this procedural area is *Janssen Pharmaceutica, Inc. v. Armond*, 866 So. 2d 1092 (Miss. 2004). In *Armond*, 56 plaintiffs treated with the pharmaceutical drug Propulsid sought joinder with respect to a series of defendants consisting of 42 prescribing physicians, the drug's manufacturer, and a hospital. The Court found that "each plaintiff/doctor combination has its own set of facts and evidence surrounding the prescribing of Propulsid, the transaction or occurrence of which is the basis for each claim." *Id.* at 1102. That the plaintiffs shared the common fact of being prescribed a certain drug did not constitute a sufficiently distinct event to link them judicially.

Mississippi has had features in its jurisprudence that have compensated in some measure for the absence of a class action provision in its codified procedure. Such factors have included liberal joinder under Rules 20 and 42 of the Mississippi Rules of Civil Procedure, the equitable class action, and the availability of punitive damages for individual claims. *See USF&G*, 911 So. 2d at 464 (quoting Richard T. Phillips, *Class Action & Joinder in Mississippi*, 71 Miss. L.J. 447, 453 (2001)). Those compensatory factors exist no more or, alternatively, exist strictly in greatly limited form. The equitable class action is no longer valid, liberal joinder of individual claims has given way to a strict construction, and tort reform enacted in the previous decade has limited the scope of punitive damage recoveries.

This chapter was prepared by Don Barrett and David McMullan, of Barrett Law Group, PA, in Lexington, Mississippi.

MISSOURI

1. COMPARISON WITH FEDERAL RULE 23

While, for many years, Missouri's Rule 52.08 regarding class actions has substantially tracked Federal Rule 23, the newly amended version of Rule 52.08, tracks Rule 23 even more closely and is essentially identical with only minor variations.[1] Thus, it is anticipated that Missouri courts will continue to use federal precedents in interpreting and applying the rule. *State ex rel. Union Planters Bank, N.A. v. Kendrick*, 142 S.W.3d 729, 736 (Mo. banc 2004); *State ex. rel. Byrd v. Chadwick*, 956 S.W.2d 369, 378 (Mo. Ct. App. 1997); *Ralph v. American Family Mutual Ins. Co.*, 809 S.W.2d 173, 175 (Mo. Ct. App. 1991). When there is no Missouri interpretation of a point relevant to Rule 52.08, federal court interpretations of Federal Rule 23 are viewed as persuasive in interpreting Rule 52.08. *Ressler v. Clay County*, 375 S.W.3d 132, 136–37 (Mo. Ct. App. 2012).

2. STANDARD OF REVIEW

a. Class Certification

Class certification determinations under Mo. Sup. Ct. R. 52.08 lie within the sound discretion of the trial court. *Hootselle v. Mo. Dep't of Corr.*, 624 S.W.3d 123, 133 (Mo. June 1, 2021), citing *State ex rel. Gen. Credit Acceptance Co., LLC v. Vincent,* 570 S.W.3d 42, 46 (Mo. banc 2019); *Union Planters,* 142 S.W.3d at 735; *State ex. rel. American Family Mutual Ins. Co. v. Clark*, 106 S.W.3d 483, 486 (Mo. banc 2003); *Karr v. Kan. City Life Ins. Co.*, 702 S.W.3d 1, 34 (Mo. Ct. App. 2024). "Because class certification is subject to later modification, a court should err in favor of, and not against, allowing maintenance of the class action." *Wright v. The Country Club of St. Albans*, 269 S.W.3d 461, 465 (Mo. Ct. App. 2008); *see also Frank v. Enviro-Tech Servs.*, 577 S.W.3d 163, 167 (Mo. Ct. App, 2019) (discussed *infra*); *Dale v. DaimlerChrysler Corp.*, 204 S.W.3d 151, 164 (Mo. Ct. App. 2006) ("[I]n the face of a motion to decertify, the party seeking class certification bears the burden of proving that all requirements of class certification are met."); *Ogg v. Mediacom, LLC*, 382 S.W.3d 108, 116 (Mo. Ct. App. 2012) (citing *Marlo v. UPS, Inc.*, 639 F.3d 942, 947 (9th Cir. 2011)).

Missouri appellate courts review an order granting or denying class action certification solely for abuse of discretion. *Craft,* 190 S.W.3d at 376, (citing *Koger v. Hartford Life Ins. Co.*, 28 S.W.3d 405, 410 (Mo. Ct. App. 2000)). An abuse of discretion occurs in this context if the decision "is clearly against the logic of the circumstance, is arbitrary and unreasonable, and indicates a lack of careful consideration." *Hootselle*, at 133, citing *State ex rel. McKeage v. Cordonnier*, 357 S.W.3d 597, 599 (Mo. banc 2012); *see also Dale*, 204 S.W.3d at 164 (abuse of discretion "occurs when a

[1] Rule 52.08 does not include a counterpart for 23(e)(5)(C) ("Procedure for Approval After An Appeal.") and 52.08(f) omits a provision regarding the timing of appeals involving United States government entities. With the exception of those minor variations and Missouri's use of "shall" rather than "must," the substantive text of the rules otherwise track each other verbatim.

court bases its decision on an erroneous conclusion of law or where there is no rational basis in [the] evidence for the ruling") (citing *Harvell v. Goodyear Tire & Rubber Co.*, 2006 OK 24 (Okla. 2006)) (emphasis added). Inasmuch as Mo. Sup. Ct. R. 52.08(c)(1) provides for de-certification of a class "before [a] decision on the merits," a court will err on the side of upholding certification in cases where it is a close question. *Wright*, 269 S.W.3d at 464–65 (Mo. Ct. App. 2008); *Dale*, 204 S.W.3d at 164 (since decertification is always possible, the court should give the benefit of the doubt to approving the class). Thus, "[t]he circuit court's ruling on whether or not to decertify a class will be upheld unless the trial court's decision constitutes an abuse of its discretion." *Ogg*, 382 S.W.3d. at 113 (citing *Smith v. American Family Mutual Insurance Co.,* 289 S.W.3d 675, 689 (Mo. Ct. App. 2009)). An abuse of discretion may also be found if the circuit court's decision is clearly against the logic of the circumstances, is arbitrary and unreasonable, and indicates a lack of careful consideration. *Id.* (citing *State ex rel. McKeage v. Cordonnier*, 357 S.W.3d 597, 599 (Mo. banc 2012)). It is important, however, for the trial court to include findings of fact and conclusions of law relevant to its class certification ruling. *Townsend v. Regis Corp.*, No. SD36671, 2020 Mo. App. LEXIS 1233, at *3–4 (Mo. Ct. App. Oct. 13, 2020) (remanding class certification denial to trial court to make findings and conclusions to permit meaningful appellate review).

In *Elsea v. U.S. Eng'g Co.*, 463 S.W.3d 409 (Mo. Ct. App. 2015), *transfer denied*, *Elsea v. U.S. Eng'g Co.*, 2015 Mo. LEXIS 108 (June 30, 2015), a class action involving medical monitoring for a class exposed to asbestos fibers during a courthouse renovation, the Missouri Court of Appeals addressed the parties' disagreement regarding how an appellate court reviews the facts of a class action case: plaintiffs asserted that "in class certification determinations, the named plaintiffs' allegations are accepted as true," while Defendants contended that the appellate court is to "take the evidence and the reasonable inferences therefrom in the light most favorable to the judgment." *Elsea v. U.S. Eng'g Co.*, 463 S.W.3d at 413. To this disagreement the court of appeals held "[i]n class certification determination, the named plaintiffs' allegations are accepted as true," *Id.* (quoting *Hale v. Wal-Mart Stores, Inc.*, 231 S.W.3d 215, 227 (Mo. Ct. App. W.D. 2007) (noting that arguments which tend to negate allegations from the petition should be ignored because such allegations are taken as true for purposes of a class certification motion), and that "the determination of class certification is based primarily upon the allegations in the petition." *Id.* at 413–14 (citing *Hope v. Nissan N. Am., Inc.*, 353 S.W.3d 68, 74 (Mo. Ct. App. W.D. 2011)). The court of appeals in *Elsea* further held that "[w]hile some evidence relating to the merits may be considered in determining whether the class certification prerequisites have been met, the court must look only so far as to determine whether, given the factual setting of the case, if the plaintiff's general allegations are true, common evidence could suffice to make out a prima facie case for the class." *Id.* at 414 (citing *Hale*, 231 S.W.3d at 222) (internal citation omitted).

3. RULE 52.08—GENERAL CONSIDERATIONS

An action may be maintained as a class action if all the prerequisites of subdivision (a) are satisfied and, in addition, one element of Mo. Sup. Ct. Rule 52.08(b) is met. *Karr v. Kan. City Life Ins. Co.*, 702 S.W.3d 1, 35 (Mo. Ct. App. 2024); *St. Peters v. Gronefeld*, 609 S.W.2d 437, 439 (Mo. Ct. App. 1980); *State ex rel. Niess v. Junkin*, 572 S.W.2d 468, 470 (Mo. banc 1978). The requirements of Mo. Sup. Ct. R. 52.08(a) include numerosity, commonality, typicality, and adequate representation. *Karr*, 702 S.W.3d at 35. "[T]he party seeking class certification has the burden of proof." *Dale v. DaimlerChrysler Corp.*, 204 S.W.3d 151, 164 (Mo. Ct. App. 2006). "This burden is satisfied if there is evidence in the record, which if taken as true, would satisfy each and every requirement of the rule." *Id.* at 164–65. "In class certification determination, the named plaintiffs' allegations are accepted as true." *Hale v. Wal-Mart Stores, Inc.*, 231 S.W.3d 215, 227 (Mo. Ct. App. 2007). The determination of class certification is based primarily upon the allegations in the petition. *Hope v. Nissan N. Am., Inc.*, 353 S.W.3d 68, 74 (Mo. Ct. App. 2011).

The Missouri Supreme Court has noted that class actions are "designed to promote judicial economy by permitting the litigation of the common questions of law and fact of numerous individuals in a single proceeding." *Union Planters*, 142 S.W.3d at 735. In close cases, the Missouri Supreme Court has emphasized that trial courts should err in favor of class certification. *Meyer v. Fluor Corp.*, 220 S.W.3d 712, 715 (Mo. banc 2007). *See also Little v. Drury Inns, Inc.*, 306 S.W.3d 577, 580 (Mo. Ct. App. 2010).

Another general consideration, neither mentioned in statute nor rule, concerns proper class definition. The Missouri Supreme Court, in 2008, indicated that requiring a proper class definition underlies each of the mandatory elements for certification. *State ex rel. The Coca-Cola Co. v. Nixon*, 249 S.W.3d 855, 860–61 (Mo. banc 2008). Although the class definition must be sufficiently definite so that it is administratively feasible to identify members of the class, it need not be so ascertainable from the definition that every potential member can be identified at the commencement of the action. *Id.* The court in *Hope* held that taking plaintiffs' allegations in their petition as true, the original putative class was ascertainable as including owners of the FX vehicles on the theory that each owner would have been or would be damaged by the "stigma" and "diminished resale value" as the plaintiffs contended, regardless of the manifestation of the defect. *Hope,* 353 S.W.3d at 79. Regarding Nissan's concern that the list of "current owners" of FX vehicles changes constantly, making the class members indiscernible, the court did not discern an abuse of discretion in the initial definition because (1) by the use of time limitations, ultimately a method of determining class membership can be determined, making the class ascertainable; (2) while it is possible that a significant number of FX owners may not feel cheated or injured in any way, at this stage the court did not have that information; and (3) the parties can identify the owners of the FX vehicles. *Id.* The court also noted that the trial court may end up altering or revoking either the class definition or the certification. *Id.* at 22. That fact does not in itself mean that the decision to certify was an abuse of discretion. *Id.*

For example, in *Elsea v. U.S. Eng'g Co.*, 463 S.W.3d 409, 423–24 (Mo. Ct. App. 2015), transfer denied, *Elsea v. U.S. Eng'g Co., 2015 Mo. LEXIS 108 (June 30, 2015)*, discussed *supra*, the court of appeals upheld a class definition as both precise and objectively ascertainable because class membership was restricted by definition to persons who had worked in the courthouse or who were "required to spend" (for example, jurors) a minimum period of time (eighty hours or ten days), and had received specified, medically significant minimum levels of exposure to asbestos fibers present in the Courthouse from 1983 to the present. 463 S.W.3d 409, 425–26 (relying on *Meyer v. Fluor Corp.*, 220 S.W.3d 712, 719 (Mo. banc 2007).

a. Rule 52.08(a) Requirements

As a threshold matter, certification of a class action requires, at a minimum, that (1) the class be so numerous that joinder of all members is impracticable, (2) questions of law or fact common to the class exist, (3) the claims of the representative parties are typical of the claims of the class, and (4) the representative parties will fairly and adequately protect the interests of the class. Rule 52.08(a). *Clark*, 106 S.W.3d at 486.

In *State ex rel. Collector of Winchester v. Jamison*, the Court overturned the circuit court's decision to strike and dismiss Winchester's class action claims in its suit against Charter Communications on the basis of § 71.675, R.S.Mo. Supp. 2009, which bars cities and towns from serving as class representatives in suits to enforce or collect business license taxes imposed on telecommunication companies. 357 S.W.3d 589, 595 (Mo. banc 2012*)*. Plaintiffs argued that because it otherwise met the requirements for serving as a class representative in suits against telecommunication companies under Rule 52.08, by enacting § 71.675, the legislature had changed the requirements for serving as a class representative under that rule. *Id.* at 590–91. The Court agreed with plaintiffs' arguments by holding that (1) Missouri's Constitution permits the legislature to amend a procedural rule of this Court, such as Rule 52.08, which governs class actions, only "by a law limited to the purpose" of so doing and that (2) Section 71.765 was not limited to amending Rule 52.08 and did not mention it by name. *Id.* at 591 (Mo. Const. Art. V, § 5). Accordingly, it held that § 71.675 violates Article V, Section 5 of the Missouri Constitution because it amends a procedural rule of this Court, Rule 52.08(a), governing who can bring class actions, but fails to do so in a law limited to that purpose (52.08) as required by Article V, Section 5 of Missouri's Constitution. *Id.* at 595.

i. Numerosity. Under Mo. Sup. Ct. R. 52.08(a)(1), to bring a class action the class must be "so numerous that joinder of all members is impracticable." Rule 52.08(a)(1). Plaintiffs need not specify an exact number of class members to satisfy the numerosity prerequisite for certification but must show only that joinder is impracticable through some evidence or *reasonable, good faith estimate* of the number of purported class members. *Dale*, 204 S.W.3d at 167. Although putative class size alone is not necessarily determinative, it is an important consideration in satisfying the numerosity requirement. *Doyle v. Fluor Corp.*, 199 S.W.3d 784, 787–88 (Mo. Ct. App. 2006) (finding joinder of over four hundred potential class members not an abuse of discretion.) "Members" may initially include persons who do not have claims or who do not wish to assert claims against the defendants unless it can be shown that most, if not all of the potential class members have no claims to be asserted by the class representatives. *Id.*

There is no hard and fast rule as to how many class members constitutes an "impracticable" amount; instead, the determination must be made on a case-by-case basis. *Dale*, 204 S.W.3d at 167. Joinder of all members is impracticable when it would be "inefficient, costly, time consuming, and probably confusing." *Id.* To support a finding of the numerosity prerequisite of Mo. Sup. Ct. R. 52.08(a)(1), the trial court can accept "common sense assumptions." *Id.* In its discretion, the trial court may resolve the issue based on briefs and affidavits, and other evidence. *Id*. Under the federal rule that Missouri's rule tracks, however, permissive joinder may generally be considered impracticable when the class numbers 40 or more. *McHugh v. United Healthcare of the Midwest*, St. Louis City Circuit Court, Cause No. 952-09095, decided October 18, 1999. The *Dale* Court recognized that class certifications have been upheld where the class is composed of as little as eighteen members. 204 S.W.3d at 168.

Numerosity refers to the number of people that are in the class as defined, not the number of ultimate claimants, and Missouri courts reject the notion that litigants must affirmatively demonstrate that any number of potential class members intend to actually participate in the suit. In *Frank v. Enviro-Tech Servs*., 577 S.W.3d 163 (Mo. Ct. App. 2019), the trial court determined that numerosity did not exist because the plaintiffs only produced two affidavits of absent class members reflecting an intent to join the suit. 577 S.W.3d at 166. Noting that "[t]he trial court is mistaken that class representatives . . . are required to provide evidence demonstrating that most or all individual putative class members wish to be a party to the suit," and that there were more than 80 people that met the class definition, the Court of Appeals found the trial court abused its discretion in failing to certify the class on this basis and remanded the matter for further consideration. *Id.*, at 168–69. Provided there are otherwise sufficient claimants that meet the class definition, absent class members are not required to "opt in" at the class certification phase. *Id.* at 169.

ii. Commonality. Commonality only requires that "questions of law or fact are common to the class." Mo. R. Civ. P. 52.08(a)(2). While relief to the various members of a class need not be uniform, the requisite commonality of law or fact must be present. *Grosser v. Kandel-Iken Builders, Inc.*, 647 S.W.2d 911, 918 (Mo. Ct. App. 1983). This does not mean that all class members must be identically situated. *Renstcher v. Carnahan*, 160 F.R.D. 114, 116 (E.D. Mo. 1995). Further, factual differences are not fatal to maintenance of the class action if common questions of law or fact exist. There only needs to be a single issue common to all class members; therefore, the requirement is easily met in most cases. *Renstcher*, 160 F.R.D. at 116; *Crain v. Missouri State Employees Retirement System*, 613 S.W.2d 912, 916 (Mo. Ct. App. 1981).

iii. Typicality. In order to meet the typicality requirement, a class representative must simply "be part of the class and possess the same interest and suffer the same injury as the class members." *Koger v. Hartford Life Ins. Co.*, 28 S.W.3d 405, 410 (Mo. Ct. App. 2000). In essence, the named plaintiff and each member of the class need only have an interest in prevailing on similar legal claims, not that all claims be identical. *Phillips v. Hallmark Cards, Inc.*, 1986 Mo. Ct. App. Lexis 4039, at *12–13 (Mo. Ct. App. Apr. 29, 1986). Where all class members are allegedly damaged in the same way and the named plaintiff's claims arise from the same conduct directed against the class members, commonality and typicality exist. *McHugh v. United Healthcare of the Midwest*, St. Louis City Circuit Court, Cause No. 952-09095 (Oct. 18, 1999). This means that a class representative must be able to assert a claim individually in order to assert the same claim on behalf of the class. *Id.* Plaintiffs who cannot assert a claim individually cannot assert it on behalf of a class. *Id. See also Harris v. Union Electric Co.,* 766 S.W.2d 80, 86 (Mo. banc. 1989) (plaintiffs who cannot assert a claim individually cannot assert it on behalf of a class); *LVNV Funding, LLC v. Mavaega*, 527 S.W.3d 128, 141 (Mo. Ct. App. 2017); *Koehr v. Emmons*, 55 S.W.3d 859, 864 (Mo. Ct. App. 2001). In class certification determinations, the court assumes the named plaintiffs' allegations are true. *Hale*, 231 S.W.3d at 227 (Mo. Ct. App. 2007).

Dale, moreover, has recognized the proposition that the class representative need not show a probability of individual success on the merits. *Dale*, 204 S.W.3d at 172. The mere fact that the respondent may not ultimately recover, depending on the various defenses that may be asserted, is irrelevant to whether his claim is typical of the claims of the class members. *Id.* As such, the *Dale* court held that the existence of an affirmative defense against a class representative does not make his claim atypical. *Id. See also Smith v. Leif Johnson Ford, Inc.*, 632 S.W.3d 798, 807 (Mo. Ct. App. 2021) (contentions of unique defenses have nothing to do with the typicality standard).

The typicality prerequisite for class certification is satisfied even when there is a variance in the underlying facts of the representative's claim and the putative claims, as long as (1) the claim arises from the same event or course of conduct of the defendant as the class claims, (2) the underlying facts are not markedly different, and (3) the conduct and facts give rise to the same legal or remedial theory. *Id.* at 171–72. "Factual variations in the individual claims will not normally preclude class certification if the claim arises from the same event or course of conduct as the class claims, and gives rise to the same legal or remedial theory." *Smith v. Leif Johnson Ford, Inc.*, 632 S.W.3d at 807 (quoting *Dale,* 204 S.W.3d at 170).

Differences in the amount of damages class members may be entitled to does not defeat typicality. In *Mitchell v. Residential Funding Corp.*, plaintiffs met the typicality requirement where the wrongs alleged against the defendants and remedies sought were "identical, the only difference being the exact monetary amount" for which each defendant was liable. 334 S.W.3d 477, 492 (Mo. Ct. App. 2010).

When determining whether a class meets the prerequisites of Mo. Sup. Ct. R. 52.08(a)(3), a court should freely give leave to amend the petition to redefine the class if the original class members do not appear to have the requisite typicality of claims, so long as persons dropped from the class are not prejudiced by the redefinition. *Grosser*, 647 S.W.2d at 917.

iv. Adequacy of representation

Adequacy of class representative. Because a class action affects the rights of absent class members, Missouri Supreme Court Rule 52.08(a)(4), like its federal counterpart, requires the trial court to make a determination that the representative parties will fairly and adequately represent the interests of the class. Mo. Sup. Ct. R. 52.08(a)(4); *Union Planters*, 142 S.W.3d at 735. *See also Doyle, v. Fluor Corp.*, 400 S.W.3d 316, 321–22 (Mo. Ct. App. 2013) (citing *Vandyne v. Allied Mortg. Capital Corp.*, 242 S.W.3d 695, 698 (Mo. banc 2008)). To this end, the court must consider whether the named representatives have any conflicts of interest that will adversely affect the interests of the class. *Id.* at 322 (citing *Vandyne*, 242 S.W.3d at 698). According to the Missouri Supreme Court, the adequacy requirement is "particularly important because the due process rights of absentee class members may be implicated if they are bound by a final judgment in a suit where they are inadequately represented by the named plaintiff." *Union Planters*, 142 S.W.3d at 735–36.

Adequacy of representation is a fact issue that must be determined under the circumstances of each case. *Craft*, 190 S.W.3d at 379. Adequacy of representation is a determination within the sound discretion of the trial court. *See Doyle,* 400 S.W.3d at 321. A true conflict of interest between the representative and the class members with respect to the subject matter of the lawsuit prevents a finding that the representative can fairly and adequately represent the class. *Craft*, 190 S.W.3d at 379. The primary consideration is that all diversified class interests and points of view are represented and that the named representatives have truly adverse interests so that all issues are actually litigated without collusion. *O'Fallon v. Bethman,* 569 S.W.2d 295, 299 (Mo. Ct. App. 1978). The fact that potential class members may have individual personal injury claims arising from the consumption of the defendants' products did not make plaintiff an inadequate class representative with respect to a claim for economic damages brought under Missouri's consumer fraud statute, known as the "Missouri Merchandising Practices Act," R.S. Mo. § 407.025. *See Craft*, 190 S.W.3d at 380 (Mo. Ct. App. 2005) (trial court properly certified a class under Missouri's consumer fraud statute arising out of defendant cigarette manufacturer's marketing of "light" cigarettes).

Merely being the relative of an employee/non-lawyer of class counsel does not *per se* disqualify the class representative. *Dale*, 204 S.W.3d at 174. Whether such individual cannot serve as a class representative due to a conflict of interest or a likelihood of such a conflict should be within the trial court's discretion, decided on a case-by-case basis. *Id.* Relying on the Missouri Supreme Court case of *Union Planters,* 142 S.W.3d at 740, the court in *Dale* further noted that "[t]he case-by-case approach is logical inasmuch as the primary concern or focus of the trial court, with respect to the adequacy prerequisite, is not the interests of the class representatives and class counsel, but the interests of the absent parties." *Id.*

In *Doyle*, the appellants, objectors opposed a certified class who suffered nuisance and damage to their real property as a result of toxins emitted from a lead smelter, asserted that the settlement was not "fair, reasonable, and adequate" because the representatives did not sufficiently represent the interests of the whole class. 400 S.W.3d at 319–21. Specifically, the appellants insisted that separate representatives should have been appointed to represent the interests of (1) each certified subclass (owners of remediated property versus owners of unremediated property) and (2) current versus previous owners. *Id.* at 322.

The *Doyle* court began by observing that adequacy of representation and fairness of settlement are determinations within the sound discretion of the trial court. *Id.* at 321. It then examined the trial court's findings to determine whether there was an abuse of discretion in its determination. *Id.* at

322. It also noted that that the trial court did its evaluation of the adequacy of representation based on the terms of the settlement. *Id.* (citing *Ring v. Metro. St. Louis Sewer Dist.*, 41 S.W.3d 487, 492 (Mo. Ct. App. 2000)). The *Doyle* court then listed the following factors that the trial court considered in its settlement approval decision: (1) the action was complex and vigorously litigated over a long period of time; (2) both parties incurred considerable expenses; (3) the settlement was a product of an arm's-length negotiation, free of fraud or collusion; (4) further litigation would consume even more time and resources, cause the class additional hardship, uncertainty, and delay in compensation, and possibly jeopardize the settlement altogether; (5) there was no guaranty [*sic*] that the plaintiffs would succeed or recover as much as the settlement offered them if the case were to proceed to trial; (6) with respect to allocation, (a) the entire area was contaminated; (b) reasonable minds can differ on how to quantify loss when viewed through a "nuisance lens;" (c) the plan provided nuisance compensation to all current and previous owners by function of duration of ownership and additional compensation for all current owners' property damage based on remediable surface area; and (d) by the time of settlement in 2012, nearly all properties in the class had undergone remediation, so the sub-class distinction created in 2005 had become largely irrelevant; and (7) the trial court balanced the merits of plaintiffs' case and the risks of trial against the terms of the settlement, considering the nature and extent of their damages with the recovery under the allocation plan, and it ultimately found the arrangement fair, reasonable, and adequate. *Id.*

The *Doyle* court found no abuse of discretion in any of the foregoing determinations by the trial court. *Id.* Additionally, it observed that all the affected properties had now been remediated, thus rendering the distinction moot and that not one of the appellants was actually aggrieved by the absence of subclass representatives. *Id.* at 322–23. The *Doyle* court held that, in sum, the trial court committed no abuse of discretion because the class representatives "quite adequately represented the entire class [. . .] and reached a settlement that was fair and reasonable weighing all relevant factors." *Id.* at 323.

In another case, Plaintiffs brought a class action questioning the validity of an ordinance (and corresponding notices of violations) governing a municipality's automated traffic control signals, commonly referred to as red-light cameras. *Damon v. City of Kansas City*, 419 S.W.3d 162, 169 (Mo. Ct. App. 2013). Defendant dismissed the underlying ordinance violations against plaintiff but did not dismiss the action against the other members of the subclass. *Id.* at 169, n.3. The Missouri Court of Appeals noted that, although no class had been certified, the defendant "cannot avoid the potential class action by merely dismissing the ordinance violation against the named member of the class." *Id.*

Adequacy of class counsel. In addressing the "adequacy" requirement, Missouri courts will also scrutinize class counsel to ensure that there is no conflict of interest that would hinder class counsel's ability to "exercise independent judgment on behalf of the class." *Union Planters*, 142 S.W.3d at 737. However, even when there is an apparent conflict of interest between class counsel and a certified class, decertification is usually *not* an appropriate remedy. *Id.* at 740–42. Rather, the preferable course is to simply replace class counsel and let the class certification stand. *Id.*

Further elucidation was given this requirement in 2008 when the Missouri Supreme Court held that class counsel was adequate despite the fact that one attorney for the class was related to a named plaintiff. *Vandyne*, 242 S.W.3d at 698.

Adequacy of representation for a defendant class is determined similarly to that for a plaintiff class. *City of Excelsior Springs v. Elms Redevelopment Corp.*, 18 S.W.3d 53, 60 (Mo. Ct. App. 2000). The named defendant representatives "must be represented by qualified counsel and they must have common interests with and not be antagonistic towards their fellow class members." *Id.*

v. Class notice is also critical to the adequacy requirement. The Missouri Court of Appeals has noted that "[i]n a class action, notice is a function of adequate representation: Notice's function is to ensure effective representation." *City of Excelsior Springs*, 18 S.W.3d at 59. If a class is cohesive in its interest, minimal notice is required." *Id.*

b. Rule 52.08(b) Requirements

To maintain a class action in Missouri, the plaintiff must prove only one of three 52.08(b) elements. These elements are identical to F.R.C.P. 23 and involve the risks of inconsistent adjudications ((b)(1)); the appropriateness of final injunctive or declaratory relief with respect to the class as a whole ((b)(2)); or the predominance of common questions of fact or law ((b)(3)).

i. (B)(1) requirements. The requirements of 52.08 (b)(1) are met if the prosecution of separate actions by or against individual members of the class would create a risk of (A) inconsistent or varying adjudications with respect to individual members of the class which would establish incompatible standards of conduct for the party opposing the class, or (B) adjudications with respect to individual members of the class which would as a practical matter be dispositive of the interests of the other members not parties to the adjudications or substantially impair or impede their ability to protect their interests. *Centerre Trust Co. v. Jackson Saw Mill Co.*, 736 S.W.2d 486, 497 (Mo. Ct. App. 1987).

Under subsection (b)(1), the interests of the class members must be substantially similar and the duty owed to each member by the defendant must not vary depending on the member. *Id.* Homogeneity of the class will allow (b)(1) certification. *Id.* Classes have been certified under Mo. Sup. Ct. R. 52.08(b)(1) in cases involving revenue bondholders and duties of a trustee as to such bondholders. *Id.*

ii. (B)(2) requirements. A plaintiff may satisfy 52.08(b)(2) by proving that the party opposing the class has acted or refused to act on grounds generally applicable to the class, thereby making appropriate final injunctive relief or corresponding declaratory relief with respect to the class as a whole. Mo. Sup. Ct. R. 52.08(b)(2). Where the state refused to refund sales taxes, the dissenting justices in *Charles v. Spradling* opined that the plaintiffs had satisfied their 52.08(b) burden under prong (2) because the state had "refused to act on grounds generally applicable to the class." 524 S.W.2d 820, 824 (Mo. banc 1975).

A class seeking primarily injunctive or declaratory relief may be certified under Mo. Sup. Ct. R. 52.08(b)(2), despite an accompanying request for compensatory damages. *Harris*, 766 S.W.2d 80. The trial court may bifurcate the case for trial to facilitate administration of the claims of the class, as was done in *Harris* at the trial level. (The original *Harris* decision was reversed by the Missouri Court of Appeals on other grounds.) *See Harris*, 622 S.W.2d 239 (Mo. Ct. App. 1981).

iii. (B)(3) requirements. A plaintiff may satisfy 52.08(b)(3) if "the court finds that the questions of law or fact common to the members of the class predominate over any questions affecting only individual members, and that a class action is superior to other available methods for the fair and efficient adjudication of the controversy."

Predominance. With respect to 52.08(b)(3), the court must first determine whether the question is "common" or "individual." *Craft*, 190 S.W.3d at 382. A question is considered "individual" if "to make a *prima facie* showing on a given question, the members of a proposed class will need to present the evidence that varies from member to member." *Id. See also Hope*, 353 S.W.3d at 81. A question is deemed "common" if "the same evidence will suffice for each member to make a prima facie showing." *Id. See also Hope*, 353 S.W.3d at 81.

The trial court must determine whether questions common to the class predominate over any individual questions. The predominance requirement does not demand every single issue in the case be common to all the class members, but only that there are substantial common issues which override the individual issues. *Hootselle*, at 134; *Karr v. Kan. City Life Ins. Co.*, 702 S.W.3d 1, 36–37 (Mo. Ct. App. 2024) ("fundamental question is whether the group aspiring to class status is seeking to remedy a common legal grievance"); *Smith v. American Family Mutual Insurance Co.*, 289 S.W.3d 675, 688 (Mo. Ct. App. 2009) (one single common issue can satisfy the predominance requirement, and the single predominant issue need not even be dispositive of the case); *Plubell v. Merck & Co., Inc.*, 289 S.W.3d 707, 712–13 (Mo. Ct. App. 2009) (a single common issue maybe the overriding one in the litigation, despite the fact that the suit also entails numerous remaining individual questions). The predominance issue may not be dispositive of the controversy or even be determinative of the liability issues involved. *Hootselle*, at 134; *Smith*, 289 S.W.3d at 675; *Clark*, 106 S.W.3d at 488. Indeed, the need for inquiry as to individual damages does not preclude a finding of predominance. *Id.* A single common issue may be the overriding one in the litigation, despite the fact that the suit also entails numerous remaining individual questions. *Id.* (citing *Conte & Newberg* § 4:25 at 172). Also, the fact that an affirmative defense may be available against certain individual class members and affect them differently does not, by itself, show that individual issues predominate. *Clark*, 106 S.W.3d at 488. The trial court can resolve individual questions, particularly those relating to damages and defenses, after making a determination on the predominant issue. *Id.*

How a court will rule on the issue of predominance depends on the allegations contained in the complaint. In *Craft*, the plaintiffs alleged that the defendant cigarette manufacturer falsely represented that "light" cigarettes delivered lower tar and nicotine and manipulated test results. 190 S.W.3d 368. The Missouri Supreme Court, in upholding the trial court's certification of a Missouri class of "light" cigarette smokers, found that the plaintiffs' allegations focused on the condition and labeling of the product at the time it was sold, and that the defendant's liability was not dependent on each consumer's individual smoking behavior. *Id.* at 382. As a result, the Court held that an individual's smoking behavior, an "individual" question, did not predominate over the "common" questions of liability. *Id.* at 383–84.

In cases where an individual factual issue may not predominate, if the allegations give rise to some form of uniform damages, such as nominal damages, predominance may be found. The Missouri Supreme Court has said predominance can be seen in actions where nominal damages would be common to all members of the class. *Green v. Fred Weber, Inc.*, 254 S.W.3d 874, 882 (Mo. banc 2008). This can be enough to satisfy the predominance requirement even where the nature and extent of individual damages would not be a common question. *Id.*

In *Hootselle*, the Missouri Supreme Court was presented with a claim by corrections officers alleging that they were not paid for certain pre- and post-shift activities related to their employment. 624 S.W.3d at 129. In opposing the class, the Missouri Department of Corrections complained that individual questions of damages predominated because officers spent varying amounts of time performing these activities, and because the proof of the time spent was unreliable. *Id.* at 134. The Supreme Court upheld the trial court's refusal to decertify the class notwithstanding the existence of these individual damage questions, noting that common questions of law or fact may be overriding even though the suit also entails numerous individual questions. *Id.* at 134.

The Missouri Court of Appeals held that a trial court granting class certification based upon unjust enrichment claims did not abuse its discretion even though elements of the plaintiffs' claims necessarily turned upon individual experiences. *Hale*, 231 S.W.3d at 225. In *Hale*, the plaintiffs alleged that defendant retailer's policies resulted in chronic understaffing and caused employees to miss promised breaks and work off the clock without compensation. *Id.* at 215. The court highlighted that the granting of class certification by the trial court was proper since the unjust enrichment claim did not go to the named plaintiff's conduct but rather to defendant's conduct. *Id.* at 226. The court also noted that Missouri does not require that common issues advance resolution of the litigation for them to predominate over the individual ones. *Id.*

Meyer v. Fluor Corp., 220 S.W.3d 712 (Mo. banc 2007), a leading case on class actions handed down by the Missouri Supreme Court in 2007, is particularly instructive on the predominance issue. In *Meyer*, the plaintiffs brought a claim for medical monitoring of a class of children allegedly exposed to lead and other chemicals generated by the defendants at their facility near Herculaneum, Missouri. *Id.* at 713–14. The trial court denied class certification, which the Court of Appeals affirmed, finding that individual issues concerning each putative class members' exposure to lead and the potential risk of harm predominated over any common questions. *Meyer ex rel. Coplin v. Fluor Corp.*, 2006 Mo. Ct. App. Lexis 499, at *10–11 (Mo. Ct. App. Apr. 18, 2006). The Missouri Supreme Court reversed, recognizing for the first time an independent claim for medical monitoring damages in Missouri. *Meyer*, 220 S.W.3d at 717 (Mo. banc 2007). Moreover, the Missouri Supreme Court held that class certification of the medical monitoring claims of children supposedly exposed to lead contamination was appropriate because the common issues of law and fact predominated over any individual issues. *Id.* at 719. Similarly, in another case involving the same defendant and its lead producing facilities, the Missouri Court of Appeals held that the trial court properly certified a class of landowners who alleged that their property diminished in value as a result of lead contamination produced by the defendants' facilities. *Doyle*, 199 S.W.3d 784. In upholding the certification of a class of landowners, the Missouri Court of Appeals noted that although there were individual questions relating to the class, the common questions relating to liability predominated over the individual questions. *Id.* at 789–90.

Furthermore, relying upon *Meyer*, the court of appeals in *Elsea v. U.S. Eng'g Co.* held that the trial court abused its discretion in finding that the predominance requirement was not met because, "like Meyer, '[i]t is the common fact of exposure to [asbestos] from a single source (Defendants' 1983-84 Courthouse air-handling unit retrofit project), at a level which Plaintiffs allege to be medically significant, "that is the common and overriding issue in Plaintiff[s'] case" and that "the individual factors identified by the circuit court are not particularly relevant because the need for monitoring is based on a common threshold of exposure." 463 S.W.3d 409, 419, 422–23 (Mo. Ct. App. 2015).

Worth noting, however, is that notwithstanding *Meyer* and *Elsea*, medical monitoring claims do need to, in fact, advance the plaintiffs' interests and address a potential future need to meet the superiority requirement. In *Moore v. Scroll Compressors, LLC*, 632 S.W.3d 810 (Mo. Ct. App. 2021), the Court of Appeals affirmed denial of class certification as to a claim seeking medical monitoring as a result of exposure to metalworking fluids. In that case, as distinguished from *Meyer* and *Elsea*, the named plaintiffs had already received all the testing that was being sought on behalf of the class and manifested a present, rather than latent, injury. *Moore*, 623 S.W.3d at 817. Additionally, because the proposed program included a provision that those who did not currently manifest evidence of an MWF-related respiratory disease—i.e., evidence of present injury—would not be eligible for monitoring, the Court determined that the class action for medical monitoring would address only present, and not latent, injuries and thus found that a class action would not be superior. *Id.* at 818.

In *State ex rel. McKeage v. Cordonnier*, plaintiffs sued defendants in a five-count petition for charging a document preparation fee for purchasing a boat. 357 S.W.3d 597, 598–99 (Mo. banc 2012). Plaintiffs sought certification of a nationwide class. *Id.* at 599. The circuit court, however, certified a class that was limited to contracts entered into within the state. *Id.* The Missouri Supreme Court held that there was predominance pursuant to Section 507.070.1(3), RSMo 2000 because (1) the allegation of potential differences in state law was insufficient to defeat the class; (2) there were sufficient common issues of fact that favor class certification, notably the purchase agreement documents required the application of Missouri law to any claim; and (3) due to a forum selection clause, all claims arising from the documents drafted by Bass Pro were required to be litigated in Greene County (whether the class member resided in or out of state). *Id.* at 601.

In *Hope v. Nissan N. Am., Inc.*, plaintiffs sued defendants regarding a cosmetic bubbling defect in the dashboard of certain vehicles. 353 S.W.3d at 72. The trial court certified the class. *Id.* On appeal, Nissan argued that plaintiff failed to show that common issues predominate for the following of plaintiffs' claims: violation of the Missouri Merchandising Practices Act (MMPA), section 407.025.3, Breach of Express Warranty, and Breach of Implied Warranty. *Id.* at 80. Regarding the MMPA, Nissan argued that common issues did not predominate in the class because (1) plaintiffs were required to show deception, ascertainable loss, and causation, and the individual issues on these elements overwhelmed common ones, and (2) for the omission claims, which require scienter, plaintiffs were required to show at a minimum that defendant had knowledge or reason to know of the defect at the time of the sale to each class member. *Id.* at 82. To these contentions, the court held the individual issues were not so numerous for purposes of the MMPA claims as to negate class certification notably (1) because the trial court can revoke certifications as the matter proceeds, and (2) because class treatment could reasonably be viewed as a superior means of adjudicating such claims as Nissan's conduct is the focus of many of the MMPA claims. The court relied on *Plubell v. Merck & Co., Inc.*, 289 S.W.3d 707, 713–15 (Mo. Ct. App. 2009), which held (1) it is the defendant's conduct, not its intent, which determines whether a violation has occurred, and thus Merck's knowledge of Vioxx's risks at the time of each member's purchase was not something that required the plaintiffs to present individualized proof; (2) because the plaintiffs alleged Merck misrepresented Vioxx throughout the entire class period, individualized inquiries into Merck's representations as to when each class member purchased Vioxx would be unnecessary; (3) evidence of each physician's or consumer's reliance on Merck's misrepresentation was not required as "reliance is not an element of deception or misrepresentation" under the MMPA's regulations and Missouri's case law; (4) MMPA does not require plaintiffs to demonstrate an "ascertainable loss" by individually showing the cost of alternative therapy or that the unlawful practice caused the class member to make the "purchase" in question, but instead the court found that the "benefit-of-the-bargain" rule alleged by the plaintiffs was "applicable in MMPA cases to meet the element of ascertainable loss." *Id.* at 82–85.

The court further held in *Hope* that the trial court abused its discretion in certifying a class for the breach of express warranty claim under Rule 52.08(b)(3) because there would have to be an individualized inquiry whether putative class members (1) read the material distributed by Nissan, (2) whether the defect in the dashboard actually manifested, (3) whether the class member was damaged as a result, and (4) whether the class member timely notified Nissan of the nonconformity. *Id.* at 89.

Finally, the court in *Hope* held that the trial court abused its discretion in certifying a class for the breach of implied warranty of merchantability claim under Rule 52.08(b)(3) because class membership would require individual determinations of whether each putative class member actually experienced manifestation of the bubbling defect, so as to be able to maintain a cause of action for breach of implied warranty of merchantability, and then, subsequently, individual inquiries into the extent of (a) damage sustained, (b) whether the alleged defect was the cause in fact or proximate cause of the damage sustained, and, finally, (c) whether each individual class member notified Nissan. *Id.* at 91–92.

In *Triplett v. Mo. Hwys. & Transp. Comm'n*, the Missouri Court of Appeals held that the trial court abused its discretion in certifying a class action with a plaintiff class consisting of all persons who sustained injuries or property damage during a five-year period as a result of wet-pavement crashes on a 1.3-mile section of Interstate 44 in Phelps County, Missouri (the I-44 section) because plaintiffs failed to prove that the common issues predominated over the individual issues in the case. 372 S.W.3d 90, 92, and 94 (Mo. Ct. App. 2012). In particular, the court in *Triplett* observed that "[b]ecause of the fact-specific nature of causation, personal injury cases, even those involving large numbers of plaintiffs, are rarely amenable to class action treatment." *Id.* at 94 (citing *Amchem Products, Inc. v. Windsor*, 521 U.S. 591 (1997)). *See also Ogg v. Mediacom, LLC*, 382 S.W.3d 108, 111 (Mo. Ct. App. 2012) (trial court did not abuse its discretion in decertifying a class on the grounds that individual issues of class standing and liability would make the class unmanageable).

Superiority. Mo. Sup. Ct. R. 52.08(b)(3) contains four factors relevant to the superiority determination. *See Craft*, 190 S.W.3d at 378–79. The superiority requirement requires the trial court to balance, in terms of fairness and efficiency, the merits of a class action in resolving the controversy against those of alternative available methods of adjudication. *Dale,* 204 S.W.3d at 181. For example, the trial court may consider the inability of the poor or uninformed to enforce their rights, and the improbability that large numbers of class members would possess the initiative to litigate individually. *Hootselle*, at *17–18; *Dale*, 204 S.W.3d at 182. However, the primary focus of the superiority analysis is the efficiency of the class action over other available methods of adjudication. *Id.* at 182.

While there may be effective alternative methods of adjudicating the controversy in question, that fact alone does not mean they are superior when balanced against resolution by class action. *Id.* at 182–83. Conversely, failure to certify an action on the sole ground that it would be unmanageable is disfavored. *Craft*, 190 S.W.3d. at 386. While manageability is a consideration that "encompasses the whole range of practical problems that may render the class action format inappropriate for a particular suit," the existence of administrative complications in managing the distribution of different damage awards to a class does not suggest that a trial court abused its discretion in finding a class manageable. *Id.* at 387. Even if the class action seems unmanageable, a class action will be held to be a superior form of adjudication where the defendants fail to both provide any legal authority to support their claim that an alternative forum is superior, and provide any rationale beyond conclusions explaining why, in the absence of such authority, they should prevail. *Id.*

Whether an administrative adjudication would provide a more advantageous procedure than a class action may depend on the type of remedy that could be awarded by the agency and the general attitude of the agency toward the issues and problems raised by the claimants. *Craft*, 190 S.W.3d at 382 (citing *Wright, Miller & Kane, Federal Practice and Procedure: Civil 2d Section* 1779, at 561 (1986)).

Finally, in *Elsea v. U.S. Eng'g Co.*, 463 S.W.3d 409, 423, a class action involving medical monitoring for a class exposed to asbestos fibers during a courthouse renovation, the circuit court denied class certification because the "circuit court found that a class action was not superior to other available methods of adjudicating a medical monitoring claim because the presence of so many individualized issues would make managing a class action inordinately difficult." In reversing the lower court, the Court of Appeals observed that "our Missouri Supreme Court has expressly concluded that 'individual factors' are not relevant in a medical monitoring claim, we again fail to see how the circuit court may rely upon 'individual factors' as a basis for denying class certification—whether as a basis for its predominance or its superiority conclusions." *Id.* at 424. In finding the superiority method was met in that case, the court of appeals in *Elsea* further observed that the circuit court is empowered to craft class participation rules designed to protect both the putative class members and the defendants; for example, there is nothing prohibiting the circuit court from establishing an "opt out" procedure whereby putative class members who do not wish to participate in medical monitoring would have the choice of "opting out" of the class action, and conversely, for those putative class members wishing to participate in the class action, the circuit court has the power to dictate measures enabling Defendants the opportunity to assert defenses to certain categories of class members within the class action. *Id.*

c. Rule 52.08(c) Requirements

Rule 52.08 simply requires that the class be provided "the best notice practicable under the circumstances, including individual notice to all members who can be identified through reasonable effort." *Doyle*, 400 S.W.3d at 324 (citing Rule 52.08(c)(2)). The notice must advise that: (1) members can opt out by a specified date, (2) the judgment will include all members who don't opt out, and (3) members may enter an appearance by counsel. *Id.* For instance, in *Doyle*, the Court also found that the trial court exercised appropriate discretion in approving the form notice with a blank date at that time in anticipation of appeal, as indeed further litigation did ensue. *Id.*

4. THE TRIAL COURT HAS DISCRETION IN CERTIFYING A CLASS

Determination of whether an action should proceed as a class action under Missouri Supreme Court Rule 52.08 ultimately rests within the sound discretion of the trial court. *Karr*, 702 S.W.3d at 34; *Plubell,* 289 S.W.3d at 711; *Doyle,* 199 S.W.3d at 787; *Union Planters*, 142 S.W.3d at 735; *Clark*, 106 S.W.3d 483. *See also McKeage*, 357 S.W.3d at 599. A trial court need not hold a full evidentiary hearing before certifying a class. *Byrd*, 956 S.W.2d at 380. When it is unclear from the petition whether class certification may be granted, however, the trial court is to allow pre-class certification discovery so that the plaintiff may be afforded the opportunity to prove the class certification prerequisites. *State ex rel. Coffman Group, L.L.C. v. Sweeney*, 219 S.W.3d 763, 767 (Mo. Ct. App. 2005). A trial court, however, does not have authority to conduct a preliminary inquiry into the merits of a lawsuit when it is determining whether the lawsuit may be maintained as a class action. *Eisen v. Carlisle & Jacquelin*, 417 U.S. 156, 177 (1974); *Meyer,* 220 S.W.3d at 715; *Craft*, 190 S.W.3d at 377. In the absence of a request for findings of fact and conclusions of law, Missouri trial courts are not required to make findings or conclusions in support of its class certification decision under Mo. Sup. Ct. R. 52.08. *Dale,* 204 S.W.3d at 163.

Under 52.08(c)(1), an order determining whether a class action is to be maintained "may be conditional and may be altered or amended before the decision on the merits." *Reinhold v. Fee Fee Trunk Sewer, Inc.*, 664 S.W.2d 599, 602 (Mo. Ct. App. 1984). Moreover, "[b]ecause class certification can be modified as the case progresses, courts should err in favor of, and not against, certifying a class." *Doyle,* 199 S.W.3d at 787–88. *See also Karen S. Little, L.L.C. v. Drury Inns, Inc.*, 306 S.W.3d 577, 580 (Mo. Ct. App. 2010).

Appellate courts in Missouri will reverse a trial court's decision to certify a class "only if its ruling is so arbitrary and unreasonable as to shock one's sense of justice and indicate a lack of careful consideration." *Plubell*, 289 S.W.3d at 711. But in a recent decision, the trial court's decision to deny class certification was reversed by the Court of Appeals. In *Lucas Subway MidMo, Inc. v. Mandatory Poster Agency, Inc.*, 524 S.W.3d 116 (Mo. Ct. App. 2017), Lucas Subway brought an action against MPA, Inc. for the unauthorized practice of law. The trial court denied class certification because it found the class to be overbroad, indefinite, and that the suit did not meet the requirements of Rule 52.08(a) and (b). The Court of Appeals reversed the trial court's decision denying class certification and remanded the action. The appellate court found that the class was not overbroad where the initial definition included members who had not been injured or did not wish to pursue claims against the defendant. Lucas Subway, 524 S.W.3d at 127.

The appellate court further found that the circuit court erred in determining the class to be a "waste of judicial resources." The refund offer and separate state action did not bar a class action on a different claim offering different remedies. *Id.* at 129.

Next, the appeal considered, and rejected, the trial court's rulings on the requirements of Rule 52.08(a).

- Numerosity. The appellate court determined that for a claim for unauthorized practice of law, satisfaction with the legal services is immaterial. While 170 persons had accepted refunds from MPA, Inc., the outstanding 1,555 purchasers are enough to satisfy the numerosity component regardless of their satisfaction with the legal services.
- Commonality and Typicality. The appellate court found it significant that all purchasers received the same form corporate minutes from MPA, Inc. and paid the same amount; although they were personalized to each company, that specialization was not enough to prevent a finding of commonality or typicality.
- Adequacy. The trial court found Lucas Subway to be an inadequate class representative because the company chose to proceed with the class action rather than accept the refund and that it would not be adequately protecting the class members. The appellate court determined, however, Lucas Subway posits additional statutory damages for the unauthorized practice of law not available under the refund. The remedy sought is therefore not duplicative and provides a benefit to the class members even with added costs of a lawsuit.

Id. at 129–31.

5. DUE PROCESS CONSIDERATIONS

Mo. Sup. Ct. R. 52.08(e) provides that "a class action may not be dismissed or compromised without the approval of the court, and notice of the proposed dismissal or compromise shall be given to all members of the class in such manner as the court directs." *See also Byrd,* 956 S.W.2d at 377.

See, however, *Ressler*, where the plaintiff filed a class action against the defendant alleging gender discrimination in compensation. 375 S.W.3d at 134. At issue on appeal was whether the trial court erred by failing to rule on the certification of the putative class action *before* considering and granting a pre-certification dispositive motion regarding the appellant's individual claims. *Id.* at 135. The Missouri Court of Appeals held that the trial court was not required to make a determination on Rule 52.08[2] certification before proceeding with dispositive motions on individual issues. *Id.* at 134 and 140. The appellate court held that a grant of summary judgment in favor of the defendant on an individual plaintiff's claims before the putative class is certified does not have any preclusive effect on the future claims of anyone that might have been included in the putative class but for plaintiff's shortcomings. *Id.* at 138. The appellate court further concluded that the claims of the putative class

[2] Rule 52.08(c)(1) states, in part, that "[a]s soon as practicable after the commencement of an action brought as a class action, the court shall determine by order whether it is to be so maintained."

members here are not before the court, and there was no prejudicial effect on their individual claims by granting the summary judgment motion. *Id.*

Notice in a class certified under Mo. Sup. Ct. R. 52.08(b)(3) must satisfy due process, which means that it must be "reasonably calculated, under all the circumstances, to apprise interested parties of the pendency of the action and afford them an opportunity to present their objections." *Byrd*, 956 S.W.2d at 385; *Clark*, 106 S.W.3d 483. The notice must contain an adequate, objective description of the proceedings so that it may be understood by the average absentee class member. *Byrd*, 956 S.W.2d at 385.

The trial court must evaluate the fairness of any proposed settlement offered on behalf of the class, and it must send proper notice to all class members before holding a fairness hearing or requiring absent class members to decide to opt out or file a claim. *Id.* at 385. If the trial court fails or refuses to exercise its discretion in such matters, a writ of mandamus may be issued to compel the trial court to do so. *Id.* at 376.

"[N]on-named class members . . . who have objected in a timely manner to approval of the settlement at the fairness hearing have the power to bring an appeal without first intervening." *Bachman v. A.G. Edwards, Inc.*, 344 S.W.3d 260, 265 n.3 (Mo. Ct. App. 2011) (citing *Devlin v. Scardelletti*, 536 U.S. 1, 10 (2005)); *see also Paulson v. Dynamic Pet Prods., LLC*, 560 S.W.3d 583, 589 (Mo. Ct. App. 2018). *Devlin* does not apply only to Rule 52.08(b)(2) class actions where class members do not have the opportunity to opt out. *Id.* It also applies to class action objectors appealing from Rule 52.08(b)(3). *Id.* Although the *Doyle* Court uncovered no Missouri case on point, it relied on well-reasoned authority from other jurisdictions holding that belated objections are deemed waived. 400 S.W.3d at 321. Where the factual and procedural history of the case spanned over a decade, the Court held the appellants' tardiness was unjustified and their point untimely. *Id.*

6. CLASS CERTIFICATION IS APPROPRIATE UNDER MISSOURI'S CONSUMER PROTECTION STATUTE

Like many states, Missouri has enacted a state consumer protection statute. The statute, referred to as the "Missouri Merchandising Practices Act," R.S. Mo. § 407.010 *et seq.*, or "MMPA," proscribes a wide array of unfair activities and is broad in scope. Missouri courts have said that the "purpose of Missouri's Merchandising Practices Act is to preserve fundamental honesty, fair play and right dealings in public transactions." *Schuchmann v. Air Services Heating & Conditioning, Inc.*, 199 S.W.3d 228, 233 (Mo. Ct. App. 2006). Specifically, the Act prohibits "deception, fraud, false pretense, false promise, misrepresentation, unfair practice or the concealment, suppression, or omission of any material fact in connection with the sale or advertisement of any merchandise in trade or commerce." § 407.020.1. The Act permits civil actions by any person who purchased or leased "merchandise primarily for personal, family or household purposes," and this appears to exclude claims brought by businesses or other non-consumers. § 407.025.1. In addition to awarding actual damages, the court may, in its discretion award punitive damages and attorneys' fees to the prevailing party. § 407.025.1. A jury must determine whether punitive damages are appropriate under the Act. *Scott v. Blue Springs Ford Sales, Inc.*, 176 S.W.3d 140 (Mo. banc 2005). Critically, a plaintiff need not prove scienter to prevail under the MMPA. *Plubell,* 289 S.W.3d at 713.

The Missouri Merchandising Practices Act specifically authorizes class actions where an unlawful practice "has caused similar injury to numerous other persons." § 407.025.2. Previously, classes certified under the MMPA were "opt-in" classes only, meaning that to be a member of a certified class under the MMPA, class members had to take affirmative steps to "opt-in" to the class. Realizing the inherent difficulties of "opt-in" classes, the Missouri legislature amended the MMPA to make classes certified under the MMPA the more traditional "opt-out" variety. *See* § 407.025.4. Under the Act, the requirements for class certification are essentially identical to the requirements under Rule 52.08 and Federal Rule 23. §407.025.3. *Plubell*, 289 S.W.3d at 712.

An illustrative case demonstrating the breadth of the MMPA in a class action context is *Plubell v. Merck*, 289 S.W.3d 707 (Mo. Ct. App. 2009). In *Plubell*, the trial court certified a state-wide class of Missouri residents who claimed Merck violated the terms of the MMPA by failing to disclose and concealing the health risks associated with Vioxx, a painkiller manufactured and sold by the defendant drug company. On appeal of the trial court's certification order, the Missouri Court of Appeals ruled that the trial court was correct in certifying the class under the MMPA. Specifically, the appellate court rejected Merck's contention that the "predominance" requirement was not satisfied because there were individualized questions with respect to each class member's purchase of Vioxx. 289 S.W.3d at 712–13. Instead, the court ruled that because the issue of whether Merck failed to disclose and concealed Vioxx's safety risk was a common question for all Missouri class members, the predominance requirement was satisfied and certification was appropriate. *See also Glen v. Fairway Independent Mortgage Corp.*, 265 F.R.D. 476, 481–82 (E.D. Mo. 2010) (federal court certified a class under the Missouri Merchandising Practices Act for failing to disclose certain information in mortgage contracts).

7. TOLLING OF STATUTE OF LIMITATIONS

Missouri courts, like federal courts, recognize that the filing of a class action may toll the statute of limitations. *Hyatt Corporation v. Occidental Fire & Casualty*, 801 S.W.2d 382, 389 (Mo. Ct. App. 1990). Note that only the pendency of a Missouri class action has a tolling effect; pending class actions in other jurisdictions do not. *City of Columbia v. Spectra Commc'ns Grp., LLC*, No. ED109769, 2022 Mo. App. LEXIS 456, at *19 (Ct. App. July 19, 2022) (citing *Rolwing v. Nestle Holdings, Inc.*, 437 S.W.3d 180, 184 (Mo. banc 2014)).

8. APPEALS UNDER RULE 52.08(F)

Under R.S. Mo. § 512.020(3) and Missouri Supreme Court Rule 52.08(f), orders granting or denying class action certification are of the type of order that may be appealed—so long as the Court of Appeals, in its discretion, permits such an appeal. R.S. Mo. § 512.020(3). *See Craft v. Philip Morris Cos., Inc.*, 190 S.W.3d 368, 376 (Mo. Ct. App. 2005); *see also Stagner v. Wells Fargo Bank, N.A.*, 632 S.W.3d 443, 446 n.1 (Mo. Ct. App. 2021) (citing *Younker v. Inv. Realty, Inc.*, 461 S.W.3d 1, 13 (Mo. App. S.D. 2015)).

A petition for permission to appeal is "timely" if it is filed "within ten days of the entry of the order of which the party complains." Mo. Sup. Ct. Rule 84.035. Without an order from the appellate court, however, the appeal is simply from an interlocutory order and is not appealable. *Karen Little, LLC v. Brinker Missouri, Inc.*, 185 S.W.3d 784, 785 (Mo. Ct. App. 2006). Pursuant to Rule 52.08(f), "[t]he filing of a petition shall not stay the proceedings in the trial court unless the trial judge or the appellate court so orders."

9. TREATMENT OF ARBITRATION CLAUSES WITH CLASS ACTION WAIVER

In *Brewer v. Missouri Title Loans, Inc.*, 323 S.W.3d 18 (Mo. banc 2010), the Missouri Supreme Court initially affirmed the trial court's judgment insofar as it held that the class arbitration waiver was unconscionable and reversed that part of the judgment ordering that the claim be submitted to an arbitrator to determine suitability for class arbitration. *Brewer v. Mo. Title Loans, Inc.* 364 S.W.3d 486, 487 (Mo. banc 2012). The Missouri Supreme Court held that the appropriate remedy was to strike the entire arbitration agreement. *Id.* The United States Supreme Court vacated *Brewer* in *Missouri Title Loans, Inc. v. Brewer*, 131 S. Ct. 2875, 179 L. Ed. 2d 1184, (U.S. 2011), and remanded the case to the Missouri Supreme Court for further consideration in light of its holding in *AT&T Mobility, LLC, v. Concepcion*, 131 S. Ct. 1740, 179 L. Ed. 2d 742 (2011). *Id.* Subsequently, in applying *Concepcion*, the Missouri Supreme Court found that the presence and enforcement of the class arbitration waiver did not make the arbitration clause unconscionable. *Id.* The Court instead applied traditional Missouri contract law in looking at the agreement as a whole to determine the conscionability of the arbitration provision. *Id.* The Court held that Brewer had demonstrated unconscionability in the formation of the agreement. *Id.* As a result, the judgment finding the class arbitration waiver unconscionable was affirmed because the entire arbitration agreement was deemed unconscionable and unenforceable. *Id.* at 496. The judgment was reversed, however, to the extent that it severed the class arbitration waiver and required an arbitrator to determine the propriety of class arbitration. The case was remanded for further proceedings.

In *Robinson v. Title Lenders, Inc.*, at issue was whether a consumer arbitration agreement containing a class action waiver was unconscionable and, therefore, unenforceable. 364 S.W.3d 505 and 506 (Mo. banc 2012). The defendant argued that its arbitration agreement containing a class waiver was enforceable and should result in the dismissal of a lawsuit brought by the borrower. *Id.* at 506. The borrower sought to have the arbitration provision or its class waiver declared unenforceable so that she could proceed with a class action suit or class arbitration against the company. *Id.* The Missouri Supreme Court held that the trial court erred in finding that the company's arbitration agreement was unconscionable based on its class waiver. *Id.* at 506–07. It further held that, "*Concepcion* indicates that, in light of the [Federal Arbitration Act's] section 2, the trial court instead should have adjudicated whether the arbitration agreement was enforceable in light of Borrower's evidence relevant to her claims regarding ordinary state-law principles that governed contracts but that did not single out or disfavor arbitration." *Id.* at 507. Thus, the Missouri Supreme Court reversed the trial court's judgment and remanded the case back to the trial court for consideration of the borrower's unconscionability claims that were not related to the arbitration agreement's class waiver. *Id.*

Similar to *Robinson*, in the case of *Lopez v. H & R Block*, 429 S.W.3d 497, 503 (Mo. Ct. App. 2014), the Missouri Court of Appeals held that "[t]he trial court clearly erred in finding the arbitration provision in the CSA unenforceable based on public policy concerns regarding class waivers." *Id.* (citing *Brewer*, 364 S.W.3d at 487–88 (holding the FAA does not permit finding an arbitration agreement unconscionable on the basis of a class action waiver alone)). Nevertheless, the *Lopez* court remanded the case to the trial court for the trial court to consider Mr. Lopez's other claims of unconscionability under ordinary state law principles, notably the sufficiency of the arbitration opt out procedure. *Id.* Subsequently, the *Lopez* case came back up on appeal again, and this time the Missouri Court of Appeals affirmed the trial court's order denying H&R Block's motion to compel arbitration of Plaintiff's claims because the plaintiff had opted out of the 2012 arbitration agreement with H&R Block. *Id.* at 228. The appellate court did not rule on whether the 2011 arbitration agreement with H&R Block was unconscionable because that issue was not before the court on appeal.

Id.

Furthermore, in *Hobbs v. TAMKO Building Products, Inc.*, the Court of Appeals held that an arbitration provision was not enforceable because defendant failed in its burden to prove a valid, enforceable agreement to arbitrate plaintiffs' disputes for the following reasons: (1) plaintiffs did not accept the arbitration agreement by merely purchasing the shingles, (2) plaintiffs never signed any document agreeing to the arbitration clause in the warranty, and that (3) plaintiffs did not form a contract with defendant by simply "wrapping its fine print around packaging the 'ultimate purchaser' will likely never see because it is torn off and discarded." 479 S.W.3d 147, 150–52 (Mo. Ct. App. 2015).

In *Ford Motor Credit Co., LLC v. Jones*, No. WD80809, 2018 Mo. Ct. App. LEXIS 272 (Mo. Ct. App. Mar. 20, 2018), the Court of Appeals was called upon to address the question of which issues were to be decided by the courts, and which issues had been delegated to the arbitrator. In that case, which involved a counterclaim on behalf of a class in the context of vehicle financing agreements, the trial court determined that Ford's arbitration agreement was unconscionable and unenforceable, and that Ford had, through its conduct, waived any right it may have to insist upon arbitration. On appeal, Ford argued that because the arbitration clause delegated "[c]laims regarding the interpretation, scope, or validity of this provision, or arbitrability of any issue," to the arbitrator, it was the arbitrator, and not the trial court, who was required to rule upon the enforceability, unconscionability, and waiver of the arbitration clause. *Ford Motor Credit*, at *17–21. Placing great significance upon the breadth of the clause in particular and the absence of any disagreement as to the formation of the agreement, the appellate court agreed and the matter was reversed and remanded to permit the arbitrator to rule upon those issues.

The question of the enforceability of a delegation provision was again raised in *Fogelsong v. Joe Machens Auto. Grp. Inc.*, 600 S.W.3d 288 (Mo. Ct. App. 2020). In that case, the Western District characterized the agreement to incorporate the rules of the American Arbitration Association as an agreement to abide by the delegation provisions contained therein. *Fogelsong*, at 298–99. The Court further noted that because this agreement to delegate questions of arbitrability to an arbitrator is itself a distinct arbitration agreement, it "should be considered separately from the underlying arbitration agreement." *Id.*, at 299. Because the challenges made to the delegation provision relied upon the same arguments challenging the arbitration agreement itself, the Court of Appeals upheld the delegation provision and reversed with instructions to stay the matter and compel arbitration. *Id.*

Finally, the Missouri Supreme Court handed down a decision regarding the proper timing of an interlocutory appeal for an order involving a motion to compel arbitration. In *Sanford v. CenturyTel of Missouri, LLC*, the Missouri Supreme Court held that an internet and phone service provider's appeal of a trial court order denying its motion to compel arbitration of a customer's claims was dismissed because the provider did not timely file its appeal within 10 days of entry of the order denying arbitration, but rather, it had filed its appeal thirty-nine days after the trial court entered its order. 490 S.W. 3d 717 (Mo. banc 2016). It further explained that because the order did not dispose of all claims in the case, it was an interlocutory order that was appealable under Mo. Rev. Stat. § 435.440 immediately upon entry and should have been brought within 10 days of the entry of that order. *Id.*

10. ATTORNEYS' FEES

In *Berry v. Volkswagen Group of Am., Inc.*, the Missouri Supreme Court upheld a trial court's award of attorneys' fees based on a lodestar amount of $3,087,320 and applying a multiplier of 2.0 for a total award of $6,174,640 for attorneys who successfully represented a class of consumers who sued

Volkswagen Group of America Inc. over defective windows. 397 S.W.3d 425, 429 (Mo. banc 2013). The Court, in a split *en banc* ruling, found the trial court had properly calculated the award for class counsel and declined to disturb it, rejecting Volkswagen's challenge to the lodestar amount and the multiplier the trial court applied. *Id.* In particular, the Court held that "the lodestar amount was within the trial court's discretion. Further, while this is the first time this court is addressing the use of a multiplier, there is no reason to usurp the longstanding principle in Missouri that our trial judges are considered experts in determining the proper amount of attorneys' fees." *Id.* at 427–28.

In determining whether the use of the multiplier was appropriate, the Court began by noting that trial courts should avoid awarding a multiplier based upon facts that it considered in its initial determination of the lodestar amount. *Berry*, 397 S.W.3d at 433 (citations omitted). The *Berry* Court then found that the trial court's use of a multiplier appropriate in this case because the trial court found (1) "[t]he fee to be received by class counsel was always contingent, unlike the fees received by counsel for Defendant;" (2) "[t]aking this case precluded class counsel from accepting other employment that would have been less risky;" and (3) "[t]he time required by the demands of preparing this cause for trial delayed work on class counsel's other work." Accordingly, the *Berry* Court held that "[t]hese findings support a finding that a multiplier was necessary to ensure a market fee that compensated class counsel for taking this case in lieu of working less risky cases on an hourly basis." *Id.*

While not in the class context, the Western District Court of Appeals considered a question of attorneys' fees under fee shifting statutes that is germane to class action practice as well. In *Ostermeier v. Prime Props. Invs. Inc.*, 589 S.W.3d 1 (Mo. Ct. App. 2019), the Court was called upon to answer the question of whether attorneys working pro bono could nevertheless apply for an award of attorneys' fees in the wake of successful litigation under the Missouri Merchandising Practices Act's fee-shifting provision. In that case, the trial court denied attorneys' fees to attorneys on an MMPA case on the basis "that plaintiff did not incur any legal fees in that plaintiff was represented by a legal aid attorney and an attorney working on a pro bono basis." *Ostermeier*, at 5. The Western District reversed with instructions to award fees, noting the important deterrent effect of fee shifting statutes and that Missouri has previously allowed attorneys' fees circumstances where the client was not directly liable for fees, finding the denial of attorneys' fees to be an abuse of discretion. *Id.* at 8.

Finally, in *Bachman v. A.G. Edwards, Inc.*, 344 S.W.3d 260, 267 (Mo. Ct. App. 2011), the Missouri Eastern District Court of Appeals held that in cases involving complex litigation or in the class action context, a one-third contingent fee award is not unreasonable.

11. DISCOVERY ON CLASS MEMBERS/COMMUNICATION WITH CLASS MEMBERS

In *Padberg v. Dish Network LLC*, No. 11-04035-CV-C-NKL, 2014 U.S. Dist. LEXIS 48025 (W.D. Mo. Apr. 8, 2014), a class action was brought against Defendant DISH Network because DISH customers temporarily lost access to the FX channel and FOX regional sports networks from October 1, 2010, to October 28, 2010. DISH attempted to depose (1) any class member on whose testimony or statements class counsel relied; and (2) absent class members selected by DISH to balance the class member testimony on which class counsel/plaintiff relied. *Id.* at *2. The court of appeals in *Padberg* denied this request, holding: "Discovery from absent class members is ordinarily not permitted. *Phillips Petroleum Co. v. Shutts*, 472 U.S. 797, 105 S. Ct. 2965, 86 L. Ed. 2d 628 (1985). The Supreme Court has held that 'burdens' like discovery are 'rarely imposed' on class members. *Id.* at 810." *Id.* at *3–4. The court in *Padberg* also did not find any "exceptional circumstances" for discovery on class members such as where class members may be deposed when they have been identified as potential witnesses or have otherwise "injected" themselves into the litigation. *Id.* at *4.

In *Domiano v. Schnucks Mkts., Inc.*, No. 4:13-CV-683-JAR, 2014 U.S. Dist. LEXIS 14718 at *3–4 (E.D. Mo. Feb. 6, 2014), a class action involving identity theft of customer's information, plaintiffs tried to prevent defendant from communicating with class members through defendant's website. Plaintiffs asserted that, through its website, defendant had created a claims program to reimburse individuals for losses related to the security breach and that such program will likely be cited as a "settlement" or "satisfaction" in future litigation. *Id.* The district court in *Schnucks* began by citing the relevant law:

> "In a class-action lawsuit, a district court may not order restraints on speech under Fed.R.Civ.P. 23(d) except when justified by actual or threatened misconduct of a serious nature." *Great Rivers Co-op. of Se. Iowa v. Farmland Indus., Inc.*, 59 F.3d 764, 766 (8th Cir. 1995) (citing Manual for Complex Litigation, Second §30.24 at 232 (1985)). "Before entry of such an order, there must be a clear record and specific findings that reflect a weighing of the need for a limitation and the potential interference with the rights of the parties." *Great Rivers Co-op. of Se. Iowa*, 59 F.3d at 766 (citing *Gulf Oil v. Bernard*, 452 U.S. 89, 101, 101 S.Ct. 2193, 2200, 68 L.Ed.2d 693 (1981)).

Based on this law, the district court in *Schnucks* held that the restriction of defendant's communications was not warranted at this stage of the litigation chiefly because "[p]laintiffs have not demonstrated that Defendant has abused the class action process such to require Plaintiffs' proposed overly burdensome sanction" and that plaintiffs have not demonstrated that Defendant has been "soliciting class members to opt out of the litigation[.]" *Id.* at 4 (citing *Great Rivers Co-op. of Se. Iowa v. Farmland Indus., Inc.*, 59 F.3d 764, 766 (8th Cir. 1995)).

Furthermore, in *Buck v. Republic Servs.*, No. 4:13cv0801 TCM, 2013 U.S. Dist. LEXIS 74468, *5–6 (E.D. Mo. May 28, 2013), a case that likewise relied on the Eighth Circuit's *Great Rivers Co-op. of Se. Iowa* decision, the district court did not issue an order restraining speech, but instead ordered defendants to provide notice to plaintiffs' counsel of any written communication they intend to send potential class members three days prior to sending the communication. *Id.* The district court then gave plaintiffs three days to file a motion with the court addressing any concerns with a hearing to follow promptly thereafter. *Id.*

12. SETTLEMENT (COMPROMISE)

When determining whether a class action settlement is fair, reasonable, and adequate, the court must consider (1) the existence of fraud or collusion behind the settlement; (2) the complexity, expense, and likely duration of the litigation; (3) the stage of the proceedings; (4) the probability of the plaintiff's success on the merits; (5) the range of possible recovery; (6) the opinions of class counsel, class representatives and absent class members. *Bachman*, 344 S.W.3d 260, 266 (Mo. Ct. App. 2011) (citing *Ring*, 41 S.W.3d at 492). Among these, "[t]he most important consideration in determining if a settlement is fair, reasonable, and adequate is the strength of the plaintiff's case on the merits balanced against the offered settlement." *Id.*

In *Doyle*, objectors maintained that the trial court abused its discretion by denying their motion for continuance and discovery, which the objectors sought purportedly to evaluate the fairness of the settlement. 400 S.W.3d at 324. To this argument, the *Doyle* court found no abuse of discretion because (1) appellants' counsel had conducted significant discovery in other suits against the same defendant; (2) voluminous environmental information was publicly available; (3) respondents provided additional discovery specifically relevant to appellant's objection concerning allocation; (4) all properties were affected, (5) distance from the smelter was simply not the parties' chosen basis for allocation under the settlement, and (6) appellants' objection to this decision did not suffer for lack of further environmental discovery. *Id.* at 325. In addition, the court held that "[w]eighing the arguable benefit of additional time for appellants' discovery against the potentially substantial prejudice to the class as a result of further delays," it was apparent that the trial court properly exercised its discretion by denying the motion. *Id.* at 13.

In reviewing the class action settlement to determine whether it is fair, reasonable, and adequate under Rule 52.08, Missouri appellate courts apply an abuse of discretion standard. *Bachman,* 344 S.W.3d 260, 265 (citing *Ring,* 41 S.W.3d at 492; *Byrd,* 956 S.W.2d at 276). Approval of the settlement of a class action is reviewed under the standard set out in *Murphy v. Carron*, 536 S.W.2d 30, 32 (Mo. banc 1976). *Id.* (citing *Byrd*, 956 S.W.2d at 276 n.3).

Objections to a settlement should be made at a time when they can be meaningfully considered to be valid. In *Paulson v. Dynamic Pet Prods., LLC*, 560 S.W.3d 583 (Mo. Ct. App. 2018), multiple overlapping class cases were resolved in Missouri following a mediation including counsel for parties in all related cases. 560 S.W.3d at 587. Following the submission and preliminary approval of the settlement to the trial court, litigants from the non-Missouri cases—who had themselves jointly proposed the settlement—objected to the settlement. *Id.* Noting that parties "should not engage in sandbagging tactics" and that the objectors participated in the mediation and had ample opportunity to voice their concerns as part of that process, the appellate court found that any objections had been waived that affirmed the trial court's approval of the settlement. *Id.* at 589, *citing O'Connell v. Sch. Dist. of Springfield R-12*, 830 S.W.2d 410, 421 (Mo. banc 1992).

13. CONCLUSION

Missouri courts will apply a thorough analysis of the various prerequisites to class certification contained in Missouri Supreme Court Rule 52.08, which is substantially identical to Federal Rule 23. However, Missouri law holds that the issue of predominance is satisfied if there is only one common issue of fact or law which is central to the case, a standard which is more liberal than most states. Classes have also been certified under Missouri's consumer protection statute, which has been broadly interpreted.

MISSOURI SUPREME COURT RULESRULES OF CIVIL PROCEDURE

PART I. RULES GOVERNING CIVIL PROCEDURE IN THE CIRCUIT COURTS

RULE 52. PARTIES

52.08. CLASS ACTIONS

(a) *Prerequisites*. One or more members of a class may sue or be sued as representative parties on behalf of all members only if:

(1) the class is so numerous that joinder of all members is impracticable;

(2) there are questions of law or fact common to the class;

(3) the claims or defenses of the representative parties are typical of the claims or defenses of the class; and

(4) the representative parties will fairly and adequately protect the interests of the class.

(b) *Types of Class Actions*. A class action may be maintained if Rule 52.08(a) is satisfied, and if:

(1) prosecuting separate actions by or against individual class members would create a risk of:

(A) inconsistent or varying adjudications with respect to individual class members that would establish incompatible standards of conduct for the party opposing the class; or

(B) adjudications with respect to individual class members that, as a practical matter, would be dispositive of the interests of the other members not parties to the adjudications or would substantially impair or impede their ability to protect their interests;

(2) the party opposing the class has acted or refused to act on grounds that apply generally to the class, so that final injunctive relief or corresponding declaratory relief is appropriate respecting the class as a whole; or

(3) the court finds that the questions of law or fact common to the class members predominate over any questions affecting only individual members, and that a class action is superior to other available methods for fairly and efficiently adjudicating the controversy. The matters pertinent to the findings include:

(A) the class members' interests in individually controlling the prosecution or defense of separate actions;

(B) the extent and nature of any litigation concerning the controversy already commenced by or against class members;

(C) the desirability or undesirability of concentrating the litigation of the claims in the particular forum; and

(D) the likely difficulties in managing a class action.

(c) *Certification Order – Notice to Class Members – Judgment – Issues Classes – Subclasses.*

(1) Certification Order.

(A) Time to Issue. At an early practicable time after a person sues or is sued as a class representative, the court shall determine by order whether to certify the action as a class action.

(B) Defining the Class – Appointing Class Counsel. An order that certifies a class action shall define the class and the class claims, issues, or defenses, and shall appoint class counsel under Rule 52.08(g).

(C) Altering or Amending the Order. An order that grants or denies class certification may be altered or amended before final judgment.

(2) Notice.

(A) For (b)(1) or (b)(2) Classes. For any class certified under Rule 52.08(b)(1) or Rule 52.08(b)(2), the court may direct appropriate notice to the class.

(B) For (b)(3) Classes. For any class certified under Rule 52.08(b)(3), or upon ordering notice under Rule 52.08(e)(1) to a class proposed to be certified for purposes of settlement under Rule 52.08(b)(3), the court shall direct to class members the best notice that is practicable under the circumstances, including individual notice to all members who can be identified through reasonable effort. The notice may be by one or more of the following: United States mail, electronic means, or other appropriate means. The notice shall clearly and concisely state in plain, easily understood language:

(i) the nature of the action;

(ii) the definition of the class certified;

(iii) the class claims, issues, or defenses;

(iv) that a class member may enter an appearance through an attorney if the member so desires;

(v) that the court will exclude from the class any member who requests exclusion;

(vi) the time and manner for requesting exclusion; and

(vii) the binding effect of a class judgment on members under Rule 52.08(c)(3).

(3) Judgment. Whether or not favorable to the class, the judgment in a class action shall:

(A) for any class certified under Rule 52.08(b)(1) or Rule 52.08(b)(2), include and describe those whom the court finds to be class members; and

(B) for any class certified under Rule 52.08(b)(3), include and specify or describe those to whom the notice under Rule 52.08(c)(2) was directed, who have not requested exclusion, and whom the court finds to be class members.

(4) Particular Issues. When appropriate, an action may be brought or maintained as a class action with respect to particular issues.

(5) Subclasses. When appropriate, a class may be divided into subclasses that are each treated as a class under this Rule 52.08.

(d) *Conducting the Action.*

(1) In General. In conducting an action under this Rule 52.08, the court may issue orders that:

(A) determine the course of proceedings or prescribe measures to prevent undue repetition or complication in presenting evidence or argument;

(B) require, to protect class members and fairly conduct the action, giving appropriate notice to some or all of the members of: (i) any step in the action; (ii) the proposed extent of the judgment; or (iii) the members' opportunity to signify whether they consider the representation fair and adequate, to intervene and present claims or defenses, or otherwise come into the action;

(C) impose conditions on the representative parties or on intervenors;

(D) require that the pleadings be amended to eliminate allegations about representation of absent persons and that the action proceed accordingly; or

(E) deal with similar procedural matters.

(2) Combining and Amending Orders. An order under Rule 52.08(d)(1) may be altered or amended from time to time and may be combined with an order under Rule 62.01.

(e) *Settlement, Voluntary Dismissal, or Compromise*. The claims, issues, or defenses of a certified class, or a class proposed to be certified for purposes of settlement, may be settled, voluntarily dismissed, or compromised only with the court's approval. The following procedures apply to a proposed settlement, voluntary dismissal, or compromise:

(1) Notice to the Class.

(A) Information That Parties Shall Provide to the Court. The parties shall provide the court with information sufficient to enable it to determine whether to give notice of the proposal to the class.

(B) Grounds for a Decision to Give Notice. The court shall direct notice in a reasonable manner to all class members who would be bound by the proposal if giving notice is justified by the parties' showing that the court will likely be able to:

(i) approve the proposal under Rule 52.08(e)(2); and

(ii) certify the class for purposes of judgment on the proposal.

(2) Approval of the Proposal. If the proposal would bind class members, the court may approve it only after a hearing and only on finding that it is fair, reasonable, and adequate after considering whether:

(A) the class representatives and class counsel have adequately represented the class;

(B) the proposal was negotiated at arm's length;

(C) the relief provided for the class is adequate, taking into account:

(i) the costs, risks, and delay of trial and appeal;

(ii) the effectiveness of any proposed method of distributing relief to the class, including the method of processing class member claims;

(iii) the terms of any proposed award of attorney fees, including timing of payment; and

(iv) any agreement required to be identified under Rule 52.08(e)(3); and

(D) the proposal treats class members equitably relative to each other.

(3) Identifying Agreements. The parties seeking approval shall file a statement identifying any agreement made in connection with the proposal.

(4) New Opportunity to Be Excluded. If the class action was previously certified under Rule 52.08(b)(3), the court may refuse to approve a settlement unless it affords a new opportunity to request exclusion to individual class members who had an earlier opportunity to request exclusion but did not do so.

(5) Class-Member Objections.

(A) In General. Any class member may object to the proposal if it requires court approval under this Rule 52.08(e). The objection shall state whether it applies only to the objector, to a specific subset of the class, or to the entire class, and also state with specificity the grounds for the objection.

(B) Court Approval Required for Payment in Connection with an Objection. Unless approved by the court after a hearing, no payment or other consideration may be provided in connection with:

(i) forgoing or withdrawing an objection; or

(ii) forgoing, dismissing, or abandoning an appeal from a judgment approving the proposal.

(f) *Appeals*. A court of appeals may permit an appeal from an order granting or denying class-action certification under this Rule 52.08, but not from an order under Rule 52.08(e)(1). An appeal does not stay the proceedings in the trial court unless the trial judge or the court of appeals so orders.

(g) *Class Counsel.*

(1) Appointing Class Counsel. Unless a statute provides otherwise, a court that certifies a class shall appoint class counsel. In appointing class counsel, the court:

(A) shall consider:

(i) the work counsel has done in identifying or investigating potential claims in the action;

(ii) counsel's experience in handling class actions, other complex litigation, and the types of claims asserted in the action;

(iii) counsel's knowledge of the applicable law; and

(iv) the resources that counsel will commit to representing the class;

(B) may consider any other matter pertinent to counsel's ability to fairly and adequately represent the interests of the class;

(C) may order potential class counsel to provide information on any subject pertinent to the appointment and to propose terms for attorney fees and nontaxable costs;

(D) may include in the appointing order provisions about the award of attorney fees or nontaxable costs under Rule 52.08(h); and

(E) may make further orders in connection with the appointment.

(2) Standard for Appointing Class Counsel. When one applicant seeks appointment as class counsel, the court may appoint that applicant only if the applicant is adequate under Rules 52.08(g)(1) and 52.08(g)(4). If more than one adequate applicant seeks appointment, the court shall appoint the applicant best able to represent the interests of the class.

(3) Interim Counsel. The court may designate interim counsel to act on behalf of a putative class before determining whether to certify the action as a class action.

(4) Duty of Class Counsel. Class counsel shall fairly and adequately represent the interests of the class.

(h) *Attorney Fees and Nontaxable Costs.* In a certified class action, the court may award reasonable attorney fees and nontaxable costs that are authorized by law or by the parties' agreement. The following procedures apply:

(1) A claim for an award shall be made by motion under Rule 74.16, subject to the provisions of this Rule 52.08(h), at a time the court sets. Notice of the motion shall be served on all parties and, for motions by class counsel, directed to class members in a reasonable manner.

(2) A class member, or a party from whom payment is sought, may object to the motion.

(3) The court may hold a hearing and shall find the facts and state its legal conclusions.

(4) The court may refer issues related to the amount of the award to a special master.

HISTORY: Adopted April 21, 1972, eff. Dec. 1, 1972. Amended Sept. 28, 1993, eff. Jan. 1, 1994;

June 21, 2005, eff. January 1, 2006. Amended April 24, 2025, eff. August 28, 2025; amended June 30, 2025, eff. January 1, 2026.

COMMENT

This is the same as Rule 23 of the Federal Rules of Civil Procedure.

Chapter authors John J. Carey and James J. Rosemergy are partners in the law firm of Carey, Danis, & Lowe, which specializes in the prosecution of class action and mass tort cases. Carey, Danis & Lowe is located in St. Louis, Missouri.

MONTANA

1. COMPARISON OF MONT. R. CIV. P. 23 TO FED. R. CIV. P. 23

On April 26, 2011, the Montana legislature revised Rule 23 of the Montana Rules of Civil Procedure to more closely conform to its federal counterpart. The rules are largely identical. Section (a) of Montana's Rule 23 is identical to the federal rule and the two contain the same four class action prerequisites. *Chipman v. N.W. Healthcare Corp.*, 288 P.3d 193, 205 (Mont. 2012). Because of the similarities between the Montana rule and the federal rule, the Montana Supreme Court has held that "[f]ederal authority on the issue of class certification is instructive." *Id.* However, Montana's Rule 23 contains a few notable differences to the federal rule.

First, on September 16, 2014, Montana adopted subdivision (i), which requires at least 50 percent of any residual funds from a class action suit to be paid to a nonprofit entity that "supports activities and programs that promote access to the Montana civil justice system." The federal rule contains no such provision. Second, subdivision (f) deviates from the federal rules and defers to the Montana Rules of Appellate Procedure for guidance on class action appeals. It allows an interlocutory appeal from an order granting or denying class certification, and, unlike the federal rule, an order rejecting a proposed class action settlement. Such appeals may be "filed within the time allowed for appeals under the Montana Rules of Appellate Procedure," but do not stay proceedings unless ordered by the district court or the supreme court. Third, subdivision (g)(1)(A) uses the phrase "*may* consider" as opposed to the federal rule's "*must* consider" when referencing factors that the court considers in appointing class counsel. Finally, subdivision (h)(4) of the federal rule—concerning appointment of a special master or magistrate to address attorney fee awards—has been left out of the Montana rule.

2. CASE LAW INTERPRETING MONT. R. CIV. P. 23

Class actions are the exception to the usual rule that litigation is conducted by and on behalf of individually-named parties only. *Sangwin v. State*, 315 P.3d 279, 283 (Mont. 2013). To be certified for a class action under Montana law, a class must meet the relevant requirements of Rules 23(a) and 23(b) of the Montana Rules of Civil Procedure. "Once Rule 23(a) is satisfied a [court] must then determine whether the class action conforms to the type of class actions available pursuant to Rule 23(b)." *Roose v. Lincoln Cty. Employee Group Health Plan*, 362 P.3d 40, 43 (Mont. 2015).

Class certification in Montana "fundamentally consists of two principles: first, the trial court must have some evidentiary basis for determining the moving party satisfied each M. R. Civ. P. 23 requirement; and, second, the trial court has broad discretion at the certification stage." *Ascencio v. Orion Int'l Corp.*, 417 P.3d 1094, 1097 (Mont. 2018).

When determining whether a proposed class and class representative meet these requirements for certification, a judge should make whatever factual and legal inquiries are necessary; to that end, the court may allow discovery and hear evidence. *Mattson v. Montana Power Co.*, 215 P.3d 675, 694 (Mont. 2009) (*Mattson II).* A "rigorous analysis" is required that "may touch the merits of the class claim," but district courts should not assess "any aspect of the merits unrelated to a Rule 23 requirement." *Cook v. Buscher Constr. and Dev., Inc.*, 2024 MT 137, ¶ 10. The Montana Supreme Court, following federal precedent, has held that Rule 23 is not merely a pleading standard and requires actual, not presumed, conformance to its requirements. *Byorth v. USAA Cas. Ins. Co.*, 2016 MT 302, ¶ 17. A request for class certification may be denied, however, based on the allegations in the pleadings alone. *See Vulles v. Thies & Talle Mgmt., Inc.*, 512 P.3d 248, 250–51 (Mont. 2021).

While the Court has not established a clear burden of proof for meeting class requirements, it has held that "the trial court must have *some evidentiary basis* for determining each Rule 23 requirement is satisfied." *Id.* (emphasis in original). A district court may not simply rely on the allegations of the parties' pleadings. *Id.* While not explicitly adopting the preponderance of the evidence standard, the Court has recognized that "[i]n recent years, the burden has trended toward more proof, with several circuits adopting the familiar preponderance of the evidence standard." *Id.* ¶ 19. "The party seeking class certification must prove 'in fact' the requirements of 23(a) and 'satisfy through evidentiary proof' any individual provision of 23(b)." *Kramer v. Fergus Farms Mutual Ins. Co.*, 2020 MT 258, ¶15. That said, "the class action proponent need not prove each element with absolute certainty." *Cook*, ¶ 10.

a. Rule 23(a) Requirements

The requirements of Rule 23(a) "ensure that the named plaintiffs are appropriate representatives of the class whose claims they wish to litigate" and "effectively limit the class claims to those fairly encompassed by the named plaintiff's claims." *Mattson v. Montana Power Co.*, 291 P.3d 1209, 1215 (Mont. 2012) (*Mattson III*); *Byorth*, ¶ 15. To be certified as a class action in Montana, the class must satisfy the requirements found in Rule 23(a)(1) through 23(a)(4). The four elements require that:

1. The class must be so numerous that joinder of all members is impractical.
2. There must be questions of fact or law common to the class.
3. The claims or defenses of the representative parties must be typical of the claims or defenses of the proposed class.
4. The representative parties will fairly and adequately protect the interest of the proposed class.

McDonald v. Washington, 862 P.2d 1150, 1155 (Mont. 1993). "The District Court must conduct a 'rigorous analysis' to determine whether each of the Rule 23(a) prerequisites is met, which 'may entail analyzing some merits issues, but only to the extent that those issues are relevant to determining whether the Rule 23 requirements are satisfied.'" *Gottlob v. Desrosier*, 2025 MT 56, ¶ 26, 421 Mont. 176, 565 P.3d 1196 (quoting *Worledge v. Riverstone Residential Group, LLC*, 2015 MT 142, ¶ 23, 379 Mont. 265, 350 P.3d 39).

i. Numerosity. To satisfy the numerosity requirement of Rule 23(a)(1), a proposed class must be "so numerous that joinder of all members is impracticable." *Sangwin*, 315 P.3d at 284. The Montana Supreme Court has held that joinder of over 1,000 injured members would be impracticable. *Gottlob v. Desrosier*, 2025 MT 56, ¶ 31, 421 Mont. 176, 565 P.3d 1196. Speculation about numerosity falls short of this standard. Montana requires that plaintiffs "present some evidence of, or reasonably estimate, the number of class members." *Diaz v. Blue Cross & Blue Shield*, 267 P.3d 756, 763 (Mont. 2011). The numerosity requirement "does not require precision." *Rogers v. Lewis & Clark County*, 513 P.3d 1256, 1263 (Mont. 2022). The Montana Supreme Court has recognized that "sheer numbers alone" do not determine whether 23(a)(1) is satisfied. *Roose*, 362 P.3d at 45.

Joinder of the class's members can be impracticable for other reasons; for instance, the potential class members may be unaware that they were treated unlawfully. Even a class of one plaintiff satisfied the numerosity requirement in *Roose* because the Court found that other parties "exist whose interests are directly affected by the outcome of this litigation." *Id.* Later, the Court clarified that in *Roose* the defendant admitted that all the insurance policies it issued contained an exclusion that violated the law and that all policyholders were entitled to equitable or injunctive relief as a result. *Byorth*, ¶¶ 24–25. Thus, the existence of other parties with interests affected by the litigation was more than mere speculation.

ii. Commonality. To satisfy the commonality requirement of Rule 23(a)(2), the class must have questions of law or fact in common. *Gottlob*, ¶ 34. "Commonality requires that the class members' claims "depend upon a common contention of such a nature that it is capable of classwide resolution—which means that determination of its truth or falsity will resolve an issue that is central to the validity of each one of the claims in one stroke." *Houser*, 458 P.3d at 1034. In *Ferguson v. Safeco Ins. Co. of America*, the Montana Supreme Court stated that, "[t]he commonality requirement is not a stringent threshold and does not impose an unwieldy burden on plaintiffs." 180 P.3d 1164, 1169 (Mont. 2008). The Court went on to hold that, "as a general rule, all that is necessary to satisfy Rule (23)(a)(2) is an allegation of standardized, uniform course of conduct by defendants affecting plaintiffs." *Id.* That said, commonality is not satisfied merely by raising a "superficial question that fails to demonstrate common injury." *Byorth*, ¶ 29. Rather "[t]o satisfy commonality, the question would have to address the common injury allegedly shared across the class." *Id.* "Total commonality is not required, meaning all questions of law or all questions of fact need not be common." *Sieglock v. Burlington Northern Santa Fe Ry. Co.*, 81 P.3d 495, 498 (Mont. 2003). The Montana Supreme Court applied *Wal-Mart Stores, Inc. v. Dukes,* 564 U.S. 338, 350 (2011), in *Chipman v. Northwest Healthcare Corp*, referencing Montana's history of relying on federal precedent when interpreting Rule 23 class certification requirements. *Chipman v. Northwest Healthcare Corp.,* 288 P.3d 193, 206. There, the Court noted that the *Wal-Mart* standard "significantly tightened the commonality requirement." *Id.* The Montana Supreme Court has not yet explicitly adopted the *Wal-Mart* standard, though it has often referred to it and applied it. *Byorth*, ¶ 26; *see also Cook v. Buscher Constr. & Dev., Inc.*, 2024 MT 137, ¶ 21, 417 Mont. 111, 551 P.3d 811; *Mattson III,* 291 P.3d at 1221–22; *Cook*, ¶ 20.

iii. Typicality. To satisfy the typicality requirement of Rule 23(a)(3) of the Montana Rules of Civil Procedure, "a plaintiff must demonstrate that the claims or defenses of the representative parties are typical of the claims or defenses of the class." *Chipman*, 288 P.3d at 208. The typicality requirement "ensures the named class members' interests align with the interest of absent class members." *Byorth*, ¶ 33; *see also In re Blue Cross and Blue Shield of Montana, Inc.*, 372 P.3d 457, 462 (Mont. 2016) (quoting *Diaz*, 267 P.3d at 764) (typicality "serves to prevent[] plaintiffs from bringing a class action against defendants with whom they have not had any dealings"). The Montana Supreme Court has stated that "[t]ypicality is not a demanding standard." *Gottlob*, ¶ 43. Typicality is satisfied if the class claims are based on "the same event, practice, or course of conduct and the same legal or remedial theory." *Byorth*, ¶ 33; *see also Sangwin*, 315 P.3d at 285 (quoting *Diaz*, 267 P.3d at 764). According to the Montana Supreme Court, typicality and commonality often overlap: "commonality looks to the questions of law or fact common to the class as a whole, while typicality focuses more closely on the named representatives' relationship to the rest of the class." *Byorth*, ¶ 34 (citing 1 William B. Rubenstein et al., *Newberg on Class Actions* § 3:31 (5th ed. 2011)); *but see Sangwin*, 315 P.3d at 286 ("Typicality refers to the nature of the claim or defense of the class representative, and not to the specific facts from which it arose or the relief sought."). The Court has indicated that the plaintiff must show that the common question under Rule 23(a)(2) "unite[s] not only the class as a whole, but also the named representatives with the absent class members." *Byorth*, ¶ 37. "There cannot be typicality sufficient to satisfy the rule unless the named representative has individual standing to raise the legal claims of the class." *Hop v. Safeco Ins. Co. of Ill.*, 2011 MT 215, ¶ 19. However, the Montana Supreme Court has recognized the "juridical link doctrine," which allows a class representative to join as defendants parties with whom the named representative did not have direct contract when the defendant "took part in a similar scheme that was sustained either by a contract or conspiracy, or was mandated by a uniform state rule." *Cook*, ¶ 24; *see also Worledge v. Riverstone Residential Grp., LLC*, 2015 MT 142, ¶ 36.

iv. Adequacy of representation. Montana Rule of Civil Procedure 23(a)(4) requires that "the representative parties will fairly and adequately protect the interests of the class." *See also In re Blue Cross*, 372 P.3d at 462. The rule "requires that the named representative's attorney be qualified and competent and able to conduct the litigation and that the named representative's interests not be antagonistic to the interests of the class." *In re Blue Cross*, 372 P.3d at 462. In *Jacobsen v. Allstate Ins. Co.*, the Court stated that "perfect symmetry of interest is not required and not every discrepancy among the interests of class members renders a putative class action untenable." 310 P.3d 452, 470 (Mont. 2013). However, "conflicts that are fundamental to the suit and that go to the heart of the litigation prevent a plaintiff from meeting the Rule 23(a)(4) adequacy requirement." *Id.* (quoting *Matamoros v. Starbucks Corp.*, 699 F.3d 129, 138 (1st Cir. 2012)). In other words, conflicts of interest "so substantial as to overbalance the common interests of the class members as a whole" would disqualify *Jacobsen* from certification. *Id.* Adequacy is closely related to commonality and typicality. *Id*, ¶ 58.

b. Rule 23(b) Class Actions

The different types of class actions that may be maintained in the State of Montana and their individualized requirements are outlined in the Montana Rules of Civil Procedure Rules 23(b)(1)-(3).

i. 23(b)(1) Inconsistent adjudication/limited fund classes. According to the Montana Supreme Court, "Rule 23(b)(1) is a narrow basis for class actions that applies only when individual adjudications threaten to create 'incompatible standards' for the opposing party's conduct or when there are limited funds available for recovery." *Knudsen*, ¶ 11. The Montana Supreme Court affirmed certification of a Rule 23(b)(1)(a) class in *Chipman*. *Chipman*, ¶ 61. *Chipman* involved a suit brought by employees against their employer arising from a dispute over the discontinuation of a sick leave buy-back program. *Id.*, ¶ 1. Analogizing to an ERISA case from the Northern District of Ohio, *Cates v. Cooper Tire and Rubber Company*, 253 F.R.D. 422 (N.D. Ohio 2008), the Court reasoned that certification under Rule 23(b)(1) was appropriate because "denying class certification could result in individual Plaintiffs bringing over 1,200 lawsuits" that could "result in varying determinations of the same factual and legal issues" and "a decision could be dispositive for the absent class members by setting binding precedent" to the prejudice of absent class members. *Chipman*, ¶ 61. It does not appear that the Montana Supreme Court has otherwise affirmed certification of a Rule 23(b)(1) class.

ii. 23(b)(2) Declaratory or injunctive relief class. Rule 23(b)(2) provides for an injunctive or declaratory relief class when "final injunctive relief or corresponding declaratory relief is appropriate respecting the class as a whole." Mont. R. Civ. P. 23(b)(2). Rule 23(b)(2) classes are mandatory classes and "relief awarded to [such] class applies to all class members regardless of whether they are knowledgeable of the litigation and regardless of whether all have suffered the precise injury that was suffered by the representative party." *Roose*, 362 P.3d at 44. The Montana Supreme Court has held that injunctive relief may be proper under Montana Rule of Civil Procedure 23(b)(3) when two requirements are met. *Houser*, 458 P.3d at 1035. "The first requirement focuses on whether the defendant's action affects everyone in the same proposed class in a similar fashion. The second requirement focuses on the 'indivisible nature' of the declaratory or injunctive relief—'the notion that the conduct is such that it can be enjoined or declared unlawful only as to all of the class members or as to none of them.'" *Id.*; *see also Knudsen*, 445 P.3d at 839.

Rule 23(b)(2) class certification requires "ongoing conduct to enjoin or declare unlawful." *Id.* at 840. In *Knudsen*, the Court held certification under Rule 23(b)(2) was inappropriate because the allegedly unlawful contract had expired and there was no showing that the defendant was planning to enter into a similar contract in the future. *Id.*

Following *Wal-Mart*, the Montana Supreme Court has indicated that a Rule 23(b)(2) class is inappropriate when "monetary relief is not incidental to the [requested] injunctive or declaratory relief." *Roose*, ¶ 28. Likewise, "when each class member would be entitled to an individualized award of monetary damages, or when each class member would be entitled to a *different* injunction or declaratory judgment against the defendant," Rule 23(b)(2) certification is inappropriate. *Id.*, ¶ 29. Recognizing the due process concerns raised, the Court in *Jacobsen* reversed certification of a Rule 23(b)(2) class for punitive damages, explaining that "[p]ermitting class-wide recovery of punitive damages before sending notice to the class and determining the extent of the class members' actual harm would allow the punitive award to be potentially based on non-injured parties." *Jacobsen,* 310 P.3d at 476.

iii. 23(b)(3) Monetary damages class. A Rule 23(b)(3) class for monetary damages may be certified if "questions of law or fact common to the class members predominate over any question affecting only individual members and [] a class action is superior to other available methods for fairly and efficiently adjudicating the controversy." Mont. R. Civ. P. 23(b)(3). Class members can generally opt out of the action and "will not be entitled to share in any monetary compensation which may ultimately be obtained." *McDonald*, 862 P.2d at 1159. An individual who opts out may pursue an individual lawsuit separate from the class action. *Id* at 407. When assessing these requirements, the Court will consider "the class members' interests in individually controlling separate actions, the extent and nature of any already existing litigation concerning the controversy, the desirability or undesirability of concentrating the litigation in a particular forum, and likely difficulties in managing a class action." *Gottlob*, ¶ 47. The primary concern of these considerations is "whether adjudication of common issues will help achieve judicial economy." *Mattson III*, 291 P.3d at 1221; *see also Cook*, ¶ 29 (judicial economy is a "fundamental concern of the Rule 23(b)(3) predominance test"). A Rule 23(b)(3) class must be "sufficiently cohesive to warrant adjudication by representation." *Cook*, ¶ 29.

A common question will predominate if it is key to the liability determination for all class members. Questions regarding individual damages are generally insufficient to defeat predominance. *Cook*, ¶ 31. In *Knudsen v. University of Montana*, the Court affirmed certification of a Rule 23(b)(3) class when it concluded that regardless of the requirement for individual damage calculations, a common question of liability existed whose answer would "'move the litigation forward and be answered the same for all class members.'" *Knudsen v. Univ. of Mont.*, 2019 MT 175, ¶ 24; *see also Kramer*, ¶ 20 (holding Rule 23(b)(3) certification appropriate when determination of common question would "'move the litigation forward and be answered the same for all class members' regardless of individualized calculations of damages"); *see also Cook*,

¶¶ 31–34 (finding predominance satisfied when "predominating issue of liability based on nondisclosure" existed, despite existence of individual issues and noting that determining predominance "is not an exact science").

When liability must be determined on an individual basis, however, predominance generally will not be met. In *Sangwin*, the Montana Supreme Court reversed the district court's determination that the predominance requirement was met because "factual questions must be answered on an individual basis before the plaintiffs will be in a position to establish liability." *Sangwin*, ¶ 37. The *Sangwin* Court agreed with the plaintiffs that "the necessity to assess damages on an individual basis does not necessarily defeat class certification" but because there was "undeniably a preliminary need for an individual determination of whether each individual qualifies as a class member," the Court held that the predominance requirement of Rule 23(b)(3) was not met. *Id.*

c. Tax Class Actions

Montana's current tax statutes specifically provide for an alternative remedy of bringing a class action pursuant to Montana Rules of Civil Procedure 23 for declaratory judgment and refunds of unlawful taxes. *See* Mont. Code Ann. § 15-1-407(2)(a), as amended in 1995. To avail themselves of this procedure, the taxpayer must follow the administrative procedures for paying the tax under protest, the action must be filed within 90 days of the representative's receipt of notice of the tax assessment or refund denial, and all class members must also have paid the tax under protest. *Id.*; *see also Samson v. State*, 948 P.2d 232, 235 (Mont. 1997) (affirming dismissal of complaint for failure to file within 90 days).

d. Montana Consumer Protection Act

In Montana, class actions are not allowed under the Montana Consumer Protection Act (MCPA). Mont. Code Ann. 30-14-101 *et seq*. The MCPA "provides a private cause of action" for violation of the Act through "[u]nfair methods of competition and unfair or deceptive acts or practices in the conduct of any trade or commerce." *Rohrer v. Knudson,* 203 P.3d 759, 763 (Mont. 2009); Mont. Code Ann. § 30-14-103. An action brought under the Montana Consumer Protection Act "may bring an individual but not a class action." Mont. Code Ann. § 30-14-133(1) (quoted in *Doll v. Major Muffler Centers, Inc.*, 687 P.2d 48, 52 (Mont. 1984)). However, if a case in federal court based on diversity jurisdiction involves an alleged violation of the Montana Consumer Protection Act, this prohibition may not apply. *See Hill v. LLR, Inc.*, 2019 WL 2404900, *9–11 (D. Mont. Mar. 8, 2019) (findings and recommendations adopted), 2019 WL 3024896, *2–5 (D. Mont. July 11, 2019); *Wittman v. CB1, Inc.*, 2016 WL 1411348, *7–8 (D. Mont. Apr. 8, 2016) (findings and recommendations adopted), 2016 WL 3093427, *5–6 (D. Mont. June 1, 2016); *see also Shady Grove Orthopedic Assocs., P.A. v. Allstate Ins. Co.* (2010), 559 U.S. 393, 130 S. Ct. 1431.

e. Notice

The certification notice provision contained in Rule 23(c)(2) of the Montana Rules of Civil Procedure serves to "protect the due process rights of all class members, specifically those who are absent." *Roose*, 362 P.3d at 47. For mandatory classes outlined by Rule 23(b)(1) and 23(b)(2) of the Montana Rules of Civil Procedure, "certification notice is discretionary; whereas notice is required for Rule 23(b)(3) damages classes." *Id.* Although the expense of class notice usually must be borne by the plaintiffs, once liability is determined, the cost of notice can be shifted to the defendants. *St. James Community Hosp., Inc. v. Dist. Court.*, 77 P.3d 534, 537 (Mont. 2003).

f. Discovery

There is no Montana law requiring unlimited discovery for the purpose of allowing a plaintiff to find other plaintiffs for a class action. *Shattuck v. Mont. First Jud.Dist. Ct.,* 2009 Mont. LEXIS 720, *3 (Mont. 2009).

g. Further Orders

The Montana Supreme Court has "specifically recognized" the District Court's continuing jurisdiction to make "appropriate orders" in the course of the litigation under Montana Rules of Civil Procedure 23(d). *State ex rel. Boyne v. Dist. Court*, 742 P.2d 464, 468 (Mont. 1987). Also, in *State ex rel. Anaconda Aluminum Co. v. Dist. Ct.*, the Court recognized that an order denying the defendants' motion to declare that the action not be maintained as a class action "may be altered or amended before a decision on the merits." 490 P.2d 351, 351 (Mont. 1971); *see also Rolan v. New West Health Servs.*, 2013 MT 220, ¶ 15 ("class action certification orders 'are not frozen once made'; instead, the District Court maintains discretion to alter the class definition as the case proceeds"); *Cook*, ¶ 35 ("class action certification orders are not frozen once made and a district court may alter or amend an order on class certification before the final judgment") (cleaned up). The Montana Supreme Court has clarified that it will read class definitions narrowly because the trial court "retains the discretion to alter or amend the class definition to include (or exclude) additional members as litigation proceeds." *Rogers v. Lewis & Clark County*, 513 P.3d 1256, 1261 (Mont. 2022).

h. Venue

Class actions in Montana must be filed in a county which, under Montana's venue statutes, Mont. Code Ann. §§ 25-2-111, *et seq*., is a proper county with respect to all named class representatives and all defendants. *State ex rel. Kesterson v. Dist. Ct.*, 614 P.2d 1050, 1052 (Mont. 1980).

i. Attorneys' Fees

In *Association of Unit Owners of Deer Lodge Condominium, Inc. v. Big Sky of Montana, Inc.*, the Montana Supreme Court held that "in a class action an award of attorney fees is 'contingent upon success and upon the existence of a fund from which the fees can be paid', and that the evaluation of settlement must be 'fair, reasonable, and in the best interests of all affected.'" 790 P.2d 967, 969 (Mont. 1990) (quoting *Waters v. City of Chicago*, 420 N.E.2d 599, 603–04 (Ill. App. 1981)). Accordingly, in *McDonald*, the Montana Supreme Court recognized the principle that members of a class "will not be required to pay any attorneys' fees or costs in the absence of monetary recovery." *McDonald*, 862 P.2d at 1159. The controlling standard for attorney fees in class actions, as in any actions, is that the amount of fees awarded be reasonable. *Gendron v. Montana University System*, 461 P.3d 115, 119. The Supreme Court of Montana recognizes that quick results do not mean an award was less earned or reasonable, and "Class Counsel's work may not necessarily end with the final approval of the Settlement Agreement." *Tafelski v. Johnson*, 2024 MT 143, ¶ 29, 417 Mont. 160, 552 P.3d 40. In *Tafelski v. Johnson*, the Montana Supreme Court upheld an award of 33.33 percent of a settlement fund in attorney fees. *Id.* ¶ 32. There, objectors argued the award would "transform Montana into a class-action magnet," but the Montana Supreme Court utilized the Gendron factors and upheld the District Court's decision. *Id.* ¶ 26.

j. Settlement

The Supreme Court of Montana has held that, "[a]pplicable case law and Rule 23 require that a settlement agreement in a class action proceeding must be approved by a district court judge after a determination that the settlement is 'fair, adequate and reasonable.'" *Pallister v. Blue Cross and Blue Shield of Montana, Inc.*, 285 P.3d 562, 567 (Mont. 2012). Accordingly, "[a] proposed settlement agreement is entitled to a presumption of fairness where: '(1) the settlement negotiations occurred at arm's length; (2) there was sufficient discovery; (3) the proponents of the settlement are experienced in similar litigation; and (4) only a small fraction of the class objected.'" *Id.* at 568. Further, "settlement approval that takes place before formal class certification or appointment of class counsel requires a higher standard of fairness." *Id.* at 568–69; *see also Hanlon v. Chrysler Corp.*, 150 F.3d 1011, 1026 (9th Cir. 1998). In such a "settlement only class action," "the heightened scrutiny required . . . mandates that there be sufficient information provided to the class representatives, any objectors, and the district court to enable the parties and the court to reach a well-informed decision of whether the proposed settlement is fair, adequate and reasonable." *Id.* at 570.

k. Appellate Review

The standard for appellate review of trial court orders concerning class action certification is abuse of discretion. *Knudsen v. Univ. of Mont.*, 445 P.3d 834, 838 (Mont. 2019). As such, the Supreme Court, "afford[s] the trial courts the broadest discretion when reviewing a decision on class certification." *Houser*, 458 P.3d at 1034. The Court in *Chipman* clarified that such abuse of discretion is clear when "the district court acted arbitrarily without conscientious judgement or exceeded the bounds of reason." 288 P.3d at 200. Accordingly, "the district court's judgement should be accorded the greatest respect because it is in the best position to consider the most fair and efficient procedure for conducting any given litigation." *Id.*

A district court abuses its discretion if its class certification order is premised on legal error. *Rogers v. Lewis & Clark County*, 513 P.3d 1256, 1261 (Mont. 2022). Findings of fact supporting a ruling under Rule 23 are reviewed under the clearly erroneous standard. *Id.* The Montana Supreme Court "is reluctant to interfere with discretionary orders in the early stages of litigation, especially as the trial court has flexibility to modify its certification orders as the litigation proceeds." *Id.*

l. Residual Funds

Rule 23(i)(3) states that, "[i]n matters where the claims process has been exhausted and residual funds remain, not less than fifty percent (50%) of the residual funds shall be disbursed to an Access to Justice Organization to support activities and programs that promote access to the Montana civil justice system." Montana joins states including California, Hawaii, Illinois, Indiana, Kentucky, Louisiana, Maine, Massachusetts, New Mexico, North Carolina, Pennsylvania, South Dakota, Tennessee, and Washington in providing such a codified approach for such distribution of residual funds.

3. LEGISLATIVE CHANGES

Montana's 67th Legislature produced no statutory changes affecting class actions.

MONTANA'S VERSION OF RULE 23

RULE 23. CLASS ACTIONS

Rule 23(a) Prerequisites. One or more members of a class may sue or be sued as representative parties on behalf of all members only if:

(1) the class is so numerous that joinder of all members is impracticable;

(2) there are questions of law or fact common to the class;

(3) the claims or defenses of the representative parties are typical of the claims or defenses of the class; and

(4) the representative parties will fairly and adequately protect the interests of the class.

Rule 23(b). Types of Class Actions. A class action may be maintained if Rule 23(a) is satisfied and if:

(1) prosecuting separate actions by or against individual class members would create a risk of:

(A) inconsistent or varying adjudications with respect to individual class members that would establish incompatible standards of conduct for the party opposing the class; or

(B) adjudications with respect to individual class members that, as a practical matter, would be dispositive of the interests of the other members not parties to the individual adjudications or would substantially impair or impede their ability to protect their interests;

(2) the party opposing the class has acted or refused to act on grounds that apply generally to the class, so that the final injunctive relief or corresponding declaratory relief is appropriate respecting the class as a whole; or

(3) the court finds that the questions of law or fact common to the class members predominate over any questions affecting only individual members, and that a class action is superior to other available methods for fairly and efficiently adjudicating the controversy. The matters pertinent to the findings include:

(A) the classmembers' interests in individually controlling the prosecution or defense of separate actions;

(B) the extent and nature of any litigation concerning the controversy already begun by or against class members;

(C) the desirability or undesirability of concentrating the litigation of the claims in the particular forum; and

(D) the likely difficulties in managing a class action.

Rule 23(c). Certification Order; Notice to Class Members; Judgment; Issues Classes; Subclasses.

(1) *Certification Order*.

(A) Time to Issue. At an early practicable time after a person sues or is sued as a class representative, the court must determine by order whether to certify the action as a class action.

(B) Defining the class; Appointing Class Counsel. An order that certifies a class action must define the class and the class claims, issues, or defenses, and must appoint class counsel under Rule 23(g).

(C) Altering or Amending the Order. An order that grants or denies class certification may be altered or amended before final judgment.

(2) *Notice*.

(A) For (b)(1) or (b)(2) Classes. For any class certified under Rule 23(b)(1) or (b)(2), the court may direct appropriate notice to the class.

(B) For (b)(3) Classes. For any class certified under Rule 23(b)(3), the court must direct to class members the best notice that is practicable under the circumstances, including individual notice to all members who can be identified through reasonable effort. The notice must clearly and concisely state in plain, easily understood language:

(i) the nature of the action;

(ii) the definition of the class certified;

(iii) the class claims, issues, or defenses;

(iv) that a class member may enter an appearance through an attorney if the member so desires;

(v) that the court will exclude from the class any member who requests exclusion;

(vi) the time and manner for requesting exclusion; and;

(vii) the binding effect of a class judgment on members under Rule 23(c)(3).

(3) *Judgment*. Whether or not favorable to the class, the judgment in a class action must:

(A) for any class certified under Rule 23(b)(1) or (b)(2), include and describe those whom the court finds to be class members; and

(B) for any class certified under Rule 23(b)(3), include and specify or describe those to whom the Rule 23(c)(2) notice was directed, who have not requested exclusion, and whom the court finds to be class members.

(4) *Particular Issues*. When appropriate, an action may be brought or maintained as a class action with respect to particular issues.

(5) *Subclasses*. When appropriate, a class may be divided into subclasses that are each treated as a class under this rule.

Rule 23(d). Conducting the Action.

(1) *In General.* In conducting an action under this rule, the court may issue orders that:

(A) determine the course of proceedings or prescribe measures to prevent undue repetition or complication in presenting evidence or argument;

(B) require—to protect class members and fairly conduct the action—giving appropriate notice to some or all class members of:

(i) any step in the action;

(ii) the proposed extent of the judgment; or

(iii) the members' opportunity to signify whether they consider the representation fair and adequate, to intervene and present claims or defenses, or otherwise come into the action;

(C) impose conditions on the representative parties or on intervenors;

(D) require that the pleadings be amended to eliminate allegations about representation of absent persons and that the action proceed accordingly; or

(E) deal with similar procedural matters.

(2) *Combining and Amending Orders*. An order under Rule 23(d)(1) may be altered or amended from time to time and may be combined with an order under Rule 16.

Rule 23(e). Settlement, Voluntary Dismissal, or Compromise. The claims, issues, or defenses of a certified class may be settled, voluntarily dismissed, or compromised only with the court's approval. The following procedures apply to a proposed settlement, voluntary dismissal, or compromise:

(1) The court must direct notice in a reasonable manner to all class members who would be bound by the proposal.

(2) If the proposal would bind class members, the court may approve it only after a hearing on finding that it is fair, reasonable, and adequate.

(3) The parties seeking approval must file a statement identifying any agreement made in connection with the proposal.

(4) If the class action was previously certified Rule 23(b)(3), the court may refuse to approve a settlement unless it affords a new opportunity to request exclusion to individual class members who had an earlier opportunity to request exclusion but did not do so.

(5) Any class member may object to the proposal if it requires court approval under this subdivision (e); the objection may be withdrawn only with the court's approval.

Rule 23(f). Appeals. Appeal may be filed from an order granting or denying class action certification under this rule, or an order finally and definitively rejecting a proposed class settlement, by notice of appeal filed within the time allowed for appeals under the Montana Rules of Appellate Procedure. An appeal does not stay proceedings in the District Court unless the district judge or supreme court so orders.

Rule 23(g). Class Counsel.

(1) *Appointing Class Counsel*. Unless a statute provides otherwise, a court that certifies a class must appoint class counsel. In appointing class counsel, the court:

(A) may consider:

(i) the work counsel has done in identifying or investigating potential claims in the action;

(ii) counsel's experience in handling class actions, other complex litigation, and the types of claims asserted in the action;

(iii) counsel's knowledge of the applicable law; and

(iv) the resources that counsel will commit to representing the class;

(B) may consider any other matter pertinent to counsel's ability to fairly and adequately represent the interests of the class;

(C) may order potential class counsel to provide information on any subject pertinent to the appointment and to propose terms for attorney fees and nontaxable costs;

(D) may include in the appointing order provisions about the award of attorney fees or nontaxable costs under Rule 23(h); and

(E) may make further orders in connection with the appointment.

(2) *Standard for Appointing Class Counsel.* When one applicant seeks appointment as class counsel, the court may appoint that applicant only if the applicant is adequate under Rule 23(g)(1) and (4). If more than one adequate applicant seeks appointment, the court must appoint the applicant best able to represent the interests of the class.

(3) *Interim Counsel.* The court may designate interim counsel to act on behalf of a putative class before determining whether to certify the action as a class action.

(4) *Duty of Class Counsel.* Class counsel must fairly and adequately represent the interests of the class.

Rule 23(h). Attorney Fees and Nontaxable Costs. In a certified class action, the court may award reasonable attorney fees and nontaxable costs that are authorized by law or by the parties' agreement. The following procedures apply:

(1) A claim for an award must be made by motion under Rule 54(d)(2), subject to the provisions of this subdivision (h), at a time the court sets. Notice of the motion must be served on all parties and, for motions by class counsel, directed to class members in a reasonable manner.

(2) A class member, or a party from whom payment is sought, may object to the motion.

(3) The court may hold a hearing and must find the facts and state its legal conclusion under Rule 52(a).

Rule 23(i). Disposition of Residual Funds.

(1) "Residual Funds" are funds that remain after the payment of all approved class member claims, expenses, litigation costs, attorneys' fees and other court-approved disbursements. This rule does not prohibit the trial court from approving a settlement that does not create residual funds.

(2) "Access to Justice Organization" means a Montana non-profit entity whose purpose is to support activities and programs that promote access to the Montana civil justice system.

(3) Any order entering a judgment or approving a proposed compromise of a class action certified under this rule that establishes a process for identifying and compensating members of the class shall provide for disbursement of residual funds. In matters where the claims process has been exhausted and residual funds remain, not less than fifty percent (50%) of the residual funds shall be disbursed to an Access to Justice Organization to support activities and programs that promote access to the Montana civil justice system. The court may disburse the balance of any residual funds beyond the minimum percentage to an Access to Justice Organization or to another non-profit entity for purposes that have a direct or indirect relationship to the objectives of the underlying litigation or otherwise promote the substantive or procedural interests of members of the certified class.

This chapter was prepared by Mac Morris of Crowley Fleck PLLP in Bozeman, Montana.

NEBRASKA

1. COMPARISON WITH RULE 23 OF THE FEDERAL RULES OF CIVIL PROCEDURE

Nebraska has no analogue to Rule 23 of the Federal Rules of Civil Procedure as it remains one of the few states that continue to employ the procedural statutes based on the Field Code of 1849. Neb. Rev. Stat. 25-319 is a broad provision authorizing the use of class actions. *Obstetricians-Gynecologists, P.C. v. Blue Cross & Blue Shield of Nebraska*, 219 Neb. 199, 208, 361 N.W.2d 550, 556 (Neb. 1985). Although the statute is broad, something more than the suggestion of a class action is necessary to fulfill the parties' requirement. *Id.* One commentator on the statute found that the Nebraska Supreme Court has construed the statute in such a way that bringing a successful class action suit in Nebraska is difficult. C.L. Robinson & Thomas H. Dahlk, *Class Actions—The Nebraska Procedure*, 61 Neb. L. Rev. 30 (1982).

The following requirements are necessary in order to bring a class action in Nebraska:

1. proper joinder;
2. no potentiality of a conflict of interest;
3. necessity; and
4. manageability.

Id. at 38. The first two requirements fall into a broader, more familiar category of commonality, the latter two into numerosity. *See Hoiengs v. County of Adams*, 245 Neb. 877, 901, 516 N.W.2d 223, 240 (Neb. 1994) (concluding that in order to justify class status treatment, the plaintiffs' claim must meet both statutory requirements of commonality and numerosity).

The statute providing for class actions includes no counterparts to Federal Rule 23(f), and certification of a class is not a final and appealable order or a special proceeding. *Keef v. State of Nebraska, Dept. of Motor Vehicles*, 262 Neb. 622, 630–31, 634 N.W.2d 751, 759 (Neb. 2001).

2. 2020 DEVELOPMENTS

There is one 2020 case involving a class action in Nebraska, *Lassalle v. State*, 307 Neb. 221, 948 N.W.2d. 725 (Neb. 2020). This class action involved a group of Department of Health and Human Services (DHHS) employees that brought a wage dispute against the State. *Id.* Lassalle, a DHHS employee, sought to take and be paid for leave hours in addition to working a full eighty hours in a pay period several times between 2016 and 2019. *Id.* Lassalle sought class certification and the State moved for summary judgment. *Id.* The lower court, overruling Lasalle's motion for class certification, recognized that there was a potential conflict of interest as certain class members who may prefer to retain accrued leave would lose the chance to do so if Lassalle prevailed. *Id.* On appeal, the Nebraska Supreme Court affirmed summary judgment in favor of the State. *Id.* As a result, the issue of class certification was deemed moot. *Id.* Lassalle could not represent a class of DHHS employees in an action against the State because the State was entitled to summary judgment, resulting in the class certification issue to be moot. *Id.* The Nebraska Supreme Court cited to the Seventh and Tenth Circuit for the proposition that summary judgment in favor of the defendants makes the issue of class certification moot, suggesting this is the first time this issue has arisen in Nebraska. *Id.*

3. 2025 DEVELOPMENTS

In 2025, the nebraska legislature passed legislative bill 241 (lb241) which, in relevant part, states, "a private entity shall not be liable in a class action resulting from a cybersecurity event unless the cybersecurity event was caused by willful, wanton, or gross negligence on the part of the private entity." No nebraska case law has yet discussed or interpreted this portion of lb241.

4. CASE LAW INTERPRETING 25-319

a. Commonality

i. Proper joinder. The members of the class must be unified in interest to the extent that the suit can be brought jointly. *Sarratt v. Lincoln Benefit Life Co.*, 212 Neb. 436, 438, 323 N.W.2d 81, 83 (Neb. 1982); *Evans v. Metropolitan Utilities District of Omaha*, 185 Neb. 464, 467, 176 N.W.2d 679, 681 (Neb. 1970) (citing *Certia v. University of Notre Dame Du Lac, Ind.*, 141 N.E. 318 (Ind. Ct. App. 1923)). In other words, a class action can be maintained where questions of law and fact are common to all and predominate over individual interests. *Hoiengs*, 245 Neb. at 902, 516 N.W.2d at 241. An action may not be maintained as a class action by a plaintiff on behalf of himself or herself and others unless he or she has the power as a member of the class to satisfy a judgment on behalf of the class as a whole. *Miller v. City of Omaha,* 253 Neb. 798, 805–06, 573 N.W.2d 121, 127 (Neb. 1998). Furthermore, an action may not be maintained as a class action by a plaintiff if the defendant is entitled to summary judgment. *See Lassalle v. State*, 307 Neb. 221, 948 N.W.2d 725 (Neb. 2020) (holding class certification became moot when defendant was entitled to summary judgment and therefore, the plaintiff could no longer represent a class against the defendant).

Note that a class representative in a class action who has failed to state a claim upon which relief can be granted was not a proper plaintiff in such action, even if the plaintiff(s) who filed the petition successfully stated the same claims and, thus, remain parties to the class action. *McGinn v. State Farm Mut. Auto Ins. Co.*, 268 Neb. 843, 849, 689 N.W.2d 802, 807 (Neb. 2004). *See also Lynch v. State Farm Mut. Auto Ins. Co.,* 275 Neb. 136, 144, 745 N.W.2d 291, 298 (Neb. 2008) (finding that because plaintiff could not maintain individual cause of action, as a matter of law, she lacked commonality with members of the purported class to act as class representative); *Davio v. Nebraska Dept. of Health & Human Servs.,* 280 Neb. 263, 270, 786 N.W.2d 655, 663 (Neb. 2010) (stating that class action cannot be used to circumvent affirmative defenses or to revive claims which are barred).

ii. Typicality and adequacy. The second requirement for bringing a class action is that claims of the representative must be typical of the class, and the representative must fairly protect the interests of the class. *Hoiengs*, 245 Neb. at 903–04, 516 N.W.2d at 242; *Blankenship v. Omaha Pub. Power Dist.*, 195 Neb. 170, 176, 237 N.W.2d 86, 90 (Neb. 1976). The test for potentiality of a conflict of interest, as stated in *Blakenship*, is to verify "if any party included in the class stands to suffer an economic loss as the result of his inclusion, the party initiating the class action will have an interest adverse to those of the party he purports to represent with the result that the action is not being brought for the benefit of all members of the class." *Blakenship,* 295 Neb. at 175–76, 237

N.W.2d at 90. It has been argued that the potentiality of a conflict of interest test is a severe hurdle to overcome even if the joinder requirement is met. *Class Actions—The Nebraska Procedure*, note 2 at 47. A non-lawyer plaintiff lacking legal counsel may be deemed inadequate to represent the interests of a class. *See McCroy v. Sprint Communications Co., L.P.*, 2002 WL 31002118, at *3 (Neb. Ct. App. 2002) (noting without comment the trial court's decertification of a class following withdrawal of plaintiffs' counsel and plaintiffs' failure to secure replacement counsel).

b. Numerosity

i. Necessity. While no mathematical test exists for the number of plaintiffs needed for a class action, the action may be improper if the same result can be reached by suing individually. *Benesch v. City of Schuyler*, 5 Neb. Ct. App. 59, 68, 555 N.W.2d 63, 68–69 (Neb. App. 1996); *Berkshire v. Douglas County Board of Equalization*, 200 Neb. 113, 262 N.W.2d 449 (Neb. 1978). Consequently, an action under Neb. Rev. Stat. 25-319 is improper if class allegations add nothing to the lawsuit and the final result would be the same whether a class action were brought or an individual action maintained.

ii. Manageability. A class action must be manageable or it will be denied. *Kosowski v. City of Betterment Corp.*, 197 Neb. 402, 405, 249 N.W.2d 481, 483 (Neb. 1977). A case would not be manageable, for instance, if distribution of the plaintiffs' award "would be extremely difficult and impractical, if not impossible, to satisfactorily reach and identify, and distribute the award to, those entitled to share in it." *Id.*

c. Conclusion

Since the 2020 developments, there is no additional case law or modifications to Nebraska's class action law. The text of Nebraska Revised Statute § 25-319 remains the same as the previous submission of the 2022 ABA Class Action survey. The tolling of the statute of limitations period during the pendency of a class action still remains unaddressed in Nebraska jurisprudence.

SECTION 25-319 OF THE REVISED STATUTES OF NEBRASKA

25-319. CLASS ACTIONS; REPRESENTATION

When the question is one of a common or general interest of many persons, or when the parties are very numerous, and it may be impracticable to bring them all before the court, one or more may sue or defend for the benefit of all.

TOLLING OF THE STATUTE OF LIMITATIONS DURING THE PENDENCY OF A CLASS ACTION

None to date.

Edward D. Hotz is of counsel with the firm of Pansing, Hogan, Ernst, and Buser, LLP in Omaha, Nebraska. Practice areas include insurance and commercial law as well as business and personal injury litigation. Maggie Brokaw is an associate with Pansing, Hogan, Ernst, and Buser, LLP.

NEVADA

1. COMPARISON WITH RULE 23 OF THE FEDERAL RULES OF CIVIL PROCEDURE

Rule 23 of the Nevada Rules of Civil Procedure mirrored its federal counterpart until the Federal Rule was amended in 2003, revising subdivisions (c) and (e) and adding subdivisions (g) and (h). Nev. R. Civ. Proc. 23 drafter's note, 2004 amendment. Despite the significant differences between the provisions now, the Nevada Supreme Court's class-certification decisions continue to rely heavily upon the analogous portions of FRCP 23. *See, e.g., Shuette v. Beazer Homes Holdings Corp.*, 124 P.3d 530, 538 (Nev. 2005).

2. 2019 AMENDMENTS

Effective March 1, 2019, the Nevada Supreme Court implemented comprehensive changes to the Nevada Rules of Civil Procedure. The amendments to Rule 23 include structural and stylistic changes and the addition of two substantive provisions: Rule 23(b) and 23(d)(2).[1] Rule 23(b) authorizes aggregation of the value of class members' claims to reach the district court jurisdictional amount. Notably, Rule 23(b) abrogates a Nevada Supreme Court decision that, albeit in dicta, declined to permit such aggregation. *See Castillo v. United Federal Credit Union*, 409 P.3d 54 (Nev. 2018). Rule 23(d)(2) authorizes the substitution of a class representative where a representative party is unable or unwilling to continue in that role.

3. INTERPRETIVE CASE LAW

Nevada's class certification requirements remained under-addressed until the Nevada Supreme Court handed down a comprehensive NRCP 23 discussion in *Shuette v. Beazer Homes Holdings Corporation* in 2005.[2] 124 P.3d 530 (Nev. 2005). In order for a litigant to obtain class certification under Nevada's Rule 23, in addition to satisfying the ordinary rules of justiciability, the litigant must satisfy each of the four requirements of subsection (a) and meet at least one of the categories in subsection (c) (formerly subsection (b)). *Shuette*, 124 P.3d at 537. The burden of proof rests with the party seeking class certification, *Cummings v. Charter Hosp.*, 896 P.2d 1137, 1140 (Nev. 1995), and

[1] The addition of a new subpart (b) and structural changes to the rule altered the letter and number designations for existing subparts. These changes will require special attention when reviewing decisions issued prior to the 2019 amendments.

[2] *Shuette* suggests that "single-family residence constructional defect cases will rarely be appropriate for class action treatment," but recognizes that "some constructional defects matters might be amenable to class action certification" and expressly acknowledges that class treatment "may be proper" in a single-defect case. *Shuette*, 124 P.3d at 544.

the district court has complete discretion to decide whether the class action is the best vehicle for a particular action. *Deal v. 999 Lakeshore Assn.*, 579 P.2d 775, 778–79 (Nev. 1978). The court must undertake a "thorough and documented" analysis and "pragmatically determine" whether "it is better to proceed as a single action, than as many individual actions, in order to redress a single fundamental wrong." *Shuette*, 124 P.3d at 537 (quoting *Deal*, 579 P.2d at 778–79) & 544. In performing this analysis, the court "should generally accept the allegations of the complaint as true" rather than requiring an "extensive evidentiary showing[.]" *Meyer v. Eighth Jud. Dist. Ct.*, 885 P.2d 622, 626 (Nev. 1994). Where applicable, the court should defer to an agency's interpretation of whether its governing statutes or regulations permit class actions if the interpretation is within the statute's or regulation's language. *Wynn Las Vegas, LLC v. Baldonado*, 311 P.3d 1179, 1182 (Nev. 2013) (en banc) (district court erred in failing to defer to Labor Commissioner's conclusion that NAC 607.200 does not permit class actions). Class certification issues become moot if the named plaintiff's claims do not survive a motion to dismiss or motion for summary judgment. *Martel v. HG Staffing*, 519 P.3d 25, 35 n.14 (Nev. 2022) (citing *Sargeant v. Henderson Taxi*, 394 P.3d 1215, 1218 (Nev. 2017)).

A court does not abuse its discretion by deferring the issue of class standing and/or representative standing until the class certification stage after sufficient discovery. *State Bd. of Regents of Nevada Sys. of Higher Educ. on Behalf of Coll. of S. Nevada v. Second Jud. Dist. Ct.*, 2023 WL 8886422, 540 P.3d 1056, at *2 (Nev. Dec. 22, 2023) (unpublished). "[O]nce a named plaintiff establishes individual standing and the pleadings do not show that the plaintiff's claim substantially differs from the claims the plaintiff alleges on behalf of others, the action may proceed to discovery and class certification, if appropriate." *Id.* (citing *D.R. Horton, Inc. v. Eighth Jud. Dist. Ct.*, 215 P.3d 697, 703–04 (Nev. 2009) and 1 William B. Rubenstein, Newberg & Rubenstein on Class Actions § 2:6, at 135–36, 148–49 (6th ed. 2022)).

NRCP 23(d)(1) permits the court to certify a class on a conditional basis. "Conditional certification notifies the parties that a court may exercise its discretion to later revoke certification in complex litigation cases." *Shuette*, 124 P.3d at 544. Because this discretion is continuous, the court "must reevaluate" and may decertify a class if any of the required elements ever becomes unsatisfied. *Id.* To improve case manageability, the court may use NRCP 23(d)(5) to certify issue classes or subclasses to, among other things, "classify and distinguish claims that are suitable for class action certification from those requiring individualized proof." *D.R. Horton, Inc.*, 215 P.3d at 704. The court's analysis of NRCP 23(a)(2) commonality and NRCP 23(c)(3) predominance "will affect whether the member 'class' is divided into subclasses and, if so, how." *Beazer Homes Holding Corp. v. Eighth Jud. Dist. Ct.*, 291 P.3d 128, 135–36 (Nev. 2012). Both NRCP 23(e)(1)(E) and NRCP 42(b) leave case management decisions on the need for separate subclass trials to the sound discretion of the district court. *Go Wireless, Inc. v. Eighth Jud. Dist. Ct.*, 555 P.3d 1161, at *2 (Nev. Sept. 6, 2024) (unpublished) (finding district court did not abuse discretion in ordering two separate trials for subclasses with dissimilar, complex commission calculations). "Individual variations in commission calculation might not suffice to defeat the legal requirement of predominance but may provide a basis justifying separate trials[.]" *Id.*

In *D.R. Horton*, the Nevada Supreme Court first held that a common-interest community association may use the NRCP 23 class action procedural device to prosecute, in its representative capacity pursuant to NRS 116.3102(1)(d), common constructional defect claims affecting real property owned by two or more of its individual members. *D.R. Horton, Inc.*, 215 P.3d 697; *accord Oxbow Constr. v. Eighth Jud. Dist. Ct.*, 335 P.3d 1234, 1239 (Nev. 2014); *Beazer*, 291 P.3d at 134–37. These decisions allowed common-interest community associations to institute litigation involving non-common elements (i.e., their members' separately owned real property located within the common interest-community) and, if the requirements of NRCP 23 were satisfied, proceed on generalized rather than individualized proof.

In response to this burgeoning area of case law, the Nevada Legislature, during its 2015 regular session, amended NRS 116.3102(1)(d) to add the following language: "The association may not institute, defend or intervene in litigation or in arbitration, mediation or administrative proceedings in its own name on behalf of itself or units' owners with respect to an action for a constructional defect pursuant to NRS 40.600 to 40.695, inclusive, unless the action pertains exclusively to common elements." This amendment took effect on February 24, 2015, and limits a common-interest community association's ability to institute constructional defect actions to common elements within the community. *High Noon at Arlington Ranch Homeowners Association v. Eighth Jud. Dist. Ct.*, 402 P.3d 639 (Nev. 2017) (applying former statute where complaint filed before statute's effective date); *Azure Manor/Rancho de Paz Homeowners Association v. U.S. Home Corp., et al.*, 2016 WL 1270995, at *2–3, n.23 (D. Nev. Mar. 31, 2016) (holding amended statute "clearly provides" it does not apply to associations that gave notice "on or before the effective date of" the amendment); *but see Platinum Unit-Owner's Association v. Residential Constructors, LLC*, 2015 WL 1186530, at *6 (D. Nev. Mar. 16, 2015) (applying amended statute retroactively despite express provision to the contrary). In 2019, the Nevada Legislature relaxed these constraints by amending NRS 116.3102(1)(d) to allow an association to pursue legal redress for additional categories of claims—none of which revert to the broad pre-2015 statutory language (i.e., affecting real property owned by two or more individual members).

While common-interest community associations have historically used NRS 116.3102(1)(d) to initiate constructional defect litigation for the individual units, which was and likely still is statutorily precluded, the current statute does not prohibit associations from using their standing under NRS 116.3102(1)(d) to pursue other types of litigation on their members' behalf. In such non-constructional defect actions, the prior case law linking NRS 116.3102(1)(d) with NRCP 23 appears to remain in force. Under those circumstances, the association "functions much like the plaintiffs in a class-action litigation" and, after satisfying all applicable NRCP 23 requirements, may pursue any certified claims through the use of generalized proof. *D.R. Horton*, 215 P.3d at 703 (quoting Restatement (Third) of Prop.: Servitudes § 6.11 cmt. a (2000)); *see also Beazer*, 291 P.3d at 134–36 (stating NRCP 23 analysis will "affect the resolution of generalized proof and other evidentiary questions and influence how trial will proceed"). Once an association declares its intent to prosecute its members' common claims as a class action, any party may ask the court to conduct a thorough NRCP 23 analysis of each claim for relief to determine whether the association can maintain a class action and "how the action should proceed." *Oxbow*, 335 P.3d at 1239 (citing *Beazer*, 291 P.3d at 136). Upon such a request, the court "must thoroughly analyze NRCP 23's requirements and document its findings." *Beazer*, 291 P.3d at 136 (quoting *D.R. Horton, Inc.*, 215 P.3d at 704) (internal quotation marks omitted); *see, e.g., D.R. Horton, Inc. v. Eighth Jud. Dist. Ct.*, 2013 WL 324270 at *2 (Nev. Jan. 25, 2013) (unpublished); *D.R. Horton, Inc. v. Eighth Jud. Dist. Ct.*, 2013 WL 3324998 at *1 (Nev. Apr. 18, 2013) (unpublished).[3] When an association brings common claims on its members' behalf pursuant to its representational capacity under NRS 116.3102(1)(d), "a [f]ailure to meet any additional procedural requirements, including NRCP 23's class action requirements, cannot strip a common-interest community association of its standing to proceed on behalf of its members." *Oxbow*, 335 P.3d at 1239 (quoting *Beazer*, 291 P.3d at 134) (internal quotation marks omitted); *see also Southern*

[3] Unpublished Nevada Supreme Court decisions do not establish mandatory precedent, but parties may cite such post-2015 decisions for their persuasive value. Nev. R. App. Proc. 36(c)(2)–(3).

Highlands Community Ass'n v. Eighth Jud. Dist. Ct., 2014 WL 5840129 at *8 (Nev. Nov. 10, 2014) (unpublished).

a. Nev. R. Civ. P. 23(a)

i. Numerosity. The Nevada Supreme Court has commented that "[t]he express language and intent of Nev. R. Civ. P. 23(a)(1) leaves no doubt that a class action may be maintained only if the class is so numerous that joinder of all members is impracticable," *Kane v. Sierra Lincoln-Mercury, Inc.*, 533 P.2d 464, 465–66 (Nev. 1975), or "the plaintiff class is so large that proceeding as a class action is the only manageable method of resolving the controversy." *Cummings*, 896 P.2d at 1140. Although no magic number has been identified as satisfying the numerosity requirement, Nevada decisions reflect that three or five plaintiffs are too few to justify a class action, but "a putative class of forty or more generally will be found 'numerous." *Shuette*, 124 P.3d at 537 (internal quotations omitted); *see also Monarch Estates Homeowners Assn. v. Eighth Jud. Dist. Ct.*, 2009 WL 3191402, at *2 (Nev. Sept. 3, 2009) (unpublished) (finding 35 sufficiently numerous).

Although early Nevada decisions indicate that the numerosity analysis is essentially a mathematical calculation, the Nevada Supreme Court's comments in *Shuette* emphasize not class size, but impracticality of joinder. The court must examine the specific facts of the case and consider "judicial economy arising from the avoidance of a multiplicity of actions, geographic dispersion of class members, financial resources of class members, the ability of claimants to institute individual suits, and requests for prospective injunctive relief which would involve future class members," as well as "other relevant factors" to determine whether NRCP 23(a)(1) is satisfied. *Shuette*, 124 P.3d at 538 (quoting *Robidoux v. Celani*, 987 F.2d 931, 936 (2d Cir. 1993)); *accord Beazer*, 291 P.3d at 135.

The Nevada Supreme Court has held the numerosity requirement serves a different function in the context of representative actions by common-interest community associations.[4] The *Beazer* court held, "in examining the numerosity requirement, . . . the court need only determine that the common-interest community association's representative action claim pertains to at least two units' owners; if so, the representative action is permissible and cannot be defeated on the ground that the represented members are insufficiently numerous." 291 P.3d at 135 (citing Nev. Rev. Stat. § 116.3102(1)(d)). However, an association must satisfy the numerosity required by NRCP 23(a)(1) should it wish to prosecute its individual members' common claims through the class-action procedure. *Beazer*, 291 P.3d at 136. Should an association fail to meet that numerosity threshold, "the case will proceed more like a . . . joinder action, or in some other fashion . . . ." *Id.*

ii. Commonality. Commonality is established by demonstrating a question of either law or fact common to all plaintiffs. The Nevada Supreme Court has stressed that this requirement must be read and applied in the disjunctive. Thus, factual differences between common legal questions are not fatal to class certification. *See Meyer*, 885 P.2d at 626 (holding that question of whether eviction-related practice of "pinning" is unlawful was sufficient to establish commonality despite disparate circumstances surrounding each individual episode of "pinning"). This is true even though the class plaintiffs may have incurred different damages. *See Johnson v. Travelers Ins. Co.*, 515 P.2d 68, 73 (Nev. 1973). Additionally, the court has repeatedly voiced that, as a general rule, due to the inherent uniqueness of each occasion of fraud and the lack of a "common thread" running through these

[4] Nevada's Uniform Common-Interest Ownership Act confers standing on common-interest community associations to litigate certain matters "in its own name on behalf of itself or two or more units' owners on matters affecting the common-interest community." *Beazer*, 291 P.3d at 134 (quoting Nev. Rev. Stat. § 116.3102(1)).

instances, "a class suit to recover damages for fraud allegedly practiced upon numerous persons is not warranted" because commonality is simply nonexistent. *Meyer*, 885 P.2d at 627; *see also Cummings*, 896 P.2d at 1140 (affirming dismissal of class action for fraud); *Johnson*, 515 P.2d at 72 (dismissing fraud class action for lack of common question of law or fact as to liability). The court has, however, left open the possibility of bringing a representative suit for collective deceit, provided that the requisite "common thread" is present. *Johnson,* 515 P.2d at 72.

iii. Typicality. "Typicality demands that the claims or defenses of the representative parties be typical of those of the class." *Shuette*, 124 P.3d at 538 (internal quotations omitted). Typicality focuses "on the defendants' actions, not on the plaintiffs' conduct." *Id.* If "each member's claim arises from the same course of events and each class member makes similar legal arguments to prove the defendant's liability," the typicality prong is satisfied despite factual variations among the individual claims. *Id.* "Defenses that are unique to a representative party will rarely defeat this prerequisite, unless they 'threaten to become the focus of the litigation.'" *Dancer v. Golden Coin, Ltd.*, 176 P.3d 271, 276 (Nev. 2008) (quoting *Shuette*, 124 P.3d at 538–39).

iv. Adequacy. In *Shuette*, the Nevada Supreme Court adopted the adequacy analysis employed by the United States Supreme Court in *Amchem Products, Inc. v. Windsor*. *Shuette*, 124 P.3d at 539. By determining whether the class members "possess the same interest and suffer the same injury" as the other class members, the court can ensure that the representative parties "fairly and adequately protect the interests of the class." *Id.* (quoting *Amchem*, 521 U.S. 591, 625–26 (1997)). In *Sargeant*, 394 P.3d 1215, the Nevada Supreme Court applied *Amchem*'s same-interest and same-injury requirements and held the plaintiff could not represent the proposed class due to conflicting interests. *Id.* at 1220. A named plaintiff's conflict arising after the settlement does not undermine her adequacy to serve as a class representative. *Murray v. Dubric*, 514 P.3d 1081 (Nev. 2022) (unpublished). Sufficient typicality under NRCP 23(a)(3) "will generally meet the adequacy requirement, [but] issues regarding the overall adequacy of representation must be determined by the district court." *Beazer*, 293 P.3d at 136 (citing *Salton City Etc. v. M. Penn Phillips Co.,* 75 Cal. App. 3d 184, 141 Cal. Rptr. 895, 899–900 (Ct. App. 1977)).

b. Nev. R. Civ. P. 23(c)

In addition to meeting the NRCP 23(a) prerequisites, Nevada plaintiffs seeking class certification must show that a class action is "logistically possible and superior to other actions," *Meyer,* 885 P.2d at 626, by satisfying one of three conditions in NRCP 23(c). The movants must demonstrate: "(1) that separate litigation by individuals in the class would create a risk that the opposing party would be held to inconsistent standards of conduct or that nonparty members' interests might be unfairly impacted by the other members' individual litigation; (2) that the party opposing the class has acted or refused to act against the class in a manner making appropriate classwide injunctive or declaratory relief; or (3) that common questions of law or fact predominate over individual questions, and a class action is superior to other methods of adjudication." *Shuette*, 124 P.3d at 539.

Nevada authority is devoid of any meaningful discussion of NRCP 23(c)(1) or (2), but the *Shuette* opinion provides substantial guidance for 23(c)(3) certification. NRCP 23(c)(3) focuses "on when common questions predominate over individual questions and the class action vehicle is a superior method for adjudication." *Id.* at 539.[5] The predominance prong "tests whether proposed

[5] "Individualized claims for monetary relief are subject to this subsection." *Beazer*, 291 P.3d at 135 n.4 (citing Wal-Mart Stores, Inc. v. Dukes, 564 U.S. 338, 363, 131 S. Ct. 2541, 2558, 180 L. Ed. 2d 374 (2011)).

classes are sufficiently cohesive to warrant adjudication by representation." *Id.* (quoting *Amchem*, 521 U.S. at 625). Although the predominance inquiry "is related to" the commonality and typicality analysis, the Nevada Supreme Court has acknowledged that "it is more demanding." *Id.* at 540. "Common questions predominate over individual questions if they significantly and directly impact each class member's effort to establish liability and entitlement to relief, and their resolution can be achieved through generalized proof." *Id.* (quoting *Amchem*, 521 U.S. at 623–24) (internal quotation marks omitted). Class treatment is the superior method for adjudicating claims when "management difficulties and any negative impacts on all parties' interests are outweighed by the benefits of class-wide resolution of common issues." *Id.* (quoting *Peltier Enterprises, Inc. v. Hilton*, 51 S.W.3d 616, 624 (Tex. App. 2000)) (internal quotations omitted). As the Nevada Supreme Court has recognized, "common issues regarding damages may still predominate even when the party opposing certification can present evidence of individual variations among the class members." *Go Wireless, Inc. v. Eighth Jud. Dist. Ct.*, 555 P. 3d 1161, at *1 (Nev. Sept. 6, 2024) (unpublished) (finding district court did not abuse discretion in expanding class despite defendants' assertion of individual variations in commission calculations at issue).

The Nevada Supreme Court has expressed "Nevada's strong public policy in favor of class action suits"— particularly Rule 23(c)(3) actions. *Picardi v. Eighth Jud. Dist. Ct.*, 251 P.3d 723, 728 (Nev. 2011) (overturned on other grounds by *Tallman v. Eighth Jud. Dist. Ct.*, 359 P.3d 113 (Nev. 2015) (relying on *AT&T Mobility LLC v. Concepcion*, 563 U.S. 321, 131 S. Ct. 1740 (2011))). The court observed that NRCP 23([c])(3) "demonstrates a state policy favoring class actions when the class members present common questions of law or fact that predominate over any questions affecting only individual members." *Id.* at 727 (alteration added) (referring to the former subsection 23(b)(3)). "Class actions serve a valuable function in Nevada's judicial system by increasing efficiency," and the "class action mechanism is important in cases involving small claims consumer cases because the *realistic* alternative to a class action is not 17 million individual suits, but zero individual suits, as only a lunatic or a fanatic sues for $30." *Id.* at 727–28 (quoting *Carnegie v. Household Intern., Inc.*, 376 F.3d 656, 661 (7th Cir. 2004)) (emphasis in original) (internal quotation marks omitted). The court also aligned itself with "the growing number of jurisdictions that favor aggregating small consumer claims." *Id.* Although *Picardi*'s arbitration-related holding has been overturned,[6] the opinion nevertheless reflects the Nevada Supreme Court's unanimous affinity for the class action device.

4. APPELLATE REVIEW

The district courts have "'broad discretion in deciding whether to certify a class action and [their] discretion will be reversed only if an abuse of discretion is shown.'" *Sargeant*, 394 P.3d at 1219 (quoting 7 AA Charles Alan Wright, Arthur Miller & Mary Kay Kane, *Federal Practice and Procedure: Civil* § 1785 (3d ed. 2005)); *accord Shuette*, 124 P.3d at 537. The Nevada Supreme Court also reviews a district court's decision to approve a class action settlement for an abuse of discretion. *Murray*, 514 P.3d 1081 (citing *Marcuse v. Del Webb Communities, Inc.*, 163 P.3d 462, 467 (Nev.

---

[6] However, the more recent decision in *Morgan v. Sundance, Inc.*, 142 S. Ct. 1708, 212 L. Ed. 2d 753 (2022) (holding FAA serves as "a bar on using custom-made rules, to tilt the playing field in favor of (or against) arbitration"), calls into question the *Tallman* court's conclusion that *AT&T Mobility LLC v. Concepcion*, 563 U.S. 333, 131 S. Ct. 1740, 179 L. Ed. 742 (2011), overturned the *Picardi* court's application of "generally applicable state contract law" to invalidate a class action waiver found in an arbitration agreement. *Picardi*, 251 P.3d 723.

2007)). The Nevada Supreme Court recently declined to articulate the standard of review for a district court's notice-related decisions. *Roe 1 v. Shepard*, 2023 WL 8251386, 539 P.3d 661, at *1, n.3 (Nev. Nov. 28, 2023) (unpublished).

5. MISCELLANEOUS COMMENTS

a. Aggregation of Class Damages for Jurisdictional Purposes

The new NRCP 23(b) expressly allows the "representative parties [to] aggregate the value of the individual claims of all potential class members to establish district court jurisdiction over a class action." This amendment resolves any aggregation concerns created by dicta in a recent Nevada Supreme Court decision. *Castillo*, 409 P.3d 54. In 2021, the Nevada Supreme Court held that *Castillo*'s aggregation holding was incorrect and that total damages sought by the class, rather than those sought by any individual class member, must be considered in determining jurisdiction. *A Cab, LLC v. Murray*, 501 P.3d 961, 970 (Nev. 2021) (citing Nev. R. Civ. P. 23(b)).

b. Merits Inquiries at the Class Certification Stage

The Nevada Supreme Court adopted the directive that "[w]hile Rule 23 'grants courts no license to engage in free-ranging merits inquiries at the certification stage[, m]erits questions may be considered to the extent—but only to the extent—that they are relevant to determine whether the Rule 23 prerequisites for class certification are satisfied.'" *Sargeant*, 394 P.3d at 1219 (quoting *Amgen Inc. v. Comm. Ret. Plans & Tr. Funds*, 568 U.S. 455, 466, 133 S. Ct. 1184, 1194–95, 185 L. Ed. 2d 308 (2013)). Where the merits of a claim "materially affect[ ] class certification," the district court does not abuse its discretion by considering the merits of the class claims during the certification process. *Id.* at 1219–20 (affirming denial of class certification based on prior resolution of labor union's grievance on same issue). In general, the court should "accept the allegations of the complaint as true" and not require an "extensive evidentiary showing" before certifying a class. *Meyer*, 885 P.2d at 626.

c. Tolling of Statutes of Limitations

In *Dancer*, the Nevada Supreme Court recognized that "NRCP provides an 'opt-out' class action construct" and, therefore, "class actions brought under NRCP 23 toll the statute of limitations on all potential unnamed plaintiffs' claims." 176 P.3d at 275. This recognition is consistent with the Court's acknowledgment in *Marcuse* that "class members are parties to the class action, even though they may be unnamed." 163 P.3d at 467 n.14. In *Archon Corp. v. Eighth Jud. Dist. Ct.*, 407 P.3d 720 (Nev. 2017), the Nevada Supreme Court rejected, on procedural grounds, Archon's request to adopt a ban on cross-jurisdictional class action tolling of the statutes of limitations.

d. Substitution of Class Representatives

The newly added Rule 23(d)(2) permits "class members an opportunity to substitute a class representative meeting the requirements of Rule 23(a)(4)" "when the representative party is unable or unwilling to continue as the class representative[.]" *See* Nev. R. Civ. P. 23(d)(2). Now, class members have the opportunity "to substitute themselves as the class representative" when the existing "class representative is unable or unwilling to continue as the class representative . . . ." *Dancer*, 176

P.3d at 275 (quoting *Birmingham Steel v. Tennessee Valley Authority,* 353 F.3d 1331, 1339 (11th Cir. 2003)) (internal quotations omitted). The purpose of this rule is to "protect[] the interests of the class, which has a separate and distinct legal status from that of the representative." *Id.* (citing *Birmingham Steel*, 353 F.3d at 1339). The ability to substitute class representatives effectively means "the representative party's rejection of an offer made under Rule 68 or other . . . offers to resolve less than all of the class claims asserted by or against the representative party" has no impact on the class interest requirements under Rule 23(a)(4). Nev. R. Civ. Proc. 23(d)(2).**e. Communications with Absent Class Members**

The Nevada Supreme Court has no published authority on the subject of communications with absent class members to date. NRCP 23(e), however, does permit broad orders in the conduct of class actions. The Rule authorizes courts to make appropriate orders "imposing conditions on the representative parties . . ." and "dealing with similar procedural matters" in a class action. Nev. R. Civ. Proc. 23(e)(1)(C) & (E). In a recent unpublished decision denying writ relief for former class members who were denied the right to intervene in a certified class action, the Nevada Supreme Court held the district court did not abuse its discretion when the defendant—after the district court entered its order certifying the class—entered into arbitration agreements with class members to exclude them from the class and eventual class settlement. *Roe 1 v. Eighth Jud. Dist. Ct.*, 2023 WL 8251456, 539 P.3d 661, at *1–2 (Nev. Nov. 28, 2023) (unpublished). Of note, one dissenting Justice, relying on the plain language of the class certification order and fundamental fairness, believed the class members who subsequently signed arbitration agreements should not have been excluded from the class settlement. *Id.* at *2 (Lee, J., dissenting); *see also Roe 1 v. Shepard*, 2023 WL 8251386, 539 P.3d 661, at *3 (noting Roes waived their litigation-waiver arguments to avoid arbitration agreements by not raising issue below).

f. Class Notice, Settlement Objectors, and Settlement Approval

Under NRCP 23(d)(3), for any class action certified under NRCP 23(c)(3), the district court "should direct to the members of the class the best notice practicable under the circumstances, including individual notice to all members who can be identified through reasonable effort." The notice must contain certain information. NRCP 23(d)(3). These notice requirements do not mandate actual notice to all class members or anything more than "sufficient information regarding the settlement's terms so as to comport with due process and NRCP 23." *Roe 1 v. Shepard*, 2023 WL 8251386, 539 P.3d 661, at *1–2 (rejecting objection regarding direct-mail notice to last known addresses that lacked social media outreach). A notice satisfies these standards when it is "'reasonably calculated' under the circumstances to afford the class members notice" of the settlement and its material terms. *Id.* at *1 (citing *Grupo Famsa v. Eighth Jud. Dist. Ct.,* 371 P.3d 1048, 1050 (Nev. 2016)).

An absent class member has standing to object to a proposed class settlement and challenge a court's settlement approval order if the settlement releases the class member's claims for less than full value. *Murray*, 514 P.3d 1081 (citing *Valley Bank of Nev. v. Ginsburg*, 874 P.2d 729, 734 (Nev. 1994)). Court-appointed class representatives from a separate but overlapping class action that ended in a judgment favorable to the class members may, in their representative capacity, object to and appeal from an order approving a class settlement on behalf of the absent class members they have been appointed to represent. *Id.* (citing *Las Vegas Police Protective Ass'n Metro, Inc. v. Eighth Jud. Dist. Ct.*, 130 P.3d 182, 189 (Nev. 2006)). The *Murray* court expressly declined "to adopt the Ninth Circuit's eight-factor test for determining whether a proposed class action settlement is fair, adequate, and reasonable at this time." *Id.* (citing *Churchill Vill., LLC v. Gen. Elec.*, 361 F.3d 566, 575 (9th Cir. 2004) and noting the difference between the settlement-approval standard under FRCP 23 and NRCP 23); *see also Roe 1 v. Shepard*, 2023 WL 8251386, 539 P.3d 661, at *2 (noting difference between settlement-approval standard under FRCP 23 and NRCP 23, specifically that NRCP 23 does not require "fair, reasonable, and adequate" finding). In affirming the district court's order approving the settlement, the *Murray* court noted the settlement came after the parties conducted significant discovery and engaged in lengthy negotiations with the assistance of a joint expert and an experienced judicial officer, and it also generated relatively few class member objections. *Murray*, 514 P.3d 1081. The district court need not make specific findings of fact regarding any settlement objections or the court's basis for approving a class action settlement. *Id.*

The author of this section, Michael J. Gayan, leads the class action team at Claggett & Sykes Law Firm. Prior to Claggett & Sykes, Mr. Gayan was a partner at the litigation firm Kemp Jones, LLP, where he and others in the firm prosecuted and defended class action claims in various fields of law, including products liability, consumer goods and services, employee compensation, data breach, antitrust violations, and residential construction defects, resulting in hundreds of millions of dollars in settlements and jury verdicts.

NEW HAMPSHIRE

1. SUPERIOR COURT RULE 16 IS SIMILAR IN MOST REGARDS TO RULE 23 OF THE FEDERAL RULES OF CIVIL PROCEDURE

In 1984, the New Hampshire Superior Court established Rule 16, the state's class action rule. The state's high court had urged it to do so in *State Employees' Association of New Hampshire v. Belknap County*, 122 N.H. 614, 448 A.2d 969 (N.H. 1982), wherein it had applied each of the several class requisites contained in then-current Rule 23 of the Federal Rules of Civil Procedure in its disposition of the appeal. Thus, Rule 16 essentially codified recent common law expressly derived from Federal Rule 23. Like the federal rule, New Hampshire's Superior Court Rule 16 requires the moving party to establish the existence of numerosity, typicality, commonality, and adequate representation (as does Fed. R. Civ. P. 23(a)), as well as predominance of common questions and superiority (as does 23(b)(3)).

New Hampshire's Supreme Court first interpreted Rule 16 in *Cantwell v. J & R Props. Unlimited, Inc.*, 155 N.H. 508, 924 A.2d 355 (N.H. 2007). In doing so, it noted that "[b]ecause [Rule 16] is similar to Federal Rule of Civil Procedure 23, we rely upon cases interpreting the federal rule as analytic aids." *Id.* at 511, 358. In *Cantwell*, and in each of its three subsequent decisions interpreting Rule 16 (*Petition of Bayview Crematory, LLC et al.*, 155 N.H. 781, 930 A.2d 1190 (N.H. 2007); *Lawrence v. Philip Morris, USA, Inc.*, 164 N.H. 93, 53 A.3d 525 (N.H. 2012); and *Eby v. State*, 2014 N.H. LEXIS 56 (N.H. June 13, 2014), New Hampshire's Supreme Court extensively relied upon federal cases interpreting Rule 23.

2. IN ITS FIRST LOOK AT RULE 16, NEW HAMPSHIRE'S HIGHEST COURT ADOPTED THE RIGOROUS ANALYSIS STANDARD

In *Cantwell, supra*, the plaintiff tenant sued his former landlord for failing to pay interest on security deposits in violation of state law. He sought classwide relief for all the landlord's similarly situated former tenants. The defendant objected to the class claims, and in response to the objection the plaintiff filed his supporting class memorandum. At this point in the litigation, though, plaintiff had yet to receive responses to his discovery requests. The trial court dismissed his class claims, ruling that he had failed to provide any evidence of commonality or typicality, beyond the mere allegations contained in the pleadings. Plaintiff's subsequent motion to compel responses to his outstanding discovery requests pertaining to the class claims was then denied as moot. Plaintiff appealed, contending that by dismissing his class claims on the ground that he failed to produce evidence to support his class allegations, and then denying his motion to compel the discovery that would have enabled him to produce this evidence, the trial court erred. The state's highest court agreed with him. This straightforward consumer case provided the impetus for the New Hampshire Supreme Court to interpret Super. Ct. Rule 16 for the first time. Its ruling focused on the evidentiary burden plaintiffs must satisfy to obtain class certification. Specifically, the Court explained that the trial court cannot simply accept the allegations of the complaint as true. Instead, in conducting its "rigorous analysis" of whether the class certification prerequisites have been satisfied, the trial court will ordinarily need to go beyond the pleadings themselves. The Cantwell decision makes it clear that plaintiffs seeking class certification cannot satisfy the Rule 16 requisites by resting on the allegations in their pleadings, but instead must ensure that "the [trial] judge []receive[s] enough evidence, by affidavits, documents, or testimony, to be satisfied that each [class certification] requirement has been met." *Id.* at 512–13 (quoting *In re Initial Public Offering Securities Lit.*, 471 F.3d 24, 41 (2d Cir. 2006)).

3. IN EACH OF ITS NEXT TWO LOOKS AT RULE 16, THE COURT CONCLUDED THE NEED FOR DEEP INDIVIDUALIZED INQUIRIES DESTROYED PREDOMINANCE

a. *Bayview Crematory*—The Need for Deep Individualized Inquiries Destroys Predominance

Not long after issuing the *Cantwell* decision, the state's highest court reviewed an order certifying for class treatment the issue of the defendants' liability for negligent infliction of emotional distress. *Bayview Crematory, supra*, arose out of the allegedly negligent handling of decedents' remains entrusted to any one of several funeral homes, each of which utilized the services of this crematory. The plaintiffs and putative class members, who were the decedents' next-of-kin, alleged that Bayview Crematory and the funeral homes breached their duties and failed to perform in accordance with the applicable standard of care, resulting in emotional suffering and damages; and that their negligent handling of the bodies of the decedents caused the plaintiffs and class members to suffer emotional distress. The trial court certified the emotional distress claim to proceed on a classwide basis.

Unsurprisingly, the class certification order was appealed. Before turning to the substantive issues before it, New Hampshire's Supreme Court announced its standard for reviewing class certification orders. Relying on federal cases interpreting Rule 23, the court essentially adopted the First Circuit's abuse of discretion standard, along with its *de novo* standard of review of purely legal questions. *Id.* at 784–85. However, it did so with the caveat that it would actually apply its state's analogous "unsustainable exercise of discretion" standard rather than the First Circuit's "abuse of discretion" standard. *Id.* at 785.

The *Bayview Crematory* court decertified the class on predominance grounds, holding that "the questions relating to the individual putative class members regarding [the negligent infliction of emotional distress] will predominate over those common to all putative class members." *Id.* at 787. It explained that issues particular to the individual class members (such as whether the class member had actually suffered physical symptoms of the alleged emotional distress—a finding that must rest on expert testimony) would outweigh the issues common to the class (such as the proper standard of care and whether defendants breached it). *Id.* at 785–87.

b. *Lawrence*—Again the Need for Deep Individualized Inquiries Destroys Predominance

Five years after deciding *Bayview Crematory*, the New Hampshire Supreme Court was again confronted with a request for class decertification on predominance grounds. In *Lawrence, supra*, plaintiff alleged Marlboro Lights cigarettes were overvalued because they did not offer any added health benefits beyond traditional cigarettes, and that the defendant tobacco company had therefore violated the state's Consumer Protection Act by falsely advertising the purported existence of added health benefits. The trial court certified a statewide class of purchasers.

The tobacco company appealed the certification order, primarily on predominance ground. New Hampshire's Supreme Court, in concluding that this light cigarettes case was not suitable for class treatment, noted that eleven out of thirteen courts confronted with this issue had reached the same conclusion (for one reason or another). *Id.* at 97. Here, the court agreed with the tobacco company's argument that perhaps not all the class members had been injured by its false advertisements. The company explained that the class members would have been exposed to plenty of public information about light cigarettes, not just its advertisements. Some of this other public information did in fact call into question whether light cigarettes actually provide added health benefits over regular cigarettes. Thus, some class members, it contended, would not have been deceived by—and therefore would not have suffered an injury from—its false advertising. *Id.* at 97. On this reasoning, the court concluded that "the information about lights to which individual class members were exposed, and what they believed, are individual issues that will predominate over common ones." *Lawrence*, 164 N.H. at 101.

4. IN ITS FOURTH AND MOST RECENT LOOK AT RULE 16, THE COURT EXPLAINED THAT THE PLAINTIFF HAS TO BE A MEMBER OF THE CLASS HE OR SHE SEEKS TO REPRESENT

In *Eby, supra*, the plaintiffs were taxpayers who alleged a statute imposing a 10 percent state tax on all gambling winnings violated fairness provisions of the State's Constitution as well as the dormant Commerce Clause. After affirming the trial court's conclusion that the gambling tax did not violate the State's Constitution, the Court considered the plaintiffs' dormant Commerce Clause claim. *Id.* at 7. The Court did not need to reach the merits of the claim. Instead, it concluded the plaintiffs lacked standing because they had failed to show any cognizable harm related to the alleged Commerce Clause violation. *Id.* Essentially, given the language of the tax statute and the record, in order to have standing an individual who had paid the gambling tax would have to either (a) be a "professional gambler"; or (b) have received his or her gambling winnings in the form of an annuity. *Id.* at 9. Since none of the plaintiffs satisfied either criteria, none had standing to assert his or her individual dormant Commerce Clause claim. *Id.* at 8. Moreover, and of particular relevance here, since none met the standing requirement as to their individual claim, none had standing to bring claims on behalf of the proposed class d. at 11–12. "'[A] class representative must be part of the class and possess the same interest and suffer the same injury as the class members.' [*Wal–Mart Stores, Inc. v. Dukes*, 131 S. Ct. 2541 (U.S. 2011)] (quotations omitted). Superior Court Civil Rule 16 sets forth a similar requirement for class representatives. *See Super. Ct. Civ. R.* 16(a)(2)." *Id.* at 11. "The fact that the petitioners brought this case as a class action does not exempt them from the requirement that they have standing." *Id.* at 12.

5. THE TRIAL COURT HAS PROVIDED GUIDANCE AS TO THE REMAINING RULE 16 REQUISITES

None of the three cases discussed above required the court to extend its Rule 16 analysis beyond a consideration of the predominance requisite to class certification. The state's trial court, though, has provided guidance as to all of the class requisites enumerated within Rule 16. *In Gibson v. Universal Underwriters Life Ins. Co.*, Hills. Cty (NH) Superior Court, No. Dist., CA 04-C-414 (N.H. Super. Ct. 2005), New Hampshire's trial court provided the following guidance in its order certifying a statewide consumer class action involving a credit insurer's alleged failure to refund unearned premiums to consumers who bought defendant's prepaid credit life insurance on their car loans but then paid off their loans prior to the expiration of the coverage period.

a. Numerosity

Rather than pleading any magic number of potential class members, the movant needs to show that joinder is impractical. "[T]he court must consider the number of members in the proposed class, their geographical distribution, and whether class members can be easily identified in determining whether the proposed class satisfies the numerosity requirement." *Gibson*, at 4 (citations omitted). If more than 40 class members exist, there is a presumption of numerosity. *Id.* In *Gibson*, the trial court concluded plaintiffs satisfied the numerosity requirement by establishing that "hundreds or perhaps thousands of consumers" existed both within and outside the state who had paid off their car loans early but not received their unearned premium refunds despite defendant's alleged contractual promise to make the refunds.

b. Commonality

The *Gibson* court next explained that "[t]he test for commonality is not demanding and is met where there is at least one issue, the resolution of which will affect all or a significant number of the putative class members." *Id.* at *5 (quoting *Mullen v. Treasure Chest Casino, LLC*, 186 F.3d 620, 625 (5th Cir. 1999). It concluded plaintiffs adequately alleged defendant had engaged in a "common course of conduct" by failing to make the unearned premium refunds on early loan payoffs, thereby satisfying the commonality requirement. *Id.* at 6.

c. Typicality

Because the plaintiffs alleged they and the class members suffered the same injury—financial harm as a result of the defendant's alleged failure to refund their unearned premiums to them—the *Gibson* court ruled they had satisfied the typicality requirement since "in trying their case, the named plaintiffs will necessarily present the claims of the absent [class members]." *Id.*

d. Adequacy

The trial court, citing Newberg, § 3.22, explained that "[t]o prove the adequacy requirement, the plaintiffs must show: 1) the absence of conflict; and 2) assurance of vigorous prosecution." *Id.* at 7. Referencing plaintiffs' supporting affidavits and their counsel's work history, the trial court concluded the adequacy requirement was satisfied as to both the class representatives and their proposed class counsel.

e. Superiority

Lastly, the *Gibson* court turned to the superiority requirement. Finding that the adjudication of the common issues identified in the case would "achieve judicial economies and practical advantages without jeopardizing procedural fairness," *Id.* at 8–9, quoting *Rothwell v. Chubb Life Ins. Co. of Am.*, 191 F.R.D. 25, 29 (D.N.H. 1998), in that the risk of hundreds of individual lawsuits each seeking to recover just a few hundred dollars—and the attendant risk of inconsistent adjudications—would thereby be eliminated, the trial court concluded plaintiffs had satisfied the superiority requirement.

6. ADDITIONAL CASE LAW CONCERNING RULE 16 IS INEVITABLE

State court class actions have only recently taken hold in New Hampshire. More plaintiffs' lawyers have discovered the advantages that may flow out of the judicious use of this procedural device. At the same time, defense lawyers have become much more inclined to aggressively challenge bids for class status and to appeal certification orders. Inevitably, additional interpretations of Rule 16 will issue from the state's highest court during the coming years. These decisions will likely provide guidance as to not only the basic class requisites, but also as to emerging issues pertaining to class certification, such as ascertainability of class membership and protection of due process rights in connection with the assessment and distribution of classwide and individual class members' damages

Moreover, the New Hampshire Supreme Court may have occasion to interpret a provision within Rule 16 that has no counterpart within the federal class action rule. Superior Court Rule 16(h) provides that if the court renders judgment in favor of the class, "the court may, in its discretion, order the defendant to pay damages into the court and require each member of the class to file a claim with the court, or order payment of damages in any other manner it deems appropriate." Perhaps the court will construe Rule 16(h) as providing statutory authorization for a fluid recovery.

RULE 16 OF THE RULES OF THE SUPERIOR COURT OF THE STATE OF NEW HAMPSHIRE

RULE 16.

(a) *Prerequisites to a class action.* One or more members of a class may sue or be sued as representative parties on behalf of all if:

(1) the class is so numerous that joinder of all members, whether otherwise required or permitted, is impracticable;

(2) there are questions of law or fact common to the class which predominate over any questions affecting only individual members;

(3) the claims or defenses of the representative parties are typical of the claims or defenses of the class;

(4) the representative parties will fairly and adequately protect the interests of the class;

(5) a class action is superior to other available methods for the fair and efficient adjudication of the controversy; and

(6) the attorney or non-attorney representative for the representative parties will adequately represent the interests of the class.

(b) *Order allowing class action.* As soon as practicable after the commencement of an action brought as a class action, the court shall determine by order whether it is to be so maintained. An order under this section may be conditional and may be altered or amended before the decision on the merits on the court's own motion or on motion of the parties. The action may be maintained as a class action only if the court finds that the prerequisites under subdivision (a) of this rule have been satisfied.

(c) *Satisfaction of jurisdictional damages limit.* For purposes of satisfying the jurisdictional damages limit of the court, the claims of the members of the class shall be aggregated.

(d) *Description of class.* The order permitting a class action shall describe the class. When appropriate the court may limit the class to those members who do not request exclusion from the class within the specified time after notice.

(e) *Notice of class action.* Following the court's order maintaining the class action, the court shall direct to the members of the class the best notice practicable under the circumstances, including individual notice to all members who can be identified through reasonable effort. The notice shall advise each member that (A) the court will exclude him from the class if he so requests by a specified date; (B) the judgment, whether favorable or not, will include all members who do not request exclusion; (C) any member who does not request exclusion may, if he desires, enter an appearance through his counsel; and contain such other information that the court deems appropriate. Unless the court orders otherwise, the representatives of the class shall bear the expense of notification and be responsible for the giving of the notice to members of the class.

(f) *Exclusion.* Any member of the plaintiff class who files an election to be excluded in the manner and in the time specified in the notice, is excluded from and not bound by the judgment in the class action. A member of a defendant class may not elect to be excluded.

(g) *Judgment.* The judgment in an action maintained as a class action, whether or not favorable to the class, shall include and describe those whom the court finds to be members of the class.

(h) *Methods of payment of damages.* If the court renders judgment in favor of a plaintiff class, the court may, in its discretion, order the defendant to pay damages into the court and require each member of the class to file a claim with the court, or order payment of damages in any other manner it deems appropriate.

(i) *Action conducted partially as class actions.* When appropriate, an action may be brought or maintained as a class action with respect to particular issues, or a class may be divided into subclasses and each subclass treated as a class. The provisions of this subdivision shall then be construed and applied accordingly.

(j) *Orders in conduct of class actions.* In the conduct of class actions the court may make and alter appropriate orders:

(1) Determining the course of proceedings or prescribing measures to prevent undue repetition or complication in the presentation of evidence or argument;

(2) Requiring, for the protection of the members of the class, or otherwise for the fair conduct of the action, that notice be given in such manner as the court may direct to some or all of the members of any step in the action, or of the proposed extent of the judgment, or of the opportunity of members to signify whether they consider the representation fair and adequate, or to appear and present claims or defenses, or otherwise to come into the action; or

(3) Dealing with similar procedural matters.

(k) *Dismissal, discontinuance, or settlement.* A class action shall not be dismissed, discontinued, or settled without the approval of the court. Notice of the proposed dismissal, discontinuance, or settlement shall be given to all members of the class in such manner as the court directs.

Josh Gardner is a partner at Gardner & Rosenberg PC. He represents plaintiffs and defendants in all types of class actions, including consumer and employment cases. He practices in Massachusetts, New Hampshire, and New York. This chapter was originally authored by Edward K. O'Brien, founder of O'Brien Law Firm, PC, located in Manchester, New Hampshire.

NEW JERSEY

1. OVERVIEW

The New Jersey class action rules are provided for in the New Jersey Court Rules 4:32-1 and 4:32-2 and largely mirror the language of Fed. R. Civ. P. 23. *Goasdone v. American Cyanimid Corp.*, 354 N.J. Super. 519, 527, 808 A.2d 159, 164 (Law Div. 2002) (citing *In the Matter of Cadillac V8-6-4 Class Action*, 93 N.J. 412, 461 A.2d 736 (1983) (*Cadillac*)). The exceptions include replacement of Fed. R. Civ. P. 23(c)'s phrase "including individual notice to all members who can be identified through reasonable effort" with "consistent with the due process of law" in New Jersey's equivalent Rule 4:32-2(b). New Jersey also provides that cost of notice may be assessed against any party or may be allocated among the parties pending final disposition of the case. Additionally, the New Jersey equivalent of Fed. R. Civ. P. 23(c)(3) adds that a (b)(3) judgment shall "to the extent practicable under the circumstances, consistent with due process of law" identify the members of the class, and that the judgment may "consistent with due process of law, confer benefits upon a fluid class." *See* Rule 4:32-2(c). These provisions have no specific counterparts in the Federal Rule.

Effective September 1, 2006, the class action rules were amended to conform to the December 1, 2003, revisions to Fed. R. Civ. P. 23. They also were reorganized so that Rule 4:32-1 largely mirrors Fed. R. Civ. P. 23(a) *and* (b), and Rule 4:32-2 largely mirrors Fed. R. Civ. P. 23(c), (d), (e), (g), and (h). The 2006 amendments did not adopt a counterpart to Fed. R. Civ. P. 23(f) providing for permissive interlocutory appeals of class certification decisions because other New Jersey rules already permit discretionary appeals to the Appellate Division, *see* Rule 2:5-6, and to the Supreme Court, *see* Rule 2:2-2. In 2022, however, Rule 2:2-3(b)(9), which governs appeals to the Appellate Division, was amended to make "orders denying or granting as a final matter class certification" appealable as of right to the Appellate Division. *See* R. 2:2-3(b)(9). Additionally, Rule 2:11-1(a) was also amended in 2022 to give preference to such appeals in the scheduling of argument or submission without argument.

Rule 4:32 is reprinted below.

2. CLASS CERTIFICATION PROCESS

New Jersey courts construe class action rules liberally. *Dugan v. TGI Fridays, Inc.*, 231 N.J. 24, 46, 171 A.3d 620, 633 (2017); *Daniels v. Hollister Co.*, 440 N.J. Super. 359, 363, 113 A.3d 796, 798 (App. Div. 2015); *Iliadis v. Wal-Mart Stores, Inc.*, 191 N.J. 88, 103, 922 A.2d 710, 718 (2007); *Gross v. Johnson & Johnson-Merck Consumer Pharm. Co.*, 303 N.J. Super. 336, 340–41, 696 A.2d 793, 795 (Law Div. 1997); *Saldana v. City of Camden*, 252 N.J. Super. 188, 196, 599 A.2d 582, 586 (App. Div. 1991). It has been held that not only do class actions save time and money for the parties and the public, and promote consistent decisions for people with similar claims, class actions also allow consumers to redress common grievances under circumstances that would make individual actions uneconomical to pursue. *Dugan*, 231 N.J. at 46, 171 A.3d at 633; *Daniels*, 440 N.J. Super.

at 363, 113 A.3d at 798; *Cartiglia v. Johnson & Johnson Co.*, 2002 WL 1009473, at *9 (Law Div. April 24, 2002) (citing *Varacallo v. Massachusetts Mut. Life Ins. Co.*, 332 N.J. Super. 31, 45, 752 A.2d 807, 815 (App. Div. 2000)); *Carroll v. Cellco Partnership*, 313 N.J. Super. 488, 498, 713 A.2d 509, 512 (App. Div. 1998) and *Cadillac*, 93 N.J. at 412, 461 A.2d at 736. Nevertheless, the burden of establishing class status is on the plaintiff, and the court is required to undertake a "rigorous analysis" to determine whether class prerequisites are met. *Carroll*, 313 N.J. Super. at 495, 713 A.2d at 512. The "rigorous analysis requirement" requires the trial court to look "beyond the pleadings [to] understand the claims, defenses relevant facts, and applicable substantive law." *Iliadis*, 191 N.J. at 107, 922 A.2d at 721 (quoting *Carroll*, 313 N.J. Super. at 495); *Dugan*, 231 N.J. at 49, 171 A.3d at 633. It also "means that a class is not maintainable merely because the complaint parrots the legal requirements of the class action rule." *Id.*

The determination of the appropriateness of class certification requires "some preliminary analysis" of the underlying theories of liability and possible defenses. *Cadillac*, 93 N.J. at 426, 461 A.2d at 743. *See also Cartiglia*, 2002 WL 1009473, at *19 (stating that the merits "are not entirely off limits when evaluating whether a class should be granted"). In deciding a class certification motion, the court must accept the allegations of plaintiff's complaint as true and must also consider the remaining pleadings, discovery (including interrogatory responses, relevant documents, and depositions), and any other pertinent evidence in the light most favorable to plaintiff but must also engage in a rigorous analysis to determine whether all requirements of class certification have been met. *Lee v. Carter-Reed Co., L.L.C.*, 203 N.J. 496, 523, 4 A.3d 561, 577 (2010); *Sutton v. Hoffman La Roche*, 2020 N.J. Super. Unpub. LEXIS 1001, at *10–11 (App. Div. May 27, 2020). The contours of a proposed class must be clearly defined so that the court can feasibly determine whether a particular individual is a member of the proposed class. *Daniels*, 440 N.J. Super. at 365, 113 A.3d at 799; *Sutton*, 2020 N.J. Super. Unpub. LEXIS 1001 at *37 ("The proposed class must be sufficiently identifiable without being overly broad and may not be amorphous, vague or indeterminate but administratively feasible to determine whether a given individual is a member of the class."). In *Daniels*, however, the court held that while R. 4:32-1 requires a clear class definition, it did not contain an implicit requirement that the class be "ascertainable" as a condition for certification. *Daniels* involved consumer fraud claims asserted against a clothing retailer that allegedly imposed an expiration date on $25 gift cards that were provided to customers that purchased at least $75 worth of defendant's merchandise. Plaintiff alleged that the gift cards either stated "no expiration date" or were silent as to when they would expire. The defendant appealed the trial court's decision to grant class certification because it argued that class members were not ascertainable by objective criteria. The appellate court rejected defendant's argument holding that there is no ascertainability requirement in low value consumer class actions because such a requirement would frustrate the objectives of the class action procedure to provide the fair and efficient administration of justice to consumers with small injuries. The court further noted that an ascertainability requirement was still unsettled by the federal circuit courts interpreting Federal Rule of Civil Procedure 23. 440 N.J. Super. at 366, 113 A.3d at 800 (explaining that "federal experimentation with the ascertainability doctrine seems far from over . . ."). The court declined to consider whether an ascertainability requirement would be imposed in other types of class actions. *Compare Narain v. George Harms Constr. Co.*, 2023 WL 3575597 (App. Div. May 22, 2023), *leave to appeal denied*, 255 N.J. 380, 301 A.3d 1282 (2023) (in suit seeking damages for water main break allegedly caused by defendant's pile-driving activity, appeals court affirmed denial of motion for class certification for failure to satisfy numerosity requirement, where the proposed class, consisting of all water utility customers in municipality over three days, was overbroad and over-inclusive because there was no way to determine which residents lost water at all, much less for three days; "although our courts do not require that every class member be ascertainable before certification is permitted, a proposed class still must be 'properly defined' 'without being overly broad'; and the class 'may not be amorphous, vague, or indeterminate and it must be administratively feasible to determine whether a given individual is a member of the class'").

3. RULE 4:32-1(A) REQUIREMENTS

The prerequisites for a class action under Rule 4:32-1(a) follow those of Fed. R. Civ. P. 23(a)–(1) numerosity, (2) commonality, (3) typicality, and (4) adequacy of representation. If these elements are met, plaintiffs must then show that one of the alternative requirements of Rule 4:32-1(b) (modeling Fed. R. Civ. P. 23(b)) is satisfied. *See Goasdone,* 354 N.J. Super. at 528, 808 A.2d at 164. The decision in *Goasdone* illustrates the application of the Rule 4:32-1(a) elements. 354 N.J. Super. at 529–30, 808 A.2d at 165 (finding prerequisites of numerosity, commonality, typicality, and adequacy met in suit seeking medical monitoring for workers exposed to benzidine, noting, *inter alia*, that commonality threshold is "relatively low," requiring only a "single common question" of fact or law, and that typicality does not require that the class representatives' claims be identical to those of all class members, but share "essential characteristics" and arise from the same event, practice or cause of conduct and same legal theory).

a. Adequacy

Adequacy of representation depends on a showing of adequacy of the representative and her counsel. *Rebish v. Great Gorge*, 224 N.J. Super 619, 623–24, 541 A.2d 237, 239 (App. Div. 1988). The focus is on the quality, not quantity, of the representation and whether the representative's interests are aligned with the class members' interests, whether the representative and class members share common objectives and legal or factual positions, and whether there is an absence of antagonistic interests between the representative and the class. *Gallano v. Running*, 139 N.J. Super 239, 246, 33 A.2d 158, 162 (Law Div. 1976), *cert. denied*, 75 N.J. 609, 384 A.2d 830 (1978). While federal courts usually require the class representative to have standing in the sense of a direct relationship with defendant, the standard in New Jersey is whether plaintiff's concern with the subject matter evidences a "sufficient stake and real adverseness" as to be typical of claims and defenses of the class. *Kronisch v. Howard Sav. Inst.*, 133 N.J. Super. 124, 137, 335 A.2d 587, 594 (Ch. Div. 1975), *remanded*, 143 N.J. Super. 423, 363 A.2d 376 (App. Div. 1976), *on remand*, 154 N.J. Super. 576, 382 A.2d 64 (Ch. Div. 1977), *affirmed in part, reversed in part*, 161 N.J. Super. 592, 392 A.2d 178 (App. Div. 1978).

In *Winslow v. Corporate Express, Inc.*, 364 N.J. Super. 128, 834 A.2d 1037 (App. Div. 2003), a class representative's prior ownership of an office supplies business did not prevent him from serving as a class representative for claims alleging violations of applicable wage laws, breach of contract and fraud, arising out of his former employer's unilateral alteration of the manner in which it calculated commissions for its salespersons. While the trial court, citing concerns akin to the "typicality" and "adequacy" requirements for class certification, disqualified him from acting as class representative because he "presumably had greater knowledge of practices in the industry . . . than other potential class representatives," 364 N.J. Super. at 143, 834 A.2d at 1046, the Appellate Division reversed, stating that plaintiff's "situation, as relates to defendant's failure to give advance notice of [the change in commission calculation method], is no different from that of any other sales representative who failed to receive such notice from defendant." 364 N.J. Super. at 144, 834 A.2d at 1047.

In *Francavilla v. Absolute Resolutions VI, LLC,* 478 N.J. Super. 171, 312 A.3d 307 (App. Div. 2024), the Appellate Division upheld an order dismissing a putative class action against a collection company alleging it had purchased consumer debt without first obtaining a license to operate as a consumer lender or sales finance company, in violation of the New Jersey Consumer Finance Licensing Act, N.J.S.A. 17:11C-1 *et seq.* The court held that the named plaintiff's claims were barred by the "entire controversy" doctrine, an equitable doctrine that "generally requires parties to an action to raise all transactionally related claims in that same action," 478 N.J. Super. at 178, 312 A.3d at 311, because the plaintiff could have raised and litigated her CFLA claims in a prior action that the defendant collection company had commenced against plaintiff, "but [the plaintiff] failed or even chose not to do so." 478 N.J. Super. at 177, 312 A.3d at 310. Because the plaintiff's individual claims were barred by the entire controversy doctrine, the appeals court agreed with "the trial court's determination that the non-viability of plaintiff's claims as an individual precludes her ability to be a class representative under Rule 4:32-1(a)(3)." 478 N.J. Super. at 182, 312 A.3d at 313.

By the same token, where the class members' claims would be subject to the entire controversy doctrine or res judicata, but the named plaintiff's claims are not, that will also prevent class certification. In *Williams-Hopkins v. Medwell, LLC,* 2024 WL 1476821 (App. Div. Apr. 5, 2024), plaintiffs were sued by a provider of medical, physical therapy, and chiropractic services for outstanding fees. Though plaintiffs answered the complaint in the first suit, they separately filed a putative class action on behalf of two classes: individuals from whom the provider had sought to collect excessive fees and/or interest, and a class of individuals whose protected health information had been improperly disclosed to the public as part of collection lawsuits by the defendant provider. Plaintiffs then moved to consolidate both actions. 2024 WL 1476821, at *2–4. In affirming the trial court's denial of class certification, the Appellate Division noted the trial court's finding that the other proposed class members identified by plaintiffs had "already been litigants in prior cases, and their cases have been disposed of . . . and none of those proposed individuals raised any of these alleged issues prior to the disposition of those cases." 2024 WL 1476821, at *8. Because the class members would be precluded from participating in the putative class action due to res judicata and the entire controversy doctrine, the named plaintiffs—who were not barred from pursuing their claims—failed to demonstrate numerosity and typicality.

b. Predominance

Under (b)(3), with respect to the predominance requirement, certification will not be defeated by the need for individual damage calculations, *Delgozzo v. Kenny*, 266 N.J. Super 169, 190, 628 A.2d 1080, 1091 (App. Div. 1993), but common questions of liability must predominate and New Jersey courts will deny certification if they do not. *See, e.g*, *Cartiglia*, 2002 WL 1009473, at *17 (class certification denied under New Jersey's product liability statute because of varying circumstances in which the prescription drug at issue was taken); *Gross*, 303 N.J. Super. at 349–50, 696 A.2d at 799 (class certification denied in part because every class member would be required to answer questions as to whether he or she relied on any of three advertisements at issue); *Carroll*, 313 N.J. Super. at 505, 713 A.2d at 517 (class certification denied because claims of fraud and negligent misrepresentation did not arise out of the same transactions); *Goasdone*, 354 N.J. Super. at 537, 808 A.2d at 169 (individual issues, *e.g.*, related to the timing and extent of each worker's exposure, health impacts and need for medical monitoring precluded certification under (b)(2) or (b)(3)); *Muise v. GPU, Inc.*, 371 N.J. Super. 13, 851 A.2d 799 (App. Div. 2004) (where there were multiple causes for a series of power interruptions, individual causation issues would predominate and a theory of common liability based on general unpreparedness was not cognizable in New Jersey); *Muise v. GPU, Inc.*, 391

N.J. Super. 90, 917 A.2d 261 (App. Div. 2007) (finding that a class limited to those who lost power due to negligent failure to replace two transformers in an aged substation satisfies predominance requirement, remanding with instruction to certify such a limited class); *Arons v. Rite Aid Corp.*, 2005 WL 975462, at *20 (Law Div. Mar. 23, 2005) (class certification denied because each class member would have to prove that he or she actually received counterfeit Lipitor given that not all Lipitor sold in time period was counterfeit). In *Goasdone*, the court elaborated that while the plaintiffs had met New Jersey's requirement for a (b)(2) case that the relief sought be predominantly injunctive (*i.e*, medical monitoring), it found that the individual issues precluded a finding of "cohesiveness" or "homogeneity" of class members' claims (*i.e.*, that defendants "had acted or refused to act on grounds generally applicable to the class"). *Goasdone*, 354 N.J. Super. at 533, 808 A.2d at 167 (noting agreement with courts finding "cohesiveness" requirement for (b)(2) cases) (citations omitted). The same individual issues prevented plaintiffs from meeting the "predominance" and "superiority" requirements for a (b)(3) claim. 354 N.J. Super. at 540–41, 808 A.2d at 171–72 (distinguishing toxic exposure case from airplane crash or hotel disaster cases where individualized issues related to causation and injury are less prevalent).

The "predominance" requirement was addressed by the New Jersey Supreme Court in *Dugan v. TGI Fridays, Inc.*, where the Court addressed two separate lawsuits in which consumers asserted that they were deceived by beverage pricing practices at the defendants' restaurants. In *Dugan*, consumers brought a putative class action against TGI Friday's alleging that the company's failure to include beverage prices in its menus violated New Jersey's Consumer Fraud Act (CFA) and Truth in Consumer Contract Warranty and Notice Act (TCCWNA). The trial court had certified a class of all persons who purchased an unpriced beverage from a New Jersey–based TGI Friday's during the relevant time period. On appeal, the Appellate Division reversed, holding that the trial court erred when it found that plaintiffs established that common issues of fact predominated over individualized issues. In the second case, *Bozzi v. OSI Rest. Partners, LLC*, consumers brought a putative class action against Carraba's alleging that the restaurant charged different prices for the same beverage during the same visit without posting the price change in violation of TCCWNA. In *Bozzi*, the trial court granted class certification and the Appellate Division declined to accept the defendant's interlocutory appeal. The New Jersey Supreme Court granted certification in both cases and consolidated them for appellate purposes.

The Supreme Court upheld the Appellate Division's decision denying class certification in the *Dugan* case but held that class certification was appropriate in the *Bozzi* case, limited to those consumers who were charged different prices for the same beverage during the same visit without notice. The Court explained that the predominance standard is "far more demanding" than the requirement that a common issue of fact or law exist. A qualitative assessment of the common and individualized issues is required rather than a mathematical quantification of whether there are more common than individualized issues. 231 N.J. at 48, 171 A.3d at 634. After explaining that *Dugan*'s CFA claim required proof that each class member suffered an "ascertainable loss," the Court explained that each class member would have to establish that he would have not ordered a beverage, or would have ordered fewer beverages, had the beverage prices been included in the menu. The Court rejected plaintiffs' attempt to rely on a market inflation or fraud on the market theory, as numerous decisions have held that ascertainable loss cannot be based on such theories of proof. Because *Dugan*'s CFA claim would require individualized proof of each class member's ascertainable loss, the Court held that individualized issues predominated over common issues. 231 N.J. at 63, 171 A.3d at 643. With respect to the *Bozzi* case, the Court held that the predominance requirement had been met because plaintiffs could present individualized proof of each class member being charged different prices for the same beverage during the same visit. 231 N.J. at 67, 171 A.3d at 646. In both *Dugan* and *Bozzi*, the Court held that there were too many individualized issues to warrant class certification of plaintiffs' TCCWNA claims. 231 N.J. at 74, 171 A.3d at 650. As the New Jersey Supreme Court subsequently confirmed, plaintiffs must establish actual harm in order to recover under TCCWNA, which often requires individualized proof. *Spade v. Select Comfort Corp.*, 232 N.J. 504, 181 A.3d 969 (2018).

The "predominance" requirement was also addressed in *Lee v. Carter-Reed Corp., L.L.C.*, in which the Court stated the determination of predominance requires a "pragmatic assessment" of various factors. In *Lee*, plaintiff brought a purported class action on behalf of New Jersey consumers who purchased the defendant's dietary supplement pill called Relacore. 203 N.J. at 504, 4 A.3d at 565. Plaintiff alleged that the defendant engaged in a multi-media marketing campaign in which it represented that Relacore would help purchasers lose weight, elevate their mood, and reduce anxiety. *Id.* Plaintiff further alleged that there was no scientific basis to support any of these marketing claims and the product did not provide any such health benefits. *Id.* Plaintiff brought a claim under the CFA and claims for breach of warranty and unjust enrichment. *Id.* The trial court denied class certification and the Appellate Division affirmed finding that individualized causation issues, such as which marketing pieces the consumers viewed and which representation (weight loss, mood elevation, or anxiety reduction) persuaded them to purchase the product, predominated over common issues of fact and law. 203 N.J. at 511–14, 4 A.3d at 569–72.

The Supreme Court reversed, finding that common issues predominated over individualized issues, and certified the class as to plaintiff's consumer fraud claim. 203 N.J. at 524–27, 4 A.3d at 578–80. In reaching this decision, the Court reversed the lower courts for not accepting as true allegations in the complaint that all of the defendant's representations about the product were false, scientifically unsupported and a "passel of lies." *Id.* Because plaintiff alleged that Relacore did not provide any of the represented health benefits, the Court held that plaintiff could prove, on a class-wide basis, that the defendant's deceptive marketing was causally related to the class's ascertainable losses. *Id.* The Court further accepted plaintiff's argument that Relacore is a "credence good"—a product that is only known to purchasers because of the proposed benefits promised by the manufacturer. *Id.* The Court explained that no rational consumer would decide to purchase Relacore without having been persuaded by at least one of the manufacturer's representations. Because of these unique factors, the Court found that common issues predominated over any individualized issues, that a class action was a superior vehicle for adjudicating the claims of the purported class, and that no manageability problems precluded certification of the proposed class. *Id.*

In *D'Andrea v. K. Hovnanian*, 2013 N.J. Super. Unpub. LEXIS 1484 (App. Div. June 18, 2013), homeowners brought a putative class action alleging construction defects in the HVAC systems in their homes that presented a fire hazard. After an evidentiary hearing including experts, the trial court granted plaintiffs' class certification motion holding that common issues related to whether the defendant's construction methods and practices violated applicable building codes predominated over individual issues. 2013 N.J. Super. Unpub. LEXIS 1484 at *6–7. On appeal, the Appellate Division affirmed finding that although the class members' homes suffered from different construction defects, common issues still predominated because the alleged defects all created the same fire safety hazard. *Id.* at *13–15.

c. Superiority

With respect to the "superiority" requirement, the Supreme Court held, in reversing a pre-discovery motion to dismiss class allegations, that the availability of up to $1,000 per violation and attorneys' fees in individual actions under The Fair and Accurate Credit Transaction Act (FACTA), was an insufficient incentive to make individual actions a superior method of adjudication. *Baskin v. P.C. Richard & Son, LLC*, 246 N.J. 157, 249 A.3d 461 (2021). Courts should consider the effect of class certification on efficient judicial management. *Cadillac*, 93 N.J. at 435–36, 461 A.2d at 748. Manageability problems may arise in the context of a nationwide class action where the court would have to apply the laws of multiple states to plaintiffs' claims. *See Carroll*, 313 N.J. Super. at 506–07, 713 A.2d at 518 (where court held in fraud case that once it determined which state law to apply, it would then be required to investigate each claim to identify which class members actually received misrepresentations or omissions of material facts); *see also Arons*, 2005 WL 975462, at *21 (courts reluctant to certify nationwide state law classes when unmanageable and raise constitutional questions where New Jersey law conflicts with other states' laws). A court may find that a class action is not superior where the degree of harm plaintiff suffered was minimal compared to the amount of damages he or she may recover, and alternative procedures are available to plaintiff to swiftly and cost-effectively litigate the claim. In *Local Banking Products, Inc. v. Kosher Bagel Munch, Inc.*, 421 N.J. Super. 268, 23 A.3d 469 (App. Div.), *cert. denied*, 209 N.J. 96, 35 A.3d 679 (2011), for example, the court refused to certify a class action under the Telephone Consumer Protection Act because an individual lawsuit was superior to a class action when plaintiff could easily bring an individual action in the small claims court and recover $500 in statutory damages, which far exceeded the actual harm that it suffered. New Jersey courts may opt to proceed with a "test case" in lieu of certifying a class leaving open the possibility that class certification ultimately may be deemed appropriate after the conclusion of the "test case." *See Kronisch*, 143 N.J. Super. at 427, 363 A.2d at 378; *Carroll*, 313 N.J. Super. at 509, 713 A.2d at 520.

d. Manageability

Manageability requirements were also addressed by the New Jersey Supreme Court in *Iliadis v. Wal-Mart Stores, Inc.*, 191 N.J. 88, 922 A.2d 710 (2007), where the Court reversed Appellate Division and trial court decisions denying class certification to a wage and hour claim brought on behalf of 72,000 current and former New Jersey Wal-Mart employees. In reversing those orders and remanding the case for entry of an order certifying the class, the Court specifically noted the "equalization function" of the class action and its "historic mission of taking care of the smaller guy." 191 N.J. at 104, 922 A.2d at 719.

Wal-Mart did not dispute that the four prerequisites of R. 4:32-1(a) were satisfied but had defeated certification below on the absence of predominance and superiority required by R. 4:32-1(b)(3) and, in particular, manageability problems in Rule 4:32-1(b)(3)(D). The Court acknowledged that Wal-Mart would have individualized defenses to many of the individual plaintiff's claims, but nonetheless found that certification was appropriate, and that "the trial court and parties' counsel can resolve the practical challenges presented by this litigation's individualized questions of law or fact." 191 N.J. at 114, 922 A.2d at 725.

In finding predominance and superiority, the Court also stated that "[d]enial of class status due to manageability concerns is disfavored. . . ." 191 N.J. at 117, 922 A.2d at 727. And that "courts should be careful not to overemphasize management difficulty considerations when contrasted with judicial economy, small claims access, and deterrence goals of the class device." 191 N.J. at 117–18, 922 A.2d at 727. The Court further found that in order to deny certification on a manageability basis, the Court had to rely on "concrete evidence of actual or likely management problems, not mere speculation. . . ." 191 N.J. at 118, 922 A.2d at 728. *But see Lopez v. 5 De Mayo Bakery, Inc.*, 2010 N.J. Super. Unpub. LEXIS 1648 (App. Div. Jul. 20, 2010) (denying class certification in a wage and hour case finding that the requirements of R. 4:32-1(a) and (b) had not been met because the purported class included different groups of employees who received varying forms of compensation, and because plaintiffs also asserted tortious conversion and emotional distress claims which required highly individualized proofs).

Subsequent to *Illiadis*, in *Int'l Union of Operating Engineers Local No. 68 v. Merck & Co., Inc.*, 192 N.J. 372, 929 A.3d 1076 (2007), the Supreme Court rejected certification of a nationwide class action on behalf of third-party health plans who alleged that they had overpaid for the prescription drug Vioxx. (Vioxx was withdrawn from the market due to cardiovascular risks that plaintiffs alleged were known by Merck and suppressed.) The payors had obtained certification of a nationwide class with both the trial court and Appellate Division approving the use of the CFA for all payors.

In reviewing the nationwide certification, the Court declined to address the propriety of applying the CFA on a nationwide basis, but instead in rejecting predominance and superiority focused on the Act's proof requirements in the context of how the various plans chose the drugs for their formularies and created the reimbursement policies applicable to each drug. "The evidence about separately created formularies, different types of tier systems, and individualized requirements for approval or reimbursement imposed on various plans' members and, to some extent, their prescribing physicians, are significant." 192 N.J. at 391, 929 A.2d at 1087.[1]

The Court went on to state that the individualized treatment of loss causation required by the CFA could not be cured by expert testimony that would be proffered to show how Merck was able to raise Vioxx's market price by failing to reveal its true safety profile because New Jersey has "rejected the fraud on the market theory as being inappropriate in any context other than federal securities fraud litigation." 192 N.J. at 392, 929 A.2d at 1088 (citing *Kaufman v. i-State Corp.*, 165 N.J. 94, 97–98, 754 A.2d 1188, 1189 (2000)). Thus, plaintiffs could not use a "fraud on the market" approach as a means to satisfy the predominance requirement.

Finally, the Court also rejected the notion that a nationwide class action would be superior, given that the case involved substantial claims that each plan would have the incentive to pursue separately. "Unlike in *Illiadis*, here we see no disparity in bargaining power and no likelihood that the claims are individually so small that they will not be pursued." 192 N.J. at 394, 929 A.2d at 1089.

Similarly, in *Beegal v. Park West Gallery*, 394 N.J. Super. 98, 925 A.2d 684 (App. Div. 2007), the Appellate Division rejected a nationwide consumer fraud claim asserted on behalf of cruise ship passengers who purchased or bid on artwork at auction while at sea. Plaintiff alleged that at such auctions, defendant had a practice of placing house bids on items that had not reached an item's "reserve" price, which actually was above the minimum price.

Certification was rejected because the facts of each auction varied, making no individual claim representative. "A jury may be required to evaluate the circumstances under which each auction was conducted and make individual factual determinations as to each plaintiff." 394 N.J. Super. at 113, 925 A.2d at 693. In other words, individual issues predominated.

In rejecting predominance, the Appellate Division also held that the CFA would not apply to each putative class members' claims because admiralty law required the use of the law of each claimant's domicile. 394 N.J. Super. at 119, 925 A.2d at 696. Alternatively, applying New Jersey's choice of law rules, the Appellate Division came to the same conclusion, *i.e.,* the law of the claimant's domicile would be applied. 394 N.J. Super. at 125, 925 A.2d at 700. After determining that the

[1] In *McNair v. Synapse Group, Inc.*, No. 06-5072, 2009 U.S. Dist. LEXIS 54908 (D.N.J. June 29, 2009), the United States District Court relied on the *International Union* decision in denying class certification in a consumer fraud case involving the defendant's practice of automatically renewing magazine subscriptions. As in *International Union,* the *McNair* court found that individual issues of causation predominated over any common issues related to the defendant's conduct. 2009 U.S. Dist. LEXIS 54908 at *25–26.

laws of the jurisdictions applied, the Appellate Division found that "[g]iven the numerous differences among the various state consumer protection laws and the absence of a plan for their presentation at trial," the plaintiffs failed to establish the predominance of legal issues. 394 N.J. Super. at 128, 925 A.2d at 701–02.

And in *Castro v. NYT Television*, 384 N.J. Super. 601, 895 A.2d 1173 (App. Div. 2006), the Appellate Division found that the trial court improperly granted class certification where common law invasion of privacy and common law fraud were the basis of each plaintiff's claim. Certification was in error because the defense of consent required individualized treatment. "[T]he proof of those claims will rest on evidence of the individual circumstances surrounding the videotaping of each patient rather than factual circumstances common to all putative class members." 384 N.J. Super. at 610, 895 A.2d at 1178.

Fink v. Ricoh Corp., 365 N.J. Super. 520, 839 A.2d 942 (Law Div. 2003), denying class certification, serves to illustrate the application of a number of the class action requirements of Rule 4:32. In *Fink*, purchasers of digital cameras brought a class action against defendant Ricoh Corp. (Ricoh) alleging that Ricoh's advertising violated the CFA. 365 N.J. Super. at 531, 839 A.2d at 948. Plaintiffs sought certification of a nationwide class comprised of "[a]ll United States purchasers of Ricoh's RDC-1 digital camera." 365 N.J. Super. at 535, 839 A.2d at 952. Although it acknowledged that class actions are "particularly appropriate" in consumer fraud cases, the court rejected class certification. 365 N.J. Super. at 536, 839 A.2d at 952. First, in a detailed analysis, the court stated that plaintiffs had not established that class treatment was warranted under the "price inflation theory" advanced by plaintiffs, largely because plaintiffs could not establish causation. 365 N.J. Super. at 537–55, 839 A.2d at 953–65. Plaintiffs had not established the numerosity and typicality requirements of Rule 4:32-1(a). The numerosity requirement was not met because plaintiffs "provided no proof as to how many purchasers read the advertisements prior to their purchase of the camera and were thereby caused to make the purchase because of" Ricoh's alleged fraud (and declined to permit additional discovery on the question in light of plaintiffs' inability to establish several other class action elements). 365 N.J. Super. at 555, 558, 839 A.2d at 965, 967. The typicality requirement was not met because, *inter alia,* there were individual questions of fact relating to each class member's claim (*e.g.,* whether a particular member read the allegedly false advertising and was caused by that to purchase Ricoh's digital camera). 365 N.J. Super. at 563, 839 A.2d at 969. The "predominance" and "superiority" requirements of Rule 4:32-1(b)(3) were also not established. The predominance requirement was not met largely due to the fact that different state laws might apply to each class member's claims. 365 N.J. Super. at 567–99, 839 A.2d at 972. Lastly, the superiority requirement was not met due to the "complexity and management problems which would be confronted by the need to apply the law of conceivably up to 50 states and the need to resolve the numerous factual issues generated for individual members of the class depending upon their state of residence." 365 N.J. Super. at 599, 839 A.2d at 598.[2]

---

[2] A similar result was reached in *Agostino v. Quest Diagnostics, Inc.*, 256 F.R.D. 437 (D.N.J. 2009), *overruled on other grounds by Maniscalco v. Brother Int'l (USA) Corp.*, 709 F.3d 202 (3d Cir. 2013), where the court denied plaintiffs' motion for class certification as to plaintiffs' consumer fraud claim because it would be unmanageable to apply the consumer fraud laws of all fifty states. *See also* Payne v. Fujifilm U.S.A., Inc., 2010 U.S. Dist. LEXIS 52808 (D.N.J. May 28, 2010) (denying class certification of breach of warranty and consumer fraud claims because it would be too unmanageable to apply the laws of all fifty states). In *In re Mercedes-Benz Tele Aid Contract Litigation*, 257 F.R.D. 46 (D.N.J. 2009), however, the United States District Court reached a different result when it certified a nationwide class in a consumer fraud case involving the purchase of vehicles with emergency response systems. After deciding that the New Jersey Consumer Fraud Act applied to all of the class members' claims, the court found that the four prerequisites of Fed. R. Civ. P. 23(a) had been met and that

In *Varacallo v. Mass. Mut. Life Ins. Co.*, 332 N.J. Super. 31, 752 A.2d 807 (App. Div. 2000), the Appellate Division presumed reliance by members of a class of consumers all of whom were shown defendant's printed sales literature from which defendant allegedly knowingly omitted material facts with the intent that others rely upon the omission. In contrast, approximately one month later in *Kaufman v. i-Stat Corp.*, 165 N.J. 94, 754 A.2d 1188 (2000), the New Jersey Supreme Court rejected plaintiff's attempt to apply the fraud-on-the-market theory as no more than a reasonable application of indirect reliance principles. The *i-Stat Corp.* Court explained that because plaintiff stated explicitly that she did not consider the defendant's financial statements but acted only on market price that she did not consider defendant's material representations in her buying decision. Accordingly, plaintiff failed to show reliance—even indirect reliance—upon the misstatements or omissions of defendant and its management because she could not rely upon that which she did not even consider. In addition to refusing to find that plaintiff showed reliance, even indirectly, the Court refused to apply the fraud-on-the-market theory (as set forth by the United States Supreme Court in *Basic v. Levinson*, 485 U.S. 224, 108 S. Ct. 978, 99 L. Ed. 2d 194 (1988)) to expand New Jersey law concerning satisfaction of the reliance element of a fraud action.

As noted above, it is now clear that New Jersey has "rejected the fraud on the market theory as being inappropriate in any context other than federal securities fraud litigation." *Int'l Union of Operating Engineers Local No. 68*, 192 N.J. at 392, 929 A.2d at 1088.

e. Notice

The notice required in a class action in New Jersey is "the best notice practicable under circumstances consistent with due process of law." *Sulcov v. 2100 Linwood Owners, Inc.*, 303 N.J. Super. 13, 36, 696 A.2d 31, 36 (App. Div. 1997). There is no mandatory individual notice requirement. *Id.* Publication or other forms of constructive notice will generally be permitted if they meet due process. *Id.* Individual notice to absentee class members will generally be the best practice even when not mandatory. *Gallano*, 139 N.J. Super. at 250, 353 A.2d at 164 (although it is not mandatory for court to order notification in a (b)(1) class action, court recommended notice to absentee class members). Such notice protects defendants as well as absentee class members, because "if plaintiffs lose on the merits, absent members will be precluded from complaining that their interests were inadequately represented." *Id.*

f. Approval of Settlements

Rule 4:32-2(e) requires that all settlements of certified class actions be approved by the court after a fairness hearing. Courts will approve proposed settlements where they are fair and reasonable to the members of the class. *Chattin v. Cape May Greene, Inc.*, 216 N.J. Super. 618, 627, 524 A.2d 841, 845 (App. Div.), *cert. denied*, 107 N.J. 148, 526 A.2d 209 (1987). Although the court may properly consider the wishes of the class members, approval is within the discretion of the court and may be granted even if individual class members do not consent to the proposed settlement. *Id.* The court may be required to take testimony at the hearing testing the fairness of any settlement proposal. In

common issues predominated over individualized issues because plaintiffs could rely on common proofs to establish individual causation. 257 F.R.D. at 89–90. The defendant's motion to decertify the class was subsequently denied. In re Mercedes-Benz Tele Aid Contract Litig., 267 F.R.D. 113 (D.N.J.), *petition denied*, 2010 U.S. App. LEXIS 8087 (3d Cir. Apr. 19, 2010).

Sutter v. Horizon Blue Cross Blue Shield of New Jersey, 406 N.J. Super. 86, 966 A.2d 508 (App. Div. 2009), the Appellate Division held that the trial court should have taken testimony at the fairness hearing, including the testimony of plaintiffs' damages expert whose opinions provided the basis for valuing the settlement proposal. The court had expressed reservations concerning the expert's opinions, and when class members objected to the fairness of the settlement, the trial court should have afforded the objectors an opportunity to cross-examine the plaintiffs' expert during the fairness hearing. 406 N.J. Super. at 102, 966 A.2d at 517–18.

In *Simmermon v. Dryvit Systems, Inc.*, 196 N.J. 316, 953 A.2d 478 (2008), the New Jersey Supreme Court dismissed an individual plaintiff's action because it was the subject of a nationwide class action that had been brought and settled in a Tennessee state court. Although the plaintiff argued that he did not receive actual notice of the out-of-state class action, and that the defendant failed to comply with R. 4:5-1(b)(2) which requires that initial pleadings disclose the existence of related actions, the Court held that it was required to give full faith and credit to the Tennessee class settlement because the settlement notification procedures complied with the standards of due process. 196 N.J. at 333–34, 953 A.2d at 487–88. The Court explained that plaintiff's challenges to the settlement should be brought in the Tennessee court. *Id.*

g. The Continued Vitality of Class Action Waivers with Arbitration Provisions

In two companion cases decided in August 2006, the New Jersey Supreme Court addressed the enforceability of class action waiver provisions in arbitration agreements, with different results. Prior decisions of New Jersey Courts had held that the right to pursue a class action alleging consumer fraud may be waived in an arbitration agreement. *Gras v. Associates First Capital Corp.*, 346 N.J. Super. 42, 49–52, 786 A.2d 886, 889–92 (App. Div. 2001), *cert. denied,* 171 N.J. 445, 794 A.2d 184 (2002); *see also Discover Bank v. Shea*, 362 N.J. Super. 200, 827 A.2d 358 (Law Div. 2001) (dismissing complaint where arbitration agreement prohibited participation in class action), *appeal dis'd on other grounds,* 362 N.J. Super. 90, 827 A.2d 292 (App. Div. 2003). In *Muhammad v. County Bank of Rehoboth Beach, Delaware*, 189 N.J. 1, 912 A.2d 88 (2006), the Court found that the class action waiver provision was unconscionable under New Jersey law because the individual consumer fraud claim involved a small amount of damages (less than $600), rendering individual enforcement difficult if not impossible. The Court found that the practical effect of the class action bar would be to prevent any challenge to the substance of the loan contract's terms, thus shielding defendants from complying with the law. Insofar as the law could only be vindicated by a class action, the public interest overrode the defendants' right to enforce the class-arbitration bar where enforcing the bar would reduce the possibility of finding competent counsel to advance such a claim. In contrast, in *Delta Funding Corp. v. Harris*, 189 N.J. 28, 912 A.2d 104 (2006), although the plaintiff did not assert class claims, the Court in *dicta* concluded that a class action waiver in a loan contract's arbitration clause was not unconscionable. Applying the fact intensive standards for unconscionability under New Jersey law, the Court found that the class action waiver was enforceable because, unlike the "low value" suit in *Muhammad*, the claims in *Delta Funding* involved substantial damages (exceeding $100,000) and statutory attorneys' fees that provided adequate incentives for the plaintiff to pursue her claim on an individualized basis. *See also Vilches v. Travelers Companies, Inc.*, 413 F. App'x 487 (3d Cir. 2011) (unpub.) (holding that a class action waiver provision in an amended arbitration policy was not unconscionable in an employment setting). In *Homa v. American Express Company*, 558 F.3d 225 (3d Cir. 2009), the Third Circuit, after determining that plaintiffs' unconscionability challenge to a class action waiver provision was governed by New Jersey law and was not preempted by the Federal Arbitration Act (FAA), remanded the issue back to the District Court to analyze under the principles set forth in *Muhammad.*

Muhammad now appears to be preempted by the subsequent United States Supreme Court decisions in *AT&T Mobility LLC v. Concepcion*, 563 U.S. 333, 131 S. Ct. 1740, 179 L. Ed. 2d 742 (2011), and *American Express Co. v. Italian Colors Restaurant*, 570 U.S. 228, 133 S. Ct. 2304, 186 L. Ed. 2d 417 (2013). In *Concepcion*, the Court held that a California Supreme Court determination (*Discover Bank*) which declared unconscionable class arbitration waiver provisions in consumer adhesion contracts where little money was at stake, to be preempted by the FAA. The Supreme Court in *American Express* reaffirmed the strong preemptive effect of the FAA on challenges to arbitration and class action waiver provisions even where plaintiffs are asserting low-value, federal statutory claims such as federal antitrust claims. In *Wolf v. Nissan Motor Acceptance Corp.*, 2011 U.S. Dist. LEXIS 66649, at *20–21 (D.N.J. June 22, 2011), the court, relying on *Concepcion*, found that plaintiff's unconscionability challenge to the class action waiver provision in the parties contract was preempted by the FAA. In *NAACP of Camden County East v. Foulke Management Group*, 421 N.J. Super. 404, 24 A.3d 777 (App. Div. 2011), the court held that *Concepcion* precluded the trial court from invalidating a class action waiver provision in an automobile contract on unconscionability or public policy grounds. The court, however, held that class action waiver and arbitration provisions in the contract were so vague and internally inconsistent that plaintiff could not be found to have agreed to those provisions and therefore, held them to be unenforceable due to lack of mutual assent. 421 N.J. Super. at 438, 24 A.3d at 798. *See also Rotondi v. Dibre Auto Group, L.L.C.*, 2014 N.J. Super. Unpub. LEXIS 1662 (App. Div. July 9, 2014) (permitting plaintiff's proposed class action to proceed because the class action arbitration provision was potentially confusing and not stated with sufficient clarity). In *Litman v. Cellco Partnership*, 655 F.3d 225, 230 (3d Cir. 2011), the Third Circuit held that in light of *Concepcion*, *Homa* has been abrogated and *Muhammad* has been preempted by the FAA. On the other hand, New Jersey courts have not completely abrogated *Muhammad*, but have limited its potential application to consumer contracts of adhesion. In *Arafa v. Health Express Corp.*, 243 N.J. 147, 233 A.3d 495 (2020), the New Jersey Supreme Court declined to apply *Muhammad* to an employment contract. *See also Siperavage v. Uber Techs., Inc.*, 2021 U.S. Dist. LEXIS 122002 (D.N.J. June 30, 2021) (rejecting plaintiff's argument that class action waiver provisions are impermissible under New Jersey law and distinguishing *Muhammad* because the contract at issue was not a consumer contract of adhesion).

The Appellate Division also recently invalidated an arbitration provision with a class action waiver in a cell phone customer agreement. *Achey v. Cellco Partnership,* 475 N.J. Super. 446, 293 A.3d 551 (App. Div. 2023), *cert. granted,* 255 N.J. 286, 300 A.3d 273 (2023), *app. dismissed by order* (N.J. July 15, 2025). The arbitration provision at issue in *Achey* contained several other provisions that the court held were unconscionable, including: (i) a six-month claim period during which customers must give notice of their claim or else waive them, thus significantly shortening the period within which customers could seek to vindicate statutory rights; (ii) a "bellwether" provision, providing for arbitration of up to five claims at a time, which would enable the defendant to unduly delay plaintiffs' claims from being heard; (iii) the lack of a tolling provision, which was unconscionable because, under the bellwether provisions, claimants could not file claims until preceding "bellwether" claims were adjudicated; and (iv) an "exculpatory" clause, which barred any claims based on statements made outside of the customer agreement and barring evidence other than the contract itself, and which deprived customers of statutory rights under the CFA. The court concluded that the "'cumulative effect' of the various unconscionable terms renders the arbitration agreement 'unenforceable for lack of mutual assent.'" 475 N.J. Super. at 456–59, 293 A.3d at 558–60.

The scope of FAA preemption as it applies to mandatory arbitration provisions in consumer contracts was addressed by the New Jersey Supreme Court in *Atalese v. U.S. Legal Services Group.*,

L.P., 219 N.J. 430, 99 A.3d 306 (2014), *cert. denied*, 576 U.S. 1004, 135 S. Ct. 2084, 192 L. Ed. 2d 847 (2015). In *Atalese*, the Court held that a mandatory arbitration provision in consumer contracts is unenforceable if the provision does not state that the consumer is waiving his or her right to sue in a court of law. The Court rejected arguments that plaintiff's objections to arbitration were preempted by the FAA under *Concepcion*. The Court explained that the arbitration provision was not receiving unequal treatment (which the FAA prohibits) because New Jersey law requires that all contract clauses in which a party is waiving a constitutional or statutory right be stated in clear and unmistakable terms. The Court based its decision on the determination that mandatory arbitration provisions waive the constitutional right to a trial by jury, which must be clearly and unmistakably set forth in the provision. *See also Dispenziere v. Kushner Cos.*, 438 N.J. Super. 11, 101 A.3d 1136 (App. Div. 2014) (holding that plaintiffs could not be compelled to arbitrate because the arbitration provision in the contract did not state that plaintiffs were waiving their right to sue); *Kelly v. Beverage Works NY Inc.*, 2014 N.J. Super. Unpub. LEXIS 2792 (App. Div. Nov. 26, 2014) (same); *Barr v. Bishop Rosen & Co., Inc.*, 442 N.J. Super. 599, 126 A.3d 328 (App. Div. 2015) (same); *Morgan v. Sanford Brown Institute*, 225 N.J. 289, 137 A.3d 1168 (2016) (holding that clauses delegating arbitrability decisions to an arbitrator are subject to the same contract requirements as arbitration clauses); *Kleine v. Emeritus at Emerson*, 445 N.J. Super. 545, 139 A.3d 148 (App. Div. 2016) (holding that an arbitration clause in a patient's nursing home contract was unenforceable because the exclusive arbitration forum required under the contract was unavailable at the time the contract was entered); *Souza-Bastos v. Federal Auto Brokers, Inc.*, 2016 N.J. Super. Unpub. LEXIS 1332 (App. Div. June 10, 2016) (upholding the trial court's denial of defendant's motion to compel arbitration because the auto sales contract documents contained contradictory and inconsistent arbitration clauses).

The continued validity of the New Jersey Supreme Court's decision in *Atalese*, that arbitration agreements are only enforceable if they specifically advise consumers they are waiving their right to sue in a court of law, may be in question due to the United States Supreme Court's decision in *Kindred Nursing Centers Ltd. Partnership v. Clark*, 581 U.S. 246, 137 S. Ct. 1421, 197 L. Ed. 2d 806 (2017). In *Kindred*, the Court addressed a Kentucky Supreme Court decision that held that the Kentucky Constitution prohibited a representative with a broad power of attorney from entering into an arbitration agreement unless the power of attorney specifically authorized the entry into arbitration agreements. The United States Supreme Court reversed, holding that the FAA prohibits courts from invalidating arbitration agreements based on legal rules "that apply only to arbitration or that derive their meaning from the fact that an agreement to arbitrate is at issue." 581 U.S. at 251, 137 S. Ct. at 1426, 197 L. Ed. 2d at 812. Because the Kentucky Court's decision "adopt[ed] a legal rule hinging on the primary characteristic of an arbitration agreement—namely, a waiver of the right to go to court and receive a jury trial," the Court held that it violated the FAA. *Id.* In *Bacon v. Avis Budget Grp., Inc.*, 2017 U.S. Dist. LEXIS 88868, at *16–17 and n.6 (D.N.J. June 9, 2017), the United States District Court questioned "whether New Jersey's pre-*Kindred* standard might fail to put arbitration agreements on an equal plane with other contracts," which would be grounds for FAA preemption. In *Kernahan v. Home Warranty Adm'r of Florida, Inc.*, 236 N.J. 301, 199 A.3d 766 (2019), the New Jersey Supreme Court addressed challenges to a mandatory arbitration clause in a home warranty contract. The trial and intermediate appellate courts declared the arbitration clause unenforceable. Defendants filed a petition for certification with the New Jersey Supreme Court, which argued in part, that *Atalese* was preempted by the FAA in light of the *Kindred* decision. During oral argument, however, defendants withdrew their argument that the *Atalese* decision should be overturned in light of *Kindred*. The Court affirmed the lower courts' decision and in dicta, suggested that the *Atalese* rule did not run afoul of *Kindred* because the *Atalese* rule was essential to determining whether there was assent, and the rule did not single out arbitration agreements. 236 N.J. Super. at 324, 199 A.3d at 780. *See also Defina v. Go Ahead & Jump 1, LLC*, 2019 N.J. Super. Unpub. LEXIS 1400, at *16–17 (holding that *Kernahan* confirmed that the *Kindred* decision did not abrogate the New Jersey Supreme Court's decision in *Atalese*). Courts, however, have clarified that *Kernahan* only validated the *Atalese* rule as it relates to consumer contracts. *See GAR Disability Advocates, LLC v. Taylor*, 365 F. Supp. 3d 522, 531 (D.N.J. 2019) (holding that *Atalese* and *Kernahan* did not apply to an arbitration clause in an asset purchase agreement). *See also Victory Entm't v. Schibell*, 2018 N.J. Super. Unpub. LEXIS 1467, at *21–23 (App. Div. June 21, 2018) (holding that *Atalese* only applied to consumer contracts); *1567 South Realty v. Strategic Contract Brands*, 2020 N.J. Super. Unpub. LEXIS 1360, at *7 (App. Div. July 9, 2020) (holding that *Atalese* did not apply to arbitration clauses in negotiated contracts between sophisticated business entities).

In *Stone v. EXOS Hum. Cap., LLC,* 2025 WL 1898969 (S.D.N.Y. July 9, 2025), a wage-and-hour case involving arbitration agreement governed by New Jersey law, a New York federal district court held that *Atalese* was preempted by the FAA. First, the court held that *Atalese*'s requirement that arbitration provisions explain that the parties are giving up the right to sue in court departs from New Jersey's usual approach to contract interpretation, which enforces unambiguous contract language even if a party might have a different subjective understanding of the term. Thus, the *Atalese* standard singles out arbitration agreements for disfavored treatment. *Id.* at *8–11. Second, the *Stone* court held that the rule in *Atalese* impermissibly "interferes with arbitration" (quoting *Concepcion*) because its insistence on a heightened "knowing and voluntary" standard for the waiver of the right to a jury trial as part of an arbitration agreement is inconsistent with the FAA's liberal policy favoring arbitration. It is no answer to say that New Jersey equally treats all agreements to waive statutory or constitutional rights because the FAA requires arbitration to be on "equal footing with *all* other contracts ... not on equal footing with a disfavored subset of contracts that have been singled out for judicial suspicion." *Id.* at *11.

In *Aguirre v. CDL Last Mile Solutions, LLC,* 2024 WL 762467 (App. Div. Feb. 26, 2024), *cert. denied,* 257 N.J. 589, 315 A.3d 1216 (2024), the Appellate Division invalidated an arbitration provision and class action waiver. It applied *Atalese* in the context of a class action lawsuit brought against a logistics and delivery services company, its principal, and another company providing payroll, "driver onboarding," and other administrative services to the delivery company, on behalf of delivery drivers alleging that they were improperly classified as independent contractors rather than as employees and seeking overtime wages and allegedly unlawful deductions taken from their pay. The independent contractor agreements contained a binding arbitration provision and class action waiver, which contained a notice at the end stating: "THIS CONTRACT CONTAINS A BINDING ARBITRATION PROVISION AND CLASS ACTION WAIVER WHICH AFFECTS YOUR LEGAL RIGHTS AND MAY BE ENFORCED BY THE PARTIES." *Id.* at *2. The agreement also contained a New York choice of law provision. *Id.* Notwithstanding the choice of law provision, the Appellate Division concluded that New Jersey law applied. Applying Section 187 of the *Restatement (Second) Conflict of Laws*, the court concluded that New Jersey had a materially greater interest with respect to disputes under the independent contractor agreements because all the plaintiffs reside and work in New Jersey, they report to a New Jersey warehouse operated by the defendant delivery company, the agreements were executed in New Jersey, and the claims implicate New Jersey laws regarding payment of wages. On the other hand, New York's only connection to the dispute was that defendants reside there. *Id.* at *5. Moreover, the court concluded that application of New York law would be contrary to a fundamental policy of New Jersey. Whereas the *Atalese* decision requires waivers to explain that the plaintiff is giving up the right to bring claims in court and have a jury resolve the dispute, New York law does not specifically require that an arbitration clause explain that agreement thereto involves a waiver of the right to a jury trial. *Id.* at *6. Applying New Jersey law, the court held that the arbitration provision did not comply with *Atalese* because, even though there were specific procedures for arbitration set forth, the provision never clearly explained that agreement to arbitrate meant foregoing the right to a jury trial in court. *Id.* at *9. Furthermore, the court held that the language of the arbitration provision clearly stated that the class action waiver applied only in the context of arbitration, with no reference to litigation in court. Because the court held that the arbitration provision was unenforceable, the court concluded that the class action waiver was inapplicable to the plaintiffs' class action lawsuit. *Id.* at *11.

The effectiveness of a class action waiver in an arbitration provision has been affirmed even when the defendant materially breached the arbitration provision in the parties' agreement by failing to pay the required administrative fees. In *Cerciello v. Salerno Duane, Inc.,* 473 N.J. Super. 249, 279 A.3d 1168 (App. Div.), *leave to appeal denied*, 252 N.J. 184, 283 A.3d 1229 (2022), the plaintiff filed an arbitration demand against the defendant automobile dealer alleging various statutory violations resulting from overcharging for title and registration fees and selling the car for more than the advertised price. After the defendant failed to pay the required administrative fees to the American Arbitration Association (AAA), the AAA declined the case. Thereafter, the plaintiff filed a putative class action complaint in Superior Court asserting similar claims. 473 N.J. Super. at 252–52, 279 A.3d at 1170–71. The trial court denied the plaintiff's motion for class certification, finding that the class action waiver was clear that the parties could not pursue any class claims in court or in arbitration. 473 N.J. Super. at 255–56, 279 A.3d at 1172–73. The New Jersey Appellate Division affirmed, agreeing with the trial court that the class action waiver provision was clear and unambiguous. Moreover, although the defendant's breach of the arbitration provision by failing to pay the AAA administrative fees precluded the defendant from being able to compel arbitration, it did not prevent enforcement of the class action waiver, which precluded the parties from pursuing class claims in arbitration or in court. 473 N.J. Super. at 258–59, 279 A.3d at 1174–75.

On the other hand, an automobile dealer could not dismiss a putative class action complaint and compel arbitration based on an arbitration provision with class action waiver in an agreement between the plaintiff and a bank that provided a car loan to the plaintiff to purchase the car. In *Sikorski v. New Jersey Ventures Partners, LLC,* 2021 WL 2774854 (App. Div. July 2, 2021), the plaintiff filed a class action complaint against the defendant car dealer, alleging various statutory violations and breach of warranty arising out of the condition of the car as delivered. The defendant moved to dismiss and compel arbitration, arguing that it was a third-party beneficiary under the loan agreement between the plaintiff and its lender. The trial court denied the motion, and the Appellate Division affirmed. *Id.* at *1–2. The court reiterated that mutual assent to arbitrate is a "cornerstone of our law on arbitration" and the party seeking to enforce an arbitration agreement "must prove that the non-moving party assented to it." *Id.* at *3. The court also rejected the argument that, in the absence of any language establishing plaintiff's consent to arbitrate claims against the defendant, arbitration is warranted because the language "did not expressly exclude" the defendant from the provision in the loan agreement, holding that such an argument turns "arbitration jurisprudence on its head." *Id.* at *4. The Appellate Division came to a similar conclusion in *Nawrocki v. J&J Auto Outlet,* 2023 WL 7274675 (App. Div. Nov. 3, 2023), in which plaintiff was allowed to maintain its class action against the defendant auto dealer. The dealer had sold the plaintiff a service contract together with the used car at issue, which service contract contained an arbitration provision and class action waiver. The service contract, however, was between the plaintiff and a third-party provider; the dealer was not a party to the service contract. 2023 WL 7274675, at *3. The court also noted that the language of the arbitration provision was not enforceable with respect to the plaintiff's statutory claims because there was no plain language explicitly waiving the ability to litigate statutory rights. *Id.*

New Jersey courts have also addressed the effectiveness of arbitration provisions with class action waivers in web-based consumer contracts. Generally, to be enforceable, reasonable notice of the existence of the provision must be given to the consumer. Thus, in *Wollen v. Gulf Stream Restoration and Cleaning LLC,* 468 N.J. Super. 483, 259 A.3d 867 (App. Div. 2021), the Appellate Division reversed the trial court's order granting a motion to dismiss and compelling arbitration of a consumer complaint against the defendant, which operated an online referral site for home renovation and contracting services. In *Wollen,* the consumer-user was prompted to create an online account and to input information about the type of services requested, location, and timing. At the end of the process, a screen notified the user that there were "matching Home Renovation Contractors in your area," and invited the user to "view matching pros" by clicking an orange button on the screen. Immediately below the button was a disclaimer that "[b]y submitting this request, you are agreeing to our Terms and Conditions." The phrase "terms and conditions" appeared on screen in blue and served as a hyperlink to a separate seven-page document. However, the phrase was not underlined, bolded, or enlarged, and there were no other explanatory phrases, advising the user to "click here to accept [or acknowledge, or read, or view] the terms and conditions." Those terms and conditions included an arbitration and class action waiver. 468 N.J. Super. at 488–91, 259 A.3d at 870–72. The Appellate Division held that the hyperlink at issue did not provide reasonable notice of the terms and conditions to a reasonably prudent internet user. There was no distinction in the font, other than the color, and the placement of the disclaimer at the bottom of the screen below the "view matching pros" button could lead the user to click the button before reading that disclaimer or to believe that the full terms would appear upon clicking the button. Most significantly, there was no requirement for the user to "affirmatively assent" by requiring the user to click to accept, or to click to acknowledge that she had viewed the terms and conditions. 468 N.J. Super. at 501–03, 259 A.3d at 878–79.

By contrast, the New Jersey federal district court upheld the validity of a class action waiver in an arbitration provision that appeared in the terms of service of an online video game, where the game's initial launch screen contained a notice in the middle of the screen that, "[b]y continuing to play, you agree to our Terms of Service," the notice appeared in white letters against a black background, the words "Terms of Service" were in blue, bolded font, and contained a hyperlink to the complete terms of service, and where other facts were present. *Ackies v. Scopely, Inc.,* 2022 U.S. Dist. LEXIS 13086, *12–13 (D.N.J. Jan. 25, 2022) (applying New Jersey law).

In *Fazio v. Altice,* __A.3d __, 2025 WL 188095 (N.J. July 9, 2025), the plaintiff, a customer who visited Altice's retail store to purchase cell phone service, was not shown the customer service agreement or any other document while in the store. Instead, he was given a receipt indicating that a "copy of all documents and agreements – including Terms & Conditions, AutoPay, handset insurance, etc." will be sent to the email address provided by the customer during creation of his account. The receipt did not specifically refer to arbitration. When the defendant moved to dismiss plaintiff's complaint alleging violations of the New Jersey's Law Against Discrimination for failing to accommodate his medical condition, it cited the arbitration provisions in the customer service agreement. Plaintiff disputed he ever received the agreement by email. At issue before the New Jersey Supreme Court was whether Altice could rely on evidence of habit or routine practice that it emailed the plaintiff a copy of the customer service agreement. The Court held that evidence of habit or routine practice was admissible to prove circumstantially that a party acted in conformity with that habit and practice. However, to give rise to a rebuttable presumption that the party did so, the evidence "must have the requisite degree of specificity, such as an affidavit that describes 'a repeated behavioral response to specific factual stimulus.'" *Id.* at *7. The Court held that the affidavit supplied by Altice's Senior Director of Business Process Management for retail stores lacked the requisite degree of specificity. The affiant claimed "familiarity" with Altice's practices without specifically stating what those practices were or how they were undertaken. For example, she did not recite what customer service representatives routinely discussed with customers nor did she state how or when or from whom emails containing the customer service agreement were routinely sent. *Id.* at *8. Altice was thus not entitled to the rebuttable presumption that it provided the plaintiff with the agreement containing the arbitration provision.

Atalese has also been applied in the context of collective bargaining agreements. In *Evans v. City of Paterson,* 2025 WL 311562 (App. Div. Jan. 28, 2025), the Appellate Division reversed a trial court order dismissing a class action brought by two firefighters alleging that the overtime provisions of the collective bargaining agreement between the City of Paterson and the Paterson Firefighters Association violated their statutory rights under the New Jersey Wage and Hour Law. *Id.* at *1. Granting the City's motion to dismiss and compel arbitration, the trial court held that, as members of the Association, plaintiffs were bound by the grievance procedures in the collective bargaining agreement, including the submission of unresolved disputes to binding arbitration. *Id.* at *1–2. In reversing the trial court's decision, the Appellate Division rejected the City's argument that *Atalese* was inapplicable because the Association was a sophisticated party. The court held that there was no reason to conclude that "employees bound by a [collective bargaining agreement] should be charged with a greater understanding of their rights than the average consumer." *Id.* at *4. The court further concluded that the collective bargaining agreement at issue lacked a clear and unambiguous explanation of rights being waived. First, the agreement stated that it "is not intended and shall not be construed as a waiver of any right or benefit to which employees are entitled by law." Second, the agreement did not disclose that arbitration would replace litigation or a jury trial and, moreover, appears to limit the right to arbitration to the Association as opposed to individual firefighters. *Id.*

h. Litigation Conduct as a Waiver of Arbitration

A pair of recent Appellate Division cases have also addressed whether a defendant's litigation conduct effected a waiver of its right to compel arbitration under an otherwise valid arbitration provision. In *Hopkins v. LVNV Funding LLC,* 481 N.J. Super. 49, 330 A.3d 1231 (App. Div. 2025), the Appellate Division reversed an order dismissing a putative class action against a consumer credit company, alleging violations of New Jersey's Consumer Finance Licensing Act, the CFA, and the federal Fair Debt Collection Practices Act. In *Hopkins,* LVNV Funding had filed a collection action against the plaintiff in the Special Civil Part of the Superior Court, Law Division. The plaintiff filed an answer and class action counterclaim and then filed a similar class action complaint against LVNV Funding as well as other companies that previously held the plaintiff's debt and moved to consolidate both cases. The defendants opposed the motion to consolidate and cross-moved to dismiss the complaint for failure to state a claim. The court granted plaintiff's motion to consolidate and partially granted defendants' motion by dismissing plaintiff's claim for unjust enrichment. The defendants answered the complaint and asserted several affirmative defenses but did not include a defense based on the parties' arbitration provision. Only after plaintiff moved to compel answers to written discovery did the defendants first move to compel arbitration, some sixteen months after plaintiff filed his complaint. *Id.* at 56–58, 330 A.3d at 1235–37.

Reversing the trial court's dismissal of the action, the Appellate Division applied the factors to be considered when assessing whether a party had waived its right to arbitrate through its litigation conduct, which were first laid out by the New Jersey Supreme Court in *Cole v. Jersey City Med. Center,* 215 N.J. 265, 72 A.3d 224 (2013). Those are (1) the delay in making the request for arbitration; (2) the filing of any motions and their outcome, particularly dispositive motions; (3) whether the delay was part of a litigation strategy; (4) the extent of discovery conducted; (5) whether the party seeking arbitration raised the right to arbitration in its pleadings or otherwise gave notice of its intent to seek arbitration; (6) the proximity to trial at the time arbitration is sought; and (7) the resulting prejudice to the other side. *Hopkins,* 481 N.J. Super. at 63, 330 A.3d at 1239–40. The Appellate Division found that a majority of the factors weighed in favor of finding that defendants had waived their right to arbitration through litigation conduct. They did not seek to enforce the arbitration provision until sixteen months after the complaint was filed and did not even raise it as an affirmative defense. Additionally, they filed a dispositive motion to dismiss on the merits "demonstrating a submission to the authority of a court to resolve the dispute." *Id.* at 64, 330 A.3d at 1240. The court also found that the defendants' decision to move to dismiss on the merits—which resulted in the dismissal of the plaintiff's unjust enrichment claim—before moving to compel arbitration was part of their litigation strategy. To that point, the court also noted that the defendants never asserted that the failure to seek arbitration sooner was a good-faith mistake. *Id.* at 64, 330 A.3d at 1240. Since no trial date had been set, that factor did not weigh in favor of waiver. And the extent of discovery taken was in equipoise because they did not seek discovery from the plaintiff but used the discovery schedule to their advantage by stipulating to an extension of the discovery period and refusing to respond to plaintiff's requests before moving to compel arbitration. Finally, the court found that the dismissal of plaintiff's unjust enrichment claim resulted in some prejudice to plaintiff, since it was "inherent[ly] unfair[] – in terms of delay, expense, or damage to a party's legal position" to force plaintiff to litigate an issue and then seek to arbitrate the same issue. *Id.* at 64–65, 330 A.3d 1240–41.

On the other hand, in *Williams v. Brick City Motors, Inc.,* 2025 WL 752096 (App. Div. Mar. 10, 2025), the Appellate Division upheld the trial court's order compelling arbitration of a dispute against a used car dealer asserting claims under the CFA and TCCWNA. In *Williams,* after the plaintiff experienced repeated issues with the check engine light in the used car he purchased from the defendant, he filed an arbitration demand with the AAA pursuant to the arbitration provisions in the purchase order and retail installment sales contract. However, the AAA stated it could not arbitrate the dispute because the defendant had not complied with its payment obligations under the AAA's Consumer Due Process protocols. Two days after receiving the AAA's notice, with no response from the defendant, the plaintiff filed a putative class action complaint in court. The defendant then moved to dismiss and compel arbitration pursuant to the arbitration provisions and class action waivers in the parties' purchase order and retail installment sales contract. At oral argument, defense counsel did not know if the payment obligations had been cured but represented to the court that the defendant sought an opportunity to cure and pursue arbitration. The trial court granted the motion to dismiss, on the condition that defendant cure its payment obligation to the AAA within fourteen days. *Id.* at *1–2. The Appellate Division agreed that the defendant had not waived its right to arbitrate through its conduct, finding that only two days elapsed between the AAA's notice and the filing of the plaintiff's complaint and that plaintiff had not incurred any deprivation or harm due to the delay in defendant's non-payment. Moreover, there was no indication that defendant's non-payment was part of any litigation strategy. (The Appellate Division did, however, reverse the trial court's dismissal of the case, holding that, under the FAA, it should instead have been stayed pending arbitration of the claims. In holding that the case should be stayed rather than dismissed, the appellate court did not distinguish between plaintiff's individual and class claims. Presumably, assuming the defendant cured its payment deficiencies with the AAA and plaintiff's individual claims, there would be no reason to stay, rather than dismiss, the class claims.)

i. Class Action Waivers Without Arbitration Provisions

Although the focus of many judicial decisions addressing the enforceability of class action waivers over the past several years have been in the context of such waivers contained within arbitration provisions, the New Jersey Supreme Court has held that class action waivers contained in agreements without arbitration provisions may also be enforceable, unless they are found to be unconscionable or invalid under general contract principles, reversing a lower court decision that had imposed a bright-line rule banning class action waivers not coupled with arbitration provisions as contrary to public policy. *Pace v. Hamilton Cove Apartments,* 258 N.J. 82, 101–02, 317 A.3d 477, 489 (2024). In *Pace,* the putative class consisted of tenants asserting fraud and violations of the CFA against the defendant landlord, alleging misrepresentations promising "elevated, 24/7 security." The landlord moved to dismiss the complaint or, in the alternative, to strike the class action allegations, based on a class action waiver contained in each tenant's lease. When the motion was denied, the landlord appealed to the Appellate Division. 258 N.J. at 89–91, 317 A.3d at 481–83. The Appellate Division affirmed the denial of the motion and established a bright-line rule that a class action waiver in a contract that does not contain a mandatory arbitration provision is unenforceable as a matter of law. 258 N.J. at 92–93, 317 A.3d at 483. The Appellate Division stressed New Jersey's policy of liberally construing class action requirements, which "for certain cases . . . are the favored method of adjudicating claims. 258 N.J. at 91–92, 317 A.3d at 483. The appellate panel acknowledged the U.S. Supreme Court's decision in *AT&T Mobility v. Concepcion,* which upheld class action waivers in arbitration agreements. However, if no arbitration agreement was present, the policy favoring arbitration was irrelevant and would not override the countervailing policy favoring resolution of disputes through class actions. *Id.* Striking down the bright-line rule adopted by the Appellate Division, the Supreme Court began by noting that class action waivers are different from arbitration provisions notwithstanding that they are frequently paired to prevent class arbitration. Nothing in *Concepcion* suggests that class waivers cannot be enforced outside the arbitration context. 258 N.J. at 98–99, 317 A.3d at 487. Nor does the fact that class actions advance important public policy goals mean that they cannot be waived, just as waivers of the right to a jury trial may be enforceable. *Id.* Underscoring the state's "strong public policy in favor of the freedom to contract," the Supreme Court found neither a statutory provision explicitly permitting class actions under the New Jersey CFA "nor a clear statement of public policy disfavoring class action waivers." 258 N.J. at 99–101, 317 A.3d at 487–89. Consequently, class action waivers standing alone are not per se unenforceable. Rather, they may be unenforceable if found to be unconscionable or invalid under general contract principles. 258 N.J. at 101–02, 317 A.3d at 489. "As a matter of general contract law, the inquiry is the same regardless of whether a contract contains an arbitration provision." *Id.* The Supreme Court proceeded to find that the class action waiver in the subject lease agreement was not unconscionable. It first noted the "simple, clear, understandable and easily readable" language of the class waiver. Second, although the lease agreement was "arguably a contract of adhesion" because it was presented in a take-it-or-leave it manner, the plaintiffs were able to consult with an attorney before signing and were free to seek out other housing if they disagreed with the lease terms. Although plaintiffs argued that a "chronic housing shortage" was sufficient to establish economic compulsion, the Court found no facts that Hamilton Cove was the only apartment complex available to plaintiffs. Finally, the class action waiver did not act as a de facto exculpatory clause, because nothing prevented the plaintiffs from pursuing individual actions under the CFA, which provides for treble damages and fee-shifting for successful claims. 258 N.J. at 102–08, 317 A.3d at 489–93.

Citron v. Cinch Real Estate Inc., 2023 WL 3573769 (App. Div. May 22, 2023), presented a somewhat hybrid situation, where a dispute resolution provision in a home warranty agreement required disputes to be resolved either in arbitration or a small claims court with jurisdiction over the dispute. The Appellate Division held that the class action waiver in the provision was enforceable. Notably, in *Citron,* the plaintiff brought a putative class action in the Law Division. Because the plaintiff did not sue either in the Small Claims Section or the Special Civil Part, the court held that the only other option available to the plaintiff was binding arbitration. 2023 WL 3573769, at *3.

j. Timing of Class Determination

The Supreme Court showed a reluctance to dismiss class allegations on a motion to dismiss before discovery in *Baskin v. P.C. Richard & Son, LLC*, 246 N.J. 157, 249 A.3d 461 (2021). In *Baskin*, the New Jersey Supreme Court reversed a trial court's dismissal of a class action complaint in a FACTA case as premature, because plaintiffs needed discovery from the defendant to establish the numerosity, predominance, and superiority requirements. Also, with a respect to the timing of a determination of class issues, in *Lopez*, the Appellate Division affirmed the trial court's denial of class certification, in part, because plaintiffs did not move for class certification "at an early practicable time," but instead waited until three years after their original complaint had been filed and a trial date had already been set. 2010 N.J. Super. Unpub. LEXIS 1648, at *18. The Appellate Division has further stated that a defendant may raise the propriety of class certification before plaintiff makes a motion for class certification. *Castro v. NYT Television*, 370 N.J. Super. 282, 300–01, 851 A.2d 88, 99 (App. Div. 2004). There is also no bright-line rule that precludes trial courts from rejecting class certification before any discovery is conducted. *Myska v. N.J. Mfrs. Ins. Co.*, 440 N.J. Super. 458, 114 A.3d 761 (App. Div.), *cert. denied*, 224 N.J. 523, 135 A.3d 144 (2016) (trial court properly struck class allegations prior to discovery where an analysis of plaintiff's allegations demonstrated that the alleged claims did not "properly lend themselves to class certification").

The Supreme Court has also held that it is not a violation of due process to try common issues of a certified class prior to litigation of individual issues. *Matter of Cadillac*, 93 N.J. at 437–38, 461 A.2d at 749.

4. RULE 4:32-1(B)(2) CERTIFICATION

In connection with the standards for a (b)(2) class action certification, in *Laufer v. The United States Life Ins. Co.*, 385 N.J. Super. 172, 896 A.2d 1101 (App. Div. 2006), the Appellate Division approved a (b)(2) class action in which the named plaintiff suffered an "ascertainable loss"—the requisite financial loss to bring a private claim under the New Jersey CFA—by reason of defendant's misleading description of its insurance policy. Even though the complaint did not allege that other putative class members had suffered any monetary harm, injunctive relief in favor of the insured class—all of whom had received defendant's misleading description of the policy in notices sent by the insurer—was held proper. The court found that even though not all members of the class had been damaged by the misleading notices, "the relief sought by the named plaintiffs . . . benefit[ed] the entire class." 385 N.J. Super. at 183, 896 A.2d at 1108. In *Cameron v. South Jersey Pubs, Inc.*, 460 N.J. Super. 156, 213 A.3d 967 (App. Div. 2019), the court addressed certification of a proposed (b)(2) class in a case involving defendants' practice of not including beverage prices in its menus. Plaintiff's complaint only sought injunctive and declaratory relief. The court explained that predominance is not a requirement for (b)(2) certification, and the appropriateness of class certification "turns on the precise nature of the remedy sought" and whether there is "cohesiveness," *i.e.* a homogeneity of the class members' claims. 213 A.3d at 982–83. The court held that certification was appropriate because plaintiff showed sufficient cohesiveness because a single injunction that prohibited the defendants' practice would provide the same requested relief to all members of the purported class. *Id.* at 988.

5. DECERTIFICATION

"The decertification of a class, in whole or in part, is one of the remedies available to a trial court under Rule 4:32-2." *Little v. Kia Motors Am., Inc.*, 242 N.J. 557, 591, 233 A.3d 377, 396 (2020). With respect to the burden of proof on decertifying a class, *Muise v. GPU, Inc.*, 371 N.J. Super. 13, 851 A.2d 799 (App. Div. 2004), placed on defendants the burden of producing evidence that class treatment was inappropriate. The Appellate Division, however, reversed the trial court, finding defendants had met the burden.

6. COUNSEL FEES AND LITIGATION EXPENSES

Rule 4:32-2(h) authorizes the court to award counsel fees and litigation expenses if authorized by law, rule or the parties' agreement. Where plaintiffs' claims are based on state statutes that contain fee-shifting provisions, New Jersey courts first calculate the lodestar in determining the amount of fees to award to the prevailing party. *Rendine v. Pantzer*, 141 N.J. 292, 334–35, 661 A.2d 1202 (1995). Courts achieve the lodestar by multiplying the number of hours reasonably expended on the litigation by a reasonable hourly rate. 141 N.J. at 334–35, 661 A.2d at 1226. Once the lodestar is calculated, and certain standards are met, New Jersey courts are also authorized to add a contingency enhancement to increase the fee award to take into account the risk assumed by the attorney that he or she would not have received payment had the lawsuit not succeeded. 141 N.J. at 338, 661 A.2d at 1228. Although the trial court can award a contingency enhancement ranging from 1 to 100 percent, the New Jersey Supreme Court has held that the typical enhancement should range between 20 and 35 percent. 141 N.J. at 343, 661 A.2d at 1231. Although the United States Supreme Court in *Perdue v. Kenny A.*, 559 U.S. 542, 130 S. Ct. 1662, 176 L. Ed. 2d 494 (2010), held that contingency enhancements in cases brought under federal fee-shifting statutes are "reserved for unusual cases," the New Jersey Supreme Court held that contingency enhancements under New Jersey fee-shifting provisions are still evaluated under the factors and standards established in *Rendine*. *See Walker v. Giuffre*, 209 N.J. 124, 140–41, 35 A.3d 1177 (2012).

7. COMMUNICATIONS WITH AND DISCOVERY FROM ABSENT PUTATIVE CLASS MEMBERS

There is no blanket prohibition against counsel's communications with absent putative class members. In *Bayshore Ford Truck v. Ford Motor Co.*, 2009 U.S. Dist. LEXIS 106567, at *29 (D.N.J. Nov. 16, 2009), *rev'd in part on other grounds*, 540 Fed. App'x 113 (3d Cir. 2013), for example, the court held that "before a class action is certified, it will ordinarily not be deemed inappropriate for a defendant to seek to settle individual claims." Trial courts, however, are required to "take steps to safeguard class members from unauthorized and misleading communications from the parties or their counsel." *In re Cmty. Bank of N. Va. & Guar. Nat'l Bank of Tallahassee Second Mortg. Loan Litig.*, 418 F.3d 277, 310 (3d Cir. 2005). This obligation stems from the court's "broad authority to exercise control over a class action and to enter appropriate orders governing the conduct of counsel and parties." *Id.* (quoting *Gulf Oil Co. v. Bernard*, 452 U.S. 89, 100, 101 S. Ct. 2193, 2200, 68 L. Ed. 2d 693, 703 (1981)). Although a trial court has the authority to impose restrictions on counsel's and parties' ability to communicate with absent putative class members, only restrictions which are necessary to correct the negative effects of improper contact should be imposed. *Id.* Before the trial court does impose restrictions on pre-certification communications with absent putative class members, the court should conduct an evidentiary hearing and allow the parties and counsel an opportunity to be heard to ensure that the chosen remedy is restricted to the minimum necessary to correct the alleged improper contact. *Id.* at 312.

With respect to discovery, in appropriate circumstances the trial court may require absent putative class members to respond to defendants' discovery requests. *Towpath Unity Tenants Ass'n v. Barba*, 182 N.J. Super. 77, 440 A.2d 51 (App. Div. 1981). In *Towpath*, where plaintiff alleged fraud in connection with the leasing of apartments, the court held that the defendant was permitted to serve twenty interrogatories on each putative class member directed at the issue of what misrepresentations the defendant allegedly made to each putative class member and the extent to which it influenced his or her decision to enter into the lease. *Id.* at 84. Such discovery will only be permitted where the defendant can demonstrate that the discovery is necessary to establish a claim or defense at issue in the litigation. *See Sulcov v. 2100 Linwood Owners, Inc.*, 303 N.J. Super. 13, 696 A.2d 31 (App. Div. 1997) (holding that the defendants were properly precluded from conducting discovery of absent putative class members because the defenses to which the discovery requests allegedly related had been abandoned).

8. INTERLOCUTORY APPEALS OF DECISIONS ON CLASS CERTIFICATION

In 2006, when R. 4:32 was amended to conform to the 2003 revisions to Fed. R. Civ. P. 23, it did not include a counterpart to Rule 23(f) providing for permissive interlocutory appeals of class certification decisions because other New Jersey rules already permitted discretionary interlocutory appeals. *See* R. 2:5-6 (appeals to the Appellate Division) and R. 2.2-2 (appeals to the Supreme Court). But these rules state the standards for interlocutory appeals in general terms and do not specifically address when interlocutory appeals of class certification decisions should be granted. In *Daniels*, the court held that appellate courts should, as a general matter, "liberally indulge applications for leave to appeal: (1) when a denial of class status effectively ends the case (because say, the named plaintiff's claim is not of a sufficient magnitude to warrant the costs of stand-alone litigation); (2) when the grant of class status raises the stakes of the litigation so substantially that the defendant likely will feel irresistible pressure to settle; and (3) when permitting leave to appeal will lead to a clarification of a fundamental issue of law." 440 N.J. Super. at 361, 113 A.3d at 797 n.1 (quotations and citations omitted).

In 2022, however, the New Jersey Court Rules were amended to make "orders denying or granting as a final matter class certification" appealable as of right to the Appellate Division. *See* R. 2:2-3(b)(9). The rule change was implemented at the suggestion of the Appellate Division, which noted that the denial or grant of class certification "have a profound impact on the progress of a case in trial court." 2022 Report of N.J. Supreme Ct. Civ. Prac. Committee, at 20. The court rules were also amended to give preference to such appeals in the scheduling of argument or submission without argument. *See* R. 2:11-1(a).

RULE 4:32 OF THE NEW JERSEY RULES OF CIVIL PROCEDURE

CLASS ACTIONS 4:32-1. REQUIREMENTS FOR MAINTAINING CLASS ACTION

(a) **General prerequisites to a class action.** One or more members of a class may sue or be sued as representative parties on behalf of all only if (1) the class is so numerous that joinder of all members is impracticable, (2) there are questions of law or fact common to the class, (3) the claims or defenses of the representative parties are typical of the claims or defenses of the class, and (4) the representative parties will fairly and adequately protect the interests of the class.

(b) **Class actions maintainable.** An action may be maintained as a class action if the prerequisites of paragraph (a) are satisfied, and in addition:

(1) the prosecution of separate actions by or against individual members of the class would create a risk either of:

(A) inconsistent or varying adjudications with respect to individual members of the class that would establish incompatible standards of conduct for the party opposing the class, or

(B) adjudications with respect to individual members of the class that would as a practical matter be dispositive of the interests of the other members not parties to the adjudications or substantially impair or impede their ability to protect their interests; or

(2) the party opposing the class has acted or refused to act on grounds generally applicable to the class, thereby making appropriate final injunctive relief or corresponding declaratory relief with respect to the class as a whole; or

(3) the court finds that the questions of law or fact common to the members of the class predominate over any questions affecting only individual members, and that a class action is superior to other available methods for the fair and efficient adjudication of the controversy. The factors pertinent to the findings include:

(A) the interest of members of the class in individually controlling the prosecution or defense of separate actions;

(B) the extent and nature of any litigation concerning the controversy already commenced by or against members of the class;

(C) the desirability or undesirability in concentrating the litigation of the claims in the particular forum; and

(D) the difficulties likely to be encountered in the management of a class action.

4:32-2. DETERMINING BY ORDER WHETHER TO CERTIFY A CLASS ACTION; APPOINTING CLASS COUNSEL; NOTICE AND MEMBERSHIP IN THE CLASS; MULTIPLE CLASSES AND SUBCLASSES

(a) **Order determining maintainability; certifying class.** When a person sues or is sued as a representative of a class, the court shall, at an early practicable time, determine by order whether to certify the action as a class action. An order certifying a class action shall define the class and the class claims, issues or defenses, and shall appoint class counsel in accordance with paragraph (g) of this rule. The order may be altered or amended prior to the entry of final judgment.

(b) **Notice.**

(1) If a class is certified pursuant to R. 4:32-1(b)(1) or (b)(2), the court may direct appropriate notice to the class.

(2) If a class is certified pursuant to R. 4:32-1(b)(3), the court shall direct to the members of the class the best notice practicable under the circumstances, consistent with the due process of law. The notice shall state the following in concise, clear and easily understood language:

(A) the nature of the action;

(B) the definition of the class certified;

(C) the class claims, issues or defenses;

(D) that a class member may enter an appearance through counsel if the member so desires;

(E) that the court will exclude from the class any member who requests exclusion, stating when and how members may elect to be excluded; and

(F) the binding effect of a class judgment on class members pursuant to paragraph (c) of this rule.

(3) The cost of notice may be assessed against any party present before the court, or may be allocated among parties present before the court, pending final disposition of the cause.

(c) **Judgment.** The judgment in an action maintained as a class action under R. 4:32-1(b)(1) or (b)(2), whether or not favorable to the class, shall include and describe those whom the court finds to be members of the class. The judgment in an action maintained as a class action under R. 4:32-1(b)(3), whether or not favorable to the class, shall, to the extent practicable under the circumstances, consistent with due process of law, describe the class and specify those who have been excluded from the class. In any class action, the judgment may, consistent with due process of law, confer benefits upon a fluid class, whose members may be, but need not have been members of the class in suit.

(d) **Partial class actions; subdivided classes.** If appropriate, an action may be brought or maintained as a class action with respect to particular issues. A class may also be divided into subclasses and each subclass treated as a class, and the provisions of this rule shall then be construed and applied accordingly.

(e) Settlement, voluntary dismissal, or compromise.

(1) (A) The court shall approve any settlement, voluntary dismissal, or compromise of the claims, issues, or defenses of a certified class.

(B) The court shall direct notice in a reasonable manner to all class members who would be bound by a proposed settlement, voluntary dismissal, or compromise.

(C) The court may approve a settlement, voluntary dismissal, or compromise that would bind class members only after a hearing and on finding that the settlement, voluntary dismissal, or compromise is fair, reasonable, and adequate.

(2) The parties seeking approval of a settlement, voluntary dismissal, or compromise under this rule shall file a statement identifying any agreement made in connection with the proposed settlement, voluntary dismissal, or compromise.

(3) In an action previously certified as a class action under R. 4:32-1(b)(3), the court may refuse to approve a settlement unless it affords a new opportunity to request exclusion to individual class members who had an earlier opportunity to request exclusion but did not do so.

(4) Any class member may object to a proposed settlement, voluntary dismissal, or compromise that requires court approval under paragraph (e)(1)(A) of this rule. An objection made under this paragraph may be withdrawn only with the court's approval.

(f) Orders in conduct of actions. In the conduct of actions to which this rule applies, the court may make appropriate orders:

(1) determining the course of proceedings or prescribing measures to prevent undue repetition or complication in the presentation of evidence or argument;

(2) requiring, for the protection of the members of the class or otherwise for the fair conduct of the action, that notice be given to some or all of the members of the class in such manner as the court may direct of (A) any step in the action, (B) the proposed extent of the judgment, or (C) the opportunity of members to signify whether they consider the representation fair and adequate, to intervene and present claims or defenses, or otherwise to come into the action;

(3) imposing conditions on the representative parties or on intervenors;

(4) requiring that the pleadings be amended to eliminate therefrom allegations as to representation of absent persons, and that the action proceed accordingly;

(5) dealing with similar procedural matters.

These orders may be combined with an order under R. 4:32-2(a) and may be altered or amended as may be desirable from time to time.

(g) Class counsel.

(1) Appointing Class Counsel.

(A) Unless a statute provides otherwise, a court that certifies a class must appoint class counsel.

(B) An attorney appointed to serve as class counsel must fairly and adequately represent the interests of the class.

(C) In appointing class counsel, the court must consider: (i) the work counsel has done in identifying or investigating potential claims in the action; (ii) counsel's experience in handling class actions, other complex litigation, and claims of the type asserted in the action; (iii) counsel's knowledge of the applicable law, and (iv) the resources counsel will commit to representing the class.

The court also may consider any other matter pertinent to counsel's ability to represent fairly and adequately the interest of the class and may direct potential class counsel to provide information on any subject pertinent to the appointment and to the proposed terms for attorney fees and nontaxable costs. The court may make further orders in connection with the appointment.

(2) Appointment Procedure.

(A) The court may designate interim counsel to act on behalf of the putative class before determining whether to certify the action as a class action.

(B) When there is one applicant for appointment as class counsel, the court may appoint that applicant only if the applicant is adequate under this rule. If more than one adequate applicant seeks appointment as class counsel, the court must appoint the applicant best able to represent the interests of the class.

(C) The order appointing class counsel may include provisions about the award of attorney fees or nontaxable costs under paragraph (h) of this rule.

(h) Attorney's Fees and Litigation Expenses. In an action certified as a class action, an application for the award of attorney's fees and litigation expenses, if fees and costs are authorized by law, rule, or the parties' agreement, shall be made in accordance with R. 4:42-9. Notice of the motion shall be served on all parties. A motion by class counsel shall be directed to class members in a reasonable manner. A party from whom payment is sought as well as any class member may object to the motion.

Jeffrey J. Greenbaum is a member of the law firm of Sills Cummis & Gross, PC, in Newark, New Jersey. Jason L. Jurkevich is of counsel with the firm. Mr. Greenbaum is the chair of the firm's class action defense practice group. He is a graduate of the University of Michigan Law School (*cum laude*) and the Wharton School of the University of Pennsylvania. He is past chair of the Class Actions and Derivative Suits Committee of the American Bar Association's Litigation Section and was a member of the ABA Task Force on Class Action Legislation. Mr. Greenbaum is also founder and former co-chair of the Class Action Litigation Committee of the New Jersey State Bar Association. Mr. Jurkevich is a graduate of the New York University School of Law and the New York University College of Arts and Science (*magna cum laude)*. The authors represent defendants in securities, consumer, and other class actions in both federal and state courts.

NEW MEXICO

1. COMPARISON WITH RULE 23 OF THE FEDERAL RULES OF CIVIL PROCEDURE

Rule 1-023 NMRA was adopted by the New Mexico Supreme Court effective July 1, 1995. In 2000, New Mexico added subparagraph F to Rule 1-023 generally following the wording of Federal Rule 23(f), but New Mexico has not yet adopted the 2003 revisions to Federal Rule 23. In 2011, New Mexico added subparagraph G to Rule 1-023 to govern the disbursement of "residual funds." At the present time, Rule 23 of the New Mexico Rules of Civil Procedure is no longer identical to Rule 23 of the Federal Rules of Civil Procedure.

New Mexico originally adopted the 1938 version of Rule 23 of the Federal Rules of Civil Procedure. Federal Rule 23 was amended substantially in 1966, but New Mexico did not adopt the amendments. In 1976, the New Mexico Supreme Court expressed frustration with New Mexico's then Rule 23. In *Valley Utilities, Inc. v. O'Hare*, 1976-NMSC-024, ¶ 2, 89 N.M. 262, 550 P.2d 274, the New Mexico Supreme Court stated:

> Class suits are governed in New Mexico by Rule 23 of our Rules of Civil Procedure . . . which was taken from the "old" (i.e., pre-1966 version of) Rule 23 of the Federal Rules of Civil Procedure. This "old" Rule 23 creates three types of classes, generally referred to as "true," "hybrid," and "spurious." (Internal citations omitted.)

While only "true" and "spurious" classes were at issue in *Valley Utilities*, the Supreme Court discussed the problems inherent in the "old" Rule 23 classification scheme and expressed concern with its continued use in New Mexico. *See generally id.* Approximately two weeks after entering its opinion in *Valley Utilities*, the New Mexico Supreme Court entered an order stating that Rules 23(A) and (C) were "revoked and vacated" effective June 15, 1976. Consequently, at that point, New Mexico had no class action rule.

In 1978, the New Mexico Supreme Court adopted a new Rule 23 and an expanded Rule 24, governing intervention. The 1978 Rule 23 contained provisions similar to Federal Rule 23, but the New Mexico rule added a subsection F which provided:

> In any proceeding under this Rule 23 no damages may be awarded to and no costs or damages may be assessed against any member of a class who was not a named party in the litigation.

The 1978 Rule 24 contained a subsection D, titled "Simplified Intervention by Members of a Class." In essence, although the procedures were somewhat cumbersome, Rule 24(d) provided a means by which, following the entry of appropriate court orders making a number of specific findings, a class member could "opt in" to a lawsuit and thereby be bound by the outcome, whether favorable or unfavorable to the class.

The net result of New Mexico's class action rules prior to July 1, 1995, was that virtually no class actions were filed in New Mexico state courts.

The first reported New Mexico decision from either the Supreme Court or Court of Appeals concerning the post-1995 version of Rule 1-023 was issued by the New Mexico Court of Appeals in November 2003. *See Salcido v. Farmers Ins. Exch.*, 2004-NMCA-006, 134 N.M. 797, 82 P.3d 968. Subsequently, on July 23, 2004, the New Mexico Court of Appeals issued three rulings regarding class action law in New Mexico.[1] *See Berry v. Fed. Kemper Life Assurance Co.*, 2004-NMCA-116, 136 N.M. 454, 99 P.3d 1166; *Brooks v. Norwest Corp.*, 2004-NMCA-134, 136 N.M. 599, 103 P.3d 39; *Enfield v. Old Line Life Ins. Co. of Am.*, 2004-NMCA-115, 136 N.M. 398, 98 P.3d 1048. Since 2004, the New Mexico Court of Appeals has continued to expand New Mexico class action jurisprudence. In April 2006, the New Mexico Supreme Court addressed the modern class action rules, *see U.S. Xpress, Inc. v. New Mexico Taxation & Revenue Dep't*, 2006-NMSC-017, 139 N.M 589, 136 P.3d 999, and recently demonstrated its commitment to expanding the case law in this evolving area of New Mexico law, *see Ferrell v. Allstate Ins. Co.*, 2008-NMSC-042, 144 N.M. 405, 188 P.3d 1156. These pronouncements are the first by the New Mexico appellate courts regarding modern class action law. As such, they provide long-awaited guidance to practitioners in New Mexico.

2. CASE LAW INTERPRETING NEW MEXICO RULE 1-023

a. Early Case Law under the Modern Rule

The first reported New Mexico decision regarding modern class action law and New Mexico's current Rule 23 was issued in November 2003. In *Salcido,*[2] 2004-NMCA-006, 82 P.3d 968, the New Mexico Court of Appeals considered the guidelines set forth in Rule 1-023(F) NMRA (2003). The appeal challenged the trial court's certification of a class on two grounds: (1) that there was no separate finding that each element was met under the requirements of Rule 23 and (2) the named plaintiffs were not members of the purported class. *Id.* ¶ 5, 82 P.3d at 969–70. The Court of Appeals recognized that it held a highly discretionary role in its review of decisions either granting or denying certification of a class and applied an abuse of discretion standard. *Id.* ¶ 7, 82 P.3d at 970. Utilizing guidelines articulated by the D.C. Circuit to guide its discretion, the New Mexico Court of Appeals stated that it will ordinarily grant review of class certification decisions where:

(1) there is a death-knell situation for either the plaintiff or defendant that is independent of the merits of the underlying claims, coupled with a class certification decision by the district court that is questionable, taking into account the district court's discretion over class certification;
(2) the certification decision presents an unsettled and fundamental issue of law relating to class actions, important both to the specific litigation and generally, that is likely to evade end-of-the-case review; and

[1] On August 13, 2004, the New Mexico Court of Appeals issued a non-published memorandum opinion on class certification. Rightmire v. Mosley (No. 23,705) (August 13, 2004). While not providing precedent, the memorandum opinion emphasizes the need for a sufficient showing for class certification and for the district court to consider whether a class action will be fair to all parties. The Court of Appeals noted that certification is not a discovery tool to recruit members of a class first and meet Rule 1-023's requirements at a later date.

[2] *Salcido* has been partially overruled by a later case, *Davis v. Devon Energy Corp.*, 2009-NMSC-048, 147 N.M. 157, 218 P.3d 75.

(3) the district court's class certification decision is manifestly erroneous.

Id. ¶ 11, 82 P.3d at 971 (citing *In re Lorazepam & Clorazepate Antitrust Litig.*, 289 F.3d 98, 105 (D.C. Cir. 2002)).

The Court of Appeals emphasized that the guidelines were not a rigid test and stated that the appellate court should avoid micromanagement of complex class action cases. *Id.* ¶ 12, 82 P.3d at 971. The Court of Appeals applied its guidelines to the trial court's certification of the class and refused to grant review of the class certification order. *Id.* ¶ 30, 82 P.3d at 975.

On July 23, 2004, the New Mexico Court of Appeals issued decisions in three class certification cases. The July 23 trilogy of cases provided the first substantive appellate guidance regarding modern Rule 1-023 in New Mexico. *See Berry*, 2004-NMCA-116, 99 P.3d 1166; *Brooks*, 2004-NMCA-134, 103 P.3d 39; *Enfield*, 2004-NMCA-115, 98 P.3d 1048. All three cases address Rule 1-023(B)(3) classes and all three are notable not only for their articulation of the general rules regarding class certification, but also because they deal with class certification issues related to nationwide multi-jurisdictional classes.

After mid-2004, the New Mexico Court of Appeals has continued to address class action issues, specifically with respect to an indirect consumer antitrust class action, *Romero v. Phillip Morris, Inc.*, 2005-NMCA-035, 137 N.M. 229, 109 P.3d 768; an employment conditions class action, *Armijo v. Wal-Mart Stores, Inc.*, 2007-NMCA-120, 142 N.M. 557, 168 P.3d 129; a life insurance policy class action, *Rivera-Platte v. First Colony Life Ins.*,[3] 2007-NMCA-158, 143 N.M. 158, 173 P.3d 765; and an unjust enrichment class action, *Sloane v. Rehoboth Mckinley Christian Health Care Services, Inc.*, 2018-NMCA-048, 423 P.3d 18. Additionally, the New Mexico Supreme Court has addressed class action suits in an administrative proceeding, *U.S. Xpress, Inc. v. N.M. Taxation & Revenue Dep't*, 2006-NMSC-017, 139 N.M. 589, 136 P.3d 999; examined the proper method by which New Mexico courts should administer multi-district class action suits, *Ferrell v. Allstate Ins. Co.*, 2008-NMSC-042, 144 N.M. 405, 188 P.3d 1156; and heard the appeal of the life insurance policy class action, *Platte v. First Colony Life Ins. Co.*, 2008-NMSC-058, 145 N.M. 77, 194 P.3d 108.

b. General Principles

The trial court has broad discretion regarding certification of a class. *See Berry,*[4] 2004-NMCA-116, ¶ 25, 99 P.3d at 1176; *Brooks*, 2004-NMCA-134, ¶ 7, 103 P.3d at 43. In exercising its discretion properly, the trial court must engage in a rigorous analysis of the Rule's requirements while keeping in mind the policy behind Rule 1-023. *Brooks*, 2004-NMCA-134, ¶ 9, 103 P.3d at 43; *Romero*, 2005-NMCA-035, ¶ 36, 109 P.3d at 777. Even when pled in the alternative, all claims should be dealt with when presented, rather than at a later time. *Enfield,*[5] 2004-NMCA-115, ¶ 23, 98 P.3d at 1052–53. Rule 1-023 is a remedial procedural device and the Court of Appeals has indicated that it will interpret the rule liberally. *Romero*, 2005-NMCA-035, ¶ 36, 109 P.3d at 777.

While an evidentiary hearing is not required, the trial court may probe behind the pleadings and forecast what evidence might be required. *Brooks*, 2004-NMCA-134, ¶ 9, 103 P.3d at 43–44;

[4] *Berry* has been overruled in part, on other grounds, by *Ferrell v. Allstate Ins. Co.*, 2007-NMCA-017, 141 N.M. 72, 150 P.3d 1022.

[5] *Enfield* has been overruled in part, on other grounds, by *Ferrell*, 2007-NMCA-017, 141 N.M. 72, 150 P.3d 1022.

Romero, 2005-NMCA-035 ¶ 38, 109 P.3d at 778; *Williams v. Stewart*, 2005-NMCA-061, ¶ 30, 137 N.M. 420, 428, 112 P.3d 281, 289. The Court of Appeals has stated a strong preference for formal and detailed findings of fact and conclusions of law addressing the elements of Rule 1-023. *Berry*, 2004-NMCA-116, ¶ 19, n.1, 99 P.3d at 1175, n.1; *Enfield*, 2004-NMCA-115, ¶ 12, n.1, 98 P.3d at 1051, n.1; *Romero*, 2005-NMCA-035, ¶ 33, 109 P.3d at 776; *but see Davis v. Devon Energy Corp.*, 2009-NMSC-048, ¶¶ 38–39, 147 N.M. 157, 169, 218 P.3d 75, 87 (stating that "[l]ike the Court of Appeals, we therefore strongly encourage the district court to enter findings of fact and conclusions of law in their class certification order[s]. However, entering findings of fact and conclusions of law is not a prerequisite to our review of the district court's certification order.").

In *Brooks*, the Court of Appeals recognized an "implicit primary" requirement whereby plaintiffs bear the burden of demonstrating the existence of an identifiable class that is "capable of ascertainment under some objective standard." 2004-NMCA-134, ¶ 20, 103 P.3d at 46 (internal citation omitted). Furthermore, standing is a "threshold legal issue to class certification." *Starko, Inc. v. Presbyterian Health Plan, Inc.*,[6] 2012-NMCA-053, ¶ 105, 276 P.3d 252, 281 (internal citation omitted). In order to prove standing, the plaintiff must demonstrate "(1) an injury in fact, (2) a causal relationship between the injury and the challenged conduct, and (3) a likelihood that the injury will be redressed by a favorable decision." *Id.* (internal citation omitted).

Because portions of New Mexico Rule 1-023 NMRA (2008, prior to amendments through May 2011) are based on the federal rules, it is helpful to consider federal case law when construing the New Mexico Rule. If a New Mexico rule of civil procedure, or a portion thereof, is identical to a federal rule of civil procedure, it is appropriate for a New Mexico court to examine federal law construing the rule to determine how the New Mexico court should construe the rule. *See, e.g.*, *Romero*, 2005-NMCA-035, ¶ 35, 109 P.3d at 777; *Brooks*, 2004-NMCA-134, ¶ 8, 103 P.3d at 43; *Benavidez v. Benavidez*, 1983-NMSC-032, ¶ 14, 99 N.M. 535, 539, 660 P.2d 1017, 1021.

The New Mexico Supreme Court, in its first pronouncement regarding the modern class action rules, considered whether exhaustion of administrative remedies was a prerequisite to courts assuming jurisdiction. *See generally U.S. Xpress*, 2006-NMSC-017, 136 P.3d 999. In a case involving a claim for tax refunds governed by the Tax Administration Act, NMSA 1978, Section 7-1-22 (1995), the trial court denied class action status because the class tax payers had not exhausted their administrative remedies. *U.S. Xpress*, 2006-NMSC-017, ¶ 4, 136 P.3d at 1001. The New Mexico Supreme Court reversed the Court of Appeals' decision finding that the statute clearly required all taxpayers to exhaust administrative remedies. *Id.* ¶ 15, 136 P.3d 1005. Thus, it was not futile to require exhaustion before the courts took jurisdiction. *Id.* ¶ 9, 136 P.3d at 1002.

Furthermore, the Court also rejected the Court of Appeals' holding that "vicarious exhaustion of administrative remedies by the named plaintiffs representing the entire class serves the same purposes the legislature intended in Section 7-1-22." *Id.* ¶ 10, 136 P.3d at 1002–03. The New Mexico Supreme Court held "[w]here the Legislature specifically mandates, exhaustion is required. Where the Legislature has not clearly required exhaustion, sound judicial discretion governs." *Id.* ¶ 12, 136 P.3d at 1004. The New Mexico Supreme Court further held that, when the legislature clearly mandates the exhaustion of administrative remedies, "[e]ach member of the class must individually exhaust, and only after individual exhaustion by each class member could the district court have jurisdiction over the class." *Id.* ¶ 13, 136 P.3d at 1004.

In 2007, the New Mexico Court of Appeals established the standard of review for determining whether plaintiffs in Minimum Wage Act litigation are similarly situated for purposes of certifying

[6] *Starko* was reversed, on other grounds, by *Starko, Inc. v. N.M. Human Servs. Dep't.*, 2014-NMSC-033, 333 P.3d 947.

a class. *See Armijo*, 2007-NMCA-120, ¶ 50, 168 P.3d at 144–45. Specifically, the Court of Appeals adopted the "ad hoc" or "two-tiered" approach followed by a majority of federal courts. *Id.* Under that approach, the court considering certification makes an initial "similarly situated" determination in which it examines whether the party seeking class status has raised "substantial allegations that the putative class members were together the victims of a single decision, policy, or plan." *Id.* ¶ 48, 168 P.3d at 144 (internal citation and quotation marks omitted). Assuming the putative class survives the first step of the analysis, the court then engages in a more rigorous "similarly situated" inquiry in which it considers the following factors:

(1) whether the class members have disparate factual and employment settings;
(2) whether the available defenses to the claims are individual to each class member; and
(3) whether there are any fairness or procedural considerations relevant to the action.

Id. (internal citations omitted). Following consideration of these factors, the court may then decide whether to allow the suit to proceed as a class action. *Id.*

In 2008, the New Mexico Supreme Court held that arbitration agreements that would prohibit participation in a class action suit for small claims are against New Mexico public policy. *Fiser v. Dell Computer Corp.*,[7] 2008-NMSC-046, ¶ 16, 144 N.M. 464, 469, 188 P.3d 1215, 1220. The Court declared the class action device to be critical in protecting consumer rights, especially when the size of the claim rendered other remedies, such as arbitration, impractical. *Id.* ¶ 12, 188 P.3d at 1219. Thus, the Court held that a choice of law provision and arbitration clause that effectively barred any remedy for a small claim were against state public policy and unenforceable. *Id.* ¶ 16, 188 P.3d at 1220.

c. Rule 1-023(A)

Plaintiffs bear the burden of showing that all four prerequisites of Rule 1-023(A) are met. *Romero*, 2005-NMCA-035, ¶ 38, 109 P.3d at 778; *Brooks*, 2004-NMCA-134, ¶ 10, 103 P.3d at 44. Failure to establish any one requirement is sufficient to deny certification. *Brooks*, 2004-NMCA-134, ¶ 10, 103 P.3d at 44. A court may not "simply presume conformance with Rule 1-023." *Romero*, 2005-NMCA-035, ¶ 39, 109 P.3d at 778.

d. Rule 1-023(B)

Plaintiffs bear the burden of showing that one of the requirements of Rule 1-023(B) is met. *Brooks*, 2004-NMCA-134, ¶ 10, 103 P.3d at 44. Plaintiffs must establish both predominance and superiority. *Id.* ¶¶ 11, 30, 103 P.3d at 44–48. Although Rule 1-023(B)(3) does not specifically define either term, it does provide several factors for courts to consider when deciding whether a plaintiff has established predominance and superiority, including:

(a) the interest of members of the class in individually controlling the prosecution or defense of separate actions;
(b) the extent and nature of any litigation concerning the controversy already commenced by or against members of the class;

[7] *Fiser* was limited by a 2014 Tenth Circuit case, *THI of New Mexico at Hobbs Center, LLC v. Patton*, in which the court held that the Federal Arbitration Act preempted finding an agreement unfair "based on a perceived inferiority of arbitration to litigation as a means of vindicating one's rights." 741 F.3d 1162, 1169 (10th Cir. 2014).

(c) the desirability or undesirability of concentrating the litigation of the claims in the particular forum;
(d) the difficulties likely to be encountered in the management of a class action.

Rule 1-023(B)(3) NMRA; *see also Ferrell*, 2008-NMSC-042, ¶ 11, 144 N.M. 405, 188 P.3d 1156, 1163. Failure to show either predominance or superiority provides the trial court with a sufficient basis to deny certification. *Brooks*, 2004-NMCA-134, ¶ 10, 103 P.3d at 44. In insurance cases, New Mexico courts have held that commonality—and thus predominance—can arise "when alleged legal deficiencies in uniform documents are common to the defined class." *Ullman v. Safeway Ins. Co.*, 995 F. Supp. 2d 1196, 2013 U.S. Dist. LEXIS 184761 (D.N.M., Dec. 31, 2013), *rev'd on other grounds*, (No. 34,897, 2017) (remanding to district court the decision to decertify class when uniform insurance documents establishing class commonality were determined legal and valid).

The issue of class manageability is relevant to both predominance and superiority. *Id.* ¶ 33, 103 P.3d at 49; *Romero*, 2005-NMCA-035, ¶ 51, 109 P.3d at 781. The trial court's discretion is paramount when it determines whether a class action is manageable. *Brooks*, 2004-NMCA-134, ¶ 34, 103 P.3d at 49; *see also Romero*, 2005-NMCA-035, ¶ 97, 109 P.3d at 795. The Court of Appeals echoed the policy that where there are small claims, but common issues of fact and law predominate and common methods of proof exist, a class action is a superior procedure. *Romero*, 2005-NMCA-035, ¶ 52, 109 P.3d at 781. In antitrust price-fixing actions, the Court of Appeals noted that refusal to certify on manageability grounds is disfavored. *Id.* ¶ 54, 109 P.3d at 782.

The *Berry* and *Enfield* cases emphasized the issues associated with a nationwide class action in the context of Rule 1-023(B)(3). *See generally Berry*, 2004-NMCA-116, 99 P.3d 1166; *Enfield*, 2004-NMCA-115, 98 P.3d 1048. As the Court of Appeals observed, determining whether common issues predominate can be more involved in the context of a nationwide class. *Berry*, 2004-NMCA-116, ¶ 51, 99 P.3d at 1182. In *Berry*, the Court of Appeals discussed three general types of difficulties in the predominance inquiry, noting that:

> First, multistate classes bring into sharp focus the Rule 1-023(B)(3)(c) requirement that courts consider the relative desirability of concentrating litigation in the particular forum. Second, the district court must ascertain what the law governing the cause of action in each state actually is and compare it with the forum state law. Having completed this difficult task, the court must decide which law to apply. Applying the wrong law raises problems of constitutional dimension. Third, if the forum state decides to apply the law of other states, the court must consider the difficulty of managing the trial of sub-classes to the same jury.

Id. (internal citations omitted).

In *Romero*, the Court of Appeals analyzed class certification in the context of an indirect purchaser antitrust class action. 2005-NMCA-035, 109 P.3d 768. The Court of Appeals recognized that class actions play a "significant role" for small claim holders. *Id.* ¶ 36, 109 P.3d at 777. The claim revolved around an alleged conspiracy to set the pricing of cigarettes in New Mexico. To demonstrate commonality, the Court of Appeals noted that plaintiffs must show that they will use common evidence as to each member of the class without focusing on extensive individualized inquiry. *Id.* ¶ 42, 109 P.3d at 779. Antitrust damages also must be based on common proof. *Id.* The Court of Appeals adopted the concept that common, generalized, logically probative methodologies to prove antitrust injury were "superficially acceptable" to meet the predominance requirement under Rule 1-023. *Id.* ¶ 90, 109 P.3d at 792. However, the Court of Appeals cautioned that what might be sufficient for certification purposes did not prove antitrust injury and that the defendants could attack the plaintiffs' methodologies as to scientific reliability and sufficiency. *Id.* ¶ 93, 109 P.3d at 793. The Court of Appeals specifically noted that certification in the *Romero* case hinged on class-wide injury and not on damages methodologies. *Id.* ¶ 94, 109 P.3d at 793. If there is class-wide injury, the Court of Appeals accepted that class members who were injured suffered some damages. *Id.*

In *Ferrell*, the New Mexico Supreme Court reversed the Court of Appeals's decertification of all but the New Mexico class members in a multi-state class action consisting of thirteen different states. 2008-NMSC-042, 188 P.3d 1156. There, the district court certified a multistate class action by Allstate insureds who alleged breach of contract against Allstate Insurance Company "for failing to include installment fees that are charged when an insured opts to pay the premium in monthly installments in the total premium calculation." *Id.* ¶ 2, 188 P.3d at 1160. The Court of Appeals subsequently reversed the district court's certification decision with respect to all but the New Mexico class members, finding that common questions of law would not predominate and the case would be unmanageable if the district court were to attempt to apply the laws of thirteen jurisdictions. *See generally Ferrell v. Allstate Ins. Co.*, 2007-NMCA-017, 141 N.M. 72, 150 P.3d 1022. Ultimately, the New Mexico Supreme Court reinstated the district court's certification decision, finding that the district court correctly determined that application of New Mexico law to the entire certified class did not present any "fatal contradictions of law." *Ferrell*, 2008-NMSC-042, ¶ 45, 188 P.3d at 1170.

The New Mexico Supreme Court's decision in *Ferrell* provided much needed guidance to New Mexico courts and practitioners. Notably, the Court clarified that "[a] decision to apply the laws of several states does not . . . necessarily foreclose class certification [if] . . . [a] court may be able to manage a class through the use of subclasses or by grouping certain issues together that can be resolved by applying one state's law." *Id.* ¶ 13, 188 P.3d at 1163. Similarly, the Court established that a potential conflict of law is insufficient to defeat class certification; rather, the party opposing certification must demonstrate an actual conflict with the laws of the relevant states. *Id.* ¶ 45, 188 P.3d at 1170. Moreover, the Court held that when deciding which state's law to apply to a particular matter, New Mexico courts should refer to the Restatement (Second) of Conflicts. *Id.* ¶ 56, 188 P.3d at 1173. Finally, the Court held that challenges to forum selection clauses in class action cases should be treated as "venue defenses," i.e., as challenges asserted under Rule 1-012(B)(3) NMRA (2008), finding that treating them as such "comports with the goals underlying [New Mexico's] class action rule." *Id.* ¶¶ 61–64, 188 P.3d at 1174–75.

The New Mexico appellate courts have continued to interpret Rule 1-023(B). In *Davis v. Devon Energy Corp.*, 2009-NMSC-048, ¶ 1, 147 N.M. 157, 218 P.3d 75, a group of royalty owners brought three separate class action suits against defendant gas producers for improperly deducting costs from royalty payments. The district court consolidated the cases for discovery and class certification procedural issues, and eventually certified three separate classes under Rule 1-023(B)(2) NMRA. However, the district court denied class certification under Rule 1-023(B)(3), finding that individualized inquiries into the royalty agreements "predominated over the common issues of law and fact." *Id.* ¶ 2, 218 P.3d at 77. The defendants sought certiorari review of granting of class certification under Rule 1-023(B)(2) and the plaintiffs sought certiorari review of the denial of class certification pursuant to Rule 1-023(B)(3). While the New Mexico Court of Appeals denied interlocutory review, the New Mexico Supreme Court granted certiorari review on both issues.

The New Mexico Supreme Court addressed the certification under Rule 1-023(B)(2), ruling that the decision to grant class certification should be upheld. *Id.* ¶ 16, 218 P.3d at 81. The Court reasoned that despite the differences in various individual contracts at issue, any argument that the differences involved the need to consider individualized proof and individualized inquiries constituted an improper attempt to incorporate the predominance requirements of Rule 1-023(B)(3) into

Rule 1-023(B)(2). *Id.* ¶ 17, 218 P.3d at 81. The Court stated that Rule 1-023(B)(2) does not contain these requirements, and only requires the defendants to have done something or refused to do something which affects the whole class. *Id.* The Supreme Court relied on the district court's ruling that the defendants took a standardized approach in calculating royalty payments as a basis for its ruling. *Id.* ¶ 19, 218 P.3d at 81–82.

The defendants also raised an argument that since the plaintiffs were seeking monetary relief, certification was improper because the basis for a Rule 1-023(B)(2) certification must be predominantly for injunctive or declaratory relief. *Id.* ¶ 20, 218 P.3d at 82. The New Mexico Supreme Court acknowledged federal precedent but did not believe that the presence of monetary relief precluded certification under (B)(2), stating that "when both the injunctive and monetary relief are of roughly equal importance, and the other requirements of certification have been met, (B)(2) certification is proper." *Id.* ¶ 23, 218 P.3d at 82–83. Otherwise, the Court would be required to weigh the importance of relief to the plaintiff. *Id.*

The Court also reversed the district court's denial of class certification under Rule 1-023(B)(3). *Id.* ¶ 28, 218 P.3d at 84. While the district court concluded that the different terms in each contract made it necessary to review each contract individually and found that "the individualized inquiries . . . predominate over any common issues of law or fact," the Supreme Court reasoned that the question to be litigated did not require an individualized inquiry, but rather a question common to all class members, and therefore the class should have been certified. *Id.* ¶¶ 26, 37, 218 P.3d at 83–86. The New Mexico Supreme Court also recently affirmed these rulings in the case of *Ideal v. Burlington Resources Oil & Gas Co. LP*, 2010-NMSC-022, 148 N.M. 228, 233 P.3d 362.

Likewise, the New Mexico Court of Appeals discussed the Rule 1-023(B) predominance requirement in *Starko*, 2012-NMCA-053, ¶ 107, 276 P.3d at 282. In that case, the court held that individual issues do not necessarily predominate over class-wide issues simply because each plaintiff suffered a different amount of economic injury. *Id.* Rather, a "single common issue may be the overriding one in the litigation, despite the fact that the suit also entails numerous remaining individual questions." *Armijo*, 2007-NMCA-120, ¶ 32, 142 N.M. at 567, 168 P.3d at 139 (internal citation omitted). The *Starko* court concluded that the plaintiffs had met Rule 1-023(B)'s predominance requirement because "in order to prevail, each class member will need a holding as to the major issues common to all." *Starko*, 2012-NMCA-053, ¶ 107, 276 P.3d at 282. Once a court has ruled in the plaintiffs' favor, the class members can then demonstrate the extent of their individual injuries. *Id.* Finally, in affirming the district court's class certification, the Court of Appeals noted that (1) no class members expressed interest in bringing separate causes of action, (2) class certification would conserve judicial resources, and (3) the number of class members was manageable. *Id.* ¶ 108, 276 P.3d at 282.

The New Mexico Court of Appeals has also addressed the effects of raising affirmative defenses in response to motions for class certification under Rule 1-023(B)(3). In *Tierra Realty Trust LLC v. Village of Ruidoso*, 2013-NMCA-030, 296 P.3d 500, residential wastewater customers brought a class action suit against defendant municipality for monetary damages stemming from alleged unreasonable rate increases in utility fees. The district court denied certification based upon the defendant's contention that issues of voluntary payment and duress, as well as the affirmative defenses of estoppel and latches, created individualized issues that predominated over common issues of the class. *Id.* ¶ 24, 296 P.3d at 508. In so holding, the district court stated that "[d]uress cannot be inferred or found on a class wide basis; rather it is a factual determination that would have to be made as to each and every residential wastewater and sewage user." *Id.* The Court of Appeals overturned the district court, finding that although the voluntary payment defense was applicable to only some class members, the argument of duress was common to the class, and questions common to the class regarding those issues predominated. *Id.* ¶ 31, 296 P.3d at 510. The court also found that the application of the affirmative defenses of estoppel and laches did not require individual inquiries that would overwhelm the common issues in the case. *Id.* ¶ 33, 296 P.3d at 510. Ultimately, the court held that the issue of the unreasonableness of uniform wastewater rates paid by every customer in the class predominated over any questions affecting individual class members and remanded the case for a finding as to superiority. *Id.* ¶¶ 33–34, 296 P.3d at 510–11.

e. Rule 1-023(E)

The New Mexico appellate courts have now considered the reasonableness of an award of attorneys' fees in the context of a class action settlement. *In re N.M. Indirect Purchasers Microsoft Corp. Antitrust Litig.*, 2007-NMCA-007, 140 N.M. 879, 149 P.3d 976. The Court of Appeals recognized that the review of a fee award involves competing interests and responsibilities and set forth four general guiding principles:

(1) The judiciary has a duty to review reasonableness and in doing so acts as a fiduciary for class members weighing the interests of the class and the interests of class counsel;
(2) A court must acknowledge the public perception of windfall fees in class actions and use judicial oversight to ensure that fees awarded to class counsel are proportional to the benefit obtained for the class;
(3) The appellate court must be mindful that it does not substitute its judgment for that of the district court; and
(4) The court must conserve judicial resources and promote judicial efficiency.

Microsoft, 2007-NMCA-007, ¶¶ 12–15, 143 P.3d at 985–86.

The Court of Appeals noted that in the particular case before it, it was only reviewing the award of attorneys' fees as provided by the settlement agreement and that the provisions in the settlement agreement are controlling, unless the terms produce a result that is unfair to the class or contrary to the policies underlying class actions. *Id.* ¶16, 143 P.3d at 986. The Court of Appeals considered the arguments raised in the case, but eventually noted that reasonableness was the ultimate question regarding an award of attorneys' fees. The Court of Appeals noted that New Mexico courts have historically used the factors found in Rule 16-105 of the Rules of Professional Conduct to examine the reasonableness of an attorneys' fee award and utilized those factors to guide its analysis of the attorneys' fee awarded pursuant to the *Microsoft* settlement. The court noted that the factors to be considered are not of equal weight and not all of the factors need to be considered. These factors are:

(1) the time and labor required, the novelty and difficulty of the questions involved, and the skill requisite to perform the legal service properly;
(2) the likelihood . . . that the acceptance of the particular employment will preclude other employment by the lawyer;
(3) the fee customarily charged in the locality for similar legal services;
(4) the amount involved and the results obtained;
(5) the time limitations imposed by the client or by the circumstances;
(6) the nature and length of the professional relationship with the client;
(7) the experience, reputation, and ability of the lawyer performing the services; and
(8) whether the fee is fixed or contingent.

Id. ¶¶ 76–78, 143 P.3d at 1004–05.

While the court in *Microsoft* spoke directly to attorneys' fees, the New Mexico Supreme Court recently cited to *Microsoft* in describing the deference to be given to district courts in any class action settlement. *See Platte*, 2008-NMSC-058, ¶ 7, 145 N.M. at 78, 194 P.3d at 109. There are two reported decisions, decided under New Mexico's earlier class action rules, that are applicable to cases filed under the current Rule 1-023. First, in *Balizer v. Shaver*, 1971-NMCA-010, ¶ 12, 82 N.M. 347, 481 P.2d 709, the Court of Appeals held that if a complaint states a claim upon which relief could be granted on behalf of the individually named plaintiffs and attempts but fails to state a claim on behalf of a class, the class claim should be dismissed in response to the defendant's motion to dismiss. Second, in *Eastham v. Public Employees Retirement Ass'n Board*, the New Mexico Supreme Court held that procedural due process required notice to members of a class whose rights would be affected by the outcome of the litigation. 1976-NMSC-046, ¶ 14, 89 N.M. 399, 553 P.2d 679. In so holding, the Court established that courts are "required to direct to class members 'the best notice practicable under the circumstances, including individual notice to all members who can be identified through reasonable effort.'" *Id.* ¶ 13, 553 P.2d at 683 (quoting *Eisen v. Carlisle & Jacquelin*, 417 U.S. 156, 173–74 (1974)).

3. MISCELLANEOUS COMMENTS

The vast majority of New Mexico's state trial court judges still have no experience with class actions, either as judges or as attorneys. The appellate courts are now starting to actively review class action cases, and the law will continue to be developed in the next few years. Most district court judges have overwhelming dockets and very little support staff. In many courts, New Mexico district court judges have a secretary and a bailiff. Law clerks for district court judges are a rarity. Accordingly, if a class action is filed in a New Mexico district court, the court in all likelihood will have no experience with class action issues or managing class action cases. Out-of-state attorneys considering filing or defending a class action in New Mexico should consult with experienced local attorneys to discuss the practicalities of filing or defending in any particular judicial district in New Mexico.

RULE 1-023 OF THE NEW MEXICO RULES OF CIVIL PROCEDURE

1-023. CLASS ACTIONS.

A. Prerequisites to a class action. One or more members of a class may sue or be sued as representative parties on behalf of all only if:

(1) the class is so numerous that joinder of all members is impracticable;

(2) there are questions of law or fact common to the class;

(3) the claims or defenses of the representative parties are typical of the claims or defenses of the class; and

(4) the representative parties will fairly and adequately protect the interests of the class.

B. Class actions maintainable. An action may be maintained as a class action if the prerequisites of Paragraph A of this rule are satisfied, and in addition:

(1) the prosecution of separate actions by or against individual members of the class would create a risk of:

(a) inconsistent or varying adjudications with respect to individual members of the class which would establish incompatible standards of conduct for the party opposing the class; or

(b) adjudications with respect to individual members of the class which would as a practical matter be dispositive of the interests of the other members not parties to the adjudications or substantially impair or impede their ability to protect their interests;

(2) the party opposing the class has acted or refused to act on grounds generally applicable to the class, thereby making appropriate final injunctive relief or corresponding declaratory relief with respect to the class as a whole; or

(3) the court finds that the questions of law or fact common to the members of the class predominate over any questions affecting only individual members, and that a class action is superior to other available methods for the fair and efficient adjudication of the controversy. The matters pertinent to the findings include:

(a) the interest of members of the class in individually controlling the prosecution or defense of separate actions;

(b) the extent and nature of any litigation concerning the controversy already commenced by or against members of the class;

(c) the desirability or undesirability of concentrating the litigation of the claims in the particular forum;

(d) the difficulties likely to be encountered in the management of a class action.

C. Determination by order whether class action to be maintained; notice; judgment; actions conducted partially as class actions.

(1) As soon as practicable after the commencement of an action brought as a class action, the court shall determine by order whether it is to be so maintained. An order under this subparagraph may be conditional, and may be altered or amended before the decision on the merits.

(2) In any class action maintained under Paragraph (B)(3) of this rule, the court shall direct to the members of the class the best notice practicable under the circumstances, including individual notice to all members who can be identified through reasonable effort. The notice shall advise each member that:

(a) the court will exclude the member from the class if the member so requests by a specified date;

(b) the judgment whether favorable or not, will include all members who do not request exclusion; and

(c) any member who does not request exclusion may, if the member desires, enter an appearance through counsel.

(3) The judgment in an action maintained as a class action under Paragraph (B)(1) or (B)(2) of this rule, whether or not favorable to the class, shall include and describe those whom the court finds to be members of the class. The judgment in an action maintained as a class action under Paragraph (B)(3) of this rule, whether or not favorable to the class, shall include and specify or describe those to whom the notice provided in Paragraph (C)(2) of this rule was directed, and who have not requested exclusion, and whom the court finds to be members of the class.

(4) When appropriate:

(a) an action may be brought or maintained as a class action with respect to particular issues; or

(b) a class may be divided into subclasses and each subclass treated as a class, and the provisions of this rule shall then be construed and applied accordingly.

D. *Orders in conduct of actions*. In the conduct of actions to which this rule applies, the court may make appropriate orders:

(1) determining the course of proceedings or prescribing measures to prevent undue repetition or complication in the presentation of evidence or argument;

(2) requiring, for the protection of the members of the class or otherwise for the fair conduct of the action, that notice be given in the manner as the court may direct to some or all of the members of any step in the action, or of the proposed extent of the judgment, or of the opportunity of members to signify whether they consider the representation fair and adequate, to intervene and present claims or defenses, or otherwise to come into the action;

(3) imposing conditions on the representative parties or on intervenors;

(4) requiring that the pleadings be amended to eliminate therefrom allegations as to representation of absent persons, and that the action proceed accordingly;

(5) dealing with similar procedural matters.

The orders may be combined with an order under Rule 1-016 NMRA, and may be altered or amended as may be desirable from time to time.

E. *Dismissal or compromise*. A class action shall not be dismissed or compromised without the approval of the court, and notice of the proposed dismissal or compromise shall be given to all members of the class in the manner as the court directs.

F. *Appeals*. The Court of Appeals may in its discretion permit an appeal from an order of a district court granting or denying class action certification under this rule if application is made to it within fifteen (15) days after entry of the order. An appeal does not stay proceedings in the district court unless the district judge or the Court of Appeals so orders.

G. *Residual funds to named organization*.

(1) For purposes of Paragraph (G)(2) of this rule, "residual funds" are

(a) unclaimed funds, including uncashed checks and other unclaimed payments, that remain after payment of all approved class member claims, expenses, litigation costs, attorneys' fees, and other court-approved disbursements or dispositions to implement the relief granted, whether the payments are drawn from a common fund or directly from the judgment debtor's own funds; or

(b) if it is impossible or economically impractical to distribute the common fund to the class at all, the entire common fund after payment of all approved expenses, litigation costs, attorneys' fees, and other court-approved disbursements or dispositions to implement the relief granted, whether the payments are drawn from a common fund or directly from the judgment debtor's own funds.

(2) Either in its order entering a judgment or approving a proposed settlement of a class action certified under this rule that establishes a process for identifying and compensating members of the class or by a subsequent order entered when residual funds are determined to exist, the court shall provide for the disbursement of residual funds, if any, to one or more of the following entities:

(a) nonprofit organizations that support projects that benefit the class or similarly situated persons consistent with the goals of the underlying causes of action on which relief was based;

(b) educational entities that provide training, teaching and legal services that further the goals of the underlying causes of action on which relief was based;

(c) nonprofit organizations that provide legal services to low income persons;

(d) the entity administering the IOLTA fund under Rule 24-109 NMRA, to support activities and programs that promote access to the civil justice system for low income residents of New Mexico; and

(e) the entity administering the pro hac vice fund under Rule 24-106 NMRA, to support activities and programs that promote access to the civil justice system for low income residents of New Mexico.

(3) Nothing in this paragraph is intended to prevent the parties to a class action from proposing, or the trial court from approving, a settlement that does not create residual funds.

As amended, effective July 1, 1995; as amended, effective May 11, 2011.

Jennifer G. Anderson graduated from the University of Michigan Law School in 1997. She has been involved in numerous federal and state class actions.

NEW YORK

1. GENERAL PRINCIPLES

Article 9 of the New York Civil Practice Law and Rules (CPLR) is substantially similar to Rule 23 of the Federal Rules of Civil Procedure (Rule 23). *Compare* N.Y. C.P.L.R. § 901(a) (McKinney 2024), *with* Fed. R. Civ. P. 23 (entitled "Class Actions"); *see also In re Colt Indus. S'holder Litig.*, 77 N.Y.2d 185, 194 (1991) (explaining that CPLR Article 9 "has much in common" with Fed. Rule 23); *Amer-A-Med Health Prods., Inc., v. O'Brien*, No. 9808/04, 2011 WL 1464145 (Sup. Ct. Nassau Cty. Mar. 31, 2011) ("CPLR Article 9 is modeled on Rule 23."). New York courts look to federal law for guidance in interpreting Article 9. *City of New York v. Maul*, 14 N.Y.3d 499, 510 (2010); *Matakov v. Kel-Tech Const., Inc.*, 84 A.D.3d 677, 679 n.1 (1st Dep't 2011) ("Federal jurisprudence is an appropriate guide when analyzing CPLR article 9 issues, because article 9 has much in common with Federal rule 23, the federal class action provision.").

CPLR § 901(a) lists the prerequisites to bringing a class action in New York, and CPLR § 902 lists the requirements for maintaining such an action. N.Y. C.P.L.R. §§ 901–02 (McKinney 2024). In addition to the four requirements of Rule 23(a)—numerosity, commonality, typicality, and adequacy—CPLR § 901(a) includes Rule 23(b)(3)'s superiority requirement as a prerequisite to maintaining a class action. *See Maddicks v. Big City Properties, LLC*, 34 N.Y.3d 116, 123 (2019); *Maul*, 14 N.Y.3d at 508; *Sperry v. Crompton Corp.*, 8 N.Y.3d 204, 211 (2007); *In re Colt Indus.*, 77 N.Y.2d at 195. As set forth below, CPLR § 901(a)(2)'s commonality requirement also encompasses Rule 23(b)(3)'s predominance requirement.

If CPLR § 901(a)'s prerequisites are met, courts must also consider the following factors pursuant to CPLR § 902 to determine whether the action can proceed as a class action:

> (1) the interest of members of the class in individually controlling the prosecution or defense of separate actions; (2) the impracticability or inefficiency of prosecuting or defending separate actions; (3) the extent and nature of any litigation concerning the controversy already commenced by or against members of the class; (4) the desirability or undesirability of concentrating the litigation of the claim in the particular forum; and (5) the difficulties likely to be encountered in the management of a class action.

N.Y. C.P.L.R. § 902(1)–(5) (McKinney 2024).

"[M]ost of these considerations [namely those discussed by CPLR § 902] are implicit in CPLR § 901." *Jackson v. Citywide Mobile Response Corp.*, 80 Misc. 3d 1113, 1124 (Sup. Ct. Bronx Cty. 2023); *see also Chaine v. Paris Limousine Servs., Corp.*, No. 20786/2010, 2011 WL 3370880, at *1 (Sup. Ct. N.Y. Cty. July 29, 2011) ("CPLR § 902's factors overlap with CPLR § 901(a)(5) and are seen as implicit in the superiority prerequisite."). Further, a court will conduct a holistic analysis when applying the CPLR § 902 factors. For example, in considering the desirability or undesirability of concentrating litigation in a particular forum pursuant to CPLR § 902(4), a court examines the time required to certify, ultimately resolve, and apportion and distribute damages in the action as well as the type of oversight required to hear the claim. *See Midland Funding L.L.C. v. Joyce*, No.

68823/09, 2010 WL 1493139, at *4 (N.Y. Civ. Ct., Kings Cty. Mar. 10, 2010) (citing *Alix v. Wal-Mart Stores, Inc.*, 16 Misc. 3d 844 (Sup. Ct. Albany Cty. 2007), *aff'd*, 57 A.D.3d 1044 (3d Dep't 2008)). As another example, potential difficulties encountered in the management of a class action include "determining the adequacy of notice to the class members, mindful of the constitutional mandate to provide that form of notice reasonably necessary to apprise the interested parties of the litigation; properly apportioning the considerable anticipated cost of the notice and supervising voluminous additional pre-trial discovery." *Alix*, 16 Misc. 3d at 865 (internal citations omitted). There is some support in the case law for the proposition that the court "may also consider the merits of the action to the extent necessary for the elimination, as early as possible, of spurious actions[.]" *Corsello v. Verizon New York, Inc.*, No. 39610/07, 2009 WL 3682595, at *16 (Sup. Ct. Kings Cty. Nov. 5, 2009) (quoting *Hoerger v. Bd. of Educ. of Great Neck Union Free Sch. Dist.*, 98 A.D.2d 274, 278 (2d Dep't 1983) , *aff'g in part,* 76 A.D.3d 941 (2010), *aff'd*, 18 N.Y.3d 777 (2012); *see also Pludeman v. Northern Leasing Sys., Inc.*, 74 A.D.3d 420, 422 (1st Dep't 2010) ("In determining whether an action should proceed as a class action, it is appropriate to consider whether the claims have merit.") (citing *Bloom v. Cunard Line, Ltd.*, 76 A.D.2d 237, 240 (1st Dep't 1980)); *cf. Dabrowski v. Abax Inc.*, 84 A.D.3d 633, 634 (1st Dep't 2011) (reviewing evidence in support of plaintiffs' motion for class certification and noting the claims have merit).

However, this inquiry "is limited to a determination as to whether on the surface there appears to be a cause of action which is not a sham." *Jenack v. Goshen Operations, LLC*, 222 A.D.3d 36, 40–41 (2023); *see also Weinstein v. Jenny Craig Operations, Inc.*, 138 A.D.3d 546, 547 (1st Dep't 2016) ("[P]laintiffs' evidence was sufficient to satisfy the minimal threshold of establishing that their claim was not a sham."); *Pludeman*, 74 A.D.3d at 422 (quoting *Kudinov v. Kel-Tech Constr. Inc.*, 65 A.D.3d 481, 482 (1st Dep't 2009)) ("such threshold determination is not intended to be a substitute for summary judgment or trial"); *Aldrich v. Leasing Sys. Inc.*, No. 602803/07, 2012 WL 3638871 (Sup. Ct. N.Y. Cty. Aug. 20, 2012) ("[I]t is important that the claims on which Plaintiffs seek to certify a class must not only have merit, but must also have buttressed evidentiary support and not rest on conclusory allegations.") (citations omitted). Other courts have placed even further limits on such an inquiry. *Burdick v Tonoga, Inc.*, 60 Misc. 3d 1212(a), at *6 (Sup. Ct. Rensselaer Cty. 2018) ("In determining the propriety of a class action, the question is not whether the plaintiffs will prevail on the merits, but rather whether the requirements of CPLR § 901 and § 902 have been met.").

The provisions of CPLR Article 9 are liberally construed in favor of certification. *Krobath v. S. Nassau Communities Hosp.,* 178 A.D.3d 805, 806 (2d Dep't 2019); *Gudz v. Jemrock Realty Co., LLC*, 105 A.D.3d 625, 626 (1st Dep't 2013), *aff'd sub nom, Borden v. 400 E. 55th St. Assocs., L.P.,* 24 N.Y.3d 382 (2014); *see also Jenack*, 222 A.D.3d at 41 ("It has long been recognized that the criteria set forth in CPLR 901(a) 'should be broadly construed . . . because it is apparent that the Legislature intended [CPLR] article 9 to be a liberal substitute for the narrow class action legislation which preceded it.'") (citation omitted); *Hurrell-Harring v. State of New York*, 81 A.D.3d 69, 72 (3d Dep't 2011) ("[A]ny error, if there is to be one, should be . . . in favor of allowing the class action." (quoting *Pruitt v. Rockefeller Ctr. Props., Inc.*, 167 A.D.2d 14, 21 (1st Dep't 1991)); *Onadia v. City of New York*, 56 Misc. 3d 309, 315 (Sup. Ct. Bronx Cty. 2017) ("The interests of justice require that in a doubtful case of any error, if there is to be one, should be committed in favor of allowing the class action."). However, a plaintiff seeking class certification "ha[s] the burden of establishing compliance with the statutory requirements for class action certification under CPLR 901 and 902." *Jenack*, 222 A.D.3d at 44; *see also Ferrari v. Nat'l Football League*, 153 A.D.3d 1589, 1591 (4th Dep't 2017) ("class action is appropriate only if all five of the requirements are met"); *Deluca v. Tonawanda Coke Corp.*, 134 A.D.3d 1534, 1535 (4th Dep't 2015) (a "plaintiff seeking class certification has the 'burden of establishing the prerequisites of CPLR 901(a) and thus establish[ing] . . .

entitlement to class certification.'") (quoting *Freeman v. Great Lakes Energy Partners, L.L.C.*, 12 A.D.3d 1170, 1171 (4th Dep't 2004)), *denying leave to appeal*, 137 A.D.3d 1633 (4th Dep't 2016); *Gomez v. Brill Sec., Inc.*, 95 A.D.3d 32, 43–44 (1st Dep't 2012) (citing *Godwin Realty Assoc. v. CATV Enters., Inc.*, 275 A.D.2d 269 (1st Dep't 2000)); *Osarczuk*, 82 A.D.3d at 855; *Smilewicz v. Sears Roebuck & Co.*, 82 A.D.3d 744, 744–45 (2d Dep't 2011); *Abdale v. N. Shore-Long Island Jewish Health Sys., Inc.*, No. 2367/13, 2016 WL 3045440, at *2 (Sup. Ct. Queens Cty. May 26, 2016) ("The plaintiff bears the burden of showing that the criteria of CPLR 901 and 902 have been satisfied."); *Andryeyeva v. New York Health Care, Inc.*, 45 Misc. 3d 820, 825 (Sup. Ct. Kings Cty. 2014) ("The party seeking class certification bears the burden of establishing the criteria prescribed in CPLR § 901(a). This burden must be met by providing an evidentiary basis for class certification.") (citations omitted); *Aldrich*, 2012 WL 3638871 ("[I]t is equally important for Plaintiffs to meet their burden of establishing the enumerated statutory criteria to proceed as a class action.") (citations omitted). *Cf. Chaine*, 2011 WL 3370880, at *1 ("Because plaintiffs have not met their burden to establish the § 901(a)(5) superiority prerequisite, this court need not reach the other four prerequisites."). Nonetheless, the party seeking class certification is entitled to "limited discovery, to determine whether the prerequisites to class certification listed in CPLR 901 are present, and to assess the feasibility considerations listed in CPLR 902 in relation to the particular facts." *Chang v. Westside 309 LLC*, 206 A.D.3d 491, 491–92 (1st Dep't 2022); *see also Kodirov v. County Home Care Referral Serv.*, No. 6870/11, 2012 WL 1605258, at *2 (Sup. Ct. Kings Cty. May 8, 2012) (party seeking class certification "must first be allowed to conduct the limited discovery necessary to adduce evidence to satisfy the requirements set forth by the CPLR."). With respect to such discovery, some courts have held that "[d]isclosure at [the] pre-certification stage is limited to . . . ascertaining only those facts which arc [sic] necessary to support an application for class status." *Martin v. Palisades Collection, LLC*, No. 116099/2010, 2012 WL 2930791, at *4 (Sup. Ct. N.Y. Cty. Jun. 27, 2012) (quoting *Gewanter v. Quaker State Oil Ref. Corp.*, 87 A.D.2d 970, 970 (4th Dep't 1982)) (internal quotation marks omitted). *Cf. Rodriguez v. Metro Cable Commc'ns*, 79 A.D.3d 841, 842 (2d Dep't 2010) (striking an interrogatory request at the class certification stage that did not assist the plaintiff in "ascertain[ing] the dimensions of the group of individuals who share plaintiff's grievance") (quoting *Smith v. Atlas Int'l Tours*, 80 A.D.2d 762, 764 (1st Dep't 1981)). These holdings seem to focus, however, on efforts by plaintiffs to seek discovery of the identities of those alleged to be harmed by defendants' conduct and whether those efforts go beyond what is necessary to determine the size and existence of a class. There is otherwise little support for existence of a rule bifurcating discovery between class certification and merits issues. *See, e.g.*, *Gibbs v. Kings Harbor Health Servs., LLC*, 190 A.D.3d 586, 587 (1st Dep't 2021) (affirming order compelling the production of documents responsive to pre-certification document requests that were "relevant to the claims of the class as a whole" and holding that "discovery should not be limited to material relevant only to the named representatives since the complaint contains allegations relating to the putative class as a whole"); *Argento v. Wal-Mart Stores, Inc.*, 66 A.D.3d 930, 932 (2d Dep't 2009) ("[O]ver the course of the next 10 months, the parties engaged in discovery relevant to both the statutory prerequisites for seeking class action certification and the merits of the action.").

"[T]he determination as to whether to certify a class is ultimately vested within the sound discretion of the trial court." *Abdale*, 2016 WL 3045440, at *2 (citing *Cooper v. Sleepy's, LLC*, 120 A.D.3d 742, 743 (2d Dep't 2014)). *Cf. Biscone v. JetBlue Airways Corp.*, 103 A.D.3d 158, 180 (2d Dep't 2012) ("Supreme Court providently exercised its discretion in denying . . . plaintiff's motion which was for leave to renew [her motion for class certification] on the basis that the plaintiff's supporting papers were insufficient."). However, in exercising that discretion, "pursuant to CPLR § 903 . . . the [trial] court should . . . describe[] the class." *O'Brien v. GEICO Ins. Co.*, 99 A.D.3d

683, 685 (2d Dep't 2012).

The Appellate Divisions, however, are "also vested with the same discretion and may exercise it even if there has been no abuse by the trial court." *Jenack*, 222 A.D.3d at 40; *Pludeman*, 74 A.D.3d at 422 (same). *Cf. Dugan v. London Terrace Gardens, L.P.*, 186 A.D.3d 12, 19–20 (1st Dep't 2020) (reversing trial court's order expanding previously certified class after "[c]onducting the analysis ourselves"). The Court of Appeals, unlike the Appellate Divisions and trial courts, reviews the lower courts' certification decisions for an abuse of discretion and may not exercise its own discretion. *Corsello v. Verizon N.Y., Inc.*, 18 N.Y.3d 777, 791 (2012), *reh'g denied*, 19 N.Y.3d 937 (2012). "In addition, CPLR § 902 allows the trial court to decertify the class at any time before a decision on the merits if it becomes apparent that class treatment is inappropriate." *Maul*, 14 N.Y.3d at 514.

2. SUMMARY OF CASE LAW FOR ANALOGS TO FEDERAL RULE 23(A) REQUIREMENTS—CPLR 901(A)(1)-(4)

a. CPLR § 901(a)(1). Numerosity

Similar to Rule 23(a)(1), CPLR § 901(a)(1) requires that "the class is so numerous that joinder of all members, whether otherwise required or permitted, is impracticable." *Maul*, 14 N.Y.3d at 508 (quoting CPLR § 901(a)); *see also Onadia*, 56 Misc. 3d at 316–17; *Bartis v. Harbor Tech, LLC*, 147 A.D.3d 51, 63 (2d Dep't 2016); *Roberts v. Ocean Prime, LLC*, 148 A.D.3d 525, 525 (1st Dep't 2017); *Hurrell-Harring*, 81 A.D.3d at 71–72; *Pludeman*, 74 A.D.3d at 421. "[C]ourts have not drawn a magic number at which the numerosity prerequisite is met." *Maor v. Hornblower New York, LLC*, No. 160993/14, 2016 WL 3240219, at *3 (Sup. Ct. N.Y. Cty. June 13, 2016). However, "it has been repeatedly held that 'the threshold for impracticability of joinder seems to be around forty'; although conversely, it has been held that the numerosity requirement will not be 'satisfied when the class comprises 21 or fewer' claimants." *Zeitlin v. New York Islanders Hockey Club, L.P.*, 49 Misc. 3d 511, 516 (Sup. Ct. Nassau Cty. 2015) (citations omitted); *see also Lewis v. Hallen Constr. Co., Inc.*, 193 A.D.3d 511, 512 (1st Dep't 2021) (holding that claim involving "at least 30 to 50 workers . . . establish[ed] the numerosity of the class"); *Picard v. Bigsbee Enter., Inc.*, No. 1984–13., 2014 WL 3639072, at *2 (Sup. Ct. Albany Cty. 2014) ("[I]t generally is accepted that a putative class of forty members is sufficiently numerous for certification."); *Weinstein v. Jenny Craig Operations, Inc.*, No. 105520/11, 2013 WL 5809397, at *3 (Sup. Ct. N.Y. Cty. Oct. 24, 2013) ("Generally, a prospective class of forty or more raises a presumption of numerosity."); *Thomas v. Meyers Associates, L.P.*, No. 651720/2011, 2013 WL1777483, at *10 (N.Y. Sup. Ct. Apr. 18, 2013) ("[The] evidence is sufficient at this point to establish that at least 40 stockbrokers worked overtime during the class period. The numerosity factor has been met."); *Martin*, 2012 WL 2930791, at *9 ("While there is no precise minimum number that satisfies the numerosity requirement for certification of a class action, a class of as few of 39 members has been approved."); *Nawrocki v. Proto Constr. & Dev. Corp.*, No. 104229/2007, 2010 WL 1531428, at *2 (Sup. Ct. N.Y. Cty. Apr. 7, 2010) (noting that numerosity is generally established when a class comprises around forty members), *aff'd*, 82 A.D.3d 534 (1st Dep't 2011) (citations omitted); *Juarez v. USA Roofing Co. Corp.*, No. 651437/13, 2016 WL 4991254 at *5 (N.Y. Sup. Ct. Sept. 16, 2016) (finding a class of 25 members did not satisfy the numerosity requirement absent any "special factors").

Courts may also analyze numerosity on a case-by-case basis, even where the requisite for the presumption is satisfied, by assessing the totality of the circumstances. *See Borden*, 24 N.Y.3d at 399 ("As to the first factor, numerosity, the legislature contemplated classes involving as few as 18 members where the members would have difficulty communicating with each other, such as where 'barriers of distance, cost, language, income, education or lack of information prevent those who are aware of their rights from communicating with others similarly situated'") (citation omitted); *Marshall v. Roselli Moving & Storage Corp.*, No. 103478/09, 2012 WL 274590, at *2 (Sup. Ct. N.Y. Cty. Jan. 23, 2012) ("Although numerosity is presumed at a level of 40 members . . . the court is to consider the particular circumstances of each case and the reasonable inferences and commonsense assumptions from the facts before it.") (internal quotation marks and citations omitted). Consideration of these circumstances will also obviate the need to show the precise number of class members. *See Kudinov*, 65 A.D.3d at 481 (1st Dep't 2009) (citing as sufficient to show numerosity, without evidence of the exact "number of workers alleged to have been underpaid," the following facts: "the number of projects, the certified payroll records and the testimony and affidavits regarding the number of workers potentially affected by the allegations"); *see also Globe Surgical Supply v. GEICO Ins. Co.*, 59 A.D.3d 129, 137–38 (2d Dep't 2008).

b. CPLR § 901(a)(2). Commonality and Predominance

"[U]nder New York State caselaw, the CPLR's commonality requirement is more stringent than FCRP [sic] 23's." *Cardona v. Maramont Corp.*, No. 602877–2007, 2014 WL 2558176, at *12 (Sup. Ct. N.Y. Cty. June 6, 2014). The reason is that § 901(a) is a synthesis of Rule 23(a)(1) and (b)(3). "A party seeking class certification must establish more than that issues exist which are common to the entire class and that they are substantial and significant; the party must show that these common issues *predominate* over unique circumstances that may pertain to each individual's situation."*Abdale*, 2016 WL 3045440, at *4 (emphasis added); *accord Maul*, 14 N.Y.3d at 508; *Small v. Lorillard Tobacco Co.*, 94 N.Y.2d 43, 53 (1999); *Osarczuk*, 82 A.D.3d at 855; *Hurrell-Harring*, 81 A.D.3d at 72; *Pludeman*, 74 A.D.3d at 421; *Roberts*, 148 A.D.3d at 526.

For example, in a suit against tobacco companies, the court denied class action treatment because issues of causation and damages could not be resolved on a common basis. *Geiger v. Am. Tobacco Co.*, 277 A.D.2d 420, 420–21 (2d Dep't 2000). *Cf. Bardsley v. Great Lakes Indus. Dev., LLC*, 206 A.D.3d 1608, 1609–10 (4th Dep't 2022) (denying subclass certification in action seeking damage awards for a variety of medical ailments allegedly caused by multi-day warehouse fire where assessing negligence would require "individualized assessments of each plaintiff's medical history"); *In re Long Island Power Auth. Hurricane Sandy Litig.*, 200 A.D.3d 1040, 1042–44 (2d Dep't 2021) (denying class certification in breach of contract action against electric company where determining causation would require "trac[ing] the various causes of the [approximately 1.1 million] class members' outages"); *Corsello*, 18 N.Y.3d at 792 (denying certification where claims against a phone company required "building-specific evidence relating to property owned by many other members of the putative class"); *Westfall*, 132 A.D.3d at 1394 (denying certification where actual exposure to blood-borne diseases required "individualized determinations with respect to each plaintiff"); *Smilewicz*, 82 A.D.3d at 744–45 (denying certification because the way in which the plaintiffs encountered defendant's allegedly deceptive and misleading return policy varied across retail locations); *Aldrich v. N. Leasing Sys., Inc.*, 168 A.D.3d 452, 455 (1st Dep't 2019) (denying certification on two causes of actions where "it will be necessary to look at each class member's lease/personal guaranty").

CPLR § 901(a)(2) does not require that class members' claims be identical or that individual issues be nonexistent. *See Jenny Craig*, 2013 WL 5809397, at *3 ("Common does not mean identical in every respect."); *see also Ferrari*, 153 A.D.3d at 1589; *Freeman v. Great Lakes Energy Partners, LLC*, 12 A.D.3d 1170, 1171 (4th Dep't 2004); *Mimnorm Realty Corp. v. Sunrise Fed. Sav. & Loan Ass'n*, 83 A.D.2d 936 (2d Dep't 1981). "Rather, it is predominance, not identity or unanimity, that is the linchpin of commonality." *Maul*, 14 N.Y.3d at 514 (internal quotation marks omitted). Thus, for example, to the extent common issues of fact and law related to liability predominate over individualized issues, a court can certify the class even though calculating class members' damages requires individualized inquiries. *See Maddicks*, 34 N.Y.3d at 124 ("[T]o focus on potential idiosyncrasies within the class claims—distinctions that speak to damages, not to liability—at this juncture would potentially be to reward bad actors who execute a common method to damage in slightly different ways."); *Borden*, 24 N.Y.3d at 399 ("[T]he amount of damages suffered by each class member typically varies from individual to individual, but that fact will not prevent the suit from going forward as a class action if the important legal or factual issues involving liability are common to the class."); *Andryeyeva v. New York Health Care, Inc.*, 33 N.Y.3d 152, 185 (2019) ("[T]he fact that damages may vary by class member does not per se foreclose class certification."); *see also Vandee v. Suit-Kote Corp.*, No. Ca 17-02093, 2018 WL 3007523, at *1 (4th Dep't June 15, 2018) (same); *Maul*, 14 N.Y.3d at 512–13 (class certified based on claims that, if true, represented "a de facto policy . . . of delaying the receipt of services" by city agency, notwithstanding that "a determination regarding appropriate placements will require a particularized inquiry of each plaintiff's requirements"); *Deluca*, 134 A.D.3d 1535–36 (certifying class where the individual class members "may have sustained differing amounts of damages," but there were "common questions of law or fact whether defendants negligently discharged chemicals into the atmosphere and whether such negligent conduct caused decreases in property values or quality of life in the affected area"); *Rebibo v. Axton Owners Inc.*, No. 105995/10, 2012 WL 5230637 (Sup. Ct. N.Y. Cty. Oct. 11, 2012) (class certified because "inquiry related to . . . when each apartment was deregulated or the last legal rent charged, is relevant to damages, and the complexity of the damage issue is not a bar to class action certification") (quoting *Pruitt v. Rockefeller Ctr. Props., Inc.*, 167 A.D.2d 14, 23 (1st Dep't 1991) (internal quotation marks omitted); *cf. Weinstein*, 138 A.D.3d at 547 ("Where, as here, 'the same types of subterfuge [were] allegedly employed to pay lower wages,' commonality of the claims will be found to predominate, even though the putative class members have "different levels of damages."'") (quoting *Kudinov*, 65 A.D.3d at 482); *Rubman v. Osuchowski*, 163 A.D.3d 1471, 1473 (4th Dep't 2018) (plaintiffs adequately plead predominance of common issues when they "alleged that the common issue is whether, by commingling the security deposits of their tenants, defendants acted unlawfully, and that the individual issues are the amount of the security deposit and defendants' entitlement to deductions therefrom"); *Access Plumbing Corp. v. 1184 Brighton Dev., LLC*, No. 34488/08, 2011 WL 1440307, at *7–8 (Sup. Ct. Kings Cty. Apr. 14, 2011) (certifying class even though the named plaintiff can assert a breach of contract claim that likely differs from other class members' claims); *Maddicks*, 34 N.Y.3d at 128 ("It would be antithetical to CPLR 901 to conclude that a statute of limitations defense applicable to some, but not all, members of a class of plaintiffs would insulate defendants from class liability.").

There is no mechanical test for determining whether commonality or predominance exists , but courts look to "whether the use of a class action would achieve economies of time, effort, and expense, and promote uniformity of decision as to persons similarly situated." *Jackson*, 80 Misc. 3d at 1120; *Burdick v. Tonoga, Inc.*, 179 A.D.3d 53, 60 (3rd Dep't 2019) (same); *Pludeman*, 74 A.D.3d at 423 (same); *Onadia*, 56 Misc. 3d at 317 (same); *Roth v. Phoenix Companies, Inc.*, 56 Misc. 3d 191, 196–97 (N.Y. Sup. Ct. 2017) (satisfying commonality where the claims "require the court to address a series of the same legal and factual questions"). *See generally Andryeyeva*, 33 N.Y.3d at 184 ("Claims of uniform systemwide violations are particularly appropriate for class certification."); *Maul*, 14 N.Y.3d at 513 ("CPLR 906(2) permits a class to 'be divided into subclasses and each subclass treated as a class.'"); *Roberts*, 148 A.D.3d at 525 (recognizing the court's power to establish subclasses where common questions predominate over individual questions concerning the amount and type of damages sustained by each individual member).

c. CPLR § 901(a)(3). Typicality

CPLR § 901(a)(3) is identical to Fed. R. Civ. P. 23(a)(3). A representative's claims are "typical" when his/her "claim derives from the same course of conduct that gives rise to the claims of the other class members and is based upon the same legal theory." *Burdick*, 179 A.D.3d at 56; *Hurrell-Harring*, 81 A.D.3d at 73 (similar); *see also Onadia*, 56 Misc. 3d at 320; *Pludeman*, 74 A.D.3d at 423; *Rebibo*, 2012 WL 5230637; *Casey v. Whitehouse Estates, Inc.*, No. 111723/11, 2012 WL 3168689, at *5 (Sup. Ct. N.Y. Cty. Aug. 6, 2012); *Morrissey v. Nextel Partners, Inc.*, No. 3194-06, 2009 WL 400030, at *10 (Sup. Ct. Albany Cty. 2009), *aff'd*, 72 A.D.3d 209 (3d Dep't 2010). A representative's claims and the claims of the other members do not need to be identical in every aspect; rather, the claims must be substantially similar. *See Marshall*, 2012 WL 274590, at *4 ("Plaintiffs' claims need not be identical to those of the class.") (citing *Branch v. Crabtree*, 197 A.D.2d 557, 557 (2d Dep't 1993)); *see also Cheng v. Oxford Health Plans, Inc.*, 84 A.D.3d 673, 675 (1st Dep't 2011) ("With respect to typicality, '[t]he requirement is satisfied even if the class representative cannot personally assert all the claims made on behalf of the class[.]'" (alteration in original) (quoting *Pruitt*, 167 A.D.2d at 22)). A representative's claims are not typical when they arise out of unique circumstances and require separate types of proof. *See Corsello*, 18 N.Y.3d at 792 (affirming decisions denying class certification on the ground that neither typicality nor commonality exists where the class claims arise out of unique contractual relationships and require individualized evidence concerning those relationships); *Aldrich*, 2012 WL 3638871 ("[T]he circumstances as to Plaintiffs' lease originations cannot possibly be typical of the putative class sought to be certified.").

Typicality does not relate to the relative amount of damages incurred by individual class members, but rather to the conduct that gave rise to those damages. *See Andryeyeva*, 33 N.Y.3d at 185 ("A difference in damage awards is an insufficient basis to deny certification as a matter of law where the class may rely on representative evidence of the class-wide violations.") (internal citation omitted); *Deluca*, 134 A.D.3d at 1536 ("[B]ecause 'the typicality requirement relates to the nature of the claims and the underlying transaction, not the amount or measure of damages, [the fact that the class representative's] damages may differ from those of other members of the class is not a proper basis to deny class certification.'") (quoting *Pruitt*, 167 A.D.2d at 22); *see also In re HSBC Bank*, 2015 WL 6698518, at *7 (proposed class representatives were typical of the class where "[t]he only differences between their claims and those of the Class [were] the number of overdraft fees that were improperly charged—i.e., damages").

d. CPLR § 901(a)(4). Adequacy

CPLR § 901(a)(4) is identical to Rule 23(a)(4). Like the federal rule, § 901(a)(4) requires that the representative plaintiff have the competence, experience, and ability to adequately prosecute the action on behalf of the class. Determining whether a plaintiff can adequately represent the class involves a three–pronged inquiry into "potential conflicts of interest between the representative and the class members, personal characteristics of the proposed class representative (*e.g.*, familiarity with the lawsuit and his or her financial resources), and the quality of the class counsel." *Cooper*, 120 A.D.3d at 743–44 (quoting *Globe Surgical Supply*, 59 A.D.3d at 144); *see also Onadia*, 56 Misc. 3d at 320–21; *Wilder v. May Dep't Stores Co.*, 23 A.D.3d 646, 648 (2d Dep't 2005); *Maor*, 2016 WL 3240219, at *7 (quoting *Ackerman v. Price Waterhouse*, 252 A.D.2d 179, 202 (1st Dep't 1998)); *Michels v. Phoenix Home Life Mut. Ins. Co.*, No. 95/5318, 1997 WL 1161145, at *11 (Sup.

Ct. N.Y. Cty. Jan. 7, 1997) (characterizing the second factor, personal characteristics of the representative, as "the ability of the class representatives to assist their counsel"). *Cf. Nawrocki v. Proto Constr. & Dev. Corp.*, 82 A.D.3d 534, 535 (Sup. Ct. N.Y. Cty. 2011) (finding that a class representative's occupation as a laborer and/or her "tenuous grasp of the English language" does not render her inadequate); *Rollin v. Frankel & Co.*, 290 A.D.2d 368, 369 (1st Dep't 2002) (finding representative plaintiffs were adequate because their relationship with their attorneys was non-collusive and they had an "adequate understanding of the case"); *Thomas*, 2013 WL 1777483, at *12 (class representative was adequate because "[h]e ha[d] no known conflicts, [wa]s knowledgeable of the facts surrounding the case, [wa]s familiar with the lawsuit, and [wa]s ready, willing, and able to assist class counsel"); *Casey*, 2012 WL 3168689, at *5–6 (same and, in addition, the class counsel has extensive experience in class action litigation); *Onadia*, 56 Misc. 3d at 321 (finding a detainee in false imprisonment case was an adequate representative of the class as he had "a general understanding of the class claims").

i. Conflicts of interest of class representative. A proposed class representative whose interests are antagonistic to, or in conflict with, those of other class members cannot adequately represent the class. *See Cooper*, 120 A.D.3d at 744 (rejecting class certification where there was evidence of disputes between class representatives and members of the proposed class); *Alix v. Wal-Mart Stores, Inc.*, 57 A.D.3d 1044, 1046–47 (3rd Dep't 2008); *Rivkin v. Heraeus Kulzer GmbH*, 289 A.D.2d 27, 28 (1st Dep't 2001) (ruling that the two individual plaintiffs were inadequate to represent the interests of the class because they lacked damages). Thus, for example, if a class representative's claims "raise any prospect that [she] will be preoccupied with defenses unique to her" the proposed class representative may be found to be inadequate. *Borden v. 400 E. 55th St. Assocs. L.P.*, No. 650361/09, 2011 WL 6446039, at *4 (Sup. Ct. N.Y. Cty. Nov. 9, 2011); *Globe Surgical Supply*, 59 A.D.3d at 145 (finding that defending against counterclaims "would preoccupy . . . and detract from . . . [the] representation of the class[,]" thus rendering the proposed class representative inadequate). A class representative with high damages is well suited to "fairly and adequately protect the interests of the proposed class." *ECD NY, Inc. v. Britt Realty, LLC*, 47 Misc. 3d 923, 928 (Sup. Ct. Kings Cty. 2015).

To ensure that there exists no conflict of interest between the class representative and the class, courts have held that "[t]he class representative must be part of the class, possess the same interest, and suffer the same injury as the class members." *CLC/CFI Liquidating Trust v. Bloomingdales Inc.*, No. 603859/03, 2007 WL 3101249, at *7 (Sup. Ct. N.Y. Cty. Sept. 7, 2007). However, "[o]nly a fundamental conflict will defeat the adequacy of representation requirement." *Jenny Craig*, 2013 WL 5809397, at *4 (quoting *Lewis v. Alert Ambulette Serv. Corp.*, No. 11-cv-442, 2012 WL 170049, at *11 (E.D.N.Y. Jan. 19, 2012) (internal quotation marks omitted)).

As a general rule, a class representative should avoid any relationship with class counsel that could give rise to what some courts have called "an appearance of impropriety." *Fiala v. Metro. Life Ins. Co.*, 52 A.D.3d 251, 859 N.Y.S.2d 426 (2008); *Meachum v. Outdoor World Corp.*, 171 Misc. 2d 354, 370 (Sup. Ct. Queens Cty. 1996). An appearance of impropriety is likely to arise where there exists a lack of independence between a class representative and class counsel. *Meachum*, 171 Misc. 2d at 370 (noting that "in any class action there is always the temptation for the attorney for the class to recommend settlement on terms less favorable to his clients because a large fee is part of the bargain") (citation omitted). Adequacy therefore "require[s] that the class representative shall have some measure of independence from the attorneys, or at least not be the alter ego of the attorneys." *Tanzer v. Turbodyne Corp.*, 68 A.D.2d 614, 620 (1st Dep't 1979). Moreover, there is an "inherent conflict of interest" when the class representative is also the class counsel. *Dank v. Sears Holding Mgmt. Corp.*, 59 A.D.3d 584, 584 (2d Dep't 2009).

Such an appearance of impropriety may arise when a class representative is related to class counsel. *See Tanzer*, 68 A.D.2d 614 at 620, (noting that most courts have held that "such close relatives to be improper representatives"); *see also Brissenden v. Time Warner Cable of New York City,* 25 Misc. 3d 1084, 1094–95 (Sup. Ct. N.Y Cty. 2009) (recognizing a lack of independence when the class representative was the sister-in-law of lead counsel). *But see Dolgow v. Anderson*, 43 F.R.D. 472, 479 (E.D.N.Y. 1968), *rev'd on other grounds*, 438 F.2d 825 (2d Cir. 1970) (sustaining class certification despite familial relationship between class representative and class counsel); *Fischer v. Int'l Tel. & Tel. Corp.*, 72 F.R.D. 174 (E.D.N.Y. 1976) (noting that plaintiff representative's class action was sustained even though representative's mother was class counsel).

Courts have also denied class certification where there exists a business relationship between the class representative and the class counsel. *See, e.g., Tanzer*, 68 A.D.2d at 620. *But see Rollin,* 290 A.D.2d at 369 (holding that class certification was a proper exercise of discretion even though the class representative was an attorney who had referred business to, and had received referrals from, class counsel).

ii. Ability of class representatives to assist their counsel. Since "class actions are to result in judgments which will bind or inure to the benefit of many persons who have not expressly authorized suit on their behalf," it's imperative that a class representative have the ability and experience to competently serve the interests of the class. *Tanzer*, 68 A.D.2d at 620. It is "important that the proposed class representative demonstrate that s/he possess an adequate understanding of the litigation, including a knowledge of the claims and progress of the litigation." *Borden*, 2011 WL 6446039, at *5. In making this determination, "[t]he court needs to hear from the representative herself in order to determine that she is able to [sic] willing and able to serve, that she has an adequate understanding of the claims in the litigation and that she is able to make decisions both in her individual capacity and fiduciary capacity for the class," which "must be established through a tender of evidence and not conclusory statements." *Id.*; *see also Abdale*, 2016 WL 3045440, at *5 (finding class representatives' conclusory affidavits not sufficient to prove that they are adequate representatives); *Rebibo*, 2012 WL 252643, at *3 ("Though counsel for plaintiffs has attested to plaintiffs' adequacy as representatives, plaintiffs themselves have not provided any affidavits confirming this attestation, nor have they verified the complaint. Thus, they have not met their burden under § 901(a).") (internal citations omitted). Testimony from the representative plaintiff can establish sufficient familiarity with the lawsuit. *Camelot Event Driven Fund v. Morgan Stanley & Co., LLC*, 201 N.Y.S.3d 922 (N.Y. Sup. Ct. 2024) (testimony from managing member of representative plaintiff fund demonstrated sufficient familiarity with the case's status and plaintiffs' responsibilities).

Also relevant to a determination of adequacy are the financial resources of the representative plaintiff. *Pruitt*, 167 A.D.2d 14 at 25; *see also Stern v. Carter*, 82 A.D.2d 321, 329 (2d Dep't 1981) ("[P]laintiff should be obligated to demonstrate financial resources to prosecute the case rigorously."). But "[w]hile the ability and willingness of a class plaintiff to bear the cost of litigation is relevant to a determination of whether the plaintiff will adequately protect the interests of the class, financial status *is but one factor to be considered*." *Pruitt*, 167 A.D.2d at 25 (emphasis added) (internal quotations omitted); *Stern*, 82 A.D.2d at 730 (noting that while the representative plaintiff's financial resources is "[r]elevant to making such a determination is the ability and willingness of the plaintiff to bear the cost of litigation such financial inquiry should not be allowed to degenerate into an oppressive means of discouraging the action, as well as a tactical defense to the class action prior to reaching the substantive issues").

A plaintiff's personal financial condition becomes irrelevant, however, where his or her attorney agrees to advance funding for the litigation. *Kozak v. Kushner Vill. 329 E. 9th St. LLC*, 232 A.D.3d 542, 545 (2024) (granting class certification where "counsel submitted an affirmation stating that they (counsel) are bearing the costs of this action"); *Wilder*, 23 A.D.3d at 648–49; *cf. Gudz* 105

A.D.3d at 626 ("We reject defendant's contention that plaintiff was required to provide an affidavit focused solely on her financial ability to adequately represent the class, which was adequately shown by counsel's assumption of the risk of costs and expenses in the litigation."). Nonetheless, if class counsel "fail[s] to meet any expenses during the pendency of the suit, the [ ] court could decertify or reduce the class in order to protect members of the class from the *res judicata* effects of a suit in which they were inadequately represented." *Stern*, 82 A.D.2d at 342.

iii. Adequacy of class counsel. Adequacy requires that class counsel "be qualified, experienced, and generally able to conduct the proposed litigation . . ." *Meachum*, 171 Misc. 2d at 358; *see also Globe Surgical Supply*, 59 A.D.3d at 144 ("In order to be found adequate in representing the interests of the class, class counsel should have some experience in prosecuting class actions."); *Fiala*, 52 A.D.3d 251 (noting that adequacy demands that class counsel possess "competence, vigor, and experience") (citation omitted); *Abdale*, 2016 WL 3045440, at *5 (denying class certification where counsel "[did] not state whether she has had any experience in prosecuting class actions").

Ethical considerations are also relevant in considering the adequacy of representation. *Meachum*, 171 Misc. 2d at 359 ("Generally, the unethical conduct condemned by the courts has been egregious misconduct or extreme examples of solicitation and champerty.") (citation omitted). Thus, while "a slight breach of ethics may be overlooked in light of the circumstances, or a reasonable, good faith belief of propriety, serious misconduct does constitute a ground for denial of class action status." *Id.*; *see also Roberts*, 148 A.D.3d at 526 (allegations arising from a partnership dispute at one of the firms proposed as class counsel did not implicate the specific attorneys seeking to be appointed class counsel).

3. SUMMARY OF CASE LAW FOR ANALOGS TO FEDERAL RULE 23(B)(3) REQUIREMENTS—CPLR (A)(5)

a. CPLR § 901(a)(5). Superiority

CPLR § 901(a)(5) adds a fifth prerequisite that closely resembles Rule 23(b)(3)'s superiority requirement: a class representative must demonstrate that the class action device is superior to other methods for adjudicating the particular controversy. *Maul*, 14 N.Y.3d at 508; *Sperry*, 8 N.Y.3d at 211; *Small*, 94 N.Y.2d at 53; *In re HSBC Bank*, 2015 WL 6698518, at *8; *Andryeyeva*, 33 N.Y.3d at 169–70.

Courts consider the "large number of potential claimants," the "close similarity of their claims," and the "relatively small potential recovery by each individual claimant" to determine if a class action suit is superior to any other methods. *Jim & Phil's Family Pharm., Ltd. v. Aetna U.S. Healthcare, Inc.*, 271 A.D.2d 281, 282 (1st Dep't 2000); *see also Fuquan F. v. Annucci*, 81 Misc. 3d 517, 522–23 (N.Y. Sup. Ct. 2023) ("Class actions are deemed a superior method for adjudication of a controversy where, as here, the members of a proposed class are indigent individuals who seek modest benefits and for whom commencement of individual actions would be burdensome."); *Stewart v. Roberts*, 163 A.D.3d 89, 94 (2018) (same); *Dugan v. London Terrace Gardens, L.P.*, 45 Misc. 3d 362, 380 (Sup. Ct. N.Y. Cty. 2013) ("Judicial resources would be taxed much more heavily in managing such numerous individual actions."); *Thomas,* 2013 WL 1777483, at *12 (superiority was satisfied "given the relatively small size of each claim, as well as fear of retaliation, many members of the class would be reluctant and unable to afford to pursue redress . . . absent class certification"). Thus, superiority is satisfied where individual damages are low relative to the costs to prosecute an action. *See Chua v. Trim-Line Hitech Constr. Corp.*, 225 A.D.3d 565, 573 (2024) ("A class action is the superior vehicle for resolving this prevailing wage dispute because plaintiffs have shown that the damages allegedly suffered by an individual class member are likely to be insignificant and that the costs of prosecuting individual actions would result in the class members having no realistic day in court"); *Jackson v. Citywide Mobile Response Corp.*, 196 N.Y.S.3d 879, 896 (N.Y. Sup. Ct. 2023) ("[T]he superiority requirement is satisfied when the damages sustained by each member of the putative class are so modest that it is unlikely that the members would institute separate actions.").

Courts also take into consideration whether individual cases will create inconsistent rulings. *See Thomas*, 2013 WL 1777483, at *12 ("The alternative of requiring possibly hundreds of individual actions is an ineffective and inefficient method, which could lead to conflicting determinations."); *Rebibo*, 2012 WL 52306378 ("[F]orcing the tenants to pursue their claims individually would be a waste of resources and could result in inconsistent decisions."). In addition, public policy considerations weigh in favor of finding superiority where class actions can induce "socially and ethically responsible behavior" by large institutions. *See Kozak*, 232 A.D.3d at 545–46.

That another method for resolving the dispute is available is not sufficient, by itself, to refute superiority. *Globe Surgical Supply*, 59 A.D.3d at 146 ("[T]he availability of an arbitration alternative does not mean such a proceeding is superior to a class action which, through the aggregation of many similar claims, provides an incentive to the legal profession to expend the resources necessary to fully litigate often complex cases such as the instant matter, including the pursuit of this very appeal."). Similarly, a class representative is not required to have exhausted available administrative remedies. *Ferrari v. Nat'l Football League*, 153 A.D.3d 1589, 1593 (2017). Superiority may not be met if putative class members have already appeared and are represented in other pending related actions, pursuing their own independent claims. *Façade Technology, LLC v. CNY Constr. 701 LLC*, 216 A.D.3d 509 (1st Dep't 2023).

However, courts have found alternative methods superior in some instances. *Gomez*, 95 A.D.3d at 44 ("Given the limited size of this class and the issues involved, there is no justification to argue the class action method is superior to other methods of adjudication."); *Morrissey v. Nextel Partners Inc.*, No. 3194-06, 2009 WL 400030, at *12 (Sup. Ct. Albany Cty. Feb. 19, 2009), *aff'd*, 72 A.D.3d 209 (3d Dep't 2010) ("[I]t is obvious that a multi-state class action lawsuit prosecuted in New York under the laws of more than two dozen different jurisdictions would not be superior to other available methods for the fair and efficient adjudication of the controversy."). When there is the option to have an administrative proceeding instead of a class proceeding, courts will consider whether the claims "call for the type of intensive individualized inquiries that are highly problematic in the context of a class-wide adjudication, but well suited for administrative review." *Picard*, 2014 WL 3639072, at *5; *see also Chaine*, 2011 WL 3370880, at *2 (finding that a class action is not superior where an administrative resolution is shown to be more efficient). *But cf. Jenny Craig*, 2013 WL 5809397, at *5 ("Plaintiffs' failure to pursue their administrative remedies is irrelevant, because the Labor Law is not the exclusive remedy to recover prevailing wages.").

Finally, the CPLR § 902 factors, noted above, "overlap with CPLR §§ 901(a)(5) and are seen as implicit in the superiority prerequisite." *Chaine*, 2011 WL 3370880, at *1; *see also Gilman v. Merrill Lynch, Pierce, Fenner & Smith, Inc.*, 93 Misc. 2d 941, 948 (Sup. Ct. N.Y. Cty. 1978).

b. Predominance

See discussion above regarding commonality and CPLR § 901(a)(2).

4. ANALOGS TO FEDERAL RULE 23(B)(1) AND (B)(2)

As shown above, CPLR § 901 establishes the numerosity, commonality, typicality, and adequacy of representation prerequisites that are also specified under Rule 23(a). *Compare* Fed. R. Civ. P. 23 (a), *with* CPLR § 901(a). However, unlike Rule 23(b)(1)-(3), CPLR § 901 neither categorizes nor distinguishes between various types of class actions. *See generally* Fed. R. Civ. P. 23 (a)–(b); CPLR §§ 901, 902; 3 Jack B. Weinstein, Harold L. Korn & Arthur R. Miller, *New York Civil Practice: CPLR* ¶¶ 901.00–909.07 (David L. Ferstendig 2d. ed. 2013). Moreover, it provides that all class actions must satisfy the predominance and superiority requirements that are encompassed by Rule 23(b)(3) for only certain class actions. *Cf.* Fed. R. Civ. P. 23 (b)(1)–(3).

CPLR § 901 does not explicitly address class actions that would fall within Rule 23(b)(1)–(2)'s categories: (1) cases in which there is a risk of inconsistent adjudications, or an impairment of interests of absent parties if individual actions are brought (Rule 23(b)(1)), and (2) actions in which injunctive or declaratory class-wide relief is appropriate (Rule 23(b)(2)). However, the legislative history of CPLR § 901 does not clearly preclude the notion that claimants can maintain more than Rule 23(b)(3) type actions under Article 9. Weinstein et al., *supra*. Further, New York State courts have relied on CPLR § 901 to certify class actions that seek injunctive or declaratory relief. *See, e.g.*, *In re Colt*, 77 N.Y.2d at 193–96 (granting certification where plaintiffs sought preliminary and permanent injunctive relief blocking a proposed merger or rescission in the event the merger did go forward); *New York City Coal. to End Lead Poisoning v. Giuliani*, 245 A.D.2d 49, 51 (1st Dep't 1997) (holding that plaintiffs' motion for class certification was properly granted where the relief sought was an injunction seeking to compel defendants to perform their duties to alleviate danger to children caused by presence of lead-based paints in multiple dwellings).

Moreover, the notice provision of CPLR Article 9—CPLR § 904—demonstrates that a litigant can bring a class action that primarily seeks injunctive relief. *See generally* CPLR § 904 (a)–(b) (providing that the form of notice in actions seeking declaratory or injunctive relief differs from the form of notice in other actions).

5. MISCELLANEOUS COMMENTS

a. No Actions to Recover a Statutory Penalty

CPLR § 901(b) bars class actions that seek "a penalty, or minimum measure of recovery created or imposed by statute," unless the statute creating such potential recovery specifically authorizes class-wide relief. *Sperry*, 8 N.Y.3d at 213 ("It is evident that by including the penalty exception in CPLR § 901(b), the Legislature declined to make class actions available where individual plaintiffs were afforded sufficient economic encouragement to institute actions (through statutory provisions awarding something beyond or unrelated to actual damages), unless a statute expressly authorized the option of class action status."); *Rudgayzer & Gratt v. Cape Canaveral Tour & Travel Inc.*, 22 A.D.3d 148, 152 (2d Dep't 2005); *Asher v. Abbott Labs.*, 290 A.D.2d 208, 208 (1st Dep't 2002); *Pires v. Bowery Presents, LLC*, 44 Misc. 3d 704, 712–13 (Sup. Ct. N.Y. Cty. 2014).

Nonetheless, many courts have certified class actions for actual damages under various penalty statutes, as long as the statutory penalty incorporated in those statutes is (1) deemed waivable and (2) waived by the class. *See, e.g.*, *Machuca v. Collins Bldg. Servs., Inc.*, 206 N.Y.S.3d 515 (N.Y. Sup. Ct. 2024) (finding statutory restriction "inapplicable where the class representative seeks to recover only actual damages and waives the penalty on behalf of the class, and individual class members are allowed to opt out of the class to pursue their punitive damages claims") (citation omitted); *Little v. Hartz Hotel Servs., Inc.*, 81 Misc. 3d 844, 847 (N.Y. Sup. Ct. 2023) (Labor Law 195) ("Where a statute imposes a nonmandatory penalty, plaintiffs may waive the penalty in order to bring the claim as a class action."); *Borden,* 24 N.Y.3d at 394 (2014) (same); *Ibarra v. 101 Park Rest.*

Corp., 140 A.D.3d 700, 703 (2d Dep't 2016); *Downing v. First Lenox Terrace Assoc.*, 107 A.D.3d 86, 89 (1st Dep't 2013); *Gudz*, 105 A.D.3d at 625; *Cox v. Microsoft Corp.*, 8 A.D.3d 39, 40 (1st Dep't 2004). As a logical corollary to this exception, it does not apply to statutes imposing *mandatory* penalties, "i.e., [penalties that are] not discretionary or contingent upon a finding of bad faith." *Asher*, 290 A.D.2d at 209; *County of Nassau v. Expedia, Inc.*, 120 A.D.3d 1181, 1182 (2d Dep't 2014). However, courts have been willing to find statutory penalty provisions waivable. *See, e.g.*, *Borden,* 24 N.Y.3d 382 (Rent Stabilization Law of 1969); *Rutella v. Craig Scott Capital, LLC*, No. 603120/14, N.Y.L.J. 1202726958417, at *1 (Sup. Ct., Nassau Cty. May 13, 2015) (Labor Law 663); *Pires*, 44 Misc. 3d 704 (Arts and Cultural Affairs Law 25.33); Thomas A. Dickerson & Colleen D. Duffy, *"Borden": A Welcome Sea Change on New York State Class Actions*, N.Y.L.J. (June 29, 2015), A4.

To determine whether a remedy is penal under CPLR § 901(b), "courts look both at how the remedy is described and how it functions in its particular statutory context." *Rubino v. HSBC Bank USA, N.A.*, 238 N.Y.S.3d 376 (N.Y. Sup. Ct. 2025). Notably, New York courts have not uniformly applied this CPLR § 901(b) exception to all statutory penalty provisions. Thus, while a plaintiff may seek class action relief under General Business Law § 349 (deceptive business practices statute) and § 350 (false advertising statute) by waiving the penalty imposed by that statute, the state courts have yet to extend this rule to class actions alleging violations of General Business Law § 340 (the "Donnelly Act," New York's Antitrust Statute), even though both statutes are silent on class actions. *See, e.g.*, *Sperry*, 8 N.Y.3d at 209; *Paltre v. General Motors Corp.*, 26 A.D.3d 481, 483 (2d Dep't 2006); *Cunningham v. Bayer AG*, 24 A.D.3d 216 (1st Dep't 2005); *Asher*, 290 A.D.2d 208; *Ho v. Visa U.S.A. Inc.*, No. 112316/00, 2004 WL 1118534, at *3 (Sup. Ct. N.Y. Cty. Apr. 21, 2004), *aff'd*, 16 A.D.3d 256 (1st Dep't 2005). Moreover, on similar grounds, this rule has yet to extend to class actions alleging violations under the Telephone Consumer Protection Act. *See, e.g.*, *Giovanniello v. Carolina Wholesale Office Machine Co., Inc.*, 29 A.D.3d 737 (2d Dep't 2006); *Rudgayzer*, 22 A.D.3d 148; *Leyse v. Flagship Capital Servs. Corp.*, 22 A.D.3d 426 (1st Dep't 2005).

Where a statutory penalty or minimum measure of recovery is deemed discretionary or waivable, then if a plaintiff decides to pursue a class action under a penalty statute, it must first offer the opportunity for class members to opt out. *See Machuca*, 206 N.Y.S.3d 515; *Thomas*, 2013 WL 1777483, at *4; *Downing*, 107 A.D.3d at 91; *Pesantez v. Boyle Envtl. Servs., Inc.*, 251 A.D.2d 11, 12 (1st Dep't 1998).

To the extent the jurisdictional prerequisites are met, litigants can avoid CPLR 901(b)'s prohibition by bringing actions in federal courts. *Shady Grove Orthopedic Assocs., P.A. v. Allstate Ins. Co.*, 130 S. Ct. 1437 (2010) (Rule 23 "creates a categorical rule entitling a plaintiff whose suit meets the specific criteria to pursue his claim as a class action. . . . Because [CPLR] 901(b) attempts to answer the same question . . . it cannot apply in diversity suits."); *see, e.g.*, *In re Packaged Ice Antitrust Litig.*, 779 F. Supp. 2d 642, 661 (E.D. Mich. 2011) (construing *Shady Grove* to apply to class actions brought under GBL § 340).

Recently, in response to the uneven applications of the statute by New York courts and to the Supreme Court's ruling in *Shady Grove*, critics have been calling for the legislature to repeal CPLR 901(b). *See Report of the Advisory Committee on Civil Practice to the Chief Administrative Judge of the Courts of the State of New York* (January 2022) ("First, under current law, where a statute imposes a penalty or minimum amount of recovery, New York law authorizes a class action only if the statute expressly permits a party to file such a lawsuit. This approach simply results in attempts to evade the § 901 restriction and prompts unnecessary litigation about the meaning of and possible waiver of many statutes' penalty or minimum recovery provisions. Equally important, the rule does not apply in federal courts in New York, which results in state-federal forum shopping."); *Proposed*

Amendments to Article 9 of the Civil Practice Law and Rules, New York City Bar, Nov. 2015, at 9–10 ("Repealing CPLR 901(b) would streamline and modernize New York State class action certification procedures, bringing them into conformity with the practice in federal courts and the courts of other states."); Thomas A. Dickerson et al., *New York State Class Actions: Making It Work-Fulfilling the Promise: Some Recent Positive Developments and Why CPLR 901(b) Should Be Repealed*, 77 Alb. L. Rev. 59, 77 (2014) ("Although there have been several recent positive developments in how New York State courts have interpreted and implemented CPLR Article 9, CPLR section 901(b) is still problematic and should be repealed in order for CPLR Article 9 to realize its salutary purpose. CPLR section 901(b) is no longer viable in prohibiting penalty class actions. Furthermore, the courts have applied it inconsistently."). Senate Bill S.7113/A.9425, introduced in May 2023, proposed repealing CPLR § 901(b), but did not advance. A new, similar bill, Senate Bill S.3661/A.1379 was introduced in the New York State 2025–2026 Judiciary Session. As of September 2025, the bill has not passed and CPLR § 901(b) remains in effect.

b. Class Action Developments under GBL § 350

New York's General Business Law § 350 regulates false advertising in business. N.Y. Gen. Bus. Law § 350 (McKinney). To assert a cause of action for false advertising pursuant to Gen. Bus. Law § 350, plaintiffs must allege that the advertisement "(1) had an impact on consumers at large, (2) was deceptive or misleading in a material way, and (3) resulted in injury" and (4) occurred in New York. *DeAngelis v. Timberpeg E., Inc.*, 51 A.D.3d 1175, 1177 (3d Dep't 2008) (citing *Andre Strishak & Assoc. v. Hewlett Packard Co.*, 300 A.D.2d 608, 609 (2d Dep't 2002) (internal quotations omitted)).

Unlike Gen. Bus. Law § 349, regulating deceptive business practices, however, asserting a claim under § 350 previously required a showing of individual reliance. *See, e.g.*, *Morrissey,* 72 A.D.3d at 216; *Klein v Robert's Am. Gourmet Food, Inc.*, 28 A.D.3d 63, 71–72 (2d Dep't 2006); *Gale v. Int'l Bus. Machs. Corp.*, 9 A.D.3d 446, 447 (2d Dep't 2004). Without the burden of proving individual reliance, which New York appellate courts have held is not subject to class-wide proof, class actions have generally been certifiable under § 349 but not under § 350. *See Morrissey*, 72 A.D.3d 209, 217.

In 2012, however, the Court of Appeals held in *Koch v. Acker, Merrall & Condit Co.* that "[j]ustifiable reliance by the plaintiff is not an element of the [§ 350] claim. . . . To the extent that the Appellate Division order imposed a reliance requirement on General Business Law §§ 349 and 350 claims, it was error." 18 N.Y.3d 940, 941 (2012); *accord Hollander v. Metropolitan Transp. Auth.*, No. 160972/13, 2015 WL 4077193, at *4 (Sup. Ct. N.Y. Cty. June 25, 2015). Apparently overruling a line of Appellate Division cases dating to 1986, the Court of Appeals declared that "[t]he standard for recovery under General Business Law § 350, while specific to false advertising, is otherwise identical to [Gen. Bus. Law §] 349." *Goshen v. Mut. Life Ins. Co. of New York,* 98 N.Y.2d 1190, 1195 n.1 (2002).

Without having to prove individual reliance, commentators have noted that "consumers should be more readily able to prosecute GBL §§ 349 and 350 claims together, either as individuals or as members of a consumer class." Thomas A. Dickerson & Jeffrey A. Cohen, *Ruling on Reliance in GBL § 350 Claims Serves as Game Changer*, N.Y.L.J. (Apr. 19, 2012). Thus, "[b]ecause the standard for recovery is identical under both GBL § 349 and GBL § 350, courts in this circuit merge analysis of the two claims. *Morales, et al., v. Sportsengine, Inc.*, 2025 WL 2662134, at *4 (S.D.N.Y. Sept. 17, 2025). In doing so, courts consider the following elements: "(1) consumer-oriented conduct that is (2) materially misleading and that (3) plaintiff suffered injury as a result of the allegedly deceptive act or practice." *Pizzaro v. Sazerac Co., Inc.,* 2025 WL 2682673, at *4 (S.D.N.Y. Sept. 18, 2025).

Since reliance is no longer an element of § 350, predominance is met where "putative class members suffered economic harm when they paid a premium based on a misleading claim, which will be determined by class-wide evidence." *Id.* at *7; *In re Kind LLC "Healthy and Natural" Litig.*, 337 F.R.D. 581, 600 (S.D.N.Y. 2021) (similar).

c. Mass Torts

Mass tort class actions involving personal injuries or property damage on account of negligence, negligent misrepresentation, trespass, nuisance, strict products liability, or violations of GBL § 349 are generally not certifiable under New York state law. *See generally* Weinstein et al., *supra.* This is because such actions tend to raise many individual questions relating to proximate cause and individual damages, which are often held to predominate over questions of law and fact common to the class. *See, e.g.*, *Westfall*, 132 A.D.3d at 1394; *Osarczuk*, 82 A.D.3d at 855; *Geiger*, 277 A.D.2d 420, 420; *Komonczi v. Fields*, 232 A.D.2d 374 (2d Dep't 1996); *Evans v. City of Johnstown*, 97 A.D.2d 1, 3 (3d Dep't 1983).

However, some mass torts are more likely to be certified than others. For example, single-incident mass torts, in which one event results in several personal injuries (*i.e.*, a plane crash), are generally less difficult to certify than multi-incident mass torts, in which several personal injuries result over a period of time (*i.e.*, products liability), because they tend to raise less individualized questions. Weinstein et al., *supra. Compare Roberts v. Ocean Prime, LLC*, 148 A.D.3d 525 (1st Dep't 2017) (certifying class action on behalf of tenants against building owners for failure to secure buildings prior to Superstorm Sandy), and *Fleming v. Barnwell Nursing Home & Health Facilities*, 309 A.D.2d 1132 (3d Dep't 2003) (certifying a mass torts class action on behalf of nursing home residents under Public Health Law § 2801-d) and *Godwin Realty*, 275 A.D.2d 269 (certifying class action on behalf of building owners against cable providers for misappropriation and conversion of electricity) with *Geiger*, 277 A.D.2d 420 (denying class certification on behalf of smokers against tobacco corporations); *see also Osarczuk*, 82 A.D.3d 855–56 ("[Q]uestions of whether the emissions of various toxic materials, over several decades, from various sources and in various ways, caused injury to the individual properties and economic loss to the property owners, cannot be resolved on a class-wide basis."); *Aprea v. Hazeltine Corp.*, 247 A.D.2d 564 (2d Dep't 1998) (denying class certification in mass tort action involving personal injuries resulting from toxic emissions); *Askey v. Occidental Chemical Corp.*, 102 A.D.2d 130 (4th Dep't 1984) (denying class certification in mass tort action involving personal injuries resulting from toxic waste); *In re New York Diet Drug Litig.*, 15 Misc. 3d 1114A (Sup. Ct. N.Y. Cty. 2007) (denying class certification in mass tort action involving personal injury). *See generally* Weinstein et al., *supra.* Nevertheless, on occasion plaintiffs have established that there are common questions of law or facts resulting from a multi-incident mass tort. *See, e.g.*, *Deluca*, 134 A.D.3d at 1535–36.

Certifying a *partial* class pursuant to CPLR § 906 (which provides that "an action may be brought or maintained as a class action with respect to particular issues," or "a class may be divided into subclasses and each subclass treated as a class") is similarly difficult to secure in this area. *See, e.g.*, *Rosenfeld v. A.H. Robins Co.*, 63 A.D.2d 11, 20 (2d Dep't 1978) ("[W]hile some factual issues could perhaps be resolved in a class action format, these issues are thoroughly intertwined with those which must be determined individually. . . . [T]he judicial economy to be reaped and the advantages for litigants of a partial class action [would] be relatively small."). However, in rejecting plaintiff's request to proceed as a partial class under § 906, the *Rosenfeld* court indicated (in dicta) that had this case involved a single-incident mass tort instead of a multi-incident mass tort, then "there would be strong reasons for certifying the proposed class, although the question of damage would necessarily have to be left for individual determination. Thus, in the case of an airplane crash, to use the most frequently cited example, it would be possible in many cases to isolate a single causative factor which was responsible for the injury or death of all of the class members." *Id.* at 16.

d. Challenges to Government Operations

The government operations rule "cautions against class certification where governmental operations are involved, since any relief granted to the named plaintiffs would adequately flow to and protect others similarly situated under principles of *stare decisis*." *New York City Coal. to End Lead Poisoning*, 245 A.D.2d at 51; *see also Sysco Metro NY, LLC v. City of New York*, 65 Misc. 3d 1234(A), 119 N.Y.S.3d 822 (N.Y. Sup. Ct. 2019); *In re Graves v. Doar*, 62 A.D.3d 874, 875 (2d Dep't 2009); *Jones v. Board of Educ. of Watertown City Sch. Dist.*, 30 A.D.3d 967, 970 (4th Dep't 2006); *cf. Pena v. Doar*, No. 401490/2012, 2012 WL 4335191, at *8 (Sup. Ct. N.Y. Cty. Sept. 14, 2012) (certification denied where the government-defendant already "formulate[d] plans to remediate [the] problems" and noting plaintiffs could renew certification if the plans fail); *In re Strauss v. City Univ. of NY*, No. 111900/112012, 2012 WL 1576457 (Sup. Ct. N.Y. Cty. Apr. 25, 2012) (denying certification because the decision will bind the respondents without certification) (citing *Baumes v. Lavine*, 38 N.Y.2d 296, 305 (1975)); *Zheng v. The City of New York*, No. 400806/11, 2011 WL 1740250 (Sup. Ct. N.Y. Cty. May 2, 2011) (Plaintiffs "have no need to bring separate actions, since NYC has agreed to apply this court's determination equally to all similarly situated. To the extent that NYC fails to similarly treat all tenant-participants in accordance with this court's ruling, plaintiffs may renew their motion for class certification at that time."); *but see Fuquan F.*, 81 Misc. 3d at 523 (certifying prisoner class in action against state department of corrections and noting that the government operations rule "concerns itself only with the inefficiency of using the class action form when the prospective rights of interested litigants can be safeguarded by other means") (citing *NYCHHC v. McBarnette*, 84 N.Y.2d 194 (1994)).

However, there are numerous exceptions to this rule. *See generally* Weinstein et al. Plaintiffs bear the burden of establishing these exceptions. *See Oak Beach v. Town of Babylon*, 100 A.D.2d 930, 930–31 (2d Dep't 1984). For example, the government operations rule will not bar class certification to the extent the plaintiff demonstrates that the governmental entity will not abide by *stare decisis*. *See Chalfin v. Sabol*, 247 A.D.2d 309, 310–11 (1st Dep't 1998) (finding that a government-defendant's failure to comply with prior orders and *stare decisis* renders the government operations rule inapplicable); *In re Lamboy v. Gross*, 126 A.D.2d 265, 273 (1st Dep't 1987); *cf. Zheng*, 2011 WL 1740250 (noting that plaintiffs can renew their motion if the defendant fails to apply the court's ruling to similarly situated individuals). Also, the government operations rule generally does not apply if plaintiffs seek nominal money damages for a defined class arising from past events. *Sysco*, 65 119 N.Y.S.3d 822, at *2; *Graves*, 62 A.D.3d at 876; *Tosner v. Town of Hempstead*, 12 A.D.3d 589, 590 (2d Dep't 2004); *Pino Alto Partners v. Erie Cty. Water Auth.*, No. 11957/2006, 2008 WL 4603469, at *6 (Sup. Ct. Erie Cty. 2008), *aff'd*, 67 A.D.3d 1375 (4th Dep't 2009). The rule may not bar certification if either the defendant fails to propose relief that would help or protect the plaintiff, or "the condition sought to be remedied by the plaintiffs poses some immediate threat that cannot await individual determinations." *New York City Coal. to End Lead Poisoning*, 245 A.D.2d at 51 (citations omitted). Similarly, the rule does not bar class actions where "a class action provides the only mechanism available to secure retroactive benefits for potential class members." *Stewart v. Roberts*, 163 A.D.3d 89, 94 (2018). This rule may also not apply "where the plaintiffs' ability to commence individual suits is highly compromised, due to indigency or otherwise." *Id.* Lastly, the government operations rule does not apply where the *municipality* is a plaintiff seeking to sue on behalf of other municipalities. *Cty. of Nassau v. Expedia, Inc.*, 41 Misc. 3d 626, 632 (Sup. Ct. Nassau Cty. 2013).

The following considerations are also relevant to determining whether or not the government operation rule bars certification: (1) whether the case involves claims of systemic deficiencies which seek widespread, systematic reform; (2) whether the absence of class action status would subject the prosecution of the case to significant discovery challenges; and (3) whether denial of class certification would give rise to the possibility of multiple lawsuits involving claims duplicative of those asserted in this action and inconsistent rulings by various courts. *Hurrell-Harring*, 81 A.D.3d at 75; *see also New York City Coal. to End Lead Poisoning*, 245 A.D.2d at 52; *Tindell v. Koch*, 164 A.D.2d 689, 695 (1st Dep't 1991); *see generally In re Colt*, 77 N.Y.2d at 195 (noting that actions against the government or a private entity that seek equitable relief should be certified if the prerequisites in CPLR § 901 and § 902 are established).

Finally, "[w]here the relief accorded to individual petitioners will provide no relief for the alleged harm affecting the whole class or will not effectively operate as precedent for the class, this 'governmental operations rule' does not bar class certification." *Smith v. Berlin*, No. 400903/2010, 2013 WL 8210836, at *6–7 (Sup. Ct. N.Y. Cty. 2013) (citing *Chalfin*, 247 A.D.2d at 311).

e. Certification Deadline

Pursuant to CPLR § 902, the plaintiff must move to certify the class within sixty days after the time to serve a responsive pleading expires. *See Gomez*, 95 A.D.3d at 39 n.3 (citing CPLR § 902); *Shah v. Wilco Sys., Inc.*, 27 A.D.3d 169, 173 (1st Dep't 2005); *Mike Bldg. & Contracting, Inc. v. Just Homes, LLC*, 27 Misc. 3d 833, 858 (Sup. Ct. Kings Cty. 2010); *cf. David B. Lee & Co. v. Ryan*, 266 A.D.2d 811, 812 (4th Dep't 1999) ("[The class certification] motion was premature because it was made before the time for service of an answer had expired."); *Cruz v. Town Sports Int'l*, No. 600695/05, 2013 WL 497330, at *4 (Sup. Ct. N.Y. Cty. Jan. 29, 2013), *aff'd*, 116 A.D.3d 539 (1st Dep't 2014); *see also Maddicks v. Big City Props., LLC*, 163 A.D.3d 501, 502 (1st Dep't 2018) (finding that "[b]ecause the [60 day limit] to make [] a [class certification] motion had not occurred, it was premature, in this case, for the court to engage in a detailed analysis of whether the requirements for class certification were met[]") (internal citation omitted), *aff'd*, 34 N.Y.3d 116, 124 (2019); *Griffen v. Gregory's Coffee Mgt. LLC*, 191 A.D.3d 600, 600–01 (1st Dep't 2021) ("it will generally be 'premature to dismiss class action allegations before an answer is served or pre-certification discovery has been taken'" (citing *Downing v First Lenox Terrace Assoc.*, 107 A.D.3d 86, 91 (1st Dep't 2013), *aff'd* 24 N.Y.3d 382 (2014)), with the only exception being when a defendant "conclusively" establishes that there is "no basis for class action relief as a matter of law"). *Compare* Fed. R. Civ. P. 23(c)(1)(A) (Class certification shall be determined "[at] an early practicable time after a person sues or is sued as a class representative[.]"). This rule "is designed to promote an early determination of whether class action relief is appropriate." *Argento*, 66 A.D.3d at 932 (citing *O'Hara v. Del Bello*, 47 N.Y.2d 363, 368 (1979)). However, "[t]he time limit for moving for class certification, set forth in CPLR § 902, applies only to a motion for the initial certification of the class." *O'Brien*, 99 A.D.3d at 684.

The CPLR § 902 "filing deadline is mandatory." *Talbi v. Boulevard Taxi Leasing, Inc.*, No. 1577/11, 2012 WL 1154777, at *4 (Sup. Ct. Queens Cty. Apr. 3, 2012); *see also Ortega v. Skyworx Contracting Inc.*, 221 A.D.3d 463, 463–64 (2023) (affirming denial of class certification where plaintiffs did not move for class certification by the filing deadline); *Cruz*, 2013 WL 497330, at *4 ("in the absence of an extension, the deadline set forth is mandatory"). Nonetheless, courts have discretion to extend this deadline prospectively or retroactively if good cause is shown. *See generally Façade Tech., LLC v. CNY Constr. 701 LLC*, 200 A.D.3d 607 (2021) (finding that class certification motion should not have been denied as untimely because plaintiff demonstrated good cause for brief, non-prejudicial delay); *Gerard v. Clermont York Assocs. LLC*, 143 A.D.3d 478 (1st Dep't 2016) (noting that a court has discretion to "deem a late-filed class certification motion timely upon a showing of good cause"); *Chavarria v. Crest Hollow Country Club at Woodbury, Inc.*, 109 A.D.3d 634 (2d Dep't 2013) (extending the 60-day time period was reasonable "based on the plaintiffs' need to conduct class certification discovery"); *MacDonell v. PHH Mortg. Corp.*, 93 A.D.3d 700, 701 (2d Dep't 2012) (noting that trial courts have broad discretion to allow limited discovery and disclosure of information pertinent to class certification and extend the deadline in CPLR § 902) (citations omitted); *Argento*, 66 A.D.3d at 932; *Galdamez v. Biordi Constr. Corp.*, 50 A.D.3d 357, 358 (1st Dep't 2008); *Talbi*, 2012 WL 1154777 (explaining that CPLR § 902's filing deadline may be extended if the plaintiff needs to conduct pre-certification discovery to establish CPLR § 901's prerequisites); *In re Cablevision Sys. Corp. S'holders Litig.*, 21 Misc. 3d 419, 431 (Sup. Ct. Nassau Cty. 2008) (noting that while failure to timely move has a bearing on adequacy of representation, "with respect to an application for attorneys' fees [as opposed to seeking certification only after a finding of liability], unless the protesting party makes a showing of actual prejudice, class action determination may be delayed until the hearing of the application[.]") (internal quotation marks omitted).

f. Communication with Absent Class Members

Pursuant to CPLR 907, courts have the authority to control pre-certification contact between defendants and putative class members. *Carnegie v. H&R Block, Inc.*, 180 Misc. 2d 67, 71–72 (Sup. Ct. N.Y. Cty. 1999); *cf. Kaplan v. Hutton Grp., Inc.*, 155 A.D.2d 227, 229 (1st Dep't 1989) (modifying an order permitting the defendant law firm to only respond to plaintiff class members' inquiries and not initiate any communication). "[A] Court has broad powers to control the course of class action litigation" under CPLR 907. *In re Colt,* 155 A.D.2d at 159–60 (citations omitted); *cf. Carnegie,* 180 Misc. 2d at 70, 71 n.5 (relying on federal precedent in interpreting CPLR Article 9, as New York courts are permitted to do, *Alfaro v. Vardaris Tech Inc.,* No. 109673/2005, 2009 WL 889951 (Sup. Ct. N.Y. Cty. Mar. 11, 2009), *aff'd and mod'f in part*, 69 A.D.3 436 (1st Dep't 2010), the court found that "[w]here communications by defendants to class members was found to constitute impermissible interference with the conduct of class litigation and/or to violate [Rule of Professional Conduct rule 4.2], federal courts have acted to restrain the abuse").

Further, "[w]here there is an ongoing business relationship, unilateral communication from the class defendant to class members is inherently coercive and misleading since the class member will need to rely on the defendant in the future . . . . The potential for abuse is even greater where . . . the relationship is one of employer-employee." *Alfaro*, 2009 WL 889951 (citations omitted) "The test for whether a party, with or without aid of its counsel, has had impermissible contact with potential members of the plaintiff class, is whether the contact is coercive, misleading, or an attempt to affect a class member's decision to participate in the litigation." *Carnegie*, 180 Misc. 2d, at *71; *accord Zeitlin v. New York Islanders Hockey Club, L.P.*, No. 002484/15, 2015 WL 2359187, at *3 (Sup. Ct. Nassau Cty. May 14, 2015); *see also Weinstein v. Jenny Craig Operations*, 132 A.D.3d 446, 446–47 (1st Dep't 2015) ("[Defendant] continued having putative class member employees sign the arbitration agreements, without informing them of the existence of this class action litigation or of their right to join this action. . . . [Trial] court properly exercised its discretion by drawing the inference that the agreements had been implemented in response to this litigation and to preclude putative class members.").

g. Duties Class Counsel Owes to Absent Class Members

Class counsel represents the interest of and owes a fiduciary duty to the entire class. However, class counsel does not have a traditional attorney-client relationship with absent class members. *See* Rules of Professional Conduct [N.Y. Comp. Codes R. & Regs. tit. 22] rule 1.7 Comment [25]. In particular, an absent class member does not have a presumptive right of access to case files of class counsel when the representation has been terminated. *Wyly v. Milberg Weiss Bershad & Schulman, LLP*, 12 N.Y.3d 400, 412–13 (2009), *aff'g*, 49 A.D.3d 85 (1st Dep't 2007).

h. Notice

Pursuant to CPLR § 904(d), plaintiffs generally bear the expense of preparing and distributing notice. *See Access Plumbing Corp.*, 2011 WL 1440307, at *9–10. However, "CPLR § 904(d) authorizes the court to shift [to defendants] the cost of providing notice to class members when the interests of justice so mandate." *Pludeman*, 74 A.D.3d at 424–25; *see also* CPLR § 904(d)(I). "In determining whether to shift the cost [of notice], the court considers the merits of the action, the defenses thereto, and the resources of the respective parties." *Pludeman*, 74 A.D.3d at 424–25 (citations omitted). Article 9's notice provisions are more flexible than those of Rule 23. Rule 23 requires "the best notice practicable under the circumstances, including individual notice to all members who can be identified through reasonable effort." Fed. R. Civ. P. 23(c)(2). However, CPLR § 904(b) requires "reasonable notice" be given to the potential class members "in such manner as the court directs" in class actions not brought primarily for injunctive or declaratory relief. *Vignola v. JDM Washington St. LLC*, 163 N.Y.S.3d 796 (N.Y. Sup. Ct. 2022) (quoting CPLR § 904(b)); *Fiala v. Metro Life Ins. Co.*, 2007 WL 2772230, at *2 (same). Class notice is not required in a class action brought primarily for injunctive or declaratory relief unless the court finds that a "notice is necessary to protect the interests of the represented parties and that the cost of notice will not prevent the action from going forward." CPLR § 904(a); *see also Jiannaras v. Alfant*, 124 A.D.3d 582, 590 (2d Dep't 2015), *aff'd*, 27 N.Y.3d 349 (2016) ("[I]n class actions which seek primarily injunctive or declaratory relief, notice of the action to the class is not required."); *Onadia*, 56 Misc. 3d at 319 (notice of claim requirements do not apply to actions brought to "vindicate a public interest") (citing *Union Free School Dist. No. 6 of Towns of Islip and Smithtown v. New York State Human Rights Appeal Bd.*, 35 N.Y.2d 371 (1974)).

In determining what constitutes reasonable notice under CPLR § 904(c), a court considers the cost of notice methods, the resources of the parties, the stake of each member in the party, and the possibility of exclusions. *See Fiala*, 2007 WL 2772230, at *2 (holding that reasonable notice is provided by publishing notice in the Wall Street Journal and the New York Post once per week for three weeks, mailing notices to a random sample of 500,000 class members, and mailing notices of the action along independent mailings); *Drizin v. Sprint Corp.*, No. 101707/02, 2005 WL 1035823, at *2 (Sup. Ct. N.Y. Cty. 2005).

i. Right of Exclusion from the Class

Rule 23(c) provides that members of a class certified under Rule 23(b)(3), unlike members of 23(b)(1) and (b)(2) classes, must be afforded an opportunity to "request exclusion" from the class (*i.e.*, the right to "opt-out" of the class). CPLR § 903 states only that "[w]hen appropriate[,] the court may limit the class to those members who do not request exclusion from the class within a specified time after notice." CPLR § 903. The notes to the rule quote the 1975 Judicial Conference Report as expressly stating that the right to opt out is favored when the entire class does not need representation for a just disposition of the case, when class members have a significant practical interest in individual control of the litigation, and when individual notice is feasible. *See generally New York State Judicial Conference Report to the 1975 Legislature in Relation to the CPLR*, Leg. Doc. 90, 208, 232, 252 (1976). Thus, CPLR § 903 appears to create either a regime in which there are classes representing all class members with no right of exclusion, or a regime in which class members have the right of exclusion. Article 9 does not refer to classes in which membership is predicated upon an affirmative election, and these so-called "opt-in" classes are not constitutionally required. *Hibbs v. Marvel Enters., Inc.*, 19 A.D.3d 232, 233 (1st Dep't 2005) ("There is no legal or constitutional principle that mandates the use of the opt-in method."); *see also Klein*, 28 A.D.3d at 66–67.

j. Settlements

"CPLR § 908 requires judicial approval for any compromise of claims brought on a class basis. In determining whether to approve a class action settlement, courts examine the 'fairness of the settlement, its adequacy, its reasonableness and the best interests of the class' members." *Ryan v. Volume Servs. Am.*, No. 652970/2012, 2013 N.Y. Misc. LEXIS 932, at *2–3 (Sup. Ct. N.Y. Cty. Mar. 7, 2013) (quoting *Fiala*, 899 N.Y.S.2d at 537). The courts will take into consideration "the likelihood of success, the extent of support from the parties, the judgment of counsel, the presence of bargaining in good faith, and the nature of the issues of law and fact." *Ryan*, 2013 N.Y. Misc. LEXIS 932, at *3 (quoting *In re Colt*, 155 A.D.2d at 160). In addition to the *Colt* factors, in the context of a proposed nonmonetary settlement of a shareholder class action suit challenging a corporate merger or acquisition, courts must also consider "whether the proposed settlement is in the best interests of the putative settlement class as a whole and whether the settlement is in the best interest of the corporation." *Gordon v. Verizon Commc'ns, Inc.*, 148 A.D.3d 146, 158 (1st Dep't 2017) (reaffirming *Colt* and adding two additional factors to "ensure appropriate evaluation of proposed nonmonetary settlements of class action suits"). "The 'best interests' test requires that the court evaluate the 'reasonableness of the 'give' and 'get' or what class members receive in exchange for ending the litigation." *In re Xerox Corp. Consol. S'holder Litig.*, 65 Misc. 3d 1201(A), 2019 WL 4400296, at *8 (Sup. Ct. N.Y. Cty. 2019) (quoting *Gordon*, 148 A.D.3d at 162). Applying this standard, the court in *In re Xerox Corp.* found that the proposed settlement was "not in the best interests of the shareholders" where the purported class members would "'get' no financial benefit," and were asked to "'give' broad releases of any derivative claims they may have." *See id.*

Notice of a proposed settlement "shall be given to all members of the class in such manner as the court directs." N.Y. C.P.L.R. 908 (McKinney 2024). "[A]t a minimum" such notice must "inform[] all class members of the pending class action, the composition of the class, the issues between the parties, the terms of the proposed settlement, how a class member may object, the time period within which such objection, if any, must be made, and, the date on which the Trial Court will hold a hearing, at which same will consider the fairness of the proposed settlement." *In re Colt,* 155 A.D.2d at 160 (citations omitted); *see also In re HSBC Bank*, 2015 WL 6698518, at *12 (finding "the notice provisions of the Settlement Agreement to be not only adequate, but comprehensive" when counsel agreed to send postcard notice to each class member that can be identified, to publish settlement notice in major newspapers, and to provide a settlement website where class members can access long-form notice). Such notice should be given to putative class members even after "the time in which to seek class certification ha[s] expired pursuant to CPLR 902." *Desrosiers v. Perry Ellis Menswear, LLC*, 139 A.D.3d 473, 473 (1st Dep't 2016), *aff'd*, 30 N.Y.3d 488 (2017). CPLR 908 applies even in the pre-certification context. *Desrosiers*, 30 N.Y.3d at 492.

While the notice requirement has been criticized recently for being expensive, extraneous, and inconsistent with federal law, *see Vasquez v. Nat'l Sec. Corp.*, 48 Misc. 3d 597, 599 (Sup. Ct. N.Y. Cty. 2015), *aff'd*, 139 A.D.3d 503 (N.Y. App. Div. 2016), the courts are leaving it up the state legislature to make any changes to the rule. *Vasquez*, 139 A.D.3d at 503 ("The legislature . . . has not amended CPLR 908 to conform to the federal statute. Although defendant-appellant raises policy arguments in support of its position, its remedy lies with the legislature and not with this Court."). When "a class is certified for settlement purposes only, the[ ] [CPLR § 901 and § 902] prerequisites—and particularly those designed to protect absentee class members—must still be met and, indeed, 'demand undiluted, even heightened, attention.'" *Klein*, 28 A.D.3d at 70 (quoting *Amchem Prods., Inc. v. Windsor*, 521 U.S. 591, 620 (1997)); *cf. Berkman v. Robert's Am. Gourmet Food, Inc.*, No. 107441/02, 2007 WL 1815990, at *3–4 (Sup. Ct. N.Y. Cty. 2007) (denying motion to certify class for settlement purposes because CPLR § 901's prerequisites were not established). Senate Bill S.3661/A.1379, introduced in April 2025 and under review by the Assembly Judiciary Committee as of September 2025, would amend CPLR § 908 to more closely track Rule 23(e).

As articulated in *Matter of Colt*, out-of-state class members have a constitutionally protected right to opt out of a settlement if the settlement requires class members to waive damage claims, or if the settlement is not completely equitable in nature. 77 N.Y.2d at 197 ("[T]he trial court did err as a matter of law by seeking to bind an absent plaintiff with no ties to New York State to a settlement that purported to extinguish its rights to bring an action in damages in another jurisdiction[]" because the trial court failed to give the absent plaintiff the opportunity to opt out). Recently, the New York Court of Appeals had the opportunity to modify this rule. *Jiannaras*, 27 N.Y.3d at 352. Declining to overrule *In re Colt*, the court held "that because the proposed settlement in this instance would deprive out-of-state class members of a cognizable property interest, the courts below properly refused to approve the settlement." *Id.* at 351. Further, the court clarified that trial courts are authorized "to expand due process rights where a class settlement would extinguish out-of-state class members' damages claims separate from class-wide equitable relief." *Id.* at 354.

Courts may approve settlements that provide discount coupons as consideration if (1) the coupons are transferable and fully assignable, (2) they are distributed directly to class members; and (3) such coupons provide real and quantifiable value. *Klein*, 28 A.D.3d at 73. In cases where it is difficult to locate class members or to distribute funds directly to them, courts may approve a *cy pres* distribution—the settlement is not distributed to class members but made available to the public at large. *Id.* at 73–74. "In a settlement context, when an aggregate class recovery cannot economically be distributed to individual class members . . . the parties, subject to court approval, may agree that undistributed funds will be distributed or disposed of for the indirect benefit of the class[.]" *Id.* at 73 (citing *Newberg on Class Actions* § 11:20 (4th ed. 2006)); *see also Fiala*, 27 Misc. 3d at 609 (approving distribution to *cy pres* beneficiary to allocate funds to national, health-related research projects); *Ousmane v. City of New York*, No. 402648/04, 2009 WL 722294, at *8 (Sup. Ct. N.Y. Cty. Mar. 17, 2009) (denying motion for a *cy pres* distribution, but providing that the issue may be restored to the calendar "[i]n the event . . . that after three years there remain funds that are still unclaimed and the parties are unable to agree as to their final disposition"); *cf. In re HSBC Bank*, 2015 WL 6698518, at *4 (providing for a *cy pres* program in the event the *pro rata* distribution of residual funds "is not feasible").

Courts may also preliminarily approve a proposed settlement if such settlement "appears to be the product of serious, informed non-collusive negotiations, has no obvious deficiencies, does not improperly grant preferential treatment to class representatives or segments of the class and falls within the reasonable range of approval." *Saska v. Metropolitan Museum of Art*, 53 Misc. 3d 1212(A), at *10 (quoting *In re Platinum*, 2014 WL 3500655, at *11 (S.D.N.Y. July 15, 2014). If the proposed settlement falls within the range of reasonableness, it "meets the requirements for preliminary approval such that notice to the Class Members is appropriate." *Id.* (citing *Illoldi v. Koi N.Y. LLC,* 2016 WL 3099372, at *1 (S.D.N.Y. May 31, 2016)).

k. Enhancement Awards

While Section 9 does not authorize service awards, "plaintiffs' requests for awards are deemed warranted to the extent that they seek reasonable compensation for time and effort expended on behalf of the class" by the class representative. *See Saska*, 53 Misc. 3d at *12 n.16. *See also* Avilez v. Pasta La Vista, Inc., 205 N.Y.S.3d 753 (N.Y. Sup. Ct. 2024) (awarding $6,500 service awards to each named plaintiff). "Such awards reward the named plaintiffs for the effort and inconvenience of consulting with counsel over the many years a case was active and for participating in discovery, including depositions." *Ryan*, 2013 N.Y. Misc. LEXIS 932, at *5 (quoting *Cox v. Microsoft Corp.*, 26 Misc. 3d 1220(A), at *4 (Sup. Ct. N.Y. Cty. 2007) (internal quotation marks omitted)); *accord Lopez v Dinex Group, LLC*, No. 155706/2014, 2015 N.Y. Misc. LEXIS 3657, at *7 (Sup. Ct. N.Y. Cty. Oct 6, 2015) (granting a service award where "[t]he named Plaintiffs expended considerable time and effort assisting Class Counsel with the case, performed significant services to Class Counsel and assumed significant risk in prosecuting this action"); *but see Saska v. Metro. Museum of Art,* 57 Misc. 3d 218, 228–32 (Sup. Ct. N.Y. Cty. 2017) (denying the requested award as without statutory authorization and noting that "while some judges in this court have approved incentive awards [*see, e.g., Chowdhury v. GK Grill LLC*, 2015 WL 8488817, at *3 (Sup. Ct. N.Y. Cty. 2015); *Lopez v. The Dinex Group, LLC*, 2015 WL 5882842, at *3 (Sup. Ct. N.Y. Cty. 2015)], this court has reservations about doing so").

l. Attorneys' Fees

CPLR 909 governs attorneys' fee awards. If a judgment "is rendered in favor of the class, the court in its discretion may award attorneys' fees to the representatives of the class . . . based on the reasonable value of legal services rendered and if justice requires, allow recovery of the amount awarded from the opponent of the class." N.Y. C.P.L.R. § 909 (McKinney 2024); *see also Flemming v. Barnwell Nursing Home & Health Facilities, Inc.*, 56 A.D.3d 162, 165 (3d Dep't 2008), *aff'd*, 15 N.Y.3d 375 (2010); *Klein*, 28 A.D.3d at 74–75; *Gordon*, 148 A.D.3d at 164–65. "When granting fees, a trial judge has broad discretion in deciding whether, and in what amount attorneys' fees should be awarded." *Schumacher v. NeoStem, Inc.*, No. 653285/12, 2014 WL 2696581, at *2 (Sup. Ct. N.Y. Cty. June 13, 2014). The overarching "principle [is] that a settlement court should have discretion to award attorney's fees in an amount commensurate with the degree of benefit obtained by the class as a result of the litigation." *Id.* at 840. "When reviewing a fee application in a class action, the court acts as a fiduciary and must protect the rights of absent class members." *Flemming*, 56 A.D.3d at 165.

Attorneys' fees are generally payable out of the judgment fund. *Loretto v. Group W. Cable*, 135 A.D.2d 444, 448 (1st Dep't 1987). Where no such fund is created, the standards applicable to fee awards are heightened. *Cf. La. Mun. Emps.' Ret. Sys. v. Cablevision Sys. Corp.*, 74 A.D.3d 1291, 1293 (2d Dep't 2010) ("[A] showing of bad faith or other improper conduct on the part of a defendant [is required] before . . . an award of fees directly against it [is approved by a court]."); *Huff v. C.K. Sanitary Sys. Inc.*, 260 A.D.2d 892, 897 (3d Dep't 1999) (Defendant's conduct was not "so extreme, oppressive or vexatious that justice cries out for counsel fees[.]"). The standards applicable to fee awards are also heightened when the parties agree to a disclosure only settlement. *See In re Allied*

Healthcare S'holder Litig., No. 652188/2011, 2015 WL 6499467, at *2 (Sup. Ct. N.Y. Cty. Oct. 23, 2015) (rejecting a fee proposal where "proposed settlement offers nothing to the shareholders except that attorneys they did not hire will receive a $375,000 fee and the corporate officers who were accused of wrongdoing will receive general releases").

"Generally, the 'Lodestar' method is employed to calculate reasonable attorney's fees, which is calculated by multiplying the reasonable hours expended on the action by a reasonable hourly rate." *Schumacher*, 2014 WL 2696581, at *2 (citing *Matakov v. Kel-Tech Const., Inc.*, 84 A.D.3d 677 (1st Dep't 2011)). But courts have held that "[w]here a settlement establishes a common fund, the percentage method is often preferable because [t]he lodestar method has the potential to lead to inefficiency and resistance to expeditious settlement because it gives attorneys an incentive to raise their fees by billing more hours." *Ryan*, 2013 N.Y. Misc. LEXIS 932, at *11 (quoting *Cox*, 26 Misc. 3d 1220(A), at *3). Nonetheless, courts that apply the percentage method usually use the lodestar/multiplier method to confirm the reasonableness of the award. *Michels v. Phoenix Home Life Mut. Ins.*, No. 95/5318, 1997 WL 1161145, at *32 (Sup. Ct. N.Y. Cty. Jan. 7, 1997); *Willson v. New York Life Ins. Co.*, No. 94/127804, 1995 N.Y. Misc. LEXIS 652, at *90 (Sup. Ct. N.Y. Cty. Nov. 8, 1995). *See also Nager v. Teachers' Ret. Sys. of the City of New York*, 57 A.D.3d 389, 390 (1st Dep't 2008) (The "Supreme Court properly used the lodestar method in determining the reasonable value of plaintiffs' attorneys' services in instituting and settling this class action, rather than applying a percentage of the value of the settlement, in view of the enormous disparity in result between the two methods[.]"). *Cf. M.F. v. Amida Care, Inc.*, 75 Misc. 3d 1209(A), at *3 ("Courts have used the lodestar method and the percentage approach as a way of cross-checking the appropriateness of the legal fees in common fund cases, but very often the percentage approach is unavailable as a cross check or used only to ensure that the fee is within the "realm of reasonableness," with lodestar methodology being presumptively reasonable.").

Under the lodestar/multiplier method, courts consider numerous factors, including (1) whether plaintiff's counsel had the benefit of a prior judgment or decree in a case brought by the government; (2) the standing of counsel at the bar—both counsel receiving award and opposing counsel; (3) the time and labor spent; (4) the magnitude and complexity of the litigation; (5) the level of responsibility undertaken; (6) the amount recovered; (7) the knowledge the court has of conferences, arguments that were presented and of work shown by the record to have been done by attorneys for the plaintiff prior to trial; (8) what it would be reasonable for counsel to charge a victorious plaintiff; (9) the contingent nature of the success; and (10) the novelty of the issues presented. *Sternberg v. Citicorp Credit Servs., Inc.*, 110 Misc. 2d 804, 810 (Sup. Ct. Nassau Cty. 1981) (citations omitted); *see also Matakov*, 84 A.D.3d at 678 (finding that plaintiff's attorneys must establish that its fees are reasonable, the level of training and skill of the individual attorneys who worked on the case, and that the work performed was reasonable and not duplicative to determine attorney's fees under the lodestar method) (quotations omitted); *GS Brooklyn Apts., LLC v. Roberts*, No. 2015-11479, 2019 WL 4849364, at *2 (2d Dep't 2019) (recognizing well-established factors including "the time and labor required; the difficulty of the questions involved; the skill required to handle the issues presented; the experience, ability and reputation of counsel; the proposed amount of fees; the benefit resulting to the client from the services; the customary fee charged for similar services; the contingency or certainty of compensation; the results obtained; and the responsibility involved").

Similar factors are also considered by the court when using the percentage of the fund methodology. *Ryan*, 2013 N.Y. Misc. LEXIS 932, at *14.

m. Attorneys' Fees for Objectors

The trial court has discretion to award attorneys' fees to objectors. More specifically, "any other person that the court finds has acted to the benefit of the class" is entitled to reasonable attorneys' fees. CPLR 909. New York's approach to attorneys' fees for objectors comports with the federal approach in Rule 23(h).

n. Lien Law

Pursuant to Lien Law § 77(1), an action to enforce a claim under a trust arising under New York's Lien Law, Article 3-A, must be brought as a class action for the benefit of all the beneficiaries of the trust. *See ADCO Elec. Corp. v. McMahon*, 38 A.D.3d 805, 806 (2d Dep't 2007); *Brooklyn Navy Yard Dev. Corp. v. J. M. Dennis Constr. Corp.*, 12 A.D.3d 630, 632 (2d Dep't 2004); *Access Plumbing Corp.*, 2011 WL 1440307, at *6; *Mike Bldg. & Contracting, Inc.*, 27 Misc. 3d at 858. Additionally, since "there can be *only one* representative cause of action" under Lien Law § 77, the "presence of . . . previously filed cases arguably precludes" a subsequently filed class case from being certified to represent the class. *Concrete Indus. One Corp. v. Empire Outlet Builders, LLC,* 71 Misc. 3d 1219(A), at *3 (N.Y. Sup. Ct. 2021).

However, "failure to bring the action as a class action is not fatal and may be cured." *Bergassi Group LLC v. Consolidated Edison Co. of NY, Inc.*, No. 56860/2012, 2013 N.Y. Misc. LEXIS 768, at *89 (Sup. Ct. Westchester Cty. Jan. 3, 2013). Courts may give leave to the plaintiffs to amend their pleadings so as to bring the claim as a class action. *Id.* Moreover, courts may waive the requirements of Section § 901(a) at its discretion. *Callender v. Shirell Air, Inc.*, 282 A.D.2d 564, 565 (2d Dep't 2001); *Marcor Constr., Inc. v. Bil-Ray Aluminum Siding of Queens, Inc.*, No.705-12, 2012 WL 5465378, at *5 (Sup. Ct. Suffolk Cty. Oct. 26, 2012) ("[F]ailure to comply with CPLR Article 9 or to seek an order waiving its application or extending the time to certify is not fatal to the action, as the representation aspects of any such action may be cured after commencement or the requirements therefor are waived by the court."). *Cf. Access Plumbing Corp.*, 2011 WL 1440307, at *9 (waiving the numerosity requirement).

o. Class-wide Arbitration and Other Arbitration Issues

Under New York law, courts may order arbitration to proceed on a class-wide basis to the extent the entity ordering arbitration neither exceeded its powers nor manifestly disregarded the law when it certified the class. *Cheng*, 84 A.D.3d at 675. For example, in *Cheng*, the First Department affirmed an American Arbitration Association (AAA) panel's decision that certified a class of physicians and ordered class-wide arbitration of their breach of contract claims against a health insurance company because "the arbitration panel neither exceeded its powers nor manifestly disregarded the law in certifying the class." *Id.* The First Department found that (1) AAA rules permit class-wide arbitration, (2) the AAA found that contract giving rise to the claim at issue does not preclude class-wide arbitration, and (3) the AAA did not disregard the law because the proposed action satisfied the typicality and predominance prongs of class certification. *Id.* at 674–75.

The manner in which New York courts apply this rule is influenced by recent United States Supreme Court decisions, beyond the parameters of this guide, relating to class action arbitration waivers, including: *Stolt-Nielsen S.A. v. AnimalFeeds International*, 559 U.S. 662 (2010); *AT&T Mobility LLC v. Concepcion*, 131 S. Ct. 1740, 1740–41 (2011); *American Express Co. v. Italian Colors Restaurant, Inc.*, 133 S. Ct. 2304 (2013); *Oxford Health Plans, LLC v. Sutter*, 133 S. Ct. 2064

(2013). *See, e.g.*, *Sci. Games Corp. v. Mohawk Gaming Enterprises LLC*, 217 A.D.3d 556, 556 (2023) (citing *Oxford Health Plans, LLC v. Sutter* and holding that "[b]ecause the parties 'bargained for the arbitrator's construction of their agreement,' an arbitral decision 'even arguably construing or applying the contract' must stand, regardless of a court's view of its (de)merits"); *Wu v. Uber Techs., Inc.*, 78 Misc. 3d 551, 567–68 (N.Y. Sup. Ct. 2022) (citing *AT&T Mobility LLC v. Concepcion* for the proposition that courts should "place arbitration agreements on an equal footing with other contracts and enforce them according to their terms") aff'd, 219 A.D.3d 1208 (2023).

In *Rutella v. Nat'l Sec. Corp.*, 172 A.D.3d 1124, 1126–27 (2d Dep't 2019), the Second Department denied a motion to compel arbitration, notwithstanding the "defendants' contention that the Agreement contained a broad and unequivocal arbitration provision that required the parties to arbitrate all disputes *without exception*." The basis for the court's holding was that the pertinent agreement contained a provision that arbitrations were to be conducted under FINRA rules. One of those rules barred enforcement of "an arbitration agreement against a member of a putative class action with respect to any claim that is the subject of the putative class action, unless, among other things, class certification is denied." Thus, given that a plaintiff was required under the agreement to prove entitlement to class certification to avoid arbitration, the filing of a class claim was not a means of circumventing that agreement.

p. Court of Claims Class Actions

Class members must "satisfy the substantive pleading requirements of Court of Claims Act § 11(b) and be a named claimant in a filed claim" as a condition precedent to maintaining a class action in the court of claims. *Weaver v. State*, 82 A.D.3d 878, 879 (2d Dep't 2011) (citing N.Y. Ct., Cl. Act § 11), *leave to appeal dismissed*, 17 N.Y.3d 778 (2011), *leave to appeal den.*, 19 N.Y.3d 804 (2012). Court of Claims Act § 11(b) provides:

> The claim shall state the time when and place where such claim arose, the nature of same, the items of damage or injuries claimed to have been sustained and, except in an action to recover damages for personal injury, medical, dental or podiatric malpractice or wrongful death, the total sum claimed. A claim for the appropriation by the state of lands, or any right, title or interest in or to lands shall include an inventory or itemized statement of fixtures, if any, for which compensation is claimed. The notice of intention to file a claim shall set forth the same matters except that the items of damage or injuries and the sum claimed need not be stated. The claim and notice of intention to file a claim shall be verified in the same manner as a complaint in an action in the Supreme Court.

N.Y. Ct., Cl. Act § 11(b) (McKinney). In *Weaver*, the Second Department affirmed a trial court decision dismissing plaintiffs' claims because the plaintiffs failed to comply with these requirements with respect to each class member. 82 A.D.3d at 879.

q. Statutes of Limitation and *American Pipe* Tolling

For causes of action accruing "within" New York, CPLR § 201 provides that "[a]n action . . . must be commenced within the time specified in this article unless a different time is prescribed by law or a shorter time is prescribed by written agreement. No court shall extend the time limited by law for the commencement of an action." CPLR § 202 provides that an action based upon a "cause of action accruing without the state"—*i.e.*, in another jurisdiction—"cannot be commenced after the expiration of the time limited by the laws of either the state or the place without the state where the cause of action accrued, except that where the cause of action accrued in favor of a resident of the state the time limited by the laws of the state shall apply."

The Court of Appeals has "long recognized that 'the various tolling provisions to the Statutes of Limitation are largely, if not exclusively, *the product of legislative design*[,]'" and, as a rule, the "'time limitations created by statute are not tolled in the absence of statutory authority' because '[c]ourts may only construe provisions made by the Legislature creating exceptions' and 'may not create such exceptions.'" *Bermudez Chavez v. Occidental Chem. Corp.*, 35 N.Y.3d 492, 504–05 (2020) (quoting *McCarthy v. Volkswagen of Am., Inc.*, 55 N.Y.2d 543, 547 (1982); *King v. Chmielewski*, 76 N.Y.2d 182, 187 (1990) (emphasis in original)).

One notable exception is *American Pipe*, where the U.S. Supreme Court held that "'commencement of [a] class suit tolls the running of the statute [of limitations] for all purported members of the class who make timely motions to intervene after the court has found the suit inappropriate for class action status.'" *Bermudez*, 35 N.Y.3d at 501 (quoting *Am. Pipe & Constr. Co. v. Utah*, 414 U.S. 538, 553 (1974) (alterations in original)). Nine years later, the U.S. Supreme Court "clarified that '[t]he filing of a class action tolls the statute of limitations as to all asserted members of the class, not just as to intervenors.'" *Id.* at 502 (quoting *Crown, Cork & Seal Co., Inc. v. Parker*, 462 U.S. 345, 350 (1983)).

In other words, "tolling applies to both those members of the putative class who, following a denial of class certification, wish to intervene and those who prefer to commence individual actions. . . . *American Pipe* tolling 'is not inconsistent with the purposes served by statutes of limitations,'" which "'are intended to put defendants on notice of adverse claims and to prevent plaintiffs from sleeping on their rights. . . . [T]hese ends are met when a class action is commenced.'" *Id.* (quoting *Crown, Cork & Seal*, 462 U.S. at 351–52). *American Pipe* and *Crown, Cork & Seal* both "allowed tolling of the statute of limitations for federal claims for the benefit of absent class members filing in a federal court following a putative class action previously filed in another court until the absent class members could no longer reasonably rely upon the previously filed putative class action to vindicate their rights." *Id.* at 503.

In *Bermudez*, the Court of Appeals "confirm[ed] nearly forty years of Appellate Division case law acknowledging" that *American Pipe* tolling applies "intra-jurisdictionally," *i.e.*, the filing of a class action within New York tolls putative class members' claims in New York. *Id.* at 506 & n.10 (collecting cases). *Bermudez* also held that *American Pipe* tolling applies "cross-jurisdictionally," *i.e.*, the filing of a class action in another jurisdiction outside New York also tolls putative class members' claims in New York. *Id.* at 503–04. The New York Court of Appeals reasoned that both Federal Rule of Civil Procedure 23 and CPLR article 9 were "intended to permit the named plaintiffs in a putative class action to act as placeholders" and "designed to avoid wasteful and duplicative litigation by eliminating the need . . . for putative class members to initiate individual claims to protect their rights" during the pendency of a class action. *Id.* at 504 (*American Pipe* tolling "give[s] effect to the legislative policy embodied in article 9" to avoid the need for putative class members to "initiate parallel individual claims in New York . . . to protect against the risk of a subsequent denial of class certification or other non-merits termination"). The Court of Appeals "emphasize[d] that tolling applies only if a defendant receives fair notice of all claims that might arise under New York law" and "the putative class action, itself, must be timely and comport with CPLR 202." *Id.* at 505–06. In so holding, the Court of Appeals noted that its recognition of *American Pipe* cross-jurisdictional tolling harmonizes any tension between two statutory schemes adopted by the legislature, CPLR articles 2 and 9, and is not an exercise of judicial discretion." *Id.* at 505.

Finally, the Court of Appeals held that *American Pipe* tolling terminates "when it is no longer objectively reasonable for absent class members to rely upon the putative class action to vindicate their rights," *i.e.*, "tolling ends—as a matter of law—when there is a clear dismissal or a putative class action" including non-merits dismissals "or a denial of class certification for any reason." *Id.* at 506–08 ("Under those circumstances, future plaintiffs are on notice that they must take steps to protect their rights because the litigation no longer compels the court to address class certification or the named plaintiffs to advance absent class members' interests").

In sum, "New York recognizes *American Pipe* tolling for absent class members of putative class actions filed in other state and federal courts" and a "'non-merits dismissal of class certification' . . . extinguishes tolling because, under New York law, tolling ceases when there is a clear dismissal of the action . . . or denial of class certification for any reason." *Id.* at 508.

CLASS ACTIONS UNDER NEW YORK CIVIL PRACTICE LAW AND RULES: ARTICLE 9 CLASS ACTIONS

§ 901. PREREQUISITES TO A CLASS ACTION

a. One or more members of a class may sue or be sued as representative parties on behalf of all if:

    1. the class is so numerous that joinder of all members, whether otherwise required or permitted, is impracticable;

    2. there are questions of law or fact common to the class which predominate over any questions affecting only individual members;

    3. the claims or defenses of the representative parties are typical of the claims or defenses of the class;

    4. the representative parties will fairly and adequately protect the interests of the class; and

    5. a class action is superior to other available methods for the fair and efficient adjudication of the controversy.

b. Unless a statute creating or imposing a penalty, or a minimum measure of recovery specifically authorizes the recovery thereof in a class action, an action to recover a penalty, or minimum measure of recovery created or imposed by statute may not be maintained as a class action.

§ 902. ORDER ALLOWING CLASS ACTION

Within sixty days after the time to serve a responsive pleading has expired for all persons named as defendants in an action brought as a class action, the plaintiff shall move for an order to determine whether it is to be so maintained. An order under this section may be conditional, and may be altered or amended before the decision on the merits on the court's own motion or on motion of the parties. The action may be maintained as a class action only if the court finds that the prerequisites under section 901 have been satisfied. Among the matters which the court shall consider in determining whether the action may proceed as a class action are:

1. The interest of members of the class in individually controlling the prosecution or defense of separate actions;

2. The impracticability or inefficiency of prosecuting or defending separate actions;

3. The extent and nature of any litigation concerning the controversy already commenced by or against members of the class;

4. The desirability or undesirability of concentrating the litigation of the claim in the particular forum;

5. The difficulties likely to be encountered in the management of a class action.

§ 903. DESCRIPTION OF CLASS

The order permitting a class action shall describe the class. When appropriate the court may limit the class to those members who do not request exclusion from the class within a specified time after notice.

§ 904. NOTICE OF CLASS ACTION

(a) In class actions brought primarily for injunctive or declaratory relief, notice of the pendency of the action need not be given to the class unless the court finds that notice is necessary to protect the interests of the represented parties and that the cost of notice will not prevent the action from going forward.

(b) In all other class actions, reasonable notice of the commencement of a class action shall be given to the class in such manner as the court directs.

(c) The content of the notice shall be subject to court approval. In determining the method by which notice is to be given, the court shall consider

I. the cost of giving notice by each method considered

II. the resources of the parties and

III. the stake of each represented member of the class, and the likelihood that significant numbers of represented members would desire to exclude themselves from the class or to appear individually, which may be determined, in the court's discretion, by sending notice to a random sample of the class.

(d) I. Preliminary determination of expenses of notification. Unless the
court orders otherwise, the plaintiff shall bear the expense of notification. The court may, if justice requires, require that the defendant bear the expense of notification, or may require each of them to bear a part of the expense in proportion to the likelihood that each will prevail upon the merits. The court may hold a preliminary hearing to determine how the costs of notice should be apportioned.

II. Final determination. Upon termination of the action by order or judgment, the court may, but shall not be required to, allow to the prevailing party the expenses of notification as taxable disbursements under article eighty-three of the Civil Practice Law and Rules.

§ 905. JUDGMENT

The judgment in an action maintained as a class action, whether or not favorable to the class, shall include and describe those whom the court finds to be members of the class.

§ 906. ACTIONS CONDUCTED PARTIALLY AS CLASS ACTIONS

When appropriate,

1. an action may be brought or maintained as a class action with respect to particular issues, or

2. a class may be divided into subclasses and each subclass treated as a class.

The provisions of this article shall then be construed and applied accordingly.

§ 907. ORDERS IN CONDUCT OF CLASS ACTIONS

In the conduct of class actions the court may make appropriate orders:

1. determining the course of proceedings or prescribing measures to prevent undue repetition or complication in the presentation of evidence or argument;
2. requiring, for the protection of the members of the class, or otherwise for the fair conduct of the action, that notice be given in such manner as the court may direct to some or all of the members of any step in the action, or of the proposed extent of the judgment, or of the opportunity of members to signify whether they consider the representation fair and adequate, or to appear and present claims or defenses, or otherwise to come into the action;
3. imposing conditions on the representative parties or on interveners;
4. requiring that the pleadings be amended to eliminate therefrom allegations as to representation of absent persons, and that the action proceed accordingly;
5. directing that a money judgment favorable to the class be paid either in one sum, whether forthwith or within such period as the court may fix, or in such installments as the court may specify;
6. dealing with similar procedural matters.

The orders may be altered or amended as may be desirable from time to time.

§ 908. DISMISSAL, DISCONTINUANCE, OR COMPROMISE

A class action shall not be dismissed, discontinued, or compromised without the approval of the court. Notice of the proposed dismissal, discontinuance, or compromise shall be given to all members of the class in such manner as the court directs.

§ 909. ATTORNEYS' FEES

If a judgment in an action maintained as a class action is rendered in favor of the class, the court in its discretion may award attorneys' fees to the representatives of the class and/or to any other person that the court finds has acted to benefit the class based on the reasonable value of legal services rendered and if justice requires, allow recovery of the amount awarded from the opponent of the class.

This chapter was originally prepared by John Sullivan, a partner in the New York office of Fried, Frank, Harris, Shriver & Jacobson LLP, assisted by Tina Chao and Maureen Lim. Alfred L. Fatale III, a partner in the New York office of Labaton Keller Sucharow LLP, provided the update to this chapter, assisted by Rachel A. Berger.

NORTH CAROLINA

1. RULE 23(A)

North Carolina Rule 23(a) provides:

> If persons constituting a class are so numerous as to make it impracticable to bring them all before the court, such of them, one or more, as will fairly insure the adequate representation of all may, on behalf of all, sue or be sued.

2. COMPARISON WITH RULE 23 OF THE FEDERAL RULES OF CIVIL PROCEDURE

From a review of North Carolina's Rule 23, it should be obvious that there are substantial differences with its federal counterpart. Specifically, there are no Rule 23(b)(3) requirements, although similar issues are posed by the courts as "factors," among others, which the trial courts should consider prior to certifying a class action.

Additional differences involve the continuing review of class certification status of an action. As the North Carolina appellate courts have recognized, there are "substantial differences" between Rule 23 of the North Carolina Rules of Civil Procedure and Rule 23 of the Federal Rules of Civil Procedure:

Substantial differences exist between the foregoing rule and its federal counterpart. Clearly, the federal rule contemplates continuing review of the class certification status of an action. Rule 23 of the North Carolina Rules of Civil Procedure contains no such provision, and we will not judicially legislate one. *Dublin v. UCR, Inc.,* 115 N.C. App. 209, 444 S.E.2d 455, 461 (N.C. Ct. App. 1994) (citations omitted).

In undertaking consideration of a class certification motion, a trial court typically may not engage in a debate over the relative merits of the parties' positions:

> Following *Eisen v. Carlisle & Jacquelin,* 417 U.S. 156 (1974), construing our Rule 23, we hold that North Carolina *trial courts have no authority to hear the merits of a case* in determining whether to certify a class. The class must be determined *solely* according to procedural criteria relevant to Rule 23. *See English v. Holden Beach Realty Corporation,*41 N.C. App. 1, 254 S.E. 2d 223, *disc. rev. denied,* 297 N.C. 609, 257 S.E.2d 217 (1979).

Crow v. Citicorp Acceptance Co., 319 N.C. 274, 354 S.E.2d 459 (N.C. 1987). Nevertheless, citing more recent authority from the Fourth Circuit Court of Appeals, the North Carolina Supreme Court has allowed that inquiry into the merits "should be made only to the extent necessary to determine whether the requirements of Rule 23 have been met. *Beroth Oil Co. v. N. Carolina Dep't of Transp.*, 367 N.C. 333, 343, 757 S.E.2d 466, 474 (2014).

3. CASE LAW INTERPRETING RULE 23 OF THE NORTH CAROLINA RULES OF CIVIL PROCEDURE

a. Prerequisites

A "class" exists under Rule 23(a) "when the named and unnamed members each have an interest in either the same issue of law or of fact, and that issue predominates over issues affecting only individual class members." *Crow*, 354 S.E.2d at 464. While the predominance prerequisite historically has not required an identity of all issues among members of a class, more recent authority suggests that the predominance requirement may involve a complex inquiry in some contexts. The North Carolina Supreme Court held in *Beroth* that a putative class of over 800 property owners, who had inverse condemnation claims against the state Department of Transportation arising from its filing of corridor maps that allegedly impaired property values, had not shown "that all 800 owners within the corridor are affected in the same way and to the same extent." *Beroth*, 357 N.C. at 343, 757 S.E.2d at 474. The Court recognized that although differences in the amount of damages do not preclude class certification "as long as the takings issue predominates," it held that in this case "the takings issue is inextricably tied to the amount of damages; the extent of damages is not merely a collateral issue, but is determinative of the takings issue itself." *Id.* at 344, 757 S.E.2d at 475. Accordingly, the Court held that individual issues would predominate over common issues of law or fact.

The other prerequisites to utilizing the class action procedure are what are commonly denominated as "numerosity," "typicality," and "adequacy of representation." *See Crow*, 354 S.E.2d at 465–67; *see also English v. Holden Beach Realty Corp.*, 41 N.C. App. 1, 254 S.E.2d 223 (N.C. Ct. App. 1979). Appellate courts in North Carolina review a trial court's order allowing class certification for abuse of discretion. *Fisher v. Flue-Cured Tobacco Cooperative Stabilization Corp.*, 369 N.C. 202, 794 S.E.2d 699 (2016); *Surgeon v. TKO Shelby, LLC*, 385 N.C. 772, 898 S.E.2d 732, 736 (N.C. 2024). In *Beroth*, the North Carolina Supreme Court further refined the standard of review applicable to the findings of fact and conclusions of law in the class certification order, concluding that although "the general standard of review is abuse of discretion," the trial court's conclusions of law are reviewed *de novo*. *Beroth*, at 388.

The named class representatives in a class action must have individual standing. *Dicesare v. Charlotte-Mecklenburg Hospital Authority*, 2017 WL 1359599 (N.C. Super. Ct. Apr. 11, 2017).

Although North Carolina courts are not bound by the "case or controversy" requirement of the United States Constitution with respect to the jurisdiction of federal courts, "similar 'standing' requirements apply 'to refer generally to a party's right to have a court decide the merits of a dispute.'" *Meadows v. Iredell Cty.*, 187 N.C. App. 785, 787, 653 S.E.2d 925, 927–28 (2007) (citation omitted). "As is obvious from the wording of [Rule 23], one who is not a member of the represented class may not bring a class action representing that class." *Id.* at 788, 653 S.E.2d at 928 (citation omitted. *See also id.* at 789, 653 S.E.2d at 929 (affirming a trial court's dismissal of a class action in part because "[the] plaintiffs were not suitable to represent the proposed class"); *Laborers' Int'l Union of N. Am., AFL-CIO v. Case Farms, Inc.*, 127 N.C. App. 312, 315, 488 S.E.2d 632, 635 (1997) ("[Rule 23] does not grant or deny standing to parties. Rather than providing a basis for standing, this statute allows a party who is entitled to sue to bring suit on behalf of itself and other parties in the form of a class action."). The North Carolina Supreme Court has discussed the so-called "pick-off exception to mootness" regarding the justiciability and adopted the logic of the Third Circuit Court of Appeals in *Richardson v. Bledsoe*, 829 F.3d 273 (3d Cir. 2016), holding that the "relation back" doctrine "may be applied to relate a now-moot individual claim back to the date of the class action complaint when the event that moots the plaintiff's claim occurs before the plaintiff has had a fair opportunity to seek class certification and provided that the plaintiff has not unduly delayed in litigating the motion for class certficiation." *Chambers v. Moses H. Cone Mem'l Hosp.*, 374 N.C. 436, 437, 843 S.E.2d 172, 173 (2020). "Therefore, 'when satisfaction of the plaintiff's individual claim [occurs] before the court can reasonably be expected to rule on the class certification motion, the plaintiff's stake in the litigation is not extinguished.'" *Id.*

i. Commonality. Rule 23(a), as interpreted by North Carolina's highest court, requires a showing that each of the named and unnamed members of the proposed class has an interest in the same issue of law *or* of fact. *Crow,* 354 S.E.2d at 464; *see also Pitts v. American Sec. Ins. Co.*, 144 N.C. App. 1, 550 S.E.2d 179 (N.C. Ct. App. 2001), *disc. rev. allowed*, 355 N.C. 214, 560 S.E.2d 133 (N.C. 2002), *aff'd without precedential value*, 356 N.C. 292, 569 S.E.2d 647 (N.C. 2002). It does not require both. "A common issue predominates when plaintiffs demonstrate that the potential class members' claims share a common issue capable of resolution 'in one stroke.'" *Dewalt v. Hooks*, 2022-NCSC-105, ¶ 12, 382 N.C. 340, 344, 879 S.E.2d 179, 183 (citing *Wal-Mart Stores, Inc. v. Dukes*, 564 U.S. 338, 350, 131 S. Ct. 2541, 180 L. Ed. 2d 374 (2011)).

Moreover, there is no requirement that any member of the proposed class share a jural relationship or so-called "community of interest" with any other member of the proposed class. *Crow,* 354 S.E.2d at 464. Whether a proper "class" exists under Rule 23(a) is a question of law. *Crow,* 354 S.E.2d at 464.

In undertaking a consideration of the propriety of a class action, the court is required to consider the allegations contained in the plaintiffs' complaint as "true," and view them in the light most favorable to the representative plaintiffs. *Crow,* 354 S.E.2d at 464–65 ("Taking the allegations of the complaint as true, it appears that . . . the plaintiffs sufficiently alleged the existence of a 'class' under Rule 23(a)").

Regarding damages, although different members of the class could indeed end up with different damages based on individual circumstances, the North Carolina Supreme Couirt has held that "these differences do not undermine the availability of a class-wide theory of generalized liability." *McMillan v. Blue Ridge Co., Inc.*, 2021-NCSC-160, ¶ 22, 379 N.C. 488, 497, 866 S.E.2d 700, 707 (2021). At the class certification stage, "the only question regards the appropriateness of class certification, not the merits of plaintiffs' claims or extent of plaintiffs' damages. . . ." *Id.*

ii. Numerosity. The "numerosity" prerequisite is satisfied by a showing that the class members are so numerous that it is impracticable to bring them all before the court. *Crow,* 354 S.E.2d at 466; N.C. R. Civ. P. 23(a). "It is not necessary that [the named representatives] demonstrate the impossibility of joining class members, but they must demonstrate substantial difficulty or inconvenience in joining all members of the class." *Crow*, 354 S.E.2d at 466; *English*, 254 S.E.2d at 229. There is no firm rule for determining when a class is so numerous that joinder is impracticable. *Crow*, 354 S.E.2d at 466; *English*, 254 S.E.2d at 229. The number of potential class members in determining what is a "numerous" class is not dependent on any arbitrary limit, but rather the circumstances of each case. *English*, 254 S.E.2d at 229.

iii. Typicality. The claims of the class representatives must be typical of the claims of the class, *see Crow*, 354 S.E.2d at 465–67; *see also English*, 254 S.E.2d at 229–31. Typicality is met if the class representative's claim "arises from the same event or practice or course of conduct that gives rise to the claims of other class members and his or her claims are based on the same legal theory." *Blitz v. Agean, Inc.*, 197 N.C. App. 296, 306, 677 S.E.2d 1, 8 (2009) (citing *Hinman v. M and M Rental Ctr.*, 545 F. Supp. 2d 802 (N.D. Ill. 2008).

iv. Superiority. The overriding factor which courts in North Carolina impose prior to the certification of a class is whether it makes sense for common issues to be litigated once, or (potentially) more than once, with the possibility of inconsistent results. Consider this mandate from the North Carolina Supreme Court:

> Our Rule 23 should receive a liberal construction, and it should not be loaded down with arbitrary and technical restrictions. . . . The rule has as its objectives "the efficient resolution of the claims or liabilities of many individuals in a single action" and "the elimination of repetitious litigation and possible inconsistent adjudications involving common questions, related events, or requests for similar relief."

Crow v. Citicorp Acceptance Co., 319 N.C. 274, 354 S.E.2d 459 (N.C. 1987) (quoting *English v. Holden Beach Realty Corp.,* 41 N.C. App. 1, 254 S.E.2d 223, 230–31 (N.C. Ct. App. 1979), *cert. denied,* 257 S.E.2d 217 (N.C. 1979) (citations omitted)).

The North Carolina Supreme Court ended its analysis of Rule 23(a) by stating:

> If the prerequisites to a class action are established . . . the decision whether a class action is superior to other available methods for the adjudication of this controversy continues to be a matter left to the trial court's discretion.

Central to this determination is whether a class action is superior to other available methods for the adjudication of the controversy. *Crow*, 354 S.E.2d at 466. "Class actions should be permitted where they are likely to serve useful purposes such as preventing a multiplicity of suits or inconsistent results." *Id.*; *see Pitts*, 550 S.E.2d at 188 ("however, the trial court must balance the useful purpose against 'inefficiency or other drawbacks'") (quoting *Crow*, 354 S.E.2d at 466). Before certifying a class, the trial court must balance the potential benefits of certifying the proposed class against any "inefficiency or other drawbacks." *Surgeon,* 898 S.E.2d at 739. "Thus, although class certification analysis ordinarily does not involve an inquiry into the merits of plaintiffs' claims, it is appropriate for a trial court to consider, as a matter of law, what remedies would be available if the plaintiffs prevailed on their claims. *Id.* Therefore, when "balancing the costs of litigation against the likely benefits," the "costs of administering a class action, compared to the plaintiffs' potential recovery, may render the class action so inefficient that it does not warrant certification. *Id.*

In claims involving statutory damages, the North Carolina Supreme Court has determined that the certification of a class damages based upon "objective, class-wide criteria" was appropriate when those damages can be determined "based on the generalized theory of alleged class-wide . . . injuries." *McMillan, supra*, at *500. "While statutory damages and attorneys' fees are among the many factors that a trial court may consider within a class action superiority determination, neither dispositively renders a certain cause of action per se unsuitable for class certification." *Id.*

When making the determination of whether a class action is superior to other methods of determination, the trial court is not limited to the consideration of the prerequisites to bringing a class action as previously set forth. *See Nobles v. First Communications, Inc.*, 108 N.C. App. 127, 132, 423 S.E.2d 312, 315 (N.C. Ct. App. 1992), *disc. rev. denied*, 333 N.C. 463, 427 S.E.2d 623 (N.C. 1993). "Some proper considerations include, but are not limited to, the amount of recovery compared to the cost of administration of the lawsuit, 'the interest of members of the class in individually controlling the prosecution or defense of separate actions,' 'the extent and nature of any litigation concerning the controversy already commenced by or against members of the class,' 'the desirability or undesirability of concentrating the litigation of the claims in the particular forum,' and 'the difficulties likely to be encountered in the management of a class action.'" *Pitts*, 354 S.E.2d at 466 (*quoting* Fed. R. Civ. P. 23(b)(3)).

The trial court's conclusion as to whether a class action is the superior method of adjudication is within its discretion and is binding on appeal absent thereof. *Pitts*, 550 S.E.2d at 189; *Crow*, 354 S.E.2d at 466; *Dewalt*, 2022-NCSC-105, ¶ 14, 382 N.C. 340, 345, 879 S.E.2d 179, 183. "Honoring that discretion is the 'touchstone for appellate review' of class certification orders." *Id.* Nevertheless, the trial court must make findings of fact to support its conclusion. *See Nobles*, 108 N.C. App. at 132–33, 423 S.E.2d at 315–16.

North Carolina's Business Court is a forum that litigates a statistically significant percentage of class actions in North Carolina, due to a party's ability to file a Notice of Designation of an action as a "mandatory complex business case" "that involve[s] a material issue related to" certain matters, including disputes involving "the law governing corporations," "securities," "antitrust law," and "intellectual property," in which the "amount in controversy . . . is at least five million dollars ($5,000,000.00)." N.C.G.S. § 7A-45.4. The Business Court's published decisions provide guidance, consistent with North Carolina appellate courts, as to the requirements for class certification under North Carolina's Rule 23. "A trial court, in its discretion, may certify a class action where the following requirements are met: (1) the existence of a class; (2) . . . the named representatives will fairly and adequately represent the interests of all class members; (3) . . . there is no conflict of interest between the representative and class members; (4) . . . class members outside the jurisdiction will be adequately represented; (5) . . . the named party has a genuine personal interest in the outcome of the litigation; (6) . . . class members are so numerous that it is impractical to bring them all before the court; and (7) adequate notice of the class action is given to class members." *In re Newbridge Bancorp Shareholder Litig.*, 2016 WL 6885882 (N.C. Super Ct. Nov. 22, 2016).

v. Dismissal. Following the "spirit of Rule 23(c)," North Carolina's Business Court has set forth the "procedures that counsel must follow in pre-certification class actions assigned to Special Superior Court Judges for Complex Business Cases when a plaintiff who has assumed a fiduciary duty by filing a class action subsequently files a voluntary dismissal. Information that, pre-certification, a party or their counsel have may be required to submit prior to the Business Court approving, pre-certification, the dismissal of a putative class action include: A statement of (1) the reason for dismissal; (2) the person gain received by Plaintiffs in any settlement; (3) a statement of any other material terms of the settlement, specifically including any terms which have the potential to impact class members; (4) a statement of any counsel fees paid to Plaintiffs' counsel by Defendants; (5) a statement of any agreement by Plaintiffs restricting their ability to file other litigation against any Defendant; and (6) a statement either detailing any potential prejudice to putative class members or representing to the Court that no prejudice exists. *See generally Bennett v. Commer. Coll. of Asheboro, Inc.,* 2016 WL 1118739 (N.C. Super. Ct. Mar. 22, 2016); *BB&T Boli Plan Trust v. Massachusetts Mut. Life Ins. Co.*, No. 09 CVS 4007, 2016 WL 1733362, at *16 (N.C. Super. Apr. 29, 2016).

vi. Appeal from denial of class certification—not interlocutory. North Carolina's appellate courts have held that the denial of class certification affects a substantial right and is therefore immediately appealable because "it necessarily determinate the action as to the unnamed plaintiffs." *Frost v. Mazda Motor of Am., Inc.*, 353 N.C. 188, 193, 540 S.E.2d 324, 327 (2000); *Elam v. William Douglas Management, Inc.*, 773 S.E.2d 574 (2015).

vii. Appeal from grant of class certification—interlocutory. An interlocutory order granting class certification is generally not immediately appealable unless it affects a substantial right. *Frost v. Mazda Motor of America, Inc.*, 353 N.C. 188, 192, 540 S.E.2d 324, 327 (2000). "The 'substantial right' test for appealability of interlocutory orders is that 'the right itself must be substantial and the deprivation of that . . . right must potentially work injury . . . if not corrected before appeal from final judgment. . . . However, no order *allowing* class certification has been held to similarly affect a substantial right such that interlocutory appeal would be permitted.'" *Id.*

viii. Settlement. North Carolina courts have observed that "[s]ettlement has long been preferred to litigation, and public policy prefers upholding good faith settlements, even without strong regard to the consideration underlying the settlement. *In re Newbridge Bancorp Shareholder Litig., supra* (citing *In re Progress Energy S'holder Litig.* 2011 WL 5967183 (N.C. Super Ct. Nov. 29, 2011)). However, the North Carolina Business Court has held that 'due to the unique due process concerns' of a class action settlement, which binds individuals not before the court to the settlement, parties cannot settle a class action without court approval." *Id.; Ehrenhaus v. Baker*, 216 N.C. App. 59, 717 S.E.2d 9 (2011). The Business Court has observed that court approval of a class action settlement is intended to:

> assure[ ] that any person whose rights would be affected by settlement has the opportunity to support or oppose it; (2) prevent . . . private arrangements that may constitute "sweetheart deals" contrary to the best interests of the class; (3) protect the rights of those whose interests may not have been given due regard by the negotiating parties; and finally (4) assure each member of the class that his or her integrity and right to express views and be heard on matters of vital personal interest has not been violated by others who have arrogated to themselves the power to speak and bind without consultation and consent.

Id. When determining the fairness, reasonableness and adequacy of a proposed class action settlement, the North Carolina Business Court has utilized the following factors: (a) the strength of the plaintiff's case; (b) the defendant's ability to pay; (c) the complexity and cost of further litigation; (d) the amount of opposition to the settlement; (e) class members' reaction to the proposed settlement; (f) counsel's opinion, and (g) the stage of the proceedings and how much discovery has been completed. *Id.*; *Ehrenhaus*, 216 N.C. App. at 73–75. The first factor "is the likelihood the class will prevail should litigation go forward and the potential spoils of victory, balanced against benefits to the class offers in the settlement." *Id.* When reviewing a proposed settlement, the trial court "must protect, to the extent practicable, the rights of passive class members, and the trial court should consider and scrutinize what the class is to receive (the 'get') and to give up (the 'give') in the settlement." *Corwin v. British Am. Tobacco PLC,* 2016 WL 635191 (N.C. Super. Ct. Feb. 17, 2016).

ix. Mootness. In 2020, the North Carolina Supreme Court, following the logic of the Third Circuit Court of Appeals in *Richardson v. Bledsoe*, 829 F.3d 273 (3d Cir. 2016), held that the "relation back" doctrine can be applied to "relate a now-moot individual claim back to the date of the class action complaint" when the event that moots the plaintiff's claim occurs before the plaintiff has had a fair opportunity to seek class certification, provided that the plaintiff has not unduly delayed in litigating the motion for class certification. *Chambers v. Moses H. Cone Mem'l Hosp.*, 374 N.C. 436, 437, 843 S.E.2d 172, 173 (2020). Therefore, "when satisfaction of the plaintiffs individual claim occurs before the court can reasonably be expected to rule on the class certification motion, the plaintiff's stake in the litigation is not extinguished, and the case is not moot." *Id.*

4. CONTACTING ABSENT CLASS MEMBERS

There is no significant North Carolina case law discussing the ground rules for communications by attorneys with absent class members. However an ethics opinion from the North Carolina State Bar has generally outlined what type of communication is permissible, broken down by three types of communications: (1) notices from the court; (2) informal communications by the litigants' counsel with prospective class members on topics prior to class certification; and (3) communications by plaintiff's counsel that ask a prospective class member if he or she wants to hire the attorney's firm. 2004 Ethics Opinion (2004 FEO 5). A Notice from the Court is authorized by law and is not a communication from a lawyer. More importantly, there is no blanket prohibition against informal communications by the litigants' counsel with prospective class members on a wide array of topics prior to class certification, although the trial court has the discretion to limit counsel's communications with potential class members pursuant to its duty to exercise control over class actions and prevent abuse. *Gibbons v. CIT Group/Sales Financing, Inc.*, 101 N.C. App. 502, 506, 400 S.E.2d 104, 106–07 (1991). Provided that such limitations should only be ordered in limited circumstances. *Id.* Finally, communications by plaintiff's counsel that ask a prospective class member if he or she wants to hire the attorney's firm are permissible provided that the communication contains the words "[t]his is an advertisement for legal services" on the outside of the envelope and at the beginning of the body of the communication. Rule 7.3(c). 2004 Ethics Opinion (2004 FEO 5).

5. OTHER REQUIREMENTS

The court may not apply North Carolina law to a nationwide class of drug purchasers claiming that manufacturers artificially inflated the price of the drug without analyzing the law of the other jurisdictions to determine whether it conflicts with North Carolina law. *Stetser v. TAP Pharmaceutical Prod., Inc.*, 165 N.C. App. 1, 598 S.E.2d 570 (N.C. App. 2004).

Aside from the existence of a "class," North Carolina class action law requires that (1) the representative plaintiffs establish that they will fairly and adequately represent the interests of all members of the class, (2) there is no conflict of interest between the representative plaintiffs and the unnamed members of the class, (3) the representative plaintiffs have a genuine personal interest in the action, (4) the representative plaintiffs adequately represent those outside the jurisdiction, (5) the class members are so numerous that it is impractical to bring them all before the court, and (6) adequate notice be given to members of the class. *Faulkenbury v. Teachers and State Employees Retirement Sys. of North Carolina*, 108 N.C. App. 357, 424 S.E.2d 420, 430 (N.C. Ct. App. 1993), *aff'd,* 335 N.C. 158, 436 S.E.2d 821 (N.C. 1993); *see Pitts*, 550 S.E.2d at 188.

Once the existence of a class has been established and the prerequisites to utilizing the class action procedure have been satisfied, it is left to the trial court's discretion to determine whether the action should proceed as a class action:

> In deciding whether an action may be maintained as a class action, the trial court is accorded a degree of discretion . . . A court has broad discretion in deciding whether to allow the maintenance of a class action and therefore also may take account of considerations not expressly dealt with in the rule in reaching a decision.

English, 254 S.E.2d at 231 (citations omitted).

While section (a) of Rule 23 does not require it, fundamental fairness and due process dictate that adequate notice, determined in the discretion of the trial court, be given to members of the class. *English*, 254 S.E.2d at 230. The court is required to direct to members of the class the best notice practicable under the circumstances. *Id.* This includes individual notice to all members who can be identified through reasonable effort. The notice must be adequate to satisfy constitutional due process requirements. *Id.* The trial court has further discretion in determining which party bears the costs of providing notices to class members. *Frost v. Mazda Motor of America, Inc.*, 353 N.C. 188,

540 S.E.2d 324, 330 (N.C. 2000).

Despite the public policy favoring arbitration, a class action lawsuit should not be compelled to arbitration where the arbitration clause is procedurally and substantively unconconscionable factors to consider in determining unconscionability include: (1) whether the arbitration clause prohibits joinder of claims and class actions, (2) whether the consumer is given the opportunity to negotiate the terms of the arbitration provision, (3) whether there is unequal bargaining power, and (4) whether a corporate defendant would not have provided its services but for the inclusion of the arbitration provision. *Tillman v. Commercial Credit Loans, Inc.*, 362 N.C. 93, 655 S.E.2d 362 (N.C. 2008).

On appeal, the standard of review employed by the appellate courts in North Carolina with respect to the review of findings of fact and conclusions of law in a class certification order, findings of fact are binding on appeal if supported by competent evidence, and conclusions of law are reviewed de novo. *Beroth*, 367 N.C. at 338, 757 S.E.2d at 471.

"Although North Carolina courts are not bound by the 'case or controversy' requirement of the United States Constitution with respect to the jurisdiction of federal courts, similar 'standing' requirements apply 'to refer generally to a party's right to have a court decide the merits of a dispute.'" *Meadows v. Iredell Cty.*, 187 N.C. App. 785, 787, 653 S.E.2d 925, 927–28 (2007) (citation omitted). "As is obvious from the wording of [Rule 23], one who is not a member of the represented class may not bring a class action representing that class." *Id.* at 788, 653 S.E.2d at 928 (citation omitted; (*see Chambers v. Moses H. Cone Mem'l Hosp.*, 814 S.E.2d 864, 867 (N.C. Ct. App. 2018) (holding class action was rendered moot by hospital's dismissal of its counterclaim against plaintiff seeking to recover unpaid balances for cost of services rendered).

As a general rule, attorneys' fees are not recoverable, either as damages or costs, absent statutory authority. *See, e.g.*, *Stillwell Enters., Inc. v. Interstate Equip. Co.*, 300 N.C. 286, 289, 266 S.E.2d 812, 814 (1980). Notwithstanding this rule, the Court of Appeals has held that a court may award attorneys' fees agreed upon in a class action, disclosure-based settlement without additional statutory authority, such that "parties to a class action may agree to a fee-shifting provision in a negotiated settlement that is . . . subject to the trial court's approval." *Ehrenhaus v. Baker*, 243 N.C. App. 17, 30, 776 S.E.2d 699, 708 (2015) (*Ehrenhaus II*); *see also In re Pike Corp. S'holder Litig.*, No. 14 CVS 1202, 2015 NCBC LEXIS 95, at *17 (N.C. Super. Ct. Oct. 5, 2015) (citing *Faulkenbury v. Teachers' & State Emps.' Ret. Sys. of N.C.*, 345 N.C. 683, 696, 483 S.E.2d 422, 430 (1997)) and *Ehrenhaus II*, 243 N.C. App. at 30, 776 S.E.2d at 708) ("The long-standing general rule . . . that a court can award attorneys' fees to a prevailing party only if the court has the statutory authority to do so[,] . . . does not govern a settlement where there is no 'prevailing party,' and . . . the parties have agreed to a fee-shifting provision in a voluntary settlement."). Under *Ehrenhaus II*, a class settlement including a valid fee-shifting procedure establishes a contractual basis for the Court's authority to award fees. *See In re Newbridge Bancorp S'holder Litig.*, No. 15 CVS 9251, 2016 NCBC LEXIS 91, at *36, 2016 WL 6885882 (N.C. Super. Ct. Nov. 22, 2016) (finding that the parties' express agreement that defendants would pay plaintiffs' counsel for their attorneys' fees, costs, and expenses established a "contractual basis for the Court's authority to make an award"); *see also In re Krispy Kreme Doughnuts, Inc. S'holder Litig.*, 2018 WL 3062205, at *4 (N.C. Super. June 20, 2018) (awarding attorneys' fee in the amount of $150,000, but denying expense request as plaintiff's fee agreements fail to comply with RPC 1.8(e) because they hold Plaintiffs harmless at the inception of the litigation from any potential liability for expenses, and that any expense recovery would violate the public policy on which RPC 1.8(e) is based).

RULE 23 OF THE NORTH CAROLINA RULES OF CIVIL PROCEDURE

RULE 23. CLASS ACTIONS

(a) *Representation.* If persons constituting a class are so numerous as to make it impracticable to bring them all before the court, such of them, one or more, as will fairly insure the adequate representation of all may, on behalf of all, sue or be sued.

(b) *Secondary action by shareholders.* In an action brought to enforce a secondary right on the part of one or more shareholders or members of a corporation or an unincorporated association because the corporation or association refuses to enforce rights which may properly be asserted by it, the complaint shall be verified by oath.

(c) *Dismissal of compromise.* A class action shall not be dismissed or compromised without the approval of the judge. In an action under this rule, notice of a proposed dismissal or compromise shall be given to all members of the class in such manner as the judge directs.

(d) *Tax class actions.* In addition to all of the requirements set out in this rule, a class action seeking the refund of a State tax paid due to an alleged unconstitutional statute may be brought and maintained only as provided in G.S. 105-241.18.

Chapter author Gary K. Shipman is the founder and senior partner of Shipman Wright & Moore, LLP, in Wilmington, North Carolina. Mr. Shipman's practice is limited to complex commercial litigation, mass torts, medical malpractice, personal injury, wrongful death, and products liability. Mr. Shipman is certified as a Civil Trial Specialist by the National Board of Trial Advocacy.

NORTH DAKOTA

1. COMPARISON WITH RULE 23 OF THE FEDERAL RULES OF CIVIL PROCEDURE

Rule 23 of the North Dakota Rules of Civil Procedure is based on the Model Class Action Rule as drafted by the National Conference of Commissioners on Uniform State Laws. Before the Model Rule became effective, North Dakota Rule 23 was identical to Rule 23 of the Federal Rules of Civil Procedure. Despite the modification, the underlying judicial philosophy of Rule 23 remains the same. *Peterson v. Dougherty Dawkins, Inc.*, 1998 ND 159, ¶ 9, 583 N.W.2d 626; *Rogelstad v. Farmers Union Grain Terminal Ass'n, Inc.*, 226 N.W.2d 370, 374 (N.D. 1975). Courts are to "interpret Rule 23 so as to provide an open and receptive attitude toward class actions." *Howe v. Microsoft Corp.*, 2003 ND 12, ¶ 7, 656 N.W.2d 285; *Rose v. United Equitable Ins. Co.*, 2002 ND 148, ¶ 6, 651 N.W.2d 683; *Saba v. County of Barnes*, 307 N.W.2d 590, 593 (N.D. 1981); *Rogelstad*, 226 N.W.2d 370 (N.D. 1975); *see also Bice v. Petro-Hunt*, 2004 ND 113, ¶ 7, 681 N.W.2d 74; *Ritter, Laber & Assoc.v. Koch Oil*, 2000 ND 15, ¶ 3, 605 N.W.2d 153 (*Ritter I*); *Ritter, Laber & Associates v. Koch Oil*, 2001 ND 56, ¶ 5, 623 N.W.2d 424 (*Ritter II*); *Ritter, Laber & Assoc.v. Koch Oil*, 2004 ND 117, ¶ 36, 680 N.W.2d 634 (*Ritter III*); *Old Broadway Corp. v. Hjelle*, 411 N.W.2d 81, 82 (N.D. 1987). Iowa is the only other state to have adopted Model Rule 23.

It is well settled that the trial court must make a determination of class certification without delving into the merits of the case. *Howe*, 2003 ND 12, ¶ 19, 656 N.W.2d 285; *Werlinger v. Champion Health Care Corp.*, 1999 ND 173, ¶ 18, 598 N.W.2d 820. A trial court may consider a motion for summary judgment whenever a class action certification is pending. *O'Conner v. Northern States Power Co.,* 308 N.W.2d 365, 369 (N.D. 1981).

2. CASE LAW INTERPRETING NORTH DAKOTA RULE OF CIVIL PROCEDURE 23

There are four requirements that must be met under North Dakota Rule of Civil Procedure 23.

1. Numerosity (23(a)(1));
2. Commonality (23(a)(2));
3. Fair and Efficient Adjudication of the Controversy (23(b)(2)(B)); and
4. Fair and Adequate Representation by the Representative Parties (23(b)(2)(C)).

Howe, 2003 ND 12, ¶ 8, 656 N.W.2d 285; *Rose*, 2002 ND 148, ¶ 7, 651 N.W.2d 683.

a. 23(a)(1). Numerosity

The proposed class must be so numerous or so constituted that joinder of all members, whether or not otherwise required or permitted, is impracticable. A class of 101 potential members was considered to be sufficiently numerous for certification. *Peterson*, 1998 ND 159, ¶ 5, 583 N.W.2d 626. A 48–member class was sufficiently large to justify certification. *Horst v. Guy*, 211 N.W.2d 723, 726-27 (N.D. 1973).

b. 23(a)(2). Commonality

The moving party must establish that there is a question of law or fact common to the case. When claims all arise from the same alleged misrepresentations and omissions made in an official statement, commonality has been met. *Peterson*, 1998 ND 159, ¶ 12, 583 N.W.2d 626. When a question of law refers to standardized conduct by the defendants toward members of a proposed class, a common nucleus of operative facts is typically presented and the commonality requirement is met. *Bice*, 2004 ND 113, ¶ 9, 681 N.W.2d 74.

c. 23(c)(1)(A)-(M). Fair and Efficient Adjudication

Any conclusion as to whether a class action provides a fair and efficient means of adjudication requires that the court consider the factors of Rule 23(c)(1)(A)–(M). Weighing the various factors is separate and independent from the ultimate inquiry whether a class can prove its claim. *Baker v. Autos, Inc.*, 2015 ND 57, ¶ 9, 860 N.W.2d 788. To determine whether a class action would be a fair and efficient adjudication of the controversy, numerous factors must be considered. N.D. R. Civ. P. 23(c)(1)(A)–(M). *Klagues v. Maintenance Eng'g*, 2002 ND 59, ¶ 8, 643 N.W.2d 45; *Peterson*, 1998 ND 159, ¶ 13, 583 N.W.2d 626. No one factor predominates and each of the 13 factors under Rule 23(c)(1) need not be satisfied before certification is appropriate. *Id.*; *Old Broadway Corp.*, 411 N.W.2d at 83; *Holloway v. Blue Cross of North Dakota*, 294 N.W.2d 902, 907 (N.D. 1980); *Vignaroli v. Blue Cross of Iowa*, 360 N.W.2d 741, 744 (Iowa 1985) ("No weight is required by the rule to be assigned by the trial court to any criteria listed, further evidencing an intent to grant considerable discretion to the trial court."). Nor must the court explicitly address all 13 factors. *Old Broadway Corp.*, 411 N.W.2d at 83; *Holloway*, 294 N.W.2d at 907; *Peterson*, 1998 ND 159, ¶ 14, 583 N.W.2d 626; *Howe*, 2003 ND 12, ¶ 9, 656 N.W.2d 283; *Rose*, 2002 ND 148, ¶ 9, 651 N.W.2d 683. However, a court's decision to certify a class must address some of the factors to provide an adequate explanation for a reviewing court to understand the basis of the decision. *North Dakota Human Rights Coalition v. Bertsch*, 2005 ND 98, ¶ 15, 697 N.W.2d 1. A trial court's decision to certify will not be overturned on appeal unless the court abused its discretion. *Mann v. North Dakota Tax Com'r*, 2007 ND 119, ¶ 31, 736 N.W.2d 464; *Bice*, 2004 ND 113, ¶ 7, 681 N.W.2d 74.

i. 23(c)(1)(A). In applying the "joint or common interest" factor of Rule 23(c)(1)(A), a court must consider whether plaintiffs "have a common and undivided interest" in the subject matter of the suit. *Werlinger*, 1999 ND 173, ¶ 50, 598 N.W.2d 820, *aff'd*, 617 N.W.2d 131 (N.D. 2000). Rule 23(c)(1)(A) contemplates a joint interest similar to the old "true" class action. *Werlinger*, 1999 ND 173, ¶ 51, 598 N.W.2d 820. However, a common interest may exist if the defendant's total liability does not depend on how the recovery of a claim is distributed among the class members. *Ritter I*, 2000 ND 15, ¶ 12, 605 N.W.2d 153; *Ritter II*, 2001 ND 56, ¶ 17, 623 N.W.2d 424 (district court's certification order as to joint and common interest was affirmed at certification stage subject to further refinement including subclasses and possible de-certification as case progressed).

ii. 23(c)(1)(B). Differing results in actions for money damages do not constitute incompatible standards under 23(c)(1)(B). Thus, factor 23(c)(1)(B) does not weigh in favor of certification unless a defendant would be unable to comply with one judgment without violating the terms of another. *Werlinger*, 1999 ND 173, ¶ 54, 598 N.W.2d 820. *See also Ritter I*, 2000 ND 15, ¶ 15, 605 N.W.2d 153. While most class certification issues under this factor deal with cases involving limited funds, the plain language of the rule does not restrict its application to such cases. *Klauges*, 2002 ND 59, ¶ 17, 643 N.W.2d 45.

iii. 23(c)(1)(C). Rule 23(c)(1)(C) focuses on the impact individual adjudications would have on class members. If adjudication as to the rights of the representatives would be very persuasive in later litigation and would, as a practical matter, likely be dispositive of the other class members' interests, the factor may be satisfied. *Bice*, 2004 ND 113, ¶ 16, 681 N.W.2d 74; *Ritter I*, 2000 ND 15, ¶ 20, 605 N.W.2d 153, *aff'd*, 2001 ND 56, 623 N.W.2d 424. Precedent plus some other practical factor can be sufficient to weigh in favor of certification under factor (c)(1)(C). *Klagues*, 2002 ND 59, ¶ 17, 643 N.W.2d 45. Thus, factor 23(c)(1)(C) can be satisfied even when there is no limited fund, as long as there are numerous common facts.

iv. 23(c)(1)(D). Rule 23(c)(1)(D) applies when the party opposing the class has acted or refused to act on grounds applicable to the class thereby making final injunctive relief or declaratory relief appropriate to the class as a whole. A district court determined that, even though no injunctive relief was sought, factor (c)(1)(D) weighed in favor of certification because the action involved declaratory type of relief in determining whether Microsoft's actions were unlawful. *Howe v. Microsoft Corp.*, No. 00-C-00328, 2002 WL 199130, at *2 (N.D. Dist. Ct. Jan. 16, 2002). Microsoft's actions were applicable to the class making declaratory relief appropriate to the class as a whole. *Id.*

v. 23(c)(1)(E). Individual claims of class members need not be carbon copies of each other for common questions to predominate. *Ritter I*, 2000 ND 15, ¶ 22, 605 N.W.2d 153. If common questions predominate to meet the requirement of factor 23(c)(1)(E), factors 23(c)(1)(G) and (K) are also satisfied. *Ritter I*, 2000 ND 15, ¶¶ 27–28, 605 N.W.2d 153.

vi. 23(c)(1)(F). Factor F calls for a determination of whether other means of adjudicating the claims and defenses are impracticable or inefficient. N.D. R. Civ. P. 23(c)(1)(F). A finding that a history of prior individual litigation did not weigh against certification was not an abuse of discretion. *Bice*, 2004 ND 113, ¶ 22, 681 N.W.2d 74. A finding that a government run refund process, which dictated that each claimant prove his/her entitlement to a refund with information that only he/she possessed, provided means other than a class action that were more practical and efficient than a class action. *Mann*, 2007 ND 119, ¶ 34, 736 N.W.2d 464.

vii. 23(c)(1)(G). The trial court must consider whether a class action offers the most appropriate means of adjudicating the parties' claims and defenses. N.D. R. Civ. P. 23(c)(1)(G). The party opposing certification has the burden to present persuasive reasoning showing that the trial court abused its discretion. *Bice*, 2004 ND 113, ¶ 23, 681 N.W.2d 74. When the only remaining controversy is the remedy to be imposed and the parties can obtain the same relief without class certification, then a class action may not be necessary for a fair and efficient adjudication. *Mann*, 2007 ND 119, ¶ 35, 736 N.W.2d 464.

viii. 23(c)(1)(H). A trial court must determine whether class members who are not representative parties have a substantial interest in individually controlling the prosecution or defense of separate actions. N.D. R. Civ. P. 23(c)(1)(H). The party opposing class certification must present persuasive reasoning showing the trial court abused its discretion in weighing and considering factor H. *Bice*, 2004 ND 113, ¶ 23, 681 N.W.2d 74.

ix. 23(c)(1)(K). The trial court must determine whether management of the class poses unusual difficulties. N.D. R. Civ. P. 23(c)(1)(K). The trial court must analyze whether a class action would involve management problems that a court would not encounter in individual litigations involving the same plaintiffs without certification as a class. *Baker,* 2015 ND 57, ¶61, 860 N.W.2d 788. Again, the party opposing certification must present persuasive reasoning showing the trial court abused its discretion in weighing and considering factor K. *Bice*, 2004 ND 113, ¶ 23, 681 N.W.2d 74.

d. 23(b)(2)(C). Fair and Adequate Representation by Representative Parties

The "fair and adequate representation" requirement includes class representatives and class counsel. N.D. R. Civ. P. 23(c)(2)(A)(B) & (C). The court must find that the attorney for the representative parties will adequately represent the interests of the class. N.D. R. Civ. P. 23(c)(2)(A). Even though one of the attorneys for the class was also a class member, the potential for conflict of interest and a possible appearance of impropriety were not sufficient to establish that the trial court abused its discretion in certifying a class. *Bice*, 2004 ND 113, ¶ 27, 681 N.W.2d 74.

Representative parties must not have a conflict of interest in the maintenance of the class and must be able to acquire adequate financial resources to assure that the interests of the class will not be harmed. N.D. R. Civ. P. 23(c)(2)(B) & (C). Research revealed no case where the representative plaintiff's ability to fairly represent the class has been seriously challenged. However, the *Rogelstad* court indicated that the standard is to have representatives who "make the vigorous, conscientious and undivided effort required to fairly and adequately protect the interests of the class." *Rogelstad*, 226 N.W.2d at 375.

When a representative's individual claim becomes moot before a class has been properly certified or before certification has been denied, dismissal of the action is required. *DeCouteau v. Nodak Mutual Insurance*, 2002 ND 182, ¶ 15–17, 636 N.W.2d 432.

3. ORDER CERTIFYING OR DENYING THE CLASS—23(D)

The order certifying or refusing to certify a class action must state the reasons for the court's ruling and the court's findings as to the various criteria. N.D. R. Civ. P. 23(c) & (d)(2); *Holloway*, 294 N.W.2d at 906; *North Dakota Human Rights Coalition*, 2005 ND 98, ¶ 15, 697 N.W.2d 1. The order of certification must describe the class, describe any subclasses, state the relief sought, and provide whether any particular issues are included. *Id.* An order certifying or refusing to certify an action as a class action is appealable. N.D. R. Civ. P. 23(d)(3). The rule permits appeals from what are otherwise nonappealable orders. *Glasow v. E.I. Du Pont de Nemours and Co.*, 2005 ND 94, ¶ 3, 692 N.W.2d 531. Denial of a motion for certification conclusively affects a substantial right and delaying the appeal would render review of the order inadequate. Thus, denial of a motion to certify is immediately appealable. *Rogelstad v. Farmers Union Grain Terminal Ass'n, Inc.*, 224 N.W.2d 544, 548 (N.D. 1974); *Ritter I*, 2000 ND 153, ¶ 3, 605 N.W.2d 153.

4. AMENDMENT OF CERTIFICATION ORDER—23(E)

The court may amend the certification order at any time before entry of judgment on the merits. N.D. R. Civ. P. 23(e)(1). The court has several options for amendment under the rule, including the authority to make any other appropriate change in the order. N.D. R. Civ. P. 23(e)(1)(E). The rule permits the court to amend a certification order by decertifying a previously certified action under the proper circumstances. *Ongstad v. Piper Jaffray & Co.*, 2008 ND 167, ¶ 19, 755 N.W.2d 877.

5. NOTICE OF ACTION—23(G)

Rule 23(g) directs that, after certification, the court shall order notification of the class members. The notification order is required to include the manner and form of notification, taking into consideration the interests of the class, the relief sought, the costs of notification and the possible prejudice to class members who do not receive notice. *Holloway*, 294 N.W.2d at 907. A federal class action judgment was not binding under the due process clause as to North Dakota plaintiffs because safeguards to guarantee sufficient notice and adequate representation were not in fact applied in light of the defendant's concession that "the required individual notice" had not been provided to them. *Palmer v. Gentek Building Products, Inc.*, 2019 ND 306 ¶¶ 21–22, 935 N.W.2d 552.

6. DISCOVERY BY OR AGAINST CLASS MEMBERS—23(J)

Discovery by or against representative parties or those appearing is governed by the rules dealing with discovery in a civil action. N.D. R. Civ. P. 23(j)(3). A court order is required to conduct discovery against a class member who is not a representative party or who has not appeared. N.D. R. Civ. P. 23(j)(1). To permit such discovery, the court considers the timing of the request, the subject matter to be covered, whether representatives of the class are seeking discovery on that subject matter and whether discovery will result in annoyance, oppression or undue burden or expense for the class members. N.D. R. Civ. P. 23(j)(2)(A), (B), (C), (D).

There are no decisions reflecting how pre-certification communications with putative class members may be treated. However, considering the post-certification protections afforded absent class members by Rule 23(j)(1) and (2), the courts may be inclined to limit such communications as necessary.

7. DISMISSAL OR COMPROMISE—23(L)

Unless certification has been denied, a district court may not dismiss any class action without following the procedural requirements of Rule 23(l). A class action may only be "voluntarily dismissed, involuntarily dismissed without adjudication on the merits, or compromised after a hearing and court approval." *Glasow*, 2005 ND 94, ¶¶ 5–7, 696 N.W.2d 531. The court has a duty to investigate the provisions of a suggested settlement agreement, including exploring the manner in which attorneys' fees are to be paid and the dollar amount for such services. *Ritter, Laber and Assoc., Inc. v. Koch Oil*, 2007 ND 163, ¶ 28, 740 N.W.2d 67 (*Ritter IV*).

8. ATTORNEYS' FEES—23(P)

Rule 23(p) states that attorneys' fees for representing a class are subject to control of the court. The district court is considered an expert in determining an award of attorneys' fees, and its decision is reviewed on a clear abuse of discretion standard. *Ritter IV*, 2007 ND 163, ¶ 28, 740 N.W.2d 67. The court must act as a fiduciary for the beneficiaries of a common fund and must consider any claim for attorneys' fees from the common fund as adverse to the interests of the class. *Id.* ¶ 35. Attorneys representing a successful class are entitled to fees from the fund as a whole, not just claimed funds;

however, a factor in determining the size of an attorneys' fees awarded can include the actual monetary distribution to the members of the class. *Id.* ¶¶ 29, 33.

9. TOLLING OF THE STATUTE OF LIMITATIONS—23(R)

The rule specifies that the statute of limitations is tolled for all class members upon the commencement of an action asserting a class action, pending a determination of class action status. N.D. R. Civ. P. 23(r). This portion of the rule codifies the case of *American Pipe and Constr. Co. v. Utah*, 414 U.S. 538 (1974). N.D. R. Civ. P. 23(r) explanatory note.

10. DUE PROCESS PROTECTION

North Dakota Rule 23 provides more due process protections than the federal rule. *Ritter II*, 2001 ND 56, ¶ 23, 623 N.W.2d 424. North Dakota Rule 23 permits mandatory class members to participate in the action under Rule 23(i)(1)(B)(iii). *Id.* Non-representative class members have the right to appear and be represented by separate counsel under 23(i)(2). *Id.* There is no corresponding protection under the federal rule. *Ritter II*, 2001 ND 56, ¶ 23, 623 N.W.2d 424. Rule 23(e)(1)(B) also authorizes courts to "eliminate from the class a member who was included in the class as certified. . . ."

This chapter was prepared by Ian R. McLean, a shareholder in the Serkland Law Firm in Fargo, North Dakota.

OHIO

The seminal case on class certification in the State of Ohio is *Hamilton v. Ohio Savings Bank*, 82 Ohio St. 3d 67 (1998). *Hamilton* redefined the standard for Ohio courts to follow in reviewing the certification question and broadened the scope of class action treatment by encouraging the use of the class action device in the consumer context. 82 Ohio St. 3d at 80.

Following *Hamilton*, the Ohio Supreme Court handed down several cases encouraging class actions. In *Cope v. Metropolitan Life Ins. Co.*, 82 Ohio St. 3d 426 (1998), the court acknowledged the propriety of certification in cases involving claims such as fraud and breach of fiduciary duty despite the need for proof of reliance as an element of such claims. 82 Ohio St. 3d at 435 ("[C]lass action treatment is appropriate where claims arise from standardized forms or routinized procedures, notwithstanding the need to prove reliance."). In *Baughman v. State Farm Mut. Auto. Ins. Co.*, 88 Ohio St. 3d 480 (2000), the court reaffirmed its position that consumer fraud cases are suitable for class treatment by holding that issues related to proof of Ohio reliance will not be destructive of typicality, adequacy, or predominance. 88 Ohio St. 3d at 486–90. In *In re Consol. Mortg. Satisfaction Cases*, 97 Ohio St. 3d 465, 2002-Ohio-6720, the court touted the propriety of the class action device as a means to address repeated or ongoing wrongdoing, irrespective of individual questions or manageability problems that might arise. ("[T]he class action is the preferable method for dealing with evidence of a party's recurring malfeasance because the ability to avoid duplicating a court's time, effort, and resources is an important and relevant consideration.") 97 Ohio St. 3d at 470.

In 2004, the Ohio Supreme Court began a reversal of its favorable treatment of class actions. First, it handed down a pair of decisions disallowing class treatment of mass tort-product liability cases. *See Wilson v. Brush Wellman, Inc.*, 103 Ohio St. 3d 538, 2004-Ohio-4884; *Howland v. Purdue Pharma L.P.*, 104 Ohio St. 3d 584, 2004-Ohio-6552. In 2006, the Court severely limited the ability to bring a class action under the Consumer Sales Practices Act. *See Marrone v. Philip Morris USA, Inc.*, 110 Ohio St. 3d 5, 2006-Ohio-2869 ¶ 2 ("A consumer may qualify for class-action certification under Ohio's CSPA only if the defendant's alleged violation of the Act is substantially similar to an act or practice previously declared to be deceptive by one of the methods identified in R.C. 1345.09(B)."). The Court has subsequently reiterated its stance on this issue and found that a claim seeking class certification that does not sufficiently allege that the act or practice has previously been declared deceptive is subject to dismissal under Ohio R. Civ. Proc. 12(b)(6). *Volbers-Klarich v. Middletown Mgmt.*, 125 Ohio St. 3d 494 (2010).

1. COMPARISON WITH RULE 23 OF THE FEDERAL RULES OF CIVIL PROCEDURE

"Fed. R. Civ. P. 23(a), (b), and (c) are identical to their counterparts in the Ohio rule." *Wilson*, 103 Ohio St. 3d at 542 n.4. As such, it is well settled that "federal authority is an appropriate aid to interpretation of the Ohio rule." *Id. See also Hamilton*, 82 Ohio St. 3d at 82 (quoting *Marks v. C.P. Chemical Co., Inc.*, 31 Ohio St. 3d 200, 201 (1987)); *Vaccariello v. Smith & Nephew Richards, Inc.*,

94 Ohio St. 3d 380, 382, 2002-Ohio-892.

2. STANDARD OF REVIEW

A trial judge has broad discretion in determining whether or not a case may be maintained as a class action. *See Marks*, 31 Ohio St. 3d at 201. However, that discretion "is not unlimited, and indeed is bounded by and must be exercised within the framework of Civ. R. 23. The trial court is required to carefully apply the class action requirements and conduct a rigorous analysis into whether the prerequisites of Civ. R. 23 have been satisfied." *Hamilton*, 82 Ohio St. 3d at 70. However, "a trial court's failure to follow preferred procedures under *Hamilton* to specify facts and reasons for conclusions under Civ. R. 23 as to whether class certification is appropriate does not, by itself, require an appellate court to reverse a judgment on class certification." *Stammco, LLC v. United Telephone Co.*, 6th Dist. Fulton No. F-11-003, 2008-Ohio-3845 ¶ 26; *See Mozingo v. 2007 Gaslight Ohio, LLC,* 9th Dist. Summit Nos. 26164 and 26172, 2012-Ohio-5157 for an example of a trial court going too far in discussing the merits in connection with class certification. In considering newly asserted claims for certification, the trial court may incorporate findings made in an earlier decision on certification. *State ex rel. Merrill v. Ohio Dept. of Natural Resources*, 11th Dist. Lake No. 2012-L-13, 2014-Ohio-1343 ¶ 16.

"In making these determinations, the trial court must not consider the merits of the case, except as necessary to determine whether the Civ. R. 23 requirements are met." *See Walker v. Firelands Community Hosp. (Oct. 5, 2001),* 6th Dist. Erie No. E-01-006, 2001 WL 1198660 (citing *Ojalvo v. Board of Trustees*, 12 Ohio St. 3d 230, 233 (1985)). In fact, "[d]etermining the merits of a claim at the class certification stage constitutes an abuse of discretion." *George v. Ohio Dept. of Human Services*, 145 Ohio App. 3d 681, 687 (10th Dist. 2001). *See also Ass'n for Hosps. & Health Sys. v. Dep't of Human Servs*., 10th Dist. Court of Claims No. 04AP-762, 2006-Ohio-67 ("Indeed, a court abuses its discretion by determining the merits of a claim at the class certification stage."); *Nagel v. The Huntington Nat'l Bank*, 179 Ohio App. 3d 126, 2008-Ohio-5741, ¶ 15 (8th Dist.); *Madyda v. Ohio Dept. of Pub. Safety*, 10th Dist. Franklin No. 20AP-217, 2021-Ohio-956, ¶ 1.

This does not mean, however, that the court cannot examine the merits for the purpose of determining whether the requirements of Rule 23 are satisfied. In *Cullen v. State Farm Mut. Auto. Ins. Co.*, 137 Ohio St. 3d 373, 2013-Ohio-4733, the Ohio Supreme Court adopted the holdings of the U.S. Supreme Court in *Comcast Corp. v. Behrend*, 569 U.S. 27, 133 S. Ct. 1426 (2013), and *Wal-Mart Stores, Inc. v. Dukes*, 564 U.S. 338, 131 S. Ct. 2541 (2011), finding that the trial court may examine the merits of a claim as part of its rigorous analysis, "but only to the extent necessary to determine whether the requirement of the rule is satisfied." 2013-Ohio-4733 ¶17.

"The party pursuing certification of a class action bears the burden of showing, by a preponderance of the evidence, that the prerequisites set forth in Civ. R. 23(A) are present, and that the action falls within one of the categories of Civ. R. 23(B)." *Grant v. Becton Dickinson & Co.*, 10th Dist. Franklin No. 02-AP-894, 2003-Ohio-2826 ¶ 23 (citing *State ex rel. Ogan v. Teater*, 54 Ohio St. 2d 235 (1978)). *See also Warner v. Waste Mgmt., Inc.,* 36 Ohio St. 3d 91, 94 (1988). Any doubts about satisfaction of the specific elements of Rule 23 "should be resolved in favor of upholding the class, subject to the trial court's authority to amend or adjust its certification order as developing circumstances demand, including the augmentation or substitution of representative parties." *See Baughman*, 88 Ohio St. 3d at 487 (2000).

"Generally, an evidentiary hearing is unnecessary for a trial court to be able to determine whether class certification is warranted. However, in those cases where the facts related to class issues are disputed, a hearing should be conducted." *Ritt v. Billy Blanks Enterprises*, 8th Dist. Cuyahoga No. 80983 2003-Ohio-3645. *See also Warner,* 36 Ohio St. 3d at 99. At least one appellate court has concluded that trial courts are permitted to issue class certification decisions without a pending motion, hearing or making the requisite findings of fact; however, "[t]his is only proper where the factual information set forth in the pleadings is detailed enough to enable the trial judge to make a class certification decision by a preponderance of the evidence." *Ward v. NationsBanc Mortg. Corp.*, 6th Dist. Erie No. E-05-040 2006-Ohio-2766 ¶ 34; *Black v. Dutiel, 5th Dist. Perry No. 10-CA3*, 2010-Ohio-4626, ¶ 17.

The Ohio Supreme Court has strongly encouraged trial courts to make specific findings as to each prerequisite of Civ. R. 23 and to specify the reasoning as to each of these findings. *See Hamilton,* 82 Ohio St. 3d at 71 ("the failure to provide an articulated rationale greatly hampers an appellate inquiry into whether the relevant Civ. R. 23 factors were properly applied by the trial court and given appropriate weight, and such an unarticulated decision is less likely to convince the reviewing court that the ruling was consistent with the sound exercise of discretion"). Increasingly, appellate courts are overturning the grant or denial of class certification, citing the trial court's failure to specify the reasons for such determination. *See, e.g., Maas v. The Penn Central Corp.,* 11th Dist. Trumbull No. 2003-T-00123 2004-Ohio-7233; *Robinson v. Johnston Coca-Cola Bottling Group, Inc.*, 153 Ohio App. 3d 764 (1st Dist. 2003). The Ohio Supreme Court recently commented that it could not overturn a trial court's class determination in the face of a detailed and thoughtful written analysis of the elements of Civ. R. 23. *See Wilson*, 103 Ohio St. 3d at 545; *Howland*, 104 Ohio St. 3d at 588.

An appellate court reviews a decision to strike class allegations for an abuse of discretion. *Baker v. Gulfport Energy Corp.*, 2020-Ohio-4825, ¶ 13.

3. REQUIREMENTS OF CIVIL RULE 23

In *Warner*, 36 Ohio St. 3d 91, the Ohio Supreme Court held that a trial judge must make seven affirmative findings before certifying a case as a class action. Two of the prerequisites are implicitly required by Civ. R. 23; the other five requirements are specifically enumerated in the rule.

a. Implied Requirements

i. Identifiable class. The first implied prerequisite is that an identifiable class must exist based on an unambiguous class definition. "[T]he requirement that there be a class will not be deemed satisfied unless the description of it is sufficiently definite so that it is administratively feasible for the court to determine whether a particular individual is a member." *Hamilton*, 82 Ohio St. 3d at 71–72. Actual identification of individual class members is not required, but "the class definition must be precise enough 'to permit identification within a reasonable effort.'" *Id.* A definition may fail the "reasonable effort" test if manual searching through thousands of files will be required to identify class members, *Margulies v. Guardian Life Ins. Co., 8th Dist. Cuyahoga No. 88056*, 2007-Ohio-1601, or if it is not administratively feasible to identify those who were injured by the challenged conduct, *Fowler v. The Ohio Edison, 7th Dist. Jefferson No. 07-JE-21*, 2008-Ohio-6587. In contrast, one Ohio appellate court has held that a defendant's claim that it would have to manually search 17,000 loan records in order to identify class members would not preclude certification absent evidence that the search could not be done within a reasonable time period. *Wachovia Nat'l Bank of Del., NA v. Ball*, 6th Dist. Huron No. H-08-022, 2010-Ohio-1479 ¶ 26.

"The test of class identifiability is whether means are specified at the time of the certification that will permit a determination whether a particular individual is a member of the class." *Petty v.*

Wal-Mart Stores, Inc., 148 Ohio App. 3d 348, 354 (2d Dist. 2002). Generally, this includes "a time frame, a place, and the specific conduct for which the class members seek redress." *Walker*, 2001 WL 1198660, at *5 (Ohio App. Oct. 5, 2001). Per the Ohio Supreme Court, a class is appropriately defined by reference to the defendant's conduct. *See Hamilton,* 82 Ohio St. 3d at 73. *See also Washington v. Spitzer Mgmt.*, 8th Dist. Cuyahoga No. 81612, 2003-Ohio-1735 ¶ 17; *Gordon v. Erie Islands Resort & Marina*, 2016-Ohio-7107, 76 N.E.3d 455, ¶ 33 (6th Dist.), *appeal not allowed,* 149 Ohio St. 3d 1432, 2017-Ohio-4396, 76 N.E.3d 1208, ¶ 33 (2017).

A proper class definition will include the period of time during which class members were harmed, *Jacobs v. First Merit Corp.,* 11th Dist. Lake No. 2013-L-012, 2013-Ohio-4308 ¶ 31, and refer to the causal connection between the alleged misconduct and the damage to the class, *Id.* at ¶ 34. *But see Rimmer v. Citifinancial, Inc.,* 8th Dist. Cuyahoga No. 99760, 2013-Ohio-5732 ¶ 46 ("[A]n end date in the class definition is not required in this case."). However, a class may include those whose claims are outside the statute of limitations, as that argument is not relevant to class certification. *Bowen v. Farmers Ins. Co., 8th Dist. Cuyahoga No. 105643*, 2018-Ohio-1638, ¶ 22.

A class definition that requires the court to examine the merits of individual claims to determine inclusion in the class is not sufficiently definite. *See Bungard v. Ohio Dep't of Job & Family Servs.*, 10th Dist. Franklin No. 05AP-43, 2006-Ohio-429. Similarly, a class definition that includes those who were charged for services "without their permission" is unacceptable because it requires an individual inquiry into whether permission was actually given. *Stammco, L.L.C. v. United Tel. Co.*, 125 Ohio St. 3d 91 (2010). A class that includes those who "attempted" to purchase a car is also defective due to the inability to definitively define "attempted." *Konarzewski v. Ganley, Inc., 8th Dist. Cuyahoga No. 92623*, 2009-Ohio-5827. A class that includes those who were "denied" an advertised car wash is similarly defective due to the need to determine, on an individual basis, which class members actually wanted the car wash, chose the defendant's business because of the advertised free car wash, and did not receive a car wash. *Clark v. Park 'n Fly*, 8th Dist. Cuyahoga No. 94379, 2011-Ohio-323, ¶ 22-P23. The court is not required to specify the method by which class members will be identified in its certification decision. *Radatz v. Fannie Mae,* 176 Ohio App. 3d 319 (8th Dist. 2008).

A class defined with respect to the central liability question (sometimes referred to as a "fail-safe" class or one-way intervention) will not be certified because of the necessity of holding "mini-hearings" on the merits of the action to determine class membership. *Cicero v. U.S. Four, Inc.,* 10th Dist. Franklin No. 07AP-310, 2007-Ohio- 6600 ¶ 28 (10th Dist. 2007). To determine whether a proposed definition creates a "fail-safe" class, the "court must decide whether the class would still exist if the defendant in the class action prevails at trial." *Miller v. Volkswagen of Am., Inc.,* 6th Dist. Erie No. E-07047, 2008-Ohio-4736 ¶ 28. "The class definition should not incorporate contested elements of liability; otherwise, class membership depends on whether the member has a valid claim on the merits." *Cach v. Young*, 7th Dist. Mahoning Nos. 15 MA 0176, 15 MA 0177, 2021-Ohio-4638, ¶ 34. *But see Burns v. Spitzer Mgmt.,* 190 Ohio App. 3d 365, 373 (8th Dist. 2010), finding a definition which "limits the class to all consumers who were allegedly charged a fee in violation of the CSPA" proper.

To the extent a trial court finds that an identifiable class does not exist under the proposed class definition, it should, *sua sponte*, modify the definition. *See Ritt,* 2003-Ohio-3645, ¶ 20 ("*Warner* not only permits but encourages the trial court to modify what is otherwise an unidentifiable class."). *See also Baughman*, 88 Ohio St. 3d at 483–84 (class definition modified by Ohio Supreme Court). In fact, "[t]he failure of the trial court to modify the class itself or to allow plaintiffs to modify it constitutes an abuse of discretion and thus a reversible error." *Ritt, supra*, 2003-Ohio-3645 ¶ 22. However, at least one court has suggested, citing *Ritt*, that a plaintiff's failure to propose an alternate definition may relieve the trial court of its responsibility. *Clark*, 2011-Ohio-323, ¶ 28.

A class composed of members who signed differing agreements with the defendant only poses challenges to class identification when the definition is overly broad. *Goree v. Northland Auto Ents.*, 8th Dist. Cuyahoga No. 108881, 2020-Ohio-3457, ¶ 49, citing *Cantlin v. Smythe Cramer Co.*, 2018-Ohio-4607, ¶ 19, 114 N.E.3d 1260 (8th Dist.).

ii. Membership in the class. The second implied prerequisite is that the class representatives must be members of the class as defined. "The class membership prerequisite requires only that 'the representative have proper standing. In order to have standing to sue as a class representative, the plaintiff must possess the same interest and suffer the same injury shared by all members of the class that he or she seeks to represent.'" *Hamilton*, 82 Ohio St. 3d at 74 (quoting 5 *Moore's Federal Practice* (3d ed. 1997), 23–57, Section 23.2[1]). *See also Pyles v. Johnson*, 143 Ohio App. 3d 720, 732 (4th Dist. 2001); *In re Rogers Litig.*, 6th Dist. Sandusky No. S-02-042, 2003-Ohio-5976 ¶ 21 (anonymity of class representatives does not affect standing).

A risk of future harm, or the cost of preventing future harm, is too hypothetical to confer standing. *Jones v. Ohio Bureau of Workers' Comp., Court of Claims No. 2010-09990*, 2011-Ohio-1855, ¶ 10. Likewise, what a court termed an "informational injury" to the class that occurred where the defendant classified shareholder distributions as dividends rather than a return of capital was insufficient to confer standing on the class representative where there was no evidence that all class members suffered an injury in fact. *Estate of Mikulski v. Toledo Edison Co.*, 6th Dist. Lucas, No. L-19-1019, 2021-Ohio-361, ¶ 34.

There is no requirement that each member of the class be able to demonstrate standing. *Rimedio v. SummaCare, Inc., 9th Dist. Summit No. 25068*, 2010-Ohio-5555, ¶¶ 43–46. The *Rimedio* court discusses at length cases in which a class has been certified despite the possibility that certain class members may not have suffered any injury.

A 2016 decision from the Ohio Supreme Court effectively overruled *Rimedio* on this point. In *Felix v. Ganley Chevrolet, Inc.*, 145 Ohio St. 3d 329, 2015-Ohio-3430, the class was defined to include those who purchased an automobile through a purchase contract containing an unconscionable arbitration provision. The Supreme Court held that the class as defined failed because there was no showing that each class member suffered an injury in fact. *Id.* at ¶ 37. While the Court did limit its holding to claims under Ohio's Consumer Sales Practices Act, subsequent appellate court decisions have interpreted *Felix* to hold that the class representative must establish that all class members have suffered a concrete injury. *Estate of Mikulski* at ¶ 34; *Estate of Mikulski v. Centerior Energy Corp.*, 8th Dist. No. 107108, 2019-Ohio-983, 133 N.E.3d 899, ¶ 45 and *Ford Motor Credit Co. v. Agrawal*, 8th Dist. No. 103667, 2016-Ohio-5928, 71 N.E.3d 671, ¶ 28.

An association has standing to bring suit on behalf of its members in specified instances. *See Ass'n for Hosps. & Health Sys.*, 10th Dist. Franklin Nos. 04AP-762 and 04-AP-763, 2006-Ohio-67.

b. Civil Rule 23(A)

i. Numerosity. Civil Rule 23(A)(1) requires that the class be "so numerous that joinder of all class members is impracticable." Civ. R. 23(A)(1). Ohio courts generally determine numerosity by examining the number of potential class members; "the number alone is sufficient to establish that the class is so numerous that joinder of all members is impracticable." *See Hamilton*, 82 Ohio St. 3d at 82. "The complaint need not allege an exact number of class members or individually identify class members to satisfy the numerosity requirement. A finding of sufficient numerosity can be based on common sense assumption." *Martin v. Services Corp. International*, 2001 WL 688896, at

*3 (Ohio App. June 20, 2001). *See also In re Rogers Litig.*, 2003–Ohio-5976 ¶ 23 ("a trial court is permitted to make common sense assumptions in order to find support for numerosity"). However, plaintiffs must ordinarily show some evidence or a reasonable estimate of the number of class members in order to satisfy this element. *See Williams v. Countrywide Home Loans, Inc.*, 2002 WL 31270283, at *3 (Ohio App. Mar. 12, 2003).

Evidence of a class of more than forty people is generally held to satisfy the numerosity requirement. *See Warner*, 36 Ohio St. 3d at 97. However, there are no specified numerical limits. In fact, subclasses have been certified with as few as twenty-three class members. *See, e.g., Marks*, 31 Ohio St. 3d 200. *But see Adkins-Bagola v. Universal Nursing Services*, 9th Dist. Summit No. 22033, 2004-Ohio-6082 (class of ten members fails numerosity test); *Black*, 2010-Ohio-4626, ¶¶ 24–25 (class of twenty-eight members fails numerosity test). At least one recent decision has held that the number must be limited to those actually harmed by defendant's conduct. *George v. R. Good Logistics, LLC*, 12th Dist. Preble Nos. CA2012-06-008, CA2012-06-009, and CA2012-06-010, 2013-Ohio-16 ¶ 26.

Finally, the Ohio Supreme Court has held that the value of the individual claims is a factor that may make joinder impracticable. *See Hamilton,* 82 Ohio St. 3d at 75. Specifically, the court reasoned that class members with small claims could not afford to file separate actions, thereby weighing in favor of certifying the class. *Cf., Shipp v. Norton Outdoor Advertising, Inc.*, 1st Dist. Hamilton No. C-210150, 2022-Ohio-216).

The *Hamilton* court further ruled that "the lack of parallel individual actions is not a bar to a finding of impracticability." *Hamilton,* 82 Ohio St. 3d at 75. However, at least one court has refused to follow this rule. *See Podany v. Real Estate Mort. Corp. Escrow Co.*, 1999 WL 1204849 (Ohio App. Dec. 16, 1999) (affirmed denial of certification finding that plaintiff failed to show numerosity since no other consumer complained of alleged wrongdoing).

ii. Commonality. "The test for commonality under Civ. R. 23(A) is typically met without difficulty." *Howland*, 104 Ohio St. 3d at 587. Courts are instructed to give commonality a permissive application. *See Hamilton*, 82 Ohio St. 3d at 82. "It is important to note that this provision does not demand that all the questions of law or fact raised in the dispute be common to all the parties." *Marks*, 31 Ohio St. 3d at 202. *See also Pyles*, 143 Ohio App. 3d at 733. Rather, commonality will exist if there is a common nucleus of operative facts or a common liability issue. *See Marks*, 31 Ohio St. 3d at 202. "The issue of whether there are any additional questions affecting only individual class members does not enter the class certification analysis until the Civ. R. 23(B)(3) requirement of predominance and superiority is applied." *Hamilton*, 82 Ohio St. 3d at 77. *See also Pyles,* 143 Ohio App. 3d at 733.

iii. Typicality. Typicality requires that the party moving for class certification establish that the claims or defenses of the representative parties are typical of the claims or defenses of the class. "However, typicality does not require an exact identity of claims." *See Baughman*, 88 Ohio St. 3d at 485. Typicality will be met even though not all claims or defenses apply to all class members. "[A] plaintiff's claim is typical if it arises from the same event or practice or course of conduct that gives rise to the claims of other class members, and if his or her claims are based on the same legal theory." *Baughman,* 88 Ohio St. 3d at 485; *Konarzewski v. Ganley, Inc.,* 8th Dist. Cuyahoga No. 92623, 2009-Ohio-5827. The fact that some of the named representative's claims may ultimately be time-barred does not destroy typicality. *Maas,* 2007-Ohio-2055 ¶ 60. Nor does individual settlement with one of the originally named defendants. *Ritt v. Billy Blanks Enterprises*, 171 Ohio App. 3d. 204 (8th Dist. 2007). Nor does the fact that the class representative was able to pass on the cost of challenged overcharges to its own customers. *Satterfield v. Ameritech Mobile Communications, Inc.*, 2017-Ohio-928, ¶ 26 (8th Dist. Cuyahoga).

"The requirement of typicality serves the purpose of protecting absent class members and promotes the economy of class action by ensuring that the interests of the named plaintiffs are substantially aligned with those of the class." *Washington,* 2003-Ohio-1735 ¶ 23 (citing *Baughman,* 88 Ohio St. 3d at 484). This purpose is met when no express conflict exists between the class representatives and the rest of the class. *See Hamilton*, 82 Ohio St. 3d at 82. A unique defense will not destroy typicality unless the defense threatens to preoccupy the class representative to the detriment of other class members. *Id.* at 77. *See also Baughman,* 88 Ohio St. 3d at 486 ("[D]efenses asserted against a class representative should not make his or her claims atypical. Defenses may affect the individual's ultimate right to recover, but they do not affect the presentation of the case on the liability issues for the plaintiff class."). "[A]bsent a serious discrepancy between the position of the representatives and that of the class, the focus of typicality should remain on the essential conforming characteristics of the defendant's actions and the claims arising therefrom." *Martin v. Grange Mutual Ins. Co.*, 11th Dist. Geauga No. 2004—G-2558, 2004-Ohio-6950 ¶ 23. "A unique defense will not destroy typicality unless it is so central to the litigation that it threatens to occupy the class representative to the detriment of the other class members." *Pevets v. Crain Communs., Inc.,* 11th Dist. Ottawa No. 01-10-023, 2011-Ohio-2700. *See also Estate of Reed v. Hadley*, 163 Ohio App. 3d 464 (4th Dist. 2005).

iv. Adequacy of representation. In Ohio, courts traditionally view the adequacy of representation requirement as a two-pronged test. The first prong involves whether the class representative is adequate. The second is whether the designated class counsel is adequate.

A class representative is adequate if his or her interests are not antagonistic to the interests of the other class members. *See, e.g., Warner*, 36 Ohio St. 3d at 98; *Marks*, 31 Ohio St. 3d at 202–03. *See also In re Rogers Litig.*, 2003-Ohio-5976 ¶ 36 (anonymity of class representatives did not affect adequacy to represent class). "A unique defense will not destroy adequacy of representation unless it is so central to the litigation that it threatens to preoccupy the class representative to the detriment of the other class members." *Martin v. Grange Mutual Ins. Co.*, 2004-Ohio-6950 ¶ 33. Likewise, the representative's decision to forego pursuit of some forms of damages that may be available does not render him or her inadequate. *Brandow v. Wash. Mut. Bank,* 8th Dist. Cuyahoga No. 88816, 2008-Ohio-1714 ¶ 27. A class representative whose claim is barred by the statute of limitations is not, by definition, a member of the class and is therefore inadequate. *Mozingo v. 2007 Gaslight Ohio, LLC,* 9th Dist. Summit Nos. 26164 and 26172, 2012-Ohio-5157, ¶ 14.

While the Ohio Supreme Court has not affirmatively decided whether the class representative's inability to finance the litigation renders the class representative inadequate, the court has suggested that if class counsel is able to finance the litigation, "there is no basis for inquiry into [the class representative's] personal finances." *See Hamilton,* 82 Ohio St. 3d at 79. In addition, Ohio's Disciplinary Rules allow reimbursement of any advancement made by class counsel to be contingent upon a successful recovery from the defendant. *See* Ohio Rules of Professional Conduct 1.5.

The trial court should also examine whether the attorneys designated as class counsel are qualified to conduct the kind of litigation being brought. *See Warner,* 36 Ohio St. 3d at 98 ("An attorney should be experienced in handling litigation of the type involved in the case before class certification is allowed."). Courts have affirmed the adequacy of counsel where it appears that "the litigation has proceeded in an orderly and ordinary fashion and the litigation has in no way suffered from lack of [counsel's] experience or funds." *See Walker,* 2001 WL 1198660, at *4. As one court noted, "the better rule is that in the absence of evidence that counsel is unable to handle complex litigation, there is no need for the trial court to require significant evidence of counsel's ability." *Blankenship v. CFMOTO Powersports, Inc.,* 166 Ohio Misc. 2d 21, 41 (Ohio C.P. 2011) (citing *Lasson v. Coleman*, 2d Dist. Montgomery No. 21524, 2007-Ohio-3443, ¶ 42).

The appointment of a deceased person as class representative is an abuse of discretion. *Winrod v. City of Lorain*, 9th Dist. Lorain No. 19CA011503, 2020-Ohio-157, ¶ 9.

c. Civil Rule 23(B)

To certify a class, one of the following three subsections of Civ. R. 23(B) must also be met. *See Hamilton*, 82 Ohio St. 3d at 71.

i. Civil Rule 23(B)(1)(a) and 23(B)(1)(b). Civ. R. 23(B)(1)(a) is satisfied if separate actions by individual class members could result in the defendant being forced to comply with incompatible standards of conduct. A class action that primarily seeks to recover monetary damages is inappropriate for certification pursuant to Civ. R. 23(B)(1)(a) because incompatible standards of conduct do not arise when the defendant is forced to pay damages in one case but not in another. *See Warner*, 36 Ohio St. 3d at 95. Nor does it arise where the court is asked to determine the legality of a standard form contract. *Toy v. Mazza,* 11th Dist. Trumbull No. 2007-T-0028, 2007-Ohio-6406 at ¶ 30. In contrast, the Ohio Supreme Court determined that Rule 23(B)(1)(A) certification was appropriate in a defendant class action where the plaintiff was seeking to restrict picketers; the court affirmed certification because individual trials could result in different and incompatible standards of conduct. *See Planned Parenthood Ass'n v. Project Jericho*, 52 Ohio St. 3d 56, 66 (1990).

In Ohio, Civ. R. 23(B)(1)(b) is recognized as a basis for certification if the funds available to satisfy all the class claims are insufficient. *See Warner,* 36 Ohio St. 3d at 95; *Planned Parenthood Ass'n,* 52 Ohio St. 3d at 66. "This section applies where only a limited amount of money is available and there is a risk that separate actions would deplete the fund before all deserving parties could make a claim." *Gottlieb v. City of South Euclid*, 157 Ohio App. 3d 250, 259 (8th Dist. 2004). "To satisfy Civ. R. 23(B)(1)(b), class action plaintiffs must, *inter alia*, establish, by specific evidence, that the total of the aggregated liquidated claims and the fund available for satisfying them, set definitely at the maximum, demonstrate the inadequacy of the fund to pay all claims." *In re Rogers Litig.*, 2003-Ohio-5976 ¶ 41. "The fact that the parties might agree to the amount of the fund and its inadequacy is insufficient." *Id.*

ii. Civil Rule 23(B)(2). Civ. R. 23(B)(2) provides for class actions where "the party opposing the class has acted or refused to act on grounds generally applicable to the class, thereby making appropriate final injunctive relief or corresponding declaratory relief respect to the class as a whole." Civ. R. 23(B)(2). A Civ. R. 23(B)(2) class has two distinct requirements that must be established. *See Wilson*, 103 Ohio St. 3d at 541.

First, "the action must seek primarily injunctive relief." *Wilson*, 103 Ohio St. 3d at 541. *See also Marks*, 31 Ohio St. 3d at 203 (injunctive relief under Civ. R. 23(B)(2) is inappropriate where primary relief sought is damages). Class certification is not precluded by the fact that money damages are sought in addition to injunctive relief. *See Hamilton*, 82 Ohio St. 3d at 86–87. *See also Santos v. Ohio Bureau of Workers Comp.*, 101 Ohio St. 3d 74, (2004) (distinguishing suit for money damages from equitable action for restitution which may include judgment for money). A finding that a class action can be maintained under Civ. R. 23(B)(3) may make it unnecessary to determine whether a class action can be maintained under Civ. R. 23(B)(2). *Konarzewski v. Ganley, Inc.*, 8th Dist. Cuyahoga No. 92623, 2009-Ohio-5827, ¶ 33. In *Cullen v. State Farm Mut. Auto. Ins. Co.*, 137 Ohio St. 3d 373 (2013), the Supreme Court noted that *Hamilton* does not allow the trial court to dispense with a rigorous analysis of whether the equitable relief sought is merely incidental to damage claims. The court went on to hold that declaratory relief that "lay[s] a foundation for subsequent determinations regarding liability or that facilitate an award of damages do not meet the requirement for certification" under (B)(2).

The Ohio Supreme Court has cautioned that "[d]isputes over whether the action is primarily for injunctive or declaratory relief rather than a monetary award neither promote the disposition of the case on the merits nor represent a useful expenditure of energy. Therefore, they should be avoided. If the Rule 23([A]) prerequisites have been met and injunctive or declaratory relief has been requested, the action usually should be allowed to proceed under subdivision ([B])(2)." *Hamilton*, 82 Ohio St. 3d at 86–87. *See also Williams v. Countrywide Home Loans, Inc.*, 6th Dist. Lucas No. L-01-1473, 2002-Ohio-5499 ¶ 38; *Asset Acceptance LLC v. Caszatt*, 11th Dist. Lake No. 2009-L-90, 2010-Ohio-1449.

Second, "the class must be cohesive." *Wilson*, 103 Ohio St. 3d at 541. In other words, "[a]lthough division (B)(2), unlike division (B)(3), contains no specific [predominance] requirement . . . it does require that a proposed class have sufficient unity so that final injunctive relief is appropriate 'with respect to the class as a whole.'" *Id.* at 547; *See also Reed Estate v. Hadley*, 4th Dist. Washington No. 06CA14, 2007-Ohio-5462 ¶ 24. In *Cullen,* the Supreme Court seems to have clarified that for "unity" to exist, the conduct must be unlawful "as to all of the class members or none of them." 2013-Ohio-4733 ¶25. *See also Cirino v. Ohio Bur. of Worker's Comp.*, 2016-Ohio-8323, 75 N.E.3d 965, ¶ 84 (8th Dist.).

"Where individual issues predominate under Civ. R. 23(b)(3), those same issues will make it impossible for a court to find that a party opposing class certification has acted on grounds generally applicable to the class." *Haas v. Behr Dayton Thermal Prod. LLC,* 2d Dist. Montgomery No. 21586, 2007-Ohio-571 ¶38. Where the class members have individual views of the severity and pervasiveness of the alleged conduct, the class is not cohesive. *Harrison v. Johnston Coca-Cola Bottling Group,* 1st Dist. Hamilton No. C-070665, 2008-Ohio-3572.

iii. Civil Rule 23(B)(3). "Civ. R. 23(B)(3) states that in order to certify a class in an action for damages, two findings must be made by the trial court. First, it must find that questions of law or fact common to the members of the class predominate over any questions affecting only individual members; and second, the court must find that a class action is superior to other available methods for the fair and efficient adjudication of the controversy." *In re Consol. Mortg. Satisfaction Cases*, 97 Ohio St. 3d at 467 (2002).

Predominance. "A predominance inquiry is far more demanding than the Civ. R. 23(A) commonality requirement and focuses on the legal or factual questions that qualify each class member's case as a genuine controversy." *Hoang v. E*Trade Group, Inc.*, 151 Ohio App. 3d 363, 368 (8th Dist. 2003). To establish predominance, "it is not sufficient that common questions merely exist; rather, the common questions must represent a significant aspect of the case and they must be able to be resolved for all members of the class in a single adjudication." *Howland*, 104 Ohio St. 3d at 587. Nonetheless, "[t]he purpose of Civ. R. 23(B)(3) was to bring within the fold of maintainable class actions cases in which the efficiency and economy of common adjudication outweigh the interests of individual autonomy." *Hamilton*, 82 Ohio St. 3d at 80. *See also Blumenthal v. Medina Supply Co.*, 139 Ohio App. 3d 283, 292, (8th Dist. 2000). Thus, "[p]redominance is a test readily met in certain cases alleging consumer or securities fraud or violations of the antitrust laws." *See Baughman*, 88 Ohio St. 3d at 489. *See also Holznagel v. Charter One Bank, FSB*, 2000 WL 1844780 (Ohio App. Dec. 14, 2000).

Common issues predominate when class claims can be established by common proof. *See Cope*, 82 Ohio St. 3d at 436 (court abused discretion in failing to certify class where misrepresentations and fraud claims involved form documents, standardized practices and procedures, common omissions, and wide-spread scheme). "It is not enough that some common questions exist; the common question must form a 'significant part' of the case, and it must be possible to resolve these common questions for all members in a single adjudication." *See Walker*, 2001 WL 1198660, at *5 (citing *Schmidt v. Avco Corp.*, 15 Ohio St. 3d 310, 313 (1984)). If the moving party cannot establish a common scheme or the court must examine the individual circumstances of each class member, individual class issues will predominate over the common ones. *See Cope,* 82 Ohio St. 3d at 435. *See also Hinkston v. Sunstar Acceptance Corp.*, 2000 WL 1886388 (Ohio App. Dec. 29, 2000); *Schmidt*, 15 Ohio St. 3d at 314. That having been said, the Ohio Supreme Court has cautioned that "[t]he mere existence of different facts associated with the various members of a proposed class is not by itself a bar to certification of that class. If it were, then a great majority of motions for class certification would be denied. Civ. R. 23(B)(3) gives leeway in this regard and permits class certification where there are facts common to the class members." *In re Consol. Mortg. Satisfaction Cases*, 97 Ohio St. 3d at 468. If generalized evidence exists that proves the claim on a class-wide basis, then the predominance element is satisfied irrespective of differences in the underlying facts. *See also Estate of Reed*, 163 Ohio App. 3d 464.

Ohio courts must not engage in a time analysis of individual versus common questions since proof of individual issues may often be more time-consuming than proof of the common ones. *See Hamilton,* 82 Ohio St. 3d at 85 ("[a] court should not 'determine predominance by comparing the time that the common issues can be anticipated to consume in the litigation to the time that individual issues will require. Otherwise, only the most complex common questions could predominate since such issues tend to require more time to litigate than less complex issues."). Generally, predominance is shown "when there exists generalized evidence which proves or disproves an element on a simultaneous, class-wide basis since such proof obviates the need to examine each class member's individual position." *See Baughman,* 88 Ohio St. 3d at 489; *Pevets*, 2011-Ohio-2700, ¶ 17. As one court recently noted, "[it] is not simply a matter of numbering the questions in the case, labeling them as common or diverse, and then counting up. It involves a sophisticated and necessarily judgmental appraisal of the future course of the litigation." *Estate of Mikulski v. Centerior Energy Corp., 8th Dist. Cuyahoga No. 94536*, 2011-Ohio-696, ¶ 12 (citations omitted).

Notably, the Ohio Supreme Court has held that if all the elements of Civ. R. 23(A) have been fulfilled, certification should not be denied based on an overly narrow construction of Civ. R. 23(B)(3). *See Ojalvo*, 12 Ohio St. 3d 230. Neither disparate damages nor a statute of limitations defense should destroy a finding of predominance. *See Hamilton,* 82 Ohio St. 3d at 81, 84; *Pyles,* 143 Ohio App. 3d at 732 and 739 ("The fact that some class members may be entitled to different relief than the representatives does not mean that their claims are not typical or that there is a conflict between the representatives and the class. . . ." Likewise, the fact that a statute of limitations may bar the claims of some, but not all, class members does not compel a finding that individual issues predominate over common ones."). *See also Estate of Reed,* 163 Ohio App. 3d at 477 (while the amount of damages will differ, "it is unreasonable to conclude that the class as a whole did not or will not suffer damages if [the class] successfully proves its claims").

Similarly, "[t]he fact that potential class members live in different states is not sufficient in and of itself to warrant the denial of class certification." *Simmons v. American Gen. Life & Accident Ins. Co.*, 140 Ohio App. 3d 503, 511 (6th Dist. 2000). While choice of law questions may impact whether common questions of law predominate, "when courts are faced with common-law state claims such as fraud, negligent misrepresentation, and negligence, they have expressed doubts that differences in state laws are so great as to preclude class treatment." *Carder Buick-Olds v. Reynolds & Reynolds, Inc.*, 148 Ohio App. 3d 635, 651 (2d Dist. 2002).

Superiority. "In determining whether a class action is a superior method of adjudication, the court must make a comparative evaluation of the other processes available to determine whether a class action is sufficiently effective to justify the expenditure of judicial time and energy involved therein." *In re Consol. Mortg. Satisfaction Cases*, 97 Ohio St. 3d at 467–68. "The key to Civ. R. 23(B)(3), 'should be whether the efficiency and economy of common adjudication outweigh the difficulties and complexity of individual treatment of class members' claims.'" *Washington,* 2003-Ohio-1735 ¶ 50 (quoting *Carder Buick-Olds*, 148 Ohio App. 3d at 649). In making this determination, the trial court should consider each of the four factors enumerated in Civil Rule 23(B)(3). *In re Consol. Mortg. Satisfaction Cases*, 97 Ohio St. 3d at 469. "Analysis of these factors ensures that the policy objectives of Civ. R. 23(B) are given weight and permits a court to balance the efficiency and economy of the class action device against the need to ensure the fair representation of the interests of otherwise unrelated entities." *Id.*

When evaluating the utility and propriety of class treatment, Ohio courts focus on the ability of a class action to permit people with small claims to have their day in court. *See Hamilton*, 82 Ohio St. 3d at 86–87. However, the fact that some class members may receive significant recoveries does not preclude certification. *Asset Acceptance LLC*, 2010-Ohio-1449.

A party's ability to spread the cost of an action over a class of individuals to more readily attack a defendant's wrongdoing is a persuasive argument that weighs in favor of certification. *See In re Consol. Mortg. Satisfaction Cases*, 97 Ohio St. 3d at 469. Similarly, "[t]he *presence* of parallel, individual actions tend to weigh *against* class certification, while the *lack* of parallel lawsuits tends to weigh in *favor* of certification." *Hamilton,* 82 Ohio St. 3d at 81 (emphasis in original). Finally, courts should recognize that there will be some difficulties incurred in the management of any class action. *See In re Consol. Mortg. Satisfaction Cases*, 97 Ohio St. 3d at 469. However, "the ability to avoid duplicating a court's time, effort, and resources is an important and relevant consideration" supporting certification. *Id.* at 470; *See also Strickler v. First Ohio Banc & Lending, Inc.*, 9th Dist. Lorain No. 12CA010178, 2013-Ohio-1221, ¶ 20 (rejecting an argument that a class action was not superior because it would require "mini-trials" where defendant did not explain how individual lawsuits would be more efficient). But in those instances "where an individual plaintiff, or a small group of plaintiffs, can obtain relief for the greater whole—certifying a class is an unnecessary expenditure of court time and energy." *Frisch's Rest., Inc. v. Kielmeyer*, 10th Dist. Franklin No. 05AP-412, 2005-Ohio-5426 ¶ 23. *See also State ex. rel. Davis v. Public Emples. Ret. Bd.*, 10th Dist. Franklin No. 04AP-1293, 2005-Ohio-6612.

In *State ex rel. Davis v. Public Employees Retirement Bd.,* 111 Ohio St. 3d 118 (2006), the Court added another factor to the Rule 23(b)(3) superiority analysis—whether there is a "need" for a class action. In a unanimous opinion, the court found that where an individual judgment would apply to all potential class members, a class action is unnecessary. In *San Allen, Inc. v. Buehrer*, 8th Dist. Cuyahoga No. 94651, 2011-Ohio-1676, ¶¶ 17–18, the court listed several decisions in which this analysis has been used, including *Frisch's Rest., Inc.,* 2005-Ohio-5426; *Smith v. State Teachers Retirement Bd.*, 1998 Ohio App. LEXIS 403; and *State ex rel. Horvath v. State Teachers Retirement Bd.,* 1995 Ohio App. LEXIS 1292. The *San Allen* court declined to apply the rule in the case before it, however, finding it inapplicable in cases where the requested relief will not automatically inure to class members.

4. NOTICE TO CLASS MEMBERS

Ohio follows the standard for class notice adopted by the United States Supreme Court in Eisen v. Carlisle & Jacquelin, 417 U.S. 156 (1974). Specifically, individual notice must be given to all class members "who are identifiable through reasonable effort." *Id.* at 175; *Gross v. The Standard Oil Co.*

45 Ohio Misc. 45, 49–50, (Ohio Ct. Common Pleas 1975). As with the notice requirements of Federal Rule 23, Ohio courts have interpreted this to require notice by mail to all class members whose names and last known addresses are available from a defendant's own business records. *West v. Carfax, Inc., 11th Dist. Trumbull No. 2008-T-0045*, 2009-Ohio-6857, ¶ 19.

While it is ordinarily the representative's responsibility to bear the cost of notice, those costs may be shifted to the defendant where (1) it can perform the task with less difficulty or expense or (2) there has been a determination of liability. *Rimmer,* 2013 Ohio 5732 ¶¶ 51–52.

5. APPELLATE REVIEW

a. Interlocutory Appeals

Ohio has suffered a tortured history as to whether or not interlocutory appeals are available for class certification rulings. In 1993, the Ohio Supreme Court held that interlocutory appeals would not be permitted for orders granting or denying class certification. *See generally Polikoff v. Adam*, 67 Ohio St. 3d 100 (1993). However, in July 1998, the Ohio legislature effectively overruled *Polikoff* by amending Ohio's final order statute to provide an immediate review of any class certification determination. Ohio Rev. Code § 2505 now provides that "an order that determines an action may or may not be maintained as a class action" constitutes a final order and may be immediately appealed. *See generally* R.C. § 2505(B)(5); *Rehoreg v. Stoneco, Inc.*, 9th Dist. Lorain No. 04CA008481, 2005-Ohio-12; *Blumenthal*, 139 Ohio App. 3d 283.

While an initial class certification decision is appealable, a decision modifying the class definition is not. *Gabbard v. Ohio Bureau of Workers' Comp.*, 10th Dist. Franklin Nos. 02-AP-976 and 02-AP-1168, 2003-Ohio-2265 ¶ 33; *Rosette v. Countrywide Home Loans, Inc.*, 8th Dist. Cuyahoga No. 86923 and 86970, 2006-Ohio-4488; *Asset Acceptance LLC v. Caszatt*, 11th Dist. Lake Nos. 2011-L-080, 2012-Ohio-1886. Similarly, orders subsequent to class certification are not appealable under R.C. § 2505(B)(5) simply because those orders apply to the class. *Coleman v. Showroom Transp., 8th Dist. Cuyahoga No. 93675*, 2010-Ohio-1439; *Lucio v. Safe Auto Ins. Co.,* 7th Dist. Monroe No. 10 MO 2, 2010-Ohio-02528. Nor is the denial of a request by members of an earlier-filed class to intervene for purposes of objecting to the settlement. *Schmidt v. AT&T, Inc.*, 8th Dist. Cuyahoga No. 94856, 2010-Ohio-5491.

Likewise, a decision denying *conditional* certification is not immediately appealable. *Oakley v. Ohio State Univ. Wexner Med. Ctr.*, 10th Dist. Franklin No. 18AP-843, 2019-Ohio 3557.

A party has 30 days to file a notice of appeal on a class certification decision, or its right to do so is waived. *See* App. R. 4(A); *Lofti-Fard v. First Fed. of Lakewood, 8th Dist. Cuyahoga No. 87207*, 2006-Ohio-3727.

When a trial court dismisses claims that include class allegations prior to class certification, the named plaintiff must appeal the dismissal on behalf of the class to preserve the claims on remand. *Midland Funding LLC v. Hottenroth*, 8th Dist. Cuyahoga No. 111328, 2023 Ohio 923.

b. Abuse of Discretion Standard

Abuse of discretion is the appropriate standard of review of a trial court's class determination. *See Hamilton*, 82 Ohio St. 3d at 70. *See also Warner*, 36 Ohio St. 3d at 99. An abuse of discretion is "more than a mere error of law or judgment, instead requiring a finding that the trial court's decision was unreasonable, arbitrary, or unconscionable." *In re Consol. Mortg. Satisfaction Cases*, 97 Ohio St. 3d at 467. *See also Strongsville Bd. Educ. v. Cuyahoga Cty. Bd. of Revision*, 53 Ohio St. 3d 254,

257 (1990) (abuse of discretion connotes "decision that is without a reasonable basis and is clearly wrong").

"[W]hile a trial court's determination concerning class certification is subject to appellate review on an abuse-of-discretion standard, due deference must be given to the trial court's decision . . . . A finding of abuse of discretion, particularly if the trial court has refused to certify, should be made cautiously." *Wilson,* 103 Ohio St. 3d at 541. *See also Hamilton,* 82 Ohio St. 3d at 70 (trial court's discretion not unlimited and "is bounded by and must be exercised within the framework of Civ. R. 23"). Appellate review must focus upon whether the trial court's decision comports with the applicable law and record evidence of the individual case. *See Warner,* 36 Ohio St. 3d at 99 ("Where the trial court completely misconstrues the letter and spirit of the law, it is clear that the court has been unreasonable and has abused its discretion."). *See also Howland*, 104 Ohio St. 3d at 589.

Since any doubts whether the elements of class certification have been met should be resolved in favor of upholding the class, *see Baughman,* 88 Ohio St. 3d at 487, "it is not uncommon for a reviewing court to reverse a trial court's denial of class certification." *Carder Buick-Olds*, 148 Ohio App. 3d at 640. "[W]hen an appellate court finds an abuse of discretion; it should not proceed to formulate the class or issue itself but should remand the matter to the trial court for such a determination." *George*, 145 Ohio App. 3d at 688 (citing *Marks*, 31 Ohio St. 3d at 201).

If the appellate court finds the class definition unworkable, it must remand to the trial court with instruction to craft a workable definition rather than attempt to formulate one itself. *Lindsay v. City of Garfield Heights,* 8th Dist. Cuyahoga Nos. 107230 and 107236, 2019-Ohio 1359 ¶ 29.

c. De Novo Review

"Insofar as a party alleges that a class notice approved by the trial court violates procedural due process, appellate courts review the matter de novo." *West,* 2009-Ohio-6857, ¶ 12.

6. MISCELLANEOUS COMMENTS

a. Types of Cases in Which Class Certification Has Been Approved

i. Mass tort and environmental claims. *See Warner v. Waste Management, Inc.*, 36 Ohio St. 3d 91 (1988).

ii. Consumer claims. *See Hamilton v. Ohio Savings Bank*, 82 Ohio St. 3d 67 (1998); *Baughman v. State Farm Mut. Auto*., 88 Ohio St. 3d 480 (2000).

iii. Defendant class. *See Planned Parenthood Ass'n v. Project Jericho*, 52 Ohio St. 3d 56, 568 N.E.2d 157 (Ohio 1990).

iv. Breach of contract. *See Ojalvo v. Board of Trustees of Ohio State Univ*., 12 Ohio St. 3d 230 (1985); *Rimedio*, 2010-Ohio-5555, P72 (noting that breach of contract cases are routinely certified).

v. Fraud and breach of fiduciary duty. *See Cope v. Metropolitan Life Ins. Co*., 82 Ohio St. 3d 426 (1998).

vi. Infliction of emotional distress. *See Walker v. Firelands Community Hosp.*, 2001 WL 1198660 (6th Dist. 2001).

vii. COVID-19. *Cross v. Univ. of Toledo*, Ct. of Cl. No. 2020-00274JD, 2021 Ohio Misc. LEXIS 43 (Apr. 26, 2021).

b. Types of Cases in Which Class Certification Has Been Denied

i. Mass tort-product liability. *See Wilson v. Brush Wellman, Inc.*, 103 Ohio St. 3d 538 (2004); *Marks*, 31 Ohio St. 3d 200.
ii. Commercial. *See Schmidt v. Avco Corp.*, 15 Ohio St. 3d 310 (1984).
iii. Consumer Sales Practices Act. *See Marrone,* 110 Ohio St. 3d 5. *See also Volbers-Klarich* at ¶ 32, finding a CSPA claim defective where the plaintiff failed to plead the "requirements of a class action pursuant to *R.C. 1345.09(B),*" specifically that "that the substantive provisions of the Act have been violated, and (1) a specific rule or regulation has been promulgated under *R.C. 1345.05* that specifically characterizes the challenged practice as unfair or deceptive, or (2) an Ohio state court has found the specific practice either unconscionable or deceptive in a decision open to public inspection." *Id.* at ¶ 26.
iv. Collateral attack of state court judgments. In a case in which Midland Credit was accused of obtaining default judgments in cases that were improperly venued, the court denied certification on the ground that it did not have the authority to vacate judgments from other courts. *Gilbert v. Midland Funding LLC*, 3d Dist. Hancock No. 5-19-11, 2019-Ohio-5295, ¶ 1.

c. Class Action Filing Tolls Statute of Limitations

The filing of a class action, whether in Ohio or in federal court, tolls the running of the statute of limitations for all members of the putative class. *See Vaccariello,* 94 Ohio St. 3d at 382–83. Accordingly, if an Ohio or federal class action fails "otherwise than upon the merits" of the case, any member of that putative class has one (1) year from the date of the denial of class certification to file his or her own suit. *Id.*

d. Unilateral Communications with Class Members Prohibited

The Ohio Supreme Court has warned that a defendant's efforts to discuss the merits of a class action with members of the class "is rife with potential for coercion," and so, unilateral communications with absent class members are prohibited. *See Hamilton*, 82 Ohio St. 3d at 76 ("[A]fter the commencement of a class action, the defendant is not permitted to engage in unilateral and unsupervised communications with potential members of the class concerning the substance of the class action[.]"). This prohibition applies to communications with putative class members as well. *See Burns v. Prudential Secs., Inc.*, 145 Ohio App. 3d 424 (3d Dist. 2001).

e. Proof of Damages

"Implicit in Rule 23's requirements is a showing that those persons sought to be included in the class have all suffered some harm to which common questions of law or fact apply." *Hoang*, 151 Ohio App. 3d at 370. While it is well settled that differing amounts of damages do not preclude class certification, *see, e.g., Hamilton*, 82 Ohio St. 3d at 81, 84; *Pyles,* 143 Ohio App. 3d at 732," [c]lass certification cases distinguish between the amount of damages, the calculation of which will not ordinarily defeat class certification, and the fact of injury and causation, which are liability elements of a claim." *Hoang,* 151 Ohio App. 3d at 369.

"The fact that statutory damages are not available in a class action indicates proof of actual damages is required before certification of an *R.C. 1345.09(B)* class action is proper." *Searles v.*

Germain Ford of Columbus, LLC, 10th Dist. Franklin No. 08AP-728, 2009-Ohio-1323.

Ohio courts have moved away from *Hamilton*'s caution that individual damages should not defeat certification toward requiring expert testimony on how damages can be calculated on a class-wide basis. *See, e.g., Waitt v. Kent State Univ.*, 10th Dist. Franklin No. 22AP-167, 2022 Ohio 4781; *Duke v. Ohio Univ.*, 10th Dist. Franklin No. 22AP-184, 2022 Ohio 4694.

f. Arbitration Clauses

The impact of the U.S. Supreme Court's decision in *AT&T Mobility, LLC v. Concepcion*, 563 U.S. 321 (2011), in which the Supreme Court struck down California's landmark decision invalidating class action bans, *Discover Bank v. Sup. Ct.*, 36 Cal. 4th 148 (2005), has significantly impacted the availability of the class action device in Ohio. The *AT&T Mobility* decision held that the *Discover Bank* rule was not one that concerned state contract law generally, but rather one that required arbitration of a broad category of claims and imposed class arbitration without the parties' consent, and thus was inconsistent with—and preempted by—the FAA. In *Wallace v. Ganley Auto Group*, 8th Dist. Cuyahoga No. 95081, 2011-Ohio-2909, the plaintiff argued that forced arbitration of claims under Ohio's Consumer Sales Practices Act was inconsistent with the Act's alleged policy of favoring class actions for the enforcement of consumer rights. Relying upon *AT&T Mobility*, the court held that even if the "CSPA contains a policy favoring class actions (an issue we need not decide), this court may not apply that policy in a way that disfavors arbitration." *Id.* at ¶ 19.

Prior to the decision in *AT&T Mobility*, the courts of Ohio were split on the enforceability of class actions bans. At least one court found that an arbitration clause that seeks to eliminate a consumer's right to proceed through a class action may be grounds, in and of itself, to strike such clause as substantively unconscionable. *See Schwartz v. Alltel Corp.*, 8th Dist. Cuyahoga No. 86810, 2006-Ohio-3353 ¶ 30 ("limitation of consumer rights found within the arbitration provision establishes a quantum of substantive unconscionability"). *But see Hawkins v. O'Brien*, 2d Dist. Montgomery No. 22490, 2009-Ohio-60, upholding a class action waiver because it did not deprive the plaintiff of any substantive statutory rights. In *Alexander v. Wells Fargo Fin. Ohio 1, Inc.*, 8th Dist. Cuyahoga No. 89277, 2009-Ohio-4873 ¶ 18, the Eighth District Court of Appeals explained that its decision in *Schwartz* should not be interpreted to preclude arbitration of any claim which eliminates the right to participate in a class action.

At issue in *Strickler*, 2009-Ohio-1422, was an arbitration agreement that contained a poorly worded attempt at a class action waiver. The arbitration agreement at issue provided that "the arbitration may not address any dispute on a 'class action' basis" and prohibited a signatory to the agreement from participating as a representative or member of any class of claimants *pertaining to any dispute subject to arbitration*." The court held that because class claims were excluded from arbitration, it followed that a signatory to the agreement could bring a class claim outside of arbitration.

In *Shakoor v. VXI Global Solutions*, 7th Dist. Mahoning No. 14 MA 59, 2015-Ohio-2587, the court held that the question of whether the contract permits an arbitrable claim to be arbitrated as a class action is one that must be answered by the court unless the agreement specifies otherwise. *Id.* at ¶ 36, citing *Bachrach v. Cornwell Quality Tool Co.,* 9th Dist. Summit No. 27113, 2014-Ohio-5778 ¶ 14 ("When a contract between parties is silent on who will decide whether a claim may be arbitrated as a class, the issue is one for the courts not the arbitrators to decide.").

In situations where a class representative is not subject to a valid arbitration agreement, but other class members may be, the existence of the arbitration provision may become an issue impacting the propriety of class certification. Most commonly, the question is whether the arbitration provision requires inquiry of each and every potential class member in order to determine whether he or she agreed to arbitrate, thereby destroying predominance of any common questions. Ohio courts are split on this issue. *See Ritt,* 2003-Ohio-3645 (where plaintiff alleged contract obtaining arbitration provision was obtained through fraud, no inquiry of individual class members is necessary and predominance requirement is satisfied); *Rimedio v. Summacare, Inc.*, 9th Dist. Summit No. 21828, 2004-Ohio-4971 ¶ 25 (named plaintiff who chose to waive arbitration clause has no interest in protecting class members who did not, thereby destroying typicality). One appellate court has held that in cases in which the class representative did not sign an arbitration agreement, the defendant does not waive the right to demand arbitration by waiting until the certification stage to raise the issue. *Gembarski v. PartsSource, Inc., 11th Dist. Portage No. 2016-P-0077*, 2020-Ohio-981, ¶ 23; *accord*, *Dumas v. N. E. Auto Credit, L.L.C.*, 8th Dist. Cuyahoga Nos. 108151, 108388, 2019-Ohio-4789, ¶ 1.

g. Certification of Limited Issues and/or Subclasses

Civ. R. 23(C)(4) allows a trial court to certify a particular issue, as necessary, that is suitable for class treatment, irrespective of whether or not the remaining issues presented satisfy the requirements of Civ. R. 23. *See, e.g., Gottlieb*, 157 Ohio App. 3d at 257 n.2 ("a trial court may grant class certification on particular issues while denying that certification on other issues"); *Martin v. Services Corp. Int'l*, 2001 WL 688896, at *4 n.3 (Ohio App. June 20, 2001). Similarly, Civ. R. 23(C)(4) gives trial courts flexibility to create subclasses to determine particular issues such as damages. *See In re Rogers Litig.*, 2003-Ohio-5976 ¶ 21, 38. *See also Martin v. Grange Mutual Ins. Co.*, 2004-Ohio-6950, ¶ 49) (trial court has "wide discretion in applying various procedural devices" to manage individual issues such as defenses and/or damages).

Certification of a particular issue or claim is discretionary with the trial court and appropriate where doing so will "materially advance" the litigation. *Marks*, 31 Ohio St. 3d at 205. It is not an abuse of discretion to deny certification of one claim where its proof will mirror that of other claims that have been denied certification; under these circumstances, certification would not materially advance the litigation. *Knoop v. Orthopaedic Consultants, 12th Dist. Clermont No. CA2006-07-048*, 2007-Ohio-1371.

h. Certification of Multi-state Classes

"To establish commonality of the applicable law, nationwide class action movants must creditably demonstrate, through an 'extensive analysis' of state law variances that 'class certification does not present insuperable obstacles.'" *Ritt*, 171 Ohio App. 3d. 204. This requires more than the use of charts showing the elements required of a claim in a particular state. *Id.*

The value of the "extensive analysis" a court needs to make this determination should not be underestimated. In *Cowit v. Cellco Partnership*, 1st Dist. Hamilton No. C-080627 and C-080677, 2009-Ohio-1596, the First District Court of Appeals upheld certification of a nationwide breach of contract class, noting that the trial court reviewed "extensive evidence" concerning the propriety of certifying a nationwide class, and given its inherent power to manage its own docket, the trial court's determination that nationwide certification was appropriate would not be disturbed on appeal.

Out-of-state consumers have standing to assert claims under Ohio's Consumer Sales Practices Act, and certification of a nationwide class of claimants is appropriate under that statute where the practices complained of emanated from within the State. *Brown v. Market Dev.,* 41 Ohio Misc. 57, 322 N.E.2d 367 (1974); *Parker v. Berkeley Premium Nutraceuticals, Inc.*, 2005 Ohio Misc. LEXIS 605 (Ohio Misc. 2005).

i. Class Action Settlements

Civ. R. 23(E) provides that no class action shall be dismissed or compromised "without approval of the court, and notice of the proposed dismissal or compromise" to all members of the class. Thus, the named parties to a certified or putative class action must obtain approval of the trial court and provide notice to all class members before a settlement of the case may go forward. This requires a finding by the trial court that the proposed settlement is fair, reasonable, and adequate.

Generally speaking, courts look to the following criteria in determining whether a settlement is fair, reasonable, and adequate: "(1) Likelihood of recovery, or likelihood of success; (2) Amount and nature of discovery or evidence; (3) Settlement terms and conditions; (4) Recommendation and experience of counsel; (5) Future expense and likely duration of litigation; (6) Recommendation of neutral parties, if any; (7) Number of objectors and nature of objections; and (8) The presence of good faith and the absence of collusion[.]" *See Beder v. Cleveland Browns, Inc.*, 114 Ohio Misc. 2d 26, 758 N.E.2d 307, 308–09 (Ohio 2001) (quoting *Newberg on Class Actions* (3d ed. 1992) 11–97, Section 11:43).

At least one court has held that, where vouchers are made available to class members as part of the settlement, the claims "take rate" or projected rate may be considered when determining the value of the settlement to the class. *West,* 2009-Ohio-6857, ¶ 19.

j. Attorneys' Fees

In *Wilken v. Wachovia Bank of Delaware, N.A.*, 6th Dist. Huron No. H-12-006, 2013-Ohio-2132, ¶ 8, the Sixth District Court of Appeals had the unique opportunity to consider an appeal from a decision that awarded less than requested attorneys' fees as part of a settlement. In that case, class counsel applied for a "clear sailing" award of fees equal to one-third of the value of the settlement, or $5.6 million, as determined by the parties. The trial court held that the settlement should be valued based on the amount actually claimed by class members, approximately $3 million, and found that the difference in fees realized because of the inflated settlement value was a "supplemental payment" from the defendant to class counsel. The Court of Appeals seemed particularly troubled by the fact that fees were to be paid from the total available to pay class members. In affirming the trial court decision, the Court of Appeals noted that "had class counsel negotiated for Wachovia to be liable for all of the attorney fees as part of the settlement agreement and thus not deduct that amount from class members' claims or had class counsel negotiated for a common fund from which the attorney fees could have been paid, we may have reached a different result." *Id.* at 30.

k. Voluntary Dismissal/Late Opt-out

At issue in *Arndt v. P & M Ltd.*, 11th Dist. Portage No. 2009-Ohio-0088, 2011-Ohio-649, ¶¶ 50–51, was the validity of a voluntary dismissal of the class representative's claims filed after the date set by the court for opting out of the class. The court treated the notice of dismissal as a request to opt out and held that court approval was required because the deadline had passed.

l. Timing of Class Certification Rulings

In Hupp v. Beck Energy Corp., 7th Dist. Monroe Nos. 12 MO 6, 13 MO 2, 13 MO 3, 13 MO 11, 2014-Ohio-4255, the court was asked to review an order granting certification of a (B)(2) class. The trial entered the order after it granted summary judgment in favor of the Named Plaintiffs. The defendant argued that doing so violated the principle against one-way intervention. The *Hupp* court disagreed, holding that the rule against one-way intervention does not apply in (B)(2) classes. *Id.* at ¶ 54. The court did caution, however, that under some circumstances, a ruling on the merits prior to certification could be prejudicial to the defendant.

m. Evidentiary Hearings

A trial court has discretion as to whether to hold a class certification hearing, and if it had sufficient information before it to rule on certification, it did not abuse its discretion by failing to hold a hearing. *Lindsay v. City of Garfield Hts., 8th Dist. Cuyahoga Nos. 108967, 109015*, 2020-Ohio-3672, ¶ 1.

Chapter author Barbara Quinn Smith has practiced in Ohio since 1991 and concentrates her practice on consumer matters. Ms. Smith can be reached at bqsmith@bqslaw.com.

OKLAHOMA

1. COMPARISON OF OKLAHOMA CLASS ACTION STATUTE WITH FED. R. CIV. P. 23

Title 12, Section 2023 of the Oklahoma Statutes is similar to Fed. R. Civ. P. 23. The most recent changes to Oklahoma's class action statute were enacted effective September 10, 2013.

Oklahoma courts may look to federal authority for "guidance and enlightenment" in their analysis of class action issues. *Dewey v. State ex rel. Oklahoma Firefighters Pension and Retirement System*, 2001 OK 40, 28 P.3d 539; *KMC Leasing, Inc. v. Rockwell-Standard Corp.,* 2000 OK 51, 9 P.3d 683, 688; *Mattoon v. City of Norman,* 1981 OK 92, 633 P.2d 735.

Oklahoma does provide for an immediate appeal of a trial court's interlocutory order on class certification. Okla. Sup. Ct. R. 1.60(g).

2. SUMMARY OF CASE LAW INTERPRETING OKLA. STAT. TIT. 12, § 2023

Plaintiffs have the burden of establishing each of the four requirements of subsection (A) and one of the requirements of subsection (B). *Sias v. Edge Communications, Inc.,* 2000 OK CIV APP 72, 8 P.3d 182, 185; *First Life Assurance Co. v. Mountain,* 1993 OK CIV APP 20, 848 P.2d 1177. For the purpose of determining whether class certification is appropriate, courts "take as true all uncontroverted allegations in the instruments of record and the undenied statements of counsel in the briefs." *Harvell v. Goodyear Tire and Rubber Co.,* 2006 OK 24, 164 P.3d 1028; *Shores v. First City Bank Corp*., 1984 OK 67, 689 P.2d 299. The Court in *KMC Leasing, Inc., supra,* said, "It is often necessary to analyze the substantive claims and defenses of the parties and the essential elements of those claims and defenses." *KMC Leasing, Inc.*, 633 P.2d at 692.

Oklahoma courts have noted that where there is a close question as to certification, certification is the appropriate ruling early in the case. "The pragmatically correct action, in the face of a close question as to certification, has been said to sustain certification because if it develops later in the course of the trial that the order is ill-advised, the order is always (prior to judgment on the merits,) subject to modification." *Perry v. Meek,* 1980 OK 451, 618 P.2d 934, 940.

In determining whether the class meets the numerosity requirement for class certification, courts will look to the facts of each case. Class size alone is not determinative. *Martin v. Hanover Direct, Inc.,* 2006 OK CIV APP 33, 135 P.3d 251, *cert. denied* (Mar. 28, 2006). Failure to adequately define a class can defeat the numerosity requirement. *KMC Leasing, Inc., supra.*

The analysis of whether there is predominance of common questions of law or fact sufficient to support class certification is a qualitative, not quantitative, analysis. When many individualized issues are crucial to the resolution of claims and defenses, those issues may preclude the common from being predominant. *Gentry v. Cotton Elec. Co-Op, Inc.,* 2011 OK CIV APP 24, 268 P.3d 534, *cert. denied* (Feb. 14, 2011). *Greghol Ltd. P'ship v. Oryx Energy Co.,* 1998 OK CIV APP 111, 959

P.2d 596, *cert. denied* (July 8, 1998).

Consistent with federal law, the existence of defenses which could apply to individual putative class members does not necessarily defeat certification. The Oklahoma Supreme Court in *Shores*, 689 P.2d at 303–04, addressed the defendant's claim that there were individual statute of limitations defenses, which should prevent class certification. The Oklahoma court stated: "The claim that there exists sufficient individual statute of limitations defenses to prevent class action certification has not found much favor with the courts dealing with these questions." The court went on to state: "As to those whose actions give rise to questions concerning this issue, the trial court may surely treat those problems in connection with individualized damage claims, or at least eliminate those affected individuals as members of the class." *Id. See also Melot Oklahoma Farm Bureau Mut. Ins. Co.,* 2004 OK CIV APP 25, 87 P.3d 644.

The Oklahoma Supreme Court has specifically considered the *existence of*, as distinguished from the *consideration of the merits of*, numerous and individualized defenses in its analysis of the typicality requirement. In *KMC Leasing*, *supra,* the Court attached significance to the fact that there were individualized defenses which would bear on liability and affirmed the Trial Court's denial of certification because of the lack of typicality. Quoting *Davoll v. Webb,* 160 F.R.D. 142, 144 (D. Colo. 1995), the Court noted:

> [I]t is often necessary to analyze the substantive claims and *defenses* of the parties and the essential elements of those claims and *defenses* . . . Nevertheless, there is a distinction between identifying the issues that the case will present for purposes of determining whether the requirements of Rule 23 have been met and deciding those issues on the merits.

In *Bunch v. KMART Corporation*, 1995 OK CIV APP 41, 898 P.2d 170, the court denied class certification for plaintiffs' fraud claims. This was an action for fraud and/or negligent misrepresentation in which plaintiffs alleged that K-Mart, in all forty-nine states in which K-Mart had automotive divisions, had fraudulently informed plaintiffs that they needed parts or service. The Court of Appeals held that because of the number of states involved and differences in the substantive law of fraud in each state, questions of law were not sufficiently common to support the certification of the class action. The court concluded that the legal relationships between K-Mart and the proposed class members would be governed by the law of each of the forty-nine states in which the automobiles were serviced and the parts were sold. Accordingly, the court concluded that the substantive law of each state would apply.

Applying Oklahoma law, the court in *Dane v. Southwestern Bell Telephone Co*., 352 F. Supp. 257 (W.D. Okla. 1972), ruled that a class action may be maintained for deceit, citing *Hall Jones Oil Corp.*, 459 P.2d 858, and *Young v. West Edmond Hunton Lime Unit*, 1954 OK 195, 275 P.2d 304, *appeal dismissed*, 349 U.S. 909, 99 L.Ed. 1245 (1955).

The Oklahoma Supreme Court in *Ysbrand v. Daimler-Chrysler Corp.,* 2003 OK 17, 81 P.3d 618, affirmed certification of a nationwide class action asserting Uniform Commercial Code claims for breach of express and implied warranty. The Court reversed certification of plaintiffs' fraud claims. Plaintiffs' breach of warranty claims arise from defendant's manufacture of over a million 1996 and 1997 model minivans equipped with front passenger airbags. Defendant argued that common issues of law or fact would not predominate because varying state laws would apply to the asserted claims and defenses, citing *KMC Leasing, Inc.*, *supra*. The Supreme Court, applying Oklahoma's "most significant relationship" test, held that Michigan, the defendant's principal place of business, had the greatest interest in the litigation of the warranty claims. The Court said, "while the interest of each home state in applying its local law is significant, Michigan's interest in the conduct of its manufacturer, and thus its connection to the warranty issues, is greater."

Although affirming nationwide class treatment of the breach of warranty claims, the Court, again applying Oklahoma's "most significant relationship test," found that class members' home states have the greatest interest in the alleged fraud claims. The Court said that "applying the law of 51 jurisdictions to the fraud claims would present an overwhelming burden which would make the class unmanageable and a class action determination of that claim inappropriate."

Recent Oklahoma cases that affirmed class certification include *Weber v. Mobil Oil Corp.*, 2010 OK 33, 243 P.3d 1, and *Cactus Petroleum Corp. v. Chesapeake Operating, Inc.*, 2009 OK 67, 222 P.3d 12.

Recent Oklahoma cases denying class certification include *Panola Independent School Dist. No. 4 v. Unit Petroleum Co.*, 2012 OK CIV APP 94, 287 P.3d 1033, *cert. denied* (Oct. 8, 2012), and *Rees v. BP America Production Co.*, 2009 OK CIV APP 37, 211 P.3d 910, 910, *cert. denied* (Apr. 13, 2009).

§ 12-2023 CLASS ACTIONS

A. PREREQUISITES TO A CLASS ACTION. One or more members of a class may sue or be sued as representative parties on behalf of all only if:

1. The class is so numerous that joinder of all members is impracticable;
2. There are questions of law or fact common to the class;
3. The claims or defenses of the representative parties are typical of the claims or defenses of the class; and
4. The representative parties will fairly and adequately protect the interests of the class.

B. CLASS ACTIONS MAINTAINABLE. An action may be maintained as a class action if the prerequisites of subsection A of this section are satisfied, if the petition in the class action contains factual allegations sufficient to demonstrate a plausible claim for relief and:

1. The prosecution of separate actions by or against individual members of the class would create a risk of:
   a. inconsistent or varying adjudications with respect to individual members of the class which would establish incompatible standards of conduct for the party opposing the class, or
   b. adjudications with respect to individual members of the class which would as a practical matter be dispositive of the interests of the other members not parties to the adjudications or substantially impair or impede their ability to protect their interests; or
2. The party opposing the class has acted or refused to act on grounds generally applicable to the class, thereby making appropriate final injunctive relief or corresponding declaratory relief with respect to the class as a whole; or
3. The court finds that the questions of law or fact common to the members of the class predominate over any questions affecting only individual members, and that a class action is superior to other available methods for the fair and efficient adjudication of the controversy. The matters pertinent to the findings include:
   a. the interest of members of the class in individually controlling the prosecution or defense of separate actions,
   b. the extent and nature of any litigation concerning the controversy already commenced by or against members of the class,
   c. the desirability or undesirability of concentrating the litigation of the claims in the particular forum, and
   d. the difficulties likely to be encountered in the management of a class action.

C. DETERMINATION BY ORDER WHETHER CLASS ACTION TO BE MAINTAINED; NOTICE; JUDGMENT; ACTIONS CONDUCTED PARTIALLY AS CLASS ACTIONS.

1. As soon as practicable after the commencement of an action brought as a class action,

the court shall determine by order whether it is to be so maintained. An order entered on or after November 1, 2009, that certifies a class action shall define the class and the class claims, issues or defenses, and shall appoint class counsel under subsection F of this section. An order under this subsection may be conditional, and may be altered or amended before the decision on the merits.

2. The order described in paragraph 1 of this subsection shall be subject to a de novo standard of review by any appellate court reviewing the order. While the appeal of the order on class certification is pending, the trial court shall retain sufficient jurisdiction over the case to consider and implement a settlement of the action should one be reached between the parties and discovery as to the class claims shall be stayed pending resolution of the appeal.

3. For any class certified under paragraph 1 or 2 of subsection B of this section, the court may direct appropriate notice to the class.

4. In any class action maintained under paragraph 3 of subsection B of this section, the court shall direct to the members of the class the best notice practicable under the circumstances, including individual notice to all members who can be identified through reasonable effort. The notice shall clearly and concisely state in plain, easily understood language:

   a. the nature of the action,

   b. the definition of the class certified,

   c. the class claims, issues or defenses,

   d. that a class member may enter an appearance through an attorney if the member so desires,

   e. that the court will exclude the member from the class if the member so requests by a specified date,

   f. that the judgment, whether favorable or not, will include all members who do not request exclusion, and

   g. that any member who does not request exclusion may, if the member desires, enter an appearance through counsel.

   Members to whom individual notice is not directed shall be given notice in such manner as the court shall direct, which may include publishing notice in newspapers, magazines, trade journals or other publications, posting it in appropriate places, and taking other steps that are reasonably calculated to bring the notice to the attention of such members, provided that the cost of giving such notice shall be reasonable in view of the amounts that may be recovered by the class members who are being notified. Members to whom individual notice was not directed may request exclusion from the class at any time before the issue of liability is determined, and commencing an individual action before the issue of liability is determined shall be the equivalent of requesting exclusion from the class.

5. The judgment in an action maintained as a class action under paragraph 1 or 2 of subsection B of this section, whether or not favorable to the class, shall include and

describe those whom the court finds to be members of the class. The judgment in an action maintained as a class action under paragraph 3 of subsection B of this section, whether or not favorable to the class, shall include and specify or describe those to whom the notice provided in paragraph 4 of this subsection was directed, and who have not requested exclusion, and whom the court finds to be members of the class.

6. When appropriate:

   a. an action may be brought or maintained as a class action with respect to particular issues, or

   b. a class may be divided into subclasses and each subclass treated as a class.

The provisions of this section shall then be construed and applied accordingly.

D. ORDERS IN CONDUCT OF ACTIONS. In the conduct of actions to which this section applies, the court may make appropriate orders:

1. Determining the course of proceedings or prescribing measures to prevent undue repetition or complication in the presentation of evidence or argument;

2. Requiring, for the protection of the members of the class or otherwise for the fair conduct of the action, that notice be given in such manner as the court may direct to some or all of the members of any step in the action, or of the proposed extent of the judgment, or of the opportunity of members to signify whether they consider the representation fair and adequate, to intervene and present claims or defenses, or otherwise to come into the action;

3. For actions filed after November 1, 2009, class membership shall be limited, unless otherwise agreed to by the defendant, only to individuals or entities who are:

   a residents of this state, or

   b. nonresidents of this state who:

      (1) own an interest in property located in this state where the property is relevant to the class action, or

      (2) have a significant portion of the nonresident's cause of action arising from conduct occurring within the state;

4. Requiring, for the sole purpose of class notice upon certification of a class, that parties to the action provide such names and addresses of potential members of the class as they possess, subject to an appropriate protective order;

5. Imposing conditions on the representative parties or on intervenors;

6. Requiring that the pleadings be amended to eliminate therefrom allegations as to representation of absent persons, and that the action proceed accordingly; and

7. Dealing with similar procedural matters.

The orders may be combined with an order under Section 2016 of this title and may be altered or amended as may be desirable from time to time.

E. DISMISSAL OR COMPROMISE. The claims, issues or defenses of a certified class may be settled, voluntarily dismissed, or compromised only with the court's approval. For motions filed after November 1, 2009, the following procedures apply to a proposed settlement, voluntary dismissal, or compromise:

1. The court shall direct notice in a reasonable manner to all class members who would be bound by the proposal;
2. If the proposal would bind class members, the court may approve it only after a hearing and on finding that it is fair, reasonable and adequate;
3. The parties seeking approval shall file a statement identifying any agreement made in connection with the proposal;
4. If the class action was previously certified under paragraph 3 of subsection B of this section, the court may refuse to approve a settlement unless it affords a new opportunity to request exclusion to individual class members who had an earlier opportunity to request exclusion but did not do so; and
5. Any class member may object to the proposal if it requires court approval under this subsection.

F. CLASS COUNSEL.

1. Unless a statute provides otherwise, a court that certifies a class shall appoint class counsel. In appointing class counsel after November 1, 2009, the court:
   a. shall consider:
      (1) the work counsel has done in identifying or investigating potential claims in the action,
      (2) counsel's experience in handling class actions, other complex litigation, and the types of claims asserted in the action,
      (3) counsel's knowledge of the applicable law, and
      (4) the resources that counsel will commit to representing the class,
   b. may consider any other matter pertinent to counsel's ability to fairly and adequately represent the interests of the class,
   c. may order potential class counsel to provide information on any subject pertinent to the appointment and to propose terms for attorney fees or nontaxable costs,
   d. may include in the appointing order provisions about the award of attorney fees or nontaxable costs, and
   e. may make further orders in connection with the appointment;
2. When one applicant seeks appointment as class counsel, the court may appoint that applicant only if the applicant is adequate under paragraphs 1 and 4 of this subsection. If more than one adequate applicant seeks appointment, the court shall appoint the applicant best able to represent the interests of the class.
3. The court may designate interim counsel to act on behalf of a putative class before determining whether to certify the action as a class action.

4. Class counsel shall fairly and adequately represent the interests of the class.

G. ATTORNEY FEES AND NONTAXABLE COSTS.

1. In a certified class action, the court may award reasonable attorney fees and nontaxable costs that are authorized by law or by the parties' agreement.

2. A claim for an award shall be made by motion, subject to the provisions of this subsection, at a time set by the court. Notice of the motion shall be served on all parties and, for motions by class counsel, directed to class members in a reasonable manner.

3. A class member, or a party from whom payment is sought, may object to the motion.

4. In considering a motion for attorney fees filed after November 1, 2009:

a. the court shall conduct an evidentiary hearing to determine a fair and reasonable fee for class counsel,

b. the court shall act in a fiduciary capacity on behalf of the class in making such determination,

c. the court may appoint an attorney to represent the class upon the request by any members of the class in a hearing on the issue of the amount of attorney fees or the court may refer the matter to a referee pursuant to Section 613 et seq. of this title,

d. if the court appoints an attorney to represent the class for the fee hearing pursuant to subparagraph c of this paragraph or refers the matter to a referee, the attorney or referee shall be independent of the attorney or attorneys seeking attorney fees in the class action, and said independent attorney or referee shall be awarded reasonable fees by the court on an hourly basis out of the proceeds awarded to the class,

e. in arriving at a fair and reasonable fee for class counsel, the court shall consider the following factors:

(1) time and labor required,

(2) the novelty and difficulty of the questions presented by the litigation,

(3) the skill required to perform the legal service properly,

(4) the preclusion of other employment by the attorney due to acceptance of the case,

(5) the customary fee,

(6) whether the fee is fixed or contingent,

(7) time limitations imposed by the client or the circumstances,

(8) the amount in controversy and the results obtained,

(9) the experience, reputation and ability of the attorney,

(10) whether or not the case is an undesirable case,

(11) the nature and length of the professional relationship with the client,

(12) awards in similar causes, and

(13) the risk of recovery in the litigation, and

f. if any portion of the benefits recovered for the class in an action maintained pursuant to paragraph 3 of subsection B of this section are in the form of coupons, discounts on future goods or services or other similar types of noncash common benefits, the attorney fees awarded in the class action shall be in cash and noncash amounts in the same proportion as the recovery for the class.

Added by laws 1984, SB 417, c. 164, § 23, eff. November 1, 1984; amended by laws 2009, HB 1603, c. 228, § 16, eff. November 1, 2009 (repealed by Laws 2013, 1st Extr. Sess., HB 1013, c. 10, § 1, emerg. eff. September 10, 2013); Amended by Laws 2011, SB 704, c. 223, § 1, eff. November 1, 2011 (superseded document available); Amended by Laws 2013, 1st Extr. Sess., HB 1013, c. 10, § 4, emerg. eff. September 10, 2013, as amended by Laws 2013, 1st Extr. Sess., HB 1013, c. 10, § 5, emerg. eff. September 10, 2013 (superseded document available).

Chapter author Michael E. Smith is a shareholder in the Oklahoma City office of Hall, Estill, Hardwick, Gable, Golden & Nelson, PC. Mr. Smith is a 1969 graduate of the U.S. Military Academy and a 1975 graduate of the University of Oklahoma College of Law. Mr. Smith specializes in complex, civil litigation, including class actions, with an emphasis in oil and gas litigation in both federal and state courts.

OREGON

1. OREGON RULE OF CIVIL PROCEDURE 32—A BRIEF HISTORY

Oregon has allowed representative claims for 140 years. *Trustees of the M.E. Protestant Church v. Adams*, 4 Or. 76, 88 (1870) (holding that "where the parties are very numerous, and it may be impracticable to bring them all before the court, one or more may sue or defend for the benefit of the whole"). Oregon courts were historically reluctant to grant class certification, agreeing with other courts that "class actions should be closely scrutinized and should be permitted only in clear cases." *Lonsford v. Bailey*, 200 Or. 497, 508, 267 P.2d 208, 214 (1954). Indeed, until recently, class actions were limited to equitable claims. *Am. Timber & Trading Co. v. First Nat'l Bank*, 263 Or. 1, 500 P.2d 1204 (1972). That changed in 1973, when the Legislative Assembly enacted a class action statute allowing for damages. *Bernard v. First Nat'l Bank of Or.*, 275 Or. 145, 149-50, 550 P.2d at 1207–08 (discussing enactment of O.R.S. § 13.220 *et seq.*). In 1978, Oregon's class action statute was converted into its present form as a procedural rule, when the Oregon Council on Court Procedures (CCP) promulgated ORCP 32.

2. COMPARISON WITH FEDERAL CIVIL RULE 23

Oregon's class action rule is more restrictive than most states' rules and was designed to address perceived class action abuses. As originally proposed, Oregon's class action statute was an exact duplicate of Federal Rule 23. *Bernard*, 275 Or. at 150–51, 550 P.2d at 1208; *Pearson v. Philip Morris, Inc.*, 208 Or. App. 501, 504, 145 P.3d 299–300 (2006) (*Pearson II*), *rev'd on other grounds*, 257 Or. App. 106 (2013) (*Pearson III*), *rev. granted*, 354 Or. 699 (2014). In response to management concerns perceived to be inherent to the federal rule, however, the Oregon Senate Judiciary Committee requested that the proponents and opponents together draft amendments, which were ultimately incorporated into the bill. *Bernard*, 275 Or. at 150–51. Reviewing this history, the Oregon Supreme Court emphasized that there "can be no doubt that the purpose of these amendments was to prevent abuses perceived under Rule 23," and that the Oregon rule "was intended to be circumscribed to a greater extent than is the case under . . . Rule 23." *Id.* at 152; 550 P.2d at 1208–09. Oregon's class action rule further departed from its federal counterpart in 1992, when the CCP discarded the three categories of class actions and instead adopted a unitary form of class action. *See* ORCP 32B. Under the new rule, the previous requirements corresponding to Federal Rules 23(b)(1), (b)(2), and (b)(3), are now only "matters pertinent" to the Court's finding that "a class action is superior to other available methods of the fair and efficient adjudication of the controversy." ORCP 32B. The Council believed the distinctions between the types of classes were causing confusion and unnecessary procedural obstacles, and that strict adherence to the requirements of each category was "unduly rigid." *See* CCP Staff Comment (1992).

3. RELIANCE ON FEDERAL CASE LAW

Because there are relatively few published decisions addressing class certification in Oregon—roughly two dozen—parties often rely on analogous federal case law in support of their respective positions. Because the 1978 adoption of ORCP 32 was based on Federal Rule 23 as it then existed, pre-1978 federal court decisions interpreting Federal Rule 23 in particular "inform" Oregon courts as to the proper interpretation of ORCP 32. *Shea v. Chicago Pneumatic Tool Co.*, 164 Or. App. 198, 206, 990 P.2d 912, 916 (1999). Likewise, where provisions of ORCP 32 contain identical language to that of Federal Rule 23, federal cases "assist in interpreting" ORCP 32, are given "considerable weight," and are "persuasive" authority. *Froeber v. Liberty Mut. Ins. Co.*, 222 Or. App. 266, 277 n.9, 193 P.3d 999, 1066 n.9 (2008) (*Froeber II*) (federal class action cases are "persuasive"); *Newman v. Tulatin Dev. Co., Inc.*, 287 Or. 47, 49–50, 597 P.2d 800, 801 (1979); *Hoy v. Jackson*, 26 Or. App. 895, 897, 554 P.2d 561, 561 (1976) (cases interpreting federal rule on which state rule is based are entitled to "considerable weight"). Also, where the Oregon courts rely on federal cases, those cases are relevant to future interpretations of ORCP 32. *Bernard*, 275 Or. at 159–60, 162–65, 550 P.2d at 1210–15 (citing federal cases).

4. CASE LAW INTERPRETING ORCP 32

A class action may be certified if the class representatives establish all requirements of ORCP 32A, show that pursuant to ORCP 32B a class action is superior to other available methods for the fair and efficient adjudication of the controversy, and (in damages actions) satisfy the notice requirements of ORCP 32H. *See* ORCP 32A, 32B, 32H. The eight factors "pertinent" to whether a class action is superior are contained in ORCP 32B and include all the requirements and factors listed in Federal Rule 23. *See* ORCP 32B. In addition, the class representative must have standing, as use of the class action device does not provide standing that does not already exist. *Ashland Drilling Inc. v. Jackson County*, 168 Or. App. 624, 628 n.1 (2000) (desire to represent others with standing who have standing to bring claims does not confer standing on representative party who otherwise lacks standing); *see also East Texas Motor Freight Sys., Inc. v. Rodriguez*, 431 U.S. 395, 403–04 (1977). Indeed, the Oregon Court of Appeals in 2015 held that if a named Plaintiff's claims are moot or there is a lack of standing before the Plaintiff seeks class certification, that the trial court must dismiss the Complaint and may not allow intervenors into the action even where they may have standing. *See Nordbye v. BRCP/GM Ellington*, 271 Or. App. 168, 184–87, 349 P.3d 639, 649–51 (2015). Similarly, Oregon courts refuse to certify class actions based on allegations of potential future harm, where there is no evidence that a class of injured plaintiffs currently exists. *State v. Johansen*, 125 Or. App. 365, 378, 866 P.2d 470, 477 (1993) (if no evidence of existing harm, claims "can be dealt with individually; they do not lend themselves to class-action remedies"). Courts strictly construe ORCP 32A's requirements but adopt a pragmatic approach to class certification: "[T]he Legislature intended to prevent cases from being certified as class actions when questions concerning individual claims would be so numerous as to impose an impractical burden upon the court thereby destroying the value of consolidation." *Bernard*, 275 Or. at 152, 550 P.2d at 1209. To obtain certification, plaintiffs must satisfy their burden through "evidence, not just representations of counsel, that a certain type of proof is available." *Pearson v. Philip Morris, Inc.*, 2006 WL 66304, *7–8 (Or. Cir. Feb. 23, 2006) (Wilson, J.) (Pearson I), *rev'd on other grounds Pearson III, supra*. This means that even though a "class certification decision is not a trial on the merits, the issues that must be resolved for the class certification determination frequently overlap with the merits of a plaintiffs' class claim." *Pearson v. Philip Morris, Inc.*, 358 Or. 88, 107–08, 361 P.3d 3 (2015).

a. Class Definition

Although not an express requirement of ORCP 32, a class definition must be established before a court can enter an order describing the class or provide notice to class members. *See* ORCP 32C(1), ORCP 32E(2); Charles Alan Wright, et al., *Federal Practice & Procedure* § 1760 (3d ed. 1998) (cited by *Bernard*, 275 Or. at 156, 550 P.2d at 1211). "The purpose of defining the class at the outset is to determine to whom notice must be sent and to facilitate the court's determination on the manageability of the action. *Bernard*, 275 Or. at 156, 550 P.2d at 1211 (citing Wright & Miller, *Federal Practice & Procedure* § 1760, at 584 (1972)). Although the class definition need not identify every class member, the definition must make class members sufficiently ascertainable from the outset so that notice and manageability determinations can be made. *Id.* Oregon courts reject attempts to circumvent definitional flaws by presuming satisfaction of the required elements and limiting class membership to those members with viable claims, holding that "such ingenuity" does not surmount the individual inquiry that will be necessary to determine which class members might recover. *Bernard*, 275 Or. at 156, 550 P.2d at 1211. Thus, a claim that depends on a class member's state of mind is uncertifiable, even if the definition limits the class to those people having a certain state of mind. *See id.* A class definition is improper where it is so broad that proving the named plaintiffs' claims will not prove the claims of any other class member. *Bernard*, 275 Or. at 156. It is also overbroad if it includes class members whose claims are time barred. *See Bellshaw v. Farmers Ins. Co. of Oregon*, 326 Or. App. 605, 619–21, 533 P.3d 40, 49–50 (2023).

b. The Requirements of ORCP 32A

The first four prerequisites of ORCP 32A are identical to those in FRCP 23(a). As a result, federal case law interpreting FRCP 23(a) is useful when examining ORCP 32A. *See Newman*, 287 Or. at 49, 597 P.2d at 801; *Froeber II*, 222 Or. App. at 277 n.9, 193 P.3d at 1066 n.9. Plaintiffs bear the burden of proving all elements of ORCP 32. *Bernard*, 275 Or. at 154, 550 P.2d 1210 ("the unquestioned rule" is that plaintiff bears burden on all ORCP 32 elements).

i. ORCP 32A(1). Numerosity. Establishing the numerosity requirement of ORCP 32A(1) involves whether "as a matter of efficient judicial administration it is impractical to have multiple parties all before the court." *Newman*, 287 Or. at 49, 597 P.2d 801. Early Oregon cases found that joinder practical in cases involving as many as 101 class members. *See, e.g.*, *Tobin v. Portland Mills Co.*, 41 Or. 269, 278–79, 68 P. 743, 746–47 (1902) (holding that 101 putative class members could be joined in one suit and therefore representative action not warranted); *Lonsford v. Burton*, 200 Or. 497, 517–20 (1954) (refusing to certify as a class action a group containing the three named plaintiffs and thirty-five other putative class members); *Bergquist v. Int'l Realty, Ltd.*, 272 Or. 416, 431 n.9 (1975) (citing *Lonsford* as lack of numerosity). More recent authority suggests that 25 to 30 class members are sufficiently numerous that joinder may be impractical. *Newman*, 287 Or. at 50, 597 P.2d 802. In establishing numerosity plaintiffs may not rely on "speculation" as to class size and must instead produce some evidence that joinder of the putative class members is impractical. *Demarco v. Edens*, 390 F.2d 836, 845 (2d Cir. 1968) (cited in by *Bernard*, 275 Or. at 154, 550 P.2d at 1210). In "class suits it is important to plead . . . and prove[] with a fair degree of certainty" that the class is "so numerous as to make it impractical to bring them before the court." *Lonsford*, 200 Or. at 510 (citation omitted). To establish impracticability of joinder, "[m]ore is required than the mere pleading of the language of" the rule." *Id.*; *Dale v. Sitel Corp.*, 502-1375, at 5 (Multnomah County Cir. Ct. June 1, 2007) (Wittmayer, J.) (refusing to certify based on lack of numerosity where "it is unknown how many members of the potential class have claims," and determining that figure requires individual inquiry); *Rogers v. RGIS LLP*, 2006 WL 4691057 (Or. Cir. 2006) (Hodson, J.) (refusing to certify; no evidence of numerosity); *Lowdermilk v. US Bank Nat'l Ass'n*, 2008 WL 4281960, *2–3 (Or. Cir. 2008) (Marsha, J) (same).

ii. ORCP 32A(2). Commonality. Oregon courts have not provided substantial guidance on what it takes to satisfy the commonality requirement of ORCP 32A(2). One Oregon court adopted a stringent test for commonality, holding that if there were any "questions of fact not common to *all* members of the proposed class," the Court should deny class certification based on a lack of commonality. *See Brown v. Lobdell*, 36 Or. App. 397, 411–12, 585 P.2d 4, 12 (1978) (class certification denied for class of persons whose tax refunds had been reduced or eliminated by an Oregon Department of Revenue set off program where Department might have various justifications for withholding different person's tax refunds and resolution of due process questions required examination of notices and procedures in each case); *see also Baker v. Portland*, 2 F. Cas. 472 (Or. Cir. Ct. 1879) (where plaintiff and class members sought relief against same defendant but under different contracts "no common interest" was present). Other published Oregon cases discussing commonality takes a more liberal approach to commonality. The court in *Alsea Veneer, Inc. v. State*, 117 Or. App. 42, 843 P.2d 492 (1992), *aff'd in part, rev'd in part on other grounds*, 318 Or. 33, 862 P.2d 95 (1993), held that differences in damages with respect to class members, or even that some class members may not be entitled to damages, does not negate commonality where there remain significant common issues. *Id.* at 53, 843 P.2d at 497. Notably, however, the broad commonality discussion in *Alsea Veneer* stems from a claim that a state statute was an unconstitutional impairment of the obligation of a contract—a unique claim that does *not* require proof of injury as an element of liability. *Id.*; *Fed'n of Parole and Probation Officers v. State*, 144 Or. App. 535, 539, 928 P.2d 335, 337–38 (1996) (listing elements). But there is a difference between demonstrating that evidence is susceptible to proof by common evidence and the evidence needed to send a case to a jury for decision on a class-wide basis. *See Delgado v. Del Monte Fresh Produce N.A., Inc.*, 260 Or. App. 480, 492 (2014), *rev. den.* 355 Or. 380 (2014). Inconsistent testimony about common practices may not defeat class certification, but rather may only be evidence a jury needs to consider in reaching a class-wide verdict. *Id.* Indeed, the Oregon Court of Appeals recently confirmed that "to satisfy the commonality requirement for class certification, [courts] 'look at whether the claimed common issues are susceptible to and appropriate for proof of common evidence.'" *Migis v. Autozone Inc.*, 282 Or. App. 774, 781 (2016) (quoting *Delgado*).

iii. ORCP 32A(3). Typicality. To satisfy typicality, plaintiffs must demonstrate that the claims of the representative plaintiffs are typical of the claims of the class. ORCP 32A(3). The stringency of the typicality requirement has varied over time. One older case held that to establish typicality the plaintiff must show that his or her interest is "so identical that the motive and inducement to protect and preserve may be assumed in each." *Lonsford*, 200 Or. at 509, 267 P.2d at 214. Another older case, by contrast, held that typicality arises where "the underlying bases for the claims are the same." *Derenco, Inc. v. Benjamin Franklin Fed. Sav. & Loan Ass'n*, 281 Or. 533, 568–69 (1978). More recent cases have expressly adopted the view of the federal courts that a representative's claim is typical if it "arises from the same event or practice of course of conduct that gives rise to the claims of members and his or her claims are based on the same legal theory." *Newman*, 287 Or. at 50, 597 P.2d at 802 (citation omitted). Like commonality, that damages might differ among class members does not bar certification, so long as the claims of all class members arise from the same course of conduct or transaction. *Alsea Veneer*, 117 Or. App. at 53. And if the plaintiff seeks to certify only certain issues, he need be typical only as to those issues, not all claims of the class as a whole. *Shea*,

164 Or. App. at 205, 990 P.2d at 916. Although individual defenses can render a representative atypical, theoretical defenses with little basis in fact will not impede certification. *Bernard*, 275 Or. at 158, 550 P.2d at 1211–12. Oregon courts do not often deny class certification based on a lack of typicality but will do so where the law (or defendants) vary between the representative and the class. *See Powell v. Equitable Sav. and Loan Ass'n*, 57 Or. App. 110, 113–15, 643 P.2d 1331, 1332–33 (1982) (if the named plaintiffs' claims are governed by law different than some other class members, the named plaintiffs' claims are not sufficiently typical for class certification); *John Deere v. Delphia*, 266 Or. 116, 121, 511 P.2d 386, 389 (1973) (no typicality where plaintiff's claims were against a different company than those of the rest of the class).

iv. ORCP 32A(4). Adequacy. Few Oregon cases address the requirements of ORCP 32A(4). Generally, "the interests of a class can be adequately protected if (1) there are no disabling conflicts of interest between the class representatives; and (2) the class, and the class is represented by counsel competent to handle such matters." *Alsea Veneer,* 117 Or. App. at 53, 843 P.2d at 498; *Sosna v. Iowa*, 419 U.S. 393, 403 (1975). Adequacy requires that the class representative show the "requisite community interest with the represented class." *John Deere*, 266 Or. at 121, 511 P.2d at 389. This requirement led several judges to dismiss class action claims based on "non-participation grounds," where the representative plaintiffs did not "meaningfully participat[e] in th[e] litigation as required by" ORCP 32. *Rivera v. U.S. Bank Nat'l Assoc.*, 0305-05045, at *5 (Multnomah County Cir. Ct. Aug. 29, 2006) (Baldwin, J.); *Rogers*, 2006 WL 4691057, at 9; *Lowdermilk*, 2008 WL 4281960, at 4 (where class representative could not recall viewing complaint before filing or testify about disputed practices, and deferred all decisions to counsel, she was inadequate). Courts will deny certification based on a lack of adequacy where a conflict of interest exists between the relief sought by the representative and the class. *See Safeway, Inc. v. Or. Pub. Employees Union*, 152 Or. App. 349, 359, 954 P.2d 196, 201 (1998) (where class representatives sought rights contrary to those of other class members, certification should be denied on adequacy grounds); *see also Pearson I*, 2006 WL 66304, at *7–8 (doubting adequacy of representative where their punitive damages claims might be so large as to preclude actual damages claims of class members, but finding issue "too remote" to deny certification); *Froeber v. Liberty Mut. Ins. Co.*, No. 00C15234, at 5–6 (Marion County Cir. Ct. Feb. 26, 2004) (Hart, J.) (plaintiffs inadequate where their interests in damages may result in increased premiums for class, as they neither provided "record evidence nor convincing logic to show that a class-wide judgment would produce a net benefit for most—or even many—class members").

v. ORCP 32A(5). Prelitigation notice requirement class actions for damages. ORCP 32A(5) mandates that in any class action for damages, the named plaintiff must demonstrate compliance with the prelitigation notice requirement contained in ORCP 32H, by showing that at least thirty days before filing a damages class action, the named plaintiff notified the potential defendant (in writing by registered or certified mail) of the particular alleged cause(s) of action, and demanded that the person correct or rectify the alleged wrong. ORCP 32H. The notice requirements of ORCP 32H do *not* apply to claims for equitable relief. *See* ORCP 32J. Moreover, a plaintiff may amend his complaint for equitable relief after thirty days to include damages claims, so long as the requirements of ORCP 32H have been satisfied in the interim. *Id.* It is unclear whether the statute of limitations on a damages claim would expire during the 30-day notice period, even if a complaint for equitable relief had already been filed. The purpose of the prelitigation notice is to allow the defendant an opportunity to remedy the alleged wrong and avoid the negative publicity associated with class actions complaint for damages. *See* Laird Kirkpatrick, *Procedural Reform in Oregon*, 56 Or. L. Rev.

539, 547 n.48 (1977) (one of the "*[m]ost significant differences*" between the federal rule and Oregon's rule is that the "Oregon Act provides that, prior to filing a class action for damages, a plaintiff must send a thirty-day pre-litigation notice that *allows the defendant to avoid the adverse publicity of a class action by voluntarily redressing the alleged* wrong with regard to all class members") (emphasis added). Accordingly, if a party intends at the outset to seek both damages and equitable relief in a class action, the proper course is to first provide thirty days' notice before *any* complaint is filed. Filing a complaint for equitable relief that expresses an intent to immediately seek damages at the expiration of the thirty-day window violates at least the spirit, if not the letter, of ORCP 32A(5), ORCP 32H, ORCP 32I, and ORP 32J. *See, e.g.*, *Pro-Fac Coop v. Alpha Nursery, Inc.*, 205 F. Supp. 2d 90, 94–95 & n.2 (W.D.N.Y. 2002) (discussing ORCP 32H notice obligation and noting that complaint was filed *after* notice was provided); *see also* Gary M. Berne & R. Alan Wright, Chapter 16, *Civil Pleadings & Practice* (Berne & Wright, CPP) at 10–11 (1994) (a defendant receiving ORCP 32I notice may consider whether to try and resolve the potential litigation before the class representative actually files a complaint).

c. ORCP 32B. Superiority

A class action will be maintained only if the court finds that proceeding as a class is superior to all other available methods for the fair and efficient adjudication of the controversy. *See* ORCP 32B. The 1992 amendments to ORCP 32 adopting a unitary class action mechanism were intended to avoid arguments concerning the category of class action for which the plaintiff should be seeking certification. Instead, the class certification process now adheres to the spirit of what Federal Rule 23 sought to achieve—a determination as to whether "a class action would achieve economies of time, effort, and expense, and promote uniformity of decisions as to persons similarly situated, without sacrificing procedural fairness or bringing about undesirable results." *Bernard*, 275 Or. at 152 n.3, 550 P.2d at 1208 n.3 (quoting Fed. R. Civ. P. 23 Advisory Committee Notes, 39 F.R.D. 69, 102–03 (1966)). The post-1992 version of ORCP 32B makes eight factors "pertinent" to the superiority analysis. ORCP 32B(1)–(8). These factors are not a certification checklist, *Shea*, 164 Or. App. 198, 206–07, 990 P.2d 912, 917 (1999), and should not be counted mechanistically as "for" or "against" certification; rather they should be weighed by the court in exercising its discretion. *Pearson I*, 2006 WL 663004, at *9. Indeed, the Court of Appeals in *Migis v. Autozone Inc.* 282 Or. App. 774 (2016), recently held that predominance of common issues was but one factor, and that if other factors collectively show superiority, a lack of predominance is not fatal. *Id.* at 782–86.

i. ORCP 32B(1). Risk of inconsistent results or impeding the ability of non-parties to protect their interests. ORCP 32B(1) is concerned with two basic issues, the first of which supports class status and second of which counsels against it: (1) whether individual adjudications would establish incompatible standards of conduct for the defendant; and (2) where results of a class action would impair or impede the interests of non-parties. *See* ORCP 32B(1)(a)–(b). Speculation is insufficient to show that the concerns of ORCP 32B(1) are an issue. The mere possibility of inconsistent verdicts does not mean that incompatible standards of conduct will result. *Pearson I*, 2006 WL 66304, at *9 (discussing ORCP 32B(1)(a), and holding that any inconsistency in verdicts "would not likely result in 'incompatible standards of conduct' for defendant"); *Lowdermilk*, 2008 WL 4281960, at 4 ("there must be a real risk of individual litigation resulting in incompatible standards of conduct"). Likewise, that a large award for the class might prevent awards for non-parties against the same defendant can "impair[] other plaintiffs' ability to protect their interests"; if that possibility is "remote," however, it will not defeat a certification motion. *Id.*; *State ex rel.*

Young v. Crookham, 290 Or. 61, 72, 618 P.2d 1268, 1274 (1980) ("class actions, in appropriate cases, provide for unitary consideration of [the effect of large punitive] damages" awards). Moreover, there must be some evidence of a realistic possibility of individual suits being filed absent certification before this factor supports certification since, in the absence of such evidence, there is no reason to believe that inconsistent results will occur. *Eisen v. Carlisle & Jacquelin*, 391 F.2d 555, 564 (2d Cir. 1968), *rev'd on other grounds*, 417 U.S. 156 (1974). One cannot simultaneously argue that there is a concrete risk of inconsistent adjudications without a class and also that a class is warranted because the claims of the class members are too small to bring in absent a class. *See id.* (plaintiff "rebutted his own argument").

ii. ORCP 32B(2). Injunctive or declaratory relief claims. ORCP 32B(2) requires the court to examine the extent to which relief sought would take the form of injunctive or declaratory relief with respect to the class as a whole. *See* ORCP 32B(2). No published Oregon cases address ORCP 32B(2), other than to observe that a claim for "equitable relief" does not implicate ORCP 32B(2) if no injunctive or declaratory relief is sought. *See Pearson I*, 2006 WL 663004, at *10.

iii. ORCP 32B(3). Predominance. ORCP 32B(3) concerns the "extent to which questions of law or fact common to the members of the class predominate over any questions affecting only individual members." ORCP 32B(3). The most significant change contained in the 1992 amendment to ORCP 32 was to remove predominance of common issues over all others as a requirement for certification of a damages class action. *Shea*, 164 Or. App. at 207, 990 P.2d at 917 (predominance issue is not the "*sine qua non* of certification of any class," but is "pertinent" to superiority). The 1992 change was patterned on recommendations from a federal subcommittee that studied practice problems under Federal Rule 23—which were not adopted by any other jurisdiction. *See* CCP Staff Comment (1992) (citing ABA Section of Litigation, Report and Recommendations of the Special Subcommittee on Class Action Improvements, 110 F.R.D. 195 (1986)). Those recommendations provide important context to the changes, however, and emphasize that, even under the unitary structure adopted by Oregon, a predominance analysis is still "unquestionably important" in deciding whether to certify. *See* Special Committee Report, 110 F.R.D. at 204. Thus, properly understood, Oregon's rule seeks only to avoid elevating form over substance and the "unduly rigid" structure of Federal Rule 23's three specific categories of class action; if individual issues predominate over common issues such that a class action is not a superior method of adjudication, certification may be denied. Indeed, no Oregon decision has ever allowed a class action to proceed where (as to the issues certified) individual issues predominate over common ones. *Cf. Shea*, 164 Or. App. at 207, 990 P.2d at 917 (if discrete issues are certified, common questions need predominate only over issues certified, not the action "as a whole").

The Oregon cases devoting the greatest attention to predominance pre-date the 1992 amendments but are nonetheless relevant in examining when individual issues become so prevalent that a class action ceases to be a superior means of resolving the dispute. For example, in *Joachim v. Crater Lake Lodge, Inc.*, 48 Or. App. 379, 617 P.2d 632 (1980), plaintiff became ill after drinking contaminated water at a national park and filed a class action against several defendants seeking to recover for her injuries. *Id.* at 381–83, 617 P.2d at 633–34. The court denied class certification on predominance grounds because the issues presented "very difficult and arduous individual proof that is disfavored" under ORCP 32, which "would be most difficult to manage in class action form." *Id.* at 392–93, 617 P.2d at 639. This type of individual inquiry was also discussed in *Bernard*, where the Oregon Supreme Court held that where personal knowledge of each class member was at issue, class treatment would deny the defendant both substantive and procedural rights. *Bernard*, 275 Or. at 159–60 (citations omitted) (predominance lacking because individual determinations of putative class members knowledge of a particular bank policy would require separate adjudications and therefore prohibits certification); *see also Brown*, 36 Or. App. at 411–12, 585 P.2d at 12 (1978) (certification denied in tax refund case where resolution of due process questions required examination of notices and procedures in each case); *Rogers*, 2006 WL 4691057 (potential for conflicting evidence for each class member "defeat[s] any benefit obtained from trying the claims as a class"). "It is not enough to allege a policy that affects an entire class; plaintiffs must establish that the policy affected class members in similar and typical ways." *Lowdermilk*, 2008 WL 4281960, at *4; *see also id.* ("because U.S. Bank's liability as to each plaintiff can only be proved through an individualized inquiry, this case is not appropriate for class certification").

Certain types of claims have likewise been held generally inappropriate for class status. For example, in *Bernard*, the court acknowledged that "without eliminating or eroding the traditional statutory elements of a fraud action, there is no possibility that common questions can predominate over individual ones." *Bernard*, 275 Or. at 163, 550 P.2d at 1215; Fed. R. Civ. P. 23 Advisory Committee Notes, 39 F.R.D. 69, 102–03 (1966) ("fraud case may be unsuited for treatment as a class action if there was material variation in the representations made or in the kinds or degrees of reliance by the persons to whom they were addressed"). Likewise, the court in *Bernard* recognized that a breach of contract claim would usually be inappropriate for class certification because it "would require an examination of each claimant's understanding of the contract and would inevitably deteriorate into multiple lawsuits unsuited for" class treatment. *Id.* at 165, 550 P.2d at 1215; *but see Derenco*, 281 Or. at 572–73, 577 P.2d at 499 (recognizing that individual knowledge can preclude class treatment of contract claims, but certifying class because evidence before the court showed lack of general class knowledge); *Froeber v. Liberty Mut.*, § D(2)(d), *supra*, at 2 ("Plaintiffs cannot prove a breach of Liberty Fire's insurance contracts [on a class-wide basis] by attacking the *methods* that Liberty Fire uses to determine the amounts that it will pay," but must instead can prove breach "only by attacking the *results* achieved in a particular case."). Indeed, tort claims are rarely suited for class treatment.

Many (but not all) claims requiring proof of individualized reliance are inappropriate for class treatment. *See Newman*, 287 Or. at 53–54, 597 P.2d at 803 ("in the present case it would appear that individual determinations of reliance would be required" and the "result would be that common questions of fact would not predominate"); *Pearson I*, 2006 WL 663004, at *10–12 (allegations of affirmative misrepresentations require reliance). Even if common questions exist, if "the establishment of the answers to those common questions [is] likely to be an individualized process," then predominance is lacking. *Dale v. Sitel*, § D(2)(a), *supra*, at 6. Whether reliance is required (and thus would defeat class certification) depends on the conduct involved and the legal theory of the loss allegedly incurred. *See Bohr v. Tillamook Cnty. Creamery Ass'n*, 321 Or. App. 213, 224–26, 516 P.3d 284, 292–93 (2022), *rev'd on other grounds*, 373 Or. 343 (2025). Where individual reliance is required, class treatment is improper and a court may strike the class allegations. *Id.*

But reliance is not always a bar to certification if the focus is on material omissions made by the defendants with a duty to disclose, rather than affirmative misstatements. *Cf. Basic, Inc. v. Levinson*, 485 U.S. 224, 242 (1988) ("Requiring proof of individualized reliance from each member of the proposed plaintiff class effectively would have prevented respondents from proceeding with a class action, since individual issues then would have overwhelmed the common ones."), *and Affiliated Ute Citizens of Utah v. United States*, 406 U.S. 128, 153–54 (1972) (failure to disclose does not require reliance); *Sanders v. Francis*, 277 Or. 593, 598–99, 561 P.2d 1003, 1006 (1977) (same); *Blue Line Farms Inc. v. Pro-Fac Co-Op., Inc.*, 2002 WL 33294579, *2 (Or. Cir. 2002) (McShane, J.). Thus, if a duty to disclose exists, class-wide reliance has been inferred from material fact omissions, in concert with uniform written statements to class members. *Blue Line*, 2002 WL 33294579, at *2;

see also Strawn v. Farmers Ins. Co of Ore., 228 Or. App. 545, 470–71, & n.10, 209 P.3d 357 (2009) (same), *aff'd in part, rev'd in part*, 350 Or. 336 (2011); *Scharfstein v. BP W. Coast Prods., LLC*, 292 Or. App. 69, 87–88, __ P.3d __ (2018) (class action for statutory damages under Unfair Trade Practices Act requires proof of loss as a result of illegal actions, but where legally required disclosures are not made, reliance is not required). The Oregon Court of Appeals has warned, however, that calling something an omission does not make it so, as "every fraud case based on material misrepresentation can be turned facilely into a material omission case." *Pearson III*, 257 Or. App. at 143. But in a notable decision (currently on review in the Oregon Supreme Court), a divided *en banc* panel of the Oregon Court of Appeals held that reliance could be proven through class-wide evidence, where there is a reasonable inference of reliance based on the facts of the particular case. *See id.* at 138.

iv. ORCP 32B(4). Class members' interest in individually controlling separate actions. ORCP 32B(4) requires assessment whether putative class members have an interest in individually controlling their actions. No published Oregon cases address ORCP 32B(4).

v. ORCP 32B(5). The extent and nature of any litigation concerning the controversy already commenced. ORCP 32B(5) requires the court to examine the "extent and nature of any litigation concerning the litigation already commenced by or against members of the class." ORCP 32B(5). There are no published decisions addressing ORCP 32B(5), although at least one trial court denied certification in part based on the fact that "essentially the same claim" was being pursued on a class basis elsewhere. *Lowdermilk*, 2008 WL 4281960, at *4–5.

vi. ORCP 32B(6). Desirability of the class forum. ORCP 32B(6) requires the court to examine the "desirability or undesirability of concentrating the litigation of the claims in the particular forum" chosen by the plaintiff. ORCP 32B(6). In addressing ORCP 32B(6), Oregon courts have recognized that, as a general rule, a "single adjudication of" common issues is "preferable to piecemeal litigation and potentially inconsistent awards" in different forums. *Alsea*, 117 Or. App. at 55, 843 P.2d at 499. Despite that general rule, at least one trial court recently held that "other avenues and procedures do exist to accomplish" the resolution of similar claims absent class treatment, including "assignments to the same Judge for case management, changes of venue to the same Circuit Court Judicial District, Assignment by the Chief Justice of a Circuit Judge to handle cases from another judicial district for administrative efficiencies, etc." *Dale v. Sitel*, § D(2)(a), *supra*, at 7.

vii. ORCP 32B(7). Manageability. The difficulties likely to be encountered in the management of a class action that will be eliminated or significantly reduced if the controversy is adjudicated by other available means is pertinent to the class certification determination. *See* ORCP 32B(7). The manageability inquiry "necessarily overlaps with that of predominance." *Pearson I*, 2006 WL 663304, at *11. An early Oregon decision summarized manageability as whether the class action, if tried, would "impede the usual business of the courts." *Hurt v. Midrex Div. of Midland Ross Corp.*, 276 Or. 925, 930, 556 P.2d 1337, 1339 (1976). Manageability "encompasses the whole range of practical problems that may render the class action format inappropriate for a particular case." *Eisen v. Carlisle & Jacquelin*, 417 U.S.156, 164 (1974). Where a "single administration is undoubtedly less difficult than would be management of the [class] claims," then ORCP 32B(7) tilts in favor of certification. *Alsea Veneer*, 117 Or. App. at 55, 843 P.2d at 499. The class action device cannot abrogate the procedural and substantive rights of a party simply to make the case manageable: "We cannot imply from the mere enactment of a class action statute . . . that the legislature intended to abrogate settled principles of substantive and procedural law simply to make the class action manageable in instances where it presently is not. Several provisions of our statute clearly indicate to the contrary." *Bernard*, 275 Or. at 160 n.5, 550 P.2d at 1212 n.5; *Froeber v. Liberty Mut.*, § D(2)(d), *supra*, at 3 (case is "hopelessly unmanageable," as "[t]rying Plaintiffs' breach of contract theory as a class action would require the Court to ignore Plaintiffs' burden to prove an actionable breach, indulge an impermissible presumption of injury, and deprive Liberty Fire of an opportunity to rebut that presumption with individualized evidence"). Manageability directly affects the superiority analysis because if a class action is not manageable, it cannot be superior. Thus, "where the plaintiff has other, less burdensome methods available by which to resolve the controversy," a class action is not superior. *Becker v. Schenley Indus., Inc.* 557 F.2d 346, 348 (2d Cir. 1977) (cited by *Newman*, 287 Or. at 51). And where governmental action may provide relief to the putative class, manageability concerns tilt against certification. *Pearson I*, 2006 WL 663304, at 11 ("Attorney General [action] . . . would eliminate many of the manageability difficulties.").

viii. ORCP 32B(8). The effect of limited class benefits. ORCP 32B(8) requires the court to examine whether the class members' claims are too small, taking into consideration the complexities of the issues and expenses of the litigation, to provide any significant relief to the class members. *See* ORCP 32B(8). There is no analogous provision to ORCP 32B(8) in the federal rules. The original statutory version of ORCP 32B(8) was taken "verbatim" from American College of Trial Lawyers, *Report and Recommendations of the Special Committee on Rule 23 of the Federal Rules of Civil Procedure* (1972) (ACTL Report), which was "highly critical of class actions as they have been conducted under Rule 23." *Bernard*, 275 Or. at 151, 550 P.2d 1208. The recommendations from that report provide the best analysis of what ORCP 32B(8) seeks to achieve in assessing superiority of class actions. ORCP 32B(8) was intended to prevent class actions from going forward where the amount of recovery for the class members was minimal when compared with the interests involved, and where the main beneficiaries of the action would be class counsel. The ACTL Report's recommendation (adopted in ORCP 32B(8)) was that Federal Rule 23 "be revised to clearly indicate that not every wrong committed in our society should be the subject of a class action." ACTL Report, at 27–28. The ACTL Report observed that many small value class actions "primarily benefit the attorneys who initiate them," and that "the public interest issue may well be so insignificant that the redress of the nine-dollar wrong should from a policy viewpoint be left to the realm of private ordering," because "scarce" judicial resources "cannot be allocated on the vindication of every individual wrong however slight." *Id.* at 27–28.

This skepticism toward small-dollar class action claims was recognized by the Oregon Supreme Court in *Bernard*, where the court noted that, although Oregon's rule allows aggregation of small value claims, it does so only where a class action was otherwise clearly called for. *Bernard*, 275 Or. at 152 & n.3, 550 P.2d at 1208–09 & n.3. The basis for this skepticism is that experience under the federal rule showed that courts too often sacrifice the procedural safeguards established by the Constitution, congressional statutes, and the Federal Rules of Civil Procedure "to make the class action manageable where it presently is not." *Id.* at 159–60 & n.5, 550 P.2d 1213 & n.5 (citations omitted). The result of that approach was "almost always confusion of thought and irrational, emotional, and unsound decisions" by "those whose intentions may be above reproach." *Id.* This skepticism does not mean, however, that small claims are always inappropriate, and will depend on the facts of each case. *See Vasquez-Lopez v. Beneficial Or., Inc.*, 210 Or. App. 553, 569–72, 152 P.3d 940 (2007) (refusing to compel arbitration in part, based on effect of class action waiver on consumers).

The intent and language of ORCP 32B(8) appear to have been misinterpreted in *Alsea Veneer*. There, the Court read the rule as suggesting that the fact that the individual Plaintiffs tried small value claims was "one of the most persuasive reasons for certification" because the amount would not cover the costs of the litigation. *Alsea Veneer*, 117 Or. App. at 55, 843 P.2d at 499. This view is the opposite of what the rule was intended to accomplish.

d. ORCP 32C. Class Certification (and Decertification) Orders

ORCP 32C(1) mirrors the language of former Federal Rule 23(c)(1) by requiring that "as soon as practicable after the commencement of an action brought as a class action" the court "shall" determine by Order "whether and with respect to what claims or issues it is to be maintained." ORCP 32 C(1). "[I]t is apparent that ORCP 32C(1) grants broad authority to trial courts to make rulings in class actions that can be tailored to the practical needs of individual cases and to a variety of circumstances," including the timing, sequence, and conditional nature of certification orders. *Greene v. Salomon Smith Barney, Inc.*, 228 Or. App. 379, 386, 209 P.3d 333, 336 (2009). The rule also recognizes the court's ability to certify as to only certain issues or claims. *Shea*, 164 Or. App. at 205, 990 P.2d at 205. ORCP 32C(1) requires that the court make findings of fact and state separately its conclusions on class certification. ORCP 32C(1).

Nonetheless, the court "has a duty to continually assess whether class treatment is appropriate" and may decertify if plaintiffs cannot "present a viable, efficient trial plan in a timely manner." *Belknap v. U.S. Bank Nat'l Ass'n*, 2007 WL 3035171 (Or. Cir. 2007) (Cinneger, J.) (decertifying class), *aff'd* 235 Or. App. 658, 234 P.3d 1041 (2010). In particular, as a case proceeds from certification toward trial, plaintiff's inability to present a viable trial plan warrants decertification. *Id.* In deciding whether to decertify a class action, the Court need not "consider each and every one of the listed factors [in ORCP 32B] in making its determination whether to allow an action to continue as a class action" and need only consider whether class treatment remains superior. *Belknap*, 235 Or. App. at 667, 234 P.3d at 1046. Finally, like its federal counterpart, Oregon's rules permit a defendant to preemptively move to strike class allegations. *See, e.g., Paul v. Providence Health Sys. Ore.*, 237 Or. App. 584, 588, 240 P.3d 1110, 1113 (2010), *aff'd* 351 Or. 587, 273 P.3d 106 (2012) (noting that trial court granted motion to strike class allegations, affirming dismissal of motion to dismiss); *Thomas v. U.S. Bank, N.A.*, 244 Or. App. 457, 474, 260 P.3d 711, 722 (2011) (affirming trial court's striking of class allegations based on collateral estoppel effect of prior decertification of similar class). That said, a defendant must make all decertification arguments before a verdict, as arguments saved for post-trial motions are too late for consideration on appeal. *See Delgado*, 260 Or. App. at 488. Likewise, one factor in determining whether a Court abuses its discretion in refusing to decertify is when the Defendant learns of the bases supporting the motion; delaying the motion until trial counsels against decertification. *Id.* at 489. *See also Migis v. Autozone, Inc.*, 282 Or. App. 774, 783 (2016) ("In keeping with the fact that a superiority determination is a matter of judicial administration, attempts to decertify late in the litigation process are disfavored.").

e. ORCP 32D. Settlement or Compromise

Unlike its federal counterpart Federal Rule 23(e), ORCP 32 provides that—even if class certification has not been granted or sought—the action may "not be voluntarily dismissed or compromised without the approval of the court, and notice of the proposed dismissal or compromise [must] be given to some or all members of the class in such manner as the court directs." ORCP 32D. The only exceptions to this notice requirement are where dismissal is (1) to be without prejudice or (2) with prejudice against the class representative only. Moreover, even settlement under these two narrow exceptions is permitted only where "there is a showing that no compensation in any form has passed directly or indirectly from the party opposing the class to the class representative or to the class representative's attorney and that no promise of such compensation has been made." *Id.* These limitations make pre-certification settlement with the named plaintiff less likely than under the federal rules. (Notice may also be required if the statute of limitations has run or may run against the claim of any class member.) The only decision to address ORCP 32D is *Froeber II*, where the court followed federal cases and approved a class action settlement releasing unpleaded claims because the underlying factual bases and injury were the same. 222 Or. App. at 276–81, 193 P.3d at 1005–08. *Froeber II* also adopted the federal approach to determining the adequacy of the settlement notice to the class, holding that so long as the notice was "'reasonably clear' and 'fairly apprised' recipients of the proposed settlement terms," it was sufficient and "need not explain all of the consequences involved" or be a "complete source of settlement information." *Id.* at 282–83, 193 P.3d at 1009.

f. ORCP 32F & L. Class Notice, Mandatory Claim Forms, and Costs

Unlike Federal Rule 23, which requires (for damages class actions) the "best notice practicable under the circumstances, including individual notice to all members who can be identified through reasonable effort," *see* Fed. R. Civ. P. 23(c)(2)(B), Oregon's notice provision requires only that notice be given "to some or all members of the class." ORCP 32F(1). Oregon's rule lists six factors providing guidance for when and how notice should be provided and when class members can opt out of the class. ORCP 32F(1). Oregon has historically used an opt-in procedure to recover in class actions. The Oregon Legislature substantially amended (and shortened) ORCP 32F in 2015. The changes reflect that the Court may approve process for payment of damages, including use of claim forms, removes the prior requirement that class members affirmatively indicate desire for share of monetary award before determination of judgment amount, and requires the Court to identify all individuals who request exclusion from class, and to generally describe the remaining class. These amendments apply only to actions in which appeals have been exhausted or expired. Plaintiff typically bears the notice costs before judgment is entered, but under ORCP 32F, a Court has the discretion to apportion notice costs if the Defendant can include notice within regular mailings to employees. ORCP 32F(2).

ORCP 32L parallels ORCP 32(f), by providing that any judgment in a certified class action—regardless of the result—must generally describe the members of the class and must specifically identify any persons who requested exclusion from the class and are not bound by the judgment.

g. ORCP 32G. Issue Classes and Subclasses

ORCP 32G expressly allows for issue classes to be certified when "appropriate," and mirrors the language of Federal Rule 23(c)(4)(a). In *Shea v. Chicago Pneumatic Tool*, the court held that where an issue class is certified, the typicality and predominance inquiries need only be made with respect to the issues certified. *See* 164 Or. App. at 205–07; 990 P.2d at 916–17. Thus, the fact that individual issues might predominate over common issues as to the action "as a whole" does not bar certification on those issues where predominance is satisfied. *Id.* Subclasses are appropriate to resolve differences among discrete categories of class members, particularly where the difference between class members involves only the amount of damages sustained (rather than the existence of liability). *Alsea Veneer*, 117 Or. App. at 54, 843 P.2d at 498. Subclasses must still "separately satisfy the requirements of ORCP 32," except for numerosity. *Pearson I*, 2006 WL 663004, at *12.

h. ORCP 32H, 32I, and 32J. Limitations on Class Actions for Damages Where the Defendant Offers a Remedy

ORCP 32H, 32I, and 32J create a specific process for bringing class actions for damages. These rules are the most significant restriction and departure from Federal Rule 23. *See* Don S. Willner, *More Justice Under Law*, 55 Or. L. Rev. 183, 191 (1976) (Oregon's thirty-day notice requirement is a "fundamental difference[]" between Federal Rule 23 and the Oregon class action rule). ORCP 32H requires that before a plaintiff may bring a class action for damages, he must give first give the defendant thirty days' notice (via certified or registered mail) of the claims plaintiff intends to bring and a demand that the defendant correct or rectify the alleged wrong. *See* ORCP 32H. ORCP 32I, in turn, precludes plaintiffs from maintaining a class action for damages if the defendant has ceased engaging in the allegedly improper activity, identified the putative class members, and offered to remedy the alleged wrong upon request. *Id.* Until 2021, no appellate case law explained ORCP 32I, but the language of the rule, trial court decisions, and its legislative history generally showed that the rule should be strictly applied where a defendant "has voluntarily addressed the alleged wrong with regard to all class members." *Kirkpatrick*, § D(2)(e), *supra*, 56 Or. L. Rev. at 547 n.48; *Gibson v. Providence Health Sys. Or.*, 2007 WL 3339229 (Or. Cir. 2007) (Litzenberger, J.) (striking class allegations pursuant to ORCP 32I), *aff'd on other grounds sub nom.*, 237 Or. App. 584, 240 P.3d 1110 (2010), *aff'd* 351 Or. 587, 273 P.3d 106 (2012); *Bravo v. Taco Bell Corp.*, 1997 WL 34650259 (Or. Cir. 1997) (Brown, J.) (staying discovery to permit opportunity to complete ORCP 32I cure); Berne & Wright, CCP, § D(2)(e), *supra*, Ch. 16 at 5–6 (1994) (rule stops "unnecessary litigation" by giving defendant the chance to give appropriate [class] relief").

In 2021, however, the Oregon Court of Appeals conducted a lengthy analysis of ORCP 32I, in *Stewart v. Albertson's, Inc.*, 308 Or. App. 464 (2021). After an exhaustive review of the history and text of the Rule, the court determined both the process for evaluating offers under ORCP 32I as well as the varying standards of review involved. As to process, the court held:

> When a trial court is called upon to evaluate a defendant's showing under ORCP 32 I, the court must make a series of determinations. It must consider the pleadings to determine the alleged wrong and the extent of available remedies under the substantive law that applies to that wrong. It must consider the defendant's evidentiary showing about the remedy offered, including resolving any factual disputes in that regard. And then it must determine whether, in light of what the substantive law treats as available and just relief, the defendant's proposed cure is the appropriate compensation, correction, or remedy under the circumstances.

Id. at 487. As to the standard of review, the court acknowledged different standards depending on the nature of the challenge to the use of ORCP 32I:

> We review the court's ultimate determination that a proposed cure provides the appropriate compensation, correction, or remedy for an abuse of discretion; however, to the extent that the court's exercise of discretion is predicated on conclusions about what a plaintiff has alleged and the available remedies for the alleged wrong, we review for errors of law; and to the extent that the ruling is predicated on factual findings about a defendant's showing as to the proposed cure, we review for any evidence in the record to support them.

Id. at 487–88. Finally, the court in St*ewart* also held that the 30-day notice provision of ORCP 32I does not require that the defendant provide the proposed cure or remedy during the 30-day window between notice and the filing of a damages action, and that a defendant may make an offer under ORCP 32I after plaintiff brings a class action for damages. *Id.* at 472–75.

Notably, ORCP 32J excludes the requirements of ORCP 32H and ORCP 32I from solely equitable claims, but also provides a right amend the complaint to seek damages without leave of court after thirty days and compliance with ORCP 32H and 32I.

i. ORCP 32M. Attorneys' Fees Awards[1]

ORCP 32M permits an attorneys' fees award to be obtained from any class recovery, so long as that recovery is divisible. *See Strawn v. Farmers Ins. Co. of Ore.*, 353 Or. 210, 216, 297 P.3d 439, 444 (2013) (*Strawn II*). The Oregon Supreme Court in *Strawn II* provided a comprehensive analysis of every aspect of attorneys' fees in class actions and provides more detail than is warranted in this summary. Anyone examining fees under ORCP 32 should review *Strawn II* in detail. Nevertheless, some general guidelines exist from *Strawn II* and elsewhere.

As a procedural rule, nothing in ORCP 32M provides an independent basis for an award of attorneys' fees in addition to the class recovery. *See Strawn*, 233 Or. App. at 406 n.3, 226 P.2d at 90 n.3. Some older cases rely on the "common benefit" doctrine as a basis for requiring a defendant to pay attorneys' fees separately from damages included in a class fund. *See Guinasso v. Pac. First Fed.*, 89 Or. App. 270, 278–79, 749 P.2d 577 (1988). The common benefit doctrine is similar to the "common fund doctrine" and involves situations where the court assesses fees against a nominal defendant—like a corporation or labor union—whose controlling members are both the beneficiaries of the class relief and the parties who will pay the fee. The common benefit doctrine has been dramatically limited, however, and now only applies where, among other criteria, "the party requesting attorney fees [has] been seeking to vindicate an important constitutional right applying to all citizens without any gain peculiar to himself." *Armatta v. Kitzhaber*, 327 Or. 250, 287, 959 P.2d 49, 69–70 (1998). Because the limitations in *Armatta* so severely restrict the common benefit doctrine, that doctrine will not usually apply in damages class actions, and a separate fee award based on *Guinasso* will be rarely, if ever, be permitted. By providing that reasonable attorneys' fees may be paid from the recovery, ORCP 32M codifies the common fund doctrine, articulated in *State Farm Mut. Auto. Ins. v. Clinton*, 267 Or. 653, 657, 518 P.2d 645 (1974) (holding that attorney whose efforts result in recovery of fund payable to various persons is entitled to payment of reasonable attorneys' fees from that fund). Oregon courts have not specifically endorsed either the percentage of recovery or the lodestar method of calculating attorneys' fees in class actions but have criticized the lodestar approach as "unduly cumbersome." *Griffin v. Tri-County Metro. Transp. Dist. of Or.*, 112 Or. App. 575, 584–85, 831 P.2d 42 (1992), *rev'd on other grounds*, 318 Or. 500, 870 P.2d 808 (1994). That said, the Supreme Court has recognized that the lodestar approach is "at least permissible" in cases with fee-shifting statutes, and that ORCP 32M allows for lodestar or percentage of fund, depending on which methodology gives a fair award under the circumstances. *Strawn II*, 353 Or. at 221 & n.7. 297 P.3d at 447 & n.7.

Although attorneys' fees for representing a class are subject to the control of the court, ORCP 32M(1)(a), any fee agreement with class counsel must be considered. *Kalman v. Currey*, 88 Or. App. 398, 405, 745 P.2d 1232, 1236–37 (1987) (citing former ORCP 32N(2)(b)); *Coulter Prop. Mgmt. v. James*, 160 Or. App. 390, 394, 981 P.2d 395 (1999) (in exercising its discretion to award attorneys' fees, trial court "had a duty to consider all relevant circumstances, including [the prevailing party's] contingent fee agreement"). This rule, like its federal counterpart, is "designed to protect the interests of the class members, who are frequently widely dispersed geographically, individually may have a small financial stake in the action and may be poorly equipped to defend their interests against those of their attorneys when the fee is determined." *Kalman*, 88 Or. App. at 405, 745 P.2d at 1236–37. For these reasons, ORCP 32M(1)(e) lists five "factors to be considered by the court in determining the fee, all of which are particularly relevant in evaluating the reasonableness of a contingent fee

[1] In 2009 the Legislature repealed ORCP 32K (barring class actions for statutory damages). The subsequent ORCP 32 provisions were renamed, shifting alphabetically by one letter. Thus, ORCP 32M used to be ORCP 32N.

payable out of a settlement fund." *Id.* Nothing in ORCP 32M suggests or requires a multiplier or a particular benchmark to arrive at a reasonable fee, and fee enhancements through the use of a multiplier are uncommon in Oregon courts. *Id.* at 404, 408, 745 P.2d at 1236–38 (rejecting fee enhancement request). That said, in *Strawn II*, the Oregon Supreme Court suggested that Courts should exclude any claim with free-shifting provisisons from the contingency aspect of any multiplier because fee-shifting statute and claims have different policy goals than common-fund attorneys' fees awards. 353 Or. at 228, 297 P.3d at 451. The Court added that generally, for complex class litigation, attorneys' fees should not exceed 20–30 percent of the recovered fund, with deviations as appropriate. *Id.* at 229–30, 297 P.3d at 452. If fees already fall within that area, no multiplier is needed. *Id.*

Class representatives in Oregon, unlike other states, bear the risk of costs in a class action that may not be borne by class counsel under the ethical rules. *Id.* at 244–45, 297 P.3d at 460. As a result, courts are more apt to provide an incentive award to compensate for that risk. *Id.*

Finally, the Oregon Court of Appeals has confirmed that, by statute, prevailing party attorneys' fees are not available against a class action plaintiff, even if otherwise permissible, and even where the Court refuses to certify the class. *Curzi v. Ore. State Lottery*, 286 Or. App. 254, 256–57 (2017) ("Under ORS 20.190(6)(a), prevailing party fees may not be assessed in a 'class action proceeding under ORCP 32.'").

j. ORCP 32N. Tolling

No published decision addresses the effect of class actions on applicable limitations periods. (One recent decision from the Court of Appeals discusses the tolling issues under ORCP 32N, but ultimately refused to rule on the issue because it deemed the issue waived. *Migis v. Autozone, Inc.*, 282 Or. App. 774 803–06 (2016).) However, at least one trial court order directly addressed ORCP 32N (formerly ORCP 32O), and citing the relevant legislative history, adhered to the federal approach established in *American Pipe & Constr. Co. v. Utah*, 415 U.S. 952 (1974), which held that the commencement of a class action tolls the applicable limitations period pending a certification decision. *See Livingston v. U.S. Bank Nat'l Ass'n*, 2009 WL 1542465 (Multnomah County Sup. Ct. Apr. 27, 2009). In *Livingston*, the Court was faced with the "stacking" issue inherent to *American Pipe* tolling—*i.e.*, whether successive class actions continue to toll the limitations period indefinitely. *See id.* at 3–4. In that case, the court was faced with a second class action filing, alleging the same claims as a prior case where certification was denied. *Id.* The Court held that the plaintiffs' claims in the second action were time-barred, because the denial of class certification in the first action commenced the running of the limitations period anew. *Id.* at 4. The court concluded that a "rule allowing plaintiffs to 'stack one class action on top of another and continue to toll the statute of limitations indefinitely would allow lawyers to file successive putative class actions with the hope of attracting more potential plaintiffs and perpetually tolling the statute of limitations.'" *Id.* (citations omitted).

k. ORCP 32O. Payment of Damages

The Oregon Legislature added ORCP 32(O) effective March 2015, which authorizes courts, as part of settlement or judgment in class action, to approve process for payment of damages, and directs court to order that at least 50 percent of amount awarded as damages but not paid to class members must be paid to Oregon State Bar for funding Legal Services Program. The new Rule also directs court to order that any remainder of amount not paid to class members be paid to an entity for purposes related to the particular class action or benefiting interests of class members.

5. DISCOVERY IN CLASS ACTIONS

No published Oregon decision addresses the scope of discovery permitted under ORCP 32, although the court in *Bernard* noted that the trial court made its certification decision based on "affidavits, depositions and documentary evidence." *Bernard*, 275 Or. at 147, 550 P.2d 1203 (1976). Discovery from class members is allowed, as "there is nothing improper about" obtaining discovery from potential class members if relevant to certification. *Dale v. Sitel*, § D(2)(a), *supra*, at 2 (refusing to strike class members' declarations obtained by defendants).

6. APPEALS OF CLASS CERTIFICATION ORDERS

Class certification decisions are not immediately appealable in Oregon. *Pearson II*, 208 Or. App. at 503, 145 P.3d at 298–99. There is no state law equivalent of Federal Rule 23(f). *Id.* at 504 & n.2, 145 P.3d at 299 n.2. Oregon's class-action appeal statute, ORS 19.225, was passed in 1973 and modeled on 28 U.S.C. § 1292(b). *Id.* at 504, 145 P.3d at 299. This means that Oregon courts interpreting ORS 19.225 rely on federal appellate interpretations of Section 1292(b) that existed before 1973 to determine whether an interlocutory appeal should be permitted. *Id.* at 504–06, 145 P.3d at 299–302. As with 28 U.S.C. 1292(b), in Oregon, there is no absolute right to seek interlocutory review, as the trial court must first certify the action for such review after finding that there are: (1) controlling questions of law, (2) as to which there is substantial ground for difference of opinion, and (3) that an immediate appeal from the Order granting certification may materially advance the ultimate termination of the litigation. *See* ORS 19.225; *Pearson II*, 208 Or. App. at 512–13, 145 P.3d at 304. The court of appeals then may, in its discretion, accept review of the appeal. ORS 19.225. There is no stay in proceedings pending review unless the trial court of court of appeals orders a stay. *Id.* It is up to the trial court to decide which issues may be certified for review, and the appellate court is limited to reviewing only those issues certified. *Shea*, 164 Or. App. at 204–05, 990 P.2d at 915–16. Notably, ORS 19.225 eschews ORCP 32's distinction between actions "brought as" a class action, and actions "maintained" as a class action, and permits a possible appeal even where the class certification was never reached. *Joarnt v. Autozone, Inc.*, 343 Or. 187, 194, 166 P.3d 525, 528 (2007).

To be "controlling," the "legal issue need not be dispositive of the litigation," but only "have a significant effect on the outcome of the litigation." *Pearson II*, 208 Or. App. at 512, 145 P.3d at 304. Likewise, to show that there is "substantial ground for difference of opinion," there is no "requirement" that the court of appeals believe the trial court "erred in its legal conclusions," only that the "order present issues about which reasonable appellate jurists could disagree." *Id.* at 512–13, 145 P.3d at 305. Similarly, whether an immediate appeal may "materially advance the ultimate termination of the litigation" is to be decided in light of Oregon's "disfavor of piecemeal appeals," and the policy that interlocutory appeals of class actions are reserved for "exceptional cases." *Id.* at 513, 145 P.3d at 304. Notably, where the primary issues remaining involve legal, rather than factual issues, interlocutory appeal is not generally appropriate because a final judgment "may be forthcoming in the form of summary judgment or some other pretrial disposition." *Id.*, 145 P.3d at 304. Thus, to obtain interlocutory review of a class certification decision, the party seeking review must show the existence of "an exceptional case in which immediate resolution of the legal issues presented by the trial court's" certification decision "will necessarily result in less expense for the parties, speedier resolution of the litigation, or more efficient use of judicial resources." *Id.* at 514, 145 P.3d at 304–05.

The standard of review for class certification findings and conclusions is mixed because class certification presents issues of both law and fact. *Alsea Veneer, Inc. v. State*, 117 Or. App. 42, 52, 843 P.2d 492, 497 (1992), *aff'd in part, rev'd in part*, 318 Or. 33, 862 P.2d 95 (1993). The trial court's factual determinations on class certification are reviewed for substantial evidence, whereas the legal conclusions are reviewed for errors of law under an abuse of discretion standard. *Id.* (citation omitted); *see also Froeber II*, 222 Or. App. at 274–76, 193 P.3d at 1004–05. In determining any error of law, the court looks "to the text and context of the rule and evidence of the intent of the Council on Court Procedures that promulgated" the rule. *See Stewart v. Albertsons, Inc.*, 308 Or. App. 464, 472 (2021). The class certification determination is entitled to "wide latitude." *Froeber II*, 222 Or. App. at 275, 193 P.3d at 1004 (citations omitted).

7. COMMUNICATIONS WITH CLASS MEMBERS

No Oregon state court decision addresses limitations or guidance on communications with absent class members. At least one federal district court case in Oregon cites the general federal standards and case law—suggesting the Court has the authority to limit such contact—and there is little reason to think the state courts would deviate from the norm. *See Cedano v. Thrifty Payless, Inc.*, 2011 WL 8609402, *12 (D. Or. 2011) (citing *Gulf Oil Co. v. Bernard*, 452 U.S. 89, 100, 101 S. Ct. 2193, 68 L.Ed.2d 693 (1981)). Likewise, Oregon courts often follow formal ABA Ethics Opinions, suggesting Oregon courts would adhere to the Formal Opinion 07-445 of the ABA Standing Committee on Ethics and Professional Responsibility, "Contact by Counsel with Putative Members of Class Prior to Class Certification" (Apr. 11, 2007) (ABA Opinion). *See, e.g., In re Conduct of Brandt*, 331 Or. 113, 143 10 P.3d 906, 924 (2000) (following ABA Ethics Opinion). Thus, Oregon practitioners should review the ABA Opinion.

RULE 32 OF THE OREGON STATE COURT RULES OF CIVIL PROCEDURE

RULE 32 CLASS ACTIONS

A. Requirement for class action. One or more members of a class may sue or be sued as representative parties on behalf of all only if:

(1) The class is so numerous that joinder of all members is impracticable;

(2) There are questions of law or fact common to the class;

(3) The claims or defenses of the representative parties are typical of the claims or defenses of the class;

(4) The representative parties will fairly and adequately protect the interests of the class; and

(5) In an action for damages, the representative parties have complied with the prelitigation notice provisions of section H of this rule.

B. Class action maintainable. An action may be maintained as a class action if the prerequisites of section A of this rule are satisfied, and in addition, the court finds that a class action is superior to other available methods for the fair and efficient adjudication of the controversy. The matters pertinent to this finding include:

(1) The extent to which the prosecution of separate actions by or against individual members of the class creates a risk of:

(a) Inconsistent or varying adjudications with respect to members of the class which would establish incompatible standards of conduct for the party opposing the class; or

(b) Adjudications with respect to members of the class which would as a practical matter be dispositive of the interests of the other members not parties to the adjudications or substantially impair or impede their ability to protect their interests;

(2) The extent to which the relief sought would take the form of injunctive relief or corresponding declaratory relief with respect to the class as a whole;

(3) The extent to which questions of law or fact common to the members of the class predominate over any questions affecting only individual members;

(4) The interest of members of the class in individually controlling the prosecution or defense of separate actions;

(5) The extent and nature of any litigation concerning the controversy already commenced by or against members of the class;

(6) The desirability or undesirability of concentrating the litigation of the claims in the particular forum;

(7) The difficulties likely to be encountered in the management of a class action that will

be eliminated or significantly reduced if the controversy is adjudicated by other available means; and

(8) Whether or not the claims of individual class members are insufficient in the amounts or interests involved, in view of the complexities of the issues and the expenses of the litigation, to afford significant relief to the members of the class.

C. Determination by order whether class action to be maintained.

(1) As soon as practicable after the commencement of an action brought as a class action, the court shall determine by order whether and with respect to what claims or issues it is to be so maintained and shall find the facts specially and state separately its conclusions thereon. An order under this section may be conditional, and may be altered or amended before the decision on the merits.

(2) Where a party has relied upon a statute or law which another party seeks to have declared invalid, or where a party has in good faith relied upon any legislative, judicial, or administrative interpretation or regulation which would necessarily have to be voided or held inapplicable if another party is to prevail in the class action, the court may postpone a determination under subsection (1) of this section until the court has made a determination as to the validity or applicability of the statute, law, interpretation, or regulation.

D. Dismissal or compromise of class actions; court approval required; when notice required. Any action filed as a class action in which there has been no ruling under subsection C(1) of this rule and any action ordered maintained as a class action shall not be voluntarily dismissed or compromised without the approval of the court, and notice of the proposed dismissal or compromise shall be given to some or all members of the class in such manner as the court directs, except that if the dismissal is to be without prejudice or with prejudice against the class representative only, then such dismissal may be ordered without notice if there is a showing that no compensation in any form has passed directly or indirectly from the party opposing the class to the class representative or to the class representative's attorney and that no promise of such compensation has been made. If the statute of limitations has run or may run against the claim of any class member, the court may require appropriate notice.

E. Court authority over conduct of class actions. In the conduct of actions to which this rule applies, the court may make appropriate orders which may be altered or amended as may be desirable:

(1) Determining the course of proceedings or prescribing measures to prevent undue repetition or complication in the presentation of evidence or argument, including precertification determination of a motion made by any party pursuant to Rules 21 or 47 if the court concludes that such determination will promote the fair and efficient adjudication of the controversy and will not cause undue delay;

(2) Requiring, for the protection of class members or otherwise for the fair conduct of the action, that notice be given in such manner as the court may direct to some or all class members of any step in the action, of the proposed extent of the judgment; of the opportunity of members to signify whether they consider the representation fair and adequate, to intervene and present claims or defenses or otherwise to come into the

action, or to be excluded from the class;

(3) Imposing conditions on the representative parties, class members, or intervenors;

(4) Requiring that the pleadings be amended to eliminate therefrom allegations as to representation of absent persons, and that the action proceed accordingly; and

(5) Dealing with similar procedural matters.

F. Notice and exclusion.

(1) When ordering that an action be maintained as a class action under this rule, the court shall direct that notice be given to some or all members of the class under subsection E(2) of this rule, shall determine when and how this notice should be given and shall determine whether, when, how, and under what conditions putative members may elect to be excluded from the class. The matters pertinent to these determinations ordinarily include: (a) the nature of the controversy and the relief sought; (b) the extent and nature of any member's injury or liability; (c) the interest of the party opposing the class in securing a final resolution of the matters in controversy; (d) the inefficiency or impracticality of separately maintained actions to resolve the controversy; (e) the cost of notifying the members of the class; and (f) the possible prejudice to members to whom notice is not directed. When appropriate, exclusion may be conditioned on a prohibition against institution or maintenance of a separate action on some or all of the matters in controversy in the class action or a prohibition against use in a separately maintained action of any judgment rendered in favor of the class from which exclusion is sought.

(2) Plaintiffs shall bear costs of any notice ordered prior to a determination of liability. The court may, however, order that defendant bear all or a specified part of the costs of any notice included with a regular mailing by defendant to its current customers or employees. The court may hold a hearing to determine how the costs of such notice shall be apportioned.

(3) No duty of compliance with due process notice requirements is imposed on a defendant by reason of the defendant including notice with a regular mailing by the defendant to current customers or employees of the defendant under this section.

(4) As used in this section, "customer" includes a person, including but not limited to a student, who has purchased services or goods from a defendant.

G. Commencement or maintenance of class actions regarding particular issues; subclasses. When appropriate an action may be brought or ordered maintained as a class action with respect to particular claims or issues or by or against multiple classes or subclasses. Each subclass must separately satisfy all requirements of this rule except for subsection A(1).

H. Notice and demand required prior to commencement of action for damages.

(1) Thirty days or more prior to the commencement of an action for damages pursuant to the provisions of sections A and B of this rule, the potential plaintiffs' class representative shall:

(a) Notify the potential defendant of the particular alleged cause of action; and

(b) Demand that such person correct or rectify the alleged wrong.

(2) Such notice shall be in writing and shall be sent by certified or registered mail, return receipt requested, to the place where the transaction occurred, such person's principal place of business within this state, or, in the case of a corporation or limited partnership not authorized to transact business in this state, to the principal office or place of business of the corporation or limited partnership, and to any address the use of which the class representative knows, or on the basis of reasonable inquiry, has reason to believe is most likely to result in actual notice.

I. Limitation on maintenance of class actions for damages. No action for damages may be maintained under the provisions of sections A and B of this rule upon a showing by a defendant that all of the following exist:

(1) All potential class members similarly situated have been identified, or a reasonable effort to identify such other people has been made;

(2) All potential class members so identified have been notified that upon their request the defendant will make the appropriate compensation, correction, or remedy of the alleged wrong;

(3) Such compensation, correction, or remedy has been, or, in a reasonable time, will be, given; and

(4) Such person has ceased from engaging in, or if immediate cessation is impossible or unreasonably expensive under the circumstances, such person will, within a reasonable time, cease to engage in such methods, acts, or practices alleged to be violative of the rights of potential class members.

J. Application of sections H and I of this rule to actions for equitable relief; amendment of complaints for equitable relief to request damages permitted. An action for equitable relief brought under sections A and B of this rule may be commenced without compliance with the provisions of section H of this rule. Not less than 30 days after the commencement of an action for equitable relief, and after compliance with the provisions of section H of this rule, the class representative's complaint may be amended without leave of court to include a request for damages. The provisions of section I of this rule shall be applicable if the complaint for injunctive relief is amended to request damages.

K. Coordination of pending class actions sharing common question of law or fact.

(1) (a) When class actions sharing a common question of fact or law are pending in different courts, the presiding judge of any such court, upon motion of any party or on the court's own initiative, may request the Supreme Court to assign a Circuit Court, Court of Appeals, or Supreme Court judge to determine whether coordination of the actions is appropriate, and a judge shall be so assigned to make that determination.

(1) (b) Coordination of class actions sharing a common question of fact or law is appropriate if one judge hearing all of the actions for all purposes in a selected site or sites will promote the ends of justice taking into account whether the common question of fact or law is predominating and significant to the litigation; the convenience of parties, witnesses, and counsel; the relative development of the actions and the work

product of counsel; the efficient utilization of judicial facilities and personnel; the calendar of the courts; the disadvantages of duplicative and inconsistent rulings, orders, or judgments; and the likelihood of settlement of the actions without further litigation should coordination be denied.

(2) If the assigned judge determines that coordination is appropriate, such judge shall order the actions coordinated, report that fact to the Chief Justice of the Supreme Court, and the Chief Justice shall assign a judge to hear and determine the actions in the site or sites the Chief Justice deems appropriate.

(3) The judge of any court in which there is pending an action sharing a common question of fact or law with coordinated actions, upon motion of any party or on the court's own initiative, may request the judge assigned to hear the coordinated action for an order coordinating such actions. Coordination of the action pending before the judge so requesting shall be determined under the standards specified in subsection (1) of this section.

(4) Pending any determination of whether coordination is appropriate, the judge assigned to make the determination may stay any action being considered for, or affecting any action being considered for, coordination.

(5) Notwithstanding any other provision of law, the Supreme Court shall provide by rule the practice and procedure for coordination of class actions in convenient courts, including provision for giving notice and presenting evidence.

L. **Form of judgment.** The judgment in an action ordered maintained as a class action, whether or not favorable to the class, must generally describe the members of the class and must specifically identify any persons who requested exclusion from the class and are not bound by the judgment.

M. **Attorney fees, costs, disbursements, and litigation expenses.**

(1) (a) Attorney fees for representing a class are subject to control of the court.

(b) If under an applicable provision of law a defendant or defendant class is entitled to attorney fees, costs, or disbursements from a plaintiff class, only representative parties and those members of the class who have appeared individually are liable for those amounts. If a plaintiff is entitled to attorney fees, costs, or disbursements from a defendant class, the court may apportion the fees, costs, or disbursements among the members of the class.

(c) If the prevailing class recovers a judgment that can be divided for the purpose, the court may order reasonable attorney fees and litigation expenses of the class to be paid from the recovery.

(d) The court may order the adverse party to pay to the prevailing class its reasonable attorney fees and litigation expenses if permitted by law in similar cases not involving a class.

(e) In determining the amount of attorney fees for a prevailing class the court shall consider the following factors:

(i) The time and effort expended by the attorney in the litigation, including the nature, extent, and quality of the services rendered;

(ii) Results achieved and benefits conferred upon the class;

(iii) The magnitude, complexity, and uniqueness of the litigation;

(iv) The contingent nature of success; and

(v) Appropriate criteria in Rule 1.5 of the Oregon Rules of Professional Conduct.

(2) Before a hearing under section C of this rule or at any other time the court directs, the representative parties and the attorney for the representative parties shall file with the court, jointly or separately:

(a) A statement showing any amount paid or promised them by any person for the services rendered or to be rendered in connection with the action or for the costs and expenses of the litigation and the source of all of the amounts;

(b) A copy of any written agreement, or a summary of any oral agreement, between the representative parties and their attorney concerning financial arrangement or fees; and

(c) A copy of any written agreement, or a summary of any oral agreement, by the representative parties or the attorney to share these amounts with any person other than a member, regular associate, or an attorney regularly of counsel with the law firm of the representative parties' attorney. This statement shall be supplemented promptly if additional arrangements are made.

N. Statute of limitations. The statute of limitations is tolled for all class members upon the commencement of an action asserting a class action. The statute of limitations resumes running against a member of a class:

(1) Upon filing of an election of exclusion by such class member;

(2) Upon entry of an order of certification, or of an amendment thereof, eliminating the class member from the class;

(3) Except as to representative parties, upon entry of an order under section C of this rule refusing to certify the class as a class action; and

(4) Upon dismissal of the action without an adjudication on the merits.

O. Payment of damages. As part of the settlement or judgment in a class action, the court may approve a process for the payment of damages. The process may include the use of claim forms. If any amount awarded as damages is not claimed within the time specified by the court, or if the court finds that payment of all or part of the damages to class members is not practicable, the court shall order that:

(1) At least 50 percent of the amount not paid to class members be paid or delivered to the Oregon State Bar for the funding of legal services provided through the Legal Services Program established under ORS 9.572; and

(2) The remainder of the amount not paid to class members be paid to any entity for purposes that the court determines are directly related to the class action or directly beneficial to the interests of class members.

[CCP 12/2/78; amended by CCP 12/13/80; amended by 1981 c.912 § 1; § H amended by CCP 12/8/84; amended by CCP 12/12/92; § F amended by CCP 12/10/94; § N amended by CCP 12/9/00; §§ F, M amended by 2003 c.576 §§ 173,259; §§ F, N amended by CCP 12/9/06, eff. Jan. 1, 2008.]; [F and L amended, and O added, by House Bill 2700 effective March 2015].

This chapter was prepared by Fred B. Burnside, a partner at Davis Wright Tremaine LLP in Seattle, Washington.

PENNSYLVANIA

1. SUMMARY

a. Rule 23(a) Requirements: Numerosity, Commonality, Typicality, and Adequacy

Pennsylvania Rules 1702(1), (2), and (3) mirror Rules 23(a)(1), (2) and (3) on numerosity, commonality, and typicality. Pennsylvania Rule 1702(4) on adequacy incorporates criteria set forth in a separate rule, Pennsylvania Rule 1709, which sets forth a standard for adequacy of representation that is substantively similar to Rule 23(a)(4). For a discussion of class action requirements, *see Samuel-Bassett v. Kia Motors America, Inc.,* 34 A.3d 1 (Pa. 2011).

b. Rule 23(b)(3) Requirements: Superiority and Predominance

The Pennsylvania counterpart to Rule 23(b)(3)'s requirement of predominance and superiority is found in Pennsylvania Rule 1708. That rule incorporates the predominance requirement, but not that of superiority. The Pennsylvania Rules do not require that the class action method be "superior" to alternative modes of suit. *Weinberg v. Sun Company, Inc*., 740 A.2d 1152, 1163 (Pa. Super. Ct. 1999), *rev'd on other grounds*, 777 A.2d 442 (Pa. 2001).

Pennsylvania Rule 1708 sets forth separate criteria to be considered by a court depending on whether monetary recovery or equitable or declaratory relief is sought. Where monetary recovery alone is sought, the court is to consider seven separate criteria, the first of which, Pennsylvania Rule 1708(a)(1–5), includes Rule 23(b)(3)'s predominance requirement as well as other requirements identical to those found in Rule 23(b)(1) and (3). However, the sixth and seventh criteria,

> (6) whether in view of the complexities of the issues or the expenses of litigation the separate claims of individual class members are insufficient in amount to support separate actions; and,
>
> (7) whether it is likely that the amount which may be recovered by individual class members will be so small in relation to the expense and effort of administering the action as not to justify a class action,

are not found in Rule 23. As discussed in the notes to Pennsylvania Rule 1708, the first additional criterion, number 6, follows federal case law, while the second, number 7, is somewhat based on Section 3(a) of the Uniform Class Action Act. The seventh criterion was an issue in *Kelly v. County of Allegheny*, 546 A.2d 608 (Pa. Super. Ct. 1988), where the court held that a class action on behalf of over 10,000 public employees was not *de minimus* so as to warrant denial of certification on the ground that the recovery of each member, $13.61, was trivial in relation to the expense and effort of maintaining a class action. *But see Klusman, supra* (denying class certification because, among other things, the maximum recovery of $3.55 was so small in view of the expenses of litigation and effort of administration that class action not justified).

Where equitable or declaratory relief alone is sought, Pennsylvania Rule 1708(b) requires a court to consider the criteria set forth in Pennsylvania Rule 1708(a)(1–5) plus the criterion, identical to Rule 23(b)(2), whether the party opposing the class has acted or refused to act on grounds generally applicable to the class, thereby making final equitable or declaratory relief appropriate with respect to the class. Where both monetary and other relief is sought, courts are required to consider all criteria in both subdivisions (a) and (b). Pennsylvania Rule 1708(c). The rule does not accord any specific weight to the listed criteria nor insist on the exclusivity of the list, thereby implying a great deal of discretion for the trial court. *Dickler v. Shearson Lehman Hutton, Inc.*, 596 A.2d 860 (Pa. Super. Ct. 1991), *appeal denied*, 616 A.2d 984 (Pa. 1992).

c. Rule 23(f). Appeals

While the federal rule contains a provision for immediate appeal of an order either granting or denying class certification, Pennsylvania case law has developed a different procedure. An order granting class certification is an interlocutory order appealable under Pa.R.A.P. 312 (by permission), while an order denying class certification is appealable as a "collateral order" under Pa.R.A.P. 313. A "collateral order" is "an order separable from and collateral to the main cause of action where the right involved is too important to be denied review and the question presented is such that if review is postponed until final judgment in the case, the claim will be irreparably lost." Pa.R.A.P. 313(b). *See Dunn v. Allegheny County Property Assessment Appeals and Review*, 794 A.2d 416, 421–23 (Pa. Commw. Ct. 2002) (discussing cases).

In the class action context, an order decertifying a class is generally an appealable collateral order. *See Doe 1 v. Franklin County*, 272 A.3d 1022, 1031 (Pa. Commw. Ct. 2022) (citing and quoting *Bell v. Beneficial Consumer Discount Company*, 348 A.2d 734, 736 (Pa. 1975)); *In re Sheriff's Excess Proceeds Litig.*, 98 A.3d 706, 719 (Pa. Commw. Ct. 2014) ("Although orders denying class action have usually been deemed appealable, 'each distinct legal issue over which an appellate court is asked to assert jurisdiction' must meet the **separability, importance** *and* **urgency** requirements in order to be immediately appealable under Pa.R.A. P. 313.") (emphasis in original) (citation omitted); *see also Sommers v. Univ. of Pittsburgh Med. Ctr.*, 185 A.3d 1065 (Pa. Super. Ct. 2018) (holding that an order decertifying a class is appealable as a collateral order, under Pa.R.A.P. 313). A trial court's order that plaintiff produce documents protected by privilege was an appealable collateral order on the issue of whether the representative parties would fairly and adequately represent the class. *Gocial v. Independence Blue Cross*, 827 A.2d 1216 (Pa. Super. 2003) (fact that class representative was married to attorney allegedly representing class raised conflict of interest concerns sufficient to require production of documents). However, there was no collateral appeal available from an order granting preliminary approval but conditioning final approval on a sufficient number of class members expressing their willingness to participate in the settlement; the appellate court held that the order implicated no sufficiently important policy interest to permit an immediate appeal. *Brophy v. Philadelphia Gas Works*, 2007 Pa. Commw. LEXIS 162 (Pa. Commw. Ct. Apr. 5, 2007); *see also Basile v. H&R Block, Inc.*, 973 A.2d 417 (Pa. 2009) (holding that defendant properly preserved its right to challenge certification of the class even though it did not timely challenge the order granting class certification, because it ultimately won a later motion for summary judgment on the merits of the dispute).

d. Other Differences from Federal Rule

i. Pennsylvania Rules 1703, 1704. These Rules provide that a class action shall be commenced "only" by the filing of a complaint with the Prothonotary in the form provided by Rule 1704. Pa. R.C.P. 1703(a), Explanatory Comment—1977. Thus, a case commenced as an individual case cannot be amended to become a class action. *Debbs v. Chrysler Corp.*, 810 A.2d 137 (Pa. Super. Ct. 2002) (trial court abused discretion when it permitted plaintiff to amend individual case with class action allegations and new parties).

ii. Pennsylvania Rule 1711. This Rule provides generally in subsection (a) that every member of the class as defined in the court's order is included in the class unless exclusion is requested by a specified date. This differs from the federal procedure which limits opting out to Rule 23(b)(3) actions. The Explanatory Note to the Rule points out that there will be times when self-exclusion should not be permitted, such as where the members of the class have joint, as distinguished from several, interests in the subject matter and their joinder is compulsory. In subsection (b), the Rule provides the court with the option to require a true opt-in procedure only in certain limited instances, such as where the individual claims are substantial and the potential members of the class have sufficient resources, experience, and sophistication in business affairs to conduct their own litigation, or under other special circumstances.

iii. Pennsylvania Rule 1712. Whereas Rule 23(c) only requires notice in actions certified under Rule 23(b)(3), Pennsylvania Rule 1712 requires notice in all class actions. The Rule provides that in certain circumstances, individual notice is not required; general notice reasonably calculated to inform members of the pendency of the action, such as through newspapers, television, radio, or certain interest groups, may suffice. Further, the Rule allocates to the plaintiff the expense of providing notice, though the defendant may be required to cooperate so as to minimize expense.

iv. Pennsylvania Rule 1714. This Rule contains a provision not found in the federal rules. It provides in subsection (a) that no class action shall be compromised, settled, or discontinued without the approval of the court after hearing. In contrast, Rule 23(e) requires court approval of resolutions only when the class has been certified.

Rule 1714(b) provides that a class action may be discontinued without notice, prior to certification, if the court finds that the discontinuance will not prejudice the members of the class. Such discontinuance must be preceded by a hearing and factually based findings that discontinuance prior to certification would not prejudice members of the class. *Silver Spring Tp. v. Pennsy Supply, Inc.*, 613 A.2d 108 (Pa. Commw. Ct. 1992).

Rule 1714(d) provides that courts may approve class action settlements that do not create residual funds.

v. Pennsylvania Rule 1716. This is a new Rule, effective July 1, 2012, which addresses residual funds in class actions. Rule 1716(a) provides that any order entering a judgment or approving the settlement or compromise of a class action must provide for the disbursement of residual funds. Rule 1716(b) states that "not less than fifty percent (50%) of residual funds in a given class action shall be disbursed to the Pennsylvania Interest on Lawyers Trust Account Board." Further, the remaining funds may be disbursed "to the Pennsylvania Interest on Lawyers Trust Account Board, or to another entity for purposes that have a direct or indirect relationship to the objectives of the underlying class action, or which otherwise promote the substantive or procedural interests of the members of the class." Pa. R.C.P. 1716(b).

vi. Pennsylvania Rule 1717. Prior Rule 1716 has been renumbered, effective July 1, 2012, as Rule 1717. This Rule specifically states the criteria to be applied by the court in determining the amount of attorney fees, a subject not specifically addressed by Rule 23, but by a section of the Class Action Fairness Act, 28 U.S.C. § 1712 (limiting fee awards in coupon settlements). The non-exclusive list of factors in the Pennsylvania Rule includes the time and effort reasonably expended, the quality of the services, the results achieved and benefits conferred upon the class or the public, the magnitude, complexity and uniqueness of the litigation and whether the receipt of a fee was contingent on success.

2. INTERPRETIVE DECISIONS

a. Definition of Class Action

Rule 1701 defines a "class action" as an action brought by or against parties as representatives of a class until the court by order refuses to certify it as such or revokes a prior certification. Pa.R.C.P. 1701(a). *See Bell v. Beneficial Consumer Discount Company*, 348 A.2d 734 (Pa. 1975) ("class is in the action until properly excluded"); *Braun v. Wal-Mart Stores, Inc.*, 60 Pa. D & C. 4th 13 (C.P. Phila. 2003) (putative class members entitled to protections of Rules of Professional Conduct and defendant not permitted to conduct *ex parte* interviews with class members). This principle is consistent with most federal court rulings. *See, e.g., Philips v. Allegheny County,* 869 F.2d 234, 237 (3d Cir. 1989) ("action filed as class action should be treated as if certification has been granted for the purposes of settlement until certification is denied"); *Kahan v. Rosenstiel*, 424 F.2d 161, 169 (3d Cir. 1970) ("suit brought as a class action should be treated as such for purposes of dismissal or compromise, until there is a full determination that the class action is not proper"); *but see* Fed. R. Civ. P. 23(e)(requiring court approval of settlements only where class has been certified).

A case commenced as an individual action cannot become a class action by amending the complaint. *Debbs v. Chrysler Corp.*, 810 A.2d 137 (Pa. Super. Ct. 2002).

b. Procedure for Class Certification

Ordinarily, a court may not address questions of certification until the pleading stage is completed and attacks on the complaint or demurrers to the substance of the claim have already been ruled upon. *Sears v. Corbett*, 49 A.3d 463 (Pa. 2012) ("a court cannot make a class action determination until the close of pleadings"); *Niemic v. Allstate Ins. Co.*, 721 A.2d 807, 810 (Pa. Super. Ct. 1988) ("upon a motion for class action certification the court considers whether a claim may be brought by a class of plaintiffs, whereas at the earlier, preliminary stage, the court must decide whether there exists a valid claim to be brought at all, no matter who the plaintiff"). An isolated exception to the rule occurred in *Adamson v. Commonwealth*, 410 A.2d 392 (Pa. Commw. Ct. 1980), where, based on a defendant's preliminary objections, the court concluded that the action would not benefit the class. This case has been described as violating the principles set forth in later cases. *Koch v. First Union Corp.*, 2002 WL 372939, *10 n.7 (C.P. Phila. Jan. 10, 2002).

In *Baldassari v. Suburban Cable TV Co. Inc.*, 808 A.2d 184 (Pa. Super. Ct. 2002), the court stated that, in a class certification hearing, the court's authority is confined to a consideration of the class action allegations, not the merits of the controversy, citing the Explanatory Note to Pennsylvania Rule 1707.

c. Burden to Show Class Certification

The burden of showing each of the elements of class certification is initially on the moving party. This burden "is not heavy and is thus consistent with the policy that decisions in favor of maintaining a class action should be liberally made." *Cambanis v. Nationwide Ins. Co.*, 501 A.2d 635, 637 (Pa. Super. Ct. 1985). The moving party need only present evidence sufficient to make out a prima facie case from which the court can conclude that the class certification requirements are met. *Debbs v. Chrysler Corp.*, 810 A.2d 137, 153–54 (Pa. Super. Ct. 2002). Where evidence conflicts, doubt should be resolved in favor of class certification. *Lewis v. Bayer AG*, 2004 WL 1146692, *7 (C.P. Phila. Mar. 19, 2004). "The prima facie burden of proof standard at the class certification stage is met by a qualitative "substantial evidence" test. *Id.* "Courts have consistently interpreted the phrase 'substantial evidence' to mean 'more than a mere scintilla,' but evidence 'which a reasonable mind might accept as adequate to support a conclusion.'" *Crepeau v. Rite Aid, Inc.*, 2005 WL 1041395, *3 (C.P. Phila. May 3, 2005), *quoting SSEN, Inc. v. Borough of Eddystone*, 810 A.2d 200, 207 (Pa. Commw. Ct. 2002).

The courts in Pennsylvania have long stressed that, in adjudicating a motion for class certification, the merits should not be considered:

> The hearing is confined to a consideration of the class action allegations and is not concerned with the merits of the controversy or with attacks on the other averments of the complaint. Its only purpose is to decide whether the action shall continue as a class action or as an action with individual parties only. In a sense, it is designed to decide who shall be the parties to the action and nothing more. Viewed in this manner, it is clear that the merits of the action and the right of the plaintiff to recover are to be excluded from consideration.

Baldassari v. Suburban Cable TV Co., 808 A.2d 184, 189–90 (Pa. Super. Ct. 2002), quoting Pa.R.C.P. 1707, Explanatory Comment. *Accord, Cavanaugh v. Allegheny Ludlum Steel Corp.*, 528 A.2d 236 (Pa. Super. Ct. 1987); *Braun v. Wal-Mart Stores, Inc.,* 78 Pa. D. & C.4th 359 (C.P. Phila. 2005) (credibility may not be the focus of a certification decision, and it would not be proper to deny certification even if court concluded that the plaintiffs had not proven their case to the satisfaction of the court sitting as if conducting a non-jury trial). However, "courts may need to examine the elements of the underlying cause of action in order to dispose of class issues properly." *Debbs v. Chrysler Corp.,* 810 A.2d at 154.

Simply alleging class status will not provide an independent basis for equity jurisdiction where there is statutorily mandated administrative remedy. In *Zarwin v. Montgomery County*, 842 A.2d 1018 (Pa. Commw. Ct. 2004), taxpayers filed a class action against the county when it attempted to collect personal property tax allegedly in breach of a mutual release agreement. The Commonwealth Court noted that "a class action is a procedural device and not a substantive right," and would not permit a class action before taxpayers first pursued their claims before the county's Board of Assessment Appeals. *Id.* at 1023.

d. Tolling Statute of Limitations

Upon the filing of a class action, the statute of limitations normally is tolled for all putative members of the class. *Cunningham v. Insurance Company of North America, Inc.*, 530 A.2d 407, 408 (Pa. 1987). Even an erroneous certification of a class equitably tolls the running of the statute of limitations. *Verrichia v. Commonwealth, Dept. of Revenue*, 639 A.2d 957, 964 n.3 (Pa. Commw. Ct. 1994).

Tolling does not occur, however, for plaintiffs who commence an action after an earlier action has been dismissed for lack of standing on the part of the class representatives where the lack of standing was apparent on the face of the complaint filed in the earlier action. *Cunningham v. Insurance Co. of North America, Inc*., 530 A.2d 407, 409 (Pa. 1987).

Pennsylvania does not recognize the doctrine of cross-jurisdiction equitable tolling. *Ravitch v. Pricewaterhouse*, 793 A.2d 939, 943 (Pa. Super. Ct. 2002), *appeal denied*, 818 A.2d 505 (Pa. 2003) (mem.). Accordingly, the filing of a class action in another state does not toll the statute of limitations as to a subsequent action filed in Pennsylvania's state court system. *See Johnson v. American Home Products Corp*., 62 Pa. D. & C. 4th 20 (C.P. Phila. 2003), *affirmed*, 847 A.2d 765 (Pa. Super. Ct. 2004) (declining to address question whether a Pennsylvania class action merged into a class action in federal court, combining class members in federal and state courts, tolls the statute of limitations as to an individual action filed in the Pennsylvania state court system).

e. Nationwide Class

In *Weinberg v. Sun Company, Inc*., 740 A. 2d 1152 (Pa. Super. Ct. 1999), *rev'd in part on other grounds*, 777 A.2d 442 (Pa. 2001), the court held that Pennsylvania courts are empowered to certify national classes based on consideration of the factors enumerated in Rule 1708. *Accord, In re Pennsylvania Baycol Third-Party Payor Litig.*, 2005 WL 852135 (C.P. Phila. April 4, 2005) (nationwide class certified for breach of warranty and unjust enrichment claims). *See also, Dearlove v. Genzyme Transgenics Corp*., 2004 WL 3053701 (C.P. Phila. Dec. 28, 2004) (class membership in fifteen states); *Foultz v. Erie Insurance Exchange*, 2002 WL 452115 (C.P. Phila. March 13, 2002) (class certified where members were from twelve different states; if necessary, court would certify subclasses based on state of residence); *Tesauro v. The Quigley Corp.*, 2002 WL 372947 (C.P. Phila. Jan. 25, 2002) (nationwide class certified for claims of breach of implied warranty of merchantability and for unjust enrichment); *Parsky v. First Union Corp.*, 51 Pa. D & C. 4th 468 (C.P. Phila. 2001) (class certified for breach of contract and breach of fiduciary duty claims; membership included investors in Pennsylvania, New Jersey, Delaware, New York). On a related issue, the Pennsylvania Supreme Court has granted certification of legal questions from the Third Circuit Court of Appeals as to whether the Pennsylvania Unfair Trade Practices and Consumer Protection Law applies to non-resident consumers when they transact with a Pennsylvania business that uses a Pennsylvania choice of law clause in all of its contracts, *Danganan v. Guardian Protection Serv.*, No. 36 WAP 2017 (Pa. Aug. 8, 2017), on certification from Third Circuit Court of Appeals.

Where a plaintiff fails to carry the initial burden of establishing that state law differences would be manageable and not overwhelm common issues, a nationwide class is not warranted. *Debbs v. Chrysler Corp*., 810 A.2d 137 (Pa. Super. Ct. 2002).

f. Numerosity

A defendant cannot defeat the numerosity requirement by arguing that the plaintiff's inability to identify the total number of class members renders the class definition overbroad. *Keppley v. School District of Twin Valley*, 866 A.2d 1165 (Pa. Commw. Ct. 2005) (proponent of class need not plead or prove actual number of class members, so long as she can define class with some precision and provide sufficient indicia that more members exist that it would be practicable to join); *Baldassari v. Suburban Cable TV Co. Inc*., 808 A.2d 184 (Pa. Super. Ct. 2002) (reversing trial court denial of certification of class of cable television subscribers who had been assessed late fees and pointing out that defendant's administrative difficulties in calculating number of subscribers did not defeat numerosity).

Numerosity was held not to be established in *Weismer v Beech-Nut Nutrition Corp.*, 615 A.2d 428, 430–31 (Pa. Super. Ct. 1992) (overly broad definition of class led to failure to satisfy numerosity; while that defect could have been corrected, court also held there was no predominance of common issues).

g. Commonality

In *Baldassari v. Suburban Cable TV Co. Inc.*, 808 A.2d 184 (Pa. Super. Ct. 2002), the trial court was held to have abused its discretion in improperly focusing on the merits of the litigation and confusing questions of liability and damages with commonality. The appellate court emphasized that "it is the strong and oft-repeated policy of this Commonwealth that, in applying the rules for class certification, decision should be made liberally and in favor of maintaining a class action." 808 A.2d at 189.

In *Liss & Marion, P.C. v. Recordex Acquisition Corp.*, 603 Pa. 198, 220 (Pa. 2009), the Pennsylvania Supreme Court affirmed the trial court's certification of the class and grant of summary judgment on plaintiff's contract claims, expressly rejecting the defendants' assertion that reliance was an element of the breach of contract claim presenting individual questions that defeated commonality and prevented class certification.

Commonality was held not to be established in *Weinberg v. Sun Co., Inc.*, 777 A.2d 442 (Pa. 2001), where the proposed class consisted of gasoline consumers with claims for false advertising. The court held that questions of fact applicable to each individual consumer would be numerous, extensive and would predominate over common issues of fact and law. *See also, Kern v. Lehigh Valley Hospital, Inc.*, 108 A.3d 1281, 1290 (Pa. Super. Ct. 2015) (holding that trial court properly "determined that the requirement for justifiable reliance as set forth in Section 201–9.2 of the UTPCPL defeats Rule 1702(2)'s requirement of commonality of facts and law between prospective class members"); *Eisen v. Independence Blue Cross*, 839 A.2d 369 (Pa. Super. Ct. 2003) (variations in coverage and insurer response to requests for precertification of chiropractic services were based on individual rather than common factors); *Weismer v. Beech-Nut Nutrition Corp.*, 615 A.2d 428, 430–31 (Pa. Super. Ct. 1992) (where proof as to one plaintiff could not suffice as proof as to all, there was no predominance of common issues); *but see Liss & Marion, P.C.*, 603 Pa. at 220 (distinguishing *Weinberg v. Sun Co.,* 777 A.2d 442 (2001), because it involved a claim for common law fraud in which reliance was indeed an element that plaintiff had to prove); *Piper v. Elkhart Brass Mfg. Co.*, 2016 Pa. Super. Unpub. LEXIS 1329 (Pa. Super. Ct. 2016) (non-precedential) (affirming trial court's conclusion that commonality not met where class members' damages could not be "determined by a mathematical or formula calculation" and could not be "considered a mechanical task"); *but see Patterson v. Fid. Nat'l Title Ins. Co.*, 2015 Pa. Dist. & Cnty. Dec. LEXIS 479 (Pa. County Ct. 2015) (Allegheny) (distinguishing *Kern v. Lehigh Valley Hospital, Inc.*, 108 A.3d 1281 and certifying class under Section 201–9.2 of the UTPCPL).

The long-running case of *Basile v. H&R Block, Inc.* illustrates the debate over commonality issues in Pennsylvania. In 1999, the Pennsylvania Superior Court reversed the trial court for abuse of discretion in refusing to certify Basile's claims under Pennsylvania's consumer protection law. 729 A.2d 574 (Pa. Super. Ct. 1999). The appellate court held that because H&R Block was a fiduciary of the plaintiffs, reliance by the class plaintiffs was implicit and established by operation of law and need not be proven on an individual basis. The decision was vacated on other grounds, 761 A.2d 1115 (Pa. 2000), and on remand, the Superior Court concluded that there was sufficient evidence to establish the elements of a confidential relationship. If that relationship were successfully demonstrated upon remand to the trial court, then reliance, inherent in a finding of fiduciary duty, would be presumed for purposes of the claims under the Pennsylvania consumer protection law. *Basile v. H&R Block, Inc.*, 777 A.2d 95, 107–08 (Pa. Super. Ct. 2001), *appeal denied*, 806 A.2d 857 (Pa. 2002). Upon remand, the trial court held that proof of a confidential relationship in those particular circumstances required individualized inquiry and decertified the class. 66 Pa. D & C 4th 57 (C.P. Phila. 2004). On appeal, the Superior Court held that by failing to challenge the trial court's class certification order at the same time it cross-appealed the grant of summary judgment, H&R Block had waived its right to do so. The Superior Court reversed the class decertification and remanded. *Basile v. H&R Block, Inc.*, 926 A.2d 493 (Pa. Super. Ct. 2007). However, this decision was reversed, and the case remanded, by the Supreme Court when it concluded that H&R Block properly preserved its right to challenge certification of the class even though it did not timely challenge the order granting class certification, because it ultimately won a later motion for summary judgment on the merits of the dispute. *Basile v. H&R Block, Inc.*, 973 A.2d 417 (Pa. 2009). On remand from the Supreme Court, the Superior Court again found that there was sufficient evidence to establish the elements of a confidential relationship and that, if this relationship was successfully demonstrated at the trial court level after remand, then reliance would be presumed as to the plaintiffs' Pennsylvania consumer protection law claims. *Basile v. H&R Block, Inc.*, 11 A.3d 992 (Pa. Super. Ct. 2010), petition for allowance of appeal granted, 610 Pa. 417 (Pa. 2012). The Supreme Court again reversed the Superior Court, however, holding that proof of a confidential relationship required individualized inquiry and that the trial court's decertification order was therefore proper. *Basile v. H&R Block, Inc.*, 52 A.3d 1202 (Pa. 2012).

Other cases discussing such issues include *Clark v. Pfizer Inc.*, 990 A.2d 17 (Pa. Super. Ct. 2010) (commonality not satisfied due to individual issues of reliance and/or causation); *Wurtzel v. Park Towne Place Associates Limited Partnership*, 2002 WL 31487894 (C.P. Phila. Nov. 5, 2002) (fraud claim certified for class action where reliance could be presumed from fiduciary relationship); *Foultz v. Erie Insurance Exchange*, 2002 WL 452115, *16 (C.P. Phila. March 13, 2002) (certified insurance bad faith claim where insurer's alleged bad faith predicated on common course of conduct); *Cwietniewicz v. Aetna U.S. Health Care, Inc.*, June Term 1998, No. 423 (C.P. Phila. Nov. 7, 2001) (class certified for claims of fraud, *inter alia*, where reliance can be presumed from common material omission); *Parsky v. First Union Corp.*, 51 Pa. D & C. 4th 468 (C.P. Phila. 2001) (certified class claim for breach of fiduciary duty; minor differences in underlying trust documents do not prevent satisfaction of commonality requirement).

Automobile defect cases may or may not present common questions depending on the facts. Class certification was granted in *Samuel-Bassett v. Kia Motors America, Inc.*, 68 Pa. D&C 4th 270 (C.P. Phila. 2004), *aff'd*, No. 3048 EDA 2005 (Pa. Super. Ct. Oct. 24, 2007), *aff'd*, 34 A.3d 1 (Pa. 2011), where the claims centered on a uniformly defective braking system in one model. However, in *Zwiercan v. General Motors Corp.*, 68 Pa. D. & C. 4th 449 (C.P. Phila. 2004), the court found predominance of common questions lacking where the allegedly unsafe seat design was included in fifty-five automobile models from nine model years and there was no showing that the same seats were in all models.

Wage and hour class actions under Pennsylvania state laws have been certified even where federal claims have not. *See, e.g.*, *Bonds v. GMS Mine Repair & Maintenance, Inc.*, 245 A.3d 1102 (Pa. Super. 2020); *see also In re Amazon.Com, Inc. Fulfillment Center Fair Labor Standards Act (FLSA) and Wage and Hour Litig.*, No. 43 EAP 2019, 2021 WL 3059773 (Pa. July 21, 2021) (answering certified questions from the United States Court of Appeals for the Sixth Circuit).

h. Typicality

"[S]ome scintilla of evidence must be present for there to be a finding of typicality." *Lewis v. Bayer AG*, 2004 WL 1146692, *21 (C.P. Phila. Mar. 19, 2004). Typicality is established when the class representative's claims arise out of the same course of conduct, involve the same legal theories and do not raise divergent goals or interests. A class representative challenging an unlawful tax met this requirement despite the trial court's ruling that any relief provided through resolution of the action would result in higher taxes to pay for revenue for that relief. *Dunn v. Allegheny County Property Assessment Appeals and Review*, 794 A.2d 416, 424–25 (Pa. Commw. 2002).

In *Delaware County v. Mellon Financial Corp.*, 914 A.2d 469, 476 (Pa. Cmwlth. 2007), the court reversed a class certification order because the class representative was subject to a "unique defense" that "could become the focus of the entire litigation and divert attention from the suit as a whole, as well as disadvantage other class members." Typicality was held not to be established in *Eisen v. Independence Blue Cross*, 839 A.2d 369 (Pa. Super. 2003), where chiropractic service providers sought class certification for allegedly improper policies and practices of health insurance companies. The court held that the differential treatment of patients—some being granted and some being denied benefits—made it unclear that the named representatives were consistently denied reimbursement. Recently, in *Farneth v. Wal-Mart Stores, Inc.*, 2017 Pa. Dist. & Cnty. Dec. LEXIS 2259 (CCP Allegheny Cty. Mar. 21, 2107), the court rejected challenges to typicality related to the named plaintiff's alleged close connection to class counsel, finding that individual reliance was not at issue because all members of the proposed class necessarily suffered damages if it was improper for the defendant to collect sales tax on purchases made with coupons.

i. Adequacy of Representation

A court may presume the lack of a conflict of interest that would make a class representative inadequate. *Gregg v. Independence Blue Cross*, 2004 WL 869063, *27 (C.P. Phila. Apr. 22, 2004).

A lack of funding by the representative plaintiff, without more, is not sufficient to warrant denial of class certification. Where an attorney for a class representative ethically advances costs and expenses to the representative, the adequate financing requirement of the certification test is met. *Weinberg v. Sun Co., Inc.*, 740 A.2d 1152, 1171 (Pa. Super. 1999), *aff'd in part and rev'd in part on other grounds*, 565 Pa. 612, 777 A.2d 442 (2001). Where counsel has agreed and is able to advance costs, a representative's own limited financial resources are not fatal to her adequacy. *Janicik v. Prudential Ins. Co. of America*, 451 A.2d 451 (Pa. Super. Ct. 1982); *Foultz v. Erie Insurance Exchange*, 2002 WL 452115, *14 (C.P Phila. March 13, 2002). But where the representative lacks the financial resources and produces no evidence of an agreement in place to assist in financing the action, adequacy may be lacking. *See Keppley v. School District of Twin Valley,* 866 A.2d 1165 (Pa. Commw. Ct. 2005).

Furthermore, an old criminal offense is not sufficient to support a finding of inadequacy of representation. Where a conviction is old and entirely unrelated to any aspect of the case at hand, it will have no bearing on this prong of class certification. *McCall v. Drive Financial Services, L.P.*, Jan. Term 2006, No. 00005 (C.P. Phila. April 10, 2009) (class representative not inadequate due to conviction occurring fifteen years prior to the commencement of the case).

The adequacy of representation prerequisite was not met where plaintiff's counsel failed to promptly move for class certification within 30 days after the last pleading was due or seek an extension, and counsel admitted he would need additional assistance but did not provide any details about the qualifications of the unknown counsel. *Buynak v. Department of Transportation,* 833 A.2d

1159, 1166 (Pa. Commw. Ct. 2003). Adequacy is also not met where a lawyer seeks to be both class representative and lead counsel for the class. *Karn v. Quick & Reilly Inc.*, 912 A.2d 329 (Pa. Super. Ct. 2006) (citing Explanatory Comment to Rule 1709). Similarly, the fact that one of the class representatives was married to attorney allegedly representing class raised conflict of interest concerns sufficient to require production of documents that plaintiff claimed were protected by the attorney-client and work-product privileges. An affidavit executed by the attorney stating that he did not have any financial interest in the action was insufficient to preclude the conflict of interest challenge by defendants. *Gocial v. Independence Blue Cross*, 827 A.2d 1216, 1223 (Pa. Super. Ct. 2003).

j. Fair and Efficient Method of Resolving Issues

Rule 1708's requirement that a class action must constitute a fair and efficient method of resolving the issues in dispute has been the subject of several cases. A trial court's decision that recovery was likely to be so small in relation to the expense and effort of administering the action as not to justify class certification was reversed in *Dunn v. Allegheny County Property Assessment Appeals and Review*, 794 A.2d 416, 427 (Pa. Commw. Ct. 2002). The appellate court pointed out that public policy considerations and the avowed purpose of the class action procedure is to permit the aggregation of small claims that would otherwise go unlitigated in individual actions. *See also, Baldassari v. Suburban Cable TV Co. Inc.*, 808 A.2d 184 (Pa. Super. Ct. 2002) (small recovery of $2.00 per class member, with aggregate potential claim of $1.2 million, warranted certification); *Kelly v. County of Allegheny*, 546 A.2d 608 (Pa. 1988) (trial court abused discretion in denying class certification on ground that average recovery would be $13.61 for each class member).

On the other hand, where class members would have substantial claims in individual cases which would be economically feasible to pursue, class certification is not appropriate. *Savage Hyundai, Inc. v. North American Warranty Services, Inc.*, 60 Pa. D. & C. 4th 156 (C.P. Phila. 2002). *But see Clemente v. Republic First Bank*, 2005 Phila. Ct. Com. Pl. LEXIS 181 at *14 (Phila. C.P. March 18, 2005) (certification proper even though named plaintiffs' damages were approximately $25,000).

Rule 1708(a)(1) requires a court to determine whether common questions predominate over any question affecting only individual members. This requirement was not met in *Keppley v. School District of Twin Valley*, 866 A.2d 1165 (Pa. Commw. Ct. 2005), where the court held predominance lacking where each class member would be required to testify concerning, among other things, their individual expectations of privacy. *See also, Kern v. Lehigh Valley Hospital, Inc.*, 108 A.3d 1281, 1290 (Pa. Super. Ct. 2015) (holding that, with respect to Section 201–9.2 of the UTPCPL, trial court did not abuse its discretion in determining "that, under Rule 1702(5), class action would not be a fair and efficient method of adjudication because individual reliance would be the predominant factor over the common issues"); *Eisen v. Independence Blue Cross*, 839 A.2d 369 (Pa. Super. Ct. 2003) (range of insurer reactions to benefit claims created variety of facts and legal claims which could not be covered by one single proceeding); *Green v. Saturn Corp.*, 2001 WL 1807390, *5–7 (Pa. Com. Pl. Oct. 24, 2001) (false advertising and misrepresentation claims would require reviewing reasons of each class member for purchasing vehicle).

More recently, in *Cardinale v. R.E. Gas Dev., LLC*, 154 A.3d 1275 (Pa. Super. Ct. 2017), the Pennsylvania Superior Court vacated the trial court's denial of class certification, which was based on a finding of lack of predominance, and remanded. The Superior Court found that plaintiffs were alleging breach of form leases, the "vast majority" of which defendant had failed to timely reject under the lease provisions, and the trial court thus erred in concluding that it would be forced to examine the potentially individualized grounds for defendant's ultimate rejection of each class member's lease.

k. Management Difficulties

Rule 1708(a)(2) governs manageability, but the consideration of potential difficulties in managing a class action is not given a great deal of weight. For example, the ability to divide a class into subclasses under Rule 1710(c) obviated any manageability issues presented where some class members would be confronted by defenses while others would not, since the defenses arose from common documents. *Wurtzel v. Park Towne Place Associates Limited Partnership*, 2002 WL 31487894 (C.P. Phila. Nov. 5, 2002). *See also, Tesauro v. The Quigley Corp.*, 2002 WL 372947 (C.P. Phila. Jan. 25, 2002) (potential choice of law issues for national class do not support denying class certification; application of other states' consumer protection laws has no relevancy at certification stage of case) (citing *Janicik v. Prudential Ins. Co. of America*, 451 A.2d 451 (Pa. Super. Ct. 1982)).

Another manageability decision is *Parsky v. First Union Corp.*, 51 Pa. D & C. 4th 468 (C.P. Phila 2001). In *Parsky*, a national class of investors brought claims for breach of contract and breach of fiduciary duty arising from alleged tax liabilities as a result of the conversion of common trust funds. In certifying the proposed class, the court held, among other things, that no manageability problems were posed by applying both New Jersey and Pennsylvania law; that there was a high risk of inconsistent decisions; and, that a recovery of less than $50,000 for most class members was low enough to preclude separate actions for each member. *See also, In re Pennsylvania Baycol Third-Party Payor Litigation*, 2005 WL 852135, *9 (C.P. Phila April 4, 2005) (court will rely on ingenuity and aid of counsel, and upon its plenary authority, to control action to solve whatever management problems the litigation may bring); *Lewis v. Bayer AG*, 2004 WL 1146692, *22 (C.P. Phila Mar. 19, 2004), where the court held that problems of administration alone should not justify denial of an otherwise appropriate class action ("given the prospect of a limited damage award and the expense of proving a medical monitoring claim," court held that a class action was the "only means asymptomatic plaintiffs ha[d] to recover medical monitoring expenses").

A defendant's threat to join additional defendants had the potential to create manageability problems, but threat itself was insufficient to preclude certification. *Foultz v. Erie Insurance Exchange*, 2002 WL 452115, *16 (C.P. Phila Mar. 13, 2002).

Where a court believed it would have to handle over a thousand separate trials on the question of individual damages, class certification was denied. *Savage Hyundai, Inc. v. North American Warranty Services, Inc.*, 60 Pa. D. & C. 4th 156 (C.P. Phila 2002).

No manageability problems were perceived by the appellate court where a number of individuals had opted out and sought to bring their own individual actions. The court held that coordination of the individual cases with the class action for discovery and other efficiently related purposes was proper. *Washington v. FedEx Ground Package System, Inc.*, 2010 WL 2119570 (Pa. Super. Ct. May 27, 2010).

l. Settlement

Pennsylvania law requires that a class action may not be settled without a hearing and court approval. PA. R. CIV. P. 1714(a). Class action settlements are not required to benefit all class members equally. *Gregg v. Independence Blue Cross*, 2004 WL 869063, *47 (Pa. Com. Pl. Apr. 22, 2004). The applicable standard for approving a class action settlement is the analysis established by the Pennsylvania Supreme Court in *Dauphin Deposit Bank and Trust Co. v. Hess,* 727 A.2d 1076, 1079–80 (Pa. 1999). Seven factors should be considered to determine whether a class action settlement should be approved:

(1) the risks of establishing liability and damages;
(2) the range of reasonableness of the settlement in light of the best possible recovery;
(3) the range of reasonableness of the settlement in light of all of the attendant risks of litigation;
(4) the complexity, expense and likely duration of the litigation;
(5) the state of the proceedings and the amount of discovery completed;
(6) the recommendations of competent counsel; and
(7) the reaction of the class to the settlement.

Dauphin, 727 A.2d at 1079–80.

A settlement in a class action lawsuit is entitled to the initial presumption that it is fair. *Gregg v. Independence Blue Cross*, 2004 WL 869063, *31 (C.P. Phila. Apr. 22, 2004). The factors required to establish this presumption are:

(1) That the settlement has been arrived at by arm's-length bargaining;
(2) That sufficient discovery has been taken or investigation completed to enable counsel and the court to act intelligently;
(3) That the proponents of the settlement are counsel experienced in similar litigation; and
(4) That the number of objectors or interests they represent is not large when compared to the class as a whole.

Milkman v. American Travelers Life Insurance Co., 2002 WL 778272, *5 (C.P. Phila. Apr. 1, 2002) (citing Herbert B. Newberg and Alba Conte, 2 *Newberg on Class Actions* § 11.41 (3d ed. 1992)). In the absence of a binding Pennsylvania rule or case law, the *Milkman* court adopted the procedure used for proposed settlement in federal class action suits. *Milkman v. American Travelers Life Insurance Co.*, 2001 WL 1807376 (C.P. Phila. Nov. 26, 2001) (adopting two-step process for approval of class action settlements set forth in *Manual for Complex Litigation*, Third, § 30.41 at 237).

An order disapproving a class settlement is immediately appealable under the "collateral order" doctrine. *See, e.g.*, *Treasurer of State of Conn. v. Ballard Spahr Andrews & Ingersoll LLP,* 866 A.2d 479, 483–84 (Pa. Commw. Ct. 2005); *Buchanan v. Century Fed. Sav. & Loan Ass'n,* 393 A.2d 704 (Pa. Super. Ct. 1978). However, an order granting preliminary approval of a class settlement but imposing certain conditions in order to obtain final approval is not appealable under the collateral order doctrine. *Brophy v. Philadelphia Gas Works*, 921 A.2d 80 (Pa. Commw. Ct. 2007).

m. Notice to Class

To be effective and binding, the notice provided to a class must pass constitutional muster. In *Wilkes v. Phoenix Home Life Mut. Ins. Co.*, 902 A.2d 366 (Pa. 2006), insureds and trustees of an insurance trust brought an action against a life insurance company to recover for misrepresentation, unfair trade practices, and breach of contract. The insurance company claimed that the res judicata effect of an out-of-state class settlement in which plaintiffs were notified of their class membership barred the suit. Reversing a lower court determination that genuine factual issues as to the adequacy of the notice precluded summary judgment on the res judicata question, the Pennsylvania Supreme Court undertook a broad collateral review and found the notice constitutionally adequate. *Id.* at 382–84. While acknowledging that inadequate notice is an exception to both res judicata doctrine and the grant of full faith and credit to out-of-state judgments, the court held that the information provided in the notice adequately warned the plaintiffs that they were included in the earlier class action litigation. *Id.*

A plaintiff's proposal that notice be posted on defendant's website was denied; potential prejudice to defendant outweighed plaintiff's desire to minimize expense of sending notice through defendant's established methods of communication as provided in Rule 1712(c). *Tesauro v. The Quigley Corp.*, 2002 WL 372947 (C.P. Phila. Jan. 25, 2002).

n. Contact with Class Members

Although no Pennsylvania appellate court has stated a bright line rule prohibiting communications with putative absent class members, several trial courts have placed significant restrictions on such communications. Pennsylvania law provides that the court may make orders to direct the conduct of parties to a class action and that notice to members of the class "may be given in such a manner as the court may direct." Pa. R.C.P 1713. In *Lewis v. Bayer, A.G.*, the trial court relied on Rule 1713 to modify communications sent by a defendant to putative absent class members. *Lewis v. Bayer A.G.*, 2002 WL 1472339, *9–10 (Pa. Com. Pl. June 12, 2002). Another Pennsylvania trial court relied on Rule 4.2 of the Pennsylvania Rules of Professional Conduct in prohibiting a defendant's communications with its current and former employees regarding the subject matter of the case, in which the employees were putative class members. *Braun v. Wal-Mart Stores, Inc.*, 2003 WL 1847695, *2 (Pa. Com. Pl. Jan. 15, 2003). Citing Pennsylvania precedent, the *Braun* court concluded that putative class members are parties to the action and are therefore entitled to the protection Rule 4.2 affords represented parties from communications by counsel representing other parties.

The Pennsylvania Superior Court has relied on Rule 1713 in addressing communications with absent members of a certified class. In *Pennsylvania Orthopaedic Society v. Independence Blue Cross*, 885 A.2d 542 (Pa. Super. Ct. 2005), health insurance companies appealed the lower court's order enjoining named medical societies/associations and all others acting on their behalf from communicating with class members about the class action settlement without prior approval by the court. The Superior Court upheld the trial court's injunction as appropriate where its order was based on a finding that "communications sent by certain lawyers and medical associates to the members of the settlement class were false, misleading, and confusing. . . ." *Id.* at 547. The injunctive order was appropriate and satisfied first amendment concerns, where "the limitation on speech furthered the compelling interest of ensuring that the class members' decisions to participate or opt out were based on an independent analysis of their own self-interest." *Id.*

In *In re Bridgeport Fire Litigation*, 8 A.3d 1270, 1294 (Pa. Super. Ct. 2010), the Superior Court reiterated its holding in *Pennsylvania Orthopaedic Society*, stating: "In *Pennsylvania Orthopaedic Society,* we adopted the *Gulf Oil Co.* rationale and held that under *Pa.R.C.P. 1713(a)(2),* a trial court presiding over a class action can control communications to class members in order to protect the class or to ensure the fair conduct of the action." As explained by the Superior Court, "in *Gulf Oil Co. v. Bernard*, 452 U.S. 89, 101 S. Ct. 2193, 68 L. Ed. 2d 693 (1981), the United States Supreme Court concluded that Federal Rule 23(d) authorized a trial court supervising a class action to enter orders limiting communications to class members to ensure the orderly administration of these complex cases." *Bridgeport*, 8 A.3d at 1293. In *Bridgeport*, the Superior Court affirmed a trial court order restraining a lawyer who left one of the firms serving as class counsel from communicating with absent members of a certified class in an effort to solicit them as clients.

o. Attorneys' Fees

Pennsylvania Rule 1717, formerly Rule 1716, sets forth the factors to be considered by a court in awarding attorneys' fees in a class action:

(1) the time and effort reasonably expended by the attorney in the litigation;
(2) the quality of the services rendered;
(3) the results achieved and benefits conferred upon the class or upon the public;
(4) the magnitude, complexity and uniqueness of the litigation; and
(5) whether the receipt of a fee was contingent on success.

See also In re Bridgeport Fire Litig., 8 A.3d 1270, 1288–89 (Pa. Super. Ct. 2010) (quoting former Rule 1716 factors and recognizing that order of factors does not indicate their priority).

Pennsylvania courts are "permitted to award a reasonable fee pursuant to a lodestar, a percentage of the common fund, or, if necessary, a hybrid approach." *Braun v. Wal-Mart Stores, Inc.*, 24 A.3d 875, 979 (Pa. Super. Ct. 2011), *aff'd on other grounds*, 106 A.3d 656 (Pa. 2015). A court may apply a "contingency enhancement, *i.e.,* a multiplier," to the lodestar calculation but "only if the lodestar does not reflect counsel's contingent risk." *Id.* (reversing trial court's award of 3.7 multiplier on lodestar amount based on finding that hourly rates of plaintiffs' attorneys reflected contingency risk and remanding for re-calculation of fees).

Where a federal statute provides the substantive rule for attorney fee-shifting, a state court award of fees is limited by that rule in state class actions under the federal fee-shifting rule. *Samuel-Bassett*, 34 A.3d at 57.

p. Effect of Arbitration Clause on Class Actions

Consumer agreements that explicitly preclude class wide litigation or arbitration are invalid since they are contrary to public policy. *Thibodeau v. Comcast Corp.*, 912 A.2d 874 (Pa. Super. Ct. 2006). In *Thibodeau,* a cable TV customer filed a class action against his cable company alleging that cable customers were illegally billed for converter boxes and remote controls that were unnecessary for basic cable service. The cable company moved to stay or dismiss on the basis of the arbitration provisions included in its subscriber agreements with the customers. The trial court held the arbitration clause was unconscionable and unenforceable because it prohibited consumer class actions. On appeal, the intermediate appellate court in Pennsylvania affirmed. The court held that a class prohibition was procedurally and substantively unconscionable under general contract principles. "It is only the class action vehicle which makes small consumer litigation possible." 912 A.2d at 885. No Pennsylvania court has yet addressed the effect on *Thibodeau* of *AT&T Mobility, LLC v. Concepcion*, 131 S.Ct. 1740, 2011 WL 1561956 (2011), the United States Supreme Court's recent decision concerning class action bans contained in consumer arbitration clauses. *But see Quilloin v. Tenet Healthsystem Philadelphia, Inc.*, 673 F.3d 221, 233 (3d Cir. 2012) (holding that *Thibodeau* is "clearly preempted under *Concepcion*").

q. Standing and Subject Matter Jurisdiction

Following the Supreme Court's decision in *TransUnion LLC v Ramirez*, 594 U.S. 413 (2021), defendants have attempted to argue that the same federal standing principles in that case apply to Pennsylvania state court class actions. But the Pennsylvania courts have rejected these arguments: "While standing in a federal court is derived from the United States Constitution, the same is not true in Pennsylvania." *First Star Bank v. Chipego,* 312 A.3d 910, 920 (Pa. Super. Ct. 2024), *quoting Johnson v. American Standard*, 607 Pa. 492, 8 A.3d 318, 327 n.9 (2010); *see also Firearm Owners Against Crime v. Papenfuse*, 261 A.3d 467, 481–82 (Pa. 2021) (distinguishing Pennsylvania's more liberal standing test from the constitutional test for standing in federal court). The Superior Court in

Chipego also rejected (emphatically) the argument that Pennsylvania courts "lacked subject matter jurisdiction" to decide violations of other states' statutes, describing the argument as "devoid of merit." *Chipego*, 312 A.3d at 917.

r. Motions for Decertification or Amendment of Class Orders

Rule 1710(d) addresses motions to revoke, alter, or amend a class certification order. In *Sommers v. UPMC*, 185 A.3d 1065 (Pa. Super. Ct. 2018), the court held that "new evidence" must be presented to activate a trial court's authority to revisit an earlier class certification decision. *Id.* at 1071 (**"Without a Later Evidentiary Development, the Trial Court Has No Authority to Revisit the Certification Order."** (emphasis in original)). In effect, this places the burden of proof on the party moving to decertify the class; as opposed to the class proponent having a continuing burden to maintain class certification.

Chapter author Michael D. Donovan is principal in Donovan Litigation Group, LLC, in Malvern, Pennsylvania. His practice focuses on class action securities, shareholder, employment, and consumer protection litigation.

RHODE ISLAND

1. COMPARISON WITH RULE 23 OF THE FEDERAL RULES OF CIVIL PROCEDURE

Rule 23 of the Rhode Island Superior Court Rules of Civil Procedure is *nearly* identical to Rule 23 of the Federal Rules of Civil Procedure. This was achieved through substantial revisions of the rule made in a 1991 amendment, by a Supreme Court order, dated and effective April 17, 1991. In 1995, another amendment made stylistic changes in paragraph (c)(2), by Superior Court order dated June 12, 1995, and approved by the Supreme Court on June 13, 1995, effective September 5, 1995. In 1998, however, the United States Supreme Court adopted Rule 23(f) of the Federal Rules of Civil Procedure, which explicitly allows the federal courts of appeals, in their discretion, to entertain immediate appeals of a federal district court grant or denial of class certification. In 2003, the United States Supreme Court also adopted Rule 23(g), which addresses appointment of class counsel, and Rule 23(h), which addresses award of attorney fees. Rhode Island has not adopted paragraphs (f), (g), or (h) of the Federal Rule.

2. CASE LAW INTERPRETING RULE 23

Rule 23 requires that the class proponent make a timely motion to certify the suit as a class action and present evidence from which the court can conclude that class certification requirements are met. *Cabana v. Littler*, 612 A.2d 678, 686 (R.I. 1992); *Cazabat v. Metropolitan Prop. & Cas. Ins. Co.*, No. KC99-544, 2001 WL 267762 (R.I. Super. Ct. Feb. 23, 2001). The court must find that a class action will fairly ensure the adequate representation of alleged parties as a condition precedent to the maintenance of a class action. *Cabana*, 612 A.2d at 685. The hearing on class certification should be held as soon as practicable, must be on the record, and may not be substituted by an unrecorded chambers conference. *Id.* The parties may not stipulate the existence of a class in lieu of an independent judicial determination made after a hearing on the record. *Id.* The initial burden by the party pleading class action is not heavy but requires more than mere conjective and conclusory allegations. *Id.* at 686. The burden requires a showing that (1) there are a sufficient number of class members to make joinder impracticable, (2) there are common legal or factual issues which can be effectively adjudicated by the court on a classwide basis, (3) the claims of the chosen representative are typical of those of the members of the class, and (4) the chosen representative and attorney will vigorously and adequately represent the interests of all class members. *Id.* at 685; *accord Clifford v. Raimondo*, 184 A.3d 673, 685 (R.I. 2018).

One of the reasons for this light burden is that an initial determination of class certification is not final. *Id.* at 686. The court can modify its order granting class certification at any time up to final judgment. *Id.* The Supreme Court will independently review plaintiff's motion to certify a class when the order was a pro forma statement granting the motion to certify class without accompanying findings of fact and without record or transcript from hearing on class certification. *Id.* at 685. The standard of review on appeal from a trial justice's decision to certify a class is the same as the standard of review of findings of fact made by a trial justice sitting without a jury. The finding is accorded great deference and will not be disturbed unless the trial justice misconceived material evidence. *Id.*; *Pereira v. Tellier*, 583 A.2d 523, 524 (R.I. 1990); *Smith v. Boyd*, 553 A.2d 131, 134 (R.I. 1989).

In ruling on a motion for class certification, a court must not decide the merits of the case. *Providence Retired Police & Firefighter's Ass'n v. City of Providence*, C.A. No. PC-11-5853, 2012 WL 1957737 (R.I. Super. Ct. May 24, 2012) (Taft-Carter, J.). Nor may courts "'conduct a preliminary inquiry into the merits of a suit in order to determine whether it may be maintained as a class action.'" *Clifford*, 184 A.3d at 685 (quoting *Eisen v. Carlisle & Jacquelin*, 417 U.S. 156, 177 (1974)). However, a court may "look past the pleadings in determining whether the requirements of Rule 23 have been satisfied." *Providence Retired Police & Firefighter's Ass'n*, 2012 WL 1957737.

The fact that not all class members actually participate in the litigation does not violate Rule 23. *Clifford*, 184 A.3d at 689 (rejecting appellees' argument that their lack of participation in the underlying litigation should have kept them from being made a part of a class that was constituted for settlement purposes only and concluding that such an argument "misconstrues the entire purpose of a class action"). Indeed, "Rule 23 does not require that each class member has participated in the underlying litigation, but requires only that the trial justice certify the class in accordance with its provisions." *Id.*

Rhode Island courts have recognized that there is a "dearth of case law in Rhode Island pertaining to class actions and Rule 23," therefore, Rhode Island courts look to interpretations of Rule 23 of the Federal Rules of Civil Procedure for guidance when interpreting Rhode Island's Rule 23. *Id.*; *see also Rhode Island Public Employees Retiree Coalition v. Raimondo*, C.A. No. P.C. 2015-1486, 2015 WL 1872189, at *4 (R.I. Super. Ct. Apr. 16, 2015), *aff'd Clifford*, 184 A.3d 673 (*Rhode Island Public Employees Retiree Coalition I*).

The Rhode Island Superior Court, looking to the First Circuit Court of Appeals, has recognized that "'[i]f it is obvious from the pleadings that the proceeding cannot possibly move forward on a classwide basis, district courts can use their authority under Federal Rule of Civil Procedure 12(f) to delete the complaint's class allegations.'" *Diore v. Synagro Woonsocket, LLC*, No. PC-2024-06059, 2025 R.I. Super. LEXIS 57, at *32 (quoting *Manning v. Boston Medical Center Corp.*, 725 F.3d 34, 59 (1st Cir. 2013)). However, striking class allegations is "'disfavored because it requires a reviewing court to preemptively terminate the class aspects of . . . litigation, solely on the basis of what is alleged in the complaint, and before plaintiffs are permitted to complete the discovery to which they would otherwise be entitled on questions relevant to class certification.'" *Id.* at *33 (quoting *Manning*, 725 F.3d at 59) (denying motion to strike class allegations).

a. Rule 23(a)

i. Numerosity. The pleading party of a class action suit must show that there are a sufficient number of class members to make joinder impracticable. *Cabana*, 612 A.2d at 685. "Class actions have been awarded judicial recognition in this jurisdiction when the interested parties to a suit are numerous." *Seibert v. Clark*, 619 A.2d 1108, 1111 (R.I. 1993) (quoting *Johnston Businessmen's Ass'n v. Aarussillo*, 274 A.2d 433, 435 (R.I. 1971)). "As a general rule, a class of forty (40) or more members raises a presumption of impracticability of joinder." *Providence Retired Police & Firefighter's*, 2012 WL 1957737 (citing *Newburg on Class Actions* § 3:12 at 198 (5th ed. 2011) and ruling that a class of 648 retirees and their spouses satisfied the numerosity requirement); *Rhode Island Public Employees Retiree Coalition I* at 5 (ruling that a class of 60,000 active and inactive employees and retirees and a class of 113 municipal entities satisfied the numerosity requirement);

Clifford, 184 A.3d at 686 (affirming the decision in *Rhode Island Public Employees Retiree Coalition I* and, in response to arguments made by certain members who were involuntarily included in the class, observing that the involuntary members asserted claims that were the same as the union plaintiffs).

The Rhode Island Supreme Court has permitted taxpayers to maintain a class action by filing a bill in equity questioning the validity of the whole tax and its assessment on every person taxed. In such circumstances the Court has ruled that equity shall take jurisdiction of suits brought by one or more taxpayers who are suing on their own behalf and on behalf of all other taxpayers, in order to avoid multiplicity of suits. *Johnston*, 274 A.2d at 435. If there is a conflict between Rule 23(a) and the statute, R.I. Gen. Laws § 44-5-27, as amended by P.L. 1968, chap. 163, sec. 2, which bars a taxpayer's suit as a class action, the rule prevails over the statute. *Id.* at 436.

ii. Commonality. The party pleading a class action must show that there is a common legal or factual issue that can efficiently be adjudicated by the court on a classwide basis. *Cabana*, 612 A.2d at 685. To that end, the proposed class representative has the burden of proving there is at least one common question of law or fact shared by the class and that the common question is not peripheral but important to most of the individual class members' claims. *Rhode Island Public Employees Retiree Coalition I* at 5. Indeed, Rhode Island courts require commonality to "'be of such a nature that it is capable of classwide resolution—which means the determination of its truth or falsity will resolve an issue that is central to the validity of each one of the claims in one stroke.'" *Clifford*, 184 A.3d at 688 (citing *Wal-Mart Stores, Inc. v. Dukes*, 149 U.S. 788 (2011). A single common question is sufficient. *Id.*; *accord Providence Retired Police & Firefighter's*, 2012 WL 1957737 (citing *Wal-Mart Stores, Inc.*, 149 U.S. 788). The commonality requirement in Rule 23(a)(2) requires more than a technical consistency among the legal and factual issues raised. It also requires that a commonality of "interest" in the action's outcome exist among prospective class members. *See Cohen v. Harrington*, 722 A.2d 1191, 1196–97 (R.I. 1999). Commonality may arise when every member of a purported class receives a document which becomes the main issue of litigation. *Hanoian v. Blue Cross and Blue Shield of Rhode Island*, C.A. No. 96-2579, 2002 WL 31097767, at *5 (R.I. Super. Ct. Sept. 18, 2002). Similarly, commonality may exist when a common question of contractual liability is present, even if individual damage assessments would be required later. *Rhode Island Public Employees Retiree Coalition I*, at *5 (citing *Decesare v. Lincoln Benefit Life Co.*, 852 A.2d 474, 488 (R.I. 2004)). Indeed, the Rhode Island Supreme Court has held that "'[t]he need for individual damages calculations . . . does not diminish the appropriateness of class action certification where common questions as to liability predominate.'" *Clifford*, 184 A.3d at 688 (quoting *Decesare*, 852 A.2d at 488). In applying the foregoing principles, the Rhode Island Supreme Court concluded that the requirement of commonality had been met when all plaintiffs had a single question in common—whether the General Assembly's enactment of a pension reform statute amounted to a violation of the rights afforded by the Rhode Island Constitution. *Id.*

iii. Typicality/Adequacy. A class plaintiff or class defendant may represent the interests of others who are absent from the court, so long as the claims of the chosen representative are typical of those members of the class and the representative and his or her attorney will vigorously and adequately represent the interests of all class members. *Cabana*, 612 A.2d at 685. "As long as the representative plaintiff and the class are injured by the same sequence of events, factual discrepancies among the various claims will not defeat typicality." *Hanoian*, 2002 WL 31097767, at *6 (citing *Baby Neal v. Casey*, 43 F.3d 48, 56 (3d Cir. 1994)); *accord Clifford*, 184 A.3d at 688 (recognizing that "[w]hen it is alleged that the same unlawful conduct was directed at or affected both the named plaintiff and the class sought to be represented, the typicality requirement is usually met irrespective of minor variations in the fact patterns underlying individual claims").

Typicality is generally presumed to be met where all class members' claims arise out of the same or similar contracts. *Providence Retired Police & Firefighter's*, 2012 WL 1957737 (citing *Mund v. EMCC, Inc.*, 259 F.R.D. 180 (D. Minn. 2009)). The class representative must have a personal stake in the controversy, an injury in fact, before they will have standing to assert the broader claims of the public at large. *Rhode Island Ophthalmological Soc. v. Cannon*, 317 A.2d 124, 130 (R.I. 1974).

The Rhode Island Supreme Court has noted that "'[a]dequate representation depends on two factors: (1) the plaintiffs' attorneys must be qualified, experienced, and generally able to conduct the proposed litigation; and (2) the plaintiff[s] must not have interests antagonistic to those of the class.'" *Clifford*, 184 A.3d at 689 (quoting *Pa. Dental Ass'n v. Med. Serv. Ass'n*, 745 F.2d 248, 262–63 (3d Cir. 1984); *accord Hanoian*, 2002 WL 31097767, at *7.

In *Clifford*, the Rhode Island Supreme Court held that the trial justice properly concluded that the typicality requirement was met when she approved a proposal to create plaintiff subclasses and appointed class representatives specifically for each of the subclasses, including a subclass of retirees thereby assuring that all union plaintiffs were represented by individuals who had alleged the same constitutional challenges to the state statute as they had alleged. 184 A.3d at 688. The Court further held that the adequacy requirement was met notwithstanding the plaintiffs' dissatisfaction with the way the attorneys for their subclass handled their claims. *Id.* at 689. In doing so, the Court relied on the Eighth Circuit's decision in *DeBoer v. Mellon Mortgage Co.*, 64 F.3d 1171, 1175 (8th Cir. 1995), which acknowledged "that the fact that the plaintiffs did not approve of the settlement did 'not of itself, demonstrate that . . . class counsel provided inadequate representation' because to 'hold as much would require decertification any time an objection is raised to a class,' which is 'certainly not the standard envisioned by Rule 23.'" *Clifford*, 184 A.3d 689 (quoting *DeBoer*, 64 F.3d at 1175).

b. Rule 23(b)

Once the initial prerequisites set forth in Rule 23(a) have been met, the Court will consider whether the class may be certified under one of Rule 23(b)'s three subsections. Consistent with United States Supreme Court jurisprudence, Rhode Island courts have recognized that "[c]lasses certified under (b)(1) and (b)(2) share the most traditional justifications for class treatment—that individual adjudications would be impossible or unworkable, as in a (b)(1) class, or that the relief sought must perforce affect the entire class at once, as in a (b)(2) class." *Rhode Island Public Employees Retiree Coalition I* at 7 (quoting *Walmart-Stores*, 131 S. Ct. at 2558).

The Rhode Island Supreme Court has acknowledged that courts generally prefer to certify classes under Rule 23(b)(1) or (2) before certifying classes under Rule 23(b)(3) because "members of a class certified under Rule 23(b)(1) or (2) cannot opt out of the action, while members of a class certified under Rule 23(b)(3) are entitled to opt out and pursue individual suits." *Decesare*, 852 A.2d at 490 (citing *DeBoer v. Mellon Mortg. Co.*, 64 F.3d 1171, 1175 (8th Cir. 1995)). Thus, certification under either Rule 23(b)1) or 23(b)(2) avoids "'unnecessary inconsistencies and compromises in future litigation.'" *Rhode Island Public Employees Retiree Coalition I*, at *7 (quoting *DeBoer*, 64 F.3d at 1171).

i. Rule 23(b)(2). Rule 23(b)(2) allows for class certification when "[t]he party opposing the class has acted or refused to act on grounds generally applicable to the class, thereby making appropriate final injunctive relief or corresponding declaratory relief with respect to the class as a whole." Rule 23(b)(2); *see also Clifford*, 184 A.3d at 686; *Cabana*, 612 A.2d at 685; *Decesare*, 852 A.2d at 488–89. The Rhode

Island Supreme Court and the advisory committee notes to the Rule have made it clear that "Rule 23(b)(2) is intended to address those cases in which broad, classwide injunctive or declaratory relief is necessary." *Decesare*, 852 A.2d at 488 (citing Advisory Committee Notes to Fed. R. Civ. P. 23(b)(2) at 128). "'Stated another way, this rule seeks to redress what are really group, as opposed to individual injuries.'" *Rhode Island Public Employees Retiree Coalition I*, at *7 (quoting *Decesare*, 852 A.2d at 488). The Rhode Island Supreme Court, adopting language from the United States Supreme Court, has said that "Rule 23(b)(2) is properly applied 'only when a single injunction or declaratory judgment would provide relief to each member of the class.'" *Clifford*, 184 A.3d at 690 (quoting *Wal-Mart Stores, Inc.*, 564 U.S. at 360). "'It will not apply to cases where 'each class member would be entitled to an individualized award of monetary damages.'" *Id.*

Classes certified under Rule 23(b)(2) are often referred to as mandatory class actions because members of the class are not afforded an opportunity to opt out. *Id.* at 486; *Rhode Island Public Employees Retiree Coalition v. Raimondo*, C.A. No. P.C. 2015-1486, 2015 WL 3648161, at *14 (R.I. Super. Ct. June 9, 2015), *aff'd Clifford*, 184 A.3d 673 (*Rhode Island Public Employees Retiree Coalition II*) (recognizing that "members of a class certified under Rule 23(b)(1) or (2) cannot opt out of the action, while members of a class certified under Rule 23(b)(3) are entitled to opt out and pursue individual suits"). The Rhode Island Superior Court has recognized that "due process does not require that [objectors] be given the opportunity to 'opt-out' of a Rule 23(b)(2) class action settlement." *Id.*

> The due process clause of the Constitution is satisfied when a Rule 23(b)(2) class action is settled without providing objectors a means of opting out because the objectors are (1) adequately represented by the named plaintiffs, (2) represented by an attorney who is qualified, (3) provided with notice of the proposed settlement, (4) given an opportunity to object to the settlement, and (5) assured that the settlement will not take effect unless the trial judge – after analyzing the facts and law of the case and considering all objections to the proposed settlement – determines it to be fair, adequate, and reasonable.

Id. (citing *Kincade v. Gen. Tire & Rubber Co.*, 635 F.2d 501, 507–08 (5th Cir. 1981), *aff'd without opinion* 893 F.2d 347 (11th Cir. 1989)).

A court may only grant class certification based upon Rule 23(b) to protect *all* the members of the class. *See Cazabat*, 2001 WL 267762, at *5–6 (denying class certification based upon Rule 23(b)(2) because defendant did not act or refuse to act on grounds generally applicable to the class as a whole and stating that injunctive relief was best decided on a case-by-case basis). To qualify under Rule 23(b)(2), a prospective class must first establish the opposing party's conduct was generally applicable to the class as a whole. However, Rule 23 does not require that every member of the proposed class actually be aggrieved by or desire to challenge the defendant's conduct. Rather, Rule 23(b)(2) requires that "each member of the proposed class would have standing to challenge the defendant's conduct if he/she so chose to because the conduct at issue is common to all class members." *Hanoian*, 2002 WL 31097767, at *8 (granting class certification based upon Rule 23(b)(2)) (internal quotations and citations omitted). In addition, a prospective class must request final injunctive or corresponding declaratory relief for the class. *Decesare*, 852 A.2d at 489. Requests for specific performance of a contract have also been "routinely recognized as an appropriate subject for Rule 23(b)(2) class certification." *Decesare*, 852 A.2d at 490 (finding equitable relief of specific performance of an annuity contract was the only relief that fully restored the class to its previous position).

In a dispute concerning a city ordinance that required Medicare-eligible retirees to enroll in

Medicare, the Rhode Island Superior Court (Taft-Carter, J.) ruled that class certification under Rule 23(b)(2) was appropriate. *Providence Retired Police & Firefighter's*, 2012 WL 1957737. In so concluding, the court recognized that the city's actions in passing the ordinance inflicted the same injury on all members of the class because, pursuant to the ordinance, all plaintiffs could lose their health insurance under their respective collective bargaining agreements if they did not enroll in Medicare. *Id.* The court also recognized that the plaintiff's complaint requested declaratory and injunctive relief and that a declaratory judgment as to the constitutionality of the ordinance would redress the harm suffered by the members of the class. *Id.* Therefore, the court concluded that the action met both prerequisites for certification of a class under Rule 23(b)(2). *Id.*

In what was likely Rhode Island's highest-profile class action, a dispute concerning the constitutionality of legislative changes to the pension benefits of approximately 60,000 retired, active and inactive state and municipal employees, the Rhode Island Superior Court (Taft-Carter, J.) ruled that class certification under Rule 23(b)(2) was appropriate. *Rhode Island Public Employees Retiree Coalition I*, at *8. In so concluding, the court recognized that the state defendants' actions in enacting legislation over the course of three years that altered retirement benefits were generally applicable to the class as a whole. *Id.* The court further recognized that plaintiffs sought injunctive relief and a declaratory judgment that the challenged statutes were unconstitutional thereby making certification under Rule 23(b)(2) appropriate. *Id.* Thus, the court recognized that "(1) the challenged conduct by the State was applicable to the entire class; (2) courts' general preference for Rule 23(b)(2) certifications rather than certification under Rule 23(b)(3); and (3) the fact that the underlying pension suits challenged the constitutionality of a complex statutory scheme," all militated in favor of certification pursuant to Rule 23(b)(2). *Rhode Island Public Employees Retiree Coalition II*, at *24. The Rhode Island Supreme Court affirmed that decision in all respects. *See Clifford*, 184 A.3d 673. In doing so, the Court addressed plaintiffs' argument that because the class action resulted in a settlement, the award paid under the settlement precluded certification under Rule 23(b)(2). *Id.* The Court held that "the award paid to all plaintiffs in the settlement is not relevant to a Rule 23(b)(2) analysis. Rather, we look to the relief sought in the class-action complaint, which is mainly declaratory and equitable relief." *Id.* The Court concluded that because any money damages would be incidental to the declaratory and equitable relief sought, the trial justice did not abuse her discretion in certifying the class under Rule 23(b)(2). *Id.*

ii. **Rule 23(b)(3).** Rule 23(b)(3) requires that a party pleading class action show that questions of law or fact common to the class members predominate over any questions affecting only individual members. *See also Clifford*, 184 A.3d at 686. If a court determines class certification under Rule 23(b)(2), it should not proceed to analyze class certification under Rule 23(b)(3). *Decesare*, 852 A.2d at 490. This is because "courts prefer that classes proceed under Rule 23(b)(2) because of its broader *res judicata* effect. Courts should proceed under Rule 23(b)(3) only when the class is heterogeneous in composition, thereby necessitating the additional procedural protections afforded by opt-out and notice." *Id.* at 490 (citations omitted); *accord Clifford*, 184 A.3d at 686 ("Due to the potential for 'individual claims brought by members opting out of a class . . . prejudicing other class members or causing inconsistencies and compromises in future litigation, courts prefer that 'classes proceed under Rule 23(b)(2) because of its broader *res judicata* effect.'" (Internal citations omitted)).

Although no precise test controls the predominance inquiry, the existence of questions peculiar to specific class members undermines the predominance element when the uncommon questions are significant and numerous. *Zarrella v. Minnesota Mutual Life Ins. Co.*, 824 A.2d 1249, 1263 (R.I. 2003) (citing *Amchem Prod., Inc. v. Windsor*, 521 U.S. 591, 622–24 (1997)); *see also Cazabat*, 2001 WL 267762, at *6–9 (denying class certification based upon Rule 23(b)(3) because "the individual questions that arise in determining liability and damages [for] each separate [class member] are too numerous to assure an efficiently run and managed trial"). The presence of non-uniform representations by a defendant's agents renders each representation inherently individualized thus undermining predominance. *See Zarrella*, 824 A.2d at 1264. Individual issues of reliance on non-uniform representations and differences in state laws also make claims unsusceptible to class treatment. *See id.* at 1264.

Rule 23(b)(3) also requires that a class action be "superior to other available methods for the fair and efficient adjudication of the controversy." Super. Ct. R. Civ. P. 23(b)(3). The Court must consider the following four factors to determine wither this requirement is satisfied: "(A) the interest of members of the class in individually controlling the prosecution or defense of separate actions; (B) the extent and nature of any litigation concerning the controversy already commenced by or against members of the class; (C) the desirability or undesirability of concentrating the litigation of the claims in the particular forum; (D) the difficulties likely to be encountered in the management of a classification." *Id.* Rule 23(b)(3)(D), "which commonly is referred to as 'manageability,' is a consideration that encompasses the whole range of practical problems that may render the class action format inappropriate for a particular suit." *Zarrella*, 824 A.2d at 1265 (internal quotations and citations omitted). A class action is unmanageable when there is a need to inquire into facts that are specific to individual class members and consider those facts in the context of varying state laws. *Id.*; *see also Hanoian*, 2002 WL 31097767, at *11 (finding the manageability required satisfied).

c. Rule 23(c)(1)

Rule 23(c)(1) governs the timeliness of a motion for class certification and provides that "[a]s soon as practicable after the commencement of an action brought as a class action, the court shall determine by order whether it is to be so maintained." Looking to federal cases on the issue of timeliness of requests for class certification, the Rhode Island Supreme Court has noted that each motion for certification must be reviewed on the facts and circumstances of the particular case and there is no set deadline by which the court must act. *Zarrella,* 824 A.2d at 1263 n.16 (citations and quotations omitted). Nevertheless, "'[t]he current practice is to determine maintability of the class and to identify and structure the class at the earliest pragmatically wise moment.'" *Rhode Island Public Employees Retiree Coalition I*, at *5 (quoting *Berman v. Narragansett Racing Ass'n*, 48 F.R.D. 333, 336 (D.R.I. 1969)).

More recently, the Rhode Island Supreme Court has reminded litigants that it has not adopted the 2003 amendments to Federal Rule 23 or its more liberal timeliness requirement. *Long v. Dell, Inc.*, 93 A.3d 988, 997 (R.I. 2014). *Compare* R.I. Super. R. Civ. P. 23(c)(1) ("As soon as practicable after the commencement of an action brought as a class action, the court shall determine by order whether it is to be so maintained.") *with* Fed. R. Civ. P. 23(c)(1)(A) ("At an early practicable time after a person sues or is sued as a class representative, the court must determine by order whether to certify the action as a class action."). Even applying the Rhode Island rule, courts have generally found motions for class certification to be timely. *See, e.g., Hanoian*, 2002 WL 31097767, at *12 (finding motion for class certification two and one half years after case filed was timely based upon specific facts and circumstances at hand); *Retired Police & Firefighter's*, 2012 WL 1957737 (finding motion for class certification timely when it was filed prior to the close of discovery); *Rhode Island Public Employees Retiree Coalition I*, at *5 (finding motion for class certification timely even when it the underlying lawsuits had been pending for five and three years, respectively).

d. Rule 23(c)(4)

Rule 23(c)(4) provides that "[w]hen appropriate (A) an action may be brought or maintained as a class action with respect to particular issues, or (B) a class may be divided into subclasses and each subclass treated as a class, and the provisions of this rule shall then be construed and applied accordingly." R.I. R. Civ. P. 23(c)(4). In *Clifford*, the Rhode Island Supreme Court concluded that the trial justice had properly divided the class of recipients of pension benefits into subclasses of active and retired employees. *Clifford*, 184 A.3d at 691. In so concluding, the Court noted that "[n]otwithstanding the validity of certifying subclasses, there is nothing that requires a trial justice to create sub-subclasses based on class members' varying and unique circumstances." *Id.* (citing *Int'l Union, United Automobile Aerospace and Agricultural Implement Workers of Am. v. General Motors Corp.*, 497 F.3d 615, 629 (6th Cir. 2007)).

e. Rule 23(d)

Rule 23(d) grants the court power to subdivide, modify, or decertify the class at any time prior to judgment and serves as a vehicle through which the court can change its initial determination as the case develops. *Cabana*, 612 A.2d at 686. This low threshold allows the class proponent to meet its burden at an early stage in order to alert all parties that the suit will proceed as a class action. *Id.* Rule 23(d) does not require notice in every class action but is used instead to ensure the adequacy of the representation of the class. *Testa v. City of Providence*, 572 A.2d 1336, 1338 (R.I. 1990). Notice is not required when there is no suggestion that representation is inadequate or problematic, when all members have common residence in the jurisdiction, when the amounts of money involved are so small that it is not economical for everyone to join suit individually or to file a separate suit, and when notice will be an unreasonable expenditure. *Id.* In addition, due process does not require that each class member must opt in to the class action, nor is it necessary for purposes of allowing class members to opt out. *Id.*

f. Rule 23(e)

Rule 23(e) provides that "[a] class action shall not be dismissed or compromised without the approval of the court, and notice of the proposed dismissal or compromise shall be given to all members of the class in such manner as the court directs."

In accordance with Rule 23(e), "[a] court must independently determine whether the proposed settlement agreement is 'fundamentally fair, adequate, and reasonable,' before granting approval." *Rhode Island Public Employees Retiree Coalition II*, at *14 (quoting *In re Heritage Bond Litig.*, 546 F.3d 667, 674–75 (9th Cir. 1008)); *Clifford*, 184 A.3d at 691 ("A class action settlement has to be fair, reasonable, and adequate."). A court's review is limited to determining whether the compromised reached is fair, reasonable and adequate when considered from the perspective of the class as a whole. *Id.* (citing *In re Baby Products Antitrust Litig.*, 708 F.3d 163, 173–74 (3d Cir. 2013)). In reviewing a proposed settlement, the court "must eschew any 'rubber stamp' approval in favor of an independent review of the settlement." *Id.* (citing *City of Detroit v. Grinnell Corp.*, 495 F.2d 448, 462 (2d Cir. 1974)). Nevertheless, courts are "'restrained by the clear policy in favor of encouraging settlements' to facilitate resolution of controversies and promote judicial economy.'" *Id.* (citing *Durrett v. Hous. Auth. of City of Providence*, 896 F.2d 600, 600–04 (1st Cir. 1990)). This is especially true in complex class action litigation. *Id.* (citing *In re Syncor ERISA Litig.*, 516 F.3d at 1101).

i. Preliminary approval of settlement. When a proposed settlement is reached, the court must determine if it is fair, adequate and reasonable. *Rhode Island Public Employees Retiree Coalition I*, at *8 (citing *In re Lupron Mktg. and Sales Practices Litig.*, 228 F.R.D. 75, 93 (D. Mass 2005)). The Rhode Island Supreme Court has observed that "[w]hile there are a number of factors a trial justice may use to decide whether a settlement is reasonable, 'the ultimate decision by the judge involves a balancing of the advantages and disadvantages of the proposed settlement as against the consequences of going to trial or other possible but perhaps unattainable variations on the proffered settlement.'" *Clifford*, 184 A.3d at 691 (quoting *Bezdek v. Vibram USA, Inc.*, 809 F.3d 78, 82 (1st Cir. 2015)). "'[A] preliminary determination establishes an initial presumption of fairness when the court finds that: (1) the negotiations occurred at arm's length; (2) there was sufficient discovery; (3) the proponents of the settlement are experienced in similar litigation; and (4) only a small fraction of the class objected.'" *Id.* (quoting *In re Gen. Motors Corp. Pick-Up Truck Fuel Tank Prods. Liab. Litig.*, 55 F.3d 768, 785 (3d Cir. 1995)). To that end, the settlement must be the product of good faith negotiations between the parties and not the product of collusion or bad faith. *Id.* (citing *R.I. Depositors Econ. Prot. Corp.*, 661 A.2d 969. 971 (R.I. 1995) and *In re Fleet/Norstar*, 935 F. Supp. 99, 105–06 (D.R.I. 1996) *supplemented*, 974 F. Supp. 155 (D.R.I. 1997)).

The court may preliminarily approve the class when a proposed settlement appears to be fair and within the range of settlements that could be worthy of final approval as fair, reasonable and adequate. Importantly, because this stage of approval is not final, the court only needs to determine whether the settlement, as proposed, merits an initial presumption of fairness. *Id.* at *9.

ii. Class actions for settlement purposes. The Rhode Island Superior Court has recognized that class actions for settlement purposes only are not inherently wrong. *Rhode Island Public Employees Retiree Coalition II*, at *13. Similar to other courts that have addressed this issue, Rhode Island courts have held that "'the absence of class certification prior to the notice of the settlement is not an absolute bar to approval.'" *Id.* at *15 (quoting *Weinberger v. Kendrick*, 698 F.2d 61, 73 (2d Cir. 1982)). However, when class actions are brought for settlement purposes only, the court must "'pay undiluted, even heightened' attention to the class certification." *Id.* at *13 (citing *Hanlon v. Chrysler Corp.*, 150 F.3d 1011, 1019 (9th Cir. 1998)). Indeed, "'[t]he dangers of collusion between class counsel and the defendant, as well as the need for additional protections when the settlement is not negotiated by a court-designed class representatives, weigh in favor of a more probing inquiry than may normally be required under Rule 23(e).'" *Id.* at *15 (quoting *Hanlon*, 150 F.3d at 1026). As other courts have recognized, "'the absence of any indication of collusion, the protracted settlement negotiations, the ability and experience of plaintiffs' counsel, the extensive discovery preceding settlement and the fact that counsel for all parties . . . had access to materials produced in discovery . . . are important indicia of the propriety of settlement negotiations.'" *Id.* (quoting *Weinberger*, 698 F.2d at 74).

iii. Notice of proposed settlement. Rule 23(e) requires that all members of a class be notified of the terms of any proposed settlement. *Rhode Island Public Employees Retiree Coalition I*, at *9. Courts have held that such a requirement is "'designed to summarize the litigation and the settlement and to apprise class members of the right and opportunity to inspect the complete settlement documents, papers, and pleadings filed in the litigation.'" *Id.* (quoting *Gates v. Rohm and Haas, Co.*, 248 F.R.D. 434, 445 (E.D. Pa. 2008)).

Nevertheless, Rhode Island courts recognize that notice is discretionary in Rule 23(b)(2) classes but that Rule 23's notice provisions must be interpreted to comply with the requirements of due process. *Id.* (citing *Johnson v. Gen. Motors Corp.*, 598 F.2d 432, 436 (5th Cir. 1979)). Thus, Rhode Island courts will exercise their discretion and will require that appropriate notice be given in certain circumstances. *Id.* For example, in a case with over 60,000 class members, the Rhode Island Superior

Court required that notices be mailed to class members and published in the Providence Journal notwithstanding that the class was certified as a Rule 23(b)(2) class. *Id.* at *10.

Generally, "the standard for the adequacy of a settlement notice in a class action under either the Due Process Clause or the Rules of Civil Procedure is reasonableness." *Rhode Island Public Employees Retiree Coalition II*, at *17 (citing *Wal-Mart Stores, Inc. v. Visa U.S.A., Inc*., 396 F.3d 96, 113 (2d Cir. 2005)). To satisfy the demands of due process, a settlement notice must be "'reasonably calculated, under all the circumstances, to apprise interested parties of the pendency of the action and afford them an opportunity to present their objections.'" *Id.* (quoting *Int'l Union, United Auto, Aerospace, & Agr. Implement Workers of Am.*, 497 F.3d 615, 629 (6th Cir. 2007)). A settlement notice that informs class members of "'the nature of the pending action, the general terms of the settlement, that complete and detailed information is available from court files and that any class member may appear and be heard at a hearing'" is sufficient to satisfy the demands of due process. *Id.* (quoting *Newberg on Class Actions*, § 8:17 (5th ed. 2014)).

iv. Fairness hearing. Class action settlement agreements are vetted by the court at fairness hearings. The purpose of a fairness hearing is to "'protect unnamed members of a class from unjust or unfair settlements affecting their rights.'" *Id.* at *1 (citing *In re Syncor ERISA Litig*., 516 F.3d 1095, 1100 (9th Cir. 2008)). The judge presiding over a fairness hearing, serves as a guardian of any absent class members who will be bound by the settlement. *Id.* (citing *Barbosa v. Cargill Meat Solutions Corp*., 297 F.R.D. 431, 445 (E.D. Cal. 2013)). A fairness hearing is not a time for a trial of the case. *Id.*

v. Procedural fairness. In reviewing the fairness of settlement agreements, courts are "'mindful of the strong judicial policy in favor of settlements, particularly in the class action context.'" *Id.* at *26 (quoting *Wal-Mart Stores, Inc*., 396 F.3d at 116)). Accordingly, Rhode Island courts recognize that "[a] presumption of fairness attaches to a proposed class settlement when that settlement is reached in arm's-length negotiations between experienced, capable counsel after meaningful discovery." *Id.* at *16 (citing *Wal-Mart Stores, Inc.*, 396 F.3d at 116); *Clifford*, 184 A.3d at 692 ("a settlement following sufficient discovery and genuine arm's-length negotiation is presumed fair"). In conducting this analysis, the court will be mindful that "'[t]he storm warnings indicative of collusion are a lack of significant discovery and an extremely expedited settlement of questionable value accompanied by an enormous legal fee.'" *Id.* at *18 (quoting *In re Lupron Mktg. and Sales Practices Litig*., 228 F.R.D. 75, 94 (D. Mass. 2005)). While the court will conduct its own independent analysis, it accords great weight to the recommendations of counsel who are most closely acquainted with the facts of the underlying litigation. *Id.* at *19 (citing *In re NASDAQ Market-Makers Antitrust Litig*., 187 F.R.D. 465, 474 (S.D.N.Y. 1998)).

vi. Substantive fairness. While Rule 23(e) provides that a class action settlement may only be approved by the court if it is "fair, reasonable, and adequate," the rule does not define those terms. Instead, Rhode Island courts are guided by standards developed by other courts. For example, in a recent decision the Rhode Island Supreme Court upheld the superior court's consideration of the "so-called *Grinnell* factors," as well as the First Circuit's modified version of the *Grinnell* factors. *Clifford*, 184 A.3d at 692 (affirming the decision in *Rhode Island Public Employees Retiree Coalition II*). In applying the *Grinnell* factors, courts consider:

> (1) the complexity, expense and likely duration of the litigation; (2) the reaction of the class to the settlement; (3) the stage of the proceedings and the amount of discovery completed; (4) the risks of establishing liability; (5) the risks of establishing damages; (6) the risks of maintaining the class action through the trial; (7) the ability of the defendants to

> withstand a greater judgment; (8) the range of reasonableness of the settlement fund in light of the best possible recovery; (9) the range of reasonableness of the settlement fund to a possible recovery in light of all the attendant risks of litigation.

Id. (quoting *In re Tyco Int'l, Ltd. Multidistrict Litig.*, 535 F. Supp. 2d 249, 259 (D.N.H. 2007), which adopted the standards articulated by the Second Circuit in *City of Detroit v. Grinnell Corp.*, 495 F.2d 448, 463 (2d Cir. 1974)). The First Circuit's modified version of the *Grinnell* factors requires courts to consider:

> (1) comparison of the proposed settlement with the likely result of litigation; (2) reaction of the class to the settlement; (3) stage of the litigation and the amount of discovery completed; (4) quality of counsel; (5) conduct of the negotiations; (6) prospects of the case, including risk, complexity, expense and duration.

Rhode Island Public Employees Retiree Coalition II, at *20 (quoting *In re Compact Disc Minimum Advertised Price Antitrust Litig.*, 216 F.R.D. 197, 206–07 (D. Me. 2003)).

Similar to other jurisdictions, Rhode Island has recognized that "'the reaction of the class to the settlement is perhaps the most significant factor to be weighed in considering its adequacy.'" *Id.* at 22 (quoting *In re Am. Bank Note Holographics, Inc.*, 127 F. Supp. 2d 418, 425 (S.D.N.Y. 2001)). Thus, "'the absence of a large number of objections to a proposed class action settlement raises a strong presumption that the terms of a proposed class settlement action are favorable to the class members.'" *Id.* (quoting *Dyer v. Wells Fargo Bank, N.A.*, 303 F.R.D. 326, 332 (N.D. Cal. 2014)). Nevertheless, "even 'majority opposition to a settlement cannot serve as an automatic bar to a settlement that a district judge, after weighing all the strengths and weaknesses of a case and the risks of litigation, determines to be manifestly reasonable.'" *Id.* (quoting *TBK Partners, Ltd. v. W. Union Corp.*, 675 F.2d 456, 462 (2d Cir. 1982)); *accord Clifford*, 184 A.3d at 693.

The stage of the proceedings and the amount of discovery completed at the time the court is asked to rule on the fairness of a proposed settlement is another important consideration. Rhode Island courts consider the scope of completed discovery "to ensure that (1) the parties have a good understanding of the strengths and weaknesses of their respective claims so that the settlement's value is based on adequate information, and (2) the parties litigated the case in an adversarial manner." *Id.* at 26 (citing *Newberg on Class Actions* § 13:50 and *McBean v. City of New York*, 233 F.R.D. 377, 386 (S.D.N.Y. 2006)); *see also, e.g., Clifford*, 184 A.3d at 693 (upholding fairness of settlement when production of documents included more than 700 gigabytes of electronic documents and 4 million pages of documents). The parties' retention of expert witnesses is also a factor weighing in favor of a finding that sufficient discovery has been completed. *Rhode Island Public Employees Retiree Coalition II*, at *27 (citing *In re Nissan Radiator/Transmission Cooler Litig.*, No. 10 CV 7493(VB), 2013 WL 4080946 (S.D.N.Y. May 30, 2013)).

In evaluating the plaintiff's risk of establishing liability and the risk of establishing damages, "'the Court need not delve into the intricacies of the merits of each side's arguments, but rather may 'give credence to the estimation of the probability of success proffered by class counsel, who are experienced in the underlying case, and the possible defenses which may be raised to their causes of action.'" *Id.* (quoting *Perry v. FleetBoston Fin. Corp.*, 229 F.R.D. 105, 115 (E.D. Pa. 2005)).

In considering the substantive fairness of a proposed settlement, courts will also consider whether the proposed settlement impacts certain groups more than others. *Id.* at *25. Importantly, "'a small minority of the class members may not be asked to bear an unduly disproportionate share of the accompanying burdens.'" *Id.* (quoting *Officers for Justice v. Civil Serv. Comm'n of the City and Cnty. of San Francisco*, 688 F.2d 615, 624 (9th Cir. 1982)). Accordingly, the Rhode Island

Superior Court has concluded that the proffered explanation that a proposed settlement did the greatest good for the greatest number of class members is an unacceptable justification for a proposed settlement. *Id.* (citing *Marcello v. Regan*, 574 F. Supp. 586, 597 (D.R.I. 1983) ("[T]he greatest good for the greatest number cannot suffice as a justification for the subversion of constitutionally-protected rights.")).

Finally, the court will evaluate whether the proposed settlement is within the range of reasonableness in light of the best possible recovery and the risks the parties would face if the case went to trial. *Id.* at *28 (citing *In re Prudential Ins. Co. Am. Sales Practice Litig. Agent Actions*, 148 F.3d 283, 322 (3d Cir. 1998)). In conducting this analysis, courts "'must be careful to judge the fairness factors against realistic, rather than theoretical, potential for recovery after trial.'" *Id.* (quoting *Sullivan v. DB Invs., Inc.*, 667 F.3d 273, 323 (3d Cir. 2011)).

3. RULE 23(D) MISCELLANEOUS COMMENTS

a. Jurisdiction

When the injunctive relief sought fails to bring a class action within the exclusive equity jurisdiction of the Superior Court, each class member must satisfy the $5,000 jurisdictional threshold required under R.I. Gen. Laws § 8-2-14. *Freitas v. First New Hampshire Mortgage Corp.*, C.A. No. 98-0022, (Hurst, J.) (Bench Decision Mar. 15, 2000); *Hanoian,* 2002 WL 31097767, at *4 (recognizing that the individual claims of purported class members were divisible and each individual claim did not exceed the $5,000, but granting jurisdiction because plaintiff sought equitable relief in the form of a mandatory injunction). Neither a request for declaratory relief seeking simple factual determinations, nor a plea for general injunctive relief, excepted class members from meeting the monetary jurisdictional requirements in a consumer class action based predominantly on breach of contract. *See id.* Similarly, in an attempted class action by plaintiffs who were seeking statutory damages regarding secured transactions, the Rhode Island Superior Court ruled that the collective plaintiffs had "distinct rights" as opposed to a "common and undivided interest[,]" and therefore the plaintiffs were required to meet jurisdictional amount-in-controversy requirement individually. *Howard v. Greenwood Credit Union*, C.A. No. PB 07-0928 (R.I. Super. Ct. Feb. 12, 2010) (Silverstein, J.). Thus, the court determined that the appropriate inquiry in determining whether a class may meet the jurisdictional requirement in the aggregate or must meet the jurisdictional requirement individually is whether "the shares of the remaining plaintiffs are increased . . . if one plaintiff cannot or does not collect his share[.]" *Id.* (quoting *Sellers v. O'Connell*, 701 F.2d 575, 579 (6th Cir. 1983)).

In 2004, the Rhode Island Supreme Court held that claims for damages under the Deceptive Trade Practice Act "either individually or in the aggregate, need not reach the $5,000 jurisdictional threshold. . . . [T]he Superior Court has jurisdiction to hear all case or class actions that allege 'any ascertainable loss' suffered as a result of unlawful trade practices" under the Deceptive Trade Practice Act. *Park v. Ford Motor Co.*, 844 A.2d 687 (R.I. 2004) (finding that even though the individual class claims did not exceed $200 per class member, the class claims should be allowed to proceed in Superior Court because the claims were brought under the Deceptive Trade Practice Act, which explicitly allows Superior Court actions no matter how large or small the claims are). On remand, the Superior Court denied plaintiff's motion to certify the class pursuant to the Deceptive Trade Practices Act, holding that class certification would be inappropriate because the purported class failed to meet the numerosity requirement. Plaintiff appealed. In a second appeal, the Supreme Court clarified its earlier ruling, holding that the Superior Court could not exercise jurisdiction over consumer class claims including claims for breach of express and implied warranties under Rule

20 of the Superior Court Rules of Civil Procedure, which provides for the joinder of parties. The Court held that these class claims each arose out of separate purchase transactions and joinder would be inappropriate. *Park v. Ford Motor Co.*, 928 A.2d 469 (R.I. 2007).

b. Summary Judgment before Class Certification

The Rhode Island Supreme Court has held that when a defendant files a motion for summary judgment before the plaintiff class is certified, the court must treat the case as though it were certified as a class action. *Long*, 93 A.3d at 996. Such a rule is consistent with the court's summary judgment jurisprudence, which requires that the court view the evidence in the light most favorable to the non-moving party. *Id.* By treating a case as a certified class action at the motion for summary judgment stage, the court may consider the injury or damages sustained by the class and is not restricted to considering only the injury or damages of the named plaintiff. *Id.* at *35 n.17 (noting that "if the class is treated as certified, for purposes of viewing the evidence in the light most favorable to the nonmoving party on summary judgment, an inference of class-wide injury should be drawn when competent evidence permits").

c. Waiver

A class action is waived when a trial justice never determines that a class action was formed and when plaintiffs fail to brief or argue the issue of class action, in addition to failing to meet 23(a) requirements. *Lee v. Nielsen*, 388 A.2d 1176 (R.I. 1978); *Berberian v. New England Tel. & Tel. Co.*, 369 A.2d 1109 (R.I. 1977).

d. Attorneys' Fees

Rhode Island law does not support the award of attorneys' fees to the representative of a non-prevailing defendant class. *Western Sur. Co. v. Lums of Cranston, Inc.*, 618 F.2d 854 (1st Cir. 1980).

e. Conflict between Rule and Statute

The requirement that a plaintiff who brings a "Quiet Title" action under R.I. Gen. Laws § 34-16-5 must name all persons with potentially adverse claims is superseded by Rule 23 when the excessive number of defendants makes it impracticable and any named defendant will fairly ensure adequate representation of all. *See Gammons v. Caswell*, 447 A.2d 361, 365 (R.I. 1982).

f. Res Judicata Effect on Individual Suits

In 2007, the Rhode Island Supreme Court held that a settlement agreement entered in a class action case from a foreign jurisdiction has preclusive effect over individual suits brought in Rhode Island even when the individual suit was pending at the time the class action was instituted, provided that the definitions of the class and of the released claims set forth in the settlement agreement show that such claims are intended to be resolved by the settlement. *Lamarque v. Fairbanks Capital Corp.*, 927 A.2d 753, 757–59 (R.I. 2007) (enforcing settlement agreement entered in class action from the United States District Court for the District of Massachusetts).

The Rhode Island Supreme Court, however, has recognized the general principle that "uncertified class actions cannot bind nonmembers of the class." *In re CVS Health Corp. Sec. Litig.*, 328

A.3d 614, 622 (R.I. 2025). Absent such privity, collateral estoppel will not preclude a subsequent suit. *Id.*

g. Scope of Permissible Collateral Attacks on Adequacy of Notice

A class member may not collaterally attack in Rhode Island courts the adequacy of the actual notice, or lack thereof, provided to her of a class action suit from another jurisdiction that precludes her from bringing individual claims. *Lamarque*, 927 A.2d at 764–65. Rather, Rhode Island law limits a collateral attack on due process grounds of a class action determination from a foreign jurisdiction to a challenge of the adequacy of the procedures applied by the court in which the class action was adjudicated for providing notice to the class members, and whether those procedures were in fact followed. *Id.* at 765.

RULE 23 OF THE RHODE ISLAND SUPERIOR COURT RULES OF CIVIL PROCEDURE

RULE 23. CLASS ACTIONS

(a) *Prerequisites to a class action.* One or more members of a class may sue or be sued as representative parties on behalf of all only if (1) the class is so numerous that joinder of all members is impracticable, (2) there are questions of law or fact common to the class, (3) the claims or defenses of the representative parties are typical of the claims or defenses of the class, and (4) the representative parties will fairly and adequately protect the interests of the class.

(b) *Class actions maintainable.* An action may be maintained as a class action if the prerequisites of subdivision (a) are satisfied, and in addition:

(1) The prosecution of separate actions by or against individual members of the class would create a risk of:

(A) Inconsistent or varying adjudications with respect to individual members of the class which would establish incompatible standards of conduct for the party opposing the class, or

(B) Adjudications with respect to individual members of the class which would as a practical matter be dispositive of the interests of the other members not parties to the adjudications or substantially impair or impede their ability to protect their interests; or

(2) The party opposing the class has acted or refused to act on grounds generally applicable to the class, thereby making appropriate final injunctive relief or corresponding declaratory relief with respect to the class as a whole; or

(3) The court finds that the questions of law or fact common to the members of the class predominate over any questions affecting only individual members, and that a class action is superior to other available methods for the fair and efficient adjudication of the controversy. The matters pertinent to the findings include:

(A) the interest of members of the class in individually controlling the prosecution or defense of separate actions;

(B) the extent and nature of any litigation concerning the controversy already commenced by or against members of the class;

(C) the desirability or undesirability of concentrating the litigation of the claims in the particular forum;

(D) the difficulties likely to be encountered in the management of a classification.

(c) *Determination by order whether class action to be maintained; notice; judgment; actions conducted partially as class actions.*

(1) As soon as practicable after the commencement of an action brought as a class action, the court shall determine by order whether it is to be so maintained. An order under

this subdivision may be conditional, and may be altered or amended before the decision on the merits.

(2) In any class action maintained under subdivision (b)(3), the court shall direct to the members of the class the best notice practicable under the circumstances, including individual notice to all members who can be identified through reasonable effort. The notice shall advise each member that (A) the court will exclude the member from the class if the member so requests by a specified date; (B) the judgment, whether favorable or not, will include all members who do not request exclusion; and (C) any member who does not request exclusion may, if the member desires, enter an appearance through counsel.

(3) The judgment in an action maintained as a class action under subdivision (b)(1) or (b)(2), whether or not favorable to the class, shall include and describe those whom the court finds to be members of the class. The judgment in an action maintained as a class action under subdivision (b)(3), whether or not favorable to the class, shall include and specify or describe those to whom the notice provided in subdivision (c)(2) was directed, and who have not requested exclusion, and whom the court finds to be members of the class.

(4) When appropriate (A) an action may be brought or maintained as a class action with respect to particular issues, or (B) a class may be divided into subclasses and each subclass treated as a class, and the provisions of this rule shall then be construed and applied accordingly.

(d) *Orders in conduct of actions.* In the conduct of actions to which this rule applies, the court may make appropriate orders: (1) determining the course of proceedings or prescribing measures to prevent undue repetition or complications in the presentation of evidence or argument; (2) requiring, for the protection of the members of the class or otherwise for the fair conduct of the action, that notice be given in such manner as the court may direct to some or all of the members of any step in the action, or of the proposed extent of the judgment, or of the opportunity of members to signify whether they consider the representation fair and adequate, to intervene and present claims or defenses, or otherwise to come into the action; (3) imposing conditions on the representative parties or on intervenors; (4) requiring that the pleadings be amended to eliminate therefrom allegations as to representation of absent persons, and that the action proceed accordingly; (5) dealing with similar procedural matters. The orders may be combined with an order under Rule 16, and may be altered or amended as may be desirable from time to time.

(e) *Dismissal or compromise.* A class action shall not be dismissed or compromised without the approval of the court, and notice of the proposed dismissal or compromise shall be given to all members of the class in such manner as the court directs.

(1) When appropriate (A) an action may be brought or maintained as a class action with respect to particular issues, or (B) a class may be divided into subclasses and each subclass treated as a class, and the provisions of this rule shall then be construed and applied accordingly.

(f) *Orders in conduct of actions.* In the conduct of actions to which this rule applies, the court may make appropriate orders: (1) determining the course of proceedings or prescribing measures to prevent undue repetition or complications in the presentation of evidence or argument; (2) requiring, for the protection of the members of the class or otherwise for the fair conduct of the action, that notice be given in such manner as the court may direct to some or all of the members of any step in the action, or of the proposed extent of the judgment, or of the opportunity of members to signify whether they consider the representation fair and adequate, to intervene and present claims or defenses, or otherwise to come into the action; (3) imposing conditions on the representative parties or on intervenors; (4) requiring that the pleadings be amended to eliminate therefrom allegations as to representation of absent persons, and that the action proceed accordingly; (5) dealing with similar procedural matters. The orders may be combined with an order under Rule 16, and may be altered or amended as may be desirable from time to time.

(g) *Dismissal or compromise.* A class action shall not be dismissed or compromised without the approval of the court, and notice of the proposed dismissal or compromise shall be given to all members of the class in such manner as the court directs.

Chapter author Nicole J. Benjamin is a shareholder at Adler Pollock & Sheehan, P.C. where she litigates complex commercial disputes and appellate matters. Ms. Benjamin represented Rhode Island's Governor, General Treasurer and Employees' Retirement System of Rhode Island before the trial court and on appeal in what was considered the state's high profile, high-stakes class action concerning the constitutionality of legislative changes to pension benefits of nearly 60,000 retired, active, and inactive state and municipal employees.

SOUTH CAROLINA

1. COMPARISON WITH RULE 23 OF THE FEDERAL RULES OF CIVIL PROCEDURE

Rule 23 of the South Carolina Rules of Civil Procedure, while derived from F.R.C.P. 23, differs significantly from its federal counterpart. The South Carolina rule incorporates the four prerequisites to class certification found in F.R.C.P. 23(a) and adds a fifth prerequisite, requiring that the amount in controversy for each member of the class be at least $100.00, except where the relief primarily sought is injunctive or declaratory in nature.

Conspicuously absent from the state rule is the language contained in F.R.C.P. 23(b). While F.R.C.P. 23(b)(3) explicitly requires the plaintiffs in certain federal class actions to show that common questions of law or fact predominate over individual questions, and that the class action device be superior to other available methods for adjudication for the class to merit certification, a class action brought under the state rule arguably imposes no formal prerequisites to class certification beyond those specified in S.C.R.C.P. 23(a). Also absent from the state rule are the provisions found in F.R.C.P. 23(f), which provides for interlocutory appeals of class certification in federal cases; F.R.C.P. 23(g), outlining criteria and procedures for the appointment of class counsel; and F.R.C.P. 23(h), addressing the procedures for awarding attorney's fees.

Two of the remaining subsections of S.C.R.C.P. 23 contain language also found in F.R.C.P. 23. S.C.R.C.P. 23(c) is identical to F.R.C.P. 23(e). S.C.R.C.P. 23(d)(1) corresponds directly with F.R.C.P. 23(c)(1). The balance of the text of S.C.R.C.P. 23 differs substantially from the federal rule. Additionally, S.C.R.C.P. 23(b)(1) and 23(b)(2) correspond with F.R.C.P. 23.1 and 23.2, respectively.

S.C.R.C.P. 23(d)(1) provides that the trial court determine whether a case should proceed as a class action "as soon as practicable." Rule 23(d)(2) authorizes the court to "impose such terms as shall fairly and adequately protect the interests of the persons on whose behalf the action is brought or defended." Rule 23(d)(3) gives the trial court authority to impose additional conditions upon the representative parties to protect absent class members, or where the class representatives prove inadequate to protect absent class members, the court may order the pleadings amended so that any resulting judgment would bind only the parties to the action, and not affect the rights of those absent class members whose rights and interests had been inadequately protected by the representative parties.

2. CASE LAW INTERPRETING RULE 23

a. Relationship between State and Federal Rule 23

There are relatively few appellate decisions construing Rule 23 of the South Carolina Rules of Civil Procedure, adopted in 1985. While there are many substantive differences between the South Carolina rule and the federal rule, the courts have nevertheless relied upon federal cases for guidance, since the state version of Rule 23 was derived from the federal rule. *See Gardner v. Newsome Chevrolet-Buick, Inc.*, 304 S.C. 328, 331, 404 S.E.2d 200, 201–02 (S.C. 1991).

The differences between the state rule and the federal rule merit further discussion. The South Carolina courts have long held that the state rule favors class actions to a greater degree than the federal rule. The South Carolina Court of Appeals, in *Premium Investment Corp. v. Green*, 283 S.C. 464, 471, 324 S.E.2d 72, 76 (S.C. App. 1984), described the federal rule as having "more stringent requirements" than the state rule. More recently, the South Carolina Supreme Court has explicitly held that that the state rule is more permissive with regard to class actions than the federal rule.

In *Littlefield v. S.C. Forestry Commission*, 337 S.C. 348, 523 S.E.2d 781 (S.C. 1999), the South Carolina Supreme Court found that the trial court had abused its discretion in denying class certification based upon federal grounds not present in the state rule. Similarly, in *Kennedy v. S.C. Retirement System*, 24 Employee Benefits Cas. (BNA) 2859 (S.C. 2000), *withdrawn on unrelated grounds and superseded by substituted opinion*, 345 S.C. 339, 549 S.E.2d 243, *rehearing denied*, 349 S.C. 531, 534 S.E.2d 322 (S.C. 2001), the Court reversed the trial court's denial of class certification based upon "judicial economy" and "necessity," finding that the lower court had impermissibly "graft[ed] requirements from federal class action case law onto our state rule analysis."

However, in *Gardner v. S.C. Dept. of Revenue*, 353 S.C. 1, 577 S.E.2d 190 (S.C. 2003), the state supreme court cited several federal cases and interpreted the "commonality" provision of S.C.R.C.P. 23(a)(2) to require that a "determinative critical issue overshadow[] all other issues." 353 S.C. at 21, 577 S.E.2d at 201. The court stated: "A representative class cannot exist where the court must investigate each plaintiff's prejudice claim where it is one of the two predominate [sic] issues in the case. Requiring such individualized examination negates the benefits of a class action suit." 353 S.C. at 22, 577 S.E.2d at 201.

While *Gardner* represents a departure from prior cases in which the South Carolina courts have expressly rejected efforts to narrow the scope of permissible class certification to the stricter federal standard, it importantly did not overrule *Littlefield* and did not address in any way the plain-language differences between the state and federal rules. The continued vitality of *Littlefield* is clearly supported in the recent case of *Grazia v. South Carolina State Plastering, LLC*, 390 S.C. 562, 703 S.E.2d 197 (S.C. 2010), in which the state supreme court reiterated the longstanding favored status of class actions under state law, quoting *Littlefield* as follows:

> Our state class action rule differs significantly from its federal counterpart. The drafters of Rule 23, South Carolina Rules of Civil Procedure (SCRCP) intentionally omitted from our state rule the additional requirements found in Federal Rule 23(B), Federal Rules of Civil Procedure (FRCP). By omitting the additional requirements, Rule 23, SCRCP, endorses a more expansive view of class action availability than its federal counterpart.

Grazia, 390 S.C. at 576–77, 703 S.E.2d at 204, quoting *Littlefield*, 337 S.C. at 354–55, 523 S.E.2d at 784 (S.C. 1999). More recently, in *Hensley v. S.C. Dept. of Social Services*, 429 S.C. 144, 838 S.E.2d 510 (2020), the state supreme court appeared to move toward a middle ground on this issue, stating: "Though our Rule 23 does not specifically require the common issues 'predominate,' there must be a proper balance between common and individualized issues in order to achieve the efficiencies the class procedure was designed to promote." *Hensley*, 429 S.C. at 152, 838 S.E.2d at 514.

b. Class Certification Generally

Neither a trial court nor an appellate court may look to the merits when determining whether to certify a class. *Tilley v. Pacesetter Corp.*, 333 S.C. 33, 43, 508 S.E.2d 16, 21 (S.C. 1998), *subsequent appeal*, 355 S.C. 361, 585 S.E.2d 292 (S.C. 2003); *Bazzle v. Green Tree Fin. Corp*., 351 S.C. 244, 267, 569 S.E.2d 349, 361 (S.C. 2002), *vacated on other grounds sub nom. Green Tree Fin. Corp. v. Bazzle*, 539 U.S. 444, 123 S. Ct. 2402, 156 L. Ed. 2d 414 (2003). Instead, the trial court must look to see whether the purported class meets the prerequisites to class certification set out in S.C.R.C.P. 23(a). Certification of a class that meets the prerequisites to certification specified in S.C.R.C.P. 23(a) is within the trial court's discretion and is reviewed under the abuse of discretion standard. *See Bazzle, supra*; *Tilley, supra*; *Waller v. Seabrook Island Property Owners Assn*., 300 S.C. 465, 468, 388 S.E.2d 799, 801 (S.C. 1990). Likewise, absent clear error of law, an appellate court will defer to the trial court's discretion in deciding to decertify a class. *Smith v. Progressive Halcyon Ins. Co.*, 2015 WL 4642794 (S.C. Ct. App. 2015) (unpublished opinion). Class certification is interlocutory and not immediately appealable. *Salmonsen v. CGD, Inc*., 377 S.C. 442, 661 S.E.2d 81 (S.C. 2008). *See also Thornton v. S.C. Elec. & Gas Co.*, 391 S.C. 297, 301–02, 705 S.E.2d 475, 478–79 (Ct. App. 2011) (where class action defendant's motion "to strike class action allegations" actually sought a ruling that the plaintiffs did not meet the prerequisites to be certified as a class, trial court order granting motion was, in effect, denial of class certification and therefore not immediately appealable). In *Salmonsen*, the South Carolina Supreme Court relied in part upon the fact that F.R.C.P. 23(f), which specifically provides for interlocutory appeals of class certification orders, has no analogous counterpart in the South Carolina rules. 377 S.C. at 452, 661 S.C.2d at 87. *See also Hensley v. South Carolina Department of Social Services,* 429 S.C. 144, 148–54, 838 S.E.2d 510, 512–15 (2020) (reversing the Court of Appeals decision allowing immediate appeal of the trial court's class certification order).

The requirement of commonality found in S.C.R.C.P. 23(a)(2) is discussed in *McGann v. Mungo*, 287 S.C. 561, 340 S.E.2d 154 (Ct. App. 1986). *McGann* makes clear that not all issues need to be common to the class to satisfy the commonality prerequisite for certification. However, to the extent that a "determinative" or "predominant" issue in a case presents individualized factual issues which tend to "negate[] the benefits of a class action suit," *Gardner v. S.C. Dept. of Revenue*, *supra*, tends to militate against class certification. More recently, in *Hensley v. S.C. Dept. of Social Services*, 429 S.C. 144, 838 S.E.2d 510 (2020), the state supreme court held that, in order to support class action status, "the existence of common questions alone is not sufficient," and that "the class action must be a better procedural mechanism for resolving the litigation than named joinder or separate litigation." 429 S.C. at 152, 838 S.E.2d at 514.

In *King v. American General Finance, Inc.*, 386 S.C. 82, 687 S.E.2d 321 (S.C. 2009), the South Carolina Supreme Court held that the trial court had committed legal error in decertifying a previously certified class based upon its finding that the named plaintiffs did not satisfy the commonality and typicality requirements contained within Rule 23(a). The state supreme court held that the trial court had misconstrued the relevant provision of the South Carolina Consumer Protection Code. The high court therefore ordered that the class be recertified and deemed continuously certified from July 2, 1998, the date of the initial order certifying the class, and remanded the case to proceed as a class action.

In *Pope v. Heritage Communities, Inc.*, 395 S.C. 404, 717 S.E.2d 765 (Ct. App. 2011), the South Carolina Court of Appeals affirmed the trial court's denial of a motion to decertify a class of condominium owners on the grounds of lack of commonality where the members of the class suffered varying degrees of damage to their units and had different amounts of damages for loss of use. The Court of Appeals reiterated the longstanding rule that where the class shares a determinative issue, the commonality requirement may be deemed satisfied and that the mere fact that not all issues are common to all class members will not defeat commonality. 395 S.C. at 422, 717 S.E.2d at 774. The Court similarly rejected the argument that the class should have been decertified on the basis of lack of typicality of the class representatives, finding evidence in the record that hat all unit owners, regardless of the manner of their use, would be excluded from the property for four months and that the named representatives were therefore typical of the class. 395 S.C. at 422, 717 S.E.2d at 775.

The adequacy prerequisite named in Rule 23(a)(4) is discussed in *Waller v. Seabrook Island Property Owners Ass'n*, 300 S.C. 465, 468, 388 S.E.2d 799, 801 (S.C. 1990). In *Waller*, the South Carolina Supreme Court held that adequacy referred to whether class representatives had interests antagonistic to other members of the class and that the determination of adequacy must be made on a case-by-case basis.

The South Carolina Supreme Court further addressed the adequacy requirement in *Ferguson v. Charleston Lincoln/Mercury, Inc.*, 349 S.C. 558, 564 S.E.2d 94 (S.C. 2002), stating: "We hold that where a single named plaintiff in a class action suit dies before class certification, the named plaintiff no longer adequately represents the class and the suit becomes moot, unless a suitable plaintiff intervenes and satisfies the requirements of Rule 23, S.C.R.C.P." 349 S.C. at 566, 564 S.E.2d at 98.

In *Gardner v. Newsome Chevrolet-Buick, Inc.*, 304 S.C. 328, 404 S.E.2d 200 (S.C. 1991), the South Carolina Supreme Court relied upon federal law construing "amount in controversy" in holding that for the purposes of determining whether the $100-per-claim threshold contained in S.C.R.C.P. 23(a)(5) was met, the trial court may not consider punitive damages and attorneys' fees. To maintain a class action seeking primarily monetary relief, each member of the class must seek at least $100 in money damages exclusive of any punitive award or attorneys' fees.

c. Class Administration by the Court and Treatment of Absent Class Members

In *Eldridge v. City of Greenwood*, 308 S.C. 125, 417 S.E.2d 532 (S.C. 1992), the South Carolina Supreme Court acknowledged that Rule 23(d) gave the trial court broad discretion in issuing orders necessary to ensure fair administration of the class action and to protect the interests of all parties. However, relying upon the U.S. Supreme Court's decision in *Gulf Oil Co. v. Bernard*, 452 U.S. 89, 101 S. Ct. 2193, 68 L. Ed. 2d 693 (1981), the South Carolina Supreme Court held that a trial court's decision to limit contact between the class representatives and class members was an abuse of discretion where the court failed to weigh the defendant's interest in limitation of contact between the class representatives and class members against the competing interests of the putative plaintiffs. There are no reported cases from the South Carolina appellate courts addressing whether and under what circumstances the defendant in a class action would be permitted to depose or otherwise contact absent class members.

The timing and manner in which notice is given to the class of the pendency of a class action is left to the sound discretion of the trial court. *Tilley v. Pacesetter Corp.*, 355 S.C. 361, 585 S.E.2d 292 (S.C. 2003). The South Carolina Supreme Court has specifically rejected the use of an "opt-in" procedure requiring prospective class members to act affirmatively to participate in a class action. *Salmonsen v. CGD, Inc.*, 377 S.C. 442, 661 S.E.2d 81 (S.C. 2008). Finding that the "opt-in" procedure "undermines the due process reasoning of Rule 23 and essentially amounts to *de facto* decertification of a class," and that the procedure "effectively eviscerates class action status," the Court concluded that an "opt-out" notification procedure is the proper method to be offered to class members. 377 S.C. at 459–60, 661 S.E.2d at 91.

d. Shareholders' Class Actions

Rule 23(b)(1) requires that the complaint in a shareholder derivative action alleges with particularity the efforts made by the plaintiff(s) to induce the desired action(s) by the directors or comparable officers of the subject corporation. The South Carolina Court of Appeals addressed the pre-suit demand requirement of Rule 23(b)(1) in *Carolina First Corp. v. Whittle*, 343 S.C. 176, 539 S.E.2d 402 (S.C. App. 2001). The Court of Appeals held that derivative-suit shareholders are required to set forth in their complaint "particularized allegations of the efforts made to demand that the board take the action that the [s]hareholders . . . seek to compel . . ." and that "[t]he particularized allegations must support an earnest, and not a simulated, effort with the managing body of the corporation to induce remedial action on their part." The generalized, conclusory allegations of the *Carolina First* plaintiffs, in which they cited demands of "certain information" and "certain actions" prior to commencing suit were deemed legally insufficient to satisfy the requirements of Rule 23(b)(1). 343 S.C. at 189–90, 539 S.E.2d at 410.

More recently, in *Walbeck v. The I'On Co., LLC*, 439 S.C. 568, 889 S.E.2d 537 (S.C. 2023), the South Carolina Supreme Court excused the plaintiffs from the demand requirement of Rule 23(b)(1) in a derivative class action brought on behalf of the members of their homeowners association against the developers of their community. Documentary evidence and witness testimony showed that the defendant companies had veto power over any actions by the HOA which, in their sole judgment, would tend to impair their rights. Therefore, any demand on behalf of the HOA would have been futile.

In *Boathouse at Breach Inlet, LLC v. Stoney*, 442 S.C. 633, 900 S.E.2d 483 (Ct. App. 2024), the South Carolina Court of Appeals recognized that a single member of a limited liability company may bring a derivative action as a "class of one" when the shareholder "(1)seeks by its pleading[s] to enforce a right of the corporation and (2) does not appear to be similarly situated to any other shareholder." 442 S.C. at 646, 900 S.E.2d at 490 (*quoting Angel Invs. LLC v. Garrity*, 2009 UT 40, 216 P.3d 944, 951 (Utah 2009)). Subsequently, in *McMillan Pazdan Smith, LLC v. Mattison*, 445 S.C. 35, 911 S.E.2d 412 (Ct. App. 2024), the Court of Appeals affirmed the trial court's finding that the plaintiff's "personal interest in increasing the value of her membership units and the conflict between her interests and the interests of [the defendant LLC] bar[red] her from acting as a representative in a derivative action." 445 S.C. at 52, 911 S.E.2d at 421.

e. Class Actions in Arbitration

In *Bazzle v. Green Tree Fin. Corp.*, 351 S.C. 244, 569 S.E.2d 349 (S.C. 2002), *vacated on other grounds sub nom. Green Tree Fin. Corp. v. Bazzle*, 539 U.S. 444, 123 S. Ct. 2402, 156 L. Ed. 2d 414 (2003), the South Carolina Supreme Court unanimously upheld two arbitral class awards with aggregate value of approximately $27 million against a finance company for violations of the state Consumer Protection Code. Rejecting the finance company's assertion that the arbitrator had exceeded his authority by allowing class-wide relief, the state supreme court held that any contractual ambiguities must be construed liberally and interpreted in favor of the non-drafting party, and that where an arbitration clause is silent with regard to permitting class actions in the arbitral forum, class-wide arbitration may be ordered if, in the trial court's discretion, it would serve efficiency and equity and would not result in prejudice. On certiorari, the United States Supreme Court rejected the finance company's argument that the Federal Arbitration Act legally precluded class arbitration, and further held that it was for the arbitrator alone to decide whether the contract permitted class arbitration. Because the Supreme Court found ambiguity in the record as to whether the arbitrator had himself decided to arbitrate the case as a class action or whether the court had imposed upon the arbitrator the decision to so arbitrate, it vacated the South Carolina Supreme Court's decision and remanded the case for the arbitrator to decide this issue of contract interpretation.

In *Simpson v. MSA of Myrtle Beach, Inc.*, 373 S.C. 14, 644 S.E.2d 663 (S.C. 2007), the South

Carolina Supreme Court held that an arbitration clause was unconscionable and unenforceable where (1) the consumer had no meaningful choice in agreeing to arbitrate her claims; (2) the agreement purported to bar the plaintiff from receiving the statutory remedies mandated by the South Carolina Unfair Trade Practices Act and the South Carolina Manufacturers, Distributors, and Dealers Act; and (3) the agreement purported to reserve to the defendant its right to pursue judicial remedies of claim and delivery, repossession, injunctive relief, or collection, and further provided that such actions shall not be stayed pending the outcome of any arbitration. Because the arbitration agreement contained in the adhesion contract was found "wholly unconscionable and unenforceable based on the cumulative effect of a number of oppressive and one-sided provisions," 373 S.C. at 34, 544 S.E.2d at 674, the Supreme Court affirmed the lower court's severance of the arbitration clause from the remainder of the contract in its entirety and denial of the defendant's motion to stay litigation pending arbitration.

In *Herron v. Century BMW*, 387 S.C. 525, 693 S.E.2d 394 (S.C. 2010), the South Carolina Supreme Court held that a car-purchase contract that included a mandatory arbitration clause prohibiting a consumer from pursuing a class action in arbitration was a contract of adhesion and that its proscription of class actions was against public policy and unenforceable. The Regulation of Manufacturers, Distributors, and Dealers Act specifically authorizes class actions to enforce its mandates, providing that "[w]hen such action is one of common or general interest to many persons or when the parties are numerous and it is impracticable to bring them all before the court, one or more may sue for the benefit of the whole, including actions for injunctive relief." S.C. Code Ann. § 56-15-110(2). Accordingly, the court held that a dealer must not be permitted to evade this portion of the statute by having its customers sign a contract of adhesion requiring their waiver of this statutory right. Subsequently, however, in *Sonic Automotive, Inc. v. Watts,* 131 S. Ct. 2872 (Mem) (2011), the Supreme Court of the United States vacated the South Carolina Supreme Court's *Herron* decision and remanded it for further consideration in light of *AT&T Mobility LLC v. Concepcion,* 563 U.S. 321, 131 S. Ct. 1740, 179 L. Ed. 2d 742 (2011). On remand, the South Carolina Supreme Court held that the dealer had failed to preserve the issue of federal preemption for appellate review. *Herron v. Century BMW*, 395 S.C. 461, 719 S.E.2d 640 (S.C. 2011).

In *York v. Dodgeland of Columbia, Inc.*, 406 S.C. 67, 749 S.E.2d 139 (S.C. App. 2013), the South Carolina Court of Appeals affirmed the lower court's order compelling arbitration of disputes arising from the alleged charging of illegal administration fees by automobile dealers. The court analyzed multiple arbitration clauses to determine whether each (1) complied with the Federal Arbitration Act; (2) evidenced intent to arbitrate; (3) was not unconscionable; and (4) was not void as a matter of public policy. The court found that while *Simpson v. MSA*, *supra*, compelled the finding that one of the arbitration clauses was unconscionable as a matter of law, every dispute at issue was within the scope of at least one valid arbitration agreement, and therefore, all of the disputes were properly subject to mandatory arbitration. Similarly, in *One Belle Hall Property Owners Assn, Inc. v. Trammell Crow Residential Co.*, 418 S.C. 51, 791 S.E.2d 286 (S.C. Ct. App. 2016), the Court of Appeals held that the arbitration clause in a shingle warranty was severable from other contract provisions containing allegedly illegal limitations and disclaimers and was therefore enforceable. Subsequently, in *Parsons v. John Wieland Homes and Neighborhoods of the Carolinas, Inc.*, 418 S.C. 1, 791 S.E.2d 128 (2016), the state supreme court held that an arbitration clause located within the contract's warranty provisions was enforceable as to all claims brought under the contract and not limited to claims covered by the warranty. Most recently, in *Grant v. Jud Kuhn Chevrolet*, 431 S.C. 279, 847 S.E.2d 806 (Ct. App. 2020), the South Carolina Court of Appeals reversed the trial court's order compelling class arbitration, finding that the arbitration clause was silent as to class treatment, and therefore did not evince agreement to submit to class arbitration.

f. Causes of Action for Which Class Actions Are Proscribed or Authorized by Statute or Rule

Class actions may not be brought under the South Carolina Retirement Systems Claims Procedures Act. S.C. Code Ann. § 9-21-40. Class actions may not be brought to recover wrongfully collected taxes. S.C. Code Ann. § 12-60-80; *Aiken v. S.C. Dept. of Revenue*, 429 S.C. 414, 839 S.E.2d 96 (2020); *Lightner v. Hampton Hall Club, Inc.*, 419 S.C. 357, 367, 798 S.E.2d 555, 560 (2017); *Drummond v. South Carolina Dept. of Revenue*, 378 S.C. 362, 662 S.E.2d 587 (2008). Class actions may not be brought pursuant to the South Carolina Unfair Trade Practices Act. S.C. Code Ann. §§ 39-5-20 and 39-5-140; *Dema v. Tenet Physician Services-Hilton Head, Inc.*, 383 S.C. 115, 678 S.E.2d 430 (2009). Class actions may not be brought pursuant to the South Carolina Consumer Protection Code, as amended. S.C. Code Ann. §§ 37-5-108, 37-5-202, 37-6-104, 37-6-113, 37-10-105, 37-23-50, and 37-23-70. Rule 23 of the South Carolina Rules of Civil Procedure is inapplicable to appeals before the South Carolina Administrative Law Court. *Allen v. South Carolina Public Employee Benefit Authority*, 411 S.C. 611, 620–21, 769 S.E.2d 666, 671–72 (S.C. 2015). In *Freeman v. J.L.H. Investments, LP*, 414 S.C.362, 778 S.E.2d 902 (2015), the South Carolina Supreme Court held that Section 56-15-110(2) of the South Carolina Dealer's Act authorizes parties to bring class actions under that chapter, and that Rule 23 and Section 56-15-110(2) present independent, alternative methods for seeking relief for the benefit of a class.

g. Fiduciary Duty of Class Counsel and Class Representatives

Class representatives assume a fiduciary duty to absent class members once a case is pled as a class action. *Premium Investment Corp. v. Green*, 283 S.C. 464, 324 S.E.2d 72 (Ct. App. 1984). The attorney who settled the case at issue in *Premium Investment Corp.* was publicly reprimanded by the South Carolina Supreme Court for settling the case for his individual client to the detriment of the absent members of the putative class. *Matter of Green*, 291 S.C. 523, 354 S.E.2d 557 (S.C. 1987).

h. Attorneys' Fees

The reasonableness of attorneys' fees awarded by a trial court to class counsel are properly determined by examining each of the factors set out in *Jackson v. Speed*, 326 S.C. 289, 486 S.E.2d 750 (1997), and those factors enumerated in Rule 1.5 of the South Carolina Rules of Professional Conduct, Rule 407, S.C.A.C.R. The trial court's fee award will be affirmed unless it is not supported by "any competent evidence." *Condon v. State*, 354 S.C. 634, 643, 583 S.E.2d 430, 435 (S.C. 2003).

In *Layman v. State*, 376 S.C. 434, 658 S.E.2d 320 (S.C. 2008), the South Carolina Supreme Court held that an attorneys' fee award that was based upon a percentage of the recovery generated for the plaintiff class was improper, excessive, and unreasonable. In *Layman*, the plaintiff class had been awarded attorneys' fees of $8,665,297.50 pursuant to the state action statute, S.C. Code § 15-77-300, which provides that reasonable attorneys' fees may be taxed as court costs against a state agency where there is a finding that the state agency acted without substantial justification in pressing a legal claim, and where there are no special circumstances that would make an award of attorneys' fees unjust. The court found that while an attorneys' fee award based upon a percentage of gross recovery would be appropriate in a fee-spreading case where the fees would be paid from a common fund recovered for the plaintiffs, the proper method for calculating an attorneys' fee award under the state action statute, a fee-shifting statute, is the lodestar method of multiplying a reasonable hourly rate by the reasonable time expended, with enhancement of the base figure with a multiplier where justified by exceptional circumstances. 376 S.C. at 457–58, 658 S.E.2d at 332. Applying the lodestar method, the court awarded class counsel $1,075,701.74. This figure represented a reduction of over $7.5 million from the lower court fee award. *Layman* is the first case in which any South Carolina court has employed the lodestar method of calculating a class action fee award.

i. Tolling during Pendency of a Class Action

In *Roof v. Swanson*, 344 S.C. 315, 543 S.E.2d 278 (S.C. App. 2001), the South Carolina Court of Appeals characterized the question of whether a statute of limitations was tolled during the pendency of a class action as one of first impression under South Carolina law, but the court did not directly address the issue, ruling that the statute of limitations in that case had run even if tolled during the pendency of the action.

More recently, in *Doe v. Bishop of Charleston*, 407 S.C. 128, 754 S.E.2d 494 (S.C. 2014), the Supreme Court of South Carolina held that even where a class action has been concluded, absent class members are entitled to due process before their claims are subject to res judicata. 407 S.C. at 137–38, 754 S.E.2d at 499. The court further held that "[d]eliberate acts of deception by a defendant calculated to conceal from a potential plaintiff that he has a cause of action toll the statute of limitations." 407 S.C. at 140, 754 S.E.2d at 500–01.

j. Multi-state Class Actions

South Carolina's "door closing statute," S.C. Code § 15-5-150, controls the eligibility of class members in a class action where the defendant is a foreign corporation. Those persons who would have no access to South Carolina state courts via individual lawsuits are likewise precluded from participating in class actions in South Carolina state courts. Section 15-5-150 prohibits South Carolina plaintiffs from representing nationwide or multi-state classes in state court. *Farmer v. Monsanto Corp.*, 353 S.C. 553, 579 S.E.2d 325 (S.C. 2003).

In *Hospitality Management Associates, Inc. v. Shell Oil Co.*, 356 S.C. 644, 591 S.E.2d 611 (S.C. 2004), the South Carolina Supreme Court upheld the lower court's denial of class certification and entry of summary judgment in favor of the defendants due to the preclusive effect of two previously entered nationwide class action settlements and the resulting judgments. The plaintiffs, whose claims arose from defective poly-butylene plumbing systems, had sought to pursue a separate opt-in class action limited to South Carolina claimants. The plaintiffs had argued that notice of the nationwide settlements to absent class members was constitutionally insufficient, and that absent class members had been inadequately represented by the representative plaintiffs and class counsel. The trial court ruled that the nationwide settlements and resulting judgments were entitled to full faith and credit, and that the settlements and judgments precluded the plaintiffs from pursuing their separate class action.

The South Carolina Supreme Court held that collateral review of a class action settlement to determine whether the settlement is entitled to full faith and credit is limited to an examination of procedural due process. The court reviewed the multimedia notice programs used in the two national settlements and expressly rejected the plaintiffs' argument that they were entitled to personal notice of the settlement rather than notice by publication. The court further found that the plaintiffs' arguments with regard to adequate representation were beyond the limits of its scope of review. Finding that there had been safeguards in place to guarantee sufficient notice to absent class members and adequate representation of absent class members' interests in the two cases which had generated the nationwide settlements, and that these safeguards had in fact been applied, the supreme court ruled that the nationwide settlements were entitled to full faith and credit and upheld the lower court's disposition of the plaintiffs' separate action, noting that "mere disagreement with the terms of a settlement cannot provide grounds for a collateral attack on a class settlement." 356 S.C. at 666, 591 S.E.2d at 623.

Subsequently, in *Cowden Enterprises, Inc. v. East Coast Millwork Distributors,* 363 S.C. 540, 611 S.E.2d 259 (S.C. App. 2005), the state Court of Appeals held that a national class action settlement barred recovery by a third-party claimant. The plaintiff in the *Cowden* case was a general contractor who had been sued by a homeowner in connection with construction defects. The contractor settled the homeowner's claim, and then sought contribution from the manufacturer of the allegedly defective materials. The manufacturer had previously entered into a national class action settlement. The homeowner had been a member of the settlement class and had not opted out of the settlement. The contractor argued that while the homeowner had, as a member of the settlement class, released the manufacturer from any and all claims in connection with alleged product defects, that release should not bar recovery by a third party in an action for contribution. The contractor relied heavily upon the fact that the express terms of the settlement agreement specifically excluded builders and contractors from the class. Rejecting the contractor's arguments, the Court of Appeals found that the national settlement was entitled to full faith and credit, and that the release of claims barred the contractor's contribution claim.

TEXT OF RULE 23 OF THE SOUTH CAROLINA RULES OF CIVIL PROCEDURE

(a) *Prerequisites to a class action.* One or more members of a class may sue or be sued as representative parties on behalf of all only if the court finds (1) the class is so numerous that joinder of all members is impracticable, (2) there are questions of law or fact common to the class, (3) the claims or defenses of the representative parties are typical of the claims or defenses of the class, (4) the representative parties will fairly and adequately protect the interests of the class, and (5) in cases in which the relief primarily sought is not injunctive or declaratory with respect to the class as a whole, the amount in controversy exceeds one hundred dollars for each member of the class.

(b) (1) *Derivative actions by shareholders.* In a derivative action brought by one or more shareholders or members to enforce a right of a corporation or of an unincorporated association, the corporation or association having failed to enforce a right which may properly be asserted by it, the complaint shall be verified and shall allege that the plaintiff was a shareholder or member at the time of the transaction of which he complains or that his share or membership thereafter devolved on him by operation of law. The complaint shall also allege with particularity the efforts, if any, made by the plaintiff to obtain the action he desires from the directors or comparable authority and, if necessary, from the shareholders or members, and the reasons for his failure to obtain the action or for not making the effort. The derivative action may not be maintained if it appears that the plaintiff does not fairly and adequately represent the interests of the shareholders or members similarly situated in enforcing the right of the corporation or association. The action shall not be dismissed or compromised without the approval of the court and notice of the proposed dismissal or compromise shall be given to shareholders or members in such manner as the court directs.

(2) *Actions relating to unincorporated associations.* An action brought by or against the members of an unincorporated association as a class by naming certain members as representative parties may be maintained only if it appears that the representative parties will fairly and adequately protect the interests of the association and its members. In the conduct of the action, the court may make appropriate orders corresponding with those described in Rule 23(d), and the procedure for dismissal or compromise of the action shall correspond with that provided in Rule 23(c).

(c) *Dismissal or compromise.* A class action shall not be dismissed or compromised without the approval of the court, and notice of the proposed dismissal or compromise shall be given to all members of the class in such manner as the court directs.

(d) *Orders in the conduct of actions.* In the conduct of actions to which this rule applies, the court may make appropriate orders:

(1) As soon as practicable, after the commencement of an action brought as a class action, the court shall determine by order whether it is to be so maintained. An order under this subdivision may be conditional, and may be altered or amended before the decision on the merits.

(2) The court may at any time impose such terms as shall fairly and adequately protect the interest of the persons on whose behalf the action is brought or defended. It may order that notice be given in such a manner as it may direct of the pendency of the action by the party seeking to maintain the action on behalf of the class. It may order that notice be given in such manner as it may direct of a proposed settlement, of entry of judgment, or any other proceedings in the action including notice to the absent persons that they may come in and present claims and defenses if they so desire.

(3) Whenever the representation appears to the court inadequate fairly to protect the interests of absent persons who may be bound by the judgment, the court may at any time impose additional conditions on the representative parties, or order an amendment of the pleadings, eliminating therefrom all reference to the representation of the absent persons, and in that event the court shall order entry of the judgment in such form as to affect only the parties to the action and those adequately represented.

(e) *Disposition of Residual Funds.*

(1) "Residual Funds" are funds that remain after the payment of all approved class member claims, expenses, litigation costs, attorneys' fees, and other court-approved disbursements to implement the relief granted. Nothing in this rule is intended to limit the parties to a class action from suggesting, or the trial court from approving, a settlement that does not create residual funds.

(2) Any order, judgment, or approved compromise in a class action under this rule that establishes a process for identifying and compensating members of the class may provide for the disbursement of residual funds. In matters where the claims process has been exhausted and residual funds remain, not less than fifty percent of residuals must be distributed to the South Carolina Bar Foundation to support activities and programs that promote access to the civil justice system for low-income residents of South Carolina. The court may disburse the balance of any residual funds beyond the minimum percentage to the South Carolina Bar Foundation to any other entity or entities for purposes that have a direct or indirect relationship to the objectives of the underlying litigation or otherwise promote the substantive and procedural interests of members of the class.

Chapter author B. Randall Dong is a graduate of Mississippi State University and the University of Virginia Law School. While in private practice, Mr. Dong represented plaintiffs in numerous class actions in state and federal courts in South Carolina. In 2006, he left private practice to join the Legal Staff of the Public Service Commission of South Carolina. In 2020, he became Legal Director of Disability Rights South Carolina.

SOUTH DAKOTA

1. DIFFERENCES BETWEEN S.D. CODIFIED LAWS § 15-6-23 AND FED. R. CIV. P. 23

South Dakota's class action statute mimics the pre-1998 federal rule exactly with but one exception: the South Dakota rule adds a fifth subsection to 23(a), which reads as follows:

> One or more members of a class may sue or be sued as representative parties on behalf of all only if . . . and (5) the suit is not against this state for the recovery of a tax imposed by Chapter 10-39, 10-39A, 10-40, 10-41, 10-43, 10-44, 10-45, 10-46, 10-46A, 10-46B, or 10-52.

2. SUMMARY OF CASE LAW INTERPRETING S.D. CODIFIED LAWS § 15-6-23

a. Rule 23(a) Requirements

i. Numerosity. *Shangreaux v. Westby*, 281 N.W.2d 590 (S.D. 1979): Plaintiff's request for certification of class including all AFDC recipients residing in South Dakota was "far too encompassing and overboard." *Id.* at 593. "SDCL 15-6-23(a) requires that there be at least some evidence of the number of class members . . ." *Id.* Consequently, plaintiff's request for certification of a class failed for not meeting the prerequisites of S.D. Codified Laws § 15-6-23. *Id.*

Trapp v. Madera Pacific, Inc., 390 N.W.2d 558 (S.D. 1986): In a class action suit brought by former and current employees against the employer, the court considered a class consisting of 136 individuals. *Id.* The court first explained that certification of a class will only be reviewed for a clear abuse of discretion by the trial court. *Id.* at 560. The evidence reflected that the majority of the members were known to the defendant through personnel records and they resided in the same area. The defendant argued that joinder could have been effected with minimal effort and inconvenience, but the court stated that although "where the number of class members is at best fairly small (*i.e.*, approximately 100), plaintiffs must demonstrate additional reasons why joinder is impracticable," the court could not conclude that the trial court abused its discretion by certifying the class of employees in this case. *Id.* at 561. As a result, the court affirmed the trial court's certification of the class. *Id.* at 562.

Schumacher v. Tyson Fresh Meats, Inc., 2004 DSD 3; Class Action against meat packers for allegedly knowingly using inaccurate prices published by the USDA to negotiate the purchase of slaughter cattle from plaintiff class at prices substantially lower than would have been economically justified had plaintiff known the accurate higher prices that defendant were receiving for their boxed beef. The court found that there were anywhere from 100 to 1000 producers that clearly met the numerosity test.

In *Duerre et, al. v. Kelper et, al.*, 2017 S.D. 8 (2017), the South Dakota Supreme Court affirmed the certification of a class as defendants in an action for declaratory and injunctive relief concerning the public's right to use or intend to use the waters and ice overlying landowners' private property for recreational purposes. On the issue of numerosity the court stated that when determining the numerosity factor for class certification, specific numbers are not required. The court held that the plaintiffs' evidence supported the trial court's conclusion that the members of the defendant class were so numerous that their individual joinder in a single action was not only impracticable, but impossible.[1]

ii. Commonality. *Trapp v. Madera Pacific, Inc.,* 390 N.W.2d 558 (S.D. 1986): There must be questions of law or fact common to the class, but not all questions of law or fact raised need to be in common. *Id.* at 561. This element is really concerned with whether the issues in the action are individual in nature and must be decided on a case-by-case basis. *Id.* In this case, the court found that the defendant raised legitimate questions regarding the individual character of some of the employees' (class members) claims by producing evidence that not all of the employees received the employment manual in dispute, certain employees were orally advised that sections of the manual did not apply to them (specifically bonuses, which were in dispute), and some employees were hired under a benefits plan different from that outlined in the manual. *Id.* (The court nevertheless affirmed the trial court's certification of the class because no abuse of discretion could be shown).

Schumacher v. Tyson Fresh Meats, Inc., 2004 DSD 5, 221 FRD 605: Although the court recognized that some class members will have a different measure of damages, may have relied upon different factual representations by the defendants, and there were a wide variety of factors that had to be taken into account in determining the price to be paid for a particular pen of cattle, the court held that Rule 23(a) of the FRCP "does not require that every question of law or fact be common to the class.

In 2017, in *Duerre v. Hepler*, 2017 S.D. 8, the court confirmed that the commonality factor does not require a class of clones, identical in all respects, but "qualitative, not quantitative," is the test.

iii. Typicality. *Shangreaux v. Westby*, 281 N.W.2d 590 (S.D. 1979): "SDCL 15-6-23(a)(3) requires that the class representative demonstrate that there are other members of the class with similar grievances." *Id.* at 593. Plaintiff's failure to identify even one person other than herself as a member of the class defeated her attempt to certify a class. *Id.* "A class cannot consist of phantom claimants." *Id.*

Trapp v. Madera Pacific, Inc., 390 N.W.2d 558 (S.D. 1986): "Obviously, this requirement is not met when the 'representative' plaintiff never had a claim of *any* type against *any* defendant." *Id.* at 561 (emphasis added). In this case, the court found it sufficient that a representative had a potential claim and that the representative's position might also be typical of other members' positions against the defendant. *Id.* "It is not necessary that each of the [members'] claims be absolute, only typical." *Id.*

Schumacher v. Tyson Fresh Meats, Inc., 2004 DSD 5, 221 FRD 605: Since the plaintiffs claimed that during the proposed class period, the defendants "unfairly" or "unjustly" profited from the errors in reporting boxed beef prices when the defendants purchased fed cattle from the plaintiffs, that was the same allegedly unlawful treatment suffered by the proposed class members. Therefore, this prong

---

[1] In this March 15, 2017, decision, the South Dakota Supreme Court ruled that what constituted a "public purpose" regarding the use of private land for recreational use, was one for the legislature, not the Court. In June of 2017, at a Special Session of the Legislature called by the Governor, a law was passed providing for public recreational use of certain waters overlying public and private property.

of the rule was satisfied.

On the issue of typicality, in *Duerre v. Hepler*, *supra,* the court held that the State's interest—a declaration that the waters overlying the plaintiff Landowners' property are open for use by the public for recreational purposes—will also advance the interests of the absent class members.

iv. Adequacy. *Trapp v. Madera Pacific, Inc.*, 390 N.W.2d 558 (S.D. 1986): "Adequate representation depends on two factors: (a) the plaintiff's attorney must be qualified, experienced, and generally able to conduct the proposed litigation, and (b) the plaintiff must not have interests antagonistic to those of the class." *Id.* at 561–62. Because the judgment conclusively determines the rights of absent class members, a court must carefully scrutinize the adequacy of representation in class actions. *Id.* at 562. Although the defendant raised substantial questions regarding numerosity and commonality, the court was unable to say that the trial court abused its discretion in certifying the current and former employees as a class. *Id.*

Thurman v. Cuna Mutual Insurance Society, 2013 S.D. 63, 863 N.W. 2d 611, 2013 WL 4177501: Although the trial court had found that there were potential factual differences between the named plaintiffs and other class members that could create conflicts of interest, the Supreme Court pointed out that the trial court had failed to identify those potential conflicts or explain why the conflicts could exist. The Supreme Court went on to hold that there was no evidence that any potential factual differences between the named plaintiffs and the other class members would result in the plaintiffs failing to protect the interests of the other class members.

In *Duerre v. Hepler*, *supra*, the State argued that the Attorney General was not authorized to represent private citizens, let alone private citizens of another state. The court held that South Dakota law, SDCL 1-11-1(1) authorized the Attorney General's Office to "appear for the state and prosecute and defend all actions and proceedings, civil or criminal, . . . in which the State may be a party or interested." In that action the court concluded "This case concerns the interests of the public at large, and in defending the action, the "Attorney General's Office is pursuing a matter in which the State is both a 'party' and 'interested.'"

v. Impracticability of joinder. *See Trapp,* 390 N.W.2d 558.

b. Rule 23(b)(3) Requirements

i. Superiority. *Trapp v. Madera Pacific, Inc.*, 390 N.W.2d 558 (S.D. 1986): "In deciding whether to allow a class action, a primary determination to be made is whether the class action is superior to, and not just as good as, other available methods for handling the controversy, and such a determination lies in an area where the trial court's discretion is paramount." *Id.* at 560. In this case, the court affirmed the class certification because no abuse of discretion was evidenced in the record. *Id.* at 562. *Also see Trapp,* below.

Thurman v. Cuna Mutual Insurance Society, 2013 S.D. 63, 863 N.W. 2d 611, 2013 WL 4177501: The Supreme Court held that the trial court had failed to consider common issues in the statute of limitation defense (*see* Predominance below) to make findings regarding which other methods of adjudication that it considered and found to be superior. It held that that trial court had failed to address why those methods were fair or an efficient use of judicial resources.

ii. Predominance. *Trapp v. Madera Pacific, Inc.,* 390 N.W.2d 558 (S.D. 1986): The case involved a class action by current and former employees of the defendant for the defendant's refusal to pay a 3 percent bonus of their respective earnings as stated in the defendant's employment manual. The court found "that the questions of law or fact common to the members of the class predominate over any questions affecting *only* individual members, *and* that a class action is *superior* to other available methods for the fair and efficient adjudication of this controversy." *Id.* at 562 (emphasis supplied).

Thurman v. Cuna Mutual Insurance Society, 2013 S.D. 63, 863 N.W. 2d 611, 2013 WL 4177501: In overruling the trial court's determination that different statute of limitation issues would be a predominate question and that "individualized proof is patently required to litigate the defendants' statute of limitation defense, the Supreme Court held that the predominance question focuses on whether the members of a class have enough in common to have their claim adjudicated together, not the defendants' potential affirmative defenses. In this case the issue was the change of the terms of the plaintiffs' credit disability policy, and the adequacy of the notice of that change that went out to some 4,461 borrowers. Since the notice that was sent was common to all borrowers and sent at the same time, the Court held that the facts as to such notice were common to the entire class.

c. Other Decisions of Interest Regarding Class Actions in South Dakota

Swanson v. Sioux Valley Elec. Ass'n, 535 N.W.2d 755 (S.D. 1995): When ruling on class action certification, the court will reverse the trial court's denial only for an abuse of discretion. *Id. See also Trapp v. Madera Pacific, Inc.*, 390 N.W.2d 558, 560–61 (S.D. 1986). In this case, the court affirmed the trial court's denial of certification because the plaintiff failed to show upon appeal any abuse of discretion by the trial court. *Id.* at 759 n.2.

Lick v. Dahl, 285 N.W.2d 594 (S.D. 1979): In this case, taxpayers, on behalf of themselves and other real property owners and taxpayers similarly situated, brought suit against the county and county treasurer. The question presented was whether a taxpayer can maintain a class action on behalf of all other taxpayers similarly situated for refunds attributable to an allegedly illegal tax. *Id.* at 599. The court first determined that such a suit would be against the state. *Id.* Having made this ruling, the court cited the two statutes under which the State of South Dakota waived sovereign immunity and allowed suits for recovery of allegedly illegal taxes paid to the state. *Id.* Because neither statute provided for class action suits for tax refunds, the court found it patently clear that any action commenced under these statutes must be brought by each individual on his or her own behalf. *Id.* at 600. The state waived its sovereign immunity only to the extent provided by the statutes; accordingly, class actions could not be employed in suits for tax refunds. *Id.*

Shangreaux v. Westby, 281 N.W.2d 590 (S.D. 1979): "Class action and conditional class action status relieve cries of mootness. . . ." *Id.* at 592. However, in this case the plaintiff's case was barred on general mootness principles. *Id.* On a second issue, the plaintiff argued that the trial court erred in denying conditional certification in order for the plaintiff to obtain statistical data showing the purported number of members in the putative class. The court recognized that the state class action statute left the timing of a determination of a class to the trial court. *Id.* Further, the timing of the decision affects discovery, summary judgment, and trial strategies. *Id.* However, if the trial court has applied S.D. Codified Laws § 15-6-23(a) and (b) to the case, its decision must be accorded great weight. *Id.* at 593. Finally, the court also recognized that "in some instances it may be desirable to permit relevant discovery before deciding whether to allow a class action, particularly when the party opposing the class action is more likely to have access to information relating to the size and nature of the alleged class." *Id.* In this case however, the court saw no need to apply this principle because the plaintiff failed to make even a minimal showing of a class pursuant to S.D. Codified Laws §15-6-23(a)(1) and (3). *Id.*

Smith v. Tobin, 311 N.W.2d 209 (S.D. 1981): Under South Dakota law, a judgment from a circuit court may be appealed only when that judgment is final rather than interlocutory. *Id.* at 210.

Because an order denying class action certification does not adjudicate all the issues of fact and law involved in a controversy, leaving no question open for final determination, such an order is interlocutory in nature and is not subject to direct appeal. *Id.* This holding overruled anything to the contrary in the court's prior decision in *Rollinger v. J.C. Penney Company,* 192 N.W.2d 699 (S.D. 1971). The court supported its holding by reasoning that a policy existed which disfavored piecemeal litigation. *Id.* In light of that policy, the court found persuasive the rationale of the United State Supreme Court in *Coopers & Lybrand v. Livesay*, 437 U.S. 463 (1978), restricting appellate review in order to prevent the debilitating effect on judicial administration caused by piecemeal appellate disposition of what was, in practical consequence, but a single controversy. *Smith*, 311 N.W.2d at 211.

In re South Dakota Microsoft Antitrust Litigation, 2003 SD 19, 657 N.W.2d 668: The trial court granted class certification for indirect-purchasers alleging antitrust violations under South Dakota law. The Supreme Court granted a discretionary appeal of the class certification issue. The Supreme Court affirmed the trial court. Although Microsoft did not dispute that the requirements of SDCL 15-6-23(a) were met, it took the position on the appeal that the plaintiff failed to meet its burden under SDCL 15-6-23(b). The Court held that the trial court had applied a "rigorous analysis" in determining whether the elements of Rule 23 had been met. On the battle of experts regarding whether damages could be calculated on a class-wide basis, the Court held that the trial court did not abuse its discretion by ruling that the Plaintiff had satisfied the requirements of Rule 23, that is whether it appeared that differences between the experts could be intelligently presented and evaluated within the framework of the class action. It was not necessary at this stage resolve a battle of experts. The Court concluded that the trial court did not abuse its discretion in granting class certification.

In re South Dakota Microsoft Antitrust Litigation, 707 N.W. 2d 85, 2005 SD 113 (*Microsoft II*): Although after the decision in *Microsoft I* (cited above), the principal action, was settled, the issue of the amount of plaintiffs' attorneys' fees was not. As part of the settlement Microsoft had agreed to pay the plaintiffs "reasonable attorney fees," however, the trial court retained jurisdiction to decide the plaintiffs' application for attorneys' fees, expenses, and costs in the amount of $2,279,286 to be paid by Microsoft to plaintiffs. The trial court had used a lodestar calculation to determine the attorneys' fees and applied a multiplier of two. An appeal was taken by Microsoft to the South Dakota Supreme Court on the multiplier and other grounds. The South Dakota Supreme Court reversed the trial court's application of a multiplier, holding that this was not a case where "exceptional success" had been attained by prevailing counsel, stating "the benefit was relatively modest given that the relief requested by Plaintiffs in their complaint, the difference between the monopoly price and the competitive price, had little perceived benefit to the majority of Class Members." The court also remanded the issue of the proper allocation and reallocation of the lodestar figure for out-of-state plaintiffs' counsel who had also been working on similar Microsoft antitrust cases in other jurisdictions but had not kept adequate records of the time allocations.[2]

Beck v. City of Rapid City, 2002 SD 104, 650 N.W.2d 520: The City of Rapid City had annexed property and collected city sales tax in the annexed area. It was later determined that the annexation was improper. A class action was brought to obtain a refund of the sales taxes paid by consumers who had purchased taxable goods and services in the improperly annexed area. The City had instituted an administrative procedure that allowed the consumers to obtain a refund of the sales taxes paid. The trial court had granted class certification and held that the alternative methods of recovery

[2] The matter was subsequently settled without further hearings on remand.

were not superior to the class action lawsuit. Citing anticipated tremendous difficulty and only limited success in notifying perspective class members, difficulty in ensuring that class members who do not opt out to actually receive their damage awards, the Supreme Court expressed its concern that the benefits of such a class action would inure, if at all, to the class counsel and the designated recipients of the class. The Court remanded the case to the trial court for further development of the record on such issues as whether there were class members who had more than nominal damages as risk; whether the class members would be effectively contacted; whether judicial efficiency would be bettered by the use of a class action, or whether any other matters pertinent to finding superiority as listed in SDCL 15-6-23(b)(3) exist.

Pourier d/b/a Muddy Creek Oil and Gas, Inc. et. al. v. South Dakota Department of Revenue and Regulation, 2010 SD 10, 778 N.W.2d 602: In prior decisions, *Pourier v. S.D. Dep't of Revenue*, 2003 SD 21, 658 N.W.2d 395, *modified on reh'g*, 2004 SD 3, 674 N.W.2d 314 (*Pourier I*), The plaintiff was granted the right to obtain the refund of certain motor fuel taxes that the Supreme Court had determined were illegally collected from an enrolled member of the Oglala Sioux Tribe. The plaintiff filed a motion for leave to amend his claims and add a class of Oglala Sioux tribal-member-customer claimants. The South Dakota Supreme Court held that the statute governing tax refund claims combined with gap-filler statute did not constitute an express waiver of the State's sovereign immunity for a class action against it.

Thurman v. Cuna Mutual Insurance Society, 2013 S.D. 63, 863 N.W. 2d 611, 2013 WL 4177501: The Supreme Court used this class action to clarify and somewhat modify the court's abuse of discretion standard of review of a trial court order denying or granting a motion to maintain a class. Historically it had held that a trial court abused its discretion when it makes an error at law. The court observed that the definition of "judicial mind" has been shortened to the point of losing much of its original meaning. It stated "[I]t is a fundamental error of judgment, a choice outside the range of permissible choices, a decision, which, on full consideration, is arbitrary or unreasonable." Quoting from *McNeil v. Superior Siding, Inc.*, 2009 S.D. 68, ¶ 6, 771 N.W.2d 345, 348 (quoting *Permann v. S.D. Dep't of Labor,* 411 N.W.2d 113, 119 (S.D. 1987)).

If, on the other hand, the question requires us to consider legal concepts in the mix of fact and law and to exercise judgment about the values that animate legal principles, then the concerns of judicial administration will favor the appellate court, and the question should be classified as one of law and reviewed de novo.

3. TOLLING OF LIMITATION PERIODS DURING PENDENCY OF CLASS ACTIONS

In 2008, the South Dakota Supreme Court determined in *Lloyd One Star v. Sisters of St. Francis, Denver, Colorado*, 2008 SD 55, 752 N.W.2d 668, that the filing of a federal class action does not toll the statute of limitations where the defendant in a separate state action was not a named defendant in the federal class action.

Neither the South Dakota Supreme Court nor the federal courts interpreting South Dakota class action statutes have addressed the question of whether a pending class action would toll an applicable statute of limitations where the defendant was a named defendant in a separate filed class action. If the issue were to come before a federal court having jurisdiction, the court may follow the United States Court of Appeals for the Eighth Circuit in *Adams Public School District v. Asbestos Corp., Ltd.*, 7 F.3d 717 (8th Cir. 1993) *rehearing den. and suggestion for rehearing en banc den.* Nov. 22, 1993, interpreting North Dakota law. Although North Dakota had passed a special statute extending the period during which claims arising from the presence of asbestos in public buildings could be brought, the federal court held that even without that statute, the *American Pipe* rule would have the effect of tolling the statute of limitation until such time as the School District opted out of the federal class action. Since South Dakota does not provide for tolling in such instances, it is likely that the Eighth Circuit would follow its decision in *Adams Public School* and likewise apply the *American Pipe* rule in South Dakota.

However, the South Dakota Supreme Court in *Peterson v. Hohm*, 2000 SD 27, 607 N.W.2d 8, refused to apply the doctrine of substantial compliance to statute of limitations issues or the doctrine of equitable tolling in the absence of the legislature adopting a savings statute. In that case an action for medical malpractice and a wrongful death action was first brought in federal court. While a motion to dismiss the federal court action on the grounds of lack of diversity for federal jurisdiction was pending, an identical action was commenced in state court, however, the statutes of limitations for both medical malpractice and wrongful death had run. The South Dakota Supreme Court affirmed the trial court's granting of Summary Judgment for the defendants on the grounds that both actions were time barred and the statutes of limitations were not tolled by the pending federal action.

SECTION 15-6-23 OF THE SOUTH DAKOTA CODIFIED LAWS

§ 15-6-23(a). *Prerequisites to a class action.* One or more members of a class may sue or be sued as representative parties on behalf of all only if

(1) the class is so numerous that joinder of all members is impracticable,

(2) there are questions of law or fact common to the class,

(3) the claims or defenses of the representative parties are typical of the claims or defenses of the class,

(4) the representative parties will fairly and adequately protect the interests of the class, and

(5) the suit is not against this state for the recovery of a tax imposed by chapter 1039, 1039A, 1040, 1041, 1043, 1044, 1045, 1046, 1046A, 10 46B, or 1052.

§ 15-6-23(b). *Class actions maintainable.* An action may be maintained as a class action if the prerequisites of § 156 23(a) are satisfied, and in addition:

(1) the prosecution of separate actions by or against individual members of the class would create a risk of

(A) inconsistent or varying adjudications with respect to individual members of the class which would establish incompatible standards of conduct for the party opposing the class, or

(B) adjudications with respect to individual members of the class which would as a practical matter be dispositive of the interests of the other members not parties to the adjudications or substantially impair or impede their ability to protect their interests; or

(2) the party opposing the class has acted or refused to act on grounds generally applicable to the class, thereby making appropriate permanent injunctive relief or corresponding declaratory relief with respect to the class as a whole; or

(3) the court finds that the questions of law or fact common to the members of the class predominate over any questions affecting only individual members, and that a class action is superior to other available methods for the fair and efficient adjudication of the controversy. The matters pertinent to the findings include:

(A) the interest of members of the class in individually controlling the prosecution or defense of separate actions;

(B) the extent and nature of any litigation concerning the controversy already commenced by or against members of the class;

(C) the desirability or undesirability of concentrating the litigation of the claims in the particular forum;

(D) the difficulties likely to be encountered in the management of a class action.

§ 15-6-23(c). *Determination by order whether class action to be maintained; notice; judgment; actions conducted partially as class actions.*

(1) As soon as practicable after the commencement of an action brought as a class action, the court shall determine by order whether it is to be so maintained. An order under this section may be conditional, and may be altered or amended before the decision on the merits.

(2) In any class action maintained under subdivision 15623(b)(3), the court shall direct to the members of the class the best notice practicable under the circumstances, including individual notice to all members who can be identified through reasonable effort. The notice shall advise each member that (A) the court will exclude him from the class if he so requests by a specified date; (B) the judgment, whether favorable or not, will include all members who do not request exclusion; and (C) any member who does not request exclusion may, if he desires, enter an appearance through his counsel.

(3) The judgment in an action maintained as a class action under subdivisions 15623(b)(1) or (2), whether or not favorable to the class, shall include and describe those whom the court finds to be members of the class. The judgment in an action maintained as a class action under subdivision 15623(b)(3), whether or not favorable to the class, shall include and specify or describe those to whom the notice provided in subdivision (2) of this section was directed, and who have not requested exclusion, and whom the court finds to be members of the class.

(4) When appropriate (A) an action may be brought or maintained as a class action with respect to particular issues, or (B) a class may be divided into subclasses and each subclass treated as a class, and the provisions of § 15623 shall then be construed and applied accordingly.

§ 15-6-23(d). *Orders in conduct of actions. In the conduct of actions to which § 15623 applies, the court may make appropriate orders.*

(1) Determining the course of proceedings or prescribing measures to prevent undue repetition or complication in the presentation of evidence or argument;

(2) Requiring, for the protection of the members of the class or otherwise for the fair conduct of the action, that notice be given in such manner as the court may direct to some or all of the members of any step in the action, or of the proposed extent of the judgment, or of the opportunity of members to signify whether they consider the representation fair and adequate, to intervene and present claims or defenses, or otherwise to come into the action;

(3) Imposing conditions on the representative parties or on intervenors;

(4) Requiring that the pleadings be amended to eliminate therefrom allegations as to representation of absent persons, and that the action proceed accordingly;

(5) Dealing with similar procedural matters.

The orders may be combined with an order under § 15616, and may be altered or amended as may be desirable from time to time.

§ 15-6-23(e). *Dismissal or compromise of class actions.* A class action shall not be dismissed or compromised without the approval of the court, and notice of the proposed dismissal or compromise shall be given to all members of the class in such manner as the court directs.

ADDITIONAL SECTION TO SOUTH DAKOTA CLASS ACTION STATUTE

§ 15-6-23.1. *Derivative actions by unincorporated associations.* In a derivative action brought by one or more members to enforce a right of an unincorporated association, the association having failed to enforce a right which may properly be asserted by it, the complaint shall be verified and shall allege

(1) That the plaintiff was a member at the time of the transaction of which he complains or that his membership thereafter devolved on him by operation of law, and

(2) That the action is not a collusive one to confer jurisdiction on a court of the state which would not otherwise have.

The complaint shall also allege with particularity the efforts, if any, made by the plaintiff to obtain the action he desires from the directors or comparable authority and, if necessary, from the members, and the reasons for his failure to obtain the action or for not making the effort. The derivative action may not be maintained if it appears that the plaintiff does not fairly and adequately represent the interests of the members similarly situated in enforcing the right of the association. The action shall not be dismissed or compromised without the approval of the court, and notice of the proposed dismissal or compromise shall be given to members in such manner as the court directs.

Michael F. Nadolski is a contributing author to American Bar Association's *The Law of Class Action: Fifty State Survey 2025* and the author of its chapter on class action law in South Dakota. This text is additionally published by Thomson Reuters as a supplement to the hard bound volumes of the prestigious *Newberg and Rubenstein on Class Actions.*

TENNESSEE

1. COMPARISON WITH RULE 23 OF THE FEDERAL RULES OF CIVIL PROCEDURE

The first five sections of Rule 23 of the Tennessee Rules of Civil Procedure, Tenn. R. Civ. P. 23.01-23.05, substantially mirror Fed. R. Civ. P. 23(a)–(e). Because Tennessee Rule 23 closely follows Federal Rule 23, Tennessee courts have found federal court opinions persuasive in this area. *See, e.g.*, *In re SmileDirectClub, Inc. Sec. Litig.*, No. M202100469COAR3CV, 2022 WL 818950, at *7–19 (Tenn. Ct. App. Mar. 18, 2022); *Wofford v. M.J. Edwards & Sons Funeral Home Inc.*, 528 S.W.3d 524, 528–34 (Tenn. Ct. App. 2017); *Carson v. DaimlerChrysler Corp.*, No. W2001-03088-COA-R3-CV, 2003 Tenn. App. LEXIS 236, at n.3 (Tenn. Ct. App. Mar. 19, 2003); *Meighan v. U.S. Sprint Comm. Co.*, 924 S.W.2d 632, 637 n.2 (Tenn. 1996); *Bayberry Assocs. v. Jones*, 783 S.W.2d 553, 557 (Tenn. 1990). While Tenn. Rule 23.03 does not follow the requirement in Federal Rule 23(c), that the court "must define the class and the class claims, issues or defenses, and must appoint class counsel under Rule 23(g)" when certifying a class, appellate courts have held that the failure to define the purported class is reversible error. *Roberts v. McNeill*, No. W2013-01072-COA-R3CV, 2014 WL 2475595, at *10 (Tenn. Ct. App. May 30, 2014) (citing Fed. R. Civ. P. 23(c)(1)(B) as persuasive authority); *see also Doe v. City of Memphis*, No. W2023-01222-COA-R3-CV, 2024 WL 4891769, at *4 (Tenn. Ct. App. Nov. 26, 2024) (noting that "courts have not hesitated to overturn orders that attempt to certify vaguely-defined classes"). Federal Rule 23(c)(2)(B) specifically requires that notice to class members "must clearly and concisely state in plain, easily understood language" the nature of the action, the definition of the class certified and the class claims, issues or defenses. The Tennessee Rule does not have this requirement.

Federal Rule 23(e) and Tennessee Rule 23.05 governing Settlement, Voluntary Dismissal, or compromise both require judicial settlement approval and prior notice to the class. Federal Rule 23(e) additionally requires that approval of any settlement or dismissal binding the class be given only after a fairness hearing and a finding that the settlement "is fair reasonable and adequate." The Federal Rule requires that the party seeking approval of the court file a "statement identifying any agreement made in connection with the" proposed settlement, voluntary dismissal, or compromise. The Tennessee rule does not have these requirements but the Tennessee Court of Appeals has stated that "the Trial Court must exercise 'the highest degree of vigilance in scrutinizing proposed settlements,' and acts as a type of fiduciary for the class members." *Posey v. Dryvit Systems,* 2005 Tenn. App. LEXIS 1, at *6 (Tenn. Ct. App. Jan. 4, 2005) (citing *Reynolds v. Beneficial Nat'l Bank*, 288 F.3d 277 (7th Cir. 2002)); *In re Pacer Int'l, Inc.*, No. M201500356COAR3CV, 2017 WL 2829856 (Tenn. Ct. App. June 30, 2017) ("We have directed trial courts to consider various factors [when presented with proposed settlements], such as 'the risk and likely return to the class of continued litigation, the range of possible outcomes and probability of each, and whether class counsel's fees are proportional to the incremental benefit conferred on the class members'" (citing *id.* at *2)).

Rule 23(f) of the Federal Rules of Civil Procedure has not been incorporated into Tennessee

Rule 23.[1] The "Tennessee Civil Justice Act," Tenn. Code Ann. § 27-1-125, however, gives parties a right to appeal class certification orders under Tenn. Rule Civ. P. 23 "if a notice is filed within ten (10) days after entry of the order," and stays the action pending the appeal.

Tenn. Rules 23.06 and 23.07 track the language in Federal Rule 23.1 and 23.2, respectively. *United Supreme Council AASR SJ v. McWilliams*, 586 S.W.3d 373, 380 (Tenn. Ct. App. 2019) ("Federal Rule of Civil Procedure 23.1(a) is nearly identical to Tennessee Rule of Civil Procedure 23.06."). Tennessee Rule 23.08 has no federal analogue.

2. PREREQUISITES AND REQUIREMENTS FOR MAINTENANCE OF A CLASS ACTION

Tennessee courts have held that class certification is a procedural privilege rather than a substantive right. *See, e.g., Bennett v. Stutts*, 521 S.W.2d 575, 577–78 (Tenn. 1975); *Hamilton v. Gibson Cty. Util. Dist.*, 845 S.W.2d 218, 225 (Tenn. Ct. App. 1992); *First Am. Nat'l Bank v. Hunter*, 581 S.W.2d 655, 659 (Tenn. Ct. App. 1978); *Emergency Med. Care Facilities P.C. v. BlueCross BlueShield of Tennessee Inc.*, No. W201702211COAR3CV, 2018 WL 6266529, at *3 (Tenn. Ct. App. Nov. 29, 2018). The proponent of the class has the burden of establishing that all of the requirements of Rule 23.01 are satisfied and the court must find that the class certification is procedurally appropriate under at least one of the three prongs of Rule 23.02. *See, e.g., Emergency Med. Care Facilities P.C.*, 2018 WL 6266529, at *3–4; *Am. Heritage Apartments, Inc. v. Hamilton Cty. Water & Wastewater Treatment Auth.*, No. E201400302SCR11CV, 2016 WL 1424458, at *16 (Tenn. Apr. 8, 2016); *Roberts IRA v. McNeill,* No. W2010-01000-COA-R9-CV, 2011 Tenn. App. LEXIS 80 (Tenn. Ct. App. Feb. 23, 2011); *Govt. Emps. Ins. Co. v. Bloodworth*, No. M2003-02986-COA-R10-CV, 2007 Tenn. App. LEXIS 404, at *12 (Tenn. Ct. App. June 29, 2007); *Hamilton*, 845 S.W.2d at 225; *Albriton v. Hartsville Gas Co.*, 655 S.W.2d 153, 155 (Tenn. Ct. App. 1983) (citing *Cash v. Swifton Land Corp.*, 434 F.2d 569, 571 (6th Cir. 1970)); *Meighan*, 924 S.W.2d at 636.

In considering a motion for class certification, the trial court must conduct a "rigorous, thorough, and careful analysis of the issues related to the standards in Tenn. R. Civ. P. 23 before certifying a class action." *Rogers v. Adventure House LLC*, 617 S.W.3d 542 (Tenn. Ct. App. 2020) (quoting *Gov't Emps. Ins. Co. v. Bloodworth*, No. M2003-02986-COA-R10-CV, 2007 WL 1966022, at *7 (Tenn. Ct. App. June 29, 2007)). The "trial court [is] required to make a rigorous and thorough analysis of [the Rule 23 requirements] and to provide a sufficient explanation of that analysis to provide an opportunity for meaningful appellate review." *Roberts*, 2014 WL 2475595 at *10 (quoting *Bloodworth*, 2007 WL 1966022 at *51). In doing so, the trial court must make clear which issues it considered and "the factors used by the court to decide to certify the class," *Bloodworth*, 2007 WL 1966022, at *31, "identify[ing] sufficient facts upon which it based its decision." *Am. Heritage Apartments*, 2016 WL 1424458, at *16. The court's order must provide "insight into [its] reasoning to allow [the appellate court] to perform our review under the relevant standard in a meaningful way." *Id.* at *33. An Advisory Commission Comment effective May 17, 2005, explains: "The court is required to make an affirmative determination as to whether or not a class action is proper in any given set of circumstances; this determination is subject to alteration at any time prior to judgment

[1] Fed. R. Civ. P. 23(f) Appeals. "A court of appeals may permit an appeal from an order granting or denying class-action certification under this rule if a petition for permission to appeal is filed with the circuit clerk within 14 days after the order is entered. An appeal does not stay proceedings in the district court unless the district judge or the court of appeals so orders." (Effective December 1, 1998.)

on the merits. Criteria governing the court's determination are spelled out in detail. The rule seeks to secure to the courts and litigants the advantages of the class action while clothing the court with power to protect all members of the class against a miscarriage of justice."

In *Wofford*, the Tennessee Court of Appeals affirmed that "the commonality test is qualitative rather than quantitative," that "[w]here a common course of wrongful conduct is alleged, commonality is most easily demonstrated," and "[a] common nucleus of facts is usually enough to satisfy the commonality requirement[.]" 2017 WL 1191298, at *2. In addition to raising common questions, the Tennessee Court of Appeals held that commonality requires that the "proceeding will generate common answers." *Rogers*, 617 S.W.3d at 561 (citing *Wal-Mart Stores, Inc. v. Dukes*, 564 U.S. 338, 350 (2011)). In *Meighan*, the Tennessee Supreme Court, referring to the second prong of Rule 23.01, concluded that the removal of one common legal question is not sufficient grounds to decertify a class if other common questions of law and fact remain. *Meighan*, 924 S.W.2d at 637. The Court also found that the existence of individual issues of law and fact "particularly regarding damages, do not negate class action certification." *Id.* (citing Rules Advisory Committee Notes to 1966 Amendments to Fed. R. Civ. P. 23).

The Tennessee Court of Appeals has found that where there is a motion for certification of a multi-state class, the court must conduct an analysis which "necessarily includes choice of law considerations . . . ; and that the question of whether common questions of law and fact predominate over individual ones requires identification of common and individual questions and a decision that the cause of action can be established by classwide proof." *Bloodworth,* 2007 Tenn. App. LEXIS 404, at *2. Moreover, although a determination on the merits is not permitted, the Court of Appeals held that the trial court must review the "substantive law applicable to the claim and determine whether the party seeking class certification presented sufficient evidence that common questions of law or fact predominate." *Id.* at *55 (citation omitted). This may include an analysis of the expert proof required to establish the claims asserted. *Id.* at *17.

Typicality is met if the "class representative's claim . . . arises from the same event, practice or course of conduct that gives rise to the claims of the other class members and if his claims are based on the same legal theory." *Wofford*, 2017 WL 1191298, at *4. Factual variations and the possibility of individualized issues with certain affirmative defenses is generally insufficient to defeat typicality. *In re SmileDirectClub, Inc., Sec. Litig.*, 2022 WL 818950, at *10 (citing *Waste Mgmt. Holdings, Inc. v. Mowbray*, 208 F.3d 288, 296 (1st Cir. 2000)). Adequacy requires that "the class representatives must have common interests with the unnamed class members and it must appear that the class representatives will vigorously prosecute the case and protect the interests of the class through qualified counsel." *Wofford*, 2017 WL 1191298, at *5.

In *Highlands Phys., Inc. v. Wellmont Health Sys.*, No. E2017-01549-COA-R3-CV, 2017 WL 6623992 (Tenn. Ct. App. Dec. 28, 2017), *permission to appeal granted* (Tenn. Mar. 14, 2018), the court reversed class certification under Rule 23.02(1). The trial court had found that prosecution of individual actions would create the risk of "inconsistent or varying adjudication." The Court of Appeals reversed, explaining that "the full reading of subsection (a) requires not only risk of inconsistent results, but that those results must also risk establishing 'incompatible standards of conduct' for the party opposing the class." *Id.* at *8. Because the plaintiff "has not sufficiently shown that these declarations and injunctions, even if asserted by various individuals outside of the class action context, create the risk of [the defendant] being sued for different and incompatible affirmative relief," class certification was improper. *Id.* at *9. Similarly, the trial court's analysis of subsection (b) was inadequate because the plaintiff "has not shown there is a substantial risk that any of the declaratory or injunctive relief sought by [the plaintiff] would infringe upon the rights of" absent class members.

The Court of Appeals in *Highlands* affirmed class certification under the remaining prongs of Rule 23.01. Specifically, the court held that a class can be certified under Rule 23.02(2) where, even though the complaint "seeks declaratory, injunctive, and monetary relief," on a "sparse" record "due to the early state of this litigation," the court could not "conclude that the primary relief sought by [the plaintiff] is not injunctive or declaratory in nature." *Id.* The Court of Appeals also affirmed certification under Rule 23.02(3), adopting the holding of *Butler v. Sears Roebuck & Co.*, 727 F.3d 796, 801 (7th Cir. 2013), that "individualized proof to assess damages of the purported class [does not] preclude a finding of predominance." *Id.* at *1. The court also explained that a class action was "superior" because "[w]e cannot see how it would be preferable to have potentially hundreds of cases with different judges in different courts dealing with these same legal and factual issues." *Id.*

On review of *Highlands*, however, the Tennessee Supreme Court vacated the ruling of the Court of Appeals as to Rule 23.02(2), holding that the trial court had not sufficiently explained its reasoning pursuant to *Meighan*, 924 S.W.2d at 632, and *Wal-Mart Stores, Inc. v. Dukes*, 564 U.S. 338, 361-62 (2011). *Highlands Phys., Inc. v. Wellmont Health Sys.*, No. E2017-01549-SC-R11-CV, slip op. (Tenn. Mar. 14, 2018) (per curiam). The Supreme Court affirmed the Court of Appeals' reversal of class certification under Rule 23.02(1) and affirmed Rule 23.02(3) certification. *Id.* The Court remanded the case back to the trial court for additional Rule 23.02(2) findings, or for further proceedings under only Rule 23.02(3). *Id.* Subsequently, the *Highlands* case went to trial and in *Highlands Physicians, Inc. v. Wellmont Health System*, 625 S.W.3d 262 (Tenn. Ct. App. 2020), the Tennessee Court of Appeals affirmed a $57 million class action jury verdict on behalf of the class of physician groups alleging breach of an agreement and related claims by a defendant hospital corporation. The court of appeals affirmed the damages verdict, affirmed class certification, affirmed the admissibility of plaintiffs' damages expert testimony, affirmed the court's pretrial summary judgment rulings, and reversed and remanded for redetermination of the attorney fee award by a jury, rather than by the judge alone. The decision is notable for its lengthy review of class action certification issues in the trial context.

A named plaintiff must have standing to assert a claim on their own behalf in order to assert that same claim on behalf of a class. *In re SmileDirectClub, Inc. Sec. Litig.*, 2022 WL 818950, at *14.

In *Griffin v. Crompton Corp.*, No. W2008-02669-COA-R3-CV, 2009 Tenn. App. LEXIS 833 (Tenn. Ct. App. Dec. 14, 2009), the Tennessee Court of Appeals held that actual, individual notice is not required to bar Tennessee plaintiffs from relitigating claims already settled in other states because the "full faith and credit clause requires that the common law doctrine of *res judicata* be applied in one state to a judgment rendered in another state." *Griffin,* 2009 Tenn. App. LEXIS 833, at *11 (quoting *First State Bank v. Wyssbrod*, 124 S.W.3d 566, 573 (Tenn. Ct. App. 2003)).

Tennessee's collateral estoppel doctrine bars relitigation of a prior class certification denial that was affirmed on appeal. *See Emergency Medical Care Facilities, P.C. v. BlueCross BlueShield of Tenn., Inc.*, 715 S.W.3d 273, 276 (Tenn. 2025). In *Emergency Medical Care*, the plaintiff voluntarily nonsuited its claims after the trial court denied class certification and the Court of Appeals affirmed and remanded. *Id.* The Tennessee Supreme Court held that while the plaintiff could have the merits of its substantive claims heard in its refiled action, collateral estoppel precluded it from litigating the class certification issue again. *Id.* at 276–77.

3. STANDARD OF REVIEW OF CLASS CERTIFICATION ORDERS

Class certification decisions are reviewed for abuse of discretion to determine whether the lower court's decision has a basis in fact and is not arbitrary, illogical, or unconscionable. *See Rogers*, 617

S.W.3d at 553; *Highlands Physicians, Inc. v. Wellmont Health Sys.*, 625 S.W.3d 262, 277–78 (Tenn. Ct. App. 2020); *Meighan*, 924 S.W.2d at 637 (citing *Sterling v. Velsicol Chem. Corp.*, 855 F.2d 1188 (6th Cir. 1988)); *Warren v. Scott*, 845 S.W.2d at 783 (Tenn. Ct. App. Sept. 4, 1992); *Hamilton*, 845 S.W.2d at 225; *Bohlinger v. Am. Credit Co.*, 594 S.W.2d at 712 (Tenn. Ct. App. Oct. 16, 1979). Reviewing courts seek to determine "(1) whether the factual basis for the decision is properly supported by evidence in the record, (2) whether the lower court properly identified and applied the most appropriate legal principles applicable to the decision, and (3) whether the lower court's decision was within the range of acceptable alternative dispositions." *Highlands Physicians*, 625 S.W.3d at 278 (quoting *Rogers*, 617 S.W.3d at 549–50). The determination of whether the trial court used the correct legal standard is reviewed *de novo*, requiring the reviewing court to consider "whether the applicable legal standards have been interpreted and applied correctly." *Bloodworth*, 2007 Tenn. App. LEXIS 404, at *34.

4. CROSS-JURISDICTIONAL AND INTRA-JURISDICTIONAL TOLLING

Tennessee does *not* recognize the doctrine of cross-jurisdictional tolling. *See Maestas v. Sofamor Danek Group, Inc.*, 33 S.W.3d 805 (Tenn. 2000), *limited perm. app. granted* (Tenn. 1999). In *Maestas,* the Tennessee Supreme Court held that Tennessee "simply has no interest, except perhaps out of comity, in furthering the efficiency and economy of the class action procedures of another jurisdiction, whether those of the federal courts or those of another state." *Maestas*, 33 S.W.3d at 808 (quoting *Wade v. Danek Med., Inc.*, 182 F.3d 281, 287 (4th Cir. 1999)). The Court was concerned that if it recognized the doctrine of cross-jurisdictional tolling, Tennessee would become a clearinghouse for stale claims from other jurisdictions. ("We cannot sanction such forum shopping.") *Id.*

In *Tigg v. Pirelli Tire Co.*, 232 S.W.3d 28 (Tenn. 2007), the Tennessee Supreme Court considered whether the plaintiffs' claims for wrongful termination were tolled by the filing of a class action in which they were putative class members until that case settled. *Id.* at 32. The Court noted that it had rejected the rule of cross-jurisdictional tolling in *Maestas* but recognized that many courts had adopted intra-jurisdictional tolling, "which tolls statutes of limitations *within* the same court system during the pendency of a class action for potential members of the class." *Id.* at 33 (emphasis in the original). The Court neither adopted nor rejected intrajurisdictional tolling in *Tigg*. Instead, it found that the previous plaintiffs failed to seek class certification within 60 days after their case was remanded to Davidson County Circuit Court pursuant to Davidson County Circuit Court Rule 26.14. *Id.* (noting that Davidson County Circuit Court Rule 26.14 requires plaintiffs to move for certification within 60 days of the removal, and the previous plaintiffs' case was pending for six years without a motion for class certification being filed). *See also Doe v. City of Memphis*, No. W2023-01248-COA-R9-CV, 2024 WL 4889005, at *4–6 (Tenn. Ct. App. Nov. 26, 2024), *perm. app. denied* (Tenn. May 28, 2025) (concluding the trial court erred in ruling that an intrajurisdictional class action complaint tolled the statute of limitations for plaintiff's GTLA claim because, while the Tennessee Supreme Court "may be open to the idea of adopting an intrajurisdictional tolling rule," it would not apply to cases involving the GTLA).

5. ATTORNEYS' FEES

The Tennessee Court of Appeals has found that under 42 U.S.C. § 1988, which requires the plaintiff to be the prevailing party in order to receive an award of attorneys' fees, a reasonable award of fees is appropriate where "actual relief on the merits of his claim materially alters the legal relationship between the parties by modifying the defendant's behavior in a way that directly benefits the plaintiff." *C.S.C. v. Knox Cty. Bd. of Educ.*, No. E2006-01155-COA-R3-CV, 2007 Tenn. App. LEXIS 337, at *17 (Tenn. Ct. App. May 25, 2007) (quoting *Farrar v. Hobby,* 506 U.S. 103, 111–12 (1992)). In *C.S.C.,* because the plaintiff class prevailed on several issues, and because the "efforts of the Plaintiff class members and their counsel have contributed to the public interest through this litigation," the Court of Appeals upheld the trial court's order granting fees to plaintiffs' counsel. *Id.* at *24–25.

The Tennessee Supreme Court has found that the Tennessee Legislature intended to remove the availability of attorneys' fees for a plaintiff in a shareholder's derivative suit brought on behalf of a for-profit corporation when the legislature adopted the Tennessee Business Corporation Act of 1986 (TBCA), *House v. Estate of Edmondson*, 245 S.W.3d 372 (Tenn. 2008). It noted that the TBCA "limits the recovery of attorney's fees in derivative actions to only successful defendants." *Id.* at 379.

6. TENNESSEE CONSUMER PROTECTION ACT CLAIMS MAY NOT BE MAINTAINED AS CLASS ACTIONS

The Tennessee Civil Justice Act amended the Tennessee Consumer Protection Act (TCPA) to prohibit class actions on behalf of consumers. *See* Tenn. Code Ann. § 47-18-109(g) ("[n]o class action lawsuit may be brought to recover damages for an unfair or deceptive act or practice declared to be unlawful by this part"). In doing so, the legislature codified the ruling of the Tennessee Supreme Court that "class certification is unavailable under the TCPA and that class certification was not appropriate in the plaintiff's claims for common law fraud and misrepresentation due to the individual nature of those claims." *Walker v. Sunrise Pontiac-GMC Truck, Inc.*, 249 S.W.3d 301, 304 (Tenn. 2008).

7. TENNESSEE CYBERSECURITY CLASS ACTIONS MAY NOT BE MAINTAINED UNLESS THE PRIVATE ENITY ENGAGED IN WILLFUL AND WANTON MISCONDUCT OR GROSS NEGLIGENCE

Taking effect on May 21, 2024, Tennessee enacted § 29-34-215, which states:

> (a) As used in this section:
>
> > (1) "Cybersecurity event" means an event resulting in unauthorized access to, or disruption or misuse of, an information system or nonpublic information stored on an information system;
> >
> > (2) "Information system" has the same meaning as defined in § 56-21003;
> >
> > (3) "Nonpublic information" means information that is not publicly available and concerns a person that, because of a name, number, personal mark, or other identifier, can be used to identify that person, in combination with the following:
> >
> > > (A) A social security number;
> > >
> > > (B) A driver license number or non-driver identification card number;
> > >
> > > (C) A financial account number or credit or debit card number;

(D) A security code, access code, or password that would permit access to the person's financial accounts; or

(E) Biometric records;

(4) "Private entity" means a corporation, religious or charitable organization, association, partnership, limited liability company, limited liability partnership, or other private business entity, whether organized for-profit or not-for-profit; and

(5) "Publicly available information" means information that is lawfully made available through federal, state, or local government records, or information that a business has a reasonable basis to believe is lawfully made available to the general public.

. . .

(b) A private entity is not liable in a class action lawsuit resulting from a cybersecurity event unless the cybersecurity event was caused by willful and wanton misconduct or gross negligence on the part of the private entity.

In *Haney v. Charter Foods N., LLC*, No. 2:23-CV-168, 2024 WL 4054361 (E.D. Tenn. Aug. 28, 2024), defendant Charter Foods attempted to raise the issue of Tenn. Code § 29-34-215(b) as part of a motion to dismiss for failure to state a claim. *Id.* at *8. The Eastern District of Tennessee considered the argument that the statute applied retroactively and plaintiffs did not sufficiently allege willful and wanton misconduct or gross negligence in the complaint. *Id.* Citing the substantive purpose of the law and the general presumption in Tennessee against retroactive application, the court found that the law did not raise the standard for action taken prior to the statute's effective date. *Id.* at *7–8 (citing *Kee v. Shelter Ins.*, 852 S.W.2d 226, 228 (Tenn. 1993)). The court thus denied defendant's motion on § 29-34-215 grounds and plaintiffs' claims were allowed to proceed. *Id.* at *8. Tennessee state courts, however, have yet to decide on the matter of potential retroactivity or interpret the statute in other application.

8. COMMUNICATIONS WITH ABSENT CLASS MEMBERS

a. Communications or Solicitations by Plaintiffs' Counsel with Putative or Absent Class Members

Rules 7.2 and 7.3 of the Tennessee Supreme Court's Rules of Professional Conduct (TRPC) govern attorney advertising and solicitation of potential clients.

TRPC 7.3 states:

(a) A lawyer shall not by in-person, live telephone, or real-time electronic contact solicit professional employment from a potential client when a significant motive for the lawyer's doing so is the lawyer's pecuniary gain, unless the person contacted:

(1) is a lawyer; or
(2) has a family, close personal, or prior professional relationship with the lawyer; or
(3) has initiated a contact with the lawyer.

. . .

(b) A lawyer shall not solicit professional employment from a potential client by written, recorded, or electronic communication or by in-person, live telephone, or real-time electronic contact even when not otherwise prohibited by paragraph (a), if:

(1) the potential client has made known to the lawyer a desire not to be solicited by the lawyer; or

(2) the solicitation involves coercion, duress, fraud, harassment, intimidation, over-reaching, or undue influence; or

(3) a significant motive for the solicitation is the lawyer's pecuniary gain and the communication concerns an action for personal injury, worker's compensation, wrongful death, or otherwise relates to an accident or disaster involving the person to whom the communication is addressed or a member of that person's family, unless the accident or disaster occurred more than thirty (30) days prior to the mailing or transmission of the communication or the lawyer has a family, close personal, or prior professional relationship with the person solicited.

. . .

(c) If a significant motive for the solicitation is the lawyer's pecuniary gain, a lawyer shall not send a written, recorded, or electronic communication soliciting professional employment from a specifically identified recipient who is not a person specified in paragraphs (a)(1) or (a)(2) or (a)(3), unless the communication complies with the following requirements:

(1) The words "Advertising Material" appear on the outside of the envelope, if any, in which a communication is sent and at the beginning and ending of any written, recorded or electronic communication.

(2) A lawyer shall not state or imply that a communication otherwise permitted by these rules has been approved by the Tennessee Supreme Court or the Board of Professional Responsibility.

(3) If a contract for representation is mailed with the communication, the top of each page of the contract shall be marked "SAMPLE" and the words "DO NOT SIGN" shall appear on the client signature line.

(4) Written communications shall not be in the form of or include legal pleadings or other formal legal documents.

(5) Communications delivered to potential clients shall be sent only by regular U.S. mail and not by registered, certified, or other forms of restricted delivery, or by express delivery or courier.

(6) Any communication seeking employment by a specific potential client in a specific matter shall comply with the following additional requirements:

(i) The communication shall disclose how the lawyer obtained the information prompting the communication;

(ii) The subject matter of the proposed representation shall not be disclosed on the outside of the envelope (or self-mailing brochure) in which the communication is delivered; and

(iii) The first sentence of the communication shall state, "IF YOU HAVE ALREADY HIRED OR RETAINED A LAWYER IN THIS MATTER, PLEASE DISREGARD THIS MESSAGE."

(7) A copy of each written, audio, video, or electronically transmitted communication sent to a specific recipient under this Rule shall be retained by the lawyer for two years after its last dissemination along with a record of when, and to whom, it was sent.

. . .

(d) Unless the contents thereof include a solicitation of employment, a lawyer need not comply with the requirements of paragraph (c) above when sending announcements of an association or affiliation with another lawyer that complies with the requirements of RPC 7.5, newsletters, brochures, and other similar communications.

In *Frye v. Baptist Mem. Hosp., Inc.*, No. 07-2708 Ma/P, 2008 U.S. Dist. LEXIS 41511 (W.D. Tenn. May 20, 2008), the defendant moved for the plaintiffs to cease communication with putative class members, arguing that a website posted by plaintiffs' counsel violated TRPC 7.2 in that it was misleading, and a letter sent by plaintiffs' counsel to potential collective action members was a direct solicitation in violation of TRPC 7.3. Looking to the United States Supreme Court's decision in *Gulf Oil Co. v. Bernard*, 452 U.S. 89 (1981), the court denied the motion, holding that, while it has broad discretion to prohibit abusive conduct in class actions, and findings of abuses may justify a communications ban, the mere possibility of abuse does not justify a ban that interferes with the formation or prosecution of a class action. *Frye*, 2008 U.S. Dist. Lexis 41511, at *12. Although the plaintiffs' initial letter did violate TRPC 7.3, plaintiffs' counsel immediately revised the website and mailed corrected versions of the letter to putative class members upon learning of the issues raised in the defendant's motion. Because these updated materials did not violate TRPCs 7.2 and 7.3, the court held that a communications ban was not warranted at such time. *Id.* at *5.

Trollinger v. Tyson Foods, Inc., No. 4:02-CV-23, 2007 U.S. Dist. LEXIS 88866 (E.D. Tenn. Dec. 3, 2007), makes several points regarding communications to putative class members. First, acknowledging the value of the internet in disseminating information to class members, the court noted that it was appropriate for plaintiffs' counsel to post class notice and other relevant court documents on its website. *Id.* at *7. The court also held that defendants could not be compelled to provide class notices to its employees, the putative class members, because inclusion of notice with pay checks would not provide the best notice practicable. *Id.* at *23.

b. Communications by Defense Counsel with Putative or Absent Class Members

Even after certification, defendants may communicate with putative class members for a variety of reasons as long as the opt-out period has not expired. *In re Southeastern Milk Antitrust Litig.*, No. 2:08-MD-1000, Dkt. No. 1698 at 4–6, (E.D. Tenn. July 29, 2011). In *In re Southeastern Milk*, the court in this case was persuaded by the defendants that it was permissible for them to attach declarations obtained from putative class members after class certification had been granted to the defense's motion to decertify the class because no lawyer-client relationship yet existed between class counsel and potential class members where opt-out was still available. As the declarants had indicated an intention not to be represented by class counsel and class notice had not yet been sent out, the court reasoned that the defense could take appropriate action to prepare its case, including taking declarations where opt-out had not yet expired.

In contrast, the court in *Abadeer v. Tyson Foods, Inc.*, No. 3:09-cv-00125, 2009 U.S. Dist. LEXIS 110685, at *14 n.3 (M.D. Tenn. Nov. 25, 2009), refused to consider affidavits the defendants had obtained without court approval from absent class members in support of the defendants' opposition to class certification.

In *Roslies-Perez v. Superior Forestry Serv., Inc.*, 652 F. Supp. 2d 887 (M.D. Tenn. 2009), a FLSA action in which defendants had repeatedly violated protective orders forbidding intimidation or contact of a similar nature with potential collective action members, their families, and potential witnesses, the court found defendants in contempt of court orders and imposed sanctions.

RULE 23 OF THE TENNESSEE RULES OF CIVIL PROCEDURE

Rule 23.01 Prerequisites to a class action. One or more members of a class may sue or be sued as representative parties on behalf of all only if (1) the class is so numerous that joinder of all members is impracticable, (2) there are questions of law or fact common to the class, (3) the claims or defenses of the representative parties are typical of the claims or defenses of the class, and (4) the representative parties will fairly and adequately protect the interest of the class.

Rule 23.02 Class actions maintainable. An action may be maintainable as a class action if the prerequisites of 23.01 are satisfied, and in addition:

(1) The prosecution of separate actions by or against individual members of the class would create a risk of

(a) inconsistent or varying adjudications with respect to individual members of the class which would establish incompatible standards of conduct for a party opposing the class, or

(b) adjudications with respect to individual members of the class which would as a practical matter be dispositive of the interests of the other members not parties to the adjudications or would substantially impair or impede their ability to protect their interest; or

(2) the party opposing the class has acted or refused to act on grounds generally applicable to the class, thereby making appropriate final injunctive relief or corresponding declaratory relief with respect to the class as a whole; or

(3) the court finds that the question of law or fact common to the members of the class predominate over any questions affecting only individual members, and that a class action is superior to other available methods for the fair and efficient adjudication of the controversy. The matters pertinent to the findings include: (a) the interest of members of the class in individually controlling the prosecution or defense of separate actions; (b) the extent and nature of any litigation concerning the controversy already commenced by or against members of the class; (c) the desirability or undesirability of concentrating the litigation of the claims in the particular forum; (d) the difficulties likely to be encountered in the management of a class action.

Rule 23.03 Determination by order whether class action to be maintained; notice, judgment; actions conducted.

(1) As soon as practicable after the commencement of an action brought as a class action, but never in a hearing without all representative plaintiffs and all defendants having been given an opportunity to be present, the court shall determine by order whether the action is to be so maintained. An order under this section may be conditional and may be altered or amended before the decision on the merits.

(2) In any class action maintained under Rule 23.02(3), the court shall direct to the members of the class the best notice practicable under the circumstances, including publication when appropriate or individual notice to all members who can be identified through reasonable effort. The notice shall advise each member that (a) the court will exclude the member from

the class if the member so requests by a specified date; (b) the judgment, whether favorable or not, will include all members who do not request exclusion; and (c) any member who does not request exclusion may, if the member desires, enter an appearance.

(3) The judgment in an action maintained as a class action under Rule 23.02(1) or Rule 23.02(2), whether or not favorable to the class, shall include and describe those whom the court finds to be members of the class. The judgment in an action maintained as a class action under Rule 23.02(3), whether or not favorable to the class, shall include and specify or describe those to whom the notice provided in Rule 23.03(2) was directed, and who have not requested exclusion, and whom the court finds to be members of the class.

(4) When appropriate (a) an action may be brought or maintained as a class action with respect to particular issues, or (b) a class may be divided into subclasses and each subclass treated as a class, and the provisions of this rule shall then be construed and applied accordingly.

Rule 23.04 Orders in conduct of actions. In the conduct of actions to which this rule applies, the court may make appropriate orders: (1) determining the course of proceedings or prescribing measures to prevent undue repetition or complication in the presentation of evidence or argument; (2) requiring, for the protection of the members of the class or otherwise for the fair conduct of the action, that notice be given in such manner as the court may direct to some or all of the members of any step in the action, or of the proposed extent of the judgment, or the opportunity of members to signify whether they consider the representation fair and adequate, to intervene and present claims or defenses, or otherwise come into the action; (3) imposing conditions on the representative parties or on intervenors; (4) requiring that the pleadings be amended to eliminate therefrom allegations as to representation of absent persons, and that the action proceed accordingly; (5) dealing with similar procedural matters. The orders may be combined with an order under Rule 16, and may be altered or amended as may be desirable from time to time.

Rule 23.05 Dismissal or compromise. A certified class action shall not be voluntarily dismissed or compromised without approval of the court, and notice of the proposed dismissal or compromise shall be given to all members of the class in such manner as the court directs. If attorney fees are sought as part of a compromise, a motion for fees must be filed and served on all parties and, for motions by class counsel, directed to class members in a reasonable manner. A class member, or a party from whom payment is sought, may object to the motion.

Rule 23.06 Derivative actions by shareholders.[2] In a derivative action brought by one or more shareholders or members to enforce a right of a corporation or of an unincorporated association, the corporation or association having failed to enforce a right which may properly be asserted by it, the complaint shall be verified and shall allege that the plaintiff was a shareholder or member at the time of the transaction of which the plaintiff complains or that the plaintiff's share of membership thereafter devolved on the plaintiff by operation of law. The complaint shall also allege with particularity the efforts, if any, made by the plaintiff to obtain the action desired from the directors or comparable authority and, if necessary, from the shareholders, or members, and the reasons for the plaintiff's failure to obtain the action or for not making the effort. The derivative action may not be maintained if it appears that the plaintiff does not fairly and adequately represent the interests of the shareholders

---

[2] In 2011, the Tennessee General Assembly amended Tenn. Code Ann. § 47-18-109 to state, "No private right of action shall be commenced under this section for any alleged unfair or deceptive act or practice involving the marketing or sale of a security as defined in the Tennessee Securities Act, § 48-2-102(17)."

or members similarly situated in enforcing the right of the corporation or association. The action shall not be voluntarily dismissed or compromised without the approval of the court, and notice of the proposed dismissal or compromise shall be given to shareholders or members in such manner as the court directs.

Rule 23.07 Actions relating to unincorporated associations. An action brought by or against the members of an unincorporated association as a class by naming certain members as representative parties may be maintained only if it appears that the representative parties will fairly and adequately protect the interests of the association and its members. In the conduct of the action the court may make appropriate orders corresponding with those described in Rule 23.04, and the procedure for dismissal or compromise of the action shall correspond with that provided in Rule 23.05.

Rule 23.08 Disposition of residual funds. Any order entering a judgment or approving a proposed compromise of a class action certified under this rule may provide for the disbursement of residual funds. Residual funds are funds that remain after the payment of all approved: class member claims, expenses, litigation costs, attorneys' fees, and other court-approved disbursements to implement the relief granted. Nothing in this rule is intended to limit the parties to a class action from suggesting, or the trial court from approving, a settlement or order entering a judgment that does not create residual funds.

It shall be within the discretion of the court to approve the timing and method of distribution of residual funds and to approve the recipient(s) of residual funds. A distribution of residual funds to a program or fund which serves the pro bono legal needs of Tennesseans including, but not limited to, the Tennessee Voluntary Fund for Indigent Civil Representation is permissible but not required.

Upon motion of any party to a settlement or judgment of a class action certified under this rule or upon the court's own initiative, orders may be entered after an approved settlement or judgment to address the disposition and disbursement of residual funds in a manner consistent with this rule.

This chapter was prepared by Kenneth S. Byrd, Betsy A. Sugar, and Ellie Olson of Lieff Cabraser Heimann & Bernstein, LLP.

TEXAS

1. COMPARISON WITH RULE 23 OF THE FEDERAL RULES OF CIVIL PROCEDURE

Texas Rule 42 is identical in most respects to Federal Rule 23. Accordingly, federal court decisions interpreting Rule 23 are "persuasive authority." *Intratex Gas Co. v. Beeson*, 22 S.W.3d 398, 403 n.4 (Tex. 2000); *General Motors Corp. v. Bloyed*, 916 S.W.2d 949, 954 n.1 (Tex. 1996). However, federal court decisions are not binding authority. *See Intratex Gas Co. v. Beeson*, 22 S.W.3d 398, 404 n.5 (Tex. 2000) (expressly noting that its holding conflicts with holding of Fifth Circuit, *Mullen v. Treasure Chest Casino*, LLC, 186 F.3d 620 (5th Cir. 1999)). The points on which Rule 42 differs in substance from Rule 23 are identified below in the discussion of specific sections.

Rule 42 departs from Rule 23 in the details, such as (1) burden on the trial court when granting or denying class certification, (2) type of notice to the class, (3) appointment of class counsel, and (4) treatment and award of attorneys' fees.

2. SUMMARY OF TEXAS CASE LAW

a. General Observations

In 2000, the Texas Supreme Court handed down a series of three decisions that clarified, and to some extent narrowed, the circumstances where a class action may be certified under Rule 42. *Intratex Gas Co. v. Beeson*, 22 S.W.3d 398 (Tex. 2000); *Southwestern Refining Co., Inc. v. Bernal*, 22 S.W.3d 425 (Tex. 2000); *Ford Motor Co. v. Sheldon*, 22 S.W.3d 444 (Tex. 2000). The Supreme Court made it quite clear that, while it views class actions favorably, it also insists that lower courts strictly comply with Rule 42 in certifying class actions. "Even though it is an efficient device, there is no right to litigate a claim as a class action. Rather, Rule 42 provides only that the court may certify a class action if the plaintiff satisfies the requirements of the rule." *Ford Motor Co. v. Sheldon*, 22 S.W.3d 444, 452–53 (Tex. 2000) (internal citation omitted). However, the trial court is not bound by class definitions submitted by the parties and may use its own definition as the needs of the case require. *Bailey v. Kemper Cas. Ins. Co.*, 83 S.W.3d 840, 848 (Tex. App.—Texarkana 2002).

Nonetheless, as at least one court of appeals has confirmed, Texas courts take a "much different approach" than that taken by other courts outside Texas—a much more "rigorous approach." *Stobaugh v. Norwegian Cruise Line Ltd.*, 105 S.W.3d 302, 311 (Tex. App.—Houston [14th Dist.] 2003).

Unlike Federal Rule 23, the trial court must hold a hearing on the issue of class certification. The hearing should not determine the merits of the case. *Intratex Gas Co. v. Beeson*, 22 S.W.3d 398, 404 (Tex. 2000). The trial court may consider matters in the record, regardless of whether they are proven in a fully evidentiary hearing. *Snyder Communs. v. Magana*, 94 S.W.3d 213 (Tex. App.—Corpus Christi, 2002); *Health & Tennis Corp. of America v. Jackson*, 928 S.W.2d 583, 587 (Tex. App.—San Antonio 1996, no writ); *Dresser Industries, Inc. v. Snell*, 847 S.W.2d 367, 376 (Tex. App.—El Paso 1993, no writ); *Clements v. League of United Latin American Citizens (LULAC)*, 800

S.W.2d 948, 952 (Tex. App.—Corpus Christi 1990, no writ). A trial court does not err in denying a motion to certify without a hearing if it has dismissed all of the individual plaintiff's claims. *Roach v. Ingram*, 557 S.W.3d 203, 226 (Tex. App. 2018), *review den.* (May 31, 2019) ("Given that we have affirmed the trial court's holdings dismissing all of the [Plaintiffs'] claims, we hold that the trial court did not err by denying the Parents' motion for class certification after dismissing all of the [Plaintiffs'] claims."). Similarly, an appellate court will not review class certification issues if the trial court has not ruled on the merits of class certification. *City of Willis v. Garcia*, 523 S.W.3d 729, 733 n.5 (Tex. App. 2017) ("The trial court has not yet determined whether the class should be certified. We express no opinion on the validity of the alleged class."), and *Wilder v. Merritt*, No. 02-16-00477-CV, 2017 WL 5494258, at *2 (Tex. App. Nov. 16, 2017) ("The Petitioners have pleaded for class-action relief, but the trial court has not certified a class.").

Prior to 2000, several courts held that a court could certify a case solely on the basis of a well-pleaded petition. *Weatherly v. Deloitte & Touche*, 905 S.W.2d 642, 647 (Tex. App.—Houston [14th Dist.] 1995, writ dism'd w.o.j.); *Vinson v. Texas Commerce Bank-Houston, N.A.*, 880 S.W.2d 820, 823 (Tex. App.—Dallas 1994, no writ); *National Gypsum Co. v. Kirbyville Independent School District*, 770 S.W.2d 621, 627 (Tex. App.—Beaumont 1989, writ dism'd w.o.j.); *Life Ins. Co. of Southwest v. Brister*, 722 S.W.2d 764, 772-73 (Tex. App.—Fort Worth 1986, no writ) (en banc). However, inconsistent holdings of the Texas Supreme Court in 2000 created confusion on this point. First it noted that a trial court *may* look beyond the pleadings. *Intratex Gas Co. v. Beeson*, 22 S.W.3d 398, 404 (Tex. 2000). Then, two months later, the court stated that "going beyond the pleadings is *necessary*." *Southwestern Refining Co., Inc. v. Bernal*, 22 S.W.3d 425, 435 (Tex. 2000) (emphasis added). Then, in 2003, the Supreme Court attempted a clarification:

> In *Bernal,* we held that in order to make a proper analysis of the Rule 42 factors, a court must go beyond the pleadings and must understand the claims, defenses, relevant facts, and applicable substantive law in order to make a meaningful determination of the certification issues. *Id.* (quoting *Castano v. Am. Tobacco Co.*, 84 F.3d 734, 744 (5th Cir.1996)). By choosing to delay analysis of [a recent decision of the Supreme Court] until another stage of litigation, the court of appeals ignored applicable substantive law crucial to understanding the claims and defenses in this case.

Union Pacific Resources Group, Inc. v. Hankins, 111 S.W.3d 69, 72 (Tex. 2003) (internal quotations omitted).

The best reconciliation of these opinions is that what the Court means by "going beyond the pleadings" requires examining something more than the petition and answer and considering whether there are legal defenses that would be fatal to the ultimate success of the lawsuit. It may not be required in every case but will be required in a case involving complex factual or legal determinations as part of class certification. As the Texas Supreme Court itself observed: "Personal injury claims will often present thorny causation and damage issues with highly individualistic variables that a court or jury must individually resolve." *Southwestern Refining Co., Inc. v. Bernal*, 22 S.W.3d 425, 436 (Tex. 2000).

Most importantly, a class must be "clearly ascertainable by reference to objective criteria." *Intratex Gas Co. v. Beeson*, 22 S.W.3d 398, 403 (Tex. 2000). A class must not be defined by subjective criteria or by an analysis of the merits of the case. *Id.* A class definition should not require a separate inquiry into each class member's state of mind to determine whether that person is a member of the class. *Ford Motor Co. v. Sheldon*, 22 S.W.3d 444, 454 (Tex. 2000). This avoids creating a "fail-safe" class that is bound only by a judgment favorable to the class, but not by a judgment in favor of the defendant. *Intratex Gas Co. v. Beeson*, 22 S.W.3d at 404–05.

The Texas Supreme Court reiterated its insistence on strict scrutiny of class certification in *Schein v. Stromboe*, 102 S.W.3d 675, 691 (Tex. 2002), when it said that "we likewise expressly refused to indulge every presumption in favor of the trial court's ruling. A trial court has discretion to rule on class certification issues, and some of its determinations—like those based on its assessment of the credibility of witnesses, for example—must be given the benefit of the doubt. But the trial court's exercise of discretion cannot be supported by every presumption that can be made in its favor." The Supreme Court later made this rule even clearer, holding that "compliance with class action requirements must be demonstrated rather than presumed." *Compaq Computer Corp. v. Lapray*, 135 S.W.3d 657, 672 (Tex. 2004).

Soon after, the Texas Supreme Court held that a trial court had failed to "perform a rigorous analysis" when it considered a defendant's assertion of the voluntary-payment rule. The district court considered that assertion, opined that its application was "unlikely" in that case, and that if it were to be applied, it was not an individual issue but could be determined as a common class-wide issue. *BMG Direct Marketing, Inc. v. Peake*, 178 S.W.3d 763, 777 (Tex. 2005). The Supreme Court held that the trial court should have included in its trial plan "how the voluntary-payment rule and the issues involved in its application could be tried class wide were the court to determine that the rule did apply," and should have considered "obstacles to class certification that the rule's application might present." *Id.*

Nonetheless, the actual standard of review of a decision on certification appears to be abuse of discretion. "Texas law, however, does not *require* a trial court to certify a class action even if the facts sufficiently satisfy rule 42. . . . This Court may reverse a trial court for abuse of discretion only if, after searching the record, it is clear that the trial court's decision was arbitrary and unreasonable." *Vincent v. Bank of America*, 109 S.W.3d 856, 864 (Tex. App.—Dallas 2003) (affirming trial court grant of certification). *Cyganek v. A.J.'s Wrecker Service of Dallas, Inc.*, 2009 WL 1942184, 5 (Tex. App.—Dallas 2009) ("Because we review an order denying class certification under an abuse-of-discretion standard, . . . the question presented is not whether the trial court reasonably could have granted certification on this record, but whether it acted arbitrarily and unreasonably by failing to do so.") (affirming trial court denial of certification).

b. Rule 42(a) [equivalent to Federal Rule 23(a)]

i. Numerosity [Rule 42(a)(1)]. Texas law does not require proof of the precise number of class members. *Phillips v. Joint Legislative Committee*, 637 F.2d 1014, 1022 (5th Cir. 1981), *cert. denied,* 456 U.S. 960 (1982); *Carpenter v. Davis*, 424 F.2d 257, 260 (5th Cir. 1970). But *some* evidence is required. Representations made by counsel at a certification hearing may be considered 'materials' for purposes of a class certification decision, but courts "decline to credit the vague speculations and unsubstantiated complaints of counsel in light of the almost complete absence of any other evidence of numerosity." *HICA Educ. Loan Corp. v. Sullivan*, 2009 WL 3210954, 3 (Tex. App.—Corpus Christi 2009).

ii. Commonality [Rule 42(a)(2)]. Common questions are those questions that, when answered as to the named plaintiff, are answered as to the class members. *Health & Tennis Corp. of America v. Jackson*, 928 S.W.2d 583, 590 (Tex. App.—San Antonio 1996, no writ); *Reserve Life Ins. Co. v. Kirkland*, 917 S.W.2d 836, 842 (Tex. App.—Houston [14th Dist.] 1996, no writ). The standard for commonality is not high. *Union Pacific Resources Group, Inc. v. Hankins*, 111 S.W.3d 69, 74 (Tex. 2003). Not all or even a great portion of the questions in the suit must be common to the class. *Microsoft Corp. v. Manning*, 914 S.W.2d 602, 611 (Tex. App.—Texarkana 1996, writ dism'd); *Wente v. Georgia-Pacific Corp.*, 712 S.W.2d 253, 255 (Tex. App.—Austin 1986, no writ); *Reserve Life Ins. Co. v. Kirkland*, 917 S.W.2d at 842. "A single common question can warrant certification." *Health & Tennis Corp. of America v. Jackson*, 928 S.W.2d at 590, citing *Microsoft Corp. v. Manning*. Moreover, the common question may be one of law *or* fact; it does not have to be both. *Health & Tennis Corp. of America v. Jackson*, 928 S.W.2d at 590. Affirmative defenses do not destroy commonality. *Microsoft Corp. v. Manning*, 914 S.W.2d at 613. However, the decision to abandon some claims in order to achieve commonality can become "one relevant factor in evaluating the requirements for class certification." *Bowden v. Phillips Petroleum Co.*, 247 S.W.3d 690, 698 (Tex. 2008); *Lon Smith & Assocs., Inc. v. Key*, 527 S.W.3d 604, 620 (Tex. App. 2017), *review denied* (June 15, 2018).

iii. Typicality [Rule 42(a)(3)]. The typicality requirement is satisfied if the class representative demonstrates that his claims have the same essential characteristics as those of the class as a whole. *Microsoft Corp. v. Manning*, 914 S.W.2d 602, 613 (Tex. App.—Texarkana 1996, writ dism'd); *Cedar Crest Funeral Home, Inc. v. Lashley*, 889 S.W.2d 325, 331 (Tex. App.—Dallas 1993, no writ). Unsurprisingly, "the class representative must be a member of the class and have individual standing to sue." *Southwestern Bell Telephone Co. v. Marketing on Hold Inc.*, 308 S.W.3d 909, 915 (Tex. 2010). The class representative's claims need not be identical to those of absent class members, only substantially similar. *Reserve Life Ins. Co. v. Kirkland*, 917 S.W.2d 836, 842 (Tex. App.—Houston [14th Dist.] 1996, no writ); *Cedar Crest Funeral Home, Inc. v. Lashley*, 889 S.W.2d at 331. All that is required is that the claims arise from the same pattern of conduct and be based on the same legal theory. *Microsoft Corp. v. Manning*, 914 S.W.2d at 613. Public policy does not deny standing to a class plaintiff that holds contractually valid assignments from other class members. *Southwestern Bell Telephone Co. v. Marketing on Hold Inc.*, 308 S.W.3d 909, 916 (Tex. 2010). More recently, the Court concluded that a plaintiff could not represent an injunctive class because she didn't have standing to seek prospective injunctive relief on her own behalf. Expanding on this, the Court also found that there were issues regarding both predominance and typicality. *USAA Casualty Insurance Co. v. Letot,* 690 S.W.3d 274 (2024). This continued a long line of cases where the Court often appears openly hostile to the idea of any class action at all.

iv. Adequacy [Rule 42(a)(4)]. Adequacy of representation is demonstrated by showing (1) that no conflict in the litigated issues exists between the representative and the class members and (2) that class counsel is sufficiently qualified and experienced to prosecute the action vigorously. *Health & Tennis Corp. of America v. Jackson*, 928 S.W.2d 583, 589 (Tex. App.—San Antonio 1996, no writ); *Microsoft Corp. v. Manning*, 914 S.W.2d 602, 614 (Tex. App.—Texarkana 1996, writ dism'd); *Weatherly v. Deloitte & Touche*, 905 S.W.2d 642, 651-652 (Tex. App.—Houston [14th Dist.] 1995, writ dism'd w.o.j.). Interests are not considered antagonistic unless they relate directly to the matters in controversy. *Health & Tennis Corp. of America v. Jackson*, 928 S.W.2d at 589 (citing *Microsoft Corp. v. Manning*). Texas law "does not require a higher standard of involvement from a proposed class representative than from an individual plaintiff." *Health & Tennis Corp. of America v. Jackson*, 928 S.W.2d at 589 (citing *Weatherly v. Deloitte & Touche*). Courts therefore look to class counsel, not the named plaintiff, to determine whether vigorous prosecution is probable. "The qualifications and experience of the class counsel is of greater consequence than the knowledge of the class representatives." *Health & Tennis Corp. of America v. Jackson*, 928 S.W.2d at 589 (citing *Microsoft Corp. v. Manning*, 914 S.W.2d at 614; *Weatherly v. Deloitte & Touche*, 905 S.W.2d at 652). If there is any doubt as to a class representative's adequacy, the trial court can easily satisfy it by requiring additional class representatives. Departing from Federal Rule 23, Texas Rule 42(c)(1) expressly states that the "court may order the naming of additional parties in order to insure the adequacy of class representation." However, deciding not to sue for certain claims—even ones that can't be certified—may raise questions about class adequacy. "A class representative's decision to abandon certain claims may be detrimental to absent class members for whom those claims could be more lucrative or valuable, assuming those class members do not opt out of the class." *Citizens Insurance Co. of America v. Daccach*, 217 S.W.3d 430 453–54 (Tex. 2007).

A class member whose interests conflict with the interests of other class members may not adequately represent a class. *State Farm Mut. Auto. Ins. Co. v. Lopez*, 156 S.W.3d 500, 556 (Tex. 2004). The mere existence of minor conflicts, however, will not prevent a class representative from adequately representing a class. *Riemer v. Texas*, 392 S.W.3d 635, 639 (Tex. 2013). For a conflict of interest to prevent class certification under rule 42(a)(4), the conflict must be fundamental and go to the heart of the litigation. *Riemer v. Texas,* 392 S.W.3d at 640–41 (potential relief in class action would not prevent settling class members from continuing to honor the settlement, and the conflict regarding the settlement did not go directly to the heart of the class action litigation); 452 S.W.3d 491 (Tex. App. 2014) (after remand following interlocutory appeal, the court denied class certification). A conflict that is merely speculative or hypothetical will not defeat the adequacy-of-representation requirement. *Emp'rs Cas. Co. v. Tex. Ass'n of School Bds. Workers' Comp. Self-Ins. Fund*, 886 S.W.2d470, 476 (Tex. App.—Austin 1994, writ dism'd w.o.j.).

c. Rule 42(b)(1) [equivalent to Federal Rule 23(b)(1)]

The Texas rule, like the Federal rule, allows a class action when prosecution of separate actions by or against individual members of the class would create a risk of either (1) inconsistent or varying adjudications with respect to individual members of the class that would establish incompatible standards of conduct for the party opposing the class, or (2) adjudications with respect to individual members of the class that would as a practical matter be dispositive of the interests of the other members not parties to the adjudications or substantially impair or impede their ability to protect their interests.

An investors' suit against former officers and directors of financial investment company which had filed for bankruptcy satisfied class action jurisdiction, because prosecution of separate actions by or against individual members of proposed class of investors would create risk of inconsistent or varying adjudications and would establish incompatible standards of conduct for party opposing class. *Adams v. Reagan*, 791 S.W.2d 284, 291 (Tex. App.—Fort Worth 1990). Invocation of this section based on a limited fund theory requires more than a mere assertion in the pleadings. *St. Louis Southwestern Ry. Co. v. Voluntary Purchasing Groups, Inc.*, 929 S.W.2d 25, 33 (Tex. App.—Texarkana 1996).

d. Rule 42(b)(2) [equivalent to Federal Rule 23(b)(2)]

A class may be certified pursuant to Rule 42(b)(2) for injunctive or declaratory purposes when the "party opposing the class has acted or refused to act on grounds generally applicable to the class." "Nonequitable monetary relief may be obtained in a (b)(2) class action only if the predominant relief sought is injunctive or declaratory." *Dairyland County Mut. Ins. Co. of Texas v. Casburg*, 63 S.W.3d 590, 592 (Tex. App.—Beaumont 2001). At least one court has permitted this section to be used against a defendant class. *Wiggins v. Enserch Exploration, Inc.*, 743 S.W.2d 332, Tex. App.—Dallas 1987).

In 2004, the Texas Supreme Court significantly changed the landscape of (b)(2) classes when it decided *Compaq Computer Corp. v. Lapray*, 135 S.W.3d 657 (Tex. 2004):

> We now turn to whether parties may evade *Bernal*[1] by seeking (b)(2) certification. Put simply, they may not. Although (b)(2) does not explicitly require predominance and superiority as (b)(3) does, (b)(2) does require a rigorous analysis of "cohesiveness." *Id.*, at 670. . . . We disagree, therefore, with the trial court's statement that '[n]amed Plaintiffs are not required to show predominance, superiority, or manageability in order to certify a class under TRCP 42(b)(2). Similarly, parties cannot evade the 'rigorous analysis' requirement by seeking (b)(2) certification.

Id. at 671.

This is an amazing job of grafting the more rigorous (b)(3) damages class standards onto (b)(2) injunctive class jurisprudence. Lest there be any doubt that it intended to make injunctive classes more difficult to certify, the Court added that "In many cases, this analysis will be identical to the 'predominance and superiority' directive undertaken by trial courts certifying (b)(3) classes." *Id.*

In a mandatory class, the Court added, a (b)(2) class "may require more cohesiveness" than a (b)(3) class. *Id.*

Thus, the Court has made it generally more difficult to certify an injunction-only class than a damages class. But the Court allows for a possible out: "Of course, if a trial court determines that notice and opt-out should be provided in the (b)(2) setting, the cohesiveness required in a (b)(2) class *need not be greater than the predominance and superiority* necessary for a class certified under (b)(3)." *Id.* (emphasis added).

Thus, at best, certification under (b)(2) of an injunctive class, where the class is not releasing any rights, is as difficult as a (b)(3) class, which is as difficult in Texas as anywhere in the nation.

e. Rule 42(b)(3) [equivalent to Federal Rule 23(b)(3)]

To maintain a lawsuit as class action under this section, the named plaintiff must show "both that the questions of law or fact common to the members of the class predominate over any questions affecting only individual members, and that a class action is superior to other available methods for the fair and efficient adjudication of the controversy." *TCI Cablevision of Dallas, Inc. v. Owens*, 8 S.W.3d 837, 842 (Tex. App.—Beaumont 2000).

In applying this section, the trial court must consider "(A) the interest of members of the class in individually controlling the prosecution or defense of separate actions; (B) the extent and nature of any litigation concerning the controversy already commenced by or against members of the class; (C) the desirability or undesirability of concentrating the litigation of the claims in the particular forum; (D) the difficulties likely to be encountered in the management of a class action." *Snyder Communications, L.P. v. Magana*, 142 S.W.3d 295, 299 (Tex. 2004).

"In evaluating whether common issues predominate, courts must identify the controlling substantive issues of the case and assess which issues will predominate to determine whether those issues are in fact common to the class. Courts must therefore determine 'whether common or individual issues will be the object of most of the efforts of the litigants and the court.' If there are some common questions of law or fact, but the focus of the litigation will be mainly on individual issues, the court cannot certify the class under Rule 42(b)(3)." *Id.* (internal references omitted). The predominance inquiry applies to common defenses as well as common claims. *Stonebridge Life Ins. Co. v. Pitts*, 236 S.W.3d 201, 206-207 (Tex. 2007). This requirement does not mean that all questions of

[1] Southwestern Refining Co., Inc. v. Bernal, 22 S.W.3d 425 (Tex. 2000)—one of the cases from 2000 discussed above.

law and fact must be identical, but that an issue of law or fact exists that inheres in the complaints of all the class members. *Entex, a Div. of Noram Energy Corp. v. City of Pearland*, 990 S.W.2d 904, 919 (Tex. App.—Houston [14 Dist.] 1999).

For example, "predominance is not defeated when the doctrines used by plaintiffs for tolling a statute of limitations involve proof common to the defendants." *Lon Smith & Assocs., Inc. v. Key*, 527 S.W.3d 604, 631 (Tex. App. 2017), *review den.* (June 15, 2018). Similarly, "[c]lass certification will not be prevented merely because damages must be determined separately for each class member. Likewise, defensive issues peculiar to different members do not destroy the entire class." *TCI Cablevision of Dallas, Inc. v. Owens*, 8 S.W.3d 837, 846 (Tex. App.—Beaumont 2000) (internal quotation omitted); *accord, Lon Smith & Assocs., Inc. v. Key*, 527 S.W.3d 604, 632 (Tex. App. 2017), *review den.* (June 15, 2018).

On the same day in May 2023, the Texas Supreme Court issued three opinions on the plaintiff's burden at class certification. Together, they auger an even higher threshold than previously existed. First, in *Mosaic Baybrook One, L.P. v. Cessor*, 668 S.W.3d 611 (Tex. Sup. 2023), the court reversed certification because the trial court did not "list or analyze the elements of Mosaic's defenses," even though the defenses were only raised in a "late amended answer submitted without leave of court three days before the certification hearing, and Mosaic did not bring them to the trial court's attention in connection with the motion for class certification, as our rules required it to do." *Id.* Certification by ambush would seem to be the rule now.

Second, in *American Campus Communities, Inc. v. Berry*, 667 S.W.3d 277 (Tex. Sup. 2023), the Court reversed certification by reaching an issue of law not before the Court—whether the property code's requirement that a "lease must contain language in underlined or bold print that informs the tenant of the remedies available under this section." Tex. Prop. Code § 92.056(g). Defendant had moved for summary judgment on this point, but the trial court denied that motion and the defendant did not appeal that ruling. Undeterred, the Court chose to reach the merits of that point and ruled for defendant, concluding that this vitiated the certification. Twisting the knife for future tenants, the Court noted that "It is surely true, as the plaintiffs point out, that omitting the required lease language might leave tenants unaware of their repair rights and therefore less likely to assert rights the Legislature has afforded them. And it is surely true that authorizing lawsuits for omission of the lease term would encourage compliance by landlords and more robustly empower tenants." *Id.* at 288.

Third, in another certification under the Property Code regarding a landlord's duty to repair, *Mosaic Baybrook One, L.P. v. Simien,* 2023 WL 3027992 (Tex. Sup. 2023), the Court used similar logic as it used in *Mosaic Baybrook One, L.P. v. Cessor,* 668 S.W.3d 611 (Tex. Sup. 2023), and *American Campus Communities, Inc.,* holding that "[w]hen a trial court's certification order reveals an incorrect understanding of a claim or defense that may have materially impacted its analysis of a certification requirement, it is not for a reviewing court to guess whether the trial court would still have exercised its discretion to certify a class had its understanding been correct." *Simien*, 2023 WL 3027992.

The courts of appeal have not hesitated to apply the strictures of the Supreme Court. For example, a court of appeals recently concluded that, although the class representatives had standing to assert a claim, it should decertify because the district court opinion did not adequately address Pentair's defenses. *Pentair Residential Filtration, LLC v. Belsome*, 2024 WL 3995436 (Tex. App.—Houston [1st Dist.] (2024)).

The Texas Supreme Court is very skeptical of the ability of a court to certify a multi-state class action that involves state law. "If the laws of fifty-one jurisdictions apply in this class action, the variations in the laws of the states and District of Columbia 'may swamp any common issues and defeat predominance.'" *Compaq Computer Corp. v. Lapray*, 135 S.W.3d 657, 672 (Tex. 2004) (citing *Castano v. Am. Tobacco Co.,* 84 F.3d 734, 741 (5th Cir.1996)). Any consideration of multi-state certification must, not surprisingly, involve a "critical analysis." *Id.* A trial court must decide conflict of laws issues before it certifies a class. *Id.,* 135 S.W.3d at 680; *State Farm Mutual Automobile Ins. Co. v. Lopez*, 156 S.W.3d 550, 557 (Tex. 2004); *Nat'l Western Life Ins. Co. v. Rowe*, 164 S.W.3d 389, 391 (Tex. 2005).

f. Rule 42(c) [comparable to Federal Rule 23(c)]

The Texas rule provides that "the court must—at an early practicable time—determine by order whether to certify the action as a class action." This is identical to Rule 23(c)(1)(a).

The Texas rule also requires far more detail than the corresponding federal rule, specifying that an order certifying a class action "must define the class and the class claims, issues, or defenses, and must appoint class counsel."

Departing from prior practice, the rule expressly requires that any order *granting or denying certification* of a class for damages under Rule 42(b)(3) must state:

(i) the elements of each claim or defense asserted in the pleadings;
(ii) any issues of law or fact common to the class members;
(iii) any issues of law or fact affecting only individual class members;
(iv) the issues that will be the object of most of the efforts of the litigants and the court;
(v) other available methods of adjudication that exist for the controversy;
(vi) why the issues common to the members of the class do or do not predominate over individual issues;
(vii) why a class action is or is not superior to other available methods for the fair and efficient adjudication of the controversy; and
(viii) if a class is certified, how the class claims and any issues affecting only individual members, raised by the claims or defenses asserted in the pleadings, will be tried in a manageable, time efficient manner.

Tex. R. Civ. P. 42(c)(1)(D).

This is an innovative and important development, because it requires that a court denying class certification conduct as rigorous an analysis as a court that certifies a class, and to give its reasoning. However, at least one court of appeals has concluded that the Texas Supreme Court's "rigorous analysis" requirement is a one-way street—that a trial court does not have to engage in rigorous analysis if it is refusing to certify a class action, but only when it rules for the plaintiff. "In *Lapray,* the supreme court was addressing a trial court's order *certifying* a nationwide class—not denying certification." *Solotko v. LegalZoom.com, Inc.*, 03-10-00755-CV, 2013 WL 3724770 (Tex. App. July 11, 2013), *review denied* (Dec. 13, 2013). This case appears to be an incorrect outlier.

The rule also confirms that certifications under (b)(1) and (b)(2) do not require notice to the class, but that a court has discretion to order notice. Tex. R. Civ. P. 42(c)(2)(A). In fact, however, the Texas Supreme Court held—after it adopted the amendment to the rule—that "trial courts considering certification under (b)(2) must consider, and due process may require, individual notice and opt-out rights to class members who seek monetary damages under any theory." *Compaq Computer Corp. v. Lapray*, 135 S.W.3d 657, 667 (Tex. 2004).

As to a (b)(3) damages class, the rule attempts to ensure that a minimal amount of information to class members is clearly provided.

The notice must concisely and clearly state in plain, easily understood language:

(i) the nature of the action;
(ii) the definition of the class certified;
(iii) the class claims, issues, or defenses;
(iv) that a class member may enter an appearance through counsel if the member so desires;
(v) that the court will exclude from the class any member who requests exclusion, stating when and how members may elect to be excluded; and
(vi) the binding effect of a class judgment on class members under Rule 42 (c)(3).

Courts have recently considered notice by text message, in addition to mail and email notice. Noting that "first-class mail, like payphones and dial-up internet, is quickly fading into obscurity," a court examined the use of text messaging as effective notice. "While e-mail is engrained in the fabric of our world's communication structure, there is no denying that it has become saturated and unwieldy. The cheery days of 'You've got mail!' are long gone. Now, our virtual mailboxes are inundated with hundreds or thousands of messages. . . . Unlike e-mail, text messages, at the very least, have eyes laid on them before being opened or ignored. . . . Accordingly, in light of the over-arching goal of providing potential class members the opportunity to join the case, the court finds that providing notice via text message serves to further the FLSA's remedial purpose." *Thrower v. UniversalPegasus, Int'l Inc.*, No. 3:19-CV-00068, 2020 WL 5258521, at *11–13 (S.D. Tex. Sept. 3, 2020); *accord, Field v. Anadarko Petroleum Corp.*, No. 4:20-CV-00575, 2020 WL 6075633, at *5 (S.D. Tex. Oct. 15, 2020). Other courts disagree. "Text messages and phone calls can present invasion of privacy concerns . . . . [I]t does not appear to be necessary here in addition to regular mail and email." *Macias v. Catapult Painting, LLC*, No. CV H-19-4856, 2020 WL 6253589, at *5 (S.D. Tex. Oct. 22, 2020).

g. Rule 42(e) [comparable to Federal Rule 23(c)]

In *Frisco Med. Ctr. v. Chestnut*, No. 23-0039 (Tex. May 17, 2024), the Texas Supreme Court extended its holding in *Citizens Ins. v. Daccach*, 217 S.W.3d 430 (Tex. 2007). "In *Daccach*, we cautioned "that Rule 42(d) cannot be used to manufacture compliance with the certification prerequisites." 217 S.W.3d at 455. Instead, Rule 42(d), "like its federal counterpart, 'is a housekeeping rule that allows courts to sever the common issues for a class trial.'" In other words, don't try using a "housekeeping" rule if the case isn't certifiable under Rule 42(b) and (c).

h. Rule 42(e) [comparable to Federal Rule 23(c)]

The Texas rule provides that a class that has been certified must be approved before it is settled, dismissed, or otherwise compromised. This tracks federal practice but makes that practice unavoidably clear.

The rule clearly does not require a hearing prior to settlement, dismissal or compromise of a case filed as a class action, but not yet certified. *Ventura v. Banales*, 905 S.W.2d 423, 426 (Tex. App.—Corpus Christi 1995, no writ). Notwithstanding this, it is better practice to advise the court of the settlement of an uncertified class and obtain a corresponding order of dismissal.

Rule 42(e) provides details for the manner in which the court reviews any settlement of a certified class. "Notice of the material terms of the proposed settlement, dismissal or compromise, together with an explanation of when and how the members may elect to be excluded from the class, shall be given to all members in such manner as the court directs." Presumably, the court has discretion whether to require notice in a settled (b)(1) or (b)(2) class, as long as the settlement has no binding effect on class members, but this issue is not resolved. Properly addressed first class mail to class members is sufficient to satisfy class members' due process rights. *Barkley v. Texas Windstorm Ins. Ass'n*, 14-11-00941-CV, 2013 WL 5434171 (Tex. App. Sept. 26, 2013).

Clearly, notice of any settlement of a (b)(3) damages class must be given to class members. Even before the 2004 amendments, notice was emphasized. *Peters v. Blockbuster*, 65 S.W.3d 295, 309 (Tex. App.—Beaumont 2001). However, "class members need not be made cognizant of every material fact that has taken place prior to the mailing of their individual notice." *Peters v. Blockbuster*, 65 S.W.3d 295, 309 (Tex. App.—Beaumont 2001) (internal citation omitted).

Notice that does not provide the class information about class counsel's attorneys' fees sought is fatally defective. *General Motors Corp. v. Bloyed*, 916 S.W.2d 949, 958 (Tex. 1996).

The rule requires a second notice in the settlement of a case where the class members have already been given notice. The "court may not approve a settlement unless it affords a new opportunity to request exclusion to individual class members who had an earlier opportunity to request exclusion but did not do so."

For any resolution that would bind class members, a hearing is mandatory, at which the court must find that the settlement, dismissal, or compromise is "fair, reasonable, and adequate."

After a class is certified, a change to the nature of the case, such as dropping some causes of action, may require notice to the class and approval by the trial court. *J.C. Penney Co., Inc., v. Pitts*, 139 S.W.3d 455, 460 (Tex. App. 2004).

Standing to object is clear. Any class member may object to any settlement for which court approval is required. However, in an apparent attempt to curb the activities of shakedown objectors who object only to line their own pockets, the rule provides that any such objection "may be withdrawn only with the court's approval."

i. Rule 42(f) [no equivalent Federal Rule]

Unnamed members of a class action are not to be considered as parties for purposes of discovery. However, one appellate court went to great lengths to accommodate a defendants' demand to take six-hour depositions (the maximum allowed by the Texas rules of civil procedure) of "six intervenors who are putative class members," even though a motion for class certification had not yet been filed, and therefore issued an order of mandamus to the trial court directing it to allow all 36 hours of planned depositions. *In re Topletz*, No. 05-17-00315-CV, 2017 WL 3634296, at *2 (Tex. App. Aug. 24, 2017).

j. Rule 42(g) [comparable to Federal Rule 23(g)]

The rule adds significant requirements to appointment of class counsel, going beyond the traditional requirement of adequacy, in much the same manner as Federal Rule 23(g). The court *must* consider (1) the work counsel has done in identifying or investigating potential claims in the action, (2) counsel's experience in handling class actions, other complex litigation, and claims of the type asserted in the action, (3) counsel's knowledge of the applicable law, and (4) the resources counsel will commit to representing the class. In addition, the court *may* consider (1) any other matter pertinent to counsel's ability to fairly and adequately represent the interests of the class, and (2) direct potential class counsel to provide information on any subject pertinent to the appointment and to propose terms for attorney fees and nontaxable costs. The latter provision appears to invite competitive bids by opposing counsel. The rule further provides that the "order appointing class counsel may include provisions about the award of attorney fees or nontaxable costs."

The rule allows the court to designate "interim counsel to act on behalf of the putative class" before making the class certification decision. This would appear to foster a race to the courthouse for competing classes, but it also may resolve that competition by making it clear who represents the class. The binding effect of this decision on a case pending in another state or federal court is likely to be minimal.

k. Rule 42(h) and (i) [comparable to Federal Rule 23(h)]

The Texas rule contains detailed provisions about award of class counsel fees, in significantly more detail than Federal Rule 23(h).

Any claim for fees must be made by motion and notice must be directed to class members. Any class member, or the defendant, may object.

The court must hold a hearing "in open court" and find facts and make conclusions of law either orally on the record or in writing.

Prior to 2003, class counsel's attorneys' fees could be calculated using either a percentage or lodestar method. *General Motors Corp. v. Bloyed*, 916 S.W.2d 949, 960–61 (Tex. 1996).

Incorporating provisions of 2003 Texas legislation, Tex. Civ. Practice & Remedies Code § 26.003, the amended rule prohibits any fee determination other than a lodestar calculation. Thus, percentage recoveries are out. However, the rule expressly allows a multiplier of 400 percent on the lodestar amount. On the other hand, the rule also allows reduction of the lodestar amount to as little as 25 percent. The logic of the latter provision is unclear, since a lodestar calculation by its very nature involves determination of a reasonable hourly fee and reasonable time spent. Thus, any reduction from the amount determined to be reasonable as a lodestar would itself appear to be unreasonable.

In a truly innovative development, also in compliance with the 2003 legislation, the rule provides for fees when there are coupons as part of the class settlement. "If any portion of the benefits recovered for the class are in the form of coupons or other noncash common benefits, the *attorney fees awarded in the action must be in cash and noncash amounts in the same proportion as the recovery* for the class." Goose, meet gander.

Two Texas courts of appeal separately interpreted this language to conclude that attorneys' fees to class counsel were precluded when the class received injunctive relief (in the form of additional disclosures) but no cash. *Rocker v. Centex Corp.*, 377 S.W.3d 907, 922 (Tex. App. 2012); *Kazman v. Frontier Oil Corp.*, 398 S.W.3d 377, 387 (Tex. App. 2013). These opinions appear clearly erroneous, as the statutory basis for these decisions did not address injunctive relief but rather damages that were paid in something other than cash ("coupons or other noncash common benefits"). Tex. Civ. Prac. & Rem. Code § 26.003(b). Rule 42(b)(2) expressly contemplates injunctive-only classes. It is noteworthy that the Texas Supreme Court granted review of *Rocker* and set aside the opinion (later remanding after the parties settled).

A probably unique provision in Rule 42 allows Texas courts to increase or decrease lodestar fees in class actions. "In awarding attorney fees, the court must first determine a lodestar figure by multiplying the number of hours reasonably worked times a reasonable hourly rate. The attorney fees award must be in the range of 25% to 400% of the lodestar figure." Tex. R. Civ. P. 42(i)(1). One case illustrates how this provision works. "A trial on attorney's fees only was held over several days in November 2016. The jury found that $812,332.50 was a reasonable fee for necessary services provided by class counsel in the trial court, and it assessed additional conditional amounts for representation on appeal. . . ." The court of appeal affirmed the decision of the trial court, which found that the class was entitled to a 'multiplier [of] 3.75 times the base lodestar . . . especially because of the risk and nature of contingent fee work, the length of time commitment required, the result obtained and the substantial and protracted costs incurred.'" *Farmers Grp., Inc. v. Geter*, No. 13-18-00187-CV, 2019 WL 5076510, at *3 (Tex. App. Oct. 10, 2019) (citing Tex. R. Civ. P. 42(i)(1)). The court of appeals affirmed an award of "$3,046,246.88 in trial attorney's fees, along with conditional appellate fees, and $486,789.97 in costs." *Farmers Grp., Inc. v. Geter*, 2019 WL 5076510, at *11. However, the Texas Supreme Court subsequently reversed on the merits and held that because the class had lost on the merits, no award of fees was proper. *Farmers Group, Inc. v. Geter*, 620 S.W.3d 702, 713 (2021).

3. MISCELLANEOUS COMMENTS

a. Settlement Class Standards

A trial court must conduct a plenary evidentiary hearing before approving a class settlement. Rule 42(e); *General Motors Corp. v. Bloyed*, 916 S.W.2d 949, 959 (Tex. 1996); *Northrup v. Southwestern Bell Telephone Co.*, 72 S.W.3d 1, 8 (Tex. App.—Corpus Christi 2001). "In making its class certification decision, the trial court can consider the pleadings and other material in the record, along with the evidence presented at the hearing. The evidence on which a trial court bases its certification ruling need not be in a form necessary to be admissible at trial." *National Western Life Ins. Co. v. Rowe*, 86 S.W.3d 285, 293 (Tex. App. 2002) (internal citation omitted).

Because of various concerns particular to class action settlements, a trial court must "independently determine that the requirements of Rule 42 have been scrupulously met, in their entirety, before approving any class action settlement." *General Motors Corp. v. Bloyed*, 916 S.W.2d 949, 955 (Tex. 1996). The Texas Supreme Court subsequently said that a trial court must make at least some Rule 42(a) determinations before it permits the named plaintiff and plaintiff's counsel to settle on behalf of the class and send notice of the settlement to the class. *McAllen Medical Center, Inc. v. Cortez*, 66 S.W.3d 227, 234 (Tex. 2001). Specifically, the Supreme Court said that a trial court is required to give "heightened scrutiny" to the class definition, to typicality of claims, and to adequacy of representation by both the named plaintiff and would-be class counsel. *McAllen Medical*, 66 S.W.3d at 234.

These rulings appear quite clear, but the binding effect of them is somewhat blunted by the fact that the actual issue before the Court was whether a nonsettling defendant could appeal a trial court order that certified a "settlement-only" class and that gave "preliminary approval" to the settlement terms. The express holding of the Court was that a nonsettling defendant had the right to appeal a preliminary approval of class counsel and notice to the class, even before the fairness hearing, "if the nonsettling defendant can show that the certification adversely affects it." *McAllen Medical*, 66 S.W.3d at 235.

The best practice is that parties should present the various Rule 42(a) matters to the trial court for actual determination, with an evidentiary presentation, before entry of an order approving notice to the class. Because certification of a "settlement-only" class and "preliminary approval" of settlement terms are without any binding effect, *McAllen Medical*, 66 S.W.3d at 234, an order setting a fairness hearing should not contain language either certifying a "settlement-only" class or purporting to "approve" the settlement preliminarily. The order should contain preliminary approval of the class definition, and preliminary findings as to typicality and adequacy of both the class representative and class counsel.

b. Reliance

Any class action that is dependent on a showing of reliance by the class members will have a very difficult row to hoe. The Texas Supreme Court's seminal opinion on reliance said this:

> The Fifth Circuit has recently observed that if 'individual reliance is necessary to prove actual damages, a class action may not be certified on this issue.' We need not and do not decide whether a class asserting a cause of action requiring proof of reliance, like the class alleged here, can ever be certified. We hold only that the plaintiffs in this case have failed to show that individual issues of reliance do not preclude the necessary finding of predominance under Rule 42(b)(4).

Schein v. Stromboe, 102 S.W.3d 675, 694 (Tex. 2002) (citing *Perrone v. General Motors Acceptance Corp.,* 232 F.3d 433, 440 (5th Cir. 2000); *accord, Spector v. Norwegian Cruise Line Ltd.*, 2004 WL 637894, *2 (Tex. App.—Hous. [1st Dist.] 2004)).

"The question the court must decide before certifying a class, after rigorous analysis and not merely a lick and a prayer, is whether the plaintiffs have demonstrated that they can meet their burden of proof in such a way that common issues predominate over individual ones." *Schein v. Stromboe*, 102 S.W.3d 675, 695 (Tex. 2002).

Having stressed the burden, the Court lessened the sting somewhat: "This does not mean, of course, that reliance or other elements of their causes of action cannot be proved class-wide with evidence generally applicable to all class members; class-wide proof is possible when class-wide evidence exists." *Id.*, 102 S.W.3d at 693. The Court nonetheless stressed that "evidence insufficient to prove reliance in a suit by an individual does not become sufficient in a class action simply because there are more plaintiffs." *Id.*

Thus, while the Supreme Court did not bar the door to class-wide proof of reliance by inferential methods, survey evidence, or similar non-individualized proof, it nonetheless continued to restrict the nature of class actions that may be brought in Texas state courts. As the Corpus Christi Court of Appeals put it, "The court did not entirely preclude class actions in which reliance was an issue, but it did make such cases a near-impossibility. . . ." *Texas South Rentals, Inc. v. Gomez*, 267 S.W.3d 228, 237 (Tex. App.—Corpus Christi 2008) (citing *Fidelity and Guar. Life Ins. Co. v. Pina*, 165 S.W.3d 416, 423 (Tex. App.—Corpus Christi 2005)).

c. Communications with Class Members

As general precepts, counsel for the plaintiff in a class action may *always* communicate with members of the class and counsel for defendant may *never* communicate with members of a certified class. Texas law follows these precepts.

Pre-certification contact by a defendant is more restricted. A court may enter orders in class actions that govern the conduct of counsel and parties, including communications between the defendant and class members. *Hampton Hardware, Inc. v. Cotter & Co., Inc.*, 156 F.R.D. 630 (N.D. Tex. 1994). A trial court is the guardian of the class it certifies and may take necessary actions to police the conduct of the proceedings before it, contrary to the detached role a court plays in ordinary civil proceedings. *H & R Block, Inc. v. Haese*, 82 S.W.3d 331, 335 (Tex. App. 2000). A trial court is vested with all powers to take any action necessary to protect the integrity of a pending class action if it learns some party or counsel is improperly attempting to interfere with the orderly conduct of the action. *Id.* at 335.

However, because an order limiting communications between a defendant and class members may be a prior restraint of speech, *Bernard v. Gulf Oil Co.*, 619 F.2d 459, 467 (5th Cir.1980), aff'd, 452 U.S. 89, 101 S. Ct. 2193, 68 L. Ed. 2d 693 (1981), a "district court should only consider the narrowest possible relief that limits speech as little as possible consistent with the rights of the parties under the circumstances. The movant does not have to show specific detriments to plaintiffs or the plaintiff class. A showing of actual harm is not necessary." *Burrell v. Crown Cent. Petroleum, Inc.*, 176 F.R.D. 239, 243 (E.D. Tex. 1997) (internal citation and quotation omitted).

It is not enough that a potentially coercive situation exists. *Burrell v. Crown Cent. Petroleum, Inc.*, 176 F.R.D. 239, 244 (E.D. Tex. 1997). An order limiting a defendant's contacts with class members must be based on "a clear record and specific findings that reflect a weighing of the need for a limitation and the potential interference with the rights of the parties." *Id.* A "trial court only has authority to limit a defendant's communications with class members to the extent such contact jeopardizes the class action before it, and the order must be carefully drawn to limit speech and other contacts, as little as possible, consistent with the rights of the parties under the circumstances." *H & R Block*, 82 S.W.3d at 337.

"As commercial speech, ex parte communications tending to discourage absent class members from joining the suit may be limited by orders grounded in good cause and issued with a heightened sensitivity for First Amendment Concerns. Courts examine four criteria to determine good cause in this context: the severity and likelihood of the perceived harm, the precision with which the order is drawn, the availability of a less onerous alternative, and the duration of the order." *Belt v. Emcare, Inc.,* 299 F. Supp. 2d 664, 668 (E.D. Tex. 2003) (internal citation omitted).

d. Res Judicata

Any claims that are not capable of class resolution may nonetheless be subject to res judicata. That is, an issue that involves "too little commonality to allow for a class to survive the predominance requirements may still be precluded for later individual action." *Citizens Insurance Co. of America v. Daccach*, 217 S.W.3d 430, 451 (Tex. 2007). In addition, although "tactical and strategic decisions to structure the lawsuit"—by abandoning some claims in order to achieve commonality—are up to the class representatives, the "choice of claims to pursue or abandon is one relevant factor in evaluating the requirements for class certification." *Bowden v. Phillips Petroleum Co.*, 247 S.W.3d 690, 697–98 (Tex. 2008).

e. Standing of the Class Representative

Above and beyond requirements that the class representative be adequate is the requirement of standing. A court has jurisdiction over a class action only if the named class representative has individual standing at the time suit is filed. *M. D. Anderson Cancer Center v. Novak*, 52 S.W.3d 704, 711 (Tex. 2001). Standing requires an actual injury. *Id.* At the same, the Texas Supreme Court affirmed existing federal jurisprudence that it was not necessary for "the named plaintiff's personal stake in the lawsuit to continue throughout the entirety of the litigation." *Id.* (quoting *Sosna v. Iowa*, 419 U.S. 393, 402 (1975)). Thus, if the named plaintiff's grievance becomes moot over time, the initial standing that vested jurisdiction in the court does not evaporate. The Supreme Court has affirmed this principle, holding that claims "capable of repetition yet evading review" were not moot. *Texas A & M Univ.-Kingsville v. Yarbrough*, 347 S.W.3d 289, 290 (Tex. 2011). In 2016, one intermediate court expounded on this point. "The Supreme Court has explained that in the absence of a class action, the 'capable of repetition, yet evading review' doctrine is limited to the situation where two elements combine: (1) the challenged action is in its duration too short to be fully litigated prior to its cessation or expiration, and (2) there is a reasonable expectation that the same complaining party would be subjected to the same action again." *City of Cleveland v. Keep Cleveland Safe*, 500 S.W.3d 438, 454 (Tex. App. 2016) (internal citations and edits omitted).

Clearly, a class representative who sues for past wrongs can represent the class to recover for those past wrongs, even if she cannot seek to enjoin future bad acts because she no longer has a continuing relationship with the defendant. *Forth v. Allstate Indemnity Co.*, 151 S.W.3d 732, 737–38 (Tex. App. 2004). In addition, the Texas Supreme Court follows the federal exception to mootness for "inherently transitory" claims "where a population as a whole retains a live claim against the defendant, but the individual membership of that population is always changing due to the short-lived nature of the claim." *Heckman v. Williamson County*, 369 S.W.3d 137, 164 (Tex. 2012). In *Heckman*, the Court reaffirmed the continuing existence of the "capable of repetition" exception to mootness as well, distinguishing the two thus: "The two are similar in that the latter, like the former, requires a claim that is short-lived. The two exceptions differ, however, in that the 'capable of repetition' exception generally applies only if the plaintiff can show that the claim is capable of repetition *as to him*." *Id.* at 164 (emphasis in original; footnotes omitted). In another exception to mootness, a defendant's waiver of the charge on which suit was based, while the motion for certification was pending, does not moot the class claims because "the picking-off exception to the mootness doctrine applies . . . ." *Growden v. Good Shepherd Health Sys.,* 550 S.W.3d 716, 727 (Tex. App. 2018). That court also held that the issue of attorney's fees for bringing a declaratory judgment claim were similarly not moot. "[A] claim for attorney fees remains a live controversy, even if the substantive claims under the [Texas Declaratory Judgment Act] become moot during the pendency of the case." *Id.*, at 728 (citing *Camarena v. Texas Employment Comm'n*, 754 S.W.2d 149, 151 (Tex. 1988)).

The Texas Attorney General has standing to bring a class action on behalf of the State, and without including named plaintiffs, under the special provision of the Texas Insurance Code, but must satisfy the standard prerequisites. *Farmers Group, Inc. v. Lubin*, 222 S.W.3d 417 423 (Tex. 2007). In this opinion, the Texas Supreme Court rejected the court of appeals holding that the Attorney General had separate *parens patriae* authority. *Id.* However, a court of appeals held that actions filed by the Attorney General under the Texas Deceptive Trade Practices Act "qualify as de facto class actions." *Thomas v. State*, 226 S.W.3d 6, 70797 (Tex. App.—Corpus Christi 2007). This opinion was delivered two weeks before the Supreme Court's *Lubin* opinion, but the two opinions do not conflict—in *Lubin*, the Supreme Court interpreted a law with a special class action provision; in *Thomas*, the court of appeals interpreted a law that gave the Attorney General standing on behalf of the people. In 2008, the same court of appeals addressed the issue specifically and held that walking like a duck (read, "class action") does not make it a duck: "a request for restitution by the Attorney General perforce converts the DTPA [Texas Deceptive Trade Practices Act] action into a class action would impede its efficient and economical procedure to secure the protection of consumers from deceptive business practices. Requiring actions brought by the Attorney General under the DTPA to meet the class certification and notice requirements would impact their efficiency and economy of those actions." *Molano v. State*, 262 S.W.3d 554, 561 (Tex. App.—Corpus Christi 2008).

f. Standing and Intervention by Absent Class Members

The Texas Supreme Court affirmed the standing of an objector to overturn a class action settlement in *General Motors Corp. v. Bloyed*, 916 S.W.2d 949 (Tex. 1996). Although the objectors had intervened in that action, intervention is not required for an objecting class member to appeal a settlement. *Northrup v. Southwestern Bell Telephone Co.*, 72 S.W.3d 1, 10 (Tex. App.—Corpus Christi 2001). On the other hand, intervention is required for an absent class member to appeal a class action that is tried to judgment. *San Juan 1990-A, L.P. v. Meridian Oil Inc.*, 951 S.W.2d 159, 164 (Tex. App.—Houston [14 Dist.] 1997, pet. denied).

When objections are raised, class counsel do not have any "responsibility to represent the dissidents apart from their class representation. In fact, to represent the dissidents in connection with their appeal would have created a conflict of interest between class counsel and the class itself. Class counsel owes no duty to promote a position inconsistent with the definition of the class or contrary to the law." *Adame v. Law Office of Allison & Huerta*, No. 13-04-670-CV, 2008 WL 2151454, at *9 (Tex. App.—Corpus Christi 2008).

g. Discovery Limits

The Texas Supreme Court has rejected both a blanket rule that all class-wide discovery should be abated until after certification and its corollary, full classwide discovery before certification. The Court instead said that trial courts should limit pre-certification discovery to the particular issues governing certification in each case, considering factors such as the importance, benefit, burden, expense, and time needed to produce the proposed discovery. *In re Alford Chevrolet-Geo,* 997 S.W.2d 173, 185 (Tex. 1999); *In re SCI Texas Funeral Serv., Inc.,* 236 S.W.3d 759, 760–61 (Tex. 2007).

This creates a tension between the plaintiff's discovery rights—seemingly limited to discovery related to class certification issues—and the Texas Supreme Court's rule that a court must go "beyond the pleadings"—which perforce may involve an inquiry into the factual merits of the case *Southwestern Refining Co., Inc. v. Bernal*, 22 S.W.3d 425, 435 (Tex. 2000); *Union Pacific Resources Group, Inc. v. Hankins*, 111 S.W.3d 69, 72 (Tex. 2003). These two requirements can be reconciled by allowing discovery of the merits of the plaintiff's case prior to certification, but prohibiting discovery directed to a classwide determination of the merits, unless of course the defendant raises classwide issues such as reliance, common defenses, and the like—which of course it will.

Rule 42(f) expressly provides that unnamed members of a class are not to be considered parties for purposes of discovery. Although this is the general practice in federal court, Texas Rule 42 makes it the rule for Texas state courts. *General Motors Corp. v. Bloyed*, 916 S.W.2d 949 (Tex. 1996).

h. Trial Plan

The Texas Supreme Court held that it is "improper to certify a class without knowing how the claims can and will likely be tried." *Southwestern Refining Co., Inc. v. Bernal*, 22 S.W.3d 425, 435 (Tex. 2000). "To make a proper analysis, going beyond the pleadings is necessary, as a court must understand the claims, defenses, relevant facts, and applicable substantive law in order to make a meaningful determination of the certification issues. Any proposal to expedite resolving individual issues must not unduly restrict a party from presenting viable claims or defenses without that party's consent. . . . If it is not determinable from the outset that the individual issues can be considered in a manageable, time-efficient, yet fair manner, then certification is not appropriate." *Id.* at 435–36 (internal citations omitted).

After *Bernal*, numerous courts interpreted this holding to require a separate formal "trial plan," but the Supreme Court corrected that interpretation in 2002: "The plaintiffs argue correctly that *Bernal* should not be read to require a 'trial plan' by that name, set out in a separate document. Rule 42 does not require adoption of a trial plan as a mere formality; rather, according to *Bernal,* the rule requires a rigorous analysis and a specific explanation of how class claims are to proceed to trial." *Schein v. Stromboe*, 102 S.W.3d 675, 689 (Tex. 2002).

A trial plan is a necessity and must consider virtually every aspect of the class claims pled and all defenses raised. The Texas Supreme Court has faulted trial plans that did not contain a rigorous analysis of (1) all causes of action, (2) how those claims will be tried, (3) every controlling substantive issue, (4) whether or how individual issues related to limitations will be determined, (5) how it would dispose of issues of reliance, (6) how it would try damages, both actual and punitive, (7) why individual issues did not predominate, and (8) why a class action is superior to other methods of resolving the dispute. *State Farm Mutual Automobile Ins. Co. v. Lopez*, 156 S.W.3d 550, 557 (Tex. 2004) (first three points); *Nat'l Western Life Ins. Co. v. Rowe*, 164 S.W.3d 389 (Tex. 2005) (remaining points).

A good example of a trial plan is contained in the Appendix to *Gill v. Exxon Mobil Corp.*, 221 S.W.3d 841, 865 *ff.* (Tex. App.—Corpus Christi 2007). (The Texas Supreme Court subsequently reversed on other grounds but did not address the lower court's trial plan. *Exxon Mobil Corp. v. Gill*, 299 S.W.3d 124 (2009).)

i. Arbitrability of Class Claims

The Texas Supreme Court has affirmed that, when a contract is silent on class actions but contains a provision requiring all disputes to be arbitrated, the decision whether to arbitrate each claim separately or as a class is one for the arbitrator and not the trial court. *In re Wood*, 140 S.W.3d 367, 369 (Tex. 2004); *followed in Sam Houston Elec. Coop., Inc. v. Berry*, 582 S.W.3d 282, 293 (Tex. App. 2017) ("[W]here a claimant seeks to bring claims on behalf of a class, an otherwise valid arbitration provision must be enforced and the issue of class certification becomes one of contract construction appropriately left to the arbitrator.").

In 2023, the Court took silence one step further, holding that a party's mere agreement to arbitrate under AAA rules "establishes a clear and unmistakable agreement to delegate arbitrability issues to the arbitrator." *TotalEnergies E&P USA, Inc. v. MP Gulf of Mexico, LLC*, 667 S.W.3d 694, 701 (Tex. Sup. 2023). From a policy standpoint, it is sophistry to infer agreement with anything about arbitration, given that a consumer rarely sees anything about arbitration in the initial agreement.

In a case where the plaintiffs claimed that the defendant had waived its right to arbitrate by filing criminal charges, participating in criminal trials, and obtaining findings of guilt, thus substantially invoking judicial process, the Texas Supreme Court disagreed, holding (against all reason) that these actions "did not substantially invoke the judicial process." *Henry v. Cash Biz, LP*, 551 S.W.3d 111, 118 (Tex.), *cert. denied,* 139 S. Ct. 184, 202 L. Ed. 2d 40 (2018). The Court expressly refused to follow Fifth Circuit precedent to the contrary. "We recognize that our opinion does not accord with the decision in *Vine v. PLS Financial Services, Inc.*, 689 Fed. App'x 800 (5th Cir. 2017) (per curiam). . . . With due respect, and recognizing that it is important for federal and state law to be as consistent as possible in this area where we have concurrent jurisdiction, we agree with the dissenting justice in *Vine*. *Id.* at 807 (Higginson, J., dissenting). We conclude, as he did, that although some lenders may be 'gaming the system' by taking actions like the lenders took there and as Cash Biz took here, more is required for waiver of a contractual right to arbitrate." *Henry*, 551 S.W.3d at 118–19.

j. Removal

Although prior to enactment of the Class Action Fairness Act of 2005 (CAFA), amount in controversy for removal purposes was determined based on the value to the plaintiff of the relief sought ("plaintiff viewpoint") and not on the cost to the defendant ("defendant viewpoint"), *Garcia v. Koch*

Oil Co. of Texas, 351 F.3d 636, 640 n.4 (5th Cir. 2003), at least one federal magistrate judge has adopted the "either viewpoint" rule. *Rasberry v. Capitol County Mut. Fire. Ins. Co.*, 609 F. Supp. 2d 594, 600–01 (E.D. Tex. 2009). It does not appear that the Fifth Circuit has addressed this issue.

The Fifth Circuit has also not addressed the burden of proof on removal after CAFA, but it appears that the burden of proving federal jurisdiction remains on the removing defendant. *Id.; Werner v. KPMG LLP*, 415 F. Supp. 2d 688, 695 (S.D. Tex. 2006); *DeHart v. BP Am., Inc.*, 2010 WL 231744 (W.D. La. 2010).

k. Counterclaims

Although a counterclaim against the named plaintiff may be proper, a counterclaim against the class is improper unless the counterclaim complies with Rule 42's criteria regarding suits against a defendant class. *Parker County v. Spindletop Oil and Gas Co.*, 628 S.W.2d 765, 769 (Tex. 1982).

l. Interlocutory Appeal

A decision by a trial court to grant or deny class certification is immediately appealable. Tex. Civ. Prac. & Rem. Code § 51.014(a)(3); *Bowden v. Phillips Petroleum Co.*, 247 S.W.3d 690, 696 (Tex. 2008).

Any such interlocutory appeal stays all other proceedings in the trial court pending resolution of that appeal. Tex. Civ. Prac. & Rem. Code § 51.014(b). This provision stays any class action proceedings in the trial court while the appeal is pending, thus preventing notice to the class, trial of the certified class, or any other form of continued trial court oversight of the class certification.

An interlocutory appeal is limited strictly to the trial court's decision to grant or deny class certification, and other certification-related orders are not usually subject to an interlocutory appeal. *See Bally Total Fitness Corp. v. Jackson*, 53 S.W.3d 352, 359 (Tex. 2001) (post-certification order granting partial summary judgment to class and denying motions to de-certify are not subject to an interlocutory appeal); and *Union Pacific Resources Group, Inc. v. Hankins*, 51 S.W.3d 738, 740 (Tex. App.—El Paso 2001) (trial court entry of a trial plan subsequent to appeal of class certification is not subject to an interlocutory appeal); *but see De Los Santos v. Occidental Chemical Corp.*, 933 S.W.2d 493, 495 (Tex.1996) (post-certification order that changed a certified class from an opt-out class to a mandatory class and that created a conflict between class and counsel altered the fundamental nature of the certification and was therefore subject to an interlocutory appeal).

The Texas Government Code also allows appeal to the Supreme Court from a court of appeals decision in an interlocutory appeal from a trial court order that certifies or refuses to certify a class. Tex. Gov't Code § 22.225(d).

m. *Cy Pres* Distributions

Although Texas law does not expressly permit distribution of class action funds through *cy pres*, at least one court has approved the use of *cy pres*, at least in the settlement context. "It allows a trial court to fashion an equitable remedy to distribute settlement funds in a class action when the costs of distribution outweigh the individual share to which each class member is entitled. Distributing litigation proceeds through *cy pres* satisfies class action goals by deterring similar conduct and disgorging the defendant of profits wrongfully obtained, and using those funds in a way that at least indirectly benefits the class members." *Northrup v. Southwestern Bell Telephone Co.*, 72 S.W.3d 16,

21–22 (Tex. App.—Corpus Christi 2002). However, that court added that because "there is no authority disallowing such settlements, we cannot say the trial court abused its discretion," *id.*, so this is not exactly conclusive authority. Recently the Texas Supreme Court rejected a petition by the State seeking to deny the use of *cy pres* and instead treat unclaimed settlement funds as abandoned property. The State argued that *cy pres* awards in class actions violate the Texas Unclaimed Property Act, and any unclaimed settlement money should instead be delivered to the state Comptroller. The Court rejected the State's argument, holding that application of the Act "cannot succeed unless class representatives' authority to act for class members under Rule 42 is disregarded." *Highland Homes Ltd. v. The State of Texas*, 448 S.W.3d 403, 412 (Tex. 2014). However, the Court noted that its ruling did not address the State's more general contention that *cy pres* awards can be abused. *Id.* at 412 ("We need not take sides on this disagreement today.").

n. Tolling

Texas recognizes *American Pipe* tolling—the filing of a putative class action in a Texas state court suspends the running of limitation for all purported members of the class. *Asplundh Tree Expert Co. v. Abshire,* 517 S.W.3d 320, 337 (Tex. App. 2017); *Clark v. ConocoPhillips Co.,* 465 S.W.3d 720, 727 (Tex. App. 2015). However, in federal courts, tolling ends when a district court denies class certification. In Texas, interlocutory orders of Texas state courts granting or denying class certification are appealable as of right, and "the judgment of a court of appeals hearing an interlocutory appeal only takes effect when the mandate issues, and the mandate need not issue while a party seeks review in the Supreme Court of Texas." *Clark v. ConocoPhillips Co.,* 465 S.W.3d at 727. Given the differences between state and federal appellate procedures, tolling extends through State Supreme Court review. *Id.*

The United States Supreme Court recently limited *American Pipe* tolling to individual claims only, not new class actions, seeing no "reason to permit plaintiffs to exhume failed class actions by filing new, untimely class claims." *China Agritech, Inc. v. Resh*, 138 S. Ct. 1800, 1811 (2018). As of the date of writing this chapter, the author could not find any Texas case that addressed this holding, although it seems certain that Texas courts would follow this ruling.

RULE 42. CLASS ACTIONS

(a) **Prerequisites to a Class Action.** One or more members of a class may sue or be sued as representative parties on behalf of all only if

(1) the class is so numerous that joinder of all members is impracticable,

(2) there are questions of law or fact common to the class,

(3) the claims or defenses of the representative parties are typical of the claims or defenses of the class, and

(4) the representative parties will fairly and adequately protect the interests of the class.

(b) **Class Actions Maintainable.** An action may be maintained as a class action if the prerequisites of subdivision (a) are satisfied, and in addition:

(1) the prosecution of separate actions by or against individual members of the class would create a risk of

(A) inconsistent or varying adjudications with respect to individual members of the class which would establish incompatible standards of conduct for the party opposing the class, or

(B) adjudications with respect to individual members of the class which would as a practical matter be dispositive of the interests of the other members not parties to the adjudications or substantially impair or impede their ability to protect their interests; or

(2) the party opposing the class has acted or refused to act on grounds generally applicable to the class, thereby making appropriate final injunctive relief or corresponding declaratory relief with respect to the class as a whole; or

(3) the questions of law or fact common to the members of the class predominate over any questions affecting only individual members, and a class action is superior to other available methods for the fair and efficient adjudication of the controversy. The matters pertinent to these issues include:

(A) the interest of members of the class in individually controlling the prosecution or defense of separate actions;

(B) the extent and nature of any litigation concerning the controversy already commenced by or against members of the class;

(C) the desirability or undesirability of concentrating the litigation of the claims in the particular forum;

(D) the difficulties likely to be encountered in the management of a class action

(c) **Determination by Order Whether to Certify a Class Action; Notice and Membership in Class.**

(1) (A) When a person sues or is sued as a representative of a class, the court must—at an early practicable time—determine by order whether to certify the action as a class

action.

(B) An order certifying a class action must define the class and the class claims, issues, or defenses, and must appoint class counsel under Rule 42 (g).

(C) An order under Rule 42 (c)(1) may be altered or amended before final judgment. The court may order the naming of additional parties in order to insure the adequacy of representation.

(D) An order granting or denying certification under Rule 42(b)(3) must state:

(i) the elements of each claim or defense asserted in the pleadings;

(ii) any issues of law or fact common to the class members;

(iii) any issues of law or fact affecting only individual class members;

(iv) the issues that will be the object of most of the efforts of the litigants and the court;

(v) other available methods of adjudication that exist for the controversy;

(vi) why the issues common to the members of the class do or do not predominate over individual issues;

(vii) why a class action is or is not superior to other available methods for the fair and efficient adjudication of the controversy; and

(viii) if a class is certified, how the class claims and any issues affecting only individual members, raised by the claims or defenses asserted in the pleadings, will be tried in a manageable, time efficient manner.

(2) (A) For any class certified under Rule 42(b)(1) or (2), the court may direct appropriate notice to the class. For any class certified under Rule 42(b)(3), the court must direct to class members the best notice practicable under the circumstances including individual notice to all members who can be identified through reasonable effort. The notice must concisely and clearly state in plain, easily understood language:

(i) the nature of the action;

(ii) the definition of the class certified;

(iii) the class claims, issues, or defenses;

(iv) that a class member may enter an appearance through counsel if the member so desires;

(v) that the court will exclude from the class any member who requests exclusion, stating when and how members may elect to be excluded; and

(vi) the binding effect of a class judgment on class members under Rule 42 (c)(3).

(3) The judgment in an action maintained as a class action under subdivisions (b)(1) or (b)(2), whether or not favorable to the class, shall include and describe those whom the court finds to be members of the class. The judgment in an action maintained as a

class action under subdivision (b)(4), whether or not favorable to the class, shall include and specify or describe those to whom the notice provided in subdivision (c)(2) was directed, and who have not requested exclusion, and whom the court finds to be members of the class.

(d) **Actions Conducted Partially as Class Actions; Multiple Classes and Subclasses.**

When appropriate

(1) an action may be brought or maintained as a class action with respect to particular issues, or

(2) a class may be divided into subclasses and each subclass treated as a class, and the provisions of this rule shall then be construed and applied accordingly.

(e) **Settlement, Dismissal or Compromise.**

(1) (A) The court must approve any settlement, dismissal, or compromise of the claims, issues, or defenses of a certified class.

(B) Notice of the material terms of the proposed settlement, dismissal or compromise, together with an explanation of when and how the members may elect to be excluded from the class, shall be given to all members in such manner as the court directs.

(C) The court may approve a settlement, dismissal, or compromise that would bind class members only after a hearing and on finding that the settlement, dismissal, or compromise is fair, reasonable, and adequate.

(2) The parties seeking approval of a settlement, dismissal, or compromise under Rule 42(e)(1) must file a statement identifying any agreement made in connection with the proposed settlement, dismissal, or compromise.

(3) In an action previously certified as a class action under Rule 42(b)(3), the court may not approve a settlement unless it affords a new opportunity to request exclusion to individual class members who had an earlier opportunity to request exclusion but did not do so.

(4) (A) Any class member may object to a proposed settlement, dismissal, or compromise that requires court approval under Rule 42(e)(1)(A).

(B) An objection made under Rule 42(e)(4)(A) may be withdrawn only with the court's approval.

(f) **Discovery.** Unnamed members of a class action are not to be considered as parties for purposes of discovery.

(g) **Class Counsel.**

(1) Appointing Class Counsel.

(A) Unless a statute provides otherwise, a court that certifies a class must appoint class counsel.

(B) An attorney appointed to serve as class counsel must fairly and adequately represent the interests of the class.

(C) In appointing class counsel, the court

(i) must consider:

— the work counsel has done in identifying or investigating potential claims in the action;

— counsel's experience in handling class actions, other complex litigation, and claims of the type asserted in the action;

— counsel's knowledge of the applicable law; and

— the resources counsel will commit to representing the class;

(ii) may consider any other matter pertinent to counsel's ability to fairly and adequately represent the interests of the class;

(iii) may direct potential class counsel to provide information on any subject pertinent to the appointment and to propose terms for attorney fees and nontaxable costs; and

(iv) may make further orders in connection with the appointment.

(2) Appointment Procedure.

(A) The court may designate interim counsel to act on behalf of the putative class before determining whether to certify the action as a class action.

(B) When there is one applicant for appointment as class counsel, the court may appoint that applicant only if the applicant is adequate under Rule 42(g)(1)(B) and (C). If more than one adequate applicant seeks appointment as class counsel, the court must appoint the applicant or applicants best able to represent the interests of the class.

(C) The order appointing class counsel may include provisions about the award of attorney fees or nontaxable costs under Rule 42(h) and (i).(h) Procedure for determining Attorney Fees Award. In an action certified as a class action, the court may award attorney fees in accordance with subdivision (i) and nontaxable costs authorized by law or by agreement of the parties as follows:

(i) Motion for Award of Attorney Fees. A claim for an award of attorney fees and nontaxable costs must be made by motion, subject to the provisions of this subdivision, at a time set by the court. Notice of the motion must be served on all parties and, for motions by class counsel, directed to class members in a reasonable manner.

(ii) Objections to Motion. A class member, or a party from whom payment is sought, may object to the motion.

(iii) Hearing and Findings. The court must hold a hearing in open court and must find the facts and state its conclusions of law on the motion. The court must state its findings and conclusions in writing or orally on the record.

(h) Procedure for determining Attorney Fees Award. In an action certified as a class action, the court may award attorney fees in accordance with subdivision (i) and nontaxable costs authorized by law or by agreement of the parties as follows:

(1) Motion for Award of Attorney Fees. A claim for an award of attorney fees and nontaxable costs must be made by motion, subject to the provisions of this subdivision, at a time set by the court. Notice of the motion must be served on all parties and, for motions by class counsel, directed to class members in a reasonable manner.

(2) Objections to Motion. A class member, or a party from whom payment is sought, may object to the motion.

(3) Hearing and Findings. The court must hold a hearing in open court and must find the facts and state its conclusions of law on the motion. The court must state its findings and conclusions in writing or orally on the record.

(i) **Attorney's Fees Award.**

(1) In awarding attorney fees, the court must first determine a lodestar figure by multiplying the number of hours reasonably worked times a reasonable hourly rate. The attorney fees award must be in the range of 25% to 400% of the lodestar figure. In making these determinations, the court must consider the factors specified in Rule 1.04(b), Tex. Disciplinary R. Prof. Conduct.

(2) If any portion of the benefits recovered for the class are in the form of coupons or other noncash common benefits, the attorney fees awarded in the action must be in cash and noncash amounts in the same proportion as the recovery for the class.

(j) Effective Date. Rule 42(i) applies only in actions filed after September 1, 2003.

Chapter author Stephen Gardner is a consultant on class action and food regulatory issues. Previously, Steve was Consumer Litigation Coordinator for Texas RioGrande Legal Aid; Of Counsel to the Dallas-based Stanley Law Group, a plaintiff firm; Director of Litigation for the Washington, DC-based advocacy group Center for Science in the Public Interest (CSPI); Of Counsel to the National Consumer Law Center; Assistant Dean of Clinical Education at Southern Methodist University School of Law; Visiting Assistant Professor of Law at Southern Methodist University School of Law; Assistant Attorney General in the Consumer Protection Division of the State of Texas; Assistant Attorney General in the Bureau of Consumer Frauds of the State of New York; Students Attorney at the University of Texas; and a staff attorney at Texas RioGrande Legal Aid.

UTAH

1. COMPARISON WITH RULE 23 OF THE FEDERAL RULES OF CIVIL PROCEDURE

Utah Rule of Civil Procedure 23 is nearly identical to Federal Rule of Civil Procedure 23. Utah has not, however, adopted a counterpart to Rule 23(f) of the Federal Rules, which permits interlocutory appellate review of certification decisions. Because the Utah rule is nearly parallel to the federal rule, decisions rendered under the federal rule are likely to be persuasive in Utah courts. *Olson v. Salt Lake City Sch. Dist.*, 724 P.2d 960, 965 n.5 (Utah 1986) (noting that, since Utah Rule of Civil Procedure 54(b) is nearly identical to the corresponding federal rule, "we rely heavily on decisions under the federal rule. . . ."); *Workman v. Nagle Constr., Inc.*, 802 P.2d 749, 751 (Utah Ct. App. 1990) (comparing court's interpretation of Utah Rule 77(d) with case law under comparable federal rule).

2. CASE LAW INTERPRETING RULE 23

a. Rule 23 in General

The Utah Supreme Court has described the rule permitting the maintenance of class actions as "one of the most far-reaching and important changes in legal procedure in many a decade. Its impact on the enforcement of consumer rights, antitrust claims, securities claims and civil rights actions, to name but a few areas, has been monumental." *Richardson v. Ariz. Fuels Corp.*, 614 P.2d 636, 640 (Utah 1980).

In Utah, class actions are considered equitable in nature. *See Plumb v. State*, 809 P.2d 734, 738 (Utah 1990); *Richardson*, 614 P.2d at 640 ("[C]lass actions have historical antecedents in rules of equity that go back several centuries in English jurisprudence. . . ."). Class actions in Utah "allow[] access to the courts for numerous claimants to request redress of claims that are too small to merit the expenses of litigation on an individual basis," *Call v. City of West Jordan*, 727 P.2d 180, 183 (Utah 1986), and such actions adjudicate the rights of people who generally "are not actively involved in the litigation or aware of specific actions taken in it." *Workman*, 802 P.2d at 753. These features of class actions require trial courts presiding over them to occupy a unique, supervisory role, *see Plumb*, 809 P.2d at 738, one critical aspect of which involves protecting the class members' interests.[1] *See id.* at 738–39. Because class actions adjudicate the rights of individuals without their

[1] The *Workman* court explained that the supervisory role assumed by courts in class actions can be avoided by using a different scheme to organize a group of litigants: "A class action is not the only means of organizing, for litigation purposes, a group of claimants whose interests appear to be aligned or similar. Such a group may form an association, a non-profit corporation, or use another means of organizing private activity. Such private organizational forms have the advantage of leaving in the claimants' hands the decisions concerning their relations between themselves, rather than placing the court in the role of defining and overseeing those relations in supervising a class." *Workman*, 802 P.2d at 753 n.6.

active participation and impose a higher burden on the court, class actions are justified only if the requirements set forth in Rule 23 are met. *See id.*

The court must "perform a rigorous analysis of whether the proposed class satisfies the requirements of Rule 23." *In Re Med. Waste Servs. Antitrust Litig.*, No. 2:03MD1546(DAK), 2006 U.S. Dist. LEXIS 19793, at *13 (D. Utah Mar. 3, 2006) (citations omitted). Any doubt should be resolved in favor of class certification. *Id.* Although the court may not inquire into the merits of a case, *id.*, the "rigorous analysis" required will frequently "entail some overlap with the merits of the plaintiff's underlying claim." *Soseeah v. Sentry Ins.*, 808 F.3d 800, 809 (10th Cir. 2015).

The party seeking class certification bears the burden of proving that certification is warranted. *Ditty v. Check Rite, Ltd.*, 182 F.R.D. 639, 641 (D. Utah 1998). A group of plaintiffs must obtain class certification before proceeding as a class. *Bentley v. West Valley City*, 2001 UT 23, ¶ 3, n.2, 21 P.3d 210; *accord L.C. v. Utah State Bd. of Educ.*, 188 F. Supp. 2d 1330, 1335 n.1 (D. Utah 2002). The court must make a preliminary determination as to "whether the suit has been brought by '[o]ne or more members of [the] class.'" *Paton v. New Mexico Highlands Univ.*, 275 F.3d 1274, 1278 (10th Cir. 2002) (alterations in original) (quoting Fed. R. Civ. P. 23(a)). If Rule 23's requirements are met, the trial court has discretion to determine whether the entire action or individual claims within the action should proceed as a class action. *Richardson*, 614 P.2d at 639. Merely asserting that the action qualifies as a class action by reciting or mimicking the language of Rule 23 is insufficient. *Id.* (citing *Jones v. Diamond*, 519 F.2d 1090, 1098 (5th Cir. 1975)). Attempting to revive dismissed individual claims by amending the complaint to assert a class action is also unlikely to succeed. *See Prince v. Bear River Mut. Ins. Co.*, 2002 UT 68, ¶ 49, 56 P.3d 524.

The decision to allow a case to proceed as a class action or to decertify a class action is within the sound discretion of the trial court. *Richardson*, 614 P.2d at 639; *Houghton v. Dep't of Health*, 2008 UT 86, ¶ 15, 206 P.3d 287. Where, however, a class certification decision rests on an interpretation of law, the district court's determination will be reviewed for correctness. *Id.*

b. Rule 23(a)

A party seeking to institute a class action in Utah must meet the following requirements: "(1) the class is so numerous that joinder of all members is impracticable, (2) there are questions of law or fact common to the class, (3) the claims or defenses of the representative parties are typical of the claims or defenses of the class, and (4) the representative parties will fairly and adequately protect the interests of the class." Utah R. Civ. P. 23(a). "In applying the rule 23[(a)] criteria, the district court must take the substantive allegations in the complaint as true. . . . However, the court need not blindly rely on conclusory allegations which parrot Rule 23. . . . While the court may consider evidence relevant to the plaintiff's claims, the court may not inquire into the merits of the case." *Jaques v. Midway Auto Plaza, Inc.*, 2010 UT 54, ¶ 26, 240 P.3d 769 (citations omitted) (internal quotation marks omitted).

i. Numerosity. The standard governing the required number of class members under Utah's Rule 23 is identical to the standard under the federal rule and inquires whether the size of the class is so large as to make joinder of the members' claims impracticable. *Ditty*, 182 F.R.D. at 641 ("The first question under [federal] Rule 23 is whether 'the class is so numerous that joinder of all members is impracticable.'"). "To satisfy this requirement, the plaintiffs need not show that joinder of all members of the class is impossible, only that it is impracticable." *Serfaty v. Int'l Automated Sys.*,

Inc., 180 F.R.D. 418, 420 (D. Utah 1998). No Utah court has established a minimum number of claimants necessary to form a class, but the Utah Supreme Court has stated that the size of the class alone is not determinative of impracticability of joinder. *Call,* 727 P.2d at 183. The United States District Court for the District of Utah has explained that it is not necessary for the plaintiffs to "identify the exact number of class members involved; courts have often used common sense assumptions to support a finding of numerosity." *Ditty*, 182 F.R.D. at 641; *Serfaty*, 180 F.R.D. at 420. For example, in the context of a securities action, "where the number of persons who bought stock during the class period is unknown, numerosity can be assumed where the number of shares traded is so great that common sense dictates the class is very large." *Serfaty*, 180 F.R.D. at 420 (quoting *Grace v. Perception Tech. Corp*., 128 F.R.D. 165, 167 (D. Mass. 1989) (internal quotation marks omitted)). Although the Utah Supreme Court has not expressly adopted the common sense standard, it has tacitly acknowledged its importance, stating that in some cases "sheer size alone" may render joinder impracticable. *Call*, 727 P.2d at 183. The court also has indicated that joinder may be impracticable where the size and membership of a class is unknown. *Id.*

ii. Commonality. Until recently, no reported Utah case had discussed the commonality requirement. However, it now appears that Utah follows the same standards set out in the Tenth Circuit under federal law:

> Commonality requires only that a single issue of fact or law be common to each class member. To have a common issue, there must be a discrete legal question of some kind. Simply asserting systematic violations of the law is not sufficient to meet the requirement of commonality, because it does not present a common question. The district court is given wide discretion in determining commonality, because it is in the best position to determine the facts of the case and the consequences of alternative methods of resolving the issues.

Jaques, 2010 UT 54, ¶ 27, 240 P.3d 769 (citations omitted) (internal quotation marks omitted).

In keeping with general federal law on the subject, the United States District Court for the District of Utah has noted that, "[i]n order to demonstrate commonality, the plaintiffs must show that there are questions of law or fact common to the class." *Ditty*, 182 F.R.D. at 642. With respect to common questions of law, the Tenth Circuit has held that simply asserting systematic violations of the law is insufficient; instead, all members of the putative class "must share a discrete legal question of some kind." *J.B. ex rel. Hart v. Valdez*, 186 F.3d 1280, 1289 (10th Cir. 1999). Where a plaintiff sought to introduce expert testimony to demonstrate "common elements of liability, antitrust injury, and damages," the United States District Court for the District of Utah held that "conclusory allegations, assumptions of liability and impact, and assurances of future solutions regarding damages" were insufficient to meet the plaintiff's strict burden of proof. *In re Med. Waste Servs. Antitrust Litig.*, 2006 U.S. Dist. LEXIS 19793, at *19–21. In a separate case, the court certified a class of plaintiffs alleging the defendant had violated federal Truth-in-Leasing regulations "by using lease agreements which contain[ed] unlawful provisions, by improperly managing escrow funds and charge-backs, by requiring Plaintiffs to purchase certain products and services as conditions of its leases, and by failing to deliver certain documentation to Plaintiffs regarding insurance and other matters." *Owner-Operator Indep. Drivers Ass'n v. C.R. England, Inc.*, No. 2:02CV950(TS), 2005 U.S. Dist. LEXIS 35099, at *2 (D. Utah Aug. 29, 2005). The court held that these matters were sufficiently common and typical to meet Rule 23's requirements. *Id.* at *6–8; *see also Houghton*, 2008 UT 86, ¶¶ 23–26 (refusing to decertify class merely because of the presence of issues involving waiver, estoppel, and accord).

Class representatives' interest must be "coextensive" with the interests of the rest of the class members, but the interest need not be identical to that of absent class members. *Tennille v. W. Union Co.*, 785 F.3d 422 (10th Cir. 2015); *accord Colo. Cross Disability Coal. v. Abercrombie & Fitch Co.*, 765 F.3d 1205, 1216 (10th Cir. 2014).

iii. Typicality. "The question of typicality . . . is closely related to the preceding question of commonality." *Ditty*, 182 F.R.D. at 642 (alteration in original) (internal quotation marks omitted) (quoting *Rosario v. Livaditis*, 963 F.2d 1013, 1018 (7th Cir. 1992)); *Jaques*, 2010 UT 54, ¶ 36. A plaintiff's claim is typical when it arises from "the same event or practice or course of conduct that gives rise to the claims of other class members and [is] based on the same legal theory." *Jaques*, 2010 UT 54, ¶ 36 (alteration in original) (internal quotation marks omitted) (quoting *Ditty*, 182 F.R.D. at 642). Further, where the named plaintiffs' claims are based on the same fact pattern and legal theory, a finding of typicality is favored and "minor factual variations will not defeat the formation of the class." *Id.* (quoting *Ditty*, 182 F.R.D. at 642).

iv. Fair and adequate protection of the interests of the class. As with the prior two requirements, federal law provides guidance on representation of the class members' interests. According to the Tenth Circuit, "[r]esolution of two questions determines legal adequacy: (1) do the named plaintiffs and their counsel have any conflicts of interest with other class members and (2) will the named plaintiffs and their counsel prosecute the action vigorously on behalf of the class?" *Rutter & Wilbanks Corp. v. Shell Oil Co.*, 314 F.3d 1180, 1187–88 (10th Cir. 2002); *see also Kapur v. USANA Health Sciences, Inc.*, No. 2:07CV177(DAK), 2007 U.S. Dist. LEXIS 77258, at *8 (D. Utah Oct. 17, 2007) (focusing on whether the plaintiff has common interests with the class members and whether the representative will vigorously prosecute the class's interests through qualified counsel); *Jaques*, 2010 UT 54, ¶ 38 (same). The competency and experience of class counsel also affects the adequate representation inquiry. *See Amchem Prods., Inc. v. Windsor*, 521 U.S. 591, 626 n.20 (1997) ("The adequacy heading also factors in competency and conflicts of class counsel."); *Ditty*, 182 F.R.D. at 642 (listing class attorney's "qualifications, experience, and ability to conduct the litigation" as a factor); *see also Williams v. Wilkinson*, 2016 WL 1459529, at *14 (10th Cir. 2016) (reciting the Tenth Circuit's practice of not certifying pro se class actions). While conflicts between members of a proposed class may prevent class certification, conflicts that are merely potential or based on speculation are insufficient to defeat certification. *See Serfaty*, 180 F.R.D. at 420. Additionally, the conflict must focus on the central issue of alleged wrongdoing rather than on the amount of damages suffered. *See id.*

c. Rule 23(b)

In addition to meeting each of the four requirements set forth in Rule 23(a), a plaintiff must meet at least one of the three criteria enumerated in Rule 23(b), which are identical to those set forth in the federal rule. No Utah case law has addressed the criteria in 23(b)(1) or (b)(2). However, the Utah Supreme Court has addressed the "predominance" and "superiority" requirements of Rule 23(b)(3).

Predominance, "[l]ike typicality, . . . also closely resembles the commonality requirement. While commonality only requires common issues of law or fact, predominance requires that the common issues predominate over any individual issues in the action. Thus, the predominance requirement is 'far more demanding' than the commonality requirement." *Jaques*, 2010 UT 54, ¶ 42 (citation omitted) (quoting *Amchem*, 521 U.S. at 624).

A showing of predominance may allow a class of plaintiffs to receive an evidentiary inference that is uniform for the entire class. *See CGC Holding Co., LLC v. Broad & Cassel*, 773 F.3d 1076, 109192 (10th Cir. 2014); *see also In re Urethane Antitrust Litig.*, 768 F.3d 1245, 1254 (10th Cir.

2014).

In determining whether superiority is met, a district court should consider the four factors set out in Rule 23(b)(3):

> (A) the interest of members of the class in individually controlling the prosecution or defense of separate actions; (B) the extent and nature of any litigation concerning the controversy already commenced by or against members of the class; (C) the desirability or undesirability of concentrating the litigation of the claims in the particular forum; (D) the difficulties likely to be encountered in the management of a class action.

Utah R. Civ. P. 23(b)(3). The Utah Supreme Court has found that these factors were met in a case where (1) "each class member's claim would be too small to be worthwhile to litigate separately"; (2) "there would be little effect on competing litigation"; (3) "resolution of the case in a single forum would be desirable to ensure consistent verdicts and to further judicial economy"; and (4) "difficulties would not likely be encountered in the management of the class action." *Jaques*, 2010 UT 54, ¶ 45.

d. Rule 23(c)(1)

The Utah Supreme Court has recognized that, "[b]ecause class action certification occurs early in the litigation, the 'scope and contour of a class may change radically as discovery progresses.'" *Id.* ¶ 1 n.1 (quoting *Prado-Steiman v. Bush*, 221 F.3d 1266, 1273 (11th Cir. 2000)). A trial court may, accordingly, "accommodate these changes by amending the certification order any time before a decision on the merits. Thus, class certification issues are often disposed of as the facts of the case are established through discovery and trial." *Id.* (citation omitted). Upon a motion to certify, decertify, or amend a class, a trial court must rigorously analyze whether the certified class continues to meet Rule 23's requirements, including doing more than offering brief and conclusory statements. *Maak v. IHC Health Services, Inc.*, 2016 UT App 73, ¶¶ 30–31, 33 (emphasizing, however, that courts are not obligated to take steps to preserve a class action). Furthermore, "when a party specifically proposes a mechanism to ameliorate concerns with class treatment, the district court must undertake a rigorous analysis and explain the basis for its decision to reject the proposed approach and to instead decertify the class." *Id.* ¶ 53.

e. Rule 23(c)(2)

Once a court has issued an order as to whether an action may be maintained as a class action, Rule 23(c)(2) requires the court to direct "the best notice practicable" to the class members, including individual notice to all members who can be identified through reasonable effort. Utah R. Civ. P. 23(c)(2).[2] The court's notice must advise the class members that (1) the court will exclude the member from the class if the member makes a request to that effect by a specified date; (2) the judgment, whether or not it is favorable to the class, will include all members who do not request exclusion from the class; and (3) members who do not request exclusion may, if they choose to do so, enter an

---

[2] One important caveat to the notice requirements contained in Rule 23(c)(2) is that they are applicable only to class actions brought under Rule 23(b)(3), not to actions for injunctive relief brought under Rule 23(b)(2). *See* Holmgren v. Utah-Idaho Sugar Co., 582 P.2d 856, 860 (Utah 1978). Thus, notice by publication may be adequate for purposes of a class action seeking only injunctive relief. *See id.*

appearance in the action through their counsel. *Id.* The court's duty to notify class members of a pending action is one of the responsibilities placed on the court to safeguard the interests of the absent class members. *Workman*, 802 P.2d at 753. In fact, "[n]otice to absent members of a plaintiff class, and an opportunity for them to disassociate themselves from the class, are critical requirements for maintenance of a class action, requirements founded in the federally guaranteed right of the absent class members to due process of law." *Id.* In recognition of the notice requirement's importance, the Utah Court of Appeals has held that a judgment entered on behalf of members of a class who have not received proper notice of a class action is void. *Id.*

f. Rule 23(e)

The nature of a trial court's supervisory role in class actions is exemplified by the requirement that the trial court must approve any settlement of a class action. Utah R. Civ. P. 23(e); *Plumb*, 809 P.2d at 738.[3] In the Tenth Circuit, four factors are considered in determining whether a proposed settlement should be approved:

> (1) whether the proposed settlement was fairly and honestly negotiated; (2) whether serious questions of law and fact exist, placing the ultimate outcome of the litigation in doubt; (3) whether the value of an immediate recovery outweighs the mere possibility of future relief after protected and expensive litigation; and (4) the judgment of the parties that the settlement is fair and reasonable.

Rutter & Wilbanks Corp., 314 F.3d at 1188 (quoting *Gottlieb v. Wiles*, 11 F.3d 1004, 1014 (10th Cir. 1993) (*abrogated on other grounds by Devlin v. Scardelletti*, 536 U.S. 1 (2002)).

Two specific rationales support the trial court's role as a monitor of the relations between class members and their counsel with respect to settlements. First, in cases where members of the class have not been identified or located, the court must guard the missing members' rights. *Plumb*, 809 P.2d at 739. Second, where class members have only minor interests in the litigation, they also may have only slight motivation to monitor the conduct of counsel and to carefully evaluate proposed settlements. *Id.* Accordingly, the requirement of court approval of settlements and dismissals can help prevent "manipulation or exploitation of the class by its counsel" and assures that the interests of all class members are considered by a neutral party before a settlement is finalized. *Id.* In sum, the "whole philosophy" of Rule 23 respecting dismissals and settlements of class actions is to protect class members from potential abuse. *Id.*

Another aspect of Rule 23(e) is the requirement that all class members be notified of any proposed dismissal or settlement. Utah R. Civ. P. 23(e). The notice provision allows a class member to "opt out" of any proposed settlement in the event the member disagrees with or is otherwise unsatisfied with the settlement: "The opt out rule associated with class action suits . . . 'is intended to protect the [individual's] interest in pursuing [his] own litigation rather than participating in a class action.'" *Bennett v. Jones, Waldo, Holbrook & McDonough*, 2003 UT 9, ¶ 37, 70 P.3d 17 (second alteration in original) (quoting *Gottlieb*, 11 F.3d at 1009). By opting out of a proposed settlement, the class member "preserve[s] his legal claims and position totally," leaving the class member "free to bring those claims in another lawsuit" and "plac[ing] him in the same legal position with the same

[3] A trial court's approval of a settlement agreement is reviewed for abuse of discretion. *See Rutter & Wilbanks Corp.*, 314 F.3d at 1186.

legal claims that he would have been in" had the class action never occurred. *Id.* ¶¶ 37–38. In *Bennett,* a class member who opted out of a settlement agreement subsequently sued counsel for the class, alleging that the attorneys breached the retainer agreement because the settlement was unfair and improper. On appeal from the trial court's dismissal of the breach of contract cause of action for failure to state a claim, the Utah Supreme Court affirmed, holding that the class member "as a matter of law . . . was not damaged by the . . . alleged breaches of the retainer agreement." *Id.* ¶ 36.[4] The same fact, *i.e.*, the class member's inability to show that he suffered damage, led the court to affirm the dismissal of his legal malpractice claim. *Id.* ¶¶ 43–44 (stating that class member "simply cannot plead and has not pled that he was damaged as a result of the . . . defendants' alleged breaches of duty because by opting out of the class action settlement, he preserved his legal position and his individual causes of action").

3. MISCELLANEOUS

a. Distinction between Class Actions and Derivative Actions

Derivative actions are governed by Rule 23A of the Utah Rules of Civil Procedure. Explaining the distinction between class actions and derivative actions, the Utah Supreme Court has stated that each type of action rests on fundamentally different substantive principles of law. *Richardson,* 614 P.2d at 638. On one hand,

> [a] class action . . . is predicated on ownership of the claim for relief sued upon in the representative of the class and all other class members in their capacity *as individuals.* Shareholders of the corporation may, of course, have claims for relief directly against their corporation because the corporation itself has violated rights possessed by the shareholders, and a class action would be an appropriate means for enforcing their claims. A recovery in a class action is a recovery which belongs directly to the shareholders.

Id. On the other hand,

> [a] derivative action must necessarily be based on a claim for relief which is owned by the stockholders' corporation. Indeed, a prerequisite for filing a derivative action is the failure of the corporation to initiate the action in its own name. The stockholder, as a nominal party, has no right, title, or interest whatsoever in the claim itself whether the action is brought by the corporation or by the stockholder on behalf of the corporation.

Id. The court also noted that, if a class action is improperly used in place of a derivative action, "grave injustices" may result, "not the least of which is the diversion of assets recovered in a lawsuit from creditors of a corporation to stockholders, thereby reversing long established substantive rules of law as to the relative priorities of the claims of creditors and stockholders to the assets of an insolvent corporation." *Id.* at 640.

b. Awards of Attorneys' Fees in Class Actions

Although Utah's general rule allows for the award of attorneys' fees only to a prevailing party and

---

[4] The court also held that the class member's decision to opt out "effectively terminated the class counsel's legal representation of him in the matter." *Id.* at ¶ 34.

only when such action is permitted by statute or contract, Utah courts will award attorneys' fees under principles of "justice and equity[,]" including in class action cases. *Doctors' Co. v. Drezga*, 2009 UT 60, ¶ 32, 218 P.3d 598 (quoting *Stewart v. Utah Pub. Serv. Comm'n*, 885 P.2d 759, 782 (Utah 1994)). Awards of attorneys' fees to be collected by a class are subject to the trial court's approval, which in turn is dependent on the trial court's determination that the award is fair and reasonable. *Plumb*, 809 P.2d at 738. Where a trial court is not satisfied that a sufficiently adversarial relationship exists between the class representatives and class counsel in a dispute involving attorneys' fees, the Utah Supreme Court recommends that the class hire or the trial court appoint special counsel for the class to act as an adversary in the fee dispute. *Id.* at 743–44.

c. Class Action Settlement Agreement Does Not Impose Special Duty to Protect Class Members

In *Sanders v. Leavitt*, the Utah Supreme Court held that the lawyers of a plaintiff class in an action seeking reform of the Utah child-welfare system did not assume a special duty to protect the members of the class from future harm by virtue of a settlement reached in the action. 2001 UT 78, ¶ 23, 37 P.3d 1052. In an action filed against the attorneys of the plaintiff class after the settlement of the class action, a father had sought to hold the attorneys liable for the death of his child, who had been a member of the class, based on the settlement agreement. *Id.* ¶ 5. The court declined to hold the attorneys responsible for the child's physical well-being or medical care. *Id.* ¶ 23.

d. Aggregation of Punitive Damages and Attorneys' Fees for Purposes of Diversity Jurisdiction

In the Tenth Circuit, members of a class may not aggregate their claims for punitive damages or attorney fees for purposes of meeting the amount of claim requirement of diversity jurisdiction. *Martin v. Franklin Capital Corp.*, 251 F.3d 1284, 1292–93 (10th Cir. 2001) (*abrogated on other grounds by Dart Cherokee Basin Operating Co., LLC v. Owens*, 135 S. Ct. 547 (2014)).

e. Standard of Review of Certification Decisions

The standard of review applicable to the grant or denial of certification of a class is abuse of discretion. *Call*, 727 P.2d at 183; *Valdez*, 186 F.3d at 1287.

f. Claim Preclusion under Rule 23

The United States District Court for the District of Utah analyzed the doctrine of claim preclusion in a Rule 23 context. *Pelt v. Utah*, No. 2:92CV639(TC), 2006 U.S. Dist. LEXIS 24523, at *27–41 (D. Utah Apr. 26, 2006). The court held that "[p]rocedural due process prohibits preclusive application of an earlier judgment to a non-party unless that party was in privity with the parties in the earlier suit." *Id.* at *27. In the context of a class action lawsuit, privity exists if the party to the class action suit adequately represented the nonparty and if this question is one of fact. *Id.* at *28–30.

g. Discovery

The United States District Court for the District of Utah confirmed that plaintiffs may not take discovery on class claims where the plaintiffs failed to move for certification of their alleged class within the time period established by the Court's local rule, which provides for 90 days after the service of a pleading that purports to commence a class action. *See Timothy v. Aqua Fin., Inc.*, No. 2:06CV921(TS), 2008 U.S. Dist. LEXIS 4489, at *3 (D. Utah Jan. 22, 2008).

h. Interlocutory Review of Class Action Certification

Notwithstanding the fact that Utah has not adopted a counterpart to Federal of Civil Procedure 23(f), which permits interlocutory appellate review of certification decisions, Utah adheres to "the guidelines established by the federal courts" in determining whether interlocutory review is appropriate. *Jaques v. Midway Auto Plaza, Inc.*, 2010 UT 54, ¶ 1 n.1. Accordingly, "interlocutory review of class action certification is appropriate when: (1) the denial of a class action would effectively end the case because the plaintiff's claim is too small to merit the cost of litigation; (2) granting a class action raises the stakes of the litigation and puts unreasonable pressure on the defendant to settle; or (3) there is a novel or unsettled issue of law." *Id.* (citing *Blair v. Equifax Check Servs., Inc.*, 181 F.3d 832, 834–35 (7th Cir. 1999)).

i. Communications with Absent Class Members

Utah courts provide little guidance regarding communications with absent class members. Notably, the Tenth Circuit has recognized that precertification limits on such communications "must be based on a 'clear record and specific findings that reflect a weighing of the need for limitation and the potential interference with the rights of the parties.'" *Zinser v. Cont'l Grain Co.*, 660 F.2d 754, 762 (10th Cir. 1981) (quoting *Gulf Oil Co. v. Bernard*, 452 U.S. 89, 90 (1981)). However, given the dearth of Utah law on this issue, counsel should research the matter carefully.

RULE 23 OF THE UTAH RULES OF CIVIL PROCEDURE

RULE 23. CLASS ACTIONS

(a) *Prerequisites to a class action.* One or more members of a class may sue or be sued as representative parties on behalf of all only if (1) the class is so numerous that joinder of all members is impracticable, (2) there are questions of law or fact common to the class, (3) the claims or defenses of the representative parties are typical of the claims or defenses of the class, and (4) the representative parties will fairly and adequately protect the interests of the class.

(b) *Class actions maintainable.* An action may be maintained as a class action if the prerequisites of Subdivision (a) are satisfied, and in addition:

(1) The prosecution of separate actions by or against individual members of the class would create a risk of:

(A) inconsistent or varying adjudications with respect to individual members of the class which would establish incompatible standards of conduct for the party opposing the class, or

(B) adjudications with respect to individual members of the class which would as a practical matter be dispositive of the interests of the other members not parties to the adjudications or substantially impair or impede their ability to protect their interests; or

(2) The party opposing the class has acted or refused to act on grounds generally applicable to the class, thereby making appropriate final injunctive relief or corresponding declaratory relief with respect to the class as a whole; or

(3) The court finds that the questions of law or fact common to the members of the class predominate over any questions affecting only individual members, and that a class action is superior to other available methods for the fair and efficient adjudication of the controversy. The matters pertinent to the findings include: (A) the interest of members of the class in individually controlling the prosecution or defense of separate actions; (B) the extent and nature of any litigation concerning the controversy already commenced by or against members of the class; (C) the desirability or undesirability of concentrating the litigation of the claims in the particular forum; (D) the difficulties likely to be encountered in the management of a class action.

(c) *Determination by order whether class action to be maintained; notice; judgment; actions conducted partially as class actions.*

(1) As soon as practicable after the commencement of an action brought as a class action, the court shall determine by order whether it is to be maintained. An order under this subdivision may be conditional, and may be altered or amended before the decision on the merits.

(2) In any class action maintained under Subdivision (b)(3), the court shall direct to the members of the class the best notice practicable under the circumstances, including individual notice to all members who can be identified through reasonable effort. The

notice shall advise each member that (A) the court will exclude him from the class if he so requests by a specified date; (B) the judgment, whether favorable or not, will include all members who do not request exclusion; and (C) any member who does not request exclusion may, if he desires, enter an appearance through his counsel.

(3) The judgment in an action maintained as a class action under Sub-division(b)(1) or (b)(2), whether or not favorable to the class, shall include and describe those whom the court finds to be members of the class. The judgment in an action maintained as a class action under Subdivision (b)(3), whether or not favorable to the class, shall include and specify or describe those to whom the notice provided in Subdivision (c)(2) was directed, and who have not requested exclusion, and whom the court finds to be members of the class.

(4) When appropriate (A) an action may be brought or maintained as a class action with respect to particular issues, or (B) a class may be divided into subclasses and each subclass treated as a class, and the provisions of this rule shall then be construed and applied accordingly.

(d) *Orders in conduct of actions.* In the conduct of actions to which this rule applies, the court may make appropriate orders: (1) determining the course of proceedings or prescribing measures to prevent undue repetition or complication in the presentation of evidence or argument; (2) requiring, for the protection of the members of the class or otherwise for the fair conduct of the action, that notice be given in such manner as the court may direct to some or all of the members of any step in the action, or of the proposed extent of the judgment, or of the opportunity of members to signify whether they consider the representation fair and adequate, to intervene and present claims or defenses, or otherwise to come into the action; (3) imposing conditions on the representative parties or on intervenors; (4) requiring that the pleadings be amended to eliminate therefrom allegations as to representation of absent persons, and that the action proceed accordingly; (5) dealing with similar procedural matters. The orders may be combined with an order under Rule 16, and may be altered or amended as may be desirable from time to time.

(e) *Dismissal or compromise.* A class action shall not be dismissed or compromised without the approval of the court. Notice of the proposed dismissal or compromise shall be given to all members of the class in such manner as the court directs.

This chapter is authored by Eric G. Maxfield and Cory A. Talbot. Mr. Maxfield is a partner in the Salt Lake City office of Holland & Hart LLP, where he practices complex commercial litigation and has defended class action lawsuits. Mr. Talbot is also a partner at Holland & Hart LLP. His complex commercial litigation practice includes class action defense.

VERMONT

1. COMPARISON OF RULE 23 WITH THE FEDERAL RULES OF CIVIL PROCEDURE

Rule 23 of the Vermont Rules of Civil Procedure is largely identical to Rule 23 of the Federal Rules of Civil Procedure. The only differences are as follows:

(1) Vt. R. Civ. P. 23(c)(1) states that an order certifying a class action may be conditional; this language has been removed from the federal rule.
(2) The contents of notice provided to class members in actions certified under subsection (b)(3) are set forth in Vt. R. Civ. P. 23(c)(2) vary somewhat from the notice requirements in Fed. R. Civ. P. 23(c)(2)(B).
(3) Vt. R. Civ. P. 23(e) provides that a class action "shall not be dismissed or compromised without the approval of the court," and requires that notice of a proposed dismissal or compromise be given to "all members of the class in such manner as the court directs." This subsection does not contain any of the other provisions in Fed. R. Civ. P. 23(e).
(4) Vt. R. Civ. P. 23 does not include the following subsections found in Fed. R. Civ. P. 23: (c)(1)(B), (c)(2)(A), (g) and (h).
(5) Vt. R. Civ. P. 23(g) sets forth the procedure for handling the disposition of residual funds after the class members' claims, expenses, litigation costs, attorneys' fees, and other court-approved disbursements have been paid.

2. CASE LAW INTERPRETING RULE 23

In Vermont, "class actions are intended to be of limited and special application, not to be casually resorted to or authorized. This is because, improperly used, they can seriously compromise many due process rights of those involved." *George v. Town of Calais*, 135 Vt. 244, 244, 373 A.2d 553, 554 (1977). *See also Salatino v. Chase*, 2007 VT 81, ¶ 11, 939 A.2d 482, 487 (reaffirming this statement in *George* and noting that it is "particularly true of the mandatory class actions authorized by Rule 23(b)(1)(B), because class members are bound by the judgment or settlement obtained even if they do not participate in the action").

The Vermont Supreme Court has admonished that "the certification decision must be made wholly apart from a consideration of the merits of the case using the standards set out under Rule 23(a) & (b)." *Alger v. Dep't of Labor & Indus.*, 2006 VT 115, ¶ 41, 181 Vt. 309, 329, 917 A.2d 508, 523. Later, the Court characterized this admonition as "a cautionary statement reminding the trial court that its task is to examine the Rule 23 criteria rather than weigh the merits of the case." *Wright v. Honeywell Int'l, Inc.*, 2009 VT 123, ¶ 12, 187 Vt. 123, 989 A.2d 539, 544. "The court must evaluate plaintiff's evidence to assure that the Rule 23 criteria have been met, but without turning the class-certification proceeding into a premature and unwieldy trial on the merits." *Id.* ¶ 15, 989 A.2d at 546.

a. Rule 23(a)

i. Numerosity. Class certification is appropriate only when "the class is so numerous that joinder of all members is impracticable." V.R.C.P. 23(a). "Impracticable does not mean impossible." *Duggan v. Bisson*, Docket No. 114-5-98 Cacv, 2000 WL 35746649 (Caledonia Co. Sup. Ct., March 14, 2000) (Cheever, J.). Although evidence of the exact size or identity of the putative class members is not necessary to satisfy this requirement, *id.*, a class will not be certified where there is no evidence of the size of the potential class. *Ran-Mar Inc. v. City of Barre,* Docket No. 378-6-02 Wncv, 2005 WL 5568526 (Washington Co. Sup. Ct., November 30, 2005) (Toor, J.). A class of twenty-three members is not too numerous to make joinder impracticable. *See George v. Town of Calais*, 135 Vt. 244, 247, 373 A.2d 553, 554 (1977).

One trial court in Vermont has followed the Second Circuit's approach to numerosity and considered the following factors, in addition to a pure numbers count, in analyzing whether the numerosity requirement was met: (1) judicial economy from avoidance of multiplicity of actions, (2) geographic dispersion of class members, (3) financial resources of class members, (4) ability of claimants to institute individual suits, and (5) requests for prospective injunctive relief which would involve future class members. *See Duggan v. Bisson*, Docket No. 114-5-98 Cacv, 2000 WL 35746649 (Caledonia Co. Sup. Ct., March 14, 2000) (Cheever, J.) (citing *Robidoux v. Celani*, 987 F.2d 931, 935 (2d Cir. 1993)).

ii. Commonality. "The test for commonality is not a particularly high one and requires plaintiffs to prove neither . . . quantitative or qualitative levels of commonality." *Sheldrake v. Skyline Corp.*, Docket No. S1269-01 CnC, 2004 WL 5626259 (Chittenden Co. Sup. Ct., March 29, 2004) (Katz, J.). "Generally, commonality exists when the proposed class members challenge the same conduct of the defendants." *Duggan v. Bisson*, Docket No. 114-5-98 Cacv, 2000 WL 35746649 (Caledonia Co. Sup. Ct., March 14, 2000) (Cheever, J.) (quoting *Marisol v. Guiliani*, 126 F.3d 372, 376 (2d. Cir. 1997)). "The commonality requirement will be satisfied if the named plaintiffs share at least one question of fact or law with the grievances of the prospective class." *Id.* (quoting *Baby Neal v. Casey*, 43 F.3d 48, 56 (3d Cir. 1994)). It is "not necessary to prove that all class members suffered actual injury; demonstrating that all class members are subject to the same harm will suffice for class certification." *Id.* Commonality is not met where individual intention is at issue. *George v. Town of Calais*, 135 Vt. 244, 247, 373 A.2d 553, 554 (1977). "It is insufficient for purposes of commonality to simply come up with some issue, however general, that the proposed class members' claims may have in common." *U.S. Bank Nat. Ass'n v. Breer*, Docket No. 717-10-12 Wncv, 2016 WL 8078143, at *3 (Washington Co. Sup. Ct., May 17, 2016) (Tomasi, J.). What matters is "not the raising of common 'questions'—even in droves—but, rather the capacity of a classwide proceeding to generate common answers *apt to drive the resolution of the litigation.* Dissimilarities within the proposed class are what have the potential to impede the generation of common answers." *Id.* (quoting *Wal-Mart Stores, Inc. v. Dukes*, 564 U.S. 338, 350 (2011)). See *Mullinnex v. Touchette*, Docket No. 493-11-18 Wrcv, 2019 WL 5549826, at *1 (Windsor Co. Sup. Ct., April 26, 2019) (Kainen, J.) (holding that whether the Department of Corrections' induction process for treating prisoners with opioid use disorders through Medication-Assisted Treatment and withdrawal of that treatment as a means of punishment meet the prevailing medical standard of care is a common issue that does not require an individualized analysis of each class member's claims), *rev'd on other grounds*, *Mullinnex v. Menard*, 2020 VT 33, 212 Vt. 432, 236 A.3d 171; *Sutton v. The Vermont Regional Ctr.*, Docket No. 100-5-17, 2022 WL 1468931, at *3–5 (Lamoille Co. Sup. Ct., April 7, 2022) (Teachout, J.) (holding that commonality is not met when each class member's relationship with the defendants and their reliance on the defendants' statements will have to be proven and cannot be established by representative plaintiffs, and where there were a variety of different contracts and different versions of contracts at issue and the facts related to proof of breach would not be the same for all members of the putative class).

iii. Adequacy of representation. The Vermont Supreme Court has not considered this issue in the context of certifying a class action. *See State v. Homeside Lending*, 2003 VT 17, 175 Vt. 239, 826 A.2d 997 (addressing the importance of adequate representation in class actions generally). A Vermont trial court noted that this requirement is "primarily . . . concerned with the competence of the plaintiff and counsel and the lack of an antagonistic interest to the class." *Sheldrake v. Skyline Corp.*, Docket No. S1269-01 CnC, 2004 WL 5626259 (Chittenden Co. Sup. Ct., March 29, 2004) (Katz, J.). The antagonism element of this requirement focuses on whether there is a danger that the representative plaintiff's interests might go against the interests of the class. *Id.*

One Vermont trial court questioned the adequacy of the representatives for a class of patients seeking to assert a claim against a physician under the Vermont Consumer Fraud Act for allegedly performing unnecessary surgery given the differences in the patients' relationship with the physician and the tension between the class representatives and the class members for whom the necessity of cataract surgery was a closer judgment call. *See Salatino v. Chase*, Docket No. S930-03 CnC, 2005 WL 5872281, *12–14 (Chittenden Co. Sup. Ct., February 28, 2005) (Pearson, J.).

iv. Typicality. The typicality requirement is satisfied "when each class member's claim arises from the same course of events and each class member makes similar legal arguments." *Duggan v. Bisson*, Docket No. 114-5-98 Cacv, 2000 WL 35746649 (Caledonia Co. Sup. Ct., March 14, 2000) (Cheever, J.) (quoting *Robidoux v. Celani*, 987 F.2d 931, 936 (2d Cir. 1993)). Minor variations in the fact patterns of the underlying individual claims will not bar a finding that this requirement is met. *Id.* In establishing this requirement, the class representative must "prove that there is a pervasive violation and that the various injuries alleged all stem from that common violation." *Id.* (quoting *Baby Neal v. Casey*, 43 F.3d 48, 58 (3d. Cir. 1994) (discussing *General Tel. Co. of Southwest v. Falcon*, 457 U.S. 147, 157–59 (1982)). Accordingly, typicality does not require that the claims of the class representative and the class be identical. *Butler v. Vermont Electric Power Co.*, Docket No. 35-1-07 Ancv, 2008 WL 4281980 (Vt. Sup. Ct., Addison Unit, Civil Division, May 14, 2008) (Toor, J.). Typicality, however, will not be found when important aspects of the putative class members are too different from one another, even within possible subclasses. *Sutton v. The Vermont Regional Ctr.*, Docket No. 100-5-17, 2022 WL 1468931, at *5 (Lamoille Co. Sup. Ct., April 7, 2022) (Teachout, J.).

A second attempt to obtain class certification in *Salatino v. Chase* was made, this time as a limited fund class action under Rule 23(b)(1)(B). The plaintiffs sought certification of a class of all patients who allegedly underwent unnecessary cataract surgery within a six-year period. The trial court concluded that the proposed class failed to meet the requirement of typicality because the claims were based on oral communications between doctor and patient, which necessarily vary from patient to patient and a complex course of conduct over a long period negates typicality. *See Salatino v. Chase*, Docket No. S930-03 CnC, 2005 WL 5872282, *2–5 (Chittenden Co. Sup. Ct., October 21, 2005) (Joseph, J.). An appeal to the Vermont Supreme Court pursuant to V.R.C.P. 23(f) was taken and the Court affirmed the order denying certification under Rule 23(b)(1)(B) on alternate grounds (see discussion under Section 2.b, herein).

b. Rule 23(b)

A class action is "maintainable only if at least one of the more onerous conditions set forth in Rule

23(b) is satisfied," in addition to the four prerequisites set forth in Rule 23(a). *Wright v. Honeywell Int'l, Inc.*, 2009 VT 123, ¶ 9, 187 Vt. 123, 989 A.2d 539, 544. The requirements for certifying a class under Rule 23(b)(3) "reflect the fact that special caution must be exercised in class actions of [that] type because of the loose affiliation among the class members, which is thought to magnify the risks inherent in any representative action. *U.S. Bank Nat. Ass'n v. Breer*, Docket No. 717-10-12 Wncv, 2016 WL 8078143, at *3 (Washington Co. Sup. Ct., May 17, 2016) (Tomasi, J.) (quotation omitted). The Vermont Supreme Court considered Vt. R. Civ. P. 23(b)(3) in a case in which the plaintiff was claiming an antitrust violation under Vermont's Consumer Fraud Act. *See Wright v. Honeywell Int'l, Inc.*, 2009 VT 123, 187 Vt. 123, 989 A.2d 539. The issue before the Court was whether the plaintiff made a sufficient showing that issues of law and fact common to the class will predominate with respect to the second element of an antitrust claim, that is, the fact of impact or injury to the members of the proposed class. The plaintiff relied upon an expert in antitrust economics to make this showing, but the trial court concluded that there were fatal flaws in the expert's methodology and refused to certify the class. The Supreme Court reversed holding that the trial court "demanded too much of plaintiff at this stage of the litigation and that plaintiff provided potentially viable methodologies to demonstrate proof of injury in fact common to the proposed class." *Id.* ¶ 22, 989 A.2d at 548. The Court also reversed the trial court's conclusion that a class action was not the superior method for resolving the controversy, noting that most courts agree that, from a manageability perspective, a class action is a superior procedure for handling thousands of class members' small claims when the predominance requirement is met. *Id.* ¶ 30, 989 A.2d at 552. In conclusion, the Court stated that "[t]he guiding principle for Rule 23(b)(3) certification is that the interests of the parties can best be served by settling their differences in one single action." *Id.* ¶31, 989 A.2d at 552.

"Predominance complements commonality by testing 'whether proposed classes are sufficiently cohesive to warrant adjudication by representation.'" *U.S. Bank Nat. Ass'n v. Breer*, Docket No. 717-10-12 Wncv, 2016 WL 8078143, at *4 (Washington Co. Sup. Ct., May 17, 2016) (Tomasi, J.) (quoting *Amchem Products, Inc. v. Windsor*, 521 U.S. 591, 623 (1997)). "As the predominance test is meant to help courts identify cases in which aggregate treatment would be efficient, it focuses on the extent to which the issues in the cases are common as opposed to individual—the more common the issues, the more likely it is that the case will be processed efficiently in the aggregate; the less common the issues, the less likely efficient resolution will be furthered by aggregation." *Id.* (quotation omitted). "This is more of a qualitative than quantitative analysis." *Id.* (quotation omitted).

Another Vermont trial court has described the predominance criterion as "a far more stringent requirement than the commonality[] and typicality factors under Rule 23(a)," and recognized that "implicit in the predominance test is the notion that the adjudication of common issues will help achieve judicial economy." *See Salatino v. Chase*, Docket No. S930-03 CnC, 2005 WL 5872281, *12–14 (Chittenden Co. Sup. Ct., February 28, 2005) (Pearson, J.) (refusing to certify a class of patients asserting claims of unnecessary surgery under Vt. R. Civ. P. 23(b)(3)); *see also Butler v. Vermont Electric Power Co.*, Docket No. 35-1-07 Ancv, 2008 WL 4281980 (Vt. Sup. Ct., Addison Unit, Civil Division, May 14, 2008) (Toor, J.) (holding predominance factor not met where an individualized determination is necessary with respect to whether each class member's claim is time-barred and on the calculation of damages; also holding that predominance did not exist for the consumer fraud sub-class due to the individualized issues regarding the timing, substance and content of the oral communications between the electric company and the landowners); *Sheldrake v. Skyline Corp.*, Docket No. S1269-01 CnC, 2004 WL 5626259 (Chittenden Co. Sup. Ct., March 29, 2004) (Katz, J.) (holding that the predominance requirement was not met in a proposed class action where the class members represent seven different states because, among other things, the determination of liability and damages will be affected by the conflicts of state law that will not be unilaterally resolved); *U.S. Bank Nat. Ass'n v. Breer*, Docket No. 717-10-12 Wncv, 2016 WL 8078143, at *4–5 (Washington Co. Sup. Ct., May 17, 2016) (Tomasi, J.) (recognizing that predominance will often not be when the substantive laws of multiple jurisdictions must be applied, and when the statute of limitations analysis turns on the discovery rule).

With respect to the superiority requirement in a Rule 23(b)(3) action, a Vermont trial court has held that this requirement was not met where "the individual legal and factual issues involved would make the management of the class devolve into multiple lawsuits needing separate trial." *Sheldrake v. Skyline Corp.*, Docket No. S1269-01 CnC, 2004 WL 5626259 (Chittenden Co. Sup. Ct., March 29, 2004) (Katz, J.). The court found that the plaintiffs and class members had alternatives available to them if class certification was denied. Specifically, the court noted that they could individually pursue their cases. Although their damage awards may not be sizable (the named plaintiffs were seeking $50,000), the court concluded that they should be able to locate competent counsel willing to take their cases because some of their claims included statutorily authorized attorneys' fees. The court also noted that the issues concerning conflicts of laws within the class would make management of the case difficult.

A second attempt for class certification was made in *Salatino v. Chase* under Vt. R. Civ. P. 23(b)(1)(B) on a "limited fund" theory for all patients who allegedly underwent unnecessary cataract surgery within a six-year period was denied by the trial court and then appealed to the Vermont Supreme Court under Rule 23(f). *See Salatino v. Chase*, 2007 VT 81, 939 A.2d 482. The Supreme Court affirmed holding that plaintiffs failed to meet their burden of showing that the total of the aggregated liquidated claims was greater than the fund available to satisfy them because the common law tort claims and the claim for attorneys' fees under the Consumer Fraud Act were still unliquidated.

In *Mullinnex v. Touchette*, Docket No. 493-11-18 Wrcv, 2019 WL 5549826, at *1 (Windsor Co. Sup. Ct., April 26, 2019) (Kainen, J.), several Vermont inmates sought class certification of claims related to the Department of Corrections' use of Medication-Assisted Treatment (MAT) for prisoners with opioid use disorders. The inmates were claiming, among other things, that the Department of Corrections' induction process for treating prisoners with opioid use disorders through Medication-Assisted Treatment and policy of withdrawing that treatment as a means of punishment violate the prevailing medical standard of care. *Id.* The court certified a class under Vt. R. Civ. P. 23(b)(1)(A), concluding that the prosecution of separate actions by "individual inmates who suffer from opioid use disorder and are subjected to an inadequate MAT induction process, . . . would establish incompatible standards of conduct" for the Department of Corrections. *Id.* at *2. On interlocutory appeal from this decision pursuant to Vt. R. Civ. P. 23(f), the Vermont Supreme Court reversed the trial court's prior ruling that the class representative had exhausted his administrative remedies and that the putative class had satisfied the exhaustion requirement based on the vicarious-exhaustion doctrine. See *Mullinnex v. Menard*, 2020 VT 33, 212 Vt. 432, 236 A.3d 171. Because the Supreme Court concluded that the class representative failed to exhaust his administrative remedies and reversed on that basis, the Court did not address the trial court's certification decision.

3. MISCELLANEOUS COMMENTS

a. Class Definition

The Vermont Supreme Court has affirmed a denial of class certification where the class definition was "too amorphous." *Alger v. Dep't of Labor & Indus.*, 2006 VT 115, ¶¶ 36–41, 181 Vt. 309, 327–

29, 917 A.2d 508, 522–23. The proposed class members must have a sufficient connection with the claim being litigated for a class action to stand. *Id.* ¶¶ 38, 41. A trial court has recognized that "the existence of [a] class is a standard preliminary question for certification" and that this is a fact dependent inquiry based on the circumstances of each case. *Sheldrake v. Skyline Corp.*, Docket No. S1269-01 CnC, 2004 WL 5626259 (Chittenden Co. Sup. Ct., March 29, 2004) (Katz, J.). In that case, the trial court refused to certify a class, in part, because there was not a definite and homogenous class. *Id. See also U.S. Bank Nat. Ass'n v. Breer*, Docket No. 717-10-12 Wncv, 2016 WL 8078143, at *3 n.5 (Washington Co. Sup. Ct., May 17, 2016) (Tomasi, J.) (noting that while Vermont's rule does not require the court to describe the classes and claims with specificity, the rule should be interpreted that way "because without that specificity, potential class members cannot effectively determine whether to opt out of the class action").

b. Identification of Class Members

The Vermont Supreme Court reversed a trial court's conclusion that a class action was not a superior method for resolving the controversy where the trial court ruled that there was "no feasible plan for identifying class members" and "allowing a novel or permissive method for identifying class member creates the potential for fraud." *Wright v. Honeywell Int'l, Inc.*, 2009 VT 123, ¶ 30, 187 Vt. 123, 989 A.2d 539, 552. The Court held that "[t]hese speculative considerations should not preclude certifying the class before plaintiff has had an opportunity to propose methods for identifying class members." *Id.*

c. Power to Adjust Class Decisions

After affirming the denial of class certification because the class definition was "too amorphous," the Vermont Supreme Court noted that the trial court "has continuing power to adjust its class decisions in light of evidentiary developments and the general progression of the case from assertion to facts." *Id.* ¶ 40. The Court then held that in view of the "early stage of this litigation, and our reversal of the trial court on the motion to dismiss, plaintiffs are not barred from seeking certification of a more precisely defined class that meets the standards of Rule 23." *Id.*

d. Notice to Class Members

Where the class has been certified pursuant to Vt. R. Civ. P. 23(b)(1) or (2), notice to the class members may be made via newspaper or trade journal publication in the court's discretion pursuant to Vt. R. Civ. P. 23(d)(2). *See Am. Trucking Ass'n, Inc. v. Conway*, 152 Vt. 383, 390–91 566 A.2d 1335, 1339 (1989).

The Vermont Supreme Court has held that the language of Vt. R. Civ. P. 23(d)(2) vests the court with discretion (albeit "substantially narrow[ed]" discretion) to provide notice to putative class members, whether or not a class has been certified. *Salatino v. Chase*, 2007 VT 81, ¶ 18, 939 A.2d 482, 489. The Court went on to hold that "notice of class-certification denial is only appropriate when the denial may affect adversely the rights of individuals not before the court. . . . Putative class members will only be prejudiced by not receiving notice that class-certification is denied when they are reasonably relying on the pending class action to protect their interests. The court's discretion to provide notice of class certification must be exercised only in that situation." *Id.* ¶¶ 23, 25 (quotation omitted).

e. Jurisdiction of Other States' Class Actions over Vermont Residents

The Vermont Supreme Court held that where a class action can impose monetary burdens on plaintiff class members that can exceed any benefits they might gain, a state court outside Vermont has personal jurisdiction only over those Vermont class members with minimum contacts with the foreign state. *See State v. Homeside Lending*, 2003 VT 17, 175 Vt. 239, 826 A.2d 997 ("Opt-out" notice to absent class members of action held insufficient to comport with due process, class representation was inadequate and did not comport with due process, and foreign class action judgment was subject to collateral attack in Vermont).

f. Discovery from Absent Class Members

A Vermont trial court has held that unnamed class members should not be treated as parties to the litigation for discovery purposes. Accordingly, "mere notice of deposition under V.R.C.P. 30(b) is unenforceable as to such persons, and all unnamed . . . class members . . . must be subpoenaed for deposition under V.R.C.P. 45." *See Duggan v. Bisson*, Docket No. 114-5-98 Cacv, 2003 WL 25826926 (Caledonia Co. Sup. Ct., May 14, 2003) (Pearson, J.).

g. Tolling the Statute of Limitations

It is generally recognized that a class action tolls the statute of limitations for individual potential class members. *See American Pipe & Construc. Co. v. Utah*, 414 U.S. 538, 554 (1974) ("[T]he commencement of a class action suspends the applicable statute of limitations as to all asserted members of the class who would have been parties had the suit been permitted to continue as a class action."); *Crown, Cork & Seal Co. v. Parker*, 462 U.S. 345, 350 (1983) ("Once the statute of limitations has been tolled, it remains tolled for all members of the putative class until class certification is denied. At that point, class members may choose to file their own suits or to intervene as plaintiffs in the pending action."). A Vermont trial court has held that when an individual class member voluntarily chooses to leave a class prior to the court's certification decision, he/she loses the tolling benefit provided by the class action. *See Sheldrake v. Skyline Corp.*, Docket No. S1269-01 CnC, 2005 WL 5895190 (Chittenden Co. Sup. Ct., June 23, 2005) (Norton, J.).

h. Mootness

In *Sullivan v. Menard*, 2019 VT 76, ¶ 9 n.2, 211 Vt. 138, 222 A.3d 79, the Supreme Court cited with approval (albeit in dicta) to the holding in *Sosna v. Iowa*, 419 U.S. 393, 401-02 (1975), that mootness as to an individual class representative does not moot the litigation if the controversy may still exist between defendant and a member of the class represented by the named plaintiff.

i. Timing and Scope of Appeal under Vt. R. Civ. P. 23(f)

In *Mullinnex v. Menard*, 2020 VT 33, 212 Vt. 432, 236 A.3d 171, several inmates filed a class action against the Department of Corrections arguing that its medication-assisted treatment program for opiod-use disorders did not meet prevailing medical standards of care. The DOC moved to dismiss for lack of subject matter jurisdiction arguing that the class representative had not exhausted his administrative remedies. *Id.* ¶ 6. The trial court denied that motion finding that the class representative satisfied the exhaustion requirement and the putative class satisfied it based on the doctrine of vicarious-exhaustion, which has been endorsed by several federal circuit courts. *Id.* ¶ 7. The trial court then certified the class and the DOC appealed both the subject matter jurisdiction and certification decisions pursuant to Vt. R. Civ. P. 23(f). *Id.* On appeal, the class representative argued that the only issue the Court could consider on a Rule 23(f) appeal is the certification decision and the appeal of the subject matter jurisdiction decision was untimely. *Id.* ¶ 9. The Supreme Court rejected these arguments. The Court explained that the vicarious-exhaustion doctrine applies only to certified classes, therefore, the trial court's decision as to its applicability was conditioned on its later certification decision. *Id.* ¶ 10. "[I]t was only upon certification of the class that the vicarious-exhaustion ruling took legal effect; had the court declined to certify the class, that language would have remained dicta." *Id.* Thus, the Supreme Court held that the interlocutory appeal of the exhaustion decision was not untimely because the issues of exhaustion and class certification are "inextricably intertwined," and the exhaustion ruling was "appropriately considered in connection with an interlocutory appeal pursuant to Rule 23(f)" because it was "bound up in the ruling on class certification."

In *Sutton v. The Vermont Regional Ctr.*, Docket No. 100-5-17, 2022 WL 12611661 (Lamoille Co. Sup. Ct., Aug. 4, 2022) (Teachout, J.), the trial court denied the representative plaintiffs' motion for permission to file an interlocutory appeal to the Vermont Supreme Court that was filed pursuant to V.R.A.P. 5(b)(1). The court did not mention or discuss Rule 23(f) in its decision (likely because the time to file an appeal under that rule had long since passed).

4. COMMUNICATIONS WITH ABSENT CLASS MEMBERS

There is only one trial court opinion in Vermont addressing the issue of communications with absent class members. *See Duggan v. Bisson*, Docket No. 114-5-98 Cacv, 2003 WL 25826926 (Caledonia Co. Sup. Ct., May 14, 2003) (Pearson, J.). In that case, the trial court was required to determine whether the defendant could depose the unnamed class members. The court held that the unnamed class members were not parties to the litigation for discovery purposes, but they were represented by class counsel once the class action was certified. Accordingly, the court endorsed the general anti-contact rule which provides that "[a] lawyer who represents a client opposing a class in a class action is subject to the anti-contact rule of this Section." *Id.* (quoting *Restatement (3d) of the Law Governing Lawyers*, § 99 cmt. I (2000)). In doing so, the trial court noted that Vermont's anti-contact rule, Rule 4.2 of the Vermont Rules of Professional Conduct, "prohibits a lawyer representing a client from communicating about a subject of the representation with a person the lawyer knows to be represented by another lawyer" and that rule "applies to all represented persons, regardless of whether they are actual parties to the existing litigation." *Id.*

RULE 23 OF THE VERMONT RULES OF CIVIL PROCEDURE

RULE 23. CLASS ACTIONS

(a) *Prerequisites to a class action.* One or more members of a class may sue or be sued in an action in a superior court as representative parties on behalf of all only if (1) the class is so numerous that joinder of all members is impracticable, (2) there are questions of law or fact common to the class, (3) the claims or defenses of the representative parties are typical of the claims or defenses of the class, and (4) the representative parties will fairly and adequately protect the interests of the class.

(b) *Class actions maintainable.* An action may be maintained as a class action if the prerequisites of subdivision (a) are satisfied, and in addition:

(1) the prosecution of separate actions by or against individual members of the class would create a risk of

(A) inconsistent or varying adjudications with respect to individual members of the class which would establish incompatible standards of conduct for the party opposing the class or,

(B) adjudications with respect to individual members of the class which would as a practical matter be dispositive of the interests of the other members not parties to the adjudications or substantially impair or impede their ability to protect their interests; or

(2) the party opposing the class has acted or refused to act on grounds generally applicable to the class, thereby making appropriate final injunctive relief or corresponding declaratory relief with respect to the class as a whole; or

(3) the court finds that the questions of law or fact common to the members of the class predominate over any questions affecting only individual members, and that a class action is superior to other available methods for the fair and efficient adjudication of the controversy. The matters pertinent to the findings include: (A) the interest of members of the class in individually controlling the prosecution or defense of separate actions; (B) the extent and nature of any litigation concerning the controversy already commenced by or against members of the class; (C) the desirability or undesirability of concentrating the litigation of the claims in the particular forum; (D) the difficulties likely to be encountered in the management of a class action.

(c) *Determination by order whether class action to be maintained; notice; judgment; actions conducted partially as class actions.*

(1) As soon as practicable after the commencement of an action brought as a class action, the court shall determine by order whether it is to be so maintained. An order under this subdivision may be conditional, and may be altered or amended before the decision on the merits.

(2) In any class action maintained under subdivision (b)(3), the court shall direct to the members of the class the best notice practicable under the circumstances, including individual notice to all members who can be identified through reasonable effort. The

notice shall advise each member that (A) the court will exclude the member from the class if the member so requests by a specified date; (B) the judgment, whether favorable or not, will include all members who do not request exclusion; and (C) any member who does not request exclusion may, if the member desires, enter an appearance through counsel.

(3) The judgment in an action maintained as a class action under subdivision (b)(1) or (b)(2), whether or not favorable to the class, shall include and describe those whom the court finds to be members of the class. The judgment in an action maintained as a class action under subdivision (b)(3), whether or not favorable to the class, shall include and specify or describe those to whom the notice provided in subdivision (c)(2) was directed, and who have not requested exclusion, and whom the court finds to be members of the class.

(4) When appropriate (A) an action may be brought or maintained as a class action with respect to particular issues, or (B) a class may be divided into subclasses and each subclass treated as a class, and the provisions of this rule shall then be construed and applied accordingly.

(d) *Orders in Conduct of Actions.* In the conduct of actions to which this rule applies, the court may make appropriate orders: (1) determining the course of proceedings or prescribing measures to prevent undue repetition or complication in the presentation of evidence or argument; (2) requiring, for the protection of the members of the class or otherwise for the fair conduct of the action, that notice be given in such manner as the court may direct to some or all of the members of any step in the action, or of the proposed extent of the judgment, or of the opportunity of members to signify whether they consider the representation fair and adequate, to intervene and present claims or defenses, or otherwise to come into the action; (3) imposing conditions on the representative parties or on intervenors; (4) requiring that the pleadings be amended to eliminate therefrom allegations as to representation of absent persons, and that the action proceed accordingly; (5) dealing with similar procedural matters. The orders may be combined with an order under Rule 16, and may be altered or amended as may be desirable from time to time.

(e) *Dismissal or Compromise.* A class action shall not be dismissed or compromised without the approval of the court, and notice of the proposed dismissal or compromise shall be given to all members of the class in such manner as the court directs.

(f) *Appeals.* The Supreme Court may in its discretion permit an appeal from an order of the Superior Court granting or denying class action certification under this rule if application is made to it within 14 days after entry of the order. An appeal does not stay proceedings in the Superior Court unless the trial judge or the Supreme Court so orders.

(g) Disposition of Residual Funds.

(1) "Residual Funds" are funds that remain after the payment of all approved class member claims, expenses, litigation costs, attorneys' fees, and other court-approved disbursements to implement the relief granted. Nothing in this rule is intended to prevent the parties to a class action from suggesting, or the trial court from approving, a settlement that does not create residual funds.

(2) Any order, judgment, or approved compromise in a class action certified under this rule that establishes a process for identifying and compensating members of the class shall provide that, in matters where the claims process has been exhausted and residual funds remain,

(A) at least fifty percent of the residual funds shall be disbursed to Vermont Legal Aid to support direct delivery of legal services to indigent persons, and

(B) the balance of remaining residual funds shall be disbursed to the Vermont Bar Foundation to support activities and programs that promote access to the civil justice system for indigent persons, or shall be disbursed to one or more nonprofit organizations or foundations which support projects that will benefit the class or similarly situated persons consistent with the objectives and purposes of the underlying causes of action on which relief was based.

Chapter author Angela R. Clark is with the firm of Dinse, P.C., in Burlington, Vermont. Ms. Clark joined the firm in September 2002, and practices exclusively in litigation, with an emphasis on professional malpractice, complex civil litigation, and appeals. Before joining Dinse, Ms. Clark spent four years serving as a trial court law clerk in Vermont and Maine.

VIRGINIA

The Rules of the Supreme Court of Virginia do not offer an analog to Federal Rule of Civil Procedure 23. As a result, "Virginia jurisprudence does not recognize class actions." *Casey v. Merck & Co.*, 722 S.E.2d 842, 846 (Va. 2012).

The unavailability of class actions in Virginia has particular relevance in the wake of *Spokeo, Inc. v. Robins*, 136 S. Ct. 1540, 1546 (2016), and its progeny, which affect the scope of standing under Article III of the United States Constitution. *Spokeo* is especially relevant to class actions because it "requires a concrete injury even in the context of a statutory violation." *Id.* at 1549. Thus, a class action cannot proceed in federal court on "a bare procedural violation, divorced from any concrete harm." *Id.*

The Supreme Court's decision in *Transunion LLC v. Ramirez*, 141 S. Ct. 2190, 2200 (2021), clarifies that *Spokeo* bars "no injury" class actions premised on statutory violations. *See id.* ("No concrete harm, no standing."). Under *Ramirez*, "[e]very class member must have Article III standing," meaning each class member must show they have been concretely harmed by a defendant's statutory violation. *Id.* at 2205, 2208. Because Virginia does not recognize class actions, when a federal class action is dismissed under *Spokeo* and *Ramirez*, class claimants cannot resort to seeking relief in Virginia courts—even if Virginia's standing requirements are less demanding.

Virginia law does permit consolidation of multiple cases in limited circumstances. Specifically, the Multiple Claimant Litigation Act provides a means to join, coordinate, consolidate, or transfer six or more civil actions.

The Multiple Claimant Litigation Act, Va. Code § 8.01-267.1 *et seq.*, permits Virginia circuit courts to join, coordinate, consolidate, or transfer civil actions upon a finding that:

(1) separate civil actions brought by six or more plaintiffs involve common questions of law or fact and arise out of the same transaction, occurrence, or series of transactions or occurrences;
(2) the common questions of law or fact predominate and are significant to the actions; and
(3) the order will promote the ends of justice and the just and efficient conduct and disposition of the actions, and is consistent with each party's right to due process of law, and does not prejudice each individual party's right to a fair and impartial resolution of each action.

Va. Code § 8.01-267.1.

In its current form, the Multiple Claimant Litigation Act permits related civil cases pending in different courts to be transferred to one court by a panel of circuit court judges designated by the Supreme Court of Virginia. Va. Code § 8.01-267.4. If the panel elects to transfer the related cases, they are deemed pending in the same court and eligible for consolidation. *Id.* § 8.01-267.2.

Whether to consolidate is within the discretion of the transferee circuit court. *Lamberton v. Lamberton*, No. 1714-03-4, 2004 WL 2032094, at *4 (Va. Ct. App. Sept. 14, 2004). A court must entertain, but is not constrained by its consideration of, the following statutory factors under Virginia Code § 8.01.267.1(3):

- the nature of the common questions of law or fact;
- the convenience of the parties, witnesses, and counsel;
- the relative stages of the actions and the work of counsel;
- the efficient utilization of judicial facilities and personnel;
- the calendar of the courts;
- the likelihood and disadvantages of duplicative and inconsistent rulings, orders, or judgments;
- the likelihood of prompt settlement of the actions without the entry of the order; and
- the likelihood of prejudice or confusion in joint trials by jury.

After a court finds that consolidation is appropriate, it may direct consolidated pretrial proceedings, conduct a joint hearing or trial regarding any or all the common questions, or simply consolidate the actions for all purposes. Va. Code § 8.01-267.3.

The court also may organize and manage the litigation "to assure fair and efficient conduct and resolution of the litigation." *Id.* § 8.01.267.1 For example:

- Courts may consolidate actions on the issue of liability. *See, e.g.*, *Bond v. Baker Roofing Co.*, 81 Va. Cir. 439, 448 (Norfolk Cir. Ct. 2010); *see also Centra Health, Inc. v. Mullins*, 670 S.E.2d 708, 718 (Va. 2009). But in order to avoid the possibility of undue prejudice to either party, the court may subsequently bifurcate the consolidated cases to determine damages. *See Bond*, 81 Va. Cir. at 448–49. The Supreme Court of Virginia has even proclaimed that bifurcation is "the most practical means" of avoiding prejudice to a party. *See Centra Health*, 670 S.E.2d at 718.

- A court also may appoint a "lead plaintiff" or "committee" to represent the larger group of consolidated plaintiffs. *See, e.g.*, *City of Chesapeake v. Cunningham*, 604 S.E.2d 420, 422 n.1 (Va. 2004) (circuit court appointed lead plaintiff to speak on behalf of combined group of 214 plaintiffs); *Gas Mart Corp. v. Bd. of Supervisors*, 611 S.E.2d 340, 342 (Va. 2005) (trial court "directed the formation of a Litigation Steering Committee to represent all complainants in the consolidated cases with respect to common issues of law and fact").

The Multiple Claimant Litigation Act allows the court to sever parties and issues if claims do not arise out of the same transaction(s) or occurrence(s) and do not satisfy the requirements of § 8.01-267.1. Va. Code § 8.01-267.5; *see, e.g.*, *Gas Mart Corp. v. Loudoun Cty. Bd. of Supervisors*, 67 Va. Cir. 159, 160 (Loudoun Cir. Ct. 2005) (noting the court had severed a claim from the consolidated case). The court may do this only on a party's motion. *See Livingston v. Cty. of Fairfax*, 78 Va. Cir. 283, 289 (Fairfax Cir. Ct. 2009).

The Multiple Claimant Litigation Act has been invoked in various types of litigation, including medical malpractice actions, *see, e.g.*, *Centra Health*, 670 S.E.2d at 709, and zoning challenges, *see, e.g.*, *Gas Mart*, 611 S.E.2d at 341. Notably, the Multiple Claimant Litigation Act does not allow for the consolidation of state and federal cases. *Mathes v. Gen. Motors, L.L.C.*, 92 Va. Cir. 158, 162 (Augusta Cir. Ct. 2015). It also does not apply to actions against manufacturers or suppliers of asbestos or products for industrial use that contain asbestos to which the provisions of § 8.01-374.1—which permits consolidation of certain asbestos personal injury claims—may apply. Va. Code § 8.01-267.9.

In addition to the Multiple Claimant Litigation Act, Virginia litigants also may consider representative suits in equity, which historically have permitted plaintiffs in equity to represent others who are similarly situated. *See, e.g.*, *Bull v. Read*, 54 Va. (13 Gratt.) 78, 86–87 (1855).

In recent years, legislators have proposed dramatically altering the class action landscape in Virginia. One proposal was to amend the Multiple Claimant Litigation Act to allow "civil action[s] brought by a plaintiff on behalf of multiple similarly situated persons." House Bill 505 (offered Jan. 12, 2022) (available at https://lis.virginia.gov/cgi-bin/legp604.exe?221+sum+HB505&221+sum+HB505). The legislation called for the Supreme Court of Virginia to promulgate rules governing such actions, which would be "no more restrictive than those contained in Rule 23 of the Federal Rules of Civil Procedure." *Id.* The bill, however, never made it out of committee in the House of Delegates. *See id.* This proposal followed a similar attempt in 2021 to allow class actions in Virginia, but the 2021 bill made it farther than its 2022 counterpart, passing the Senate before dying in committee in the House. Senate Bill 1180 (offered Jan. 13, 2021) (available at https://lis.virginia.gov/cgi-bin/legp604.exe?212+sum+SB1180&212+sum+SB1180). No such legislation was proposed in the 2023 session.

In the 2024 session, a proposal with even greater proposed changes to Virginia law passed both the House and Senate but was vetoed by the Governor. This proposal would have created an entirely new Code section "relating to civil actions filed on behalf of multiple persons; class actions." House Bill 418 (offered Jan. 8, 2024). Rather than calling for the promulgation of Rules to reflect Federal Rule of Civil Procedure 23, this bill set forth the substantive rules and procedures that would permit class actions in Virginia state court. The bill largely tracked the substance of Federal Rule of Civil Procedure 23, but it also deviated from that federal Rule in several respects. Some of the more significant changes proposed to become Virginia law include:

- No ability to request an interlocutory appeal from an order granting or denying class-action certification, as permitted under Fed. R. Civ. P. 23(f).
- Exempting the certification of any Virginia Consumer Protection Act claim from having to satisfy the equivalent to Fed. R. Civ. P. 23(b)(1), (b)(2), or (b)(3), so long as the proposed class satisfied the equivlant to Fed. R. Civ. P. 23(a) (numerosity, commonality, typicality, and adequacy).
- Appearing to create an independent right to seek attorneys' fees upon pursuing a class action, unlike Fed. R. Civ. P. 23(h) which merely establishes the process a court must follow when attorneys' fees are otherwise permitted by law.
- Requiring that any class action settlement that compensates class members must provide for the distribution of residual funds, which is not required by Fed. R. Civ. P. 23.
- When two or more overlapping class actions are filed, creating a procedure where a panel of judges would decide where those overlapping class action cases should be transferred.

This was the first bill in recent history, which would have permitted class actions in Virginia state court, to pass both the House and Senate. The Governor vetoed the bill at the conclusion of the 2024 legislative session.

The Virginia chapter was prepared by Bryan A. Fratkin and Travis C. Gunn of McGuireWoods LLP. Bryan co-leads McGuireWoods' class action practice group, focusing his national practice on consumer financial services litigation under the various "alphabet soup" statutes. He represents large financial institutions involved in credit card, auto finance, banking, and mortgage litigation, alleging violations of the Fair Credit Reporting Act, Fair Debt Collection Practices Act, Servicemembers Civil Relief Act, Truth in Lending Act, Credit Repair Organizations Act, Equal Credit Opportunity Act, Bankruptcy Discharge Injunction and Stay, and state law consumer protection statutes. Travis is counsel who defends clients against putative class and mass actions across various industries, defending against consumer litigation, state attorney general matters, significant personal injury and wrongful death claims, and general commercial litigation.

WASHINGTON

1. WASHINGTON'S SUPERIOR COURT CIVIL RULE 23

Long before adoption of the current Civil Rules, the Washington code allowed class actions. *See* RCW § 4.08.070, *repealed by* 1985 Wash. Laws, ch. 68, § 1. *See Wm. D. Perkins & Co. v. Diking Dist. No. 3*, 162 Wash. 227, 228, 298 P. 462 (1931) (discussing code provision for actions in representative capacity). Washington adopted its current Civil Rule 23 in 1967 and modeled it on the recently adopted Federal Rule of Civil Procedure 23.

2. COMPARISON WITH RULE 23 OF THE FEDERAL RULES OF CIVIL PROCEDURE

Until amendments in 2006 added a provision concerning disposition of residual funds (discussed below), Civil Rule 23 was "an exact counterpart" of the pre-1998 Rule 23 of the Federal Rules of Civil Procedure. *Johnson v. Moore*, 80 Wash. 2d 531, 532, 496 P.2d 334, 335 (1972); *see also Lacey Nursing Ctr., Inc. v. Washington Dep't of Revenue*, 128 Wash. 2d 40, 46–47, 905 P.2d 338, 341 (1995) (CR 23 is "identical" to Fed. R. Civ. P. 23). As a result, Washington courts determining whether to certify a class action frequently seek guidance from cases applying Fed. R. Civ. P. 23, which are "highly persuasive." *Schnall v. AT&T Wireless Serv. Inc.*, 171 Wash. 2d 260, 270, 259 P.3d 129, 133 (2011). Washington has not adopted the significant amendments to Federal Rule of Civil Procedure 23 promulgated in 2003, 2007, and 2018. Washington courts continue to look to pre-amendment federal case law for guidance in construing Washington Civil Rule 23. *Jones v. Home Care of Wash., Inc.*, 152 Wash. App. 674, 682–83 & n.3, 216 P.3d 1106, 1109–10 & n.3 (2010) (citing federal cases that "apply the earlier version of FRCP 23(e) which is similar to CR 23(e)").

3. CASE LAW INTERPRETING CIVIL RULE 23.

"[T]he goals underlying a class action" include "efficiency, deterrence, and access to justice." *Moore v. Wash. Health Care Auth.*, 181 Wash. 2d 299, 305, 332 P.3d 461, 464 (2014). A court should certify a proposed class only if it satisfies all four requirements of CR 23(a) and one of the subsections of CR 23(b). *Washington Educ. Ass'n v. Shelton Sch. Dist.*, 93 Wash. 2d 783, 789, 613 P.2d 769, 773 (1980). In addition, the named representative of the class must have standing, *Johnston v. Beneficial Management Corp.*, 85 Wash. 2d 637, 645, 538 P.2d 510, 516 (1975); *Doe v. Spokane and Inland Empire Blood Bank*, 55 Wash. App. 106, 115, 780 P.2d 853, 859 (1989), and a justiciable claim against the defendant. *Mullen v. North Pac. Bank*, 25 Wash. App. 864, 879, 610 P.2d 949, 958 (1980) (denying class certification where representative's claim was barred by statute of limitations); *Johnston*, 85 Wash. 2d at 644–45, 538 P.2d at 516 (same). Because the procedural mechanism of a class action "does not confer standing that a plaintiff does not otherwise have in an individual capacity," a class representative "cannot litigate a claim against a defendant who the representative cannot sue individually." *Doe*, 55 Wash. App. at 115, 780 P.2d at 859. "[A]n individual named as a party in a class action cannot assert the action merely because the class has a claim if [the individual] does not." *Williams v. City of Spokane*, 199 Wash. 2d 236, 248, 505 P.3d 91 (2022) (quoting *Wash. Educ. Ass'n v. Shelton Sch. Dist. No. 309*, 93 Wash. 2d 783, 790, 613 P.2d 769 (1980)). Similarly, to have a justiciable claim appropriate for certification, a named plaintiff must have "a live claim at the time the suit was filed and at the time the trial court certifie[s] the class." *Burman v. State*, 50 Wash. App. 433, 440, 749 P.2d 708, 713 (1998) (citing *Sosna v. Iowa*, 419 U.S. 393, 402 (1975)). But a defendant in Washington may not render moot a plaintiff's claim in a class action through an offer of judgment under CR 68, even if the unaccepted offer affords the named plaintiff complete relief. *Gorden v. Lloyd Ward & Assocs., P.C.*, 180 Wash. App. 552, 323 P.3d 1074, 1078–79 (2014). *Compare Jones v. Windermere Real Estate Services Co.*, 19 Wash. App. 2d 1004 (2021) (unpublished) (where named plaintiffs accept offer of judgment to settle the "above titled cause," doing so settled all claims and barred appeal of earlier class certification denial).

Washington courts have applied CR 23 with varying degrees of rigor. One early CR 23(b)(2) case asserted that Washington courts "favor a liberal interpretation of CR 23, rather than a restrictive one." *Brown v. Brown*, 6 Wash. App. 249, 256, 492 P.2d 581, 586 (1971). But the case law since then trends toward a more rigorous standard, requiring "strict conformity" with CR 23. *Lacey Nursing Ctr.*, 128 Wash. 2d at 47, 905 P.2d at 341; *DeFunis v. Odegaard*, 84 Wash. 2d 617, 622, 529 P.2d 438, 441 (1974); *Schwendeman v. USAA Cas. Ins. Co.*, 116 Wash. App. 9, 17, 65 P.3d 1, 5 (2003) ("strict conformity" with CR 23 required).

The trend towards more rigorous analysis of Rule 23's requirements reflects concern that the class action mechanism, although "advantageous and important in our system of justice," can be abused. *Darling v. Champion Home Builders Co.*, 96 Wash. 2d 701, 706, 638 P.2d 1249, 1252 (1982). "The potential abuse of the class action process includes stirring up litigation, solicitation of funds, the maintenance of an action by counsel, exertion of undue influence on class members to opt out, and misrepresentations creating false impressions of the action and the court's rule." *Id.* Because of this potential for abuse, many Washington opinions emphasize that "'actual, not presumed conformance with Rule 23(a)' remains indispensable, and that a 'rigorous analysis' is called for." *Oda v. State*, 111 Wash. App. 79, 92, 44 P.3d 8, 15 (2002) (quoting *General Tel. Co. v. Falcon*, 457 U.S. 147, 160–61 (1982)); *Schwendeman*, 116 Wash. App. at 17, 65 P.3d at 5 ("trial court must engage in rigorous analysis to ensure prerequisites of the rule have been met"); *Weston v. Emerald City Pizza LLC*, 137 Wash. App. 164, 168, 151 P.3d 1090, 1092 (2007) ("rigorous analysis" required). One Washington Court of Appeals has reiterated the U.S. Supreme Court's observation that "Rule 23 does not set forth a mere pleading standard. A party seeking class certification must affirmatively demonstrate his compliance with the Rule—that is, he must be prepared to prove that there are *in fact* sufficiently numerous parties, common questions of law or fact, etc." *Admasu v. Port of Seattle*, 185 Wash. App. 23, 34 & n.18, 340 P.3d 873, 878 & n.18 (2014) (quoting *Wal-Mart Stores, Inc. v. Dukes*, 131 S. Ct. 2541, 2551 (2011)) (emphasis in original).

But the Washington Supreme Court has also said that "[a]n appellate court resolves close cases in favor of allowing or maintaining the class." *Nelson v. Appleway Chevrolet, Inc.*, 160 Wash. 2d 173, 188–89, 157 P.3d 847, 854 (2007) (citing *Sitton v. State Farm Mut. Auto. Ins. Co.*, 116 Wash. App. 245, 250, 63 P.3d 198, 204 (2003)). Further, the Court has said that because "[a] class is always subject to later modification or decertification by the trial court, . . . the trial court should err in favor of certifying the class." *Moeller v. Farmers Ins. Co. of Wash.*, 173 Wash. 2d 264, 278, 267 P.3d 998, 1004 (2011) (citations omitted); *Chavez v. Our Lady of Lourdes Hospital at Pasco*, 190 Wash. 2d

507, 515, 415 P.3d 224, 229 (2018) ("courts should err in favor of certifying a class because the class is always subject to the trial court's later modification or decertification"). This abuse of discretion standard applies both to orders certifying a class and decertifying a class. *Lundquist v. Seattle School District No. 1*, 2025 WL 1368086, at *6 (Wash. Ct. App. May 12, 2025).

A trial court's decision regarding class certification is discretionary and will not be overturned "absent a manifest abuse of discretion." *Eriks v. Denver*, 118 Wash. 2d 451, 466, 824 P.2d 1207, 1215 (1992); *see also Lacey Nursing Ctr.*, 128 Wash. 2d at 47, 905 P.2d at 341; *Moeller*, 173 Wash. 2d at 278, 267 P.3d at 1004; *Admasu*, 185 Wash. App. at 30, 340 P.3d at 876. A class certification order will survive appellate review if "it appears from the record that the court considered all the criteria of CR 23." *Eriks,* 118 Wash. 2d at 467, 824 P.2d at 1215. *See Nelson*, 160 Wash. 2d at 190, 157 P.3d at 855 (record must show that the trial court "properly considered all CR 23 criteria"). On the other hand, "[n]otwithstanding the rule of liberal interpretation, it is clear that the class action rule does not contemplate automatic affirmance whenever a trial court certifies a class." *Oda*, 111 Wash. App. at 92, 44 P.3d at 14; *Weston*, 137 Wash. App. at 168, 151 P.3d at 1092. In particular, the trial court must articulate the basis for any class certification decision. The Washington Supreme Court has overturned certification orders on the ground that "[t]he trial court's refusal to certify the plaintiff or defendant class without appropriate consideration and articulate reference to the criteria of CR 23 was an abuse of discretion." *Washington Educ. Ass'n*, 93 Wash. 2d at 793, 613 P.2d at 775; *see also Oda*, 111 Wash. App. at 93, 44 P.3d at 15 (reversing trial court's certification because its findings did "little more than recite the language of the rule"); *Miller v. Farmer Bros. Co.*, 115 Wash. App. 815, 822, 828, 64 P.3d 49, 54, 57 (2003) (reversing because of failure to make findings on impracticability of joinder and superiority); *Chavez*, 190 Wash. 2d at 517, 415 P.3d at 230 (reversing denial of certification, noting the trial court's failure to make findings on the record results in no deference to the trial court's decision); *Worley v. Cedar Recycling, Inc.*, 2022 WL 2132711, at *14 (Wash. App. June 14, 2022) (reversing denial of class certification because of failure to make factual findings showing lack of typicality); *but see Hill v. Garda CL Northwest, Inc.*, 198 Wash. App. 326, 341, 394 P.3d 390, 399 (2017) (findings sufficient for class certification where court "signaled that it had considered the individual issues and determined that this one was common to all class members and would predominate").

In determining whether a plaintiff has satisfied the criteria of CR 23, "a trial court may certainly look past the pleadings" so that it can "make a meaningful determination of the certification issues." *Oda*, 111 Wash. App. at 94, 44 P.3d at 16. Indeed, going beyond the pleadings "is necessary, as a court must understand the claims, defenses, relevant facts, and applicable substantive law in order to make a meaningful determination of the certification issue." *Id.* (quoting *Castano v. American Tobacco Co.*, 84 F.3d 734, 744 (5th Cir. 1996)). Thus, "it is proper for the court to consider all the evidence in the record" that is "relevant to the issue of whether the requirements of CR 23 were met." *Schwendeman*, 116 Wash. App. at 21 n.34, 65 P.3d at 7 n.34. At the same time, a certification decision must be "made independently, with no consideration of the merits of the claims" and must "articulate on the record its consideration of each of the factors under CR 23." *Sorrel v. Eagle Healthcare, Inc.*, 110 Wash. App. 290, 299–300, 38 P.3d 1024, 1029 (2002). Plaintiffs bear the burden of establishing that certification is appropriate, *Miller*, 115 Wash. App. at 820, 64 P.3d at 53, even if the court decides the certification question on a defendant's motion to strike class allegations, *see Walker v. Wenatchee Valley Truck & Auto Outlet, Inc.*, 155 Wash. App. 199, 206, 229 P.3d 871, 875 (2010) (noting trial court's granting of motion to strike class allegations).

The ban on considering the merits of the named plaintiff's claim has created confusion among Washington appellate courts as to what deference (if any) should be given to a named plaintiff's class—as opposed to individual—allegations. In *Oda*, the trial court accepted as true all allegations in the complaint, including the class allegations upon which plaintiff bears the burden of proof at the certification stage. *See Oda*, 111 Wash. App. at 923, 44 P.3d at 15. The court of appeals rejected that approach, holding that blind acceptance of the plaintiff's allegations undermines the "rigorous analysis" required by CR 23. *Id.* at 93–94, 99–100, 44 P.3d at 18–19 (plaintiffs did not offer evidence of discrimination beyond their own, and their "accounts *cannot be assumed* to represent a common and typical course of conduct") (emphasis added); *see also Weston*, 137 Wash. App. at 173, 151 P.3d at 1095 (refusing to accept allegations of commonality as true and denying certification based on lack of evidence of commonality). Other Washington courts, however, have held that, in "making the initial class certification determination, the trial court takes the substantive allegations of the complaint as true." *Smith v. Behr Process Corp.*, 113 Wash. App. 306, 320 n.4, 54 P.3d 665 (2002); *see also Miller*, 115 Wash. App. at 820, 64 P.3d 49 (citing *Smith*). The Washington Supreme Court has not yet addressed the apparent conflict in these approaches to the class certification inquiry. *See* James Wm. Moore et al., *Moore's Federal Practice* § 23.82[2], at 23–338 (3d ed. 2006) ("On a motion for class certification, the court does not accept the *class allegations* of the complaint as true, as a court would in connection with a Rule 12(b)(6) motion to dismiss. Instead, the court must make whatever factual inquiries are necessary.") (emphasis added).

Although the court should not consider the merits of a claim when deciding whether to certify a class, "a trial court retains discretion, for purposes of judicial economy, to delay ruling on a motion for class certification until after hearing dispositive motions." *Sheehan v. Central Puget Sound Regional Transit Authority*, 155 Wash. 2d 790, 807, 123 P.3d 88, 97 (2005) (citing *Washington Educ. Ass'n v. Shelton School Dist. No. 309*, 93 Wash. 2d 783, 789, 613 P.2d 769 (1980)). *Sheehan* rests on the premise that pre-certification dispositive motions may result in dismissal of the action and thus "protect both the parties and the court from needless and costly further litigation." *Sheehan,* 155 Wash. 2d at 807, 123 P.3d at 97 (quoting *Wright v. Schock*, 742 F.2d 541, 544 (9th Cir. 1984)). The Ninth Circuit authority on which *Sheehan* relies, however, has made "the defendant's consent a precondition to a dispositive ruling prior to certification"; while this condition is "easily satisfied when it is the defendant that makes the motion to dismiss or for summary judgment," defendants often have ample reason to object to a pre-certification dispositive motion from plaintiffs. Moore et al., *Moore's Federal Practice*, § [2]23.81, at 23–336 (3d ed. 2005) (citing *Wright*, 742 F.2d at 543–44). Without comment on this issue, the Washington Supreme Court has decided cases in which a trial court granted summary judgment to plaintiffs on cross-motions filed before resolving class certification issues. *See, e.g., Zachman v. Whirpool Acceptance Corp.*, 120 Wash. 2d 304, 841 P.2d 27 (1992) (cross-motions for summary judgment before certification; affirming partial summary judgment in favor of plaintiffs); *Drinkwitz v Allied Techsystems, Inc.,* 140 Wash. 2d 291, 996 P.2d 582 (2000) (same); *see also Williams*, 199 Wash. 2d at 248 (class certification decision need not always precede other merits determinations, including standing).

a. CR 23(a)(1)—Numerosity

A court may certify a class only if the members of the class are so numerous that it is impracticable for each of them to bring their claims individually before the court. Although plaintiffs need not show "that it would be impossible to join all members of the proposed class, they must show it would be extremely difficult or inconvenient." *Miller v. Farmer Bros. Co.*, 115 Wash. App. 815, 821, 64 P.3d 49, 53 (2003). Washington courts look to "the circumstances of the individual case" to determine whether a class is numerically viable. *Orland and Tegland, Wash. Prac. Civil Rule* 23 at 538 (4th ed. 1992). "As a general rule, joinder is impracticable where a class contains at least 40 members." *Chavez*, 190 Wash. 2d at 520, 415 P.3d at 232.

b. CR 23(a)(2)—Commonality

To merit certification, a case must present questions of law or fact common to the class. CR 23(a)(2). "CR 23 does not require 'that the shared questions of law or fact be identical' as to each individual class member." *Pellino v. Brink's Inc.*, 164 Wash. App. 668, 683, 267 P.3d 383, 392 (2011) (citing *Miller*, 115 Wash. App. at 824, 64 P.3d at 55). In *Brown v. Brown*, 6 Wash. App. 249, 255, 492 P.2d 581, 585 (1971), for example, the trial court denied CR 23(b)(2) certification to a class of utility customers challenging a utility's practices in terminating service because of payment arrearages. The court of appeals reversed. Although "it [could] not be denied that different facts and perhaps different questions of law exist within the potential class," the court of appeals held that "all . . . potential class members suffer under the same alleged arbitrary and discriminatory conduct . . . and all are potentially subject to having their service cut off for non-payment of bills or deposits." *Id.* Further, a single common issue can satisfy the commonality requirement. *Hill v. Garda CL Northwest, Inc.*, 198 Wash. App. 326, 341, 394 P.3d 390, 399 (2017).

But a finding of commonality "is not justified merely because class members share a legal theory of recovery." *Miller*, 115 Wash. App. at 824, 64 P.3d at 55. Accordingly, Washington courts have denied certification based on a lack of commonality where proof of a claim would require demonstration of facts particular to each plaintiff. *See, e.g., Panorama Residential Protective Ass'n v. Panorama Corp.*, 28 Wash. App. 923, 934, 627 P.2d 121, 129 (1981). Similarly, because a plaintiff "bears the burden of establishing CR 23's requirements," a failure to provide evidence of a common course of conduct requires denial of class certification. *See Weston v. Emerald City Pizza LLC*, 137 Wash. App. 164, 151 P.3d 1090, 1095 (2007) (reversing class certification based on lack of commonality); *Davies v. Philip Morris U.S.A., Inc.*, 2006 WL 1600067, at *3 (Wash. Super. 2006) ("commonality is defeated when, despite common questions, the answers vary with each individual").

The commonality requirement presents "a question of law for the court to determine at the class certification stage; it is not a question for the jury in determining liability." *Anfinson v. FedEx Ground Package Sys. Inc.*, 174 Wash. 2d 851, 874, 281 P.3d 289, 301 (2012). Thus, a jury instruction is improper if it allows the defendant to argue in closing in a wage and hour class action that commonality requires proof of liability as to *all* class members and that, if the proof falls short as to only one class member, the verdict must be for the defendant. Such an instruction erroneously "would have precluded plaintiffs from relying on evidence that was true for most, but not all, members of the class." *Id.* at 875, 281 P.3d at 301. Further, the instruction improperly "suggest[ed] to the jury that [plaintiff's] burden was to demonstrate to the jury that each and every member of the plaintiff class was an employee [rather than an independent contractor] without also making clear that this could be accomplished through the use of representative evidence." *Id.* The court of appeals in the same case made clear that, if the defendant believes commonality is lacking at trial, it should seek decertification—not argue the issue to the jury based on the alleged absence of uniform evidence as to each class member. *Anfinson v. FedEx Ground Package Sys. Inc.*, 159 Wash. App. 35, 67–68, 244 P.3d 47–48 (2010). Indeed, the Court of Appeals in *Lundquist* affirmed a trial court order decertifying a class action based on a post-summary judgment ruling finding that commonality was lacking. 2025 WL 1368086, at *6–7 (holding that plaintiff's decision to seek partial summary judgment on "two of the 18 policies within the class demonstrates that the court would be required to evaluate non-common evidence of intent as to each contract. . . . Because the court must examine individualized evidence to interpret each policy, the trial court did not abuse its discretion" in decertifying "under CR 23(a)(2)").

c. CR 23(a)(3)—Typicality

A court may certify a class only if the claims or defenses of the representative parties are typical of the claims or defenses of the class. CR 23(a)(3). The Washington decisions tend to blur the distinctions among the related requirements of commonality, typicality, and adequacy of representation. *See Oda*, 111 Wash. App. at 89, 44 P.3d at 13 ("The requirements of commonality and typicality tend to merge, and are often addressed as a single issue."); *see also Doe*, 55 Wash. App. at 119, 780 P.2d at 861 (discussing typicality and adequacy as related concepts). Unique defenses applicable to the named plaintiff may render the plaintiff atypical and inadequate. *Turk v. USAA*, 6 Wash. App. 2d 1033, 2018 WL 6523324, at *8 (2018) (unpublished) (citing *Hisle v. Todd Pacific Shipyards Corp.*, 113 Wash. App. 401, 426–27, 54 P.3d 687, 700 (2002) (considering trial court decision finding no typicality because defendant had defenses to named plaintiffs' claims that did not apply generally to the class; reversing after rejecting defenses on their merits). But Washington courts will allow substitution of a new class representative if the existing class representatives are found atypical or inadequate, without the need for an amended pleading and a renewed class certification motion. *See Elter v. United Servs. Auto. Ass'n*, 17 Wash. App. 2d 643, 654–55, 487 P.3d 539, 546 (2021).

Where class representatives can show they would "face[] harm from disclosure of their [personal] information, including harassment and potential loss of economic opportunity," disclosure of the class representatives' identities may not be necessary to establish typicality or adequacy, so long as there are sufficient indicia that that named plaintiffs share the same interests as the class. "The superior court did not need to know the class representatives' names; rather, it was provided with detailed declarations under penalty of perjury stating that the class members . . . would suffer the same injury and brought the same claims as their respective classes." *Doe L v. Pierce Cnty.*, 7 Wash. App. 2d 157, 203–04, 433 P.3d 838, 862 (2018).

d. CR 23(a)(4)—Adequacy of Representation

The named class representative must fairly and adequately represent the interests of the class. This means at least that the class representative and the members of the class must have claims against the same defendants. *Doe*, 55 Wash. App. at 118, 780 P.2d at 861. Further, the interests of the proposed class representative must not conflict with the interests of the class. In *DeFunis v. Odegaard*, 84 Wash. 2d 617, 619–21, 529 P.2d 438, 440–41 (1974), plaintiff sought certification of a class of all applicants denied admission by the University of Washington Law School as a result of minority admission preferences. Because members of the proposed class competed for admissions, and their interests therefore conflicted, the court found that the named plaintiff could not adequately represent all class members. *Id.* at 622–23, 529 P.2d at 441–42. Where circumstances permit, however, a conflict of interest among class members may be cured by certifying a small number of subclasses, each with an adequate representative. *See O'Brien v. Shearson Hayden Stone, Inc.*, 90 Wash. 2d 680, 687, 586 P.2d 830, 835 (1978). "'[M]inor conflicts' will not defeat class certification," *Nobl Park, L.L.C. of Vancouver*, 122 Wash. App. 838, 847, 95 P.3d 1265, 1271 (2004), but unique defenses applicable to the named plaintiffs render them both atypical and inadequate, *see Turk*, 2018 WL 6523324, at *8.

The class representative must retain competent class counsel, subject to the trial court's approval. The trial court will not approve counsel who has conflicting interests with respect to various class members or who "lacks the necessary experience in light of the complexity of the action." *Marquardt v. Fein*, 25 Wash. App. 651, 656–57, 612 P.2d 378, 381 (1980). Pro se plaintiffs may not serve as class representatives, since they "may not pursue claims on behalf of others in a representative capacity." *Khalid v. Microsoft Corp.*, 14 Wash. App. 2d 1055, 2020 WL 6037123, at *12 (2020) (unpublished) (citing *Simon v. Hartford Life, Inc.*, 546 F.3d 661, 664 (9th Cir. 2008)).

e. CR 23(b)

CR 23(b) offers three alternative approaches to class certification. Although "[i]t is not impossible that an action merits certification under all three sections of the rule, . . . it is surely rare, and such occasions require a more definite and clear order" explaining the basis for certification as to each subsection of CR 23(b). *Sitton v. State Farm Mut. Auto. Ins. Co.*, 116 Wash. App. 245, 63 P.3d 198, 204 (2003).

i. CR 23(b)(1). Washington appellate courts have devoted little attention to certification under CR 23(b)(1), except to observe that certification under that subsection is "designed to avoid prejudice to the defendant or absent class members," *Sitton*, 116 Wash. App. at 252, 63 P.3d at 203, and that "subsection (b)(1) is reserved for actions where individual adjudications would be impossible or unworkable," *Dolan v. King Cty.*, 13 Wash. App. 2d 1054, 2020 WL 2395167, at *11 (2020) (unpublished). No published Washington case affirms a contested class under CR 23(b)(1). *See Sitton*, 116 Wash. App. at 251–53, 63 P.3d at 203–04 (reversing CR 23(b)(1) certification); *Johnson v. Morris*, 87 Wash. 2d 922, 930, 557 P.2d 1299, 1305 (1976) (trial court refused to certify under CR 23(b)(1)). Because CR 23(b)(1) classes are mandatory (i.e., class members have no right to opt out), due process concerns allow damage claims to be resolved for members of such classes only if the alleged damages are incidental to claims for declaratory or injunctive relief. *Sitton*, 116 Wash. App. at 252, 63 P.3d at 203; *Nelson v. Appleway Chevrolet, Inc.*, 160 Wash. 2d 173, 190, 157 P.3d 847, 855 (2007) (quoting *Sitton*).

ii. CR 23(b)(2). CR 23(b)(2) permits certification of a class seeking injunctive relief against a party who has acted on grounds generally applicable to the class. "The courts have a tendency to relax the common questions of law or fact requirement when they are dealing with a CR 23(b)(2) action for injunctive or declaratory relief." Orland and Tegland, *Wash. Prac. Civil Rule* 23 at 542 (4th ed. 1992). Washington courts may not certify a Rule 23(b)(2) action for declaratory relief "[w]here the declaration merely forms the basis for monetary relief." *Eriks v. Denver*, 118 Wash. 2d 451, 466, 824 P.2d 1207, 1215 (1992). In these circumstances, certification is properly sought under the more demanding requirements of CR 23(b)(3). Despite this, a class certified under CR 23(b)(2) may seek damages "incidental" to the primary claim for injunctive or declaratory relief, i.e., damages "that flow directly from liability to the class as a whole on the claims forming the basis for injunctive or declaratory relief." *Sitton*, 116 Wash. App. at 252, 63 P.3d at 203 (quoting *Allison v. Citgo Petroleum Corp.*, 151 F.3d 402, 415 (5th Cir. 1998)). Where a plaintiff "asks the court to declare his rights under [a] statute," the plaintiff may invoke certification under CR 23(b)(2) even if the plaintiff also requests a monetary recovery. *Nelson v. Appleway Chevrolet, Inc.*, 160 Wash. 2d at 190, 157 P.3d at 855.

Damages properly pursued by a CR 23(b)(2) class must be in essence "a group remedy, rather than an individual one"; if the computation of damages "will require individualized determinations about each class member's circumstances," the damages "are not incidental" and a court may not certify under CR 23(b)(2). *Sitton*, 116 Wash. App. at 253, 63 P.3d at 203–04. *See also Nelson*, 160 Wash. 2d at 189, 157 P.3d at 855 (citing *Sitton* with approval). If, however, computation of monetary relief "relies entirely on objective facts, without need for individual assessments of each class member's circumstances," a court may certify under CR 23(b)(2) and still allow pursuit of monetary relief. Consistent with the express language of the rule, the Washington courts have held that a plaintiff need not show the predominance of common issues to obtain certification under CR 23(b)(2). *Nelson v. Appleway Chevrolet, Inc.*, 129 Wash. App. 927, 949, 121 P.3d 95, 106 (2005), *aff'd* 160 Wash. 2d 173, 157 P.3d 847 (2007).

Several reported Washington decisions have certified CR 23(b)(2) classes challenging government action. *See, e.g., Darrin v. H.D. Gould*, 85 Wash. 2d 859, 863, 540 P.2d 882, 885 (1975) (class for constitutional claims of girls excluded from high school football teams solely on basis of gender); *Johnson v. Moore*, 80 Wash. 2d 531, 536, 496 P.2d 334, 337 (1972) (class of individuals held in Seattle city jail "on suspicion" without a prompt hearing before a magistrate); *Dore v. Kinnear*, 79 Wash. 2d 755, 767, 489 P.2d 898, 905 (1971) (class of taxpayers seeking to enjoin Department of Revenue from basing property taxes on reevaluated property values). Washington courts also have certified CR 23(b)(2) classes challenging the constitutionality of a statute. *See, e.g., Zimmer v. City of Seattle*, 19 Wash. App. 864, 869, 578 P.2d 548, 551 (1978) (class comprised of children taken into custody by police officers relying on statute allowing removal of minors from prurient circumstances); *Hanson v. Hutt*, 83 Wash. 2d 195, 203, 517 P.2d 599, 604 (1973) (class of woman employees challenging constitutionality of statute denying them unemployment benefits for quitting because of pregnancy).

iii. CR 23(b)(3). A court may certify a class under CR 23(b)(3) only if questions of law and fact common to the class predominate over individual questions of law and fact and if a class action is superior to other available methods for the fair and efficient adjudication of the controversy. The "predominance requirement is more exacting and stringent than the commonality requirement" under CR 23(a). *Schwendeman v. USAA Cas. Ins. Co.*, 116 Wash. App. 9, 20, 65 P.3d 1, 6 (2003). "Simply stating the existence of commonalities does not prove predominance," absent a showing that those commonalities predominate over the individual issues. *Schnall v. AT&T Wireless Serv. Inc.*, 171 Wash. 2d 260, 270, 259 P.3d 129, 133 (2011). Instead, "the relevant inquiry is whether the issue or issues shared by the class members are the dominant, central, or overriding issues." *Miller*, 115 Wash. App. at 825, 64 P.3d at 56; *see also Admasu*, 185 Wash. App. at 31, 340 P.3d at 877 (quoting Miller). A single "overriding" issue may satisfy both commonality under CR 23(a)(2) and predominance under CR 23(b)(3). *Hill v. Garda CL Northwest, Inc.*, 198 Wash. App. 326, 341, 394 P.3d 390, 399 (2017).

"To determine whether common issues predominate over individual ones, a trial court pragmatically examines whether there is a common nucleus of operative facts in each class member's claim." *Chavez*, 190 Wash. 2d at 516, 415 P.3d at 229–30; *see also Schwendeman*, 116 Wash. App. at 20, 65 P.3d at 6 (same). Although "[c]omplete unanimity of position and purpose is not required among members of a class," *King v. Riveland*, 125 Wash. 2d 500, 519, 886 P.2d 160, 171 (1994), courts will not certify proposed classes pressing claims for which plaintiff-specific proof is required. In *Lacey Nursing Ctr., Inc. v. Washington Department of Revenue*, 128 Wash. 2d 40, 51–52, 905 P.2d 338, 43–44 (1995), for example, the court reversed certification of a class of nursing homes seeking tax refunds because the refund statute required individual proof of the amount each plaintiff was overtaxed. Similarly, in *Schwendeman*, the court held that determining whether a replacement part was of "like kind and quality" as required under an insurance contract would "require consideration of so many variables that the questions are more individualized than common to all class members." *Schwendeman*, 116 Wash. App. at 23, 65 P.3d at 8. In *Admasu*, the court of appeals affirmed a class certification denial in an inverse condemnation case because "each affected property owner must establish that his or her property has suffered a diminution in value because of the government action in order to demonstrate liability," making individual issues predominate even in the face of "[g]eneralized evidence of diminished value." *Admasu*, 185 Wash. App. at 32, 340 P.3d at 877. On the other hand, predominance "is not defeated merely because individual factual or legal issues exist; . . . [a] single common issue may be the overriding one in the litigation, despite the fact that the suit also entails numerous remaining individual questions." *Chavez*, 190 Wash. 2d at 519, 415 P.3d at 231(quotation marks omitted, citations omitted). As a result, in *Chavez* the Supreme Court reversed a denial of class certification because "individual issues . . . do not override the central, predominant issue of whether [the employer defendant] failed to ensure its nurses could take breaks and record missed breaks." *Id.*

In deciding whether common issues predominate, courts may use CR 23(c)(4) "to narrow the issues to be resolved as part of the class action," leaving individual issues to be resolved after disposition of the class case. *Sitton*, 116 Wash. App. at 255, 63 P.3d at 205. In such a case, the trial court must provide a means to decide whatever individual issues remain after class adjudication, taking care to respect the defendant's right to require "plaintiffs to prove individual causation," where applicable, and "to advance its defenses" on an individual basis. *Id.* at 258 63 P.3d at 206. In *Sitton*, the court of appeals explored several alternative approaches to this issue, including appointment of a master, certification of small subclasses, and decertification after adjudication of the class issues. *Id.; see also Davies*, 2006 WL 1600067, at *3 (class action is "simply a procedural device that allows class-wide issues to be tried in an economical fashion. It is not a means by which the Plaintiff is relieved of proving its case. It is not a means by which the Defendant is denied an opportunity to present its defense").

In *Schnall v. AT&T Wireless Services Inc.*, 171 Wash. 2d 260, 259 P.3d 129 (2011), the Washington Supreme Court addressed the impact of choice of law considerations on predominance, joining the "overwhelming number of federal courts" in holding that individual issues predominate in cases seeking the potential application of 50 states' laws to a nationwide class. *Id.* at 271, 259 P.3d at 134 (citations omitted; emphasis omitted). Discussing predominance under the Washington Consumer Protection Act, the Court also held that, in affirmative misrepresentation cases under the statute, plaintiffs must show the injury complained of "would not have happened if not for defendant's [unfair or deceptive] acts." *Id.* at 278, 259 P.3d at 137 (citation omitted, quotation marks omitted). It remanded for the trial court to consider whether "the causality element of plaintiffs'" statutory consumer protection claims defeated predominance for a proposed class of Washington residents. *Id.* at 280, 259 P.3d at 138.

CR 23(b)(3)'s "superiority" factor requires that a class action "be superior to other available methods for fair and efficient adjudication." *Schwendeman*, 116 Wash. App. at 28, 65 P.3d at 10. This "'requires that a class action be *superior* to other methods for the fair and efficient adjudication of the controversy," not "*just as good as*, other available methods.'" *Schnall*, 171 Wash. 2d at 275, 259 P.3d at 136 (citations omitted) (emphasis in original). Factors relevant to this determination include the interest of class members in controlling their own actions, the extent and nature of litigation already commenced, the desirability of concentrating claims in a particular forum, and the difficulties likely to be encountered in managing a class action. CR 23(b)(3). Superiority "is a highly discretionary determination that involves consideration of all the pros and cons of a class action as opposed to individual lawsuits." *Miller*, 115 Wash. App. at 828, 64 P.3d at 57. Where the proposed class is widely dispersed and the case would require many individual inquiries, "a class action would be difficult and unruly to manage" and therefore fail the superiority requirement of CR 23(b)(3). *Schwendeman*, 116 Wash. App. at 29, 63 P.3d at 11. Further, if similar cases have gone to trial on an individual basis, that fact may indicate a class action is not a superior procedural device. *See Admasu*, 185 Wash. App. at 35 & n.26, 340 P.3d at 879 & n.26 (no abuse of discretion in finding "a class action where the plaintiffs would likely allocate individual damages based on a class-wide diminution in value is not superior to individual actions where the plaintiffs would prove property-specific diminution in value," especially given history of individual litigation). "But the fact that individual issues might take some time to resolve does not make the class action unmanageable." *Chavez*, 190 Wash. 2d at 521, 415 P.3d at 232. Nor does the ability to proceed in small-claims court defeat superiority, at least where the issues in the litigation "implicate important public safety issues." *Id.* at 523–24, 415 P.3d at 233.

f. CR 23(c)(2) & (d)(2)—Notice

CR 23(c)(2) requires that "the best notice practicable under the circumstances" be given to the members of any class certified under CR 23(b)(3). In addition, CR 23(d)(2) gives the court discretion to require notice "of any step in the action, or of the proposed extent of the judgment, or of the opportunity of members to signify whether they consider the representation fair and adequate." The rules leave the content and form of the notice up to the court.

The "appropriate procedure for giving notice of a class action" lies in the trial court's discretion. *Wright v. Jeckle*, 121 Wash. App. 624, 629 n.1, 90 P.3d 65 (2004). But the trial court must adopt means of delivering class notice that one "might reasonably adopt" when "desirous of actually informing the absentee." *Summers v. Sea Mar Community Health Centers*, 29 Wash. App. 2d 476, 541 P.3d 381 (2024) (quoting *Mullane v. Cent. Hanover Bank & Trust Co.*, 339 U.S. 306, 315 (1950)). In *Summers*, for example, the court of appeals found a notice program sufficient where it included "first class mail when addresses were known and . . . e-mail when e-mail addresses were known, establishing a website and toll-free telephone number, and using online advertising on Facebook and Instagram in English and Spanish." *Summers*, 29 Wash. App. 2d at 494–95, 541 P.3d at 391–92. The low response rate (in *Summers*, a claims rate of only 0.5 percent) was not "necessarily an indicator of inadequate notice," *id.* at 496, 541 P.3d at 392, especially because the settlement "anticipat[ed] and mitigate[ed] the difficulty of notice by providing for cy pres relief" rather than just distributing settlement benefits in response to claims, 29 Wash. App. 2d at 498, 541 P.3d at 394.

Even when it simultaneously informs the class of a proposed settlement, a notice need not contain every detail concerning the class action. "Initial notices to class members need not contain all information and details of class membership or terms of settlement. A notice is sufficient if it provides general notice of the action, class membership requirements, and provides information by which interested persons can obtain a copy of the settlement." *Nobl Park, L.L.C. of Vancouver*, 122 Wash. App. 383, 847, 95 P.3d 1265, 1270 (2004). Applying these principles, the court of appeals in *Nobl Park* found a party bound by provisions in a Tennessee class action settlement agreement, even though the party "chose not to request a copy of the . . . Settlement or to review the exclusion requirements." *Id.*

In class actions involving class members' confidential affairs, courts can implement class notice procedures to safeguard privacy interests. In *Wright*, for example, the court of appeals held that notice to a class of fen-phen consumers suing their physician would not compromise patients' privacy interests where a mailing service received only sealed envelopes containing the class notice and a list of names, with no information as to the nature of the litigation. 121 Wash. App. at 631, 90 P.3d at 68–69.

g. CR 23(e)—Settlement

"[T]he primary concern" of Rule 23(e), which deals with class action settlements, is "the protection of those class members, including the named plaintiffs, whose rights may not have been given due regard by the negotiating parties." *Pickett v. Holland America Line-Westours Inc.*, 145 Wash. 2d

178, 188, 35 P.3d 351, 356 (2001), *cert. denied sub nom. Bebchick v. Holland America Line-Westours Inc.,* 536 U.S. 941 (2002). The requirements to satisfy Rule 23(e) are "for the most part procedural, requiring a notice of proposed settlement be given to class members and that they be given an opportunity to object to the settlement." *Id.* At the same time, Washington courts have recognized that class action settlements, "are susceptible to certain types of abuses," which require a "court overseeing a class action [to] maintain[] a higher degree of control in order to protect the class and absentee class members." *In re Firestorm 1991*, 106 Wash. App. 217, 222–23, 22 P.3d 849, 851 (2001). Unlike some other states, Washington has not adopted the "private attorney general" doctrine, and attorney fees therefore are not awarded in class actions (or any other actions) absent a statutory or contractual basis. *See Wright v. Jeckle*, 121 Wash. App. 624, 632–33, 90 P.3d 65, 69 (2004).

A trial court should approve a proposed settlement if it "is determined to be fair, adequate, and reasonable." *Pickett*, 145 Wash. 2d at 188, 35 P.3d at 356. Washington courts have adopted a non-exhaustive list of eight factors to be used in this determination: (1) the likelihood of success by plaintiffs; (2) the amount of discovery or evidence; (3) the settlement terms and conditions; (4) recommendation and experience of counsel; (5) future expense and likely duration of litigation; (6) recommendation of neutral parties, if any; (7) number of objectors and nature of objections; and (8) the presence of good faith and the absence of collusion. *See id.* at 188–89, 35 P.3d at 356 (citing Herbert B. Newberg & Alba Conte, *Newberg on Class Actions* § 11.43 "General Criteria for Settlement Approval" (3d ed. 1992)). The trial court's review "must be limited to the extent necessary to reach a reasoned judgment that the agreement is not the product of fraud or overreaching by, or collusion between, the negotiating parties, and that the settlement, taken as a whole, is fair, reasonable and adequate to all concerned." *Pickett*, 145 Wash. 2d at 189, 35 P.3d at 356. Once the trial judge rules on a settlement, its decision is accorded great weight "because he is exposed to the litigants, and their strategies, positions and proofs. He is aware of the expense and possible legal bars to success. Simply stated, he is on the firing line and can evaluate the action accordingly." *Id.* at 189, 35 P.3d at 357. But "[c]ourts apply heightened scrutiny when assessing class settlements negotiated prior to class certification." *Summers v. Sea Mar Community Health Centers*, 29 Wash. App. 2d 476, 499–500, 541 P.3d 381, 394 (2024) (quotation marks omitted, citations omitted).

Because of due process concerns, class settlements generally cannot release claims of absent class members unrelated to the matters at issue in the case being settled. Having said that, "[a] class settlement agreement may preclude a party from bringing a related claim in the future even though the claim was not presented and might not have been presentable in the class action," as long as "the released claim is based on the identical factual predicate as that underlying the claims in the settled class action." *Summers*, 29 Wash. App. 2d at 405–05, 541 P.3d at 396 (quotation marks omitted, citations omitted).

Any class member objecting to a settlement must raise all objections in the trial court or forfeit the right to review on appeal because "reviewing unpreserved objections for the first time on appeal deprives class members of their right to be apprised of the nature of any objection to the class settlement." *Deien v. Seattle City Light*, 26 Wash. App. 2d 57, 527 P.3d 102, 106–07 (2023). "[T]he court may deny without prejudice the approval of a settlement agreement, explaining the deficiencies that foreclosed such approval and allowing the parties an opportunity to address the settlement's shortcomings." *Id.* at 107.

Class settlement distribution receives the same scrutiny as the settlement itself—it must be fair, reasonable, and adequate. *See In re Firestorm 1991*, 106 Wash. App. at 223, 22 P.3d at 851. The trial court's distribution plan will be reversed only upon a showing of an abuse of discretion. *See id.* Indeed, a trial court may even require a repayment from a class member if a mistake in allocation has occurred because "it is not precluded from modifying a distribution plan in a way that will enhance an equitable distribution, so long as it is fair and just in light of the prevailing circumstances." *Id.* at 225, 22 P.3d at 853.

Once a party opts out of a class settlement—even if acting as a class representative—the party "has no standing to object to the settlement, its fairness or lack thereof," or as to the manner of notification of settlement. *Aguirre v. AT&T Wireless Servs.*, 109 Wash. App. 80, 85, 33 P.3d 1110, 1112 (2001). On the other hand, the court of appeals has held that even after settling individual claims, a putative class representative may appeal a class certification denial, on the theory that the representative's "individual claim on the merits is separate from his claim that he is entitled to represent a class." *Schwendeman v. USAA Cas. Ins. Co.*, 116 Wash. App. 9, 17, 65 P.3d 1, 4–5 (2003) (release addressing only individual claims did not extinguish right to appeal denial of class certification); *but see Jones v. Windermere Real Estate Services Co.*, 19 Wash. App. 2d 1004 (2021) (unpublished) (where named plaintiffs accept offer of judgment to settle the "above titled cause," they settled all claims and barred appeal of earlier class certification denial).

In contrast to the Federal Rule, Washington's CR 23(e) may require notice of a settlement to absent class members even if the parties settle on an individual basis. In deciding whether to require notice, a trial court should consider the possibility of prejudice to absent class members. *Jones v. Home Care of Wash., Inc.*, 152 Wash. App. 674, 682–83, 216 P.3d 1106, 1109–10 (2009). In this respect, Washington law follows federal law before the 2003 amendments to Federal Rule of Civil Procedure 23. In *Pugh v. Evergreen Hospital Medical Center*, 177 Wash. App. 348, 356, 311 P.3d 1253, 1256 (2014), the court of appeals held "a suit brought by [a union] in its associational capacity" on behalf of its members could be settled without court approval under CR 23(e).

"Judgments in class action lawsuits [in other states] are entitled to full faith and credit absent a due process violation or jurisdictional defect." *Chan Healthcare Group P.S. v. Liberty Mut. Fire & Ins. Co.*, 192 Wash. 2d 516, 522, 431 P.3d 484, 487 (2018); *see also Nauheim v. Volkswagen Grp. of Am., Inc.*, 2 Wash. App. 2d 1062 (2018) (unpublished) (class action settlement and judgment extinguish claims of all class members). But if a class member shows the class representative in the foreign case "did not adequately represent Washington class members," making the judgment constitutionally infirm, Washington courts "would not give full faith and credit to the judgment." *Chan Healthcare Group*, 192 Wash. 2d at 523, 431 P.3d at 488. Washington courts will enforce broad releases included in settlements of foreign class actions, even when a class member seeks to "avoid its contractual commitment by bringing claims on behalf of others" as assignee. *Folweiler Chiropractic PS v. Safeco Ins. Co. of Am.*, 19 Wash. App. 2d 1101, at *1–3 (2021) (unpublished).

h. CR 23(f)—Disposition of Residual Funds

CR 23(f) details how to disburse residual funds in a class action, i.e., funds remaining after the payment of all approved class member claims, expenses, litigation costs, attorneys' fees, and other court-approved disbursements. *See* CR 23(f)(1). Effective September 1, 2017, the rule requires that fifty percent of any residual funds be disbursed to the Legal Foundation of Washington to support activities and programs promoting access to the civil justice system for low-income residents of Washington. CR 23(f)(2). The remaining fifty percent of residual funds may be provided to either the Legal Foundation of Washington or, in the alternative, to "any other entity for purposes that have a direct or indirect relationship to the objectives of the underlying litigation or otherwise promote the substantive or procedural interests of members of the certified class." *Id.*

Although CR 23(f) applies to any residual funds derived from class relief, whether by settlement or judgment, Rule CR 23(f) does not require that a settlement provide or allow for a residual fund.

Instead, the rule is not "intended to limit the parties to a class action from suggesting, or the trial court from approving, a settlement that does not create residual funds." CR 23(f)(1). *See also* Comment to CR 23(f) (CR 23(f) does not "alter the ability of the parties, subject to court approval, to formulate settlement agreements that leave no residual funds remaining for distribution"). Thus, even after promulgation of Rule 23(f), parties remain free to negotiate an agreement that disposes of all settlement funds, even through a reversion to the settling defendant, and thus avoids the creation of a residual.

4. COMMUNICATIONS WITH ABSENT CLASS MEMBERS

Washington appellate courts have not articulated any clear standards to guide trial courts in deciding whether to limit communications with absent class members. The Washington Supreme Court last considered the propriety of communicating with absent class members in two cases decided the same day in 1982, both involving communications by a plaintiff (or plaintiff's counsel) with absent class members. In *Darling v. Champion Home Builders Co.*, 96 Wash. 2d 701, 706, 638 P.2d 1249, 1252 (1982), the trial court followed a King County local rule (no longer in existence) and entered an order forbidding the parties and their lawyers from "communicat[ing] concerning such [class] action with any potential or actual class member not a formal party to the action without the consent of and approval of the communication by order of the Court." On the plaintiff's appeal, the Supreme Court reversed, holding the trial court needed to make "findings of fact [and] conclusions of law to support the order," as well as "a clear record reflecting the court's weighing of the need for a limitation and the potential interference with the rights of the parties." *Darling*, 96 Wash. 2d at 707, 638 P.2d at 1252. And in *Johnston v. Beneficial Management Corp.*, 96 Wash. 2d 708, 638 P.2d 1201 (1982), the Court considered an order finding plaintiff's counsel in contempt because, after settlement, he sent class members a reminder of the deadline for submitting claims, in violation of a pretrial order restraining communications with absent class members. The Court vacated the contempt finding, holding it "reasonable" to conclude "the settlement agreement superseded the original protective order"; as a result, since counsel had the obligation to send class notice, the Court "cannot say [the reminder] notice was excessive." *Johnston,* 96 Wash. 2d at 715, 638 P.2d at 1205.

Although *Darling* and *Johnston* remain good law, they provide little practical guidance. By contrast, three decades of federal jurisprudence have addressed class communications in detail, generally following *Gulf Oil Co. v. Bernard*, 452 U.S. 89 (1981). (The Washington Supreme Court cited *Bernard* in *Darling* and declined to follow it—but nevertheless appeared to adopt its reasoning.) For example, in *Saucedo v. NW Management and Realty Services*, 2013 WL 163425 (E.D. Wash. Jan. 15, 2013), the district court recognized "that defendants are generally permitted to interview putative class members *ex parte* before a class is formally certified . . . on the theory that putative class members do not become represented by counsel until the class is actually certified." *Id.* at *1. But the district court forbade contact with absent class members about their immigration status, finding it "not particularly relevant" to class certification and "inherently coercive." *Id.* at *2. By contrast, the district court denied a request to limit defendant's communications with absent class members in *Bell v. Addus Healthcare, Inc.*, 2007 WL 2752893 (W.D. Wash. Sept. 19, 2007), where the plaintiff failed to show the defendant "used abusive or coercive practices during the interviews in question." *Id.* at *3.

In short, Washington follows the general rule allowing either party to contact absent class members before class certification. But it also follows the general rule permitting courts to restrict communications on an appropriate showing of abusive or coercive practices.

5. MISCELLANEOUS

CR 23 does not address the form or content of a class definition. The Washington Supreme Court has made clear, however, that a class definition must be framed so that disposition of the named plaintiff's claims can fairly bind a cohesive class. In *Mader v. Health Care Authority*, 149 Wash. 2d 458, 468–69, 70 P.3d 931, 936 (2003), the court held that a class definition was a "manifest abuse of discretion" where, as defined, the class encompassed only a fraction of the people who would be entitled to relief under "the essence" of plaintiffs' theory. On the other hand, "[t]he class should not be defined by criteria that are subjective or that require an analysis of the merits of the case." *Kihuria v. Consumer Legal Servs. Am., Inc.*, 5 Wash. App. 2d 1001, 2018 WL 4087600, at *6 (2018) (unpublished) (rejecting ascertainability argument on the ground that class was objectively defined); *see also Elter*, 17 Wash. App. 2d at 658 n.2, 487 P.3d at 547 n.2 (no ascertainability requirement under CR 23). The class definition has significant downstream consequences beyond the issue of class certification. For example, the court of appeals has recognized that where a subgroup is expressly excluded from a class definition, and the defendant prevails, collateral estoppel does not bar the excluded subgroup from seeking class relief at a later date on the same theories. *Mendoza v. Expert Janitorial Servs., LLC*, 11 Wash. App. 2d 32, 39–40, 450 P.3d 1220, 1224–25 (2019) (rejecting virtual representation doctrine on the facts).

Class actions are available to pursue statutory claims, even if the statute appears to afford relief only to individuals who sue. Thus, in *Doe v. Dept. of Corrections*, 197 Wash. App. 609, 629–30, 391 P.3d 496, 506 (2017), the court of appeals held that plaintiffs could pursue class claims even though the relevant statute allowed relief only "on motion and affidavit" by an aggrieved party. "[T]he representative plaintiffs stand in for all other members of the class; those members are treated as parties to the litigation." *Id.* As a result, "even statutes the legislature phrases in individual terms allow for class actions." *Id.*

In *Campeau v. Yakima HMA LLC*, __ Wash. 2d __, 551 P.3d 1037, 1040 (2024), the Washington Supreme Court "decline[d] to determine whether *American Pipe* tolling is available in Washington, deciding it would "await a case that more squarely confronts that question." *But see Pickett v. Holland America Line-Westours Inc.*, 145 Wash. 2d 178, 194–95, 35 P.3d 351, 359 (2001), *cert. denied sub nom. Bebchick v. Holland America Line-Westours Inc.*, 536 U.S. 941 (2002) (appearing to recognize tolling under *American Pipe & Construction Co. v. Utah*, 414 U.S. 538, 551 (1974), as a matter of Washington law). The court in *Campeau* nevertheless tolled the limitations period for a newly filed class action where a union brought an earlier case seeking the same class relief for its members under a theory of associational standing but "associational standing fails, [the] association's member files a follow-on class action, and all of the other elements of equitable tolling have been met." *Campeau*, 551 P.3d at 1042.

Damages class actions in Washington can proceed based on theories of aggregate damages recovery. "When liability has already been established, it is not necessary for each plaintiff in a class action to prove the amount of damages on an individualized basis." *Moore v. Wash. Health Care Auth.*, 181 Wash. 2d 299, 307–08, 332 P.3d 461, 465 (2014). "[I]t is not unusual, and probably more likely in many types of cases, that aggregate evidence of the defendant's liability is more accurate and precise than would be so with individual proofs of loss." *Id.* at 308, 332 P.3d at 466 (quoting Alba Conte & Herbert B. Newberg, *Newberg on Class Actions,* § 10:2, at at 479 (4th ed. 2002)). Thus, in a case involving the State's wrongful denial of health care coverage, the Court allowed plaintiffs to prove damages by" statistically estimat[ing] their healthcare costs by comparing the [class] with State employees who did receive health benefits." *Id.*

Before the U.S. Supreme Court decided *AT&T Mobility, LLC v. Concepcion*, 131 S. Ct. 1740

(2011), the Washington Supreme Court refused to enforce a contract clause requiring arbitration if the clause included a waiver of the right to proceed on a class basis. In the context of a Washington Consumer Protection Act (CPA) claim for a small amount of money, the Court found such a class action waiver to be "an unconscionable violation of this State's policy to 'protect the public and foster fair and honest competition,' . . . because it drastically forestalls attempts to vindicate consumer rights." *Scott v. Cingular Wireless*, 160 Wash. 2d 843, 854, 161 P.3d 1000, 1006 (2007). The Ninth Circuit has held that the Federal Arbitration Act preempts the rule announced in *Scott* and requires enforcement of a class action waiver contained within an arbitration clause. *Coneff v. AT&T Corp*., 673 F.3d 1155, 1159–60 (9th Cir. 2012). On the other hand, the Washington Supreme Court has clarified that preemption principles do not require enforcement of an arbitration clause deemed unconscionable under traditional principles of contract law. *Gandee v. LDL Freedom Ents., Inc.*, 176 Wash. 2d 598, 610, 293 P.3d 1197, 1203 (2013). And where the Federal Arbitration Act does not apply, then Washington courts will strike class action waivers as substantively unconscionable if enforcement will frustrate fundamental public policy. *Oakley v. Domino's Pizza LLC*, 23 Wash. App. 2d 218, 233–35, 516 P.3d 1237, 1245–46 (2022) (holding FAA did not apply to transportation worker and class action waiver in employment dispute was unconscionable under Washington law).

The Washington Court of Appeals has followed the U.S. Supreme Court's lead in holding that a court cannot compel parties to engage in class arbitration where "the parties [have] not agreed to arbitrate on a class-wide basis." *Hill v. Garda CL Northwest Inc.*, 169 Wash. App. 685, 698–99, 281 P.3d 334, 341 (2012) (citing *Stolt-Nielsen S.A. v. Animal Feeds Int'l Corp.*, 130 S. Ct. 1758, 1775 (2010)). The Washington Supreme Court reversed, finding the arbitration clause in *Hill* unconscionable and unenforceable, without reaching the court of appeals' holding regarding the necessity of consent to class arbitration. *See Hill v. Garda CL Northwest Inc.*, 179 Wash. 2d 47, 308 P.3d 635 (2013). More recently, the Court of Appeals has held that courts, rather than arbitrators, should usually decide issues of arbitrability, including whether the agreement allows for class arbitration. *Romney for Estate of Romney v. Franciscan Med. Grp.*, 199 Wash. App. 589, 595–96, 399 P.3d 1220, 1224–25 (2017) (holding agreement's silence on class arbitration barred arbitration). A defendant seeking to enforce a clause providing only for individual arbitration must timely object to class arbitration or risk waiving that objection. *Id.* at 601–08, 399 P.3d at 1227–29 (finding waiver of objection and directing "trial court to enter an order sending the putative class to a single arbitrator under the terms of the agreements"). Further, parties may agree to delegate the resolution of arbitrability issues to the arbitrator, and Washington courts will enforce that delegation. *See, e.g., Raven Offshore Yacht Shipping, LLP v. F.T. Holdings, LLC*, 199 Wash. App. 534, 538, 400 P.3d 347, 349 (2017) (enforcing delegation clause in rules of the Maritime Arbitration Association of the United States); *Woolley v. el Toro.com, LLC*, 17 Wash. App. 2d 1037, 2021 WL 1788526, at *4 (2021) (unpublished) (enforcing delegation of arbitrability issues in rules of American Arbitration Association).

The Washington Supreme Court has also refused to enforce a forum-selection clause where the designated forum did not allow for class actions and the plaintiff had asserted a Washington CPA claim. "[A] forum selection clause that seriously impairs the plaintiff's ability to go forward on a [CPA] claim of small value by eliminating class suits in circumstances where there is no feasible alternative for seeking relief violates public policy and is unenforceable." *Dix v. ICT Group, Inc.*, 160 Wash. 2d 826, 837, 161 P.3d 1016, 1022 (2007).

Defendants cannot shift the burden of attorneys' fees in a putative class action using RCW 4.84.250, which provides that a trial court shall award attorney fees to the prevailing party in "any action for damages where the amount pleaded" is $10,000 or less "if the plaintiff recovers nothing, or if the recovery, exclusive of costs, is the same or less than the amount the defendant offered to settle." *Gordon v. Robinhood Financial, LLC*, __ Wash. App. 2d __, 547 P.3d 945, 957 (2024). Even where the named plaintiff's individual claim seeks less than $10,000 and fits squarely within the statute, "[i]nterpreting RCW 4.84.250 as applying to class action lawsuits could and likely would interfere with the orderly administration of such actions. Partly because class action lawsuits are complex cases where millions of dollars are often at stake, we believe the legislature did not intend for RCW 4.84.250 to apply to such lawsuits." *Id.* But if a court strikes the class allegations and the case proceeds individually, RCW 4.84.250 does apply, and courts may award a defendant attorneys' fees. *Greenlee v. Frye's Electronics, Inc.*, 136 Wash. App. 1054, 2007 WL 211210, *1–4 (2007).

RULE 23 OF THE WASHINGTON SUPERIOR COURT CIVIL RULES

RULE 23. CLASS ACTIONS

(a) *Prerequisites to a class action.* One or more members of a class may sue or be sued as representative parties on behalf of all only if (1) the class is so numerous that joinder of all members is impracticable, (2) there are questions of law or fact common to the class, (3) the claims or defenses of the representative parties are typical of the claims or defenses of the class, and (4) the representative parties will fairly and adequately protect the interests of the class.

(b) *Class actions maintainable.* An action may be maintained as a class action if the prerequisites of section (a) are satisfied, and in addition:

(1) The prosecution of separate actions by or against individual members of the class would create a risk of

(A) inconsistent or varying adjudications with respect to individual members of the class which would establish incompatible standards of conduct for the party opposing the class, or

(B) adjudications with respect to individual members of the class which would as a practical matter be dispositive of the interests of the other members not parties to the adjudications or substantially impair or impede their ability to protect their interest; or

(2) The party opposing the class has acted or refused to act on grounds generally applicable to the class, thereby making appropriate final injunctive relief or corresponding declaratory relief with respect to the class as a whole; or

(3) The court finds that the questions of law or fact common to the members of the class predominate over any questions affecting only individual members, and that a class action is superior to other available methods for the fair and efficient adjudication of the controversy. The matters pertinent to the findings include: (A) the interest of members of the class in individually controlling the prosecution or defense of separate actions; (B) the extent and nature of any litigation concerning the controversy already commenced by or against members of the class; (C) the desirability or undesirability of concentrating the litigation of the claims in the particular forum; (D) the difficulties likely to be encountered in the management of a class action.

(c) *Determination by order whether class action to be maintained; notice; judgment; actions conducted partially as class actions.*

(1) As soon as practicable after the commencement of an action brought as a class action, the court shall determine by order whether it is to be so maintained. An order under this subsection may be conditional, and may be altered or amended before the decision on the merits.

(2) In any class action maintained under subsection (b)(3), the court shall direct to the

members of the class the best notice practicable under the circumstances, including individual notice to all members who can be identified through reasonable effort. The notice shall advise each member that (A) the court will exclude the member from the class if the member so requests by a specified date; (B) the judgment, whether favorable or not, will include all members who do not request exclusion; and (C) any member who does not request exclusion may, if the member desires, enter an appearance through counsel.

(3) The judgment in an action maintained as a class action under subsection (b)(1) or (b)(2), whether or not favorable to the class, shall include and describe those whom the court finds to be members of the class. The judgment in an action maintained as a class action under subsection (b)(3), whether or not favorable to the class, shall include and specify or describe those to whom the notice provided in subsection (c)(2) was directed, and who have not requested exclusion, and whom the court finds to be members of the class.

(4) When appropriate, (A) an action may be brought or maintained as a class action with respect to particular issues, or (B) a class may be divided into subclasses and each subclass treated as a class, and the provisions of this rule shall then be construed and applied accordingly.

(d) *Orders in conduct of actions.* In the conduct of actions to which this rule applies, the court may make appropriate orders: (1) determining the course of proceedings or prescribing measures to prevent undue repetition or complication in the presentation of evidence or argument; (2) requiring, for the protection of the members of the class or otherwise for the fair conduct of the action, that notice be given in such manner as the court may direct to some or all of the members of any step in the action, or of the proposed extent of the judgment, or of the opportunity of members to signify whether they consider the representation fair and adequate, to intervene and present claims or defenses, or otherwise to come into the action; (3) imposing conditions on the representative parties or on intervenors; (4) requiring that the pleadings be amended to eliminate therefrom allegations as to representation of absent persons, and that the action proceed accordingly; (5) dealing with similar procedural matters. The orders may be combined with an order under rule 16, and may be altered or amended as may be desirable from time to time.

(e) *Dismissal or compromise.* A class action shall not be dismissed or compromised without the approval of the court, and notice of the proposed dismissal or compromise shall be given to all members of the class in such manner as the court directs.

(f) *Disposition of residual funds.*

(1) "Residual Funds" are funds that remain after the payment of all approved class member claims, expenses, litigation costs, attorneys' fees, and other court-approved disbursements to implement the relief granted. Nothing in this rule is intended to limit the parties to a class action from suggesting, or the trial court from approving, a settlement that does not create residual funds.

(2) Any order entering a judgment or approving a proposed compromise of a class action certified under this rule that establishes a process for identifying and compensating members of the class shall provide for the disbursement of residual funds. In matters

where the claims process has been exhausted and residual funds remain, not less than fifty percent (50%) of the residual funds shall be disbursed to the Legal Foundation of Washington to support activities and programs that promote access to the civil justice system for low income residents of Washington State. The court may disburse the balance of any residual funds beyond the minimum percentage to the Legal Foundation of Washington or to any other entity for purposes that have a direct or indirect relationship to the objectives of the underlying litigation or otherwise promote the substantive or procedural interests of members of the certified class.

Chapter authors Stephen M. Rummage and Fred B. Burnside are partners in the Seattle office of Davis Wright Tremaine LLP, where their practices focus on complex, class action, and appellate litigation.

WEST VIRGINIA

1. COMPARISON OF WEST VIRGINIA RULE 23 WITH FEDERAL RULE 23

Rule 23 of the West Virginia Rules of Civil Procedure, adopted on April 6, 1998 and revised effective January 1, 2025, is essentially identical to Rule 23 of the Federal Rules of Civil Procedure, except for Fed. R. Civ. P. 23(f) and 23(g). *State ex rel. Erie Fire Ins. Co. v. Madden,* 515 S.E.2d 351 (W. Va. 1998). Prior to that date West Virginia used a variation of the 1938 Federal Rule 23. As a result, no decisions regarding class issues in West Virginia dealt explicitly with issues arising under 23(b)(3) (superiority, predominance) or 23(b)(1) and (2). *Burks v. Wymer*, 172 W. Va. 478, 307 S.E.2d 647 (1983).

In *In re W. Va. Rezulin Litigation v. Hutchinson*, 214 W. Va. 52, 585 S.E.2d 52 (2003), the Supreme Court of Appeals held that the pre-1998 factors in determining class certification were no longer sufficient. The new rule required a different analysis: provided that the requirements of numerosity, commonality, typicality and adequacy of representation and any of the three requirements of Rule 23(b) were met, the class should be certified. *Rezulin* was followed by *Love v. Georgia-Pacific Corp*., 214 W. Va. 484, 590 S.E.2d 677 (2003), *Ways v. Imation Enterprises Corp*., 214 W.Va. 305, 589 S.E.2d 36 (2003), *Gulas v. Infocision Mgmt. Corp*., 215 W. Va. 225, 599 S.E.2d 648 (2004), and *State of West Virginia ex rel. Chemtall, Inc. v. Madden*, 216 W. Va. 443, 607 S.E.2d 772 (2004), all of which reaffirmed that new guidelines exist for class actions in West Virginia.

2. CASE LAW INTERPRETING RULE 23

Certification of a class under Rule 23 may only be granted when the party seeking certification has satisfied all four prerequisites of Rule 23(a)—numerosity, commonality, typicality, and adequacy of representation—and one of the three subdivisions of Rule 23(b). *Chemtall, Inc*., 216 W. Va. at 453, 607 S.E.2d at 782. *See also Rezulin*, 214 W. Va. at 64, 585 S.E.2d at 64. The party who seeks to establish the propriety of a class action has the burden of proving that the pre-requisites of Rule 23 have been satisfied. *Rezulin*, 214 W. Va. at 64, 585 S.E.2d at 64 (quoting *Jefferson County Bd. of Educ. v. Jefferson County Educ. Ass'n,* 183 W. Va. 15, 22, 393 S.E.2d 653, 660 (W. Va. 1990)). Similarly, the party who seeks to establish the propriety of a class action also has the burden of proving that the statutory prerequisites of a class action have been satisfied. Syl. pt. 5, *Ways v. Imation Enterprises Corp*., 214 W. Va. 305, 589 S.E.2d 36 (2003). Whether the requirements for a class action exist rests within the sound discretion of the trial court. *Id.* (quoting Syl. pt. 5, *Mitchem v. Melton*, 167 W. Va. 21, 277 S.E.2d 895 (1981)). Nothing in the language or history of Rule 23 gives a court any authority to conduct a preliminary inquiry into the merits of a suit to determine whether it may be maintained as a class action. *Rezulin,* 214 W. Va. at 63, 585 S.E.2d at 63. However, a trial court will be charged with clear error and an abuse of discretion if it does not undertake a consideration of questions of merit that are *essential* to a thorough analysis of whether the prerequisites of

Rule 23 are satisfied. *State ex rel. West Virginia Univ. Hosp., Inc. v. Gaujot*, 242 W. Va. 54, 63, 829 S.E.2d 54 (2019) (emphasis added). The trial court cannot capriciously or arbitrarily refuse a class action if it meets the requirements of Rule 23. *Evans,* 168 W. Va. at 224, 283 S.E.2d at 855. An order by the trial court refusing to certify a class action under Rule 23 is appealable. *Mitchem v. Melton*, 167 W. Va. 21, 32, 277 S.E.2d 895, 901 (1981). The West Virginia Supreme Court of Appeals will review a circuit court's order granting or denying a motion for class certification under an abuse of discretion standard. *Gulas,* 215 W. Va. at 227, 599 S.E.2d at 650. It is an abuse of discretion for the trial court to deny certification and dismiss the class action without appropriate consideration and articulation of how the movant failed to establish the Rule 23 criteria. *Evans,* 168 W. Va. at 224, 283 S.E.2d at 855.

Where a party seeks to proceed as a class representative under Rule 23 and where issues related to class certification are present, reasonable discovery related to class certification issues is appropriate, particularly where the pleadings and record do not sufficiently indicate the presence or absence of the requisite facts to warrant an initial determination of class action status. *Gulas,* 215 W. Va. at 229, 599 S.E.2d at 652, *Love*, 214 W. Va. at 488, 590 S.E.2d at 681. In *Love*, the circuit court abused its discretion in denying the appellant's motion to conduct discovery on class certification. *Accord, Gulas*, 215 W.Va. 225, 599 S.E.2d 648, reversing denial of class certification for the purpose of allowing discovery. To bring a class action lawsuit, at least one named plaintiff must have standing with respect to each claim asserted, and the burden of establishing standing is on the plaintiff(s). Syl. pt. 1, *State ex rel. W. Va. Univ. Hosp. – East, Inc. v. Hammer*, 246 W. Va. 122, 866 S.E.2d 187 (2021). Finally, a class certification order should be detailed and specific in showing the rule basis for the certification and the relevant facts supporting the legal conclusions. *Chemtall Inc*., 216 W. Va. at 454, 607 S.E.2d at 783.

a. Rule 23(a)

i. Numerosity. Numerosity is an absolute pre-requisite to maintaining a class action suit. *Rezulin,* 214 W. Va. at 64, 585 S.E.2d at 64. The standard under West Virginia practice is whether persons constituting the class are so numerous as to make joinder impractical. *Jefferson County Bd. of Educ*., 183 W. Va. at 22, 393 S.E.2d at 660. The test for impracticability of joining all members does not mean impossibility but only difficulty or inconvenience of joining all members. *Mitchem*, 167 W. Va. at 33, 277 S.E.2d at 902. Before a class can be certified pursuant to Rule 23 it is imperative that the class be identified with sufficient specificity so that it is administratively feasible for the court to ascertain whether a particular individual is a member. *State ex rel. Metropolitan Life Ins. Co. v. Starcher*, 196 W. Va. 519, 526, 474 S.E.2d 186, 190 (1996). A class action cannot be maintained if it is too ill defined, amorphous, or fails in objective terms to describe the class with necessary specificity. *Id.* at 523.

ii. Commonality. Commonality is an absolute prerequisite to the certification of a class action. *Rezulin,* 214 W. Va. at 64, 585 S.E.2d at 64. The rights asserted against or on behalf of those making up the class must be of the character specified in the rule. *Jefferson Cty. Bd. of Educ*., Syl. pt. 5, 183 W. Va. 15, 393 S.E.2d 653. A common nucleus of operative fact or law is usually enough to satisfy the commonality requirement, as the commonality threshold is not high and requires only that the resolution of common questions affect all or a substantial number of class members. Syl. pt. 11, *Rezulin,* 214 W. Va. 52, 585 S.E.2d 52 (2003). *See also Chemtall Inc*., 216 W. Va. at 452, 607 S.E.2d at 781.

iii. Typicality. A class representative must be a member of the class he or she represents. *Bd.*

of Educ. of Monongalia Cty. v. Starcher, 176 W. Va. 388, 391, 343 S.E.2d 673, 676 (1986). A representative party's claim or defense is typical if it arises from the same event, practice, or course of conduct that gives rise to the claims of other class members. *Rezulin,* 214 W. Va. at 68, 585 S.E.2d at 68. A representative's claims need only be typical of the other class members' claims, not identical, and if the representative's claim arises out of the same legal or remedial theory, factual variations will normally not be sufficient to preclude class treatment. *Id. Accord, Ways*, 214 W. Va. at 313, 589 S.E.2d at 44. A change in the status of a class representative does not require the court to dismiss a class action on the basis of mootness. *Miller v. Sencindiver*, 170 W. Va. 288, 290, 294 S.E.2d 90, 92 (1982). "[A] class action will not become moot, even though the named petitioners' status changes or they lose their stake in the outcome of the litigation, if the issue is capable of repetition and yet will evade review because all potential petitioners will inevitably experience a change in status." *Rissler v. Giardina*, 169 W. Va. 558, 562, 289 S.E.2d 180, 183 (1982).

iv. Adequacy. The adequacy requirement of Rule 23(a)(4) of the West Virginia Rules of Civil Procedure serves two purposes. First, the adequacy of representation inquiry tests the qualifications of the attorneys to represent the class. Second, it serves to uncover conflicts of interest between the named parties and the class they seek to represent. Syl. pt. 5, *Chemtall Inc.,* 216 W. Va. 443, 607 S.E.2d 772. *See also Rezulin*, 214 W. Va. at 69, 585 S.E.2d at 69. The court will protect the absent members of a class if the entire merits of the controversy are placed in issue. *Robertson v. Hatcher*, 148 W. Va. 239, 135 S.E.2d 675 (1964). However, those who elect to opt-out of the class are not deemed to be absent members and lose standing to challenge any settlement reached by those who choose to remain in the class action. *Bd. of Educ. of Monongalia County*, 176 W. Va. 388, 391, 343 S.E.2d at 676.

b. Rule 23(b)

Although prior to April 6, 1998, Rule 23 of the West Virginia Rules of Civil Procedure did not contain 23(b), the West Virginia Supreme Court of Appeals, in *Burks,* addressed nearly identical factors under circumstances in considering the appropriateness of certifying a "spurious" class action. *Burks,* 172 W. Va. at 481, 307 S.E.2d at 657.

Also, the Supreme Court of Appeals discussed two of the three Rule 23(b) requisites in *Rezulin,* noting that the term "generally applicable" in Rule 23(b)(2) should be read to mean that the party opposing the class does not have to act directly against each member of the class. Rather, the key is whether the actions of the party opposing the class would affect all persons similarly situated, so that the acts apply generally to the whole class. *Rezulin*, 214 W. Va. 52, 585 S.E.2d 52. To be certified under Rule 23(b)(3), a class must first satisfy both the predominance test and the superiority test. *Perrine v. E.I. Du Pont De Nemours and Co*., 225 W. Va. 482, 694 S.E.2d 815 (2010). Under the predominance test, a trial court is required to find that questions common to the class predominate over questions affecting individual members. *Id.* at 526. Under the superiority test, a trial court must compare the class action with other potential methods of litigation. *Id.* at 527. For class certification, the trial court must undertake a thorough analysis to determine whether the predominance and superiority requirements have been satisfied pursuant to Rule 23(b)(3). *State ex rel. Surnaik Holdings of WV, LLC v. Bedell*, 244 W. Va. 248, 852 S.E.2d 748, 761 (2020). The thorough analysis includes: "(1) identifying the parties' claims and defenses and their respective elements; (2) determining whether these issues are common questions or individual questions by analyzing how each party will prove them at trial; and (3) determining whether the common questions predominate." *Id.* Further, the trial court must analyze the predominance requirement by keeping its main purpose in mind:

ensuring that the class action would protect "economies of time, effort, and expense, and promote uniformity of decision" without producing unfair or undesirable results. *Id.*

Rule 23(b)(3)'s predominance criterion is a corollary to the commonality requirement of Rule 23(a)(2)—while commonality requires a showing of common questions, predominance requires a showing that the common questions of law or fact outweigh individual questions. *Rezulin,* 214 W. Va. 52, 585 S.E.2d 52. The West Virginia Supreme Court of Appeals has rejected the notion that a claim for punitive damages is inappropriate for class action certification because allegations regarding the defendants' conduct and the resulting harm must be individually examined. *In re Tobacco Litig.,* 218 W. Va. 301, 624 S.E.2d 738 (2005).

c. Rule 23(c)

In *GMS Mine Repair and Maintenance, Inc. v. Miklos*, the West Virginia Supreme Court of Appeals was asked to determine whether class discovery should proceed when a defendant files or intends to file a motion for summary judgment on the purported class representative plaintiff's individual claim. 238 W. Va. 707, 798 S.E.2d 833 (2017). While noting that Rule 23(c)(1) of the West Virginia Rules of Civil Procedure mandates class certification "as soon as practicable" the Court held that "[w]here the interests of judicial efficiency and economy warrant, a circuit court may defer ruling on class certification under Rule 23(c)(1) of West Virginia Rules of Civil Procedure until a motion for summary judgment directed to the purported class representative's claim is decided." *Id.* at Syl. pt. 3. The Court reasoned that "if a plaintiff's case clearly lacks merit and can be disposed of quickly, the court and parties avoid the expense of adjudicating a class suit." *Id.* at 842 (citing William B. Rubenstein, *Newberg on Class Actions*, § 7.8, p.37 (5th ed. 2013). Although limited discovery may be necessary during the summary judgment stage, it would be "counterintuitive to allow class discovery to proceed where a court has elected to defer ruling on class certification until it first decides a motion for summary judgment." *Id.* Accordingly, the Court further held that "[w]hen a circuit court elects to defer ruling on the issue of class certification pending its decision on a motion for summary judgment, class discovery should be stayed until such time as the court decides the motion, unless the non-moving party has demonstrated that significant prejudice will result from a discovery stay. Whether a party has demonstrated significant prejudice will necessarily require the circuit court to consider the procedural posture of the case and fairness to the parties in conjunction with the objective of advancing the goal of a just, speedy, and inexpensive determination of every action." *Id.* at Syl. pt. 4 (internal citations omitted).

3. COMMUNICATIONS WITH ABSENT CLASS MEMBERS

West Virginia generally prohibits defendants from communicating with absent class members. Rule 23(c)(2) of the West Virginia Rules of Civil Procedure states that the "court shall direct members of the class to the best notice practicable under the circumstances . . ." and that the "notice shall advise each member that (A) the court will exclude the member from the class if the member so requests by a specified date; (B) the judgment, whether favorable or not, will include all members who do not request exclusion; and (C) any member who does not request exclusion may, if the member desires, enter an appearance through counsel."

Therefore, if any member of the class fails to request exclusion by the specific date, the attorney(s) for the named plaintiff(s) becomes his or her counsel if no other counsel enters an appearance on behalf of the member through Rule 23(c)(2)(C). Either way the member is deemed to be represented by counsel.

Rule 4.2 of West Virginia Rules of Professional Conduct prohibits attorneys from communicating “about the subject of the representation with a party the lawyer knows to be represented by another lawyer in the matter,” unless with the other lawyer’s consent. As a result, it appears Rule 4.2 would prohibit defense counsel from communicating with absent class members.

West Virginia case law in this area is almost non-existent. In *Shingleton v. ICT Group, Inc.* (unpublished opinion; 2003 WL 22835735), the Berkeley County Circuit Court denied a defendant’s Motion which sought to allow communication with class members. The Court’s Order stated: “[The Defendant] does not cite any caselaw in support of its Motion, and the Court finds the overwhelming weight of authority to the contrary.” The Circuit Court cited to *Cobell v. Norton*, a United States District Court case from the District of Columbia which held: “After a court has certified a case as a class action and the time for exclusions has expired, the attorney for the named plaintiff represents all class members who are otherwise un-represented by counsel. Defense counsel must observe the rules of ethical conduct in these circumstances and communicate with the opposing parties through their attorney, who is counsel for the class.” 212 F.R.D. 14 (D.C. 2002). Although this decision is not binding on any other circuit court in West Virginia, the reasoning seems consistent with the rules discussed above.

4. MISCELLANEOUS COMMENTS

Since the adoption of amended Rule 23, few decisions have been handed down by the West Virginia Supreme Court of Appeals interpreting West Virginia’s class action rule. In *State ex rel. Erie Fire Ins. Co. v. Madden,* 204 W. Va. 606, 515 S.E.2d 351 (1998), on a writ of prohibition, the court refused to recognize the doctrine of juridical link under the specific facts of the case. *Madden*, 515 S.E.2d at 354–56. The doctrine of juridical link had never before been recognized in West Virginia.

RULE 23 OF THE WEST VIRGINIA RULES OF CIVIL PROCEDURE

RULE 23. CLASS ACTIONS.

(a) **Prerequisites**. One or more members of a class may sue or be sued as representative parties on behalf of all members only if:

(1) the class is so numerous that joinder of all members is impracticable;

(2) there are questions of law or fact common to the class;

(3) the claims or defenses of the representative parties are typical of the claims or defenses of the class; and

(4) the representative parties will fairly and adequately protect the interests of the class.

(b) **Types of class actions**. A class action may be maintained if Rule 23(a) is satisfied and if:

(1) Prosecuting separate actions by or against individual class members would create a risk of:

(A) inconsistent or varying adjudications with respect to individual class members that would establish incompatible standards of conduct for the party opposing the class; or

(B) adjudications with respect to individual class members that, as a practical matter, would be dispositive of the interests of the other members not parties to the individual adjudications or would substantially impair or impede their ability to protect their interests.

(2) the party opposing the class has acted or refused to act on grounds that apply generally to the class, so that final injunctive relief or corresponding declaratory relief is appropriate respecting the class as a whole; or

(3) the court finds that the questions of law or fact common to the class members predominate over any questions affecting only individual members, and that a class action is superior to other available methods for the fair and efficient adjudication of the controversy. The matters pertinent to the findings include:

(A) the members' interests in individually controlling the prosecution or defense of separate actions;

(B) the extent and nature of any litigation concerning the controversy already begun by or against class members;

(C) the desirability or undesirability of concentrating the litigation of the claims in the particular forum;

(D) the likely difficulties in managing a class action.

(c) **Certification order; notice to class members; judgment; issues classes; subclasses.**

(1) **Certification Order.**

(A) **Time to issue.** At an early practicable time after a person sues or is sued as a class representative, the court shall determine by order whether to certify the action as a class action.

(B) **Defining the class; appointing class counsel.** An order that certifies a class action shall define the class and the class claims, issues, or defenses, and shall appoint class counsel under Rule 23(g).

(C) **Altering or amending the order.** An order that grants or denies class certification may be altered or amended before final judgment.

(2) **Notice.**

(A) **For (b)(1) or (b)(2) Classes.** For any class action certified under Rule 23(b)(1) or (b)(2), the court may direct appropriate notice to the class.

(B) **For (b)(3) Classes.** For any class certified under Rule 23(b)(3)—or upon ordering notice under Rule 23€(1) to a class proposed to be certified for purposes of settlement under Rule 23(b)(3)—the court shall direct to class members the best notice that is practicable under the circumstances, including individual notice to all members who can be identified through reasonable effort. The notice may be by one or more of the following: United States mail, electronic means, or other appropriate means. The notice shall clearly and concisely state in plain, easily understood language:

(i) the nature of the action;

(ii) the definition of the class certified;

(iii) the class claims, issues, or defenses;

(iv) that a class member may enter an appearance through an attorney if the member so desires;

(v) that the court will exclude from the class any member who requests exclusion;

(vi) the time and manner for requesting exclusion; and

(vii) the binding effect of a class judgment on members under Rule 23(c)(3).

(3) **Judgment.** Whether or not favorable to the class, the judgment in a class action shall:

(A) for any class certified under Rule 23(b)(1) or (b)(2), include and describe those whom the court finds to be class members of the class; and

(B) for any class certified under Rule 23(b)(3), include and specify or describe those to whom the Rule 23(c)(2) notice was directed, who have not requested exclusion, and whom the court finds to be class members.

(4) **Particular issues.** When appropriate, an action may be brought or maintained as a class action with respect to particular issues.

(5) **Subclasses.** When appropriate, a class may be divided into subclasses that are each

treated as a class under this rule.

(d) **Conducting the actions.**

(1) **In general.** In conducting action under this rule, the court may issue orders that:

(A) determine the course of proceedings or prescribe measures to prevent undue repetition or complication in presenting evidence or argument;

(B) require—to protect class members and fairly conduct the action—giving appropriate notice to some or all class members of:

(i) any step in the action;

(ii) the proposed extent of the judgment; or

(iii) the members' opportunity to signify whether they consider the representation fair and adequate, to intervene and present claims or defenses, or to otherwise come into the action;

(C) impose conditions on the representative parties or on intervenors;

(D) require that the pleadings be amended to eliminate allegations about representation of absent persons, and that the action proceed accordingly; or

(E) deal with similar procedural matters.

(2) **Combining and amending orders.** An order under Rule 23(d)(1) may be altered or amended from time to time and may be combined with an order under Rule 16.

(e) **Settlement, voluntary dismissal or compromise.** The claims, issues, or defenses of a certified class—or a class proposed to be certified for purposes of settlement—may be settled, voluntarily dismissed, or compromised only with the court's approval. The following procedures apply to a proposed settlement, voluntary dismissal, or compromise:

(1) **Notice to the class.**

(A) **Information that parties shall provide to the court.** The parties shall provide the court with information sufficient to enable it to determine whether to give notice of the proposal to the class.

(B) **Grounds for a decision to give notice.** The court shall direct notice in a reasonable manner to all class members who would be bound by the proposal if giving notice is justified by the parties' showing that the court will likely be able to:

(i) approve the proposal under Rule 23(e)(2); and

(ii) certify the class for purposes of judgment on the proposal.

(2) **Approval of the proposal.** If the proposal would bind class members, the court may approve it only after a hearing and only on finding that it is fair, reasonable, and adequate after considering whether:

(A) the class representatives and class counsel have adequately represented the class;

(B) the proposal was negotiated at arm's length;

(C) the relief provided for the class is adequate, taking into account:

(i) the costs, risks and delay of trial and appeal;

(ii) the effectiveness of any proposed method of distributing relief to the class, including the method of processing class-member claims;

(iii) the terms of any proposed award of attorney fees, including timing of payment; and

(iv) any agreement required to be identified under Rule 23(e)(3); and

(D) the proposal treats class members equitably relative to each other.

(3) **Identifying agreements.** The parties seeking approval shall file a statement identifying any agreement made in connection with the proposal.

(4) **New opportunity to be excluded.** If the class action was previously certified under Rule 23(b)(3), the court may refuse to approve a settlement to afford a new opportunity to request exclusion to individual class members who had an earlier opportunity to request exclusion but did not do so.

(5) **Class-member objections.**

(A) **In General.** Any class member may object to a proposal under this subdivision (e). The objection shall state whether it applies only to the objector, to a specific subset of the class, or to the entire class, and also state with specificity the grounds for the objection.

(B) **Court Approval Required for Payment in Connection with an Objection.** Unless approved by the court after a hearing, no payment or other consideration may be provided in connection with:

(i) forgoing or withdrawing an objection, or

(ii) forgoing, dismissing, or abandoning an appeal from a judgment approving the proposal.

(f) **Class counsel.**

(1) **Appointing class counsel.** Unless a statute provides otherwise, a court that certifies a class shall appoint class counsel. In appointing class counsel, the court:

(A) shall consider:

(i) the work counsel has done in identifying or investigating potential claims in the action;

(ii) counsel's experience in handling class actions, other complex litigation and the types of claims asserted in the action;

(iii) counsel's knowledge of the applicable law; and

(iv) the resources that counsel will commit to representing the class;

(B) may consider any other matter pertinent to counsel's ability to fairly and adequately represent the interests of the class;

(C) may order potential class counsel to provide information on any subject pertinent to the appointment and to propose terms for attorney fees and nontaxable costs;

(D) may include in the appointing order provisions about the award of attorney fees or nontaxable costs under Rule 23(h); and

(E) may make further orders in connection with the appointment.

(2) **Standard for appointing class counsel.** When one applicant seeks appointment as class counsel, the court may appoint that applicant only if the applicant is adequate under Rule 23(g)(1) and (4). If more than one adequate applicant seeks appointment, the court shall appoint the applicant best able to represent the interests of the class.

(3) **Interim counsel.** The court may designate interim counsel to act on behalf of a putative class before determining whether to certify the action as a class action.

(4) **Duty of class counsel.** Class counsel shall fairly and adequately represent the interests of the class.

(g) **Attorney fees and nontaxable costs.** In a certified class action, the court may award reasonable attorney fees and nontaxable costs that are authorized by law or by the parties' agreement. The following procedures apply:

(1) A claim for an award shall be made by motion under Rule 54(d)(2), subject to the provisions of this subdivision (h), at a time the court sets. Notice of the motion shall be served on all parties and, for motions by class counsel, directed to class members in a reasonable manner.

(2) A class member, or a party from whom payment is sought, may object to the motion.

(3) The court may hold a hearing and shall find the facts and state its legal conclusions.

(4) The court may refer issues related to the amount of the award to a special commissioner.

(h) **Residual funds.** When the claims process has been exhausted in class actions and residual funds remain, then fifty percent (50%) of the amount of the residual funds shall be disbursed to Legal Aid of West Virginia. The court may, after notice to counsel of record and a hearing, distribute the remaining fifty percent (50%) to one or more West Virginia non-profit organizations, schools within West Virginia universities or colleges, or foundations, which support programs that will benefit the class consistent with the objectives and purposes of the underlying causes of action upon which relief was based.

This chapter was prepared by Joseph Beeson and Craig Beeson of the firm Robinson & McElwee in Charleston, West Virginia.

WISCONSIN

1. COMPARISON WITH RULE 23 OF THE FEDERAL RULES OF CIVIL PROCEDURE

In Wisconsin, class action procedure is governed by Wis. Stat. § 803.08, a rule that was substantially amended effective June 1, 2018, pursuant to a December 21, 2017, order of the Wisconsin Supreme Court. Before its amendment in 2018, Wis. Stat. § 803.08 was a relatively brief, one-sentence rule sometimes referred to as the "19th-century Field Code." The old § 803.08's language did not closely track Rule 23, but case law interpreting it adopted many federal class action concepts, including commonality, adequacy, and numerosity. *See Cruz v. All Saints Healthcare Sys., Inc.*, 2001 WI App 67, ¶ 12. The recently amended § 803.08 now more closely tracks Rule 23 and incorporates many of its requirements. Indeed, much of the new § 803.08 is considered a "direct copy and paste" from Rule 23. *See* Michael D. Leffel, Elizabeth A.N. Haas, & Aaron R. Wegrzyn, *A Primer: Wisconsin's New Class Action Statute*, 91 Wisconsin Lawyer 4, 4 (Apr. 2018).

Before 2018, Wisconsin had two sets of class action procedures, which were set forth in two different rules: Wis. Stat. § 803.08, the "general" class action rule, and Wis. Stat. § 426.110, the "consumer" class action rule, which applied to class actions involving the Wisconsin Consumer Act, the Federal Consumer Credit Protection Act, and certain other claims involving consumer credit transactions. The 2018 amendments created a single set of class action procedures more closely aligned to Rule 23. As a result, many of Rule 23's procedural elements are now included within Wis. Stat. § 803.08, while the procedural language that was previously part of Wis. Stat. § 426.110—specifically, subsections (5) through (13)—has been repealed. Nevertheless, Wis. Stat. § 426.110 still includes certain notice, damages, and award of fees and costs provisions that are pertinent to claims brought under that statute.

In many ways, the incorporation of Rule 23's provisions into § 803.08 in 2018 was consistent with prior Wisconsin class action practice, which looked to Rule 23 case law as persuasive authority when construing the pre-2018 version of the rule. *See, e.g., Wilson v. Continental Ins. Co.*, 87 Wis. 2d 310, 316, 274 N.W.2d 679, 682 (1979); *Browne v. Milwaukee Bd. of Sch. Dirs*., 69 Wis. 2d 169, 183, 230 N.W.2d 704, 711 (1975); *Kiser v. Jungbacker*, 2008 Wis. App. 88, ¶¶ 15, 18 n.6.

The new § 803.08 largely follows the structure of Rule 23. For example, Wis. Stat. § 803.08(1), like Rule 23(a), lays out four prerequisites for certifying a class: (a) numerosity, (b) commonality, (c) typicality, and (d) adequacy.

Also, consistent with Rule 23(b), Wis. Stat. § 803.08(2) identifies the types of class actions that may be maintained and addresses the issues of predominance and superiority. Similarly, like Rule 23(c)(1), Wis. Stat. § 803.08(3) addresses the timing, content, and amendment of court orders certifying a class. Wis. Stat. § 803.08(4), like Rule 23(c)(2), addresses notice to class members. Likewise, Wis. Stat. § 803.08(5) describes what must be contained in judgments entered in certified class action cases, tracking the language of Rule 23(c)(3). Wis. Stat. § 803.08(6), like Rule 23(c)(4), addresses when a class action may be brought or maintained with respect to particular issues. Like Rule 23(c)(5), Wis. Stat. § 803.08(7) governs the creation of subclasses. And Rule 23(d), like Wis.

Stat. § 803.08(8), addresses the types of orders a court may issue in a class action. Similarly, like Rule 23(e), Wis. Stat. § 803.08(9) sets forth the procedures for providing notice to the class and obtaining court approval of a settlement, voluntary dismissal, or compromise in a class action. Like Rule 23(f), Wis. Stat. § 803.08(11) governs the right to appeal from orders granting or denying class certification. Furthermore, like Rule 23(g), Wis. Stat. § 803.08(12) governs the procedure and standards for appointing class counsel as well as the duties of class counsel. Finally, like Rule 23(h), Wis. Stat. § 803.08(13) addresses attorney fees and nontaxable costs.

New § 803.08 diverges from Rule 23 in two significant ways. First, Wis. Stat. § 803.08(10) addresses the use of "residual funds" that may remain in some cases after payment of the class members' claims and class counsel's court-approved attorney fees, litigation costs, disbursements and other expenses. This rule "carries forward Order No. 15-06, issued by the Wisconsin Supreme Court on June 24, 2016, which requires that 'not less than 50 percent' of any residual funds be directed to support noncriminal legal services for low-income and indigent people in Wisconsin." By comparison, Rule 23 does not directly address the use of residual funds. Leffel, *supra* at 8. Second, Wis. Stat. § 803.08(14) prohibits the filing of state-tax-related class actions against the state of Wisconsin. *Id.*

2. CASE LAW INTERPRETING WISCONSIN STATUTE § 803.08 GENERALLY

There are an increasing number of appellate decisions in Wisconsin interpreting new Wis. Stat. § 803.08, which became effective July 1, 2018.

In 2019, the Wisconsin Court of Appeals decided *Harwood v. Wheaton Franciscan Servs., Inc.*, 2019 WI App 53. In *Harwood*, the Court of Appeals affirmed a trial court's certification of a class action involving alleged overcharges for hospital records. In reviewing the trial court's order, the Court of Appeals applied a discretionary standard of review, holding that a trial court's certification decision will be affirmed so long as it "applied the correct law to the facts of record and reached a reasonable decision." *Id.* at ¶ 41.

When considering the four prerequisites of the new Wis. Stat. § 803.08, the Court of Appeals confirmed longstanding Wisconsin case law holding "it is in the public interest as declared by the legislature to permit class actions when the [§ 803.08] prerequisites are satisfied." *Id.* at ¶ 54, citing *Mercury Records Prods., Inc. v. Economic Consultants, Inc.*, 91 Wis. 2d 482, 490, 283 N.W.2d 613 (Ct. App. 1979). Then, turning to the first prerequisite of the new § 803.08(1), numerosity, *Harwood* held the requirement was satisfied when there were 42 potential class members. *Harwood*, 2019 WI App. at ¶ 55. Similarly, it concluded there was sufficient evidence to affirm the trial court's conclusions that the other three § 803.08(1) prerequisites—commonality, typicality, and adequacy—were satisfied. *Id.* at ¶¶ 56, 57.

After affirming the trial court's decision on the four prerequisites of § 803.08(1), the Court of Appeals readily disposed of the defendant's arguments concerning predominance and superiority under § 803.08(2). As to predominance, the Court of Appeals held that the requirement was plainly satisfied because the class representatives and class members were asserting the same legal claims. *Id.* at ¶ 58. Similarly, the Court of Appeals decided that the superiority element was satisfied, noting that "case law is clear that public policy favors class actions especially where the amount in controversy is so small that the wronged party is unlikely ever to obtain judicial review of the alleged violation without a class action." *Id.* For these reasons, *Harwood* concluded that the trial court properly exercised its discretion to grant class certification. *Id.* at ¶ 66. Finally, the Court of Appeals followed the Seventh Circuit's decision in *Mullins v. Direct Digital*, 795 F.3d 654 (7th Cir. 2015) and rejected the Third Circuit's adoption of "heightened ascertainability standards" in cases like *Marcus v. BMW of North America, LLC*, 687 F.3d 583 (3d Cir. 2012). *Harwood*, 2019 WI App 53, ¶ 64.

Similarly, in 2021, the Wisconsin Court of Appeals affirmed a trial court's decision granting class certification in *Hammetter v. Verisma Systems, Inc.*, 2021 WI App 53. As in *Harwood*, the plaintiffs in *Hammetter* alleged they were overcharged for medical records. Citing its 2019 *Harwood* decision, the Court of Appeals again confirmed that trial courts have "broad discretion" when deciding class certification motions. *Id.* at ¶ 9 (citing *Harwood*, 2019 WI App 53, ¶¶ 5, 41). The Court of Appeals then considered the various elements set forth in the new § 803.08, including numerosity, commonality, typicality, adequacy, predominance, and superiority. *Hammetter*, 2021 WL 3235323 at ¶¶ 10–28. Ultimately, as in *Harwood*, the Court of Appeals had little difficulty affirming the trial court's decision to certify the class. *Id.* at ¶ 42.

In another 2021 decision arising from a putative class action involving overcharges for medical records, *Shannon v. Mayo Clinic Health Sys.–Nw. Wisconsin Region, Inc.*, 2021 WI App 49, ¶ 1, the Court of Appeals again applied the language of the new § 803.08 to determine whether the trial court had properly granted class certification. In *Shannon*, however, the Court of Appeals reversed the trial court's class certification decision because the plaintiff's complaint and class definition focused on the wrong defendant. Specifically, the plaintiff alleged she had been overcharged for medical records by Mayo Clinic Health System-Northwest Wisconsin Region Inc. (Northwest), but those allegations were simply wrong. In fact, the plaintiff had been overcharged by a different entity, Mayo Clinic Health System-Red Cedar (Red Cedar). Northwest had merged with Red Cedar, which assumed Northwest's liabilities. The Court of Appeals reversed the trial court's order certifying the class against Northwest because it was factually undisputed that Northwest never overcharged the plaintiff (or anybody else) for medical records. *Id.* at ¶ 22.

In a third 2021 decision involving a class action arising from alleged overbilling for medical records, the Wisconsin Court of Appeals affirmed another trial court's grant of class certification under the new § 803.08. *Rave v. SVA Healthcare Servs., LLC*, 2021 WI App. 36. In *Rave*, the trial court certified the proposed class after concluding that the plaintiff had satisfied the requirements of § 803.08. *Id.* ¶ 5. On appeal, the defendant argued that the prerequisites for class certification were not satisfied because the named plaintiff's claims allegedly gave rise to "unique" defenses involving waiver, voluntary payment, and statute of limitations. *Id.* ¶ 10. However, the trial court rejected those arguments, concluding that those defenses, even if "unique," would not defeat class certification because they would not be a "major focus" of the litigation. *Id.* (citing 1 William B. Rubenstein, *Newberg on Class Actions* § 3:45 (5th ed.)). The Wisconsin Court of Appeals affirmed the trial court's decision, concluding that the typicality and adequacy requirements of § 803.08 were satisfied. *Id.* at ¶ 12 ("[W]e are not convinced that [these defenses] will be a 'major focus' in this litigation.") (citing *Koos v. First Nat'l Bank of Peoria*, 496 F.2d 1162, 1164 (7th Cir. 1974) (holding that typicality is defeated only when "a major focus of the litigation will be on an arguable defense unique to the named plaintiff")).

In 2023, the Wisconsin Court of Appeals decided *Fotusky v. ProHealth Care, Inc.*, 2023 WI App 19, another case brought as a class action alleging violations of Wisconsin's law governing medical record charges. In *Fotusky*, the Court of Appeals reversed a trial court's decision granting class certification, finding that the trial court had erroneously exercised its discretion by certifying the alleged class. Specifically, the trial court erred by including attorneys who sought their clients' medical records within the certified class because attorneys did not fall within the definition of individuals protected by the relevant Wisconsin statute. The Court of Appeals clarified that this "does not mean that class certification is ultimately inappropriate in this matter." *Id.* at ¶ 33. Rather, it was necessary to remand the case to the trial court to reanalyze whether class certification is appropriate for a redefined class that did not include attorneys.

Likewise, during 2023, the Wisconsin Court of Appeals issued two unpublished, non-precedential decisions overturning circuit court orders granting class certification. *Freeman v. SL Greenfield, LLC*, 2023 WI App 44 (per curiam), ¶ 30; on *Nat'l Collegiate Student Loan Tr. 2007-4 v. Seldal*, 2023 WI App 50, ¶¶ 43, 45. In both cases, the Court of Appeals concluded that that the certification orders lacked sufficient detail needed to comply with Wis. Stat. § 803.08(11)(a), which requires that all class certification orders be included in "a written decision setting forth all reasons why the action may be maintained [as a class action] and describing all evidence in support of the determination."

In 2025, the Wisconsin Court of Appeals revisited both cases. In the *Freeman* case, on remand, a newly assigned trial court judge issued a thirteen-page written order reinstating the earlier court order certifying the class. *Freeman v. SL Greenfield, LLC*, 2025 WI App 30. On appeal, the Court of Appeals affirmed the remand court's grant of class certification, rejecting the defendant's arguments that the commonality and predominance elements were not satisfied. *Id.* at ¶ 27–29. The Court of Appeals also rejected the defendant's argument that class certification was improper because 1,500 members of the proposed class had signed agreements that waived their rights to participate in a class action. The Court of Appeals concluded that the defendant's waiver argument was an affirmative defense that was itself waived when the defendant failed to file a timely responsive pleading at the outset of the case. *Id.* at ¶ 32.

In *Nat'l Collegiate Student Loan Tr. 2007-4*, on remand, the circuit court denied class certification, concluding that the plaintiff had failed to point to any evidence that would apply to the class as a whole on the key question of whether student loans had been lawfully assigned to the defendant. *Id.* at ¶ 25. The Wisconsin Court of Appeals affirmed, concluding that the circuit court had properly exercised its discretion when deciding the certification question.

The Wisconsin Supreme Court also issued a 2025 decision involving a class action filed by state corrections officers seeking compensation for time spent in the correctional facilities before and after their shifts. *McDaniel v. Wisconsin Dep't of Corr.*, 2025 WI 24. The trial court had certified the class, but the Wisconsin Court of Appeals "reversed because—in its view—the class would lose on the merits." *Id.* at ¶ 1. The Wisconsin Supreme Court reversed the Court of Appeals, making clear "that a court should not consider the viability of a class's claim on the merits when assessing the class-certification requirements of commonality and typicality." *Id.* After analyzing issues of commonality, typicality, predominance and superiority, the Supreme Court affirmed the trial court's decision to grant class certification and remanded the case to the trial court for further proceedings.

There are many Wisconsin decisions that interpret the old (pre-July 1, 2018) class action rule. Despite the old rule's use of the disjunctive, in 1974, the Wisconsin Supreme Court construed it to present "only one set of criteria"—namely, commonality, adequate representation, and numerosity:

(1) The named parties "must have a right or interest in common with the persons represented";
(2) The named parties "must fairly represent the interest or right involved so that the issue may be fairly and honestly tried"; and
(3) It must be "impracticable to bring all interested persons before the court."

Schlosser v. Allis-Chalmers Corp., 65 Wis. 2d 153, 169, 222 N.W.2d 156, 165 (1974) (*Schlosser I*) (quoting *Lozoff v. Kaisershot*, 11 Wis. 2d 485, 488, 105 N.W.2d 783, 785 (1960)). As this earlier class action case law confirms, the class action doctrine "was devised to simplify litigation, to make more convenient the administration of justice both for the parties and the court, and to avoid a multiplicity of suits in those cases where the rights and liabilities of many persons similarly affected or interested could be fairly determined in the action." *Pipkorn v. Vill. of Brown Deer*, 9 Wis. 2d 571,

577, 101 N.W.2d 623, 626 (1960).

The determination of whether an action may proceed as a class action "involves a weighing of the benefits to be gained from disposing of the entire controversy in one proceeding against the difficulties inherent in a single action." *Schlosser v. Allis-Chalmers Corp.*, 86 Wis. 2d 226, 233–34, 271 N.W.2d 879, 883 (1978) (*Schlosser II*) (citations omitted). "In other words, a court must determine whether the issues common to the named plaintiffs and the class members are outweighed by the issues particular to the individual class members." *Goebel v. First Fed. Sav. & Loan Ass'n of Racine*, 83 Wis. 2d 668, 684, 266 N.W.2d 352, 360 (1978). "The trial court's view of the merits is not a proper basis on which to deny class certification." *Tietsworth v. Harley-Davidson, Inc.*, 2003 WI App 75, ¶ 27 (citing *Cruz*, 2001 WI App 67, ¶¶ 11–24), *rev'd on other grounds*, 2004 WI 32.

3. CASE LAW INTERPRETING PARTICULAR REQUIREMENTS FOR CLASS ACTION

a. Numerosity

In 2019, the Wisconsin Court of Appeals held that the numerosity requirement of Wis. Stat. § 803.08(1) was satisfied when there were 42 potential class members. *Harwood*, 2019 WI App 53 at ¶¶ 55.

In *Browne*, 69 Wis. 2d at 171, the court certified a class of approximately 150 school district employees. Similarly, the court in *Goebel*, 83 Wis. 2d at 683, certified a class of 369 borrowers.

Two late nineteenth-century cases plumbed the limits of numerosity. In *Hodges v. Nalty*, the court held that it would be impracticable to join 75 members of a proposed class: "[a] line must be drawn somewhere, and, while it may be difficult to draw the line at any precise number, we hold that 75 is a sufficient number, in a case like the present, to justify the court in allowing one or more to sue for all." 104 Wis. 464, 468, 80 N.W. 726, 728 (1899) (citing *Phipps v. Jones*, 20 Pa. 260 (1853)). The court distinguished *George v. Benjamin*, 100 Wis. 622, 630, 76 N.W. 619, 622 (1898), which stated that a group of 31 persons was not "very numerous," as that term was used in the predecessor to § 803.08. *Id.* Ultimately, however, "[n]o numerical test can be formulated nor should such a test alone determine the issue." *Pipkorn*, 9 Wis. 2d at 579.

b. Commonality

"Under the commonality requirement, a class must show that '[t]here are questions of law or fact common to the class.'" *McDaniel v. Wisconsin Dep't of Corr.*, 2025 WI 24, ¶ 20 (quoting Wis. Stat. § 803.08(1)(b)). "Even one common question is enough." *Id.* A common question is one that is capable of classwide resoltution, which means that answering the question "will resolve an issue that is central to the validity of each one of the claims in one stroke." *Id.* (quoting *Wal-Mart Stores, Inc. v. Dukes*, 554 U.S. 338, 359 (2011)). Although the Wisconsin Supreme Court quoted *Dukes* in its decision, it made clear that it was "follow[ing] the *Amgen* approach." *Id.* at ¶¶ 24–26 (quoting *Amgen Inc. v. Conn. Ret. Plans & Tr. Funds*, 568 U.S. 455 (2013). Specifically, the *McDaniel* court emphasized the following language from the *Amgen* decision: "Although . . . a court's class-certification analysis must be 'rigorous'. . . [the federal rule] grants courts no license to engage in free-ranging merits inquiries at the certification stage." *Id.* at ¶ 27 (citing *Amgen*, 586 U.S. at 465–66). "The test for common interest is whether all members of the purported class desire the same outcome of the suit that the alleged representatives of the class desire." *Hogan*, 157 Wis. 2d at 379 (quoting *Mercury Records,* 91 Wis. 2d at 490). "It is not necessary that the position of each member of a class be identical," *Goebel,* 83 Wis. 2d at 684, or arise from common title, *Schlosser I,* 65 Wis. 2d at 170 (citing John Norton Pomeroy, *Equity Jurisprudence* § 269 (5th ed. 1941)), and "members of the class need not share all interests. . . ." *Mercury Records*, 91 Wis. 2d at 490 (citing *State ex rel. Harris v. Larson*, 64 Wis. 2d 521, 525, 219 N.W.2d 335, 338 (1974)). Rather, there need only be "'a community of interest among them in the questions of law and fact involved in the general controversy, or in the kind and form of relief demanded and obtained by or against each individual member of the numerous body. . . .'" *Goebel*, 83 Wis. 2d at 684 (citation omitted) (quoting *Schlosser I*, 65 Wis. 2d at 171). In most cases, this community of interest originates from the fact that the separate claims of individuals comprising the class arose by means of the same unauthorized, unlawful, or illegal act or proceeding. *Schlosser I*, 65 Wis. 2d at 171 (quoting *Pomeroy* § 269); *cf. Fazio v. Dept. of Employee Trust Funds*, 2005 WI App 87, ¶¶ 19–25 (finding lack of common interest where annuity-value-based and account-value-based beneficiaries under state retirement system became entitled to death benefits pursuant to separate and independent statutory sections), *aff'd* 2006 WI 7.

"In the interest of simplifying the lawsuit and avoiding a multiplicity of litigation, a class action is proper even if each member of the class has a separate cause of action for money damages." *Mercury Records*, 91 Wis. 2d at 490 (citing *Hicks v. Milwaukee County*, 71 Wis. 2d 401, 406, 238 N.W.2d 509, 513 (1976)); *Cruz*, 2001 WI App 67, ¶ 16; *Schlosser I*, 65 Wis. 2d at 174–75 (citing *Milwaukee Fire Fighters Ass'n v. Milwaukee*, 50 Wis. 2d 9, 20, 183 N.W.2d 18 (1971)). In *Hammetter*, 2021 WL 3235323 at ¶ 13, the defendants argued that the commonality element could not be satisfied because some class members were eligible to receive up to $1,000 in exemplary damages for "negligent" statutory violations, while others might receive up to $25,000 in exemplary damages if the alleged violations were shown to be "willful." *Hammetter* rejected this argument because there was no evidence showing different mental states and also because "the potential need for individual damages determinations later in the litigation 'does not justify the denial of certification.'" *Hammetter*, 2021 WL 3235323 at ¶ 13, citing *Mullins v. Direct Digit., LLC*, 795 F.3d 654, 671 (7th Cir. 2015) ("It has long been recognized that the need for individual damage determinations at [the damages] stage of the litigation does not itself justify the denial of certification.").

c. Adequacy/Typicality

"Under the typicality requirement, a class must show that '[t]he claims or defenses of the representative parties are typical of the claims or defenses of the class.'" *McDaniel*, 2025 WI 24, ¶ 41 (quoting Wis. Stat. § 803.08(1)(c)). "A representative's claim is typical if "it arises from the same event or practice or course of conduct that gives rise to the claims of other class members and [is] based on the same legal theory." *Id.* (quoting *Lacy v. Cook Cnty.*, 897 F.3d 847, 866 (7th Cir. 2018)).

In its 2021 *Hammetter* decision, the Wisconsin Court of Appeals held that when considering adequacy, "the primary criteria are: (1) whether the plaintiffs or counsel have interests antagonistic to those of absent class members; and (2) whether class counsel are qualified, experienced and generally able to conduct the proposed litigation." *Hammetter v. Verisma Sustems, Inc.*, 2021 WI App 53, at ¶ 21, quoting *Cruz*, 2001 WI App 67, ¶ 18. Similarly, "[t]he question of typicality . . . is not whether the claims of [the class representatives] are identical in every way with every other potential class member but whether their claims are typical." *Id.* at ¶ 20. *Hammetter* concluded that the typicality requirement was satisfied because the claims alleged by the class representatives and putative class members arose from the same general practice or course of conduct, were based on the same legal theories, and had the same essential characteristics. *Id.*

d. Predominance and Superiority

When deciding whether to certify a class, Wisconsin courts also consider issues of predominance and superiority. Wis. Stat. § 803.08(2). Specifically, courts consider whether "the questions of law or fact common to class members predominate over any questions affecting only individual members," and whether "a class action is superior to other available methods for fairly and efficiently adjudicating the controversy." Wis. Stat. § 803.08(2)(c). One of the factors that courts consider when deciding issues of predominance and superiority is whether the class action will be manageable. Wis. Stat. § 803.08(2)(c)(4).

"When analyzing predominance, a court must ask whether 'common, aggregation-enabling, issues in the case are more prevalent or important than the non-common, aggregation-defeating, individual issues.'" *McDaniel v. Wisconsin Dep't of Corr.*, 2025 WI 24, ¶ 46 (quoting *Tyson Foods, Inc. v. Bouaphakeo*, 577 U.S. 442, 453). Questions of individualized damages do not defeat predominance. *Id.* at ¶ 47.

"Under the superiority requirement, a court must determine whether 'a class action is superior to other available methods for fairly and efficiently adjudicating the controversy.'" *Id.* at ¶ 57 (quoting Wis. Stat. § 803.08(2)(c)). "In the end, the circuit court is in the best position to understand whether it can handle a class action in its courtroom. And we give deference to the circuit court's decision." *Id.* at ¶ 64.

In its 2021 *Hammetter* decision, the Wisconsin Court of Appeals considered defendants' argument that the class action mechanism was not superior because an "individualized inquiry" would be required to determine whether the defendants' alleged statutory violations were "negligent" or "knowing and willful" with regard to each individual class member. *Hammetter*, 2021 WI App 53 at ¶ 27. The Court of Appeals rejected defendants' superiority challenge, concluding that a defendant's state of mind could be examined for a particular "identified time period" rather than on an individualized basis for each class member. *Id.* The Court of Appeals also explained that the trial court had the discretion under § 803.08(7) to create subclasses, if necessary, to address these issues. *Id.* Finally, the Court of Appeals explained that "[i]n the interest of simplifying the lawsuit and avoiding a multiplicity of litigation, a class action is proper even if each member of the class has a separate cause of action for money damages." *Id.* (quoting *Harwood*, 2019 WI App 53, ¶ 54).

Likewise, in another 2021 decision, the Court of Appeals rejected defendant's superiority and predominance arguments. *Rave v. SVA Healthcare Servs., LLC*, 2021 WI App 36. In *Rave*, the defendant argued that the trial court's decision "completely failed to address" its superiority and predominance arguments when granting class certification. *Id.* at ¶ 18. The Court of Appeals rejected this argument and affirmed, noting that the trial court's eleven-page decision explained that "[i]n deciding this motion, the [c]ourt has considered SVA's lengthy and comprehensive submissions, including its supplemental briefing," and later stated that "[a]fter thoroughly considering the parties' submissions, the [c]ourt concludes that Rave and class counsel have met the requirements for class certification." *Id.* As the Court of Appeals further explained: "To the extent that the circuit court did not expressly address each issue that SVA raised, it implicitly deemed them unpersuasive. That determination is supported by the record." *Id.* (citing *Harwood*, 388 Wis. 2d 546, ¶ 48 (noting that "if the [circuit] court 'fails to set forth its reasoning in exercising its discretion . . . the appellate court should independently review the record to determine whether it provides a basis for the [circuit] court's exercise of discretion'" (citation omitted))).

4. TOLLING OF LIMITATIONS DURING PENDENCY OF A CLASS ACTION

Section 893.13(2) of the Wisconsin Statutes provides:

> A law limiting the time for commencement of an action is tolled by the commencement of the action to enforce the cause of action to which the period of limitation applies. The law limiting the time for commencement of the action is tolled for the period from the commencement of the action until the final disposition of the action.

No published Wisconsin decision has construed this statute in the context of a class action. In *Sajdak v. Michaels Pipeline Constr.*, 109 Wis. 2d 697, 327 N.W.2d 723 (Ct. App. 1982), an unpublished (non-precedential) decision, the court held that in the absence of legislative intent to the contrary, the tolling statute did not apply to a cause of action that had accrued prior to the statute's effective date (July 1, 1980). The court stated in *dictum*, however, that if the tolling statute were applicable, it would toll the limitation period "from the commencement [of the class action in which the current plaintiffs were absent members] until the final disposition of the action." *Id.*

Likewise, no appellate courts in Wisconsin have considered the United States Supreme Court authority that has established the well-recognized rule that, as a matter of law, the filing of a class action tolls the statute of limitations for putative class members. *See American Pipe & Construction Co. v. Utah*, 414 U.S. 538 (1974) (involving a Rule 23 class action). However, Wisconsin courts have long applied Rule 23 case law when interpreting Wis. Stat. § 803.08. *See, e.g., Wilson*, 87 Wis. 2d at 316; *Browne*, 69 Wis. 2d at 183; *Kiser*, 2008 Wis. App 88, ¶¶ 15, 18 n.6.

5. NOTICE OF CLASS CLAIMS AGAINST GOVERNMENT ENTITIES

Lawsuits against a Wisconsin governmental body, including class actions, generally must be preceded by substantial compliance with Wisconsin's Notice of Claims statute, Wis. Stat. § 893.80. *But see Felder v. Casey*, 487 U.S. 131 (1988) (involving application of § 893.80 to federal civil rights claims). Because such a Notice must present the identities and claims of all claimants, the Wisconsin Court of Appeals has held that a class action involving "unnamed claimants, is never possible against the government. . . ." *Townsend v. Neenah Jt. School Dist.*, 2014 WI App 117, ¶ 1. In *Townsend*, the Court of Appeals held that a single claimant could not assert a claim under the Notice of Claims statute on behalf of other claimants in the way that a single plaintiff may sue on behalf of others who are similarly situated. *Id.* at ¶ 13. But nothing bars a "mass action" type of class action against the government, so long as all claimants give notice before suing. *Id.* at ¶ 2. Thus, when a notice identified the claimants by name, address, and claim amounts, and was signed by an attorney asserting that he represented all the claimants, the class action should have been allowed to proceed. *Id.* at ¶ 31. By contrast, notice given to the city of Milwaukee of claims by named persons "and other persons similarly situated" was insufficient as to the unnamed claimants because of the Notice of Claims prerequisite to filing a lawsuit against the city. *Markweise v. Peck Foods Corp.*, 205 Wis. 2d 208, 219–24, 556 N.W.2d 330, 330–32 (Ct. App. 1996), 205 Wis. 2d at 219–24 (reversing grant of class certification) (citations omitted).

The new language of Wis. Stat. § 803.18(14), which became effective July 1, 2018, specifically bars class actions against the state of Wisconsin concerning state tax issues.

6. ARBITRATION CLAUSES PROHIBITING CLASS CLAIMS

In *Coady v. Cross Country Bank, Inc.*, 2007 WI App 26, ¶ 1, *review denied*, 2007 WI 114, the Wisconsin Court of Appeals held that a credit card agreement containing a mandatory arbitration clause that forbade class-wide arbitration was unconscionable. The bar against class-wide arbitration "contributed" to this conclusion. *Id.* ¶¶ 43, 47. *But see AT&T Mobility LLC v. Concepcion*, 563 U.S. 333, 352 (2011) (holding that the Federal Arbitration Act preempts state rule that arbitration provision disallowing class-wide arbitration is unconscionable). In *Cottonwood Financial, Ltd. v. Estes*, 2012 WI App 12, ¶ 2, the Court of Appeals, on remand from the Wisconsin Supreme Court for reconsideration in light of *Concepcion*, adhered to that case and reversed its previous decision that had followed *Coady*. *Accord*, *Drogorub v. Payday Loan Store of WI, Inc.*, 2013 WI App 13, ¶¶ 24–25 (unpublished decision) (general choice-of-law clause does not demonstrate clear intent to displace federal arbitration law). *But see Wisconsin Auto Title Loans Inc. v. Jones*, No. 2011AP2482, 2013 WL 425449 (Wis. App. Feb. 5, 2013) (certifying to Wisconsin Supreme Court issue of whether trial court ruling that arbitration clause is unconscionable, in part due to class action waiver, is permitted under *Concepcion*; consumers argue, *inter alia*, that *Concepcion* does not apply to actions originating in state court).

In *Pruett v. WESTconsin Credit Union*, 2023 WI App 57, the Wisconsin Court of Appeals affirmed the denial of a credit union's motion to compel arbitration in a putative class action, holding that the credit union lacked the authority to add an arbitration clause and class action waiver to an existing account agreement because the plaintiff did not agree to that addition. The court rejected the credit union's argument that it could rely on a change-of-terms provision, which allowed the agreement's terms to be changed on 60 days' notice, because including a new arbitration clause and class action waiver was not a "change" to the agreement's existing terms, but instead was an "addition" to those terms. *Id.* at ¶ 34.

In *Freeman v. SL Greenfield, LLC*, 2025 WI App 30, the Wisconsin Court of Appeals rejected the defendant's argument that class certification was improper because 1,500 members of the proposed class had allegedly signed agreements that waived their rights to participate in a class action. The Court of Appeals concluded that the defendant's waiver argument was an affirmative defense that was itself waived when the defendant failed to file a timely responsive pleading at the outset of the case. *Id.* at ¶ 32.

7. STANDING TO APPEAL COMMON FUND FEE AWARD TO CLASS COUNSEL

In *Kiser v. Jungbacker*, 2008 WI App. 88, ¶ 1, the court held that defendants, who had entered into a settlement agreement creating a common fund for the benefit of plaintiff class members, lacked standing to appeal an award of fees and out-of-pocket expenses to class counsel from that common fund. The defendants premised standing on the facts that they were general partners and the class members were limited partners in a commercial real estate investment limited partnership that was liquidated under the terms of the settlement agreement, and argued that they had a "fiduciary obligation to the class to ensure that the most money possible could end up in the limited partners' pockets." *Id.* ¶ 12. The court rejected that argument, holding that "[a]ny fiduciary relationship that once existed between [defendants] and the class is over. In this dispute, they are adversaries, pure and simple." *Id.* ¶ 20. The court added that while the trial court "has a judicial duty to ensure that the award of costs and fees is reasonable," that duty is not a "fiduciary" one running from the court to the class members. *Id.* ¶ 18.

8. CLASS CLAIMS IN ADMINISTRATIVE PROCEEDINGS

According to a Wisconsin Attorney General's opinion, "[t]he Wisconsin Open Housing Law permits, but does not require, the Department of Industry, Labor and Human Relations to receive and process class action complaints of housing discrimination." 70 Wis. Op. Att'y Gen. 250–51 (1981). The opinion is based in part on the statutory definition of "discriminate" and "discrimination" as "to segregate, separate, exclude or treat any person *or class of persons* unequally . . . because of sex, race, color, . . ." as well as similar holdings under anti-discrimination laws in other states. *Id.* at 252 (citing Wis. Stat. § 106.50(1m)(h) (italics added)).

9. DEFENDANT CLASSES UNDER DECLARATORY JUDGMENT ACT

In *Ewer*, 2012 WI App 64, ¶¶ 48–50, the court held that the requirement under the Declaratory Judgments Act, Wis. Stat. § 806.04(11), that "all persons shall be made parties who have or claim any interest which would be affected by the declaration," does not preclude certification of a defendant class. Rather, "the Declaratory Judgments Act 'should be construed together with [the statute on class actions] and [therefore] it does not exclude the procedure of representative defense of the interests of a class from an action for declaratory relief.'" *Ewer*, 2012 WI App 64, ¶ 50 (quoting *Lozoff*, 11 Wis. 2d at 489). Thus, it was unnecessary to join all 1,602 members of an association of property owners in an action to construe a provision of the association's bylaws relating to annual assessments. *Id.* However, when suing the State of Wisconsin or an agency or officer thereof for a declaration of rights or obligations under a statute, or that a statute is unconstitutional and therefore cannot be enforced, plaintiffs are well advised to utilize a defendant class comprised of those State, county and municipal officials who have potential enforcement authority under the statute, in order to thwart such officials from claiming that they are not obligated to abide by the declaration of a trial court in a case in which the actors were not named as individual defendants.

10. UNIQUE PROVISION REGARDING REFUND OF OR DAMAGES ASSOCIATED WITH A TAX

Wis. Stat. § 803.08 was amended, effective March 1, 2012, to prohibit any class action, whether against the state or any other party, if the relief sought includes the refund of or damages associated with a tax administered by the state. 2011 Wis. Act 68 § 51. The amended rule applied to any action filed on or after the effective date. *Id.* § 52. That provision was carried forward in the new Wis. Stat. § 803.08, in subsection (14).

Wisconsin appellate courts have yet to construe this amendment. Of particular interest is whether the broad language, "damages *associated* with a tax," together with the amendment's application to class actions against *any* party, precludes class actions against parties *other* than the State, the Department of Revenue, and its officials claiming damages that are arguably "associated" with a tax administered by the state—e.g., damages arising from improper collection of sales or use tax by manufacturers, wholesalers, or retailers. In other words, how broadly will the courts construe the term "associated"?

The legislative history of the amendment is sparse, which is typically the case in Wisconsin. The amendment was a part of 2011 Wisconsin Act 68, the focus of which is to limit the powers and prescribe certain duties and procedures of the Wisconsin Department of Revenue. The Wisconsin Legislative Council Act Memo on 2011 Wis. Act 68 describes the Act as making "numerous changes to the duties of the Department of Revenue." A sponsor of the underlying Senate Bill (S.B. 23, 2011-

2012 Leg., 1st Spec. Sess. (Wis. 2011)) testified at a Senate committee hearing:

> This bill seeks to provide fairness, justice, and impartiality for business and individual taxpayers. Our state's tax system is complex and taxpayers should have a resource in the Department[,] not an adversary.***
>
> The goal of this bill is to restore trust and confidence in Wisconsin's tax collection system. Taxpayers and businesses need to know that tax laws will be enforced consistently and efficiently, and this bill is a major step forward in that direction.

In short, the Act is essentially a "taxpayer rights" law. With particular reference to the amendment of the class action rule, the Fiscal Estimate for S.B. 23 commented: "[c]lass action lawsuits involving states [sic] taxes are rare, but the bill would eliminate the risk of potentially large, though infrequent judgments."

11. COMMUNICATIONS WITH ABSENT CLASS MEMBERS

Wisconsin appellate courts have not specifically addressed the permissibility of and any limitations on communications by class counsel with absent class members either before or after certification. Particularly in the pre-certification context, putative class counsel who undertake to communicate with putative absent class members are clearly subject to pertinent rules of professional conduct regulating "Transactions with Persons Other than Clients" and "Information About Legal Services." *See* Wisconsin SCR 20:4.1-20:4.4, 20:7.1-20:7.3. Depending on the context of the communication, at least some of these ethical rules remain relevant after certification. An absent class member is not a "client" of class counsel. Indeed, an absent class member may retain his or her own counsel with respect to the class action and may take legal positions conflicting with those of class counsel and the class representatives notwithstanding certification.

12. CONCLUSION

The revised Wisconsin class action rule, Wis. Stat. § 803.08, has filled holes in the prior rule and will continue leading to interpretations and additional case law that will assist judges and practitioners in matters involving class action procedure.

SECTION 803.08, WISCONSIN STATUTES

(1) Prerequisites. One or more members of a class may sue or be sued as representative parties on behalf of all members only if the court finds all of the following:

(a) The class is so numerous that joinder of all members is impracticable.

(b) There are questions of law or fact common to the class.

(c) The claims or defenses of the representative parties are typical of the claims or defenses of the class.

(d) The representative parties will fairly and adequately protect the interests of the class.

(2) Types of class actions. A class action may be maintained if sub. (1) is satisfied and if the court finds that any of the following are satisfied:

(a) Prosecuting separate actions by or against individual class members would create a risk of either of the following:

1. Inconsistent or varying adjudications with respect to individual class members that would establish incompatible standards of conduct for the party opposing the class.

2. Adjudications with respect to individual class members that, as a practical matter, would be dispositive of the interests of the other members not parties to the individual adjudications or would substantially impair or impede their ability to protect their interests.

(b) The party opposing the class has acted or refused to act on grounds that apply generally to the class, so that final injunctive relief or corresponding declaratory relief is appropriate respecting the class as a whole.

(c) The court finds that the questions of law or fact common to class members predominate over any questions affecting only individual members, and that a class action is superior to other available methods for fairly and efficiently adjudicating the controversy. The matters pertinent to these findings include all of the following:

1. The class members' interests in individually controlling the prosecution or defense of separate actions.

2. The extent and nature of any litigation concerning the controversy already begun by or against class members.

3. The desirability or undesirability of concentrating the litigation of the claims in the particular forum.

4. The likely difficulties in managing a class action.

(3) Certification order.

(a) Time to issue. At an early practicable time after a person sues or is sued as a class representative, the court must determine by order whether to certify the action as a class action.

(b) Defining the class; appointing class counsel. An order that certifies a class action must define the class and the class claims, issues, or defenses, and must appoint class counsel under sub. (12).

(c) Altering or amending the order. An order that grants or denies class certification may be altered or amended before final judgment.

(4) Notice.

(a) For sub. (2) (a) or (b) classes. For any class certified under sub. (2) (a) or (b), the court may direct appropriate notice to the class.

(b) For sub. (2) (c) classes. For any class certified under sub. (2) (c), the court must direct to class members the best notice that is practicable under the circumstances, including individual notice to all members who can be identified through reasonable effort. The notice must clearly and concisely state in plain, easily understood language, all of the following:

1. The nature of the action.

2. The definition of the class certified.

3. The class claims, issues, or defenses.

4. That a class member may enter an appearance through an attorney if the member so desires.

5. That the court will exclude from the class any member who requests exclusion.

6. The time and manner for requesting exclusion.

7. The binding effect of a class judgment on members under sub. (5).

(5) Judgment. Whether or not favorable to the class, the judgment in a class action must do one of the following:

(a) For any class certified under sub. (2) (a) or (b), include and describe those whom the court finds to be class members.

(b) For any class certified under sub. (2) (c), include and specify or describe those to whom the notice under sub. (4) was directed, who have not requested exclusion, and whom the court finds to be class members.

(6) Particular issues. Notwithstanding ss. 805.05 (2) and 805.09 (2), when appropriate, an action may be brought or maintained as a class action with respect to particular issues.

(7) Subclasses. When appropriate, a class may be divided into subclasses that are each treated as a class under this rule.

(8) Conducting the action.

(a) In general. In conducting an action under this section, the court may issue orders that do any of the following:

1. Determine the course of proceedings or prescribe measures to prevent undue repetition or complication in presenting evidence or argument.

2. Require — to protect class members and fairly conduct the action — giving appropriate notice to some or all class members of any of the following:

   a. Any step in the action.

   b. The proposed extent of the judgment.

   c. The members' opportunity to signify whether they consider the representation fair and adequate, to intervene and present claims or defenses, or to otherwise come into the action.

3. Impose conditions on the representative parties or on intervenors.

4. Require that the pleadings be amended to eliminate allegations about representation of absent persons and that the action proceed accordingly.

5. Deal with similar procedural matters.

(b) Combining and amending orders. An order under sub. (8) (a) may be altered or amended from time to time and may be combined with an order under s. 802.10.

(9) Settlement, voluntary dismissal, or compromise. The claims, issues, or defenses of a certified class may be settled, voluntarily dismissed, or compromised only with the court's approval. All of the following procedures apply to a proposed settlement, voluntary dismissal, or compromise:

(a) The court must direct notice in a reasonable manner to all class members who would be bound by the proposal.

(b) If the proposal would bind class members, the court may approve it only after a hearing and on finding that it is fair, reasonable, and adequate.

(c) The parties seeking approval must file a statement identifying any agreement made in connection with the proposal.

(d) If the class action was previously certified under sub. (2) (c), the court may refuse to approve a settlement unless it affords a new opportunity to request exclusion to individual class members who had an earlier opportunity to request exclusion but did not do so.

(e) Any class member may object to the proposal if it requires court approval under sub. (9); the objection may be withdrawn only with the court's approval.

(10) Disposition of residual funds.

(a) In this subsection:

1. "Residual funds" means funds that remain after the payment of all approved class member claims, expenses, litigation costs, attorney fees, and other court-approved disbursements in an action under this section.

2. "WisTAF" means the Wisconsin Trust Account Foundation, Inc.

(b) 1. Any order entering a judgment or approving a proposed compromise of a class action that establishes a process for identifying and compensating members of the class shall provide for disbursement of any residual funds. In class actions in which residual funds remain, not less than 50 percent of the residual funds shall be disbursed to WisTAF to support direct delivery of legal services to persons of limited means in non-criminal matters. The circuit court may disburse the balance of any residual funds beyond the minimum percentage to WisTAF for purposes that have a direct or indirect relationship to the objectives of the underlying litigation or otherwise promote the substantive or procedural interests of members of the certified class.

2. This subsection does not prohibit the trial court from approving a settlement that does not create residual funds.

(11) Interlocutory appeal of class certification.

(a) When practicable after the commencement of an action brought as a class action, the court shall determine by order whether it is to be so maintained. If the court finds that the action should be maintained as a class action, it shall certify the action accordingly on the basis of a written decision setting forth all reasons why the action may be maintained and describing all evidence in support of the determination. An order under this subsection may be altered, amended, or withdrawn at any time before the decision on the merits. The court may direct appropriate notice to the class.

(b) An appellate court shall hear an appeal of an order granting or denying class action certification, or denying a motion to decertify a class action, if a notice of appeal is filed within 14 days after entry of the order. During the pendency of an appeal under this subsection, all discovery and other proceedings shall be stayed, except that the trial court shall retain sufficient jurisdiction over the case to consider and implement a settlement of the action if a settlement is reached between the parties.

(12) Class counsel.

(a) Appointing class counsel. Unless a statute provides otherwise, a court that certifies a class must appoint class counsel.

(b) 1. In appointing class counsel, the court must consider all of the following:

a. The work counsel has done in identifying or investigating potential claims in the action.

b. Counsel's experience in handling class actions, other complex litigation, and the types of claims asserted in the action.

c. Counsel's knowledge of the applicable law.

d. The resources that counsel will commit to representing the class.

2. In appointing class counsel, the court may do any of the following:

a. Consider any other matter pertinent to counsel's ability to fairly and adequately represent the interests of the class.

b. Order potential class counsel to provide information on any subject pertinent to the appointment and to propose terms for attorney fees and nontaxable costs.

c. Include in the appointing order provisions about the award of attorney fees or nontaxable costs under sub. (13).

d. Make further orders in connection with the appointment.

(c) Standard for appointing class counsel. When one applicant seeks appointment as class counsel, the court may appoint that applicant only if the applicant is adequate under sub. (12) (a) and (d). If more than one adequate applicant seeks appointment, the court must appoint the applicant best able to represent the interests of the class.

(d) Interim counsel. The court may designate interim counsel to act on behalf of a putative class before determining whether to certify the action as a class action.

(e) Duty of class counsel. Class counsel must fairly and adequately represent the interests of the class.

(13) Attorney fees and nontaxable costs. In a certified class action, the court may award reasonable attorney fees and nontaxable costs that are authorized by law or by the parties' agreement. All of the following procedures apply:

(a) A claim for an award must be made by motion, subject to the provisions of this subsection, at a time the court sets. Notice of the motion must be served on all parties and, for motions by class counsel, directed to class members in a reasonable manner.

(b) A class member, or a party from whom payment is sought, may object to the motion.

(c) The court may hold a hearing and must find the facts and state its legal conclusions under s. 805.17 (2).

(d) The court may refer issues related to the amount of the award to a referee, as provided in s. 805.06.

(14) Prohibition against certain class actions. No claim may be maintained against the state or any other party under this section if the relief sought includes the refund of or damages associated with a tax administered by the state.

SECTION 426.110, WISCONSIN STATUTES

(1) Either the administrator, or any customer affected by a violation of chs. 421 to 427 and 429 or of the rules promulgated pursuant thereto or by a violation of the federal consumer credit protection act, or by conduct of a kind described in sub. (2), may bring a civil action on behalf of himself or herself and all persons similarly situated, for actual damages by reason of such conduct or violation, together with penalties as provided in sub. (14), reasonable attorney fees and other relief to which such persons are entitled under chs. 421 to 427 and 429. The customer filing the action must give prompt notice thereof to the administrator, who shall be permitted, upon application within 30 days, to join as a party plaintiff. For purposes of apportionment of cost, the administrator need not be a party to the action.

(2) Actions may be maintained under this section against any person who in making, soliciting or enforcing consumer credit transactions engages in any of the following kinds of conduct:

(a) Making or enforcing unconscionable terms or provisions of consumer credit transactions;

(b) False, misleading, deceptive, or unconscionable conduct in inducing customers to enter into consumer credit transactions; or

(c) False, misleading, deceptive, or unconscionable conduct in enforcing debts or security interests arising from consumer credit transactions.

(3) Notwithstanding this chapter, no class action may be maintained for conduct proscribed in sub. (2) or for a violation of s. 423.301, 424.501, 425.107, 426.108 or 427.104 (1) (h) unless the conduct has been found to constitute a violation of chs. 421 to 427 and 429 at least 30 days prior to the occurrence of the conduct involved in the class action by an appellate court of this state or by a rule promulgated by the administrator as provided in ss. 426.104 (1) (e) and 426.108 specifying with particularity the act or practice in question.

(4) (a) At least 30 days or more prior to the commencement of a class action for damages pursuant to the provisions of this section, any party must:

1. Notify the person against whom an alleged cause of action is asserted of the particular alleged claim or violation; and

2. Demand that such person correct, or otherwise remedy the basis for the alleged claim.

(b) Such notice shall be in writing and shall be sent by certified or registered mail, return receipt requested, to such person at the place where the transaction occurred, such person's principal place of business within this state, or, if neither will effect actual notice, the department of financial institutions.

(c) Except as provided in par. (e), no action for damages may be maintained under this section if an appropriate remedy, which shall include actual damages and may include penalties, is given, or agreed to be given within a reasonable time, to such party within 30 days after receipt of such notice.

(d) Except as provided in par. (e), no action for damages may be maintained under this section upon a showing by a person against whom the alleged claim or violation is asserted that all of the following exist:

1. All customers similarly situated have been identified, or a reasonable effort to identify such other consumers has been made;

2. All customers so identified have been notified that upon their request such person shall make the appropriate remedy;

3. The remedy requested by such customers has been or in a reasonable time will be given; and

4. Such person has ceased from engaging, or if immediate cessation is impossible under the circumstances, such person will, within a reasonable time, cease to engage in any acts on which the alleged claim is based.

(e) An action for injunctive relief may be commenced without compliance with par. (a). Not less than 30 days after the commencement of an action for injunctive relief, and after compliance with par. (a) the customer may amend his or her complaint without leave of court to include a request for damages. The appropriate provisions of par. (c) or (d) shall be applicable if the complaint for injunctive relief is amended to request damages.

(4m) Actions commenced under this section shall be conducted under the procedures set forth in s. 803.08.

(14) A merchant shall not be liable in a class action for specific penalties under s. 425.302 (1) (a), 425.303 (1), 425.304 (1), 425.305 (1) or 429.301 (1) for which it would be liable in individual actions by reason of violations of chs. 421 to 427 and 429 or of conduct prescribed in sub. (2) unless it is shown by a preponderance of the evidence that the violation was a willful and knowing violation of chs. 421 to 427 and 429.No recovery in an action under this subsection may exceed $100,000.

(15) A plaintiff who prevails shall be awarded a reasonable attorney's fee. Notwithstanding s. 425.308 (2), reasonable attorney's fees in a class action shall be determined by the value of the time reasonably expended by the attorney rather than by the amount of the recovery on behalf of the class. A legal aid society or legal services program which represents a class shall be awarded a reasonable service fee in lieu of reasonable attorney's fees, equal in amount to the amount of the attorney's fees as measured by this subsection.

(16) The administrator, whether or not a party to an action, shall bear the costs of notice except that the administrator may recover such costs from the defendant.

The contents of this chapter were reviewed and edited by Douglas P. Dehler, who is a shareholder at O'Neil, Cannon, Hollman, DeJong & Laing, S.C., located in Milwaukee, Wisconsin.

WYOMING

Rule 23 of the Wyoming Rules of Civil Procedure is virtually identical to Rule 23 of the Federal Rules of Civil Procedure. Because Wyoming's procedural rules are patterned after the federal rules, Wyoming courts generally consider federal precedent on the rules to be persuasive authority. *Lamar Outdoor Adver. v. Farmers Co-Op Oil Co.*, 2009 WY 112, ¶ 12, 215 P.3d 296, 301 (Wyo. 2009) (holding that, "[b]ecause the Wyoming Rules of Civil Procedure are patterned after the Federal Rules of Civil Procedure, federal court interpretations of their rules are highly persuasive in our interpretation of the corresponding Wyoming rules."). Although the Wyoming Supreme Court has not yet construed any provisions of Wyoming's class action rule, practitioners can expect that Wyoming courts will find federal cases implementing the federal class action rule highly persuasive.

1. CASE LAW INTERPRETING RULE 23

There are no Wyoming Supreme Court cases interpreting and applying the provisions of Wyo. R. Civ. P. 23.

2. MISCELLANEOUS COMMENTS

The Wyoming Supreme Court has held that small claims cannot be aggregated for the purpose of meeting the jurisdictional limit of the district courts. *Mutual of Omaha Ins. Co. v. Blury-Losolla*, 952 P.2d 1117 (Wyo. 1998). Prior to 2011, district courts in Wyoming had jurisdiction over claims of $7,000 or more. County courts had exclusive jurisdiction for claims less than $7,000. Following the federal precedent as set forth in *Zahn v. International Paper Co.*, 414 U.S. 291 (1973), and *Snyder v. Harris*, 394 U.S. 332 (1969), the Wyoming Supreme Court held that individual class claimants may not participate in a class action lawsuit in district court unless each individual class members' claim exceeds $7,000 at the commencement of the lawsuit. *See Mutual of Omaha*, 952 P.2d at 1121–22. Although the Supreme Court did not directly so hold, language in the opinion strongly suggests that county courts did not have jurisdiction to entertain class actions in Wyoming. *See Mutual of Omaha*, 952 P.2d at 1120–21.

Effective July 1, 2000, the county court system was replaced with circuit courts. Wyo. Stat. § § 5-9-101 to -154. This statutory change provided concurrent jurisdiction with district courts to $7,000. Wyo. Stat. § 5-9-128 (2000). For the year 2000, this extended to district courts concurrent jurisdiction for claims under $7,000, permitting small claims to be brought in a class action in district court. Effective July 1, 2001, however, the Wyoming legislature reinstated the *exclusive* jurisdictional limitation for circuit courts to $7,000, resurrecting the prior law which provided that district courts do not have jurisdiction for claims less than $7,000. 2001 Wyo. Sess. Laws, Ch. 40, § 1; Wyo. Stat. § 5-9-128 (2001). Effective July 1, 2001, therefore, the rule set forth by the Wyoming Supreme Court in *Mutual of Omaha Ins. Co. v. Blury-Losolla*, 952 P.2d 1117 (Wyo. 1998), is once again valid and class actions involving relatively small individual claims may not be maintained in Wyoming.

Effective July 1, 2011, the legislature increased the circuit court's exclusive jurisdictional limits from $7,000 to $50,000. 2011 Wyo. Sess. Laws, Ch. 196, § 1.

3. ANALYSIS

Wyoming's current class action rule, W.R.C.P. 23, closely mirrors the federal rule. It was most recently revised in February 2017 to reflect the changes made to the Federal Rules of Civil Procedure. Specifically, the rule now outlines specific procedures for settlement, voluntary dismissal, or compromise, requirements for class counsel, and provisions regarding attorney's fees and nontaxable costs.

Wyoming has no Supreme Court cases construing its rule. Only a couple of class action cases have been before the Court, and none have involved the rule or its procedural requirements.

Of significance to practitioners is that circuit courts (formerly county courts) have exclusive civil jurisdiction when the amount in controversy is equal to or less than $50,000. Wyo. Stat. § 5-9-128 (2025). Any individual claim for $50,000 or less must be brought in circuit court. The Supreme Court also held that circuit courts do not have jurisdiction to entertain class action lawsuits. *Mutual of Omaha Ins. Co. v. Blury-LoSolla*, 952 P.2d 1117 (Wyo. 1998). Consequently, as a general rule class actions in Wyoming can only be brought in the district court and each class member must have an individual claim exceeding $50,000.

There are a few jurisdictional statutes granting a district court jurisdiction over smaller amounts, which may affect the availability of class actions in Wyoming. For example, the Wyoming Royalty Payment Act, §§ 30-5-301 *et. seq*., grants the district court jurisdiction over claims arising under the Act regardless of the amount in controversy. Wyo. Stat. § 30-5-303. A class action under this Act can be brought even if the individual claims are for less than $50,000. This has led to a number of recent state class actions involving oil and gas royalty payment disputes. However, none of these cases has, to date, led to the issuance of a Supreme Court decision construing Wyoming's class action rule.

RULE 23 OF THE WYOMING RULES OF CIVIL PROCEDURE

RULE 23. CLASS ACTIONS

(a) *Prerequisites.* One or more members of a class may sue or be sued as representative parties on behalf of all members only if:

(1) the class is so numerous that joinder of all members is impracticable;

(2) there are questions of law or fact common to the class;

(3) the claims or defenses of the representative parties are typical of the claims or defenses of the class; and

(4) the representative parties will fairly and adequately protect the interests of the class.

(b) *Types of Class Actions.* A class action may be maintained if Rule 23(a) is satisfied and if:

(1) prosecuting separate actions by or against individual class members would create a risk of:

(A) inconsistent or varying adjudications with respect to individual class members that would establish incompatible standards of conduct for the party opposing the class; or

(B) adjudications with respect to individual class members that, as a practical matter, would be dispositive of the interests of the other members not parties to the individual adjudications or would substantially impair or impede their ability to protect their interests;

(2) the party opposing the class has acted or refused to act on grounds that apply generally to the class, so that final injunctive relief or corresponding declaratory relief is appropriate respecting the class as a whole; or

(3) the court finds that the questions of law or fact common to class members predominate over any questions affecting only individual members, and that a class action is superior to other available methods for fairly and efficiently adjudicating the controversy. The matters pertinent to these findings include:

(A) the class members' interests in individually controlling the prosecution or defense of separate actions;

(B) the extent and nature of any litigation concerning the controversy already begun by or against class members;

(C) the desirability or undesirability of concentrating the litigation of the claims in the particular forum; and

(D) the likely difficulties in managing a class action.

(c) *Certification Order; Notice to Class Members; Judgment; Issues Classes; Subclasses.*

(1) *Certification Order.*

(A) *Time to Issue.* At an early practicable time after a person sues or is sued as a class representative, the court must determine by order whether to certify the action as a class action.

(B) *Defining the Class; Appointing Class Counsel.* An order that certifies a class action must define the class and the class claims, issues, or defenses, and must appoint class counsel under Rule 23(f).

(C) *Altering or Amending the Order.* An order that grants or denies class certification may be altered or amended before final judgment.

(2) *Notice.*

(A) *For (b)(1) or (b)(2) Classes.* For any class certified under Rule 23(b)(1) or (b)(2), the court may direct appropriate notice to the class.

(B) *For (b)(3) Classes.* For any class certified under Rule 23(b)(3), the court must direct to class members the best notice that is practicable under the circumstances, including individual notice to all members who can be identified through reasonable effort. The notice must clearly and concisely state in plain, easily understood language:

(i) the nature of the action;

(ii) the definition of the class certified;

(iii) the class claims, issues, or defenses;

(iv) that a class member may enter an appearance through an attorney if the member so desires;

(v) that the court will exclude from the class any member who requests exclusion;

(vi) the time and manner for requesting exclusion; and

(vii) the binding effect of a class judgment on members under Rule 23(c)(3).

(3) *Judgment.* Whether or not favorable to the class, the judgment in a class action must:

(A) for any class certified under Rule 23(b)(1) or (b)(2), include and describe those whom the court finds to be class members; and

(B) for any class certified under Rule 23(b)(3), include and specify or describe those to whom the Rule 23(c)(2) notice was directed, who have not requested exclusion, and whom the court finds to be class members.

(4) *Particular Issues.* When appropriate, an action may be brought or maintained as a class action with respect to particular issues.

(5) *Subclasses.* When appropriate, a class may be divided into subclasses that are each treated as a class under this rule.

(d) *Conducting the Action.*

(1) *In General.* In conducting an action under this rule, the court may issue orders that:

(A) determine the course of proceedings or prescribe measures to prevent undue repetition or complication in presenting evidence or argument;

(B) require—to protect class members and fairly conduct the action—giving appropriate notice to some or all class members of:

(i) any step in the action;

(ii) the proposed extent of the judgment; or

(iii) the members' opportunity to signify whether they consider the representation fair and adequate, to intervene and present claims or defenses, or to otherwise come into the action;

(C) impose conditions on the representative parties or on intervenors;

(D) require that the pleadings be amended to eliminate allegations about representation of absent persons and that the action proceed accordingly; or

(E) deal with similar procedural matters.

(2) *Combining and Amending Orders.* An order under Rule 23(d)(1) may be altered or amended from time to time and may be combined with an order under Rule 16.

(e) *Settlement, Voluntary Dismissal, or Compromise.* The claims, issues, or defenses of a certified class may be settled, voluntarily dismissed, or compromised only with the court's approval. The following procedures apply to a proposed settlement, voluntary dismissal, or compromise:

(1) The court must direct notice in a reasonable manner to all class members who would be bound by the proposal.

(2) If the proposal would bind class members, the court may approve it only after a hearing and on finding that it is fair, reasonable, and adequate.

(3) The parties seeking approval must file a statement identifying any agreement made in connection with the proposal.

(4) If the class action was previously certified under Rule 23(b)(3), the court may refuse to approve a settlement unless it affords a new opportunity to request exclusion to individual class members who had an earlier opportunity to request exclusion but did not do so.

(5) Any class member may object to the proposal if it requires court approval under this subdivision (e); the objection may be withdrawn only with the court's approval.

(f) *Class Counsel.*

(1) *Appointing Class Counsel.* Unless a statute provides otherwise, a court that certifies a class must appoint class counsel. In appointing class counsel, the court:

(A) must consider:

(i) the work counsel has done in identifying or investigating potential claims in the action;

(ii) counsel's experience in handling class actions, other complex litigation, and the types of claims asserted in the action;

(iii) counsel's knowledge of the applicable law; and

(iv) the resources that counsel will commit to representing the class;

(B) may consider any other matter pertinent to counsel's ability to fairly and adequately represent the interests of the class;

(C) may order potential class counsel to provide information on any subject pertinent to the appointment and to propose terms for attorney's fees and nontaxable costs;

(D) may include in the appointing order provisions about the award of attorney's fees or nontaxable costs under Rule 23(g); and

(E) may make further orders in connection with the appointment.

(2) *Standard for Appointing Class Counsel.* When one applicant seeks appointment as class counsel, the court may appoint that applicant only if the applicant is adequate under Rule 23(f)(1) and (4). If more than one adequate applicant seeks appointment, the court must appoint the applicant best able to represent the interests of the class.

(3) *Interim Counsel.* The court may designate interim counsel to act on behalf of a putative class before determining whether to certify the action as a class action.

(4) *Duty of Class Counsel.* Class counsel must fairly and adequately represent the interests of the class.

(g) *Attorney's Fees and Nontaxable Costs.* In a certified class action, the court may award reasonable attorney's fees and nontaxable costs that are authorized by law or by the parties' agreement. The following procedures apply:

(1) A claim for an award must be made by motion under Rule 54(d)(2), subject to the provisions of this subdivision (h), at a time the court sets. Notice of the motion must be served on all parties and, for motions by class counsel, directed to class members in a reasonable manner.

(2) A class member, or a party from whom payment is sought, may object to the motion.

(3) The court may hold a hearing and must find the facts and state its legal conclusions under Rule 52(a).

(4) The court may refer issues related to the amount of the award to a master, as provided in Rule 54(d)(2)(D).

Patrick R. Day originally prepared this chapter. Mr. Day is a partner with the law firm of Holland & Hart, LLP. The 2026 edition was reviewed for updates by Christine L. Jordan, an associate at the firm of Hirst Applegate, LLP, in Cheyenne, Wyoming.

ABOUT THE CONTRIBUTORS

COORDINATING EDITORS

Elizabeth J. Cabraser, Esq.
Fabrice Vincent, Esq.
LIEFF CABRASER HEIMANN & BERNSTEIN, LLP
275 Battery Street, 29th Floor
San Francisco, CA 94111
415-956-1000
ecabraser@lchb.com
fvincent@lchb.com

Jahan C. Sagafi, Esq.
OUTTEN & GOLDEN, LLP
One California Street, 12th Floor
San Francisco, CA 94111
415-638-8800
jsagafi@outtengolden.com

Howard S. Suskin, Esq.
JENNER & BLOCK, LLC
353 N. Clark Street
Chicago, IL 60654
312-923-2604
hsuskin@jenner.com

Fred B. Burnside, Esq.
DAVIS WRIGHT TREMAINE LLP
920 Fifth Avenue, Suite 3300
Seattle, WA 98104-1610
206-757-8016
fredburnside@dwt.com

STATE EDITORS

Alabama

James P. Pewitt, Esq.
JAMES P. PEWITT, LLC
Two North Twentieth
2 20th Street North, Suite 925
Birmingham, AL 35203
205-874-6686
attorneypewitt@gmail.com

Alaska

Jeff Feldman, Esq.
UNIVERSITY OF WASHINGTON SCHOOL OF LAW
Box 353020
William H. Gates Hall - Room 342
Seattle, WA 98195
206-543-0600
feldmanj@uw.edu

Arizona

Nicole Maroulakos Goodwin, Esq.
GREENBERG TRAURIG LLP
2375 East Camelback Road, Suite 800
Phoenix, AZ 85016
602-445-8454
nicole.goodwin@gtlaw.com

Arkansas

Byron J. Walker
Ryan Smith
ROSE LAW FIRM
120 East Fourth Street
Little Rock, AR 72201-2893
501-377-0351
bwalker@roselawfirm.com
rsmith@roselawfirm.com

California

Elizabeth J. Cabraser, Esq.
Fabrice N. Vincent, Esq.
LIEFF CABRASER HEIMANN & BERNSTEIN, LLP
275 Battery Street, 29th Floor
San Francisco, CA 94111
415-956-1000
ecabraser@lchb.com
fvincent@lchb.com

Jahan C. Sagafi, Esq.
OUTTEN & GOLDEN, LLP
One California Street, 12th Floor
San Francisco, CA 94111
415-638-8800
jsagafi@outtengolden.com

Colorado

Jessica P. Marsh, Esq.
WILLIAMS WEESE PEPPLE & FERGUSON, PC
1801 California Street, Suite 3400
Denver, CO 80202
303-861-2828
jmarsh@williamsweese.com

Connecticut

Richard S. Order, Esq.
UPDIKE, KELLY & SPELLACY, PC
225 Asylum Street, 20th Floor
Hartford, CT 06103
860-548-2659
rorder@uks.com

Delaware

Bruce E. Jameson, Esq.
Eric J. Juray, Esq.
John G. Day, Esq.
Caitlin E. Whetham
PRICKETT, JONES & ELLIOTT, PA
1301 N. King Street
Wilmington, DE 19801
302-888-6500
bejameson@prickett.com
ejjuray@prickett.com
jgday@prickett.com
cewhetham@prickett.com

District of Columbia

Aaron J. Marks, Esq.
Benjamin D. Brown, Esq.
COHEN, MILSTEIN, SELLERS & TOLL, PLLC
1100 New York Avenue NW
Suite 500 West
Washington, DC 20005-3964
202-408-4600
stoll@cohenmilstein.com
amarks@cohenmilstein.com

Florida

Jason K. Kellogg, Esq.
LEVINE KELLOGG LEHMAN SCHNEIDER & GROSSMAN, LLP
100 Southeast Second Avenue, 36th Fl.
Miami Tower
Miami, FL 33131
305-403-8788
jk@LKLSG.com

Edward A. Marod, Esq.
GUNSTER YOAKLEY & STEWART, P.A.
777 South Flagler Drive
Suite 500 East
West Palm Beach, FL 33401
561-655-1980
emarod@gunster.com

Georgia

Kevin A. Maxim, Esq.
THE MAXIM LAW FIRM, P.C.
1718 Peachtree Street N.W., Suite 599
Atlanta, GA 30309
404-924-4272
kmaxim@maximlawfirm.com

Hawaii

Robert M. Hatch, Esq.
BRONSTER FUJICHAKU ROBBINS
1003 Bishop Street, Suite 2300
Honolulu, HI 96813
808-524-5644
rhatch@bfrhawaii.com

Idaho

Hon. Peter G. Barton
Ada County Courthouse
Chambers Room 5177
200 W. Front Street
Boise, ID 83702
208-287-7524

Illinois

Ryan R. Bradley
Kathryn Johnson-Monfort
HEYL, ROYSTER, VOELKER & ALLEN, P.C.
301 N. Neil Street, Suite 505
Champaign, IL 61820
217-239-3629
RBradley@heylroyster.com
kjohnsonmonfort@heylroyster.com

Indiana

Richard E. Shevitz, Esq.
Vess A. Miller, Esq.
COHEN MALAD, LLP
One Indiana Square, Suite 1400
Indianapolis, IN 46204
317-636-6481
rshevitz@cohenmalad.com
vmiller@cohenmalad.com

Iowa

Susan A. Low, Esq.
LAW OFFICES OF SUSAN A. LOW
311 42nd Street
Des Moines, IA 50312
515-897-1685
salow@iabar.org

Kansas

Hammons P. Hepner
SHARP LAW, LLP
4820 West 75th Street
Prairie Village, KS 66208
913-901-0505
hhepner@midwest-law.com

Kentucky

Marjorie A. Farris, Esq.
STITES & HARBISON
400 West Market Street, Suite 1800
Louisville, KY 40202-3352
502-681-0496
mfarris@stites.com

Louisiana

Pearl Robertson
Emma K. Schwab
IRPINO AVIN & HAWKINS
2216 Magazine Stree
New Orleans, LA 70130
504-525-1500
probertson@irpinolaw.com
eschwab@irpinolaw.com

Maine

Gavin McCarthy, Esq.
Matthew Altieri, Esq.
PIERCE ATWOOD, LLP
Merrill's Wharf
254 Commercial Street
Portland, ME 04101
207-791-1170
gmccarthy@pierceatwood.com
maltieri@pierceatwood.com

Maryland

Matthew T. Wagman, Esq.
Bridget Brodie, Esq.
MILES & STOCKBRIDGE PC
100 Light Street
Baltimore, MD 21202
410-727-6464
mwagman@milesstockbridge.com
bbrodie@MilesStockbridge.com

John Parker Sweeney
Andrew J. Narod
Timothy Willman
BRADLEY ARANT BOULT CUMMINGS LLP
1615 L Street, NW
Washington, DC 20036
202-393-7150
jsweeney@bradley.com
anarod@bradley.com
twillman@bradley.com

Massachusetts

Laurence A. Schoen, Esq.
Kevin McGinty, Esq.
Matthew Stein, Esq.
MINTZ LEVIN COHN FERRIS GLOVSKY & POPEO, PC
One Financial Center
Boston, MA 02111
617-542-6000
lschoen@mintz.com
kmcginty@mintz.com
mstein@mintz.com

Michigan

Dennis K. Egan, Esq.
KOTZ, SANGSTER, WYSOCKI, PC
36700 Woodward Ave., Suite 202
Bloomfield Hills, MI 48304
313-259-8784
degan@kotzsangster.com

Minnesota

J. Gordon Rudd, Jr., Esq.
David Cialkowski
ZIMMERMAN REED LLP
1100 IDS Center
80 South 8th Street
Minneapolis, MN 55402
612-341-0400
gordon.rudd@zimmreed.com
david.cialkowski@zimmreed.com

Mississippi

Don Barrett, Esq.
David McMullan
BARRETT LAW GROUP, PA
404 Court Square North
P.O. Box 927
Lexington, MS 39095
662-834-9168
dbarrett@barrettlawgroup.com
dmcmullan@barrettlawgroup.com

Missouri

John J. Carey, Esq.
James J. Rosemergy, Esq.
CAREY, DANIS & LOWE
8235 Forsyth Blvd., Suite 1100
St. Louis, MO 63105
314-725-7700
jcarey@careydanis.com
jrosemergy@careydanis.com

Montana

Mac Morris, Esq.
CROWLEY FLECK, PLLP
1915 South 19th Avenue
Bozeman, MT 59718
406-556-1430
wmorris@crowleyfleck.com

Nebraska

Edward D. Hotz, Esq.
Maggie L. Brokaw, Esq.
PANSING, HOGAN, ERNST AND BACHMAN LLP
10250 Regency Cir. #300
Omaha, NE 68114-3728
402-397-5500
ehotz@pheblaw.com
MBrokaw@pheblaw.com

Nevada

Michael J. Gayan, Esq.
CLAGGETT & SYKES LAW FIRM
4101 Meadows Lane, Suite 100
Las Vegas, NV 89107
702-323-8649
mike@claggettlaw.com

New Hampshire

Josh Gardner, Esq.
GARDNER ROSENBERG, P.C.
One State Street, 4th Floor
Boston, MA 02109
617-390-7570
josh@gardnerrosenberg.com

New Jersey

Jeffrey J. Greenbaum, Esq.
Jason Jurkevich, Esq.
SILLS CUMMIS & GROSS, PC
One Riverfront Plaza
Newark, NJ 07102-5400
973-643-5430
jgreenbaum@sillscummis.com
jjurkevich@sillscummis.com

New Mexico

Jennifer G. Anderson, Esq.
MODRALL SPERLING
500 Fourth Street NW, Suite 1000
Albuquerque, NM 87102
505-848-1800
jga@modrall.com

New York

Alred L. Fatale III, Esq.
LABATON KELLER SUCHAROW
140 Broadway
New York, NY 10005
212-907-0884
afatale@labaton.com

North Carolina

Gary K. Shipman, Esq.
SHIPMAN & WRIGHT, LLP
575 Military Cutoff, Suite 106
Wilmington, NC 28405
910-762-1990
gshipman@shipmanlaw.com

North Dakota

Ian R. McLean, Esq.
SERKLAND LAW FIRM
10 Roberts St. N., P.O. Box 6017
Fargo, ND 58108
701-232-8957
Imclean@serklandlaw.com

Ohio

Barbara Quinn Smith, Esq.
LAW OFFICES OF BARBARA QUINN SMITH
9853 Johnnycake Ridge Road, Suite 106
Mentor, OH 44060
440-354-4010
bqsmith@bqslegal.com

Oklahoma

Michael E. Smith, Esq.
HALL, ESTILL, HARDWICK, GABLE,
GOLDEN & NELSON PC
100 N. Broadway, Suite 2900
Oklahoma City, OK 73102
405-553-2821
mesmith@hallestill.com

Oregon

Fred B. Burnside, Esq.
DAVIS WRIGHT TREMAINE LLP
1920 Fifth Avenue, Suite 3300,
Seattle, WA 98104-1610
206-757-8016
fredburnside@dwt.com

Pennsylvania

Michael D. Donovan, Esq.
DONOVAN LITIGATION GROUP LLC
1885 Swedesford Road
Malvern, PA 19355
610-647-6067
mdonovan@donovanlitigationgroup.com

Rhode Island

Nicole J. Benjamin, Esq.
ADLER POLLOCK & SHEEHAN, P.C.
100 Westminster Street, 16th Floor
Providence, RI 02903
401-274-7200
nbenjamin@apslaw.com

South Carolina

B. Randall Dong, Legal Director
DISABILITY RIGHTS SOUTH CAROLINA
3710 Landmark Dr., Suite 208
Columbia, SC 29204-4034
803-782-0639
dong@disabilityrightssc.org

South Dakota

Michael F. Nadolski, Esq.
LYNN, JACKSON, SHULTZ & LEBRUN, P.C.
110 N. Minnesota Ave., Suite 400
Sioux Falls, SD 57104
605-342-2592
mnadolski@lynnjackson.com

Tennessee

Kenneth S. Byrd
Betsy A. Sugar
Ellie Olson
LIEFF CABRASER HEIMANN & BERNSTEIN, LLP
222 2nd Avenue South, Suite 1640
Nashville, TN 37201
615-313-9000
kbyrd@lchb.com
bsugar@lchb.com
eolson@lchb.com

Texas

Stephen Gardner
53 Verano Loop
Santa Fe, NM 87508
214-549-3627
steve@consumerhelper.com

Utah

Eric Maxfield, Esq.
Cory A. Talbot, Esq.
HOLLAND & HART LLP
222 South Main Street, Suite 2200
Salt Lake City, UT 84101
801-799-5800
egmaxfield@hollandhart.com
catalbot@hollandhart.com

Vermont

Angela R. Clark, Esq.
DINSE PC
209 Battery Street
P.O. Box 988
Burlington, VT 05402
802-864-5751
aclark@dinse.com

Virginia

Bryan A. Fratkin
Travis C. Gunn
McGuireWoods LLP
Gateway Plaza
800 East Canal Street
Richmond, VA 23219
804-775-1000
bfratkin@mcguirewoods.com
tgunn@mcguirewoods.com

Washington

Stephen M. Rummage, Esq.
Fred B. Burnside, Esq.
Davis Wright Tremaine LLP
1920 Fifth Avenue, Suite 3300
Seattle, WA 98104-1610
206-757-8016
206-622-3150
steverummage@dwt.com
fredburnside@dwt.com

West Virginia

Joseph S. Beeson, Esq.
Craig S. Beeson, Esq.
Robinson & McElwee PLLC
400 Fifth Third Center
700 Virginia Street East
P.O. Box 1791
Charleston, WV 25326
304-347-8326
jsb@ramlaw.com
csb@ramlaw.com

Wisconsin

Douglas P. Dehler
O'Neil, Cannon, Hollman, DeJong & Laing S.C.
111 E. Wisconsin Avenue
Suite 1400
Milwaukee, WI 53202
414-276-5000
doug.dehler@wilaw.com

Wyoming

Christine L. Jordan
Hirst Applegate, LLP
1720 Carey Avenue, Suite 400
P.O. Box 1083
Cheyenne, WY 82003
307-632-0541
CJordan@hirstapplegate.com

Printed by Libri Plureos GmbH in Hamburg,
Germany